AUTHORS, ILLUSTRATORS, AND REPRESENTATIVE BOOKS

1989　JON SCIESZKA
*The True Story of the
Three Little Pigs*
ILLUSTRATED BY LANE SMITH

1989　LAURENCE YEP
Rainbow People
ILLUSTRATED BY DAVID WIESNER

1989　ED YOUNG
*Lon Po Po: A Red Riding
Hood Story from China*

1988　PAUL FLEISCHMAN
*Joyful Noise: Poems for
Two Voices*
ILLUSTRATED BY ERIC BEDDOWS

1988　ELOISE GREENFIELD
Nathaniel Talking
ILLUSTRATED BY JAN SPIVEY
GILCHRIST

1988　VIRGINIA HAMILTON
*Anthony Burns:
The Defeat and Triumph
of a Fugitive Slave*

1987　RUSSELL FREEDMAN
Lincoln: A Photobiography

1987　JOHN STEPTOE
*Murafo's Beautiful
Daughters:
An African Tale*

1987　JANE YOLEN
Owl Moon
ILLUSTRATED BY JOHN
SCHOENHERR

1986　NICHOLASA MOHR
Going Home

1985　PATRICIA MACLACHLAN
Sarah, Plain and Tall

1985　CHRIS VAN ALLSBURG
The Polar Express

1982　TOSHI MARUKI
Hiroshima No Pika

1981　YOSHIKO UCHIDA
Jar of Dreams

1970s

1978　PAUL GOBLE
*The Girl Who
Loved Wild Horses*

1977　KATHERINE PATERSON
Bridge to Terabithia

1977　DAVID MCCORD
One at a Time

1976　JEAN FRITZ
*What's the Big Idea,
Ben Franklin?*
ILLUSTRATED BY MARGOT TOMES

1976　BYRD BAYLOR
Hawk, I'm Your Brother
ILLUSTRATED BY PETER PARNALL

1976　MILDRED TAYLOR
*Roll of Thunder Hear
My Cry*

1975　TOMIE DEPAOLA
Strega Nona

1975　NATALIE BABBITT
Tuck Everlasting

1975　SHARON MATHIS
The Hundred Penny Box

1975　LAURENCE YEP
Dragonwings

1974　VIRGINIA HAMILTON
M. C. Higgins the Great

1973　SUSAN COOPER
The Dark Is Rising

1972　ARNOLD LOBEL
Frog and Toad Together

1971　MISKA MILES
Annie and the Old One
ILLUSTRATED BY PETER PARNALL

1971　MURIEL FEELINGS
*Moja Means One:
Swahili Counting Book*
ILLUSTRATED BY TOM FEELINGS

1970　BETSY BYARS
Summer of the Swans

1960s

1969　JOHN STEPTOE
Stevie

1968　DON FREEMAN
Corduroy

1968　URSULA K. LE GUIN
Wizard of Earthsea

1967　VIRGINIA HAMILTON
Zeely
ILLUSTRATED BY SYMEON SHIMIN

1964　MAURICE SENDAK
*Where the Wild
Things Are*

1964　LLOYD ALEXANDER
The Book of Three

1962　MADELEINE L'ENGLE
A Wrinkle in Time

1962　EZRA JACK KEATS
The Snowy Day

Literature and the Child

SEVENTH EDITION

LEE GALDA
UNIVERSITY OF MINNESOTA

BERNICE E. CULLINAN
NEW YORK UNIVERSITY

LAWRENCE R. SIPE
UNIVERSITY OF PENNSYLVANIA

WADSWORTH
CENGAGE Learning™

Australia • Brazil • Japan • Korea • Mexico • Singapore • Spain • United Kingdom • United States

Literature and the Child, **Seventh Edition**
Lee Galda, Bernice E. Cullinan,
Lawrence R. Sipe

Education Editor: Christopher Shortt

Developmental Editor: Tangelique Williams

Assistant Editor: Caitlin Cox

Editorial Assistant: Linda Stewart

Media Editor: Ashley Cronin

Marketing Manager: Kara Parsons

Marketing Communications Manager:
Martha Pfeiffer

Content Project Manager: Tanya Nigh

Creative Director: Rob Hugel

Art Director: Maria Epes

Print Buyer: Rebecca Cross

Rights Acquisitions Account Manager, Text:
Bob Kauser

Rights Acquisitions Account Manager, Image:
Robyn Young

Production Service: Joan Keyes, Dovetail
Publishing Services

Text Designer: Marsha Cohen

Photo Researcher: Bill Smith Group

Copy Editor: Susan M. Gall

Cover Designer: Marsha Cohen

Cover Illustrator: James Ransome

Compositor: Lachina Publishing Services

For product information and technology assistance, contact us at
Cengage Learning Customer & Sales Support, 1-800-354-9706.

For permission to use material from this text or product,
submit all requests online at **www.cengage.com/permissions**.
Further permissions questions can be e-mailed to
permissionrequest@cengage.com.

Library of Congress Control Number: 2009922839

ISBN-13: 978-0-495-60239-2

ISBN-10: 0-495-60239-6

Wadsworth
10 Davis Drive
Belmont, CA 94002-3098
USA

Cengage Learning is a leading provider of customized learning solutions with office locations around the globe, including Singapore, the United Kingdom, Australia, Mexico, Brazil, and Japan. Locate your local office at **www.cengage.com/global**.

Cengage Learning products are represented in Canada by Nelson Education, Ltd.

To learn more about Wadsworth, visit **www.cengage.com/wadsworth**.

Purchase any of our products at your local college store or at our preferred online store **www.ichapters.com**.

Printed in the United States of America
1 2 3 4 5 6 7 13 12 11 10 09

Brief Contents

Contents

PART ONE
Children & Books

Chapter 1
Children's and Adolescent Literature — 3

Chapter 2
Literature in the Lives of Young Readers — 31

PART TWO

Genres in Literature for Young Readers

Chapter

3

Picturebooks: A Unique Format in Children's Literature   53

4

Poetry and Verse   137

5

Folklore: A Literary Heritage   173

6
Fantasy and Science Fiction   205

7
Contemporary Realistic Fiction   229

Chapter 8
Historical Fiction
253

Chapter 9
Biography and Memoir
283

12

Response-centered, Literature-based Instruction in Intermediate Grades and Middle School   345

Preface

The books we read help shape our lives. Perhaps this has never been more true than today, when the constant flow of information, the pressure to respond to communications instantly, the multiple demands on time and attention all lead to a lack of time for contemplation. Time with books *is* time for contemplation. Whether we are experiencing fictional worlds through narrative, seeing the world with fresh eyes through poetry, or discovering new ideas through nonfiction, books offer us time to curl up and read—and think. This makes our job as authors a constant tension between spending time reading and thinking about those great books, and sitting down to write about them! And because there are so many wonderful books, it is difficult to choose which to focus on. How fortunate we are to have these challenges as authors, just as we have them as teachers, librarians, parents, and readers.

• • ABOUT THE • • SEVENTH EDITION

Just as books shape the lives of those who read them, books have shaped this seventh edition as well, and in many ways. The first edition of *Literature and the Child*, written by Bee Cullinan and published almost thirty years ago, is the foundation upon which this edition rests, and subsequent editions have influenced the structure of this seventh edition as well. For example, the enthusiastic response to the "Close Look at" feature introduced in an earlier edition prompted us to expand the number of those to three in each of the genre chapters.

Feedback from those who use this text caused us to expand the children's literature database as well. We have kept all of the books from the sixth edition and added new books and new information for this seventh edition, including publication dates, awards, and indicators of cultural diversity. The book-specific website at www.cengage .com/education/galda offers students a variety of study tools and resources such as chapter outlines, web links, self-assessments, and tools including forms. Materials for instructors include an electronic version of the Instruc-

tor's Manual and PowerPoint slides. The new premium website offers additional materials including access to the expanded children's literature database, to the video conversations with children's book authors and illustrators that were available with the sixth edition, and InfoTrac® exercises. Go to www.cengage.com/login to access these premium resources.

WebTutor™ Toolbox for WebCT™ and or Blackboard® provides access to all the content of this text's rich book companion website from within your course management system. Robust communication tools—such as course calendar, asynchronous discussion, real-time chat, a whiteboard, and an integrated e-mail system—make it easy for students to stay connected to the course.

Every edition is shaped by the field, and reflects the field not only in the books that are included in each but also in the manner in which we discuss them. Culturally diverse literature is enjoying a more robust growth than in the past, and students and teachers are no longer surprised by finding excellent books that reflect varied cultural perspectives. Thus, we have eliminated the separate chapter on building a culturally diverse collection and integrated much of that information in Chapters 1 and 2 of this edition. Diverse books have always been central to the genre chapters, so that is not new in this edition, but the booklists at the end of each do now contain an icon (☀) marking diversity, so that it is immediately apparent. We have also added publication dates to the booklists. As in the previous edition, we will update the booklists on the website for the life of this edition.

In this edition, we moved the chapter on response to literature from the last to the first section. Having it follow the introductory chapter reinforces our position that the great enterprise of literature involves both books *and* readers. Thus, the first section includes an introduction to the books followed by an introduction to readers and reader response. The second, and longest, section focuses, as in past editions, on the major kinds of literature for young readers. In this edition, we have consolidated the two picturebook chapters of previous editions into one, extended chapter. This allowed us to save space and cut redundancy and provide you with more, and more detailed, information about picturebooks just as the world of picturebooks is expanding in many ways. Other changes include the development of a "brief history" of literature in general and of each genre; these appear in Chapters 1 and 3 through 10. By doing this, we were able to ground our discussion of what is new in the field within an understanding of what came before. The final section, consisting of the two "in the classroom" chapters, has been updated, and still reflects best practices in teaching with literature.

Another way in which this edition is influenced by earlier editions is the cover art. James Ransome, who painted the cover for the third edition, has created another beautiful cover for the seventh. Perhaps the most important change for this edition is the addition of a new author, Lawrence R. Sipe, University of Pennsylvania, who brought his expertise in picturebooks to this new edition. Lauren Aimonette Liang authored the Instructor's Manual for this edition, just as she did for the sixth, and also contributed her expertise in middle-grade reading and responding to Chapter 12.

• • ACKNOWLEDGEMENTS • •

The new contributions of Larry and Lauren, the continuing influence of Bee Cullinan's foundational early editions, and the work of Rebecca Rapport and Sarah Hansen on the sixth edition help make *Literature and the Child* seventh edition both current and scholarly. Beth Brendler developed the website to bring it up to date and even more informative than it was in the sixth edition. Both Beth and Kara Coffino, Ph.D. candidates and teaching assistants at the University of Minnesota, have worked with me in our university classrooms to develop quizzes and PowerPoint presentations that enhance the use of this text. They and Rebecca Rapport also were wonderful advisers when I needed opinions about the revisions, as well as great people with whom to discuss books. Thanks also to poet David Harrison for helping me with poetic terminology. Sherise Ross, graduate assistant at the University of Minnesota, and Jessica Whitelaw and Tara McGowan, graduate assistants at the University of Pennsylvania, were terrific help with the almost insurmountable task of keeping up with references. I couldn't have made our deadline without them! Once again, Cathy Zemke, ever patient and cheerful, helped me overcome the mysteries of formatting and saved many an hour by knowing exactly which button to push.

Those people who helped produce this seventh edition also reflect the "old" and the "new." Although Dan Alpert is no longer the editor, his profound influence on the fifth and sixth editions is still evident in the seventh. Chris Shortt, our new editor, has been most supportive and enthusiastic. Tangelique Williams, development editor, has been with us since the fifth edition and her even hand and calm manner helps keep everyone on schedule and productive. Joan Keyes, of Dovetail Publishing Services, is simply terrific, and having her continue her role as production manager for this new edition, the third with which she has been associated, has been invaluable. Susan Gall, copyeditor, brought a keen eye and an equally keen sense of humor to this formidable task, especially when she tackled the reference lists. Ashley Cronin, technology project manager; Linda Stewart, editorial assistant; Caitlin Cox, assistant editor; Tanya Nigh, content project manager; and Maria Epes, art director executive, have all contributed immensely to the complete product—book and ancillaries.

We also acknowledge the many good ideas that our reviewers provided to us. It is always gratifying to have reviewers like the text, and it's really wonderful to have them not only like the text, but give us new, good ideas. Thank you to:

Eileen Hinders, University of Memphis
Jennifer Geringer, University of Northern Colorado
Mingshui Cai, University of Northern Iowa
Susannah Richards, Eastern Connecticut State University
Kathleen Tice, University of Texas at Arlington
Ian Wojcik-Andrews, Eastern Michigan University
Tammy Milby, Virginia Commonwealth University
Ken Schatmeyer, Wright State University

We also thank the children's literature instructors who responded to our online survey:

Jamie C. Naidoo, University of South Carolina
Zelda McMurtry, Arkansas State University
Veronica Moore, Southwestern Community College
Kristine Mohring, Ottawa University
Peg Moneypenny, Trinity International University
Esther Fusco, Hofstra University
Grace Leyhane, Dowling College
Sheryl Shipley, Northwest State Community College
Tracy Reynolds, University of Missouri–St. Louis
Jean Potter, Seton Hill University
Robert Gamble, D'Youville College
Rebecca Wilson, Bethel College
Laraine Croall, South Louisiana Community College

Suzi O'Brien, Northeast Iowa Community College
Kathleen J. Sanders, Fort Hays State University
Ronald S. Reigner, University of West Georgia
Peggy Hill, Arkansas Northeastern College
April Van Camp, Indian River Community College
Barbara Bleeker, Emporia State University
Anne Balay, Indiana University Northwest
Ann Adkins, Dana College
Kathleen Cummings, Suffolk County Community College
Susan Garness, Minot State University
Katherine Bucher, Old Dominion University
Dr. Rachael Hungerford, Lycoming College
Annette Wannamaker, Eastern Michigan University
Barb Witteman, Concordia University, St. Paul
Mary Alice Barksdale, Virginia Tech University
Cheryl Johnston, Monroe County Community College
Barb Tengesdal, University of Mary
Nancy Harrington, Westfield State College
Barbara A. Lehman, Ohio State University
Tena Litherland, University of Tennessee
Rebecca Rapport, University of Minnesota
Lisa Krall, Bemidji State University
Rita Buchoff, University of Central Florida
Sally Smith, Hofstra University
Gail Yunk, Loras College
Janice Cappelletti, McKendree University
Bernadyn Suh, Dowling College
Kay Drake, Elon University
Natalie Patchell, Kalamazoo Valley Community College
Diane Neal, Bluffton University
Carolee Ritter, Southeast Community College
Sonja Burnett, Arkansas Northeastern College
Jo Ann Garrett, North Greenville University
Linda Hoyer, Madonna University
Andrea Neptune, Sierra College
M.J. McGowan, University of Nebraska–Lincoln
Dominic A. Nuciforo, Sr., University of Central Florida
Katherine Byrn, University of Minnesota
Richard L. Henderson, University of the Incarnate Word
Linda Dunham, Oral Roberts University
Vivian Johnson, Marygrove College

Betty Watson, Harding University
Belinda Eggen, University of South Carolina
LynnAnn Wojciechowicz, South Mountain Community College
Julia Foust, Utah State University
Kristiina Montero, Syracuse University
Roberta Tragarz, Santiago Canyon College
Walter Johnson, Cumberland County College
Stan Steiner, Boise State University
Sherry DuPont, Slippery Rock University
Deborah L. Norland, Luther College
Louise Stearns, Southern Illinois University at Carbondale
Carrie Hintz, Queens College
Karen Gentsch, East Texas Baptist University
Nadene A. Keene, Indiana University Kokomo
Barbara Hershberger, Maranatha Baptist Bible College
Dawn Putney, University of West Georgia
Dawna Lisa Butterfield, University of Central Missouri
Mary Dwiggins, Millikin University
Amy Getty, Grand View College
Linda Tetzlaff, Normandale Community College
Janice Gardner, Peninsula College
Louanne Jacobs, Alabama A&M University
Claudia Reder, California State University, Channel Islands
Pam Adams, Dordt College
Robert Sweetland, Wayne State College
Kathryn Henkins, Mt. San Antonio College
Marcia Huntington, Everett Community College
Pat Austin, University of New Orleans
Joyce Herbeck, Montana State University
James O'Keefe, Diablo Valley College
Maureen Siera, St. Martin's University
Marcia Huntington, Everett Community College
Cheryl Johnston, Monroe County Community College

Finally, the many students, teachers, friends, and casual acquaintances with whom I talk about books helped shape me as a reader, and through me, helped shape this text. Among them all, my family remains my touchstone resource. Thank you to Gini, Morgan, and Henry for your book tips and your over-the-phone book club conversations. Thank you, Tony, Anna, and Adam, for everything.

Lee Galda

About the Authors and Illustrator

Lee Galda

After teaching in elementary- and middle-school classrooms for a number of years, Lee Galda received her Ph.D. in English Education from New York University. A former professor at the University of Georgia, she is now a professor at the University of Minnesota where she teaches courses in children's and young adult literature. Lee is a member of the International Reading Association, the American Library Association, and the United States Board on Books for Young People, working on various committees related to literature. She was children's books department editor for *The Reading Teacher* from 1989 to 1993, a member of the 2003 Newbery Committee, a member of the 2007–2008 International Reading Association Book Award Selection Committee, and a member of the USBBY Bridge to Understanding Award Committee in 2008 and 2009. She sits on the review boards of several professional journals and on the editorial boards of *Children's Literature in Education* and *Language Arts*. Author of numerous articles and book chapters about children's literature and response, she was lead author of the first chapter on children's literature appearing in the *Handbook of Reading Research (Volume III)*. Lee lives in Minneapolis, Minnesota, with her husband, two dogs, a cat, and a fish named Jaws.

Bernice E. Cullinan

Bernice E. Cullinan is known both nationally and internationally for her work in children's literature. She has written more than 30 books on literature for classroom teachers and librarians, including *Literature and the Child, Poetry Lessons to Dazzle and Delight*, and *Three Voices: Invitation to Poetry across the Curriculum*. She also has written a book for parents, *Read to Me: Raising Kids Who Love to Read*. Dr. Cullinan is editor in chief of *Wordsong*—the poetry imprint of Boyds Mills Press, a Highlights for Children Company and has collected poems written by the recipients of the National Council of Teachers of English Award for Poetry in *A Jar of Tiny Stars*. She served as president of the International Reading Association, was inducted into the Reading Hall of Fame and The Ohio State University Hall of Fame, and selected as the recipient of the Arbuthnot Award for Outstanding Teacher of Children's Literature. Dr. Cullinan lives in New York City.

Lawrence R. Sipe

Lawrence R. Sipe is an associate professor in the University of Pennsylvania's Graduate School of Education, where he teaches courses in children's and adolescent literature and conducts research on young children's responses to picturebooks. He taught in primary and elementary classrooms for six years, including a two-year stint in an isolated one-room school in the province of Newfoundland, Canada. He also was the coordinator of professional development for K–6 teachers for a school board in Newfoundland for 13 years. His Ph.D. is in Children's Literature and Emergent Literacy from Ohio State University, where he studied with Janet Hickman, who was herself a student of Charlotte Huck. Currently he is in his 13th year at the University of Pennsylvania. His awards include Outstanding Dissertation of the Year from the International Reading Association, the Outstanding Dissertation Award from the College Reading Association, the Promising Researcher Award from the National Council of Teachers of English, and the Early Career Achievement Award from the National Reading Conference. He has also won several awards for teaching, including the Teaching Excellence Award for the province of Newfoundland; the Graduate School of Education Teaching Award; and the Lindback Award for Distinguished Teaching from the University of Pennsylvania. He is the North American editor of the journal *Children's Literature in Education*. His book *Storytime: Young Children's Literary Understanding in the Classroom* was published in 2008 by Teachers College Press.

James Ransome

James Ransome is an award-winning illustrator of nearly 40 books. James' most recent books are *What Lincoln Said*, a young-reader biography of Abe Lincoln, and *Helen Keller*, the 6th book James has collaborated on with his wife, Lesa Cline-Ransome. A graduate of Pratt Institute, James recently completed three large murals for the National Underground Railroad Museum in Cincinnati, Ohio. His most recent awards are for *Sky Boys* which received the 2006 Boston Globe–Horn Book Award Honor Book for Picture Book, and the ALA Notable Book Award. Other awards include the Coretta Scott King award, NAACP, IBBY, and the Simon Wiesenthal Museum of Tolerance Award. James is a professor at Syracuse University. He lives in Rhinebeck, New York with his wife, Lesa, and four children. More information about James and his work can be found at www.jamesransome.com.

children & Books

PART 1

Children's and Adolescent Literature

At the moment the royal procession reached the Yamakage Bridge, Balsa's destiny took an unexpected turn.

She was crossing the commoners' bridge downstream, the Aoyumi River visible through gaps between the planks. Never a pleasant sight, today it was particularly terrifying—swollen after the long autumn rains, its muddy brown waters topped with churning white foam. The rickety bridge swayed precariously in the wind.

Balsa, however, stepped forward without hesitation.

—NAHOKO UEHASHI,
Moribito: Guardian of the Spirit, p. 1

The opening words of the 2009 Batchelder Award–winning **Moribito: Guardian of the Spirit** (I), written by Nahoko Uehashi and translated from the Japanese by Cathy Hirano, immediately grabs readers, pulling them into this fantasy adventure story, which has already been translated into many languages and adapted for an animated series for television in Japan, as well as a popular manga series.

The Batchelder Award honors the most outstanding translated book of the year and calls attention to the increasing globalization of the literature available for children and young adults. Step into any children's bookstore and you will find books from many countries, many cultures, many points of view, just waiting to be read. Whether you walk through the purple door at The Wild Rumpus, an independent children's bookstore in Minneapolis, or through the red door at The Red Balloon, an independent children's bookstore in St. Paul, you find books, and children, everywhere. On this late January day, the windows of The Wild Rumpus are filled with books about winter, with Cynthia Rylant's **Snow** (P), illustrated by Minneapolis artist Lauren Stringer, predominant. Little ones come with their mothers for story hour; today, several of them are leaving with a copy of Jonathan Bean's lovely picturebook **At Night** (N–P), winner of the Boston Globe–Horn Book Award, or the new Caldecott Medal winner, Susan Marie Swanson's **The House in the Night** (P), illustrated by Beth Krommes. Elementary school children appear after school, looking for the next good book to read. Today, some of them are laughing at Marla Frazee's funny picturebook, **A Couple of Boys Have the Best Week Ever** (P), a Caldecott Honor book. Older elementary readers are looking at Sally Nicholls's heartbreaking novel **Ways to Live Forever** (I), some have a copy of Cornelia Funke's **Inkdeath** (I–A), the final book in her popular trilogy, and others have discovered **Savvy** (I), a

Newbery Honor novel by a new author, Ingrid Law. Kathi Appelt's Newbery Honor–winning *The Underneath* (I) is passed around as well, with those who have read it recommending it enthusiastically. Several are delighted to find Jacqueline Woodson's *Peace, Locomotion* (I) because they liked *Locomotion* (I) so much. Those who like scary fantasy are thrilled that the store has copies of Neil Gaiman's Newbery Medal winner, *The Graveyard Book* (I–A). Adolescents, trying not to show how much they enjoy the experience, browse the shelves, picking up a book, reading a bit, and then going on to another until they've found what they like. Several of them are clustered around Shaun Tan's *Tales from Outer Surburbia* (A), reading bits aloud and marveling at the pictures, while others are asking for Melina Marchetta's *Jellicoe Road* (A), winner of the Printz Award.

Many of the adults who come into the store are looking for these recently announced Newbery, Caldecott, Printz, Batchelder, Siebert, and King, and other award–winning books. Scenes like this are replicated across the country as young readers and their parents flock to bookstores to find a book to delight in.

Both the beauty and the joy of a fresh snowfall are portrayed in text and illustrations in **Snow**.

It seems that children's books and young adult literature are alive and well, thriving in fact. Indeed, in 2008 many publishing houses found that young readers' fiction was the most profitable part of their business! There are thousands of wonderful books just waiting to be put into the hands of young readers. This text will help you learn about those books.

In this chapter, we present a brief history of the development of children's and adolescent literature, and then move to a detailed description of the literature today. We explore the major types of literature, or *genres*, as well as current trends and issues. We then consider the challenge of selecting literature today, presenting basic criteria for considering literary quality and cultural content in books. We discuss educational mandates, standards, and censorship issues, then conclude with a brief description of some of the many resources for selecting books. In Chapter 2 we consider the readers of literature and some general theoretical constructs that describe how readers read and respond to texts. In Chapters 3 through 10, we present detailed information about the major genres in children's and adolescent literature. Finally, in Chapters 11 and 12 we describe teachers and children working with literature, from primary through middle school levels. But first, we define literature for young readers.

Defining Literature for Children and Adolescents

A basic definition of literature for children and adolescents might state that it encompasses books written for this particular audience; we add that it can also include books that children and adolescents enjoy and have made their own. In short, this literature consists of books that children and adolescents read. In this textbook, we focus on those books written for and marketed to an audience of young readers. This audience begins at birth and ends at adulthood, which is, for the purposes of this text, age eighteen. Although our primary focus is on literature for young readers from birth through middle school, we do also discuss some of the trends in and major contributions to literature for older adolescents as well. We indicate the general age range of the books that we discuss in this text with the following designations:

N = Nursery (birth to age five)

P = Primary (ages five to eight)

I = Intermediate (ages eight to twelve)

A = Advanced (ages twelve to eighteen)

Many books, however, appeal in different ways to a wide range of ages, so there is considerable overlap in these designations. Today, we are fortunate to have a wealth of wonderful books from which to select. The field has grown tremendously in the almost three hundred years since John Newbery opened his bookstore.

A Brief History of Literature for Children and Adolescents

● ● ●   THE EARLY YEARS   ● ● ●

In 1744, John Newbery (1713–1767) opened a bookstore in St. Paul's Churchyard, London, where he published and sold books for children. Up until that time, children had been given chapbooks (crudely printed little books sold by peddlers or chapmen), battledores (folded sheets of cardboard covered with crude woodcuts of the alphabet or Bible verses), and hornbooks (small wooden paddles with lesson sheets tacked on with strips of brass and covered with a transparent sheet of cow's horn). These materials, like other books of their day, were meant to instruct children.

One of Newbery's early books, *A Little Pretty Pocket-Book: Intended for the Instruction and Amusement of Little Master Tommy and Pretty Miss Polly*, contained the alphabet, proverbs, and rules of behavior. In 1765, Newbery published *The Renowned History of Little Goody Two Shoes*, a bittersweet story of orphan Marjorie Meanwell, who is overcome with gratitude when a clergyman and his wife buy her a pair of shoes. Newbery's books were meant to teach children proper behavior, but did not threaten them with the standard fire and brimstone if they did not behave.

At first, most children's books came to the United States from England. At first, they were intended for instruction, but it soon became clear that the books nurtured children's imagination. Lewis Carroll's *Alice's Adventures in Wonderland* (1865/1992), was soon reprinted in English-speaking countries all over the world. The revolutionary quality of Lewis Carroll's two books, *Alice's Adventures in Wonderland* and *Through the Looking Glass* (1871/1977), derives from the fact that they were written purely to give pleasure to children. There is not a trace of a lesson or moral in the books. Other books from the same period, such as George MacDonald's *At the Back of the North Wind* (1871/1989) and Charles Kingsley's *The Water Babies* (1863/1995), which described a make-believe world alongside a real one, are still read today.

Nathaniel Hawthorne is considered the author of the first American book written specifically for children,

A Wonder Book for Boys and Girls (1851/1893). England, however, continued as a major source of literature for North American children for generations and led the way to global publishing. American children made no distinction among British and American books or those from other countries. They read Carlo Collodi's *Pinocchio* (1833/1993) from Italy, Johanna Spyri's *Heidi* (1881/1945) from Switzerland, Selma Lagerlöf's *The Wonderful Adventures of Nils* (1906–1907/1991) from Sweden, and Antoine de Saint-Exupéry's *The Little Prince* (1943) from France with equal enthusiasm.

The first child labor laws, which were passed in 1907, freed children to go to school. As more children learned how to read and write due to universal first- through eighth-grade public schools, the quantity and the types of books published for them rapidly increased. At the same time, new technologies helped reduce publishing costs, and the public generosity of charitable individuals allowed public library systems to develop rapidly, putting books in the hands of vast numbers of children worldwide. Literature written especially for children became profitable, and publishers began to establish departments of children's books.

THE TWENTIETH CENTURY

In 1919, the U. S. publishing house Macmillan launched a department devoted entirely to children's books. Louise Bechtel Seaman, who had worked as an editor of adult books and taught in a progressive school, was appointed department head. In 1922, the John Newbery Award was established by the American Library Association, followed by the Randolph Caldecott Award in 1938. (See Appendix A for a complete list of the winners and honor books.) In 1922, Helen Dean Fish became the first children's book editor at Frederick A. Stokes and Company, and in 1923, May Massee took the leadership of the children's book department at Doubleday. In 1924, *The Horn Book Magazine* was published by the Bookshop for Boys and Girls in Boston under the guidance of Bertha Mahony and Elinor Whitney. In 1933, May Massee moved from Doubleday to open a children's books department at Viking. Other publishers began to open children's books departments, and children's literature blossomed into the twentieth century. Modern picturebooks began to develop during the 1920s and 1930s; from the 1940s through the 1960s, children's and young adults' books became an increasingly important part of libraries, schools, homes, and publishing houses. The spread of public libraries with rooms devoted to children's and adolescents' reading interests opened the floodgates, inviting an eager audience to read books and magazines and to listen to stories told aloud. Leonard Marcus traces the history of children's literature in the United States in *Minders of Make-Believe: Idealists, Entre-*

preneurs, and the Shaping of American Children's Literature. Figure 1.1 contains some milestones in the history of literature for children and young adults.

The field of children's books changed considerably during the last half of the twentieth century as it slowly began to reflect the diversity that marks North America and to include more literature from around the world. Early publications sought to instill a seemingly unified community's values in the young, to socialize them, and to teach them. This approach has changed to reflect a broad spectrum of social values that come from many cultures and cross international boundaries. The percentage of culturally diverse books in relation to the entire corpus of books published each year remained woefully low, however, despite the increasing diversity of our population. In 1975, disturbed by the lack of picturebooks that reflected diversity, Harriet Rohmer established Children's Book Press, devoted to the publication of bilingual picturebooks that reflected a diversity of cultural experiences. Other small presses, such as Just Us Books, founded in 1988, were established to address the lack of diversity in the field, and forward-thinking editors such as Phyllis Fogelman, at Dial, encouraged and supported the work of several now-notable African American authors and illustrators (Marcus, 2008).

A study conducted in the final decade of the twentieth century confirmed that the number of children's books that present pluralistic, balanced racial and ethnic images of children seldom paralleled census figures (Bishop, 1994). Although the number of U. S. residents from parallel cultures (Hamilton, 1993) had increased dramatically, few books representing those groups were published between the 1960s and 1980s. In 1994, Bishop found that only 3 to 4 percent of the children's books published in 1990, 1991, and 1992 related to people of color. Since 1999, less than 3 percent of books published each year were by or about people of color (Hansen-Krening, Aoki, and Mizokawa, 2003). Considering that more than five thousand books for children and early adolescents were published in the United States alone each year, there were not enough books that reflected diversity published in any given year.

The situation was similar in terms of international literature. Although books published in English-speaking countries were often available internationally, less than 1 percent of books published in the United States were books that had been translated (Tomlinson, 2002; see also Stan, 2002, and Tomlinson, 1998). Books that contained characters who are gay, lesbian, bisexual, or transgendered were also few and far between, as were books that contained characters with exceptionalities.

In spite of the paltry number of books that embrace diversity, we made some progress. Whereas it was difficult in the 1960s and 1970s to find books that presented girls and women in what at the time were "nontraditional" roles, that was not the case at the end of the twentieth

Figure **1.1**

Milestones in Literature for Children and Adolescents

1865	Lewis Carroll, *Alice's Adventures in Wonderland*	1943	Esther Forbes, *Johnny Tremain*
1902	Walter de la Mare, *Songs of Childhood*	1950	C. S. Lewis, *The Lion, the Witch, and the Wardrobe*
	Rudyard Kipling, *Just So Stories*		Elizabeth Yates, *Amos Fortune: Free Man*
	E. Nesbit, *Five Children and It*	1952	Ben Lucien Burman, *High Water at Catfish Bend*
	Beatrix Potter, *The Tale of Peter Rabbit*		Mary Norton, *The Borrowers*
1904	J. M. Barrie, *Peter Pan*		E. B. White, *Charlotte's Web*
1908	Kenneth Grahame, *The Wind in the Willows*	1954	Lucy M. Boston, *The Children of Green Knowe*
	L. M. Montgomery, *Anne of Green Gables*		Rosemary Sutcliff, *The Eagle of the Ninth*
1922	Margery Williams, *The Velveteen Rabbit*		J.R.R. Tolkien, *The Fellowship of the Ring*
1924	A. A. Milne, *When We Were Very Young*	1958	Philippa Pearce, *Tom's Midnight Garden*
1934	Jean de Brunhoff, *The Story of Babar*	1962	Ezra Jack Keats, *The Snowy Day*
	P. L. Travers, *Mary Poppins*		Madeleine L'Engle, *A Wrinkle in Time*
1936	Edward Ardizzone, *Little Tim and the Brave Sea Captain*	1963	Maurice Sendak, *Where the Wild Things Are*
1938	Marjorie Kinnan Rawlings, *The Yearling*	1964	Lloyd Alexander, *The Book of Three*
1939	Ludwig Bemelmans, *Madeline*		Robert Cormier, *The Chocolate War*
	T. S. Eliot, *Old Possum's Book of Practical Cats*		Roald Dahl, *Charlie and the Chocolate Factory*
1940	Maud Hart Lovelace, *Betsy-Tacy*		Louise Fitzhugh, *Harriet the Spy*
	Eric Knight, *Lassie Come-Home*		Irene Hunt, *Across Five Aprils*
1941	Robert McCloskey, *Make Way for Ducklings*	1967	Virginia Hamilton, *Zeely*
	H. A. Rey, *Curious George*		S. E. Hinton, *The Outsiders*

century. Rather, female characters in contemporary realistic fiction reflected a profound change in society's perceptions of roles for women and girls. Social class as presented in contemporary fiction also seemed to have been slightly transformed, with a greater number of books in which the characters are poor or working class, but again, the numbers did not reflect the census figures.

Although literature by and about people of color remained a small percentage of all publications, publishing houses devoted to publishing these books continued to increase in number. Publishing houses that focus on culturally diverse literature—such as Children's Book Press, Lee & Low Books, Piñata Books, and Arte Público, among others—promised a continued increase in the number of books by and about people of color. Lee & Low Books celebrated their success with *A Tenth Anniversary Celebration of Multicultural Publishing* (2003). Publishers such as North-South Books and Kane/Miller were in the forefront of the effort to bring translated books to an American audience, with sometimes spectacular success. For example, Chih-Yuan Chen's *Guji Guji* (P), first pub-

lished in Taiwan, where it won the Hsin Yi Picture Book Award, was a *New York Times* bestseller when it became popular in North America. Publishers' contact information appears in Appendix C.

Stunning talent, market recognition, stalwart publishers, and the cultural and social changes in the last few decades of the twentieth century have come together to create a demand for quality books from parallel cultures that will continue into the future (Bader, 2003b). In a three-part series of articles in *The Horn Book Magazine*, Barbara Bader (2002, 2003a, b) describes the gradual growth of literature from parallel cultures. Rudine Sims Bishop's brilliant *Free Within Ourselves: The Development of African American Children's Literature* details the struggles and triumphs of those committed to bringing African American literature to young readers. Special recognition of authors and illustrators of particular parallel cultures, such as the Coretta Scott King Awards (for African American literature) and the Pura Belpré Awards (for Latino literature), were established in 1970 and 1996, respectively, and are administered by the American Library Association. The

1968	Ursula Le Guin, *A Wizard of Earthsea*		2003	Kate DiCamillo, *The Tale of Despereaux*
	Paul Zindel, *The Pigman*		2004	Russell Freedman, *The Voice That Challenged a Nation: Marian Anderson and the Struggle for Equal Rights*
1971	Virginia Hamilton, *The Planet of Junior Brown*			
	Robert C. O'Brien, *Mrs. Frisby and the Rats of NIMH*		2005	Lynne Rae Perkins, *Criss Cross*
				Jacqueline Woodson, *Show Way*
1972	Richard Adams, *Watership Down*		2006	Gene Luen Yang, *American Born Chinese*
1976	Mildred Taylor, *Roll of Thunder, Hear My Cry*			Markus Zusak, *The Book Thief*
1977	Katherine Paterson, *Bridge to Terabithia*		2007	Sherman Alexie, *The Absolutely True Diary of a Part-Time Indian*
1978	Janet and Allan Ahlberg, *Each Peach Pear Plum*			Christopher Paul Curtis, *Elijah of Buxton*
1983	Anthony Browne, *Gorilla*			Brian Selznick, *The Invention of Hugo Cabret*
1985	Patricia MacLachlan, *Sarah, Plain and Tall*			Peter Sís, *The Wall: Growing Up Behind the Iron Curtain*
1988	Paul Fleischman, *Joyful Noise*			Shaun Tan, *The Arrival*
1993	Lois Lowry, *The Giver*		2008	Kathi Appelt, *The Underneath*
1997	Karen Hesse, *Out of the Dust*			Carin Berger, *The Little Yellow Leaf*
1998	J. K. Rowling, *Harry Potter and the Sorcerer's Stone*			Mark Reibstein, *Wabi Sabi*
	Louis Sachar, *Holes*			
1999	Walter Dean Myers, *Monster*			
2000	Philip Pullman, *The Amber Spyglass*			
2001	Marc Aronson, *Sir Walter Ralegh and the Quest for El Dorado*			
	Marilyn Nelson, *Carver: A Life in Poems*			
	David Wiesner, *The Three Pigs*			

history of these awards reflects increasingly robust publication. The King has expanded from the original single award for an author to awards for both authors and illustrators, including Honor awards. The Belpré has always honored both authors and illustrators, but, since 2009, is an annual, rather than biennial, award. Winners of these and other awards are listed in Appendix A.

At the same time that literature for children was becoming increasingly diverse, young adult literature was enjoying a robust renaissance. The genre began in earnest in the 1960s with the publication of novels such as Robert Cormier's *The Chocolate War* (A), S. E. Hinton's *The Outsiders* (A), Paul Zindel's *The Pigman* (A), Robert Lipsyte's *The Contender* (A), and Judy Blume's *Forever* (A), among others. The subsequent resurgence of adolescent literature was marked by the establishment of the Michael L. Printz Award in 2000; this award is administered by the American Library Association.

Similarly, the increasing attention paid to nonfiction in the final decades of the twentieth century is reflected in the establishment of the Robert F. Sibert Award for outstand-

ing informational books, administered by the American Library Association, and the Orbis Pictus Award, administered by the National Council of Teachers of English.

Literature for young readers continued to evolve along many dimensions in both content and form. The continued popularity of series books, the increase of books for emerging readers, young adult fiction that cast an unrelenting eye on life, the rise of graphic novels, the popularity of *crossover* books, and other developments marked the transition from twentieth to twenty-first centuries. Although there may not be anything "new" in literature for young readers, there are certainly many books that brought us the "unexpected," from Sendak's *Where the Wild Things Are* (N–P), which shocked many adults with its "scariness," to Lois Lowry's *The Giver* (A), a dystopian novel with an unexpectedly bizarre twist (Hearne, 2006). We summarize the history of each genre in Chapters 3–10.

Today's literature for children and adolescents is marked by increasingly varied content, continued experimentation with innovative formats and literary techniques, and with expanding—or blurring—the boundaries

Teaching Idea 1.1

Distinguish among Fantasy, Contemporary Realism, and Historical Fiction

Choose three picturebooks (use the booklists at the end of Chapters 3, 6, 7, and 8)—one fantasy, one contemporary realistic fiction, and one historical fiction. If you can find three with similar themes, your comparisons will be richer. Read the books aloud and compare them on relevant points, including genre, characters, plot, setting, theme, and any important details. Ask students to answer the following questions, using both the text and the illustrations to explain their answers:

✿ Which stories could really have happened? How do you know?

✿ Which story could not really have happened? How do you know?

✿ Which story is contemporary, set in today's world? How do you know?

✿ Which story is historical? How do you know?

✿ How are these stories alike?

✿ How are these stories different?

Next, help students generate some descriptors of each of the three genres.

of genre and audience. Technological innovations have spurred experimentation in illustration as well, with artists expanding the idea of what is possible in a book for young readers. Teaching Idea 1.1 describes a way to help young readers compare old and new books so they can understand how children's books have changed over the years.

Children's and Adolescent Literature Today and Tomorrow

The content of this literature is as broad as the hopes, fears, dreams, experiences, and interests of the audience it reaches. It reflects the increasing diversity and globalization of the lives of young readers. This literature also demonstrates the amazing talent of those who write and

illustrate books for young readers, who find unique ways of presenting their imaginative visions.

Literature for young readers is also diverse in terms of genre, or type. One basic distinction is between narratives and other structures such as exposition, description, argumentation, or non-narrative poetry. *Narratives* tell a story; they often have a *character* or characters who encounter some kind of problem and work to resolve it. The narrative is developed through the *plot*—the temporal events or actions that lead to the solution of the problem—which progresses to a *climax*, or solution to the problem, and sometimes, but not always, ends with a *resolution*, or closure to the story. Figure 1.2 summarizes literary elements and how they function in narratives. Texts that are not narratives do not tell a story, but rather may present information through argumentative, descriptive, expository, or persuasive language—in short, nonfiction. They may be poetry, presenting an experience, thought, or emotion.

Another way to categorize literature is by *genre*, as we do in Figure 1.3 on page 12. A genre is a category of composition that has such defining characteristics as type of characters, setting, action, and overall form or structure. The defining characteristics of each genre help us recognize the organization of the discipline of literature, provide a framework for talking about books, and help guide our selection. In this text, we explore the format of picturebooks as well as the genres of poetry, folklore, fantasy, science fiction, realistic fiction, historical fiction, biography and memoir, and nonfiction.

Distinguishing features help readers recognize genres. For example, *poetry* is marked by condensed language that contains various poetic devices to call attention to something in a fresh way. Ancient stories that were told by word of mouth are known as *folklore*. *Fantasy* stories could not happen in the real world; *science fiction* might happen in the future. Stories focusing on events that could happen in the real world today are works of *contemporary realistic fiction*; realistic stories set in the past are called *historical fiction*; and stories that tell the tale of a person's life are *biography* or *memoir*. Books that present information are called *nonfiction*. In the case of *picturebooks*, the content might be any of the aforementioned genres; the distinguishing feature is the format, the importance of the art in how the book conveys meaning.

Within these general distinctions, however, lies amazing variation. Some writers deliberately cross the rather arbitrary boundaries of genre presented previously by, for example, setting a story in both contemporary and historical times, or using fantasy devices or folkloric elements in contemporary or historical fiction. Within many of these genres, readers can find subgenres such as mystery stories, romances, quest tales, sports stories, and adventure stories. Humorous stories as well as serious stories populate each genre, as do series books. Some authors even blend fiction

Figure **1.2**

Literary Elements and How They Function in Narrative

Narratives contain certain literary elements that authors and illustrators work with to create memorable stories. They include setting, characterization, plot, theme, and style.

Setting

Setting is the time and place in which the story events occur. In most stories, the setting is important and thoroughly described. In others, the setting is less important, with few details. Picturebooks with vague settings in the text offer artists the opportunity to create images that present their own vision of the physical surroundings of the story. In other stories, setting is very important; details about a particular city, a part of the country, a historical period, or an imaginary place affect the development of the characters and the plot.

Characterization

Characterization refers to the means by which an author establishes credibility of character. Characters are the personalities that populate literature. Like people, main characters—protagonist(s) and antagonist(s)—are multidimensional, with varied strengths and weaknesses, and dynamic, growing and changing over time. This change or development is most often due to the events that occur as the characters seek to resolve some kind of problem. Authors develop characters by describing how they appear, what they do or say, what others *say* about or to them as well as what others *do* to them, and by what the narrator reveals. In picturebooks, character is also interpreted by illustrators who reveal appearance, thoughts, and actions.

Plot

Plot refers to the sequence of story events. In fiction for children, the plot is often a straightforward chronology, but sometimes authors use flashbacks, episodic plots, or alternating plots, especially those writing for an adolescent audience. Flashbacks provide background information about earlier events that led to the creation of the problem the character faces. Episodic plots highlight particular events in characters' lives, and alternating plots enable authors to tell parallel or contrasting stories from different points of view.

The plot usually revolves around a central conflict or conflicts. Common conflicts include: self against self, in which the main character engages in an internal struggle; self against other, in which the struggle is between the main character and one or more others; self against society, in which the main character combats societal pressures or norms; and self against nature, in which the main character struggles with the forces of nature. In most fiction for children, the conflict is positively, or at least hopefully, resolved by the end of the story; fiction for adolescents often ends with an unclear or a less-than-happy resolution.

Theme

A *theme* is a central, unifying idea, a thread that stitches the story together. Often a theme is the reason authors write in the first place: a story allows them to say what they want to say about something important. Most stories have several interwoven themes. Interpretation of themes varies among readers; each internalizes it in an individual way.

Style

Style is how an author writes—the vocabulary, syntax, and structure that create the story. A tale is all in the telling, so style is all-important. The style needs to reflect the time, place, and characters through dialogue that sounds natural and descriptions that are vivid and fresh.

Point of view is part of style. Many stories are told through the voice of the main character, who reports events in a first-person narrative, solely from his or her point of view. This allows readers to understand thoroughly the thoughts of that character and often provokes a strong identification with that character. Another point of view, third-person limited, limits the information that is conveyed to what a particular character could logically know, but it does so in a more detached tone, using third-person rather than first-person pronouns. Omniscient narrators, ones who are all-knowing, can reveal the thoughts and inner feelings of several characters. They can move about in time and space to report events from an unbiased position. This point of view allows readers to know a great deal about what all the characters are thinking and doing. It also puts more distance between the reader and the main character because the reader is viewing the protagonist through the narrator's eyes rather than viewing the story world through the protagonist's eyes. Authors generally select one point of view and stick with it throughout the story, although some alternate between two or among several narrators. In a well-written story, the point of view provides a perspective that enriches the story.

Poets and authors who work with nonfiction also work with elements of style as they seek to illuminate the concept or idea that unifies their work. In the chapters that follow, we discuss the unique qualities of the literary elements that define each genre.

Genres in Children's and Young Adult Literature

Category	Brief Description
Poetry and Verse	Condensed language, expression of imaginative thoughts and perceptions, often containing rhythm and other devices of sound, imagery, figurative language.
Folklore	Traditional stories, myths, legends, nursery rhymes, and songs from the past. Oral tradition; no known author.
Fantasy	Stories set in places that do not exist, about people and creatures that could not exist or events that could not happen.
Science Fiction	Based on extending physical laws and scientific principles to their logical outcomes, usually futuristic.
Contemporary Realistic Fiction	Stories could happen in the real world; characters seem real; contemporary setting.
Historical Fiction	Stories reconstruct life in the past, using realistic actual or fictional characters, events, and historical setting.
Biography/Memoir	An account of a person's life, or part of a life history by someone else or the person him- or herself.
Nonfiction	Informational books that explain a subject or concept using facts about the real world.
Picturebooks	A format in which art and text (if any) are interdependent. All genres appear in picture books.

and nonfiction. This text shows you how to recognize different genres and the variation within them. Following, we discuss each genre, presenting some examples of books that exemplify each genre, and then go on to consider more examples in greater depth in Chapters 3 through 10. Teaching Idea 1.2 presents ways to help young readers distinguish among the genres of fantasy, contemporary realistic fiction, and historical fiction using story picturebooks.

Genres of Literature for Children and Adolescents

• • PICTUREBOOKS • •

Picturebooks are a format, not a genre, a unique combination of text and art. In other words, this format includes examples from many different literary genres. Biography, for example, is intriguingly represented by *Dark Fiddler: The Life and Legend of Nicolo Paganini* (I) by Aaron Frisch with illustrations by Gary Kelley. Jen Bryant's *A River of Words: The Story of William Carlos Williams* (I), illustrated by Melissa Sweet, is not only a terrific biography, but also a Caldecott Honor book. Light fantasy for younger readers is exemplified by *Elephants Never Forget!* (N–P) by Anushka

Ravishankar, who has been called the "Dr. Seuss" of India. Another delightfully illustrated book for younger readers, containing clever rhymes and sparse text, is *Posy* (N–P) by Linda Newberry, illustrated by Catherine Rayner. Wordless books, such as *Wonder Bear* (P) by Tao Tyeu, use silkscreen and water-based ink to convey a magical, exuberant world where anything is possible.

Picturebooks of related poems, such as *Stitchin' and Pullin': A Gee's Bend Quilt* (P–I) (Patricia McKissack, illustrated by Cozbi A. Cabrera), also continue to be popular. Nikki Giovanni's *Hip Hop Speaks to Children: A Celebration of Poetry* (P–I–A) includes contributions by six illustrators and forty-four poets (ranging from Langston Hughes and W.E.B. Du Bois to contemporary poets), and includes a CD with readings of the poems. Joyce Carol Thomas won a King Honor award for her poetry in *The Blacker the Berry* (P), while Floyd Cooper's illustrations earned him the King Illustrator award.

Informational picturebooks of various types have increased in both number and quality. A wonderful example is *The Way We Work: Getting to Know the Amazing Human Body* (I) by David Macaulay. *Monarch and Milkweed* (P–I), by Helen Frost, illustrated by Leonid Gore, describes one of nature's most harmonious relationships between a butterfly and the specific plant it feeds on.

In the last fifteen to twenty years, pictures have changed both physically and conceptually. In terms of physical appearance, the rise of computer technology

Teaching Idea **1.2**

Compare Picturebooks of Past and Present

Ask students to gather picturebooks of the past from parents, grandparents, relatives, neighbors, friends, librarians, antique book dealers, flea markets, or garage sales. If possible, visit a museum or library collection of historical children's books to examine the books at close range. If you cannot locate early books, select reprinted classics, such as *The Tale of Peter Rabbit*. Choose some of the early Newbery and Caldecott Medal winners available at your public library. Collect several recent picturebooks, preferably award winners, to compare with the old. Prepare a comparison chart similar to the following.

	Old Title	New Title
Color		
Style of Art		
Relation to Story		
Quality of Art as Art		
Attractiveness		
Visual Appeal		
Portrayal of Children		

Questions to Ask about the Books

✿ What do you think about the art?

✿ Is the art coordinated with the text?

✿ What differences in the use of color, media, or other artistic elements do you notice?

✿ What are the children like in the early books? In later books?

After completing the chart, discuss the differences the students found.

that allows artists to "draw" and produce color with digital media such as Adobe Photoshop has dramatically changed the potentials for picturebook illustration. As well, picturebooks have changed physically because of the ways in which they have begun to become hybrid blends of graphic novels, Japanese manga, comic books, film, and other forms of art that utilize both words and visual images to convey meaning. One of the great events in picturebooks in the last few years has been the awarding of the Caldecott Medal to *The Invention of Hugo Cabret*, a book by Brian Selznick containing more than five hundred pages of text and hundreds of pictures. (See Chapter 3, where we discuss these physical changes in more detail.)

Picturebooks have also changed conceptually in the last few years. Children seem more tolerant of ambiguous endings, books that make references to other texts, and books that play with the seemingly solid distinction between fiction and reality. These picturebooks are labeled with the broad term *postmodern*.

Why would these types of picturebooks be important? New types of texts teach children different things

about reading. Just as historical fiction and poetry are different types of texts that children must learn to read differently, so, too, do postmodern picturebooks force readers to read in new ways. For example, readers learn to be satisfied with ambiguous endings; to accept multiple interpretations; to play with stories instead of taking them at face value; and to understand the humor of combining different texts together. In these ways, postmodern picturebooks give children the opportunity to become more critical and thoughtful readers. See Chapter 3 for further discussion of these highly entertaining and sophisticated picturebooks, and for a list of exemplars.

• • POETRY AND VERSE • •

Poetry is the shorthand of beauty; its distilled language captures the essence of an idea or experience and encompasses the universe in its vision. Emerson suggests that poetry says the most important things in the simplest way. A lot of poetry is rhythmic and rhymed, appealing to the ear as well as to the mind and emotions, but many wonderful poems are in free-verse or concrete forms as well.

*With a dual text containing the cat's story and haiku in both English and Japanese, Mark Reibstein explores the ancient Japanese concept of Wabi Sabi. Ed Young's brilliant collage illustrations for **Wabi Sabi** create a profound sense of the multilayered depth of life.*

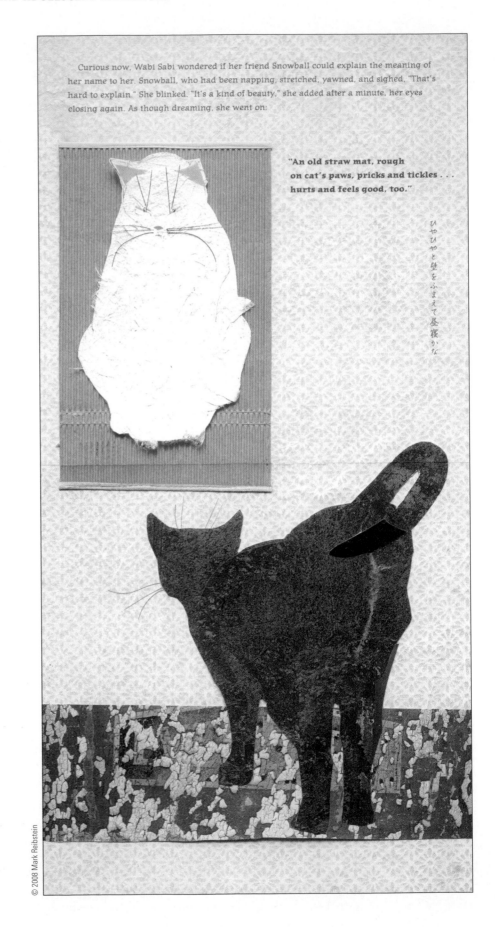

Curious now, Wabi Sabi wondered if her friend Snowball could explain the meaning of her name to her. Snowball, who had been napping, stretched, yawned, and sighed, "That's hard to explain." She blinked. "It's a kind of beauty," she added after a minute, her eyes closing again. As though dreaming, she went on:

"An old straw mat, rough
on cat's paws, pricks and tickles . . .
hurts and feels good, too."

ひやひやと壁をふまえて昼寝かな

Carin Berger's spare yet evocative illustrations in **The Little Yellow Leaf** *demonstrate a restrained use of stylized graphic design that perfectly matches the sparse text.*

The best poetry and verse—from nonsense rhymes and limericks through lyrical and narrative poetry—shape an experience or idea into thoughts extraordinary.

Poetry not only varies across form, but also across audience and content. Paul Fleischman's Newbery Medal–winning *Joyful Noise: Poems for Two Voices* (I), a collection of poems about insects, has delighted countless teachers and young readers for more than twenty years with its witty word play and brilliant use of sound to evoke meaning. Kristine O'Connell George's *Fold Me a Poem* (P–I), stunningly illustrated by Lauren Stringer, offers young readers the opportunity to savor both words and images in a picturebook containing a series of poems inspired by origami. Marilyn Nelson creates a full biography through poetry in *Carver: A Life in Poems* (A), and Andrea Cheng tells a poignant story in her verse novel, *Where the Steps Were* (I). Avis Harley employs varied forms of poetry in *The Monarch's Progress: Poems with Wings* (I).

An increase in the number of books of poetry published each year reflects an increase in interest over the past twenty-five years. Parents have discovered that poetry lulls children to sleep at night. Teachers have discovered that poetry encourages reading, expands oral language development, provides techniques for young writers to experiment with, and enriches experiences across the curriculum. Researchers have found that poetry learned by heart in childhood stays in the mind for a lifetime. Today, publishers who once published only one or two poetry books per year create entire divisions devoted to poetry. We explore poetry in Chapter 4.

• • FOLKLORE • •

Folklore is composed of stories passed down through generations by word of mouth. As such, they have no known author. As people told the stories to one another, they changed and molded them to suit their fancy. Eventually, collectors such as Charles Perrault and the Brothers Grimm wrote the stories down. Over time, other retellers have continued to shape the stories. Folklore reflects the values of the culture in which it grew; it encompasses universal experiences as shaped by individual cultures.

Folklore comes in many forms, including *nursery rhymes* such as those from Mother Goose; *folktales* and *fairy tales* such as the Brer Rabbit stories or Cinderella

© 2008 Beth Krommes

*Susan Marie Swanson was inspired by the pattern of traditional cumulative poems for **The House in the Night**, a contemporary good-night book. Beth Krommes's Caldecott Medal–winning scratchboard and watercolor illustrations highlight the relationship between darkness and light.*

tales; *tall tales* exaggerating the strength and riches of America, such as John Henry and Paul Bunyan; *fables*—simply told, highly condensed morality tales—such as "The Boy Who Cried Wolf"; *mythology*, which explains the origins of the Earth and the relation between humans and gods; *pourquoi stories*, which explain why things are as they are; *hero tales, epics*, and *legends*, such as Robin Hood and Beowulf; and *folksongs*.

Folklore comes from around the world, and what is available today reflects an increasingly international view. Similarly, as the composition of North America has become increasingly multicultural, folklore for children has expanded beyond a predominantly Western European tradition to include folklore of many cultures. Virginia Hamilton's posthumously published picturebook retelling of a Gullah tale, **Bruh Rabbit and the Tar Baby Girl** (P), illustrated by James Ransome, is a wonderful addition to a growing number of books that are retellings of African American tales. Classic stories such as **Beowulf** (I–A), retold and illustrated by James Rumford, continue to delight young readers. Paul Fleischman has

highlighted the multiple cultural origins of the classic Cinderella tale in **Glass Slipper, Gold Sandal** (I). We discuss folklore in Chapter 5.

• • FANTASY • •

Fantasy is imaginative literature distinguished by characters, places, or events that could not happen in the real world. Animals can talk, inanimate objects have feelings, time follows the author's rules, and humans accomplish superhuman feats. Fantasy ranges from picturebooks containing talking animal stories for very young children to complex novels for older readers that explore universal truths. Although fantasy stories could not possibly happen in reality, their carefully constructed plots, well-developed characters, and vivid settings cause readers to suspend disbelief.

The fantasy genre continues to grow as modern fantasy writers create powerful stories redolent with the legacy of folklore and ancient tales. From E. B. White's well-loved **Charlotte's Web** (P–I) to the success of **Harry**

Potter and the Sorcerer's Stone (ɪ) and the subsequent books in the series, the genre of fantasy is thriving. The final book in Philip Pullman's **His Dark Materials** trilogy, *The Amber Spyglass* (ᴀ), won Great Britain's prestigious Whitbread Book of the Year Award in 2001. In 2004 Kate DiCamillo won the Newbery Medal for her fantasy *The Tale of Despereaux* (ᴘ–ɪ). Kathi Appelt's *The Underneath* (ɪ), a National Book Award finalist and Newbery Honor winner, explores love and hate, vengeance and mercy. Writers continue to create stories that transport readers to a world of the imagination, and young readers continue to clamor for their books. F. E. Higgins's *The Black Book of Secrets* (ɪ), first published in the United Kingdom, is a wonderful combination of mystery, adventure, and fantasy in a historical setting, with great appeal to young readers. Fantasy series books continue to be immensely popular as well. We explore fantasy in Chapter 6.

• • SCIENCE FICTION • •

Science fiction is an imaginative extrapolation of fact and theory: stories project what could happen in the future through a logical extension of established theories and scientific principles. Science fiction describes worlds that are plausible and that could exist someday. Scientific advances cause writers to speculate about the consequences of those advances; science fiction is the result. For example, space travel led to stories of space colonies and intergalactic wars. Garbage pileups led to stories of people and places drowning in garbage.

Nancy Farmer's *The House of the Scorpion* (ᴀ), winner of both a Printz Honor and a Newbery Honor, is an outstanding example of contemporary science fiction. Farmer presents a future world in which cloning has become a way for the rich and powerful to prolong their own lives, and drug trafficking has created countries ruled by drug lords. Lois Lowry spells out another possible future world in *The Giver*, *Gathering Blue*, and *Messenger* (ᴀ). *The Giver* is one of the most popular science fiction books with teachers and students alike. Suzanne Collins's *The Hunger Games* (ᴀ) is a very popular novel in which a dystopian society sacrifices teenagers through mortal combat. Neal Shusterman's *Unwind* (ᴀ) involves a world in which teenagers age backward—retroactive abortion. A discussion of science fiction appears in Chapter 6.

• • CONTEMPORARY REALISTIC FICTION • •

Contemporary realistic fiction is set in modern times with events, settings, and characters that could occur in the real world. Authors create characters, plots, and settings that stay within the realm of possibility, and many readers respond to these stories as if the characters were actual people.

Realistic fiction grapples with a wide range of human conditions and emotions. Writers address contemporary problems such as hunger, divorce, drugs, and homelessness as well as themes such as growing up, making friends, and falling in love. Both picturebooks and novels address the experiences of today's world, as Patricia Reilly Giff does in *Pictures of Hollis Woods* (ɪ–ᴀ). There is also humorous contemporary realistic fiction, such as Marla Frazee's picturebook *A Couple of Boys Have the Best Week Ever* (ᴘ), a Caldecott Honor book. In this case, the sly humor lies in the illustrations.

Contemporary realistic fiction contains books that are about sports, adventure stories and animal stories, mysteries and romances. Many of the series books that young readers devour are also realistic fiction, such as Sara Pennypacker's **Clementine** series and Judy Blume's **The Pain and the Great One** series. Contemporary realistic fiction writers today write knowingly from many cultures and lifestyles, as in Sherman Alexie's *The Absolutely True Diary of a Part-Time Indian* (ᴀ), a portrayal of the life of a teenager straddling life on the reservation and at the all-white school he attends. The frequent illustrations, ostensibly created by the protagonist, illuminate both character and situation in this funny, poignant novel that was a National Book Award winner. We discuss contemporary realistic fiction in Chapter 7.

• • HISTORICAL FICTION • •

Historical fiction tells stories set in the past; it portrays events that actually occurred or possibly could have occurred. Authors create plot and character within an authentic historical setting. Once a genre in which history was retold from an all-white, and usually all-male, point of view, today we are fortunate to have skilled authors writing from careful research and from various cultural perspectives. Historical fiction ranges from stories set in prehistoric times to those reflecting the issues and events of the twentieth century. The stories are usually told through the perspective of a child or adolescent who is living life in a particular time and place. Collectively, historical fiction for children and young adults now represents a broad range of voices and cultures.

Although much historical fiction is written for intermediate and advanced readers, such as Laurie Halse Anderson's *Chains* (ᴀ), Sharon Draper's *Copper Sun* (ᴀ), and Christopher Paul Curtis's *Elijah of Buxton* (ɪ), there also are many fine picturebooks—such as Karen Hesse's *Spuds* (ᴘ), illustrated by Wendy Watson—that bring the past to life for younger readers. We discuss historical fiction in Chapter 8.

• • BIOGRAPHY • •
AND MEMOIR

Biography tells about a real person's life. The subjects of biography are usually people who are famous, such as national leaders, artists, sports figures, writers, or explorers, but there are also many biographies and memoirs that are about "ordinary" people who do extraordinary things. Like historical fiction, biography has become increasingly diverse; today, the stories of many people from many cultures and parts of the world are available for young readers. These stories are told both in picturebooks and in lengthy texts.

Every biography bears the imprint of its author; although the story of the person's life provides the basic facts, the writer selects, interprets, and shapes elements to create an aesthetic work. Tonya Bolden's *M. L. K.: Journey of a King* (I–A), winner of the Orbis Pictus Award, is a combination of carefully selected archival photographs and compelling writing that merge to present the man behind the hero. In *The Life and Death of Adolf Hitler* (A), James Cross Giblin presents a chilling portrait of one of history's worst villains.

Like biographies, autobiographies and memoirs are stories of a person's life, but they are written by the subjects themselves. Over the years, a number of memoirs from children's and young adult authors have been produced. Chris Crutcher's *King of the Mild Frontier: An Ill-Advised Biography* (A) and Walter Dean Myers's *Bad Boy* (A), among others, offer readers insight into how the lives of these authors shaped the books those readers enjoy. Peter Sís's *The Wall: Growing Up Behind the Iron Curtain* (I), winner of the Sibert Award, is a brilliant visual depiction, supported by text, of his childhood and young adulthood in Prague. The book explores his quest for freedom, and freedom of expression, as it shaped his artistic life. We discuss biographies and memoirs in Chapter 9.

• • NONFICTION • •

Nonfiction books are informational sources that explain a subject. Children are naturally curious about the world they inhabit. They observe and explore, question and hypothesize about how this world works. Nonfiction outnumbers fiction in most children's libraries and is available for children from preschool through the advanced grades.

Nonfiction presents information in a variety of formats: as picturebooks and photo essays, as how-to manuals, and as descriptive or expository texts. Alphabet and counting books, once intended only for the very young, now have sophisticated formats in which artists demonstrate their talents. Books designed to inform have evolved into books designed to inform and delight.

Nonfiction covers diverse topics, ranging from dinosaurs to endangered species, cathedrals to igloos, triangles to probability, history to philosophy, artistic design to book construction. Most contemporary nonfiction books are works of art as well as works of fact. For example, Kadir Nelson's *We Are the Ship: The Story of the Negro Baseball League* (A) reflects Nelson's passion for the game and the men who played it in both text and illustration. Winner of the Sibert Award for nonfiction, this book also received the King Book Award and was a King Illustrator Award Honor book. Lisa Westberg Peter's *Our Family Tree: A Story of Evolution* (P), illustrated by Lauren Stringer, is also beautiful as well as informational.

Informational books about any topic you might imagine appear on library shelves. The interests of contemporary society, current events, and new insights into history, science, art, or other disciplines appear in nonfiction for young readers. In addition to concept books for young readers, discussed in Chapter 3, and authentic biographies, discussed in Chapter 9, we explore other nonfiction in Chapter 10.

These examples demonstrate the depth and breadth that marks literature for young readers today. We continue to see innovations in what our talented writers and illustrators offer to these readers, including experimentation with genre and technique, blurring of audience boundaries, increasing diversity and globalization, and contemporary topics.

Current Trends

• • BUILDING ON THE PAST • •

In 2000, Roger Sutton, editor-in-chief of *The Horn Book Magazine*, asked several literary critics to hypothesize just how children's literature might look in the new millennium. He also asked a number of writers to choose one book from the twentieth century that he or she would most like to see survive into the twenty-second century. Among those selected were Robert McCloskey's *Make Way for Ducklings* (P), selected by Natalie Babbitt; Philippa Pearce's *Tom's Midnight Garden* (I), selected by Susan Cooper; Frances Hodgson Burnett's *The Secret Garden* (I), selected by Lois Lowry; T. H. White's *The Once and Future King* (A), selected by Jane Yolen; E. B. White's *Charlotte's Web* (I), selected by Katherine Paterson; and Natalie Babbitt's *Tuck Everlasting* (I–A), selected by Tim Wynne-Jones. Other professionals in the field of children's and adolescent books selected one hundred books that shaped the twentieth century. A selection from this list appears in the Booklist at the end of this chapter. Anita Silvey (2004), a former editor for Houghton Mifflin and of *The Horn Book Magazine*, has created her own list in *100 Best Books for Children*, although she couldn't resist adding a few extra titles at the end! How fortunate we are that it is so difficult to select only one hundred.

At the end of the first decade of the twenty-first century, reissues—new editions of previously published books, as opposed to "revisions" or "excerpting"—of "classic" books continue to be popular. Roger Duvoisin's **Veronica** (P) books are available to delight young readers, as are many of the picturebooks that he illustrated for others. Eve Titus's *Anatole* (P), recently reissued on the fiftieth anniversary of its original publication, and *Anatole and the Cat* (P), both illustrated by Paul Galdone—and both Caldecott Honor books—bring the intrepid little Parisian mouse to today's children. Jeanette Winter's outstanding presentation of a story of the Underground Railroad, *Follow the Drinking Gourd* (P–I), was reissued in 2008, twenty years after its original publication. Beloved **Little Golden Books** are reissued as well, often in collections, and historian Leonard Marcus has traced the influence of them on American children's literature in *Golden Legacy: How Golden Books Won Children's Hearts, Changed Publishing Forever, and Became an American Icon Along the Way.*

Older readers, too, benefit from reissues of old favorites. Square Fish Press offers a number of classic stories, such as Madeleine L'Engle's *Meet the Austins* (I–A) and its sequels, in new paperback editions. Marguerite Henry's classic horse stories *King of the Wind* and *Misty of Chincoteague* (I–A) are also currently available, along with Walter Farley's *The Black Stallion* (I–A). Timeless favorites such as these add richness to the array of outstanding books available to today's young readers.

The short story also continues to be popular, especially in adolescent literature. Walter Dean Myers's *145th Street Stories* (A) has been reissued, with a companion collection, *What They Found: Love on 145th Street* (A). The intertwined stories told by multiple narrators present a place and its people with a subtle complexity. Not all short story collections are written as interconnected stories. Sharon Flake's *Who Am I Without Him? Short Stories about Girls and the Boys in Their Lives* (A) speaks to older adolescents through multiple narrators that present varied views of heterosexual relationships. Lori Marie Carlson's edited volume, *Moccasin Thunder: American Indian Stories for Today* (A), contains ten stories by contemporary Native American authors who explore varied aspects of life for contemporary Indian adolescents. Gary Soto's *Facts of Life* (I–A) offers ten stories about pivotal moments in the lives of Latino preadolescents and adolescents living in California. Jennifer Armstrong based her collection *Shattered: Stories of Children and War* (A) around the theme of war. The twelve stories in this powerful book speak eloquently about the effects of war on children. Avi selected twenty-four short stories from both the past and present in his collection for younger readers *Best Shorts: Favorite Short Stories for Sharing* (I).

EXPERIMENTING WITH GENRE AND TECHNIQUE

Creative authors and illustrators ignore prior constraints and convention to expand genre, age-level appropriateness, and formats. Where does Louis Sachar's Newbery Medal–winning *Holes* (I) belong? Is it fantasy or realistic, historical or contemporary? Is it a spoof or a coming-of-age story? Is Brian Selznik's Caldecott Medal book *The Invention of Hugo Cabret* (I) a picturebook, even though it is thicker than some novels? Are the many wonderful novels in verse, such as Jackie Woodson's *Locomotion* (I), Karen Hesse's *Out of the Dust* (A), and Helen Frost's *The Braid* (A), realistic fiction or are they poetry? And do we have a book of poetry or a biography in Marilyn Nelson's *Carver: A Life in Poems* (A)? Where do graphic novels, such as Neil Gaiman's new version of his popular *Coraline* (I–A), fit? They are not picturebooks, but they are stories told through illustration and text, so perhaps they are. These and many other examples demonstrate the creative power of writers and illustrators who are shaping new ways to communicate with young readers.

With increasing frequency, the postmodern novel is becoming a staple of adolescent literature as authors blur genre boundaries by including aspects of more than one genre in their work and push the stylistic envelope with innovative narrative forms (Hunt, 2007). Innovative narrative techniques did not begin with Walter Dean Myers's *Monster* (A), the first Printz Award winner, but this novel certainly stands as an example of the increased experimentation with narrative techniques that marks adolescent literature today. Narrative techniques such as multiple voices and unreliable narrators are increasingly present in books for young readers, especially adolescents.

Innovative literary techniques also appear in books for younger readers. David Almond's *Skellig* (I–A), winner of the 2001 Printz Award, and some of his subsequent books contain magical realism, a literary device usually associated with adult authors from South America in which the boundary between realism and fantasy is blurred so as to make readers accept the fantastic as reality. Laura Amy Schlitz offered children a new format when she wrote the Newbery Medal winner *Good Masters! Sweet Ladies! Voices from a Medieval Village* (I), which is not really a set of short stories, but is perhaps best described as a set of verbal portraits meant to be read either silently or aloud before an audience. The Library of Congress calls this book a collection of one-person plays. Lois Lowry's innovative *The Willoughbys* (I) is a humorous parody of many old classics, with high melodrama and a perfectly happy ending.

Conceptually, picturebooks have undergone dramatic changes. The very concept of "story" has been radically altered in what are commonly termed *postmodern* picturebooks. This word is difficult to define and is used by theorists in a variety of ways, but the types of picturebooks we might call "postmodern" seem to have some identifiable characteristics. Examples of these picturebooks are *Black and White* (P–A) (David Macaulay, 1990), *The Stinky Cheese Man and Other Fairly Stupid Tales* (P–A) (Jon Scieszka, 1992), and David Wiesner's (2001) version of *The Three Pigs* (P–A).

Sipe and McGuire (2008), combining and synthesizing the work of several scholars, list six characteristics of postmodern picturebooks:

1. Blurring the distinctions between "high culture" and popular culture, the categories of traditional literary genres, and the boundaries among author, narrator, and reader.

2. Subversion of literary traditions and conventions, and undermining the traditional distinctions between the story and the outside "real" world.

3. Intertextuality—texts referring to other texts—is present in all writing, but in postmodern texts, this layering of texts is made explicit and often results in strange and amusing juxtapositions.

4. Multiplicity of meanings, so that there are many possible pathways through the story, a high degree of ambiguity, and endings that are often ambiguous and open-ended.

5. Playfulness, in which readers are invited to manipulate the text, "enter" it and control it, and generally subvert the story.

6. *Self-referentiality*, a term that refers to the types of stories that refuse to allow readers to have what Louise Rosenblatt calls a "lived-through" experience of the story. Instead, the story pushes readers away, as if to say, "What you are reading is not real—remember that it's just a story."

In Japan, graphic novels, in the form of manga, have been popular for many decades, and the increasing globalization of children's and adolescent literature brought them to the attention of North American readers (Michaels, 2004). Older children and adolescents responded with great delight. Although Art Spiegelman's **Maus** books were not intended for an adolescent audience, young readers quickly made them their own. Other popular adult authors, such as Neil Gaiman in his **Sandman** series, have produced graphic novels that enthrall young readers, such as Gaiman's recent recast of *Coraline* (I–A).

The graphic novel, with its resemblance to a long and complicated comic book, has come into its own as another form of art that combines words and visual images in synergistic ways. A graphic novel, Gene Luen Yang's *American Born Chinese* (A), won the Printz Award in 2007. It was also a National Book Award finalist. This alone signals a new respect for a sophisticated art form that many had dismissed as "light reading." In fact, many of the newest graphic novels, such as David Almond's graphic novel within a novel, *Savage* (A), Brian K. Vaughan's *Pride of Baghdad* (A), and Don Wood's *Into the Volcano* (I–A) have extremely serious themes and plots and have given inspiration to those who work in the world of picturebooks. In our opinion, the enormous potential of this new form has yet to be realized.

Just as the distinctions among various literary genres are becoming less clear, the distinction among the formats of comics, graphic novels, and picturebooks are blurring. We predict that this trend will continue until the distinctions become less and less useful, and we begin to think of picturebooks, comics, and graphic novels as forms of "sequential art" (Eisner, 2008). Australian Shaun Tan was awarded a Boston Globe–Horn Book Special Citation for Excellence in Graphic Storytelling for his stunning *The Arrival* (I–A). This gorgeous book is part wordless picturebook, part graphic novel, wholly imaginative, and eloquently speaks to the immigrant experience.

● ● BLURRING AUDIENCE ● ●
BOUNDARIES

Picturebooks are not just for small children anymore. There seem to be increasingly more picturebooks whose intended audience is clearly older readers. *Woolvs in the Sitee* (I–A), by Margaret Wild with illustrations by Anne Spudvilas, is highlighted in Chapter 3, along with several other outstanding examples of books in picturebook format that have an older set of readers in mind. Picturebooks, one of the robust forms of literature for children, have expanded their horizons to include older readers.

With the resurgence of adolescent literature came the resurgence of what we call "crossover" books, books that are written for adolescents that adults read and books written for adults that adolescents adopt as their own. Crossover books continue to be popular. For example, Yann Martel's *The Life of Pi*, which won Great Britain's coveted Booker Prize, delights many young readers. Mark Haddon's *The Curious Incident of the Dog in the Night-Time* (A) was published in two editions—one for adults and one for adolescents (Wynne-Jones, 2004). It won the 2003 Whitbread Book of the Year Award and is told from the point of view of a young protagonist with Asperger's syndrome. Markus Zusak's *The Book Thief* (A) crossed audience lines as many adult book clubs read and discussed this powerful novel set in World War II Germany, not caring at all that it was marketed as a young adult novel.

• • INCREASING DIVERSITY • •
OF CONTENT

New ideas and topics always appear in literature, as literature itself reflects what is happening in our changing world. Today's books present challenging content by exploring diverse, contemporary ideas and experiences, including specific cultural experiences as well as aspects of popular culture. M. T. Anderson, known for the brilliant style in *Feed* (A), the science fiction novel that explores the ramifications of popular culture, gives adolescent readers a very different experience in his far-reaching crossover novels, *The Astonishing Life of Octavian Nothing, Traitor to the Nation, Volume I: The Pox Party* and *The Astonishing Life of Octavian Nothing, Volume II: The Kingdom on the Waves* (A). These weighty novels, and those to come, present a searing story of racial exploitation and discrimination that turns a cold eye on American history and its mythology. Sharon Draper's *Copper Sun* (A) depicts slavery in graphic detail, not flinching from the ramifications of a young African woman being "given" to a white male as a birthday present. Louise Erdrich's *The Birchbark House, The Game of Silence*, and *The Porcupine Year* (I) offer a Native American view of the expansion of the United States.

Today, we find ever more books in every genre that deal explicitly with a wide range of serious content and from increasingly varied perspectives. Laurie Halse Anderson's popular novel *Speak* (A) offers readers the diary of an emotionally disturbed and sarcastically witty young woman as she is struggling to recover from a major trauma. Books like Patricia McCormick's *Cut* (A) and Chris Lynch's *Inexcusable* (A) take readers into the minds of adolescents who are spiraling out of control. David Levithan's *Boy Meets Boy* (A) allows adolescents to consider sexuality from varied perspectives. From sex to drugs to violence to racial hatred to just about anything you can imagine—literature is full of ideas that are worth talking about.

The upsurge in the popularity of adolescent literature and the many innovative writers producing books for adolescent readers extended its audience. Now, review journals such as *The Horn Book Magazine* distinguish between young adult fiction for middle school readers and that for high school readers. Indeed, this distinction became necessary because of the edgier nature of books for older adolescents. Generally, the fiction for younger adolescents is less intense and graphic.

Literature reflects the interests and concerns of the culture that produces it. Currently, the United States is focused on the people and places in the Middle and Far East. Although in the past there were excellent books set in these countries, such as Suzanne Fisher Staples's *Shabanu* and *Haveli* (A), there has been a recent increase in books set in that region or about people who have fled from that region. *Running on Eggs* (A), a story of friendship between a Jewish girl and a Palestinian girl by Anna Levine, is a positive picture of possibilities for friendship and peace. Daniella Carmi's *Samir and Yonatan* (I–A) also explores Palestinian-Israeli friendship but is less hopeful. Ibtisam Barakat's *Tasting the Sky: A Palestinian Childhood* (I–A) is a memoir recounting her experiences as a young girl caught up in war. Naomi Shihab Nye, a Palestinian American writer, has given us *Sitti's Secrets* (P–I), a lovely picturebook describing an Arab American girl's visit to her Palestinian relatives; her novel *Habibi* (I–A) is based on the same premise but graphically explores the political and social realities of living in Palestine. Her book of poetry, *19 Varieties of Gazelle* (I–A), is again focused on Palestine and offers older readers a glimpse of a culture that is on the brink of being shattered. Deborah Ellis sets her books, including *The Breadwinner* (I), in contemporary Afghanistan. Literature for young readers continues to reflect the concerns of society, both political and social, reflecting the diversity of our increasingly global society.

• • GLOBAL PERSPECTIVES • •

In the late fall of 2002, the International Children's Digital Library (ICDL) was launched, a joint project of the Human-Computer Interaction Laboratory at the University of Maryland and the Internet Archive in San Francisco. By early 2004 there were almost four hundred books online, with plans for an additional ten thousand more by 2009 (Cummins, 2004). Although the system is not yet perfect, the ICDL's goal of providing free access to children's books from around the world to the children of the world is magnificent.

We now have an increasingly robust global literature. International coedition publishing ventures, in which the same book is published simultaneously in several different countries, are developed annually at the Bologna Book Fair, the Frankfurt Book Fair, the London Book Fair, and the Guadalajara Book Fair. International publishing poses special problems, as there are conflicting ideas about how different cultural practices should be presented in "imported" editions. Recently, however, publishers are realizing that keeping the flavor of the original language and customs is more important and that young readers can and do manage unusual words. If a book is culturally "sanitized," readers lose the opportunity to participate in another's world. Organizations such as the International Board on Books for Young People (IBBY), with members from around the world, also help sustain a global perspective. IBBY has national sections in many countries, such as the United States Board on Books for Young People (USBBY). IBBY sponsors the Hans Christian Andersen Awards, an international, prestigious award given annually for writing and illustration.

Members of USBBY, the International Reading Association, the National Council of Teachers of English, and the American Library Association produce books about international literature, such as USBBY's *Children's Books from Other Countries*, edited by Carl Tomlinson and *The World through Children's Books*, edited by Susan Stan. Annual annotated bibliographies such as "Notable Books for a Global Society" from the International Reading Association and that compiled by the ALA's Association for Library Service to Children's International Relations Committee, as well as the USBBY/CBC Outstanding International Books list, keep readers current.

In the United States, books set in other countries include those written by American authors. This practice has long been a part of literature for young readers, and most contemporary writers take great pains to research their material carefully so that they present as accurate a picture of life in another country as they are able. Patricia McCormick's *Sold* (A) is a good example of this type of book, with its powerful portrayal of the experience of a young Nepalese girl sold into a life of prostitution in India. While the accurately depicted circumstances of Lakshmi's life are unbearable, her indomitable spirit never flags.

Books from other English-speaking countries are the most plentiful type of international literature. Canada, Great Britain, and Australia produce the majority of imported books to the United States (Stan, 2002). In most cases, these books are published in the United States, usually, but not always, a little while after publication in the home country. Irishman Eoin Colfer's best-selling **Artemis Fowl** series was a runaway success in America. His 2008 novel *Airman* (I–A) is a rip-roaring adventure set on islands off the Irish coast. Siobhan Parkinson's novel set in Ireland, *Blue Like Friday* (I–A), explores family dynamics and friendship in a manner that crosses national boundaries. Mimi Grey's *Traction Man Meets TurboDog* (P), a companion to her popular *Traction Man Is Here* (P), a Boston Globe–Horn Book Award winner, appeals to young readers in many countries other than her native England, with its spirited graphics and text. Helen Ward's *Varmints* (I), hauntingly illustrated by Marc Craste, is an imaginative science fiction picturebook from England that poses questions important to young readers everywhere. Venezuelan Menena Cottin offers young readers an intriguing experience in *The Black Book of Colors* (P), illustrated by Rosana Faria and translated by Elisa Amado. Raised black line drawings on black paper, accompanied by both Braille and English text, offers sighted readers an

opportunity to "see" color in a new way and to experience making meaning through their fingertips.

Translated books are less plentiful, less than one percent annually, but awards such as the American Library Association's Mildred L. Batchelder Book Award encourage a truly international exchange. A translation of Josef Holub's *An Innocent Soldier* (A) won that award. Other recent translated books include Jean-Claude Mourlevat's *The Pull of the Ocean* (I), a haunting social fable reminiscent of the story of Tom Thumb, and Mirjam Pressler's *Let Sleeping Dogs Lie* (A), a welcome addition to her several other novels for young readers that have been translated from German.

● ● COMMERCIALISM ● ● AND TECHNOLOGY

Audiobooks for young readers are a lucrative market. Publishing houses such as Random House and HarperCollins are increasing their production of audiobooks, and parents, teachers, and librarians are thinking and talking about their place in the world of children's reading (Varley, 2002). Listening to a book is certainly not the same as reading it, but listening to a wonderful recording of a great book offers its own opportunities for engagement, literary appreciation, and comprehension. Listening to Listening Library's full-cast recording of Philip Pullman's **His Dark Materials** trilogy is as amazing an experience as reading the books. Audiobooks have become so popular that *The Horn Book Magazine* reviews them in a special section that follows their book reviews. The American Library Association publishes an annual list of Notable Children's Recordings as well.

The American Library Association also publishes an annual list of Notable Children's Videos, designating twenty in 2008. Filmmakers, too, have successfully adapted several popular books, such as J. K. Rowling's **Harry Potter** series and Lemony Snicket's **A Series of Unfortunate Events**, Chris Van Allsburg's *The Polar Express*, and Kate DiCamillo's *Because of Winn-Dixie* and *The Tale of Despereaux*.

Commercialism continues to spread. The end of the twentieth century and the early years of the twenty-first century have been a time of dramatic change in the publishing world. We've seen mergers, buyouts, conglomerations, the establishment of new publishers, disagreements among writers and publishers vying for electronic rights, and a continuous search for that one "big book" that will sell millions of copies and ensure financial success. Economics drives business in bookstores and in publishing. Once upon a time, the person who owned the publishing company also ran the company, made the publishing decisions, and knew the authors personally. No more. Big business practices make warm and friendly personal relationships between publishers and authors less likely. The same kind of change is apparent in the bookselling industry as well. Many independent bookstores have vanished; big chains prevail, although the recent "indie" movement among independent bookstores across the nation is promising for the health of the industry.

Still today, there is often more to a picturebook than just words and pictures. Books come with finger puppets and a finger puppet theater, felt board pieces to stuff into the tummy of the old lady who swallowed a fly, and dress-up outfits or animals to cuddle with. Some of the worst books published today are those that are tie-ins to popular television series. In addition to books, we have computers, film, videos, CD-ROM products, videodiscs, microcomputer software, interactive games, book-group blogs, and other Internet activities for a visually oriented audience. The ALA provides an annual list of great websites for kids (go to www.ala.org/ala/alsc; follow the links).

The Challenge of Selecting and Using Literature for Children and Adolescents

Books can play a significant role in the life of the young, but the extent to which they will do so depends on the adults surrounding them. Books and children aren't made of Velcro; they don't stick to each other without a little help from significant others, including parents, grandparents, teachers, librarians, community leaders, volunteers, and others who come into contact with them. Adults are responsible for determining a child's literary heritage by selecting and presenting nursery rhymes, traditional tales, beautiful poetry, arresting picturebooks of all kinds, great novels, and riveting nonfiction. This selection process is neither easy nor without pitfalls. Knowing the literature is important. Knowing children and their community is equally important.

• • CONSIDERING • • LITERARY EXCELLENCE

Selecting books to offer to young readers is a multidimensional task. For teachers and librarians, this process is even more difficult because they are selecting a large number of books to use with many children from varied backgrounds. Because of the diversity and richness in children's literature today, readers' experiences with books can be infinitely varied. With so much to choose from, we as teachers and librarians can select high-quality

literature: books that use interesting language in creative ways, develop important ideas, are potentially interesting to children, and (through picturebooks) contain artistically excellent illustrations. Characteristics of excellence in each genre are summarized in Figure 1.4. We elaborate on and explore these characteristics in Chapters 3 through 10. In this text, we focus on "literary quality," as we believe that the books we put into the hands of young readers should be the best we have to offer. We also acknowledge, as Deborah Stevenson has pointed out, that " 'good' is a tremendously complicated and shifting idea" (2006, p. 511), given that readers' needs and experiences as well as cultural values and practices always influence our definition of "good."

• • EVALUATING • • CULTURAL CONTENT

Diversity is a complex notion. Too often those in the mainstream make the mistake of thinking that cultural diversity refers only to people who are different from them, but everyone belongs to a culture, and in fact, to several cultural communities. Our cultures are woven from many diverse strands; we all live in families and communities that draw on a wealth of knowledge and skills to help them function (Moll, 1994). Cultural diversity is wider than race, ethnicity, gender, sexual preference, or exceptionalities; it also involves values, attitudes, customs, beliefs, and ethics. From this perspective, all children's books could be considered culturally diverse in relation to one another. However, because for so long literature for young readers was a literature of the white middle class, it is necessary to pay special attention to books coming from people who are not representative of that group. Selecting good books that reflect a diversity of nationalities, races, and ethnicities, contain a wide configuration of family structures, explore diverse sexual orientations, make readers think about issues of class and gender, and contain characters with exceptionalities that shape their worlds means that young readers will have a wider, more realistic view of how lives are lived in our global society.

Today, all genres contain books from a variety of cultural perspectives, which means that it is now possible to make diversity a central tenet of any literature collection. There are many aspects to consider when selecting books to build a culturally diverse collection. For example, consider the role of culture in a book. Some books have characters that are from a variety of ethnicities or cultures, and often indicate diversity through visual information, such as skin color, eye shape, hair color and style, or the presence of a wheelchair, but present no cultural content. You might think of books of this type as "painted faces" books. If the inclusion of culturally diverse characters is gratuitous or stereotyped, select another book. Sometimes, however, the diversity subtly reinforces the idea

Characteristics of Good Books by Genre

Genre	Text	Illustration
Poetry	Condensed, evocative language	Interprets beyond literal meaning
Folklore	Patterned language, fast-paced plot Sounds like spoken language	Interpretive of the tale and cultural origins
Fantasy	Believable, consistent, logical world Clearly defined conflict Strong characterization	Extends fanciful elements Reflects characterization and events
Science fiction	Speculative extrapolation of scientific possibility vivid and logical Strong characterization	Visualizes imaginative worlds Enhances characterization and plot
Contemporary realistic fiction	Story is plausible Well-defined conflict Strong characterization	Enhances characterization and plot
Historical fiction	Setting affects plot and character Authenticity of details and language	Enhances setting, characterization, and plot
Biography/Memoir	Authentic, vivid representation	Authentic images of life segments
Nonfiction	Clarity, accuracy Stimulating writing	Clarifies and extends facts and concepts Artful design

that we live in a culturally diverse world, one populated by people of different colors, people in wheelchairs, people who live in a variety of situations. Norman Juster's *The Hello-Goodbye Window* (P), illustrated by Chris Raschka and winner of the Caldecott Medal, features an interracial family, but being interracial is not the focus of the book, or of the companion book, *Sourpuss and Sweetie Pie* (P). Culture, as such, is not an important aspect of this book, but the theme of the strength of family is broadened by the diversity depicted.

Other books are about "culture as a concept." Their theme or unifying idea is that culture is important, that people are different yet the same, and, often, that both differences and commonalities need to be acknowledged. Many of these books explicitly state this idea, such as Mem Fox's *Whoever You Are* (P), Aliki's *Marianthe's Story: Painted Words/Spoken Memories* (P), or Jacqueline Woodson's *The Other Side* (P–I).

Other books are "culturally rich," depicting experiences that are explicitly embedded in a particular culture, with setting, plot, and characters inextricably tied to culture (Bishop, 1997, 2007), such as Francisco Jiménez's *La Mariposa* (P–I) or Walter Dean Myers's *Blues Journey* (I–A), illustrated by Christopher Myers. Culturally rich books allow readers to look through a window at characters similar to or different from themselves, to recognize their own culture or learn about another. These books offer young readers the opportunity for a more-than-superficial experience with diverse characters and concepts.

Regardless of the role culture plays in a book, the depiction of culture should be accurate, authentic, and free from stereotypes. Good literature portrays what is unique to an individual culture. It accurately portrays the nuances and variety of day-to-day living in the culture depicted. It does not distort or misrepresent the culture it reflects (Bishop, 1997). At the same time, most stories are about the experience of an individual character, not necessarily representative of a cultural "norm." As Barbara Bader points out, "It is important, too, to have the cultural details be right, although just what *is* right is not always easy to determine. People's experiences and understandings of their experiences vary. Cultures are large, and individuals within cultures are distinct—even in cultures that don't stress individualism. Blatant misinformation and the perpetuation of demeaning stereotypes are one thing, minor mistakes are another" (2007, p. 420).

Determining authenticity, accuracy, and the absence of stereotypes can be difficult. Fortunately, there are a number of resources that can help you make good decisions about which books to include in your collection. The Multicultural Booklist Committee of the National Council of Teachers of English (NCTE) periodically prepares *Kaleidoscope*, an annotated bibliography of multicultural books (defined as books about people of color residing in the United States, Africa, Asia, South and Central America, the Caribbean, Mexico, Canada, and England) as well as books that focus on intercultural or interracial issues. As they read and evaluate books, the committee eliminates those that demonstrate stereotyped images in text or illustration, demeaning or inaccurate use of language, and inaccuracies in text or illustration. The committee does not consider books multicultural when culture is mere tokenism or when it is reflected through the gratuitous inclusion of a sprinkling of words from another language or an occasional character of color in the illustrations (Bishop, 1994).

Problems with perspective are another concern of the committee, and they are a source of debate among the children's literature community. Some argue that anyone outside a particular cultural group cannot hope to write with the understanding and knowledge of an insider and therefore should not try. Some grant that being an outsider makes it more difficult, but contend that good writers such as Paul Goble transcend their outsider status. A good book will "contribute in a positive way to an understanding of the people and cultures portrayed" (Bishop, 1994), whether its author is an insider or an outsider to the culture. However, it helps to note the perspective of the author when deciding on the quality of any book. In *Stories Matter: The Complexity of Cultural Authenticity in Children's Literature*, editors Dana Fox and Kathy Short (2003) have collected a number of previously published articles that explore this issue.

Books representing a particular culture must represent it accurately and, in most cases, with depth. Look for books that avoid stereotypes, portray the values and the cultural group in an authentic way, use language that reflects cultural group usage, and validate readers' experiences while also broadening vision and inviting reflection. As you begin to evaluate books for their cultural authenticity, think about aspects listed in Figure 1.5. You can also consult some of the many sources listed in Figure 1.6.

In Chapters 3 through 10, we discuss the criteria for quality literature in each genre and give examples of books that are among the best of the genre. When appropriate, we also evaluate books on criteria that speak to the quality of the cultural content. If you think of the genre criteria summarized in Figure 1.4 and elaborated in Chapters 3 through 10 as one lens through which to view children's books critically, think of cultural content as a second lens, one that is additional to, rather than a replacement for, the genre criteria. Each informs the other, and any book can and should be evaluated in terms of both its quality as an example of its genre and its cultural content.

Further, we can evaluate a collection of books—whether in a classroom, a school library, or a public library—in terms of both the depth and breadth of the diversity that it represents. It is up to all of us to select individual books that are of the highest merit, both in

Considering Culturally Diverse Literature

- The book is an excellent piece of literature.
- The book depicts diversity as an important but not gratuitous backdrop in a nonstereotyped manner, **or**
- The book explores cultural differences and similarities in an accurate and sensitive manner, **or**
- The book explores a particular culture accurately, demonstrating diversity within as well as across cultures if appropriate, and avoiding stereotypes.
- The book is a positive contribution to an understanding of the culture portrayed.

literary and in cultural terms, and to make sure that a collection is culturally diverse, no matter who the readers are. All readers need outstanding books that are also richly diverse.

It is important to build a diverse collection because culturally diverse books portray the uniqueness of people while demonstrating a common humanity that connects us all. Human needs, emotions, and desires are similar; books can help us appreciate the similarities as well as celebrate the uniqueness of cultural groups. North America, once considered a melting pot where cultural differences disappeared, is more like a patchwork quilt today—patches of varying colors, textures, shapes, and sizes, all held together by a common thread of humanity (Jackson, 1992).

Children's books offer opportunities for building background knowledge and understanding about the world. Picturebooks, poetry, folklore, realistic and historical fiction, biographies, and nonfiction that demonstrate cultural diversity are available for a wide range of readers. With the help of these books, we can work toward the goal of cross-cultural understanding.

STANDARDS, MANDATES, TESTS, AND TIME TO READ

Although there are many joys in sharing books with young readers, there are also many challenges. One such challenge is finding time in the school day to read with

Figure
1.6

Resources for Considering Culturally Diverse Literature

The following is a selection of the many books that you might want to consult when selecting culturally diverse literature.

Bishop, Rudine Sims, *Free Within Ourselves: The Development of African American Children's Literature*

Fox, Dana, and Kathy Short, *Stories Matter: The Complexity of Cultural Authenticity in Children's Literature*

Harris, Violet, *Teaching Multicultural Literature in Grades K–8*

_____, *Teaching with Multiethnic Literature, K–8*

Helbig, Althea, and A. R. Perkins, *Many Peoples, One Land: A Guide to New Multicultural Literature for Children and Young Adults*

Horning, Kathleen, Ginny Moose Kruse, and Megan Schliesman, *Multicultural Literature for Children and Young Adults*

Kaleidoscope (available through the National Council of Teachers of English and now in its fourth edition)

Lehr, Susan, *Beauty, Brains and Brawn: The Construction of Gender in Children's Literature*

Miller-Lachmann, Lynn, *Our Family, Our Friends, Our World*

Pratt, Linda, and Janice Beaty, *Transcultural Children's Literature*

Quintero, Elizabeth, and Mary Kay Rummel, *American Voices: Webs of Diversity*

Smith, Henrietta, *The Coretta Scott King Awards: 1970–2004*

Stan, Susan, editor, *The World through Children's Books*

Tomlinson, Carl, editor, *Children's Books from Other Countries*

A committee of the International Reading Association also generates a list, "Notable Books for a Global Society," published annually in the February issue of *The Reading Teacher*. See also www.usbby.org for a listing of excellent new international titles.

students. In the past few years, our schools have been under extreme scrutiny, and teachers under extreme pressure. We have standards in most states that describe what schoolchildren should be able to do at each grade level. This is a good thing, when the standards are sound, as we all should know the goals that we are trying to reach. National organizations, too, have set national standards. The International Reading Association and the National Council of Teachers of English worked together to create Standards for the English Language Arts, which can be found at the websites of those organizations (www.reading.org and www.ncte.org). If you examine these standards, you will find that many of them can best be met through the combination of children's literature and good teaching. The point is that children's literature can help you teach so that your students meet the standards.

Whereas standards can be beneficial and can serve to promote reading, too many national and state-mandated tests can work against the inclusion of children's literature in the curriculum. When a high-stakes test looms, and both a teacher's job and the students' futures are on the line, time to read seems to evaporate. Yet reading a variety of texts for a variety of purposes does serve students well, even when they are taking tests. Generally, students who read the most are also among the best readers and the best test-takers. Creative teachers, knowing that they have an

obligation to prepare their students to do their best but not wanting to allow standardized tests to take over their curriculum, often teach their students how to take the tests—how to read and answer questions—much as they teach their students how to read and understand a genre of literature. Tests, like literary genres, have structures and formats that can be taught so that they are familiar to students. When treated in this manner, preparing for these tests becomes simply another unit.

It is vital that we do not let testing take over our teaching, for if time to read and savor books disappears, there will be fewer avid readers. Books are the secret ingredient that keep children doing the hard work of learning to read, learning to read fluently, and learning to read with comprehension. Much of the recent research on motivation indicates that children's literature plays a central role in engaging readers (Pressley et al., 2003). Reading engaging books, and thinking, writing, and talking about them with others also provide opportunities for students to develop the higher-order thinking skills that will enable them to be successful citizens of the twenty-first century (Galda & Graves, 2006).

For these reasons, and others mentioned at the beginning of this chapter, it is important that we offer wonderful books to our students so that they view books as a vital part of their lives. We must be careful in what we choose.

Even when we are cautious, however, it is not unusual to have a book "challenged" by a parent, community member, or even administrator. Challenges to your students' right to read are called *censorship*.

• • CENSORSHIP • • AND SELECTION

Books about virtually any topic or issue in the world are found in children's and especially adolescent literature. For example, Laurie Halse Anderson's main character in *Speak* (A) remains silent for most of the novel but finally reveals that she has been sexually abused and identifies her attacker. Walter Dean Myers's *Monster* (A) involves the murder of a Korean storekeeper and the trial of a teenage boy for that murder. The wide range of topics covered in children's and adolescent literature gives young people access to a comprehensive picture of their world; it also invites serious attempts to censor what they read. Many people feel that children should not face difficult issues; others believe that difficult issues should be presented in books that reflect the real world children face. Sometimes an author's realistic portrayal of language or customs disturbs adults, as in Kris Franklin's *The Grape Thief* (I–A), which caused some argument about whether the ethnic slurs present in the book as used by the characters in the 1920s small-town setting—were too nasty or not nasty enough to be realistic.

Even books that seem quite harmless, such as Beatrix Potter's *The Tale of Peter Rabbit* (N–P), can cause some adults to want to keep them from children. In the case of *Peter*, many felt that it was sexist because the girls were good and the boy got to have all the fun, and they wanted the book removed from nursery schools in London. The outpouring of challenges to the use of the **Harry Potter** books, and fantasy in general, occurred because many people believe that magic is not fantasy at all, but real, and as such is the work of evil. The point is that although we all have beliefs and preferences, we cannot prevent others from reading, viewing, or listening to the material they choose. That is what the First Amendment is all about. The ALA's Office for Intellectual Freedom publishes a list of frequently challenged books. *Hit List for Children 2* and *Hit List for Young Adults 2* provide resources for withstanding challenges to the targeted books.

Most professional organizations, such as the ALA, the International Reading Association (IRA), and the National Council of Teachers of English (NCTE), believe that parents have the right to decide what their own children read but not the right to tell other people's children what they should read. Sometimes books that teachers and librarians choose for school study provoke criticism from parents or community members. Often parents simply request that their child not read a particular book; it is

easy to make provisions for that. Sometimes, however, an individual parent, school board member, or member of the larger community will request that no child be allowed to read a particular book; this is a bigger problem.

Suppressing reading material is *censorship*, a remedy that creates more problems than it solves. Choosing reading material that does not offend our taste, however, is *selection*—not censorship. Censorship is the attempt to deny others the right to read something the censor thinks is offensive. Selection is the process of choosing appropriate material for readers according to literary and educational judgments.

The NCTE (1983, p. 18) differentiates between selection and censorship in five dimensions: (1) Censorship *excludes* specific materials; selection *includes* specific material to give breadth to collections. (2) Censorship is *negative*; selection is *affirmative*. (3) Censorship intends to *control* the reading of others; selection intends to *advise* the reading of others. (4) Censorship seeks to *indoctrinate and limit access* to ideas and information, whereas selection seeks to *educate and increase access* to ideas and information. (5) Censorship looks at specific aspects and *parts of a work in isolation*, whereas selection examines the relationship of *parts to each other and to a work as a whole*.

The controversy surrounding many books is rooted in a blatant attempt to impose censorship, to limit student access to materials, and to impose the religious and political views of a small segment of society on those whose views may differ. The IRA (www.reading.org), the NCTE (www.ncte.org), the ALA (www.ala.org), and the National Coalition Against Censorship (www.ncac.org) condemn attempts by self-appointed censors to restrict students' access to quality reading materials. Professional associations and most school districts have established procedures for dealing with attempts at censorship. School media specialists or principals need to have a standard process to follow if a book is challenged.

All these organizations have wonderful websites that provide information and guidance about censorship. Go to those websites and familiarize yourself with their information. For example, the NCTE publishes *Guidelines for Selection of Materials in English Language Arts Programs*, in which they advocate for a clear, written policy that reflects local interests and issues for the selection of materials in any English language arts program. Because selection must be tied to community standards, there is no one set of guidelines, but rather general principles: material must have a clear connection to established educational objectives and must address the needs of the students.

NCTE's Anti-Censorship Center (www.ncte.org/ action/anti-censorship) offers a wealth of information about what to do if a book is challenged. There is a site for reporting a censorship incident, as well as a listing of

Electronic Databases for Children's and Adolescent Literature

www.acs.ucalgary.ca/~dkbrown/
A reliable source with a search function for literature resources. Located at the University of Calgary, Canada.

www.ala.org
Access the American Library Association and the awards they administer, as well as the annual lists of notable books, videos, and websites.

www.bookwire.com
Switch back and forth among *School Library Journal*, *Publisher's Weekly*, and *Library Journal* book reviews. You'll visit this website frequently.

www.britannica.com
Access the *Encyclopaedia Britannica*. Full-text articles free of charge.

www.carolhurst.com
Carol Hurst is an informed book person. She posts lively discussions of books to use with suggested thematic units, as well as other pertinent information.

www.cbcbooks.org
Maintained by the Children's Book Council, this site is full of information, including links to author and illustrator sites.

www.childrensliteraturenetwork.org
Contains just about everything you would want in a children's literature website, including links to other good sites.

www.cynthialeitichsmith.com/index.html
Bibliographies of diverse literature and other resources.

www.dawcl.com/
Database of Award-Winning Children's Literature. Search by historical period, gender of protagonist, publication date, format, age of reader, ethnicity, genre, language, setting, keyword, or awards. Lists and brief annotations.

www.education.wisc.edu/ccbc/
The Cooperative Children's Book Center contains reviews of more than fifty thousand books; ccbc-net is an interesting discussion list.

www.loc.gov
The Library of Congress is the place to find book titles by a specific author. Click on "Using Library Catalog" and "Other Libraries' Online Catalog." Conduct a simple search by "last name of author, first name." Click on "Search."

www.lib.muohio.edu/pictbks/search/
Database from Miami University, searchable by keyword or Boolean search to find annotations of more than five thousand picturebooks.

www.nationalgeographic.com
National Geographic has several interactive activities, such as finding the hidden animals in a forest and learning about them.

www.ncte.org
Access the National Council of Teachers of English and the awards they administer.

www.pitt.edu/~dash/folktexts.html
Online versions of many folktales and myths.

www.reading.org
Access the International Reading Association and the awards they administer.

www.teenreads.com/index.asp
Teenagers' reviews of adolescent literature, plus the "ultimate teen reading list."

www.ucalgary.ca/~dkbrown/
Children's literature web guide at University of Calgary. Award winners, annual best books, information on book discussions, teaching ideas, reader's theatre, and authors on the web.

See also Appendix B.

---

sites that contain news reports of censorship. A listing of helpful online resources includes instructions on how to obtain a series of written rationales for the most commonly challenged books, as well as the site for Students' Right to Read, which gives detailed procedures for responding to challenges, including a copy of the "Citizen's Request for Reconsideration of a Work." This form asks those who complain about a book for detailed information through questions that stress the sound educational reasons that the book was selected by the teacher or school.

If a book you have chosen is challenged, don't panic. Get the complaint in writing and take it to your media specialist, principal, or other appropriate school-based person. The most important thing to remember is to select wisely—know your resources for making good selections as well as your reasons for selection.

• • RESOURCES FOR • • SELECTING LITERATURE

The voluminous body of high-quality children's and adolescent literature shows that the field attracts talented writers and illustrators. Creative people respond to and change their world; innovation is abundantly evident in the children's book world. The number of books published continues to grow, which makes selection even more difficult. Our job as teachers, librarians, and parents is to select the best from the vast array of books. The primary goal of this textbook is to help you recognize good literature and to develop your ability to select quality material. Resources that you will find useful are review journals, awards lists, and other material that calls attention to literature for children. As poet Walter de la Mare stated, "Only the rarest kind of best is good enough for children" (1942, p. 9).

Review Journals

Sources of information about new children's and adolescent literature include review resources: *Booklinks, Booklist, Bulletin of the Center for Children's Books (BCCB), The Horn Book Magazine,* the *Horn Book Guide, Publisher's Weekly,* and *School Library Journal.* Although not primarily review journals, *Language Arts, The Reading Teacher, Journal of Children's Literature,* and *Journal of Adolescent and Adult Literacy* contain useful book reviews as well. Descriptions of these and other resources are found in Appendix B.

Book Awards

Many awards, such as the Newbery, Caldecott, and Coretta Scott King Awards, are based on experts declaring that the winners are the outstanding examples of children's literature for the year. The awards have significant educational, social, cultural, and financial impact. Books that receive these awards are read by millions of children around the world. In the United States alone, every public and school library will purchase the appropriate books that win major awards. Winning one of these awards, therefore, also guarantees considerable financial reward for the author, illustrator, and publisher. The awards receive widespread media attention, and winning authors and illustrators receive numerous speaking invitations. A list of the winners and honor books of the major awards, both national and international, appears in Appendix A. There are also many lists of outstanding books published each year, such as the American Library Association's "Notables" list for both children's books and young adult literature. Other, more specific lists are noted in the chapters that follow.

Websites

Teachers and students can access an infinite amount of current information about children's books, authors, illustrators, professional publications, teaching ideas, library collections, conferences, and other activities through the World Wide Web. You need only access to the Internet, a search engine such as InfoTrac College Edition, and a few key terms: "children's literature," "adolescent literature," "young adult literature," "children's books," "children's authors," or "children's illustrators" should get you started. You will find numerous websites to help you find out about children's and adolescent literature. Many of them, such as the Children's Literature Network (www.childrens literaturenetwork.org), will have live links to other sites, including authors' sites.

Many authors have a home page; typing an author's name into a search engine will usually get you there. At the home page you can initiate a conversation, ask questions, learn about the authors' new books, and find out about their speaking appearances. Many publishers have programs online that provide access to teaching ideas, books, and author information. Several publishers sponsor online interviews with authors, illustrators, librarians, teachers, book reviewers, and editors. See Figure 1.7 for some helpful Internet sites.

• • • SUMMARY • • •

The story of children's and adolescent literature intertwines with the social, political, and economic history of the world. Children's and adolescents' books are shaped by prevailing views of what adults believe children should be reading, but also by the amount of time children have to explore books and by competing sources of entertainment available to children. Today, we have a wealth of literature for children and adolescents. We have moved from crude horn books and religious tracts to books of artistic and literary excellence. Young readers are the beneficiaries of this wealth.

Given the history and durability of children's and adolescent literature, the future will certainly be interesting. No doubt we will have more international literature; more culturally diverse writers and artists will present their culture more accurately; global economics will play a stronger role; readers will have ready access to interviews with authors and illustrators on the World Wide Web; and projects such as the IDCL will help bring literature to all children. The many talented writers and illustrators who fill our lives with wonderful books will continue to do so, and new talent and new permutations of genre will never cease to emerge. At the same time, attempts at censorship will increase, as will pressures on schools and libraries in the form of lack of funding, mandated high-stakes testing, and increasing numbers of children who need food, clothes, and stability as well as books. Our world is changing, and literature for children and adolescents will change with it. For now, we have wonderful books to offer our young readers.

Exploring the field of literature for children and adolescents can seem overwhelming at first, but knowledge about books is addictive. The more you know, the more you want to know and to share with young readers. With each new day there is more to know. This textbook will help you begin to explore the wonderful world of books. Enjoy!

Selections from One Hundred Books That Shaped the Century

Four librarian book experts (Karen Breen, Ellen Fader, Kathleen Odean, and Zena Sutherland) chose one hundred books that shaped the twentieth century ("One Hundred Books That Shaped the Century," 2000). An asterisk (*) indicates that the *book* was a unanimous first-round selection. A double asterisk (**) indicates that the *author* was a unanimous first-round selection but that there were differences of opinion over which work(s) to include.

* Cormier, Robert, *The Chocolate War*
Crews, Donald, *Freight Train*
Dahl, Roald, *Charlie and the Chocolate Factory*
dePaola, Tomie, *Strega Nona*
* Fitzhugh, Louise, *Harriet the Spy*
Fleischman, Paul, *Joyful Noise: Poems for Two Voices*
Fox, Paula, *The One-Eyed Cat*
* Frank, Anne, *The Diary of a Young Girl*
* Freedman, Russell, *Lincoln: A Photobiography*
** Fritz, Jean, *And Then What Happened, Paul Revere?*
Gág, Wanda, *Millions of Cats*
Garden, Nancy, *Annie on My Mind*
* George, Jean Craighead, *Julie of the Wolves*
** Hamilton, Virginia, *M. C. Higgins, the Great*
** _____, *The People Could Fly: American Black Folktales*
Hesse, Karen, *Out of the Dust*
Hinton, S. E., *The Outsiders*
Hoban, Tana, *Shapes and Things*
* Keats, Ezra Jack, *The Snowy Day*
Kerr, M. E., *Dinky Hocker Shoots Smack!*
* Konigsburg, E. L., *From the Mixed-Up Files of Mrs. Basil E. Frankweiler*
Le Guin, Ursula, *A Wizard of Earthsea*
* L'Engle, Madeleine, *A Wrinkle in Time*
* Lewis, C. S., *The Lion, the Witch, and the Wardrobe*

* Lobel, Arnold, *Frog and Toad Are Friends*
** Lowry, Lois, *Anastasia Krupnik*
** _____, *The Giver*
** Macaulay, David, *Cathedral*
** _____, *The Way Things Work*
* MacLachlan, Patricia, *Sarah, Plain and Tall*
Marshall, James, *George and Martha*
Martin, Bill, Jr., and John Archambault, *Chicka Chicka Boom Boom*
** McCloskey, Robert, *Make Way for Ducklings*
McKinley, Robin, *The Hero and the Crown*
McKissack, Patricia, *Mirandy and Brother Wind*
* Milne, A. A., *Winnie-the-Pooh*
Minarik, Else, *Little Bear*
Myers, Walter Dean, *Fallen Angels*
* O'Dell, Scott, *Island of the Blue Dolphins*
* Paterson, Katherine, *Bridge to Terabithia*
Paulsen, Gary, *Hatchet*
Pearce, Philippa, *Tom's Midnight Garden*
* Potter, Beatrix, *The Tale of Peter Rabbit*
Raschka, Chris, *Yo! Yes?*
Raskin, Ellen, *The Westing Game*
Scieszka, John, *The Stinky Cheese Man and Other Fairly Stupid Tales*
* Sendak, Maurice, *Where the Wild Things Are*
* Seuss, Dr., *The Cat in the Hat*
Silverstein, Shel, *Where the Sidewalk Ends: Poems and Drawings*
** Steig, William, *Sylvester and the Magic Pebble*
Steptoe, John, *Stevie*
Taylor, Mildred, *Roll of Thunder, Hear My Cry*
Tolkien, J.R.R., *The Hobbit*
** Van Allsburg, Chris, *The Polar Express*
** Voigt, Cynthia, *Homecoming*
Wells, Rosemary, *Max's First Word*
* White, E. B., *Charlotte's Web*
* Wilder, Laura Ingalls, *Little House in the Big Woods*
Zindel, Paul, *The Pigman*
Zolotow, Charlotte, *William's Doll*

Literature in the Lives of Young Readers

But the dam still stood, its great bulk defying the puny efforts of the Minnipins.

Glocken could not believe his eyes. His hand went out to the Whisper, and he struck it again, this time from the other side. And then again. And again. And again. And still the dam stood.

Until suddenly—it simply disappeared.

One moment it was there defying them. And the next moment it had gone into a thousand cracks. And the earth, the stone, the washed-limestone simply went to powder and slid away. With a roar, the released river shot out from under them, roaring down the valley, roaring across the waste, roaring to freedom!

In his excitement Glocken struck the Whisper one last time. There was a sudden fearful crack! Over their heads.

Then the whole mountain fell down on top of them.

—Carol Kendall,
The Whisper of Glocken, *p. 218*

Anna, her head bent forward so that her dark hair makes a tent around her face and the book she is reading, is totally engrossed in the world of **The Whisper of Glocken** (1). When she gets to the part where Silky finds a little gray creature and calls him Wafer, she looks up, sighs, and says, "Mom, Wafer is a perfect name for a gray kitten." She then goes back to her reading, once more lost to the world. Later, when she is finished with the book, she talks about it, wondering aloud how the Minnipins had the courage to leave their valley and venture out into the bigger world, questioning whether she would be that brave. From one book she's found the perfect name for her new gray kitten, has experienced a dangerous journey into an unknown land, and has thought about her personal courage, all without leaving her own living room.

She's been doing this forever. She careened down a hill in a buggy with Max, Rosemary Wells's captivating rabbit, even as she chewed the corners of the sturdy board book. She went with another Max in his private boat to the land of the wild things, played in the rain with Peter Spier's children, and learned to understand the natural world through Joanne Ryder's imaginative nonfiction. She's laughed, cried, absorbed information, experienced danger, engaged in adventures, solved mysteries, and learned a great deal about the world and about herself as she's read book after book. Anna's a lucky child. She's been engaged with wonderful books all of her life.

© Lee Galda

Anna is totally absorbed in the book she is reading. A frequent traveler in the world of books, she knows the pathway well.

Memories of special books stay with us all our lives. The experiences we have during our lives shape and are shaped by the books that are important to us. Like Anna, many who love to read get so engrossed in their books that the real world disappears.

The Power of Literature

Avid readers read poetry to stir their souls, narrative fiction to help them discover who they are, and nonfiction to help them understand their worlds. The importance of reading good books is apparent in both theory (Nodelman, 1996, 1997; Galda, Ash, & Cullinan, 2000; Rosenblatt, 1938/1976; Sipe, 2008) and research (Cunningham & Stanovitch, 1998). Interest in books supports the engagement and motivation that it takes to become a successful reader (Guthrie & Wigfield, 2000). Those, like Anna, who engage with books from a young age and become avid readers have an academic advantage that continues to support their success, regardless of intelligence or circumstances. Avid reading really does make you smarter (Cunningham & Stanovitch, 1998, p. 14).

Reading literature contributes to language growth and development. When children and adolescents read or hear stories read to them, they learn new vocabulary. They encounter a greater variety of words in books than they will ever hear in spoken conversation or on television. Each reader builds an individual storehouse of language possibilities and draws on that wealth when speaking, writing, listening, and reading. Literature also develops readers' facility with language because it exposes them to carefully crafted poetry and prose. Young people who read literature have a broad range of experiences and language to put in their storehouse; they have greater resources on which to draw than do people who do not read.

Outstanding literature helps readers become better writers as well. When students read a lot, they notice what writers do. They see that writers choose from a variety of language possibilities in their writing. When readers

© Lee Galda

A rich array of books and the freedom to read and discuss them helps create avid readers.

write, they borrow the structures, patterns, and words from what they read.

Reading literature promotes skill and growth in reading. Engaging stories, poetry, and information appeal to readers and entice them to read. The more they read, the better they get. The better they read, the more they learn. The more they learn, the more curious they become. And the more curious they become, the more they read. Thus good books provide a way for young people to become motivated and engaged readers.

This love of reading leads to readers seeking out exciting stories, interesting information, and compelling poems; they turn to reading as a source of knowledge, pleasure, and enlightenment. Thus, literature enables young people to explore and understand their world. It enriches their lives and widens their horizons. They learn about people and places on the other side of the world as well as ones down the street. They travel back and forth in time to visit familiar places and people, to meet new friends, to see new worlds, to discover new ideas. They can increase their knowledge, explore their own feelings, shape their own values, and imagine lives beyond the ones they live.

Literature prompts readers to explore their own feelings. Avid readers gain insight into human experience and begin to understand themselves better. When they explore their own feelings, they also understand why others react as they do. Writer Jill Payton Walsh argues that "we cannot understand ourselves at all until we under-

stand ourselves 'longways.' This is the [narrative] mode of understanding that stories promote" (2007, p. 251). Indeed, Nodelman (1996, 1997) and Nodelman & Reimer (2003) argue that it is crucial that children have books that offer them varied depictions of what it is to be human and the tools to understand that there are many ways of being for all people. Nodelman also comments that reading literature gives children a much broader view of the way the world works than the narrow band of normality offered by television and popular culture. Literature enables us to see beyond the messages given to us daily by our own culture. Thus, while some scholars valorize popular culture for the relevance it has to children's lives (Dyson, 2003; Carrington & Luke, 2003), we believe that this is a short-sighted approach. Such scholars also argue that children's literature is an elitist, middle-class phenomenon, not realizing or acknowledging how controlled by hegemonic interests the texts of popular culture are. All young readers need and deserve a rich diet of literature.

Many wonderful books are available to enrich the lives of millions of children and adolescents worldwide, readers who are diverse in their ethnicity, religion, nationality, and social and economic status, but united by commonalities of youth. Literature provides insights into the realities and dreams of young people and of the authors and illustrators who depict those dreams and realities. It reflects life throughout the course of time and across national boundaries. Literature keeps people's dreams alive, presenting a vision of what is possible, helping to shape readers' views of the world. Frye (1970), like Rosenblatt (1938/1976), underscores the role of literature in "educating" the imagination. He argues that the fundamental job of the imagination in ordinary life is to produce, out of the society we *have* to live in, a vision of the society we *want* to live in. In this sense, we live in two worlds: our ordinary world and our ideal world. One world is around us, the other is a vision inside our minds, born and fostered by the imagination, yet real enough for us to try to make the world we see conform to its shape. Literature fuels this imagination. Glenna Davis Sloan (2009) provides an excellent summary of Frye's work, arguing for the continued relevance of his ideas as they relate to literature for young readers. As Robert Coles argues, literature can enrich the moral, intellectual, social, and spiritual lives of young readers (Coles, 1989).

Many speak to the potential of literature:

Any child who finds the healthy escapism of books—one that enlarges the mind rather than narrows it—has gained a lifelong ally. Every human spends a portion of his or her life searching for solace: a kindred spirit, a non-judgmental friend, a sympathetic mirror showing dreams and possibilities. At birth, our parents fill this need. Next, a favorite stuffed animal may take on the same burden, or a pet. How wonderful for a child to discover a similar respite in books that do not preach obvious lessons but instead hold up a mirror revealing something we suspected, but had not yet articulated. At their best, children's books shed light on our inner selves and the world around us, leading us down rabbit holes and over rainbows. (Robinson, 2008, p. 34)

Books are a powerful force in the lives of young readers. Even in today's world of standards, accountability, testing, and electronic media, books form the vital core of an education for the twenty-first century. The richness and diversity that typifies literature today means that teachers, librarians, parents, and young people have a wealth of books from which to select. The power of books to open new worlds, to cause readers to think in new ways—in short, to transform their ways of knowing—makes books the greatest single resource for educating our children to become contributing members of our society.

In Chapter 1, we introduce the world of books for young readers. In Chapters 3 through 10, we explore varied genres of literature for children and adolescents, and in Chapters 11 and 12, we present some effective ways to engage young readers in the classroom and beyond. Here, we describe a transactional view of reading, and then consider the readers themselves, for it is through

Profile

Louise Rosenblatt

Louise Rosenblatt was a remarkable woman with exceptional talent. Her work, which presents theories about the nature of reading and the literary experience, substantially shaped the teaching of literature in schools and colleges.

Rosenblatt brought a scholarly approach to literary criticism, combined with an active concern for the teaching of literature. At a time when it was assumed that the reader's role was to passively receive a meaning from a text, she stressed the idea of the reader actively making meaning by engaging in a transaction with the text, bringing background, interests, and purposes to bear. She also stressed the difference between reading and responding with attention to what is being lived through (an aesthetic experience) and reading with attention focused on what is to be taken and used for a purpose, an "efferent" reading.

Rosenblatt graduated with honors from Barnard College, Columbia University, and went on to receive her doctorate in comparative literature from the Sorbonne. Postdoctoral work in anthropology with Franz Boas and Ruth Benedict at Columbia University inspired her feeling for the contributions of diverse cultures that encourage the creation of a democratic American society, a feeling that permeates her seminal work, *Literature as Exploration*, published in 1938 and currently in a fifth edition. Rosenblatt's primary professorship was at New York University, where she directed the doctoral program in English education. She received a John Simon Guggenheim Fellowship in 1943, the Great Teacher Award from New York University in 1972, the Distinguished Service Award from the National Council of Teachers of English in 1973, and the National Conference on Research in English Lifetime Award in 1990. She was inducted into the Reading Hall of Fame by the International Reading Association in 1992 and the National Council of Teachers of English honored her with a full day of programs to celebrate the fiftieth anniversary of the publication of *Literature as Exploration*. This and her many other works, including *The Reader, the Text, the Poem* (1994), have profoundly influenced how we read and understand literature and the teaching of literature.

Louise Rosenblatt was married to Sidney Ratner, scholar in philosophy and history, for more than sixty years. She died in 2005 at one hundred years of age.

response that young readers engage with books and powerful things happen. We then explore the role of the text in the response process, ending with a consideration of how both texts and readers reflect the beliefs and attitudes of the contexts in which they are produced and read.

A Transactional View of Reading Literature

A *transactional* view of reading postulates that meaning does not reside in the text alone, waiting for a reader to unearth it, but rather is created in the transaction that occurs between a text and a reader. As a reader reads, many factors guide the selection and construction of meaning including personal experiences, abilities, knowledge, feelings, preferences, attitudes, cultural assumptions, and reasons for reading. At the same time, the text itself—the words on the page—guides and constrains the meaning that a reader builds. No matter what kind of book they are reading, readers build meaning that is shaped by the text, even as they shape the meaning. The construction of meaning is a transaction in which text and reader act on each other.

Iser (1978) argues that when we read we engage in anticipation and retrospection: we both anticipate what will happen based on our prior reading, and we look back and revise our ideas about what we have read in light of what we have just read. Thus, good readers move back and forth when they read. Good readers also know that no text contains all they need to know; they realize that they themselves must fill in the gaps or indeterminacies in the text from their own knowledge of the world. This kind of reading is very much influenced by personal experience: the closer a text is to a reader's own experience of the world, the easier it is to read; the farther away, the more work a reader must do in order to understand the worldview from which the text is written (Iser, 1978).

Rosenblatt (1938/1976; 1978), Britton (1970), and Langer (1995) describe two primary ways to approach a text: aesthetic and efferent (Rosenblatt) stances, spectator and participant stances (Britton), and reading toward a horizon of possibilities versus reading toward a point (Langer). Although there are differences in the theories that each have developed, they all agree that there are different approaches to and outcomes from reading. Readers approaching a text from an aesthetic stance (Rosenblatt, 1978) read for the experience, for the opportunity to enter the story world. Although this experience is often visceral and "real," it is virtual rather than actual, requiring not action on the part of the reader but, rather, thought and

emotional connection. This kind of reading offers readers the opportunity to contemplate, to reflect on the ideas presented in the text and their reactions to those ideas, and to develop their own values (Britton, 1970). As a young reader said, "When I was reading I was thinking, what would I do if this happened to me?" (Galda, 1982). In contrast, approaching a text from an efferent stance (Rosenblatt, 1978) means reading for information, for knowledge to use to act in the world. Generally, readers would approach a poem or fictional narrative from a primarily aesthetic stance, a biography or other nonfiction work from a primarily efferent stance. However, rarely are these stances purely one or the other. Rather than being polar opposites that are exclusive of each other, they exist along a continuum, with an aesthetic stance often containing elements of the efferent, and an efferent stance often containing elements of the aesthetic.

For example, if we read a beautiful poem, we would enjoy the experience of the reading but also note the way the poet has crafted those experiences. Reading a piece of historical fiction results in being in that historical story world for the duration of the reading, but probably also results in knowing some facts about that particular time in history. Reading a well-crafted piece of nonfiction offers the opportunity to learn about a particular aspect of our world (perhaps birds) and then to use this knowledge (in this case to identify birds), but the reader also experiences an aesthetic response to the subject, language, format, design, and illustrations. The important point here is that differences in the predominant stance that is adopted lead to different ways of reading and to more or less successful realization of the potential that waits between the covers of any book. Stance helps determine the response that readers develop over time as they read.

It is important to note that, according to Rosenblatt, the stance lies in the reader, not the text. In other words, although some texts may lend themselves to reading from an aesthetic stance, stance is not "in" a text. Poetry and literary texts that are fiction are, from Rosenblatt's point of view, most effectively read and understood when the reader first adopts an aesthetic stance. After this, the reader (or a classroom of readers) can talk about the text's structure, its major images, and the way the author's craft has influenced their reading. In other words, Rosenblatt envisions that readers will first adopt an aesthetic stance and follow this by adopting an efferent stance. Rosenblatt believes that the most complete and mature understandings and interpretations of text involve both stances, though she also stresses the importance of beginning with the aesthetic stance when reading stories and poems. Reading and understanding nonfiction is primarily an efferent task, although most successful readers will also read aesthetically, especially given the outstanding quality of nonfiction for young readers today.

This first grader used both words and pictures to respond to the many nonfiction books he is reading about the natural world. The efferent and the aesthetic are both evident in his response.

Building on the notion of an actively engaged reader described by Rosenblatt, Britton, and Iser, Langer (1995), Benton (1992), and others discuss how reading is *temporal* in nature because the linear processing of language means that readers read over time (rather than instantaneously). Further, as readers move through their reading time, they make predictions and engage in retrospection as they think about the meaning they have created in light of the new ideas they are developing (Benton, 1992). Langer (1995) describes active readers as first being out and stepping into a text, then being in and moving through, perhaps being in and stepping out to think, and, when finished reading, stepping out and thinking about the reading experience, regardless of text or stance. Other cognitive activities that occur across time during aesthetic reading are creating mental images, interacting with the text (as in identifying with characters in narrative fiction), and valuing the text, either through questioning or acquiescing to the ideas presented (Benton, 1992). The journey through the world of story that Rosenblatt, Langer, and Benton describe was summed up nicely by a ten-year-old who declared, "I love books that inhale me!" (Galda, 1982).

The valuing of ideas encoded in a text relates to the *social and cultural dimensions* of reading and responding. Although it is easy to think of reading literature as a private, personal activity, it is actually thoroughly embedded in the social and cultural milieu of the author, the reader, and the reading itself. The creators of texts—the authors—bring to their writing the sum of who they are, and who they are is the result of the expectations of their social and cultural groups. The texts they create reflect these ideologies, existing "within a complex network of ideas and images and cultural values" (Nodelman, 1997, p. 5), just as readers bring their own cultural assumptions with them as they read.

Fish (1980) proposed that readers read in various "interpretive communities" of readers, with each community helping to shape attitudes and beliefs, as well as preferences and ways of interacting with any given text in a particular situation. Readers in communities generally do what they have to do—share their responses with a book group, write a paper, make a diorama, give a report—and these post-reading tasks help shape the way they read. Reading in order to discuss with peers results in responses that are not only the product of an individual reader's transaction with an individual text, but also of that reader's knowledge that he or she will be sharing with others in a specific, community-sanctioned manner. Reading in order to answer the low-level recall questions that comprise many computerized reading programs pushes readers to read everything in a manner that allows them to retain discrete facts, which is problematic when reading poetry and fiction, as discussed previously. Every interpretive community has both explicit and implicit rules for what "counts" as response.

Teachers and scholars (Carter, 2005; Sumara, 1996) point out that, although reading is often public, especially in schools, private reading—reading done with books of one's choice, in a place of one's choice, with no post-reading task to complete—is not only important for readers, but also appropriate for what Carter calls "interior" books (2005). Even private reading, however, is steeped in cultural assumptions and social routines.

Whether private or public, when readers engage with books, the experience can be *transformational*. Engaged reading increases knowledge and helps build values and attitudes (Britton, 1970; Galda, 1998; Rosenblatt, 1978; Sipe, 2000). Reading beautifully crafted nonfiction increases knowledge exponentially. Seeing things as yet unseen, coming to understandings of experienced phenomena, even figuring out how things work, transforms the knowledge that readers call upon to make sense of the world around them. Reading poetry and stories allows readers to bring texts into their lives in a way that helps them define and shape their lives. Reading books in which they recognize themselves or come to know others offers readers the opportunity to reconstruct themselves, to understand themselves and others. These transactional, temporal, social, and cultural aspects of reading and responding to literature intertwine as readers engage with texts in ways that can be transformational. This is where the power of books lies—in the opportunity for transformation that reading affords.

Readers

Who readers are determines how they read. Instead of absorbing "one right meaning" from a text (an elusive concept at best), readers construct meaning as they read based on their own background knowledge, experiences, and skills (Goodman, 1985; Rosenblatt, 1938/1976, 1978). A text that makes one reader cry might bore another; a book read as a ten-year-old brings a different kind of response when read again as a thirteen-year-old; and the cultural values that permeate a text will trigger varying responses in culturally diverse readers. Even though the text remains the same, readers are constantly changing, and therefore will have differing responses depending on their life experiences. Even on re-reading, we never experience the same text in quite the same way. Think, for example, of Shel Silverstein's popular *The Giving Tree* (I). Many readers find this book a charming depiction of selfless love; the tree gives her all to the boy. Others, however, find this an expression of selfishness; the boy takes everything the tree gives and asks for more, giving little in return. Both groups read the same text, and view the same illustrations, but construct entirely different meanings.

As Iser (1978) and others have argued, who readers are and what they have experienced influence their responses to the books they read. The places they have been, the people they know, the attitudes they hold, who they are, what they know, and the way they present themselves to the world all influence how readers read and respond. While there are several category systems that serve to describe frequent responses by a variety of readers, research also has shown that individuals seem to have characteristic ways of responding. For example, three fifth-grade girls with similar backgrounds and schooling were quite different in their approaches to books, but each was individually consistent (Galda, 1982). Four first- and second-grade students showed remarkably different response styles; for example, one reader demonstrated sensitivity toward the feelings of the story characters and another used the story as a springboard for oral performance (Sipe, 1998). Beach, Thein, and Parks (2008) have described how adolescent readers approach

texts in ways that reflect who they are and what they have experienced.

Hickman's (1981) groundbreaking work on response in elementary schools gave us a glimpse at what it might look like, as presented in Teaching Idea 2.1.

For many years, researchers have sought to postulate general response patterns. For example, Bogdan (1990) describes three basic types of response to literature: stock response, kinetic response, and spectator response, although her use of the term is different from Britton's use of the same term. For Bogdan, *stock response* involves evaluating a text in terms of whether its worldview, ideology, and so on conform to the reader's own worldview. In this type of response, readers say something is good or bad based on their own view of how things are or should be and whether the book does or does not support their

Teaching Idea 2.1

Recognizing Response when You See It

Hickman (1981, p. 346) described seven different types of responses that occurred in the elementary classrooms she observed across the course of a school year. Her observations remind us that a response does not have to be an activity, but ranges from individual thoughtfulness to a simple sharing with another to a formal activity. She saw children engaged in

- ✿ Listening behaviors, such as laughter and applause.
- ✿ Contact with books, such as browsing, intent attention.
- ✿ Acting on the impulse to share, reading together.
- ✿ Oral responses such as storytelling and discussion.
- ✿ Actions and drama such as dramatic play.
- ✿ Making things such as pictures, games, or displays.
- ✿ Writing using literary models, summarizing, and writing about books.

Provide your students ample time, an opportunity to linger for a while in the spell of a good book. Provide them with structured response activities, such as the Teaching Ideas that are in every chapter in this text. And provide them with a supportive environment in which to engage with books and make them their own.

view. A response such as "I don't think that books about magic should be in school libraries" would be a stock response. Kinetic response consists of evaluation of a book in terms of whether it packs an emotional punch for the reader, as in "I loved this book because it made me cry." Spectator responses, for Bogdan, evaluate a book on formal structure, use of images, patterns, and language—all traditional literary elements, such as "I thought this book was great because of the striking use of metaphors." Bogdan argues that none of these responses is wrong but that they are all incomplete, that readers need to learn to respond in all three ways.

In his work with young readers, Sipe (2008) has determined that there are five basic ways children respond to picture storybooks. First, some analyze in the traditional manner of talking about the language, characters, plot, setting, theme, and mood of the story. Second, they may make intertextual connections to other texts such as books, movies, videos, and so forth. Third, children also make personal connections, drawing the self to the story or the story to the self. Fourth, they may make "transparent" responses that indicate that, for the moment, the children are "in" the story world (as when they "talk back" to the characters in the text). Finally, children may display "performative" responses that use the story as a platform in imaginative play.

Readers also learn to make connections between their own experiences and knowledge and those portrayed in story or presented in nonfiction. These links between text and world, as Cochran-Smith (1984) describes, not only help readers understand the texts they read, but also allow them to use what they read to understand their own lives. A six-year-old who is living in a new city and, upon seeing a vine-covered building on a corner, asks, "Mommy, are we in Paris?" is using her experience with Ludwig Bemelmans's *Madeline* (N) to understand where she is now living.

Thus, readers use their prior life experiences to understand literature, but they also use literature to illuminate and make sense of their own lives. For example, a combination first/second-grade class, upon hearing Charlotte Huck's *Princess Furball* (P) read aloud by their teacher, engaged in a long discussion (prompted by the frontispiece, which depicts the funeral of Princess Furball's mother) of death and how it affected them. Some children spoke of relatives (grandmothers, uncles, and aunts) who had died and how it had affected them. The children's mood during this discussion was not sorrowful or depressed; on the contrary, the experience of interpreting the frontispiece of *Princess Furball* had enabled them to work through and interpret their own lives in light of the book they were hearing (and seeing).

These ways of categorizing responses flow from the theoretical descriptions of reader response and reflect the observed behavior of readers. The important thing to note is that readers *do* things as they interact with books, and those things they do help shape the meaning they create.

How young readers respond to books is, of course, learned; past experience with books influences how readers read and respond. As Fish (1980) argues, often this relates primarily to the contexts in which these experiences occurred. The readers described by Bogdan or Sipe or any of the many researchers offering us categories of response have all learned to respond as they do through their interaction with others around books. For example, years of reading stories in classrooms in which the teacher asks questions that prompt recall of specific information from stories and poems will force young readers away from their naturally aesthetic responses into a less-productive efferent stance. One parent, for instance, talking about how her son learned to hate reading in school, described how he first reads the questions that he has to answer at the end of each reading selection, and then scans the story or poem to find the answers to those questions. Of course, he misses the story or poem, and never connecting means that he misses the pleasure that aesthetic reading can bring. Another middle-school boy, an avid reader of long, complex animal fantasies at home, felt that he had become a "poor" reader because of his performance on the tests in a popular computer-based reading program. He had learned to read fiction for the virtual experience; the tests asked him to read efferently, for very specific and often unimportant details. Consequently, he chose less complex novels for his school reading. Readers who take great delight in nonfiction and seek it out, only to have adults dismiss this kind of reading material as not important, eventually come to think of themselves as nonreaders. It is only through positive experiences with an array of books that the tremendous benefits of avid reading described by Cunningham and Stanovich (1998) are realized.

Readers who have had an array of pleasurable experiences with books will spontaneously compare stories, share information, knowledgeably discuss authors, and bring their ideas about how literature works and their experiences with other texts to their reading. Many researchers such as McGinley and Kamberelis (1996); Sipe (1999); Many and Wiseman (1992); Short and Pierce (1990); Galda, Rayburn, and Stanzi (2000); Maloch (2002); Martinez-Roldan (2003); McIntyre, Kyle, and Moore (2006); Wood, Roser, and Martinez (2001); Pantaleo (2008); Sipe (2008); and Roser, Martinez, Fuhrken, et al. (2000), have documented the richness of young readers' responses when they are in an environment that encourages exploration and consideration of books.

Experience with reading also encompasses the actual texts with which young readers have engaged. Once they understand that thinking about one book in comparison to another, or making "intertextual links," is not only interesting but also productive, readers of all ages engage in forging connections among books. When reading the Egielski version of *The Gingerbread Boy* (P), which takes place in New York City, first graders noted the similarities and differences in this version and the more traditional versions (like the one by Galdone) where the setting is rural. They noticed that instead of a "little old man and a little old woman," the makers of the gingerbread boy were a young couple. They also noticed that the construction workers that chase the gingerbread boy in the Egielski version were "like farmers." Here they were making an intertextual connection based on what Vladamir Propp (1958) calls "character function": construction workers are nothing like farmers, *except* that they chase the gingerbread boy in a group, just like the farmers. The children also commented that perhaps the Egielski version was "the original version." When the teacher asked them why they supposed it was the original version, one of them reasoned, "Well, probably they lived in the city and made a gingerbread boy and lost him. And then when they got older, they retired to the country and tried again. And that would make these two gingerbread boys [the one from the Egielski version and the one from the Galdone version] brothers!" Thus, the children were using their knowledge of another version of *The Gingerbread Boy* to interpret the text at hand; moreover, they were stitching the two stories together by postulating that the couple in the Egielski version was the same as the couple in the Galdone version, only younger!

The second-grade readers in Lisa Stanzi's class immediately took up her invitation to make an intertextual link, and with great enthusiasm. They spent the bulk of the school year weaving links between the many texts they were reading. In this way they came to many different realizations about literature. They decided that different stories might have the same themes, that characters in different stories might be both the same and different, and that some dinosaur books were factual while others wove together both fact and fiction, to name just a few of the ideas they developed as they read and compared texts (Galda, Rayburn, and Stanzi, 2000). Most importantly, they learned to use their experiences with previously read texts to understand new texts. Older readers, especially those with a rich reading diet, also rely on intertextual links to develop their understanding of new texts. Author Jane Yolen (1981) has said that "stories lean on stories," and J.R.R. Tolkien (1938/1964) wrote that "there are no new stories, only a cauldron of stories into which we dip as we write." Of course, these links encompass the texts all readers encounter in movie, song, video, and other electronic sources as well. Teaching Idea 2.2 offers suggestions for creating links across texts.

Teaching Idea 2.2

Creating Links across Stories

Talking about characters enables students to make comparisons among characters from various stories. These comparisons can lead to generalizations about character types that readers will meet as they read widely. Discussing plot results in identification of various kinds of plots and in understandings about archetypal plots that underlie literature. Finding similarities and differences in the underlying conflicts of stories also helps readers make connections among books, just as considering themes can bring the recognition that different authors treat the same general theme, but in infinitely varied ways. Readers who explore how literature works learn to look at books as works of art crafted by a writer.

Some questions that you can consider as you read and respond with your students include:

✿ Plot: What are the key events? How are they structured? How does this relate to other books we have read?

✿ Character: How do we learn about the characters? What are they like and how are they developed? Are they similar to other characters in books we have read? Do they have similar problems? Similar reactions to problems?

✿ Setting: How are characters and events influenced by the time and place in which the story takes place? How does this affect their similarity or differences with other characters we know?

✿ Theme: What are the big ideas that hold the story together? Are there other stories that you know that have similar themes?

Once they are reading for themselves, readers' reading abilities also influence the act of reading. Fluent readers read with an ease that enables them to concentrate fully on the text they are reading; those who struggle with words often miss the meaning. In a discussion of Madeleine L'Engle's *A Wind in the Door* (A), a complex science fantasy that contains some difficult-to-pronounce proper nouns, one reader remarked that he had been doing well until he tried to figure out all the names, when he became mixed up. Another reader then told the group how he had "replaced" the names with familiar ones because it "did not make any difference" to the story (Galda, 1990, 1992).

Different concepts about literature certainly influence response. What readers know about literature—its creation, its forms, its purposes, and its effects—as well as their experience with particular texts, influences the meaning they create. Understanding how literature works, and having multiple experiences with multiple texts, helps readers understand each new text encountered. Again, the context in which readers read and respond makes a difference in the way they respond; supportive contexts allow children to stretch their ideas. Lehr (1991), for example, found that young children who are in literature-rich classrooms and have many experiences reading and discussing literature over time in a supportive context can, and do, discuss themes and character motivation and make generalizations about stories—behaviors usually associated with older children. Galda, Rayburn, and Stanzi (2000) demonstrated the depth of understanding evident in the discussions of second-grade readers in a safe, supportive literature-based classroom. After reading Patricia MacLachlan's *Arthur, for the Very First Time* (I) in November, and again in January, the second graders discussed what "looking through the faraway end," a piece of advice given to the main character, might mean. The discussion was brief. Three months later, in April, Amarachi ran up to one of the researchers, who had just entered the room, and said, out of the blue, "I know why you might want to look through the faraway end. Well, I was looking through my binoculars at a bird in a tree. When I looked through the close-up end, I saw the bird, but when I looked through the faraway end, I saw the whole tree." (p. 1). This eight-year-old had tucked the story into her heart and, three months later, brought it together with a bit of life experience to understand how altering perspective changes everything.

Who readers are includes the cultural values and assumptions that they have developed over time. We all are influenced by others, as each person is shaped by the social and cultural worlds that surround them. For example, most American readers respond negatively to the idea of arranged marriage and positively to books that portray this custom in a negative light (Stewart, 2008). Yet, the attitude toward arranged marriage is cultural, as author Suzanne Fisher Staples (2008) points out when she recounts a discussion about arranged marriage with some of her Pakistani acquaintances in which they asked her, "Do you really send your children out to do the most important thing in their life without the wisdom of their elders?" These women would view a negative portrayal of arranged marriage with alarm. The point is not the validity of either opinion about arranged marriage, but the undeniable cultural influence on response to a book that portrays arranged marriage. Even young children bring cultural attitudes and assumptions with them as they read. Urban kindergarteners, on hearing Beatrix Potter's *The Tale of Peter Rabbit* (N), made that Edwardian classic relevant for themselves by bringing their own cultural attitudes and assumptions to the text. For example, they called Peter a "chip off the old block" because Peter disobeys, just as his father went into Mr. McGregor's garden and got killed. They also interpreted Mrs. Rabbit as a "harried single mother" with three children, one of whom (Peter) was always getting into trouble. One of them poignantly said, "My dad's in jail, but my grandma helps take care of us." They were pointing out that Peter's father wasn't on the scene, just as some of their own fathers were absent. Nevertheless, they also pointed out that they had extended family to help take care of them, unlike poor Mrs. Rabbit, who seems to be all alone. They were able to compare and contrast Peter's family situation with their own because they had clear ideas about their own cultural identities.

Reading interests and preferences also influence response, and we can make some generalizations about young readers' interests and preferences, about what they *might like* to read or what they *actually select* to read, but within each generalization lies a lot of individual variation. Many children, regardless of age, enjoy humor. Primary-grade children often enjoy stories with animal characters and are usually fond of folklore. There is a period of time during the elementary years when many readers are engrossed in mysteries. As children enter the intermediate grades and solidify friendships outside their immediate families, they often like to read realistic stories about children "just like" themselves, especially stories that are exciting and full of action. Older children and adolescents often diverge in their interests along gender lines, with girls preferring romance and contemporary realistic novels and boys preferring nonfiction and fantasy/science fiction. There is some evidence that girls tend to prefer the "discourse of feeling" in books that emphasize the feelings and relationships of the characters, whereas boys tend to prefer the "discourse of action," where an exciting plot is key (Cherland, 1992). Of course, the greater society also impacts young readers' preferences, as the recent surge in delight in fantasy demonstrates.

Young readers who do not yet purchase books for themselves or older readers who do not buy books are at the mercy of the adults who offer books to them. Sometimes, the books that adults offer are not the same as the books that readers prefer. A number of studies point to the discrepancy between awards for literary quality, such as the Caldecott, Newbery, and Printz, selected by adults, and awards for popularity, decided by young readers. Two awards that reflect the choices of young readers (although the initial selection of books and the awards are administered by adults), are Children's Choices and Young Adult Choices. The Booklist at the end of this chapter contains titles of books recently selected by young readers for these awards. Teaching Idea 2.3 offers a suggestion for exploring your own responses to literature for young readers.

Teaching Idea 2.3

Adult Readers, Young People's Texts

Perry Nodelman's article, "Reading across the Border," in the May/June 2004 issue of *The Horn Book Magazine* explores some of the differences between adult "experts" reading children's books and children reading those same books. You are probably somewhere between a childlike reader and an expert, as you are just learning about the world of children's and adolescent literature. Read what Nodelman has to say and think about how you read. Do you read as a reader or as a teacher? Can you read to understand and appreciate a book before you think about how you might use that book? In what ways might your response to a book differ from the response of a young reader? How might you build on these differences for effective teaching?

As each individual reader matures and reads an increasing number of books with an increasing degree of understanding, the preferences of that individual will change along lines that reflect the individual's interests, development, and experiences (Galda, Ash, and Cullinan, 2000; Sebesta and Monson, 2003). As readers' preferences change, so too do their overall responses to literature. When children read widely, they seem to develop an appreciation for a broad range of characters, styles, and genres, regardless of their own specific preferences.

While readers certainly change, as both people and readers, over the course of their development, at any age a rich diet of books to read and a supportive context in which to read them affords readers the best chance to become avid, thoughtful, responsive readers for life. This kind of reader, however, goes well beyond being "inhaled by books." Lewis (2000) argues that being a thoughtful reader involves going beyond personal response and considering the social and political dimensions of texts, an idea that revolutionizes the way we might teach literature.

Texts

The richness of literature available for children and adolescents means that every reader can find books with which they engage deeply. Picturebooks and graphic nov-

els enrich the lives of their readers with their carefully crafted visual and verbal texts. For most children, picturebooks are their primary connection to fine art, and one of the ways they learn to "read" pictures, as well as a source for varied models of language. The impact of a rich diet of picturebooks on children's literate lives is profound. Children who live with poetry in their lives turn to poetry again and again for pleasure, delight, and sometimes solace. Poems offer readers strong images, feelings, and ideas in language that calls attention to itself. Readers respond to poetry in visceral ways and learn to delight in language play. Folklore helps modern children understand the basic principles of cultures around the world, offering absolutes of good and evil, recurring patterns and motifs, and basic structures that are foundational for building an understanding of the family of stories. Fantasy offers readers the opportunity to explore big issues in the world in a way that is manageable and can be a force for moral and spiritual growth. Science fiction allows readers to consider ethical dilemmas that may result from physical and technological advances. Realistic fiction presents stories that allow readers to reflect on their own lives. So, too, does historical fiction help readers reflect on life in the past and on the idea that history was created and lived by people not unlike themselves. Biography offers much the same, allowing readers to come to know biographical subjects as human beings impacted by and having influence on their society. Nonfiction offers readers the opportunity to both learn about and reflect on the world they live in. All of these genres have something unique and universal to offer engaged readers, and increasingly reflect varied cultural experiences and viewpoints.

How, then, do we determine quality of text? As we discuss in Chapter 1, quality certainly involves a multi-layeredness, or openness to multiple interpretations, and an absence of superficiality. Nodelman (1996) puts it this way: What distinguishes the most important literature is its "ability to engender new interpretations from its readers" (p. 187). Who we are as readers and the quality and variety of the texts we have experienced help us build our own personal "canons" of valuable literature, no matter who we are.

• • CULTURALLY DIVERSE • • LITERATURE

We know that it is vital that young readers have the opportunity to see both themselves and others different from themselves in the books they encounter. The opportunities for diverse readers to see themselves in literature as well as to learn about others, to find their own values depicted as well as to consider new values, to find books a source of both comfort and challenge, are available when young readers have the opportunity to read and respond to a rich

Teaching Idea 2.4

Making Connections: Learning about Yourself

Begin the year by asking students to write down several characteristics that describe themselves, as well as several likes and dislikes. If you plan ahead, you can ask questions that will enable them to think about certain aspects of their lives before they read the books you have selected. As you read books depicting varied cultural groups and experiences, explicitly talk about the similarities between the experiences, emotions, attitudes, relationships, and personalities that students find in the book and those they find in their lives. Periodically ask students to write about what they have learned about various characters and what they have learned about themselves. For example, it might surprise some students to realize how terrible it would be not to be able to go to school or to be separated from a sibling. As an end-of-year activity, ask students to revisit and revise their original descriptions of themselves.

dict of literature. Teaching Idea 2.4 suggests how readers can use diverse literature to learn about ourselves.

As we discussed previously, readers shape their view of the world and of themselves partly through the books they read, and the texts themselves are an integral part of this shaping. If children never see themselves in books, they receive the subtle message that they are not important enough to appear in books and that books are not for them. Conversely, if children see only themselves in the books they read, the message is that those who are different from them are not worthy of appearing in books. Further, stereotyped images of an ethnic group, gender, nationality, region, religion, or other subculture are harmful not only to the children of that group but also to others who then get a distorted view. By the same token, "essentializing" cultures by depicting certain "universal" qualities as reflecting all members of a culture also presents a skewed viewpoint. Rich depictions of multiple ways of being part of a culture make diverse literature a rich source of experience for all readers.

Author Jane Kurtz has written many books that are set in Ethiopia, where she spent her childhood. In our interview with her posted on the website, she talks about how after returning to America and beginning her family and career, she put Ethiopia behind her, only to return to it through her writing. Her experience, and her books,

such as *Jakarta Missing* (I) and *Faraway Home* (P), have implications regarding the issue of cultural authenticity discussed in Chapter 1. Jane is not Ethiopian, but she spent her childhood there. She is American, but she didn't grow up here. Describing her "culture" is complicated, just as is describing anyone's culture in simplistic terms.

Literature can act as both mirror and window for its readers (Galda, 1982), and Sims Bishop (1997) has applied this metaphor to culturally diverse literature in particular. Although it is true that literature allows readers to envision themselves and those different from themselves, perhaps the best books offer an experience that is more like looking through a window as the light slowly fades. At first one sees clearly through the window into another's world—but gradually, as the light dims, one's own image becomes reflected as well (Galda, 1998). Children's books at their best highlight the unique characteristics of the cultures represented by their characters but also speak to universal emotions. With them, we can understand, recognize, and appreciate differences; call attention to commonly held values and experiences and those that differ; and promote empathy, respect, and a sense of common humanity. Thinking about, talking about, and developing an understanding of others are natural outgrowths of reading diverse literature, especially when readers discuss their reading with others. Figure 2.1 contains a list of some of the resources you might use to find a rich array of diverse literature.

An example of powerful response to an engaging text is evident in the conversation of a diverse group of fourth- and fifth-grade students discussing Christopher Paul Curtis's Newbery Honor–winning story of the experiences of an African American family, *The Watsons Go to Birmingham—1963* (I). This book captured the interest of every single student, those who liked and did not like to read, those who were African American and those who were not, those who spoke English as a second language and those who did not. The guest reader and students read the final chapter together, aloud. After a few moments of quiet, as everyone digested the ending, the talk began. They talked about how the characters of Kenny and Byron changed across the course of the book, and then about what Byron said to Kenny about fairness: "Kenny, things ain't ever going to be fair. How's it fair that two grown men could hate negroes so much that they'd kill some kids just to stop them from going to school? How's it fair that even though the cops down there might know who did it nothing will probably ever happen to those men? It ain't. But you just gotta understand that that's the way it is and keep on steppin'."

One boy asked, but *why* would the police not arrest the people who killed the little girls if they knew that they did it, and the conversation exploded with cries of "That's not fair." They offered thoughts about prejudice

Figure
2.1

Resources for Finding and Studying Culturally Diverse Literature

The following is a selection of the many books and articles that you might want to consult when selecting and studying culturally diverse literature.

Bader, Barbara, How the Little House Gave Ground: The Beginnings of Multiculturalism in a New, Black Children's Literature. *The Horn Book Magazine*, November/December 2002

_____, Multiculturalism Takes Root. *The Horn Book Magazine*, March/April 2003

_____, Multiculturalism in the Mainstream. *The Horn Book Magazine*, May/June 2003

Fox, Dana, and Kathy Short, *Stories Matter: The Complexity of Cultural Authenticity in Children's Literature*

Hadaway, Nancy L., and Marian J. McKenna, *Breaking Boundaries with Global Literature*

Harris, Violet, *Teaching Multicultural Literature in Grades K–8*

_____, *Teaching with Multiethnic Literature, K–8*

Helbig, Althea, and A. R. Perkins, *Many Peoples, One Land: A Guide to New Multicultural Literature for Children and Young Adults*

Henderson, Laretta, *Ebony Jr! The Rise, Fall, and Return of a Black Children's Magazine*

Horning, Kathleen, Ginny Moose Kruse, and Megan Schliesman, *Multicultural Literature for Children and Young Adults*

Kaleidoscope (multiple editions available through the National Council of Teachers of English)

Miller-Lachmann, Lynn, *Our Family, Our Friends, Our World*

Pinsent, Pat, *Children's Literature and the Politics of Equality*

Pratt, Linda, and Janice Beaty, *Transcultural Children's Literature*

Quintero, Elizabeth, and Mary Kay Rummel, *American Voices: Webs of Diversity*

Rogers, Theresa, and Anna O. Soter, *Reading across Cultures: Teaching Literature in a Diverse Society*

Sims Bishop, Rudine, *Free Within Ourselves: The Development of African-American Children's Literature*

Smith, Henrietta, *The Coretta Scott King Awards: 1970–2004*

Stan, Susan, editor, *The World through Children's Books*

Tomlinson, Carl, editor, *Children's Books from Other Countries*

A committee of the International Reading Association also generates a list, "Notable Books for a Global Society," published annually in the February issue of *The Reading Teacher*. See also www.usbby.org/biblioctte.html for a listing of excellent new international titles.

---

and hatred, about the Klan, about an event in their city ten years earlier in which a cross was burned in the yard of a black family who had moved into a white suburb. The conversation moved on to corrupt law enforcement in the 1960s, police brutality then and now, and racial profiling, something that was currently on television and in the papers. They finished by considering the various responses to the influx of immigrants and refugees in their city, with one child asking, "If the United States has a war in the country they [the immigrants] came from, would they get mad at us and make a war here?" (Galda, 2007). These young readers took Curtis's book into their hearts and used it to make sense of the imperfect world around them even as they were using what they knew to makes sense of the book, and they were working together to expand their understandings of their own and others' experiences. They did this by thoughtfully considering

the ideas about racial discrimination and power that Curtis offered in his text. These ideas are the ideology embedded in the story.

• • IDEOLOGY • •

Lewis's (2000) call for moving beyond the personal to consider the social and political dimensions of reading and responding is a call to encourage young readers to discover the ideology, the "assumptions" in a text. This is difficult to do if the ideology in a text reflects one's own because then it seems an obvious "truth" rather than an assumption. Sometimes, when the ideology of a text is markedly different from that of a reader, the reader reacts with resistance to the text. This is often the case when varied readers are reading literature from other cultures, as we discuss shortly. Stephens (1992) claims that simply encouraging young readers to engage with a text through identification, or "being inhaled," is actually dangerous, as then they never learn to recognize the ideologies in a text, especially those that are implicit. Literature is an expression of cultural values, but whose values, in addition to those of the author, are being expressed? Cultures, as we discussed previously, are not uniform, and not everyone believes the same thing or sees things the same way. For example, as we discuss in Chapter 8, many picture books and novels for young readers extol the bravery and resourcefulness of the pioneers who settled the West; Manifest Destiny as a national ethos permeates these stories. Other books take a different perspective, presenting the inexorable march westward as the destruction of culture after culture. Different ideologies make a significant difference.

Once we understand that texts express, both explicitly and implicitly, an ideology—cultural assumptions and attitudes that the author expresses consciously or unconsciously—we can become aware of how texts manipulate readers and of how our own ideologies shape our responses to texts. Ideology in both text and readers is socially constructed. For example, the anti-war sentiment of the Vietnam era—the assumption that war is bad—permeates Collier and Collier's *My Brother Sam Is Dead* (A), written during that era. Charlotte Zolotow's *William's Doll* (P) reflects the heightened consciousness of gender stereotypes that the feminist movement precipitated. The cultural assumption in many of these books, while appealing to those who agree with it, is nevertheless an ideology.

As society changes, so do books for young readers. Sutherland (1985) argues that authors approach social and cultural norms and ideologies in one of three ways: assent, which reflects those norms; advocacy, which promotes particular practices; and attack, which denounces particular practices (Sipe, 1999). We might describe the Collier novel as advocating the anti-war stance of the peace movement while at the same time attacking the pro-war stance of the political establishment. Zolotow advocates for young boys being allowed to cross gender barriers and play with dolls, although she does not attack those who engage in more traditional male sports.

Some of our cherished "classics," such as Louisa May Alcott's *Little Women* (A) or Carol Ryrie Brink's *Caddie Woodlawn* (A), are interesting to consider in terms of ideology. Jo, in Alcott's novel, is different from most girls, and generations of readers have loved her for that. However, she eventually accepts the role that society insists upon and abandons many of her dreams for the love of a good man. Caddie, in Brink's novel, also gives up her freedom so that she can grow up to be a young woman, just as her mother and society want her to do. Thus, these books and others like them seem to value the adventuresome and

the rebellious in girls, while disallowing those qualities as those girls become young women.

Apol claims that texts written for children are:

deeply tied to the ideologies of a culture and a time. Children's literature is a form of education and socialization, an indication of a society's deepest hopes and fears, expectations and demands. It presents to children the values approved by adult society and (overtly or covertly) attempts to explain, justify, and even impose on its audience what could be considered "correct" patterns of behavior and belief. Whether deliberate or not, children's literature functions as a form of social power, for adults control most, if not all, of a child's reading. Adults write, edit, publish, market, and purchase books; they select, read, and even teach them to children. And in each of these capacities, the choices made by adults are motivated: adults want children to read particular books for particular reasons. (1998, p. 34)

She, like Lewis (2000), argues for helping young readers learn to approach texts from a critical perspective.

Because readers rely on their own experiences and the assumptions and attitudes that they have developed as a result of those experiences, it is not surprising that, when the reader's assumptions are generally similar to the ideology of the text, most readers do not even notice the presence of these ideas. However, when they are different from those expressed in the text, readers challenge the text in different ways. Research on readers responding to texts has dubbed this behavior "resistance."

Sipe and McGuire (2006) document how kindergarten, first-, and second-grade children resist texts in six distinct ways. Some children push texts away when they differ from texts they already know. Others resist when the type of text is not that which they prefer. Children who expect texts to reflect the reality that they themselves have experienced will resist texts that present a different reality; they will also resist a text that inscribes a potentially painful reality. Some children also resist texts if they cannot identify with the characters. Finally, children resist texts that they perceive are somehow faulty in their craft, language, or illustration. Other research on response documents similar resistance in older readers (Encico, 1994; Hemphill, 1999; Lewis, 1997).

Studies of resistance often focus on readers engaging with multicultural texts. Although adults might want young readers to embrace cultural pluralism or to "experience" historical attitudes and events, resistance to texts, however ideologically problematic, does indicate that readers are not simply passively accepting the text but are actively engaged in thinking about and even talking back to the text, the very behavior that Lewis (2000) calls for. Readers resist texts for any number of reasons.

Figure
2.2

Goals of a Response-Centered Curriculum

A response-centered curriculum helps students:

- Develop a lasting love of reading.
- Establish the lifelong reading habit.
- Feel secure in their responses to literature.
- Make connections between literature and life.
- See connections among texts.
- Recognize commonalities among responses.
- See variations of meaning in stories and poems.
- Recognize different purposes for reading.
- Engage in both aesthetic and efferent reading.
- Recognize different types of reading material.
- Learn about language and how it is used.
- Understand how words work.
- Appreciate the beauty of things well said.
- Grasp subtleties of language.

Ways to achieve these goals are:

- Encourage students to interact with books.
- Provide time to read and explore.

- Give time to talk, write, draw, and dramatize.
- Provide time to collaborate with peers.
- Plan time to explore similarities and differences in responses.
- Accept and encourage diversity of ideas among readers.
- Give students a choice of material to read.
- Give students a choice of ways to respond.
- Provide ways to respond joyously.
- Provide a variety of books.
- Stimulate motivation to read.
- Give book talks to generate enthusiasm.
- Integrate reading with other areas.
- Help students find language to express responses.
- Help students realize their potential as learners, as language users, and as readers.
- Give students the opportunity to learn about themselves and their world through books.

For example, as Beach, Thein, and Parks (2007) describe, white readers of multicultural texts often resist the ideologies in those texts. Möller and Allen (2000) describe the "engaged resistance" of some African American readers of Mildred Taylor's *The Friendship* (I), who found the depictions of intolerance and prejudice too painful to read. Beach, Thein, and Parks (2008) document how classroom practice modified students' stances toward texts. Likewise, we now turn to the contexts in which readers respond to text, as these contexts have a great deal of influence on those responses.

Contexts

Learning occurs in a social context that depends on interaction, and literature plays an important role in that context. Children gain experience with life and literature in the company of others. How readers read and how they respond to the books they read is influenced by the con-

texts in which they are reading. Hearing a bedtime story is different from hearing a story at the library's story hour; reading on a rainy Saturday afternoon in the most comfortable chair in the house is different from reading from eight-thirty to nine every morning at a school desk. Reading in a space that has plenty of books, that provides time to read them, and that includes other readers who support developing ideas is much different from reading for homework or contests, and much different from reading privately. Figure 2.2 presents some goals of a response-centered curriculum.

Young people become engaged readers when we surround them with opportunities to read and respond to a variety of genres, styles, and authors; when we appreciate individual differences and offer opportunities to explore and share diverse responses; and when we provide time and encouragement for responding in a variety of ways. Rosenblatt (1938/1976) argues that the *experience* of the book must come first, with teachers then building on readers' connections to a text through various activities, one of which is discussion. Talking about books encourages readers to articulate their own responses to

Teaching Idea 2.5

Book Buddies

There are many different ways to shape a community of readers, one of which is Book Buddies. Sharing books with other readers benefits older and younger students. When students talk about books, it increases their understanding and improves their ability to express themselves orally. It also offers the opportunity to hear what another reader thinks, and thus enlarge their own responses. A Book Buddies program is one aspect of a classroom or school-wide community.

Classmate Book Buddies

To implement Book Buddies in your classroom:

✥ Have students choose partners; one reads aloud, or they both read silently.

✥ After they have finished reading, partners discuss the book quietly.

✥ Discussions are generally open-ended, with no teacher prompts.

Cross-Age Book Buddies

To implement cross-age Book Buddies, connect with another teacher in a grade level two or three years higher than yours, and proceed as follows:

✥ The older students come to visit and get acquainted with your students.

✥ The older students receive training in how to select books, read aloud, engage in discussion, and plan appropriate follow-up activities (if desired).

✥ Book Buddies meet on a regular schedule to read together and talk about what they read.

Figure 2.3

Questions for Critical Readings by Teachers

When you read, be aware of how much you assume about the way things are, or ought to be, in the stories you read. Assumptions about life profoundly influence an individual's response to text, shaping those responses without our awareness. The following questions are one way to begin recognizing how your own ideology shapes you as a reader, and how ideologies are encoded in the books you read.

1. What explicit messages does the text present? What are the implicit, or underlying, assumptions? How do they relate to each other?

2. What parts of the story are "obvious" or "natural" to you? Which assumptions do you find yourself agreeing with? Consider why you feel this way.

3. What parts of the story do you find yourself resisting? What assumptions do you disagree with? Consider why you feel this way.

4. What are some possible ways to interpret this text? How do your own experiences and beliefs influence these interpretations?

These questions are taken from Laura Apol's "But what does this have to do with kids?": Literary theory and children's literature in the teacher education classroom. *Journal of Children's Literature, 24*(2), p. 38. They do not represent all of the questions she poses in the article; read it in its entirety for more comprehensive suggestions.

books and to find out how other readers responded. In many cases, talking about books adds new dimensions to individual responses, as the ideas of others provide new perspectives. As one young reader remarked, "I never thought about it that way, but now it makes a lot of sense"—a sentiment that anyone who has discussed books with friends can understand. When young readers share books with peers and adults in collaborative, supportive contexts, they develop positive feelings about books and about themselves as readers. The social and cultural context in which young readers grow and learn shapes their view of the world and the role of literature in it. Readers belong to a community, in fact to varied communities of readers and in these interpretive communities they learn different ways of approaching a text, different ways to

think about a text, and different ways to talk about a text (Fish, 1980). One such interpretive community might be Book Buddies, as described in Teaching Idea 2.5.

Sipe (1999) points out that contexts are multiple, ranging from the immediate context—perhaps the classroom library with comfortable pillows and attractive bookshelves—to the wider context of the classroom and its interpretive community, to the even wider context of the reader's social world and cultural background, including popular culture. Langer (1995) describes reader-based literature instruction based on transactional theory and research on response. Lewis (2001) details how power, status, and cultural norms shape what occurs in one particular classroom. Apol (1998), Nodelman (1996), Nodelman and Reimer (2003), and others argue for classroom communities in which teachers and children participate in critical readings of texts. Figure 2.3 presents some of the questions that Apol suggests might lead readers, including teachers, to move beyond their personal responses.

We know now that even very young children are capable of making meaningful connections with text and responding in ways that are both deeply felt and critically astute (Cochran-Smith, 1984; Lehr, 1991; McGee, 1992; Sipe, 2008). And there is ample evidence, much of which is cited previously, that readers continue to do so as they mature, encountering new texts in the context of classroom and world, and adding them to the "family of stories" (Stott, 1987) that they know. Perhaps the most intriguing development in the research literature is a realization of just how important context is as it shapes how readers read the texts they encounter. Chapters 3 through 10 explore the texts of children's and adolescent literature. In Chapters 11 and 12 we turn once again to one important context in which children read them—the classroom.

• • • • SUMMARY • • • •

Reading is a transaction that occurs between a reader and a text and is embedded within multiple sociocultural contexts. All readers actively construct meaning, under the guidance of a text, bringing experiences with life and literature to any act of reading. The text guides them as they use prior understandings to construct new meaning. Texts are also shaped by sociocultural contexts and reflect either implicitly or explicitly the values that their authors have developed. The ideologies of both texts and readers, and of the contexts in which writing and reading occurs, play an important role in shaping meaning as readers either accept or resist the ideas presented in a text by judging that idea in terms of their own values while also reading in a socially sanctioned manner.

Booklist

※ Indicates some aspect of diversity

Children's Choices, 2008 (published in 2007)

GRADES K–2 (P)

Arnold, Tedd, *Fly Guy #4: There Was an Old Lady Who Swallowed Fly Guy*

Bateman, Donna, *Deep in the Swamp*, illustrated by Brian Lies

Christelow, Eileen, *Five Little Monkeys Go Shopping*

Cooper, Helen, *Delicious!*

Donnio, Sylviane, *I'd Really Like to Eat a Child*, illustrated by Dorothée de Monfreid

Eaton, Maxwell, *Best Buds*

Fox, Diane, and Christyan Fox, *Tyson the Terrible*

※ Geist, Ken, and Julia Gorton, *Three Little Fish and the Big Bad Shark*

Gran, Julia, *Big Bug Surprise*

Grey, Mini, *Ginger Bear*

Hills, Tad, *Duck, Duck, Goose*

Lloyd-Jones, Sally, *How to Be a Baby by Me, the Big Sister*, illustrated by Sue Heap

※ Manning, Mick, and Brita Granstrom, *Dino-Dinners*

※ McGuirk, Leslie, *Tucker's Spooky Little Halloween*

Morgan, Michaela, *Bunny Wishes*, illustrated by Caroline Jayne Church

Rockhill, Dennis, *Polar Slumber*

※ Schaefer, Lola M., *Frankie Stein*, illustrated by Kevan Atteberry

Steffensmeier, Alexander, *Millie Waits for the Mail*

Tankard, Jeremy, *Grumpy Bird*

Watt, Mélanie, *Chester*

Wheeler, Lisa, *Dino-Hockey*, illustrated by Barry Gott

Yolen, Jane, *How Do Dinosaurs Go to School?*, illustrated by Mark Teague

GRADES 3–4 (I)

Ablow, Gail, *A Horse in the House and Other Strange but True Animal Stories*, illustrated by Kathy Osborn

Byars, Betsy, Betsy Duffey, and Laurie Myers, *Dog Diaries*, illustrated by Erik Brooks

Criswell, Patti Kelley, *The Book Club Kit*, illustrated by Ali Douglass

Dadey, Debbie, *The Worst Name in the Third Grade*

DK Publishing, editor, *Dinosaurium*

_____, *Night Sky Atlas*

Edwards, Wallace, *The Painted Circus*

Evans, Lady Hestia, *Mythology*, edited by Dugald A. Steer

Farndon, John, *Do Not Open*

Goldish, Meish, *Dogs*, illustrated with photographs

Hardcastle, Henry, and Dugald A. Steer, *Explorer: A Daring Guide for Young Adventurers*, illustrated by Alastair Graham, edited by Milivoj Ceran

Harrington, Jane, *Extreme Pets!*

Heiman, Diane, and Liz Suneby, *See What You Can Be*, illustrated by Tracey Wood

Hillman, Ben, *How Big Is It?*

Holm, Jennifer L., and Matthew Holm, *Babymouse: Camp Babymouse*

_____, *Babymouse: Heartbreaker*

Jango-Cohen, Judith, *Real-Life Sea Monsters*, illustrated by Ryan Durney

Keenan, Sheila, *Animals in the House*
Landau, Elaine, *Big Cats*
Low, William, *Old Penn Station*
Mash, Robert, *Extreme Dinosaurs*, illustrated by Stuart Martin
Monroe, Mary Alice, *Turtle Summer*, photographs by Barbara Bergwerf
Morse, Jenifer, *Scholastic Book of World Records 2008*
Murrie, Steve, and Matthew Murrie, *Every Minute on Earth*, illustrated by Mary Anne Lloyd
National Geographic Society, *Sea Monsters: A Prehistoric Adventure*
Osborne, Mary Pope, *Monday with a Mad Genius*, illustrated by Sal Murdocca
Petrucha, Stefan, *Nancy Drew Graphic Novels #9: Ghost in the Machinery*, illustrated by Sho Murase
Repchuk, Caroline, editor, *The Amazing Spider-Man Pop Up*
Ruffin, Frances E., *Medical Detective Dogs*, illustrated with photographs
_____ , *Military Dogs*, illustrated with photographs
Sandler, Michael, *Race Horses*, illustrated with photographs
Searl, Duncan, *Wolves*, illustrated with photographs
Sobol, Donald J., *Encyclopedia Brown Cracks the Case*
☀ Sommer, Carl, *Spike the Rebel!*, illustrated by Enrique Vignolo
☀ _____ , *The Richest Poor Kid*, illustrated by Jorge Martinez
☀ Sommer, Carl, Jorge Martinez, and Greg Budwine, *Dare to Dream!*, illustrated by Kennon James
Spinelli, Eileen, *Summerhouse Time*, illustrated by Joanne Lew-Vriethoff
Stine, R. L., *Goosebumps Graphix 3: Scary Summer*, illustrated by Ted Naifeh, Dean Haspiel, and Kyle Baker
White, Trudy, *Could You? Would You?*
Yeh, Phil, *Dinosaurs Across America*

GRADES 5–6 (I–A)

Alter, Stephen, *The Phantomisles*
Buckingham, Royce, *Demonkeeper*
Child, Lauren, *Clarice Bean, Don't Look Now*
David, Laurie, and Cambria Gordon, *The Down-to-Earth Guide to Global Warming*
Doeden, Matt, *Crazy Cars*
Evans, John D., *Diary of a Renaissance Man*
Gee, Joshua, *Encyclopedia Horrifica*
Gerasole, Isabella, and Olivia Gerasole, *The Spatulatta Cookbook*
Golding, Julia, *The Secret of the Sirens*
Gore, Al, *An Inconvenient Truth*
Grandits, John, *Blue Lipstick*
Holm, Jennifer L., *Middle School Is Worse than Meatloaf*, illustrated by Elicia Castaldi
Kadohata, Cynthia, *Cracker!*
Kelley, K. C., *Hottest NASCAR Machines*
Krensky, Stephen, *Ghosts*
Marillier, Juliet, *Wildwood Dancing*
Messinger, Carla, with Susan Katz, *When the Shadbush Blooms*, illustrated by David Kanietakeron Fadden

Myracle, Lauren, *Twelve*
Paulsen, Gary, *Lawn Boy*
Pemberton, Bonnie, *The Cat Master*
Prevost, Guillaume, *The Book of Time*, translated by William Rodarmor
Salmansohn, Karen, *Girl Wonders*
Selznick, Brian, *The Invention of Hugo Cabret*
Smith, Jeff, *Bone #5: Rock Jaw*
_____ , *Bone #6: Old Man's Cave*
☀ Storrie, Paul D., *Beowulf: Monster Slayer*, illustrated by Ron Randall
☀ _____ , *Yu the Great*, illustrated by Sandy Carruthers
Thompson, Colin, *The Short and Incredibly Happy Life of Riley*, illustrated by Amy Lissiat
White, Ruth, *Way Down Deep*
☀ Woodson, Jacqueline, *Feathers*
Zee, Ruth Vander, and Marian Sneider, *Eli Remembers*, illustrated by Bill Farnsworth

Young Adult Choices 2008 (A) (published in 2007)

Atwater-Rhodes, Amelia, *Wolfcry*
Bagert, Brod, *Hormone Jungle: Coming of Age in Middle School*
Bowsher, Melodie, *My Lost and Found Life*
☀ Boyne, John, *The Boy in the Striped Pajamas*
Brugman, Alyssa, *Being Bindy*
Bryant, Jen, *Pieces of Georgia*
Cohn, Rachel, and David Levithan, *Nick & Norah's Infinite Playlist*
Del Vecchio, Gene, *The Sword of Anton*
Friend, Natasha, *Lush*
Giles, Gail, *What Happened to Cass McBride?*
Lockhart, E., *The Boy Book*
_____ , *Fly on the Wall*
Lowell, Pamela, *Returnable Girl*
Meyer, Stephenie, *New Moon*
☀ Namioka, Lensey, *Mismatch*
Patterson, James, *School's Out—Forever*
Paulsen, Gary, *The Amazing Life of Birds*
Peters, Kimberly Joy, *Painting Caitlyn*
Rallison, Janette, *It's a Mall World After All*
Richardson, E. E., *The Intruders*
Runyon, Brent, *Maybe*
Sachar, Louis, *Small Steps*
Shepard, Sara, *Pretty Little Liars*
Shusterman, Neal, *Everlost*
Sleator, William, *Hell Phone*
Stone, Tanya Lee, *A Bad Boy Can Be Good for a Girl*
Thayer, Ernest L., *Casey at the Bat*, illustrated by Joe Morse
Vail, Rachel, *You, Maybe: The Profound Asymmetry of Love in High School*
Westerfeld, Scott, *Specials*
Young, Steve, *15 Minutes*

Genres in Literature

for Young Readers

Chapter

3

Picturebooks: A Unique Format in Children's Literature

The integrity, the dignity, the quiet strength of Rosa Parks turned her no into a YES for change.

—NIKKI GIOVANNI,
Rosa*, illustrated by*
Bryan Collier, unpaged

During read-aloud time, Bev has been discussing picturebooks that exemplify various types of heroes with her third graders. These Philadelphia children—all African Americans—have heard stories of courage (***Henry's Freedom Box***, P–I), self-sacrifice (***Martin's Big Words***, P–I), and folk heroes (***John Henry***, P–I). Today, Bev has chosen to read Nikki Giovanni's ***Rosa*** (P–I). As they examine the front cover, the children notice two things. Jamal says that the "white man with the cap" "looks like he's angry at the woman," and Debra notices that "it looks like there's a halo around the woman's head." The children have already identified the central conflict in the story, and their comments suggest a developing sense of its theme, which is racial inequality. Bev always spends time examining the front and back covers, endpapers, and title page with the children because she feels that these elements of the picturebook provide the best introduction to the story rather than her own "purpose-setting" questions.

As Bev reads the dedication page, the children understand the idea of dedicating a book to someone and comment that Giovanni's dedication of the book to her sister "courageously facing down lung cancer" shows that the sister is a hero, too. As she reads, Bev explains that there was a time when black people and white people could not sit on buses together. The children are incredulous when they hear that black people had to sit in the back of the bus or stand. Alexis suddenly remembers that she knows something about the story: "I remember someone named Rosa and she wouldn't give up her seat on the bus." On the fifth opening of the book, they notice that the illustration is the same as the one on the front cover. When Bev reads the text, which describes the bus driver's angry confrontation with Rosa Parks, Alexis says, "I knew it—she's Rosa Parks, and she's not goin' to give up her seat!" As the story continues to tell of Rosa's arrest and the resulting bus boycott, the children hear of Dr. Martin Luther King's involvement, and many children make personal comments that show their knowledge of Dr. King's resolve to make life better for African Americans. Keith mentions that there is a picture of Dr. King in his home's living room. The children also make intertextual connections to ***Martin's Big Words*** and remember that Dr. King was "shot and killed." When the book closes with the results of the Supreme Court decision that segregation—in schools, on buses, and everywhere else—is wrong, the children want to talk about how white people still treat African Americans intolerantly. Although this is not an easy conversation for Bev, who is white, she understands that the book has touched a resonant chord for the children and encourages them to continue to talk. She has created the space for children to feel comfortable talking about these issues by explicitly mentioning issues of race.

On the last page of the story, the children again notice the "halo" around Rosa Parks, and several compare her to a "saint." Patricia remembers that at the end of *Martin's Big Words* there is an illustration with candles burning in front of an image of Dr. King and makes a beautiful connection: "This is like *Martin's Big Words* because it's like Martin Luther King was a saint, and so is Rosa."

Bev's plan is to continue the theme of heroes with a read-aloud of *Something Beautiful* (P–I), the story of a little girl who realizes that by changing her attitude about her neighborhood, she can make a positive difference. In this way, Bev will continue the idea of heroes by giving children the opportunity to talk about how they might be heroes, not by actions that would appear in newspaper headlines but by smaller actions that will make the world a better place.

Thus, both the words and illustrations of *Rosa* have added another dimension to the children's understanding of heroes: heroes can exhibit determination and "quiet strength" in the face of injustice and intolerance. The book has also invited exploration of several other aspects of the civil rights movement and has elicited serious discussion of social inequities, which will continue during the rest of the year. All of this from a thirty-two-page picturebook!

What Is a Picturebook?

For as long as there have been written texts, there have been illustrations that accompany them. Ancient Egyptian, Middle Eastern, and Asian scrolls contain both words and pictures; and medieval European manuscripts frequently include visual images along with texts. *Illustrated* books, in other words, have a very long history and many precedents; however, *picturebooks* (we use the compound word to differentiate them from books with pictures, or illustrated books) are something quite different and relatively recent. Unlike an illustrated book, in a picturebook the words cannot tell the story alone. The words tell us things that are not in the pictures, and the pictures tell us things that the words overlook. This, in short, is what picturebooks do; the central idea is the essential unity, harmony, or "synergy" (Sipe, 1998) of the words and illustrations. Each is as important as the other; unlike in illustrated books, where the visual images are clearly subordinate to the words. Indeed, there are picturebooks with few or no words at all; in these wordless picturebooks, the visual images carry the narrative by themselves. Awards given for picturebooks can be based on either the text, as is the Charlotte Zolotow Award for outstanding writing in

a picturebook, or the illustrations, in the case of the Caldecott Medal. Lists of the Zolotow and Caldecott winners are found in Appendix A.

Whether wordless or composed of text and illustration, picturebooks occupy a unique place in the world of children's literature. Because we classify picturebooks according to format rather than content, they actually span other genres. We have picturebooks that are also folklore, fantasy and science fiction, contemporary realistic fiction, historical fiction, or nonfiction—including informational books, concept books, and biographies—as well as poetry and song. Figure 3.1 summarizes the different genres found in picturebook format, and Teaching Idea 3.1 offers ideas for exploring these genres with children.

Picturebooks not only span a number of genres; they also span a wide range of ages. They are available for the

Picturebook Genres

Fiction

Fiction includes folklore, fantasy and science fiction, realistic fiction, and historical fiction.

✿   Characters are dynamic and dimensional as well as fanciful (fantasy, science fiction); dynamic and dimensional as well as believable (realistic fiction, historical fiction); or flat, static, stock (folklore).

✿   The story is set in the real world of the past (historical fiction), the real world of present times (realistic fiction), an imagined world of the future (science fiction), or in a fanciful world (fantasy and folklore).

✿   The events of the story are plausible and logical in the real world of the present (realistic fiction), in the real world of the past (historical fiction), in a fanciful world (folklore, fantasy), or in a future world (science fiction).

Nonfiction

Nonfiction includes informational books, concept books, and biographies.

✿   The book presents details about a concept (concept book), facts about a topic, or a realistic report about a person's life (biography).

✿   Content is verifiable.

Poetry or Song

✿   The language is verse, poetry, or song lyrics.

Teaching Idea 3.1

Using Picturebooks to Help Students Learn about Literature

Because picturebooks span the range of genres and include examples of outstanding writing, they can be used to teach students—from kindergarten though high school—whatever you want them to learn about literature. If we read picturebooks aloud and talk about them without ever talking about their literary quality, we miss a wonderful opportunity to help students learn how literature works. Here are some things to think about in planning literature lessons using picturebooks:

✿ What do you want students to learn?

✿ What books do you have in your classroom library that will help you teach this concept?

✿ What kinds of activities can you do with students that will help them explore this concept?

✿ How can you build on initial understandings as you go on to read more books with your students?

youngest readers as well as for adolescents. From board books that present simple concepts or tell simple stories to books that pose significant questions and explore complex issues, picturebooks have an important place in children's lives. Barbara Bader notes this when she defines *picturebooks* as "text, illustrations, total design; an item of manufacture and a commercial product; a social, cultural, historical document; and, foremost, an experience for a child" (1976, p. 1).

If, for example, you are working with younger students and want to help them make the basic distinction between fact and fiction, then you will want to collect picturebooks about the same topic that are fiction, fact, or factual information embedded in fiction. For example, you could collect imaginative stories about dinosaurs, expository nonfiction about dinosaurs, and narrative nonfiction (information set within a story frame) about dinosaurs. Read the books with your students and talk about them, noting characteristics of each in a chart that allows you to list what is fictional and what is factual. If you are working with older students, they can take a more sophisticated look at this same idea by talking about what is "true" and what is "plausible" in the historical fiction they read.

Or you might want to look at how authors and illustrators develop characters and at how characters grow and

change over the course of a story. If so, then you would select picturebooks with strong, engaging characters. You can help students learn to think about theme, or big ideas, by selecting picture storybooks and asking them to tell you the "most important word" in the story. After collecting their answers, you can lead them into a discussion of those words, which turns naturally into a discussion of theme. You can study metaphor, allusions, foreshadowing, parallel plots—whatever you care to study—using picturebooks. The possibilities are almost endless.

To help you get started, you might want to consult *Using Picture Storybooks to Teach Literary Devices* by Susan Hall (Oryx Press, 1990); *Looking through the Faraway End: Creating a Literature-based Reading Curriculum with 2nd Graders* by Lee Galda, Shane Rayburn, and Lisa Stanzi (International Reading Association, 2000); Mary R. Jalongo's *Young Children and Picture Books*, Second Edition (National Association for the Education of Young Children, 2004); and *A Picture Book Primer: Understanding and Using Picture Books* by Denise Matulka (Libraries Unlimited, 2008), as well as the various genre chapters in this textbook.

The Evolution of Picturebooks

In the form we know them now, picturebooks were virtually invented by the talented illustrator Randolph Caldecott in the 1870s and 80s. This is the person for whom the American Library Association's highest award for picturebook illustration, the Caldecott Medal, is named. What was new about Caldecott's "toy books" for children, as they were called?

Instead of merely illustrating a text that could stand perfectly well by itself, Caldecott invented a form in which both words and pictures were equally important—and necessary—to tell the story. His illustrations were not lovely embellishments, but an integral part of the whole experience of his books. For example, one of his most famous children's books took the nonsense rhyme "Hey, Diddle, Diddle" and injected it with new life through his illustrations, which are still admired and enjoyed today. The last line of the rhyme, "And the dish ran away with the spoon," is accompanied by an illustration of the dish (a male) dancing with the spoon (his girlfriend) to the tune of the cat playing the fiddle, and a whole assemblage of dishes and plates joining in the celebration. Another illustration shows the dish and spoon romantically snuggling beside each other on a bench. But this is not all: on the following page, disaster has struck. In the center of the illustration the dish lies, broken in pieces, and the other dishes and plates are wailing with mourning. On the right-hand

*Randolph Caldecott's **Hey Diddle Diddle** depicts the dish and the spoon romantically running off together.*

*The last illustration of **Hey Diddle Diddle** shows the tragic results: the spoon's parents have obviously been greatly angered by the attentions of the dish toward their daughter.*

side of the illustration, a knife and fork (the spoon's father and mother, respectively) flank the devastated spoon, haughtily leading her away. We're invited to speculate that the knife and fork didn't think the dish was worthy of their daughter and that they took violent action against him! By themselves, the words tell us nothing of a romantic involvement between the dish and spoon, let alone the tragic result of their love. In other words, this set of illustrations greatly expands and extends our understanding and enjoyment of the words. Today's picturebooks may look different, due to the great advances in printing reproduction techniques, but the essence remains the same.

Randolph Caldecott, along with illustrators Walter Crane and Kate Greenaway, showed that books for children with many colorful illustrations could be quite successful. At the turn of the century, Beatrix Potter published her first picturebook, *The Tale of Peter Rabbit* (1902). As literacy rates improved and more children became readers, and as printing techniques for reproducing illustrations made great progress, the stage was set for a veritable explosion of children's picturebooks in the 1920s, here in the United States. Some milestones of children's picturebook publishing since then are listed in Figure 3.2. All of these picturebooks are considered classics, are still in print, and continue to sell well.

In the late 1930s and early 1940s, picturebooks like *Goodnight Moon* (N–P) began to focus on the everyday lives of children rather than on fantasy and fairy tales. This trend continues to the present day, though of course fantasy and anthropomorphized animals are still an important feature of many picturebooks.

Until the 1950s and 1960s, the presence of children of color and children from diverse cultures in picturebooks was rare, and what representations there were tended to be stereotypical and racist. *The Snowy Day* (N–P) by Ezra Jack Keats (1962), himself not an African American, was the first picturebook with an African American protagonist to win the Caldecott Medal. John Steptoe's *Stevie* (P) (1969) is generally recognized as one of the first picturebooks to represent the everyday lives of African American children from an insider's perspective. An essay by Nancy Larrick, "The All-White World of Children's Books" (1965) called attention to the dearth of representations of children of color. The situation has improved, though the overwhelming percentage of picturebooks published today still do not contain images of children of color or of ethnicities other than European Americans (Martin, 2004). A few publishers (for example, Arte Público Press and Lee & Low) specialize in books that represent the wide diversity of races and ethnicities in the United States today.

Further advances in color reproduction techniques in the 1960s and early 1970s made it possible for printing companies to separate the colors in illustrations, so that illustrators did not have to do this themselves. Prior to this, illustrators had to create a separate illustration for each color they used—an unbelievable amount of labor! This advance alone increased the number of picturebooks and illustrators produced. Today, we are living in the golden age of color reproduction techniques, where any illustration, no matter what medium has been used to produce it, can be used in a picturebook.

Milestones in the History of Picturebooks

1878   *The House That Jack Built* and *The Diverting History of John Gilpin* by Randolph Caldecott
1902   *The Tale of Peter Rabbit* by Beatrix Potter
1928   *Millions of Cats* by Wanda Gág
1930   *The Little Engine that Could* by Watty Piper
1933   *The Story of Babar* by Jean de Brunoff
1936   *The Story of Ferdinand* by Munro Leaf, illustrated by Robert Lawson
1937   *And to Think I Saw It on Mulberry Street*, Dr. Seuss's first book
1938   Creation of the Caldecott Medal by the American Library Association—this greatly spurred the interest in (and availability of) picturebooks
1939   *Madeline* by Ludwig Bemelmans
       Mike Mulligan and His Steam Shovel by Virginia Lee Burton
1941   *Make Way for Ducklings* by Robert McCloskey
1942   Simon & Schuster begin publishing the Little Golden Books, which marketed picturebooks at a price low enough (25 cents) for almost every family to afford.
1947   *Goodnight Moon* by Margaret Wise Brown, illustrated by Clement Hurd
1955   *Harold and the Purple Crayon* by Crockett Johnson
1957   *The Cat in the Hat*, Dr. Seuss's most famous book
1962   *The Snowy Day* by Ezra Jack Keats
1963   *Where the Wild Things Are*, Maurice Sendak's most famous book
1967   *Brown Bear, Brown Bear, What Do You See?* by Bill Martin (Eric Carle's first picturebook)
1969   *Stevie* by John Steptoe (one of the first picturebooks to represent African American children from the perspective of an African American author/illustrator)

In this chapter, we first look closely at the art of picturebooks, beginning with the elements that are common to all visual art, as well as the various styles of art that illustrators employ to create meaning with pictures. We then consider the special aesthetic qualities specific to picturebooks and how picturebooks are put together from cover to cover as carefully designed art objects. We then turn to consider the language of picturebooks—how writers employ techniques of narrative fiction, nonfiction, and poetry to create meaning with words. We also pose criteria for evaluating picturebooks based on the elements and qualities we have discussed.

In the next section of the chapter, we explore the various types of picturebooks, ranging from simple board books and concept books for very young children all the way to picturebooks that have intellectual and aesthetic appeal to much older readers. We also discuss several common themes or issues in contemporary picturebooks. Lastly, we address teaching and learning with picturebooks in the classroom. In this chapter, we also take a close look at three exemplary books: *Monkey*

and Me (N–P) by Emily Gravett, for very young readers; Nikki Giovanni's *Rosa* (P–I) illustrated by Brian Collier, for intermediate readers; and *Woolvs in the Sitee* (A), a collaboration between author Margaret Wild and illustrator Anne Spudvilas intended for older readers. We also include profiles of each of these illustrators.

✳   ✳   ✳

A CLOSE LOOK AT

Rosa

A good picturebook can always be read on several levels. Nikki Giovanni's *Rosa* (P–I), illustrated by Bryan Collier, tells the familiar story of Rosa Parks (1913–2005), whose refusal to give up her seat to a white person on a bus in Montgomery, Alabama, in December 1955 was one of the landmarks of the civil rights movement. In simple but elegantly subtle language, Giovanni tells Rosa's story, with allusions to other important civil rights events. Collier's illustrations also deserve careful examination and portray Rosa Parks as a revered icon in this history. Collier also includes details that invite readers to pursue further study of the whole civil rights movement. Thus, this book can be read and enjoyed by a wide range of ages, from the primary through elementary grades.

The central event of the whole story is captured dramatically on the front dust jacket, which is identical to the front board cover. We see an arresting close-up of the confrontation between Rosa and the bus driver. From the top right of the picture space, the bus driver glares down at Rosa, the brim of his stiff cap pointing directly at her. Only the top half of Rosa's head is depicted, from her carefully parted black hair to the bottom of her wire-rim eyeglasses. Her eyes and eyebrows suggest calm but intense determination. Rosa's head is surrounded by a round design of irregular rectangles in thick gold paint, suggesting a glowing halo. Even the front cover, therefore,

suggests her saintlike qualities, as well as the eventual triumph of justice and freedom over repression.

The front endpapers show a crowded bus, in shades of monochromatic dark (almost black) purple, with Ms. Parks seated beside another African American who holds a newspaper with the headline "The Life of Emmett Till," referring to the horrific story of a fourteen-year-old's brutal murder and mutilation at the hands of white racists who believed he had insulted a white woman. This event, which also galvanized support for the civil rights movement, had happened in August of the same year. This is one of the details that Giovanni also refers to later in the story. Rosa Parks's refusal to give up her seat came "only weeks" after the trial in which all of Emmett's "killers were freed" near the end of September. Also present in the front endpapers is the familiar symbol of the Confederacy, with its X-shaped design of thirteen stars, representing the thirteen states that fought against the

Profile

Bryan Collier

Bryan Collier's childhood was spent in a small town on the eastern shore of Maryland. He was the youngest of six children in his family. Like many future artists, he developed an interest in art at an early age, and both his parents and teachers encouraged him. He began painting seriously at the age of fifteen, developing his own style of watercolor and collage, which won several awards. He enrolled in the prestigious Pratt Institute in New York City, winning a scholarship in a national talent competition. He graduated from Pratt in 1989 with honors.

Despite this success, however, it took Bryan a long time—seven years—to break into the world of children's publishing with his book *Uptown* (P–I), which is a celebration of the vibrant life of Harlem; *Uptown* won both the Ezra Jack Keats Book Award and the Coretta Scott King Award for Illustration. Prior to this, he showed his commitment to encouraging young artists by volunteering at the Harlem

Horizon Studio and Harlem Hospital Center, then went on to become the program director. At the Hospital Center, he worked with young people who had experienced traumatic events, helping them to express their feelings and achieve healing through making art. He feels a great responsibility to be a positive role model for children and teenagers, and believes that art can play an important role in building kids' self-esteem and steering them "away from negative influences." As a successful full-time illustrator who resides in New York, he now works on his own art as well as visiting schools and libraries. He also directs mural programs throughout the city, retaining his determination to help young people improve their lives through art.

Bryan's intensity extends to his chosen style of collage and watercolor; he comments, "Collage is more than just an art style. Collage is all about bringing different elements together. Once you form a sensibility about connection, how different elements relate to each other, you deepen your understanding of yourself and others." In *Freedom River* (P–I), a story based on an ex-slave named John

Parker who successfully guided slaves across the Ohio River from Kentucky into freedom, his exciting and accomplished paper and fabric collage illustrations add an emotionally intense dimension to this already powerful story. *Freedom River* won a Coretta Scott King Honor Award for Illustration.

Rosa, the story of Rosa Parks's role in the civil rights movement, featured in a Close Look section, was done in collaboration with the poet Nikki Giovanni. Bryan's illustrations, coupled with Giovanni's poignant language, garnered the Coretta Scott King Award and a Caldecott Medal.

Bryan's website, www.bryancollier .com, contains biographical information, examples of all his picturebooks, and his film and television credits (one of his murals was featured on *Sesame Street*!), as well as his many awards and exhibitions of his work. This is an artist who truly has a social conscience, believes wholeheartedly in the power of art, and whose sincerity and dedication are evident in his art as well as his life.

Rosa saw that the section reserved for blacks was full, but she noticed the neutral section, the part of the bus where blacks or whites could sit, had free seats.

The left side of the aisle had two seats and on the right side a man was sitting next to the window. Rosa decided to sit next to him. She did not remember his name, but she knew his face. His son, Jimmy, came frequently to the NAACP Youth Council affairs. They exchanged pleasantries as the bus pulled away from the curb.

Rosa settled her sewing bag and her purse near her knees, trying not to crowd Jimmy's father. Men take up more space, she was thinking as she tried to squish her packages closer. The bus made several more stops, and the two seats opposite her were filled by blacks. She sat on her side of the aisle daydreaming about her good day and planning her special meal for her husband.

◄━◇◇◇━►

Bryan Collier draws attention to Rosa Parks by placing her near the center of the illustration in **Rosa.** *A newspaper with the headline "The Life of Emmett Till" suggests the terrible story of an African American teenager who was brutally killed for allegedly whistling at a white girl.*

Union in the Civil War. This illustration is repeated on the fourth opening of the story, but in full color.

The dedication, frontmatter, and title page, with a background of warm yellow, contain a rectangular illustration of Rosa, smiling broadly as she seems to step off a bus. Her left hand holds the bus rail, and her right hand is raised vertically in a gesture that can be interpreted either as a simple wave or a saint's benediction. This illustration also suggests the triumph at the end of this serious story.

The great majority of the openings of this book consist of illustrations that cross the gutter, so that three-fourths of the page is illustration and one-fourth is a column of varying colors overprinted with the words of the text. This arrangement gives room for both Giovanni and Collier to share in telling the story. Collier's accomplished watercolor and collage images do not merely illustrate the story but add considerably to its power and extend it. The openings alternate between positioning the illustration to the left and the print to the right, and vice versa, adding to the visual interest.

Alabama's state capitol building is a recurring image in Collier's illustrations, appearing four times. This build-

ing holds great significance as a background for the story because it was on the steps of this edifice that Jefferson Davis was sworn in as president of the Confederacy. Until fairly recently, the Confederate flag flew just below the American flag on the staff surmounting the capitol dome, and there are still disputes about whether this potent symbol of the Confederacy should be represented anywhere on the building. In this way, Collier reminds readers/viewers of the connection between the Civil War and the civil rights events that happened almost one hundred years afterward.

The pattern of three-quarters illustration and one-quarter text is dramatically broken on the thirteenth opening, which consists of a double-page spread of many people, some holding American flags, and the text, which explains that there were people who walked to work rather than taking buses for almost a year to protest Rosa's arrest and the injustice of having to sit at the back of public transportation. The illustration seems to be set in Selma, Alabama, and not in Montgomery because of the presence of the Edmund Pettus Bridge in Selma, which in 1965 was the scene of violence toward African Americans who were marching from Selma to Montgomery and were brutally attacked by state troopers wielding billy clubs and tear gas. This illustration is a double-gatefold, which readers can open to reveal a four-page illustration of many people, steadfast in their resolve, and the text that explains the Supreme Court's 1956 ruling that "segregation of the buses, like segregation at schools, was illegal." At the extreme right of this impressive illustration is the image of the state capitol, still with its Confederate flag flying beneath the American flag, suggesting the conflict between the federal and state laws.

The last opening contains another iconic image of Rosa, surrounded by the same golden sunburst as on the front cover; she is looking down at several children, who hold their hands out to her as if venerating her and seeking her blessing. The book ends with the back endpapers, rendered in the same monochromatic dark purple as the front endpapers, with an image of a bus passing a house, and leaflets and posters in support of Ms. Parks and the bus boycott.

Collier's illustrator's note states that he made trips to both Montgomery and Selma, during which he felt the intense heat of the summer. He wanted his paintings to "have a yellow, sometimes dark, hue. I wanted the reader to feel in that heat a foreshadowing, an uneasy quiet before the storm." He also states that it was his intent to make Rosa look "as if light is emanating from her."

Naturally, not all the details of this book will be explored by teachers of young children, but the potential is there for the book to provide an entrée into a serious study of the civil rights movement.

Considering the Artistic Quality of Picturebooks

Artists have many resources and techniques at their disposal. They can choose a medium, technique, and style that fit the text they are illustrating, or they can choose texts for which their unique style is suitable. When the right art is combined with a memorable text, the result is a superb book.

✴ ✴ ELEMENTS OF VISUAL ART

Art in children's picturebooks involves the entire range of media, techniques, and styles used in all art. The *medium* (the plural is *media*)—the material used in the production of a work—may be watercolors, oils, acrylics, ink, pencil, charcoal, pastels, tissue paper, construction paper, ace-

tate sheets, real objects (such as fabric or leaves), or any other material that artists employ. The technique might be painting, etching, woodcut or linoleum block printing, airbrush, collage, photography, or many other means. Currently, an increasing number of illustrators use computer software specifically intended for the production of digital images. Some illustrations are thus produced without any of the more traditional means. William Low's illustrations for *The Day the Stones Walked* (P–I), about the last days of the Easter Island civilization, seem to be rendered in oil pastels, but a note at the back of the book tells us that they were done completely "on the computer using Adobe Photoshop." Other illustrations are the product of a sensitive combination of traditional media and the tools of the computer. For example, a note in *Wave* (N–P) informs readers that "The illustrations in this book were rendered in charcoal and acrylics and digitally manipulated." The individual artist combines medium and technique in his or her own particular style to evoke setting, establish character, convey theme, display information, explain a concept, or create a mood.

When illustrating a picturebook, artists decide what media and techniques they will use, and they make other aesthetic choices as well. They must decide about color, style, and composition in their illustrations. They must make choices about line, shape, placement on a page, the use of negative space, and texture. Artists work with the basic elements of art (line, shape, color, and texture) and with the principles of design (rhythm, balance, variety, emphasis, spatial order, and unity) to create a unified image that conveys meaning.

✴ ✴ LINE ✴ ✴

Line is a mark on paper or a place where different colors meet. Each stroke starts with a dot that grows into a line that may be slow and rolling, sleek and fast, quiet or frenetic, flowing or angular. Line is perhaps the most expressive element in the artist's arsenal. Artists create lines that move in the direction in which they want to focus the viewer and pull the eye in a particular direction. Lines can suggest delicacy (thin lines) or stability (thick lines). Artists use the angle, width, length, and motion of line to express the meaning they want to convey. David Diaz, Rosemary Wells, Peter Sís, David Wiesner, Suzy Lee, Kadir Nelson, and Brian Selznick all use line in different and effective ways.

One use of line is to create a series of thin parallel lines that are then crossed at right angles with another set of lines. This technique, called *cross-hatching*, gives the impression of energy or intensity. A classic example of cross-hatching is found in Maurice Sendak's *Where the Wild Things Are* (N–P), where most of the illustrations contain a great deal of cross-hatching in thin lines of black ink that overlay the watercolor images. The effect is particularly noticeable on the endpages of this picturebook, which seem to represent a series of colorful overlapping leaves or flowers. The addition of cross-hatching over the entire surface of the illustration gives readers a feeling of excitement: What could be hiding behind this screen of foliage? If you try to imagine what the illustration would look like without any cross-hatching, you will understand that it would seem rather flat and uninteresting, despite the different colors. It's the cross-hatching that gives the illustration its vibrancy. A more recent example of the extensive use of cross-hatching to add energy and excitement to the illustrations is found in Susan Swanson's *The House in the Night* (N–P), a Caldecott Medal winner, where Beth Krommes's black-and-white cross-hatched images, colored by touches of yellow, provide a vibrant counterpoint to the repetitive, cumulative text, which is almost hypnotically calm.

Mo Willems uses line to create a memorable character in *Don't Let the Pigeon Drive the Bus!* and its several sequels (P). Soft textured black lines (rendered with crayon) convey motion, and emotion, as the pigeon's

dream is left unfulfilled but not forgotten. Willems won a Caldecott Medal for this book. Eric Rohmann uses thick black lines to define his characters, depict movement, and propel readers from one page to another in his Caldecott Medal–winning book, *My Friend Rabbit* (N–P). For *Not a Box* (P), Antoinette Portis's thick black and red lines convey the imaginative world of children playing with cardboard boxes; what adults see is rendered with the black lines, whereas the red lines make visible what children are imagining (a rocket ship, a racing car, or a robot). Arthur Geisert masterfully employs the precision of thin etched lines to create the meticulously detailed and hilarious illustrations in *Hogwash* (P–I). Robert Sabuda in Marguerite Davol's *The Paper Dragon* (P–I) and Holly Meade in Minfong Ho's *Hush! A Thai Lullaby* (P) also use cut paper as line.

Richard Michelson's *As Good as Anybody* (I–A) is a moving and uplifting story about the friendship between Dr. Martin Luther King, Jr., and Rabbi Abraham Joshua Heschel and their joint commitment to justice and equity for all people. Raul Colón's illustrations for this picturebook use subtle lines that are lighter than

Martin organized a protest march from Selma to Montgomery. "Decent people know that prejudice is wrong," he said, "but many are too frightened to speak out."

Six hundred Negroes joined Martin, but the police blocked their way and attacked them with dogs and clubs.

Martin did not give up. "We cannot walk alone," he said, "and we cannot turn back."

He put out a call for all of God's children to join the march.

Raul Colón's accomplished illustrations for **As Good as Anybody** *add drama and a sense of movement with curving lines that cover the figures of civil rights marchers, police, and dogs.*

the background colors to give a sense of movement and definition to the subdued palette and hazy shapes. In a scene depicting dogs attacking Freedom Marchers on the road from Selma to Montgomery, Alabama, for example, Colón adds a great deal of energy to the illustration through subtle curved and swirling lines that accentuate the clothing of the police and the marchers as well as the movement of the police dogs. This use of line is a common feature of Colón's style.

In *Scribble* (N–P), Deborah Freedman's fantasy of a child who magically follows her scribbled cat into another drawing, the lines perfectly mimic the playfulness and uninhibited nature of children's drawings. We can almost see the hurried, pulsating movements of Scribble, the cat, as they are embodied in the lines quickly and chaotically drawn with black Magic Marker.

Molly Bang uses thick lines and color that become thicker and more brilliant when emotions are heightened in *When Sophie Gets Angry—Really, Really Angry . . .* (P). In this story, the little girl, Sophie, is initially outlined in a sunny yellow, but as she loses her temper the line registers her fury and gradually turns a flaming red. When Sophie actually has a screaming fit, multiple rich red pulsating lines surround her and create the impression that she is about to explode. As Sophie runs off into the woods, her anger gradually subsides, and she returns home her old self, with a sunny yellow outline.

• • COLOR • •

Artists like Molly Bang use color—or the lack of it—to express character, mood, and emotion. Color conveys warmth or coolness, personality traits, indifference or engagement, and other feelings. Color can vary in *hue*—ranging across the rainbow of colors—and *intensity*. Subdued colors can express weariness, boredom, and serenity, whereas intense (or *saturated*) colors evoke feelings of energy, vibrancy, and excitement. Colors can also vary in *value*, or the amount of light and dark. A range of values creates drama or movement; an absence of contrast creates a quiet or solemn mood. A *shade* of a color is created by adding black to the pure hue, whereas a *tint* results when white (or water, in the case of watercolors or acrylics) is added.

Lisbeth Zwerger limits her palette to rustic tones in Grimm's *Hansel and Gretel* (P). She conveys foreboding through somber clothing, dark lines on faces, and backgrounds of brown, ecru, and gray. Similarly, Allen Say employs a very limited range of shades in gray and brown to emphasize the desolation and loneliness of

© 1999 Molly Bang

Thick, pulsing lines of color help Molly Bang portray Sophie's emotions in **When Sophie Gets Angry—Really, Really, Angry . . .**

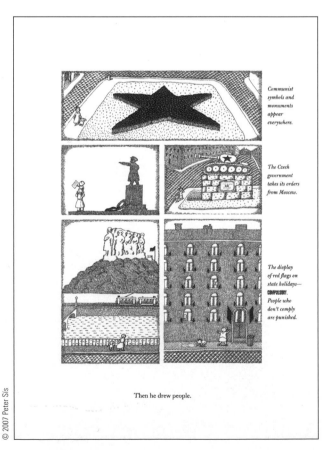

© 2007 Peter Sís

In **The Wall,** *Peter Sís uses red to suggest the oppressions of Communism.*

Sís's fanciful depiction of the Prague Spring, in full color, contrasts dramatically with the other illustrations in black, white, and red in **The Wall**.

inhabitants of the U.S. World War II internment camps for Japanese people in *Home of the Brave* (I–A). A limited palette, however, does not necessarily convey bleakness: the muted shades of color in a limited range of values in Jonathan Bean's *At Night* (N–P) are appropriate for the gentle and quiet story of a little girl who sleeps on the roof of her apartment building during the summer months. In contrast, in Christopher Myers's hip, urban version of Lewis Carroll's nonsense poem *Jabberwocky* (P–I–A), the colors are almost all saturated hues of neon colors, adding to the energy of the intense basketball game played by the hero (the "beamish boy") and the Jabberwock, who is imagined as an enormously tall and menacing basketball player. Carll Cneut's vibrant illustrations for Marilyn Singer's *City Lullaby* (P) depict busy city life through warm, saturated colors.

Peter Sís's strategic use of color in *The Wall: Growing Up Behind the Iron Curtain* (I–A) draws a dramatic contrast between the dull and fearful atmosphere of Prague during communist rule and the exuberance of the introduction of mainstream Western popular culture.

In this autobiographical picturebook, Sís uses an intense hue of red to symbolize the repressions of communism in otherwise black-and-white drawings. Whenever creativity and imagination are highlighted, however, Sís's palette becomes much more expansive, reaching a high point as he describes the "Prague Spring," where the communist authorities allowed more freedom of expression in art, music, and literature, culminating in The Beatles' rock music and the daring poetry of Allen Ginsberg. In the double-page spread that illustrates the Prague Spring, Sís uses a combination of truly psychedelic colors and intense hues to convey the excitement of that short-lived time period.

Although illustrating a story of the Holocaust, Wendy Watson uses muted colors and tones of gold that create a hopeful, positive feeling in her illustrations for Karen Hesse's *The Cats in Krasinski Square* (I). In John Light's *The Flower* (I), Lisa Evans's illustrations reflect the change in mood from the dull and lonely life of a boy who lives in a big city (rendered in a very narrow range of values of shades of gray and brown) to one of

*The front board cover of **The Flower** suggests the contrast between the dullness of a boy's life in a city and the spot of brightness and joy brought by a flower.*

quiet joy as he discovers a book full of pictures of flowers, which are depicted in colorful tints of pinks, reds, and greens. As he searches in vain for a flower, the palette again turns gray, until he discovers an old packet of flower seeds in a junk shop. As the planted seeds grow, the palette brightens along with his mood and the mood of the story to reflect the hope that the city might one day be filled with flowers.

Jeanette Winter also uses subdued colors in *The Librarian of Basra: A True Story from Iraq* (P), but not to reflect the mood of her story. Instead, she contains the emotional impact of this war story by framing her illustrations in colors. A rich gold frames the first third, depicting the buildup to the war; a muted lavender frames the middle third, in which the books are saved as Basra burns; and a periwinkle blue frames the final third, in which the librarian waits for peace, guarding her books.

• • SHAPE • •

Shape is an area or form with a definite outline. It, along with line, directs the viewer's eye and suggests feelings and ideas. Shapes can be geometric (circles, triangles, squares), abstract (suggestive, less well-defined shapes,

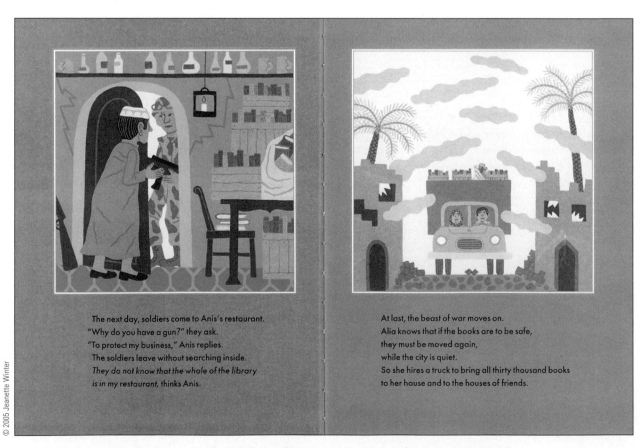

The next day, soldiers come to Anis's restaurant.
"Why do you have a gun?" they ask.
"To protect my business," Anis replies.
The soldiers leave without searching inside.
They do not know that the whole of the library is in my restaurant, thinks Anis.

At last, the beast of war moves on.
Alia knows that if the books are to be safe,
they must be moved again,
while the city is quiet.
So she hires a truck to bring all thirty thousand books
to her house and to the houses of friends.

*Jeanette Winter contains the emotions in **The Librarian of Basra**, a story of war and courage, by framing her illustrations in soft colors.*

In this double-page spread from **Show Way**, *the theme that runs through the story is emphasized by the common geometric shapes used in quilting*

Shapes (positive space) Background (negative space)

such as clouds), or realistic and representational. Shape can contribute to the volume or three-dimensional quality of an illustration. In some illustrations, shapes seem to jut out from the front, or plane, of the picture, coming toward the viewer. Artists make decisions about the placement of shapes (positive space) on the background (negative space).

Manuel Monroy extends Jorge Luján's spare, poetic text—in Spanish, with an English translation by Elisa Amado below the Spanish, set in a smaller, different-colored font—in **Rooster/Gallo** (N–P), a mythic hymn to the dawn. The colors are dramatic, and the shapes of rooster, beak, and star are a rhythmic accompaniment to the lyrical text.

Hudson Talbott's illustrations for Jacqueline Woodson's **Show Way** (P–I) rely heavily on the geometric shapes that are characteristic of quilts, which feature prominently in Woodson's history of her own family from slave times until the present. In the books of Saxton Freymann and Joost Elffers (such as **Dog Food**, **Fast Food**, and **Baby Food**, all N–P), the shapes of cleverly carved assemblages of fruits and vegetables delight all readers. Who would have thought that a piece of cauliflower could be carved into a fluffy white poodle? The

strong and beautifully photographed shapes take center stage in these lively books. The combination of strong geometric shapes of blast furnaces and other machinery used in the steel-making industry with the rounded shapes of workmen give much visual interest to **Steel Town** (I) written by Jonah Winter and illustrated by Terry Widener, resulting in a visual style similar to that of the American artist Thomas Hart Benton. Lois Ehlert highlights geometric shapes in many of her books, including **Color Zoo** (N) and **Oodles of Animals** (N). Her books are marked by bright colors, clear lines, and shapes that seem to jump off the page. Shape is an essential element of Ellen Stoll Walsh's **Mouse Paint** (P), Ashley Bryan's **Let It Shine** (P–I), and Steve Jenkins's **Living Color** (I). In these three books, shape combines with color to produce vivid illustrations.

Yuyi Morales's **Little Night** (P), a Golden Kite Award winner, is an excellent example of the use of shape to indicate mood and feeling. As Mother Sky prepares Little Night for bed, Little Night mischievously hides at every stage—bathtime, dressing in sleeping attire, snack time, and hair combing. In all the illustrations for this dreamy and magical picturebook, there is hardly a shape that is not composed of rounded curves. Thus, as Molly Bang

*The flowing curves and rounded shapes in the illustrations for **Little Night** give a sense of comfort and peace to the story of a little girl's bedtime.*

suggests (see page 71), the round, curved shapes give the mood of comfort, softness, and warmth as Mother Sky gently proceeds through the bedtime rituals. How inappropriate sharp, angular shapes would be in this calm and loving story! In addition, the color palette for this bedtime book is appropriately muted, combining with the shapes to produce a dreamlike atmosphere.

Chris Raschka combines the elements of simple line, shape, and color to depict music visually in ***John Coltrane's Giant Steps*** (P-1). Using the soft pastel colors of three shapes—raindrops, snowflake, and box—superimposed on one another like notes of music, and a cat of thick black line for a melody, Raschka explores the energy of this piece of music with the energy of his art.

*Chris Raschka uses shape, color, and strong line to visually portray a famous piece of music in **John Coltrane's Giant Steps.***

• • TEXTURE • •

Some illustrations seem smooth, others rough. Some, like collage, do have a rough texture in the original art, whereas in others texture is entirely visual. Texture conveys a sense of reality; interesting visual contrasts or patterns suggest movement and action, roughness, or delicacy.

Denise Fleming uses an unusual process to create illustrations for *Barnyard Banter* (N–P), *Lunch* (N–P), *In the Small, Small Pond* (N–P), *Where Once There Was a Wood* (P–I), *The Everything Book* (N–P), and *The Cow Who Clucked* (P–I). She pours colored cotton pulp through hand-cut stencils, which results in handmade paper images. The art is satisfyingly textured and more softly edged than most cut-paper illustrations. The softness of the paper tempers the intense colors and active composition to make her art appealing to children and fascinating to adults.

Lois Ehlert's *Red Leaf, Yellow Leaf* (P–I), with its use of real objects, such as strips of burlap, string, and twigs, has a marvelous combination of textures that delight the eye. Another master of the use of real objects, Jeannie Baker creates the illusion of a landscape through the use of real sand, bits of moss, vines, leaves, and tree bark in *Where the Forest Meets the Sea* (P–I). The use of these organic objects creates such an illusion of texture that readers want to touch the pages. Javaka Steptoe's exuberant collage illustrations for Karen English's *Hot Day on Abbott Avenue* (P) are textured with layers of tissue paper and construction paper on painted planks of wood, and his use of various materials gives us a sense of the different texture of each person's hair, from spiky and straight to smooth and flowing. David Diaz's textured collages for Eve Bunting's story *Smoky Night* (I–A) convey the turmoil, fear, and anxiety caused by riots. Diaz uses material that reflects the events in the text: wooden matches texturize the illustration for fire; plastic bags and hangers symbolize the looting of the dry cleaners. Diaz won the Caldecott Medal for this book. Barbara Reid's unique plasticine illustrations in picturebooks such as *The Subway Mouse* (P) demonstrate her ability to convey a great range of textures, from the soft fur of a mouse to the rough concrete walls of a subway to the smooth shiny surface of ripe blackberries.

It was their favourite time of day.

35

Barbara Reid's expert use of plasticene and real objects creates a multitude of textures in her illustrations for **The Subway Mouse.**

In the Caldecott Medal book *Snowflake Bentley* (P–I)—Jacqueline Briggs Martin's biography of William Bentley, a photographer of natural phenomena—Mary Azarian's hand-colored woodcuts have a folksy, down-home quality that is appropriate for this story, which takes place in the Vermont countryside at the end of the nineteenth century. As we look at the rustic woodcuts, we can almost feel the rough wood furnishings, the scratchy wool knits, and the coarse weave of the lumber jacket. We can see the diversity of textures of fields and flowers, and of course the beauty of the snowflakes that became Bentley's favorite subject matter.

Texture can be achieved by painters as well, as in Francois Roca's illustrations for Jonah Winter's ***Muhammad Ali: Champion of the World*** (I). Roca manages to convey the warm smoothness of skin, the silkiness of boxing shorts, and the shiny softness of boxing gloves with the medium of oil paint. Stephanie Anderson's watercolor illustrations for George Ella Lyon's ***Weaving the Rainbow*** (P) are smooth, beautiful landscapes and textured close-up images of the sheep, the weaver, her wool, and the beautiful cloth she weaves.

● ● DESIGN ● ●

Artists use the basic elements of art to create meaning and feeling; they manipulate the elements through principles of design to express their unique visions. Artists work to achieve unity, or a meaningful whole, through *composition of their art*. To achieve unity, artists make use of balance, repeated rhythms, variety, emphasis, and spatial order. Balance means giving equal weight to the lines, shapes, textures, and colors in a picture; without it the picture seems awkward (Greenberg & Jordan, 1991, 1993, 1995). *Repetition* in art helps achieve visual harmony and balance, whereas *variety* sets up a paradox or a progression that leads the eye from one point to another. Artists draw attention to a particular part of their piece by emphasizing size, placement, color, or line; these elements work together to force the viewer's eyes to focus on a particular place in an illustration.

For example, examine the front cover of April Jones Prince's ***What Do Wheels Do All Day?*** (P–I) illustrated by Giles Laroche. Repetition is certainly present, in the many circles of wheels and gears, however variety is also much

Fall brought their first shearing.
Then as the days turned cold
their winter wool grew in.
It kept them warm right through the snow.

*The wool of the sheep is so textured that it seems as though we could reach out and touch it, in George Ella Lyon's **Weaving the Rainbow**, with watercolors by Stephanie Anderson.*

Repetition and Variety
Why S O unversely Pleasing

Why disappearing

© 2006 Giles Laroche

Giles Laroche's beautifully rendered front dust jacket cover for **What Do Wheels Do All Day?** *by April Jones Prince exemplifies the best of all the elements of visual design.*

in evidence—no two wheels are the same, either in size or color. There is a balance between more simple wheels, such as the one in the upper right-hand corner, and more complex ones, such as the circular gear mechanism and the large wheel at the bottom left, with its multiple colors and smaller circles inside larger ones. In addition, the range of vibrant colors is balanced. The cool colors, such as blue and green, are balanced by the spectrum of warm colors, such as yellow, orange, and red. The curved lines of the wheels are balanced by the straight spokes in several of the circles. The use of negative and positive space is pleasing; some wheels seem to overlap with each other, giving a three-dimensional effect. The background (the negative space) is light beige with a texture much like sandpaper, contrasting effectively with the darker and brighter colors of the wheels. Finally, the curved lines of the title and the author's and illustrator's names are pleasingly integrated into the total design. The main word in the title, "Wheels," jumps out at us because it is presented in a larger font than the rest of the title, as well as being red, in contrast to the black used for the rest of the title. The combination of all these elements results in a superbly designed cover that invites us into the book.

In her book *Picture This: How Pictures Work* (2002), Molly Bang describes the formal principles of design; we have summarized them here:

◉ Smooth, flat, horizontal shapes present a sense of stability and calm. (p. 42)

◉ Vertical shapes are more exciting and active, implying energy and reaching. (p. 44)
◉ Diagonal shapes are dynamic, implying motion or tension. (p. 46)
◉ The upper half of a picture connotes freedom, happiness, triumph, and spirituality. (p. 54)
◉ The bottom half connotes threat, heaviness, sadness, and constraint. (p. 56)
◉ An object in the upper half carries "greater pictorial weight" and emphasis. (p. 56)
◉ The center of the page is the point of "greatest attraction." (p. 62)
◉ The edges and corners of the picture are the ends of the picture world. (p. 66)
◉ White or light backgrounds feel safer than dark backgrounds. (p. 68)
◉ Pointed shapes frighten; rounded shapes or curves comfort and feel safe. (p. 70)
◉ The larger an object is, the stronger it feels, whereas the smaller an object is, the weaker or more insignificant it seems. (p. 72)
◉ We link the same or similar colors more readily than the same or similar shapes. (p. 76)
◉ Contrasts enable us to see. (p. 80)

Artists such as Molly Bang work with these principles to compose their illustrations so that a reader's eye is guided by the art as the artist intends. In a similar way, Mark Gonyea's two books, *A Book about Design: Complicated Doesn't Make It Good* (I) and *Another Book about Design: Complicated Doesn't Make It Bad* (I) present similar design elements in ways that primary and intermediate students can understand, using many simple and effective examples.

Margaret Chodos-Irvine's *Ella Sarah Gets Dressed* (N) is full of soft, bright colors and rounded shapes that help tell the happy story of a spunky little girl who knows exactly what she wants to wear, no matter what anyone else suggests. The focus is on Ella Sarah—we can't see all of the mother's, father's, or sister's figures because they are out of the plane of the picture. In one double-page spread, there are five images of her getting dressed: pants, dress, socks (two of them), and shoes, arranged in a curve across the expanse of white space, with text placed near the appropriate image. The next spread shows her putting on her big red hat, which actually breaks the plane of the top of the picture, signifying the triumph of this independent little girl.

The text becomes part of the illustration in *Hot Day on Abbott Avenue*, mentioned previously. In an illustration of the girls playing double dutch jump rope, the artist has left room for the words of the rhyme to be printed in curved lines that follow the curves of the rope. This integration of text and picture results in a pleasing circular

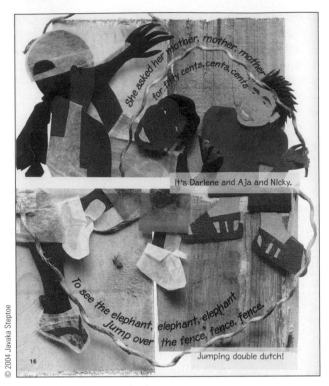

It's Darlene and Aja and Nicky.

she asked her mother, mother, mother for fifty cents, cents, cents

To see the elephant, elephant, elephant Jump over the fence, fence, fence.

Jumping double dutch!

16

© 2004 Javaka Steptoe

*In **Hot Day on Abbott Avenue**, Javaka Steptoe's collage illustrations include the words of the story as an integral part of his design, by curving them parallel to the girls' jump rope.*

© 2006 Rachel Isadora

*The excitement and exuberance of a preschool child's day are delightfully suggested by Rachel Isadora's vivid pastel illustrations for **Uh-Oh!**.*

design that gestures toward the rhythmic energy of the girls playing their game.

• • MEDIA AND TECHNIQUE • •

Artists make choices about the media and techniques they use. As mentioned earlier, *media* refers to the material used in the production of a work. *Technique* refers to the method artists use to create art with the chosen medium. Artists can work with virtually any medium— various types of paper, clay, wood, metal, watercolors, oils, gouache (a thick tempera paint), fabric, acrylics, ink, graphite pencil or colored pencil, charcoal, pastels— or with any combination of media. A combination of media in the same book is referred to as *mixed media*. For example, the publishing information for Steve Johnson's and Lou Fancher's exquisite illustrations for Maya Angelou's *Amazing Peace* (p–i) lists "oil, acrylic, and fabric on canvas" as the media used. Artists may use the same medium for several books, but produce a very different effect by using different techniques. Other artists employ different media that seem appropriate for different books. As well, no two artists use the same medium in the same way.

Stephen T. Johnson uses pastels to create gentle, delicately colored drawings in Lenore Look's *Love as Strong as Ginger* (p–i), whereas the pastel drawings in Rachel Isadora's *Uh-Oh!* (n) are full of intense, highly saturated color to complement the story of a toddler's day. Chris Van Allsburg's masterful use of pastels changes from book to book. In *The Wreck of the Zephyr* (i), Van Allsburg's illustrations give the impression of great calm and stillness; but in *The Polar Express* (p–i) and *The Stranger* (p–i), there is a luminous quality to the images that highlights the excitement and mystery in the stories.

David Shannon uses acrylics in his humorous signature illustrations for *No, David!*, *David Goes to School*, and *David Gets in Trouble* (all n–p). R. Gregory Christie's use of acrylic with colored pencil illustrations for Tonya Bolden's *The Champ: The Story of Muhammad Ali* (p–i) emphasizes the head and hands of this boxer famous for his intellectual stance on war as well as for his boxing ability. Trina Schart Hyman achieves yet another effect with acrylics in her meticulously detailed, realistic illustrations for Katrin Hyman Tchana's *Sense Pass King: A Story from Cameroon* (i). The illustrations are also filled with the folk motifs and natural beauty of northwestern Cameroon.

Watercolor is a favorite medium of many artists. Meilo So's watercolor illustrations for Janet Schulman's *Pale Male: Citizen Hawk of New York City* (i–a) convey both the serenity of New York's Central Park and the hustle and bustle of the city, and in a completely different palette, Phil Huling reflects the vibrancy of the Mexican setting in Eric Kimmel's *Cactus Soup* (P). Emily Arnold McCully's watercolors in *Squirrel and John Muir* (P) depict the beauty of Yosemite as well as the relationship between Muir and a young girl who learns from him how to observe nature. E. B. Lewis, Ted Lewin, and Jerry Pinkney each have a distinctive style of watercolor illustration, as can be seen in *The Legend of the Cape May Diamond* (I) and *Across the Alley* (I) (Lewis); *Horse Song: The Naadam of Mongolia* (I) and *The Always Prayer Shawl* (I) (Lewin); and *The Little Red Hen* (P) and *Little Red Riding Hood* (P) (Pinkney). See Teaching Idea 3.2 on page 81 for further discussion of these three very accomplished watercolorists.

Artists also use a variety of techniques in addition to painting, such as etching, linoleum block printing, airbrush, collage, stitching, computer art, and photography. Ken Robbins's hand-tinted photographs in *Bridges* (P–I) create an ethereal artistic effect that not only adds to the information about bridges but also conveys their romance; his photographs for *Seeds* (P) are informational. Those in Maya Ajmera and John Ivanko's *Be My Neighbor* (N–P) also are clear and focused on conveying information, as are Michael Doolittle's photographs for Susan Goodman's *Skyscraper: From the Ground Up* (P–I). Frank Serafini's series of nature books, *Looking Closely through the Forest*, *Looking Closely along the Shore*, *Looking Closely across the Desert*, and *Looking Closely inside the Garden* (all P–I) present close-up shots and invite readers to speculate on what larger object the close-up might be a part of. Turning the page reveals the secret, along with some information. For example, in *Looking Closely across the Desert*, we see a mysterious maroon circle with bumps and the words "What do you see? A pincushion? Monster skin? What could it be?" The page turn reveals a photograph of a prickly pear cactus.

In Martin Waddell's *Tiny's Big Adventure* (N–P), John Lawrence's lush engravings in blues and golds extend the mood of the story, as do Barry Moser's more somber-colored wood engravings for Virginia Hamilton's *Wee Winnie Witch's Skinny: An Original African American Scare Tale* (I). Mary Azarian uses woodcuts to good effect in *A Gardener's Alphabet* (N–P) and in Jacqueline Briggs Martin's *Snowflake Bentley* (P–I). Jim Meyer's stunning woodcuts, which beautifully evoke the beauty of the northern wilderness in Phyllis Root's *If You Want to See a Caribou* (P–I), are another example of the effective use of this time-intensive and difficult medium.

Trina Schart Hyman combines lush landscapes and folk designs in her acrylic illustrations for Sense Pass King.

© 2004 Jim Meyers

Jim Meyer is a master of the exacting art of colored woodcuts, as shown in his illustrations for **If You Want to See a Caribou** *by Phyllis Root.*

Two related media that produce very intriguing illustrations are represented by the work of Brian Pinkney and Chris Gall. Pinkney (who is Jerry Pinkney's son) specializes in scratchboard. Using thick cardboard that has a heavy black coating, Pinkney employs various sharp tools to scratch away the areas he wants to appear white and finishes by hand-coloring the images. The result is visually interesting because of the bold contrasts of the black-and-white portions of the illustration, overlaid with color. Fine examples of Brian Pinkney's scratchboard media and technique are found in **Duke Ellington**, **The Adventures of Sparrowboy**, and **Wiley and the Hairy Man** (all P–I). In a similar way, Chris Gall hand-engraves clay-coated board and applies his vibrant colors digitally with Adobe Illustrator. The tools he uses to scrape away the coating of clay are similar to Pinkney's, but they produce thicker, more forceful lines in contrast to Pinkney's fine and more flowing lines. Gall's work is well represented by **America the Beautiful**, **Dear Fish**, and **There's Nothing to Do on Mars** (all P–I).

Many artists use collage materials but create different effects using a variety of techniques and supplies. Rachel Isadora brushes oil paints on thick palette paper, which she allows to dry and then cuts into the shapes of people and objects in **Yo, Jo!** (P–I). In this way, it is reminiscent of Eric Carle's collage style, which employs a similar method of prepainting sheets of tissue paper, letting them dry, and then cutting out the shapes for his illustrations (see **The Art of Eric Carle**, 1996, for an excellent description of the process). Isadora also includes bits of newspaper or magazine texts and pieces of patterned wallpaper to add interest to her work. Holly Meade uses torn-paper collages in **Sleep, Sleep, Sleep: A Lullaby for Little Ones Around the World** (N–P) by Nancy Van Laan. Ed Young uses crisply cut collage shapes in **Seven Blind Mice** (P–I). Steve Jenkins is perhaps the master of the type of collage style, which relies on many types and colors of handmade paper, as shown in **Sisters and Brothers**, **Animals in Flight**, **Actual Size**, and **Prehistoric Actual Size** (P–I). Jenkins's studio contains literally thousands of papers in a great variety of colors and textures, so that he can choose exactly the right type and hue for the image he is constructing, whether it be the smooth skin of a snake, the fur of a bear, or the soft down of a newly born chick. Christopher Myers uses ink and gouache with cut and torn pieces of collage in **Harlem** (P–I) by Walter Dean Myers. Simms Taback uses mixed media—watercolor, gouache, pencil, ink, and photography—and collage on craft paper in **Joseph Had a Little Overcoat** (N–P–I). Susan Roth illustrates **Hard Hat Area** (P) with collage overlaid on a photomontage of the skyline of New York City, and Kyrsten Brooker combines oil paints and collage in Patricia McKissack and Onawumi Jean Moss's **Precious and the Boo Hag** (P). Raul Colón's illustrations, a combination of watercolor washes, etching, colored pencils, and litho pencils, are easily recognized in his many picturebooks, for example Pat Mora's tall tale **Doña Flor** (P–I) and Jonah Winter's **Roberto Clemente: Pride of the Pittsburgh Pirates** (I), Bryan Collier's

© 1997 Brian Pinkney

Brian Pinkney's signature style of scratchboard is demonstrated beautifully in **The Adventures of Sparrowboy**.

© 2008 Chris Gall

The clay engraving technique used by Chris Gall in **There's Nothing to Do on Mars** *is similar to Brian Pinkney's scratchboard, though Gall's lines are thicker and more definite.*

brilliant combinations of paint and paper or fabric collage are discussed in his Profile and the Close Look at *Rosa* on pages 59–62.

As we mentioned in the introduction to this chapter, computers are making an impact in illustration for picturebooks. Although computer-generated art was initially considered inferior, enormous advances have been made in technology. Now, with proper training one can draw with a penlike stylus and approximate any medium, which then appears on a monitor; the images can be corrected, adjusted, and enhanced. After an initial period where artists seemed infatuated with the new technology and treated it as an end in itself rather than subordinat-

ing it to their aesthetic purposes, they are now using it in more sophisticated ways (Salisbury, 2007). Such artists as Janet Stevens and Mo Willems make use of the computer to great effect. In Mo Willems's Caldecott Honor–winning *Knuffle Bunny: A Cautionary Tale* (N–P) and *Knuffle Bunny Too* (N–P), Willems digitally incorporates his brightly colored cartoon characters into sepia-toned photographs. Janet Stevens used the computer to enhance her original art in Anne Miranda's *To Market, to Market* (P), and the resulting illustrations are full of energy.

Figure 3.3 presents examples of the variety of media and techniques found in picturebooks, as well as suggestions for exploring media with children.

Media and Techniques Used in Picture Books

In the following list, we begin with the name of the illustrator and include the author's name following the title if the author is someone other than the illustrator. We mention only one or two books for each illustrator, but their other books might include similar art. Also review the chapter text for other ideas. Some publishers now state the media, technique, and typography used in their books. Check the copyright page of each book for this information. Following each list, there are some suggestions for activities you can do with children to explore these media further. Please note that some of the entries are preceded by an asterisk, which indicates that that book is multicultural.

Acrylic

✳ Austin, Michael, *Martina the Beautiful Cockroach: A Cuban Folktale* by Carmen Agra Deedy (2007) (p–i)

Beeke, Tiphanie, *I'm Going to Grandma's* by Mary Ann Hoberman (2007) (n–p)

Cooney, Barbara, *Miss Rumphius* (1985) (p–i)

Egielski, Richard, *The End* by David LaRochelle (2007) (p)

✳ Gomez, Elena, *Mama's Saris* by Pooja Makhijani (2007) (p–i)

✳ Gonzalez, Maya Christina, *Nana's Big Surprise: Nana, Qué Sorpresa!* by Amada Irma Pérez (2007) (p)

Hall, August, *When I Met the Wolf Girls* by Deborah Noyes (2007) (p)

Keller, Laurie, *Do Unto Otters: A Book About Manners* (2007) (p)

Klise, M. Sarah, *Imagine Harry* by Kate Klise (2007) (n–p)

Pilkey, Dav, *Paperboy* (1999) (p)

Pratt, Pierre, *Roar of a Snore* by Marsha Diane Arnold (2007) (n–p)

Shannon, George, *No, David!* (1998) (n–p)

_____, *Rabbit's Gift* by Laura Dronzek (2007) (n–p)

_____, *David Goes to School* (1999) (n–p)

Diluted acrylic can be painted onto transparencies and several monoprints can be made from these in the copier. Children can then experiment by painting on the copies.

Cut Paper and Collage

Baker, Jeanne, *Home* (2004) (p–i)

✳ Bryan, Ashley, *Beautiful Blackbird* (2003) (n–p)

Barner, Bob, *Penguins, Penguins, Everywhere!* (2007) (n–p)

Carle, Eric, *The Very Hungry Caterpiller* (1981) (n–p), painted tissue paper

Fleming, Denise, *On the Day You Were Born* (1995) (n–p)

✳ Isadora, Rachel, *Yo, Jo!* (2007) (n–p)

Jenkins, Steve, *Biggest, Strongest, Fastest* (1995) (p–i), commercially handmade paper

Keats, Ezra Jack, *The Snowy Day* (1985) (n–p)

Laroche, Giles, *What Do Wheels Do All Day?* by April Jones Prince (2006) (n), bas relief cut-paper collage

Lionni, Leo, *Frederick's Fables* (2005) (n–p)

✳ Meade, Holly, *Hush! A Thai Lullaby* by Minfong Ho (1996) (n–p)

McCarthy, Mary, *A Closer Look* (2007) (n–p)

Walsh, Ellen Stoll, *Mouse Shapes* (2007) (n–p)

✳ Wisniewski, David, *Rain Player* (1991) (p–i)

Young, Ed, *Seven Blind Mice* (1992) (n–p)

Use tissue paper, construction paper, magazines, newspaper, wallpaper, and gift wrap to make book illustrations, collages, mosaics, and paper sculptures.

Computer-generated or Computer-augmented Art

Auch, Mary Jane and Herm Auch, *Beauty and the Beaks: A Turkey's Cautionary Tale* (2007) (p)

Nash, Scott, *Rainy Day* by Patricia Lakin (2007) (n–p)

Pelletier, David, *The Graphic Alphabet* (1996) (p)

Willems, Mo, *Knuffle Bunny Too: A Case of Mistaken Identity* (2007) (n–p)

Use a computer program to create art. Illustrate a picture book or a poetry book with it.

Gouache

Bang, Molly, *When Sophie Gets Angry—Really, Really, Angry . . .* (1999) (n–p)

Falconer, Ian, *Olivia Helps with Christmas* (2007) (n–p)

Kalman, Maira, *Max in Hollywood, Baby* (1992) (p)

Priceman, Marjorie, *Zin! Zin! A Violin* by Lloyd Moss (2000) (p–i)

Gregory, Christie R., *Jazz Baby* by Lisa Wheeler (2007) (n–p)

Manders, John, *The Perfect Nest* by Catherine Friend (2001) (p)

✳ Paschkis, Julie, *Glass Slipper, Gold Sandal: A Worldwide Cinderella* by Paul Fleischman (2007) (p)

Yaccarino, Dan, *Every Friday* (2007) (n–p)

_____, *Who Will Sing a Lullaby?* by Dee Lillegard (2007) (n–p)

Yee, Wong Herbert, *Abracadabra!: Magic with Mouse and Mole* (2007) (p–i)

Using black or white crayons, children can make an under-drawing or outline, and then paint over it in gouache or tempera to fill in the spaces not waxed with crayon.

Graphite and Pencil

Browne, Anthony, *My Brother* (2007) (n–p)

Dale, Penny, *Jamie and Angus Together* by Anne Fine (2007) (p)

Ramá, Sue, *Fix It, Sam* by Lori Ries (2007) (n–p)

Van Allsburg, Chris, *Jumanji* (1981) (p–i)

_____ , *Zathura* (2002) (p–i)

Yee, Wong Herbert, *Who Likes Rain?* (2007) (n), colored pencil

Provide children with pencils of varying softness and hardness and experiment with different stroke techniques to show how artists develop tone and shading.

Mixed Media

☀ Blackall, Sophie, *Red Butterfly: How a Princess Smuggled the Secret of Silk out of China* by Deborah Noyes (2007) (p), Chinese ink and watercolor

Breen, Steve, *Stick* (2007) (n–p)

Briggs, Raymond, *The Puddleman* (2006) (n–p), colored pencil and gouache

Church, Caroline Jayne, *Digby Takes Charge* (2007) (n–p), acrylic and collage

Debon, Nicolas, *The Red Sash* by Jean E. Pendziwol (2005) (p–i), gouache and mixed media

Denton, Kady MacDonald, *A Second Is a Hiccup: A Child's Book of Time* by Hazel Hutchins (2007) (p), watercolor and spot art

☀ Diakité, Baba Wagué, *Mee-Ann and the Magic Serpent* (2007) (p), paintings on glazed tile

☀ Diaz, David, *Smoky Night* by Eve Bunting (1994) (p)

Duke, Kate, *The Tale of Pip and Squeak* (2007) (n–p), watercolor and gouache

Dunbar, Polly, *Penguin* (2007) (n–p), outlined drawings in mixed media

Fleming, Denise, *The Cow Who Clucked* (2006) (n), colored cotton fiber, hand-cut stencils, and squeeze bottles

Gorbachev, Valeri, *Red Red Red* (2007) (p), pen-and-ink and watercolor

Gore, Leonid, *Danny's First Snow* (2007) (p), acrylic and pastel

Grey, Mini, *The Adventures of the Dish and the Spoon* (2006) (p)

Hillenbrand, Will, *What a Treasure!* by Jane Hillenbrand (2006) (n)

☀ Isadora, Rachel, *The Princess and the Pea* (2007) (n–p), oils on patterned paper

Jackson, Shelley, *The Chicken-Chasing Queen of Lamar County* by Janice N. Harrington (2007) (n), paintings plus blend of printed paper, fabric, photos, and other items

James, Ann, *Ready, Set, Skip!* by Jane O'Connor (2007) (n), pencil and watercolor

Johnson, Stephen T., *Alphabet City* (1995) (p–i), pastel, watercolor, gouache, and charcoal

☀ Johnson, Steve and Lou Fancher, *Amazing Peace: A Christmas Poem* by Maya Angelou (2008) (p–i), oil, acrylic, and fabric on canvas

Juan, Ana, *The Jewel Box Ballerinas* by Monique de Varennes (2007) (p–i), acrylic and crayon

Kellogg, Steven, *Clorinda Takes Flight* by Robert Kinerk (2007) (p–i)

☀ Meade, Holly, *Sky Sweeper* by Phyllis Gershator (2005) (p–i), collage and paint with delicate lines

☀ McDermott, Gerald, *Raven: A Trickster Story from the Northwest* (1993) (p), gouache and colored pencil

McFarland, Richard, *Grandfather's Wrinkles* by Kathryn England (2007) (p–i), pencil, watercolor, and pastel

Milgrim, David, *Time to Get Up, Time to Go* (2006) (n), digital pastels

Myers, Christopher, *Blues Journey* by Walter Dean Myers (2003) (p–i)

☀ _____ , *Harlem* by Walter Dean Myers (1997) (p–i)

☀ Nelson, Kadir, *Henry's Freedom Box* by Ellen Levine (2007) (p–i), pencil, watercolor, and oil paint

Niland, Deborah, *Annie's Chair* (2006) (n–p), gouache and digital art

Perkins, Lynne Rae, *Pictures from Our Vacation* (2007) (p–i), pen-and-ink and watercolor

Peterson, Dawn, *Helen, Ethel & the Crazy Quilt: Based on the 1890 Letters Between Helen Keller and Ethel Orr* by Nancy Orr Johnson Jensen (2007) (p–i), archival photographs, watercolor, and actual artifacts

Reiser, Lynn, *Hardworking Puppies* (2006) (n–p), Sharpie markers, White-Out, watercolor, scissors, tape, and a copy machine

Seeger, Laura Vaccaro, *Dog and Bear: Two Friends, Three Stories* (2007) (n–p), ink pen, and paint

Small, David, *Once Upon a Banana* by Jennifer Armstrong (2006) (p), line and watercolor

Sneed, Brad, *The Boy Who Was Raised by Librarians* by Carla Morris (2007) (p), watercolor and gouache

(continued)

Mixed Media, continued

Stevens, Janet, *Tops and Bottoms* (1995) (P)

Taback, Simms, *There Was an Old Lady Who Swallowed a Fly* (1997) (P)

_____, *Joseph Had a Little Overcoat* (1999) (P), watercolor, gouache, pencil, ink, and collage

✳ Talbott, Hudson, *Show Way* by Jacqueline Woodson (2005) (I), chalk, watercolor, and muslin

Varon, Sara, *Chicken and Cat* (2006) (N), digital and ink art

✳ Young, Ed, *My Mei Mei* (2006) (P), gouache, pastel, and collage

After exploring a variety of media with children and looking at a variety of mixed media picture books, ask them how many different combinations they can come up with and then try some of these out to illustrate a story. Have them bring various materials from the recycling bin at home and see how these might be included in an illustration.

Oil Paintings

✳ Caravela, Elena, *A Night of Tamales & Roses* by Joanna H. Kraus (2007) (P)

de Monfried, Dorothée, *I'd Really Like to Eat a Child* by Sylviane Donnio (2007) (P–I)

Goossens, Philippe, *Sam Tells Stories* by Thierry Robberecht (2007) (N–P)

Hallensleben, Georg, *Fox* by Kate Banks (2007) (N)

✳ Ransome, James E., *The Old Dog* by Charlotte Zolotow (1995) (P–I)

Zelinsky, Paul, *Rapunzel* (1997) (P–I)

_____, *Rumpelstiltskin* (1986) (P–I)

Oils can damage clothing and may even be dangerous for some children if they are allergic to the chemicals involved. It is probably best to consult with an art teacher before exposing children to oil paint.

Outline Drawing and Comic Strip

deGroat, Diane, *Last One in Is a Rotten Egg!* (2007) (N–P)

McLeod, Bob, *SuperHero ABC* (2006) (N), comic-book illustration

Phillips, Louise, *I Heard a Little Baa* by Elizabeth MacLeod (2007) (N, board book)

Thomas, Jan, *What Will Fat Cat Sit On?* (2007) (N–P)

Write characters' dialogue in speech balloons. Illustrate the action. Examine different framing techniques and how they affect the flow of the narrative.

Pastels, Crayon, and Charcoal

Owens, Mary Beth, *Panda Whispers* (2007) (N–P)

Phelan, Matt, *Very Hairy Bear* by Alice Schertle (2007) (N–P)

Pigni, Guido, *The Story of Giraffe* by Ronald Hermsen (2007) (P)

Pinel, Hervé, *I'm Bored!* by Christine Schneider (2004) (N–P)

Rayyan, Omar, *To Catch a Burglar* by Mary Casanova (2007) (P–I)

Shapiro, Michelle, *A Piece of Chalk* by Jennifer Ericsson (2007) (N–P)

Williams, Sam, *Tummy Girl* by Roseanne Thong (2007) (N–P)

Yee, Wong Herbert, *Who Likes Rain?* (2007) (N–P)

Use crayons, pastels, water crayons, charcoal, and markers and try them out on a variety of textured papers. Include crayon scratch drawings and any other combination of media.

Pen-and-Ink

Gravett, Emily, *Meerkat Mail* (2007) (N–P)

✳ Kwon, Yoon-duck, *My Cat Copies Me* (2007) (N–P), brush calligraphy

Rogers, Gregory, *Midsummer Knight* (2007) (P–I)

van Haeringen, Annemarie, *Little Donkey and the Birthday Present* by Rindert Kromhout (2007) (N–P)

Examine different ways artists use pen-and-ink for outlining and shading, and have children see if they can reproduce some of these techniques in their own illustrations.

Photographs or Photomontage

Crews, Nina, *Below* (2005) (N), photomontage

Fisher, Valorie, *Moxy Maxwell Does Not Love Stuart Little* by Peggy Gifford (2007) (P–I)

✳ Global Fund for Children, *Global Babies* (2007) (N–P), board book

✳ Jiménez, Moisés and Jiménez, Armondo, *ABeCedarios: Mexican Folk Art ABCs in English and Spanish* by Cynthia Weill and K. B. Basseches (2007) (N–P), photographs of wood sculpture

Rotner, Shelley, *Senses at the Seashore* (2006) (N)

Stanton, Brian, *Dog* by Matthew Van Fleet (2007) (N), board book

Give children disposable cameras and have them take photographs to illustrate stories or informational pieces about their own life and neighborhood.

Scratchboard and Engraving

Pinkney, Brian, *The Faithful Friend* by Robert D. San Souci (1995) (P–I)

✳ _____, *Duke Ellington: The Piano Prince and His Orchestra* by Andrea Davis Pinkney (1998) (P–I)

_____, *Peggony-Po: A Whale of a Tale* by Andrea Davis Pinkney (2006) (P)

Crayon scratch drawings can be a fun way to explore this technique.

Watercolor

Brooks, Karen Stormer, *Piggy Wiglet* by David L. Harrison (2007) (N–P)

☀ Daly, Niki, *Happy Birthday, Jamela!* (2006) (P)

Davenier, Christine, *Has Anyone Seen My Emily Greene?* by Norma Fox Mazer (2007) (N–P)

☀ Dodson, Bert, *Kami and the Yaks* by Andrea Stenn Stryer (2007) (P–I)

☀ Domi, *Napi Goes to the Mountain* by Antonio Ramirez (2006) (P)

☀ Glick, Sharon, *Perros! Perros! Dogs! Dogs!: A Story in English and Spanish* by Ginger Foglesong Guy (2007) (N–P)

Henkes, Kevin, *A Good Day* (2007) (N–P)

_____, *Owen* (1993) (N–P)

Jeffers, Oliver, *Lost and Found* (2006) (N–P)

Jorisch, Stéphanie, *Granddad's Fishing Buddy* by Mary Quigley (2007) (P)

Kennedy, Anne, *Callie Cat, Ice Skater* by Eileen Spinelli (2007) (N–P)

King, Stephen Michael, *Piglet and Papa* by Margaret Wild (2007) (N–P)

☀ Lewis, E. B., *Night Boat to Freedom* by Margot Theis Raven (2006) (P)

_____, *Pitching in for Eubie* by Jerdine Nolen (2007) (P)

Mammano, Julie, *Rhinos Who Rescue* (2007) (N–P)

Parker, Robert Andrew, *Across the Blue Pacific: A World War II Story* by Louise Borden (2006) (P–I)

Pinkney, Jerry, *The Ugly Duckling* (1999) (P)

Polacco, Patricia, *The Butterfly* (2000) (I)

☀ Reiser, Lynn, *My Way/A mi manera: A Margaret and Margarita Story* (2007) (P–I)

Roberts, David, *The Dumpster Diver* by Janet S. Wong (2007) (P)

☀ Say, Allen, *Tea with Milk* (1999) (P–I)

Shulevitz, Uri, *Snow* (1998) (P)

Tallec, Olivier, *This Is a Poem that Heals Fish* by Jean-Pierre Siméon (2007) (N–P)

Tafuri, Nancy, *The Busy Little Squirrel* (2007) (N–P)

Tjong-Khing, Thé, *Where Is the Cake?* (2007) (N–P)

Tusa, Tricia, *Fred Stays with Me!* by Nancy Coffelt (2006) (P)

☀ Ungar, Richard, *Even Higher* (2007) (P)

Weisner, David, *Flotsam* (2006) (P–I)

_____, *Sector 7* (1999) (P–I)

☀ Williams, Vera B., *A Chair for My Mother* (1982) (P)

Provide children with cardboard strips of varying widths and have them experiment with the different strokes they can achieve. Dipping Q-tips in watercolor and stamping them on paper can be a fun way to experiment with pointillism. Show them how to graduate washes in different colors mixed with water and how various colors are mixed.

Woodcuts and Other Printing Techniques

Azarian, Mary, *Snowflake Bentley* by Jacqueline Briggs Martin (1998) (P–I)

Emberley, Ed, *Drummer Hoff* by Barbara Emberley (1967) (N–P)

Meyer, Jim, *If You Want to See a Caribou* by Phyllis Root (2004) (P)

☀ Louie, Catherine, with calligraphy and chop marks by Wang Fei, *Legend of the Chinese Dragon* by Marie Sellier (2007) (P–I)

Matthews, Tina, *Out of the Egg* (2007) (N–P)

Use linoleum blocks, wood blocks, potato halves, Styrofoam, cardboard, sandpaper, and yarn. Create shapes to dip into paints and stamp onto paper. Make relief prints, etchings, cardboard cuts, and potato prints.

Styles of Art

An artist's style is what makes his or her work recognizable as unique to that artist. Style refers to a configuration of artistic elements (line, shape, color, texture, and artistic medium) that together constitute a specific and identifiable manner of expression (Cianciolo, 1997). Although artists display individual styles, they are also situated in a wider context of various established traditions of art that influence their idiosyncratic styles. Some artists consciously imitate traditional styles of individual artists or schools of art. D. B. Johnson's **Henry** books (*Henry Hikes to Fitchburg*, *Henry Builds a Cabin*, *Henry Climbs a Mountain*, and *Henry Works*) as well as his *Four Legs Bad, Two Legs Good!* (P–I) give a nod to the Cubist style of Georges Braque and Pablo Picasso, and Neil Waldman's *The Starry Night* (I) expertly renders scenes from New York City in Vincent Van Gogh's instantly recognizable style. Rachel Isadora's *ABC Pop!* (N) draws heavily on the 1960s pop art style of Roy Lichtenstein. Leo and Diane Dillon's illustrations for the biblical text *To Everything There Is a Season* (I–A) evoke the universality of the words by imitating fifteen different styles of traditional art, ranging from ancient Egyptian, Greek, and

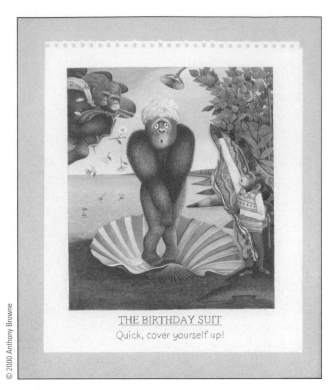

*Anthony Browne frequently parodies the works of famous paintings in the history of art. Here, in **Willy's Pictures**, he refers to Botticelli's* The Birth of Venus.

Roman art to medieval European woodcuts to fourteenth-century Pueblo art. Even more ambitiously, Jon Scieszka and Lane Smith's *Seen Art?* (I–A) follows a young boy named Art through the Museum of Modern Art in New York, as he passes sixty-four famous paintings and sculptures. More humorously, Anthony Browne parodies the styles of twenty-four different painters in *Willy's Pictures* (I–A), amusingly inserting images of gorillas and other primates instead of people. Laurent de Brunhoff's *Babar's Museum of Art* (P–I–A) parodies many styles as well, with elephants substituted for people. Elisa Gutierrez's *Picturescape* (P–I–A), a finely crafted wordless picturebook, is a fantasy about a boy who takes a trip to an art museum and magically enters paintings by twelve famous Canadian painters. (The book has its own website, www.picturescape.ca, which has information about the twelve painters and their work.) Indeed, there is a growing number of picturebooks that either parody or imitate the style of particular artists, specific paintings, or specific cultural time periods where an artistic style was prevalent. These types of picturebooks can be used to teach children the history of art (Sipe, 2001).

Nevertheless, each artist strives for his or her own unique style. In addition to reflecting the individuality and artistic strength of the artist, style is influenced by the content and mood of the text as well as by the intended

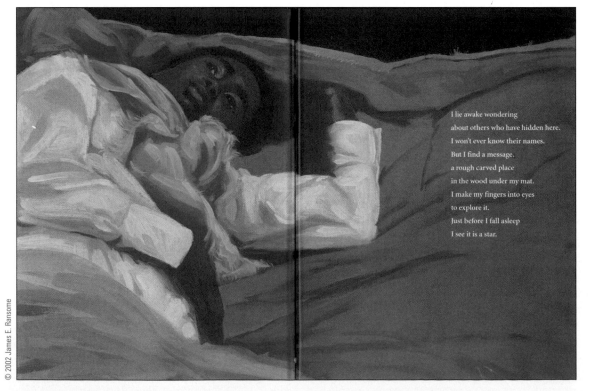

*The painterly style of James Ransome is well displayed in this illustration from **Under the Quilt of Night**, where the individual bold brushstrokes are clearly visible.*

Teaching Style to Children

It may seem as if style is a slippery concept to teach; however, students quickly learn to recognize the individual styles of artists, especially those artists who employ a consistent style in most of their books. After encountering a few books illustrated by Tomie dePaola, for example, students can spot a new dePaola book from across the room! They may not be able to articulate what makes his books so easily recognizable, but we can help students put into words what they have already noticed unconsciously. Here are a few suggestions for teaching the idea of style.

- First, start with two illustrators who have fairly consistent yet very different styles, such as Tomie dePaola and Jerry Pinkney. Then talk with the students about what makes work by these two illustrators so different. Discussion might result in these observations:

  - dePaola uses an outline style, often in dark brown (sepia), in either watercolor or diluted acrylic paint. His people are full of rounded shapes, and the facial features are often suggested by dots for eyes and minimal lines for nose and mouth. His colors are almost always tints—a pleasing pastel palette. Colored shapes are always surrounded by outlines. He commonly includes features such as fluffy white clouds and religious symbols, as well as hearts and doves in his illustrations.

  - Pinkney draws in pencil first (this is called the underdrawing), and then paints over the pencil drawing with vibrant watercolors. The pencil, however, still remains visible. His shapes and figures are not done in outline style. His renderings of people are much more realistic than dePaola's:

they look like carefully done portraits, and every face and body is different, like real people's faces and bodies. Indeed, he carefully poses models who wear the clothing he intends to depict in his preliminary drawings. His colors tend to be bright and saturated, and because the shapes are not outlined, colors often "bleed" and blend into one another. He rarely includes "signature" features, in contrast to dePaola.

- Second, after you have compared and contrasted several illustrators whose styles are quite different, try something a little more difficult: have the students examine the illustrations of two artists who are similar, but distinct, for example Jerry Pinkney and Ted Lewin.

Pinkney and Lewin both use watercolors, however Pinkney's underdrawing of pencil always shows through, whereas Lewin's work, without any underdrawing, appears less spontaneous. As well, Pinkney has a "loose" watercolor style, using a fair amount of water, and his backgrounds are usually suggested by dappled shade and light that suggests impressionist painting. In contrast, Lewin's watercolor style is "tighter," with more discernible clear outlines and more controlled use of the brush. The effect is that Lewin's illustrations look more detailed and finished. Both illustrators are master watercolorists, but a close look at their work reveals very different styles. When you have finished closely examining Pinkney and Lewin's work, take a look at E. B. Lewis's watercolors, which seem to lie somewhere between Pinkney's loose style and Lewin's tight style.

---

audience (Cianciolo, 1976). In very general terms, a *painterly* style refers to works of art in which individual brushstrokes are immediately visible, as in the bold use of oil paints by James Ransome in his illustrations for *Under the Quilt of Night* (I) and *Pele* (I). This contrasts with styles that are smoother or more "finished" in appearance, where the individual brushstrokes are blended together so that they are not noticeable except on very close inspection.

Some artists' styles remain constant across many books, so that their work is immediately recognizable. The styles of Tomie dePaola and Jerry Pinkney, for example, are remarkably uniform across their many picturebooks (see Teaching Idea 3.2). Other artists may vary their styles to suit the subject matter or setting of the story. In the illustrations for *Saint Valentine* (I), Robert Sabuda chose small squares of colored paper to give the effect of mosaic,

a common artistic technique in ancient Rome, the setting for the book. For the medieval setting of *Arthur and the Sword* (P–I), Sabuda imitated the effect of medieval stained glass by painting on clear acetate, and then photographing the translucent illustrations with strong light shining behind them. In *King Tutankhamen's Gift* (I), he painted on papyrus in the formalized style of ancient Egypt. Diane Stanley is another artist who sometimes employs a particular style to complement stories she illustrates, as in *Joan of Arc* (medieval European miniatures, I); *Shaka, King of the Zulus* (South African beadwork, I); and *Fortune* (ancient Persian miniatures, I).

Artistic styles available in books for children are thus many and varied. Next, we discuss some styles that are frequently found in picturebooks for children and adolescents.

Kadir Nelson's realistic oil paintings underscore the power of the African American men that Ntozake Shange presents in **Ellington Was Not a Street.**

● ● REPRESENTATIONAL ART ● ●

Representational art consists of literal, realistic depictions of characters, objects, and events. Paul Zelinsky creates exquisite, realistic oil paintings in the style of the French and Italian Renaissance painters to illustrate the Grimm's fairy tale **Rapunzel** (P–I). Beautifully rendered settings and emotionally evocative portraits of the leading characters add drama and dimension to the old tale. Ted Lewin is an illustrator whose watercolors are often so realistic that they resemble color photographs, as in **One Green Apple** (I), Eve Bunting's moving story of a young immigrant Muslim girl who makes her first steps in becoming friends with her U.S. classmates during a field trip. Lewin also captures the excitement of a county fair at night in his brilliantly realistic watercolors for **Fair!** (P–I). Jan Peng Wang's beautiful realistic paintings provide detail and elaborate character in Paul Yee's moving story, **A Song for Ba** (I). Ntozake Shange's poetic remembrance of some of the African American men who changed the world, **Ellington Was Not a Street** (P–I), is brought to life by Kadir Nelson's realistic oil paintings. Nelson's work in this book received a Coretta Scott King Award.

● ● SURREALISTIC ART ● ●

Surrealistic art contains "startling images and incongruities" that often suggest an "attitude or mockery about conventionalities" (Cianciolo, 1976, p. 40). Surreal pictures are often composed of the kinds of images experienced in dreams or nightmares or in a state of hallucination. Chris Van Allsburg's surrealistic paintings in **Jumanji** (I)

The surrealistic and whimsical qualities of David Wiesner's exquisite detailed watercolors for **Flotsam** *are shown to their best effect in this colorful illustration.*

extend the clever challenge of the text and are full of garishly funny details. Anthony Browne's surrealist paintings in his many books, such as *Changes* (P) and *Voices in the Park* (P–I), enhance the ideas he conveys in the texts. In David Wiesner's wordless books, such as *Tuesday* (P–I), and *Flotsam* (P–I), strange phenomena occur, and totally surreal events unfold in the skies or under water. Lane Smith's surrealist illustrations for several of Jon Scieszka's books, including *The Stinky Cheese Man and Other Fairly Stupid Tales* (P–I–A) match the bizarre, subversive stories.

• • IMPRESSIONISTIC ART • •

Impressionist artists emphasize light and color; they create a fleeting impression of reality. They may break an image into many small bits of color to mimic the way the eye perceives and merges color to create images. The result is often reminiscent of dappled sunlight. Jerry Pinkney's watercolor illustrations often convey this beautiful dappled effect, for example in the lush jungle backgrounds of Julius Lester's *Sam and the Tigers* (P–I). Ed Young's *Lon Po Po* (N–P–I) and Emily Arnold McCully's *Mirette on the High Wire* (P) both won Caldecott Medals for their beautiful, impressionistic paintings. Jerome Lagarrigue's impressionistic paintings in Janice Harrington's *Going North* (P–I) beautifully depict the experiences of a young African American girl and her family in the 1960s as they drive from Alabama to Nebraska, seeking a better life "up north."

• • FOLK ART • •
AND NAIVE ART

Folk art is a broad designation for the style of artistic expression of a particular cultural group. Folk art may simplify, exaggerate, or distort reality, but it does so in a way that is characteristic of the traditional art of a culture, often through the use of traditional motifs, symbols, and techniques.

There are as many folk art styles as there are folk cultures. Many artists illustrate folktales told in the style of a particular culture using the characteristics, motifs, and symbols found in the art of that culture, as Gerald McDermott does in many picturebooks, including *Zomo the Rabbit* (West African, P), *Raven* (Pacific northwest Native American, P), *Coyote* (American southwest Native American, P), and *The Stonecutter* (Japanese, P). Anita Riggio and You Yang's illustrations for Pegi Dietz Shea's *The Whispering Cloth* (P–I) are *pa'ndaus*, Hmong tapestries that contain traditional symbols and images. Holly Berry relies on traditional Romanian folk art designs to illustrate Sabina Rascol's retelling of the classic Romanian tale *The Impudent Rooster* (P–I).

© 1995 Anita Riggio

She helped Grandmother grow chilies and coriander.
Mai searched for empty glass bottles. When she
put them upside down in the ground around her hut,
they sparkled.
This is how Mai lived for many years.

The texture of the pa'ndau, *a tapestry with traditional symbols and images embroidered by Hmong women, creates uniquely beautiful illustrations for* The Whispering Cloth.

Naive art is often difficult to distinguish from folk art; indeed a particular style of art may be described interchangeably as folk or naive art. Martin Jarrie's illustrations for *ABC USA* (I–A) are a good example of the blurring of folk art and naive art. Naive art may look technically unsophisticated, but it is usually marked by

© 2005 Martin Jarrie

Martin Jarrie's amusing and seemingly naive style of painting for ABC USA *shows his sophisticated use of color and design.*

High above the trees, birds soared on the wind. Down by the trees, the ladies played with their young children. Nobody blew over.

28

In **How the Ladies Stopped the Wind**, *Gunnella's simple naive style is matched by the folktale quality of the story.*

an artist's clear, intense emotions and visions. Artists may be self-taught or may give the impression of ignoring traditional academic standards of art. For example, Martin Jarrie is an internationally recognized artist and illustrator, and there is nothing unsophisticated about his art; he simply makes use of the conventions of folk and naive art. These conventions include adherence to frontal posture or profile and a disregard for traditional representation of anatomy and perspective. Backgrounds, including trees, plants, and flowers, are rendered simply, and there is often a lack of three-dimensional perspective. Naive art presents the essence of experiences and objects in a deceptively simplified fashion, using clearly recognizable forms for people and places.

Gunnella's oil paintings for Bruce McMillan's *How the Ladies Stopped the Wind* (P) use rounded and simplified shapes with little shading to portray the humans and animals in this folk story. Ashley Bryan, in *Let It Shine* (P–I), an exuberant illustrated version of three spirituals (P–I), uses flat, unshaded frontal or profile depictions of people, a flattened perspective, and vivid colors. In Monica Gunning's *Not a Copper Penny in Me House* (P–I), Frané Lessac creates brilliantly colored naive paintings that capture the charm and simplicity of

life on the island of Jamaica. The vivid images conveyed in the words of the poems are perfectly complemented by the richly detailed naive pictures.

• • OUTLINE STYLE • •

Outline style art emphasizes line and often reduces features to simplified shapes. A special type of outline style, cartoon art, often uses exaggeration in two dimensions to create caricature (Cianciolo, 1976). The artist may employ such cartoon techniques as slapstick and may use ludicrous distortions of characteristics to depict absurdities and incongruities of situations so as to evoke laughter or at least a smile. Both adults and children are regularly exposed to outline style art through comic strips, political cartoons, and, of course, animated films and videos. Because of its exaggerated expressive qualities, outline style art communicates most directly and can often be understood without words or very sparse text. The cartoon outline art of comic books is perfectly adapted to the picturebook format in George O'Connor's *Kapow!* (P–I), the story of a boy and his friends who pretend to be superheroes.

There used to be a tendency to disparage outline style art, perhaps because of its connection to cartoons, comic

In **Kapow!** *by George O'Connor, the cartoon illustrations complement the story of a boy and his friends playing superhero games.*

books, comic strips, and animated films. Outline style art has become more sophisticated, however, and is increasingly popular with artists and readers. Many of our greatest children's illustrators were clearly inspired by cartoon art, and they continue to work in that style. Outline style, though, is an umbrella term for any art in which shapes are clearly delineated by lines. Such brilliant author-illustrators as Maurice Sendak, creator of *Where the Wild Things Are* (N–P), William Steig, creator of *Sylvester and the Magic Pebble* (P–I), Tomi Ungerer, creator of *The Moon Man* (P–I), and James Marshall, creator of a comic version of *Goldilocks and the Three Bears* (P), all use their various outline styles to create award-winning books. Rosemary Wells, author of *Max's Bunny Business* (N–P) and the many other Max books, uses her cartoon humor to tell of the escapades of the mischievous boy bunny, Max.

Olivier Dunrea's cartoon ink and watercolor art in *Peedie* and *Boo-Boo* (P) is beautifully drawn and full of energy and the humor of surprise. In his **David** books, David Shannon uses full-color outline style to create a portrait of a perfectly believable but impossible little boy. The simple and energetic outline style of Mo Willems's **Pigeon** books (*Don't Let the Pigeon Drive the Bus!*, winner of the Caldecott Medal, *The Pigeon Finds a Hot Dog!*, *Don't Let the Pigeon Stay Up Late*, and *The Pigeon Wants a Puppy*), as well as *Knuffle Bunny*, a Caldecott Medal book and *Knuffle Bunny, Too* (P) is a perfect accompaniment for his minimalist texts. Emily Arnold McCully is a master of outline style, as shown in *Cat Jumped In!*

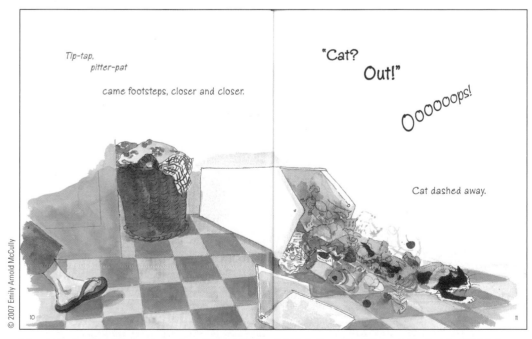

The sophisticated outline style employed by Emily Arnold McCully in Tess Weaver's **Cat Jumped In!** *defines the basket of laundry and the pieces of garbage spilling from the can the cat has just upended.*

(N–P) by Tess Weaver, where the loose watercolor style is "anchored" and given shape by the thin black ink outlines. Another master, David Small, won the Caldecott Medal for his illustrations for Judith St. George's *So You Want to Be President?* (I–A). Small's many books with his wife, Sarah Stewart, such as *The Friend* (P), have helped bring outline style into a new, sophisticated realm. Similarly, Ian Falconer's **Olivia** books (N–P) display a very delicate outline style that manages to convey an enormous range of actions, feelings, and thoughts. All of these outline styles, each quite different from one another, show how varied this style can be in picturebook art.

• • COMBINING STYLES • •

Some artists purposefully combine styles to produce intriguing illustrations. For example, Pamela Patrick's pastel illustrations for Richard Ammon's *An Amish Year* (I) are an interesting juxtaposition of realistic and impressionistic styles. Human figures, especially faces, are rendered in almost photographic realism, whereas landscape foregrounds and backgrounds are drawn in an impressionistic style that includes many strokes of different colors that combine to suggest a sun-drenched field or meadow. In Chris Gall's *Dear Fish* (P–I) outline style combines with surrealism to match the story. While at the beach for the day, a boy writes a letter beginning "Dear Fish," inviting the fish to come for a visit on dry land. The resulting magical chaos—a barracuda takes the place of a baseball bat; a shark replaces a bucking bronco; a school of fish invades a school classroom; and a blue whale acts as a hot air balloon to give passengers the ride of their life—is perfectly matched by the combination of styles.

All these many styles of art—representational, surrealistic, impressionistic, folk and naive, and outline style—are found in picturebooks. Teaching Idea 3.3 offers ideas for studying the style of a favorite illustrator, and Figure 3.4 suggests professional resources for studying illustrators and illustrations in picturebooks.

© 2000 Pamela Patrick

*Although the faces and figures in Pamela Patrick's illustrations for **An Amish Year** by Richard Ammon are quite realistic, the backgrounds, especially the field and trees, have a distinctly impressionistic style.*

Chris Gall's bold outline style uses surrealism with exciting results in his illustrations for **Dear Fish**.

Teaching Idea 3·3

Study the Art of Your Favorite Illustrator

Many artists develop a characteristic way of presenting ideas visually; some vary their style according to the text. Read-aloud books by the illustrators discussed in this chapter or in Pat Cummings's *Talking with Artists*, volumes 1 and 2, ask listeners to respond to the art. Later, see if they can recognize the artist's style when you cover up the names and titles. Play "Name that Illustrator": Hold up an illustration and ask, "Who is the illustrator?"

Collect several books by one illustrator and compare them. Is the art similar across books? Does the art represent a distinct approach? Ask students to describe each illustrator's work and to use examples of the work to illustrate their points.

The following are some illustrators you might want to consider:

Debra Frasier (cut paper, collage, mixed media)
Variety of moods, vibrant energy, total design

Patricia Polacco (watercolor, ink)
Warm, inviting, integrated with story

Peter Sís (watercolor, pen and ink)
Emotional, lots of detail, stories within art

Tomie dePaola (folk and naive art)
Strong outlines, sturdy people, hearts, birds

Chris Van Allsburg (surrealism)
Ranges from pencil to full color, bull terrier in every book

Jan Brett (representational)
Uses intricate borders

Eric Carle (collage)
Bold color, strong line

Ted Rand (representational)
Varies light and shadow throughout his books

Lauren Stringer (acrylics)
Rich colors and rounded shapes

Illustrations and Illustrators: A Suggested Bookshelf for Teachers

The following books may be useful to you as you learn more about illustrations for picturebooks and the artists who produce them, as well as the uses of picturebooks in the classroom. The list is arranged in order from the latest-published books to the ones published earliest.

Marcus, L. S. (2008). *Pass It Down: Five Picture-Book Families Make Their Mark*. New York: Walker & Company

Marcus traces the work of members of five influential families in the world of picturebooks: Crews/Jonas; Hurd; Myers; Pinkney; and Rockwell.

Evans, Dilys. (2008). *Show & Tell: Exploring the Fine Art of Children's Book Illustration*. San Francisco: Chronicle Books

In this beautifully crafted book, Evans takes twelve eminent picturebook illustrators/authors and writes insightful comments about both their art and their lives.

Charles, Z., and L. Robinson, (2008). *Over Rainbows and Down Rabbit Holes: The Art of Children's Books*. Amherst, MA: Eric Carle Museum of Picture Book Art

Featuring thirteen illustrators from classics such as Arthur Rackham and Edmund Dulac to contemporary masters such as Chris Van Allsburg and David Wiesner, this gorgeous book will acquaint readers with the best illustrations for children over a broad span of time.

Thompson, Terry. (2008). *Adventures in Graphica: Using Comics and Graphic Novels to Teach Comprehension, 2–6*. Portland, ME: Stenhouse

This very practical book will be interesting to educators who want to know how to use "graphica" (Thompson's own term) in teaching children critical thinking skills and visual literacy.

No author noted. (2008). *The Best Children's Books of the Year: 2008 Edition. Books Published in 2007*. Distributed by Teachers College Press, New York.

This very carefully considered list, which has been produced for some years, is now available through Teachers College Press and will reach a well-deserved wider audience. It contains annotated lists of books (divided by age and topic) chosen by a committee of Bank Street instructors, and covers books from preschool through young adult.

No author noted. (2007). *Artist to Artist: 23 Major Illustrators Talk to Children about Their Art*. Amherst, MA: Eric Carle Museum of Picture Book Art

The title for this book (whose proceeds benefit the Eric Carle Museum of Picture Book Art in Amherst, MA) says it all: each of the artists writes in a way that is accessible to children while also captivating adults with interesting details about their motivations to become illustrators and their artistic styles.

Marcus, L. S., J. B. Curley, and C. Ward, (2007). *Children Should Be Seen: The Image of the Child in American Picture Book Art*. Amherst, MA: Eric Carle Museum of Picture Book Art

This volume is a treasure trove of eighty-four contemporary American artists and focuses on the changing images of children and childhood present in their picturebooks.

From Cover to Cover: Artistic and Design Elements Specific to Picture Storybooks

In this section, we continue our discussion of artistic features by concentrating on elements that are particular to picture storybooks. To help you conceptualize these features more clearly, we will be frequently referring to three very different picturebooks, *Henry's Freedom Box* (P–I), *Trainstop* (P–I–A), and **Don't Let the Pigeon Drive the Bus!** (N–P), as well as several other examples of excellent picturebook art and design. *Henry's Freedom Box* (hereafter referred to as *Henry*) retells the true story of one slave's ingenious and courageous escape to freedom by mailing himself in a box to a free state. *Trainstop* is an imaginative

wordless fantasy about a girl's adventure on a city train as she gets magically transported to the countryside where she helps rescue an inhabitant of a village of tiny people. **Don't Let the Pigeon Drive the Bus!** (hereafter referred to as *Pigeon*) is a hilarious recounting of a pigeon's unsuccessful attempts to convince the reader to let it drive a bus, bringing to mind the various strategies preschoolers will use to achieve a goal: nagging, reasoning, bribing, whining, and throwing tantrums.

• • BREVITY • •

Most picturebooks differ dramatically from novels by being relatively brief. The standard length is thirty-two pages, such as in *Trainstop* or *Pigeon*. Some authors and illustrators need a little more to tell their story completely: *Henry* is forty pages long. Some need a little less (see the Close

Carter, J. B., Ed. (2007). *Building Literacy Connections with Graphic Novels: Page by Page, Panel by Panel.* Urbana, IL: National Council of Teachers of English

A companion piece to the Thompson book listed earlier, this book's contributors focus on teaching English using graphic novels to middle school and high school students.

No author noted. (2007). *Knock, Knock!* New York: Dial Books for Young Readers

A companion to *Why Did the Chicken Cross the Road?* (below), this picturebook contains fourteen more illustrators' works. Only one artist—Chris Raschka—appears in both books, so together the books present work by twenty-seven different illustrators.

Salisbury, Martin. (2007). *Play Pen: New Children's Book Illustration.* London: Laurence King

If you're interested in international children's picturebooks, this is a book you will consult again and again. Salisbury includes insightful biographies and discussions of the work of thirty-six international illustrators.

No author noted. (2006). *Why Did the Chicken Cross the Road?* New York: Dial Books for Young Readers

This age-old question is answered by fourteen illustrators, giving us a large sample of the range of contemporary illustration.

Blake, Quentin (2006). *Magic Pencil: Children's Book Illustration Today.* London: The British Council and the British Library

This lavishly illustrated book, with a foreword by Quentin Blake and an informative essay on the history of British children's illustration by Joanna Carey, contains information about thirteen British illustrators for children and includes reproductions of many of their works.

No author noted. (2005). *The Art of Reading: Forty Illustrators Celebrate Reading Is Fundamental's 40th Anniversary.* New York: Dutton Books

This is another feast for the eyes: forty illustrators from around the world write about their lives as artists and include original art inspired by their favorite books as children. Sales of the book benefit the organization Reading Is Fundamental (RIF), which has put millions of books in children's hands.

Aldana, Patricia, Ed. (2004). *Under the Spell of the Moon: Art for Children from the World's Great Illustrators.* Toronto, Ontario: Groundwood Books

This is an international collection of thirty-two illustrators whose work represents the best in children's illustration. Each illustrator is showcased by reproductions of double-page spreads from their books. This is an artistic feast, sponsored by the International Board on Books for Young People (IBBY).

Frohardt, Darcie Clark (1999). *Teaching Art with Books Kids Love.* Golden, CO: Fulcrum Resources

This useful book encourages teachers to connect famous fine artists with picturebooks that imitate or parody their styles, and to help children make art that is related to these styles.

Look at *Monkey and Me* (N–P) on page 105). What you will notice is that the number of pages is almost always a multiple of eight. This is because of the printing process; generally, eight pages are printed on each side of very large sheets of paper. When these pages are folded and cut, the sixteen pages (counting both sides) are called a *signature*, and generally two signatures are bound together for a picturebook. Leaving aside several pages for the title page, dedication page, and publishing information, you can see that there are a limited number of pages left. Pages are rarely numbered in picturebooks, so that two facing pages are referred to as *openings* or *double-page spreads*. The left-hand side of the opening is called the *verso*, and the right-hand side is called the *recto* (think "recto" = "right"). The "first opening" is the double-page spread where the text of the story begins. Writing (and illustrating) a picturebook is similar to writing a sonnet; every word must count, and every illustration must be used to its fullest advantage because there is a limited amount of space. See Teaching Idea 3.4 for ideas on teaching children to examine what illustrators choose to include and what they choose to omit.

⋅ ⋅ ELEMENTS ⋅ ⋅
"SURROUNDING"
THE STORY

Every part of the picturebook, literally from cover to cover, is used to convey meaning and contributes to our perception of it as one complete artistic whole. The *dust jacket* surrounds the front and back covers, folded inside the covers at the front and back to keep it in place. The front inner *flap* of the dust jacket often gives a general description of the story as an enticement to the reader, and the back inner flap often gives information about the author

Teaching Idea 3.4

What Do Illustrators Choose to Illustrate—and What Do They Omit?

Because picturebook artists do not have a great many double-page spreads (the average number is sixteen in most picturebooks), they must choose what scenes or events they are going to illustrate and what they will leave to the reader's imagination.

Try this activity with students: Assemble a text set of retellings of the same story in picturebook format. For example, you could use the story of *Jack and the Beanstalk*.

Jack and the Beanstalk

✿ Steven Kellogg (1997)

✿ John Howe (1998)

✿ Matt Tavares (2006)

First, read the story from a book of fairy tales, without showing any illustrations, to familiarize students with the plot. Then read the versions illustrated by Kellogg, Howe, and Tavares.

1. What choices did the illustrators make for the front and back covers? The endpages?

2. What illustration appears on the title page?

3. What scenes or events in the story did each illustrator choose to include? What was omitted from one version that is present in another?

Other trios that would work well for this activity include:

Rapunzel

✿ Trina Schart Hyman (1982)

✿ Paul Zelinsky (1997)

✿ Maja Dusikova (2000)

The Ugly Duckling

✿ Jerry Pinkney (1999)

✿ Steve Johnson and Lou Fancher (2007)

✿ Bernadette Watts (2007)

---

and illustrator. The front and back covers themselves (called the *case*) are either thick cardboard or cloth-covered board. The covers may be identical to the dust jacket, or they may have a different illustration. In *Trainstop*, the dust jacket and the front and back covers are subtly different. The dust jacket of this book depicts a train with the city in the background, and the title of the book on a horizontal stripe of the train, along with a girl looking out of one of the train windows. The front and back board covers show the train with a strip of green grass beside the tracks and the same girl with a surprised look on her face; as well, the title word is missing from the train. Thus, the differences between the dust jacket and the case prefigure the girl's adventure.

Some front and back covers contain only the title of the book, stamped or printed on the case, as in *Woolvs in the Sitee* (I–A) (see the Close Look on page 124). In addition, some books (like *Trainstop*) have a dust jacket or case that contains one continuous illustration. In other books, the front cover and front dust jacket contain one illustration whereas the back cover and back dust jacket depict another illustration. In *Henry*, the front cover shows Henry, an African American boy, sitting outdoors, silhouetted against a blue sky and tiny birds, whereas the back cover resembles part of a wooden box. In this way, Kadir Nelson, the illustrator, conveys Henry's longing for

freedom on the front cover, whereas the back cover shows us the method he will use to escape from slavery.

Contemporary dust jackets and covers are often enriched by sophisticated printing techniques. For example, *Trainstop*'s jacket and board covers feature the use of thin coatings of mylar, a clear plastic, to highlight the windows of the train; this, of course, makes the windows look more realistic because they reflect light like glass. In addition, the title word is not only covered in mylar, but also is embossed, raising the letters slightly for a three-dimensional effect. The letters of the title and names of the author and illustrator are also covered in mylar in *Henry*, drawing our attention to them and causing them to appear closer to us than the matte surface of the underlying illustration of Henry.

When we open a picturebook, the first things we see are the front *endpages* (sometimes called endpapers). The part of the endpage that adheres to the inside of the cover is called the *pastedown*, and the part that is like a normal page is called the *flyleaf*. Every hardcover book has endpages because they are used to attach the covers to the rest of the pages in the book. In picturebooks, however, special attention is often paid to the endpages because they are like the closed curtains on the stage of a theater before a performance begins. Picturebook endpages may be plain or illustrated, but even if there is a plain color, there is a reason for this choice; the color may correspond to the palette used in the book, or it may give a hint about the mood of the story. Both *Trainstop* and *Henry* have plain-colored endpages, but the colors have a definite relationship with the stories. In *Henry*, the endpages are a warm shade of metallic bronze, which harmonizes well with the palette used throughout the book and also suggests the hope and overcoming of adversity in the story. *Trainstop* has green endpages that are the same color as both the bright grass of the countryside and the little girl's slacks. For the ochre-colored endpages in the Caldecott-winning *The Hello, Goodbye Window* (P–I), illustrator Chris Raschka spent hours matching hand-painted color swatches to printer's samples to find the perfect color to harmonize with his palette for the images in the book.

Other endpages are illustrated. Moreover, some front endpages are identical to the back endpages, and other back endpages are different from the front. For example, in *Pigeon*, the front endpages present us with a pigeon, eyes closed, and a "thought bubble" containing multiple images of the pigeon driving a bus. The back endpages are similar, except that the pigeon seems to be thinking about driving a large red tractor-trailer truck. Thus, the endpages in this book give us a hint about the pigeon's aspirations at the beginning and the end of the story. Another good example of differently illustrated front and back endpages is found in Matthew Baek's *Be Gentle with the Dog, Dear!* (N–P), the story of a toddler who learns that her expressions of affection are sometimes a bit too physically hurtful for the family dog. The front endpages show Elisa, the toddler, chasing Tag; the erratic dotted line suggests the chaotic route the chase has taken. The other family pet, a kitten, lies curled up observing the chase. At the end of the story, Elisa turns her attention to the kitten, and the back endpages show her energetically chasing the kitten while Tag looks on. Here again, the front and back endpages frame the story by suggesting the beginning and the ending. Therefore, when you read picture storybooks to students, it's a good idea to take a look at both the front and back endpages before you start reading the story and see if they are different in any way. All of these options are the result of careful choices by the author, illustrator, editor, and designer, and we can speculate about these choices with students.

Upon turning the flyleaf, we come to either the *half-title page* or the *title page*. The half-title page has only the title of the book—a famous example of a half-title page is found in *Where the Wild Things Are*, with its stark title against white space. The next page (the full-title page) usually contains the title, the names of the author and illustrator, the name of the publisher, the city in which the publisher has its office, and the date the book was published. Some picturebooks (like *Henry* and *Trainstop*) dispense with the half-title page and go straight to the full title page. In *Pigeon*, the story actually begins with the title page, which contains not only the title but a speech bubble from the bus driver, asking readers to "watch things for me" to make sure that the pigeon doesn't drive his bus.

The next page of the typical picturebook contains the *front matter*—all the fine print about the copyright, ISBN number, Library of Congress cataloging data—the print almost nobody ever reads. There is often a *dedication page* as well. Sometimes, the fine print occurs at the very end of the book; then it's called the *publishing information*. Some of the fine print is worth reading because there is often a note informing the reader about what art medium or media were used to produce the illustrations. The publishing information on the last page of *Henry* notes that "The artwork was created with pencil, watercolor, and oil"; a similar note in the front matter of *Trainstop* tells us that "The illustrations are watercolor, gouache, and ink."

All of these elements occur before we actually get to the beginning of the story! It's tempting to skip over them, or at most to talk briefly just about the cover illustration and title and predict what the story might be about. But this would be a mistake. William Moebius (1986) perceptively comments that skipping all these surrounding elements and going straight to the story would be like arriving at the opera after the overture is finished. Just as the opera overture contains musical motifs and themes that will occur throughout the opera, thus giving us an idea of what to expect, so the surrounding elements of the picturebook contain much information for prediction and speculation about the characters, plot, setting, mood, and theme of the story.

At this point, you may be feeling as if you are learning a new language—all these special terms may be a bit overwhelming. Remember that you might introduce these elements to students over the course of examining many books, perhaps over an entire school year. Also remember that we must never underestimate the ability of even young children to learn this terminology and use it themselves. For example, if you casually say, "Here are the endpages" when you show them to students, they will pick up this language and use it when they discuss other books. Educators who make a point of talking about all these surrounding elements with students before actually beginning the story are surprised by how much information and food for thought are generated that help the students understand and interpret the story better. In other words, discussion about the surrounding elements is not a frill or a waste of time: this discussion sets the stage for children's literary and aesthetic understanding and is often a better preparation for the story than "purpose-setting" questions. Trust the picturebook itself to be its own best introduction, and trust the children to use their speculations, predictions, and questions to assist them as they interpret the story.

• • THE RELATIONSHIP • •
OF WORDS AND PICTURES

At the beginning of this chapter, we mentioned that the pictures and words in a picturebook are both necessary to tell the story. Another way of thinking about this is that a picturebook actually has three stories—the story told by the sequence of pictures; the story told by the words; and the *complete* story told by both the words and the pictures (Nodelman & Reimer, 2003). Reading a picturebook is as much a matter of "reading" the illustrations as it is reading the words. Words tell us things that the pictures omit, and vice versa. Pictures may extend the meaning of the words. For example, in *Henry*, when the protagonist marries and has children, the text mentions that "Henry knew they were very lucky. They lived together even though they had different masters." The illustration that accompanies this text shows the interior of a house, with a cozy fire in the fireplace, a colorful quilt on the wall, and Henry playing the banjo while his three children cuddle on their mother's lap. The illustration does much to extend our understanding of their domestic tranquility: it shows *how* they are "lucky."

According to Nodelman (1988), words "limit" the illustrations by telling us what to pay attention to and how to interpret them. In *Pigeon*, the pigeon is shown with one wing placed over its chest. The accompanying words are "True story." Thus, we're led to interpret the pigeon's physical gesture as a "cross my heart and hope to die" expression of honesty.

The art in some books not only reflects and extends the text but also presents visual information that creates a story within a story. Marla Frazee does this brilliantly in *Roller Coaster* (P–I), in which she tells multiple side stories through her illustrations. In the text, the book tells the story of a roller coaster ride, focusing on one young girl who has never ridden a roller coaster before: her initial trepidation, joyful ride with her big brother, and desire to do it over again. The illustrations tell several stories, all of them humorous. For example, behind the girl and her brother in line are three big men, bulging with muscles and, in one case, fat. The biggest one, in a muscle shirt with a tattoo on his arm, doesn't even make it onto the ride; he abandons his friends to sit and watch. The other two nonchalantly get on, arms casually draped on the sides of the car, sunglasses in place—until the first downhill, when they grab the seat in front of them (and one of them loses his cap). They hang on for dear life, close their eyes (and lose their sunglasses), and grimace until they get off, clutching their stomachs. In this case, the illustrations tell much, much more than the single story told by the text.

Mordicai Gerstein both wrote and illustrated the Caldecott Medal–winning *The Man Who Walked Between the Towers* (P–I). As he tells in words the story of the young French aerialist, Philippe Petit, who in 1974 danced on a tightrope strung between the World Trade Center towers, he also tells it in pictures. With both words and pictures, he depicts Petit's determination and his joy for life, so that readers can understand why Petit performed such a daring, and illegal, feat. Gerstein goes well beyond mere visual

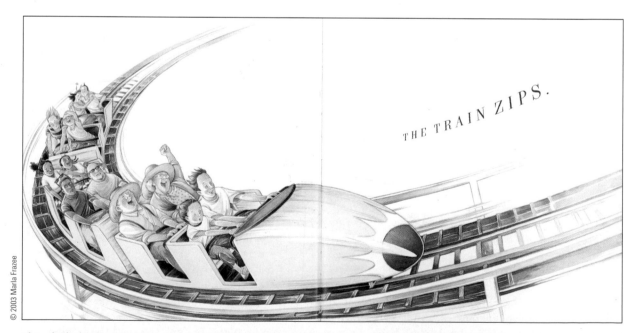

© 2003 Marla Frazee

If you look closely at the illustrations, you can see who is afraid, who is having fun, and who is ready to be sick—small stories within a story are told entirely through the illustrations in **Roller Coaster***.*

As the rising sun lit up the towers, out he stepped onto the wire.

Through his clever use of perspective, Mordicai Gerstein helps readers feel what it might be like to be up high above New York. If you have vertigo, don't read **The Man Who Walked Between the Towers!**

reflection. The illustrations extend the text in such a way that readers feel what it might be like to be almost pulled over the edge by a falling cable, just as they feel what it might be like to step out onto a cable five-eighths of an inch thick, 1,340 feet above the earth. Without the illustrations, neither the danger nor the thrill of walking between the towers would be as immediate or as powerful.

In some cases, the illustrations in picturebooks provide a much richer, broader context than the words can possibly convey. For example, in *Henry*, the last double-page spread ends the story with Henry emerging from his box, having finally arrived in Philadelphia, a city where he would be a free man. One detail of the illustration rewards close inspection: the ceramic pitcher, resting on a wooden stand, at the extreme left. On the pitcher there is an image of a slave kneeling on one knee, his hands bound in chains, with the words "Am I not a man and a brother?" The image was the emblem of the Society for Effecting the Abolition of the Slave Trade, which was formed in 1787, well over 50 years before Henry's courageous escape from slavery in 1849. The image has been famous for a long time; it was reproduced on pieces of pottery and in newspapers, and the firm Wedgwood produced it as a cameo, which women purchased and wore as a necklace. The image also appeared in a broadside printing of John Greenleaf Whittier's poem "Our Countrymen in Chains," in 1837, a condemnation of slavery. Kadir Nelson's illustration thus hints at this long history of abolitionist sentiment through this seemingly insignificant detail, as well as placing Henry's story in a fascinating historical context. The words of

Kadir Nelson's background for the culminating illustration in Ellen Levine's **Henry's Freedom Box** *contains a pitcher whose message turns out to have a fascinating history of its own.*

the story could not possibly convey this amount of detail; however, the illustration invites us to research the meaning behind this image on the pitcher, leading to much greater understanding.

The words in a picturebook can also have visual qualities that underline or extend their literal meaning. In *Pigeon*, the illustration of the pigeon's tantrum is accentuated by the large, bold letters of the words "LET ME DRIVE THE BUS!!!" in all capital letters. The "look" of the font chosen for the book is important to examine because it, too, is the result of a conscious choice by the designer. In *Henry*, for example, the title is rendered in a font that looks as if it were designed in the nineteenth century, the same time period in which the story is set.

The relationships of words and pictures can also be ironic, subversive, or even completely contradictory. Marla Frazee's hilarious text and illustrations for *A Couple of Boys Have the Best Week Ever* (P–I), a Caldecott Honor book, often stand in this type of relationship. For example, when James visits his friend Eamon "with just a couple of his belongings," the illustration depicts James standing in front of an enormous pile of boxes, baskets, and duffel bags stuffed to overflowing. The boys go to day camp together, and when they get back home at the end

of the day, the text comments that "the campers would decide to practice quiet meditation downstairs," while the accompanying illustration shows them boisterously and competitively playing a video game. See Teaching Idea 3.5 for more examples of this type of ironic or contradictory text–picture relationship.

The positioning of words and pictures on the openings of a picturebook is also part of the word–picture relationship. Some text is printed in an outlined *text box*, which is simply placed on top of an unimportant part of the illustration. Other text is printed in a column beside the illustration, or under it or over it in a blank space. In other cases, the words are printed directly over the illustration, again taking care not to obscure a crucial part of the illustration. Often, artists will leave a light-colored or white area in the illustration itself so that the words can be printed easily. In this case, the words are printed in black or a dark-colored ink. In other cases, where the background of the illustration is very dark, the words will be printed in white. Examine *Henry*, and you will see that every one of these techniques is used. This adds variation and interest to the story.

● ● SIZE AND SHAPE ● ● OF THE BOOK AND THE ILLUSTRATIONS

The *trim size* (the final dimensions of the pages of the book) varies according to the subject matter of the book and its purposes. Beatrix Potter is famous for remarking that she made her books rather small so that they could be easily held by little hands. Beyond this, designers work with authors and illustrators to determine whether a book will be in "portrait" or "landscape" form. If a story will contain many broad vistas, landscape form is appropriate. If, on the other hand, the story will contain many close-ups of human beings, portrait form is sensible. In *Trainstop*, the horizontal quality of the train, the rectangular windows that are longer than they are wide, and the countryside vista all make a landscape format appropriate. For Suzy Lee's *Wave* (N–P), a wordless book about a little girl's day at the shore, the pronounced horizontal line of the beach and the ocean are conveyed by the trim size—when the book is opened, the length is far more than three times the width, giving the illustrator plenty of space to depict the large expanse of sand, ocean, and sky. By contrast, *Henry*, with its many dramatic close-up illustrations of characters, uses a portrait orientation to the best advantage.

Illustrations can stretch across both pages of an opening, thus giving the artist a large space in which to work. An even larger space is provided if the illustrations "bleed" to the edges of the page. The illustrator can also decide to have one or many illustrations on an opening. In *Pigeon*,

The clever ironic juxtapositions of illustrations and words add to the sly humor of Marla Frazee's A Couple of Boys Have the Best Week Ever.

Teaching Idea 3.5

Pictures and Words in Picturebooks

To really understand and interpret a picturebook, children must "read" the illustrations as well as the words and integrate the knowledge they gain from both pictures and words. We can't assume that all children (or adults) will do this naturally, so we can explicitly teach it. The following examples of word–picture relationships are from Kevin Hawkes's *The Wicked Big Toddlah* (p–i), a hilarious modern-day tall tale about a baby from Maine (thus the "toddlah," imitating the Maine accent) who is as tall as a big tree. Consider a few of the illustrations in this book in terms of what the pictures and the words tell us.

> **Text**: The narrator says that when she and her brothers visited the new baby in the hospital, he "grabbed hold of my finger."

The technique you might employ is to read the text without showing the picture and ask students to talk about whether they have ever seen a baby grasp someone's finger. Then show the illustration and ask how their interpretation has changed.

> **Illustration**: Shows a group of people at the hospital, including the mother, father, and "Uncle Bert," and an array of balloons with messages: "Ayuh, It's a Buoy" and "It's anuthah Mainah." The top third of the illustration shows an enormous fist and forearm stretching almost the whole way across the double-page spread. The little girl (the narrator) is being hoisted into the air, and the baby's huge fist envelops her entire hand and part of her arm. Of course, the illustrations also tell us that the baby is from Maine, something the text never mentions.

What the text describes is a normal circumstance with a normal-sized baby: babies often grab people's fingers. The illustration, however, gives this common action an entirely new meaning!

A Second Example from the Same Book

> **Text**: The narrator says that Toddie (the huge baby) likes taking baths and playing with boats.

> **Illustration**: Shows Toddie, waist deep in the ocean, hoisting a lobster boat and two lobster fishermen out of the water with one hand and a rowboat in the other. Toddie's relatives are approaching him with a rubber dinghy with the label "S. S. Bathtime," and one of the figures in the dinghy is holding a mop with a bucket full of soapy water.

If you read the text, students will have associations with playing with toy boats in their bathtubs, either remembering themselves doing this or seeing another baby engaged in the same activity. When they see the illustration, the meaning naturally changes: the "boats" are full-sized, real boats in the illustration, corresponding to Toddie's huge size, and "taking baths" has a new meaning, too—Toddie is going to be scrubbed with a mop. From the looks of it, bathtime is going to take a long, long while!

A Third Example

In this case, you might consider showing the illustration first, asking the students to describe the details they see, and then read the text.

> **Illustration**: Shows Toddie in a huge hammock, sleeping outdoors. A rope is attached to the hammock, and Mother (inside the house, in her bed) is pulling the hammock to and fro. "Uncle Bert" is sitting near Toddie's head, playing bagpipes, and the rest of the relatives (six of them) are sitting on Toddie's enormous stomach, with their mouths wide open.

> **Text**: The narrator says that everyone sings to make Toddie go to sleep and that his uncle "plays a soft lullaby."

The "soft lullaby" that would soothe a normal baby would not even be heard by Toddie—he needs blaring bagpipes instead! Talking with students in this way makes them aware of the ironies of the illustrations versus the text. They can understand that a great deal of the humor of the book depends on the interesting relationship of words and pictures in *The Wicked Big Toddlah*. If you single out a few pages every so often when you read aloud to students and talk with them about what the illustrations tell them versus what the words tell them, this will alert them to the possible ironies, subversions, and potential humor of other books' text–picture relationships. This book, of course, represents only one of the many relationships that text and pictures can have. Words and illustrations can extend each other or amplify each other. The words never tell us *exactly* what the picture shows, nor vice versa. Other good books to try this with are *Rosie's Walk* (n–p) by Pat Hutchens; *Officer Buckle and Gloria* (p–i) by Peggy Rathman, and *A Couple of Boys Have the Best Week Ever* (p–i) by Marla Frazee.

all of these choices contribute to the interest of the design of the book. At one point (the tenth opening), illustrator Mo Willems has chosen to divide the opening into eight boxes, delineated by slightly different background colors, for multiple illustrations of the pigeon's barrage of persua-

sive techniques. In *Henry*, except for four openings where a text panel reduces the size of the illustration slightly, Kadir Nelson uses double-page-spread full bleeds, which convey the intensity of emotion and the dramatic quality of the story most effectively. In *Wave*, mentioned previously, every one of the illustrations takes up the entire double-page spread with full bleed, effectively conveying the infinity of the horizon line.

When illustrations have borders, either constituted by thin lines, white space, or thicker strips of color that look like picture frames, the effect is to render the illustration a bit less intense because we feel less as if we are "in" the illustration than if it bled to the edge of each side of the page. Notice that in *Trainstop* there are only two full bleeds, which both indicate large expanses of space: first, when the girl is running behind ten tiny people to begin her rescue of a person caught in a tree, and second, at the end of the story when, after the tiny people bring her a small tree as a gift, the scene broadens to include a panorama of the city, with several other trees, suggesting that the little people have made other visits to the city from their magical country. Most of the images in *Trainstop* are framed by thick black lines and the white space surrounding the images. "Breaking" the frame occurs on the fifth opening, in which a tiny person signals the train to stop with a large banner. In this illustration, part of the banner extends beyond the black line border, and the top of the train and its horn also break the frame. Breaking the frame often accentuates action or drama, and in this case, the train's size and speed, as well as the rapidly waving banner, are indicated by this technique. Breaking the frame can also signal a change of some kind. The illustrations in *Where the Wild Things Are* begin breaking the frame just at the point where the story changes from a realistic narration of Max's naughtiness to the magical fantasy of a forest growing in his room. Thus, the change from realistic fiction to fantasy is suggested by the frame break.

Illustrations that have no straight lines for borders but appear to "float" against a white background are called *cut-outs*. In *Henry*, there is an excellent example of cut-outs on the seventeenth opening, where a series of four borderless illustrations show Henry's box (with a view of him inside) being moved to and fro by two men, who want to use it to sit upon. The lack of a border for these cut-outs adds to the impression of topsy-turvy freedom of movement.

An artist may choose to include several illustrations on one page that show action or what Schwarcz (1982) calls "continuous narration"; in other words, the sequence of small illustrations is intended to convey motion or to be interpreted as a rapid sequence of actions. The sequence of eight illustrations on the tenth opening of *Pigeon*, mentioned previously, is an example of continuous narration.

Similarly, *Trainstop* has several instances of continuous narration. For example, on the verso of the tenth opening, there is a sequence of six illustrations. First, we see a close-up of the girl's hand trying to reach the tiny person who is stuck in the tree, but not getting quite close enough. Second, the girl is puzzling out what to do. Third,

Mo Willems's deftly simple series of vignettes in **Don't Let the Pigeon Drive the Bus!** *suggests a progression of Pigeon's unsuccessful persuasive techniques.*

*In **Trainstop**, Barbara Lehman makes excellent use of the technique of continuous narration as she tells the story of a girl who rescues some tiny people in a magical land.*

a tiny person pulls on the bottom edge of her slacks to get her attention. Fourth, she bends down to listen to him. Fifth, she holds him in the palm of her hand. Sixth, she stretches up to the tree, and the additional height provided by the tiny person allows her to reach his friend and rescue him.

• • ILLUSTRATION • • SEQUENCE

In contrast to paintings, which stand by themselves, picturebook illustrations have a critical relationship with the illustrations that come before and after them. The sequence of illustrations (with the accompanying words) is what makes the picturebook a special type of art. The variation as the sequence proceeds can take many forms. The perspective can change from close-up to far away. One of the most dramatic moments in **Henry** occurs when Henry worries about whether his wife and children will be sold to another master. At this point in the story, the illustration pans in for an extreme close-up of Henry's face, which takes up almost all of the opening. In this way, the illustrator conveys Henry's deep anxiety.

The viewpoint of the viewer can also change, from seeing the scene from the same level as the characters, or viewing the scene from above or below. A number of Chris Van Allsburg's picturebooks are notable for

their changes in perspective from one illustration to the next, adding to the surrealistic quality of many of his stories. (Look, for example, at the dramatic sequence of perspectives in **Jumanji**.) The sequence can also move from a large double-page spread illustration to a series of small illustrations in the next opening. More importantly, the sequence of openings should be considered to be like watching a slow-motion film, though with the opportunity of turning back and revisiting a page rather than the relentless succession of images in a film. The mood of the story (or individual characters) may change during the illustration sequence from light and carefree to serious and reflective. In other words, the sequence of illustrations and words must support the plot and characterization.

Taking a look at part of the sequence of **Trainstop**, we see that the title page illustration shows a little girl and her parents about to walk down steps, and on the dedication page, we see them waiting in the station. The following double-page spread contains two illustrations; on the verso, we see the girl sitting contentedly by herself while her parents read the newspaper, and other passengers sleep, read books, work on their laptop computers, or use their cell phones. The recto shows a close-up view of only the little girl, looking out the train window, with a dull gray, beige, and brown city landscape as a background. In the next spread, the verso shows the train going through a tunnel, while the recto contains four rectangular illustrations of the girl, again looking out the window. The upper left rectangle is quite similar to the previous illustration, with the dull city landscape, and the upper right and lower left rectangles depict the train's swift passage through the dark tunnel. The lower right, however, changes perspective; we as viewers are now outside the train, and we see the girl's face looking excitedly through the window. This is followed by the next spread, which again changes perspective as the large rectangular illustration on the verso gives us our first glimpse of a country landscape, with trees, a windmill, houses, and towers. The recto shows a similar landscape, but we see the girl from the back, her hands pressed against the glass of the window. Thus, the sequence leads us seamlessly from the entrance to the train station to the waiting area. Then we are inside the train, first with a wide-angle view of the whole car of passengers; next we see a close-up of the girl looking out the window. The perspective thus keeps changing, giving us a variety of views while also advancing the plot.

PAGE TURNS

Another element of picturebooks that receives very careful attention from authors and illustrators is what Barbara Bader (1976, p. 1) refers to as "the drama of the turning of the page." As the previous section on sequence indicates, no opening or double-page spread stands alone; turning from one opening to the next is part of the pleasure of reading/viewing a picturebook. In illustrator Remy Charlip's words, "A thrilling picture book not only makes beautiful single images or sequential images, but also allows us to become aware of a book's unique physical structure by bringing our attention, once again, to that momentous moment: the turning of the page" (quoted in Selznick, 2008, pp. 403–404). Because picturebooks are so brief, what is omitted is just as important as what is included. Talking about what might have happened between one opening and the next therefore gives students the opportunity to make inferences and to speculate. For example, in *Pigeon*, the reader is continually engaged in answering the pigeon's pleas: on one opening, the pigeon asks if it can drive the bus and on the next opening, it says "Please?" Readers may infer that we have refused Pigeon's request. On another opening, Pigeon says that his cousin drives a bus "almost every day." In the next opening, Pigeon says, "True story." Children in one classroom, when asked what might have happened between these two openings, suggested that they might say, "We don't believe you—you probably don't even have a cousin!" or "You're lying!" Research (Sipe & Brightman, in press) has shown that, given the opportunity, even young children make inferences about characters' actions, thoughts, and

feelings, and create dialogue when asked what might happen during the page turns between two openings. They also notice changes in perspective ("It looks like we've moved away from the pigeon"), speculate about how much time might have elapsed between openings ("The pigeon probably takes a long while to get over his tantrum"), or how the setting might have changed from one opening to the next ("Maybe the pigeon went to another part of the parking lot"). If students are accustomed to discussing books in an open, interactive manner, they will take on the challenge of speculating about page turns, and this speculation will result in greater understanding of the coherence of the story, as well as their deeper interpretive and inferential capacities.

THE CHALLENGE OF THE GUTTER

Yet another concern of picturebook illustrators, authors, and designers is that when illustrations cross both sides of the double-page spread, attention must be paid to the *gutter*, the middle of the spread where the pages are bound. If it crosses the gutter, a small bit of the illustration is lost in the binding. Thus, in planning the illustration, the artist needs to make sure that nothing important is located in the gutter. For example, an artist would rarely position a human figure or an animal in the gutter. As you look at picturebook illustrations that do cross the gutter, think about how the artist has designed the illustration so that the gutter is not obscuring an important part of the image. Also, words almost never cross the gutter because some of the letters would be hidden. So designers must ensure that the gutter does not interfere with our reading of the text. Notice how the double-page spread on the third opening of *Henry* depicts Henry and his mother standing at the bedside of their master, who is dying. The illustration is perfectly arranged so that the gutter does not interfere with the images of any of the characters: the master and Henry are on the verso and the mother stands off by herself on the recto. Even the bedposts are not split by the gutter. In fact, the placement of Henry and his mother on opposite sides of the page suggests their approaching separation, as Henry must go to work for the master's son.

THE TYPES OF EDITIONS FOR PICTUREBOOKS

In all this discussion, it's important to note that we used the *trade edition* of the picturebook—the edition you would find in the children's section of a bookstore. There is also the *library edition*, the *soft-cover* (or paperback) *edition*, and the versions of picturebooks found in reading anthologies. In the library edition, the dust jacket is frequently omitted, so if the dust jacket contains a different illustration from the board covers, this element is lost. In the case of paperback editions of picturebooks, there is never a dust jacket, and endpages are frequently omitted. In anthologies, if picturebooks are reproduced, a number of elements are always omitted, and the sequence of the illustrations is sometimes shortened or otherwise changed. In anthologies, as well, page turns are changed so that the careful attention to the "drama of the turning of the page" is also lost. In all these cases,

losing an element of the picturebook means losing the opportunity of talking about its possible meaning with students and the way it contributes to the picturebook as an integrated art object. Thus, we recommend, when possible, using the trade edition because it is the fullest expression of the artistic design of the whole picturebook. See Figure 3.5 for a list of professional resources on picturebook design, and Figure 3.6 (on page 100) for a list of specific questions to help you evaluate the overall design of picturebooks.

Figure   **3.5**

An Annotated List of Books about Picturebooks: Picturebook Design and Children's Responses

This list is arranged chronologically rather than alphabetically to give a sense of the development of book-length treatments of picturebooks over time. This list is for practitioners who want to learn more about picturebook theory and design, and who also want to know more about children's incredibly sophisticated responses to these books.

Nodelman, Perry. (1988). *Words about Pictures: The Narrative Art of Children's Picture Books*. Athens: University of Georgia Press

This book was one of the first book-length treatments of picturebooks from an academic perspective, and is still one of the best. Nodelman lucidly describes the relationship of text and pictures as one that is frequently characterized by ironic tension. An ambitious comprehensive theoretical approach.

Doonan, Jane. (1993). *Looking at Pictures in Picture Books*. Stroud, Glouchestershire: Thimble Press

Brief but packed with theoretically sound techniques for analyzing picturebooks; contains extensive examples.

Kiefer, Barbara. (1995). *The Potential of Picturebooks*. Englewood Cliffs, NJ: Prentice-Hall

Written from the perspective of an educator with an arts education background, this beautifully composed book has a wealth of information about art techniques/media, the history of picturebooks, and the use of picturebooks in classrooms, as well as careful analysis of the picturebook as an aesthetic object.

Lewis, David. (2001). *Reading Contemporary Picturebooks: Picturing Text*. New York: Routledge Falmer

Lewis packs a great deal into this slim volume. It is notable for his exploration of the "ecology" of the picturebook, in which every part (including word–picture relationships) relates to every other part, much the same way each part of the physical environment has a relationship to every

other part. Lewis also very usefully discusses Kress and Van Leeuven's *Grammar of Visual Design* and applies it specifically to picturebooks.

Nikolavja, Maria, and Carole Scott. (2001). *How Picturebooks Work*. New York: Garland Publishing

Another very ambitious and comprehensive theoretically based approach. Especially noteworthy for its typology of word–picture relationships. Considers a wide range of international picturebooks.

Arizpe, Evelyn, and Morag Styles. (2003). *Children Reading Pictures: Interpreting Visual Texts*. New York: Routledge Falmer

Includes discussions of visual literacy and text–picture relationships but is primarily a careful report of a large, two-year research study with English children, ages four to eleven, in seven primary schools, representing a large range of sociocultural diversity. The focus is on children's responses to picturebooks by Anthony Browne and Satoshi Kitamura.

Martin, Michelle. (2004). *Brown Gold: Milestones of African-American Children's Picture Books, 1845–2002*. New York: Routledge

The first book to focus exclusively on African American picturebooks, this volume takes a historical approach to contextualize the development of the representation of African Americans over 150 years.

Salisbury, Martin. (2004). *Illustrating Children's Books: Creating Pictures for Publication*. London: Quarto

Similar to Shulevitz's 1985 book *Writing with Pictures: How to Write and Illustrate Children's Books*, this beautifully illustrated guide for illustrators is packed with insights and information for a wider audience, including teachers and other practitioners who want to discover more about

(continued)

(continued)

the current state of children's book illustration, including picturebooks; illustration for older children; and nonfiction illustration.

Matulka, Dense. (2008). *A Picture Book Primer: Understanding and Using Picture Books*. Westport, CN: Libraries Unlimited

The title says it all: if you want an introductory text on understanding picturebook design and terminology, this book will help you get started.

Sipe, Lawrence R. (2008). *Storytime: Young Children's Literary Understanding in the Classroom*. New York: Teachers College Press

The result of twelve years of research with kindergarteners as well as first and second graders and their teachers, this book offers a comprehensively grounded theory of young children's literary understanding of picture storybooks.

Sipe, Lawrence R., and Sylvia Pantaleo. (2008). *Postmodern Picturebooks: Play, Parody, and Self-Referentiality*. New York: Routledge Falmer

This edited volume, the first to focus specifically on postmodern picturebooks, contains sixteen chapters from contributors who represent the fields of English, library science, and education, and who also hail from the United Kingdom, Scandanavia, Canada, the United States, and Australia—thus, it is both multidisciplinary and international in scope.

Pantaleo, Sylvia. (2008). *Exploring Student Response to Contemporary Picturebooks*. Toronto: University of Toronto Press

In this volume, Pantaleo discusses her extensive research over four years with first and fifth graders reading and interpreting postmodern picturebooks, as well as explaining how the children used what they learned in their own writing.

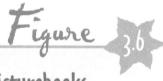

Figure 3.6

Considering Quality in the Overall Design and Artistry of Picturebooks

Overall Design

✿ Is the overall design of the book—including the dust jacket, front and back board covers, endpages, title and dedication pages, and the sequence of openings for the story—coherent and integrated?

✿ Is the trim size—the overall size and proportions of the book—appropriate for the subject or story?

✿ How is the challenge of the gutter handled in each opening? Are any important parts of the illustration obscured by the gutter?

✿ How are page turns handled? Is there a surprise or a shift that invites us to infer what happened between the openings? Is there an opportunity to make inferences about what occurs during the page breaks?

✿ Does the sequence of openings that tell the story through words and pictures seem to flow smoothly, or does it jerk around and cause confusion?

✿ How do the individual openings work in sequence?

✿ If there are several illustrations in one opening, are they related in a way that is easy to follow?

✿ Is the choice of font—shape and size—appropriate for the story being told? How is the text visually integrated with the illustrations—in text boxes, overprinting, beside, over or under the illustration?

Text–Picture Relationships

✿ Has thought been given to how both pictures and words can tell the story?

✿ How do the words and pictures integrate to produce a story that is more than either text or pictures could tell alone?

✿ Are there a variety of ways text and pictures relate to each other? Do pictures and text extend each other or amplify on each other? Do they stand in an intentionally ironic or contradictory relationship with each other? Do the pictures merely repeat what the words say, or do they add something? Do the words merely repeat what the pictures show, or do they add something?

Individual Illustrations

✿ According to the principles of art and design, are the individual illustrations well constructed?

✿ Is there balance, proportion, repetition, and variety in the colors and shapes?

✿ Does the artist's line correspond to the tone/mood/feeling conveyed in the story?

✿ Do the shapes correspond to the tone/mood/feeling conveyed in the story?

✿ Is the overall style of the illustration congruent with or complementary to the tone/mood/feeling conveyed in the story?

Elements of Narrative in Picture Storybooks

Picture storybooks, as the name implies, tell a story, and contain the traditional elements of narrative: setting, characterization, plot, theme, and style of writing. The narratives that picture storybooks tell may be folklore, fantasy, contemporary realistic fiction, or historical fiction. Whatever the type of narrative, we evaluate the text quality of the literary elements—setting, character, plot, theme, and style. The literary criteria may vary somewhat according to content, as we discussed in Chapter 1. The illustrations in picture storybooks provide visual representations, elaborations, or extensions of the setting, characters, and plot that are presented in the text. The illustrations also reflect the theme and the mood of the text.

• • SETTING • •

Setting—the time and place of a story—is often presented succinctly in the text of picturebooks, given that visual details about time and place can be portrayed clearly and economically through the illustrations. Good folklore settings reflect ethnic and cultural traditions associated with the origins of tales. Settings in contemporary or historical fiction reflect details appropriate to the time and place. In Michael Bania's ***Kumak's Fish: A Tall Tale from the Far North*** (ᴘ), the Arctic setting is clear in both text and pictures. Her light watercolor washes outlined in ink with plenty of white space highlight the icy setting, as do the details of place and the Inupiat people. Similarly, Julie Downing's watercolor and pastel illustrations and Linda Sue Park's text in ***The Firekeeper's Son*** (ᴘ–ɪ) capture the culture of rural nineteenth-century Korea, when the practice of lighting bonfires on successive mountaintops assured the Korean emperor that the coast had not been invaded by marauders from another country.

• • CHARACTERIZATION • •

Characterization—establishing characters—varies according to genre in picture storybooks. In folklore, characters are usually stereotypes—the good princess, the brave prince, the wicked stepmother. In well-written realistic or fantasy narratives, the characters are well-developed personalities that often show some evidence of growth and change over the course of the story. Many fantasy picturebooks contain talking animal characters with habits, behaviors, thoughts, and feelings that are human rather than animal. Realistic books, whether contemporary or historical, contain recognizably human characters. Whether animal or human, characters in picture storybooks are most often children or adolescents, depending on the intended audience. They reflect the actions, thoughts, and emotions of children and adolescents in the narration, the dialogue, and the art. Well-developed characters in picture storybooks are active rather than passive; they interact with their story worlds to solve their own problems.

Characters are realized through both the text and the art. As the text describes a personality trait, the art interprets that trait and presents a portrait of the character.

Sang-hee looked around.
A few huts made of wood and mud.
A few cows.
A few chickens, a few dogs.
It did not look like an important village.

"Our part of Korea is like a dragon with many humps," his father said. "The humps are the mountains—the first hump facing the sea, the last hump facing the king's palace.
"Our mountain is the first hump.
"Our fire is the first fire."

© 2004 Julie Downing

*The pastoral setting of medieval Korea is artfully suggested by Julie Downing's pastel and watercolor illustrations for Linda Sue Park's **The Firekeeper's Son**.*

As the story progresses, the art reflects characters' emotions and the growth and change that occurs. Jacqueline Woodson uses words to develop her characters, young Ada Ruth and her grandma, with whom Ada Ruth stays home when Mama goes north to Chicago to earn money during World War II. E. B. Lewis uses watercolor paintings to visually convey Ada Ruth's emotions, as well as the time and place. The combination of words and pictures creates the memorable story, *Coming on Home Soon* (P), a Caldecott Medal book.

• • PLOT • •

In picture storybooks, plot—the sequence of events—is usually presented in a straightforward chronological order. Plot usually centers on a problem or conflict, generally a problem that children recognize and relate to. As the character works to solve the problem, the plot unfolds into an event or series of events that lead to a solution. The action of the story is apparent in both the text and the illustrations. As we discussed earlier, sometimes the illustrations offer a subplot that the text does not. Peggy Rathman's text in the Caldecott Medal–winning *Officer Buckle and Gloria* (P) tells only part of the story. The story behind the story, and the humor, is carried entirely by her illustrations.

• • THEME • •

Theme, a major overriding idea that ties the whole together, often reflects a child's or adolescent's world. Picturebooks for younger children are often organized around the theme of growing up—increasing independence and self-reliance, increasing ability, increasing understanding. Memorable themes are neither blatantly stated, as in an explicit moral to a story, nor so subtle that they elude young readers. The theme evolves naturally from plot and character, and permeates the illustrations. Helen Recorvits's *My Name Is Yoon* (N–P), illustrated by Gabi Swiatkowska, gently traces the ways in which a young Korean girl becomes accustomed to the tasks of American schooling. Both the rebellion and the resiliency of young immigrants are portrayed in this story. Other picturebooks featuring Yoon and her adaptation to life in the United States are *Yoon and the Christmas Mittens* and *Yoon and the Jade Bracelet* (both N–P).

• • STYLE • •

Style of language is essential to quality in a picturebook; because words are limited, they must be carefully chosen. Most picturebooks for young readers contain rich language—well beyond the reading ability of the intended audience—because they are meant to be read aloud. Picturebooks are most often introduced to babies, toddlers, or preschool children by an adult reading *to* the child. The language in most picturebooks for younger children is language that adults can read and that children can understand.

Many educators underestimate the ability of young children to understand the language of picturebooks that are read to them; even difficult vocabulary is often understood through a combination of the context of the story and the illustrations. A wonderful example of this understanding is from Beatrix Potter's classic, *The Tale of Peter*

*Loren Long's acrylic illustrations for **I Dream of Trains** are moody and solemn, a perfect accompaniment for the story of an African American boy's dream of escape from a life of drudgery in the rural south.*

Rabbit (N–P). At the point when Peter is being chased by Mr. MacGregor, he gets caught by his coat buttons in a gooseberry net. Sparrows, according to Potter's text, "flew to him in great excitement and implored him to exert himself." Contemporary urban kindergarteners had no difficulty in understanding this sophisticated language: "It means the sparrows are trying to help him to keep trying—they're saying, don't give up, Peter, you can do it!" (Sipe, 2002). Potter was wise in never "writing down" to children and in trusting them to comprehend and infer meaning from her stories.

Most picturebooks are not meant for beginning reading material. Those that are should still contain language that is interesting, even if simple, and that is a pleasure to read aloud. For older readers, the text can be more complex. In any case, good picture storybooks have interesting words used in interesting ways, with language that builds excitement, creates images, and has an internal rhythm and melody. If it sounds natural when read aloud, it is probably well written.

The choice of words helps create the *mood* of the text. Books can be humorous or serious, lighthearted or thoughtful. The style of art must match the mood of the text. It might, for example, be inappropriate to illustrate books about a serious theme with bright, happy colors. Most of Loren Long's illustrations for Angela Johnson's *I Dream of Trains* (P–I) are somber and serious, in shades of gray and brown. However, the colors warm up when the narrator, an African American boy, associates the sounds of trains with leaving his life in the rural South for the greater freedom and hope associated with going north. Thus, the varying moods of the story are captured by the changing palette of the illustrations. Sometimes the unity of text and illustrations happens in unexpected ways. For example, the graphic novel series **Maus** (A) contains gripping stories of the Holocaust, yet is illustrated very effectively with cartoons that present animal characters.

Types of Picturebooks

The types of picturebooks we describe in the following sections are arranged roughly in a developmental sequence, from books for very young children to books that have appeal for much older readers. It is important, however, to note that *any* picturebook can be studied by older readers in terms of its overall design, quality of illustration, and the ways words and pictures complement each other. For example, *Charley Harper ABC's* (N–P) by Charley Harper is a board book with a very straightforward arrangement: on each verso, there is a letter, with a sentence: "A is for ape," "B is for bird," and so on. Each recto contains an illustration for the corresponding letter. Nothing could be simpler, and yet Charley Harper (1922–2007) was one of the best-known graphic artists of the modern era, and his stylized illustrations are masterpieces of design. Thus,

*The elegant and stylized renditions of animals and birds in **Charley Harper ABC's** make it easy for children to recognize the figures, while at the same time giving adults a wonderful experience of Harper's minimalist technique.*

even such a seemingly simple book for an audience of young children can be appreciated by older readers. The same holds true for any high-quality picturebook.

You should also be aware that the various categories may blur into one another; for example, many board books present simple concepts or are alphabet books, so that it is impossible truly to distinguish them from one another. Additionally, many standard picturebooks do not translate well into board books. *Mr. Gumpy's Outing* (P–I) by John Burningham, though a superb picturebook, does not work well as a board book. Eric Carle's classic *The Very Hungry Caterpillar* (N–P), however, has been quite successfully turned into a board book.

• • PICTUREBOOKS FOR • • YOUNG CHILDREN

As children mature and their worlds expand, the number of books available to them also expands. Children in the preschool and primary grades have their choice of concept books, alphabet and counting books, books that support their early attempts at independent reading, and books that relate to every facet of their world.

Board Books and Participation Books

Board books appeal to infants and toddlers up to three years of age; the books are often six to twelve pages long, made of sturdy cardboard. There are also cloth books, shape books, pudgy books, lift-the-flap books, toy books, and plastic bathtub books. Books of this type, appropriate for children in the picture identification stage, are also good for those in the earliest stages of reading. *Max's First Word* (N) by Rosemary Wells, is a favorite board book. Big sister Ruby tries time and again to get Max to say a word. He responds only with "Bang." Just to surprise Ruby and show that he is no dummy, when she holds up an apple, Max says, "Delicious." Children point to pictures and label them, creating meaning from texts.

A combination board book and fascinating participation book by Rufus Butler Seder, *Gallop!* (N–P) is a "runaway success" because every time a page is turned, the animals seem to move; Seder's *Swing!* (N–P) is likewise an animated book with a story about playing baseball. A similar interesting participation book is *Magic Moving Images Animated Optical Illusions* (N–P) by Colin Ord, in which an acetate overlay, provided in the book, brings images such as a moving horse or a waving flag to life.

It's never too early for children to see images by well-known painters who have contributed to the history of art. In Julie Merberg and Suzanne Bober's series of board books using reproductions of famous paintings, such as *Sunday with Seurat*, *A Magical Day with Matisse*, *A Picnic with Monet*, and *Dancing with Degas* (N–P–I), the paintings are accompanied by brief rhyming couplets. In *Sunday with Seurat*, the painter's most well-known canvas, *A Sunday on La Grande Jatte*, the text opposite the

Bathers find a place to lie
and watch the
sailboats gliding by.

*Reproductions of Georges Seurat's paintings are matched by succinct poems in **Sunday with Seurat** by Julie Merberg and Suzanne Bober.*

¿Cuánto?

© 1991 Barbara Joosse

*The words and pictures in both the English and Spanish versions of the popular **Do You Love Me, Mama?** portray loving reassurance.*

much shorter and especially created for the board book format. Other board books appear in the Booklist at the end of the chapter.

Participation books provide concrete visual and tactile materials for children to explore: textures to touch, flaps to lift, flowers to smell, and pieces to manipulate. A classic by Dorothy Kunhardt, *Pat the Bunny* (N) asks children to look in a mirror, play peek-a-boo, and feel a scratchy beard; babies love touching this book. Eric Carle's *The Very Busy Spider* (N), reissued as a twenty-four-page board book, has brightly colored collages and tactile renderings of the spider's growing web. Young children enjoy saying the repetitive phrases with the onomatopoeic sounds and feelings of the spider web. *Dog* (N) by Matthew Van Fleet enables young children to pull tabs that cause many dogs to wag their tails, shake, and scratch themselves. Young children also love lift-the-flap books that reveal the location of animals, such as *Ruff! Ruff! Where's Scruff?* (N) by David Carter. Other lift-the-flap books such as *Peekaboo Panda and Other Animals* and *Peekaboo Puppy and Other Pets* (both N–P) contain flaps, which when lifted give the answers to riddles. These and other excellent participation books are included in the Booklist at the end of the chapter.

✳ ✳ ✳

A CLOSE LOOK AT

Monkey and Me

It's common for young children to play with their stuffed animals, and the little girl in this picturebook imaginatively visits several other animals with her stuffed monkey. The book is only twenty-eight pages long, compared to the standard thirty-two. With her spare text and lively illustrations, British author/illustrator Emily Gravett does not need any more pages to tell her story. The dust jacket (identical to the board cover) shows off Gravett's elegantly simple drawing, with the girl holding a smiling monkey whose curved, outstretched arms seem to embrace the hand-lettered title. Together, the title and the monkey's arms form an elliptical shape that frames the author's name. The monkey's elongated tail is accentuated by continuing off the left side of the front cover and onto the back cover. The front endpapers show a sequence of illustrations of the little girl getting dressed and ready for her adventures with Monkey, thus beginning the story. There is clever use of the dedication page with its publishing information and the facing title page: Gravett depicts Monkey holding a poster with the publishing information and the little girl (unnamed throughout the story, which is narrated by her) holding a poster with the title and some scribbled drawings. The left side of the next opening continues this story with the words "Monkey and me

image reads, "On a sunny Sunday in the park,/families play until it's dark,/strolling or sitting under/the trees, enjoying the river's/cooling breeze."

Fruit (N–P) by Sara Anderson contains memorable illustrations that help young children identify both shapes and colors of common fruits; and *Global Babies* (N) contains wonderful photographs of babies from many countries around the world. Donald Crews created *Inside Freight Train* (N), a sturdy board book with sliding doors that open on each railroad car. Children's fascination with trains starts early and continues for many years. This book is a treasure. Children also enjoy books about children and parents. *¿Me quieres, mama?* (N) is a Spanish version of the very popular *Do You Love Me, Mama?*. David Shannon, Kevin Henkes, Mo Willems, and Ian Falconer have all created board books based on the well-beloved characters in their picture storybooks. Shannon, for example, has published the **Diaper David** series (*David Smells!*, N); Henkes uses characters from his mouse books (*Wemberly's Ice-Cream Star*, N); Willems has produced humorous board books based on his Pigeon character (*The Pigeon Loves Things that Go!*, N; and *The Pigeon Has Feelings, Too!*, N); and Falconer has used Olivia, his pig character, in *Olivia Counts* (N) and *Olivia's Opposites* (N). These board books are not simply picture storybooks converted into board books; they are [repeated three times],/We went to see" accompanied by three illustrations of the girl with a firm grasp on Monkey's forearm. The right-hand side of the opening continues with a larger illustration of the girl with Monkey in yet another position of its flexible arms, legs, and tail, and the words "We went to see some . . ." Gravett makes excellent use of the page turns in this book because, in each case, the ellipsis encourages readers to turn to the next opening to discover what the girl and Monkey "went to see"—it's a procession of penguins, some with their baby chicks. The word "PENGUINS!" is in a very large font with an exclamation point. Readers attending to details will notice that the girl's arms and legs on the previous page (arms outstretched and one leg stiffly held up in the air) exactly echo the position of the lead penguin's arms and legs on the following opening.

The stage is thus set for the comfortably predictable quality of both illustrations and text. The next opening also contains the words "Monkey and me," repeated three times, and "We went to see some . . ." inviting us to turn the page to see three lively "KANGAROOS!" with the word again in a very large font and three bounding kangaroos. As well, the illustrations of the girl show her holding Monkey partly inside her red-and-white striped shirt, in the same way the kangaroos hold their babies, and leaping in the same bouncy rhythm as the kangaroos. The predictable structure continues with the same words accompanied by an illustration of the girl, holding Monkey and hanging upside down, so readers can predict that the following illustration of the animals they "went to see" are "BATS!" The next animals the pair visit are "ELEPHANTS!", followed by the most energetic illustrations

Profile

Emily Gravett

Emily Gravett is a relative newcomer to the world of children's books, but she has already made quite an impact. This author/illustrator grew up in Brighton, England, in a family that valued the arts—her mother was an art teacher and her father a printmaker. But although she enjoyed drawing when she was a youngster, it didn't occur to her until much later that she might become a professional artist. She was a quiet child, enjoying reading. In her late teens and early twenties, she spent eight years living on the road in impoverished circumstances, which certainly changed her outlook on life! When her daughter Oleander was born, the only thing that would quiet the infant was for Emily to read to her. She kept a journal full of drawings and doodles. Finally, despite her lack of good high school credentials, she persuaded the University of Brighton to let her study art. Her first book, *Wolves* (P–I–A), which was written and illustrated when she was studying at the university, won the Kate Greenaway Medal—the British equivalent of the Caldecott Medal—and she's been busy ever since. In interviews,

she seems somewhat surprised and puzzled (but absolutely delighted) by her sudden success in children's publishing.

Her books almost always have some personal connection to her own life. For example, *Monkey and Me*, which is featured in our Close Look, was based on the daughter of a friend of hers who was a very "bouncy" child and couldn't sit still for very long. Emily wanted to make a book that this child could relate to. *Meerkat Mail* (P–I), which tells the story of a meerkat named Sunny who decides to go on a trip because he is tired of his large family, contains many postcards sent by Sunny to his family. It's no surprise to find that Emily is "obsessed" with making and receiving postcards. *Meerkat Mail* also owes its existence in part to Emily's long time traveling on the road, with no fixed address. In *Little Mouse's Big Fears* (P), which Emily describes as a "self-help book," a mouse records and learns to overcome his fears. She says that the mouse is a lot like her. Emily's wit and facility with visual humor comes to the fore in *The Odd Egg* (P).

Her style is spontaneous and emphasizes flowing lines. She is known for leaving a lot of white space in her

work, which is a refreshing change from much of the overdone, "busy" illustration we see in today's picturebooks. Most of her illustrations are done with pencil and watercolor wash; she says that she likes the fresh look of pencil rather than the more studied line of pen and ink. Her books often make something out of very little: who would have thought that "orange," "pear," "apple," "bear," and "there" could be the only words in a charming story for young children (*Orange Pear Apple Bear*, N–P)? In other words, there is a very attractive economy in both her illustrations and language, making them accessible to beginning readers. However, there is also a subtlety and cleverness that appeal to older children as well.

Emily now lives in a cottage outside Brighton with her partner Mik who is a plumber, their daughter, and several pets. She has an attractive website, www.emilygravett.com, which is interactive and fun for both children and adults. The website lists several more books that she is currently working on. It seems as if this wanderer has finally found her vocation as an author/illustrator whose work has already delighted thousands of children, teachers, and parents.

The exuberant flowing lines of the text and the illustrations in this double-page spread from Emily Gravett's **Monkey and Me** *prepare the reader for the little girl's visit to kangaroos on the following page.*

in the book when they visit "MONKEYS!" After all this activity, we are not surprised to see a page opening showing a tired-looking girl and Monkey with all limbs drooping, and the words "Monkey . . . and . . . me [repeated three times], We went . . ." The ellipses slow readers down, imitating the drowsy girl, and the last page of the story shows the sleeping girl at a table, her head resting on her arm, having barely finished a meal, and her other arm still holding Monkey. Gravett surprises us with an image of a real monkey peeking over the table's edge, prompting us to speculate how much of this story was real and how much was fantasy. Did the girl take a trip to the zoo? Did she merely imagine the whole sequence of animal visits? The back endpapers nicely recapitulate the story sequence, with a line of penguins, a kangaroo, bats, elephants, and monkeys.

What makes this repetitive, highly structured book interesting is the way in which all of the illustrations of the girl and Monkey imitate the motion and actions of the animals we see on the following page; on the opening before the "ELEPHANTS!" for example, the girl is drawn much larger than the other illustrations, with her head tucked beneath her stooped back and her right arm extended, imitating an elephant's trunk and lumbering gait.

Gravett's palette and design are as simple as the words of the story. She limits herself to shades of brown and gray, except for the bright red of the girl's striped shirt, all rendered in pencil and watercolor. As well, the large amounts of white space surrounding all the illustrations suggest freedom of movement and activity, appropriate for the exuberance of the girl's adventure.

Concept Books

Concept books, which are simple nonfiction books, appeal to a wide audience. Young children learn about the world through engaging concept books. For very young children, Kaaren Pixton's series of virtually indestructible books, such as *Things with Wings* and *Farm Charm* (N) present pictures of different sorts of birds, insects, and animals with no words so that caregivers can engage children in labeling and talking about the pictures. Preschool and primary-grade children are developing their concept of time, and Geraldine McCaughrean's *My Grandmother's Clock* (N–P), illustrated by Stephen Lambert, will help them do that. This is a simple story, redolent with the affection between grandmother and granddaughter, that looks at time from a much larger perspective than minutes and hours.

Actual Size and *Prehistoric Actual Size* (P–I) are books that Steve Jenkins created to help children understand the concept of size. His inspiration for *Actual Size* originated when observing his son comparing his hand to a cast of a gorilla's hand during a visit to the San Diego Zoo. The book contains pictures of the eyeball of a giant squid and the head of an Alaskan brown bear, among other animals. Each page includes the height and weight

© 2004 Steve Jenkins

The huge **gorilla** and the **pygmy mouse lemur** both have hands a lot like ours.

gorilla: 5½ feet tall, 600 pounds   mouse lemur: 2½ inches tall, 1 ounce

*Steve Jenkins's illustrations in **Actual Size** help all readers to grasp the concept of relative size.*

of each animal; additional information about each animal is included in the back of the book. ***Prehistoric Actual Size*** capitalizes on children's fascination with ancient insects, animals, and birds. We can see the actual size of the teeth of the forty-five-foot long Giganotosaurus, possibly the "largest predator that ever lived on land."

Concept books contribute to a child's expanding knowledge and language by providing numerous examples of an idea. Some books present abstract ideas, such as shape, color, size, or sound, through many illustrations, as Tana Hoban does in ***Cubes, Cones, Cylinders, and Spheres*** (N–P). Hoban, a master of the art of concept books and a skilled photographer, uses no words in the book about shapes. Instead, she uses crystal-clear photographs of objects that children could find in their own environment. Children enjoy working with this book and often experiment with creating images using shapes and color on their own. Petr Horacek combines the concepts of colors and different types of animals in ***Butterfly, Butterfly*** (N–P) and adds further interest with die-cut holes. Animals, colors, and the idea of camouflage are all present in Satoru Onishi's ***Who's Hiding?*** (P).

Some books tell stories that focus on specific concepts or involve the viewer by asking questions. Steve Jenkins and Robin Page challenge a broad range of readers to expand their knowledge about the function of body parts in ***What Do You Do with a Tail Like This?*** (P–I). The authors include information about each animal in the back of the book.

Exploring the concept of kindergarten itself, Rosemary Wells put together a treasure when she collected hundreds of songs, activities, games, counting, alphabet songs, measuring, and science projects all in one book, ***My Kindergarten*** (P). This is an ideal book for kindergarten teachers, parents, grandparents, or anyone who has children in the first year of school. Other outstanding concept books appear in the Booklist at the end of the chapter.

Alphabet Books

Alphabet books serve many useful purposes, only one of which is related to learning the alphabet. Children ages two to four years old point to pictures and label objects on the page; five-year-olds may say the letter names and the words that start with each letter; six-year-olds may read the letters, words, or story to confirm their knowledge of letter-sound correspondence. However they are read, alphabet books help children develop an awareness of words on the page; they increase language learning and serve as a pleasurable activity for children.

We never need to settle for a mediocre alphabet book because magnificent ones are available, such as Alison

Drawing on the style of pop art, especially the work of Roy Lichtenstein, allows Rachel Isadora to simply yet effectively illustrate ABC Pop!.

Jay's *ABC* (N–P), Lisa Campbell Ernst's *The Turn-Around, Upside-Down Alphabet Book* (N–P), Andy Rash's *Agent A to Agent Z* (P), *Max's ABC* (N) by Rosemary Wells, *ABC Pop!* (N–P) by Rachel Isadora, Steve Johnson's *Graphic Alphabet* (N–P), and Brian Floca's *The Racecar Alphabet* (N–P). Jon Agee's *Z Goes Home* (N–P) combines fun with bold graphics as it follows the journey of Z, heading home across a bridge, eating a donut, and so on until it arrives home, the Z in the City Zoo. Ross MacDonald treats the alphabet humorously in *Achoo! Bang! Crash! The Noisy Alphabet* (P). Children who are just becoming interested in superheroes will love Bob McLeod's *Super-Hero ABC* (P).

In Helen Oxenbury's classic *ABC of Things* (N), the elongated shape and simple format appeal to young readers. Each double-page spread contains both uppercase and lowercase letters, one or more words beginning with the letters, and objects associated with the letters. Children enjoy the way the illustrations place the objects in humorous situations, such as a cat and a cow sitting on a chair while a crow carries in a cake full of candles.

Some authors use the ABCs to structure the information they want to present. For example, Kristin Joy Pratt uses the alphabet for *A Walk in the Rain Forest* and *A Swim Through the Sea* (P). Similarly, Paul Kratter's *The Living Rain Forest* (P) is as much about tropical rain forests as it is an alphabet book. David McLimans's Caldecott Medal–winning book, *Gone Wild* (P–I), is a fascinating inquiry into endangered animals from A to Z. These books are organized by the alphabet, but don't really focus on the alphabet as such. Martin Jarrie's *ABC USA* (P–I) contains much information about the United States and its culture ("J is for jazz" and "L is for Liberty Bell"). Deborah Lee Rose's *Into the A, B, Sea: An Ocean Alphabet* (P–I) with Steve Jenkins's outstanding paper collage illustrations contains many animals and plants, all linked with a continuous rhyme, and also includes a short description of each creature at the end of the book. Alphabet books for older readers are discussed later in this chapter, and other excellent alphabet books appear in the Booklist at the end of the chapter.

Counting Books

Some counting books help children learn numbers, numerical concepts, days of the week, months of the year, and the four seasons. Anita Lobel does all that and wraps it in an engaging story in *One Lighthouse, One Moon* (P–I). Many counting books are available for the nursery and primary grades, starting with those that use simple pictures to illustrate the progression from 1 to 10, such as Rachel Isadora's *1 2 3 Pop!* (P) and *Charley Harper 123's* (P), illustrated by one of the best-known graphic artists. Lynn Reiser's *Ten Puppies* (N) illustrates paired integers whose sum is ten with adorable puppies that make young readers want to look closely at the *nine* pink tongues and *one* blue tongue as they count. Reading Maurie Manning's *The Aunts Go Marching* (N), a cheerful, engaging text with plenty of things to count, leads children into singing

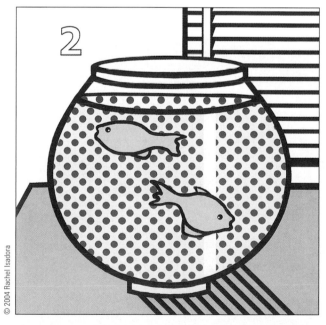

The illustrations in Rachel Isadora's 1 2 3 Pop! make it easy for young children to count objects.

along, movement, and counting out loud. Leo and Diane Dillon's delightful *Mother Goose: Numbers on the Loose* (P) highlights rhymes with numbers, and readers will enjoy counting the representations of objects and people in the illustrations. For example, in "Baa, baa black sheep," the "three bags full" are carried by a procession of characters across the double-page spread.

Other counting books go far beyond ten or count in sets, such as *Anno's Counting Book* (P–I), which moves from zero to twelve and from January to December. Mitsumasa Anno begins his counting book with an empty landscape that becomes a small village with twelve houses, twelve adults, and twelve children who go to church at twelve noon and see twelve reindeer in the sky. Stephen Johnson's *City by Numbers* (N–P) pulls young readers into visualizing the shapes of numbers with illustrations that demonstrate how to look to find number shapes in the world around us.

Philip Yates builds on children's interest in Egypt in *Ten Little Mummies: An Egyptian Counting Book* (P), in which the ten little mummies leave the tomb and go to play in the desert, where they disappear, one by one. Molly Bang's delightful *Ten, Nine, Eight* (N–P), recently reissued, also counts backward; as a father helps his daughter at bedtime, they count down from ten toes to one sleepy child all ready for bed. The illustrations depict bedtime activities that invite young readers to find the numbered objects and to enjoy the loving story. Carll Cneut's vibrant, busy illustrations combine with Marilyn Singer's rhymed text in *City Lullaby* (P) to present a humorous story of a baby who slumbers through "10 horns beeping," "9 phones ringing," "8 dogs barking" . . . until, in the surprise ending, "1 bird

begins to twitter" and the baby awakens. Counting books help children develop concepts of quantity and numerical order through fine visual portrayal of number concepts. The best illustrations for young children avoid distracting clutter so that the objects to be counted can be identified and counted without confusion. In books for older children the illustrations can be more complex. More counting books appear in the Booklist at the end of the chapter.

Picturebooks of Poetry and Song

Some picturebooks present an artist's visual interpretation of a song, poem, or verse. In these books, the artist arranges the text across the pages, often with only one or two lines per page, and then illuminates each thought expressed by the text. The lyrical language of the text should be both interesting to and understandable by the intended audience. Brief, rhythmic verses, narrative verses, and children's and folk songs make excellent picturebook texts. Some books contain several separate texts; others present single poems or songs.

In beautifully designed picturebooks of poetry and song, the arrangement of the text across the pages reflects the natural breaks in the meaning and sound of the original. Illustrations depict both action and feeling, matching the mood established by the author, as interpreted by the artist. Lynne Rae Perkins's *Snow Music* (P) is a perfect example of a beautifully designed picturebook containing a single poem. Tracey Campbell Pearson charmingly illustrates Robert Louis Stevenson's poem *The Moon* (P–I) in loose, dreamy watercolors whose setting seems to be the rocky coast of Maine. Each double-page spread illustrates

The loose watercolor and outline style of Tracey Campbell Pearson aptly illustrates Robert Louis Stevenson's peaceful poem **The Moon** *in this wordless double-page spread.*

It was Kitten's first full moon.
When she saw it, she thought,
There's a little bowl of milk in the sky.
And she wanted it.

Kevin Henkes captures the brightness of the full moon with simple lines and a muted black-and-cream palette in **Kitten's First Full Moon.**

a line or phrase from the poem, while the back endpages reprint the entire text. Eugene Field's classic nonsense poem ***Wynken, Blynken, and Nod*** (P) is visualized magically in Giselle Potter's whimsical naive art. Marla Frazee brings new life to a Woody Guthrie song with her clever and energetic illustrations for ***New Baby Train*** (P), and Chris Gall adds beautiful visual images to Katherine Lee Bates's patriotic song ***America the Beautiful*** (P–I). Holly Meade's exuberant hand-painted woodcut illustrations for David Elliott's ***On the Farm*** (P) are a wonderful accompaniment for the individual poems about farm animals on each double-page spread.

Storybooks

Whether in board book form or typical picturebook format, stories for the very young have a simple plot line, are about familiar childhood experiences, and contain clear illustrations. Toddlers who enjoy participation books also enjoy simple stories, Mother Goose rhymes, counting rhymes and alphabet jingles, and other rhythmic texts. Lively rhymes and attractive acrylic illustrations in ***I'm Going to Grandma's*** (N–P) by Mary Ann Hoberman and illustrated by Tiphanie Beeke, suggest the excitement of going to grandmother's house for a sleepover visit. Preschoolers will also appreciate reminders of parents' unconditional love, as in Emily Jenkins's ***Love You When You Whine*** (N–P), as a mother cat patiently reassures her child that she loves her even when she doesn't say "please"

or when she screams "Lollipop!" over and over while waiting with her mother in line at the bank.

As toddlers turn pages and point to pictures in books, they develop concepts about books and how they work. Simple storybooks introduce children to stories and help them learn about narrative by capturing and holding their interest even if they have short attention spans; these books often are the ones children turn to again and again. Kevin Henkes's Caldecott Medal–winning book, ***Kitten's First Full Moon*** (N), is a quiet story of one kitten's adventure as she tries to drink the bowl of milk that she mistakenly thinks is waiting for her in the full moon. Expressive pictures and a brief, lyrical text hold the attention of young listeners. The illustrations are black and white, with thick black lines and soft shading that both define Kitten's shape and personality and highlight the full moon. Henkes's simple words and simple lines combine to form a story that is satisfying to young readers.

Amy Schwartz captures the life of one young boy in ***What James Likes Best*** (N), which is not always what the adults in his life would think he would like. Schwartz presents four simple stories about everyday events, followed by the question "What did James like best?" and four possible answers, drawing young children into participating in the storytelling. Young children also enjoy the humorous search of Jack for the snorer who disturbed his sleep in ***Roar of a Snore*** (N–P) by Marsha Diane Arnold. Other favorite topics of young children include common everyday activities, as in ***Time to Get Dressed!*** (N) by Elivia

Savadier, in which a little boy wants to dress himself but still needs help.

Mo Willems tells the classic tale of the "blankie" or "lovey" lost and found again in *Knuffle Bunny: A Cautionary Tale* (N–P), a Caldecott Medal book. Young listeners identify with the child who misplaces her bunny and then utters her very first words when it is finally found. Older children enjoy the humor too. There are many more simple storybooks and poems that appeal to children who are not yet ready for long stories. These books generally have brief texts and engaging illustrations. Examples of stories for very young children appear in the Booklist at the end of the chapter.

• • BOOKS FOR • •
EMERGING READERS

As children mature, their taste for books matures; their cognitive and linguistic capabilities increase as well as their need for books. Learning to read and being able to unlock the secrets of a printed page mark an important step toward maturity. Many books are available for developing readers, including those we have already discussed. There are also special kinds of storybooks—wordless books, predictable books, and beginning-to-read books as well as illustrated, easy chapter books—that support children's attempts at independent reading.

Wordless books are appropriate for children of all ages who are developing a sense of story and are learning language rapidly. Predictable books are ideal material for the child who is beginning to pay attention to print. Beginning-to-read books are perfect for children who have just become independent readers but still need the support of simple but interesting texts. Picture storybooks, books of poetry and song, and nonfiction books continue to play an important role in a child's reading as well.

Wordless Books and Books with Very Sparse Text

Wordless books tell a story through illustration alone, though of course the title of a wordless book often contains important clues regarding what the story will be about; moreover, many wordless books incorporate words in the illustrations, often in the form of street signs or other public text. Young children who do not yet read can retell a story from looking at the pictures; beginning readers, through their developing concept of *story*, are able to narrate the story with character and narrator voices. Older, struggling readers can grasp the story elements in wordless books. All students can use wordless books as a springboard to writing and oral storytelling. Good wordless storybooks contain all the important elements found in all good storybooks—except for the dialogue and narration, which are supplied by the reader. A word-

less book such as *Breakfast for Jack* (P) by Pat Schories tells the charming story of a little boy who gets out of bed and feeds the family cat, but forgets to feed his dog Jack. Luckily, the boy remembers just as he goes out the door along with the rest of his family. Three other wordless picturebooks about Jack are *Jack and the Missing Piece*, *Jack and the Night Visitors*, and *Jack Wants a Snack* (all P). Some good wordless books appear in the Booklist at the end of the chapter.

Wordless books provide an excellent opportunity to explore how stories work. Children produce narration for wordless books; their ideas can be written down by an adult or tape-recorded and used for reading instruction material. If young children are narrating a wordless book, they can watch their own words being written and learn intuitively the relation between print and sound. This means of teaching, called the language experience approach, provides a meaningful foundation for reading, especially when accompanied by a strong read-aloud program based on good literature. Older students, too, benefit from using wordless books as a foundation for their own oral language or writing. The story they create from a wordless picture storybook is *their* story—they have composed it—and it is therefore easier for them to read.

Barbara Lehman's *The Red Book* (P–I), a Caldecott Honor winner, is, appropriately, bright red. The watercolor, gouache, and ink illustrations, with their straightforward, geometric shapes, present the story of a young girl who finds a red book in the snow on the city sidewalk, picks it up, and takes it to school. When she opens the book, she sees a map of islands. The illustrations then zoom into a close-up of the island on which a boy walks along a beach, and he finds a red book in the sand. When he opens the book, he sees a city and, as the pictures zoom in again, the girl. They gaze at each other, entranced. The girl leaves school, buys many balloons, and sails off to meet the boy on the island, dropping the red book. They do meet, and end up in the pages of the dropped book, together. At least until a boy on a bike picks up the lost book. With its clever plot, expressive characters, and exploration of the power of books and the imagination, this wordless book is a treasure. In *Museum Trip* (P–I), Lehman also explores the entering of other worlds when a boy gets lost in a museum and is able to shrink in size and explore a maze he has seen in a book. Lehman's *Rainstorm* (P–I), also a wordless book, is a fantasy about a wealthy, lonely boy who discovers a magical passage to an island off the coast from his house, where he plays joyfully with other children, and eventually brings them back through the same passage to his own house. Another of Barbara Lehman's wordless books, *Trainstop* (P–I), is described in detail previously. All of these wordless books celebrate the power of the imagination and the blurring of realism and fantasy, and are a great stimulus to writing and an inspiration to children's creative capacities.

*In **Rainstorm**, Barbara Lehman needs no words to convey a boy's magical passage from an island lighthouse to his home on the shore.*

Chicken and Cat (P) by Sara Varon, relates Cat's visit to Chicken in a big city in wordless cartoon format. This amusing story includes Cat's initial fascination with the interesting things to do in the city and Cat's growing discontent with the drab urban landscape. The witty storyline, with its resolution (Cat helps Chicken plant a garden to improve the view) will appeal to a range of readers. Another funny wordless book, ***You Can't Take a Balloon into the National Gallery*** (P–I–A) by Jacqueline Preiss Weitzman and Robin Preiss Glasser, gives readers several subplots, as well as a background activity, art, geography, maps, people, architecture, and humorous detail. In ***Invisible*** (P–I), Katja Kamm amusingly explores how things and people can disappear against backgrounds of the same color or pattern. Students of all ages can enjoy David Wiesner's book ***Sector 7*** (P–I) and Jeanne Baker's ***Window*** and ***Home*** (P–I–A), each for different reasons. Charlotte Dematons gives children a lot to look at in ***The Yellow Balloon*** (N–P), as the illustrations, through a series of aerial views, present the world travels of an escaped balloon. The visually stunning ***Yellow Umbrella*** (P–I) by Dong Il Sheen and Jae-Soo Lieu, though it contains no words, is accompanied by a CD with music to play while turning the pages.

All students learn about story structure and form when they translate the pictures of a wordless storybook into language. The structure of the story, along with the character development, provides a good model for writ-

ers, but students can also explore the visual characterization, setting, and theme that wordless books provide. Note that many wordless books are extremely sophisticated in terms of their content and structure, and are appropriate for older readers as well as precocious youngsters.

Predictable or Patterned Books

Predictable books have a strong rhythmic pattern in the language. This helps children anticipate what is going to happen next and predict the next word to come. Many four- and five-year-old children can make predictions and use their knowledge of phonics to read books on their own after hearing them read aloud once or twice. In ***The Seals on the Bus*** (N–P) Lenny Hort replicates the pattern of a familiar song, turning the wheels on the bus into the seals on the bus who go "errp, errp, errp" all around the town. In ***Cold Little Duck, Duck, Duck*** (N–P), Lisa Westberg Peters uses a similar pattern of repetition. A little duck comes to the pond only to find it still frozen. The text is written in large letters: "One miserable and frozen spring: brisk brisk brisk. A cold little duck flew in: Brr-ack Brr-ack Brr-ack. Her pond was stiff and white: creak creak creak." The interesting sounds Peters repeats make children want to read along. Emily Gravett's ***Orange Pear Apple Bear*** (N–P) contains only five words, with the illustrations providing heavy support for the streamlined plot, which involves a

© 2005 Emily Gravett

Orange, pear, apple, bear

*Emily Gravett's warm and amusing illustrations help children identify the words in **Orange Pear Apple Bear**.*

bear who finds, and eventually eats, each of the fruits in the title of the story. Bob Shea's delightful *Dinosaur vs. Bedtime* pits a young dinosaur against a pile of leaves, "talking grownups," and the dinosaur always wins. But when it comes to bedtime, the little dinosaur becomes too tired to resist. The repetitive nature of this book, with the satisfying conclusion, makes it a natural for going to bed.

Predictable books are structured using strong language patterns, such as repeated phrases, rhyme, and rhythm; cumulative story structures that add, or accumulate, information; and familiar concepts, songs, or sequences (like days of the week). Detailed illustrations reinforce the language patterns and provide a visual reproduction of the text. Dayle Ann Dodds's *Where's Pup?* (N–P) contains simple text consisting of two- and three-word sentences, rhyming words, and a limited vocabulary, yet manages to tell an engaging story that young children can actually read on their own. Children will delight in the last page, which unfolds several times to reveal where Pup is located. Pierre Pratt's colorful illustrations provide a context that both engages and supports young readers. In *Red Sled* (N–P), Patricia Thomas signals by the title that the book will be composed of pairs of rhyming words that tell the story of a boy and his father who go sledding and finish their winter's evening by having some hot chocolate and going to bed. Characteristics of predictable books are listed in Figure 3.7.

Reading involves sampling, predicting, and confirming (Goodman, 1985; Smith, 1978). Fluent readers build hypotheses about text meaning as they read. They predict a probable meaning based on the information sampled,

and then confirm it by checking to see if it makes sense, matches the letter-sound correspondence in the print, and sounds like real language. For beginning readers, patterned books are ideal fare because they match expectations every step of the way. Poetry also meets the criteria. Through rhythm, repetition, and rhyme, Jane Yolen creates a story in *How Do Dinosaurs Say Goodnight?* (P) that uses

Figure 3.7

Characteristics of Predictable, Patterned Stories

Predictable, patterned stories support children as they learn to read. The best of these books have many, if not all, of the characteristics listed here:

✿ Natural-sounding language

✿ Literal illustrations of the content

✿ Simple and direct story line

✿ Repeated phrases and repetitive refrains

✿ Rhyming words

✿ Cumulative patterns of events

✿ Content that appeals to children

✿ Plot that is understandable to children

But where is the
green sheep?

Here is the car sheep,
and here is the train sheep.

*The rhyming, rhythmic verse in **Where Is the Green Sheep?** supports new readers as they read all by themselves.*

dinosaurs to capture childlike behavior. Beginning readers chime in the second time through the book and soon can read it on their own. Other outstanding patterned books appear in the Booklist at the end of the chapter.

Patterned, predictable books help beginning readers confirm their knowledge of sound–letter correspondence. Often the books have an illustration followed by a single line of text. For example, Mem Fox's *Where Is the Green Sheep?* (N–P), illustrated by Judy Horacek, contains patterned, lilting, rhyming statements with art that precisely reflects the language until, toward the end of the story, readers are cautioned to turn the page quietly because the green sheep is fast asleep.

Beginning-to-Read Books

Beginning-to-read books are those that children who have just become independent readers can enjoy on their own; they combine controlled vocabulary with creative storytelling. Good beginning-to-read books have strong characterization, worthy themes, and engaging plots. The sentences are generally simple, with few embedded clauses, and the language is often direct dialogue. Lines of text are printed so that sentence breaks occur according to natural phrases; meaningful chunks of language are grouped together.

Illustrations depict the characters and action in ways that reflect and extend the text, which contains a limited number of different words and tells an interesting story. Arnold Lobel's classic series, including *Frog and Toad Are Friends* (N–P), is a favorite with newly independent read-

ers. Frog and Toad, humanlike characters in animal form, solve understandable problems with naiveté and wit.

Cynthia Rylant, a wizard with words, creates *Henry and Mudge* (P), a warm and wonderful series of stories about a large dog and the boy who loves him. Illustrations depict the action and provide emotional details about the characters. Rylant chooses words wisely; her stories are so well written that they are a pleasure to read. Denys Cazet's **Minnie and Moo** series has a loyal following of young readers. In *Minnie and Moo: Will You Be My Valentine?* (P) the humor is high and the text easy for young readers to decode. Kevin Henkes's *Old Bear* (P) gently relates the dreams of a bear during its long winter hibernation, culminating in the arrival of spring.

Appealing to a slightly older audience, Pamela Duncan Edwards pares down two historical moments in *The Wright Brothers* and *Boston Tea Party* (both I). Pamela employs two mice in each book to add asides of humor and significant facts to the overall stories.

Highly illustrated chapter books, although they are not true picturebooks, are an important part of a young child's development as an independent reader. Cynthia Rylant's **Cobble Street Cousins** series, Paula Danziger's **Amber Brown** series, and many others discussed in Chapter 7 offer young readers the opportunity to read longer, more complex texts that are still supported by illustrations.

As children grow in their reading ability, they move beyond listening to picturebooks and working with easy-to-read materials on to chapter books and then toward full-length texts. However, even though children outgrow reading about Frog and Toad and other characters from

Teaching Idea 3.6

Study the Body of an Author's or Illustrator's Work: Chris Van Allsburg

Any author or illustrator with five or more books is a candidate for an author or illustrator study. Here we show how a study of Chris Van Allsburg might look.

Collect Chris Van Allsburg's picturebooks. Pass them out to small groups of two or three students, and then have the groups position themselves in chronological order according to the books' copyright dates. Students sit in a circle in this chronological order. Provide time for students to read and explore each book. Students introduce their book and comment about the illustrations and text. (You can record this information if desired.) Next, have students find connections among these books. How are the writing and art similar? How did Allsburg's work change over the years? Are there any thematic similarities? Where is the dog in each book? The possible questions are endless. A chart similar to the example below can help students keep track of their ideas.

Title	Publication Date	Illustration Style	Genre	Setting	Theme or Important Message	Point of View or Perspective	Spot the Dog
The Garden of Abdul Gasazi	1979						
Jumanji	1981						
Ben's Dream	1982						
The Wreck of the Zephyr	1983						
The Mysteries of Harris Burdick	1984						
The Polar Express	1985						
The Stranger	1986						
The Z Was Zapped	1997						
Two Bad Ants	1998						
Just a Dream	1990						
The Wretched Stone	1991						
The Widow's Broom	1992						
The Sweetest Fig	1993						
Bad Day at Riverbend	1995						
Zathura	2002						
Probuditi!	2006						

✧ Students fill in the publication date.

✧ Students place a check in the column indicating that they have found the dog in each book, and note where.

their early reading experiences, they remember their happy, successful encounters with these books. These strong, positive experiences propel them into more positive connections with literature. As they grow in their familiarity with the many books available to them, children will begin to develop a list of "favorite" authors and illustrators. Teaching Idea 3.6 uses the example of Chris Van Allsburg, a popular author with primary, intermediate, and advanced readers, to present a way to study the body of an author's or illustrator's work.

Children in the preschool and primary grades continue to enjoy hearing well-written picture storybooks, books of poetry and song, and nonfiction books read aloud. Each year there is a crop of wonderful books just waiting to be placed in the hands, minds, and hearts of both young children and older ones as well.

• • NONFICTION • • PICTUREBOOKS

Nonfiction picturebooks include informational books designed to provide readers with knowledge about a particular topic, concept books that seek to present a particular concept in a way that young readers can understand, and biographies based on factual information about a subject. The text should be accurate, organized in a manner appropriate to both the information presented and the intended audience, designed in an attractive and appropriate fashion, and written and illustrated with verve and style.

Nonfiction picturebooks reach a broad range of students, enabling students at many different ability levels to access information. Producing picturebooks appropriate to a young reader's age or to a struggling older reader's ability creates a special challenge for nonfiction writers, who have to find ways to explain a subject simply enough to be understood and still be accurate. Nonfiction picturebooks for older, more advanced readers can present more complex, detailed information.

Nicola Davies's **Surprising Sharks** (P), intended for a primary-grade audience, presents many different sizes and shapes of sharks, pointing out some of the surprising results of adaptation as well as the commonalities of anatomy and behavior. The text is humorous and informative, and the bright colors and clever art of James Croft add to both the humor and the information. This book blends accuracy with fun, a perfect combination for the subject and the intended audience.

In his picturebook biographies, Don Brown displays his gift for conveying information about his subjects through a brief but straightforward text and carefully composed illustrations. In **Odd Boy Out: Young Albert Einstein** (P), Brown presents the genius as an introspective child who struggled in school, effectively selecting events and details to narrate and most often illustrating Einstein alone, with closed or downcast eyes.

• • POSTMODERN • • PICTUREBOOKS

Since about 1990, picturebooks that are decidedly unusual have piqued the interest of children and adults alike. These picturebooks may contain multiple narratives of the same incident (such as Anthony Browne's **Voices in the Park**, P–I), or interlocking narratives that it is the reader's job to connect to one another, as in David Macaulay's **Black and White** (P–I–A). In many of these postmodern picturebooks, characters talk directly to the reader. In **Do Not Open This Book!** (P–I) by Michaela Muntean, the pig who is in the process of writing a book keeps telling us not to turn the page, but of course, we do, and it's the pig's interactions with us that make the story amusing. In Mélanie Watt's **Chester** (P–I), the story consists of the author/illustrator's attempts to tell a story about a mouse; but she is continually interrupted by her cat Chester, who inserts

*Mélanie Watt clearly has her work cut out for her as she tries to gain control over her story from one of her characters, **Chester** the cat.*

his own ideas for the story (of course starring him, not the mouse) on every page. *Chester's Back!* (P–I) provides a hilarious and equally postmodern sequel. Postmodern picturebooks often refer to many other texts; that is, they are heavily intertextual. For example, in *Ivan the Terrier* (P–I) by Peter Catalanotto, the title character keeps barging in on other stories: the dog invades the stories of "The Three Billy Goats Gruff," "The Three Bears," "The Three Little Pigs," and "The Gingerbread Boy." Part of the pleasure of this book is the idea that stories are permeable to one another. In David Wiesner's version of *The Three Pigs* (P–I–A), for example, the pigs are literally blown out of their own story by the wolf's huffing and puffing, and enter a series of other stories before they return to their own tale. In Lauren Child's delightful *Who's Afraid of the Big Bad Book?* (P–I), Herb, the main character, enters his own badly damaged book of fairy tales, and has adventures with many fairy tale characters, including Goldilocks, the Three Bears, Hansel and Gretel, and Cinderella. Allan Ahlberg's *Previously* (P–I), with illustrations by Bruce

Ingman, tells a story backward, with intertextual links and visits to a similar list of commonly known tales, ending the book with "Once upon a time."

Rather than enticing the reader to enter the world of the story, many of these postmodern picturebooks push the reader away, as if to say, "Remember this is not true—it's just a story." Emily Gravett's *Wolves* (P–I–A) is an example of such a self-referential book. When a rabbit gets eaten by a wolf, the narrator breaks into the story with the comment, ". . . no rabbits were eaten during the making of this book. It is a work of fiction," and proceeds to provide an "alternative ending" for squeamish readers. Finally, some postmodern picturebooks play with the conventions of picturebooks themselves. In Jon Scieszka's collection of hilarious parodies of traditional fairy tales, *The Stinky Cheese Man and Other Fairly Stupid Tales* (P–I–A), the table of contents falls on the story characters, knocking one of the stories entirely out of the book. Jack, the narrator (we don't know for sure whether he is Jack from "Jack and the Beanstalk" or Jack from the rhyme "Jack and Jill went up the hill") moves

Figure 3.8

Some Notable Postmodern Picturebooks

Ahlberg, Janet, and Allan Ahlberg. (1986). *The Jolly Postman or Other People's Letters*. Boston: Little, Brown

Browne, Anthony. (1998). *Voices in the Park*. New York: DK Ink

_____. (2004). *Into the Forest*. Cambridge, MA: Candlewick

Catalanotto, Peter. (2007). *Ivan the Terrier*. New York: Atheneum Books

Child, Lauren. (2000). *Beware of the Storybook Wolves*. New York: Scholastic

_____. (2002). *Who's Afraid of the Big Bad Book?* New York: Hyperion

Feiffer, Jules. (1997). *Meanwhile*. New York: HarperCollins

Felix, Monique. (1988). *The Story of a Little Mouse Trapped in a Book*. La Jolla, CA: Green Tiger

Grey, Mini. (2005). *Traction Man is Here*. New York: Knopf

_____. (2006). *The Adventures of the Dish and the Spoon*. New York: Knopf

_____. (2008). *Traction Man Meets Turbo Dog*. New York: Knopf

Hawkins, Colin, and Jacqui Hawkins. (2004). *Fairytale News*. Cambridge, MA: Candlewick

Hopkinson, Deborah. (2008). *Abe Lincoln Crosses a Creek*. Illustrated by John Hendrix. New York: Random House

Lehman, Barbara. (2004). *The Red Book*. Boston: Houghton Mifflin

_____. (2006). *Museum Trip*. Boston: Houghton Mifflin

Macaulay, David. (1990). *Black and White*. Boston: Houghton Mifflin

_____. (1995). *Shortcut*. Boston: Houghton Mifflin

Muntean, Michaela. (2006). *Do Not Open This Book!* New York: Scholastic

Scieszka, Jon. (1994). *The Book That Jack Wrote*. New York: Viking

_____. (1992). *The Stinky Cheese Man and Other Fairly Stupid Tales*. New York: Viking

Vail, Rachel. (1998). *Over the Moon*. Illustrated by Scott Nash. New York: Orchard Books

Van Allsburg, Chris. (1995). *Bad Day at Riverbend*. Boston: Houghton Mifflin

Watt, Mélanie. (2007). *Chester*. Toronto, Ontario: Kids Can Press

_____. (2008). *Chester's Back!* Toronto, Ontario: Kids Can Press

Wattenberg, Jane. (2000). *Henny Penny*. New York: Scholastic

Whatley, Bruce. (2001). *Wait! No Paint!* New York: HarperCollins

Wiesner, David. (2001). *The Three Pigs*. New York: Clarion

Wilson, April. (1999). *Magpie Magic*. New York: Dial

the back endpage forward so that the Giant, who is chasing him, "will think the book is over." The satisfaction of these types of picturebooks is our delighted shock that both the conventions of stories and the conventions of the picturebook format are playfully subverted.

Both young and older readers must do a lot more active reading and thinking in these books than in picturebooks with more standard plots and structures. Moreover, such picturebooks make us self-aware of our own thought processes as we encounter elements that contradict or defy our own expectations. In this way, postmodern picturebooks teach readers to be consciously aware of their own knowledge of stories and how they work. These books are decidedly not just for older readers; research proves that young children can understand, interpret, and appreciate their violations of literary conventions (Pantaleo, 2008; Sipe, 2008). See Figure 3.8 for a list of more postmodern picturebooks.

• • PICTUREBOOKS • • FOR OLDER READERS

As we've discussed previously, an increasing number of picturebooks are targeted to a wide range of readers; and some are intended specifically for an audience of older readers (Pearson, 2005). In the past, most picturebooks were published primarily for students in preschool and primary grades. Today, publishers offer a variety of picturebooks that appeal to older students, such as picturebooks for struggling readers, second-language bilingual books, graphic picturebooks and graphic novels, as well as nonfiction picturebooks. These books appeal to visually sophisticated students; they are also accessible to struggling readers who learn more easily using books with more pictures and sparser text. Students learning English also learn more easily using picturebooks and other illustrated texts.

"Wordless" does not necessarily mean simple; in fact, wordless books can be very sophisticated, appealing primarily to an older audience. A good example is Thé Tjong Khing's *Where Is the Cake?* (I–A), which, although wordless, presents an intricate cast of characters and weaves together many stories. Older readers will enjoy making sense of all the seemingly disparate narratives and the relationships among the many characters. Istvan Banyai's *The Other Side* (I–A) is an exceptionally interesting wordless book that takes a look at the same scene from different perspectives and is quite challenging for even sophisticated readers/viewers.

*The front and back dust jacket covers for **The Other Side** by Istvan Banyai suggest the dual perspectives that form the theme of the book.*

Like counting books for younger readers, some books for older readers present information organized numerically. Peter Sís, a recipient of the MacArthur "genius" award, created *The Train of States* (I–A), which presents the fifty American states as train cars, in the order in which they became states. Every state is pictured as a train car in which you find the capital, state flower, presidents, and lots of other information. In fact, many of Sís's picturebooks are intriguing for older readers, such as *The Wall, The Three Golden Keys, Tibet Through the Red Box,* and *The Tree of Life* (all I–A). *The Buck Stops Here: The Presidents of the United States* (I–A) by Alice Provensen, starts with, "First and Foremost, Washington, Our best beloved President One." This book presents the

presidents numerically in rhyming style. The illustrations add historical information about each president.

Alphabet books are not exclusive to primary grades either. Avis Harley uses the alphabet to present poetic forms in *Fly with Poetry* (I–A). In alphabetical order, she defines a poetic form and presents a poem in that form to explain exactly what she means. For example, she explains what an acrostic poem is and then presents a poem in that form. Other acrostic ABC books for older readers include *Summer: An Alphabet Acrostic* (P–I) and *Winter: An Alphabet Acrostic* (P–I), both by Steven Schnur and illustrated by Leslie Evans's lovely hand-colored linoleum block prints. In a much more amusing way, *M is for Mischief* (I) by Linda Ashman, illustrated

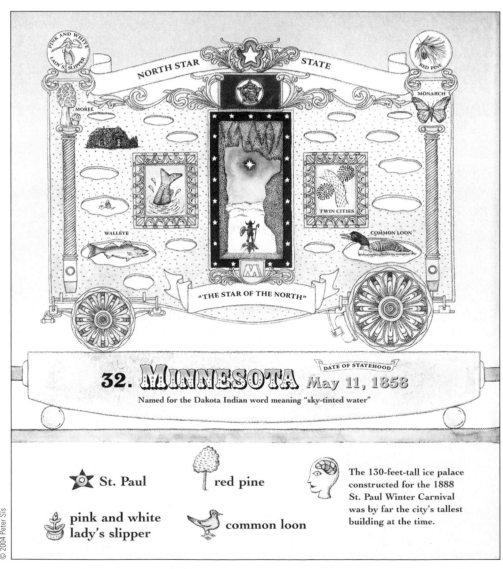

*Peter Sís's **The Train of States** provides much visual and verbal information about the states in a format pleasing to a wide range of readers.*

The colored linoleum-cut illustrations for **Winter: An Alphabet Acrostic** *by Steven Schnur,
illustrated by Leslie Evans, beautifully convey the warm light of a fireside read-aloud.*

with Nancy Carpenter's exuberant pictures, contains clever poems about naughty children from "Angry Abby" to "Zany Zelda."

Other authors use the alphabet as a structure for information. *The Queen's Progress: An Elizabethan Alphabet* (I–A) lures readers by providing alphabetical bite-sized nuggets of information about the reign of Elizabeth I. Reflecting the Elizabethan Age, the illustrations complement the text. Another example is Arthur Yorinks's *The Alphabet Atlas* (I–A). This alphabetical atlas transforms geography into stunning quilted artwork. Its beauty inspires students to want to write and illustrate their own alphabetical atlas.

Q Is for Quark: A Science Alphabet Book and *G Is for Googol: A Math Alphabet Book* (I–A), written by David M. Schwartz, are directed to upper-grade students. Some teachers use these books to complement their math and science curricula by providing a "letter-a-day" read-aloud experience or by reinforcing a topic such as "D" for DNA when it connects to the subject students are studying. The two books make complicated topics friendly and fun. "D" for DNA, for example, employs plain, simple language and silly drawings that make DNA comical and intriguing rather than boring and difficult to understand. Teaching students how to say "rhombicosidodecahedron" (the biggest polyhedron, with 240 faces) adds linguistic sparkle to a geometry lesson because it becomes a fun word to say and "show off" to others.

Just as there are counting and alphabet books for older readers, there are also pop-up books that appeal to a wide range of students. A tour de force of a pop-up ABC book is Marion Bataille's *ABC3D* (all ages), which students of all ages will be amazed by. *Brooklyn Pops Up* (all ages) is an engineering marvel that shows landmarks in Brooklyn, New York, including Coney Island, Grand Army Plaza, and the Brooklyn Museum of Art. Several artists and pop-up designers worked on the book, including Maurice Sendak and pop-up master Robert Sabuda. Sabuda's stunning *Alice's Adventures in Wonderland, The Wonderful Wizard of Oz, The Chronicles of Narnia*, and *Winter's Tale* (all I) appeal to intermediate audiences. Sabuda and his partner Matthew Reinhart have produced amazing informational pop-up books in their **Encyclopedia Prehistorica** series, including *Dinosaurs, Sharks*, and

Mega-Beasts (I–A). Another master of pop-ups is David Carter, whose books tend to be more abstract, though equally astonishing, as in *One Red Dot*, *Blue 2*, *600 Black Spots*, and *Yellow Square* (all I–A). Christopher Bing seamlessly weaves history and art into a rare treasure in *The Midnight Ride of Paul Revere* (I). Bing's masterpiece goes well beyond the familiar narrative poem, and it takes several viewings to grasp even a portion of the information contained in the pictures.

Jon Scieszka wrote and Lane Smith illustrated books difficult to categorize but delightful to read: they had fun with *Math Curse* and in 2007 produced *Science Verse* (I). Author and illustrator permeate the topics of math and science with humor; readers devour both books. *Science Verse* is a zany series of poems that parody the styles of Joyce Kilmer, Edgar Allan Poe, Lewis Carroll, Robert Frost, and many others. Each book comes with a CD featuring Scieszka and Smith reading each piece aloud.

Blurring Forms/Formats

Picturebooks have much in common with other forms of what artist Will Eisner (1985) calls "sequential art" or what Terry Thompson (2008) calls "graphica," such as comic books, graphic novels, and films. In all of these art forms, there is a sequence of visual images, and there is also a verbal component, with either written or spoken words that accompany the visual images. In addition, all require both words and pictures working in concert and synergy to communicate their meanings. The last number of years have seen a hybridization of these forms and formats that is quite exciting for both older and younger readers. A very high-profile example of this hybridization was the awarding of the 2008 Caldecott Medal to Brian Selznick's *The Invention of Hugo Cabret* (I–A). You'll

*The protagonist of **The Invention of Hugo Cabret** demonstrates his skill at repairing movable toys for an exacting shopkeeper in Brian Selznick's evocative black-and-white images.*

recall that the Caldecott Medal is given by the American Library Association "to the artist of the most distinguished American picture book for children" (quoting the ALA website, www.ala.org). At first glance, *The Invention of Hugo Cabret* (hereafter referred to as *Hugo*) looks like a novel: it's more than five hundred pages long. Opening it, we see that it contains sections of text and long sequences of black-and-white illustrations, though the words are never printed on the same page as the illustrations. Is this a picturebook? According to the Caldecott committee, it is! This decision by the committee marks a new way of conceptualizing picturebooks; it means that it is no longer easy (or perhaps even useful) to draw rigid distinctions among graphic novels, comic books, picturebooks, and films. The layout of *Hugo* resembles a graphic novel, cells in a very long comic book, or a series of stills from a film presented in slow motion. The recognition given to *Hugo* may spur those who write and illustrate literature for children and adolescents to even greater inventive departures from the traditional format of the picturebook.

Another excellent example of the blurring of forms and formats is Shaun Tan's *The Arrival* (I–A), a beautifully illustrated wordless book that tells the story of an immigrant to a country whose culture and language are quite different from his own. We learn along with the immigrant about the new culture, and rejoice with him when he is able to afford to send for his wife and young daughter to come to be with him. On the last page, the exquisite illustrations show the youngster giving another recent immigrant directions. *The Arrival* combines the forms of the wordless picturebook and the graphic novel in a wonderful work of art that might have given *The Invention of Hugo Cabret* some stiff competition for best picturebook; unfortunately, it was ineligible, due to being published first in Australia. Shaun Tan's newest book, *Tales from Outer Suburbia* (I–A), is a series of "illustrated stories" around the common theme of encountering the new and surprising in the humdrum life of the suburbs.

Recently there have been increasing numbers of graphic picturebooks or graphic novels in which the story is told through a combination of cartoons with speech bubbles and, sometimes, a brief narrative text below each cartoon. Dav Pilkey's **Captain Underpants** (P–I) series and the **Babymouse** (P–I) series by Jennifer and Matthew Holm are popular with younger readers, and adolescents are captivated by many graphic novels, such as Art Spiegelman's **Maus** (A) books, for example, *Maus: A Survivor's Tale*. Nicolas Debon uses this format to present his biography of artist Emily Carr in *Four Pictures by Emily Carr* (I–A), in which he tells his entire story through cartoon art and speech bubbles with handwritten text.

In an integrated, literature-based curriculum, students explore topics in nonfiction picturebooks that convey relevant information geared to their interest level.

A recent immigrant's struggle to communicate in order to find a place to live is perfectly conveyed without words in Shaun Tan's **The Arrival.**

The publishing trend has been to produce more reader-friendly books with increased illustration and less densely packed texts. Picturebooks for older students are longer, have more complex text and themes, and deal with topics that are more abstract and more intellectually demanding. We discuss nonfiction picturebooks in Chapters 9 and 10.

There are other picture storybooks for older students that explore themes and events that are not suited for a younger audience. For example, in Patricia Polacco's *Pink and Say* (I–A), African American Pinkus saves Sheldon's life as they fight side by side on a Civil War battlefield. Pinkus takes his wounded white soldier friend to his own home, where his grandmother nurses Sheldon back to health. Despite his generous acts, Pinkus is hanged at Andersonville jail soon after arriving there as a Confederate prisoner. Ann Turner's *Nettie's Trip South* (I–A) is another picturebook for older readers that helps them emotionally engage with the implications of slavery. Tom Feelings's *Middle Passage* (A) needs no words to convey the horrors of the slave trade.

The late Virginia Hamilton published a collection of twenty-four American black folktales. One of those stories, *The People Could Fly* (I–A), is considered her finest. Fortunately, it is now published as a stand-alone book with all-new illustrations by Leo and Diane Dillon. The combination of text and illustration is so convincing that readers almost believe the story to be true even while they understand the metaphorical meaning of flying. A perfect companion for this picturebook is Alice McGill's *Way Up and Over* (I–A), illustrated by Jude Daly, which tells a similar story of African American slaves flying away from their master.

Other topics that are clearly beyond the range of younger readers are more commonly presented in contemporary picturebooks than they were just a decade ago. These topics include: suicide in *I Never Knew Your Name* (A) by Sherry Garland, illustrated by Sheldon Greenberg's stylized oil paintings; the grim realities of the Vietnam War in *Patrol: An American Solider in Vietnam* (A) with powerful free verse by Walter Dean Myers and illustrated with Ann Grifalconi's ominous and evocative collages; and extensive and psychologically complex biographies of famous people, such as Charles R. Smith's twelve-chapter free verse version of Muhammad Ali's life, *Twelve Rounds to Glory* (I–A), illustrated with Bryan Collier's unforgettable paint and collage images. These are just a few of the picturebooks whose topics are clearly intended for an audience of older readers. Books with sophisticated black or macabre humor, such as *Mr. Maxwell's Mouse* by Frank Asch and illustrated with Devin Asch's mordantly dark images (I–A), are only appropriate for a mature audience. These and more picture storybooks that are appropriate for older readers are discussed in Chapters 5 through 8.

Graphic picturebooks and novels have become popular with upper elementary and adolescent readers. The visual nature of these books is especially appealing to many students. Marcia Williams created two graphic picturebooks: *Tales from Shakespeare* and *Bravo, Mr. William Shakespeare!* (I–A). Each book contains seven of Shakespeare's most popular plays. The first contains *Romeo and Juliet, A Winter's Tale, Macbeth, A Midsummer Night's Dream, Julius Caesar, Hamlet,* and *The Tempest.* The second contains *As You Like It, Richard III, Antony and Cleopatra, Much Ado about Nothing, Twelfth Night, King Lear,* and *The Merchant of Venice. King* (A) by Ho Che Anderson, subtitled *A Comics Biography of Martin Luther King, Jr.*, combines black-and-white comic book cells with larger illustrations that have speech bubbles and sparing but effective use of color in mixed media for a powerful and unforgettable visual and literary experience. Other not-to-be-missed graphic novels for older readers include *Persepolis 1* and *2* (I–A) by Marjane Satrapi and Gene Luen Yang's *American Born Chinese* (A). The latter won the Michael Printz Award for Young Adult Fic-

tion. *The Magical Life of Long Tack Sam* (A), an illustrated memoir by Ann Marie Fleming, uses a combination of old photographs, historical documents, and drawings to tell the fascinating story of her great-grandfather, who was one of the most famous Chinese magicians. *Fun Home: A Family Tragicomic* by Alison Bechdel (A), deals with her childhood and coming of age, addressing such serious topics as her growing awareness of being lesbian, the suicide of her father, and her father's sexual abuse of teenage boys. *500 Essential Graphic Novels* (A) by Gene Kannenberg, Jr., is an excellent resource for this proliferating format. In the realm of comic books, an equally impressive array is present in **The Best American Comics** series (A) for 2006, 2007, and 2008.

Little Vampire Goes to School (I) by French author Joann Sfar, was a Children's Choices Award Winner in 2004. This book is an interesting mix of cartoon style and creepy content and is appealing to many readers, including reluctant ones. Avi's graphic picturebook, *Silent Movie* (I–A), illustrated by C. B. Mordan, is, appropriately, black and white and told only through images and title cards. The rags-to-riches immigrant story, complete with villain, appealing young child and mother on their own, and happy ending is perfect fare for the silent movie and the audience. The melodrama is a wonderful stimulus for some extended dramatic writing.

Picturebooks have a special place in the lives of children and adolescents. Children and adolescents make connections between the books they read and the life they live because these books reflect every aspect of their expanding world.

✳   ✳   ✳

A CLOSE LOOK AT
Woolvs in the Sitee

There are few contemporary picturebooks for older readers that have as powerful an impact as *Woolvs in the Sitee* (I–A) by the Australian team of Margaret Wild and Anne Spudvilas. The title alone unsettles us; the phonetic spelling, which continues throughout the book, accentuates the chaos and deeply disturbing tone of the book, which will provide many opportunities for mature readers' speculations and inferences. Set in an unnamed, perhaps futuristic urban area, *Woolvs* is narrated by Ben, a young teenager who is terribly afraid to even step outside his own derelict building, so afraid is he of the "woolvs" whom he thinks prowl the city where he used to live happily with his family. Now an orphan, he lives alone, his only friend a neighbor, "Missus Radinski," an older woman who fails (or pretends to fail) to perceive the danger of the ominous "woolvs" that roam the streets. Are the "woolvs" figments of Ben's disordered imagination? Or are they metaphors for the distrust, fear, and terror that are everyday features of urban life, even in our contemporary cities, where the fabric of society is so tattered that no one trusts anyone else?

The front and back dust jacket of this book read as one continuous illustration. The top half has a black background, with the names of the author and illustrator in red and the title, crudely hand-lettered, in stark white. Just visible on the top half of the back dust jacket are the words "they spare no won," a phrase that occurs repeatedly in the book. The bottom half of the front and back dust jacket contains similar disquieting phrases, on a red background. Clearly, this is not going to be a light-hearted book. The cloth board cover is plain black, and the endpapers (front and back) are an equally somber black, with child-like scribbled drawings of wolves. The title page has a red background, with illegible handwritten words. The reader turns to the first opening, which begins,

> *There are woolvs in the sitee. Oh yes!*
> *in the streets. in the parks. in the allees.*
> *. . .*

And soon they will kum.
. . .
No won is spared.

The palette for the illustrations is appropriately dark and foreboding, in tones of black and sick yellows, with occasional splashes of brighter colors that only add to the eerie quality of the story. Ben says, "I longs for bloo skys. I longs for it to rane. But the seesons are topsee-turvee. Nothing is rite," suggesting that something cataclysmic—a nuclear war? A severe societal upheaval?—has reduced the city where once the streets were his "rivers, these parks my vallees" to a ruin where only an occasional person rides by on a bicycle, looking over his shoulder in apprehension. One day, seduced by a blue-painted wall, he thinks things are back to normal and runs out of the building, only to be paralyzed by fear of the "woolvs." "Missus Radinski" rescues him, and drags him back inside. Then the worst happens: Missus Radinski disappears. Ben has to summon up all his courage to look for her, all the while terrified of the "woolvs." He gathers a few things in a knapsack and goes looking for her, his heart "jak-hammering." But he is determined that he "will no longer

Profile

Margaret Wild

One of the most prolific and distinguished writers of children's literature in Australia, Margaret Wild was born in South Africa in 1948 but has lived "down under" since 1972. She has written more than forty books for children, from picturebooks to young adult fiction. Wild is a private person and does not share much of her personal life with the public.

Wild has never shrunk from topics and issues that some might consider taboo for children's books. She has dealt with death, dying, and the mourning process; divorce; anxiety; the betrayal of friendship; bullying; and the Holocaust—all in picturebook format. Her book *Jenny Angel* (P–I), about a little girl whose brother is dying, was inspired by Wild's brother's death when he was seven years old. *Fox* (I–A), one of Wild's most thought-provoking picturebooks, concerns Fox's rage and jealousy over the friendship

between Magpie (whose wing has been injured in a forest fire) and Dog. When Magpie forsakes Dog to sit on Fox's back because Fox's speed makes her feel like she is flying, Fox takes a terrible revenge: he leaves her in the middle of the desert, where her only recourse is to begin hopping painfully home to Dog. The ambiguous ending (will Dog forgive her betrayal of their friendship?) is softened slightly by the back endpapers, which, in contrast to the scene of fiery devastation on the front endpapers, depict a green regenerating forest. Despite these serious themes, however, Wild's books are never ultimately depressing; on the contrary, they are full of hope and the examples of protagonists who overcome adversity and end up making good decisions. In our Close Look at *Woolvs in the Sitee*, for example, the protagonist musters up courage and determination to look for a lost neighbor, despite his fears and anxieties.

Serious topics do not exhaust Wild's creativity: *Loosey Goosey* (about a young goose who is afraid to fly

and needs reassurance from her mother, N–P); *Kiss, Kiss* (featuring a young hippo who scampers out to play without remembering to kiss his mother good-bye, N–P); and *Tom Goes to Kindergarten* (the adventures of a young panda on the first day of school, N–P) will delight preschoolers and early primary-age children with anthropomorphized animals.

Wild is not above taking an irreverent and upbeat look at subjects that are frequently presented in an overly sentimental way. In *Our Granny*, for example, the title character is interested in plumbing; goes to the gym to get rid of her "wobbly bottom"; and exhibits a joie de vivre and feistiness that are missing from many younger adults' lives.

Wild has two children and currently lives in Sydney, one of Australia's most vibrant cities, where she enjoys the quiet pleasures of visiting cafes, listening to music (especially opera), and reading.

The sinister mood and the despair of the teenager in Margaret Wild's **Woolvs in the Sitee** *are powerfully conveyed in Anne Spudvilas's illustrations. The invented spelling suggests that Ben has been unable or unwilling to go to school for quite a while, causing readers to wonder why.*

let the woolvs forse me to scrooch." On the last, almost unbearably poignant opening, he turns to the reader, his face a combination of fear and determination, and says, "Joyn me." So the story ends.

What are we to make of this apocalyptic and desperate narrative? Older readers will find endless opportunities to hypothesize about both what caused this situation and what will become of Ben. Why is Ben so afraid? Is his childish spelling the result of his having been unable, or too afraid, to go to school for many years? Is any of this real, or is he an unfortunate victim of paranoid schizophrenia? How are we to respond to his plea to "joyn" him? The book offers no answers, with its sinister tone and unrelenting sadness. Spudvilas's full-bleed illustrations are the perfect complement to the ominous text, which is printed over the illustrations in black or white depending on the color of the backgrounds. The only hope offered in this haunting book is the luminous white background of the last opening, with its pale blue and orange tints and Ben's courageous face, gazing at us with imploring eyes.

This book will explode older readers' ideas that picturebooks are for little children, and will elicit deep and provocative discussion.

Considering Quality Picturebooks

There are many things to consider when evaluating the quality of a picturebook: the quality of the text, if there is any; the quality of the art; and the quality of the overall design of the book. There are so many outstanding picturebooks from which to choose that it is never necessary to give an inferior book to a reader. We have already considered aspects of text, art, and overall design. In Figure 3.9, we offer some general guidelines pertaining to fiction, nonfiction, and poetry and song for you to think about as you select picturebooks. These guidelines will help you determine what you might want to talk about with your

Figure
3.9

Checklist for Considering Quality Picturebooks in Various Genres

All Picturebooks

✿ Language is rich, with interesting words used in interesting ways.

✿ Illustrations are artistically excellent.

✿ Size, shape and overall design of the book are appropriate to the subject or story.

Fiction

✿ Text and illustrations establish the mood, setting, characters, and theme of the story.

✿ Illustrations expand on the story appropriately and do not merely duplicate what is described in the text.

✿ Layout and design are visually appealing.

Nonfiction

✿ Text and illustrations are accurate.

✿ Text and illustrations are organized in an appropriate manner.

✿ Text and illustrations are attractive, and show verve and style.

Poetry and Song

✿ Language is lyrical.

✿ Illustrations match the feeling established by the text.

---

students as you help them learn about the art of the picturebook and how it manifests itself in various genres.

In addition to the guidelines presented in Figure 3.9, you might want to go back to Figure 3.6 on page 100 to consider the artfulness of the book as a whole. What is the relationship between the illustrations and the text? How do the illustrations support or extend the text? Are the medium, technique, and style appropriate to the text? How do the elements of design work to enhance the meaning, in both individual pictures and across the book as a whole? What makes the book special?

Learning about Picturebook Art in the Classroom

Children learn how to think and talk about the art of picturebooks by reading and responding to outstanding picturebooks. If they are guided by teachers like Bev from the opening vignette, they will learn to notice the careful use of words; the way color, shape, texture, and line are used; and the varied styles, media, and techniques that artists choose.

Children who encounter excellent picturebooks learn how to read not only the words but also the pictures. They pay close attention to what they see, often discovering things in the illustrations that most adults would miss. Just as children notice the writer's craft, they notice

the artist's craft and discuss it. In fact, a good question to ask students after reading a picturebook is "What do you notice?" Kiefer (1986) listened to students of all ages talk about what they noticed about elements of design in picturebooks. First graders discussed line, shape, texture, and color with ease; older students considered the expressive qualities of illustrations. In every case, teachers provided time for children to explore books, to discover and develop individual responses, and to share those responses with others. Teachers also provided a wide selection of books and gave children varied opportunities for response while sharing their knowledge of the elements of language and visual art, as well as their own critical aesthetic responses. Another powerful question begins, "Why do you suppose . . ." For example, "Why do you suppose the designer chose red endpapers for this book?" or "Why do you suppose we never see the wicked stepmother's face in Nancy Ekholm Burkert's version of ***Snow White***?" These types of questions invite children to give their opinion and interpretation, and to make high-level inferences, rather than suggesting, however subtly, that there is one and only one right answer.

We often think of selecting books that contain similar themes, structures, or literary devices. We can also select books that demonstrate similarities and differences in visual art. Careful selection of these "text sets" (Harste, Woodward & Burke, 1984) can lead students to compare the use of line and color, for example, or to note how different artists use texture, light, and space. A thoughtful selection of books that demonstrate particular qualities of visual art can educate students' eyes as well as their minds and hearts. Students can also explore art first-hand, by working with various media and techniques.

Text sets consisting of variants of the same story, each containing illustrations by a different artist, are also useful in teaching children to compare and contrast both visual artistic styles and the words of the story themselves. Young children will often critique a story for not being exactly the same as the first variant with which they are acquainted. For example, one kindergarten class was incensed that *The Gingerbread Boy* by Paul Galdone was called *The Gingerbread Man* in the version by Carol Jones. If teachers keep reading variants of the same story to children, though, this allegiance to their initial experience of the story drops away, and they come to realize that stories (and the illustrations for those stories) are protean, changeable, and can be present in many different forms. Sipe (2001), for example, read five different picturebook variants of *Rapunzel* to a combination first/second-grade class and found that they naturally compared and contrasted the variants. As well, the children gradually built up a sophisticated idea of what is necessary for a Rapunzel tale to be identified as such, and what is optional. This helps children develop higher-level thinking skills and allows them to meaningfully link stories to one another. Chapter 5, on traditional literature, contains lists of variants of folktales and fairy tales that teachers can use in this way.

Children come to school full of images and ideas, with the imagination to expand on them. By providing them with the opportunity to explore the thousands of wonderful picturebooks that are available, we can feed their imaginations and encourage them to think about the symbol systems of language and art that we use to convey our ideas. Wonderful examples of this are captured—not surprisingly—in picturebooks. Rita Golden Gelman's *Doodler Doodling* (P–I), illustrated by Paul Zelinsky, begins with a young girl, sitting at her school desk, playing with words and images—doodling. As her imagination takes flight, her word play and her drawings become funnier and more complex. *The Dot* and *Ish* (P), by Peter Reynolds, both explore the perseverance of children who doubt their ability to be creative, and who become confident artists. *Art* (P) by Patrick McDonnell, exuberantly celebrates the imaginative artwork of a boy named—perhaps predictably—Art. Scott Magoon's *I've Painted Everything!* (P–I) humorously deals with the "stuck" feeling that artists of all types occasionally feel. D. B. Johnson's Cubist-influenced illustrations for Daniel Pinkwater's *Bear's Picture* (P–I) are the perfect accompaniment for the story of a bear who is criticized by "fine, proper gentlemen" for striking out in a new direction in his painting. All of these books can be understood as metaphors for the artistic process of the writers, illustrators, editors, and designers who create wonderful picturebooks.

"Besides," said the first fine, proper gentleman,
"that is a silly picture."
"Nobody can tell what it is supposed to be," said
the second fine, proper gentleman.

"I can tell," said the bear,
adding some green splotches.

D. B. Johnson's Cubist-influenced illustrations for Daniel Pinkwater's **Bear's Picture** *combine with the words of the story to communicate the struggle of artists to follow their own paths.*

Common Themes in Picturebooks and Types of Picturebooks

In the lengthy Booklist following, we have grouped picturebooks by the most common themes that are present in this wide-ranging and ever-changing format. Although some themes may be more appropriate for younger or older children, we have avoided labeling them in this way because we believe that the groupings may be suitable for a broad range of readers. The thematic groupings may be helpful as you plan units of study that are organized around certain ideas or issues, giving you suggestions for picturebooks that you might use as part of your curricular decisions. The Booklist also includes notable examples of the main types of picturebooks.

• • • SUMMARY • • •

Picturebooks hold a special place in the lives of children who read them. These books are the first exposure to fine art for many children. They can enrich children's worlds by providing opportunities for experiences through pictures and print. Illustrators use a full range of artistic elements and styles as they create picturebooks, seeking to interpret an author's words through their art. There are picturebooks in all genres, each of which pose particular constraints as well as possibilities. When we experience excellent picturebooks and share them with our students, we are educating their—and our—imaginations.

In her article "Half the Story: Text and Illustration in Picturebooks" in the January/February 2004 issue of *The Horn Book Magazine*, Anne Hoppe, herself an editor of picturebooks, describes the unique relationship between writer and artist, text and illustration. Read her article and then think about the picturebooks with which you are familiar, asking yourself how the illustrations reflect and extend the text. See also the March/April 1998 issue of *The Horn Book Magazine*, which is devoted entirely to picturebooks.

In his conversation with us, James Ransome talks about his creative process, how he works with someone else's ideas and words to create illustrations to bring them to life and make them his own. In our visit to Debra Frasier's studio, she shows us how she develops her own ideas through words and pictures. Visit the companion website to watch both of these interviews and think about how the process differs when an artist is interpreting the words of someone else as opposed to his or her own words. Discuss this, using books you have read as examples. If you have read the Anne Hoppe article, consider what she has to say as well.

Booklist

※ Indicates some aspect of diversity

THEMES: THE SOCIAL WORLD

FAMILY

Bang, Molly, *In My Heart* (2006) (N)

※ Bertrand, Diane Gonzales, *We Are Cousins/Somos Primos*, illustrated by Christina E. Rodriguez (2008) (N–P)

Browne, Anthony, *My Brother* (2008) (N–P)

_____, *My Mom* (2005) (N–P)

_____, *My Dad* (2001) (N–P)

Bunge, Daniela, *The Scarves* (2006) (P)

Bunting, Eve, *Hurry! Hurry!*, illustrated by Jeff Mack (2007) (N)

※ Cisneros, Sandra, *Hairs/Pelitos*, illustrated by Terry Ybanez (1997) (P–I)

Coffelt, Nancy, *Fred Stays with Me!*, illustrated by Tricia Tusa (2007) (P)

Cruise, Robin, *Only You*, illustrated by Margaret Chodos-Irvine (2007) (N–P)

Crum, Shutta, *A Family for Old Mill Farm* (2007) (N–P)

※ Cunnane, Kelly, *For You Are a Kenyan Child*, illustrated by Ana Juan (2006) (P)

※ Daly, Niki, *Happy Birthday, Jamela!* (2006) (P)

Davies, Nicola, *White Owl, Barn Owl*, illustrated by Michael Foreman (2008) (P–I)

※ Diakité, Penda, *I Lost My Tooth in Africa*, illustrated by Baba Wagué Diakité (2006) (P)

Duke, Kate, *The Tale of Pip and Squeak* (2007) (N–P)

※ Global Fund for Children, *Global Babies* (2007) (N–P)

Gravett, Emily, *Meerkat Mail* (2007) (N–P)

Holmberg, Bo R., *A Day with Dad*, illustrated by Eva Eriksson (2008) (P)

※ Isadora, Rachel, *What a Family!* (2006) N–P)

Jenkins, Emily, *Love You When You Whine*, illustrated by Sergio Ruzzier (2006) (N)

Joosse, Barbara M., *Mama, Do You Love Me?*, illustrated by Barbara Lavallee (1991) (N–P)

※ Kraus, Joanna H., *A Night of Tamales & Roses*, illustrated by Elena Caravela (2007) (P)

※ Makhijani, Pooja, *Mama's Saris*, illustrated by Elena Gomez (2007) (P–I)

Markle, Sandra, *A Mother's Journey*, illustrated by Alan Marks (2006) (P)

Matthews, Tina, *Out of the Egg* (2007) (N–P)

McAllister, Angela, *Mama and Little Joe*, illustrated by Terry Milne (2007) (N–P)

Moses, Sheila P., *Sallie Gal and the Wall-a-kee Man*, illustrated by Niki Daly (P–I)

Nolen, Jerdine, *Pitching in for Eubie*, illustrated by E. B. Lewis (2007) (P)

Pennypacker, Sara, *Clementine*, illustrated by Marla Frazee (2008) (P)

Perkins, Lynn Rae, *Pictures from Our Vacation* (2007) (P)

✳ Ramirez, Antonio, *Napi Goes to the Mountain*, illustrated by Domi (2006) (P)

Ransom, Jeanie Franz, *What Do Parents Do? (When You're Not Home)*, illustrated by Cyd Moore (2007) (N–P)

Ries, Lori, *Fix It, Sam*, illustrated by Sue Ramá (2007) (N–P)

Sturges, Philemon, *How Do You Make A Baby Smile?*, illustrated by Bridget Strevens-Marzo (2007) (N–P)

✳ Stryer, Andrea Stenn, *Kami and the Yaks*, illustrated by Bert Dodson (2007) (P–I)

Tinkham, Kelly A., *Hair for Mama*, illustrated by Amy June Bates (2007) (P–I)

Wild, Margaret, *Piglet and Papa*, illustrated by Stephen Michael King (2007) (N–P)

✳ Woodson, Jacqueline, *Coming on Home Soon*, illustrated by E. B. Lewis (2004) (P)

Yaccarino, Dan, *Every Friday* (2007) (N–P)

✳ Young, Ed, *My Mei Mei* (2006) (P)

Grandparents

✳ Dorros, Arthur, *Abuela*, illustrated by Elisa Kleven (1997) (P)

_____, *Isla*, illustrated by Elisa Kleven (1999) (P)

England, Kathryn, *Grandfather's Wrinkles*, illustrated by Richard McFarland (2007) (P–I)

Fox, Mem, *Wilfred Gordon McDonald Partridge*, illustrated by Julie Vivas (1989) (P)

Hoberman, Mary Ann, *I'm Going to Grandma's*, illustrated by Tiphanie Beeke (2007) (N–P)

Johnson, Angela, *When I Am Old with You*, illustrated by David Soman (1993) (P)

Lindbergh, Reeve, *My Little Grandmother Often Forgets*, illustrated by Kathryn Brown (2007) (N–P)

Lyon, George Ella, *One Lucky Girl*, illustrated by Irene Trivas (2000) (P)

McMullan, Kate, *Papa's Song*, illustrated by Jim McMullan (2003) (N)

✳ Pérez, Amada Irma, *Nana's Big Surprise: Nana, Qué Sorpresa!*, illustrated by Maya Christina Gonzalez (2007) (P)

Quigley, Mary, *Granddad's Fishing Buddy*, illustrated by Stéphanie Jorisch (2007) (P)

Siblings

Brown, Lisa, *How to Be* (2006) (N)

Funke, Cornelia, *The Wildest Brother*, illustrated by Kerstin Meyer (2008) (N–P)

✳ Isadora, Rachel, *Yo, Jo!* (2007) (N–P)

Hutchins, Pat, *The Very Worst Monster* (1988) (P)

_____, *Where's the Baby?* (1999) (P)

Lloyd-Jones, Sally, *How to Be a Baby . . . By Me, the Big Sister*, illustrated by Sue Heap (2007) (P)

Page, Robin, *Sisters and Brothers: Sibling Relationships in the Animal World*, illustrated by Steve Jenkins (2008) (N–P)

Polacco, Patricia, *My Rotten, Red-Headed Older Brother* (1998) (P)

✳ Williams, Vera B., *"More More More" Said the Baby* (1996) (P)

FRIENDSHIP

Bley, Anette, *And What Comes After a Thousand?* (2007) (P–I)

Bruel, Robert O., *Bob and Otto*, illustrated by Nick Bruel (2007) (P)

Bunge, Daniela, *Cherry Time* (2007) (P)

Bynum, Janie, *Nutmeg and Barley: A Budding Friendship* (2006) (N–P)

Chodos-Irvine, Margaret, *Best Best Friends* (2006) (N–P)

Consentino, Ralph, *The Marvelous Misadventures of . . . Fun Boy* (2006) (N–P)

Coombs, Kate, *The Secret-Keeper*, illustrated by Heather M. Solomon (2006) (P)

✳ Garza, Carmen Lomas, *In My Family/En mi familia* (1997) (P)

Hillenbrand, Jane, *What a Treasure!*, illustrated by Will Hillenbrand (2006) (N)

Hills, Tad, *Duck & Goose* (2006) (N)

Jeffers, Oliver, *Lost and Found* (2005) (N–P)

Kellogg, Steven, *Best Friends* (1986) (P–I)

Kindersley, Anabel, and Barnabas Kindersley, *Children Just Like Me* (1995) (P–I)

Kromhout, Rindert, *Little Donkey and the Birthday Present*, illustrated by Annemarie van Haeringen, translated by Marianne Martens (2007) (N–P)

Lehman, Barbara, *Rainstorm* (2007) (N–P)

Lin, Grace, *Lissy's Friends* (2007) (P–I)

Lobel, Arnold, *Frog and Toad Are Friends* (1970) (P–I)

_____, *Frog and Toad Together* (1972) (P–I)

_____, *Days with Frog and Toad* (1979) (P–I)

McCarty, Peter, *Fabian Escapes* (2007) (N–P)

Niland, Deborah, *Annie's Chair* (2006) (N)

✳ Reiser, Lynn, *My Way/A mi manera* (2007) (P)

✳ _____, *Margaret and Margarita/Margarita y Margaret* (1993) (P)

Sakai, Komako, *Emily's Balloon* (2006) (N)

Seeger, Laura Vaccaro, *Dog and Bear: Two Friends, Three Stories* (2007) (N–P)

Shannon, George, *Rabbit's Gift*, illustrated by Laura Dronzek (2007) (N–P)

Silverman, Erica, *Cowgirl Kate and Cocoa: School Days*, illustrated by Betsy Lewin (2007) (P–I)

Stein, Mathilde, *Mine!*, illustrated by Mies van Hout (2007) (N–P)

Weeks, Sarah, *Pip Squeak*, illustrated by Jane Manning (2008) (P–I)

Willems, Mo, *Knuffle Bunny Too: A Case of Mistaken Identity* (2007) (N–P)

_____, *I Am Invited to a Party!* (2007) (N–P)

_____, *My Friend Is Sad* (2007) (N–P)

_____, *There Is a Bird on Your Head!* (2007) (N–P)

_____, *Today I Will Fly!* (2007) (N–P)

BEDTIME

Bergman, Mara, *Oliver Who Would Not Sleep!*, illustrated by Nick Maland (2007) (N–P)

Brown, Margaret Wise, *Goodnight Moon*, illustrated by Clement Hurd (1947) (N)

Butler, John, *Can You Growl Like a Bear?* (2007) (N–P)

Kanevsky, Polly, *Sleepy Boy*, illustrated by Stephanie Anderson (2006) (N)

McMullan, Kate, *Papa's Song*, illustrated by Jim McMullan (2003) (N)

Morales, Yuyi, *Little Night* (2007) (N–P)

Oxenbury, Helen, *Goodnight, Good Morning* (1991) (N)

Rathman, Peggy, *Goodnight, Gorilla* (1994) (N)

Shulevitz, Uri, *So Sleepy Story* (2006) (N)

Waddell, Martin, *Sleep Tight, Little Bear*, illustrated by Barbara Firth (2006) (N)

FREEDOM

☀ Adler, David, *A Picture Book of Sojourner Truth* (2001) (I)

☀ _____, *Martin Luther King Jr.: Free at Last* (1986) (A)

☀ Levine, Ellen, *Henry's Freedom Box*, illustrated by Kadir Nelson (2007) (P–I)

☀ Raven, Margot Theis, *Night Boat to Freedom*, illustrated by E. B. Lewis (2006) (I)

☀ Wetherford, Carole Boston, *Moses: When Harriet Tubman Led Her People to Freedom*, illustrated by Kadir Nelson (2006) (I)

☀ Woodson, Jacqueline, *Show Way*, illustrated by Hudson Talbott (2007) (I)

HOLIDAYS

deGroat, Diane, *Last One in Is a Rotten Egg!* (2007) (N–P)

Falconer, Ian, *Olivia Helps with Christmas* (2007) (N–P)

McNamara, Margaret, *The Luck of the Irish*, illustrated by Mike Gordon (2007) (P–I)

Ungar, Richard, *Even Higher* (2007) (P)

Wells, Rosemary, *Max Counts His Chickens* (2007) (N–P)

THEMES: THE EMOTIONAL WORLD

FEELINGS

Aliki, *Feelings* (1986) (N–P)

Atkins, Jeannine, *Anne Hutchinson's Way*, illustrated by Michael Dooling (2007) (P–I)

Bang, Molly, *When Sophie Gets Angry—Really, Really Angry . . .* (2004) (N–P)

de Varennes, Monique, *The Jewel Box Ballerinas*, illustrated by Ana Juan (2007) (P–I)

Fleming, Denise, *Mama Cat Has Three Kittens* (2002) (N–P)

Henkes, Kevin, *A Good Day* (2007) (N–P)

_____, *Chrysanthemum* (1991) (N–P)

Hermsen, Ronald, *The Story of Giraffe*, illustrated by Guido Pigni (2007) (P)

Lakin, Patricia, *Rainy Day*, illustrated by Scott Nash (2007) (N–P)

Menchin, Scott, *Taking a Bath with the Dog and Other Things that Make Me Happy* (2007) (N–P)

Rosenthal, Amy Krouse, *One of Those Days*, illustrated by Rebecca Doughty (2006) (P–I)

Shannon, David, *No, David!* (1999) (N–P)

Steig, William, *Pete's a Pizza* (1998) (N–P)

FEARS

Allen, Jonathan, *I'm Not Scared* (2008) (N–P)

Arnold, Tedd, *There Was an Old Lady Who Swallowed Fly Guy* (2007) (P–I)

Fine, Anne, *Jamie and Angus Together*, illustrated by Penny Dale (2007) (P)

Graves, Keith, *The Unexpectedly Bad Hair of Barcelona Smith* (2006) (N–P)

Klise, Kate, *Imagine Harry*, illustrated by M. Sarah Klise (2007) (N–P)

Kwon, Yoon-Duck, *My Cat Copies Me* (2007) (N–P)

McPhail, David, *Boy on the Brink* (2006) (P)

Pitzer, Susanna, *Not Afraid of Dogs*, illustrated by Larry Day (2006) (N–P)

Sendak, Maurice, *Mommy?*, paper engineering by Matthew Reinhart; scenario by Arthur Yorinks (2006) (N–P)

RESOURCEFULNESS

☀ Farmer, Nancy, *Clever Ali*, illustrated by Gail de Marcken (2006) (I)

☀ McKissack, Patricia, *Flossie and the Fox*, illustrated by Rachel Isadora (1986) (N–P–I)

Pinkney, Andrea Davis, *Peggony-Po: A Whale of a Tale*, illustrated by Brian Pinkney (2006) (P)

Spinelli, Eileen, *Heat Wave*, illustrated by Betsy Lewin (2007) (P)

Steig, William, *Brave Irene* (1986) (N–P–I)

Wheeler, Lisa, *Castaway Cats*, illustrated by Ponder Goembel (2006) (N–P)

IMAGINATION

Briggs, Raymond, *The Puddleman* (2004) (N–P)

Crews, Nina, *Below* (2006) (N–P)

Liao, Jimmy, *The Sound of Colors* (2006) (P)

Portis, Antoinette, *Not a Box* (2006) (N)

Schneider, Christine, *I'm Bored!*, illustrated by Hervé Pinel (2006) (N–P)

Van Allsburg, Chris, *Bad Day at Riverbend* (1995) (I–A)

_____, *The Garden of Abdul Gasazi* (1979) (I–A)

_____, *Jumanji* (1981) (I)

_____, *The Mysteries of Harris Burdick* (1984) (I–A)

HUMOR

Armstrong, Jennifer, *Once Upon a Banana*, illustrated by David Small (2006) (P)

Breen, Steve, *Stick* (2007) (N–P)

Casanova, Mary, *Some Dog!*, illustrated by Ard Hoyt (2007) (P–I)

Catalanotto, Peter, *Ivan the Terrier* (2007) (N–P)

Chaconas, Dori, *Virginnie's Hat*, illustrated by Holly Meade (2007) (N–P)

Church, Caroline Jayne, *Digby Takes Charge* (2007) (N–P)

Cronin, Doreen, *Click, Clack, Moo: Cows that Type*, illustrated by Betsy Lewin (2000) (P–I)

Denise, Anika, *Pigs Love Potatoes*, illustrated by Denise Christopher (2007) (N–P)

Dodds, Dayle Ann, *Teacher's Pets*, illustrated by Marylin Hafner (2006) (P)

Donnio, Sylviane, *I'd Really Like to Eat a Child*, illustrated by Dorothée de Monfried (2007) (P–I)

Flaherty, A. W., *The Luck of the Loch Ness Monster: A Tale of Picky Eating*, illustrated by Scott Magoon (2007) (N–P)

Friend, Catherine, *The Perfect Nest*, illustrated by John Manders (2007) (N–P)

Gran, Julia, *Big Bug Surprise* (2007) (N–P)

Grey, Mini, *The Adventures of the Dish and the Spoon* (2007) (P)

Harrington, Janice N., *The Chicken-Chasing Queen of Lamar County*, illustrated by Shelley Jackson (2007) (P)

Johnson, Paul Brett, *On Top of Spaghetti* (2006) (N–P)

Jones, Sylvie, *Who's in the Tub?*, illustrated by Pascale Constantin (2007) (N)

Keller, Laurie, *Do Unto Otters: A Book About Manners* (2007) (P)

Kellogg, Steven, *Prehistoric Pinkerton* (1987) (N–P)

Khalsa, Dayal Kaur, *How Pizza Came to Queens* (1995) (N–P)

Kitamura, Satoshi, *Me and My Cat* (2000) (N–P)

Krensky, Stephen, *Big Bad Wolves at School*, illustrated by Brad Sneed (2007) (N–P)

Landström, Lena, *Boo and Baa Have Company*, illustrated by Olof Landström; translated by Joan Sandin (2006) (N–P)

Lodge, Bernard, *Custard Surprise*, illustrated by Tim Bowers (2008) (P–I)

Mahy, Margaret, *The Great White Man-Eating Shark: A Cautionary Tale*, illustrated by Jonathan Allen (1990) (P)

Macaulay, David, *Why the Chicken Crossed the Road* (1987) (P)

Meddaugh, Susan, *Hog-Eye* (1995) (P)

Offill, Jenny, *17 Things I'm Not Allowed to Do Anymore*, illustrated by Nancy Carpenter (2006) (P–I)

Pennypacker, Sara, *The Talented Clementine*, illustrated by Marla Frazee (2008) (P–I)

Rocco, John, *Wolf! Wolf!* (2007) (P–I)

Root, Phyllis, *Aunt Nancy and the Bothersome Visitors*, illustrated by David Parkins (2007) (P–I)

Sierra, Judy, *Thelonius Monster's Sky-High Fly Pie*, illustrated by Edward Koren (2006) (P–I)

Steig, William, *Pete's a Pizza* (1998) (N–P)

Stevens, April, *Waking Up Wendell*, illustrated by Tad Hills (2007) (P)

Stevens, Susan Crummel, *Ten-Gallon Bart*, illustrated by Dorothy Donohue (2006) (P)

Swallow, Pamela Curtis, *Groundhog Gets a Say*, illustrated by Denise Brunkus (2005) (P)

Tomas, Jan, *What Will Fat Cat Sit On?* (2007) (N–P)

Watt, Mélanie, *Chester* (2007) (P–I)

_____, *Chester's Back!* (2008) (P–I)

Weaver, Tess, *Cat Jumped In!*, illustrated by Emily Arnold McCully (2007) (N–P)

Weston, Carrie, *If a Chicken Stayed for Supper*, illustrated by Sophie Fatus (2007) (N–P)

Willems, Mo, *Edwina, The Dinosaur Who Didn't Know She Was Extinct* (2006) (N)

_____, *Don't Let the Pigeon Stay Up Late!* (2006) (P)

_____, *Don't Let the Pigeon Drive the Bus!* (2003) (P)

_____, *The Pigeon Finds a Hot Dog* (2004) (P)

THEMES: THE NATURAL WORLD

NATURE

Aston, Dianna, *A Seed Is Sleepy*, illustrated by Sylvia Long (2007) (N–P)

_____, *An Egg Is Quiet*, illustrated by Sylvia Long (2006) (N–P)

Baker, Jeannie, *The Hidden Forest* (2005) (N–P)

_____, *Window* (1991) (N–P)

Ehlert, Lois, *Leaf Man* (2005) (N–P)

Gore, Leonid, *Danny's First Snow* (2007) (P)

Henkes, Kevin, *A Good Day* (2007) (N)

Lyon, George Ella, *Come a Tide*, illustrated by Stephen Gammell (1990) (N–P)

Perkins, Lynne Rae, *Snow Music* (2003) (N–P–I)

Rotner, Shelley, *Senses at the Seashore* (2005) (N)

Schertle, Alice, *Very Hairy Bear*, illustrated by Matt Phelan (2007) (N–P)

Stein, David Ezra, *Leaves* (2007) (N–P)

Tafuri, Nancy, *The Busy Little Squirrel* (2007) (N–P)

Winter, Jeanette, *The Tale of Pale Male: A True Story* (2007) (P–I)

Yee, Wong Herbert, *Tracks in the Snow* (2007) (N)

Yolen, Jane, *Owl Moon*, illustrated by John Schoenherr (1987) (P–I)

FOOD

Anderson, Sara, *Fruit* (2007) (N–P)

Arnold, Caroline, *Wiggle and Waggle*, illustrated by Mary Peterson (2007) (P–I)

Degen, Bruce, *Jamberry* (1995) (N–P)

Ehlert, Lois, *Eating the Alphabet: Fruits & Vegetables from A to Z* (1998) (N–P)

Friedman, Ina R., *How My Parents Learned To Eat*, illustrated by Allan Say (1987) (P–I)

Lakin, Patricia, *Max & Mo Go Apple Picking*, illustrated by Brian Floca (2007) (N–P)

✳ Soto, Gary, *Too Many Tamales*, illustrated by Ed Martinez (1993) (P)

MAGIC AND MYSTERY

Adler, David A., *Bones and the Birthday Mystery*, illustrated by Barbara Johansen Newman (2007) (P–I)

De Felice, Cynthia, *One Potato, Two Potato*, illustrated by Andrea U'Ren (2006) (P–I)

Kline, Suzy, *Horrible Harry Cracks the Code*, illustrated by Frank Remkiewicz (2008) (P–I)

Smith, Alexander McCall, *Max & Maddy and the Chocolate Money Mystery*, illustrated by Macky Pamintuan (2007) (P–I)

_____, *Max & Maddy and the Bursting Balloons Mystery*, illustrated by Macky Pamintuan (2007) (P–I)

Yee, Wong Herbert, *Abracadabra!: Magic with Mouse and Mole* (2007) (P–I)

FAIRY TALE AND FANTASY

Bateman, Teresa, *Fiona's Luck*, illustrated by Kelly Murphy (2007) (P–I)

Cech, John, *The Elves and the Shoemaker*, illustrated by Kirill Chelushkin (2007) (P–I)

Cole, Brock, *Good Enough to Eat* (2007) (P)

✳ Daly, Niki, *Pretty Salma: A Little Red Riding Hood Story from Africa* (2007) (P–I)

✳ Deedy, Carmen Agra, *Martina the Beautiful Cockroach: A Cuban Folktale*, illustrated by Michael Austin (2007) (P–I)

✳ Diakité, Baba Wagué, *Mee-Ann and the Magic Serpent* (2007) (P–I)

✳ Fleischman, Paul, *Glass Slipper, Gold Sandal: A Worldwide Cinderella*, illustrated by Julie Paschkis (P)

Hamilton, Martha, and Weiss, Mitch, *Priceless Gifts: A Folktale from Italy*, illustrated by John Kanzler (2007) (P–I)

✳ Isadora, Rachel, *The Princess and the Pea* (2007) (N–P)

LaRochelle, David, *The End*, illustrated by Richard Egielski (2007) (P)

Lorbiecki, Marybeth, *Paul Bunyan's Sweetheart*, illustrated by Renée Graef (2007) (P–I)

Nadimi, Suzan, *The Rich Man and the Parrot*, illustrated by Ande Cook (2007) (P–I)

Nesbit, E., *Lionel and the Book of Beasts*, illustrated by Michael Hague (2006) (P)

☀ Noyes, Deborah, *Red Butterfly: How a Princess Smuggled the Secret of Silk Out of China*, illustrated by Sophie Blackall (2007) (P)

Pinkney, Jerry, *Little Red Riding Hood* (2007) (P)

Rogers, Gregory, *Midsummer Knight* (2007) (P–I)

☀ Sellier, Marie, *Legend of the Chinese Dragon*, illustrated by Catherine Louis; calligraphy and chop marks by Wang Fei (2007) (P–I)

☀ Storace, Patricia, *Sugar Cane: A Caribbean Rapunzel*, illustrated by Raul Colón (2007) (P–I)

Yorinks, Arthur, *The Witch's Child*, illustrated by Jos. A. Smith (2007) (P–I)

INFORMATIONAL TEXTS

Applegate, Katherine, *The Buffalo Storm*, illustrated by Jan Ormerod (2007) (P)

Brown, Don, *Dolley Madison Saves George Washington* (2007) (P–I)

Fletcher, Susan, *Dadblamed Union Army Cow*, illustrated by Kimberly Bulcken Root (2007) (P–I)

Hopkinson, Deborah, *Sky Boys: How They Built the Empire State Building*, illustrated by James E. Ransome (2006) (P)

Hughes, Pat, *Seeing the Elephant: A Story of the Civil War*, illustrated by Ken Stark (2007) (P–I)

Jensen, Nancy Orr Johnson, *Helen, Ethel & the Crazy Quilt: Based on the 1890 Letters Between Helen Keller and Ethel Orr*, illustrated by Dawn Peterson (2007) (P–I)

Johnson, Angela, *Wind Flyers,* illustrated by Loren Long (2007) (P–I)

Judge, Lita, *One Thousand Tracings: Healing the Wounds of World War II* (2007) (P–I)

Levitin, Sonia, *Junk Man's Daughter*, illustrated by Guy Porfirio (2007) (P–I)

☀ McCully, Emily Arnold, *The Escape of Oney Judge: Martha Washington's Slave Finds Freedom* (2007) (P–I)

Markle, Sandra, *A Mother's Journey*, illustrated by Alan Marks (2006) (P–I)

McNulty, Faith, *If You Decide to Go to the Moon*, illustrated by Steven Kellogg (2005) (P)

Micklethwait, Lucy, *A Child's Book of Art* (1993) (P–I)

Mills, Claudia, *Being Teddy Roosevelt*, illustrated by R. W. Alley (2007) (P–I)

Morrison, Taylor, *Wildfire* (2006) (I)

Page, Robin, *How Many Ways Can You Catch A Fly?*, illustrated by Steve Jenkins (2008) (P–I)

_____, *Move!*, illustrated by Steve Jenkins (2006) (P–I)

_____, *What Do You Do with a Tail Like This?*, illustrated by Steve Jenkins (2003) (P–I)

Quan, Elizabeth, *Once Upon a Full Moon* (2007) (P–I)

Robbins, Ken, *Pumpkins* (2007) (P)

Raschka, Chris, *John Coltrane's Giant Steps* (2002) (N–P)

Sandin, Joan, *At Home in a New Land* (2007) (P–I)

Schlitz, Laura Amy, *Good Masters! Sweet Ladies! Voices from a Medieval Village*, illustrated by Robert Byrd (2007) (P–I)

BOOKS FOR OLDER CHILDREN AND ADOLESCENTS

☀ Adler, David, *A Picture Book of Sojourner Truth* (1994) (A)

☀ _____, *Martin Luther King, Jr.: Free at Last* (1986) (A)

Browne, Anthony, *Piggybook* (1987) (I)

_____, *The Tunnel* (1997) (I)

☀ Bruchac, Joseph, *Crazy Horse's Vision*, illustrated by S. D. Nelson (2007)(A)

Bunting, Eve, *Fly Away Home*, illustrated by Ronald Himler (1991) (I–A)

☀ _____, *Smoky Night*, illustrated by David Diaz (1994) (A)

_____, *The Wall*, illustrated by Ronald Himler (1990) (A)

☀ Feelings, Tom, *The Middle Passage* (1995) (A)

☀ _____, *Soul Looks Back in Wonder* (1993) (A)

☀ Giovanni, Nikki, *Rosa*, illustrated by Bryan Collier (2007) (I–A)

☀ Hopkinson, Deborah, *Sweet Clara and the Freedom Quilt*, illustrated by James E. Ransome (2003) (I)

Innocenti, Robert, *Rose Blanche* (1985) (A)

Macaulay, David, *Black and White* (1990) (A)

☀ Maruki, Toshi, *Hiroshima No Piku* (1982) (A)

☀ Polacco, Patricia, *Pink and Say* (1994) (I–A)

☀ Say, Allen, *Grandfather's Journey* (1993) (I–A)

Sciezka, Jon, *Math Curse*, illustrated by Lane Smith (1995) (I–A)

_____, *Science Verse*, illustrated by Lane Smith (2004) (I–A)

_____, *The Stinky Cheese Man and Other Fairly Stupid Tales*, illustrated by Lane Smith (1992) (I–A)

Sendak, Maurice, *Outside Over There* (1989) (A)

Sís, Peter, *The Wall: Growing Up Behind the Iron Curtain* (2007) (I–A)

_____, *The Tree of Life: Charles Darwin* (2003) (I–A)

Steig, William, *Caleb and Kate* (1986) (A)

Van Allsburg, Chris, *Bad Day at Riverbend* (1995) (I–A)

_____, *The Wretched Stone* (1991) (I–A)

Yolen, Jane, *All Those Secrets of the World*, illustrated by Leslie Baker (1993) (A)

☀ _____, *Encounter*, illustrated by David Shannon (1996) (I)

TYPES OF BOOKS

CONCEPT BOOKS

Beaty, Andrea, *Iggy Peck, Architect*, illustrated by David Roberts (2007) (P)

Ehlert, Lois, *Color Farm* (1990) (N)

_____, *Color Zoo* (1989) (N)

_____, *Red Leaf, Yellow Leaf* (1991) (N)

Gonzalez, Maya Christina, *My Colors, My World/Mis colores, mi mundo* (2007) (N–P)

Hoban, Tana, *Shapes, Shapes, Shapes* (1996) (N)

_____, *Exactly the Opposite* (1990) (N)

_____, *Of Color and Things* (1996) (N)

Hutchins, Hazel, *A Second is a Hiccup*, illustrated by Kady MacDonald Denton (2007) (N)

Johnson, Angela, *Lily Brown's Paintings*, illustrated by E. B. Lewis (2007) (N–P)

Jonas, Ann, *Color Dance* (1989) (N)

Kamm, Katja, *Invisible* (2006) (N)

Martin, Bill, Jr., *Brown Bear, Brown Bear, What Do You See?*, illustrated by Eric Carle (2007) (N)

_____, *Polar Bear, Polar Bear, What Do You Hear?*, illustrated by Eric Carle (1997) (N)

Onishi, Satoru, *Who's Hiding?* (2007) (N)

Owens, Mary Beth, *Panda Whispers* (2007) (N–P)

Seeger, Laura Vaccaro, *First the Egg* (2007) (N–P)

_____, *Black? White! Day? Night! A Book of Opposites* (2006) (N)

Walsh, Ellen Stoll, *Mouse Shapes* (2007) (N–P)

_____, *Mouse Paint* (1989) (N–P)

COUNTING

Bailey, Linda, *Goodnight Sweet Pig*, illustrated by Josée Masse (2007) (N–P)

Giganti, Paul, Jr., *How Many Snails? A Counting Book*, illustrated by Donald Crews (1988) (N)

Grossman, Virginia, *Ten Little Rabbits*, illustrated by Sylvia Long (1991) (N)

Isadora, Rachel, *1 2 3 Pop!* (2000) (N)

Johnson, Steve, *City by Numbers* (1998) (N–P)

Katz, Michael Jay, *Ten Potatoes in a Pot and Other Counting Rhymes*, illustrated by June Otani (1990) (N–P)

Reiser, Lynn, *Hardworking Puppies* (2006) (P)

Donaldson, Julia, *One Ted Falls Out of Bed*, illustrated by Anna Currey (2007) (N)

ALPHABET

✳ Ada, Alma Flor, *Gathering the Sun: An Alphabet in Spanish and English*, illustrated by Simon Silva (1997) (P)

Agee, John, *Z Goes Home* (2003) (P)

Diehl, David, *Sports A to Z* (2007) (N–P)

Ehlert, Lois, *Eating the Alphabet* (1989) (N–P)

Fisher, Leonard Everett, *The ABC Exhibit* (1991) (N)

Fleming, Denise, *Alphabet Under Construction* (2002) (N–P)

Johnson, Steve, *Alphabet City* (1995) (P)

Kitamora, Satoshi, *From Acorn to Zoo: And Everything in Between in Alphabetical Order* (1995) (N–P)

Lester, Mike, *A Is for Salad* (2000) (N)

MacDonald, Suse, *Alphabatics* (1986) (P)

Martin, Bill, Jr., and John Archambault, *Chicka Chicka Boom Boom*, illustrated by Lois Ehlert (1989) (N–P)

Mayer, Bill, *All Aboard: A Traveling Alphabet* (2008) (N–P)

McLeod, Bob, *SuperHero ABC* (2006) (N)

Merriam, Eve, *Halloween ABC*, illustrated by Lane Smith (1995) (P)

Owens, Mary Beth, *A Caribou Alphabet* (1988) (N–P)

Rankin, Laura, *The Handmade Alphabet* (1991) (N–P)

Rash, Andy, *Agent A to Agent Z* (2004) (P)

Ryden, Hope, *Wild Animals of Africa ABC* (1988) (N–P)

Seeger, Laura Vaccaro, *The Hidden Alphabet* (2003) (N–P)

Shannon, George, *Tomorrow's Alphabet*, illustrated by Donald Crews (1996) (N)

✳ Weill, Cynthia, and K. B. Basseches, *ABeCedarios: Mexican Folk Art ABCs in English and Spanish*, photographs by Moisés Jiménez and Armando Jiménez (2008) (N–P)

Wells, Rosemary, *Max's ABC* (2006) (N)

PARTICIPATION

Alhberg, Allan, *The Bravest Ever Bear*, illustrated by Paul Howard (1999) (N–P)

Alhberg, Janet, and Allan Ahlberg, *Each Peach Pear Plum* (1999) (N)

Carle, Eric, *The Very Busy Spider* (1989) (N)

✳ Isadora, Rachel, *Babies* (1990) (N)

Kunhardt, Dorothy, *Pat the Bunny* (2001) (N)

Ljungkvist, Laura, *Follow the Line Through the House* (2007) (N–P)

_____, *Follow the Line* (2006) (N–P)

PATTERNED

Beaumont, Karen, *Move Over, Rover!*, illustrated by Jane Dyer (2006) (N–P)

Bunting, Eve, *Hurry! Hurry!*, illustrated by Jeff Mack (2007) (N)

Fleming, Denise, *The Cow Who Clucked* (2006) (N)

Gorbachev, Valeri, *Red Red Red* (2007) (N–P)

Guarino, Deborah, *Is Your Mama a Llama?*, illustrated by Steven Kellogg (1989) (N)

Klinting, Lars, *What Do You Want?*, translated by Maria Lundin (2007) (N)

Martin, Bill, Jr., *Brown Bear, Brown Bear, What Do You See?*, illustrated by Eric Carle (2007) (N)

_____, *Polar Bear, Polar Bear, What Do You Hear?*, illustrated by Eric Carle (1997) (N)

Martin, Bill, Jr., *Chicka Chicka Boom Boom*, illustrated by Lois Ehlert (1989) (N–P)

Rosen, Michael, *We're Going on a Bear Hunt* (1989) (N–P)

Varon, Sara, *Chicken and Cat* (2006) (P)

Walsh, Ellen Stoll, *Mouse Paint* (1989) (N)

Zelinsky, Paul O., *The Wheels on the Bus* (1990) (N–P)

RHYME

Anderson, Peggy Perry, *Chuck's Truck* (2006) (N–P)

Arnold, Marsha Diane, *Roar of a Snore*, illustrated by Pierre Pratt (2006) (N–P)

Edwards, David, *The Pen that Pa Built*, illustrated by Ashley Wolff (2007) (N–P)

Grey, Mini, *Ginger Bear* (2007) (N–P)

Lies, Brian, *Bats at the Beach* (2006) (P)

Martin, Bill, Jr., *Fire! Fire! Said Mrs. McGuire*, illustrated by Vladimir Radunsky (2006) (P)

Mazer, Norma Fox, *Has Anyone Seen My Emily Greene?*, illustrated by Christine Davenier (2007) (N–P)

McLaughlan, Patricia and Emily MacLaughlan Charest, *Once I Ate a Pie* (2006) (P)

MacLeod, Elizabeth, *I Heard a Little Baa*, illustrated by Louise Phillips (1998) (N)

O'Connor, Jane, *Ready, Set, Skip!*, illustrated by Ann James (2007)(N)

Prince, April Jones, *What Do Wheels Do All Day?*, illustrated by Giles Laroche (2006) (N)

Smee, Nicola, *Clip-Clop* (2006) (N)

Siméon, Jean-Pierre, *This Is a Poem that Heals Fish*, illustrated by Olivier Tallec (2007) (N–P)

Thong, Roseanne, *Tummy Girl*, illustrated by Sam Williams (2007) (N–P)

Wheeler, Lisa, *Castaway Cats*, illustrated by Ponder Goembel (2006) (N–P)

Yee, Wong Herbert, *Who Likes Rain?* (2007) (N–P)

POETRY, VERSE, AND SONG

Bang-Campbell, Monika, *Little Rat Makes Music*, illustrated by Molly Bang (2008) (P–I)

Banks, Kate, *Max's Words*, illustrated by Boris Kulikov (2006) (N–P)

Brown, Margaret Wise, *Where Have You Been?*, illustrated by Leo and Diane Dillon (2004) (P)

Brown, Marc, *Play Rhymes* (1987) (P)

Cali, Davide, *Piano Piano*, illustrated by Eric Heliot (2007) (P)

Cooper, Elisha, *Beach* (2006) (P)

Davies, Jacqueline, *The Night Is Singing*, illustrated by Kyrsten Brooker (2006) (N)

✳ Griego, Margot C., Betsy L. Bucks, Sharon S. Gilbert, and Laura H. Kimball, eds. and translators, *Tortillitas Para Mamá and other Nursery Rhymes/Spanish and English*, illustrated by Barbara Cooney (1981) (P)

Greenfield, Eloise, *Night on a Neighborhood Street*, illustrated by Jan Spivey Gilchrist (1991) (P–I)

_____, *Under a Sunday Tree*, illustrated by Amos Ferguson (1988) (P)

Hughes, Langston, *The Book of Rhythms*, illustrated by Matt Wawiorka (2000) (P)

Larios, Julie, *Yellow Elephant: A Bright Bestiary*, illustrated by Julie Paschkis (2006) (N–P)

☀ Nikola-Lisa, W., *Bein' with You This Way*, illustrated by Michael Bryant (1995) (P)

☀ Longfellow, Henry Wadsworth, *Hiawatha*, illustrated by Susan Jeffers (1983) (I–A)

_____, *The Midnight Ride of Paul Revere*, illustrated by Christopher Bing (2001) (I–A)

_____, *Paul Revere's Ride*, illustrated by Ted Rand (1990) (I–A)

Mayo, Margaret, *Roar!*, illustrated by Alex Ayliffe (2006) (N)

Spier, Peter, *The Fox Who Went Out on a Chilly Night* (1994) (I)

Tashiro, Chisato, *Five Nice Mice*, translated by Sayko Uchida and Kate Westerlund (2007) (P)

☀ Wheeler, Lisa, *Jazz Baby*, illustrated by R. Gregory Christie (2007) (N–P)

Yolen, Jane, and Andrew Fusek Peters, *Here's a Little Poem: A Very First Book of Poetry*, illustrated by Polly Dunbar (2007) (N–P)

Zemach, Margot, *Hush Little Baby* (1997) (P)

WORDLESS

Anno, Mitsumasa, *Anno's Journey* (1993) (I–A)

Baker, Jeannie, *Home* (2004) (P–I–A)

_____, *Window* (1991) (P–I–A)

Banyai, Istvan, *Zoom* (1998) (I–A)

_____, *Re-Zoom* (1999) (I–A)

_____, *The Other Side* (2005) (I–A)

dePaola, Tomie, *Pancakes for Breakfast* (1978) (N)

Faller, Regis, *The Adventures of Polo* (2006) (N–P)

_____, *Polo the Runaway Book* (2007) (N–P)

Goodall, John, *Little Red Riding Hood* (1988) (P)

Hutchins, Pat, *Changes, Changes* (1971) (N)

Jenkins, Steve, *Looking Down* (1995) (N–P)

Kamm, Katja, *Invisible* (2006) (N)

Keats, Ezra Jack, *Pssst! Doggie* (1973) (N)

Koren, Edward, *Behind the Wheel* (1972) (N)

Khing, T. T., *Where Is the Cake?* (2007) (N–P)

Lehman, Barbara, *Museum Trip* (2006) (P)

_____, *The Red Book* (2004) (P–I)

Martignacco, Carole, *The Everything Seed: A Story of Beginnings* (2006) (P)

Mayer, Mercer, *Frog Goes to Dinner* (2003) (N–P)

_____, *Frog Where Are You?* (2003) (N–P)

_____, *One Frog Too Many* (2003) (N–P)

McCully, Emily Arnold, *Picnic* (2003) (N)

Seeger, Karen Vaccaro, *First the Egg* (2007)(N)

Sís, Peter, *Dinosaur!* (2000) (N)

☀ Tan, Shaun, *The Arrival* (2007) (I–A)

Varon, Sara, *Chicken and Cat* (2006) (N)

Wiesner, David, *Free Fall* (1988) (P–I)

_____, *Flotsam* (2006) (P–I)

_____, *Sector 7* (1999) (P–I)

_____, *Tuesday* (1991) (P–I)

In his careful welter of dried leaves and seeds,
soil samples, quartz pebbles, notes-to-myself, letters,
on Dr. Carver's bedside table
next to his pocket watch,
folded in Aunt Mariah's Bible:
the Bill of Sale.
Seven hundred dollars
for a thirteen-year-old girl named Mary.

—MARILYN NELSON,
"Bedside Reading" in
Carver: A Life in Poems, *p. 41*

When Lila finishes reading "Bedside Reading" the room is silent as the eighth-grade students understand that the girl, Mary, was George Washington Carver's mother. Lila has been reading a handful of poems aloud each day, and the discussion has been lively. Students have argued about what kind of a book *Carver* (A) is—poetry to be sure, but also historical fiction, perhaps, or possibly even a biography. At this point they seem to have agreed that it is both poetry and biography, and are now wondering if this could be called a novel in verse, like Karen Hesse's *Out of the Dust* (A), which several of the students in class have read. Lila welcomes this discussion, but also wants her students to consider the content of the poem they have just heard. Words such as *love, slavery, loneliness,* and *belief* soon push the discussion to a consideration of how alone Carver must have felt, how difficult it was to be an educated black man in the late nineteenth century in America, even with a position at Tuskegee Institute. They go back to the poems "My People" and "Odalisque" and talk about the difficulty of being different, something they have all experienced, or at least worried about. Eventually, Lila guides the discussion to a consideration of what they are coming to understand about George Washington Carver and his life, how he is now much more than the "peanut man"—now that they understand something about his spirit because of Marilyn Nelson's poems.

Poetry is a window to the soul. Perhaps it stirs the soul of the reader, engaged by a poem. Perhaps it echoes the soul of the poet, whose choice of words and ideas and emotions offer a glimpse. Perhaps, in this case, it is also the soul of the subject of the poems. George Washington Carver is revealed as a deeply spiritual man living a life of service, struggle, and abiding love. At its best, poetry offers readers the opportunity to explore emotions, ideas, and the extraordinary use of language.

precise + evocative form

Defining Poetry

Defining poetry is perhaps the most difficult thing about poetry. It is easier to say what poetry does than to describe what it is. We know that poetry can make us chuckle or laugh aloud, startle us with insight, or surprise us with its clarity. Some poems express feelings that we did not even know we had until we read them, presenting the familiar in a way that surprises. Then we say, "Yes, that's just the way it is!" Poetry deals with the essence of life and experience. "Poems have a unique sense of contained energy, made as they are from words used in the most precise and evocative form," say anthologists Michael and Peter Benton. "Poems have their effects upon us as much by sounds, rhythms, associations, shapes, and forms as by lexical definition" (2008, pp. 136–137). Although good prose and poetry share many of the same stylistic devices, poetry is marked by the "saturation" of its language.

Poets themselves are often the best source for a definition of poetry. Robert Frost (1939) notes that "a poem begins in delight and ends in wisdom." Poetry, says poet Gregory Corso (1983, p. 11), is "the opposite of hypocrisy." Poet Ron Koertge agrees with Emily Dickinson that writers of poetry need to "tell all the Truth, but tell it slant" (2006, p. 539). Poetry combines rich meaning with sounds of language arranged in an interesting form. Poet J. Patrick Lewis calls it "ear candy." Poets select words and arrange them carefully to call attention to experiences in a fresh, new way. Samuel Taylor Coleridge distinguished between prose, "words in their best order," and poetry, "the best words in the best order." Poetry has an economy of form that prose rarely contains. Eve Merriam once remarked that poetry is like a can of frozen juice, becoming prose only when diluted.

Many poets write poems about poetry. Bobbye Goldstein's *Inner Chimes: Poems on Poetry* (P–I–A) contains several poems about poetry. In "Inside a Poem," from *It Doesn't Always Have to Rhyme* (P–I), Eve Merriam captures the essence of poetry and reveals some of its characteristics. She says poetry has a beat that repeats, words that chime, an inner chime, and images not imagined before. Eleanor Farjeon gives a more elusive definition in *Poems for Children* (P–I) when she says that it is "Not the rose, but the scent of the rose." Poet Kristine O'Connell George writes about herself as a writer in "The Blue Between" in Paul B. Janeczko's *Seeing the Blue Between: Advice and Inspiration for Young Poets* (A).

THE BLUE BETWEEN

Everyone watches clouds,
naming creatures they've seen.
I see sky differently,

I see the blue between—
The blue woman tugging
her stubborn cloud across the sky.
The blue giraffe stretching
to nibble a cloud floating by.
A pod of dancing dolphins,
cloud oceans, cargo ships,
a boy twirling his cloud
around a thin blue fingertip.

In those smooth wide places,
I see a different scene.
In those cloudless spaces,
I see the blue between.

KRISTINE O'CONNELL GEORGE

Poets and critics also often distinguish between poetry and verse. Noted poet and anthologist Myra Cohn Livingston argued that there was a clear difference; generally, the variation in emotional intensity distinguishes verse and poetry, with verse being much less intense than poetry. Anthologist Liz Rosenberg puts it succinctly: "Shel Silverstein . . . worked in a tradition of light verse. . . . [but] has moments of poetry in his light verse, just as Shakespeare deliberately plants ditties in the midst of his great poetic plays. But by and large verse and poetry are two separate creatures, like the difference between standup comedy and *A Midsummer Night's Dream*" (2005, p. 375). Verse, then, is amusing but not intense, whereas poetry is intense, an intricate combination of the sounds, meanings, and arrangement of words to call attention to something in a fresh, compelling manner. In this chapter we explore both poetry and verse for young readers.

A Brief History of Poetry for Young Readers

Verse written especially for children appears in folklore, with Mother Goose verses some of the earliest poetic forms to delight the ears and tickle the tongues of children. Whereas doggerel, sentimental lines, riddles, and traditional rhymes were plentiful, poetry written especially for children began to appear only in the nineteenth century.

Some truly great works, though written for adults, preceded the flowering of poetry written for children. For example, the English poet William Blake (1757–1827) captured the spirit of childhood in verse. The poems in *Songs of Innocence and Experience* (1789) portray the human mind with a childlike quality. Blake's poems show the child as refreshingly curious and responding intuitively to unfathomable beauty.

Profiles

David McCord, 1977

*P*oetry, like rain, should fall with elemental music, and poetry for children should catch the eye as well as the ear and the mind. It should delight; it really has to delight. Furthermore, poetry for children should keep reminding them, without any feeling on their part that they are being reminded, that the English language is a most marvelous and availing instrument.

David McCord is considered the dean of children's poets. His collected works appear in *One at a Time*. Other popular collections of his work appear in *Every Time I Climb a Tree* and *For Me to Say*. "Nature abounds in McCord's poetry," noted David A. Dillon (1978), "and the reader is treated to a sensual feast of sights, sounds, and touch, captured as a result of the poet's careful observation of common things which many of us fail to notice[:] colors, speeds, sizes, textures, shapes" (p. 379). David McCord was the first recipient of the NCTE Award for Excellence in Poetry for Children.

Aileen Fisher, 1978

*P*oetry is a rhythmical piece of writing that leaves the reader feeling that life is a little richer than before, a little more full of wonder, beauty, or just plain delight.

"Since the early 1930s," commented Lee Bennett Hopkins (1978), "Aileen Fisher . . . has reached and touched thousands upon thousands of children with her warm, wise and wonderful writing" (p. 868). A nature poet, Fisher lived as a child on forty acres of land near the Iron Range on the Upper Peninsula of Michigan. She returned to the country as an adult to write full-time. Her popular books include *Sing of the Earth and Sky: Poems about Our Planet and the Wonders Beyond*; *Always Wondering*; *The House of a Mouse*; *Like Nothing at All: Out in the Dark and Daylight*; *Rabbits, Rabbits*; and *Anybody Home?*.

Karla Kuskin, 1979

*I*f there were a recipe for a poem, these would be the ingredients: word sounds, rhythm, description, feeling, memory, rhyme, and imagination. They can be put together a thousand different ways, a thousand, thousand . . . more.

An artist as well as a poet, Karla Kuskin designed the medallion for the NCTE poetry award; when she won the same award three years later, friends teased her about designing awards she would win. "Her pictures and her verse and poetry," noted Alvina Treut Burrows (1979), "are brimming over with the experiences of children growing up in a big city" (p. 935). Fittingly, Kuskin's poetry appears in New York subways as part of the Poetry in Motion program. Her most popular books include *Near the Window Tree: Poems and Notes*; *Dogs and Dragons, Trees and Dreams: A Collection of Poems*; *The Upstairs Cat*; *The Sky Is Always in the Sky*; and *I Am Me*. Her anthology, *Moon, Have You Met My Mother?*, is a collection of all her poems.

The opening quotations for these profiles are from the poets' acceptance speeches for the NCTE poetry award. (The speech is given in November of the year the award is received.)

Ann Taylor (1782–1866) and Jane Taylor (1783–1824) published *Original Poems for Infant Minds by Several Young Persons* in 1804. These verses reflected a childlike spirit despite subtle lessons. "Twinkle, twinkle, little star" is a song that children sing today. This and other early poems, such as "Mary Had a Little Lamb" (1830) by Sarah Josepha Hale and "Will You Walk into My Parlor? Said the Spider to the Fly" in *Fireside Verses* by Mary Howitt (1799–1888), were dispersed so widely it is difficult to remember that they are not folklore.

Most nineteenth-century poets had a strong desire to teach lessons, but some went beyond preachy moralistic verses. A few early English poets portrayed life from a child's point of view and sang the pleasures of childhood as children might have seen them. Some of these include Edward Lear, *A Book of Nonsense* (1846); Robert Louis Stevenson, *A Child's Garden of Verses* (1885); and A. A. Milne, *When We Were Very Young* (1924), and *Now We Are Six* (1927). An American, Clement C. Moore, wrote *A Visit from St. Nicholas* (1823), a poem that is a rarity because it is free from the didactic teachings of the time. It is now generally known as "The Night before Christmas." The tradition begun by William Blake led to poetic conventions we draw upon today.

Despite the arguments between those who insisted on "official school poetry" from authors such as Robert Frost and Emily Dickinson (Thomas, 2007), in the last half of the twentieth century poetry for children flourished, with poets such as Aileen Fisher, David McCord, Eve Merriam, Myra Cohn Livingston, John Ciardi, and

A late twentieth-century phenomenon, the verse novel for children began in 1993 with Virginia Euwer Wolff's *Make Lemonade* (A). Verse novels are narrative in structure, contain the condensed language found in poetry, and are usually intensely focused on characters' feelings (Campbell, 2004, p. 614). Most scholars agree that Karen Hesse's Newbery Award brought mainstream attention to the verse novel, increasing with a National Book Award for Virginia Euwer Wolff's *True Believer* (A) and a Printz Award for Angela Johnson's *The First Part Last* (A). Since that time, many writers have experimented with verse novels, with more than a dozen published for adolescents in 2004 alone. We look at verse novels closely later in this chapter.

In 1977, the National Council of Teachers of English (NCTE) established an award to honor poets who write for children. The award, established in memory of Bee Cullinan's son Jonathan (born 1969, died 1975), recognizes the outstanding contribution of a poet who writes expressly for children. Charles S. Huck, Alvina Burrows, John Donovan, and Sister Rosemary Winkeljohann helped define the criteria for excellence in poetry for children and developed the procedures used to select the recipients of the award. The award is given for the entire body of a poet's work for children. This was an annual award from 1977 through 1982, but the committee realized they would soon run out of poets; in 1983, a new policy was instituted to present the award every three years. The combined works of the poets who have received the award thus far form the foundation for poetry study in the field of children's literature. Brief profiles of the NCTE award winners—David McCord, Aileen Fisher, Karla Kuskin, Myra Cohn Livingston, Eve Merriam, John Ciardi, Lilian Moore, Arnold Adoff, Valerie Worth, Barbara Juster Esbensen, Eloise Greenfield, X. J. Kennedy, Mary Ann Hoberman, Nikki Grimes, and Lee Bennett Hopkins appear throughout this chapter.

After ten poets had received the NCTE Award for Excellence in Poetry for Children, Cullinan conducted a national survey to discover children's favorite poems by

When *Joyful Noise* won the Newbery Award, it helped solidify the important place that poetry holds in literature for young readers.

Karla Kuskin providing young readers with opportunities for delight. Brief profiles of all these poets appear in this chapter. Some classics, such as Langston Hughes's work, continue to speak to young readers. Hughes's *The Dream Keeper and Other Poems* (A) is currently available in a beautiful seventy-fifth anniversary edition, illustrated by Brian Pinkney.

Other authors, such as Shel Silverstein and Jack Prelutsky, were both prolific and successful, as were others who penned the "urchin verse" that children so delighted in (Thomas, 2007). There were also three Newbery Awards given to poets. The first went to Nancy Willard in 1982 for *A Visit to William Blake's Inn: Poems for Innocent and Experienced Travelers* (I), the second to Paul Fleischman in 1989 for *Joyful Noise: Poems for Two Voices* (I–A), and the third to Karen Hesse in 1998 for her verse novel, *Out of the Dust* (A). In 2002, Marilyn Nelson received a Newbery Honor for *Carver: A Life in Poems* (A), and in 2006 Jack Prelutsky became the first children's poet laureate in the United States.

The National Council of Teachers of English Award for Excellence in Poetry for Children, designed by Karla Kuskin, 1976. (Kuskin knew that Jonathan loved to climb trees and read books. She combined both interests in the medallion.)

Children's top five favorites from early NCTE award-winning poets appear in **A Jar of Tiny Stars**.

This picturebook contains a single poem by Walter Dean Myers, which celebrates the community of Harlem. The stunning collage art by Christopher Myers adds illuminating depictions of the people and the place.

each award recipient. Children's top five favorites for each poet appear in *A Jar of Tiny Stars* (P–I) with all proceeds supporting the NCTE poetry award.

Today, we find poetry in many formats, ranging from picturebooks containing a single poem to those containing several poems by either one (individual) or many poets (collective), all of which focus on one topic. The latter are termed *specialized anthologies.* Longer anthologies can be "specialized" as well, usually containing works by several poets on one subject. Longer anthologies can also be individual, containing all or part of the collected works of a particular poet. "Generalized/collective" anthologies contain works by many poets on several subjects. All of these types of anthologies allow young readers to browse through poetry and discover favorites.

Single-volume picturebooks of poetry with beautiful illustrations provide excellent opportunities to explore poetry as visually interpreted by fine artists, as we discuss in Chapter 3. This can lead to some surprises. For example, illustrator Christopher Myers takes a single text, Lewis Carroll's *Jabberwocky* (I–A), to a new place by illustrating it in a unique, contemporary fashion as a basketball game.

Christopher Myers also collaborates with his father, writer Walter Dean Myers, on stunning books such as the Caldecott Honor– and Coretta Scott King Award–winning *Harlem.* This powerful poem explores the strength and depth of this vibrant community while the collage art illuminates Harlem's spirit. Other book-length single poems include Alice Walker's *Why War Is Never a Good Idea* (I), illustrated by Stefano Vitale, and Giselle Potter's stunning visual interpretation of the Eugene Field classic *Wynken, Blynken, and Nod* (N).

Picturebooks that are also specialized anthologies may be created by one poet, as in Joyce Carol Thomas's *The Blacker the Berry* (I), illustrated by Floyd Cooper; Jack Prelutsky's *Good Sports: Rhymes about Running, Jumping, Throwing, and More* (P–I); and Jane Yolen's *Color Me a Rhyme: Nature Poems for Young People* (I), illustrated by Jason Stemple. They also may contain the selected works of several poets, as in Lee Bennett Hopkins's *Wonderful Words: Poems about Reading, Writing, Speaking, and Listening* (I), or Hopkins's *Sky Magic* (I). Some of the best of these books are structured so that the poems build on one another to create a book that is tightly woven, as exemplified by Joyce Sidman's individual specialized anthology *The World According to Dog: Poems and Teen Voices* (A). Sidman's poems capture the essence of four-legged friends and their relationships with the teens who love them in images that empower advanced readers to almost reach out and pet the dogs featured in the anthology. Sidman uses a variety of forms to create "sorry" poems in another specialized anthology, *This Is Just to Say: Poems of Apology and Forgiveness* (A).

Specialized anthologies are popular; the plethora of collections of poems and verses about holidays, school, monsters, dinosaurs, horses, sports, family, love, death, and many other topics bear witness to this. Excellent anthologists such as Lee Bennett Hopkins, Paul Janeczko, Myra Cohn Livingston, Liz Rosenberg, Dorothy and X. J. Kennedy add immeasurably to our wealth of poetic resources available with their collective specialized anthologies. Liz Rosenberg speaks to advanced readers in *Roots and Flowers: Poets and Poems for Family* (A), an anthol-

ogy of the works of several poets who use strong images to describe bonds between family members. She and Deena November collaborated on *I Just Hope It's Lethal: Poems of Sadness, Madness, and Joy* (A), another anthology that appeals to adolescent readers.

Palestinian-American poet Naomi Shihab Nye's *19 Varieties of Gazelle: Poems of the Middle East* (A) contains sixty poems that bring the sights, sounds, smells, and tastes of Palestine to adolescent readers while also serving as a commentary on the tragedy of 9/11. Her *Honeybee: Poems & Short Prose* (A) is a blend of more than eighty poems and prose paragraphs that explore prejudice, war, peace, kindness, and Arab Americans.

The collective, generalized anthology by X. J. Kennedy and Dorothy Kennedy, *Talking Like the Rain* (P–I) contains poems arranged under informative headings. The book is a pleasure to skim, read, or savor. David McCord's individual general anthology, *One at a Time* (P–I), is an impressive volume containing most of his

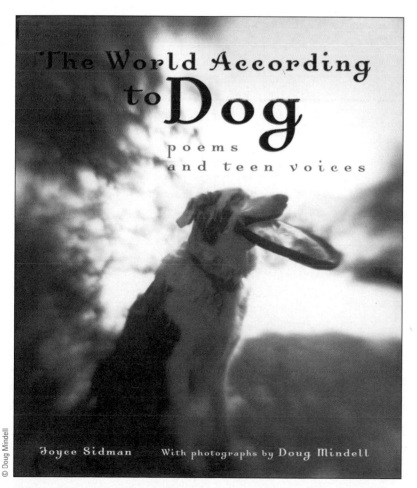

Older readers enjoy the familiar bond between person and pet, even if they don't have a dog of their own.

© 2002 Naomi Shihab Nye

The poems in this attractive volume evoke the sights, sounds, and culture of the Middle East.

Figure 4.1

Checklist for Assessing Quality in Poetry

Individual poems demonstrate

✧ Content is interesting to and understandable by intended readers.

✧ Language is innovative, with careful word choices and use of poetic devices to enhance meaning.

✧ Form or structure helps readers understand more about the poetic subject or mood.

Anthologies demonstrate

✧ Purposeful selection of quality poetry.

✧ Arrangement that is logical.

✧ Inclusiveness of a range of poetry.

poetry. McCord's wit and thoughtful perception sing through the music of his words, creating a timeless resource for cultivating poetic taste and encouraging children to read poetry for pleasure. Karla Kuskin's collected works, *Moon, Have You Met My Mother?* (P) and Valerie Worth's *All the Small Poems and Fourteen More* (P) provide invaluable resources for adults who share poetry with primary-grade students.

Considering Quality in Poetry and Poetry Anthologies

We value poems that have stood the test of time, and poetry books that have won significant awards and have received positive reviews from literary critics. Most of all, however, we treasure poems that speak to our sense of delight, wonder, recognition, or emotional state. The final test, after all, is the level of engagement of the reader. When evaluating individual poems for young readers, consider how well they speak to their intended audience,

the quality of their use of language, and the aptness of their form. The intended reader should easily be able to understand the content of a poem, and it should prove meaningful to him or her as well. Outstanding poets know how to use language in ways that enhance meaning. So, too, do poets structure a poem in a manner in which the form conveys meaning.

We judge anthologies of poetry both by the quality of the individual poems they contain and by the overall structure and content of the entire collection. Excellent anthologies have "a generous *inclusiveness* which acknowledges [the range] of poems students may enjoy, feel provoked by, remember, and, maybe, find valuable" (Benton & Benton, 2008, p. 137). The arrangement of poetry in an anthology and the overall impact of the arrangement also determine the quality. Figure 4.1 suggests some criteria to use as you evaluate books of poetry. Keep the criteria in mind as you search for excellent poetry books to delight young readers.

● ● CONTENT THAT ● ● SPEAKS TO READERS

Research tells us that young readers like poetry that they can understand. Of course they do! This does not mean, however, that poetry for children or adolescents has to

Profiles

Myra Cohn Livingston, 1980

*T*rained as a traditionalist in poetry, I feel strongly about the importance of order imposed by fixed forms, meter, and rhyme when I write about some things; yet free verse seems more suitable for other subjects. It is the force of what I say that shapes the form.

Myra Cohn Livingston was highly respected for her "commitment to the need for higher standards for children's creative writing" (Porter, 1980, p. 901). She published approximately eighty books of poetry or writings about poetry. Her work includes such titles as *Riddle-Me Rhymes, Lots of Limericks, Call Down the Moon*, and *Poem-Making: Ways to Begin Writing Poetry.*

Eve Merriam, 1981

*T*here is a physical element in reading poetry out loud; it's like jumping rope or throwing a ball. If we can get teachers to read poetry, lots of it, out loud to children, we'll develop a generation of poetry readers, we may even have some poetry writers, but the main thing [is], we'll have language appreciators.

It is the physical thrill of poetry "that Eve Merriam want[ed] children to experience for themselves" (Sloan, 1981, p. 958). She felt that "children, like poets, are intrigued by the wonderful things that words can do: how their sounds mimic what is being described, how puns are possible, how language can be made . . . to 'natter, patter, chatter, and prate'" (p. 958). Merriam's poetry is widely anthologized. Some of her books include *It Doesn't Always Have to Rhyme; There Is No Rhyme for Silver; The Singing Green: New and Selected Poems for All Seasons;* and *Higgle Wiggle: Happy Rhymes.*

John Ciardi, 1982

*P*oetry and learning are both fun, and children are full of an enormous relish for both. My poetry is just a bubbling up of a natural foolishness and the idea that maybe you can make language dance a bit.

"There is magic in the poetry John Ciardi has written for children," said Norine Odland (1982, p. 872). She felt that the "humor in his poems allows a child to reach for new ways to view ordinary things and places in the world" (p. 872). John Ciardi began writing poetry for his own children. His first book was *The Reason for the Pelican.* Other favorites include *You Read to Me, I'll Read to You; You Know Who; The Monster Den: Or Look What Happened at My House—and to It; The Man Who Sang the Sillies;* and *I Met a Man.*

The opening quotations for these profiles are from the poets' acceptance speeches for the NCTE poetry award. (The speech is given in November of the year the award is received.)

---

be simple or lighthearted. The emotions expressed in poetry run the gamut from humor to delight to despair. Indeed, many poems originally intended for adults have found their way into young readers' anthologies—and into their hearts. Readers of all ages find content engaging when it relates to their own interests and experiences. Because young readers have so many varied interests and experiences, we cannot really judge the subject of a poem because readers vary so widely. We can, however, evaluate the presentation of that content. Here are two poems that explore the same general content—the absence of a father from a child's life—written from two different perspectives, a young child's and a young adult's point of view.

The first, from the book *Fathers, Mothers, Sisters, Brothers* (N–P), by Mary Ann Hoberman, is understandable by young children.

MY FATHER

My father doesn't live with us.
It doesn't help to make a fuss,
But still I feel unhappy, plus
I miss him.

My father doesn't live with me.
He's got another family;
He moved away when I was three.
I miss him.

I'm always happy on the day
He visits and we talk and play;
But after he has gone away
I miss him.

MARY ANN HOBERMAN

Contrast the feeling of loneliness in this poem with that same feeling in a poem found in Paul Janeczko's anthology *Looking for Your Name: A Collection of Contemporary Poems* (A).

THE ABSENT FATHER

Perhaps a wish, perhaps a memory
  of rocking in your arms.

Reaching up to you
  expecting to be lifted to the sky.

Riding piggyback. Playing Trust Me:
standing straight and falling back and you would
    catch—
    no, that was Uncle Dan.

Hiking down a grassy slope, across a dusty field
to a huge yellow tent, roped and staked,
and inside: girls in pink
swivel on circling elephants, trapeze families
swing from the roof, wide-mouthed clowns
pratfall, lunge at us in the front row—
    me and Uncle Jerry.

Summer days at the ocean, I learn the math
of waves, the pulse of tide
    with Mother.

With you, what voyage?
What event or conversation, you and I?
What skill, what lore?

Not learning to ride a bike
or skate or read or write
or dance or sing in any language
or play a finger game or pray—

For a moment, you put down your paper,
let me kiss your cheek good night.
But nothing! Nothing
to remember I learned to live
to love us by.

LEE SHARKEY

Both of these poets speak of loneliness, of missing a close relationship with a father, yet they are very different in the *way* they speak about it, with Sharkey presenting a much more complex notion of what is missed than Hoberman does. The topic of both poems is understandable to all levels of readers. The manner in which the content is presented—the voice that speaks the words and the way they are spoken—is understandable only to the intended reader.

When selecting poems we must not underestimate the verbal and emotional intelligence of young readers.

Further, if we are looking for poetry to fit a particular curricular topic, be sure the poetry is excellent. No topic is worth exploring through poetry unless the poetry is excellent. For example, books such as Jane Yolen's *Fine Feathered Friends: Poems for Young People* (P) combine beauty with information. The photographs by her son, illustrator Jason Stemple, and the poetry are spectacular, and the information that appears in inserts is accurate and engaging. On a similar topic, Kristine O'Connell George's lyrical poems in *Hummingbird Nest: A Journal of Poems* (I) capture the poet's experience of watching a hummingbird make a nest, lay eggs, and raise her babies. Barry Moser's delicate watercolors are visual complements to the images the words create. Francisco X. Alarcon's bilingual *Animal Poems of the Iguazu/Animalario del Iguazu* (P) uses humor and beauty to allow the creatures of the Iguazu rainforest to plead for continued existence. Maya Christina Gonzalez's mixed-media illustrations draw the eye with color and texture that bring the rainforest to life.

Joyce Sidman's *Butterfly Eyes and Other Secrets of the Meadow: Poems* (I) combines beautiful language in various poetic forms, all of which are riddles, with stunning illustrations by Beth Krommes, as it explores the hidden world of a meadow. Douglas Florian's cycle of seasonal books, *Summersaults* (P), *Autumblings* (P), *Winter Eyes* (P), and *Handsprings* (P) capture the spirit of each season with word play, humor, and striking watercolor illustrations. David Elliott's *On the Farm* (P) offers brief, insightful observations of familiar animals.

• • LANGUAGE THAT • • ENHANCES MEANING

Scholars have noted that with poetry what matters is not so much "what" it means as "how it says what it means" (Nodelman, 1996). Outstanding poems capture readers' attention with innovative ways to use words. Nothing about poetic language is mundane or prosaic. Poets choose words carefully to describe objects, events, feelings, or ideas in new and surprising ways. Although their words, like their subjects, may be familiar ones, poets select and arrange them purposefully to capture our imagination. The experience conveyed in poetry may be commonplace, but it becomes extraordinary when seen through the poet's eye. Those who enjoy jazz, for example, will find new ways to think about that music when reading Walter Dean Myers's *Jazz* (I), vibrantly illustrated by Christopher Myers; and those who have never listened to jazz will find themselves wanting to do so after experiencing these poems.

The language of poetry startles us into seeing with wide-open eyes just how extraordinary are our thoughts and experiences, even those seemingly ordinary sub-

Figure **4.2**

Some Commonly Used Poetic Techniques

Alliteration The repetition of initial consonant sounds at close intervals

Assonance The repetition of vowel sounds at close intervals

Connotation The individual emotional implications or private meaning of a word

Consonance The repetition of internal consonant sounds at close intervals

Denotation The commonly understood or public meaning of a word

Imagery Words that appeal to the senses

Lyric poetry A poetic statement of mood or feeling

Metaphor An implied comparison of unlike things

Meter A beat or measure in a line of poetry

Narrative poetry A poem that tells a story; several poems that, taken together, tell a story

Onomatopoeia Words that sound like their meanings

Personification Human traits given to inanimate objects

Repetition Using a word or sound over and over for effect

Rhyme Words whose ending sounds are alike. May occur at end of lines (**end rhyme**) or from the end of one line to the beginning or middle of the next (**link rhyme**)

Rhythm A recurring pattern of strong and weak beats in language

Simile A stated comparison of unlike things using *like* or *as*

Symbol A word that stands for more than its denotative meaning

jects as those studied in school. Jon Scieszka and illustrator Lane Smith brought their trademark humor and brilliant collaboration to the making of *Math Curse* (I) and *Science Verse* (I). J. Patrick Lewis, also a master at writing poetry on various school topics, created *Scien-Trickery: Riddles in Science* (I), a text in which the answers to his science riddles are hidden on the pages. His *The Brother's War: Civil War Voices in Verse* (A), for older readers, presents the horrors of a difficult chapter in American history. Other recent poetry books that celebrate things we learn about in school include Betsy Franco's *Mathmatickles!* (I).

Sometimes the language that poets use contains strong rhythm and rhyme to express meaning; others write in free verse in which there is no regular rhyme or rhythm, but rather a specific structure built to reinforce meaning. Many use alliteration, assonance, or onomatopoeia to express their ideas; others do not. The elements of sound—whichever a poet chooses to use—are so important in poetry that it is often said that a poem cannot be truly understood until it is read aloud. Sometimes what a poet wants to convey is best expressed through figurative language, such as metaphor, simile, and personification, or through vivid imagery; sometimes, though, this would be inappropriate. In all poetry, however, word choice and arrangement is central because the connotation, or what a word suggests, is often as important as the denotation, or the literal meaning of a word. How these carefully selected

words are arranged also affects the sound of a poem and helps to shape the connotations of individual words. These and other poetic techniques, listed and defined in Figure 4.2, are the linguistic tools of a poet's trade, and success or failure can be judged by how carefully the poet has selected and used these tools. We explore how various poets use these devices later in this chapter. Teaching Idea 4.1 on page 148 offers suggestions for exploring line breaks in free verse with students.

In excellent anthologies, poems generally contain an array of poetic devices to support meaning, although some anthologies may highlight particular poetic devices. Jack Prelutsky provides sophisticated vocabulary and brilliant word play in *My Dog May Be a Genius* (I). Arnold Adoff's many free verse collections, such as *Sports Pages* (I) and *Chocolate Dreams: Poems* (I), or books such as Valerie Worth's *Animal Poems* (P) and Patricia McKissack's *Stitchin' and Pullin': A Gee's Bend Quilt* (I), allow young readers to think about how free verse works.

• • STRUCTURE THAT • • SUPPORTS MEANING

In well-constructed poems, the shape and patterns of words, lines, and stanzas, indeed of whole poems, says something about what the poem means. Poets structure their poems to reveal more about their subjects than words alone can. Skillful poets use form in sophisticated

Teaching Idea **4.2**

Choral Reading with Poems for Multiple Voices

One effective way of introducing choral speaking to your class is to use poems that are written for multiple voices, such as Paul Fleischman's *I Am Phoenix*; *Joyful Noise: Poems for Two Voices*; and *Big Talk* (all I). These poems are printed so that it is apparent when solo or combined voices are meant to be used. Even with these cues, it still requires some practice to be able to read well. When students work with these poems, they being to realize the close connection between sound and meaning, and they learn to work together to produce the sound that most effectively captures the meaning they want to convey.

Many poems, not just those written for multiple voices, work well for choral reading. Put one of your favorite poems on an overhead, then explore how different ways of reading the same poem can create different effects. Even a simple tempo or stress change alters the effect and often the meaning of the poem. Here are some ways to explore the connections between meaning and sound in poetry.

- ✺ Vary the tempo. Read faster or slower and discuss the effects.

- ✺ Experiment with stress, discussing which words might be emphasized, and why.

- ✺ Play with tone; some poems seem to call for a deep, somber tone, whereas others need a light tone.

- ✺ Try different groupings of voices. Poems can be read in many ways—in unison, with choruses, using single voices paired with other single or blended voices, or cumulatively, with voices blending to an increasingly powerful effect.

After you have worked with several poems this way, encourage students to experiment in small groups with choral speaking as a way to explore meaning and sound in poetry.

the prose version, and say it much more specifically . . . by creating patterns . . . that depend on these exact words being said in this exact order" (1996, p. 195).

Gwendolyn Brooks creates pattern through alliteration, assonance, rhyme, and careful word placement in "We Real Cool," a poem from her anthology *Selected Poems* (A).

> WE REAL COOL.
> THE POOL PLAYERS.
> SEVEN AT THE GOLDEN
> SHOVEL.
>
> *We real cool. We*
> *Left school. We*
>
> *Lurk late. We*
> *Strike straight. We*
>
> *Sing sin. We*
> *Thin gin. We*
>
> *Jazz June. We*
> *Die soon.*
>
> GWENDOLYN BROOKS

Nodelman (1996) notes that the repetition of "we" both establishes the rhythm and allows for the significance of its absence at the end of the last line.

Word order, or patterns, helps create meaning, calling attention to the words themselves as well as the images

they create. Whether this order is in part dictated by particular forms, as we discuss later in this chapter, or entirely by meaning, it is perhaps the core of poetry—the only words arranged in the only way possible to convey the poet's idea, and thus to trigger new ideas in the reader.

• • WORDS AS PICTURES • •

Word placement, or how words are juxtaposed or separated, helps create meaning as we have discussed above. Poets also have at their disposal several poetic devices including *connotation*, *figurative language*, and *imagery*. Writers use all of these poetic devices to suggest that the words mean more than meets the eye or ear. As in "We Real Cool," something left unsaid is often as important as what is on the page.

Poetry often carries several layers of meaning and, as is true of other literature, is subject to different interpretations. The meaning readers create relates directly to what their experience prepares them to comprehend; who we are determines what we can understand. While the words that poets choose do have a public, shared meaning, or *denotation*, the *connotations* that surround those words are both public and private. It is often the resonance of a particular word in the heart of a reader that creates a powerful poetic experience. With the words *stained glass*, Georgia Heard calls up connotations of spirituality, beauty, and peacefulness when she suggests through metaphor that the dragonfly's wings are stained glass in *Creatures of Earth, Sea, and Sky: Poems* (I):

DRAGONFLY

It skims the pond's surface
searching for gnats, mosquitoes, and flies.
Outspread wings blur with speed.
It touches down
and stops to sun itself on the dock.
Wings flicker and still:
stained-glass windows
with sun shining through.

GEORGIA HEARD

Although also found in prose, figurative language—metaphor, simile, and personification—often saturates the language of poetry. Complex comparisons using the devices of metaphor and simile, which compare one thing to another or view something in terms of something else are frequent in poetry. The comparison in a simile is stated and uses the words *like* or *as* to draw the comparison. A comparison in a metaphor is inferred; something is stated as something else, such as the dragonfly's wings being called stained-glass windows.

As poets create vivid experiences and use language metaphorically, they help us see or feel things in new way, as in this poem from Eve Merriam's *It Doesn't Always Have to Rhyme* (I):

METAPHOR

Morning is
a new sheet of paper
for you to write on.

Whatever you want to say,
all day,
until night
folds it up
and files it away.

The bright words and the dark words
are gone
until dawn
and a new day
to write on.

EVE MERRIAM

This poem functions as both a perfect example of its title and as a wonderful way of looking at the possibilities inherent in a new day, a sentiment uttered to the point of triteness by many other writers and speakers but seen as fresh through Merriam's metaphor.

Personification refers to representing a thing or abstraction as a person. When we say "Fortune smiled on us" or "If the weather permits," we are giving human qualities to an idea—fortune—and to the weather. Poets often give human feelings or thoughts to plants and animals. In her poem "Crickets," Valerie Worth uses personification to make ideas more vivid or unusual when she says that crickets "talk" and dry grass "whispers." Langston Hughes uses personification in "April Rain Song" when he advises to let the rain "kiss" you and "sing you a lullaby." Notice how Sarah Hansen uses both simile and personification to craft a new way to think about morning in "Rising," found in Lee Bennett Hopkins's *Sky Magic* (I).

RISING

Like a fresh loaf
Sun rises,
Tempting dawn
To break
Her golden crust.

Taste morning!

SARAH HANSEN

The sun, infused with a distinctly human energy, "tempts" dawn to break. No longer is sunrise merely the consequence of earth's rotation, but it is the sun's motivation to coax morning into existence. Like Hansen's readers, the sun is brimming with agency. She makes things happen, and in many ways, large or small, we can relate to that. Personification, at its best, invites us not only to observe the plants, animals, and inanimate objects populating our world, but to connect with them in ways that reveal or clarify our own thoughts, feelings, and behaviors.

Poets create *imagery* by using words that arrest our senses; we can imagine that we almost see, taste, touch, smell, or hear what they describe. Little escapes the poet's vision; nothing limits the speculations upon what he or she sees. In a poem from *All the Small Poems and Fourteen More* (P), Valerie Worth creates a fresh vision of a common flower through metaphor and imagery:

DANDELION

Out of
Green space,
A sun:
Bright for
A day, burning,
Away to
A husk, a
Cratered moon:

Burst
In a week
To dust:
Seeding
The infinite

Lawn with
Its starry
Smithereens.

VALERIE WORTH

Comparing the dandelion to a "sun" and a "cratered moon" calls up visions of hot yellow and cool, creamy gray. Words such as *green space, bright, burning,* and *husk* create an image of the flower in the phases of its life cycle, and "starry smithereens" forever changes the way we view the humble weed that grows everywhere.

Barbara Juster Esbensen creates vivid word pictures in *Words with Wrinkled Knees* (I):

Touch it with your
pencil
Splat!   The word lands   wet
and squat
upon the page   F R O G

Feed it something light
With wings   Here's one!
Tongue flicks   bright
wing   caught!
Small poem
gone

BARBARA JUSTER ESBENSEN

This and the other poems in this collection go beyond the skillful use of imagery to describe an object, place, or person, and give readers an opportunity to consider not just the thing itself, but the word that represents it. The frog, and the word itself, is "squat," "wet," with "flicking tongue," while the prey, "light" with "bright wings," is a "small poem."

Strong images allow readers to have—through language—experiences and ideas that perhaps they have never before known. Imagery helps readers stretch their sensory selves. In *Toasting Marshmallows* (I), Kristine O'Connell George uses imagery to describe the sights and sounds of camping in the woods—a subject that appeals to many children. A close look at her *Fold Me a Poem* (P–I), beautifully illustrated by Lauren Stringer, shows how a poet's words create pictures that inspire both illustrator and reader to go beyond the usual.

✳   ✳   ✳

A CLOSE LOOK AT

Fold Me a Poem

Kristine O'Connell George composed the thirty-two free verse poems in *Fold Me a Poem* (P) because she realized how alike origami and poetry were. Perfect words used well create an image, emotion, or idea in a poem, just as the precise folds of origami create wondrous things out of a simple sheet of paper. George uses perfect words to create images, mostly animals, that appeal to many children. Through these images the imagination in her poet's mind spills onto the pages to be interpreted by Lauren Stringer's vibrant illustrations. For example, "Wind Storm" implores "Hurry,

Dragon

Dragon!
Behave yourself.

Remember:
You are
made of
paper.

In Kristine O'Connell George's **Fold Me A Poem**, *Dragon has certainly decimated the origami menagerie!*

animals!/Get inside the barn./My brother/just turned on/ the fan." and the illustration depicts a pair of hands hastily placing origami animals in a cardboard box while the cat pounces on another and a paper lion leaps toward safety. The sly humor in the fifteen syllables of "Dragon" represents the tone of the entire book: "Dragon!/Behave yourself./ Remember:/You are/made of/paper." Stringer's illustration adds to the humor by depicting a dragon stretching across a full-bleed, double-page spread, with decimated origami animals strewn around the edges.

George's poems, all "small," reflect the spareness of the Japanese tradition. With Stringer's expressive origami animals, created in order to paint the illustrations almost leaping off the page, *Fold Me a Poem* becomes an enticing poetry book for young readers as well as an example of the marriage of art and text that marks an outstanding picturebook.

Poetic Structures

Poems look different from prose writing; there is a lot more white space. Within that extra white space, however, are an astounding variety of poetic forms. Generally, we speak of two basic types of poetry—narrative and lyric— but there are a plethora of poetic forms that poets play with, either to tell a story to express emotion or to amuse with simple verse.

• • NARRATIVE POETRY • •

Narrative poems tell a story, sometimes in amazingly few lines and sometimes at length. Narrative poems can take many forms, ranging from unstructured free verse to tightly structured ballads. Think about stories from childhood that you first heard through poetry. Perhaps "Casey at the Bat," "Hiawatha," "Paul Revere's Ride," or another poem comes to mind. Many readers enjoy narrative verse, and this is not surprising—they enjoy and are familiar with stories of all kinds. A book-length narrative poem (one that is longer than a picture book) is called an epic, but most contemporary story poems for young readers are relatively short and relate only one or a few episodes.

Narrative Poems

Narrative poetry sets a story with characters, plot, and theme—like any other story—into a poetic framework, which can make even a humble story memorable. Poets experiment with the narrative form. Books such as Joyce Carol Thomas's picturebooks, *Gingerbread Days, Brown Honey in Broomwheat Tea*, and *I Have Heard of*

a Land (P), or Nikki Grimes's *Oh, Brother!* (P), contain a series of short poems that, taken together, tell a story. Eloise Greenfield contributes narrative poetry in *Night on Neighborhood Street*, as does Nikki Grimes in *Come Sunday*; *Danitra Brown, Class Clown* (P); and *What Is Goodbye?* (I). Jack Prelutsky's *The Headless Horseman Rides Tonight: More Poems to Trouble Your Sleep* (I) is also a classic example of narrative poetry, and *Tales from Gizzard's Grill* (I) by Jeanne Steig offers poetry for children exploring the narrative form.

Ballads

Ballads are a specific form of narrative poetry, with "rules" for poets to follow. Within these rules, they tell a story relating a single incident or thought. Some poets use dialogue to tell a story in repeated refrains. There are folk ballads and literary ballads. Folk ballads have no known author; they have become anonymous and are handed down in song. "John Henry" is a well-known folk ballad. Myra Cohn Livingston's *Abraham Lincoln: A Man for All the People* (I) extols the trials and tribulations of Lincoln's life. Livingston's *Keep on Singing: A Ballad of Marion Anderson* (I) focuses on the triumphs of the great singer. As ballads are essentially story in song, many modern vocalists express themselves through ballads.

Verse Novels

Verse novels are another way to tell a story through poetry. Like ballads and other narrative poems, verse novels tell stories through poetry but most often consist of a series of one- or two-page poems rather than a single long poem The individual poems within the verse novel may be narrative themselves, but often they are not. Rather, the story is constructed through the arrangement and accumulation of emotions and events presented in individual poems, usually through the first-person voice of one or more characters. The immediacy inherent in first-person narration makes the poems intensely emotional.

There is some controversy about whether verse novels are really poetry. They certainly resemble poetry, with condensed language saturated with poetic devices. Campbell (2004) points out that the rhythms found in verse novels are more often that of ordinary speech than of formal metrics, but this is true of much other poetry as well. The best verse novels go well beyond the criticism of being merely prose chopped into short lines.

Verse novels, like so many other literary forms, do not fit neatly under one general category. They do all tell a story, but vary widely within that description. Some verse novels consist of free verse, as in Karen Hesse's *Out of the Dust* (A), Lindsay Lee Johnson's *Soul Moon Soup* (A), Andrea Cheng's *Where the Steps Were* (I), and Janet

Wong's *Minn and Jake* (I), but poets also explore various forms of poetry to great effect. Ron Koertge's *Shakespeare Bats Cleanup* (A), Sharon Creech's *Love That Dog* (I) and the sequel *Hate That Cat* (I), Nikki Grime's *Bronx Masquerade* (A), and Jacqueline Woodson's *Locomotion* (I) and the sequel *Peace, Locomotion* (I) contain poems in a variety of forms, with the narrators experimenting with a form as they are learning how poetry can help them come to terms with an emotional crisis in their lives. In *Love That Dog* (I) and *Hate That Cat* (I), the narrator, Jack, uses poems by various writers as models as he struggles to come to terms with the death of his beloved pet. His biggest inspiration is Walter Dean Myers's poem, "Love That Boy," and the writer behind it.

In *The Braid* (A), set in Scotland and Nova Scotia in the nineteenth century, Helen Frost uses narrative poems in two alternating voices—sisters separated by the North Atlantic—interspersed with "praise poems" that sing of something named in the narrative poems. The praise poems are linked by last and first lines, and the narrative poems are linked by the last words of each line and the first words of each line in the following poem. This complex structure echoes the closeness of the "braid" that the sisters carry with them as a symbol of their love. Elizabeth Alexander and Marilyn Nelson work within a sonnet form while also innovating on that form in *Miss Crandall's School for Young Ladies & Little Misses of Color* (A). Multiple voices of students and Floyd Cooper's illustrations combine to tell the story of the violent history of this school begun in Connecticut in the 1830s.

As discussed previously, Marilyn Nelson's *Carver: A Life in Poems* (A) tells the story of Carver's life through free verse poems, arranged to carry the narrative forward. The book is also biographical, so perhaps we might label it as a "biographical verse novel." Margarita Engle's *The Poet Slave of Cuba: A Biography of Juan Francisco Manzano* (A) is another riveting biography in verse. Stephanie Hemphill's Printz Honor–winning *Your Own, Sylvia: A Verse Portrait of Sylvia Plath* (A) is also biographical. Hemphill writes in a range of verse forms and voices, with approximately 150 poems arranged to give insight into the life and work of a great poet.

⋅ ⋅ LYRIC POETRY ⋅ ⋅

Rather than telling a story, lyric poetry is a statement of mood or feeling. It offers a direct and intense outpouring of thoughts and emotions. Any subjective, emotional poem can be lyric, but most lyric poems are melodic and are expressive of a single mood. As its Greek name indicates, a lyric was originally sung to the accompaniment of a lyre. Like ballads, lyric poems are songs, as is the first stanza of Eleanor Farjeon's "Morning Has Broken," from her book *The Children's Bells: A Selection of Poems* (P–I):

MORNING HAS BROKEN

Morning has broken
*   like the first morning*
Blackbird has spoken
*   like the first bird.*
Praise for the singing!
*   Praise for the morning!*
Praise for them, springing
*   fresh from the Word!*

ELEANOR FARJEON

Many poems are lyrical because of their singing quality and their expression of intense emotion. Songs are often the first lyric poems children hear. For *Hush Songs: African American Lullabies* (N–P–I), Joyce Carol Thomas collected traditional songs sung by cradling mothers and caring fathers to lull a child to sleep. A soothing melody sung with comforting words works its magic on sleepy children:

ALL THE PRETTY LITTLE HORSES

Hush-a-bye
Don't you cry
Go to sleep
My little baby

When you wake
You shall have
All the pretty little horses

ANONYMOUS

Walter Dean Myers captures the feelings and emotions of Harlem residents during the 1940s in *Here in Harlem: Poetry in Many Voices* (A), an excellent example of lyric poetry for advanced readers. Myers's descriptions of the pride, heartache, aspiration, determination, and elation felt by the people of Harlem resonate in the text; his words depict an emotional world in which the experiences of individuals shout—and sometimes whisper—across borders of time, speaking directly to modern readers' sensitivities. Eloise Greenfield offers primary-grade students lyric poetry in *Honey, I Love and Other Love Poems* (I).

⋅ ⋅ A VARIETY OF FORMS AND VOICES ⋅ ⋅

There are many poetic forms that are clearly defined, although poets alter conventional and traditional forms often as they manipulate word meanings. Poets experiment with form. In *A Wreath for Emmett Till* (A), Marilyn Nelson worked within the strict form of the sonnet, a fourteen-line poem with a strict rhyme scheme, in this case Petrarchan. Moreover, she wrote the poem as a "heroic crown" of sonnets, which contains fifteen interlinked sonnets, in which the last line of one becomes the first line of the next, with the final sonnet consisting of the first lines of the preceding fourteen. In her introduction to the book, she comments on how this form helped to insulate her, helped her to contain the sorrow and pain of the 1955 lynching of this young black man. Her choice of form was dictated by the content of the poem, as was Helen Frost's choice in *The Braid* (A), discussed earlier.

Form is the focus of recent anthologies that celebrate the rich variety of forms that are available to today's poets.

Concrete Poetry

We saw how Jane Yolen structured her skyscraper poem so that the shape contributed to meaning. Concrete poetry uses the appearance of words on a page to suggest or illustrate the poem's meaning. Children call these poems *shape* (or picture) *poems*. The actual physical form of the words depicts the subject, so the work illustrates itself, as shown below in Joan Bransfield Graham's "Popsicle." Note how Chris Raschka's torn-paper collage adds humor and whimsy but does not interfere with the shape of the poem itself.

"Popsicle," along with many other examples of shape poems, appears in Paul Janeczko's indispensable *A Poke in the I: A Collection of Concrete Poems* (I). *Doodle Dandies: Poems That Take Shape* by J. Patrick Lewis and *Splish Splash* and *Flicker Flash* by Joan Bransfield Graham (P) are also terrific resources for young readers discovering concrete poems. Joyce Sidman's *Meow Ruff* (P) is full of onomatopoeia and other poetic devices, and the words are hidden in Michelle Berg's innovative illustrations. John Grandits writes for older readers in *Blue Lipstick: Concrete Poems* (A), as he employs humor and inventiveness to explore being a high school girl.

Douglas Florian often uses form to convey meaning in his poems. When writing about a sawfish in his anthology

POPSICLE
Joan Bransfield Graham

```
P o p s i c l e
P o p s i c l e
t i c k l e
tongue fun
l i c k s i c l e
s t i c k s i c l e
p l e a s e
don't run
d r i p s i c l e
s l i p s i c l e
melt, melt
t r i c k y
s t o p s i c l e
p l o p s i c l e
hand   all
         s
         t
         i
         c
         k
         y
```

17

Chris Raschka's torn-paper collages add whimsy to Paul Janeczko's collection of concrete poems in A Poke in the I: A Collection of Concrete Poems.

Could do with legs!
Just think what we
Our pearly eggs.
Upstream we spawn
We somersault!
We vault!
We jump!
Our leaps astound!
We bound!
We spring!

The Salmon

Florian's words and image work together to evoke the movement of the fish in **In the Swim.**

In the Swim (I), he arranges his lines in a zigzag pattern to make his words "saw" down the page. His salmon poem hurtles diagonally upward across the page, reinforcing the fish's dramatic movement.

Limericks

Limerick, a form of light verse, has five lines and a rhyme scheme of a-a-b-b-a. Usually, the first, second, and fifth lines (which rhyme) have eight beats, whereas the third and fourth (which rhyme) have six. Limericks appeal to young readers because they poke fun and have a definite rhythm and rhyme. Edward Lear (1812–1888) is credited with making limericks popular, although he did not create the form. Limericks often make fun of people who take themselves too seriously.

Readers with a good sense of humor devour limericks. Some limericks have been passed down by word of mouth, becoming folklore when their original authorship is forgotten. One such is:

> A flea and a fly in a flue
> Were imprisoned, so what could they do?
> Said the fly, "Let us flee."
> Said the flea, "Let us fly."
> So they flew through a flaw in the flue.

ANONYMOUS

Many young readers enjoy Myra Cohn Livingston's **Lots of Limericks** (P–I), James Marshall's **Pocketful of Nonsense** (P-I), and Arnold Lobel's **The Book of Pigericks** (P–I).

Haiku and Cinquain

The word haiku means "beginning." Haiku frequently refer to nature, to a particular event happening at one moment, and to an attendant emotion or feeling, often of the most fragile and evanescent kind. This Japanese verse form consists of three lines and seventeen syllables: the first line contains five syllables; the second line, seven; and the third, five. A haiku usually focuses on an image that suggests a thought or emotion. Experimenting with the form is much more than counting syllables; meaning should be central. Paul Janeczko notes that haiku often feature nature in rural areas, but he sought out haiku that show the natural beauty of everyday city streets in his collection **Stone Bench in an Empty Park** (A).

Poets who master the haiku form sometimes stretch its boundaries by varying the five-seven-five syllable count while maintaining the essence of its meaning. Kobayashi Issa, a noted Japanese poet, demonstrates in **Don't Tell the Scarecrow: And Other Japanese Poems** (I) the beauty of haiku in these two variations:

Where can he be going
In the rain,
This snail?

Little knowing
The tree will soon be cut down
Birds are building their nests in it.

ISSA

G. Brian Karas arranged and illustrated haiku from Kobayashi Issa in *Today and Today* (P), a poetic view of one year in the life of a contemporary family. Other poetry books that help young readers explore haiku include Sylvia Cassedy and Kunihiro Suetake's *Red Dragonfly on My Shoulder* (P–I), Nikki Grimes and Javaka Steptoe's *Pocketful of Poems* (P–I), and Paul B. Janeczko and J. Patrick Lewis's *Wing Nuts: Screwy Haiku* (I).

Linda Sue Park uses the Korean variant of haiku in her book *Tap Dancing on the Roof: Sijo (Poems)* (I). The twenty-six poems in this anthology reflect the traditional sijo structure, three lines of fourteen to sixteen syllables each in which the first introduces the idea, the next lines develop it, and the final line gives it an unexpected or ironic twist. As Park says in an introductory note, however, sijo in English are sometimes divided into six shorter lines, and her collection contains both versions.

A cinquain consists of five unrhymed lines usually in the pattern of two, four, six, eight, and two syllables each.

A simplified variation has five lines with one, two, three, and four words, with the fifth line just one word that is a synonym for the title.

Haiku and cinquain are probably the first abstract poetry that young readers experience. Because the symbolism and imagery of haiku and cinquain are elusive for many children, students need to have wide exposure to other forms before they meet these. Even then, they need a lot of experience exploring the form.

Other Forms

Young readers enjoy reading and writing poems in a variety of other forms as well. Mask, or persona, poems are written from the point of view of an object or animal—anything that's not human. Myra Cohn Livingston writes from the point of view of her bed in "What My Bed Says" from *O Sliver of Liver and Other Poems* (I).

WHAT MY BED SAYS

You squirm and settle down in me
when the day goes.
I feel the ends of your toes
naked and free
from shoes and socks, and I cover
all the laughter and tears of your day.
Here in my snug world you stay,
and the dreams we discover

october

The wind rearranges the leaves,
as if to say, "Much better *there*,"
and coaxes others off their trees:
"It's lots more fun in the air."

Then it plays tag with a plastic bag,
and with one gust uncombs my hair!

Linda Sue Parker creates humor by personifying the wind in **Tap Dancing on the Roof: Sijo (Poems)**.

in the dark patterns of the night
make us feel as one.
Then comes another sun,
and its first light
tears us apart, for you wake and turn
from me, battered, wrinkled, in folds.
Leave then—see what the day holds
and share it with me when you return.

M Y R A   C O H N   L I V I N G S T O N

Paul Janeczko's collection **Dirty Laundry Pile: Poems in Different Voices** (P), illustrated by Melissa Sweet, offers many examples of mask poems.

Janeczko is also the editor of a selection of apostrophe poems, poems addressed to things such as bugs, statues, buildings, or toothbrushes. **Hey, You!: Poems to Skyscrapers, Mosquitoes, and Other Fun Things** (I), illustrated by Robert Rayevsky, presents humorous, whimsical, and serious poems such as Rebecca Kai Dotlich's "Whispers to the Wall," which is about the Vietnam Veterans Memorial.

W H I S P E R S   T O   T H E   W A L L

You are him from Maine,
him, from Montana,
and every him from sea
to sea and back.
Stewart, Kelly, York:
you are all of those,
who shrimped on boats,
flew planes
studied, wrote,
collected, kissed.

The brave ones spill
across your face;
an indelible trace
of young sons
who played baseball,
cards, guitars.
Thompson, Sanchez, Vance;
you know their favorite dish,
their first romance.

On silent nights, do they tell you
of boyhoods and Beatles,
bruised knees and hearts,
birthdays missed . . .
those who shrimped on boats,
flew planes,
studied, wrote,
collected, kissed.

R E B E C C A   K A I   D O T L I C H

J. Patrick Lewis and Paul B. Janeczko teamed up to compose a series of renga, or linked verse, in **Birds on a Wire** (I), a clever introduction to this specialized form that young readers will want to try. Janeczko's **A Kick in the Head: An Everyday Guide to Poetic Forms** (I), with illustrations by Chris Raschka, is a collective specialized anthology that also offers examples and explanations of a variety of poetic forms. Here, we take a close look at this outstanding collection.

A   C L O S E   L O O K   A T

A Kick in the Head: An Everyday Guide to Poetic Forms

As Janeczko states in his introduction, poets enjoy the challenge that the rules of particular forms provide. This pleasure comes from both following and breaking the rules to new effect. Young readers also enjoy figuring out how things work, and this collection demonstrates just that with twenty-nine different poetic forms. The book begins with simple forms such as the couplet, and moves to more complex forms such as sonnets and pantoums. With each, Janeczko presents an appropriate example and a simple, brief statement of the "rule" for the form. This clear structure allows young readers to know exactly what to expect as they turn the pages. The design is such that the name of the form and a small hand-drawn diagram that represents it appears in the upper outside corner of the pages. The limerick, for example, is depicted by a bouncing ball leaving a trail of five lines, with the third and fourth lines shorter than the first, second, and fifth— just like a limerick!

Janeczko's selections are often humorous and always engaging. For the sonnet form, for example, he presents a classic Shakespearean sonnet and pairs that with a contemporary version of the *same* sonnet. By doing so, he makes the sonnet form accessible to contemporary, young readers. The explanatory note indicates that there are two forms of the sonnet, explains the form presented here, and links it to the previously described forms of couplet and quatrain. Gary Soto's "Ode to Pablo's Tennis Shoes," as an example of an ode, is a choice much more appealing than the classic Grecian urn.

Chris Raschka's bright watercolor and torn-paper collages capture the essence of the poetic examples. On the page on which an "epitaph" poem is explained, for example, the illustration for the two-word first example depicts the brief poem on a tombstone. The second example, "An Epitaph for a Book Editor" by J. Patrick Lewis, is illustrated with a tombstone covered with editing marks. This anthology combines inspired choice, eye-catching,

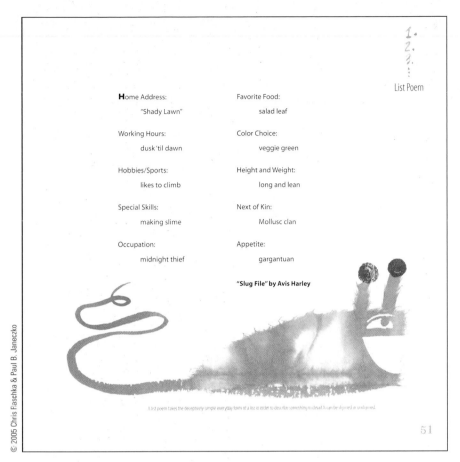

Home Address:

　　"Shady Lawn"

Working Hours:

　　dusk 'til dawn

Hobbies/Sports:

　　likes to climb

Special Skills:

　　making slime

Occupation:

　　midnight thief

Favorite Food:

　　salad leaf

Color Choice:

　　veggie green

Height and Weight:

　　long and lean

Next of Kin:

　　Mollusc clan

Appetite:

　　gargantuan

List Poem

"Slug File" by Avis Harley

A list poem takes the deceptively simple everyday form of a list in order to describe something in detail. It can be rhymed or unrhymed.

51

*In **A Kick in the Head**, Avis Harley's humor works well with Chris Raschka's whimsy in this list poem.*

meaningful illustrations, and outstanding design, and is very appealing to intermediate-grade readers who are interested in figuring out how poetry works.

Like Janeczko's *A Kick in the Head: An Everyday Guide to Poetic Forms* (I), Avis Harley's *Fly with Poetry: An ABC of Poetry* (I), *Leap into Poetry: More ABC's of Poetry* (I), and *The Monarch's Progress: Poems with Wings* (I) present clever examples of a variety of forms with brief explanatory notes that help readers—and writers—learn the conventions of the forms.

Poetry in the Classroom

Having a good collection of poetry available for young readers is the first step in helping them to know and love poetry. Although knowing and loving poetry has its own internal rewards, there are also academic benefits to engaging with poetry.

Poetry draws young readers into listening. Students pay attention to poetry because it plays with the sounds of language; uses interesting, intriguing words; and deals with fascinating topics. Poetry increases readers' language resources. We all learn the language we hear; if we hear ordinary conversational language, we will use ordinary conversational language when we speak. If we hear poetic language, we will use poetic language in our writing and speaking.

Poetry is excellent material for developing phonemic awareness, the ability to segment and manipulate speech sounds. Children learn to discriminate sounds, hear parts of words, and make connections between sounds they hear and letters they see. Because poetry and verse are often patterned, predictable, and repetitive, children know what a word should be and probably is going to be. When they recognize beginning consonants, they are likely to say the right word. Alliteration and rhyme help beginning readers decode print.

Poetry helps students learn how to write by giving them a storehouse of words and patterns to draw from

Profiles

Barbara Juster Esbensen, 1994

As a child growing up in Madison, Wisconsin, I read everything in sight and drew pictures on anything that looked like it needed decoration. I wrote stories with my two best friends, and we all intended to be writers. When I was fourteen-and-a-half, my teacher looked at a poem I had written and told me I was "a writer." When she introduced me to poets like Amy Lowell, Stephen Vincent Benét, and Emily Dickinson, she literally changed my life. Until then, I had not known that it was possible to use words in such exciting ways.

What impressed the NCTE Poetry Award Committee about Barbara Juster Esbensen's work was "the clarity of [her] images, the differentness of [her] images" (Greenlaw, 1994, p. 544). When asked if her work as an artist influenced her poetic images, Esbensen said, "I'm sure that I'm looking all the time. I'm sure of that because I am an artist, and that's what I have really been doing all my life. I'm a looker! And I'm an exaggerator . . . I tell children you are allowed to say things that are absolutely off-the-wall in poetry" (p. 544). Esbensen's poetry anthologies for children include *Cold Stars and Fireflies*, *Words with Wrinkled Knees*, and *Who Shrank My Grandmother's House?*.

Eloise Greenfield, 1997

There's a desperate need for more black literature for children, for a large body of literature in which black children can see themselves and their lives and history reflected. I want to do my share in building it.

Eloise Greenfield has played a significant role in contributing to African American literature in several genres; her poetry books are frequently cited by teachers and scholars. She received ALA Notable citations, the Coretta Scott King Award, and the Mary McLeod Bethune Award for her work, particularly for *Honey, I Love and Other Love Poems* and *Nathaniel Talking*. "[Greenfield's] poetry reflects or comments on the specific cultural experience of growing up African American in this society," noted Rudine Sims Bishop (1997, p. 632), "but the topics and themes—love, family, neighbors, dreams, the joy of living, the resilience of the human spirit—reach out to all children."

X. J. Kennedy, 2000

Rhyme and meter have been in the doghouse of adult poetry lately, and some have claimed that children, too, don't like such old-fangled devices. But children do. This makes me glad, for I have never been able to write what is termed 'free verse'. I love the constant surprise one encounters in rhyming things, and the driving urge of a steady beat.

For years, X. J. Kennedy wrote poetry for children but kept it in the bottom drawer of his desk until Myra Cohn Livingston asked him to send some of it to her editor, Margaret McElderry. McElderry published his first book of poetry for children, *One Winter Night in August*. Since then, Kennedy has authored more than a dozen collections of verse for children. Daniel L. Darigan (2001) observed, "[Kennedy's] topics are timely and accessible, his use of the language sophisticated, and his humor leads children and adoring adults into a genre that often gets overlooked and ignored. Children who read his collections as well as his anthologies will receive a better understanding of what poetry is and the joys it holds for them" (p. 298).

---

in their own writing. Playing with various poetic forms allows students to explore various options. This often pushes students to work within a structure, something that is both challenging and reassuring. The clearly visible framework of poetry helps students understand.

Poetry helps students learn to think by showing them how to look at their world in a new way. It presents fresh perspectives on life and upends stereotyped ways of thinking. Poetry builds on paradox, ambiguity, and contradictions; it sets these features in stark relief so they become apparent to naive readers.

Building a poetry collection takes time. Begin with those books that speak to you as a reader, knowing that you will want to add many more based on your students' needs and interests. All readers have personal favorites they like to read from, poets they return to again and again. Just as some books are clearly for younger or older readers—because the way the content is presented helps determine the audience—poetry can also appeal to a wide range of ages. Just as young readers vary widely in their interests, abilities, and experiences, your collection should do the same.

Profiles

Mary Ann Hoberman, 2003

*V*isual language . . . is for writers. So are word games and word play. Just think of what you can do with words. . . . Each time you discover the perfect word for your purpose, each time you shape a sentence, each time you awaken a reader's imagination, you will feel fulfilled. (Quoted in Ernst & McClure, 2004)

Mary Ann Hoberman is a master of rhyme, rhythm, and wordplay. She began publishing for children in 1957 with *All My Shoes Come in Twos*. Since then, Hoberman has created lasting favorites, including *A House Is a House for Me*; *Fathers, Mothers, Sisters, Brothers: A Collection of Family Poems*; and *The Llama Who Had No Pajama: 100 Favorite Poems*.

Nikki Grimes, 2006

*W*hen I grow up," I thought, "I'll write books about children who look and feel like me." (Quoted in *Something About the Author*, 2007)

Poet, novelist, and picturebook author, Nikki Grimes has received many honors as the author of approximately fifty published books. In most of these she did, indeed, write about children like the child she had been. Her poetry speaks to the heart in stark yet beautiful language. She began publishing for young readers in 1977 and is beloved for her books of poetry, which include *Meet Danitra Brown*; *Danitra Brown Leaves Town*; *Danitra Brown, Class Clown*; *My Man Blue*; *A Pocketful of Poems*; *Bronx Masquerade*; *It's Raining Laughter*; *What Is Goodbye?*; and *Oh, Brother!*.

Lee Bennett Hopkins, 2009

*P*oetry and I fit together. I can't imagine being without it. Were it in my power I would give poetry to every single child everywhere. (Meet the Author/Illustrator Archives, www.booksense.com)

Lee Bennett Hopkins is a prolific anthologist and writer. His many anthologies offer children the opportunity to experience wonderful poetry written about a variety of topics and ideas. His autobiography in poetry, *Been to Yesterdays: Poems of a Life*, received the Christopher Medal and a Golden Kite Honor. Among his latest anthologies are *America at War: Poems Selected by Lee Bennett Hopkins* and *Sky Magic*. Mr. Hopkins has also endowed two awards for poets, the Lee Bennett Hopkins Poetry Award, presented annually since 1983, and the Lee Bennett Hopkins/International Reading Association Promising Poet Award, presented every three years since 1995.

Unless otherwise noted, the opening quotations for these profiles are from the poets' acceptance speeches for the NCTE poetry award. (The speech is given in November of the year the award is received.)

Reading reviews in professional journals and noting the winners of the NCTE poetry award will keep you up-to-date on poetry for children. Look at the poetry books that have won awards such as the Caldecott, Newbery, or Printz, and also look at Children's Choices or Young Adult Choices to see what young readers are enjoying. There are also some wonderful resources available that are full of ideas for exploring poetry with young readers. These are listed in Figure 4.3.

Researchers have studied the kinds of poems young readers like, as well as the kinds of poems teachers like to read to them. Not surprisingly, the poems they hear influence what kinds of poems they like. Research (Fisher & Natarella, 1982; Terry, 1974) found that children in their studies liked

- Contemporary poems
- Poems they could understand
- Narrative poems
- Poems with rhyme, rhythm, and sound
- Poems that related to their personal experiences

However, what young readers prefer and what they can learn to appreciate in the company of others and an enthusiastic teacher are often very different.

McClure (1985) found that classroom experiences change children's responses to poetry. In supportive environments, children respond more positively to a wider variety of poetry, showing that teachers' attitudes and practices make a tremendous difference. In other words, what you do with poetry in the classroom determines how your students respond to poetry.

A case study focusing on the classroom poetry experiences of a fourth- and fifth-grade class in the Midwest also supports the idea that children may change their poetry preferences when their school experiences support their exploration of the genre (Hansen, 2004). After six months of classroom poetry experiences, during which

Figure **4.3**

Resources for the Poetry Teacher

Appelt, Kathi, *Poems from Homeroom: A Writer's Place to Start* (A)

Booth, David, and Bill Moore, *Poems Please! Sharing Poetry with Children* (P–I)

Brown, Bill, and Malcolm Glass, *Important Words: A Book for Poets and Writers* (I–A)

Chatton, Barbara, *Using Poetry across the Curriculum* (P–I)

Cullinan, Bernice, Marilyn Scala, and Virginia Schroder, with Ann Lovett, *Three Voices: An Invitation to Poetry across the Curriculum* (P–I)

Denman, Gregory, *When You've Made It Your Own: Teaching Poetry to Young People* (I–A)

Esbensen, Barbara Juster, *A Celebration of Bees: Endless Opportunities for Inspiring Children to Write Poetry* (P–I)

Fletcher, Ralph, *Poetry Matters: Writing a Poem from the Inside Out* (P–I)

Fox, Mem, *Radical Reflections: Passionate Opinions on Teaching, Learning, and Living* (P–I)

Graves, Donald, *Explore Poetry: The Reading/Writing Teacher's Companion* (P–I)

Grossman, Florence, *Listening to the Bells: Learning to Read Poetry by Writing Poetry* (I–A)

Harrison, David L., and Bernice Cullinan, *Easy Poetry Lessons That Dazzle and Delight* (P–I)

Heard, Georgia, *Awakening the Heart: Exploring Poetry in Elementary and Middle School* (I–A)

_____, *For the Good of the Earth and Sun: Teaching Poetry* (I–A)

_____, *Writing toward Home: Tales and Lessons to Find Your Way* (I–A)

Hewitt, Geof, *Today You Are My Favorite Poet: Writing Poems with Teenagers* (A)

Hopkins, Lee Bennett, *Pass the Poetry, Please* (I)

_____, *Pauses: Autobiographical Reflections of 101 Creators of Children's Books* (P–I)

Janeczko, Paul, *The Place My Words Are Looking For: What Poets Say About and Through Their Work* (I–A)

_____, *Poetry from A to Z: A Guide for Young Writers* (I–A)

_____, *Poetspeak: In Their Work, About Their Work: A Selection* (I–A)

_____, *Seeing the Blue Between: Advice and Inspiration for Young Poets* (I–A)

Kennedy, X. J., and Dorothy M. Kennedy, *Knock at a Star: A Child's Introduction to Poetry* (P)

Kuskin, Karla, *Dogs and Dragons, Trees and Dreams* (P)

Larrick, Nancy, *Let's Do a Poem: Introducing Poetry to Children Through Listening, Singing, Chanting, Impromptu Choral Reading, Body Movement, Dance, and Dramatization; Including 98 Favorite Songs and Poems* (P–I)

Livingston, Myra Cohn, *Climb into the Bell Tower* (I–A)

_____, *Poem-Making: Ways to Begin Writing Poetry* (I–A)

McClure, Amy, with Peggy Harrison and Sheryl Reed, *Sunrises and Songs: Reading and Writing Poetry in an Elementary Classroom* (I–A)

Nye, Naomi Shihab, *Salting the Ocean: 100 Poems by Young Poets* (A)

---

students explored poetry with enthusiastic teachers, students' appreciation for varied techniques and devices such as free verse and simile increased. They also became more articulate about what they liked and disliked about specific poems after participating in the classroom poetry experiences.

Hearing students relate in their own words how their poetry preferences broadened as a result of their school experience offers the most compelling reasons to bring poetry into the classroom. "I used to only like to read funny poems," Sam reflected during his last poetry session, "but now I like to read and write ALL poetry." Ty

also felt changed by the classroom poetry sessions: "I used to hate poetry and now I know it's more than just . . . roses are red violets are blue." Many students shared Ty's feeling that learning about the different kinds of poetry helped them like the genre more. Jin felt that this understanding directly affected his attitude toward writing poetry: "I never liked poetry but now I have a lot more interest in it because I know that there are many different kinds of poetry and so there are a lot of choices to write a poem so you have a big selection." Pat also noted, "I've learned about the names of a specific style and onomatopoeia, alliteration and now I like it more."

Poetry grows increasingly popular as more poetry is published in appealing formats. The International Reading Association's (IRA) annual Children's Choices lists show that children consistently select poetry books as among their favorites. Delight in poetry prevails amid opportunities to choose from hundreds of other picture-books, novels, and nonfiction.

We may not know why a particular poem appeals to young readers, but we do know that poems read aloud with enthusiasm are likely to become their favorites. Teachers' selections soon become children's choices. Results of the IRA Teachers' Choices project show that teachers frequently choose poetry as their favorite books for teaching. Teachers choose poems that reflect our multicultural heritage, poems with beautiful language, and poems that help them teach subject-area content. When teachers select poems they like, their enthusiasm is apparent to their students.

Immerse, or as poet Ralph Fletcher (2000) says, "marinate" students in poetry—lots of poetry over lots of time. Students need to feel comfortable using the books you have gathered; talk about the books and display their covers to attract readers. Shelve poetry with other books by the same author or about the same subject. Your students need time and space to browse, to pull out several

Teaching Idea **4.3**

Fifteen Minutes, Fifty Poems!

Teachers who write poetry have students who write poetry. Let them see you write! This teaching idea is perfect for those fifteen-minute intervals between specials or as a warm-up activity before a language arts lesson. Teachers find that it works well with both primary and more advanced students.

Before the Lesson

✿ Be sure each student has a poetry notebook (a blank composition notebook) and a pencil.

✿ Prepare a poetry notebook for yourself as well.

✿ Place an overhead projector in a location where all students will be able to see its projection from their desks.

During the Lesson

✿ Invite students to sit at their desks with their poetry notebooks and pencils.

✿ Dim the lights to create a "writing" mood.

✿ Tell students that you have a poem on your mind; invite them to watch as you try to capture it in words.

✿ Talk out loud as you project your writing on the overhead projector. Scribble out words. Sketch ideas in the margins. Consider line breaks and talk about how you will use them to convey meaning.

✿ Keep writing, even if you are not sure what words will come next. Remember, you are modeling for students what to do if they become "stuck" while writing. Demonstrate how to play with language until your words match your thoughts.

✿ Stop at a point when you are visibly excited about what you will next compose. Tell students that your poem simply cannot wait to emerge on paper and that you must spend the next ten minutes writing silently in your poetry notebook.

✿ Invite students to write poems in their poetry notebooks as you write in yours.

✿ Continue writing in your poetry notebook as students work independently. It will be tempting to circulate to observe students at work, but students need to observe *you* writing. When they glance up from their notebooks during moments of frustration, they will need to see that their teacher is a writer—and that writers persevere, even when the words do not come easily. They will also need to see you smile to yourself when you write something "really good"; they will do the same when they write words that please them. Your actions teach your students how to *be* poets—keep your pencil moving!

After the Lesson

✿ When students ask you (and they most likely will) if they can bring their poetry notebooks outside for recess or home for the weekend, say yes! Your fifteen minutes of modeling will lead students to create a multitude of poems that they may share with you, with friends, or with the class. The more you model, the more your students will write. The more poems your students write, the more poetic devices and forms they will notice in the poems they read. It is a cycle that sweeps children into exploring and experimenting with language. Teachers have the power to set the cycle in motion.

Resources for Teachers

Graves, Donald, *Explore Poetry: The Reading/Writing Teacher's Companion*

Grossman, Florence, *Listening to the Bells: Learning to Read Poetry by Writing Poetry*

McClure, Amy, with Peggy Harrison and Sheryl Reed, *Sunrises and Songs: Reading and Writing Poetry in an Elementary Classroom* volumes at once, and to compare poems or look for favorites. Give students time to browse through the poetry collection during a free period; encourage them to read poetry for their independent reading.

Young readers learn to love poetry when they explore it freely. Unfortunately, some learn to dislike poetry because a teacher insists they search for elusive meanings or rhyme schemes that make no sense to them. Close attention to students' comments can supply a basis for thought-provoking questions that will lead them to discover the substance of poetry for themselves. The object is to develop a positive response to the music of words; detailed analysis detracts from the splendor. Explanation that destroys appreciation is no improvement over misconceptions. Appropriate discussions of poetry take readers back into the experience of a poem, not away from it. Young readers, however, do love to discover how things—like poetry—work, so let their questions be your guide.

Poetry is best understood when it is read aloud, and students need to understand how to read this new style of written language. Work with students to teach them how to read poetry aloud; it is not the same as reading prose. Illustrate the differences by reading poetry aloud in a number of ways. Read it by pausing at the end of every line regardless of the punctuation. Then read it from a prose format to demonstrate the impact of line breaks.

Read poetry in a manner that highlights the meaning. Listening to a poem read aloud well brings insight into how poetry works, what a poem might mean to another reader, techniques for oral interpretation, and strategies for reading that can be employed silently. Learning these techniques gives young readers tools for their own reading; they develop an understanding of the importance of how a poem sounds. Teaching Idea 4.3 offers ideas for helping students explore poetry.

Poets themselves have good suggestions for young readers. When Eve Merriam accepted the NCTE poetry award, she encouraged children with these words:

Read a lot. Sit down with anthologies and decide which pleases you. Copy out your favorites in your own handwriting. Buy a notebook and jot down images and descriptions. Be specific; use all the senses. Use your whole body as you write. It might even help sometimes to stand up and move with your words. Don't be afraid of copying a form or convention, especially in the beginning. And, to give yourself scope and flexibility, remember: It doesn't always have to rhyme.

You don't need gimmicks, elaborate plans, or detailed instructions. You do need lots of poetry books, time to savor them, and pleasurable poetry experiences.

Poetry is a valuable tool for fully realizing life's many and varied experiences. It allows us to participate in the imaginative experience of others and thereby better understand our own experiences. The more readers participate, the more they create, and the more personal and enjoyable the experience of poetry becomes. The rewards are more than worth the effort.

• • • • SUMMARY • • • •

Listening to, reading, and writing poetry helps us learn about the world, about ourselves, and about the power and potential of language. Poets write about everything, using devices of sound and meaning to present their own unique visions. Poetry comes in varied forms and is available in many formats. Young readers are attracted to poetry, and teachers can build on this attraction, providing experiences with poetry that will lead children to enjoy poetry and thus to consider how poetry works. Children who experience a poetry-rich environment will become lifelong readers and writers of poetry.

Although books are arranged primarily under age of intended audience, many books of poetry can be enjoyed across ages.

✳ Indicates some aspect of diversity

Poems for Preschool Readers

✳ Bryan, Ashley, *Sing to the Sun: Poems and Pictures* (1992)

Calmenson, Stephanie, *Kindergarten Kids: Riddles, Rebuses, Wiggles, Giggles, and More!* (2005)

Cullinan, Bernice, Andi MacLeod, and Marc Nadel, *A Jar of Tiny Stars: Poems by NCTE Award-Winning Poets* (1996)

✳ Delacre, Lulu, *Arrorró, Mi Niño: Latino Lullabies and Gentle Games* (2004)

Field, Eugene, *Wynken, Blynken and Nod* (1889)

Hoberman, Mary Ann, *A House Is a House for Me* (1978)

_____, *Fathers, Mothers, Sisters, Brothers: A Collection of Family Poems* (1991)

Johnson, David A., *Snow Sounds: An Onomatopoeic Story* (2006)

Kennedy, X. J., and Dorothy Kennedy, *Talking Like the Rain* (1991)

McCord, David, *One at a Time* (1974)

☀ Mora, Pat, *The Desert Is My Mother/El Desierto Es Mi Madre* (1994)

Prelutsky, Jack, *Circus* (1974)

☀ Thomas, Joyce Carol, *Hush Songs: African American Lullabies* (2000)

Worth, Valerie, *All the Small Poems and Fourteen More* (1994)

Poems for Primary-Grade Readers

☀ Adoff, Arnold, *Black Is Brown Is Tan* (1973)

☀ Alarcon, Francisco X., *Animal Poems of the Iguazu/Animalario del Iguazu* (2008)

☀ Cassedy, Sylvia, *Red Dragonfly on My Shoulder: Haiku* (1992)

Ciardi, John, *You Read to Me, I'll Read to You* (1962)

Elliott, David, *On the Farm* (2008)

Farjeon, Eleanor, *Poems for Children* (1951)

Fisher, Aileen, *Always Wondering* (1991)

Florian, Douglas, *Summersaults* (2002)

_____, *Autumblings* (2003)

_____, *Winter Eyes* (1999)

_____, *Handsprings* (2006)

George, Kristine O'Connell, *Fold Me a Poem* (2005)

_____, *Little Dog and Duncan* (2002)

_____, *Little Dog Poems* (1999)

Goldstein, Bobbye, *Inner Chimes: Poems on Poetry* (1992)

Graham, Joan Bransfield, *Flicker Flash* (1999)

_____, *Splish Splash* (1994)

☀ Greenfield, Eloise, *Honey, I Love and Other Poems* (1998)

☀ _____, *Nathaniel Talking* (1988)

☀ _____, *Night on Neighborhood Street* (1991)

Greenfield, Eloise, and Jan Spivey Gilchrist, *The Friendly Four* (2006)

☀ Grimes, Nikki, *Come Sunday* (1996)

☀ _____, *Danitra Brown, Class Clown* (2005)

☀ _____, *A Dime a Dozen* (1998)

☀ _____, *Hopscotch Love: A Family Treasury of Love Poems* (1999)

☀ _____, *Meet Danitra Brown* (1994)

☀ _____, *My Man Blue: Poems* (1999)

☀ _____, *Stepping Out with Grandma Mac* (2000)

☀ _____, *Pocketful of Poems* (1957)

Hopkins, Lee Bennett, *Good Books, Good Times!* (1990)

_____, *Side by Side: Poems to Read Together* (1988)

☀ Issa, Kobayashi, et al., *Today and Today* (2007)

Janeckzo, Paul B., *Dirty Laundry Pile: Poems in Different Voices* (2001)

Kuskin, Karla, *Moon, Have You Met My Mother?: The Collected Poems of Karla Kuskin* (2003)

_____, *Soap Soup and Other Verses* (1992)

Lobel, Arnold, *The Book of Pigericks: Pig Limericks* (1983)

Marshall, James, *Pocketful of Nonsense* (2003)

McCord, David, *One at a Time* (1974)

Moore, Lilian, *I Thought I Heard the City* (1969)

_____, *Something New Begins: New and Selected Poems* (1982)

☀ Newsome, Effie Lee, *Wonders: The Best Children's Poems of Effie Lee Newsome*, compiled by Rudine Sims Bishop (1999)

Prelutsky, Jack, *Circus* (1974)

Sidman, Joyce, *Meow Ruff* (2006)

☀ Smith, Hope Anita, *Keeping the Night Watch* (2008)

Stevenson, James, *Candy Corn: Poems* (1999)

_____, *Cornflakes: Poems* (2000)

_____, *Popcorn: Poems* (1998)

_____, *Sweet Corn: Poems* (1995)

☀ Thomas, Joyce Carol, *Brown Honey in Broomwheat Tea* (1993)

☀ _____, *Gingerbread Days* (1995)

_____, *I Have Heard of a Land* (1998)

☀ _____, *Hush Songs: African American Lullabies* (2000)

Worth, Valerie, *All the Small Poems* (1987)

_____, *Peacock and Other Poems* (2002)

_____, *Animal Poems* (2007)

Yolen, Jane, *Alphabestiary: Animal Poems from A to Z* (1995)

_____, *Color Me a Rhyme: Nature Poems for Young People* (2000)

_____, *Sky Scrape/City Scape: Poems of City Life* (1996)

☀ _____, *Street Rhymes around the World* (1992)

_____, *Fine Feathered Friends* (2004)

Poems for Intermediate Grade Readers

Adoff, Arnold, *Chocolate Dreams: Poems* (1989)

_____, *Eats: Poems* (1979)

_____, *Sports Pages* (1986)

_____, *Street Music: City Poems* (1995)

☀ Cassedy, Sylvia, *Red Dragonfly on My Shoulder: Haiku* (1992)

☀ Cheng, Andrea, *Where the Steps Were* (2008)

Creech, Sharon, *Love That Dog* (2001)

_____, *Hate That Cat* (2008)

Esbensen, Barbara Juster, *Dance with Me* (1995)

_____, *Echoes for the Eye: Poems to Celebrate Patterns in Nature* (1996)

_____, *Who Shrank My Grandmother's House?: Poems of Discovery* (1992)

_____, *Words with Wrinkled Knees: Animal Poems* (1986)

Farjeon, Eleanor, *The Children's Bells* (1951)

Fleischman, Paul, *Joyful Noise: Poems for Two Voices* (1988)

_____, *Big Talk: Poems for Four Voices* (2000)

_____, *I Am Phoenix: Poems for Two Voices* (1985)

Florian, Douglas, *Beast Feast* (1998)

_____, *Bing Bang Boing: Poems and Drawings* (1994)

_____, *In the Swim: Poems and Paintings* (1997)

_____, *Laugh-eteria: Poems and Drawings* (1999)

_____, *Mammalabilia: Poems and Paintings* (2000)

_____, *Summersaults: Poems and Paintings* (2002)

_____, *On the Wing: Bird Poems and Paintings* (1996)

Froman, Robert, *Seeing Things: A Book of Poems* (1974)

George, Kristine O'Connell, *Toasting Marshmallows: Camping Poems* (2001)

_____, *Swimming Upstream: Middle School Poems* (2002)

_____, *Hummingbird Nest: A Journal of Poems* (2004)

☀ Giovanni, Nikki, *Knoxville, Tennessee* (1994)

☀ _____, *Spin a Soft Black Song: Poems for Children* (1985)

☀ Gollub, Matthew, *Cool Melons—Turn to Frogs! The Life and Poems of Issa* (2005)

☀ Greenfield, Eloise, *Honey, I Love and Other Love Poems* (1972)

☀ Grimes, Nikki, *Pocketful of Poems* (1957)

_____, *What Is Goodbye?* (2004)

Harley, Avis, *Fly with Poetry: An ABC of Poetry* (2000)

_____, *Leap into Poetry* (2001)

_____, *The Monarch's Progress: Poems with Wings* (2008)

Harrison, David, *The Boy Who Counted Stars: Poems* (1994)

_____, *Somebody Catch My Homework: Poems* (1993)

_____, *A Thousand Cousins: Poems of Family Life* (1996)

_____, *Easy Poetry Lessons That Dazzle and Delight* (1999)

Heard, Georgia, *Creatures of Earth, Sea, and Sky: Poems* (1992)

Hopkins, Lee Bennett, *Hand in Hand: An American History through Poetry* (1994)

_____, *Home to Me: Poems across America* (2002)

_____, *My America: A Poetry Atlas of the United States* (2000)

_____, *Sky Magic* (2008)

✴ Issa, Kobayashi, *et al. Don't Tell the Scarecrow* (1969)

Janeczko, Paul B., *Brickyard Summer: Poems* (1989)

_____, *Dirty Laundry Pile: Poems in Different Voices* (2001)

_____, *Hey, You! Poems to Skyscrapers, Mosquitoes, and Other Fun Things* (2007)

_____, *A Kick in the Head: An Everyday Guide to Poetic Forms* (2005)

_____, *A Poke in the I: A Collection of Concrete Poems* (2001)

_____, *That Sweet Diamond: Baseball Poems* (1998)

Janeczko, Paul B., and J. Patrick Lewis, *Wing Nuts: Screwy Haiku* (2006)

_____, *Hey, You!: Poems to Skyscrapers, Mosquitoes, and Other Fun Things* (2007)

Kennedy, X. J., *Exploding Gravy: Poems to Make You Laugh* (2002)

_____, *The Forgetful Wishing Well: Poems for Young People* (1985)

_____, *Fresh Brats* (1990)

Kurtz, Jane, *River Friendly, River Wild* (1999)

✴ Lewis, J. Patrick, *Black Swan White Crow: Haiku* (1994)

_____, *Doodle Dandies: Poems that Take Shape* (1998)

_____, *A Hippopotamusn't and Other Animal Verses* (1990)

_____, *Ridicholas Nicholas: Animal Poems* (1995)

_____, *Scien-Trickery: Riddles in Science* (2004)

_____, *Mathmatickles!* (2007)

Lewis, J. Patrick, and Paul B. Janeczko, *Birds on a Wire: Or a Jewel Tray of Stars* (2008)

Livingston, Myra Cohn, *Lots of Limericks* (1991)

_____, *Abraham Lincoln: A Man for All the People* (1993)

_____, *Keep on Singing: A Ballad of Marion Anderson* (1994)

_____, *Sky Songs* (1984)

_____, *Space Songs* (1988)

Lobel, Arnold, *The Book of Pigericks: Pig Limericks* (1983)

Marshall, James, *Pocketful of Nonsense* (2003)

✴ Medina, Jane, *My Name Is Jorge: On Both Sides of the River* (1999)

Merriam, Eve, *It Doesn't Always Have to Rhyme* (1964)

Morrison, Lillian, *The Sidewalk Racer and Other Poems of Sports and Motion* (1977)

Myers, Christopher, *Jabberwocky* (2007)

✴ Myers, Walter Dean, *Brown Angels* (1993)

✴ _____, *Harlem* (1997)

✴ _____, *Jazz* (2006)

Park, Linda Sue, *Tap Dancing on the Roof: Sijo (Poems)* (2007)

Prelutsky, Jack, *Beneath a Blue Umbrella* (1987)

_____, *Dragons Are Singing Tonight* (1993)

_____, *For Laughing Out Loud: Poems to Tickle Your Funnybone* (1991)

_____, *The Frogs Wore Red Suspenders: Rhymes* (2007)

_____, *The Headless Horseman Rides Tonight* (1992)

✴ _____, *If Not for the Cat: Haiku* (2004)

_____, *My Dog May Be a Genius* (2008)

_____, *The New Kid on the Block* (1984)

_____, *A. Nonny Mouse Writes Again!: Poems* (1993)

_____, *A Pizza the Size of the Sun: Poems* (1996)

_____, *Scranimals* (2006)

Scieszka, Jon, *Math Curse* (1995)

_____, *Science Verse* (2004).

Sidman, Joyce, *Butterfly Eyes and Other Secrets of the Meadow: Poems* (2006)

Silverstein, Shel, *Falling Up: Poems and Drawings* (1996)

_____, *A Light in the Attic* (1981)

_____, *Where the Sidewalk Ends* (1974)

✴ Sneve, Virginia Driving Hawk, *Dancing Teepees: Poems of American Indian Youth* (1989)

Steig, Jeanne, *Consider the Lemming* (1988)

_____, *Tales from Gizzard's Grill* (2004)

✴ Thomas, Joyce Carol, *The Blacker the Berry* (2008)

_____, *Hush Songs: African American Lullabies* (2000)

Walker, Alice, *Why War Is Never a Good Idea* (2007)

Willard, Nancy, *A Visit to William Blake's Inn: Poems of Innocent and Experienced Travelers* (1981)

Wong, Janet S., *Behind the Wheel: Poems about Driving* (1999)

_____, *Knock on Wood: Poems about Superstitions* (2003)

_____, *Night Garden: Poems from the World of Dreams* (2000)

_____, *The Rainbow Hand: Poems about Mothers and Children* (1999)

Yolen, Jane, *Once Upon Ice: and Other Frozen Poems* (1997)

_____, *Snow, Snow: Winter Poems for Children* (2005)

_____, *Water Music: Poems for Children* (1998)

_____, *Weather Report: Poems* (1993)

Poems for Adolescent Readers

✴ Alexander, Elizabeth, and Marilyn Nelson, *Miss Crandall's School for Young Ladies & Little Misses of Color: Poems* (2007)

✴ Angelou, Maya, *Soul Looks Back in Wonder* (1993)

✴ Bierhorst, John, *In the Trail of the Wind: American Indian Poems and Ritual Orations* (1971)

✴ Brooks, Gwendolyn, *Bronzeville Boys and Girls* (1956/2007)

✴ _____, *Selected Poems* (2006)

Fletcher, Ralph, *I Am Wings: Poems about Love* (1994)

_____, *Relatively Speaking: Poems about Family* (1999)

✴ Giovanni, Nikki, *Shimmy, Shimmy, Shimmy Like My Sister Kate: Looking at the Harlem Renaissance Through Poems* (1996)

Grandits, John, *Blue Lipstick: Concrete Poems* (2007)

Hopkins, Lee Bennett, *Been to Yesterdays: Poems of a Life* (1995)

_____, *America at War: Poems Selected by Lee Bennett Hopkins* (2008)

✴ Hughes, Langston, *The Block*, selected by Lowery S. Sims and Daisy Murray Voigt (1995)

✴ _____, *The Dream Keeper: And Other Poems* (2007)

Janeczko, Paul B., *Stone Bench in an Empty Park* (2000)

_____, *Looking for Your Name: A Collection of Contemporary Poems* (1993)

_____, *Wherever Home Begins: 100 Contemporary Poems* (1995)

Janeczko, Paul B., and Naomi Shihab Nye, *I Feel a Little Jumpy around You: A Book of Her and His Poems Collected in Pairs* (1996)

✴ Johnson, Angela, *The Other Side: Shorter Poems* (1998)

✴ _____, *Running Back to Ludie* (2001)

Lewis, J. Patrick, *The Brother's War: Civil War Voices in Verse* (2007)

Livingston, Myra Cohn, *Abraham Lincoln: A Man for All the People: A Ballad* (1993)

✴ _____, *Keep on Singing: A Ballad of Marion Anderson* (1994)

☀ _____, *Let Freedom Ring: A Ballad of Martin Luther King, Jr.* (1992)

☀ Myers, Walter Dean, *Here in Harlem: Poems in Many Voices* (2004)

☀ Nelson, Marilyn, *A Wreath for Emmett Till* (2005)

☀ _____, *Carver: A Life in Poems* (2001)

Nye, Naomi Shihab, *Honeybee* (2008)

_____, *Is This Forever, or What? Poems and Paintings from Texas* (2004)

☀ _____, *19 Varieties of Gazelle: Poems of the Middle East* (2002)

☀ _____, *The Space Between Our Footsteps: Poems and Paintings from the Middle East* (1998)

_____, *What Have You Lost?* (1999)

Rosenberg, Liz, *Light-Gathering Poems* (2000)

_____, *Roots and Flowers: Poets and Poems on Family* (2001)

Rosenberg, Liz, and Deena November, *I Just Hope It's Lethal: Poems of Sadness, Madness, and Joy* (2005)

Sidman, Joyce, *The World According to Dog: Poems and Teen Voices* (2003)

☀ Soto, Gary, *Canto Familiar* (1995)

☀ _____, *Fire in My Hands* (1990)

_____, *Neighborhood Odes* (1992)

Vecchione, Patrice, *Revenge and Forgiveness: An Anthology of Poems* (2004)

_____, *The Body Eclectic: An Anthology of Poems* (2002)

Novels in Verse

Creech, Sharon, *Hate That Cat* (2008)

_____, *Love That Dog* (2001)

Creech, Sharon, and Margarita Engle, *The Poet Slave of Cuba: A Biography of Juan Francisco Manzano* (2006)

Frost, Helen, *The Braid* (2006)

☀ Grimes, Nikki, *Bronx Masquerade* (2002)

Hemphill, Stephanie, *Things Left Unsaid* (2005)

_____, *Your Own, Sylvia: A Verse Portrait of Sylvia Plath* (2007)

Hesse, Karen, *Out of the Dust* (1997)

☀ _____, *Witness* (2001)

Janeczko, Paul B., *Worlds Afire* (2004)

Johnson, Angela, *The First Part Last* (2003)

Johnson, Lindsay Lee, *Soul Moon Soup* (2002)

Koertge, Ron, *Shakespeare Bats Cleanup* (2003)

☀ Nelson, Marilyn, *Carver: A Life in Poems* (2001)

☀ Soto, Gary, *Fearless Fernie: Hanging Out with Fernie and Me* (2002)

Testa, Maria, *Becoming Joe DiMaggio* (2002)

☀ Williams, Vera B., *Amber Was Brave, Essie Was Smart: The Story of Amber and Essie Told Here in Poems and Pictures* (2001)

Wong, Janet, *Minn and Jake* (2003)

☀ Woodson, Jacqueline, *Locomotion* (2003)

☀ _____, *Peace, Locomotion* (2009)

☀ Wolff, Virginia Euwer, *Make Lemonade* (1993)

_____, *True Believer* (2001)

General Anthologies

Cole, Joanna, *A New Treasury of Children's Poetry: Old Favorites and New Discoveries* (1984)

Cullinan, Bernice, *A Jar of Tiny Stars: Poems by NCTE Award-Winning Poets* (1996)

Hall, Donald, *The Oxford Book of Children's Verse in America* (1985)

Kennedy, X. J., and Dorothy Kennedy, *Talking Like the Rain: A First Book of Poems* (1992)

☀ Nye, Naomi Shihab, *This Same Sky: A Collection of Poems from Around the World* (1992)

☀ _____, *Salting the Ocean: 100 Poems by Young Poets* (2002)

Prelutsky, Jack, *The Random House Book of Poetry for Children* (1983)

Folklore: A Literary Heritage

Watch out behind you, Bruh Wolf! Better look out for Bruh Rabbit when next the day leans over and night falls down.

—VIRGINIA HAMILTON,
Bruh Rabbit and the Tar Baby Girl,
illustrated by James Ransome, unpaged

Dan's first/second-grade class in Minnesota has just heard Virginia Hamilton's **Bruh Rabbit and the Tar Baby Girl** (P) read aloud. This tale from the South Carolina Sea Islands was just what they needed to warm them up on this cold January day. James Ransome's sun-washed illustrations add to the warmth as well as the humor of the tale, and everyone was giggling by the time Dan finished reading the story. Comments such as "Served him right!" and "He got tricked himself!" indicate the degree of involvement of these young listeners.

Dan chose this particular book to read aloud because it meets three of the goals he has set for the winter months. He is collaborating with the art teacher to help students learn how to recognize the work of different illustrators, one of whom is James Ransome. This book is a bit different from most of Ransome's work because it is painted in watercolors rather than oils and of animal rather than human characters, so it will expand their understanding of Ransome's art. Dan also is trying to encourage his students to pay close attention to the words they read and hear, and then to use them in their own speaking and writing. Virginia Hamilton's use of Gullah words and phrases has delighted the students, and they will probably all go home tonight and tell their parents that dawn is really "dayclean" and evening is "daylean." Finally, Dan and his class are going to study trickster tales from around the world, and this is a great introduction to a classic African American trickster, a perfect way to begin their study of trickster tales—one of the most engaging types of folklore. Dan wants to help his students understand that all stories are part of a larger "family" of stories that share certain characteristics, that writers often borrow the elements and structure of old tales when they write, and that oral tales, the kind that many of the children hear at home, are the beginnings of the more polished written stories that they can produce themselves.

From just one thirty-two-page folktale comes the opportunity to learn about folklore, about art, about language, about an American culture, and about literature itself—as well as the occasion for a great deal of delight. Dan will go on to use a variety of trickster tales to not only delight his students, but to build upon their oral skills through storytelling and drama, to encourage their own writing, and to reflect on the many cultures that have produced these tales—cultures that the students in his class bring with them to school every day. Folklore offers him these unique opportunities for teaching and learning.

Defining Folklore

Creating stories is an essential part of being human. The oldest of stories—folklore, or traditional literature—includes those nursery rhymes, folktales, myths, epics, legends, fables, songs, and ballads that have been passed down by storytellers for hundreds, even thousands, of years to enlighten and entertain generations of listeners, young and old. Today, when we think of stories, we often think of books, of stories that are created by an author and written down, frozen just as they are for all time. However, long ago, before most people could read or write, stories were told aloud to captivated listeners. Each time a teller told the tale, it was revised and reborn. Many of these tales have survived over the centuries, eventually finding their way into the books we share with children; some are still shared today through the ancient art of storytelling. It is important to remember, though, that they all began as oral stories.

There are many different types of folklore available to young readers: nursery, or Mother Goose, rhymes; folktales such as talking animal stories, noodlehead tales, fairy tales, and tall tales; fables; myths and pourquoi stories; hero tales, such as epics and legends; and folk songs. Today, we can select from all of these types of folklore, from a wide variety of cultural traditions, and from stunning books in which the stories are retold and illustrated by some of our finest authors and artists. This abundance, however, has not always been the case.

A Brief History of Folklore for Young Readers

No one knows who the first teller of any particular story was, only that with countless tellers, over long periods of time, the stories evolved into the written, literary tales that we know today. An accomplished teller of tales, Jane Yolen explains that "the oldest stories were transmitted and transmuted, the kaleidoscope patterns of motif changed by time and by the times, by the tellers and by the listeners, by the country in which they arose and the countries to which they were carried. The old oral tales were changed the way culture itself changes, the way traditions change, by an erosion/eruption as powerful in its way as any geological force." (2000, p. 22)

Stories of the folk of many different world cultures explained why the world is as it is, showed that wishes could come true, gave hope to the young and the powerless, made even the fiercest fiend vulnerable, proved that good could vanquish evil, and taught all who listened how to live and work in harmony. Lise Lunge-Larsen (2004) suggests that "folktales grow out of the shadowy borderland between what is known and what is unknown. Or as ancient maps warned: Beyond here there be dragons."

Storytelling began with the songs and tales early societies composed to describe their daily work. "The first primitive efforts," notes storyteller Ruth Sawyer (1962, pp. 45–46), "consisted of a simple chant set to the rhythm of some daily tribal occupation such as grinding corn, paddling a canoe or kayak, sharpening weapons for hunting or war, or ceremonial dancing." As they speculated about the power of nature, the forces behind it, and human behavior, the people of primitive societies created stories to explain the unexplainable. These were the stories that grew into hero legends, pourquoi tales, and myths. When the ancient Greeks, for instance, were frightened by thunder, they invented a story about an angry god who shook the heavens. When they did not understand how and why the sun moved, they imagined a god who drove a chariot across the sky. With the passage of time and the growth of tribes, the desire to preserve ancestral stories increased, and the folklore that had been passed from one generation to the next became our cultural heritage. Love, hate, heroic acts, values, morality, and other human qualities and concerns play an important part in myths of all cultures.

At one time, common belief held that all folklore emerged from one prehistoric civilization. The Grimm brothers, who collected tales from all over Germany, ascribed to this view, speculating that as people migrated, they took their stories with them. This theory would account for regional differences in folktales, such as the evolution of West Africa's trickster Ananse the spider to Anansi in the Caribbean and then to Aunt Nancy in the United States. As folklorists studied the tales of many diverse cultures, however, it became apparent that some stories must have originated spontaneously in a number of separate places, which would account for the hundreds of variants of the Cinderella tale told all over the world. Today, cultural anthropologists believe that both theories about the origin of folktales are correct. Folklore scholars Iona and Peter Opie (1974) note that no one theory "is likely to account satisfactorily for the origin of even a majority of the tales. Their wellsprings are almost certainly numerous, their ages likely to vary considerably, their meanings—if they ever had meanings—to be diverse" (p. 18). What we do know is that people everywhere tell and listen to stories and have done so for a long, long time.

The transition from oral retelling to printed versions of folktales dates back centuries. Some Eastern stories appeared in print as early as the ninth century. In Europe, Straparola (1480–1557) gathered one of the earliest and most important collections of traditional tales in mid-sixteenth-century Venice in *Piacevoli Notti*, volumes 1 and 2 (published in 1550 and 1553). The work contains twenty folktales, including "Beauty and the Beast" and "Puss in Boots." Straparola's work was followed by Basile's *Pentameron* (*Entertainment for the Little Ones*) in seventeenth-century Naples. Perrault's French publication of *Histoires ou Contes du Temps Passé, avec des Moralités* (*Stories or Tales of Times Past, with Morals*) in 1697, helped folk literature flourish in Europe. Perrault included "Sleeping Beauty," "Little Red Riding Hood," "Cinderella," and "Puss in Boots" along with other familiar tales in his collection, including many nursery rhymes that are still popular today.

As in all folklore, we do not have conclusive evidence of the origins of nursery rhymes, but we do know that these rhymes were linked with various political and social events (Opie & Opie, 1951). Many of the rhymes probably have a simple origin. They may have been created to teach children to count, to learn the alphabet or the days of the week, to share important customs and beliefs, or to remind them to say their prayers; others were probably intended simply for amusement. The literary name "Mother Goose" was probably first associated with Charles Perrault's 1697 publication. The frontispiece shows an old woman spinning and telling stories and is labeled *Contes de ma Mère l'Oye* (*Tales of My Mother Goose*). Today, the name Mother Goose is associated primarily with nursery rhymes and no longer with the folktales first recorded in the late 1600s.

Folktales have deep literary roots. During the eighteenth century, La Fontaine's *Fables*, Countess d'Aulnoy's *Fairy Tales*, and Madame de Beaumont's *Beauty and the Beast* were published. Toward the end of the eighteenth century, philologists such as the brothers Grimm studied folklore to find out about customs and languages in different societies. The German brothers traveled through the countryside asking people to tell stories they remembered. The Grimms eventually wrote a German dictionary and a book of grammar, but they are best remembered for their retellings of the stories they heard. The two volumes of the first edition of *Kinder- und Hausmärchen* were published in the early nineteenth century.

German Popular Stories, an English translation of the Grimms' tales illustrated by George Cruikshank, became an instant success when it was published in 1823. It raised the respectability of the old tales among scholars and educators, who had held them to be "an affront to the rational mind" (Opie & Opie, 1974, p. 25). Following the popularity of the Grimm brothers' tales, enthusiasm for collecting folklore spread around the world. Joseph

Jacobs and Andrew Lang collected folktales in England; Jacobs's *English Fairy Tales* includes many well-loved stories, and Lang's series, in which the books are identified by color—*The Blue Fairy Book*, for example—continues to serve as a primary source of British tales. During the mid-1800s, Norse scholars Peter Christian Asbjornsen and Jorgen E. Moe collected most of the Scandinavian tales we have today.

Although most adults today recognize the importance of sharing folklore with children, some try to censor the tales because they feel they are too sexist or too violent. Historically, though the tales were shared orally by all classes of people for many centuries, by the 1600s, many adults did not approve of them, finding the stories crude, brutal, dishonest, and of questionable moral value—certainly not appropriate for children. Jack Zipes (1979) points out that "the tales were often censored and outlawed during the early phase of the rise of the middle classes to power because their fantastic components which encouraged imaginative play and free exploration were contrary to the precepts of capitalist rationalization and the Protestant ethos" (p. 196).

It wasn't until the end of the nineteenth century that the tales were no longer generally considered dangerous to young minds and became widely available in print, but even well into the twentieth century arguments about their worth continued, with librarian Anne Carroll Moore a vociferous champion of the old stories (Marcus, 2008).

The beloved American writer Wanda Gág translated and illustrated the Grimms' stories in her *Tales from Grimm* (I) in 1936 and *More Tales from Grimm* (I) in 1947. Maurice Sendak handsomely illustrated Lore Segal's translation *The Juniper Tree and Other Tales from Grimm* (A) in 1973, a collection containing many gritty tales suitable for adolescent readers. Many others have retold and illustrated single tales from the Grimm brothers, such as *Snow White and the Seven Dwarfs* (I), translated by Randall Jarrell and illustrated by Nancy Ekholm Burkert. In *The Annotated Brothers Grimm*, Maria Tatar translates thirty-seven of the 210 tales, along with nine adult tales, from the Grimms' final edition of the stories, giving readers valuable background information for each. George Webbe Dasent's translation of *East o' the Sun and West o' the Moon* (I) into English retains the vitality of spoken language. Many of the same tales appear in Ingri and Edgar Parin d'Aulaire's *East of the Sun and West of the Moon* (I), which contains illustrations echoing Norwegian folk art. Nancy Willard converted the tale into a dramatic play (A) of the same name, illustrated by Barry Moser. More recently, Lise Lunge-Larsen has collected Norwegian troll stories in *The Troll with No Heart in His Body* (I), with rough-textured woodcuts by Betsy Bowen that echo the age of the tales. Isaac Bashevis Singer's collections of Yiddish tales, in such books as *Naftali the Storyteller and His Horse, Sus* (P–I), and *When Shlemiel Went to Warsaw and Other Stories* (I), are inspired by old Jewish stories he heard as a boy in Warsaw.

In the 1960s and 1970s, interest in folklore from other than western European cultures began to grow, and in the almost fifty years since, the genre has grown to include stories from many countries and from various cultural traditions in North America. Although there are still more retellings of stories from the western European tradition, young readers now have access to tales from Australia to Zaire. Those tales include stories that Africans brought with them to America and retold as they struggled with slavery, to those brought by recent immigrants from all corners of the world, to those from Native American cultures across the continent. With this new richness of cultural traditions came important questions surrounding cultural authenticity and appropriation (Bader, 2006), with many calling for the importance of acknowledging sources and respecting cultural origins.

Stories such as Virginia Hamilton's stunning collections *The People Could Fly: American Black Folktales* (A) and *In the Beginning: Creation Stories from around the World* (A), Ed Young's illustrations of single stories from China such as *Lon Po Po: A Red-Riding Hood Story from China* (P–I) and Ai-Ling Louie's *Yeh Shen: A Cinderella Story from China* (P–I), Joseph Bruchac's retellings of Native American tales such as *Between Earth and Sky: Legends of Native American Sacred Places* (I–A), and Isabel Schon's *Doña Blanca and Other Hispanic Nursery Rhymes and Games* (P) greatly enrich the choices for young readers. Collections such as Shirley Climo's *Monkey Business: Stories from Around the World* (I), illustrated by Erik Brooks, enable young readers to savor tales from varied places, in this case Africa and Madagascar, the Americas, and Asia. The collection contains fourteen tales, a scattering of proverbs, fables, myth, legend, and folktale, and the sources are documented in the concluding commentary. Although he does not include source notes, Sam McBratney's *One Voice, Please: Favorite Read-Aloud Stories* (I), illustrated by Russell Ayto, offers fifty-six tales of wise men, fools, and tricksters from across the world. Denys Johnson-Davies retells *Gaha the Wise Fool* (I), with illustrations of hand-sewn tapestries by two Cairo tent makers, Hag Hamdy Mohamed Fattoub and Hany El Saed Ahmed. Patricia Santos Marcantonio sets her retellings in the American southwest in *Red Ridin' in the Hood: And Other Cuentos* (I–A), illustrated by Renato Alcarcao. This collection contains eleven stories, a glossary for the sprinkling of Spanish words, and detailed, if satirical, full-page drawings.

Whatever the explanation of the origins or purposes of the tales, it is clear that similar archetypes—images,

Ed Young's evocative paintings bring to life this Red Riding Hood story from China.

plot patterns, themes, or character types that recur in the oldest stories—appear in the myths, legends, and folktales of all people across time and in all places. For example, the normal process of maturing finds its psychological expression in the archetype of the hero's quest—slaying the dragon or winning a princess. Traditional heroes from many cultures share similar traits: they often have unusual births, leave home to go on a quest, have magical help, have to prove themselves through many trials, and are richly rewarded for their heroism. Other familiar character examples that reappear in many tales include the good mother (fairy godmother), the bad mother (wicked stepmother or old witch), and the evil underside of every person (the shadow). The same archetypes of these primal stories appear in realistic and fantasy novels; characters continue to battle the forces of evil to ensure the survival of good.

Folklore gave us the stories that underlie so many modern stories, the stories of the people, all the people, which continue to play a vital role in the lives of children. The bravery, loyalty, and daring embodied in some of these tales continue to thrill young readers, while the humor and exaggerations of other tales make them laugh.

Folklore from the world over also helps young readers understand the universal family of stories, providing them with many examples of common human values.

Considering Quality in Folklore

These old tales are at their best when the style of the written story reflects the oral origins of the tale. Vivid phrases and catchy rhymes capture the attention of a listener, and these remain in good retellings. Listen for language that sounds natural when read aloud—that contains imagery, melodious rhythms, and the cadences of speech. Oral origins mean that most folklore gets into the action, or plot, immediately. Characters are delineated sparingly, such as the stereotypical beautiful princess, and settings are vague, such as the oft-used *Once upon a time*. The themes of these stories represent age-old values and beliefs that formed the basis for how ancient peoples lived in the world; they should be readily apparent to young readers.

Stories that maintain the cultural integrity of early versions best represent those cultures. Excellent retellings note the cultural origins of the tale and often cite their sources, so look for this information in the books you select. Artists present an immense amount of cultural detail in their illustrations—detail that the honed language of folklore may not provide. Further, artists have a unique opportunity to create their own visions because the oft-told tales present only general descriptions of setting and character.

Figure 5.1

Considering Quality in Folklore

Language

✿ Echoes spoken language, with rich, natural rhythms.

✿ Reflects the cultural integrity of early retellings.

✿ Preserves the straightforward structure of oral stories.

✿ Explores significant universal themes.

Illustrations

✿ Serve as examples of artistic excellence.

✿ Complement and extend the narrative.

✿ Offer authentic cultural detail.

Look for artistically excellent illustrations that complement and extend the narrative and accurately reflect the cultural heritage of the tale. When evaluating folklore, look for qualities of authenticity and excellence in language, theme, and illustration, as presented in Figure 5.1.

We now turn to an examination of a familiar trickster tale retold by one of America's most gifted storytellers and illustrated by an outstanding artist.

Profile

Virginia Hamilton

 ooks can and do help us to live; and some may even change our lives.

The late Virginia Hamilton has been lauded as the most important author for children. Indeed, in her groundbreaking work, she created more than forty books, ranging from folklore and biography to historical fiction, contemporary realistic fiction, and fantasy—all of which reflected her African American roots, her unflinching willingness to tackle difficult subjects, and

above all her unsurpassed talent as a writer. This talent as well as her innovative contributions to literature for children was recognized by numerous awards. *M. C. Higgins the Great* was the first book ever to win both the National Book Award and the Newbery Medal. She won several Newbery Honor and Coretta Scott King Awards, and in 1992 was honored with the Hans Christian Andersen Medal, the "Nobel prize" in children's literature. She was also awarded the Laura Ingalls Wilder Award for lifetime achievement, and was the first writer of children's literature to receive a MacArthur "genius" grant.

Her notable works of folklore include *The People Could Fly: American Black Folktales*; *In the Beginning: Creation Stories from around the World*; *Her Stories: African American Folktales, Fairy Tales, and True Tales*; *When Birds Could Talk and Bats Could Sing: The Adventures of Bruh Sparrow, Sis Wren, and Their Friends*; *A Ring of Tricksters: Animal Tales from America, the West Indies, and Africa*; *The People Could Fly: The Picturebook*; and *Bruh Rabbit and the Tar Baby Girl*.

James Ransome's bright colors, carefully placed characters, and strong horizontal lines at the bottom of the page create an image that makes readers open the cover. They won't be disappointed.

*　*　*

A CLOSE LOOK AT

Bruh Rabbit and the Tar Baby Girl

James Ransome's brilliant artistic interpretation and Virginia Hamilton's exciting text make **Bruh Rabbit and the Tar Baby Girl** (P) a special book. In it Hamilton retells the familiar trickster tale as it is told by the Gullah people of the South Carolina Sea Islands.

Hamilton's gift with language is evident from the opening of the story with the words "It was a far time ago." She tells her story with a perfect balance of distinctive Gullah dialect and standard written English. The Gullah constructions that she chooses to use are all understandable to young readers, who are captivated by the unusual words. Such words as *Bruh, tricky-some, nary, scarey-crow, daylean, croker sack,* and *dayclean* are understandable within the context of the story and in their relation to standard written English or their descriptive proper-

ties. Sentences such as "Guess me, somebody been into my peanuts" or "For true, somebody been here" convey the thoughts of the characters, the events of the story, and the flavor of the Gullah dialect. Indeed, the link between the written text and the oral genesis of the original tale is a close one. You can hear the storyteller's voice in Hamilton's prose as the lazy rabbit "sneakity-sneaks" along until—"WHOOM!"—he sees the scarey-crow. The text simply begs to be read aloud, as a good retelling of an oral story should.

Ransome's watercolor with pen-and-ink illustrations are beautiful. Further, they not only reflect the events of the tale but create a detailed setting, develop the stock characters, and extend the humor. We know this will be a lighthearted story from the front cover because of the way the title and the author's name curve around the huge sun that fills the center of the page, anchored by the brown wooden fence and green grass running horizontally across the bottom, as well as the predominance of yellow and gold. The two title characters—the rabbit

The humor of this story is evident in the sight of Bruh Rabbit, with a sheepish look in his eye, perched on the back of the Tar Baby Girl.

and the tar baby girl—are centered on the page, directly in front of the sun. The fence, the briars that are visible behind it, and the size of the sun are the first hints of the setting.

Ransome continues to develop the setting in the endpages. As we open the book, we see, literally, a bird's-eye view of a countryside scene; the particular bird has a bonnet on her head. There's an old frame house, with a typical southern chimney and roof, a pond with ducks being watched by an alligator almost hidden in the bushes, and bluish mountains off in the distance. Everything is green, except where the grass has worn away to the orange-brown dirt. In this scene Ransome also begins to develop the characters. We see Bruh Wolf at work in his garden, while Bruh Rabbit is racing down the path from his burrow door toward the pond, fishing pole and bucket in hand. On the next page, opposite the title page, we see Bruh Rabbit throwing horseshoes, and on the dedication page he is fishing while Bruh Wolf pushes a wheelbarrow in the background. Before the story even begins, it is clear from the illustrations that Bruh Rabbit likes to have fun. The character development and the humor continue as we see Bruh Rabbit asleep in the first two pictures, and then Bruh Wolf working hard on his scarey-crow.

The seamless integration of text and illustration makes *Bruh Rabbit and the Tar Baby Girl* an outstanding example of a picturebook retelling of a classic folktale. Ransome's touching dedication of the book to the late Virginia Hamilton and the endnote about the origins of the tale add to the impact of the book.

Patterns in Folklore

Students who read widely soon recognize recurring patterns in the folklore of many countries. As characters, events, and resolutions recur in their reading, students begin to recognize the conventions, motifs, and themes that form these tales. They then use this literary knowledge in their subsequent reading and writing. Teachers and librarians can help students recognize these patterns if they provide exposure to a wide array of stories that exemplify characteristic structures.

• • CONVENTIONS • •

Literary devices called *conventions* are the cornerstones of folktales. One of the easiest conventions for children to recognize and use in their own writing is the story frame, such as the one that begins with "Once upon a time" and ends with "They lived happily ever after." Opening variations such as "Long ago and far away" or "Once there was and once there was not," which are used by storytellers in some cultural groups, contribute to children's ability to generalize the patterns; seeing a different frame serve the same purpose helps children appreciate the flexibility of the device. Early in their literary education, children search for formulaic patterns in language, plots, and characters that they can identify.

The repeated use of the number three is another familiar convention in the western European tradition. In addition to three main characters—three bears, three billy goats, three pigs—there are usually three events. "Goldilocks and the Three Bears" contains three bears, of course, but also three more sets of three: three bowls of porridge, three chairs, and three beds. Goldilocks tries each bowl of porridge and each chair and bed before deciding which is "just right." Many other folktales feature three tasks, three adventures, three magical objects, three trials, or three wishes. The number seven appears frequently, too, as in "Snow White and the Seven Dwarfs," "The Seven Ravens," and "The Seven Swans." In stories from other cultural groups, such as Native American tales, the convention might be four rather than three because the four seasons anchor many Native American tales.

• • MOTIFS • •

A *motif* is a recurring salient element, the smallest unit used to classify tales: the intentional repetition of a word or phrase, an event or unit of action, characters, objects, or ideas that run through a story. Motifs have been used by folklorists to categorize and analyze tales, as in Stith Thompson's five-volume *Motif-Index of Folk-Literature* (1955–1958). Many stories share similar stock characters (for example, the youngest son, the trickster), many contain magical objects (such as flying carpets, cooking pots, or boots and other footwear), and many include episodes in which characters sleep for a very long time or make wishes. Beasts and frogs are really princes, and evil creatures and human beings are easily tricked. These are the folklore elements that make these stories so appealing to children from one generation to the next. Margaret Read MacDonald and Brian W. Sturm have created *The Storyteller's Sourcebook: A Subject, Title, and Motif Index to Folklore Collections for Children, 1983–1999* (2001), a valuable resource for teachers and librarians who want students to compare folktale variants and their motifs.

Many stories contain a number of different motifs that students can identify when comparing folktales. Cinderella stories often contain a small shoe, a flight from a ball, a youngest daughter who is ill-treated, a prince, a wicked stepmother, and a fairy godmother. Characters—gods, witches, fairies, tricksters, noodleheads, or stepmothers—behave in stereotypical ways, so readers learn to predict how they will act in certain situations. A representative human (such as a busybody or a country bumpkin) is often used to stand for a trait or character type.

A second kind of motif focuses on magical objects, spells, curses, or wishes as the center of the plot. Beans tossed carelessly out a window lead the way to a magical kingdom in "Jack and the Beanstalk." "The Magic Porridge Pot" and its variants hinge on a secret ritual. Sometimes the magical element is a spell or enchantment. Both Snow White and Sleeping Beauty are victims of a witch's evil curse and are put to sleep until a kiss from a handsome prince awakens them. In some stories, the evil spell causes a transformation; only love and kindness can return the frog, donkey, or beast to its former state. "The Frog Prince," "The Donkey Prince," "The Seven Ravens," "The Six Swans," "Jorinda and Joringel," and "Beauty and the Beast" are all transformation tales.

A third type of motif involves trickery, or outwitting someone else. A spider man is the trickster in African and Caribbean tales, a rabbit in West African tales, and a tortoise in the Brazilian tale *Jabuti the Tortoise* (P–I), by Gerald McDermott. Trickery and cunning also appear in French and Swedish folktales, such as "Stone Soup" and "Nail Soup," and in Jon Muth's Far Eastern version, *Stone Soup* (P–I), featuring three Buddhist monks instead of soldiers. The wiliest trickster of all, Brer Rabbit, is almost always able to outsmart his larger opponents, except when he himself is tricked.

• • THEMES • •

Themes in folktales, obvious although not stated explicitly, express the values of the people who created them and reflect their philosophy of life. The theme in a folktale revolves around a topic of universal human concern. Time and time again, the struggle between good and evil is played out: hate, fear, and greed contrast with love, security, and generosity. The themes are usually developed through stock characters who personify one trait. For example, the bad fairy in "Sleeping Beauty," the witch in "Hansel and Gretel," and the stepmother in "Snow White" all represent evil. Each is destroyed, and the virtuous characters triumph. Such themes are reassuring; we would all like to believe that good prevails and evil is punished. In enchantment and transformation tales, the struggle between good and evil materializes as a contrast between surface appearances and deeper qualities of goodness. A beautiful princess sees the goodness of the prince hidden beneath the loathsome or laughable guise of a beast, frog, or donkey, or a prince sees beauty beneath the dirt and rags of a young woman. In other stories, such as some versions of "Sleeping Beauty," the entire world lies under an evil spell, veiled and hidden from clear view until goodness triumphs.

Another theme, that of the quest, centers on the hero's search for happiness or lost identity, which he undertakes in order to restore harmony to life. The hero succeeds only after repeated trials, much suffering, and extended separation, and he often exhibits courage, gallantry, and sacrifice. Teaching Idea 5.1 offers suggestions for exploring themes in folklore with students.

Teaching Idea 5.1

An Exploration of Theme in Folklore

Reading a wide range of folklore helps students develop a sense of its basic elements. Gradually, they become aware of various archetypes and motifs in the folklore they read and are able to identify images, characters, and patterns that occur frequently. To develop an awareness of the dominant themes in folklore, ask students to identify the important lessons conveyed through the tales and to list them along with the titles of the stories. Compare their discoveries with those of other students. Ask students which themes and stories appeal to them most. Why do these big ideas resonate? What do they say about what students value and believe to be true? About who they are? Some books that contain evocative themes include the following:

Hero's Quest

Hodges, Margaret, *St. George and the Dragon: A Golden Legend*

McKinley, Robin, *The Outlaws of Sherwood*

McVitty, Walter, *Ali Baba and the Forty Thieves*

Pyle, Howard, *The Story of King Arthur and His Knights*

Rumford, James, *Beowulf: A Hero's Tale Retold*

Good versus Bad

San Souci, Robert D., *The Talking Eggs: A Folktale from the American South*

Steptoe, John, *Mufaro's Beautiful Daughters*

Yolen, Jane, *Tam Lin: An Old Ballad*

Young, Ed, *Lon Po Po: A Red-Riding Hood Story from China*

Transformations and the Power of Love

Brett, Jan, *Beauty and the Beast*

Cooper, Susan, *The Selkie Girl*

Ormerod, Jan, and David Lloyd, *The Frog Prince*

Steptoe, John, *The Story of Jumping Mouse*

Yagawa, Sumiko, *The Crane Wife*, translated by Katherine Paterson

Types of Folklore

Folklore has many categories. Those most commonly available to young readers include nursery rhymes; folktales such as animal tales, noodlehead tales, fairy tales, and tall tales; fables; myths; hero tales such as epics and legends; and folk songs. Beginning in infancy and continuing through the primary grades, children delight in nursery rhymes. As they grow and develop a literary background, they begin to understand and enjoy folktales, tall tales, myths, legends, and the simple stories and morals of fables.

• • NURSERY RHYMES • •

Mother Goose and other nursery rhymes form the foundation of many children's literary heritage. Surprising as that may sound, the rhythm and rhyme of the language as well as the nursery rhyme's compact structure and engaging characters produce bountiful models for young children learning language. As they chant the phrases, mimic the nonsense words, and endlessly recite the alliterative rhymes and repetitions, children develop phonemic awareness—the ability to segment sounds in spoken words, something that is a prerequisite to phonics instruction and proficient reading. Exposure to nursery rhymes improves children's phonological skills and thereby their later reading ability (MacLean, Bryant, & Bradley, 1987). More important, children delight in language play. Poet Walter de la Mare claimed that Mother Goose rhymes "free the fancy, charm the tongue and ear, delight the inward eye, and many of them are tiny masterpieces of word craftsmanship. . . . They are not only crammed with vivid little scenes and objects and living creatures, but, however fantastic and nonsensical they may be, they are a direct shortcut into poetry itself" (1962, p. 21). Children learn about characters, themes, and structures that become the foundation for subsequent literary education.

Nursery rhymes know no regional, ethnic, cultural, or language boundaries. People around the world have crooned similar verses to their young children. The magic of Mother Goose is still handed down by word of mouth, though there are many collections available. When selecting books to share with children, it is important to choose versions that maintain the original, robust language.

Characteristics

The *rhythmic words* of nursery rhymes strengthen a child's sense of language. The cadence of the language—its beat, stress, sound, and intonation—reflects the oral origins and charms the listener's ear. It is almost impossible to keep from bouncing when hearing:

> Ride a cock horse
> to Banbury Cross
> to see a fine lady
> upon a white horse.

A second characteristic of nursery rhymes is the *imaginative use of words and ideas*. Nothing is too preposterous! Children delight in the images conjured up by:

> Hey diddle, diddle,
> The cat and the fiddle,
> The cow jumped over the moon;
> The little dog laughed
> To see such sport,
> And the dish ran away with the spoon.

These verses feed the fancy, spark creativity, and stretch imagination: three wise men of Gotham go to sea in a bowl; an old woman is tossed up in a basket nineteen times as high as the moon; another old woman lives in a shoe with her entire brood of children. Anything can happen in nursery rhymes.

A third characteristic, *compact structure*, establishes the scene quickly and divulges the plot at once. In four short lines, we hear an entire story:

> Jack Sprat could eat no fat,
> His wife could eat no lean,
> And so between them both, you see,
> They licked the platter clean.

As in all folklore, the consolidation of action and the economy of words result from the rhymes being said aloud for many generations before being set in print. As the verses were passed from one teller to the next, they were honed to their present simplicity.

The *wit* and *whimsy* of the characters also account for the popularity and longevity of Mother Goose. Children appreciate the obvious nonsense in:

> Gregory Griggs, Gregory Griggs,
> Had twenty-seven different wigs.
> He wore them up, he wore them down,

> To please the people of the town;
> He wore them east, he wore them west,
> But he never could tell which he loved best.

Surprise endings provide clever resolutions and enhance the humor, as in:

> Peter, Peter, pumpkin eater,
> Had a wife and couldn't keep her;
> He put her in a pumpkin shell,
> And there he kept her very well.

Collections of Nursery Rhymes

Such old favorites as Alice and Martin Provensen's *The Mother Goose Book*, Blanche Fisher Wright's *The Real Mother Goose*, Arnold Lobel's *The Random House Book of Mother Goose*, and Iona and Peter Opie's *Tail Feathers from Mother Goose* (N–P) provide many familiar and some less familiar rhymes to share. More recently, Rosemary Wells and Iona Opie worked together to produce *My Very First Mother Goose*, *Mother Goose's Little Treasures*, and *Here Comes Mother Goose* (N–P). Leo and Diane Dillon's *Mother Goose: Numbers on the Loose* (P) is a verbal and visual treasure. Nina Crews has added a lively urban collection, *The Neighborhood Mother Goose* (P–I). *The Charles Addams Mother Goose* (A), with its darkly droll, comic illustrations, will appeal to older students who will see the familiar rhymes in a totally novel way.

Authors, editors, and publishers, aware of the international makeup of our population and the global village view of our world, search for new books to reflect that vision. Patricia Polacco includes verses and images from her Russian grandmother in *Babushka's Mother Goose*; Nancy Van Laan depicts a mother and a child from seven different continents in *Sleep, Sleep, Sleep: A Lullaby for Little Ones Around the World*; and Jane Yolen selects from an international palette in *Sleep Rhymes Around the World* (N–P). For their collection *Chinese Mother Goose Rhymes* (N–P), illustrator Ed Young and editor Robert Wyndham have chosen rhymes from the Chinese oral tradition that may sometimes seem familiar even to modern American children. *¡Pío Peep! Traditional Spanish Nursery Rhymes* (N), by Alma Flor Ada and F. Isabel Campoy, with English adaptations by poet Alice Schertle, is a bilingual collection of rhymes that may be well known to Latino children and will appeal to children from other cultures as well.

FOLKTALES

Folktales have delighted young and old for countless generations. These stories, which include talking animal stories, noodlehead tales, fairy tales, and tall tales, are narratives in which heroes and heroines triumph over adversity by demonstrating virtues like cleverness or bravery, or loveable vices like supreme silliness. Their themes, obvious though not always stated explicitly, express the values of the people who created them. Authors Alice McGill and Virginia Hamilton have both retold the African-American slave tale, in which slaves "fly" to freedom, in language that captures the spirit of people longing to be free. Hamilton's retellings appear in her collected stories in *The People Could Fly: American Black Folktales* (A), illustrated by Leo and Diane Dillon, and in a sumptuous picturebook version, also illustrated by the Dillons, *The People Could Fly* (I). Alice McGill's version, *Way Up and Over Everything* (P), illustrated by Jude Daly, presents the same story to a younger audience. All three versions are powerful statements of the solace of imagined freedom.

Characteristics

Folktales have an artistic yet simple form that derives from the oral tradition. The *plot structure* is clean and direct. The first paragraph establishes characters and setting, the body develops the problem and moves toward the climax, and the ending quickly resolves the problem without complications. Folktales are, in fact, minidramas. See Teaching Idea 5.2 for ideas for involving students in folklore theatre.

The plot of a folktale unfolds with little ambiguity: the good characters are supremely good, the evil ones are outrageously evil—and justice prevails without compromise. The conflict is identified early, and only incidents that build on the problem or add complexity to it have survived oral transmission. Problems are resolved decisively, with little denouement, resulting in classic happily-ever-after endings. Margaret Willey's books set in the far north woods, *Clever Beatrice: An Upper Peninsula Conte* and *Clever Beatrice and the Best Little Pony* (P–I), which introduce a spunky and very capable young girl who first outsmarts a giant and then a lutin—a cunning little man— are excellent examples of tales that fit this pattern.

Because folktales are more concerned with situation than personality, characters are delineated economically and usually exemplify one salient trait. These one-dimensional stock characters crystallize in the form of the foolish, the wise, the wicked, or the virtuous. All perform in predictable ways and rarely change throughout the course of a story.

The language—direct, vivid vernacular—is uncluttered by awkward constructions or convolutions. Gail E. Haley's retelling of *Mountain Jack Tales* (I) reflects the Appalachian regional dialect of their origin. Colloquialisms add to the flavor and reflect the heritage of the tale; they are tempered to the tongue, having been honed and polished through centuries.

Although folktales use precise language, the verbal *setting* remains geographically vague; the stories take place

Teaching Idea 5.2

Create a Folklore Performance

Folklore is ideal material for readers' theatre, puppetry, or choral reading. Folktales contain simple plot lines, a limited cast of well-defined characters, and decisive endings, making them ideal for young scriptwriters and dramatists. To create a folklore performance with your students:

1. Ask book groups to choose several folktales to read.

2. Generate criteria for selecting a good story for dramatizing. What elements make stories easier to tell?

3. Have them choose their favorite folktale that fits the selection criteria to share through creative drama.

4. Prepare a script for readers' theatre, a puppet play, or choral reading.

5. Practice and share the performance with others.

Figure 5.2

Folktale Characteristics

✿ Characters represent such traits as cleverness, bravery, or supreme silliness.

✿ Characters are delineated economically.

✿ Plot lines are direct and uncluttered by side issues (this varies by culture).

✿ Stories contain very little ambiguity.

✿ Conflict is identified early.

✿ Resolution is decisive.

✿ Themes express the values of the people who created them.

✿ Language is a direct, vivid vernacular.

✿ Setting and time are vague, other than as depicted in illustrations.

An old tale is given a clean, fresh look with Lisbeth Zwerger's artistic interpretation of **The Bremen Town Musicians**.

in unidentified times, in places defined by minimal detail, allowing illustrators to let their imaginations soar. Folktales know no geographical or temporal boundaries; they come to life everywhere for each new generation of children. Figure 5.2 summarizes folktale characteristics.

Types of Folktales

TALKING ANIMAL TALES In this type of tale, animals talk with human beings or with one another. Like human characters, the talking animals may be good or evil, wise or silly. Those who are good and wise are rewarded. Young children especially enjoy talking animals. Perennial favorites include "The Three Little Pigs," "The Three Billy Goats Gruff," "Henny Penny," "Brer Rabbit," and the Anansi spider stories. Jessica Souhami retells a traditional tale from India in *No Dinner! The Story of the Old Woman and the Pumpkin* (N–P). With the help of her granddaughter, the old woman outsmarts a bear, wolf, and tiger that want to eat her for dinner. Lisbeth Zwerger illustrates the classic Grimm tale, *The Bremen Town Musicians* (P), translated

by Anthea Bell, in which a dog, cat, rooster, and donkey outwit robbers and find a home.

Children appreciate the humorous situations and rhythmic language of Eric Kimmel's retelling of the West African trickster tale *Anansi Goes Fishing* (P), an exemplary talking animal tale, as is his tale *Anansi and the Moss-Covered Rock* (P), with Janet Stevens's humorous illustrations of the scheming spider and all the animals he tricks and is tricked by. Native American tribal tales also have tricksters, such as the coyote and raven. Gerald McDermott's *Coyote: A Trickster Tale from the American Southwest* tells the story of a prideful, comic mischief-maker with "a nose for trouble." The rabbit in *Brother Rabbit: A Cambodian Tale* (P–I), by Minfong Ho and Saphan Ros, is clever enough to repeatedly outsmart the hungry crocodile. Animal tricksters such as these are common in stories from many different cultures. Julius Lester (2004) writes that "a prime characteristic of the trickster tale is the absence of morality. Uncle Remus said, 'Creatures don't know nothing about that's good and that's bad. They don't know right from wrong. They see what they want and they get it if they can, by hook or crook'" (p. 114). Perhaps tricksters and their stories are so appealing to children for just that reason: tricksters will do anything to get what they want.

Brer Rabbit trickster stories traveled from Africa and Jamaica to the American rural South, and were originally popularized by storyteller Joel Chandler Harris. Van Dyke Parks's outstanding renditions of these traditional tales include *Jump! The Adventures of Brer Rabbit*; *Jump Again! More Adventures of Brer Rabbit*, and *Jump on Over! The Adventures of Brer Rabbit and His Family* (P–I), all illustrated by Barry Moser. Julius Lester's retellings *The Tales of Uncle Remus: The Adventures of Brer Rabbit*; *More Tales of Uncle Remus: Further Adventures of Brer Rabbit, His Friends, Enemies, and Others*; and *Further Tales of Uncle Remus* (I–A) are also marked by melodious language that reflects the authentic speech patterns of the culture that gave rise to the stories. *The Butter Tree: Tales of Bruh Rabbit* (I), retold by Mary Lyons and illustrated by Mireille Vautier, and Hamilton's *Bruh Rabbit and the Tar Baby Girl* (P) show that Brer Rabbit is just as sly as ever.

Margaret Hodges retells *Dick Whittington and His Cat* (P), with illustrations by Melisande Potter, a picture-book that is sure to charm a new generation. Shirley Climo retells a story from the Philippines in *Tuko and the Birds: A Tale from the Philippines* (P), illustrated by Francesco X. Mora, in which a gecko is a nuisance to the other animals. Other talking animal stories appear in the Booklist at the end of the chapter.

NOODLEHEAD TALES Humorous noodlehead stories focus on characters who are pure-hearted but lacking in good judgment. In *Noodlehead Stories from Around the World* (I), Moritz A. Jagendorf describes a noodlehead as a simple blunderer who does not use good sense or learn from experience. Storyteller Colleen Salley's *Epossomandus* (P) and *Epossomandus Saves the Day* (P), both illustrated by Janet Stevens, engage young listeners as they laugh at the antics of the characters and cheer Epossomandus on. Jessica Souhami's *Sausages* (N–P) is a funny retelling of the classic three wishes tale, one that pairs foolish characters with magic, just as in *The Fisherman and His Wife* (P), retold by Rachel Isadora with illustrations that set the tale of the foolish couple in a generic African country setting. Every cultural group has noodlehead stories that provoke hearty laughter: the wise men of Gotham in England, the fools in the Jewish ghetto of Chelm in

Rachel Isadora sets this classic tale in an African countryside.

Poland, Juan Bobo in Puerto Rico, the Connemara Man in Ireland, and the Montieri in Italy. Other examples of noodlehead stories are listed in the Booklist at the end of the chapter.

FAIRY TALES Fairy tales are magical narratives replete with supernatural beings, such as trolls, ogres, dragons, elves, and fairies; they also feature humans, such as the youngest son; poor, widowed mothers; and wicked half-sisters. They originated long ago from the oral tradition, but today are primarily written down or told for the amusement and enlightenment of children. Though fairy tales are structured like other folktales, their deeply magical character sets them apart. Wee people, fairy godmothers, and other magical beings intervene to make things happen. Enchantment aside, these stories paint an ideal vision of life based on the hope that virtue will be recognized and hard work rewarded, while greed and wickedness are punished. Fairy tales show us that courage, honesty, and resourcefulness are valued.

There are a prodigious number of fairy tales available to young readers, including Rachel Isadora's beautifully illustrated retelling of the Grimm brother's *The Twelve Dancing Princesses* (P). Interestingly, Isadora sets this story from the Germanic tradition in a generic African countryside. Stephen Mitchell's *Genies, Meanies, and Magic Rings: Three Tales from the Arabian Nights* (I), illustrated by Tom Pohrt, is a clever retelling of these magical stories. Aaron Shepard's *One-Eye! Two-Eyes! Three-Eyes!: A Very Grimm Fairy Tale* (P) is accompanied by droll illustrations by Gary Clement that delight primary-grade readers. *Little Red Riding Hood* (P) is beautifully retold and illustrated by Jerry Pinkney, while Laura Amy Schlitz offers a less well-known tale in *The Bearskinner: A Tale of the Brothers Grimm* (I), illustrated by Max Grafe, in which the virtues of endurance and heroism are highlighted. Jeanne Steig retells six popular European tales, including "Little Red Riding Hood" and "Rumpelstiltskin," that she makes her own by sprinkling them with witty verse. Lise Lunge-Larsen's collection, *The Hidden Folk: Stories of Fairies, Dwarves, Selkies, and Other Secret Beings* (P–I–A), with lushly patterned, folkloric scratchboard illustrations by Beth Krommes, is a comprehensive introduction to the folk characters who populate many European fairy tales. Jane Yolen shares a dozen tales of strong women in *Not One Damsel in Distress: World Folktales for Strong Girls* (I), and Judy Sierra has gathered enchanting tales in *Nursery Tales Around the World* (N–P). Other examples of fairy tales and their variants are listed in the Booklist at the end of the chapter.

TALL TALES Tall tales are primarily indigenous to the United States and are a peculiarly American form of folktale. They are a combination of history, myth, and fact.

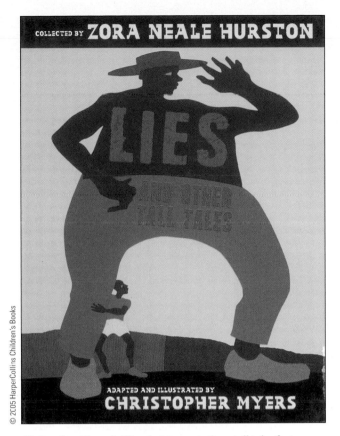

© 2005 HarperCollins Children's Books

Christopher Myers brilliantly interprets these tall tales first collected by Zora Neale Hurston.

Tall tales gave the early American settlers symbols of strength, and offset with a little humor the harsh realities of an untamed land. The exaggerated strength and blatant lies in tall tales added zest and lightened a life of hard labor. As the settlers built a new country, they created heroes who were the mightiest, strongest, and most daring lumberjacks, railroad men, coal miners, riverboat drivers, and steel workers possible.

Many heroes of tall tales were real people, but their improbable stories have made them larger than life. Davy Crockett, Daniel Boone, and Johnny Appleseed accomplished feats no mortal would dare. John Henry, Pecos Bill, and Mike Fink exemplify the brawn and muscle required to develop America. Children love the exaggerations that mark the tall tales. They laugh when Paul Bunyan's loggers tie bacon to their feet and skate across the huge griddle to grease it. The thought of Slewfoot Sue bouncing skyward every time her bustle hits the ground produces giggles. And when the infant Pecos Bill falls out of the covered wagon, children can picture the abandoned baby scrambling toward the coyote mother, who eventually raises him with the rest of the coyote pack. The heroes in tall tales are all-powerful, so readers know they will

Note how the sources of the intertwined Cinderella tales are made distinct by background color and design as well as labels in Paul Fleischman's **Glass Slipper, Gold Sandal: A Worldwide Cinderella,** *stunningly illustrated by Julie Paschkis.*

overcome any problem. The suspense is in *how* the problem will be solved.

Julius Lester describes the mighty battle between a steam drill and the legendary hero in *John Henry* (P–I), illustrated by Jerry Pinkney. Steven Kellogg's tall tale biography, *Johnny Appleseed* (P–I), and Reeve Lindbergh's poetic version, *Johnny Appleseed: A Poem* (P–I), illustrated by Kathy Jakobsen, both tell the story of John Chapman, who traveled across the Allegheny Mountains planting apple orchards. Alvin Schwartz gathered his entertaining and informative research into the language, superstition, and folk history of America's legendary past in many books, including *Whoppers: Tall Tales and Other Lies; Witcracks: Jokes and Jests from American Folklore*, and *Flapdoodle: Pure Nonsense from American Folklore* (I–A). Glen Rounds presented many larger-than-life stories of Paul Bunyan and Babe in his book *Ol' Paul the Mighty Logger* (P–I). Not all the heroes are male: Robert D. San Souci collected twenty tales about strong women in *Cut from the Same Cloth: American Women of Myth, Legend, and Tall Tale* (I).

Years ago author Zora Neale Hurston collected a slightly different kind of tall tale—outrageous lies—and

Christopher Myers has adapted and illustrated them in *Lies and Other Tall Tales* (P–I), Hurston's stories are a beautiful example of the power of language in these old tales. The style reflects the original language, while the illustrations create a visual community of the black tellers of the tales. These and other tall tales are listed in the Booklist at the end of the chapter.

Variants of Folktales

Although the origins of folktales are clouded in prehistory, variants can be traced to many cultures. Contemporary writers and artists breathe new life into the many versions of ancient folktales. Many stories have hundreds of variants from countries all over the world. Comparing the motifs, characters, and themes of the different versions can be a very illuminating activity for readers. Here we briefly discuss "Cinderella," "Sleeping Beauty," "Rumpelstiltskin," and "Jack and the Beanstalk." There are many other variants to explore.

CINDERELLA Folklorist M. R. Cox, a pioneer in folklore research during the 1890s, described the Cinderella motif in his book for adults, *Cinderella: Three Hundred and Forty-Five Variants* (1893). In the foreword to the Cox collection, Andrew Lang states, "The märchen [fairy tale] is a kaleidoscope: the incidents are the bits of coloured glass. Shaken, they fall into a variety of attractive forms; some forms are fitter than others, survive more powerfully, and are more widely spread" (p. x). Today, we know that there are more than 1,500 variants of this timeless tale. Paul Fleischman has gathered thirty-six variants of this story from seventeen cultures across the world in his clever *Glass Slipper, Gold Sandal: A Worldwide Cinderella* (I), stunningly illustrated by Julie Paschkis. Pieces of the tale are strung together as one continuous story, reflecting many variants. Accompanying art incorporates appropriate cultural details (and a small label) that reflect the origin of the specific text, placed on a background color that differs for each culture. The result is a kaleidoscope of stories, reflecting both the variety and the constancy of this well-loved tale.

The romantic rags-to-riches story of "Cinderella" based on Charles Perrault's version has been illustrated by many noted artists, including Marcia Brown, Susan Jeffers, and Errol Le Cain. Perrault's fairy godmother, coach, and lush costumes are familiar to most children. Barbara McClintock's retelling of Perrault's *Cinderella* (P) includes richly detailed illustrations both of the French court and a loyal little gray cat who is rewarded at the end of the tale. In the less-familiar German version by the Brothers Grimm, *Cinderella* (I A), illustrated by Nonny Hogrogian, the story takes on a macabre tone. In order to make their feet fit into the tiny glass slipper, the sisters take drastic measures: one cuts off her toe and the other cuts off her heel. In the end they are blinded by vengeful doves. Other versions include Appalachian, Chinese, Creole, Yiddish, Egyptian, English, Indonesian, Irish, Korean, Persian, Spanish American, and Vietnamese, as well as Native American versions such as *The Turkey Girl: A Zuni Cinderella Story* (I), retold by Penny Pollock and illustrated by Ed Young, and the Algonquin variant, *The Rough-Face Girl* (I). Here, we take a close look at this beautiful variant of this worldwide story.

*   *   *

A CLOSE LOOK AT

The Rough-Face Girl

Rafe Martin retells the Algonquin version of Cinderella in *The Rough-Face Girl* (I), illustrated by David Shannon. In this retelling, both the Algonquin culture and the voice of the storyteller are apparent in illustrations and text. The book begins with a note from Martin describing his source and commenting on the universal desire for justice.

The simple structure of an oral tale is preserved in this retelling. The story begins with a simple statement of setting and moves immediately to the problem: only the woman who can see the Invisible Being can marry him. On the third page, we are introduced to the characters: a poor man with three daughters, two cruel and heartless, one sweet and submissive. The story then moves immediately to the action, briefly detailing the unsuccessful attempts of the haughty sisters to convince the Invisible Being's sister that they have seen him, and the subsequent triumph of the Rough-Face Girl. This economy of detail reflects the oral origins of the tale; brief statements of setting and the use of stereotypical characters allow the teller to get right to the exciting part—the action—thus holding the attention of the audience.

The language, too, reflects the oral origins of the tale. The story makes use of dialogue and of prosodic features that indicate tone and volume when the sister of the Invisible Being speaks:

> "All right, then," she said quietly, "if you think you've seen him, then tell me, WHAT'S HIS BOW MADE OF?" And suddenly her voice was swift as lightning and strong as thunder!

There is also repetition. The Rough-Face Girl asks her father the same question that her older sisters have already asked, she makes the same journey they did, and she is asked the same questions by the sister. Yet sharp contrasts are also made apparent. Her father has nothing to give her, the villagers laugh at her as she walks by in her odd clothing, and she answers the questions correctly and marries the Invisible Being. By repeating the events and the dialogue, the storyteller heightens the drama of the tale.

The voice of the storyteller comes through the words, but the culture of the people comes through both the words and the beautiful full-color realistic paintings that illustrate this tale. The first page, on which the setting is introduced in one sentence, exemplifies how text and illustrations work together to form this tale. Above the text is a painting of an Algonquin village. If you look closely, you can see men in canoes and men carrying game; women carrying water, tending fires, scraping skins, and cooking; and children playing. Surrounding the village are tall pines and firs, and mist is rising from the lake. Thus, in one line the story is set, and the setting is elaborated in the detailed illustration. In subsequent illustrations we see wigwams and their symbolic decorations, details of clothing, and the beautiful natural images that inspired much of Algonquin folklore. These images speak of the people and the culture that first told this haunting tale. We also see the pride and meanness of the two sisters, the humility of the Rough-Face Girl, and the awesome nature of the Invisible Being. The illustrations not only

century French poet, adapted many of Aesop's fables into verse form. Brian Wildsmith illustrated several of these, including *The Hare and the Tortoise* (P).

The source of early collections from the East is the Indian "Panchatantra" (literally, five *tantras*, or books), known to English readers as the "Fables of Bidpai" or "Jataka Tales." The Jatakas are stories of the Buddha's prior lives, in which he took the form of various animals. Each story is intended to illustrate a moral principle. *Foolish Rabbit's Big Mistake* (P–I), by Rafe Martin, is an early version of a "sky is falling" tale, with frenetic action vividly illustrated by Ed Young. B. G. Hennessy retells *The Boy Who Cried Wolf* (P) and adds dialogue to the story. Boris Kulikov's watercolor and gouache illustrations span time by, for example, mixing articles of clothing from wildly varied time periods, adding humor even though the wolf is always frightening.

Several collections of fables for younger children are available, but some question whether young children understand the subtle abstractions. Because fables are short and are told in simple language, some adults mistakenly give fables to children who are too young to comprehend or fully appreciate them. Researchers have found that seven-year-olds often miss the point of widely used fables (Pillar, 1983). Because fables are constructed within the oblique perspective of satire, allegory, and symbolism, their intent may elude young children's literal understanding. Examples of individual and collected fables appear in the Booklist at the end of the chapter.

MYTHS AND POURQUOI STORIES

The special group of stories we call myths developed as humans sought to interpret both natural phenomena and human behavior. They were used to answer fundamental questions concerning how human beings and their world were created. Myths express the beliefs and religious customs of ancient cultures and portray their visions of destiny. Unlike other stories, myths relate to one another; taken together, they build a complex picture of an imaginative world (Frye, 1970). They are once-sacred stories that feature capricious gods and goddesses who were believed to control people's everyday lives. Many myths are so integral to Western culture that they appear as literary allusions, as discussed in Teaching Idea 5.3.

Northrop Frye (1970) traces the origins of all literature back to one central story: how man once lived in a golden age (also referred to as the garden of Eden, the Hesperides, and a happy island kingdom in the Atlantic), how that world was lost, and how we someday may be able to get it back again (pp. 53, 57). Penelope Farmer (1979), translator of many myths, describes their purpose this way: "Myths have seemed to me to point quite distinctly—yet without ever directly expressing it—to some kind of unity behind creation, not a static unity, but a forever shifting breathing one. . . . The acquisition by man of life or food or fire has to be paid for by the

---

Teaching Idea 5.3

Search for Mythical Allusions

Students who read widely recognize frequently used *allusions* (references to a literary figure, event, or object) drawn from mythology. Classical allusions—such as Pandora's box, an Achilles heel, the Midas touch, the Trojan horse, and the face that launched a thousand ships—appear in our language, literature, and culture; they are part of our common vocabulary. A winged horse (Pegasus) appeared on old gas station signs, Mercury delivers flowers, Vulcan repairs tires, and many of us wear our Nike shoes to work or play every day.

The English language reflects origins in Greek, Roman, and Norse myths: *erotic* comes from Eros, *titanic* comes from the Titans, and *cereal* comes from Ceres. The days of the week also derive from myths: Sunday = Sun-day; Monday = Moon-day; Tuesday = Tiu's-day; Wednesday = Odin's-day; Thursday = Thor's-day; Friday = Freya's-day; Saturday = Saturn's-day. In *Words from the Myths*,

Isaac Asimov presents many words that have their origins in myths. To encourage students to learn more about allusions:

1. Have students notice words, symbols, and allusions to myths as they read newspapers, magazines, and books, and as they watch television and movies.

2. Instruct them to keep a list of words and mythological referents.

3. Have them find out who Odysseus, Medea, Achilles, Antigone, Oedipus, Hector, and other mythical characters are and why their names are important to us today.

4. Have students post the allusions on a bulletin board as they find them. Who can find the most unusual?

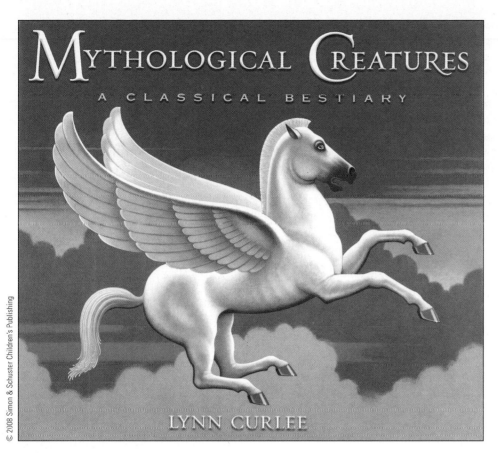

Lynn Curlee's magnificent Pegasus is only one of sixteen tales and images of classical Greek mythical creatures.

acceptance of death—the message is everywhere, quite unmistakable. To live is to die; to die is to live" (p. 4).

The great archetypal theme of life and death appears again and again throughout the stories told by all cultures. Children are familiar with the bare branches and frozen ground of winter giving way to the rebirth of flowers and trees in the spring. Most of them have buried a seed in the ground and watched for it to sprout. In images and symbols, mythic themes reappear under many guises that children can recognize through their study of myth. Literature throughout the ages echoes the themes of the ancient myths.

The literary value of myths lies in their exciting plots, memorable characters, heroic actions, challenging situations, and deep emotions. They are compelling stories of love, carnage, revenge, and mystery. At the same time, they transmit ancient values, symbols, customs, art, law, and language. Isaac Asimov explores the roots of hundreds of mythic images in *Words from the Myths* (I), a handy reference for students interested in etymology. Penelope Proddow compiled *Art Tells a Story: Greek and Roman Myths* (I–A), a collection of myths accompanied by photographs of the artwork they inspired. *Gods, Goddesses and Mon-*

sters: A Book of World Mythology (A), by Sheila Keenan, provides information about mythic characters from countries all around the globe. Lynn Curlee's *Mythological Creatures: A Classical Bestiary: Tales of Strange Beings, Fabulous Creatures, Fearsome Beasts & Hideous Monsters from Ancient Greek Mythology* (I) brings to vivid life sixteen mythical creatures of ancient Greece.

In myths, as in all folklore, a great deal depends on the telling. Much also depends on the illustrating, and myths offer artists an excellent opportunity for presenting their own interpretation of some elemental stories. Katrin Hyman Tchana's *Changing Woman and Her Sisters: Stories of Goddesses from Around the World* (I), illustrated with collage portraits by Trina Schart Hyman, is an anthology of tales from ten different cultures ranging from Navajo to Buddhist, ancient Sumer to Ireland. The extensive source material illuminates the origins of the tales.

All cultures have creation myths, and these stories are popular and are suitable for students in elementary and middle school. They describe the origin of the earth and the phenomena that affect it. Some books are collections of creation myths from around the world; others focus on myths from one culture. Jacqueline Morley collected eleven creation myths in *Egyptian Myths* (I), illustrated by Giovanni Caselli. Her graceful retellings focus on the struggle between good and evil, the creation of the world, and the relationships between gods and humans. Virginia Hamilton's definitive collection, *In the Beginning: Creation Stories from around the World* (I–A), gives students many different cultures' explanations of how the world began and how people were created.

The simplest myths are *pourquoi* stories, from the French word for "why." They tell how the earth began and why the seasons change, how animals got their colors and why they behave as they do. We humans lose our fear of things we can name and explain. "Given a universe full of uncertainties and mysteries, the myth intervenes to introduce the human element: clouds in the sky, sunlight, storms at sea, all extra-human factors such as these lose much of their power to terrify as soon as they are given the sensibility, intentions, and motivations that every individual experiences daily" (Grimal, 1965, p. 9).

Why the Sky Is Far Away: A Nigerian Folktale (N–P), by Mary-Joan Gerson, illustrated by Carla Golembe, and *Why Mosquitoes Buzz in People's Ears: A West African Tale* (P), by Verna Aardema, illustrated by Leo and Diane Dillon, are two excellent examples of African pourquoi tales. Native Americans also have many stories to explain animals' traits, human conduct, and natural phenomena. Joseph Bruchac's stories, such as *The First Strawberries* (P) and *How Chipmunk Got His Stripes: A Tale of Bragging and Teasing* (P), as well as Paul Goble's *The Gift of the Sacred Dog* (I), will give students an idea of the significance of this type of story to North American tribes. More pourquoi tales are listed in the Booklist at the end of the chapter.

Greek and Roman Mythology

Myths are only tenuously related to historical fact and geographical location, but they played an important role in the lives of the ancients, especially in the art, music, architecture, and culture of ancient Greece. The Greeks believed that gods and goddesses controlled the universe. Zeus, the most powerful god, controlled the weather— the lightning and thunder—and ruled over all the other gods who lived on Mount Olympus and the mortals who lived around it. Greek myths are replete with wondrous monsters. Young readers are fascinated by these half-human, half-beast creatures that frightened early people and wreaked havoc on their lands. Just as young children delight in tales of witches and giants, older students, too, love to read about Medusa, who grew hissing snakes on her head instead of hair; Cerberus, the huge three-headed dog; and the horrible one-eyed Cyclops.

Stories of individual heroes tell of great adventures, tests, victories, and losses. They feature relationships between gods and mortals and show how life must be lived with morality and conscience. Countless myths focus on the love between a god or goddess and a mortal, like that between Psyche and Cupid. Students familiar with this myth recognize its presence in many modern romances.

Superior retellings of Greek myths include Shirley Climo's *Atalanta's Race: A Greek Myth* (I–A), illustrated by Alexander Koshkin. In *Olympians: Great Gods and Goddesses of Ancient Greece* (I–A), Leonard Everett Fisher presents handsome portraits and describes the origins and characteristics of the deities. In *King Midas* (I–A), illustrated by Isabelle Brent, Philip Neil brings the king's sorrowful curse to life. Jane Yolen's *Wings* (I–A) tells the story of Daedalus, a mortal who is exiled to the island of Crete. Jeanne Steig's collection, *A Gift from Zeus: Sixteen Favorite Myths* (A), is retold in vivid language and enhanced by the wittily gruesome illustrations of William Steig.

Mythology from Other Cultures

Equally rich stories exist in other cultures. The tales that grew from the cold, rugged climate of northern Europe burn with man's passionate struggle against the cruelty of nature and the powerful gods and monsters that ruled the harsh land.

In *Favorite Norse Myths* (I–A), Mary Pope Osborne explains how the universe began, according to the creation story of Norway. She quotes from the *Poetic Edda,* the oldest written source of Norse mythology. In it, Odin, the Norse war god, trades an eye for all the world's wisdom. Thor, god of thunder, defeats a vicious giant with a hammer, and mischief-maker Loki creates trouble wherever he goes. Padraic Colum, an Irish poet and master storyteller, first published *The Children of Odin: The Book of Northern Myths* (I) in 1920; his classic collection remains available today. Ingri and Edgar Parin d'Aulaire have told these bold stories in *Norse Gods and Giants* (I–A), an entertaining account based on Norse mythology.

Although Greek, Roman, and Norse mythologies have traditionally been the most studied and the most readily available, today we have access to books of mythology from many cultures. Mythology from Africa has taken its place alongside European stories, and hauntingly beautiful versions of Native American and Inuit myths are being published with increasing frequency. Ngangur Mbitu and Ranchor Prime have collected the myths of Africa in *Essential African Mythology* (I). Isaac Olaleye describes a contest on a rainfield in Africa in *In the Rainfield: Who Is the Greatest?* (P–I), illustrated by Ann Grifalconi. Wind, fire, and rain are portrayed as regal Africans competing to determine who is the greatest. Richard Lewis retells the Aztec myth that explains how music came to earth in *All of You Was Singing* (I–A), a poetic version that is infused with his own imagination. Ed Young's illustrations combine Lewis's images, Aztec cultural motifs, and his own vision. The result is a stunningly beautiful book that echoes the splendor of creation. John Bierhorst has gathered many other Aztec tales in *The Hungry Woman: Myths and Legends of the Aztecs* (A). Myths from many cultures are listed in the Booklist at the end of the chapter.

• • HERO TALES: • •
EPICS AND LEGENDS

Hero tales focus on the courageous deeds of superhuman mortals in their struggles against one another as well as against gods and monsters. The heroes embody universal human emotions and represent the eternal contest between good and evil. Hero tales contribute to an appreciation of world history and literature, to an understanding of national ideals of behavior, and to our understanding of valor and nobility.

Epics are usually written in verse and consist of a cycle of tales that center on a legendary hero. Some well-known epics of the Western world include that of Beowulf, King Arthur and Camelot, and Robin Hood, as well as the account of the Trojan War retold in Homer's *Iliad* and *Odyssey*. Language is often key in setting the drama of the tales, as is evident from the first line of Robert Sabuda's *Arthur and the Sword* (I): "Long ago in a time of great darkness, a time without a king, there lived a fair boy called Arthur." The elegant language foretells the majesty in the story. *Merlin and the Making of the King* (I–A), retold by Margaret Hodges and illustrated by Trina Schart Hyman, introduces three of the famous Arthurian legends that chronicle Arthur's life from his birth until his death. The dramatic tales are accompanied by equally dramatic illustrations surrounded by tiny flowered borders inspired by illuminated manuscripts. Kevin Crossley-Holland has written an authoritative resource on Camelot, Arthur, his knights, and the history of chivalry in *The World of King Arthur and His Court: People, Places, Legend and Lore* (A), a book that gives historical knowledge of England at the time Arthur may have lived as well as information about the Arthurian ideal created by storytellers through the ages. The illustrations by Peter Malone, inspired by medieval art, clarify the information provided by the text.

The epic of the hero Gilgamesh, who travels the world with his friend Enkidu fighting monsters, is the oldest known recorded story in the world. In the foreword to her retelling, *Gilgamesh the Hero* (I–A), Geraldine McCaughrean relates that the story was carved onto twelve tablets that were smashed into thousands of shards over thousands of years. The story of this ancient Sumerian king of Mesopotamia (now Iraq), which may not be complete, was painstakingly restored by scholars. Gilgamesh,

though a powerful hero, suffers terribly: "Gilgamesh knelt on the bank of the pool vomiting his misery in great retching sobs. He beat his torn fists on the ground and howled like a wild animal" (p. 88). Like the theme of so many others to follow, his story ends, "He walked through darkness and so glimpsed light" (p. 95).

Gilgamesh's father, Lugalbanda, is the hero in Kathy Henderson's retelling, *Lugalbanda: The Boy Who Got Caught Up in a War* (A), illustrated by Jane Ray. This Sumerian epic, recorded on tablets about 4,500 years ago, is another of the oldest stories in the world. This retelling comes from the many fragments of stories from ancient Iraq and includes notes and an introduction. Now we take a close look at the retelling of the story of another warrior hero, Beowulf.

✳ ✳ ✳

A CLOSE LOOK AT
Beowulf

Beowulf: A Hero's Tale Retold (A) by James Rumford is a magnificent retelling of the epic first recorded in about 800 A.D. The endnote gives readers a brief history of the tale itself and the language that it was first written down in—Old English, or Anglo Saxon. Rumford notes that the poem was "lost" when English became heavily dominated by French, and not rediscovered until the eighteenth century. The language history is important because Rumford chose to retell this epic in words that can be traced back to their Anglo-Saxon origins, or at least usage (in the case of "dragon," "ogre," and "giant"), with the exception of "they," "their," and "them," all from Old Norse.

Rumford begins and ends his tale by speaking directly to the audience, much as the old bards would have done: "Listen! For I will sing of Beowulf. . . ." The subsequent tale is straightforward, spare, and passionate. Rumford includes the original names of characters and places, and inserts two important statements in Old English, always with the pronunciation in brackets following the first usage. This judicious use of Old English as well as his use of words descended from that language extend the power of the retelling. The two statements that he reproduces in Old English are in red, and they mark the beginning and end of Beowulf's story. "Beowulf is min nama" is how the hero announces himself, and the language and structure of this sentence alerts readers and listeners that Beowulf is the important character here. Similarly, Beowulf's final words, "Ic him aefter sceal," mark the end of his story.

Rumford's pen-and-ink and watercolor illustrations are beautiful, even as they supply details of time and place. The three sections of the story—the slaying of the ogre, Grendel, the subsequent battle with the ogre's mother, and the final battle with the dragon—are visually separated by different colors (green, blue, gold) in the background full-bleed, double-page-spread paintings. Superimposed on the background paintings are both text and illustration panels, framed in narrow black line. The first letter of the first word of each section is reminiscent of ancient illuminated manuscripts and is the same blood red as the two Anglo-Saxon statements. In the first two sections, the dragon who eventually slays the hero lurks behind text and illustration panels, a stunning visual foreshadowing.

This ancient epic speaks to young readers today with its revelation of loyalty, courage, friendship, and honor. A hero, a slayer of evil, Beowulf is even more a man whose sense of honor took him from his hearthside, even though he was old and white-haired, into his final battle with a dragon that threatened the land he protected and loved as its king.

Hero tales that are not technically epics are often referred to as *legends*. Legendary heroes may be real or imaginary people. Even if legends have some factual basis, they are often so fanciful that it becomes difficult to tell where fact stops and imagination takes over. Many storytellers elaborated on reports of their hero's exploits until the stories became full-blown legends that interwove fact and fiction yet contained a grain of truth at their core.

In *La Llorona/The Weeping Woman: An Hispanic Legend Told in Spanish and English* (I–A), Joe Hayes retells the Hispanic legend of La Llorona (the Weeping Woman), the jilted wife who turned her rage against her beloved children and is still believed to wander the banks of the river where she died of grief after she drowned them. Hayes asserts that no one knows whether the story is true, but in notes to the reader at the end of the book he writes, "When children ask me if I believe in La Llorona, I answer as I do whenever I'm asked about a story: I don't think the things I told you really did happen, but if you think about the story you can find a lot of truth in it." In Demi's tale *The Hungry Coat: A Tale from Turkey* (I), Nasrettin Hoca, a legendary wise Turkish hero, teaches an old friend and his guests, "If you want to look deeply, look at the man and not at his coat. You can change the coat, but you cannot change the man." Students will appreciate the humor in Demi's tale

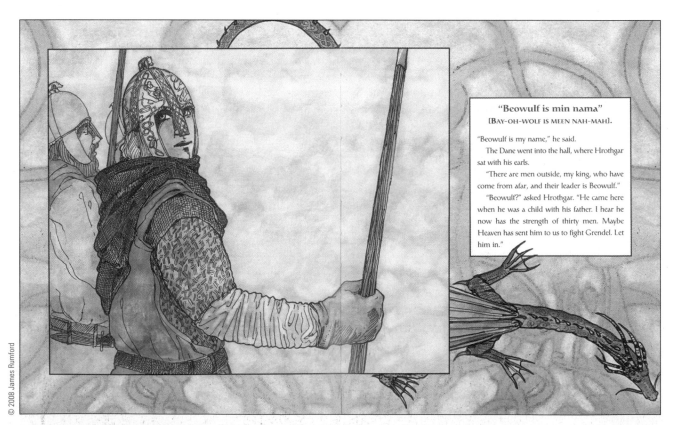

"Beowulf is min nama"
[BAY-OH-WOLF IS MEEN NAH-MAH].

"Beowulf is my name," he said.
The Dane went into the hall, where Hrothgar sat with his earls.
"There are men outside, my king, who have come from afar, and their leader is Beowulf."
"Beowulf?" asked Hrothgar. "He came here when he was a child with his father. I hear he now has the strength of thirty men. Maybe Heaven has sent him to us to fight Grendel. Let him in."

James Rumford incorporates gorgeous design, detail in image, and a bit of foreshadowing in the background as he retells the epic **Beowulf**.

James Rumford

ℰach book has been a new and rewarding experience. Writing and illustrating children's books—I can't think of a better way to spend the rest of my life.

James Rumford had a rich and varied career as a Peace Corps volunteer, Fulbright lecturer, and owner and publisher of a small press when he began publishing children's books in the late 1990s. Books such as *Seeker of Knowledge: The Man Who Deciphered Egyptian Hieroglyphs*

and *Traveling Man: The Journey of Ibn Battuta* were joined by his Siebert Honor–winning *Sequoyah: The Cherokee Man Who Gave His People Writing*. Like his other books, *Beowulf: A Hero's Tale Retold* demonstrates his mastery as a storyteller and an artist.

enhanced by her illustrations, inspired by Turkish art. Demi's *The Legend of Lao Tzu and the Tao Te Ching* (I) is another outstanding tale of an international hero. Mary Quattlebaum chose a legendary character from historical Virginia for *Sparks Fly High: The Legend of Dancing Point* (P), in which Colonel Lightfoot outsmarts the devil, complete with source notes. Julius Lester's *The Old African* (A), illustrated by Jerry Pinkney, is a powerful verbal and visual portrait of the horrors and the courage of the Middle Passage, a legend based on stories from Ybo Landing, Georgia.

Legends also grow around places and phenomena. Barbara Juster Esbensen's poem about the aurora borealis, *The Night Rainbow* (P), presents images from many cultures, including white geese, dancers, whales, and battles. Esbensen also provides scientific explanations as well as information about the legends in this celebration of the northern lights. *The Sons of the Dragon King: A Chinese Legend* (I–A), retold and illustrated by Ed Young, shows how the many tribes of China were combined into one by the Dragon King and his nine sons, and thus an entire culture is influenced by an ancient story.

• • FOLK SONGS • •

Songs serve as powerful vehicles for both shaping and preserving our cultural heritage. Ballads and folk songs inform and unify people. Work songs, often developed as a diversion from boredom, capture the rhythm and spirit of the labor in which their creators were engaged. They sing of the values and lifestyles of the people who laid the railroads, dug the tunnels and canals, sailed the ships, and toted the bales.

Folklorist Benjamin A. Botkin (1944) observed in *A Treasury of American Folklore* that we sing folk songs for self-gratification, power, or freedom (pp. 818–819). We also sing songs to lighten our labor, fill our leisure time, record events, and voice praise or protest. Civil rights

marchers led by Martin Luther King, Jr. were united by the experience of singing "We Shall Overcome" together.

We use songs to teach young children to count or to say the ABCs and, most often, to soothe them and sing them to sleep. Joyce Carol Thomas collected African American songs for *Hush Songs: African American Lullabies* (N–P–I), illustrated by Brenda Joysmith. These songs have worked their sleepy-time magic for generations. Jane Hart compiled 125 songs in her splendid *Singing Bee! A Collection of Favorite Children's Songs* (N–P–I), which is beautifully illustrated by Anita Lobel. She augments the nursery rhymes, lullabies, finger plays, cumulative songs, holiday songs, and activity songs with piano accompaniments and guitar chords. Lobel uses historical settings, eighteenth-century garb, and stage production scenes to illustrate the traditional songs.

Children celebrate their own culture or learn about others through song; they can even learn a second language through song. The best published versions include guitar or piano scores, historical notes, and appropriate illustrations that coordinate with the text. Lulu Delacre selected and illustrated *Arroz con Leche: Popular Songs and Rhymes from Latin America* (P), with English lyrics by Elena Paz and musical arrangements by Ana-Maria Rosada. Jose-Luis Orozco selected, arranged, and translated Latin American songs for *De Colores and Other Latin American Folk Songs for Children* (P), illustrated by Elisa Kleven. David Diaz highlights the single song "De Colores/Bright with Colors" (P) in his beautifully illustrated celebration of love and peace. Gary Chalk chose humorous illustrations depicting events of the American Revolution to accompany the original verses of "Yankee Doodle" in *Yankee Doodle* (P). Gerald Milnes shares traditional songs, rhymes, and riddles from the mountains of West Virginia in *Granny Will Your Dog Bite and Other Mountain Rhymes* (I–A). Other authors of folk songs include Robert Quackenbush, Aliki, Glen Rounds, John Langstaff, and Peter Spier.

Teaching Idea 5.4

Identify Folkloric Style

Contemporary stories are often written in a folkloric style: they contain elements, themes, or recurring patterns found in folklore. Read aloud and discuss fiction containing folklore elements, motifs, or allusions to illustrate the idea. Encourage book discussion groups to continue the search for transformations, magic objects, wishes, trickery, and other folklore conventions. Do the following to help students learn about folkloric style:

✿ Collect stories written in folkloric style.

✿ Discuss folklore elements. What characteristics suggest that a work is folklore?

✿ Have students work in groups to discover folklore elements.

✿ Discuss the devices, allusions, and patterns found. Make a list of commonly used folklore elements.

✿ Encourage students to use the elements in stories they write.

Many of the literary variants discussed in Chapter 5 are good materials to use, as are the books listed below:

Arnold, Caroline, *The Terrible Hodag and the Animal Catchers*

Bang, Molly, *Dawn*

_____, *The Paper Crane*

Cowley, Joy, *The Wishing of Biddy Malone*

Della Chiesa, Carol, *Adventures of Pinocchio*

French, Fiona, *Anancy and Mr Dry-Bone*

Gregory, Valiska, *Through the Mickle Woods*

Isaacs, Anne, *Swamp Angel*

Melmed, Laura Krauss, *Rainbabies*

Nolen, Jerdine, *Big Jabe*

Paterson, Katherine, *The King's Equal*

Wisniewski, David, *The Warrior and the Wise Man*

• • FRACTURED FAIRY TALES AND LITERARY FOLKLORE • •

Many writers, especially those who write fantasies, have been influenced by the structure, motifs, problems, and characters of tales from the oral tradition. Hans Christian Andersen, Rudyard Kipling, Oscar Wilde, and contemporary author Jane Yolen among others have created their own literary fairy tales and pourquoi stories, sometimes referred to as "fakelore," stories patterned after traditional tales. Other writers create parodies and fractured versions of favorite tales. David Wiesner's *The Three Pigs* (P–I) relies on the fact that readers know something about the original tale so that they can fully enjoy the pigs' plight and ingenious means of escape in his story. Jon Scieszka's *The True Story of the Three Little Pigs* (P–I), illustrated by Lane Smith, is told from the point of view of a harmless-looking and misunderstood wolf.

Older readers enjoy novel-length, embellished retellings of familiar folktales such as Cinderella in *Ella Enchanted*, by Gail Carson Levine. Writers also are inspired by mythology. Gerald McDermott's *Creation* (P–I–A) and Phyllis Root's *Big Momma Makes the World* (N–P–I) echo Genesis and other cultures' creation myths while inventing their own joyous celebrations of the

beginning of life. In *Wings* (P–I–A), Christopher Myers tells the modern story of Ikarus Jackson, who proudly flies using his powerful wings just as did his namesake in Greek mythology. We discuss these and other narratives based on folklore traditions in Chapter 6, Fantasy and Science Fiction. Teaching Idea 5.4 gives suggestions for helping children identify folkloric style in more contemporary stories that are not from the oral tradition.

Folklore in the Classroom

Because folklore is a foundation for future literary understanding, it is important for children and young adults to spend time reading from the vast body of folklore. We shortchange children if we deny them the background information necessary for understanding the countless references to folklore in contemporary books and society. Children who do not comprehend the significance of the wolf in folklore will not understand the meaning of the wolf-shaped bush in Anthony Browne's *Piggybook* (P–I), nor will they appreciate the humor of folktale parodies, such as Jon Scieszka's *The True Story of the Three Little Pigs*. Children enjoy knowing that common phrases like "sour grapes" and "slow and steady wins the race" come from Aesop's fables and that "Pandora's box" and "the Midas touch" originated in Greek mythology.

Good teachers give children opportunities to *discover* recurring patterns; they do not *tell* them what to recognize. Teachers who facilitate students' discovery of archetypes find that the primal patterns, themes, and characters become the structural framework for viewing all literature as one story. The most effective approach is to immerse students in traditional stories until they begin to recognize similarities, distinguish patterns, and make predictions. Children who have heard many folktales will tell you that they often begin "Once upon a time" and end "They lived happily ever after," that the good people win, and that the youngest son gets the prin-

cess. These responses show that children recognize the motifs, themes, and story conventions of folklore. Older readers who have been introduced to basic folktales and pourquoi stories will understand the roots of hero tales and mythology as well.

Folklore provides an opportunity for increasing multicultural understanding; it reflects the values, hopes, fears, and beliefs of many cultures. By recognizing recurring themes in folklore from around the world, we can begin to build a bridge of understanding among all people. The oral origins of folklore make it a wonderful resource for storytelling and language development. Dramatic readings or performances offer one venue for creativity. Teaching Idea 5.5 presents suggestions on how to select stories for telling and becoming a storyteller. Children

Teaching Idea 5.5

The Ancient Art of Storytelling

Teachers and students can become proficient storytellers of the tales they enjoy most, the ones that say the most about who they are and what they believe and value. To hear how the best storytellers tell tales that engage their audiences, students can listen to tapes such as those by Robert Munsch, Michael Parent, or the many actors, such as Robin Williams and Denzel Washington, who tell tales for the Rabbit Ears series *We All Have Tales*. Rafe Martin tells the story of *The Rough-Face Girl* on *Rafe Martin Tells His Children's Books* (Yellow Moon Press), and James Earl Jones has recorded the stories in Virginia Hamilton's *The People Could Fly*.

The Student Storyteller

1. With an audience in mind (maybe children in another class below theirs), students can pour over folklore looking for the perfect tale to tell. It may be one that has cultural significance to them or one that is particularly funny or exciting or that mirrors their values.

2. After discovering the ideal tale, students should read it aloud a few times to really hear the language and become familiar with the characters and plot. They should also recognize the climax and the slower parts of the tale.

3. Students should then memorize any recurring refrains and learn important events to recognize the pattern of the story.

4. After putting the book aside, students should practice telling the story a few times, making the story theirs.

5. Then students should decide how to introduce the story to the audience to help them get ready to listen.

6. Students can then tell the story often, to as many people as they can.

A good way to begin with younger students is to focus on a tale that has a cumulative structure in which each incident grows from the preceding one, as in "This Is the House that Jack Built" and "The Old Woman and Her Pig." Jeanette Winter's *The House That Jack Built* (N–P) uses rebuses in the text so that even younger children can predict what is coming next. These stories are often called "chain tales" because each part of the story is linked to the next. The initial incident reveals both central character and problem; each subsequent scene builds on the previous one, continuing to a climax and then unraveling in reverse order or stopping with an abrupt surprise ending. Cat is so very hungry in Meilo So and Sara Cone Bryant's Indian folktale, *Gobble, Gobble, Slip, Slop: A Tale of a Very Greedy Cat* (P–I) that he eats everything and everyone he encounters, with ridiculous results. Chain tales often have repetitive phrases like "Run, run as fast as you can. You can't catch me. I'm the Gingerbread man," from "The Gingerbread Boy" and its variants, "Johnny Cake," "The Pancake," and "The Bun." It is easy for young children to grasp the structure of these tales, and the telling is almost always humorous.

There are also many storytelling resources available, including *The Way of the Storyteller* by Ruth Sawyer (1962); *The Story Vine: A Source Book of Unusual and Easy-to-Tell Stories from around the World* by Anne Pellowski (1984); *Tell Me a Tale: A Book about Storytelling* by Joseph Bruchac (1997); and *Pete Seeger's Storytelling Book* by Pete Seeger and Paul DuBois (2000).

who are familiar with folklore also learn to use similar patterns and conventions in their own writing, borrowing and exploring folkloric frameworks and characters for their own personal stories.

SUMMARY

Folklore began as stories and poems told across the generations, as people sought to entertain, to explain the world, and to pass down their cultural values and beliefs. Folklore helps us understand not only ourselves but people from other cultures and other times. Folktales, fables, hero tales, myths, and songs add depth to our literary knowledge.

Each type of folklore has its own characteristics. Rhythmic nursery rhymes enchant young children. Folktales—which include fairy tales, talking animal stories,

noodlehead tales, and tall tales—have universal themes and motifs, and appear in different guises around the world. Fables incorporate explicit moral statements that are intended to guide behavior. Myths explain the origins of the world, natural phenomena, and human behavior. Hero tales reveal cultural beliefs and values. Folk songs celebrate the values and circumstances of those who first sang them.

Teachers in all grades recognize that folklore, in addition to being a source of pleasure for students of all ages, is a valuable resource for developing language, learning about literature, and learning about other cultures. As it did in the past, folklore today continues to educate and entertain. Above all else, these are stirring stories that have entertained listeners for centuries because they are filled with harrowing adventures and horrific monsters as well as mythic and everyday heroes who triumph in the end. When teachers share these memorable stories with their students, they link them to people in the distant past from all corners of the world.

Booklist

✳ Indicates some aspect of diversity

Folklore from the World's Geographical Regions

WORLDWIDE COLLECTIONS

✳ Climo, Shirley, *Monkey Business: Stories from around the World* (2005) (I)

✳ Fleischman, Paul, *Glass Slipper, Gold Sandal: A Worldwide Cinderella* (2007) (I)

✳ Hamilton, Virginia, *The Dark Way: Stories from the Spirit World* (1990) (A)

✳ _____, *In the Beginning: Creation Stories from around the World* (1988) (A)

✳ Keenan, Sheila, *Gods, Goddesses and Monsters: A Book of World Mythology* (2000) (A)

✳ Kherdian, David, *Feathers and Tails: Animal Fables from Around the World* (1992) (P–I)

✳ McBratney, Sam, *One Voice, Please: Favorite Read-Aloud Stories* (2008) (I)

✳ Norman, Howard, *Between Heaven and Earth: Bird Tales from around the World* (2004) (I)

✳ Rosen, Michael, *How the Animals Got Their Colors: Animal Myths from around the World* (1991) (P–I)

✳ Shannon, George. *More True Lies: 18 Tales for You to Judge* (2001) (I–A)

✳ Sierra, Judy, *Nursery Tales around the World* (1996) (N–P)

✳ Tchana, Katrin Hyman, *Changing Woman and Her Sisters: Stories of Goddesses from Around the World* (2006) (I–A)

✳ Van Laan, Nancy, *Sleep, Sleep, Sleep: A Lullaby for Little Ones around the World* (1995) (N)

✳ Yolen, Jane, *Mightier Than the Sword: World Folktales for Strong Boys* (2003) (I)

✳ _____, *Not One Damsel in Distress: World Folktales for Strong Girls* (2000) (I)

✳ _____, *Sleep Rhymes around the World* (1994) (N–P)

✳ _____, *Street Rhymes around the World* (1992) (I)

NORTH, SOUTH, AND CENTRAL AMERICA

✳ Aardema, Verna, *Borreguita and the Coyote: A Tale from Ayutla, Mexico* (1991) (P–I)

✳ Ada, Alma Flor, *Mediopollito/Half-Chicken* (1995) (P–I)

✳ _____, *Three Golden Oranges* (1999) (P–I)

✳ Anaya, Rudolfo, *My Land Sings: Stories from the Rio Grande* (1999) (I)

✳ Bernier-Grand, Carmen T., *Juan Bobo: Four Tales from Puerto Rico* (1994) (P–I)

✳ Bierhorst, John, *The People with Five Fingers: A Native Californian Creation Tale* (2000) (P–I)

✳ _____, *Is My Friend at Home? Pueblo Fireside Tales* (2000) (P–I)

✳ Bruchac, Joseph, *Between Earth and Sky: Legends of Native American Sacred Places* (1996) (I)

✳ _____, *The Boy Who Lived with the Bears and Other Iroquois Stories* (1995) (I)

✳ _____, *Gluskabe and the Four Wishes* (1995) (P–I)

✳ _____, *The Story of the Milky Way: A Cherokee Tale* (1995) (P–I)

※ Brusca, María Cristina, and Tona Wilson, *When Jaguars Ate the Moon and Other Stories about Animals and Plants of the Americas* (1995) (P–I)

※ Gerson, Mary-Joan, *People of Corn: A Mayan Story* (1995) (P–I)

※ Goble, Paul, *Adopted by the Eagles: A Plains Indian Story of Friendship and Treachery* (1994) (P–I)

※ _____, *Crow Chief: A Plains Indian Story* (1992) (P–I)

※ _____, *Iktomi and the Coyote* (1998) (I)

※ Gonzalez, Lucia, *The Bossy Gallito: A Traditional Cuban Folktale* (1994) (P)

※ Hamilton, Virginia, *Her Stories: African American Folktales, Fairy Tales, and True Tales* (1995) (I–A)

※ _____, *The People Could Fly: American Black Folktales* (1985) (A)

※ _____, *The People Could Fly: The Picture Book* (2007) (I–A)

※ _____, *When Birds Could Talk and Bats Could Sing: The Adventures of Bruh Sparrow, Sis Wren, and Their Friends* (1996) (I–A)

※ Hayes, Joe, *La Llorona/The Weeping Woman: An Hispanic Legend Told in Spanish and English* (2004) (I–A)

Hodges, Margaret, *Dick Wittington and His Cat* (2006) (P)

Irving, Washington, *The Legend of Sleepy Hollow* (2007) (I–A)

※ Jaffe, Nina, *The Golden Flower: A Taino Myth from Puerto Rico* (1996) (P)

※ Joseph, Lynn, *The Mermaid's Twin Sister: More Stories from Trinidad* (1994) (I–A)

Kilaka, John, *True Friends: A Tale from Tanzania* (2006) (P)

※ Kimmel, Eric A., *The Two Mountains: An Aztec Legend* (2000) (P–I)

※ Lester, Julius, *John Henry* (1994) (P–I)

※ Lyons, Mary E., *The Butter Tree: Tales of Bruh Rabbit* (1995) (I)

※ Marcantonio, Patricia Santos, *Red Ridin' in the Hood: And Other Cuentos* (2005) (I–A)

※ McDermott, Gerald, *Arrow to the Sun: A Pueblo Indian Tale* (1974) (P–I)

※ _____, *Raven: A Trickster Tale from the Pacific Northwest* (1993) (P–I)

※ McGill, Alice, *Way Up and Over Everything* (2008) (P)

※ McKissack, Patricia C., *The Dark-Thirty: Southern Tales of the Supernatural* (1992) (A)

※ Morales, Yuyi, *Just a Minute: A Trickster Tale and Counting Book* (2003) (N–P)

Moses, Will, *Johnny Appleseed: The Story of a Legend* (2001) (I)

※ Philip, Neil, *Horse Hooves and Chicken Feet: Mexican Folktales* (2003) (I)

※ Pinkney, Jerry, *Little Red Riding Hood* (2007) (P–I)

※ Rockwell, Anne, *The Boy Who Wouldn't Obey: A Mayan Legend* (2001) (P–I)

※ Rodanas, Kristina, *Dance of the Sacred Circle: A Native American Tale* (1994) (I)

※ _____, *Dragonfly's Tale* (1991) (P)

※ Root, Phyllis, *Aunt Nancy and the Bothersome Visitors* (2007) (P)

※ Ross, Gayle, *How Turtle's Back Was Cracked: A Traditional Cherokee Tale* (1995) (P–I)

Salley, Coleen, *Epossumondas Saves the Day* (2006) (P)

San Souci, Robert D., *The Faithful Friend* (1995) (P–I)

_____, *Six Foolish Fishermen* (2000) (P–I)

※ _____, *Sukey and the Mermaid* (1992) (P–I)

※ _____, *The Talking Eggs* (1989) (P–I)

※ Sierra, Judy, *Wiley and the Hairy Man* (1996) (P–I)

※ Stevens, Jane, *Old Bag of Bones: A Coyote Tale* (1996) (P)

※ Van Laan, Nancy, *In a Circle Long Ago: A Treasury of Native Lore from North America* (1995) (I–A)

※ _____, *With a Whoop and a Holler: A Bushel of Lore from Way Down South* (2001) (I)

EUROPE, AFRICA, AND THE MIDDLE EAST

※ Aardema, Verna, *The Lonely Lioness and the Ostrich Chicks* (1996) (P)

※ _____, *Misoso: Once upon a Time: Tales from Africa* (1994) (I–A)

※ _____, *Bringing the Rain to Kapiti Plain: A Nandi Tale* (1981) (P)

※ _____, *Why Mosquitoes Buzz in People's Ears: A West African Tale* (1975) (P)

※ Bryan, Ashley, *Lion and the Ostrich Chicks* (1986) (I)

※ _____, *Ashley Bryan's African Tales, Uh-Huh* (1998) (I)

※ _____, *Beautiful Blackbird* (2003) (P)

※ Doyle, Malachy, *Tales from Old Ireland* (2000) (I–A)

※ Gerson, Mary-Joan, *Why the Sky Is Far Away: A Nigerian Folktale* (1994) (N–P)

※ Gregor, C. Shana, *Cry of the Benu Bird: An Egyptian Creation Story* (1996) (P–I)

※ Haley, Gail E., *A Story, a Story* (1970) (P–I)

※ Huck, Charlotte, *The Black Bull of Norroway: A Scottish Tale* (2001) (P–I)

※ Huth, Holly Young, *The Son of the Sun and the Daughter of the Moon: A Saami Folktale* (2000) (P–I)

Isadora, Rachel, *The Fisherman and His Wife* (2008) (P)

※ _____, *Twelve Dancing Princesses* (2007) (P)

Johnson-Davies, Denys, *Goha the Wise Fool* (2005) (I)

※ Kimmel, Eric A., *The Adventures of Hershel of Ostropol* (1995) (I)

※ _____, *Count Silvernose: A Story from Italy* (1996) (P–I)

※ Lupton, Hugh, *Pirican Pic and Pirican Mor* (2003) (P)

※ Mitchell, Stephen, *Genies, Meanies, and Magic Rings: Three Tales from the Arabian Nights* (2007) (I)

※ Mollel, Tololwa M., *Subira Subira* (2000) (P–I)

※ _____, *Shadow Dance* (1998) (P–I)

※ _____, *The Orphan Boy: A Maasai Story* (1990) (P–I)

※ Morley, Jacqueline, *Egyptian Myths* (1999) (I–A)

※ Onyefulu, Obi, *Chinye: A West African Folk Tale* (1994) (P–I)

※ Paye, Won-Ldy, and Margaret Lippert, *Mrs. Chicken and the Hungry Crocodile* (2003) (P–I)

※ _____, *Head, Body, Legs: A Tale from Liberia* (2002) (P–I)

※ Philip, Neil, *Celtic Fairy Tales* (1999) (I–A)

※ Sierra, Judy, *The Beautiful Butterfly: A Folktale from Spain* (2000) (P–I)

※ Singer, Isaac, *Zlateh the Goat and Other Stories* (1966) (I)

※ _____, *When Shlemiel Went to Warsaw and Other Stories* (1968) (I)

Schlitz, Laura Amy, *The Bearskinner: A Tale of the Brothers Grimm* (2007) (I)

Shepard, Aaron, *One-Eye! Two-Eyes! Three-Eyes!: A Very Grimm Fairy Tale* (2006) (P)

※ Souhami, Jessica, *The Leopard's Drum: An Ashanti Tale from West Africa* (1995) (P)

_____, *Sausages* (2006) (P)

※ Taback, Simms, *Joseph Had a Little Overcoat* (1999) (P)

※ Tchana, Katrin, *Sense Pass King: A Story from Cameroon* (2002) (I)

※ Washington, Donna, *A Pride of African Tales* (2004) (I)

※ Wisniewski, David, *Elfwyn's Saga* (1990) (I)

※ _____, *Golem* (1996) (I)

※ Yolen, Jane, *Tam Lin: An Old Ballad* (1990) (I)

CENTRAL ASIA

✳ Brett, Jan, *The Mitten: A Ukrainian Folktale* (1989) (P)
✳ Demi, *Firebird* (1994) (P–I)
✳ _____, *The Hungry Coat: A Tale from Turkey* (2004) (I)
✳ Hastings, Selina, *The Firebird* (1992) (P–I)
✳ Hogrogian, Nonny, *One Fine Day* (1971) (P)
✳ Ransome, Arthur, *The Fool of the World and the Flying Ship: A Russian Tale* (1968) (P–I)
✳ Shah, Idries, *The Old Woman and the Eagle* (2003) (P–I)
✳ _____, *Neem the Half-Boy* (1998) (P–I)
✳ _____, *The Boy without a Name* (2000) (P–I)
✳ _____, *The Clever Boy and the Terrible, Dangerous Animal* (2000) (P–I)

THE FAR EAST

✳ Climo, Shirley, *Tuko and the Birds: A Tale from the Philippines* (2008) (P)
✳ Demi, *The Empty Pot* (1990) (P)
✳ _____, *The Magic Boat* (1990) (P–I)
✳ Greene, Ellin, *Ling-Li and the Phoenix Fairy: A Chinese Folktale* (1996) (P–I)
✳ Ho, Minfong, and Saphan Ros, *The Two Brothers* (1995) (P–I)
✳ _____, *Brother Rabbit: A Cambodian Tale* (1997) (P–I)
✳ Kajikawa, Kimiko, *Yoshi's Feast* (2000) (P–I)
✳ Kimmel, Eric, *Three Samurai Cats: A Story from Japan* (2003) (I)
✳ Muth, Jon, *Stone Soup* (2003) (P–I)
✳ Paterson, Katherine, *The Tale of the Mandarin Ducks* (1990) (I)
✳ Xiong, Blia, *Nine-in-One Grr! Grr!: A Folktale from the Hmong People of Laos* (1989) (P–I)
✳ Yep, Laurence, *Tongues of Jade* (1991) (I–A)
✳ Young, Ed, *Seven Blind Mice* (1992) (P)
✳ _____, *The Sons of the Dragon King: A Chinese Legend* (2004) (I–A)
✳ _____, *The Lost Horse: A Chinese Folktale* (1998) (I)

Nursery Rhymes

Books in this section are appropriate for nursery–primary readers unless otherwise noted.

Addams, Charles, *The Charles Addams Mother Goose* (1967) (A)
Crews, Nina, *The Neighborhood Mother Goose* (2004) (P–I)
dePaola, Tomie, *Tomie dePaola's Mother Goose* (1985)
Downes, Belinda, *A Stitch in Rhyme: A Nursery Rhyme Sampler with Embroidered Illustrations* (1996)
Galdone, Paul, *Three Little Kittens* (1986)
✳ Griego, Margot C., Betsy Bucks, Sharon Gilbert, and Laurel Kimball, *Tortillas para Mama and Other Nursery Rhymes: Spanish and English* (1981) (P–I)
Lobel, Arnold, *Random House Book of Mother Goose* (1986)
Marcus, Leonard, and Amy Schwartz, *Mother Goose's Little Misfortunes* (1990)
_____, *Old Mother Hubbard and Her Wonderful Dog* (1991)
Opie, Iona, *Here Comes Mother Goose* (1999)
_____, *My Very First Mother Goose* (1996)
_____, *Tail Feathers from Mother Goose: The Opie Rhyme Book* (1988)
Opie, Iona, and Peter Opie, *The Oxford Dictionary of Nursery Rhymes* (1951)
_____, *I Saw Esau: The Schoolchild's Pocket Book* (1992)

✳ Polacco, Patricia, *Babushka's Mother Goose* (1995)
Slier, Debby, *The Real Mother Goose: Book of American Rhymes* (1995)
Sutherland, Zena, *The Orchard Book of Nursery Rhymes* (1990)
Watson, Clyde, *Wendy Watson's Mother Goose* (1989)
Yolen, Jane, *Jane Yolen's Mother Goose Songbook* (1992)

Folktales

TALKING ANIMALS

Books in this section are appropriate for primary–intermediate readers unless otherwise noted.

✳ Faulkner, William J., *Brer Tiger and the Big Wind* (1995) (I–A)
Grimm, Jacob, and Wilhelm Grimm, *The Bremen Town Musicians* (2007) (P)
✳ Hamilton, Virginia, *Bruh Rabbit and the Tar Baby Girl* (2003) (P)
✳ Knutson, Barbara, *Sungura and Leopard: A Swahili Trickster Tale* (1993)
✳ Lester, Julius, *The Tales of Uncle Remus: The Adventures of Brer Rabbit* (1987) (I–A)
✳ _____, *More Tales of Uncle Remus: Further Adventures of Brer Rabbit, His Friends, Enemies, and Others* (1988) (I–A)
✳ _____, *Further Tales of Uncle Remus: The Misadventures of Brer Rabbit, Brer Fox, Brer Wolf, the Doodang, and Other Creatures* (1990) (I–A)
✳ McDermott, Gerald, *Zomo the Rabbit: A Trickster Tale from West Africa* (1992)
✳ _____, *Coyote: A Trickster Tale from the American Southwest* (1994)
✳ McGill, Alice, *Sure as Sunrise: Stories of Bruh Rabbit & His Walkin' Talkin' Friends* (2004)
✳ Parks, Van Dyke, *Jump Again! More Adventures of Brer Rabbit* (1987)
✳ _____, *Jump on Over! The Adventures of Brer Rabbit and His Family* (1989)
✳ Parks, Van Dyke, and Malcolm Jones, *Jump! The Adventures of Brer Rabbit* (1986)
✳ Rascol, Sabina, *The Impudent Rooster* (2004)
✳ So, Meilo, *Gobble, Gobble, Slip, Slop: A Tale of a Very Greedy Cat* (2004)

Fairy Tales

Grimm, Jacob, and Wilhelm Grimm, *The Annotated Brothers Grimm*, translated and edited by Maria Tatar (2004) (A)
✳ _____, *The Twelve Dancing Princesses* (2007) (P)
Lunge-Larsen, Lise, *The Hidden Folk: Stories of Fairies, Dwarves, Selkies, and Other Secret Beings* (2004) (I–A)
Manna, Anthony, and Christodoula Mitakidou, *Mr. Semolina-Semolinus: A Greek Folktale* (1997) (I)
Perrault, Charles, *Beauty and the Beast*, adapted by Nancy Willard (1992) (I)
✳ _____, *Beauty and the Beast*, adapted by Jan Brett (1989) (P)
_____, *Cinderella*, adapted by Barbara McClintock (2005) (P)
Smith, James, *Book of a Thousand Days* (2007) (I)
Steig, Jeanne, *A Handful of Beans: Six Fairy Tales* (1998) (I–A)
Willey, Margaret, *Clever Beatrice* (2001) (P–I)
_____, *Clever Beatrice and the Best Little Pony* (2004) (P–I)

Tall Tales

Arnold, Caroline, *The Terrible Hodag and the Animal Catchers* (2006) (P–I)
☀ Hurston, Zora Neale, *Lies and Other Tall Tales* (2005) (I)
Johnson, Paul Brett, *Old Dry Frye: A Deliciously Funny Tall Tale* (1999) (P–I)
Kellogg, Steven, *Paul Bunyan* (1984) (P)
———, *Pecos Bill* (1986) (P)
☀ Lester, Julius, *John Henry* (1994) (P)
Osborne, Mary Pope, *American Tall Tales* (1991) (P–I)
San Souci, Robert D., and Jane Yolen, *Cut from the Same Cloth: American Women of Myth, Legend, and Tall Tale* (1993) (I)
Walker, Paul Robert, *Big Men, Big Country: A Collection of American Tall Tales* (1993) (A)

Fables

Books in this section are appropriate for primary–intermediate readers unless otherwise noted.

Anno, Mitsumasa, *Anno's Aesop: A Book of Fables by Aesop and Mr. Fox* (1989)
☀ Bierhorst, John, *Doctor Coyote: A Native American Aesop's Fables* (1987)
Brett, Jan, *Town Mouse, Country Mouse* (1994)
☀ Climo, Shirley, *The Little Red Ant and the Great Big Crumb: A Mexican Fable* (1995)
☀ Demi, *A Chinese Zoo: Fables and Proverbs* (1987)
☀ Galdone, Paul, *The Monkey and the Crocodile: A Jataka Tale from India* (1969)
☀ Heins, Ethel, *The Cat and the Cook: And Other Fables of Krylov* (1995)
Hennessy, B. G., *The Boy Who Cried Wolf* (2006)
MacDonald, Suse, and Bill Oakes, *Once upon Another: The Tortoise and the Hare/The Lion and the Mouse* (1990)
☀ Martin, Rafe, *Foolish Rabbit's Big Mistake* (1985)
McDermott, Gerald, *The Fox and the Stork* (1999)
Pinkney, Jerry, *Aesop's Fables* (2000)
Stevens, Janet, *The Tortoise and the Hare: An Aesop Fable* (1984)
———, *The Town Mouse and the Country Mouse: An Aesop Fable* (1987)
Ward, Helen, *The Hare and the Tortoise: A Fable from Aesop* (1999)
———, *Unwitting Wisdom: An Anthology of Aesop's Fables* (2004)
Young, Ed, *Seven Blind Mice* (1992)

Myths

Books in this section are appropriate for intermediate–advanced readers.

Climo, Shirley, *Atalanta's Race: A Greek Myth* (1995)
———, *Stolen Thunder: A Norse Myth* (1994)
Curlee, Lynn, *Mythological Creatures: A Classical Bestiary* (2008) (I)
Fisher, Leonard Everett, *The Olympians: Great Gods and Goddesses of Ancient Greece* (1984)
Fleischman, Paul, *Dateline: Troy* (1996)
Hutton, Warwick, *Odysseus and the Cyclops* (1995)
———, *Persephone* (1994)
———, *Theseus and the Minotaur* (1989)

Orgel, Doris, *Ariadne, Awake!* (1994)
Osborne, Mary Pope, *Favorite Norse Myths* (1996)
Philip, Neil, *King Midas* (1994)
Steig, Jeanne, *A Gift from Zeus: Sixteen Favorite Myths* (2001)

Pourquoi Tales

AFRICAN

Books in this section are appropriate for primary–intermediate readers.

Aardema, Verna, *Princess Gorilla and a New Kind of Water* (1988)
———, *Why Mosquitoes Buzz in People's Ears: A West African Tale* (1975)
Gerson, Mary-Joan, *Why the Sky Is Far Away: A Nigerian Folktale* (1994)
Knutson, Barbara, *Why the Crab Has No Head* (1987)
———, *How the Guinea Fowl Got Her Spots* (1990)
Lester, Julius, *How Many Spots Does a Leopard Have? And Other Tales* (1989)
Troughton, Joanna, *How Stories Came into the World: A Folk Tale from West Africa* (1991)

NATIVE AMERICAN

Books in this section are appropriate for primary–intermediate readers.

Connolly, James E., *Why the Possum's Tail Is Bare and Other North American Indian Nature Tales* (1985)
Esbensen, Barbara Juster, *Ladder to the Sky: How the Gift of Healing Came to the Ojibway Nation* (1989)
Goble, Paul, *Her Seven Brothers* (1988)
———, *Star Boy* (1983)
———, *Mystic Horse* (2003)
Lattimore, Deborah Nourse, *Why There Is No Arguing in Heaven: A Mayan Myth* (1989)
Martin, Rafe, *The Boy Who Lived with the Seals* (1993)
Oughton, Jerrie, *How the Stars Fell into the Sky: A Navajo Legend* (1992)
Troughton, Joanna, *How the Birds Changed Their Feathers: A South American Indian Folktale* (1976)
———, *How Rabbit Stole the Fire: A North American Indian Folktale* (1986)
Vogel, Carole Garbuny, *Legends of Landforms: Native American Lore and the Geology of the Land* (1999)

Hero Tales

Books in this section are appropriate for intermediate–advanced readers unless otherwise noted.

Crossley-Holland, Kevin, *Beowulf* (1968)
———, *The World of King Arthur and His Court: People, Places, Legend and Lore* (1998)
☀ Demi, *The Legend of Lao Tzu and the Tao Te Ching* (2007) (I)
Gretchen, Sylvia, *Hero of the Land of Snow* (1990)
☀ Henderson, Kathy, *Lugalbanda: The Boy Who Got Caught Up in a War* (2006) (A)
Hodges, Margaret, *The Kitchen Knight: A Tale of King Arthur* (1990)
———, *St. George and the Dragon* (1984)

Hodges, Margaret, *Merlin and the Making of the King* (2004)

Hodges, Margaret, and Margery Evernden, *Of Swords and Sorcerers: The Adventures of King Arthur and His Knights* (1993)

Jaffrey, Madhur, *Seasons of Splendour: Tales, Myths, and Legends of India* (1985)

✳ Lester, Julius, *The Old African* (2005) (A)

Lunge-Larsen, Lise, *The Race of the Birkebeiners* (2001)

✳ McCaughrean, Geraldine, *Gilgamesh the Hero* (2002)

McKinley, Robin, *The Outlaws of Sherwood* (1988)

Perham, Molly, *King Arthur: The Legends of Camelot* (1993)

Philip, Neil, *Tale of Sir Gawain* (1987)

✳ Quattlebaum, Mary, *Sparks Fly High: The Legend of Dancing Point* (2006) (P)

✳ Running Wolf, Michael B., and Patricia Clark Smith, *On the Trail of Elder Brother: Glous'gap Stories of the Micmac Indians* (2000)

Sabuda, Robert, *Arthur and the Sword* (1995)

San Souci, Robert D., *Young Guinevere* (1993)

_____, *Larger Than Life: The Adventures of American Legendary Heroes* (1991)

Williams, Marcia, *King Arthur and the Knights of the Round Table* (1996)

Yolen, Jane, *Camelot* (1995)

✳ Young, Ed, *Monkey King* (2001)

Folklore Variants

Books in this section are appropriate for primary–intermediate–advanced readers in a study of variants.

CINDERELLA

✳ Climo, Shirley, *The Egyptian Cinderella* (1989)

✳ _____, *The Irish Cinderlad* (1996)

✳ _____, *The Korean Cinderella* (1993)

✳ Fleischman, Paul, *Glass Slipper, Gold Sandal: A Worldwide Cinderella* (2008)

Greaves, Margaret, *Tattercoats* (1990)

✳ Hayes, Joe, *Little Gold Star/Estrellita de Oro: A Cinderella Cuento* (2000)

Hooks, William, *Moss Gown* (1987)

Huck, Charlotte, *Princess Furball* (1989)

Jacobs, Joseph, *Tattercoats* (1989)

Jungman, Ann, *Cinderella and the Hot Air Balloon* (1992)

✳ Louie, Ai-Ling, *Yeh Shen: A Cinderella Story from China* (1982)

Lowell, Susan, *Cindy Ellen: A Wild Western Cinderella* (2000)

Martin, Rafe, *The Rough-Face Girl* (1992)

Perrault, Charles, *Cinderella and Other Tales from Perrault* (1989)

San Jose, Christine, *Cinderella* (1994)

✳ San Souci, Robert D., *Sootface: An Ojibwa Cinderella Story* (1994)

✳ _____, *Cendrillon: A Caribbean Cinderella* (1998)

✳ _____, *Cinderella Skeleton* (2000)

✳ Silverman, Erica, *Raisel's Riddle* (1999)

FROG PRINCE

Cecil, Laura, *Frog Princess* (1995)

Isadora, Rachel, *The Princess and the Frog* (1989)

Ormerod, Jan, and David Lloyd, *The Frog Prince* (1990)

Scieszka, Jon, *The Frog Prince Continued* (1991)

Tarcov, Edith H., *Frog Prince* (1974)

JACK TALES

Briggs, Raymond, *Jim and the Beanstalk* (1970)

Compton, Kenn, and Joanne Compton, *Jack the Giant Chaser: An Appalachian Tale* (1993)

Fleischman, Sid, *McBroom and the Beanstalk* (1978)

Haley, Gail E., *Mountain Jack Tales* (1992)

_____, *Jack and the Fire Dragon* (1998)

Howe, John, *Jack and the Beanstalk* (1989)

Kellogg, Steven, *Jack and the Beanstalk* (1991)

Osborne, Mary Pope, *Kate and the Beanstalk* (2000)

Wildsmith, Brian, and Rebecca Wildsmith, *Jack and the Meanstalk* (1994)

RED RIDING HOOD

Crawford, Elizabeth D., *Little Red Cap* (1983)

de Regniers, Beatrice Schenk, *Red Riding Hood* (1972)

Ernst, Lisa Campbell, *Little Red Riding Hood: A Newfangled Prairie Tale* (1995)

Hyman, Trina Schart, *Little Red Riding Hood* (1983)

Langley, John, *Little Red Riding Hood* (1995)

Perrault, Charles, *Little Red Cap*, adapted by Lisbeth Zwerger (1987)

Pinkney, Jerry, *Little Red Riding Hood* (2007)

✳ Young, Ed, *Lon Po Po: A Red-Riding Hood Story from China* (1989)

Zeifert, Harriet, *Little Red Riding Hood* (2000)

RUMPELSTILTSKIN

✳ Hamilton, Virginia, *The Girl Who Spun Gold* (2000)

Jacobs, Joseph, *Tom Tit Tot* (1965)

Stanley, Diane, *Rumpelstiltskin's Daughter* (1997)

Zelinsky, Paul (reteller), *Rumpelstiltskin* (1989)

Zemach, Harve, *Duffy and the Devil: A Cornish Tale* (1973)

THREE LITTLE PIGS

Bucknall, Caroline, *Three Little Pigs* (1986)

Hooks, William H., *The Three Little Pigs and the Fox* (1989)

Marshall, James, *The Three Little Pigs* (1989)

Moser, Barry, *The Three Little Pigs* (2001)

Scieszka, Jon, *The True Story of the Three Little Pigs* (1989)

Trivizas, Eugene, *Three Little Wolves and the Big Bad Pig* (1993)

Wiesner, David, *The Three Pigs* (2001)

Zemach, Margot, *The Three Little Pigs: An Old Story* (1988)

COLLECTIONS OF VARIANTS AND FRACTURED FAIRY TALES

Anno, Mitsumasa, *Anno's Twice Told Tales: The Fisherman and His Wife and The Four Clever Brothers* (1993)

Brooks, William, *A Telling of the Tales* (1990)

Galloway, Priscilla, *Truly Grim Tales* (1995)

King-Smith, Dick, *The Topsy-Turvy Storybook* (1992)

Scieszka, Jon, *The Stinky Cheese Man and Other Fairly Stupid Tales* (1992)

Fantasy and Science Fiction

fiction [readers] will ever find" and demands a great deal from its readers (1996, p. 16). Hunt (2007) argues that fantasy speaks to young readers in a special way. "Above everything else—the terrific plotting, the nifty world-building, the sense of awe and wonder and magic—the potent appeal of fantasy for me was that while so many of the mundane, ordinary things of life were controlled by adults, the *really* important things—the fate of the universe, the battle between good and evil—were left in the capable hands of children" (2007, p. 645).

Both fantasy and science fiction are imaginative narratives that explore alternate realities. Fantasy suspends scientific explanations and natural laws; it contains some element of character, setting, or plot not found in the natural world as it asks age-old questions about life, goodness, and balance. Science explores scientific possibilities, asking and answering the question "If this, then what?" Both fantasy and science fiction are often set in worlds that do not correspond to present realities, but science fiction differs from fantasy in that the future realities it depicts are based on extrapolation from scientific principles.

Of course, it is sometimes difficult to draw the line between what is scientifically possible and what is not, and some critics talk about "science fantasy" books in which the line between the fantastic and a scientific possibility is a fine one. Madeleine L'Engle's *A Wrinkle in Time*, *A Wind in the Door*, and *A Swiftly Tilting Planet* (A) all involve travel through time and space. Is this fantasy? Or, because this travel is theoretically possible, is it science fiction? What is truly important is that L'Engle's powerful novels, however one chooses to classify them, offer readers opportunities to think about the power of love in a deeper, more profound way than our daily lives permit.

A Brief History of Fantasy and Science Fiction

Children had little time to be children in the mid-nineteenth century. Social and economic conditions dictated that many young people work, often in horrendous circumstances. The society that tolerated grim conditions for children developed a literature that provided a fantasy escape from the harsh workaday world while still giving a justification for the work ethic. Much of that fanciful literature came from England, and hardworking American children welcomed it with open arms.

Alice's Adventures in Wonderland (1865) and *Through the Looking Glass* (1871) by Charles Dodgson are the first significant works of fantasy for children. Dodgson, a clergyman and scholarly math professor at

Oxford, chose the pen name Lewis Carroll to avoid being identified with books for children, ironically the very reason that he is remembered today. Legend says that Dodgson often told stories to the three Liddell girls, daughters of a friend. One afternoon, Alice, one of the sisters, asked for a story with nonsense. The story she heard that day became world famous: Dodgson wrote it out for her the following Christmas, and it was then published with John Tenniel's brilliant illustrations. Contemporary artists offer their own interpretations of this still-popular fantasy, as demonstrated by Lisbeth Zwerger's *Alice in Wonderland* (I), first published in 1999 and reissued in 2008.

Fantasy flourished in the twentieth century, with publication of books such as the classic story-play *Peter Pan* by J. M. Barrie (1904), Beatrix Potter's *The Tale of Peter Rabbit* (1902), Frank Baum's *The Wizard of Oz* (1900), and J. R. R. Tolkien's *The Hobbit* (1938). These were followed by C. S. Lewis's *The Chronicles of Narnia* (1950), E. B. White's *Charlotte's Web* (1952), Lloyd Alexander's *The Book of Three* (1964) and Susan Cooper's *The Dark Is Rising* (1973). The "series" book in the fantasy genre was increasingly frequent, and books such as Philip Pullman's **His Dark Materials** (I–A) series, J. K. Rowling's **Harry Potter** (I–A) series, and J. R. R. Tolkien's **Lord of the Rings** (I–A) trilogy are so popular that they have been made into movies, fueling the "fantasy renaissance" we have today.

Considering Quality in Fantasy and Science Fiction

As with all quality narrative literature, good fantasy and science fiction—whether they are serious explorations of the human condition or a playful exploration of an alternate reality—tell an interesting story and have well-developed characters, an engaging plot, and an identifiable theme—all presented through a well-crafted style. Authors manipulate these elements to create a fantasy world. If the writer is successful, readers willingly suspend disbelief. We judge the quality of a writer's private vision by how thoroughly it convinces us of its reality, by how long it haunts our memory, and by how deeply it moves us to new insights. As Baker points out, "Every great fantasy is great in its own way, . . . because real insight and artistic originality must be unique to its author" (2006, p. 624). Within that originality, however, it is possible to recognize certain qualities that usually are present in excellent fantasy and science fiction. Criteria for evaluating fantasy and science fiction appear in Figure 6.1.

interesting story
well developed characters
engaging plot
identifiable theme
well crafted
Chys

Figure 6.1

Considering Quality in Fantasy and Science Fiction

✿ The story meets the criteria for excellence in narrative fiction.

✿ The fantasy world is detailed and believable within the context of the story.

✿ The story events are imaginative, yet logically consistent within the story world.

✿ The characters are multidimensional, with consistent and logical behavior.

✿ The writing is rich, and the structures are clear.

✿ The themes are meaningful, causing readers to think about life.

Teaching Idea 6.1

Teaching Genre: Setting in Fantasy and Science Fiction

Good fantasy writers establish believable settings by carefully presenting them in intricate detail. Because the reader must envision the fantasy world, a writer's words ought to stimulate pictures in the mind's eye. Some writers add a map or make a scale drawing of an area; some paint scenes that are so vivid you can smell them.

Read outstanding fantasies to savor the descriptive language used to establish setting. If you work with young students, read aloud scenes and ask them to create dioramas, paintings, or three-dimensional scenes of the ones described. Ask students to describe in writing the scene they envision. Discuss these and other examples of vivid writing in a writing workshop to show effective techniques, and then ask young writers to create their own vivid settings.

Following is a list of suggested books and pages where you will read vivid scenes:

Farmer, Nancy, *The House of the Scorpion*, see chapter 33, p. 324, "The Boneyard."

Grahame, Kenneth, *Wind in the Willows*, see p. 9, the passage that begins "The Mole had been working . . ."

Jacques, Brian, *Redwall*, see the frontispiece: "Redwall stood foursquare along the marches of the old south border, flanked on two sides by Mossflower Wood's shaded depths . . ."

Jansson, Tove, *Tales from Moominvalley*, see p. 11: "The brook was a good one . . ."

White, E. B., *Charlotte's Web*, see p. 13: "The barn was very large. It was very old. It smelled of hay and it smelled of manure. It smelled of the perspiration of tired horses and the wonderful sweet breath of patient cows."

• • SETTING • •

No matter how fantastic they are, settings become believable when an author provides rich details that enable a reader to envision them. Some authors set their stories entirely in an alternate reality, providing detailed verbal "maps" of fantasy worlds, often with accompanying visual depictions. Others gradually lead readers from a fictional real world into a richly detailed fantasy world through some device, such as a magic door, a magic object, or the belief of realistic characters in the fantasy setting. In science fiction the setting is some time in the future, a future shaped by a present-day scientific possibility that has been realized. It may be, for example, a world overcrowded due to medical advances, or one in which genetic engineering has run amuck, or a world that has been devastated by global warming. Effective settings are detailed and believable within the context of the story. Teaching Idea 6.1 suggests ideas for examining some believable settings with your students.

• • PLOT • •

Even though events might not be realistic, what happens in a story must be logically consistent within the story world. If characters move through time, they do so for a reason; they may walk through a door, press a magic button, or visit a particular place. If the fantastic operates in the real world, then there must be consistency in how real people are affected by the fantastic events. In science fiction the plot is usually driven by the problems that scientific advances have created for the characters in the story world.

• • CHARACTERS • •

Main characters in excellent fantasy and science fiction are multidimensional personalities who behave consistently, respond to events in a believable fashion, and grow and change across the course of the story. There is strong unity of character and plot: characters both influence and are influenced by the events in the story. If a character that lives in a realistic story world enters a fantasy situation, the character does not magically change, but remains consistent across both worlds. Characters in science fiction struggle with scientific advances as they try to live in a future world. Even if characters are superheroes in a story, they are so carefully delineated that readers easily accept their otherworldly powers.

⋅ ⋅ STYLE ⋅ ⋅

How a writer chooses to tell a story—through structure, syntax, and word choice—makes the difference between a mediocre book and an excellent one. Some of the best writing in books for young readers appears in fantasy and science fiction. Style works to establish the setting; rich images and vivid figurative language help readers envision the created world. Style makes the characters and the plot believable; authentic dialogue and clear structure help readers build characterizations and follow the action. Well-written stories have clear structures supported by vivid, interesting images and rich language.

⋅ ⋅ THEME ⋅ ⋅

Although some fantasy and science fiction is lighthearted, many other books have serious themes of great import. The monumental struggle between good and evil, what it means to be human, and the consequences of pride are all examples of recurring fantasy themes. The themes in science fiction are similar to those in fantasy, but also challenge readers to consider the emotional, psychological, and mental effects of scientific advances. In both cases, these themes weave throughout the story, logically radiating from character and plot. At their best, these stories ask questions that arise naturally from the unity of character and action and are meaningful for readers, causing them to ask questions about life. Excellent fantasy and science fiction carry "us from the concrete to the abstract, from a satisfying narrative experience to a moment of articulate wisdom" (Baker, 2006). A Close Look at Kathi Appelt's *The Underneath* (I) demonstrates these characteristics of quality.

✳ ✳ ✳

A CLOSE LOOK AT

The Underneath

The very first words of this story draw the reader in, for who can resist a lonely cat, especially if they notice that there are two very small kittens on the cover. Within the first few pages, several "characters" are introduced and questions are raised that propel readers immediately into

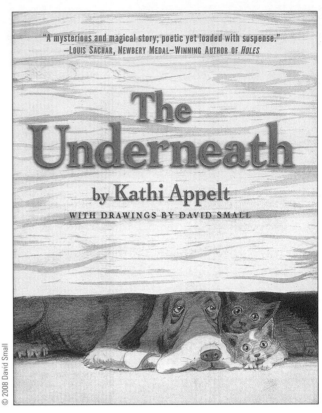

Kathi Appelt weaves a closely braided tale of love and hate, forgiveness and revenge, that holds young readers spellbound from beginning to end.

the story. There are the cat and her unborn kittens; an old, lonely hound; an ancient serpent; a man, emotionally wounded in childhood, who is filled with hate; and the piney woods, themselves a character.

The setting, seemingly an antagonist in the story, is lushly depicted—with trees detailed by name, and careful descriptions of the forest floor and the waters that surround it. The tall, ancient loblolly pine rises above the rest even though it is hollowed and cracked by lighting strikes and age. "This pine," Appelt tells us, "did not fall to the earth or slide into the creek. Not then. And not now. It still stands." And thus we are alerted to both the strength and the vulnerability of this particular tree. Other kinds of trees, and the waters, too, are named and described in such detail that Bayou Tartine, Petite Tartine, and Sorrowful Creek become familiar places in which many wild creatures, but especially snakes and alligators, and the man called Gar Face, make their home.

The characters are both varied and memorable, with each demonstrating particular qualities. Gar Face, for example, is unutterably mean, chaining and beating his hound, killing not only for money but for pleasure, yet he is also slightly sympathetic as we know of his miserable childhood, his disfigurement, and his isolation as an adult. The calico cat radiates love even as she radiates purrs, meeting the need of the lonely old hound for a loving companion, and the hound rewards her, and her kittens, with loyalty. Together, they are a family. The cat and the hound watch over the kittens from underneath the porch of Gar Face's house, warning them to stay out of his view. The kittens themselves are completely vulnerable, with individual personality traits that make them recognizably "human." The ancient serpent, woven from Native lore, seems at first to be pure evil, but even she loved her long-lost daughter. The immense alligator king, who lies in the marshes between the Tartines, a menace to everything that comes his way, has a saving grace: he is wise. Thus, each character represents a unique quality, but all have at least one other dimension.

The plot is complex, with each character's stories weaving together to form a complete and satisfying whole. We follow the angry fixation of Gar Face in his battle with the alligator king; the courage of the calico cat as she saves her kitten's life; the determination with which that kitten, Puck, seeks to reunite with his family, his sister Sabine, and Ranger the hound. Woven around these strands are the stories of Grandmother Moccasin and her daughter Night Song, who left her mother to love Hawk Man and their own daughter. And the trees, too, have their own story, one even more ancient than the grandmother and the alligator. These narrative strands intertwine in a way that is inevitable, so carefully foreshadowed that a second reading reveals just how tightly woven this novel is.

An omniscient narrator enables the structure of the book to be based on multiple narrative strands, and also allows the development of characters as we see into the minds and hearts of them all. The story, woven as it is from rage and abuse, hate and violence, but also love and loyalty, is surprisingly beautiful. The language is lyrical, begging to be read aloud, and the story is life-affirming in the depiction of the triumph of love. Over all of the events stand the trees—ancient, wise, and telling their own stories—stories that resonate with ancient themes of love and hate, life and death, stories that have been and will be told as long as those ancient trees stand, and beyond.

The World of Fantasy

Fantasy such as *The Underneath*, which explores the human condition, is often deeply serious. This type of fantasy, sometimes called "high" fantasy, lies closely beside ancient folklore and contains archetypal themes. It explores the struggle between good and evil or follows a quest for personal identity. More lighthearted, playful fantasy uses a veil of unreality to disguise the real world in some way. The fantastic element may be as simple as animals that act like humans or as complex as fully developed miniature worlds that reflect real life with a small twist. Fantasy writers, playfully and seriously, use such devices as time slips and magic, fully developed fantasy settings, or supernatural characters to create the fantasy. By creating a fantasy, writers are able to explore complex issues with a depth that might be too disturbing when considered in realistic settings. The metaphorical nature of fantasy allows young readers to consider ideas about things such as prejudice, death, war, the consequences of beauty, and other serious matters in a manageable way. The seriousness of the questions that

Profile

Kathi Appelt

I feel particularly committed to children and the difficult odds facing them in this country. One of my own personal missions is to change what we call children—that is, I would like to see them called a "priority" rather than a "resource." I don't feel we've done a very good job with our resources and I don't like the connotation that children are something that can be mined or exploited. Rather, they should be something that gets our top attention, something that receives our most intensive care and love.

The author of more than thirty books for children and young adults, Kathi Appelt published her first book for children in 1986 and the next eighteen between 1993 and 2000. A gifted writer, she creates books as diverse as her lyrical, picturebook texts in verse, nonfiction, poetry for adolescent readers and writers, short stories, and *The Underneath*, her first novel. She has won Pick of the Lists and Teachers' Choice Awards and has had her books selected by the American Library Association for their Best Books for Young Adults and Quick Picks for Reluctant Readers lists. *The Underneath* is a 2008 National Book Award finalist and a Newbery Honor winner.

Kathi serves on the faculty at Vermont college of Fine Arts in their MFA in Writing for Children and Young Adults Program, and occasionally teaches a course in creative writing at Texas A&M, her alma mater. Contact Kathi at www .kathiappelt.com.

a story raises determines whether a fantasy is "light" or "high." In either case, authors create their fantasy selecting from a variety of literary devices.

In Shaun Tan's *The Arrival* (I–A), a lengthy graphic picturebook for older readers that is discussed in Chapter 3, Tan uses fantasy to heighten the emotional impact of an immigrant entering a new culture. Just as the character is bemused by new customs, fashions, places, and people, readers also are forced to notice the surroundings because everything is new to readers as well—the new world is a fantasy world. In his Caldecott Award–winning *Flotsam* (P–I), David Wiesner asks readers to consider, and reconsider, the possibilities of the world under the sea. When the main character, who seems to have the habit of looking closely at things, finds an old camera washed up on the beach, new worlds and possibilities open to him as he looks at the photographs that were on the film in the camera. Fantasy, whether in novel or picturebook format, serious or lighthearted, asks readers to open their eyes and imagine.

Many fantasy writers use the device of time slips, or characters traveling through time, to create and sustain the fantasy in their stories. Still others use magic of some kind to propel the action. These devices help create a fantasy world and can be found in all types of fantasy, including animal fantasy, stories of miniature worlds, quest tales, and literary lore.

In some stories, time is the element that is carried beyond the realm of everyday experience, as characters move between their current reality and other times and places. For many writers, the past and future are part of the present; by challenging our understanding of time as sequential, these authors are making a statement about the meaning of time itself. One such writer, Eleanor Cameron (1969), describes a globe of time in which the past, present, and future are perceived as a whole.

Authors of fantasy invent a dazzling variety of devices to permit their characters to move in and out of conventional time. The children in C. S. Lewis's *The Lion, the Witch, and the Wardrobe* (I) enter the land of Narnia through a wardrobe door; while they are in Narnia, time does not pass in their real world. John Scieszka plays with time in his **Time Warp Trio** series (I) in which Joe, Fred, and Sam, ordinary boys all, manage to travel through time to a series of unlikely places. The very popular series has more than sixteen books, including *It's All Greek to Me* and *Marco? Polo!*, and they are all lighthearted fun.

Several time-slip fantasies focus on a central character going through a difficult adjustment period; loneliness, alienation, and extraordinary sensitivity seem to be associated with time travel. In Philip Pullman's award-winning trilogy, *The Golden Compass*, *The Subtle Knife*, and *The Amber Spyglass* (A), Lyra and Will travel between worlds as well as through time as they engage in their epic quest.

Magic is also a basic ingredient in fantasy. Often the magic is mixed with humor, and readers respond avidly to both. Children recognize the possibilities that magic entails; they willingly enter a world that does not operate by natural law. Bruce Coville's **Magic Shop** series (I) uses the device of a shop that caters to would-be magicians to allow realistic characters to enter fantasy worlds. Dragons figure prominently in *Jeremy Thatcher, Dragon Hatcher* (I), and talking toads are featured in *Jennifer Murdley's Toad* (I). A personal fairy—with a bad attitude—creates the magic in Liz Kessler's *Phillipa Fisher's Fairy Godsister* (I), illustrated by Katie May. Another kind of magic is that constructed by writers such as Neil Gaiman—ghost stories. In the Newbery Honor–winning *The Graveyard Book* (A), illustrated by Dave McKean, Gaiman combines a ghost story with a coming-of-age novel that is spellbinding, even to the point of tears at the artful ending.

Natalie Babbitt's classic fantasy, *Tuck Everlasting* (I), postulates a magic spring that, like the water so long sought by explorer Ponce de Leon, bestows eternal life. The magical water has given eternal life to the Tuck family, and young Winnie Foster discovers their secret. What she learns about the impact of eternal life on the Tucks influences the decision she makes—not to drink from the spring. The magic in this tale allows Babbitt to explore some important life questions. Young readers discuss this story with great seriousness, pondering such questions as those listed in Teaching Idea 6.2.

There are an increasing number of books that make use of magical realism, blurring the line between contemporary realistic fiction and fantasy, just as years ago Jane Yolen blurred the line between historical fiction and fantasy through the use of a time slip in her Holocaust novel, *The Devil's Arithmetic* (A). The magical realism of David Almond's *Skellig* (A), a beautifully haunting, moving tale, involves a being that seems to be an angel, at least to the two young protagonists who see and talk with him. How you categorize this book and most of the others that he has written depends on your perception of who Skellig was and where you place magical realism. For some, this is a fantasy novel; for others, it is grippingly realistic. His novels are discussed in both Chapter 7 and Chapter 8.

J. K. Rowling's **Harry Potter** series (I–A) contains a vast array of magic devices, such as Harry's famous Quidditch broom, owls that deliver mail, invisibility cloaks, and a map that shows people and their locations. The books are also firmly anchored in the well-developed fantasy world of the Hogwarts School of Witchcraft and Wizardry, which is peopled by teachers and students who practice an assortment of bizarre and intriguing magic. All of this magic is carefully placed, and the actions within the fantasy world are ultimately logical. Rowling never violates the rules she creates, and readers devour these books with a passion rarely seen.

Teaching Idea 6.2

Everlasting Questions

Powerful discussions arise from reading *Tuck Everlasting* by Natalie Babbitt. Here are some suggested book discussion group topics:

- Would you want to live forever? What age would you choose to be?
- If someone promised you everlasting life, would you do what was required to obtain it? What would you do with your life?
- Why does Winnie Foster confide in the toad?
- How does the toad help Winnie make up her mind about drinking the spring water, which promises eternal life?
- What does the man in the yellow suit represent?
- How does the Tuck family feel about Winnie Foster?
- Do you think Winnie made the right choice?
- What would you say to Winnie if you could meet her?
- Is killing someone ever justified?

Those who enjoyed **Harry Potter** ought to be fans of Chris Mould's *Something Wickedly Weird: The Wooden Mile* and *Something Wickedly Weird: The Icy Hand* (I). Eleven-year-old Stanley Buggles learns that something is odd in Crampton Rock, with a talking pike, three-legged dogs, pirates, a werewolf, and the odd behavior of the villagers. Lots of action and details revealed in pen-and-ink illustrations promise that this series will be both funny and popular.

In Cornelia Funke's trilogy *Inkheart, Inkspell,* and *Inkdeath* (all A), the magic, fittingly, is in a book that draws young Meggie and her father into its story world. As the story world becomes more chaotic and dangerous, it is clear that the characters in that world are out of the control of the author. Funke's perfect ending holds promise for every reader about to enter the world of story. Thirteen-year-old Alcatraz Smedry is the hero of the free world, a secret continent, and struggles against the rule of evil librarians in Brandon Sanderson's *Alcatraz Versus the Evil Librarians* (I–A). The adventures continue in *Alcatraz Versus the Scrivener's Bones* (I–A) as he encounters "vengeful undead" librarians while trying to find his missing grandfather. Sanderson combines action with character development and a good splash of the ridiculous.

The settings, characters, and action in these books put them clearly in the fantasy realm. It's more difficult to categorize Eva Ibbotson's *The Dragonfly Pool* (I–A), with illustrations by Kevin Hawkes. The setting, an imaginary European country just before World War II, is pure invention, but the social and political details included in the story are real. The characters are unique, the action is intense, and the style is marked with dry humor. These stories, and others like them, enchant young readers, whisking them away into alternate realities; they could also be characterized as animal fantasy, miniature world stories, quest tales, and literary lore.

• • ANIMAL FANTASY • •

Animal fantasy attributes human thought, feeling, and language to animals. Children like to see animals dressed like people and believe in them readily. Actually, young children are often willing to invest any kind of creature or object with human characteristics. Because books that extend and enrich this normal developmental tendency strike a responsive chord in children, animal fantasy in picturebook form is well loved. Like the folktale, it becomes part of children's literary experiences before they make clear distinctions between fact and fancy. This early pleasure in animal fantasy often continues as children mature into readers who devour fantasy novels.

Some of the most memorable characters from children's literature populate animal fantasy. Naïve Wilbur of *Charlotte's Web* (I) by E. B. White, incorrigible Toad of Toad Hall of *The Wind in the Willows* (I) by Kenneth Grahame, Peter Rabbit, and Babar are some classics of this genre. Today's readers enjoy these classic tales as well as new stories, such as Kate DiCamillo's **Mercy Watson** (P) series of transitional readers, illustrated by Chris Van Dusen, in which Mercy, a pig, behaves as a human, and her human owners treat her as such!

Jill Barklem's **Brambly Hedge** series presents realistic, everyday events as experienced by a community of mice. The detailed, beautiful illustrations create a setting that heightens the pleasure. Avi's **Tales from Dimwood Forest** series, which includes *Poppy, Poppy and Rye, Ragweed: A Tale for Dimwood Forest,* and *Ereth's Birthday* (I), follows the adventures of one special mouse, Poppy, and her friends. As they seek to make a safe home in Dimwood Forest, they encounter many dangers from humans and other predators. The combination of humorous dialogue, notable characters, and a vividly detailed setting makes these books perfect for readers who enjoy animal fantasy and are ready for short novels. Once they have read this series, many will want to go on to Brian Jacques's **Redwall** (I–A) books, a multivolume series that provides high adventure, memorable characters, and intriguing descriptions of battles and weapons, all within an animal fantasy.

Because this series is so extensive, many children never run out of good books to read!

The Improbable Cat (I), a small but rather dark animal fantasy by Allan Ahlberg, tells the tale of a family that is quite taken with a sweet gray kitten who appears one day. As the cat rapidly grows to an enormous size, it soon takes over the lives of everyone except David and his infant brother. They are the only ones who have not stroked the cat, and because of this they can resist it. Upper elementary-grade readers enjoy talking about just what the cat symbolizes.

Lynne Jonnell's *Emmy and the Incredible Shrinking Rat* (I) and *Emmy and the Home for Troubled Girls* (I), both with art by Jonathan Bean, are fast-paced, funny, and immensely readable. The protagonist, ten-year-old Emmy, saves herself and her parents from the wicked magic of her evil nanny, Miss Barmy, in the first book, with the help of her soccer star best friend, Joe. In the second book, she and Joe are attempting to rescue the missing girls who were shrunk and trapped by Miss Barmy before she attempted to do the same to Emmy. All of this is possible because Emmy can talk to and understand rats, and one magic rat can shrink her, with a bite, so that she can visit the underground world of the rodents as well as defeat the evil nanny. The problem is, she just wants to be a normal ten-year-old girl, but she most definitely is not. In *Masterpiece* (I), illustrated by Kelly Murphy, Elise Broach creates a memorable character out of another interesting creature, a kitchen beetle. Marvin the beetle's kindness toward eleven-year-old Jack takes them both into the world of art forgery and theft, a big adventure, and a remarkable friendship.

Tor Seidler's *Gully's Travels* (I), illustrated by Brock Cole, is just right for young readers who enjoy chapter books liberally sprinkled with sketches. Gulliver, a dog, is an engaging, multidimensional character who has some improbable but satisfying adventures before learning to love his new family and surroundings. The focal animal in Joy Cowley's *Chicken Feathers* (I), illustrated by David Elliot, is an irascible hen named Semolina who talks to her boy, Josh. Of course, Josh's parents do not believe that she can talk, and they worry so much about him that he begins to pretend that she does not talk, but things spiral out of control. His mother's enforced hospital stay, a new baby sister, a fox in the proverbial hen house, early manifestations of adolescent feelings, and a grandmother he's a bit afraid of set the stage for a perfectly happy ending for Josh and his loving family.

Animal fantasies for older readers often create an allegorical world in which the nature of the human condition is explored. Such books as *The Underneath* (I), by Kathi Appelt, *The Mob: Feather and Bone Chronicles* (A), by Clem Martini, and *Watership Down* (A), by Richard Adams, use animal fantasy to comment on human frailties

Semolina is not your ordinary hen, but then Josh is not your ordinary boy, either, in this humorous yet serious tale of caring for and trusting in others, even when they're chickens.

and foibles. In *Watership Down* we confront, among other issues, the consequences of war. In *The Mob* we explore how social organizations must examine traditional rules in the light of new challenges. Kenneth Oppel's novels in his **Silverwing** saga—*Silverwing*, *Darkwing*, *Firewing*, and *Sunwing* (I–A) consider courage, loyalty, prejudice, and honor; contain echoes of traditional tales; and portray gripping adventures in a fantasy world in which bat communities serve as metaphors for humanity.

• • MINIATURE WORLDS • •

Every cultural group has its folkloric sprites, elves, trolls, hobbits, or leprechauns, which go unseen about houses and villages. Tales about these small beings charm audiences, young and old alike. Just as older readers continue to enjoy animal fantasy as they move in to longer books, they also continue to respond to the call of miniature worlds. There is something compelling about smallness that pulls readers into a story world. What and how do small people eat, dress, move about? How does smallness transform daily life as we know it? What extra challenges does it pose? Miniature worlds, like animal fantasy, fascinate readers interested in details. Stories set in miniature worlds might take a lighthearted look at what life in miniature would be like, or seriously explore human needs and desires. Fantasies about toys or miniature beings highlight human emotions by displaying them in action on a miniscule scale. From Arriety in *The Borrowers* (I) by Mary Norton to the Minnipins in *The Gammage Cup* and *The Whisper of Glocken* (I) by Carol Kendall, the best and worst in human nature are magnified by the small size of the characters. Carnegie Medalist Terry Pratchett has been producing books in his popular **Discworld** series (A) for more than 25 years. Pratchett is a master at combining suspense and humor, and these stories do not disappoint.

• • LITERARY LORE • •

The literary tale, a story crafted by a writer who intentionally imitates the traditional qualities of ancient folklore, has become increasingly popular over the past several years. Teaching Idea 6.3 offers suggestions for exploring these tales with students. As discussed in Chapter 5, these

stories are not cultural variants of well-known folktales, but rather the deliberate construction of a writer intending to imitate, embellish, or alter traditional folktales. Today, there are many full-length novels with characters and action based on traditional lore, elaborated to create a wholly original version of a traditional tale.

Jon Scieszka's *The True Story of the Three Little Pigs* and *The Stinky Cheese Man* (I) are well-loved examples of this type of story for younger readers. Increasingly, writers for middle-school and young-adult readers have created stories that weave around traditional tales. Zoe Alley retells five wolf stories in *There's a Wolf at the Door* (P), to the delight of young readers. A text that is full of funny one-liners, a comic-strip format, and varied, humorous illustrations by R. W. Alley make this a terrific book to share.

For older readers, Robin McKinley's *Beauty* (A), an early example of an elaborated tale based on folklore, has been followed by *Rose Daughter* and *Spindle's End* (A). Older readers can appreciate Donna Jo Napoli's mastery of style in such books as *Crazy Jack*, *Beast*, *Spinners*, *Zel*, and *The Magic Circle* (A). Gail Carson Levine's *Ella Enchanted* (I), a delightful twist on the Cinderella tale, won a Newbery Honor. Elizabeth Bunel's *A Curse Dark as Gold* (A) is an elaboration of the Rumpelstiltskin tale, complete with gritty details of small-town life and unflinching observations about loyalty, pride, and determination. Shannon and Dean Hale's *Rapunzel's Revenge* (I–A) is a graphic novel that depicts a spunky sixteen-year-old heroine with some guy named Jack . . . guess who! Nathan Hale's illustrations further both action and character development.

Jane Yolen is one of the masters of literary lore. Her novels in **The Young Merlin Trilogy** re-create the legend of King Arthur with her own deft touches. In *Sword of the Rightful King: A Novel of King Arthur* (I), she re-creates the story of Excalibur with a new twist, creating ultimately human characters out of the stuff of legend. Kevin Crossley-Holland's trilogy, *The Seeing Stone, At the Crossing Places*, and *King of the Middle March* (I–A), moves between the often uncomfortable, filthy reality of the Middle Ages and the magical world described in the legend of King Arthur. These novels are a unique blend of historical fiction and fantasy. Philip Reeve re-imagines part of King Arthur's story in *Here Lies Arthur* (A). Another gifted writer who retells ancient tales, Gerald Morris brings to life both the Middle Ages and the famous story of the doomed love of Tristram and Iseult in *The Ballad of Sir Dinadan* (A). He also has an Arthurian series, which includes *The Princess, the Crone, and the Dung-Cart Knight* (I–A), a magical, sometimes funny, bittersweet tale.

Even more ancient legends are at the core of other examples of literary lore. Mary Pope Osborne's **Tales from the Odyssey** series retells and embellishes well-known stories from Homer's epic poem. *The One-Eyed Giant*,

---

Teaching Idea 6.3

Literary Tales and Folkloric Themes

It is easy to confuse literary tales with folklore because the two genres are quite similar. Modern writers intentionally use folkloric elements in their stories, and sometimes they do this so well that their work is often mistaken for folktales. For example, Hans Christian Andersen captures the essence of folktales so artfully that it's hard to distinguish his work from the massive body of anonymous traditional literature. Other authors, such as Donna Jo Napoli, Jane Yolen, and Kevin Crossley-Holland, build on essential elements of well-known folklore, and craft novel-length stories around their central core. As you read literary tales with your students, build on their knowledge of folklore elements and discuss those that they notice in the literary tales they are reading. After you have read several literary tales with your students, ask them to consider the following questions:

☆ What folklore elements do the tales contain?

☆ How subtly does the author weave in the folklore elements? Give an example.

☆ Compare a literary tale to the original piece of folklore on which it was modeled.

☆ Discuss the differences between the original and the elaborated tale.

The Land of the Dead, Sirens and Sea Monsters, The Gray-Eyed Goddess, and *Return to Ithaca* (I) are written with verve and style in a manner that appeals to middle-grade readers. These same readers enjoy Rick Riordan's **Percy Jackson and the Olympians** series, in which children of the ancient Greek gods go on quests and struggle with their powers. *The Lightning Thief* (I) is the first book in the series; it introduces readers to an array of characters. A unique combination of humor, mythological allusions, and adventure, this series is great fun.

Books for older readers abound. Adele Geras's *Troy* (A) casts the story of the siege of Troy from the perspective of two young handmaidens living through it, complete with humorous comments from the gods and goddesses who are manipulating people and events. Her *Ithaka* (A), sequel to *Troy*, tells of Penelope's long wait for Odysseus. Michael Cadnum brings classic legends from Ovid to life in *Starfall: Phaeton and the Chariot of the Sun* (A). Jean Thesman bases her novel *Singer* (A) on an ancient Gaelic tale. These writers echo the sounds from storytellers' tongues of ages past.

• • QUEST TALES • •

Many stories that we call literary lore, including those discussed previously, are also quest tales. T. A. Barron's **The Lost Years of Merlin** series (A) is a magnificent quest based on legend. His series, including *The Great Tree of Avalon: Child of the Dark Prophecy* (A), *Shadows of the Stars* (A), and *The Eternal Flame*, is set in a wholly imagined world that was created when Merlin planted a seed and the tree of Avalon sprang into being. Barron is a riveting storyteller.

Franny Billingsley, winner of the Boston Globe–Horn Book Award, builds on ancient Selkie (seal maiden) tales in *The Folk Keeper* (A), a hauntingly beautiful story of a young girl who disguises herself as a boy in order to keep herself safe as a folk keeper, a person who controls the damage that the folk can create when they are hungry and unhappy. When she moves to a wild island to control the folk there, she discovers her own heritage and her true powers, even as she is forced to acknowledge her femininity as she matures and falls in love. This quest tale epitomizes the depth of emotion and complexity of ideas that mark high fantasy.

Archetypal quest themes from folklore become vividly evident in high fantasy. Quest stories that are most memorable describe characters' outer and inner struggles and may involve Herculean journeys during which they overcome obstacles and vanquish. Quests often become a search for an inner, rather than an outer, enemy. Inner strength is required as characters are put to a variety of challenges that often seem endless and unbeatable. It is the indomitable goodness of character that prevails.

Books such as *The Book of Three* from Lloyd Alexander's beloved series **The Prydain Chronicles** (I), which has been reissued in beautiful matched editions, continue to enchant young readers eager to test their metaphorical mettle against all odds. Cornelia Funke, author of *The Thief Lord* (I) and *Dragon Rider* (I), tells the story of young Igraine, daughter of two magicians, who wants desperately to be a knight. *Igraine the Brave* (I) is full of high spirits and good cheer, and she's a very spunky hero. Christopher Paolini's series **Inheritance Cycle**, which includes *Eragon* (A), *Eldest* (A), *Brisingr* (A), and a fourth book not yet titled, creates an alternate reality, new languages, and memorable characters who engage in an epic battle between good and evil.

Some of the most remarkable quest tales published in the recent past are Philip Pullman's **His Dark Materials** trilogy (A). Readers are introduced to Lyra, the young and engaging protagonist, in *The Golden Compass*. Lyra is an interesting blend: she is both a street urchin and the highly intelligent daughter of eminent and powerful people. She thinks herself an orphan but soon discovers, to her horror, who her mother and father really are. Lyra sets out on her quest to save herself and the children who are being kidnapped and sent north to be the victims of a horrible experiment. By the end of the story, she has come to realize that her quest is bigger than this, and she unhesitatingly steps into a new world, determined to carry on. Continue she does, in *The Subtle Knife*, where she meets her partner, Will, a hero not unlike herself but from a different world. They pursue their quest, moving between worlds, aided by witches and angels, running from the evildoers of the church, until the triumphant ending of *The Amber Spyglass*. This series has it all: child heroes, alternate worlds, time slips, magic objects, fantastic creatures, imagination at its height. It is all anchored in an overarching theme of the struggle between good and evil, mirrored in the poet John Milton's story *Paradise Lost*, and the overwhelming power of love. *Once Upon a Time in the North* (A) tells the story of the character Lee Scoresby that occurs just before the time of **His Dark Materials**. In this novel Scoresby crashes, gets involved in political struggles, and meets the unforgettable Iorek Byrnison for the first time.

Nancy Farmer taps the ancient stories of the northlands in her three-volume series *The Sea of Trolls, The Land of the Silver Apples*, and *The Islands of the Blessed* (all I). Jack, an apprentice Bard, is actually an unwilling hero, a young boy who is thrust into his quest by a series of events that shatter his assumptions about life. Set in Britain in 790 A.D., these stories also depict the clash between Christianity, the "new" religion, and the ancient lore of the Druids, as well as the hostility between the British and the Norsemen.

Ursula LeGuin's **Earthsea Cycle** (A) and the books in the **Annals of the Western Shore** series (A) offer stirring stories of heroes searching for and finding themselves and their talents. *Powers* (A), third in the series, tells the story of young Gavir, raised as a slave in a wealthy family, who has powers he does not understand. When tragedy destroys the life he has known, he flees, embarking on a dangerous journey that leads, eventually, to his discovery of his essential self. Elizabeth Wein imagined a boy, half-British and half-Aksumite (Ethiopian), grandson of the immortal King Arthur, and created the Arthurian/Aksumite cycle in *The Winter Prince, A Coalition of Lions, The Sunbird, The Lion Hunter,* and *The Empty Kingdom* (all A). The setting is so vivid in these novels that it seems real, making it difficult to distinguish these quest tales from historical fiction.

A close look at Kate DiCamillo's *The Tale of Despereaux: Being the Story of a Mouse, a Princess, Some Soup, and a Spool of Thread* (P–I) reveals a story that is a combination of animal fantasy, literary lore, and quest tale.

✳　✳　✳

A CLOSE LOOK AT

The Tale of Despereaux

Kate DiCamillo's *The Tale of Despereaux: Being the Story of a Mouse, a Princess, Some Soup, and a Spool of Thread* (P–I), winner of the 2004 Newbery Medal, is an engaging, multilayered story that asks fundamental questions about life. On the surface this is a story about a very small mouse with very large ears, his love for a princess, his quest through the dungeon to rescue her, and a mostly happily-ever-after ending. Beneath the surface tale, important questions about love, honor, perfidy, self-worth, and determination combine to elevate the story to one that explores the human heart with great seriousness.

The story begins with the birth of a small mouse with large ears and wide-open eyes—our hero, Despereaux. It is soon apparent that he is not like the other mice, preferring to read instead of eat the pages of books in the castle library, becoming enchanted by the music that he hears, and eventually breaking all mouse codes by revealing himself to humans—the king and Princess Pea—and even talking with them. For this he is banished to the rat-infested dungeon by the other mice, denounced by his own father, and led to his doom by his brother. The story then pauses and goes backward, introducing the rat Chiaroscuro, who is fascinated by light, which is not a ratlike thing, and who has inadvertently caused the demise of the queen by falling from a chandelier into her soup, scaring her to death. DiCamillo then pauses and goes backward again, telling the story of Miggory Sow, a slow and unbeautiful girl who has been sold as a servant by her father and ends up working in the castle. Miggory, however, has a heart's desire—

to be a princess—and the rat Chiaroscuro uses this desire to gain revenge on the humans who have banished him to the dungeon. Together they kidnap the princess and hide her in the dungeon. Despereaux rescues her at great peril, Chiaroscuro is repentant, Miggory Sow is reunited with her father, and all is well, if not perfect.

The setting is in many ways a generic castle, but the imagery is so evocative that the reader feels the darkness and smells the stench of the dungeon, while also hearing the music and seeing the light of the castle. The kitchen, where two important scenes take place, is easy to visualize, as are the dark, dark stairs leading to the dungeon. Through DiCamillo's description of Despereaux's descent, we feel his despair when he arrives at the bottom of the steps:

> He got to his feet and became aware of a terrible, foul, extremely insulting smell. The dungeon, reader, stank. It stank of despair and suffering and hopelessness. Which is to say that the dungeon smelled of rats. And it was so dark. Despereaux had never before encountered darkness so awful, so all-encompassing. (p. 73)

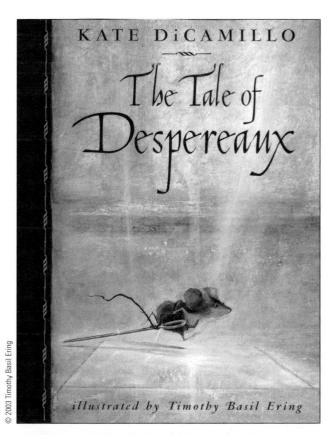

Kate DiCamillo's story of an unlikely hero with big ears not only pleased the young boy who asked her to write it but also went on to please many others and win the 2004 Newbery Medal.

Profile

Kate DiCamillo

W hen I write, I sometimes stop and cup my hands, as if I am drinking water. I try, I want desperately to capture the world, to hold it for a moment in my hands.

Kate DiCamillo's writing career began with a childhood lie. Not exactly a *lie*, she was quick to explain in a speech she delivered at the University of Minnesota. A *misunderstanding*, really. Having found a story in a children's magazine that she particularly liked, a young Kate transcribed the words in her own notebook. When her family found the notebook, they were impressed with the story. They asked if she had written it. Her answer, of course, was *yes*. She had written that story—in the literal sense of the word. That *was*

her handwriting! News circulated quickly: Kate was talented. Caught in a snowball of assumptions, Kate knew the only way to keep from disappointing her family, friends, and teachers was to actually begin writing. Her *own* stories. According to DiCamillo, *looking* at the world is an essential step in capturing the stories surrounding all of us.

DiCamillo's ability to read the world and to translate its details into stories has been widely appreciated by audiences. Her first novel, *Because of Winn-Dixie* (I), was a Newbery Honor book. *The Tiger Rising* (I) was a 2001 National Book Award finalist. She won the 2004 Newbery Medal for her fantasy *The Tale of Despereaux: Being the Story of a Mouse, a Princess, Some Soup, and a Spool of Thread*.

It was while drafting the manuscript for *Despereaux* that DiCamillo happened to be traveling by

airplane. On board the airplane, she sat next to a passenger who asked her what she did for a living. She dreaded this question. At a time when the world seemed filled with tumult and despair, writing a fantasy novel felt inconsequential, silly even. She explained she was writing a story. The passenger pressed her to explain what the story was about. A mouse. A story about a mouse. Later, the passenger found DiCamillo in the terminal and encouraged her to keep writing her story, that a story might offer just what the world needed: a ray of hope. DiCamillo agreed that stories could help people survive in the world. "The world is dark, and light is precious," begins *Despereaux*. "Come closer, dear reader. You must trust me. I am telling you a story."

Watch an interview with Kate on our companion website and visit her website at www.katedicamillo.com.

DiCamillo clearly cares about her characters, and this empathy helps charm the reader. Despereaux is the hero on a quest, and, as in all good quests, his mettle is tested, allowing him to grow and develop from a small mouse who faints into a brave hero. The sweetness of Despereaux's love for the princess, his pleasure in music and books, and his wavering but ultimately resolute determination to rescue the princess raise the mouse above a stock hero and elevate his quest beyond the confines of a fairy tale. When he returns to the dungeon to save the princess, he gathers his courage by telling himself a story.

Chiaroscuro, the rat, is a villain, but a villain with weaknesses, and it is difficult not to sympathize with him, at least a little. Miggory Sow is selfish, not too bright, and clumsy, but she has had a hard life and thus evokes some sympathy as well. The others are stock characters, but each has a bit of personality. The king loves music, his daughter, and his late wife, but he is obstinate and rather silly. The princess is sweet and charming, but she is also demanding and imperious; her heart harbors unsavory emotions. The cook is wonderful—inciting mouse murder in one scene, feeding Despereaux her special soup in another. Though clearly not real, these characters each reflect the combination of darkness and light that rests in the human heart.

The plot structure in *Despereaux* is unusual in that it is not linear. The story is divided into four "books," with the first being a linear recounting of Despereaux's life from birth through his descent into the dungeon. "Book the second" begins several years before the birth of Despereaux, with the birth of Chiaroscuro, and chronicles his fascination with light and the eventual death of the queen. "Book the third" goes back in time yet again, beginning with the death of Miggory's mother and recounting her squalid life with her father and subsequently her time as a servant. This book ends in the present, with Chiaroscuro and Miggory planning the abduction of the princess, while Despereaux listens in. "Book the fourth: Recalled to the Light," takes the action forward from there, culminating in the happy ending. By using such markers of time as "Again, reader, we must go backward before we can go forward," DiCamillo helps her readers follow the sequence of events. The intricacy of the plot, with the strands of three lives interweaving to propel the plot to the climax, is carefully, perfectly, and satisfyingly realized.

The book is distinguished in many ways, one of which is the use of the narrator's personal asides to bring readers into the story, even as they are sent off to the dictionary to enlarge their vocabulary:

Reader, you may ask this question; in fact, you must ask this question: Is it ridiculous for a very small, sickly, big-eared mouse to fall in love with a beautiful human princess named Pea? (p. 32)

The narrator's voice is funny, haughty, and often sarcastic, yet serves to remind readers that this fantasy may seem to be about a mouse and a princess, but relates directly to our lives. DiCamillo's use of imagery and symbolism, such as in the constant interplay between dark and light, heightens the impact of her tale. She names the rat "Chiaroscuro" as a way to highlight the idea that he was, in fact, not all bad, but rather a combination of good and evil, light and darkness. Not only does the name serve as a symbol, it is integral to the action of the story, as the rat's obsession with light precipitates the queen's death as well as his own eventual redemption. Other images of light and dark appear throughout the story, echoing the epic struggle between good and evil that fill stories of high fantasy.

Important questions about love, honor, perfidy, self-knowledge, and determination permeate the story. How powerful is love? How does honor spur action? How does one forgive someone for doing one a great harm? How does one stand up for what one believes in, despite the approbation of others? Where does one find the strength to begin a quest despite overwhelming fear? These and other questions are asked and answered, and linger long in readers' thoughts.

The book is also carefully designed. Timothy Basil Ering's beautiful pencil illustrations decorate the text and remind us that our hero is, after all, only a small mouse with big ears. The book's old-fashioned cover and deckle-edged pages complement the classic feel of the tale.

Themes in Science Fiction

As with fantasy, some science fiction is lighthearted; it relies on technological advances, such as space travel, to create the story. Many children are introduced to science fiction through some of these lighter stories. Science fantasy, that blend of fantasy and science fiction that is often set in other worlds but is uncomplicated by elaborate scientific theories, provides a good entree for beginning science fiction readers. As they read and enjoy these stories, they will become interested in moving on to more complex stories that explore significant issues. Young readers enjoy Jane Yolen's *Commander Toad* (P) series, as well as such books as Betsy Duffey's *Alien for Rent* (P–I) or Louis Sachar's *Marvin Redpost: A Flying Birthday Cake?*

(I), all humorous science fantasy. Other science fiction for younger readers is more serious, while still not overly complex. In *The Green Book* (I), a beautifully written story by Jill Paton Walsh, young Pattie takes her green-covered blank book with her when she and her family escape from the dying planet Earth. When they arrive at their new settlement, Pattie and her friends explore their new world, Shine. Their courage and perseverance lead the community to find a way to exist, and Pattie's book becomes the place where the community can write the story of their survival. The occasional soft illustrations by Lloyd Bloom help describe what life is like in Shine. Most science fiction is written for older readers, and these stories offer the same kind of deep questioning that fantasy offers, although in this case, the questions asked relate to scientific possibilities.

Most category systems, including ones for dividing science fiction into types, are arbitrary; many novels fit into more than one classification. There are, however, at least three major themes treated in science fiction—mind control, life in the future, and survival—that each often dominate a particular book even when all are present.

• • MIND CONTROL • •

Several science fiction writers deal with themes of mind control, telepathy, ESP, and other forms of communication across time and space. As computers, television, and other forms of communication reach more and more people across the globe, and advances in medicine make possible genetic and nervous system alterations, the potential increases for mind control on a grand scale.

One early example is John Christopher's **White Mountain** trilogy. This series about extraterrestrial invaders of Earth appeals to today's readers in the upper elementary grades. *The White Mountains*, *The City of Gold and Lead*, and *The Pool of Fire* (I–A), are set in the twenty-first century in a world ruled by the Tripods, dreaded robots. When humans are fourteen, the Tripods implant steel caps in their skulls that keep them submissive, docile, and helpless. Christopher's narrative impels readers to ponder the values of life and science.

Lois Lowry's *Messenger* (A) continues her exploration of the possibilities of controlled communities that began in *The Giver* and continued in *Gathering Blue* (A). In this final book in the trilogy, Lowry brings together characters from the first two books and creates a new hero, a young boy named Matty, who is on the brink of discovering his true power. Lowry's dystopian novels probe issues of mind control, individuality, honor, and courage in a future world, the seeds of which are visible today.

The futuristic dystopia in M. T. Anderson's *Feed* (A) may not be as futuristic as we might hope. In this story

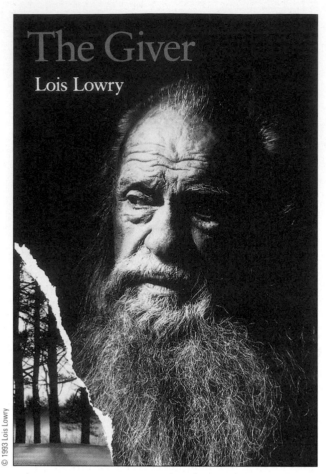

The Giver, the receiver of memories in a planned community, tries to hand down those memories to his successor and thereby changes the community forever.

world, consumer profiling has run amuck, and more than half the American population has a transmitter implanted in the brain to feed information to corporations eager to sell what people, especially teenagers, want, and what they want is controlled by the feed that they get. This unusual examination of the consequences of mind control offers young readers the opportunity to think about what they really need and want.

• • LIFE IN THE FUTURE • •

Some science fiction examines anthropological and sociological aspects of life in the future and considers questions of individual commitment and ethical behavior. These include the results of aggression and competition as opposed to peace and cooperation, a consideration of what it means to be human, the quality of life in an increasingly crowded world, and the ethical and social consequences of medical advances. Comparisons among cultures at different levels of development and finding one's purpose in life are also ideas that science fiction writers explore.

Margaret Peterson Haddix explores sociological themes—in this case population control—in her **Shadow Children** series, *Among the Hidden*, *Among the Betrayed*, *Among the Imposters*, and *Among the Barons* (I–A). The future world that she creates is crowded, so crowded that the government has mandated that only two children can be born to any one family. The mandate is not always followed, however, and third, or shadow, children live their lives in hiding, never knowing who or what might betray them. These stories are filled with engaging young characters who have many of the same hopes and dreams as contemporary readers.

The Sterkarm Handshake (A) by Susan Price, winner of the 1999 *Guardian* Fiction Prize, blends the future and the past. The Elves, time travelers from the twenty-first century, return to the sixteenth century to plunder the rich natural resources of the border country between England and Scotland. When Andrea, a twenty-first-century anthropologist, takes Per, her sixteenth-century lover, through time in order to save his life, she creates an unmanageable situation. Cultures clash, both societies and individuals, and there are no easy answers. The sequel, *A Sterkarm Kiss* (A), continues the adventure.

Mary Pearson considers the ethical and social implications of advanced medical technology in *The Adoration of Jenna Fox* (A), raising questions that are similar to those that permeate Peter Dickinson's classic, *Eva* (A). Jenna sets out to discover exactly what happened to her in the days following an automobile accident that should have killed her. Neal Shusterman tells the story of three teens struggling against their society in *Unwind* (A), a society in which unwanted teenagers undergo "retroactive abortion" so that their body parts can be used for transplants. The three teens escape, looking for safety, and embark on three journeys of self-discovery. Victoria Forester explores one possible result of intolerance for those who are "different," even if these differences are the result of unusual talents, in *The Girl Who Could Fly* (I) in which Piper fights family, church, and society for her right to be different.

Teaching Idea 6.4 describes a way to get students to think about the effects of scientific advances in their own lives and how these advances might influence their own futures.

• • SURVIVAL • •

Both gloomy and hopeful views of the future are apparent in the literature of survival. Although most nuclear scenarios are extremely depressing, an entire body of books exists that shows children surviving a nuclear war.

Teaching Idea **6.4**

Science Changes the World

Many people believe that each small change in our world results in a chain reaction of alterations. We cannot foresee subsequent modifications, nor can we control them. Some may bring good results; others, undesirable ones. Science fiction writers take the possibility of change to its ultimate extreme.

After reading several science fiction novels that use new scientific and technological advances as the premise for their futuristic depictions, discuss how these writers extrapolate from a possibility to a fully realized depiction of what might happen. Such books as *Feed*, *The House of the Scorpion*, *The Giver*, *The Exchange Student*, *Dancing with an Alien*, and *Singularity* (A) will promote interesting discussions. Then ask students to consider both the pros and cons of the new technology they use and to describe an application of that technology in a possible future world. How might such technology affect life?

This can become an interesting writing exercise if you ask students to select one piece of technology, imagine the furthest limits of its application, and create a future scenario that describes what might happen.

Postnuclear holocaust books such as Louise Lawrence's ***Children of the Dust*** (A) offer young readers the opportunity to consider deep, abiding questions. L. J. Adlington's ***Cherry Heaven*** (A) creates a futuristic society that parallels the Holocaust, and S. A. Bodeen's ***The Compound*** (A) explores what it means to live in a compound for years. Is it truly living? Are those in the compound truly human?

Stories about survival are not limited to the horrors of life after a nuclear war. The problems of life as it is today—the overcrowding, the pollution, the extinction of animal and plant species, and the question of an adequate food supply—provide science fiction writers with unlimited opportunities to project how humans will survive on earth. Some propose that the new frontier lies in outer space. Others propose that if we remain here on Earth, the new frontier might provide examples of what we could do to make Earth more livable.

The Ear, the Eye, and the Arm (A), by Nancy Farmer, deals with life in the year 2194 when people live in armed fortresses and in tunnels under toxic waste dumps. Thirteen-year-old Tendai and his younger sister and brother are kidnapped and forced to work in miserable surroundings. Their parents engage the Ear, Eye, and Arm detective agency to find them, but the detectives get near to the children only moments after they have moved on. The mystery and close calls keep readers turning the pages to find out what happens.

A future in which the sea is reclaiming the land, genetic engineering has erased most individual differences, and the intellectual pursuit of archaeology is close to illegal is the setting for Jan Mark's ***Useful Idiots*** (A). There are many levels of struggle for survival. One is the physical one, in which human beings confront the awesome power of nature's storms and seas, trying to keep nature at bay. Another is the struggle for the survival of science, in this case the science of history and archaeology. Like the Lowry trilogy, Mark's novel presents a future in which the government tries to control what people know about the past. Survival of cultures is yet another layer, as the Aboriginal, or "Inglish," people who inhabit the sea's edge in what used to be England struggle to maintain both their history and their independence. Finally, the physical and emotional survival of the protagonist is also at stake in this fast-paced mystery, which is set in a future world that no one wants to see.

Author of the popular **Underland Chronicles** (A), Suzanne Collins's ***The Hunger Games*** (A) is the first in a series about dystopian society in which teenagers are sacrificed through mortal combat with others. Survival, fierce family love, loyalty, and romance combine to create a riveting story with a remarkable female hero.

A close look at Nancy Farmer's ***The House of the Scorpion*** (A), winner of both a Printz Honor Award and a Newbery Honor Award, describes how one author asks important questions about mind control, the future, and survival by weaving a compelling tale.

✳ ✳ ✳

A CLOSE LOOK AT

The House of the Scorpion

Nancy Farmer's *The House of the Scorpion* (A) is an example of science fiction at its best. Building on the scientific possibility of cloning to prolong life and on the social possibility of drug cartels making political deals in order to create their own laws and countries, Farmer creates a future in which wealthy, powerful drug lords "farm" their own clones for future organ harvesting.

Matteo Alacran is the clone of El Patron, drug lord of the state of Opium and ruler of the Alacran Empire. Farmer's novel chronicles Matteo's maturation from a six-year-old who doesn't understand why he can't leave his house to his eventual discovery of his origins and status, his mistreatment at the hands of the ruling family and their friends, his dramatic escape, and his final return.

Farmer carefully details her setting, the mountains and desert along the sliver of the Colorado River that separates the southwestern tip of Arizona from Mexico. The mountains and sky, the endless fields of poppies that produce the opium that supports the Alacrans, the heat and sun and dust of the southwestern desert are all described so vividly that one sees, feels, and tastes what Matt does. El Patron's estate and the oasis to which Tam Lin takes Matt are also vividly depicted, a virtual map drawn in the head of the reader. This vivid setting allows readers both to visualize the story world and to realize that this world looks quite like our world today; in fact, it is identical except for the poppy fields.

Matt, the protagonist, is a complex and dynamic character who grows and changes across the course of the story. He is in charge of his own destiny even at six, when he breaks a window with a cooking pot in order to talk and play with the children who discover him locked in his house in the middle of the fields. This "birth" into the real world triggers his dawning understanding of what he is and his gradual realization of what that means. He comes to understand that most people around him consider him a beast, with "Property of the Alacran Estate" tattooed on his foot, and treat him as such. He discovers that he was born from a cow. And finally he realizes the extent of the evil of El Patron and understands that he himself will be killed in order for El Patron to continue to live. Confronted with these horrifying facts, he responds as any child would with anger, denial, and bewilderment. Finally, however, Matt acts with resolve to resist the fate planned for him.

He is the epitome of a resilient child. When he is imprisoned in a room full of chicken litter, he creates games, makes friends with roaches, and keeps his spirit alive despite his despair. Surrounded by people with twisted morals, he sometimes stumbles into anger and revenge, but he carefully creates a soul for himself, building on the love of Celia, who took care of him as a baby; the example of Tam Lin, the bodyguard who cares for Matt; and his love for Maria, daughter of one of El Patron's supporters. By the time he escapes, it is not surprising that he has the resources to confront new dangers and challenges or that he is determined, once he returns to Opium, to change it for the better.

This novel is not only science fiction but also adventure story and quest. The bulk of it occurs on the Alacran estate, where the action centers around Matt coming to realize the situation he is in as he grows from boy to young man. As the central conflict is revealed, smaller conflicts that heighten the tension occur. Matt is abused by one of the servants and taunted by others, especially Tom, who vies against him for the heart of Maria. These

Nancy Farmer creates an all-too-believable futuristic setting and forces readers to consider some complex questions in **The House of the Scorpion.**

subplots increase the distance between Matt, the beast, and others who are fully human. When Matt escapes from Opium, he finds himself in dangerous circumstances, yet these dangers allow him to prove his courage and resolve. This ending section of the book reflects the age-old quest story: Matt leaves home, albeit a home that wasn't very welcoming, and goes out into the world, only to return a changed and better person.

The world that Farmer creates is a brutal one, full of ugliness, horrifying to contemplate. Contrasted with that world is the friendship between Matt and Tam Lin, and Matt's love for Maria. Matt himself also stands in contrast, as his soul seems indomitable; it enables him to survive the brutality of body and spirit that he endures. These carefully crafted contrasts throw light on the questions that Farmer explores. Her careful use of language, including Spanish words and phrases appropriate to the region, and vivid descriptions of characters, places, and events, add to the power of her story.

What does it mean to be human? Who is more fully human, the clone or the drug lord and his compatriots? Is humanity an accident of birth or the result of one's conduct in the world? What does it mean to know yourself and chart one's own course in spite of great odds? The beast is, ironically, the most human of them all. All these questions, and more, add dimension and texture to Farmer's deft characterization and complex plot. The age-old struggles between good and evil, powerful and powerless are depicted here in terms of the future, a future that comes closer every day (Galda, 2002).

Both fantasy and science fiction offer many opportunities to explore powerful questions about life. One of the themes that students who have read these books often discuss is self-knowledge. This is not at all surprising given that this audience is frequently concerned with discovering who they are, who they want to be, and who they might become. Teaching Idea 6.5 offers some suggestions for writing prompts or discussion questions that can lead to a consideration of how characters such as Puck, Despereaux, and Matteo discovered who they were, decided what they wanted to be, and acted on this self-knowledge.

Fantasy and Science Fiction in the Classroom

For many children, fantasy is the first literature they love. Children in preschool and primary grades love books with animal characters who act like human beings. Children have no trouble understanding what the stories are about and what questions they raise about real life. As they mature, children experience many kinds of literature. Sometime during the elementary school years, some children become enraptured with realistic fiction, giving themselves completely over to this genre. Others become avid consumers of nonfiction and biography. Some continue to enjoy fantasy, moving from picturebooks to more fully developed narratives.

As children mature they either move toward science fiction and fantasy or learn to avoid them entirely in their personal selection of books (Sebesta & Monson, 2003). Those who like these genres love them passionately, and those who do not are just as passionate. For some young readers, these genre preferences may last the rest of their lives; others will become more eclectic with development and will once again enjoy fantasy. The record-breaking popularity of J. K. Rowling's **Harry Potter** (I–A) series has enticed many readers to fantasy and perhaps converted some of them into avid readers of fantasy. It has certainly spawned increased interest in writing and publishing fantasy, and there is an abundance of outstanding books from which to choose.

Once children have enjoyed and made their own the many picturebooks that are also fantasy, it is an easy step into longer, more complex stories. Many children will find these stories on their own, moving naturally from books like Mem Fox's *Possum Magic* (N–P) to such books as E. B. White's *Charlotte's Web* (I), Natalie Babbitt's *Tuck Everlasting* (I), or Kate DiCamillo's *The Tale of Despereaux: Being the Story of a Mouse, a Princess, Some Soup, and a Spool of Thread* (P–I). As children move into adolescence and develop as readers and thinkers, they discover the intellectual enchantment of Ursula Le Guin's **Earthsea** novels, ponder the questions of Nancy Farmer's *The House of the Scorpion* (A), or relive ancient stories with such books as Adele Geras's *Troy* (A). They are intrigued by the powerful questions that fantasy and science fiction writers ask and answer.

Teaching Idea 6.5

Thematic Exploration: Self-Knowledge

In *The Underneath*, Puck is foiled every step of his journey home, yet he keeps going, keeps his hope alive even though he is not sure that he is strong or clever enough to succeed, as his sister would be. In *The Tale of Despereaux: Being the Story of a Mouse, a Princess, Some Soup, and a Spool of Thread*, Despereaux finds himself at odds with his community. Rather than hide from humans, he visits with them; rather than eat books, he reads them; and he can hear music. In *The House of the Scorpion*, Matteo soon discovers that, unlike the other Alacran family and friends, he has been cloned and born from a cow. His differences are all too apparent. These heroes realize their differences and weaknesses and discover their strengths. As you read, discuss passages from these books in which the heroes discover something about themselves and act on it. Ask students to write or talk about the following general questions:

✿ What did (the protagonist) discover about himself in this passage?

✿ How did (the protagonist's) actions reflect his increasing self-knowledge?

✿ What are some of the special things that define you as a person?

✿ Have you ever felt as different from others as (the protagonist) felt?

Nancy Farmer

According to the Shona, the Africans among whom we lived, I had been visited by a shave (pronounced "shah-vay"), or wandering spirit. Shaves come from people who haven't received proper burial rites. They drift around until they find a likely host, possess whoever it is, and teach him or her a skill. In my case I got a traditional storyteller. Now I am a full-time professional storyteller myself.

Nancy Farmer was forty years old when she first began writing. "I had been reading a novel by Margaret Forster," Farmer told *Something about the Author*, "and thought: *I could do that.* Three hours later I emerged with a complete story. The experience was so surprising and pleasant I did it again the next day." In an online biography, Farmer said she knew her first story "wasn't

good, but it was fun." Although her first stories were not award-winning pieces, they did spark in Farmer a passion that would lead her to write acclaimed novels. "Since that time [in my forties], I have been absolutely possessed with the desire to write. I can't explain it," Farmer commented in her online biography, "only that everything up to then was a preparation for my real vocation."

Farmer's preparation was rich. She spent her childhood living and working in the hotel her family owned in Arizona. "I remember cages of lions and wolves in the parking lot. Once, when I was nine, the circus vet invited me to attend an elephant autopsy and he discovered that the animal had two hearts. Life there was a wonderful preparation for writing" (www.barnesandnoble.com/writers).

As an adult, Farmer served for two years as a Peace Corps volunteer in India. She also spent many years working as a scientist in Africa. "The

character, viewpoint and zany sense of humor of the people I met there have had a major effect on my writing," she said (Peacock, 2000, p. 57).

Farmer won a Newbery Honor for *The Ear, the Eye, and the Arm*, a science fiction novel set in Zimbabwe. Audiences also applauded her science fiction novel, *The House of the Scorpion*, which was a Newbery Honor book, a National Book Award winner, and a Printz Honor book. "One of my main themes," Farmer told *Locus* magazine, "is self-reliance, the ability to compete against odds and to beat them. A lot of kids' books have somebody who learns to come to terms with some dreadful situation, and it's all about them continuing to suffer at the end of the book. I don't want to write 'victim' books. I want a triumph, a hero or heroine, and that's what I write about." Contact her at www.nancyfarmerwebsite.com.

Some children, however, will leave fantasy behind as they grow older and will never discover the joys of science fiction unless they are helped into these genres by knowledgeable teachers. In many cases reading aloud is the very best way to encourage readers to expand their interests. A read-aloud program offers young readers the opportunity to experience books that move beyond magic into thoughtful considerations of some of life's most important questions. The books that we discuss and list in this chapter are both well written and thought-provoking, and most are excellent choices to read aloud, both to pique and to fuel developing interest in these genres.

Fantasy and science fiction books can also be read and discussed by literature groups, an idea that is discussed in Chapter 12. These books fit well into genre studies as well as within many thematic units. The kinds of questions about values, self, good and evil, and courage that fantasy and science fiction writers consider are also themes in contemporary realism and historical fiction. Looking at books from various genres that contain similar themes can be a powerful reading experience.

Benefits of fantasy and science fiction include the flexibility and expansion of the imagination that they

encourage and the important questions that they push readers to consider. As children read stories about people and events that are real and familiar to them, they also need to read stories that make them wonder, that cause them to reassess values and ideals, and that stretch their souls. Fantasy and science fiction can do just that.

• • • SUMMARY • • •

Fantasy is concerned with beings, places, or events that could not occur in the real world. Science fiction is concerned with the impact of present-day scientific possibilities on the world of the future. In both genres we find many excellent stories that are well written, that present multidimensional characters engaging in exciting plots, and that contain profound themes. Although some children move naturally from their favorite picturebook fantasies into more complex fantasies and science fiction, some need to be helped into the more complex books by their teachers. In either case the rewards are well worth the effort.

Animal Fantasy

☀ Adams, Richard, *Watership Down* (1974) (A)
☀ Ahlberg, Allan, *The Improbable Cat* (2004) (I)
Appelt, Kathi, *The Underneath* (2008) (I)
Avi, *The End of the Beginning: Being the Adventures of a Small Snail (and an Even Smaller Ant)* (2004) (P–I)
_____, *Ereth's Birthday* (2000) (I)
_____, *Perloo the Bold* (1998) (I)
_____, *Poppy* (1997) (I)
_____, *Poppy and Rye* (1999) (I)
_____, *Ragweed: A Tale for Dimwood Forest* (2000) (I)
☀ Barklem, Jill, *Brambly Hedge* (1980) (P)
Bell, Clare, *Ratha's Creature* (2007) (A)
Bond, Michael, *Paddington Here and Now* (2008) (P–I)
Broach, Elise, *Masterpiece* (2008) (I)
Cowley, Joy, *Chicken Feathers* (2008) (I)
DiCamillo, Kate, *Mercy Watson Goes for a Ride* (2006) (P)
_____, *The Tale of Despereaux: Being the Story of a Mouse, a Princess, Some Soup, and a Spool of Thread* (2003) (P–I)
☀ Grahame, Kenneth, *The Wind in the Willows* (1961) (I)
Hearne, Betsy, *Wishes, Kisses, and Pigs* (2001) (I)
Holm, Jennifer, and Matthew Holm, *Babymouse: Puppy Love* (2007) (P–I)
☀ _____, *Babymouse: Skater Girl* (2007) (P–I)
Howe, James, *Bunnicula* (1979) (I)
☀ Jacques, Brian, *Lord Brocktree* (2001) (A)
☀ _____, *Marlfox* (1999) (A)
☀ _____, *Redwall* (1998) (A)
Jonnell, Lynne, *Emmy and the Incredible Shrinking Rat* (2007) (I)
_____, *Emmy and the Home for Troubled Girls* (2008) (I)
☀ King-Smith, Dick, *Babe, the Gallant Pig* (1985) (I)
☀ _____, *Martin's Mice* (1988) (I)
☀ Lofting, Hugh, *The Story of Doctor Dolittle* (1997) (P–I)
Lisle, Janet Taylor, *Highway Cats* (2008) (I–A)
☀ Milne, A. A., *Winnie-the-Pooh* (1954) (I)
Oppel, Kenneth, *Darkwing* (2007) (I)
_____, *Firewing* (2003) (I)
_____, *Silverwing* (1999) (I)
_____, *Sunwing* (2000) (I)
☀ Potter, Beatrix, *The Tale of Peter Rabbit* (1902) (P)
☀ Said, S. F., *Varjak Paw* (2005) (I)
Seidler, Tor, *Gully's Travels* (2008) (I)
Selden, George, *Cricket in Times Square* (1997) (I)
_____, *Old Meadow* (1987) (I)
_____, *Tucker's Countryside* (1989) (I)
Speck, Katie, *Maybelle in the Soup* (2007) (P–I)
White, E. B., *Charlotte's Web* (1952) (I)
Zuckerman, Linda, *Taste for Rabbit* (2007) (A)

Miniature Worlds, Time Slips, Unreal Worlds, and Magic/Magical Realism

☀ Almond, David, *Heaven Eyes* (2001) (I)
☀ _____, *Kit's Wilderness* (2001) (A)
☀ _____, *Skellig* (1999) (A)
Babbitt, Natalie, *Jack Plank Tells Tales* (2007) (I)
_____, *Search for Delicious* (1969) (I)
_____, *Tuck Everlasting* (1975) (I)
Bell, Hilari, *The Goblin Wood* (2004) (I)
_____, *Last Knight: A Knight and Rogue Novel* (2007) (I)
_____, *Rogue's Home* (2008) (I)
Bosse, Malcolm, *Cave Beyond Time* (1980) (A)
☀ Bruchac, Joseph, *The Dark Pond* (2004) (I)
Carroll, Lewis, *Alice in Wonderland*, illustrated by Lisbeth Zwerger (2008) (I)
Cassedy, Sylvia, *Behind the Attic Wall* (1983) (A)
_____, *Lucie Babbidge's House* (1989) (A)
Clement-Moore, Rosemary, *Prom Dates from Hell* (2007) (A)
Collins, Suzanne, *Gregor and the Code of Claw* (2007) (I)
Conrad, Pam, *The Tub People* (1996) (P)
_____, *Zoe Rising* (1996) (I)
Coville, Bruce, *Jennifer Murdley's Toad* (1992) (I)
_____, *Jeremy Thatcher, Dragon Hatcher* (1991) (I)
Creech, Sharon, *Castle Corona* (2007) (I)
☀ Cross, Gillian, *Nightmare Game: Book Three* (2007) (A)
_____, *The Dark Ground: Book One* (2004) (A)
Curry, Jane Louise, *Dark Shade* (1998) (A)
☀ Dahl, Roald, *Charlie and the Chocolate Factory* (1964) (I)
☀ _____, *James and the Giant Peach* (1961) (I)
☀ _____, *Matilda* (1988) (I)
Delaney, Joseph, *Night of the Soul Stealer* (2007) (I)
Duey, Kathleen, *Skin Hunger* (2007) (A)
Ferris, Jean, *Once upon a Marigold* (2002) (A)
Elliott, Patricia, *Ambergate* (2007) (A)
Fleischman, Paul, *Time Train* (1991) (P)
_____, *Weslandia* (1999) (P)
French, Vivian, *The Robe of Skulls* (2008) (I)
Gaiman, Neil, *The Graveyard Book* (2008) (A)
Gardner, Lyn, *Into the Woods* (2007) (I)
Going, K. L., *Garden of Eve* (2007) (I)
☀ Hamilton, Virginia, *The Magical Adventures of Pretty Pearl* (1983) (A)
Harding, Frances, *Well Witched* (2008) (I)
Higgins, F. E., *Black Book of Secrets* (2007) (I)
Hobbs, Will, *Go Big or Go Home* (2008) (I)
Ibbotson, Eva, *The Haunting of Granite Falls* (2004) (I)
_____, *The Dragonfly Pool* (2008) (I–A)
James, Mary, *Shoebag* (1990) (I)
☀ Jansson, Tove, *Finn Family Moomintroll* (1989) (I)
☀ Jones, Diana Wynne, *House of Many Ways* (2008) (I)
☀ _____, *The Merlin Conspiracy* (2004) (A)
Joyce, William, *George Shrinks* (1985) (P)
Juster, Norton, *The Phantom Tollbooth* (1961) (I)
Kendall, Carol, *The Gammage Cup* (1959) (I)
_____, *The Whisper of Glocken* (2000) (I)
Kessler, Liz, *Philippa Fisher's Fairy Godsister* (2008) (I)
Kimmell, Elizabeth Cody, *Suddenly Supernatural: School Spirit* (2008) (I)
Kindl, Patrice, *Goose Chase* (2001) (I)
☀ King-Smith, Dick, *The Water Horse* (1998) (I)

Knox, Elizabeth, *Dreamquake: Book Two of the Dragonhunter Duet* (2007) (A)

Koertge, Ron, *Strays* (2007) (A)

Lanagan, Margo, *Red Spikes* (2007) (A)

✴ Lewis, C. S., *The Lion, the Witch, and the Wardrobe* (1950) (I)

Lisle, Janet Taylor, *Afternoon of the Elves* (1989) (A)

_____, *Lampfish of Twill* (1991) (A)

Maguire, Gregory, *What-the-Dickens: The Story of a Rogue Fairy* (2007) (I)

✴ Mahy, Margaret, *Alchemy* (2003) (A)

McKinley, Robin, *Dragonhaven* (2007) (A)

Moore, Perry, *Hero* (2007) (A)

Mould, Chris, *Something Wickedly Weird: The Wooden Mile* (2008) (I)

_____, *Something Wickedly Weird: The Icy Hand* (2008) (I)

Newbery, Linda, *At the Firefly Gate* (2007) (I)

✴ Norton, Mary, *The Borrowers* (1953) (I)

✴ Oppel, Kenneth, *Airborn* (2004) (A)

✴ Pearce, Philippa, *Tom's Midnight Garden* (1958) (I)

Peterson, John, *The Littles* (1967) (I)

Pierce, Meredith Ann, *Treasure at the Heart of Tanglewood* (2001) (I)

Pierce, Tamora, *Shatterglass* (2003) (I)

_____, *Street Magic* (2001) (I)

Pinkwater, Daniel, *Neddiad* (2007) (I)

✴ Pratchett, Terry, *A Hat Full of Sky* (2004) (I–A)

✴ _____, *Johnny and the Bomb* (2007) (I)

✴ _____, *Nation* (2008) (A)

✴ _____, *The Wee Free Men* (2003) (I)

Prevost, Guillaume, *Book of Time* (2007) (I)

Price, Charlie, *Lizard People* (2007) (A)

Prineas, Sarah, *The Magic Thief* (2008) (I)

Prue, Sally, *Cold Tom* (2001) (I)

_____, *The Devil's Toenail* (2001) (I)

✴ Rowling, J. K., *Harry Potter and the Chamber of Secrets* (1999) (I)

✴ _____, *Harry Potter and the Deathly Hallows* (2007) (I–A)

✴ _____, *Harry Potter and the Goblet of Fire* (2000) (A)

✴ _____, *Harry Potter and the Half-Blood Prince* (2005) (I–A)

✴ _____, *Harry Potter and the Order of the Phoenix* (2003) (A)

✴ _____, *Harry Potter and the Prisoner of Azkaban* (1999) (I–A)

✴ _____, *Harry Potter and the Sorcerer's Stone* (1998) (I)

Rubenstein, Gillian, *Under the Cat's Eye: A Tale of Morph and Mystery* (2001) (A)

Russon, Penni, *Breathe* (2007) (A)

Sanderson, Brandon, *Alcatraz Versus the Evil Librarians* (2007) (A)

_____, *Alcatraz Versus the Scrivener's Bones* (2008) (A)

Scieszka, Jon, *Marco? Polo!* (2006) (I)

_____, *It's All Greek to Me* (1999) (I)

Sfar, Joann, *Professor's Daughter* (2007) (I)

Shusterman, Neal, *Full Tilt* (2003) (A)

Slade, Arthur, *Dust* (2003) (I)

✴ Smith, Cynthia Leitich, *Tantalize* (2007) (A)

Steig, William, *Sylvester and the Magic Pebble* (1969) (P)

Stewart, Paul, and Chris Riddell, *Hugo Pepper* (2007) (I)

✴ Tan, Shaun, *The Arrival* (2007) (I)

Tomlinson, Heather, *Aurelie: A Faerie Tale* (2008) (A)

Townley, Roderick, *The Great Good Thing* (2001) (I)

_____, *Into the Labyrinth* (2002) (I)

Van Allsburg, Chris, *The Garden of Abdul Gasazi* (1994) (I)

_____, *Jumanji* (1981) (I)

_____, *The Wreck of the Zephyr* (1983) (I)

Vande Velde, Vivian, *Stolen* (2008) (A)

White, Ruth, *Way Down Deep* (2007) (I)

Weston, Robert Paul, *Zorgamazoo* (2008) (I)

Wiesner, David, *Flotsam* (2006) (P–I)

_____, *Sector 7* (1999) (P–I)

_____, *Tuesday* (1999) (P–I)

✴ Wilce, Ysabeau, *Flora Segunda: Being the Magical Mishaps of a Girl* (2007) (A)

Wilson, N. D., *100 Cupboards* (2007) (I)

Literary Lore and Quest Tales

Abbott, Ellen Jensen, *Watersmeet* (2009) (I–A)

Alexander, Lloyd, *The Black Cauldron* (1965) (I)

_____, *Book of Three* (1964) (I)

_____, *The Castle of Llyr* 1966) (I)

_____, *Foundling and Other Tales of Prydain* (1973) (I)

_____, *Golden Dream of Carlo Cuchio* (2007) (I)

_____, *The High King* (1968) (I)

_____, *The Rope Trick* (2002) (I)

_____, *Taran Wanderer* (1967) (I)

Alley, Zoe, *There's a Wolf at the Door* (2008) (P)

Barron, T. A., *Fires of Merlin* (2007) (A)

_____, *The Great Tree of Avalon: Child of the Dark Prophecy* (2004) (A)

_____, *The Great Tree of Avalon: The Eternal Flame* (2006) (A)

_____, *The Great Tree of Avalon: Shadows of the Stars* (2005) (A)

_____, *Lost Years of Merlin* (2007) (A)

_____, *Mirror of Merlin* (2007) (A)

_____, *Seven Songs of Merlin* (2006) (A)

_____, *Wings of Merlin* (2007) (A)

Bass, L. G., *Sign of the Qin: Outlaws of the Moonshadow Marsh, Book One* (2004) (I–A)

Billingsley, Franny, *The Folk Keeper* (1999) (A)

Bunel, Elizabeth, *A Curse Dark as Gold* (2008) (A)

Cadnum, Michael, *Starfall: Phaeton and the Chariot of the Sun* (2004) (A)

Cooney, Caroline, *Enter Three Witches: A Story of Macbeth* (2007) (A)

Cooper, Susan, *The Dark Is Rising* (1973) (A)

_____, *Greenwitch* (1973) (A)

_____, *The Grey King* (1974) (A)

_____, *Over Sea, Under Stone* (1966) (A)

_____, *Silver on the Tree* (1977) (A)

Crossley-Holland, Kevin, *At the Crossing Places* (2002) (I)

_____, *King of the Middle March* (2004) (I–A)

_____, *The Seeing Stone* (2001) (I)

✴ Dickinson, Peter, *Angel Isle* (2007) (A)

✴ Divakaruni, Chitra Banerjee, *The Conch Bearer* (2003) (I)

Dunmore, Helen, *The Tide Knot* (2008) (I)

DuPrau, Jeanne, *The Diamond of Darkhold* (2008) (I)

Farmer, Nancy, *The Sea of Trolls* (2004) (I–A)

_____, *The Land of the Silver Apples* (2007) (I–A)

_____, *The Islands of the Blessed* (2009) (I–A)

Fisher, Catherine, *The Oracle Betrayed* (2003) (A)

_____, *Snow-Walker* (2003) (A)

✴ Funke, Cornelia, *Dragon Rider* (2004) (A)

✴ _____, *Igraine the Brave* (2007) (I)

✴ _____, *Inkdeath* (2008) (I)

☀ _____, *Inkspell* (2005) (ɪ)
☀ _____, *Inkheart* (2003) (ɪ)
☀ _____, *The Thief Lord* (2002) (ᴀ)
☀ Furlong, Monica, *Colman* (2004) (ᴀ)
☀ _____, *Juniper* (2004) (ᴀ)
☀ _____, *Wise Child* (2004) (ᴧ)
Geras, Adele, *Ithaka* (2006) (ᴀ)
_____, *Troy* (2001) (ᴀ)
Hale, Shannon, and Dean Hale, *Rapunzel's Revenge* (2008) (ɪ–ᴀ)
Hodges, Margaret, *The Kitchen Knight: A Tale of King Arthur* (1990) (ᴘ–ɪ)
_____, *Merlin and the Making of a King* (2004) (ᴘ–ɪ)
Hoffman, Alice, *Green Angel* (2003) (ɪ)
Kaaberbol, Lene, *The Shamer's Daughter* (2000) (ᴀ)
Le Guin, Ursula, *The Farthest Shore* (1972) (ᴀ)
_____, *Gifts* (2004) (ᴀ)
_____, *Powers* (2007) (ᴀ)
_____, *Tehanu: The Last Book of Earthsea* (1990) (ᴀ)
_____, *The Tombs of Atuan* (1971) (ᴀ)
_____, *Voices* (2006) (ᴀ)
_____, *A Wizard of Earthsea* (1968) (ᴀ)
Lester, Julius, *Cupid* (2007) (ᴀ)
Levine, Gail Carson, *Ella Enchanted* (1997) (ɪ)
_____, *Ever* (2008) (ᴀ)
_____, *The Two Princesses of Bamarre* (2003) (ɪ)
☀ Lewis, C. S., *The Horse and His Boy* (1954) (ɪ)
☀ _____, *The Last Battle* (1956) (ɪ)
☀ _____, *The Lion, the Witch and the Wardrobe* (1950) (ɪ)
☀ _____, *The Magician's Nephew* (1955) (ɪ)
☀ _____, *Prince Caspian* (1951) (ɪ)
☀ _____, *The Silver Chair* (1953) (ɪ)
☀ _____, *The Voyage of the Dawn Treader* (1952) (ɪ)
Lisle, Janet Taylor, *The Ruby Key* (2008) (ɪ–ᴀ)
_____, *The Lost Flower Children* (1999) (ɪ)
Marillier, Juliet, *Wildwood Dancing* (2007) (ᴀ)
McKinley, Robin, *The Blue Sword* (1982) (ᴀ)
_____, *The Hero and the Crown* (1985) (ᴀ)
_____, *Beauty* (1999) (ᴀ)
_____, *Rose Daughter* (1997) (ᴀ)
_____, *Spindle's End* (2000) (ᴀ)
Morris, Gerald, *The Ballad of Sir Dinadan* (2003) (ᴀ)
_____, *Parsifal's Page* (2001) (ɪ)
_____, *The Princess, the Crone, and the Dung-Cart Knight* (2004) (ɪ–ᴀ)
_____, *The Savage Damsel and the Dwarf* (2000) (ᴀ)
_____, *The Squire, His Knight, and His Lady* (1999) (ᴀ)
_____, *The Squire's Tale* (1998) (ᴀ)
Murdock, Catherine Gilbert, *Princess Ben* (2008) (ᴀ)
Napoli, Donna Jo, *Beast* (2000) (ᴀ)
_____, *Breath* (2003) (ᴀ)
_____, *Crazy Jack* (1999) (ᴀ)
_____, *The Magic Circle* (1993) (ᴀ)
_____, *The Prince of the Pond* (1992) (ɪ)
_____, *Spinners* (1999) (ᴀ)
_____, *Zel* (1996) (ᴀ)
Osborne, Mary Pope, *The Gray-Eyed Goddess* (2003) (ɪ)
_____, *The Land of the Dead* (2002) (ɪ)
_____, *The One-Eyed Giant* (2002) (ɪ)
_____, *Return to Ithaca* (2004) (ɪ)
_____, *Sirens and Sea Monsters* (2003) (ɪ)
Paolini, Christopher, *Brisingr* (2008) (ᴀ)
_____, *Eldest* (2005) (ᴀ)
_____, *Eragon* (2003) (ᴀ)
Pierce, Meredith Ann, *The Darkangel* (1982) (ᴀ)

_____, *A Gathering of Gargoyles* (1984) (ᴀ)
Pierce, Tamora, *Alanna, the First Adventure* (1983) (ᴀ)
_____, *The Emperor Mage* (1997) (ᴀ)
_____, *In the Hand of the Goddess* (1984) (ᴀ)
_____, *Lioness Rampant* (1988) (ᴀ)
_____, *Magic Steps* (2000) (ᴀ)
_____, *Squire* (2001) (ᴀ)
_____, *Trickster's Choice* (2003) (ᴀ)
_____, *Wild Magic* (1992) (ᴀ)
_____, *Wolf Speaker* (1994) (ᴀ)
_____, *The Woman Who Rides Like a Man* (1986) (ᴀ)
☀ Pullman, Philip, *The Amber Spyglass* (2000) (ᴀ)
☀ _____, *I Was a Rat* (2000) (ɪ)
☀ _____, *The Golden Compass* (1995) (ᴀ)
☀ _____, *Once Upon a Time in the North* (2008) (ᴀ)
☀ _____, *The Subtle Knife* (1997) (ᴀ)
Riordan, Rick, *The Battle of the Labyrinth* (2008) (ɪ)
_____, *The Lightning Thief* (2005) (ɪ)
_____, *Titan's Curse* (2007) (ɪ)
Rodda, Emily, *Rowan of Rin* (2001) (ɪ)
Scieszka, Jon, *The Stinky Cheese Man and Other Fairly Stupid Tales* (1992) (ɪ)
_____, *The True Story of the Three Little Pigs* (1989) (ɪ)
Spinner, Stephanie, *Quiver* (2002) (ᴀ)
Springer, Nancy, *I Am Mordred: A Tale from Camelot* (1998) (ᴀ)
_____, *I Am Morgan LeFay: A Tale from Camelot* (2001) (ᴀ)
_____, *Rowan Hood: Outlaw Girl of Sherwood Forest* (2001) (ɪ)
Swope, Sam, *Jack and the Seven Deadly Giants* (2004) (ɪ)
Taylor, G. P., *Shadowmancer* (2004) (ᴧ)
Thesman, Jean, *Singer* (2004) (ᴀ)
Thompson, Kate, *The Last of the High Kings* (2008) (ɪ–ᴀ)
_____, *New Policeman* (2007) (ɪ)
☀ Tolkien, J. R. R., *The Hobbit* (1937) (ᴀ)
☀ _____, *The Lord of the Rings* (1954–1955) (ᴀ)
Ursu, Anne, *Siren Song: The Cronus Chronicles, Book Two* (2007) (ɪ)
☀ Wein, Elizabeth, *A Coalition of Lions* (2003) (ᴀ)
☀ _____, *The Empty Kingdom* (2008) (ᴀ)
☀ _____, *The Lion Hunter* (2007) (ᴀ)
☀ _____, *The Sunbird* (2004) (ᴀ)
☀ _____, *The Winter Prince* (1993) (ᴀ)
Yolen, Jane, *The Dragon's Boy* (2001) (ɪ)
_____, *Hobby* (1999) (ɪ)
_____, *Merlin* (1998) (ɪ)
_____, *Passager* (1998) (ɪ)
_____, *Sword of the Rightful King* (2003) (ɪ)

Science Fiction

Adlington, L. J., *Cherry Heaven* (2008) (ᴀ)
Anderson, M. T., *Feed* (2002) (ᴀ)
Bodeen, S. A., *The Compound* (2008) (ᴀ)
Brooks, Kevin, *Being* (2007) (ᴀ)
Christopher, John, *City of Gold and Lead* (1967) (ᴀ)
_____, *The Pool of Fire* (1970) (ᴀ)
_____, *When the Tripods Came* (1988) (ᴀ)
_____, *The White Mountains* (1967) (ᴀ)
Clements, Andrew, *Things Not Seen* (2002) (ᴀ)
Collins, Suzanne, *The Hunger Games* (2008) (ᴀ)
☀ Cross, Gillian, *New World* (1994) (ᴀ)
☀ Dickinson, Peter, *Eva* (1988) (ᴀ)
DuPrau, Jean, *The City of Ember* (2003) (ɪ–ᴀ)

DuPrau, Jean, *The People of Sparks* (2005) (I–A)
Engdahl, Sylvia Louise, *Enchantress from the Stars* (1970) (A)
_____, *The Far Side of Evil* 1971) (A)
✳ Farmer, Nancy, *The Ear, the Eye, and the Arm* (1994) (A)
_____, *The House of the Scorpion* (2002) (A)
Forester, Victoria, *The Girl Who Could Fly* (2008) (I)
Gaiman, Neil, and Michael Reaves, *InterWorld* (2007) (A)
Gilmore, Kate, *The Exchange Student* (1999) (A)
Grunwell, Jeanne Marie, *Mind Games* (2003) (I)
Haddix, Margaret Peterson, *Among the Barons* (2003) (I–A)
_____, *Among the Betrayed* (2002) (I–A)
_____, *Among the Hidden* (1998) (I–A)
_____, *Among the Imposters* (2001) (I–A)
✳ Hautman, Pete, *Hole in the Sky* (2001) (A)
✳ Hughes, Monica, *The Golden Aquarians* (1995) (I)
✳ _____, *Invitation to the Game* (1990) (A)
✳ _____, *Keeper of the Isis Light* (1981) (A)
Jennings, Richard, *Ferret Island* (2007) (I)
✳ Lawrence, Louise, *Children of the Dust* (2002) (A)
L'Engle, Madeleine, *A Swiftly Tilting Planet* (1978) (A)
_____, *A Wind in the Door* (1973) (A)
_____, *A Wrinkle in Time* (1962) (A)
Lennon, Joan, *Questions* (2008) (I)
Logue, Mary, *Dancing with an Alien* (2008) (A)
Lowry, Lois, *Gathering Blue* (2000) (A)
_____, *The Giver* (1993) (A)
_____, *Messenger* (2004) (A)
✳ Mark, Jan, *Useful Idiots* (2004) (A)

McCaffrey, Anne, *Dragondrums* (1979) (A)
_____, *Dragonsinger* (1977) (A)
_____, *Dragonsong* (1976) (A)
Nix, Garth, *Abhorsen* (2003) (A)
_____, *Lirael* (2001) (A)
_____, *Sabriel* (1995) (A)
O'Brien, Robert C., *Mrs. Frisby and the Rats of NIMH* (1971) (I)
_____, *Z for Zachariah* (1975) (A)
Paton Walsh, Jill, *The Green Book* (1982) (I)
Pearson, Mary, *The Adoration of Jenna Fox* (2008) (A)
Price, Susan, *The Sterkarm Handshake* (2000) (A)
_____, *A Sterkarm Kiss* (2004) (A)
✳ Reeve, Philip, *A Darkling Plain* (2007) (A)
✳ _____, *Mortal Engines* (2001) (A)
✳ _____, *Predator's Gold* (2003) (A)
✳ _____, *Starcross* (2007) (I)
Rex, Adam, *True Meaning of Smetday* (2007) (I)
✳ Rubenstein, Gillian, *Galax-Arena: A Novel* (1993) (I)
Sedgwick, Marcus, *Floodland* (2001) (I)
Service, Pamela, *Tomorrow's Magic* (2007) (I)
Seuss, Dr., *The Lorax* (1971) (P)
Shusterman, Neal, *Unwind* (2007) (A)
Sleator, William, *Singularity* (1985) (A)
Stead, Rebecca, *First Light* (2007) (I)
Thompson, Kate, *Origins* (2007) (I–A)
Waugh, Sylvia, *Who Goes Home?* (2003) (I–A)
Westerfield, Scott, *Extras* (2007) (A)

Contemporary Realistic Fiction

"I want to show you something," I told Steven. I reached into my pocket for the crumpled-up W picture I had taken out of my backpack before I'd left. "I've had it since I was six."

We sat on a ledge, our feet dangling, and he smoothed the picture on his knee, stared at it, then looked over at me.

"We had to find pictures with W words," I said.

"It's a wishing picture," he said slowly, "for a family."

I could feel my lips trembling. Oh, Mrs. Evans, I thought, why didn't you see that?

"It's too bad you didn't come when you were six." He smiled. "I knew you had to stay with us when you let me win that checkers game."

His hair was falling over his forehead and his glasses were crooked, almost hiding his eyes. I thought of the X-picture day and walking out of school. I thought of sitting in the park on a swing, my foot digging into the dirt underneath.

"I run away sometimes," I said. "I don't go to school."

He kicked his foot gently against the ledge, his socks down over his sneakers.

"Someone called me incorrigible."

Now that I'd begun, I didn't know how to stop. "Kids never wanted to play with me. I was mean. . . ."

Steven pulled his glasses off and set them down on the ledge next to him. He rubbed the deep red mark in the bridge of his nose.

I stopped, looking out as far as I could, miles of looking out. For a moment I was sorry I'd told him. But he turned and I could see his eyes clearly, and I wondered if he might be blinking back tears. I wasn't sure, though. He reached out and took my hand. "You ran in the right direction this time, didn't you?"

And that was it. He knew all about me, and he didn't mind.

—PATRICIA REILLY GIFF,
Pictures of Hollis Woods, pp. 123–125

Sarah had to stop a few times to wipe the tears from her eyes as she read this climactic scene aloud to her fourth-grade class. Several students wipe away tears too, but they don't seem at all ashamed. The moving story of the foster child, Hollis, and her missed opportunity to be part of a loving family has captured them all. They have been talking about family, and loving relationships, and what it is like for Hollis never to have experienced them. They have been talking about how Josie, an elderly artist with whom Hollis eventually goes to live, helps her understand that she is a good person with a special talent. And now they are about to discover why Hollis ran away from her one chance at being part of a family, fled the love and understanding that were offered to her.

When they hear the end of the scene, in which Steven and Hollis are about to have an accident, they erupt with comments and questions: "Oh, no! Steven is going to die!" "Giff's been hinting at this all along, this about the truck." "It's not Hollis's fault! It's not!" "How can this happen to her?" Ms. Hansen lets the comments flow freely for a minute, then brings the class back together. She begins, "I can tell that you were all engrossed in the scene as I was reading. I was even crying, wasn't I? I heard someone say that Giff has been hinting at this event. Was that you, Joelle? You're right; she has been hinting at this. This kind of hinting is called foreshadowing. How did she foreshadow this accident with the pickup?" Various students tell her about parts of the story in which either Steven or his father talks about his lack of skill as a driver and the danger of the road up the mountain. Ms. Hansen then changes the focus a bit, commenting, "I also heard someone say, 'How could this happen to her?' and I felt that way, too. What had just happened to Hollis before they got into the truck?" The class continues to talk, noting how Hollis had finally realized that Steven cared for her even though she wasn't perfect and how that seemed like a big breakthrough for her. They have been discussing how little she liked or valued herself, and this scene seemed to resolve some of that. And then the accident occurs. "We could say that this is ironic," comments Ms. Hansen, "that just when Hollis realizes that the Regan family really does like her for who she is, she and Steven crash in the truck. What do you think will happen next? Remember, we already know that she runs away from them. Take a few minutes to write in your response log and speculate on what happens. There are only forty-one pages left before we see how Giff ends it herself."

Characterization is the soul of great literature. When readers connect with the emotions of the characters in a book, they experience the events of the story as though they were happening to them. Thus, through the magic of fiction, children accumulate the experience of many lives and grow wise beyond their years. These fourth graders empathized with the loneliness and despair of Hollis as the story unfolded, and at this point they are so involved that this climactic event evoked their cries of protest. Fortunately for them, a happy ending is only pages away.

Defining Contemporary Realistic Fiction

Realistic fiction has a strong sense of actuality. Its plausible stories are about people and events that could actually happen. Good *contemporary* realistic fiction illuminates life, presenting social and personal concerns in a fully human context as it is experienced today or in the very recent past. The line between contemporary and historical is ever shifting and understood differently by readers of different ages. Here, we consider books written about life in the late twentieth and early twenty-first centuries to be contemporary realistic fiction.

Realistic fiction portrays the real world in all its dimensions: it shows the humorous, the sensitive, the thoughtful, the joyful, and the painful sides of life. By its very nature, it deals with the vast range of sensitive topics prevalent in today's world. Lloyd Alexander (1981) reminds us that stories explore polarities, such as love and hate, birth and death, joy and sorrow, loss and recovery. Life's raw materials, questions, and polarities appear most starkly in realistic fiction. Consequently, controversy often surrounds realistic fiction for children and adolescents.

Good stories do not resolve complex problems with easy answers; they consider these problems with the seriousness they require. Because literature reflects the society that creates it, children's contemporary realistic fiction reflects many of the problems that our society is concerned with today. It also reflects the things that we value in our lives: love, personal integrity, family, and friends. Thus, although many realistic novels grapple with realistic problems, many are also stories of courage in which people transform their lives into something worthwhile by drawing on their inner strength. Others are accounts of ordinary people living ordinary lives; their stories are illuminated through the careful consideration of a talented author.

No definition of *realism* is simple, and to say that realism is fiction that could happen in the real world—as opposed to fantasy, which could not—is simplistic. Every work of fiction, like the stories we tell ourselves, is part fanciful and part realistic. We selectively remember and reshape events of our past and present; the same thing happens in books. A realistic story is an author's vision of what might really happen (the plot) in a particular time and place (the setting) to particular people (the characters). Fantasy offers young readers the opportunity to consider elemental questions. Contemporary realistic fiction offers the opportunity for young readers to think about and measure their own lives; we might say that

Teaching Idea 7.1

Keep a Writer's Notebook

Authors of realistic fiction develop plot lines in which they portray real people with real feelings. To do this, they observe themselves and others living their lives and record their observations in journals—not only when they are working on a story, but every day.

Ask your students to collect material for future stories by recording their observations in small notebooks that they can carry around with them.

1. Have students start notebooks of their own by recording events that happen to them. Have them describe events they observe, as well as their feelings about what they see happening.

2. After they have kept the notebook for a period of time, have them go back through their notes and highlight items that might lead to a story. At the same time, read what established authors have to say about where they get their ideas for writing. The July/August issue of *The Horn Book Magazine* always contains the acceptance speech of that year's Newbery winner; in these speeches, authors frequently talk about why they wrote their books.

3. Have students discuss in groups what ideas might lead to interesting stories, then they can proceed to write.

4. Find resources that will help you and your students develop a writer's notebook. Ralph Fletcher's *Writer's Notebook* is an excellent place to begin, as is Janet Wong's book for younger readers, *You Have to Write*.

contemporary realistic fiction can put us in touch with our lives. Teaching Idea 7.1 shows how students can use a writer's notebook to keep track of their own observations of life as they live it, compiling ideas that they might one day turn into a realistic story.

A Brief History of Contemporary Realistic Fiction

One of the interesting aspects of this genre is that it becomes a different genre—historical fiction—with the passage of time. Because of this, early works of contemporary realistic fiction are now considered historical fiction, or "historical realism" as some label them. Keeping this in mind, looking at what was contemporary in the past shows us that children then would have had more opportunity to be "edified" and "instructed" while reading realistic fiction than to fall in love with a character. As children's book publishing developed in the late eighteenth century, the earlier focus on religious education gave way to fanciful stories for entertainment. Despite the desire for pure pleasure in stories, authors generally tucked lessons in as well. At the end of the eighteenth century, children in books were polite, diligent, dutiful, and prudent, just the opposite of Hollis Woods. Well-behaved boys and girls searched relentlessly for information and guidance whereas parents, teachers, ministers, and librarians were unquestioned as sources of information and translators of God's prescription for behavior.

In an attempt to expand the bookselling market started by John Newbery, some publishers commissioned people to write expressly for children. Most of the writers were women such as Maria Edgeworth (1767–1849). Maria wrote stories to entertain her seventeen siblings, revised them, and copied them over in ink (Goldstone, 1984, p. 48). One of Edgeworth's stories, *The Purple Jar*, illustrates how books such as this encouraged children to obey elders. After the American Revolution, writers composed stories that attempted to develop a sense of national pride. Books for children featured adventure stories of travel on the American frontier and courageous battles with the Indians. The books were still didactic, with the American ethic of "work hard and make good" embedded in the stories they told. And they were all from a white American point of view.

In the first half of the nineteenth century, Samuel Goodrich, who believed books could guide children along the right path, collaborated with other writers such as Nathaniel Hawthorne to produce the **Peter Parley** series, a forerunner of the series book that is so popular today. Once begun, series books flourished. Jacob Abbott's series, **Rollo's Tour in Europe**, reads like a travelogue, with wise Uncle George serving as mentor to young Rollo. Rollo eventually returns to America, satisfied that he hails "from a land superior to those inhabited by foreigners" (Jordan, 1983, pp 48–49).

The desire to indoctrinate children in the American work ethic was evident in a series begun by Horatio Alger in 1868. In more than one hundred stories, male characters acquired power and wealth through great effort, courage, and impeccable morality. At this time, books for boys and girls differed. Boys' books were filled with adventure, travel, and the desire to succeed; girls' books centered around homemaking, caring for others, and piety.

Gradually, a new type of literature appeared in which characters were portrayed more realistically. Boy characters, but not girls, began to act more realistically, even devilishly. Those girls who did break the mold almost always reverted to standard gender roles. For example, although most of the female characters in Louisa May Alcott's *Little Women* (1868) are portrayed in conventional roles, Jo was a breath of fresh air compared to most female characters of the time. By the end of the book, though, even Jo has moved toward becoming a wife and mother, understanding that her writing will suffer for it, as it does in the sequel. With the publication of Margaret Sidney's *The Five Little Peppers and How They Grew* in 1880, girls had a series of family stories to enjoy, albeit a sentimental one in which generosity, humility, and proper manners are rewarded in a family with little money but lots of love. Around the same time, many inexpensive, aesthetically weak, mass-produced series written to formula were devoured by children in spite of adult objections. Edward Stratemeyer was perhaps the foremost producer of series with his plot outlines and hired writers. His **Hardy Boys** and **Bobbsey Twins** were immensely popular, and updated versions of his **Nancy Drew** books still sell well today.

Although most contemporary realistic fiction for young readers was set in America, as provincialism waned, children were able to read about characters from other lands in books such as Mary Mapes Dodge's *Hans Brinker; or The Silver Skates* (1865) and Johanna Spyri's *Heidi* (1884).

In the early twentieth century, adventure stories for boys and home stories for girls continued, giving way in the middle of the century to a new realism in books for young readers. This new realism appeared in books for readers of all ages, with books such as Louise Fitzhugh's *Harriet the Spy* (I) and Judy Blume's *Are You There God? It's Me, Margaret* (I) captivating children and sometimes shocking adults. Adolescent literature began to explode in 1967 through 1968 with the publication of S. E. Hinton's *The Outsiders* (A), closely followed by Paul Zindel's *The Pigman* (A), Robert Lipsyte's *The Contender* (A), the anonymously written *Go Ask Alice* (A), Judy Blume's *Forever* (A), Robert Cormier's *The Chocolate War* (A), and other novels for adolescent readers. Thus, social concerns such as violence, sex, drugs, and difficult life decisions became literary issues. Publication of "social issues" books was dramatically curtailed in the 1980s when censorship intensified (Marcus, 2008), while the 1990s saw a boom in publishing children's books and a stunningly varied approach to form, style, and issues.

Beginning in the 1960s and 1970s, waning in the 1980s, and increasing from the 1990s to the present, we have benefited from an accumulating number of books that embrace all types of diversity, and variations within cultures, portraying unique characters who live in the world of today. There were few books that presented girls and women in what, at the time, were "nontraditional" roles during the years prior to the late 1960s; that

Julie Schumacher takes a clear-eyed look at the ripple effects of depression in **Black Box***.*

is not the case today. Female characters in contemporary realistic fiction reflect the profound change in society's perceptions of gender roles. Consideration of social class continues to be a part of realistic fiction, although now class issues are questioned rather than softened with platitudes. Although literature by and about people of color remains a much too small percentage of all publications, publishing houses devoted to publishing these books are increasing in number. At the same time, select publishers are working to bring international books to the attention of an American audience, either from other English-speaking countries or in translation. Books about characters with exceptionalities also are increasing in number, as are books that explore cultural differences, sexual orientation, mental illness, and other contemporary concerns.

As the world changes, literature changes with it. The stories that today's young readers have available encompass both familiar types of stories—such as animal stories, adventure stories, or sports stories, available for many years—and new themes that are increasingly important to

contemporary readers. Romance has taken on a gritty realism, school stories now sometimes encompass violence, coming-of-age stories reflect drug use and the dissolution of families. War stories, always with us as war has always been with us, are set in new locations, such as Afghanistan and Iraq, and terrorism plays a role in realism. Contemporary realism challenges ideas about race, class, and gender, about sexual orientation, exceptionalities, and lifestyles. Today, contemporary realistic fiction reflects the contemporary world with its joys, triumphs, and dangers—it is a passport to experiences in all parts of the world.

Considering Quality in Contemporary Realistic Fiction

We can think of contemporary realistic fiction, like many other genres, in terms of the setting, characters, plot, theme, and style. If the book is illustrated, the quality of the art is important as well. Specific considerations for realistic fiction include the plausibility of characters, plot, and setting.

• • SETTING • •

Authors of realistic stories choose a time and place that actually do or could possibly exist as a setting. The setting may be general or specific, depending on the needs of the story. Sometimes the setting may be a backdrop to the story, with little influence on characters or action. Often, however, the setting is important. A small town might be the very reason why a young character desires to be free; an ocean, a forest, or a desert might be an antagonist that challenges a character to survive. Schools or cities that are large and anonymous might provoke feelings of invisibility and isolation in characters; and cultural values and standards might challenge a character. Settings in contemporary realism work in many ways. When evaluating a setting, look for a vivid, realistic setting and note how it functions in the story.

• • CHARACTERIZATION • •

Characters in realistic fiction reflect human beings we know; they exhibit the powers and failings of a real person in a real world. Like real people, they change over time as they affect and are affected by the world surrounding them. When evaluating characterization in realistic fiction, look for main characters that are believable, authentic, and not stereotypical, are fully developed as multidimensional human beings, and show change or development during the course of the story.

• • PLOT • •

The central conflict in a realistic fiction story is one that is probable in today's world and that matters to today's children. When selecting realistic fiction, look for plot structures that are appropriate for the target audience and events that are probable given the setting and characters of the story. Note how the action is influenced by the characters and how these events impact the characters as well.

• • THEME • •

Themes in realistic fiction generally reflect important issues of contemporary society. Although no one book will—or should—reflect every current issue, there are often multiple themes in contemporary realistic fiction. A story about coming of age, for example, might also explore family relationships. peer pressure, and/or cultural tensions. Books in which the protagonist struggles with some physical challenge might also raise issues of loneliness or self-discovery. Many books today explore social and political issues while also focusing on individual yet universal concerns. Well-developed themes are intrinsic to the narrative.

• • STYLE • •

As in any book, the writing should be superb. Structure should support character development and plot. The dialogue in realistic fiction should reflect today's language forms, including current slang and appropriate dialect variations, yet not be overwhelming. Style that engages the reader and includes realistic dialogue that reflects the characters and their cultural milieu is vital to the development of setting, characterization, plot, and theme.

Figure 7.1 summarizes the criteria for evaluating a work of contemporary realistic fiction.

A close look at Patricia Reilly Giff's *Pictures of Hollis Woods* (I–A) demonstrates how the qualities of excellence in contemporary realistic fiction come together to create a memorable story.

* * *

A CLOSE LOOK AT
Pictures of Hollis Woods

Patricia Reilly Giff's *Pictures of Hollis Woods* (I–A) is an outstanding example of contemporary realistic fiction. Winner of a 2003 Newbery Honor, this book exemplifies the criteria for excellence in realistic fiction. It engages young readers in a search for love and acceptance that is sure to affect the way they regard their own lives.

Figure 7.1

Considering Quality in Contemporary Realistic Fiction

- The story exemplifies characteristics of excellence in narrative fiction.
- A vivid, realistic setting should support the events of the story.
- The characters are credible and nonstereotypical.
- The main characters are multidimensional, and they change and develop over time.
- The problems are believable and are solved in realistic, culturally grounded ways.
- The intended age group can understand the plot structure.
- There is a theme that is applicable to readers' lives, and it is intrinsic to the story.
- The dialogue and thoughts of the characters sound natural, with dialect and diction that do not overwhelm the reader.

The story is set in two different places: the primary setting is the Regans' summer home by the East Fork of the Delaware River; Josie's house is the secondary setting. Both settings are described vividly, with a great deal of visual imagery that makes both come alive for the reader. Josie's house is full of color and odd bits and pieces of her long life. The Delaware house is old, somewhat decrepit, and full of warmth and color. The river and the mountain that the house rests beside are also clearly depicted, and much of the action takes place there. The warmth and comfort of the houses, and the beauty of their surroundings, are important to the development of character and plot.

The story is told as a series of flashbacks that are interspersed with Hollis's ongoing life with Josie, until the final climax. These flashbacks are triggered by Hollis's perusal of the pictures that she drew during her summer with the Regans. As she looks and remembers, we learn of her past life, how she came to spend the summer with the Regans, how she gradually became a part of their family, and why she left them. This plot line is juxtaposed with her growing love for Josie and her decision to stay with her. Tragically, Josie's deteriorating mental health precipitates yet another move for Hollis, and she flees with Josie to the only other place she has ever felt loved—the Delaware River house. It is there, in the middle of winter, the day after Christmas, that the two parts of her life come together and the conflict is resolved.

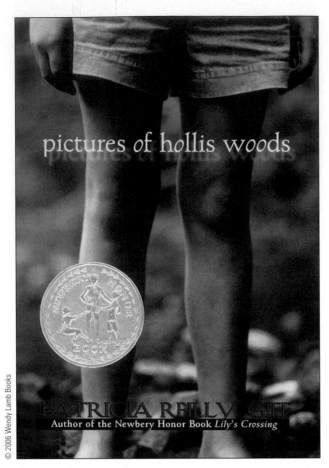

Patricia Reilly Giff creates a heartbreakingly real story in **Pictures of Hollis Woods.**

The conflict in the story is primarily an internal one, as Hollis struggles with herself, caught between her intense longing for family yet afraid of the potential for pain that loving others opens us up to. Minor conflicts between Hollis and her former foster mothers and case-workers help set up her character as a difficult child, but her internal dialogue allows us to understand that her actions spring from this desire to be loved. Finally, the climax of her story with the Regans, when she and her foster brother Steven crash while trying to drive down the mountain, pits the two children against this formidable force of nature, a conflict that has been foreshadowed throughout her time with them.

Because we experience the story through Hollis's point of view, and in part through her direct memories, we feel immediate sympathy for her. From the outset, we see her as a loving child in untenable circumstances. Like the heroes in the ancient Greek dramas, she carries within herself the seeds of her own downfall. Her habit of running away from foster homes is repeated with the Regans when Hollis feels responsible for the crash and again when she flees with Josie. Her intense lifelong desire for a fam-

ily has led her to idealize family life, and that idealization causes her to feel guilty about her role in the arguments that Steven and his father have, even though they have nothing to do with Hollis. The seeds of her redemption are also within her. Hollis is an artist, and it is through her drawings that she comes to understand her life. Her own vision, realized in her art, allows her to see those whom she loves with a clarity that is perhaps not typical of a twelve-year-old. These tight causal connections between character and plot create a unity of character and action that helps make this a very compelling novel.

Hollis is a primary character, but Giff also pays close attention to Josie and the Regans as well, creating characters that we recognize as human beings, complete with foibles as well as strengths, characters we would like to know. Just as Hollis does, we come to love these people in her life.

Giff's lyrical, intensely visual style is filled with imagery so strong that colors and shapes are almost palpable. Hollis sees the world in precise colors: French blue, iridescent silver, the yellow kitchen, the mix of greens and grays and blues of the river and the mountain. This imagery allows Giff to develop the setting, the character of Hollis, the unity of character and action that is evident in the novel, and the themes that permeate the novel.

Themes are multilayered. The sustaining metaphor of art as a clearer vision of life becomes the vehicle through which Hollis grows and changes. Through this sustaining metaphor, Giff also explores what it means to be a family; the importance of loving and being loved and how to love oneself; belonging; how actions lead to consequences; and how the misinterpretations of actions and events can lead to destruction rather than redemption. This ultimately triumphant story of the power of art and love to transform life stays in the hearts of readers long after they read the final words, through which they look with Hollis at the last picture, the one that doesn't exactly match the W picture she's been holding on to for so long:

> But the picture, and why it doesn't match the first one, the W picture: It's because I'm holding my sister, Christina, six weeks old, in my arms. . . . So there are five of us now: a mother, a father, a brother, and two sisters. A family. (p. 166)

Ways to Think about Contemporary Realistic Fiction

Like other genres, realistic fiction includes a variety of literature. One variation is in format. There are contemporary realistic fiction stories that are what second-, third-, and fourth-grade readers call "chapter books," books that are created especially for those readers who are moving toward being able to read and comprehend increasingly complex novels. These chapter books often come in series. We also find contemporary realistic fiction represented by many novels in verse, discussed in Chapter 4, in which realistic stories are the content, with verse the style through which the content is presented. Contemporary realistic fiction comes in graphic novel form as well, in which pictures and text work together to tell a story. Most contemporary realistic fiction for young readers is in the form of picture storybooks, short stories, or novels.

Contemporary realistic fiction contains various distinctive types of stories, which include adventure and survival stories, mysteries, animal stories, sports stories, and others that contemporary readers enjoy and ask for. These categories are not discrete; many books fall into more than one. Because children often ask for books by saying that they want "an adventure story," or "a real story about animals," it is useful to think about contemporary realistic fiction in this manner.

Another useful way to consider contemporary realistic fiction is by theme. There are several dominant themes—coming of age, peer relationships, family relationships—that appear over and over again in fresh ways. We begin our discussion of contemporary realistic fiction by first considering some of the formats that are available today, then move to types of stories, and finally we address this genre in terms of theme.

• • POPULAR FORMATS • •

Chapter Books in Series

Books that contain the same characters in varying situations across many different books are called *series books*. The best of these books contain memorable, vivid characters that readers remember from book to book. Series books are very popular with readers young and old. Many children like to read series books; their familiarity makes readers comfortable. Feitelsen, Kita, and Goldstein (1986) studied the effects of reading series books on first-grade readers. They found that series books facilitate reading comprehension because the reader knows the character and setting, the framework, and the background of the story. Knowing the characters and what to expect from them makes reading easier; it's like meeting a good friend again. Series books also motivate reluctant readers. Knowing that there are other books in the series increases the anticipation; if the first book was good, then the next one is sure to be enjoyable as well. In addition to the many contemporary realistic fiction series, many popular series books are from other genres as well—fantasy, science fiction, and historical fiction, not to mention biography and nonfiction.

Here, we consider a special type of series book, contemporary realistic fiction stories that are written for readers who are transitioning from brief, simple texts into longer, more complex texts. We call these "chapter books," or "transitional chapter books," many of which are available as series books that support transitioning readers.

The easy-readers series books such as Cynthia Rylant's **Henry and Mudge** and **Mr. Potter and Tabby** books (P), or Arnold Lobel's classic **Frog and Toad** series (P) are designed to support newly independent readers with their large type, careful word placement, and supportive illustrations. We discuss some of those books in Chapter 3. Longer books, such as Megan McDonald's **Judy Moody** series (P), Paula Danziger's **Amber Brown** books (P), and Patricia Reilly Giff's **Polk Street School** series (P) are popular with young readers who are outgrowing **Frog and Toad** and **Henry and Mudge** and are eager to move on to "chapter books." The supportive illustrations, simple texts, usually episodic chapters, and familiar cast of characters (once the first book is read) allow newly independent readers to rise to the challenge of longer texts.

Michele Edwards's **Jackson Friends** series (P–I) is narrated by a young African American girl who attends a contemporary American magnet school, and young readers relate to the multicultural school environment that Edwards creates. These same readers enjoy the **Gym Shorts** series, written by Betty Hicks with illustrations by Adam McCauley. This series consists of short chapter books that follow a fourth-grade boy, Henry, and his friends who love sports. Pencil sketches by Adam McCauley decorate each spread and support the text. *Basketball Bats* and *Goof-Off Goalie* (P) are the first two books in the planned series. Peter Catalanotto and Pamela Schembri's **Second Grade Friends** series offers yet another choice for newly independent readers. In *The Veteran's Day Visitor* (P), the third book in the series, readers consider some of the less comfortable aspects of aging and the bittersweet joys of having a close relationship with an older person. Lois Lowry's *Gooney Bird Greene*, *Gooney Bird and the Room Mother*, and *Gooney the Fabulous* (P), with illustrations by Middy Thomas, are humorous looks at life in the second grade for a one-of-a-kind youngster.

Young readers who are comfortable with slightly longer texts still enjoy series books. They enjoy being able to recognize the characters in Annie Barrows's *Ivy and Bean Take Care of the Babysitter* (P), the fourth book in the **Ivy and Bean** series, with illustrations by Sophie Blackall. Kimberly Willis Holt's *Piper Reed, Navy Brat* (P) introduces readers to nine-year-old Piper, irrepressible and full of spunk, and most will be eager to go on to *Piper Reed: The Great Gypsy* (P). Peggy Gifford's *Moxie Maxwell Does Not Love Stuart Little* and *Moxie Maxwell Does Not Love Writing Thank-You Notes* (P–I), blend humor and family stories in a satisfying chapter book format. In Gail Gauthier's *A Girl, a Boy, and a Monster Cat* and *A Girl, a Boy, and Three Robbers* (P–I), Brandon and Hannah develop a true friendship as they learn to play together after school while Brandon's mother is at work. Joe Cepeda's cartoon illustrations capture the humor and liveliness of the pair.

The first book in Sara Pennypacker's series, ***Clementine*** (P) was a *New York Times* bestseller. The engaging protagonist is both hysterically funny and extremely lovable, and Marla Frazee's inspired illustrations reflect both extremes. *The Talented Clementine* and *Clementine's Letter* (P) continue the adventures of a young girl finding her own voice in her loving family and the wider world of school. We now take a close look at ***Clementine***.

✳ ✳ ✳

A CLOSE LOOK AT

Clementine

As in many works of contemporary realistic fiction, character drives the everyday life stories in Sara Pennypacker's ***Clementine*** (P) and the books that follow. Eight-year-old Clementine lives with her little brother, artist mother, and father in the basement apartment of the building that her father manages. Her school and the building that she lives in are integral settings that serve to reveal character and advance the plot. Partially because her father is the building manager—although you might think that Clementine would do so anyway—she knows everyone in the building and has her own way of describing them all—not always flattering. This tells the reader a lot about Clementine's character, as does the fact that that she and her mother look out of their ground-level kitchen window and Clementine knows who comes and goes by their feet. Similarly, in school, the interactions she has with her principal reveal a great deal about her personality.

Her best friend, Margaret, a bit more than a year older, lives in the building with her mother and older brother (who is *not* Clementine's boyfriend, as she is careful to remind us). Clementine's helpful nature is apparent when Margaret cuts a chunk of her own hair trying to get glue out of it. Clementine offers to help, with disastrous results. Then she helps again by coloring Margaret's rather bald scalp with lovely orange curls, just like her own. When the permanent marker curls don't make Margaret's mother happy, Clementine cuts off her own hair in sympathy and Margaret uses the green permanent marker to make curls for her. Clementine never blames Margaret, not even when she is engaged in a discussion with the principal. In fact, Clementine worries about the principal because the principal thinks that Clementine is not pay-

ing attention, which Clementine always does—just not to the things her teachers want her to focus on. In fact, Clementine pays such careful attention that she solves a problem that her father is baffled by. It seems that Clementine possesses her own brilliance.

The language play is laugh-out-loud funny. When Clementine is trying to find a name for a pet, she goes into the bathroom to find a good word; her new cat's name, "Moisturizer," is much better than the name she gave to a former kitten, "Laxative." Chafing under her "fruit name," she refers to her little brother with a series of vegetable names: Radish, Pea Pod, Celery. Her first-person narration reveals her character, with an almost breathless retelling of her adventures. Clementine, like Ramona, is a dynamo. Just one glimpse at the cover illustration, with Clementine standing on one hand, the other pressed to the wall, both feet pressed to opposite walls, tongue out, and red curls awry, tells young readers that they want to be her friend.

As we noted previously, series books are not only written for young readers until they become able to handle extended texts with ease, but they remain popular with

Clementine is a character—both literally and figuratively—in this chapter book in a series by Sara Pennypacker.

readers through adulthood. In the sections that follow, we discuss other popular series books; for more information on series books, refer to Chapters 6, 8, 9, and 10 as well.

Novels in Verse

We consider novels in verse as poetry in Chapter 4, but some are also contemporary realistic fiction. Sharon Creech's *Love That Dog* (I) is a beautifully told story of a young boy who at first resists his teacher's attempts to get him to write poetry. As the year progresses, he learns to express himself through poetry, and we watch as he comes to terms with the loss of a beloved companion. The sequel, *Hate That Cat* (I), continues his story as he opens himself up to loving a new pet. Lindsay Lee Johnson uses poetry to tell the story of Phoebe, abandoned by both mother and father, in *Soul Moon Soup* (I–A). This hauntingly beautiful novel follows Phoebe as she discovers her inner resources and the healing power of art and nature.

Steven Herrick's *Naked Bunyip Dancing* (A), with illustrations by Beth Norling, is a novel in verse from Australia that explores the often humorous trials and joys of self-discovery as the students in Class 6C begin to learn about things that are strange "school subjects" for them—Bob Dylan, poetry, belly dancing, yoga—and discover their hidden talents as they prepare for an end-of-the-year concert.

In *Locomotion* (I–A), Jacqueline Woodson tells the story of eleven-year-old Lonnie Collins Motion who lost both of his parents in a fire. He lost his little sister, too, even though she survived the fire, because they were placed in different foster homes. His pervasive grief and loneliness begin to lift when his teacher gives him a great gift—she asks him to "write it down before it leaves your brain," and Lonnie begins to write his life in free verse. This exquisite award-winning book and its sequel, *Peace, Locomotion* (I–A), reminds us of the power of words to shape our lives. Teaching Idea 7.2 offers suggestions for using contemporary realistic fiction to help students consider what they can learn about themselves.

Graphic Novels

Novels with graphics that are a significant part of the storytelling are yet another format that young readers enjoy and, fortunately for them, more graphic novels are being produced. In 2007, Sherman Alexie's *The Absolutely True Diary of a Part-Time Indian* (A) won the National Book Award. Jacqueline Wilson's *Best Friends* (I) is an uncompromising look at how adults make decisions and children have to live with them. The story is told through a deft combination of art and speech, with the characters of Gemma and her friend Alice very realistic in their anguish about being parted and in their determination to remain "best friends forever," even as they learn to make other friends.

Teaching Idea **7.2**

Thematic Connections: Discovering the Self

In *Pictures of Hollis Woods*, Hollis is engaged in a journey of self-discovery. Ask your students to list the things that Hollis discovers about herself and how she did so. Then ask them to compare their own journeys of self-discovery with Hollis's. Is their own easier? More difficult? Have they completed it? Do they think they will? Other books that lend themselves to this same question are *Soul Moon Soup, Shakespeare Bats Cleanup, Heartbeat,* and *Locomotion.* Compare the ways that art helps the protagonists of *Soul Moon Soup, Heartbeat,* and *Pictures of Hollis Woods* heal themselves, and the way that writing helps the protagonists of *Shakespeare Bats Cleanup* and *Locomotion.* Ask students to think about some of the things each of them can do that might help them come to know themselves and heal their own emotional wounds.

Award-winning picture book artist Don Wood's venture into the graphic novel form, *Into the Volcano* (I–A), is an adventure/survival story and a mystery vividly brought to life through the detailed, colorful illustrations and snappy dialogue. There's even a bit of science thrown in as two unlikely heroes, brothers Duffy and Sumo, travel through a volcano on the island nation of Kocalaha.

Another book for older readers, *Skim* (A), with words by Mariko Tamaki and drawings by Jillian Tamaki, explores Wicca, suicide, depression, sexual orientation, love, and various social challenges as they exist in a private girls' high school. The stunning, seamless integration of text and illustration was recognized with a spot on the *New York Times* best-illustrated list for 2008.

Picturebooks, Short Stories, and Novels

Although chapter books in series, novels in verse, and graphic novels add innovation to the body of contemporary realistic fiction, most of this genre is in more traditional picturebook, short story, or novel formats. Unless otherwise noted, the books we discuss following are primarily short stories or novels, with some picturebooks, which we discuss thoroughly in Chapter 3, included as appropriate. These stories range widely in style, theme, and structure, creating a rich array of books to entice young readers into the world of contemporary realistic fiction. We turn to that array with a consideration of some of the distinct types of fiction found in contemporary realism.

• • DISTINCTIVE TYPES • •

In addition to varied formats, contemporary realistic fiction contains different types, or subgenres, of stories as well. Some frequently found in the genre and asked for by young readers include adventure and survival stories, realistic animal stories, mysteries, and sports stories.

Adventure and Survival Stories

Marked by especially exciting, fast-paced plots, adventure and survival stories captivate readers, who are eager to discover what happens. Often the central problem is a conflict between person and nature. The best adventure stories also contain multidimensional characters who control much of the action and who change as a result of the action. Many young readers who enjoy a compelling plot prefer adventure stories. *Into the Volcano* (I–A), discussed previously, is a good example of a graphic novel that is an adventure/survival story.

Gary Paulsen's *Hatchet* (I–A) is still one of the most popular adventure stories today. Engaged readers also enjoy *Brian's Winter* and *Brian's Return* (I–A), in which Paulsen explores possible endings to this exciting adventure story set in the woods of northeastern Canada. These novels focus on Brian's conflict with nature, but also include some internal conflict as Brian struggles with himself in an attempt to cope with his parents' divorce. In Tor Seidler's *Brothers Below Zero* (I), sibling rivalry results in two brothers struggling to stay alive in a terrible snowstorm, with the interpersonal conflict leading to the conflict with nature.

Sharon Creech's novel *The Wanderer* (I–A), a Newbery Honor book, revolves around several conflicts: internal struggles with the self, struggles between individuals, and a struggle with nature—in this case the sea. Sophie, thirteen, is sailing across the ocean with her uncles and two thirteen-year-old cousins, Cody and Brian, when a tremendous storm threatens their lives and calls forth courage that they did not know they possessed. Told in a series of journal entries from Sophie and Cody, this is a complex, beautifully crafted story.

In *Red Midnight* (I), Ben Mikaelsen's young protagonist, twelve-year-old Santiago, and his younger sister demonstrate great courage and resourcefulness as they flee Guatemala after guerrilla soldiers attack their village. The overland adventure soon gives way to their struggle with the ocean as they try to reach the United States by sea kayak. Also struggling to survive the horrors of war, Chanda and her siblings, Iris and Soly, are caught up in a rebel invasion of their grandmother's village in a fictitious African countryside in Allan Stratton's *Chanda's Wars*, sequel to *Chanda's Secrets* (A). As Iris and Soly are forced into military slavery, the contrast between the inhumanity of their situation and the strength of their characters is apparent.

Animal Stories

Animal stories are about realistic relationships between human beings and animals, most commonly horses or dogs, or about realistic animal adventures. When they focus on an animal-human relationship, this relationship is usually a vehicle for maturation by the central human character. Good animal stories have engaging characters that grow and change as a result of their experience with an animal. Many of these books are very moving, often provoking a strong emotional response.

The protagonist of Kate DiCamillo's *Because of Winn-Dixie* (I), ten-year-old India Opal Buloni, loves her new dog from the first moment she sees him in the Winn-Dixie grocery store. His canine companionship eases her longing for her mother, helps her develop friendships in her new town, and opens up communication with her taciturn father.

Phyllis Reynolds Naylor's *Shiloh* (I–A) is an outstanding example of a realistic animal story. Winner of the 1992 Newbery Medal, *Shiloh* presents a profound ethical dilemma as experienced by eleven-year-old Marty Preston, who rescues and then falls in love with a stray dog that has been abused. His family and community expect him to return the dog to his rightful owner, even though Judd has mistreated Shiloh. Marty, however, feels that a higher principle supports his keeping the dog. Intermediate-grade readers, in the midst of developing their own moral code as they begin to encounter ideas and experiences that cause them to think about values, can do so in the safety of the story world of *Shiloh*.

Although technically fantasy, because the first-person narration comes from the protagonist of *Chancey of the Maury River* (I–A), and the protagonist is a horse, this sentimental horse story by Gigi Amateau rings true to life, especially for anyone who has loved a horse and been loved in return. The focal animal in Helen Frost's *Diamond Willow* (I) is a dog. Set in interior Alaska, this story blends an animal story and a survival tale, with some magical realism as well.

Mysteries and Thrillers

A mystery is marked by suspense: Will the mystery be solved? The focus in a mystery story is a question—Who did it? Where is it? What happened?—and the action centers on finding the answer to that question. The best mysteries revolve around an intriguing problem and contain well-developed characters who work to solve the problem. They feature fast-paced action and a logical solution foreshadowed through the careful presentation of clues.

Nancy Werlin distinguishes between mysteries and thrillers, which "tend to be about nasty people doing bad, illegal, and/or unethical things" (2006, p. 529). Many children go through a phase in which mysteries are all they want to read; adolescents often devour thrillers. Fortunately, there are some excellent mysteries for children of all ages, many of which are also series books.

Young readers who love mysteries are happy to find that mysteries are often also series chapter books. Elizabeth Levy, Donald Sobol, Seymour Simon, and Marjorie Sharmat are some of the writers who have provided younger readers with brief, exciting mysteries that satisfy their desire to figure things out. As these young readers mature, they continue to enjoy series, such as the very popular **Sammy Keyes** (I) books, by Wendelin Van Draanen. In *Sammy Keyes and the Psycho Kitty Queen*, Sammy finds a dead cat on her thirteenth birthday and gets involved in solving yet another mystery. She is a super sleuth with a great sense of humor who navigates with verve the life of a young adolescent.

Blue Balliett's first novel, *Chasing Vermeer* (I), is a puzzle, an adventure, and a mystery that needs solving. From the beginning of this intriguing novel, Balliett invites readers to participate in helping the three young protagonists solve the mystery of the missing Vermeer, and they are more than willing to give it a try. The second and third books in this series, *The Wright 3* and *The Calder Game* (I), are equally intriguing. In *The Calder Game* the action moves to England when Calder Pillay travels there with his father. When Calder goes missing, his friends Tommy and Petra, and elderly neighbor Mrs. Sharp, fly over to help find him. There are a few too many coincidences in all of these books, but the fast-paced action pulls young readers along and the theme of creative thinking appeals as well.

These and other books, such as Trenton Lee Stewart's *The Mysterious Benedict Society and the Perilous Journey* (I), second in a series, keep intermediate-grade children reading and guessing, and provide alternatives to augment the many formula mystery series, such as the time-tested **Nancy Drew** and **Hardy Boys** books. An interesting mystery from Great Britain, Alex Shearer's *Canned* (I) is unpredictable and funny, as well as gruesome and exaggerated, introducing Fergal and Charlotte, eccentric children who form a tentative partnership when they discover unusual contents in the unlabeled cans that they both collect. Carl Hiaasen combines mystery, environmental protection, and knee-slapping humor in *Hoot* (I), a Newbery Honor book. Andrea Beaty's *Cicada Summer* (I) is a thought-provoking, gripping multilayered story. In Siobhan Dowd's *The London Eye Mystery* (I–A), twelve-year-old Ted and his older sister join together to solve the mysterious disappearance of their cousin, Salim. Ted turns out to be a terrific detective, as the effects of his

Asperger's syndrome, one of which is a very logical brain, work to his advantage.

Joan Lowry Nixon's psychic mysteries and Lois Duncan's eerie novels satisfy older readers, and Mary Downing Hahn's novels are always intriguing. Her latest, *All the Lovely Bad Ones* (I–A), is a ghostly mystery that, if you don't believe in ghosts, moves into fantasy as she keeps readers on edge until the climax. E. L. Konigsburg's *Silent to the Bone* (A), Carol Plum-Ucci's *The Body of Christopher Creed* (A), and Robert Cormier's chilling *The Rag and Bone Shop* (A) also provide adolescent mystery fans with intriguing books to read and think about. Norma Fox Mazer's psychological thriller, *The Missing Girl* (A) gets into the minds of five sisters who are being stalked, with one eventually kidnapped and imprisoned by a very dangerous man; the man's point of view alternates with those of three of the sisters in this chilling tale. Nancy Werlin's *The Rules of Survival* (A) is a perfect example of how the tension of fear can catch and keep a reader turning the pages. Kevin Brooks's *Black Rabbit Summer* (A) is filled with social commentary as two teens disappear. One is wealthy and popular, the other poor and ignored, and the responses to the two disappearances reflect a stunning indifference to "ordinary" people. *The Boxer and the Spy* (A), by Robert Parker, combines mystery and a sports story as the protagonist, Terry, trains as a boxer and investigates a friend's apparent suicide.

Sports Stories

As demonstrated by *The Boxer and the Spy*, good sports stories are almost always more than just stories about a sport. In sports stories, the action revolves around a sport and the thrills and tensions that accompany that particular sport. Like mysteries, many sports stories are series books as well, such as the **Gym Shorts** series mentioned previously. A small but increasing number of sports books with girls as central characters have broadened the scope of the genre; some sports stories examine social issues such as sexism or racism. Matt de la Peña's *Mexican White Boy* (A) tackles issues of family structure, identity, racism, and social class as the biracial protagonist moves between his barrio home and the private school where he plays baseball. The best of these books, such as Walter Dean Myers's *Slam!* (A), balance the descriptions of the sport with the development of the story, in which the central character grows in some way due to the challenges he or she faces because of participation in the sport. Often, sports serve as a metaphor for life.

Rich Wallace writes sports stories that especially appeal to older adolescent males. His *Wrestling Sturbridge* (A) explores life in a small Pennsylvania town, the trials of adolescence, and the anxiety and exhilaration of being a member of a top-notch wrestling team in a sports-crazy town. That same small town is also the setting for *Shots on Goal*, about an underdog high-school soccer team; *Playing without the Ball: A Novel in Four Quarters*; and his short-stories-cum-novel, *Losing Is Not an Option* (A). Wallace's riveting descriptions of the sports and his outstanding character development make his books excellent examples of this genre. Chris Crutcher is another master of the sports story genre. In *Whale Talk* (A) Crutcher deftly combines a story about swimming with an exploration of male friendships and high school social stratification in a gripping coming-of-age story. John Coy does much the same in *Box Out* and *Crackback* (A), in which the sport is a frame for the protagonists confronting difficult issues and decisions about life.

Rather than describing how sports shape a child's life, Ron Koertge explores how being unable to continue a beloved sport shapes a young boy's life in *Shakespeare Bats Cleanup* (I–A). Combining poetry and sports in a moving contemporary story, Koertge presents a young man driven to writing by boredom. He is home with mononucleosis, unable to play baseball, and he begins to read and write poetry, trying out different poetic forms. He uses his writing to come to terms with the recent death of his mother and with his changing role among his peers when his illness leaves him too weak to resume his role as baseball star. A novel in verse, a sports story, and a portrait of a young man growing up as he creates a new identity for himself, this novel represents the richness and complexity of contemporary realistic fiction. We now turn to exploring this genre through theme.

Themes in Contemporary Realistic Fiction

The themes in contemporary realistic fiction are as many and varied as life itself. In fact, events in authors' own lives may influence what they write, as pointed out in Teaching Idea 7.3. To make it even more confusing, most books explore more than one theme. How would you classify *Pictures of Hollis Woods*? Is it a story about family, coming of age, friendship, or self-discovery? It is all of these and more, depending on the story an individual reader creates during reading. Despite this, it is helpful to group books loosely by themes, as young readers often want to read several books that relate to a single theme; many teachers, too, enjoy constructing thematic units (discussed in Chapters 11 and 12) with their students. The thematic Teaching Ideas, such as Teaching Idea 7.2 on page 239, are examples of how to make these connections.

Teaching Idea 7.3

Study an Author's Work and Life

Choose an author who writes realistic fiction, either novels or picture storybooks, and has also written an autobiography. With your students, read the autobiography and some of the realistic fiction books and discuss how events in the author's life influenced his or her books. For example, there is a clear link between Cynthia Rylant's early years and some of her early picturebooks and novels, and the same is true of Patricia Polacco. In her autobiography, Lois Lowry makes clear connections between her life and her writing, as do Chris Crutcher, Jack Gantos, and Walter Dean Myers.

The following are some questions you might want to pursue:

✳ What were the major influences in the author's life?

✳ How did events from the author's life influence her or his writing?

✳ What parallels can you find between her stories and her life?

✳ What does the author say about the relation between his life and his art?

Common themes in realistic fiction for children center on a variety of issues embedded in the larger process of growing up, developing peer relationships, and coping with often demanding family relationships. Themes in contemporary realistic fiction change as society changes, as art reflects life. Writers explore the issues that interest them in stories both tragic and humorous.

• • COMING OF AGE • •

Not surprisingly, some of the most popular books for children and adolescents are about growing up. Because our society has few formalized rites of passage, the way to adulthood is not always clear for our children; they must mark their own paths. Books that portray a character struggling toward adulthood allow readers to see themselves reflected, and provide a rehearsal for real life. There are numerous picture storybooks for primary-grade readers that depict realistic characters trying to cope with growing up. Many of these books deal with children's increasing independence from adults and with the fear and delight that accompany that independence. We discuss these in Chapter 3.

Older readers continue to struggle for independence, often confronting conflicting feelings, difficult moral choices, and personal challenges along the way. Young people are engaged in a process of constructing their identity, trying to find out who they are, what they like and do not like, and what they will and will not do. They are passionately preoccupied with themselves and may look to literature for solutions to escape from their preoccupations. They enter into books in ways they cannot with television or film; reading is a far more personal and creative experience. When students want to understand themselves, they can use stories to help them do so, experiencing lives vicariously and thinking about how they might act.

Many of the series books discussed earlier explore growing up—some, like the **Clementine** series, with humor. Other writers turn to humor as well. Louis Sachar underscores the funny yet poignant process of growing up in novels for intermediate-grade readers, such as *There's a Boy in the Girls' Bathroom* (I) and his Newbery Medal winner, *Holes* (I). This book breaks many of the rules—it is both contemporary and historical; the characters are ludicrous; the circumstances are implausible; there are too many coincidences; and it's not truly realistic—which serves only to heighten the humor. By the end of the story, readers are cheering for Stanley Yelnats and laughing as they do. Stephanie Tolan's Newbery Honor–winning *Surviving the Applewhites* (I–A) tells the story of the redemption of a difficult boy when his grandfather forces him to be homeschooled by the very odd Applewhite family, which results in some extremely hilarious consequences. The humor in the story is in counterpoint to the serious consideration of a young man finding himself.

Humor is relatively scarce in contemporary realistic fiction for adolescent readers, however, with most books exploring serious issues from a serious perspective. Amjed Qamar, for example, creates a compelling character, fourteen-year-old Nazia, in *Beneath My Mother's Feet* (A), a haunting coming-of-age novel set in Karachi, Pakistan. When her father loses his job and her brother steals her dowry, Nazia and her mother have to go to work as housecleaners, a significant change in status. As Nazia struggles to adjust to her new life, she begins to realize that she has choices to make and that each choice carries a cost. Urdu words heighten the setting, and a glossary is thoughtfully included.

Phyllis Reynolds Naylor's long-running series of **Alice** books is a study in the process of forging an identity. The early books were perfect for intermediate-grade readers; the later novels in the twenty-three book series are for young adults. *Almost Alice* (A) takes on the challenge of a close friend's unplanned pregnancy and Alice's struggle with self-doubt. In Angela Johnson's *The First Part*

Last (A), sixteen-year-old Bobby becomes a father and realizes what that means. Told from Bobby's first-person point of view, this complex novel speaks to the rarely considered bond between a teenage father and his child.

Romance is often part of growing up, and the beginnings of romantic feelings for another is a strand in many novels for intermediate-grade readers, the best of which have multilayered themes. Martha, the protagonist in Kevin Henkes's *Olive's Ocean* (I), a Newbery Honor winner, is twelve; she is about to spend the summer at her grandmother's house in Cape Cod when she is given a diary entry written by Olive, a recently deceased classmate, in which Olive had written that she had hoped to become Martha's friend. This affects how Martha thinks about herself, her life, her peers, and the world. As she wonders about what might have been, she is thrust into what will be, as she awakens to her first crush and to the truth that her beloved grandmother is getting old. Martha's realization that she is not the center of the universe is compellingly perceptive. In the Newbery Award–winning *The Higher Power of Lucky* (I), Susan Patron lovingly portrays a young girl who is living with her stepmother in a small desert town, in a trailer, and wondering just where she fits into the world. Over the course of the story, she discovers just what her "higher powers" are. By the end she seems ready to embark on the work of becoming an adult, secure in the knowledge that she is loved by her guardian, Brigitte.

Lynne Rae Perkins won the Newbery Award for her beautiful coming-of-age novel *Criss Cross* (I–A), in which three fourteen-year-old neighbors—Debbie, from Perkins's *All Alone in the Universe* (I–A), Hector, and Lenny—are on the brink of moving from childhood into adolescence as their paths crisscross over the spring and summer. Thirty-eight vignettes, narrated primarily by either Debbie or Hector, come together in a quiet, beautifully told story. Set in a small town, perhaps in the recent past, this, like *Olive's Ocean*, is a gentle, contemplative novel.

Sharon Flake uses the medium of the short story in *Who Am I without Him? Short Stories about Girls and the Boys in Their Lives* (A) to explore identity development. This is a hard-hitting look at the dynamics of love relationships for black adolescents. In the ten first-person narratives that make up this collection, we see girls both weak and strong as they are engaged in figuring out how romantic relationships can work in today's world.

• • PEER RELATIONSHIPS • •

Part of growing up—and part of romance—involves learning to interact with ever-widening worlds and with a wide variety of people. Books that explore peer relationships mirror many of the concerns that young readers have about their own lives. Today's books explore a wide range of relationships among peers: some characters are noble, some are loyal, but most are simply ordinary beings. Because young people value acceptance by their friends, they are highly susceptible to peer pressure. The literature reflects their vulnerability and their strengths. Understandably, a number of realistic books dealing with peer relationships are set in school or revolve around a school-related problem. Many picture storybooks involve peer relationships; making new friends, going to school, and learning to share are some of the things that children learn to do as they widen their circle of friends. These books are discussed in Chapter 3.

Many books about peer relationships are series chapter books that offer humor and satisfaction as well as reassurance that boys and girls are not alone in their feelings. These "school stories," many of which we discussed previously, form a solid foundation for the more complex stories and relationships that students will encounter as they mature. Novels for intermediate and advanced readers are sometimes humorous as well. Esme Raji Codell's *Sahara Special* and *Sing a Song of Tuna Fish: Hard-to-Swallow Stories from Fifth Grade* (I) are wonderfully funny school stories. Steven Herrick's *Naked Bunyip Dancing* (I), discussed previously as a novel in verse, reveals the emotions of students in one class, often humorously, and Andrew Clements offers a funny story about twin boys who are beginning the sixth grade in *Lost and Found* (I).

Kathe Koja's *Buddha Boy* (A) explores the price of popularity through the unexpected friendship between Justin, a popular boy, and Jinsen, considered a freak by the boys who control the social scene at school. As Justin discovers Jinsen's wonderful artistic talent and learns more about his beliefs, he realizes that Buddha Boy is someone he admires. When Justin stands up for Jinsen, his shame at his own complicity in and anger at the meanness of others is wholly believable. Madeleine George looks at issues surrounding body image in her story of an unlikely friendship between a fat girl and an anorexic girl in *Looks* (A).

Friendships in and out of school are the subject of many books for young readers. Grace Lin's *The Year of the Rat* (I) presents the distress that Pacy feels when her best friend moves and her new friends don't really act like friends. Pacy is Chinese and she is acutely aware of the fact that she is now the only Asian American student in the school. Kevin Henkes's *Bird Lake Moon* (I) is a quiet book that follows two young boys as they tentatively begin a friendship during a summer vacation even as they are each struggling with serious family problems—divorce in one case and death in the other. Jacqueline Woodson's Newbery honor book, *After Tupac and D Foster* (A) depicts a close friendship among three young adolescent girls and their close connection to the music of Tupac Shakur, whose lyrics inspire the girls to discover their own "big purpose" in life.

As children mature, their relationships become more complex. Often the unevenness of the onset of adolescence creates gulfs between good friends: one is interested in the opposite sex, one isn't; one is physically mature, one isn't. Adolescence also brings with it increasing pressures to experiment with the dangerous side of life—drugs and alcohol, sex, brushes with the law—and books for advanced readers often contain characters who struggle with a personal crisis as they seek to stand up for what they value and at the same time maintain their friendships. Sharon Draper explores popularity, peer pressure, and hazing in *The Battle of Jericho* (A). Jericho is thrilled to be asked to become a member of the most prestigious club in school. When the initiation becomes frightening and dangerous, he begins to question what he is doing, but it's too late.

• • FAMILY RELATIONSHIPS • •

Family relationships are also important to children and adolescents, and contemporary books present a varied picture of family life and probe new dimensions of realism. These books portray not only two-parent families but also communal, one-parent, and extended families, families headed by divorced or separated parents, families headed by homosexual parents, and children living alone without adults. There have always been books in which each family member stays in culturally assigned roles. As these roles have evolved and changed, so too have books for young readers.

Family stories have changed in other ways as well. Fathers receive increasing attention in books for children and adolescents: where they had once been ignored, they are now recognized as viable literary characters. Fictional mothers now run the full range of likeable to despicable characters, just as they do in real life. Stories about siblings have also changed with the times: children growing up in the same home must learn to share possessions, space, and parents or guardians. Contemporary novels also consider such subjects as sibling rivalry or learning to accept stepsisters or stepbrothers. In addition to happy, well-adjusted children from safe, loving homes, there are children who are victims of child abuse, abandonment, alcoholism, neglect, and a whole range of society's ills. These characters are often cynical, bitter, disillusioned, and despondent, but also can be courageous and strong.

Not all families are perfect, even when they try, as Gary Schmidt depicts in *Trouble* (I–A). The Smith family has a perfect life—a beautiful house in a beautiful setting, important ancestors, and three achievement-oriented children. The oldest, Franklin, is admired by all, most of whom fail to notice that he is arrogant and a bully, especially in the way he treats his younger brother, Henry. When Franklin is terribly injured in an automo-

Profiles

Patricia Reilly Giff

I want to write books that children will laugh over even if their own lives are not happy, books that say ordinary people are special.

Patricia Reilly Giff's characters, full of authentic spunk, adroitly demonstrate how ordinary people are special in everyday ways. The genuineness of Giff's characters reflects her tendency to build books around the people in her life. Giff hopes her books inspire young readers to write the stories of their own lives: "I want [children] to make the connection that books are people's stories, that writing is talking on paper, and I want them to write their own stories. I'd like my books to provide that connection for them" (Bantam Doubleday Dell, n.d.).

Giff has written prolifically since 1979, producing more than seventy books for children. Her popular series include *Kids of the Polk Street School, New Kids at the Polk Street School,* and *Polka Dot, Private Eyes.* She has won Newbery Honor Awards for *Lily's Crossing* and *Pictures of Hollis Woods.*

Sara Pennypacker

I start by making up a character. I make this character very real. I imagine what she likes for breakfast, what he thinks is unfair in this world, how she fits into her family, what he loves to do most. Then, when I feel I know and care about this character, I ask him or her, "What's wrong?" And I try to imagine what he or she might answer.

Sara Pennypacker loves to write, but she has a problem: She gets too many ideas. She says they are everywhere, and tells young writers to keep a writer's notebook and take it with them everywhere; she does. She also does a lot of revising, wanting her books to be as perfect as possible. She says that each Clementine book takes close to a year to write.

There are now three Clementine volumes. The fourth book in the **Clementine** series, *Clementine: Friend of the Week*, will be published in 2009. Sara has also taken over the **Flat Stanley** series beginning with *Flat Stanley's Worldwide Adventures #2*, also to be released in 2009. Visit her at www.sarapenny packer.com.

Walter Dean Myers

*W*alter Dean Myers began writing when he was a child. That's no surprise, given that he was (and still is) also a voracious reader. His first book for young readers was published in 1969, and he began writing full time in 1977. He has now published more than seventy books for children and adolescents, ranging from poetry to picturebooks to realistic fiction, historical fiction, biography, and nonfiction. An honored writer, he has won five Coretta Scott King Awards, the Margaret A. Edwards Award, and the Virginia Hamilton Award. His groundbreaking novel, *Monster*, received the first Printz Award for young adult literature; it was also a National Book Award finalist. Visit Walter Dean Myers at www.walterdeanmyers.net.

---

bile accident and his older sister withdraws to her room, Henry begins to understand that trouble can find anyone, anywhere.

Nikki Grimes explores the idea of home and family in *The Road to Paris* (I–A), winner of a Coretta Scott King Honor Award, in which young Paris is separated from her brother, Malcolm, when they are abandoned yet again by their mother. Sent to a foster family that lives outside of New York City, which had always been her home, biracial Paris initially has trouble fitting in and making friends; she certainly is not going to learn to love her new family. Of course, she eventually does, and she also learns to feel proud of her own accomplishments and make friends. When her mother reappears, repentant and seemingly responsible, Paris must make a difficult decision—does she join her mother and be reunited with her beloved brother, or does she stay with the foster family she has come to feel a part of?

Hilary McKay's Casson family saga concludes in *Forever Rose* (A), the fifth book in the series. In this story eleven-year-old Rose is feeling anxious about her older siblings growing up and moving away. As she comes to realize that she can't halt the inexorable march toward adulthood, she realizes that everything will be different, but perhaps also good. The situation that Rits, a thirteen-year-old Dutch boy, finds himself in is much more dire than Rose Casson's. His mother is in a mental institution, his father is off with his girlfriend, and Rits is sent to a depressed and neglectful uncle's house for the summer. In spite of this, the humor in Mariken Jongman's *Rits* (A), realized through the protagonist's approach to the world, makes this a buoyant, moving story.

The second installment in Jeanne Birdsall's chronicles of the Penderwick family, *The Penderwicks on Gardam Street* (I), finds the family at home and the girls determined to keep their father from introducing a stepmother into their lives. As they implement their "save daddy" plan, they are also busy with growing up and other chores. Both funny and tender, this novel by Jeanne Birdsall is charming. The protagonist of Claudia Mills's *The Totally Made-Up Civil War Diary of Amanda MacLeish* (I) is struggling with turmoil at home, desperately wishing that her parents would stay together, that things would be like they used to be. This struggle is mirrored in the school assignment that she is working on, a diary of a fictional girl whose brothers fight on opposite sides of a war.

Jeff Kinney's *Diary of a Wimpy Kid* (I–A) is very popular, with its hand-printed format and cartoons punctuating every page. With *Diary of a Wimpy Kid: Rodrick Rules* (I–A), we follow Greg into middle school, with his adolescent angst exacerbated by older brother Rodrick and tattletale younger brother, Manny. Underneath it all, Greg's obvious sense of humor keeps him, and the book, lighthearted.

A more serious look at what it means to be a family is found in Berlie Doherty's *The Girl Who Saw Lions* (A). Rosa's mother wants to adopt a child of Tanzanian heritage, and Rosa is worried about what that will mean for her. In Tanzania, Abela's mother dies of AIDS and she is smuggled into England by her uncle, who intends to sell her, but when she wanders into a school, Abela is saved from that fate. Eventually, she and Rosa become sisters. Told through first-person narratives of Rosa and Abela, and Abela's third-person adult narrative, the story is unflinching in its depiction of the horrors that Abela suffered.

Family forms and reforms, and, sometimes, new relationships are forged. In Naomi Hirahara's *1001 Cranes* (A), twelve-year-old Angela Kato is sent to Los Angeles to live with her aunt and grandparents because her parents are on the brink of divorce. Of course, she does not want to go, and so arrives with a great deal of resentment. She works in the family's flower shop where they sell 1001 crane displays. As time passes, Angela's resentment melts and her self-esteem grows, and she develops a relationship with her prickly grandmother.

• • CURRENT ISSUES: • • DRUGS AND VIOLENCE

As the world changes, themes in literature change with it. Today, drug use is an ever-increasing concern. Melvin Burgess explores this in his novel *Smack* (A), and Walter Dean Myers does the same in *The Beast* (A). Yet another contemporary issue is violence, in and out of school, and Jamie Adoff's *Names Will Never Hurt Me* (A) is unsparing in its depiction of the daily humiliations and power plays that seem to trigger some of that violence. The four teenage voices that tell this story are all too real. Walter Dean Myers explores the same idea in *Shooter* (A), in which he presents readers with a school board's "Threat Analysis" report, consisting of newspaper articles, interviews with students,

the shooter's journal, and police and medical examiner's reports. This multilayered look at violence in high schools, like Adoff's book, provokes important conversations.

War and the consequences of war have sparked several novels for middle- and high-school readers. As in John Marsden's *Tomorrow, When the War Began* (A), an unnamed enemy invades a country in Meg Rosoff's *How I Live Now* (A), winner of the 2005 Printz Award. Life as she knows it changes dramatically for fifteen-year-old Daisy, an American girl sent to England to live with four cousins on their farm, as the children are evacuated. The war serves as a crucible for Daisy, and she grows from being self-absorbed to generous, from child to young adult. The turmoil in Afghanistan is the backdrop for Deborah Ellis's *The Breadwinner* and *Parvanna's Journey* (I), highlighting both the horrible circumstances of that country and the courageous resilience of children. The war on terror forms the background for Cory Doctorow's *Little Brother* (A), a chilling look at the encroachment of individual freedom that accompanied the government's response to the attacks of 9/11. Beverley Naidoo's *The Other Side of Truth* (I–A), a Carnegie Award winner, is the spellbinding story of two children who flee from Nigeria to London after their mother is killed. At first, their life in London is almost as dangerous as staying in Nigeria would have been.

• • CURRENT ISSUES: • • RACE AND CLASS

In *The Absolutely True Diary of a Part-Time Indian* (A), Sherman Alexie depicts the hopes and dreams of fourteen-year-old Junior, who leaves the "rez" to attend a white school in a well-to-do nearby town. Issues of race, class, and exceptionality make this novel both funny and painful, but ultimately triumphant. Jacqueline Woodson writes compellingly about race and poverty in novels such as *Miracle's Boys* (A). Judith Ortiz Cofer in *Call Me Maria* (I–A); Joseph Bruchac in *The Heart of a Chief* (A); Cynthia Leitich Smith in *Indian Shoes* (I); Gary Soto in *Buried Onions* (A); and Laurence Yep in *Thief of Hearts* (A) explore race, poverty, and prejudice, and their influence on characters' lives. Walter Dean Myers's many books touch on race, and often poverty, in one way or another as he explores growing up as an African American. Here, we take a close look at one of his books, *Monster* (A).

✳ ✳ ✳

A CLOSE LOOK AT
Monster

The first Printz Award winner, Walter Dean Myers's *Monster* (A), was also a finalist for the National Book Award and a winner of the Coretta Scott King Award. The novel has

© 1999 Walter Lean Myers

*Walter Dean Myers's **Monster** won the first Printz Award for young adult literature.*

"true," then perhaps he did not participate in the robbery that ended in murder. If his film script is "true," then it seems that the justice system is stacked against him: "You're young, you're Black, you're on trial. What else do they need to know?" asks his attorney. The story is filled with visual imagery, heightened by the sensation of looking at the trial through the lens of a camera. Further, Steve is concerned with how he looks to others, how he seems to them, a concern springing from hearing the prosecutor call him a monster. By the end of the novel, Steve is not sure what he is.

Through the devices of Steve's journal and camera lens, Myers forces us to consider the difference between "not guilty" and "innocent." He also makes us think about the culpability of the justice system and the cultural milieu that surrounds Steve both in his home community of Harlem and in the jail and courthouse. In the final analysis, do we see Steve as a monster because he is a young, black male, or do we see him as a victim? What is the "truth" of this story?

• • CURRENT ISSUES: • • CULTURAL DIFFERENCES

Many of today's children straddle two cultures—the one they were born into and the one they are living in—and this is the theme of several novels for young readers. The issue of cultural dislocation and biculturalism is not a simple one, and there are no simple answers given in Andrea Cheng's *Honeysuckle House* (I), the story of two young Chinese American girls and their families. When fourth grader Sarah is assigned the role of special friend to Tina, a newly arrived immigrant from China, Sarah resents her. She is justly upset at her teacher's assumption that a shared first-culture heritage will make the girls friends. As Sarah and Tina get to know each other, they do become friends, but not because they are both of Chinese origin. This story explores growing up and the immigrant experience, complete with incidents of subtle racism and the trauma of adjusting to new family circumstances.

Uma Krishnaswami looks at biculturalism from a different perspective in *Naming Maya* (I–A). In this story, a young Indian American girl travels from New Jersey to Chennai, in southern India, when her mother must return to sell her father's house. Not only does Maya have to contend with leaving her home and reconnecting with her friends in Chennai, but she is traveling with her mother, and they haven't really spoken much since her parents' bitter divorce. Once in India, Maya discovers a lot about herself and her family, and also learns that she can be herself in two very different parts of the world. A different look at this same issue, Jane Kurtz's *Jakarta Missing* (I–A) explores the realities of adjusting to life in the United States after living in Africa, and how this

a unique structure, a realistic character with a compelling voice and a realistic problem, and multilayered themes.

Stylistically, *Monster* is exceptional, due in large part to its unique structure as a combination of journal entries from Steve, the main character, and the script for the film that Steve imagines making of his experiences as he is on trial for murder. This structure allows the reader both intimate and distanced looks at Steve as a person and the events that precipitated the experience he is overwhelmed by; it also allows Myers to demonstrate how Steve is unable to find or face the "truth" of his own story. The book opens with an attention-grabbing line, "The best time to cry is at night, when the lights are out and someone is being beaten up and screaming for help," set in a font that resembles hand-printing. The second chapter introduces the film script as we see Steve sitting in his cell. The font varies in style, size, and thickness to represent various parts of the script including the "opening credits" that imitate the "roll" of movie credits.

The style and structure enable Myers to present Steve as both a credible and an unreliable narrator, thus allowing Myers to leave it up to the reader to determine Steve's guilt or innocence. If Steve's journal entries are adjustment varies tremendously. Not everyone, it seems, can be happy in one place.

Two picturebooks, Aliki's *Marianthe's Story: Painted Words, Spoken Memories* (P) and Helen Recorvitz's *My Name Is Yoon* (P), consider how young children adjust to life in an American school when they move with their families from another country. Although these books are suitable for primary-grade children, they can certainly be the beginning of a conversation about the topic with older children as well. Jackie Brown's *Little Cricket* (I) recounts the story of a twelve-year-old Hmong girl who flees her home in Laos for a refugee camp in Thailand and three years later immigrates to St. Paul, Minnesota, with her older brother and grandfather. Their adjustment to life in America is not easy. The protagonist of Kashmira Sheth's *Blue Jasmine* (I) is also twelve, and she misses her home in India terribly when she and her family relocate to Iowa City, Iowa. Both of these books offer realistic yet hopeful depictions of the challenges that learning to live in a new culture can create.

An Na's Printz Award–winning *A Step from Heaven* (A) tells the story of Young Ju's wrenching departure from Korea and her beloved grandmother, her childhood and adolescence in the United States, and her eventual triumph over her abusive father and the grinding poverty that has plagued her family. Told in a series of short, present-tense, first-person narratives, this story has an immediacy that almost compels readers to feel the emotions with which Young Ju wrestles.

● ● CURRENT ISSUES: ● ●
SEXUAL ORIENTATION

Just as issues of sexual identity have become part of the dialogue in the United States, they have also become part of literature for young readers. Although there are a few picturebooks for younger readers that attempt to help children develop tolerance for different lifestyles, none are without flaws. There are, however, a number of excellent contemporary realistic novels for adolescent readers that explore issues of sexuality.

Sexuality, both straight and gay, is an issue in the lives of many of the several adolescent narrators of Ellen Wittlinger's *What's in a Name?* (A), a powerful collection of interlocking stories; it is also a recurring theme in E. R. Frank's *Life Is Funny* (A), another collection of interlocking stories that spans seven years in the lives of diverse adolescents.

Jacqueline Woodson's *From the Notebooks of Melanin Sun* and *The House You Pass on the Way* (A) grapple with the issues that surround homosexuality and race in contemporary culture. Three new novels take a look at gay high school life. Brent Hartinger's *Geography Club* (A) is a bitingly funny and perceptive account of how a diverse group of GLBT students find one another and figure out how to get together without arousing suspicion—by forming the most boring school club they could imagine. David Levithan, in *Boy Meets Boy* (A), creates a setting in which homosexuality is no big deal, a setting in which he can then explore typical high school love relationship issues, only with gay characters. David LaRochelle's *Absolutely, Positively Not . . .* (A) is both humorous and heartwarming as sixteen-year-old Steven realizes that he is gay and that it is okay to be gay. The reactions of his friends and family are amazingly supportive.

● ● CURRENT ISSUES: ● ●
EXCEPTIONALITIES

A small but growing number of books for children demonstrate society's increasing awareness of the emotional and physical demands and accomplishments of those with exceptionalities. The trend in the field has shifted from nearly absolute neglect, to the appearance of occasional secondary characters, to the occasional book in which the main character has special needs. In today's literature, people's attitudes toward individuals with special needs are not always positive and do not always improve. At the same time, however, we also find many books in which characters with, for example, mental disabilities are loved and cherished by their families. Early novels such as Betsy Byars's *Summer of the Swans*, Katherine Paterson's *Preacher's Boy*, Lois Lowry's *The Silent Boy*, and Marlene Fanta Shyer's *Welcome Home, Jellybean* (I–A) all subtly underscore the humanity of those many people treat as different. See "The Portrayal of Mental Disability in Children's Literature: An Ethical Appraisal" (Mills, 2002) for a lucid discussion of both the history of literature portraying exceptionalities and a discussion of how we should assess that literature.

Contemporary realistic fiction portrays many kinds of exceptionalities: physical, mental, and emotional. In the Printz Honor book *Stuck in Neutral* (A), an unusual and disturbing novel, Terry Trueman takes readers inside the mind of Shawn, a very bright boy with very bad cerebral palsy—he cannot control his muscles, which means he cannot speak. Those around him think that he is profoundly developmentally disabled, but instead he has the gift of almost total recall of everything he hears. He's afraid that his father is planning to kill him, and he's telling us his story. Trueman informs readers in an afterword that he has a son who is very much like the protagonist in this novel. In a companion novel, *Cruise Control* (A), Trueman tells the other story, the story of the healthy and talented brother and his conflicted feelings about living with a brother like Shawn. A third novel, *Inside Out* (A), is a disturbing portrait of a young man with adolescent-onset schizophrenia.

Mark Haddon won the 2003 Whitbread Book of the Year Award for his portrayal of a young man with Asperger's syndrome, a form of autism, in *The Curious Incident of the Dog in the Night-Time* (A). Haddon wisely decides to tell Christopher's story through Christopher's own eyes, and readers are privy to both the obsession and the brilliance of his mind. As he pursues the solution to the mystery behind the killing of his neighbor's dog, he discovers things about his parents that destroy the world as he has always known it. At the same time, he discovers his own strength. Interestingly, this crossover book is marketed for both adult and adolescent audiences. In Siobhan Dowd's *The London Eye Mystery* (A), discussed previously, the protagonist has Asperger's syndrome, and his logical, literal brain helps him successfully solve the mystery.

Some books explore specific learning disabilities. Jack Gantos writes from the point of view of a young boy with attention deficit hyperactivity disorder (ADHD) in the popular **Joey Pigza** books (I). Gantos's breathless run-on sentences leave readers almost as frantic as Joey. The first-person point of view allows peers and adults to glimpse what life might be like for children with this disorder. *Joey Pigza Loses Control* is a 2001 Newbery Honor book; *I Am Not Joey Pigza* (I) is a surprise fourth book in what was billed as a trilogy. The protagonist of Patricia Reilly Giff's *Eleven* (I) can't read words, is afraid of the number eleven, and finds an old newspaper clipping that triggers fragments of frightening memories. Because he is unable to read, he enlists a new girl at school, an avid reader, to help him uncover the secrets of his past.

The categories under which we loosely group contemporary realistic fiction are only a convenient way to discuss this genre. Every book belongs in multiple categories, be it format, subgenre, theme, or a specific issue. Taken as a whole, contemporary realistic fiction is as richly diverse as our society, reflecting the varied lives of young people today.

Contemporary Realistic Fiction in the Classroom

Young readers enjoy contemporary realistic fiction, and this genre is often a way to entice reluctant readers to taste the joys of a good book. These books are often passed around from reader to reader as children discover themselves in the pages. Such books can also open windows on other people and other worlds, offering children the opportunity to "try on" other lives for the period of time it takes them to read a book and to ponder it later. Reading contemporary realistic fiction stories that are set in different locales, contain characters that are culturally diverse, and explore the lives of a variety of people helps young readers learn about others. Knowing people from diverse cultures through books is a first step toward building understanding and tolerance. It is also a first step toward recognizing our common humanity—the wishes, fears, and needs we all share, regardless of culture.

Any well-stocked classroom library contains many contemporary realistic fiction titles. These books should represent a wide range of reading levels, a diversity of authors, and a range of types and themes. Comparing books of similar types or themes can help students learn about literature as they closely examine how different authors approach comparable tasks. Reading a wide range of books can also help students develop knowledge of their own preferences. Having many titles on hand means that teachers can readily incorporate realistic fiction in thematic units, building on students' interests or curricular demands by making available numerous appropriate and timely books.

Fine contemporary realistic fiction rings with truth. It offers readers multiple lenses through which to view the world and themselves, allowing them to become finer people—more compassionate, more knowledgeable, more heroic than they are in real life. Realistic fiction can be the mirror and the window in which we readers see our better selves.

• • • SUMMARY • • •

Books of contemporary realistic fiction are plausible stories set in today's world. The characters often seem like people we know, and the plots consist of events and actions that can and do occur in everyday life. Realistic fiction includes subgenres such as adventure stories, animal stories, mysteries, and sports stories. Several series are extremely popular with young readers, each with a memorable character who ties the books together. Contemporary realism explores a number of themes, including growing up, peer and family relationships, and other contemporary, sometimes sensitive, issues. Children enjoy realistic fiction, and teachers find these books an essential part of a classroom library.

Booklist

✳ Indicates some aspect of diversity

Adventure and Survival

Creech, Sharon, *The Wanderer* (2000) (I–A)
✳ Crews, Donald, *Shortcut* (1992) (P)
Dillon, Eilis, *The Lost Island* (1954/2006) (I)
✳ George, Jean Craighead, *Julie of the Wolves* (1972) (A)
_____, *My Side of the Mountain* (1959) (A)
McCaughrean, Geraldine, *White Darkness* (2007) (A)
✳ Mickelson, Ben, *Red Midnight* (2002) (I)
✳ Morpurgo, Michael, *Kensuke's Kingdom* (1999) (I–A)
Paulsen, Gary, *Brian's Return* (1999) (I–A)
_____, *Brian's Winter* (1996) (I–A)
_____, *Dog Song* (1985) (I–A)
_____, *Hatchet* (1987) (I–A)
Philbrick, Rodman, *The Young Man and the Sea* (2004) (I–A)
Salisbury, Graham, *Lord of the Deep* (2001) (I–A)
Seidler, Tor, *Brothers Below Zero* (2002) (I)
Smith, Roland, *Peak* (2007) (I)
Wilson, N. D., *Leepike Ridge* (2007) (I)

Animal Stories

Bauer, Marion Dane, *Ghost Eye* (1992) (A)
DiCamillo, Kate, *Because of Winn-Dixie* (2000) (I)
Farley, Walter, *The Black Stallion* (1947/2008) (I–A)
Haas, Jessie, *Runaway Radish* (2001) (I)
Hearne, Betsy, *The Canine Connection: Stories about Dogs and People* (2003) (A)
Henry, Marguerite, *Misty of Chincoteague* (1947) (I)
Hurwitz, Johanna, *One Small Dog* (2000) (I)
Levin, Betty, *Look Back, Moss* (1998) (I)
Naylor, Phyllis Reynolds, *Shiloh* (1991) (I–A)
Rodowsky, Colby, *Not My Dog* (1999) (P–I)

Current Issues: Race and Class

✳ Alexie, Sherman, *The Absolutely True Diary of a Part-Time Indian* (2007) (A)
✳ Aliki, *Marianthe's Story: Painted Words, Spoken Memories* (1998) (P)
✳ Brown, Jackie, *Little Cricket* (2004) (I)
✳ Bruchac, Joseph, *The Heart of a Chief* (2001) (A)
✳ Cheng, Andrea, *Honeysuckle House* (2004) (I)
✳ Cofer, Judith Ortiz, *Call Me Maria* (2006) (I–A)
✳ Krishnaswami, Uma, *Naming Maya* (2004) (I–A)
✳ Kurtz, Jane, *Jakarta Missing* (2001) (I–A)
✳ Myers, Walter Dean, *Monster* (1999) (A)
✳ Na, An, *A Step from Heaven* (2001) (A)
✳ Perkins, Mitale, *Monsoon Summer* (2004) (I–A)
✳ Recorvitz, Helen, *My Name Is Yoon* (2003) (P)
✳ Sheth, Kashmira, *Blue Jasmine* (2004) (I)
✳ Smith, Cynthia Leitich, *Indian Shoes* (2002) (I)
✳ Soto, Gary, *Buried Onions* (2006) (A)
✳ Woodson, Jacqueline, *Miracle's Boys* (2000) (A)
✳ Yep, Laurence, *Thief of Hearts* (1997) (A)

Current Issues: Drugs and Violence

✳ Adoff, Jamie, *Names Will Never Hurt Me* (2004) (A)
✳ Antieau, Kim, *Broken Moon* (2007) (A)
✳ Burgess, Melvin, *Smack* (1998) (A)
✳ Felin, M. Sindy, *Touching Snow* (2007) (A)
✳ Myers, Walter Dean, *The Beast* (2003) (A)
✳ _____, *Shooter* (2004) (A)
✳ Woods, Brenda, *Emako Blue* (2004) (I–A)

Current Issues: War and the Consequences of War

✳ Cooney, Caroline B., *Diamonds in the Shadow* (2007) (A)
✳ Dorros, Arthur, *Under the Sun* (2004) (A)
✳ Ellis, Deborah, *The Breadwinner* (2004) (I)
✳ _____, *Parvanna's Journey* (2004) (I)
✳ Marsden, John, *Tomorrow, When the War Began* (1993) (A)
✳ _____, *While I Live* (2007) (A)
✳ Rosoff, Meg, *How I Live Now* (2004) (A)

Mystery Stories/Thrillers

Balliett, Blue, *Chasing Vermeer* (2004) (I)
Beaty, Andrea, *Cicada Summer* (2008) (I)
Bloor, Thomas, *The Memory Prisoner* (2000) (A)
Bowler, Tim, *Storm Catchers* (2003) (A)
Brooks, Kevin, *Black Rabbit Summer* (2008) (A)
Byars, Betsy, *The Dark Stairs: A Herculeah Jones Mystery* (1994) (I)
Cormier, Robert, *The Rag and Bone Shop* (2001) (A)
✳ Dowd, Siobhan, *The London Eye Mystery* (2008) (I–A)
Feinstein, John, *Cover Up: Mystery at the Super Bowl* (2007) (I)
Fienberg, Anna, *Number 8* (2007) (A)
Hahn, Mary Downing, *All the Lovely Bad Ones* (2008) (I–A)
Hiaasen, Carl, *Hoot* (2008) (I)
Konigsburg, E. L., *From the Mixed-Up Files of Mrs. Basil E. Frankweiler* (1967) (I)
_____, *Silent to the Bone* (2000) (A)
Lester, Julius, *When Dad Killed Mom* (2001) (A)
Parker, Robert, *The Boxer and the Spy* (2008) (A)
Plum-Ucci, Carol, *The Body of Christopher Creed* (2000) (A)
Raskin, Ellen, *The Westing Game* (1978) (I)
Stewart, Trenton Lee, *The Mysterious Benedict Society and the Perilous Journey* (2008) (I)
Van Draanen, Wendelin, *Sammy Keyes and the Hollywood Mummy* (2001) (I)
_____, *Sammy Keyes and the Psycho Kitty Queen* (2004) (I)
_____, *Sammy Keyes and the Skeleton Man* (1998) (I)
Werlin, Nancy, *Double Helix* (2004) (A)
_____, *The Rules of Survival* (2008) (A)

Sports Stories

Coy, John, *Box Out* (2008) (A)
_____, *Crackback* (2007) (A)
Crutcher, Chris, *Deadline* (2007) (A)
_____, *Ironman* (1995) (A)

_____, *Whale Talk* (2001) (A)
☀ de La Peña, Matt, *Mexican Whiteboy* (2008) (A)
Deuker, Carl, *Gym Candy* (2007) (A)
_____, *Night Hoops* (2000) (A)
Koertge, Ron, *Shakespeare Bats Cleanup* (2003) (I–A)
Lipsyte, Robert, *The Contender* (1997) (A)
_____, *Yellow Flag* (2007) (A)
Lynch, Chris, *Iceman* (1994) (A)
_____, *Shadow Boxer* (1993) (A)
☀ Myers, Walter Dean, *Slam!* (1996) (A)
Powell, Randy, *Run If You Dare* (2001) (A)
_____, *Three Clams and an Oyster* (2002) (A)
Russo, Marisabina, *House of Sports* (2002) (I)
Wallace, Rich, *Losing Is Not an Option* (2003) (A)
_____, *Playing without the Ball: A Novel in Four Quarters* (2000) (A)
_____, *Shots on Goal* (1997) (A)
_____, *Wrestling Sturbridge* (1996) (A)
☀ Zusak, Marcus, *Fighting Ruben Wolfe* (2000) (A)

Stories about Coming of Age

☀ Alexie, Sherman, *The Absolutely True Diary of a Part-Time Indian* (2007) (A)
☀ Atkins, Catherine, *Alt Ed* (2003) (A)
Bauer, Cat, *Harley, Like a Person* (2000) (A)
Bauer, Joan, *Hope Was Here* (2000) (A)
_____, *Rules of the Road* (1998) (A)
_____, *Stand Tall* (2002) (A)
Bauer, Marion Dane, *On My Honor* (1986) (A)
Blume, Judy, *Are You There God? It's Me, Margaret* (1970) (I)
Brooks, Bruce, *All That Remains* (2001) (A)
☀ Brooks, Martha, *True Confessions of a Heartless Girl* (2002) (A)
Clements, Andrew, *Frindle* (1996) (I)
☀ _____, *The Janitor's Boy* (2000) (I)
_____, *The Landry News* (1999) (I)
Corbet, Robert, *Fifteen Love* (2002) (A)
Creech, Sharon, *Chasing Redbird* (1997) (A)
_____, *Granny Torrelli Makes Soup* (2003) (I)
_____, *Love That Dog* (2001) (I)
_____, *Walk Two Moons* (1994) (I–A)
Cummings, Priscilla, *Red Kayak* (2004) (I–A)
Dessen, Sarah, *The Truth about Forever* (2004) (A)
Duffey, Betsy, *Cody Unplugged* (1999) (P–I)
Fergus, Maureen, *Exploits of a Reluctant (But Extremely Good-looking) Hero* (2007) (I)
☀ Flake, Sharon, *Who Am I without Him? Short Stories about Girls and the Boys in Their Lives* (2004) (A)
Fleischman, Paul, *Whirligig* (1998) (A)
Fox, Paula, *The One-Eyed Cat* (1984) (I)
Frank, E. R., *Life Is Funny* (2000) (A)
Gantos, Jack, *Jack on the Tracks: Four Seasons of Fifth Grade* (1999) (I)
Gauthier, Gail, *Saving the Planet and Stuff* (2003) (A)
Graves, Bonnie, *Taking Care of Trouble* (2002) (P)
☀ Hamilton, Virginia, *Plain City* (1993) (A)
Hannigan, Katherine, *Ida B: . . . And Her Plans to Maximize Fun, Avoid Disaster and (Possibly) Save the World* (2004) (I)
☀ Hartinger, Brent, *Geography Club* (2003) (A)
Henkes, Kevin, *Olive's Ocean* (2003) (I)
Horniman, Joanne, *Mahalia* (2003) (A)
☀ Johnson, Angela, *The First Part Last* (2003) (A)
☀ _____, *Gone from Home: Short Takes* (1998) (A)
☀ Kim, Derek Kirk, *Good as Lily* (2007) (A)
Koertge, Ron, *Margaux with an X* (2006) (A)

_____, *Stoner and Spaz* (2002) (A)
Koja, Kathe, *The Blue Mirror* (2004) (A)
Konigsburg, E. L., *The Outcasts of 19 Schuyler Place* (2004) (A)
Lowry, Lois, *Rabble Starkey* (1987) (A)
_____, *A Summer to Die* (1977) (A)
Mass, Wendy, *Leap Day* (2004) (I–A)
McKay, Hilary, *The Exiles* (1991) (I–A)
_____, *The Exiles at Home* (1993) (I–A)
_____, *The Exiles in Love* (1998) (I–A)
☀ Myers, Walter Dean, *Monster* (1999) (A)
☀ _____, *145th Street Stories* (2000) (A)
Naylor, Phyllis Reynolds, *Almost Alice* (2008) (A)
_____, *Dangerously Alice* (2007) (A)
_____, *Lovingly Alice* (2004) (I)
Nelson, Theresa, *Ruby Electric* (2003) (I–A)
☀ Nilsson, Per, *Heart's Delight* (2003) (A)
Oneal, Zibby, *In Summer Light* (1985) (A)
Patron, Susan, *The Higher Power of Lucky* (2008) (I)
☀ Rennison, Louise, *Angus, Thongs and Full-Frontal Snogging: Confessions of Georgia Nicholson* (1988) (A)
☀ Rosenberry, Vera, *Vera Rides a Bike* (2004) (P)
Sachar, Louis, *Holes* (1998) (I)
Spinelli, Jerry, *Star Girl* (2002) (A)
Tolan, Stephanie, *Surviving the Applewhites* (2002) (I–A)
Weeks, Sarah, *Guy Time* (2000) (I)
☀ Williams-Garcia, Rita, *Every Time a Rainbow Dies* (2001) (A)
Wolff, Virginia Euwer, *True Believer* (2001) (A)
Zeises, Lara, *Contents Under Pressure* (2004) (I–A)
Zephaniah, Benjamin, *Gangsta Rap* (2004) (I–A)
☀ Zusak, Marcus, *Getting the Girl* (2001) (A)

Stories about Family Relationships

Avi and Rachel Vail, *Never Mind! A Twin Novel* (2004) (I)
Birdsall, Jeanne, *The Penderwicks on Gardam Street* (2008) (I)
Brooks, Bruce, *Vanishing* (1999) (I)
Brooks, Martha, *Being with Henry* (2000) (A)
Cart, Michael, *Necessary Noise: Stories about Our Families as They Really Are* (2003) (A)
☀ Cheng, Andrea, *The Key Collection* (2003) (P–I)
Clements, Andrew, *The School Story* (2001) (I)
Conly, Jane Leslie, *Trout Summer* (1995) (I)
_____, *While No One Was Watching* (1998) (I–A)
Couloumbis, Audrey, *Getting Near to Baby* (1999) (I)
Creech, Sharon, *Heartbeat* (2004) (I)
☀ _____, *Ruby Holler* (2002) (I)
Dessen, Sarah, *Dreamland* (2000) (A)
☀ Fine, Anne, *The Jamie and Angus Stories* (2002) (P)
Fleischman, Paul, *Seek* (2001) (A)
☀ Fletcher, Ralph, *Uncle Daddy* (2001) (I)
Flinn, Alex, *Nothing to Lose* (2004) (A)
Giff, Patricia Reilly, *Pictures of Hollis Woods* (2002) (I–A)
☀ Grimes, Nikki, *The Road to Paris* (2008) (I–A)
☀ Hamilton, Virginia, *Second Cousins* (1998) (I)
Henkes, Kevin, *The Birthday Room* (1999) (I)
Hermes, Patricia, *Cheat the Moon: A Novel* (1998) (I–A)
☀ Hirahara, Naomi, *1001 Cranes* (2008) (A)
Holt, Kimberly Willis, *Keeper of the Night* (2003) (A)
☀ Johnson, Angela, *Songs of Faith* (1998) (I)
☀ Johnson, Lindsay Lee, *Soul Moon Soup* (2002) (I–A)
Kinney, Jeff, *Diary of a Wimpy Kid* (2008) (I–A)
_____, *Rodrick Rules (Diary of a Wimpy Kid)* (2008) (I–A)
Koss, Amy Goldman, *Stranger in Dadland* (2001) (I)
☀ Kurtz, Jane, *Jakarta Missing* (2001) (I–A)

Lisle, Janet Taylor, *How I Became a Writer and Oggie Learned to Drive* (2002) (I)

※ McKay, Hilary, *Forever Rose* (2008) (A)

※ _____, *Saffy's Angel* (2002) (A)

Mills, Claudia, *The Totally Made-Up Civil War Diary of Amanda MacLeish* (2008) (I)

※ Namioka, Lensey, *Yang the Third and Her Impossible Family* (1995) (I–A)

※ Nelson, Vaunda Micheaux, *Possibles* (1995) (A)

Paterson, Katherine, *The Great Gilly Hopkins* (1978) (I–A)

_____, *Jacob Have I Loved* (1980) (A)

_____, *The Same Stuff as Stars* (2002) (I)

Pennebaker, Ruth, *Both Sides Now* (2000) (A)

Plummer, Louise, *A Dance for Three* (2000) (A)

Powell, Randy, *Tribute to Another Dead Rock Star* (1999) (A)

※ Ryan, Pam Muñoz, *Becoming Naomi Leon* (2004) (I)

Rylant, Cynthia, *Missing May* (1992) (I–A)

Schumacher, Julie, *Black Box* (2008) (A)

_____, *Grass Angel* (2004) (I)

Sones, Sonya, *One of Those Hideous Books Where the Mother Dies* (2004) (I–A)

_____, *What My Mother Doesn't Know* (2001) (A)

Thesman, Jean, *Calling the Swan* (2000) (A)

※ Woodson, Jacqueline, *Miracle's Boys* (2000) (A)

Stories about Peer Relationships

※ Alexie, Sherman, *The Absolutely True Diary of a Part-Time Indian* (2007) (A)

Anderson, Laurie Halse, *Speak* (1999) (A)

_____, *Twisted* (2007) (A)

Banks, Kate, *Lenny's Space* (2007) (I)

Bauer, Marion Dane, *The Double-Digit Club* (2004) (I)

Bloor, Edward, *Crusader* (1999) (A)

_____, *Tangerine* (1997) (A)

Bradby, Marie, *Some Friend* (2004) (I)

Bradley, Alex, *Hot Lunch* (2007) (A)

Brande, Robin, *Evolution, Me & Other Freaks of Nature* (2007) (A)

Brashares, Ann, *The Second Summer of the Sisterhood* (2003) (A)

_____, *The Sisterhood of the Traveling Pants* (2001) (A)

Castellucci, Cecil, *Plain Janes* (2007) (A)

※ Choldenko, Gennifer, *If a Tree Falls at Lunch Period* (2007) (I)

Codell, Esme Raji, *Sahara Special* (2003) (I)

_____, *Sing a Song of Tuna Fish: Hard-to-Swallow Stories from Fifth Grade* (2004) (I)

Crutcher, Chris, *Staying Fat for Sarah Byrnes* (1993) (A)

Dessen, Sarah, *Someone Like You* (1998) (A)

Doherty, Berlie, *The Girl Who Saw Lions* (2008) (A)

Dowell, Frances O'Roark, *Phineas L. MacGuire . . . Gets Slimed!* (2007) (P–I))

_____, *The Secret Language of Girls* (2004) (I)

※ Draper, Sharon, *The Battle of Jericho* (2003) (A)

Easton, Kelly, *White Magic: Spells to Hold You* (2007) (I)

※ Fine, Anne, *Jamie and Angus Together* (2007) (P–I)

※ Flake, Sharon, *Broken Bike Boy and the Queen of 33rd Street* (2007) (I)

Fletcher, Ralph, *Flying Solo* (1998) (I)

Fredericks, Mariah, *Love* (2007) (I)

Gauthier, Gail, *A Girl, a Boy, and a Monster Cat* (2007) (P–I)

George, Madeleine, *Looks* (2008) (A)

※ Gipi, *Garage Band* (2007) (A)

Going, K. L., *Fat Kid Rules the World* (2003) (A)

※ Graff, Lisa, *The Thing About Georgie* (2007) (I)

※ Hamilton, Virginia, *Bluish* (1999) (I)

Hautman, Pete, *Stone Cold* (1998) (A)

※ Herrick, Steven, *Naked Bunyip Dancing* (2008) (A)

Hickey, Caroline, *Cassie Was Here* (2007) (I)

Juby, Susan, *Another Kind of Cowboy* (2007) (A)

Kantor, Melissa, *Confessions of a Not It Girl* (2004) (A)

Kerr, M. E., *What Became of Her* (2000) (A)

Kerrin, Jessica Scott, *Martin Bridge: Sound the Alarm!* (2007) (P–I)

Kimmell, Elizabeth Cody, *Visiting Miss Caples* (2000) (I–A)

Koja, Kathe, *Buddha Boy* (2003) (A)

_____, *Kissing the Bee* (2007) (A)

Korman, Gordon, *No More Dead Dogs* (2000) (I)

Koss, Amy Goldman, *The Girls* (2000) (I–A)

※ Lin, Grace, *The Year of the Rat* (2008) (I)

MacLeod, Doug, *I'm Being Stalked by a Moonshadow* (2007) (A)

McGhee, Alison, *Snap* (2004) (I)

※ McKay, Hilary, *Indigo's Star* (2003) (A)

Moriarty, Jaclyn, *The Year of Secret Assignments* (2004) (A)

Nelson, Theresa, *The Empress of Elsewhere* (1998) (I)

O'Connor, Barbara, *Fame and Glory in Freedom, Georgia* (2003) (I)

O'Dell, Kathleen, *Ophie Out of Oz* (2004) (I)

Paterson, Katherine, *Bridge to Terabithia* (1977) (I)

※ _____, *Flip-Flop Girl* (1994) (I)

Perkins, Lynn Rae, *All Alone in the Universe* (1999) (I–A)

_____, *Criss Cross* (2005) (I–A)

Pyle, Kevin C., *Blindspot* (2007) (I)

Sachar, Louis, *Marvin Redpost #7: Super Fast, Out of Control!* (2000) (P)

_____, *There's a Boy in the Girls' Bathroom* (1987) (I)

※ Seuling, Barbara, *Robert and the Happy Endings* (2007) (P–I)

※ Sneve, Virginia Driving Hawk, *Lana's Lakota Moons* (2007) (I)

※ Sonnenblick, Jordan, *Zen and the Art of Faking It* (2007) (A)

※ Soto, Gary, *Mercy on these Teenage Chimps* (2007) (I)

Spinelli, Jerry, *Eggs* (2007) (I)

Tarshis, Lauren, *Emma-Jean Lazarus Fell Out of a Tree* (2007) (I)

Vande Velde, Vivian, *Remembering Raquel* (2007) (A)

※ Walter, Mildred Pitts, *Suitcase* (1999) (I)

Weaver, Will, *Defect* (2007) (A)

Wiles, Deborah, *Aurora County All-Stars* (2007) (I)

Williams, Dar, *Amalee* (2004) (I)

Wilson, Jacqueline, *Best Friends* (2008) (I)

Wittlinger, Ellen, *Parrotfish* (2007) (A)

※ Woodson, Jacqueline, *After Tupac and D Foster* (2008) (A)

※ _____, *I Hadn't Meant to Tell You This* (1994) (A)

※ _____, *Last Summer with Maizon* (1990) (A)

※ Yee, Lisa, *Millicent Min, Girl Genius* (2003) (I)

※ Yumoto, Kazumi, *The Friends* (1996) (A)

Zevin, Gabrielle, *Memoirs of a Teenage Amnesiac* (2007) (A)

※ Zimmer, Tracie Vaughn, *Reaching for Sun* (2007) (I)

Chapter

8

Historical Fiction

The priest put his hand on my shoulder. "The steward," he said, "has declared you a wolf's head."

"A wolf's head!" I gasped, horrified.

"Do you understand what it means?"

"That . . . I'm considered not human," I said, my voice faltering. "That anyone may . . . kill me. Is that why they pulled down our house?"

"I suppose."

"But . . . why?"

The priest sat back and gave himself over to thought. In the dim light I studied his face. He seemed distraught, as if the pain of the whole world had settled in his soul.

"Father," I ventured, "is it something about my mother?"

He bowed his head. When he looked up it was to gaze at me. "Asta's son, unless you flee, you won't live long."

"But how can I leave?" I said. "I'm bound to the land. They'll never give me permission to go."

He sighed, reached forward, and placed the side of one frail hand aside my face. "Asta's son, listen to me with the greatest care. When I baptized you, you were named . . . Crispin."

"I was?" I cried.

"It was done in secret. What's more, your mother begged me not to tell you or anyone. She chose to simply call you 'Son.'"

"But . . . why?" I asked.

—Avi,
Crispin: The Cross of Lead, pp. 31–32

*9*eremy's sixth-grade students are as full of questions as Crispin was. Comments and queries fly around the room. "He thought he didn't have a name! Why didn't he know he had a name?" "'Asta's son' was what he thought his name was!" "Why did they burn his house down?" "Why did he have to give up his ox?" "What's a death tax?" "How can he belong to the land?" "Is he a slave?" After a minute or so, Jeremy brings the class to order, asking them to take out their response journals for *Crispin* and write down the two or three biggest questions they have. After they have finished, he asks for volunteers to share a question and, as each does so, asks the class for some predictions as to the answers. He records the questions and predictions on a transparency so that the class will be able to revisit them as they are gradually answered in the book and in other reading about the Middle Ages that they are doing. Jeremy then turns back to the book and continues to read until the end of the chapter.

In historical fiction, the events of the past are told as the stories of people who seem real to us. As history becomes a story about someone we know and even care about, it gives us the opportunity to vicariously experience life in the past and to consider historical events as issues that had real consequences for the people who lived them, rather than as abstract concepts. These students are beginning to study the Middle Ages in social studies, and Jeremy is using literature to help that distant time come alive. Stories such as *Crispin: The Cross of Lead* (I–A) and its sequel, *Crispin: At the Edge of the World* (I–A) help them connect with their history lessons in a way no textbook can.

Defining Historical Fiction

History is a story, the story of the world and its people and of cultures that rise and fall across time. Historical fiction tells the stories of history; as a distinct genre, it consists of imaginative narratives grounded in the facts of our past. It is not biography (discussed in Chapter 9), which focuses on the life of an individual; historical fiction has a wider scope. Historical fiction differs from nonfiction (discussed in Chapter 10) in that it does not focus on facts, but uses them to re-create a time and place; outstanding authors weave the facts into the fabric of a fictional story. Historical fiction is realistic—the events could have occurred, and the people portrayed could have lived (and sometimes really did)—but it differs from contemporary realistic fiction in that the stories are set in the past rather than the present. As Christopher Ringrose describes it, "The alternative world one is invited to enter has an additional dimension: one of time as well as space" (2007).

Some books that we now classify as historical fiction began as contemporary realism; the years between original publication and today have made the story historical. Some historical fiction stories are more factual than others, such as when authors include real events and people in their imaginative stories. Irene Hunt's *Across Five Aprils* (A), a classic story of the Civil War, is filled with names, dates, newspaper accounts of real battles, and realistic political and social detail woven into a moving story.

Some authors set their stories in times past but do not specifically connect them with any particular historical events or people, just as Avi did with the **Crispin** (I–A) books. Still, these authors know a great deal about the time and place in which their stories are set. In the interview with Avi on the companion website for this text, he discusses the books and poems that he read, the way he wrote to imitate the language of the time, and how he distilled everything into the final, artistic form. Authentic, vivid details make good stories also good history. Karen English creates a vivid picture of life in the Deep South of the 1950s in *Francie* (I–A), a Coretta Scott King Honor book that explores issues of racism, human worth, and dignity that transcend time and place. Shenaaz Nanji's *Child of Dandelions* (A) is filled with strong sensory details of life in Uganda during the early 1970s.

Other stories are based on memories of the authors' own lives or the lives of their ancestors. Mildred Taylor's Logan family saga, including the Newbery Medal–winning *Roll of Thunder, Hear My Cry* (A), is based on the stories of her family, but the events of their lives have been sifted, artistically arranged, and presented as engaging stories. Louise Erdrich writes about her own family's history in *The Birchbark House*, *The Game of Silence*, and *The Porcupine Year* (I), recounting the moving story of the life of a young Ojibwe girl and her family living in the upper Midwest during the mid-nineteenth century. Based on research by the author's mother and sister, these novels are full of the homely details of life in one Ojibwe group in that time and place. We look closely at *The Porcupine Year* in this chapter. In the Newbery Medal–winning *Bud, Not Buddy* (I), Christopher Paul Curtis creates memorable secondary characters who are based on his grandfathers, but he notes in his afterword that he learned most of what he knows about the Depression through research. Linda Sue Park, a Korean-American writer, won the Newbery Medal for *A Single Shard* (A), a novel about a medieval Korean boy who becomes a master potter. Although her ancestors were Korean, she still had to do a great deal of research to be able to capture the place and time accurately. Family experience may have triggered all of these novels, but it took significant research and talented writers to turn those memories into good historical fiction.

Historical fiction sometimes surprises readers because it can also take the form of an adventure story, as in Iain Lawrence's *The Convicts*, *The Cannibals*, and *The Castaways* (I), Sally Gardner's *The Red Necklace* (A), or Julia Golding's *The Diamond of Drury Lane: A Cat Royal Adventure*, set in England. Historical fiction can also be a mystery, as in Jen Bryant's *The Trial* (I–A) or Philip Pullman's popular **Sally Lockhart** series, *The Ruby in the Smoke*, *The Shadow in the North*, *The Tiger in the Well*, and *The Tin Princess* (I–A). Sometimes historical fiction is also a romance novel, as in Dianne Gray's *Together Apart* (A), or it may be an animal story, as in Rosemary Wells's adaptation, *Lassie Come-Home* (I). It may be written in poetic form, as in Karen Hesse's *Out of the Dust* (A) or Jen Bryant's *Ringside, 1925: Views from the Scopes Trial* (A). It may contain fantasy elements, like the time travel in Jane Yolen's *The Devil's Arithmetic* (A); the connection of stories occurring in two different times, as in Susan Cooper's *Victory* (I); or the mythical kingdom in Eoin Colfer's *Airman* (A). Historical fiction also appears as series chapter books, as in Patricia McKissack's **Scraps of Time**, in which each book recounts the story behind an African American family's keepsakes. What makes these books historical is their historical setting and the importance of that setting to the story.

No matter what form it takes, outstanding historical fiction shows that history is created by people, that people experience historical events in individual ways, that people living now are tied to those who lived in the past through a common humanity, and that human conditions of the past shape our lives today. Historical fiction offers readers the opportunity to travel across time and place and thus to find themselves.

A Brief History of Historical Fiction

As the United States developed as a country, writers told the story of that development in historical fiction for young readers. Books such as Carol Ryrie Brink's *Caddie Woodlawn* (I), winner of the 1936 Newbery Medal, and Laura Ingalls Wilder's 1938 Newbery Honor–winning *On the Banks of Plum Creek* (I) were popular with children and librarians alike. Historical fiction became even more popular during the years of World War II (Marcus, 2008). Walter Edmonds's *The Matchlock Gun* (I), set in the precolonial era in upstate New York, won the 1942 Newbery Award, followed by Elizabeth Janet Gray's *Adam of the Road* (I) in 1943, and Esther Forbes's *Johnny Tremain* (I–A) in 1944. In the two decades that followed, many of the Newbery winners and honor books were historical fiction, including Scott O'Dell's *Island of the Blue Dolphins* (I–A), a haunting story about a young native girl, which was one of the first successful attempts to enlarge the generally white, European perspective present in most historical fiction for young readers. This perspective often resulted in the presence of racism or sexism in these novels, reflecting not only the historical setting, but the attitudes of the author at the time of writing.

In the 1960s, with the civil rights movement in full swing, books for young readers began to change as new voices appeared. Writers such as Virginia Hamilton, Mildred Taylor, Yoshiko Uchida, and Joseph Bruchac brought new points of view to historical fiction. Gradually, the genre came to reflect the history of everyone in the United States—African American, Native American, Asian American, and Latino as well as European—with stories of the lives of ordinary girls and boys, rich and poor, urban and rural, captivating a new audience of readers.

The latter half of the twentieth century also saw a number of writers, such as Lucy Boston, Philippa Pearce, Penelope Farmer, Jan Mark, and several others, who incorporated the fantasy element of the time slip into otherwise historical novels.

Historical fiction series, such as the **Royal Diaries** (1), **Dear America** (1), **American Adventures** (1), and **American Girl** (1), were developed and marketed to attract even greater numbers of young readers to historical fiction. These books have created an interesting debate among children's literature scholars. Some of these books, such as Siobhan Parkinson's *Kathleen: The Celtic Knot* (1) and Jane Kurtz's *Saba: Under the Hyena's Foot* (1) are very well done, written by outstanding authors and filled with a masterful blend of historical fact and period detail within an engaging fictional story. Kathryn Lasky's *Elizabeth I: Red Rose of the House of Tudor* (1), which presents Elizabeth's life in the years immediately preceding the death of her father, Henry VIII, is another series book that stands on its own merits as an excellent piece of historical fiction. Some other series books are less well documented and may present misinformation to young readers. Native American scholars and children's book critics have faulted Ann Rinaldi's *My Heart Is on the Ground: The Diary of Nannie Little Rose, a Sioux Girl, Carlisle Indian School, PA 1880* (1) for glossing over the horrors of the Indian schools in nineteenth-century America. On balance, however, these series, with their engaging format, offer young readers an important introduction to reading historical fiction. The best of them also offer readers a glimpse of life as it was lived by a historical, albeit fictional, child, someone whose voice is rarely heard in other histories.

In 1982 Scott O'Dell, a noted writer of award-winning historical fiction, established the Scott O'Dell Award for Historical Fiction, to be given to a writer from the United States for a meritorious book published the preceding year. O'Dell hoped that this award would interest new writers in working within the historical fiction genre, and thus provide young readers more books that would help them understand the historical background that has helped shape their world. It seems that his desire has been realized, for historical fiction seems to be enjoying continued popularity; many new novels set in the past are published for young readers each year. Historical fiction has, if anything, gained in popularity, and currently many seasoned and fresh writers are producing wonderful narratives that continue to engage young readers.

Considering Quality in Historical Fiction

The best historical stories come from good storytellers who are well acquainted with the facts; good historical fiction is grounded in facts but not restricted by them. An author may use historical records to document events, but the

Figure 8.1

Considering Quality in Historical Fiction

Historical Accuracy

✤ Events and attitudes are consistent with historical evidence and appropriate to the time period

✤ Social issues are portrayed honestly, without condoning racism and sexism.

Literary Quality

✤ The work meets the criteria for all good narratives.

✤ The setting is integral to the story and evokes a vivid historical time consistent with historical and geographical evidence.

✤ The language patterns are historically authentic and in keeping with the mood and characterization, yet still understandable to readers.

✤ Characters are well developed—with feelings, values, and behavior that reflect the historical period.

✤ The plot is based on authentic facts that are subordinate to the story itself.

✤ The theme echoes larger historical concerns.

Illustrations, if present, enhance an understanding of plot, setting, and characterization through the use of realistic details.

facts only serve as a framework for the story. The trick is to make that material such a part of the background—in the setting, the events, the characterizations, the language, and the ideas—that readers may not consciously notice most of them, yet they are fundamental in shaping the story. Good historical fiction meets the criteria for *all* good narratives: it has well-developed characters and integral themes; it tells an engaging story with well-crafted language; and, in the case of picturebooks, it contains beautiful and accurate art. Beyond this, it meets criteria that are particular to the genre. Figure 8.1 is a summary of things to think about when considering quality in historical fiction.

• • HISTORICAL ACCURACY • •

Historical fiction should be consistent with historical evidence; narrative events and characters' attitudes and beliefs should be appropriate to the time portrayed. The story, though imaginative, must remain within the limits of the chosen historical background, avoiding distortion and anachronism. Historical accuracy, however, presents an interesting dilemma, one related to the discussion of ideology in Chapter 2. Although we can know "facts" about our past, we know these facts only in light of the present. As mentioned previously, every generation of historians, to some degree, interprets the past by using the concerns of their own experiences and their present lives as a lens. For example, a book like Esther Forbes's classic Revolutionary War story, *Johnny Tremain* (A), written during a time of great patriotic fervor, is not at all critical of war. James Lincoln Collier and Christopher Collier's *My Brother Sam Is Dead* (A), written during the Vietnam conflict (1974), presents a very different picture of the same war (Taxel, 1984). Both stories deal with the same set of "facts," but their implications are radically different because they are written from different perspectives, perspectives influenced by the time and place that shaped the writing. Any presentation of history is an interpretation, but good historical fiction creates as true a picture of the past as an author can craft. Historical "accuracy," then, is always influenced by who the author is and when the author is writing, and by how the author understands the historical experience within his or her own life.

Historical accuracy can create problems with racism and sexism. When writing about periods of time in which racism and sexism were a significant part of the culture, authors must take care to portray these social issues honestly while at the same time not condoning them. In Ann Turner's *Nettie's Trip South* (I–A), the issue of slavery is foregrounded; it is slavery that marked the South before the Civil War, and it is slavery that sickens young Nettie. In *Walks Alone* (I), Brian Burks describes the often-vicious approach to the Apache taken by the U.S. Army. Jerry Spinelli's *Milkweed* (A) and Gary Schmidt's *Mara's Stories: Glimmers in the Darkness* (I–A) depict the racism and violence of Nazi-occupied Europe but do so in a way that helps readers understand how horrible it was as well as appreciate the personal courage of those caught up in the Holocaust. Historical fiction may have to portray racism and sexism for historical accuracy, but the stories themselves should not be racist or sexist.

Noteworthy historical novels do not overgeneralize; they do not lead the reader to believe, for example, that all Native Americans or all young women in the Middle Ages are similar to characters in any one story. Each character is unique, just as each of us is, and although the novelist focuses on one person in a group, it should be clear that the character is only one person, not a stereotype.

Teaching Idea 8.1

Writing Connection: Descriptive Techniques

Select several historical fiction books to compare literary descriptions of historical settings. Then:

- ✿ Read aloud several books that describe the same region or historical period.

- ✿ Ask students to compare selections and illustrations.

- ✿ Discuss with students which descriptions are more evocative, and which use the most sensory details.

- ✿ Ask students to decide which books help them understand the place and time best.

- ✿ Have students use the techniques they have discussed to create original descriptions of a real place they know.

Any number of books with vivid settings, grouped by period or place, are appropriate. Often the historical fiction that you select can be complemented by nonfiction and other genres.

• • SETTING • •

Setting is a crucial element in evaluating historical fiction because setting distinguishes this genre most dramatically. The setting must be authentic and consistent with historical and geographical evidence. Clear and vivid details of setting enable readers to create mental images of the time and place in which the events occur. Historical milieu is integral to the plot of historical fiction; it determines characters' beliefs and actions. Just as setting in fantasy and science fiction helps make those stories believable, setting in historical fiction helps make those stories seem real. Often, the particular setting of a story mirrors the larger political and social setting in which the story occurs. Teaching Idea 8.1 describes a way to explore settings and help students learn about descriptive writing.

• • CHARACTERIZATION • •

Characters in historical fiction should believe and behave in a manner that is in keeping with the times in which they live. Authors who attribute contemporary values to historical figures run the risk of creating an *anachronism*, mistakenly placing something in the wrong historical period. Sometimes this is difficult to determine. When Karen Cushman's *Catherine, Called Birdy* (A) was published, several critics took Cushman to task for creating a character who was a literate female living in the Middle Ages. Women, they said, were not literate and, what's more, didn't act independently. In fact, most women indeed were not literate and were completely under the control of men. However, some noted historical figures were different, and it is these whom Catherine most resembles. She is not meant to represent "all" medieval women, but rather to stand as one specific, fictional woman. She is different, but not anachronistic; she is possible, reflecting feelings, behavior, values, and language of the time, as well as her individuality. Indeed, several historical fiction novels published in the past ten years, such as Kevin Crossley-Holland's *Crossing to Paradise* (A), feature spirited and courageous young women who challenge historical stereotypes without being anachronistic.

• • PLOT AND THEME • •

History is filled with a tremendous amount of raw material for exciting plots and themes. Events must be plausible, if not actual; they should help propel the narrative line. For example, Christopher Paul Curtis's *Elijah of Buxton* (I), a Newbery Honor book, is set in an actual place and based on true events. A master storyteller, Curtis took these historical facts and wove a heartbreaking yet also hilarious story of a young boy coming to understand what it meant to live freely in a settlement in Ontario, Canada, while his people were enslaved in the United States, just a few miles away. In Mildred Taylor's *Roll of Thunder, Hear My Cry* (I–A), a Newbery Award–winner, the rural Mississippi area where the Logan family lives, with its dominant culture of racism, reflects the larger picture of race in America at that time. As African Americans across the country struggled for a humane, just existence, so do the characters in the novel.

Themes that are developed through facts and narrative usually reflect both a macrocosm of the era (for example, a war for independence) and the microcosm of the story (for example, a struggle for personal independence). In the best historical fiction, the theme is evident in both the individual story and the larger historical context.

• • STYLE • •

Language should be in keeping with the period and the place, particularly in dialogue. However, today's readers have difficulty understanding archaic language. Accomplished authors synthesize language that has the right tone or sound for a period but is understandable to contemporary readers. Rosemary Sutcliff explains how she works appropriate language into her writing:

> I try to catch the rhythm of a tongue, the tune that it plays on the ear, Welsh or Gaelic as opposed to Anglo-Saxon, the sensible workmanlike language which one feels the Latin of the ordinary Roman citizen would have translated into. It is extraordinary what can be done by the changing or transposing of a single word, or by using a perfectly usual one in a slightly unusual way: "I beg your pardon" changed into "I ask your pardon." . . . This is not done by any set rule of thumb; I simply play it by ear as I go along. (1973, pp. 307–308)

The character's thoughts should also reflect the time and place. Any metaphors, similes, or images that describe what a character is thinking or feeling must be appropriate to the setting. In Michael Dorris's *Morning Girl* (I), set in 1492 on a Bahamian island that will soon be visited by Christopher Columbus, Morning Girl, a young Taino, thinks about her brother:

> The world fits together so tightly, the pieces like pebbles and shells sunk into the sand after the tide has gone out, before anyone has walked on the beach and left footprints.
> In our house, though, my brother was the footprints. (p. 14)

Morning Girl's world is bounded by the sand and the sea; it is fitting that she should think of life in those terms. Authentic language patterns and word choices that are in keeping with the mood and characterization help create excellent historical fiction.

• • ILLUSTRATIONS • •

In recent years, a number of excellent historical fiction picturebooks have been published. These books contain not only well-written, riveting stories but also beautiful illustrations that support and enhance the story. Illustrations in picturebooks of historical fiction must meet the criteria for quality of illustration in any picturebook. In addition, they must be historically accurate, providing realistic details of life in that historical period as well as reflecting and interpreting character and action. Excellent illustrations enhance the story and use realistic details to reflect an understanding of the setting, plot, and characterization.

Although Jacqueline Woodson's *Show Way* (P–I) received a Newbery Honor Award for her text, Hudson Talbott's illustrations are also brilliant. The picturebook traces the history of Woodson's family over nine generations, from slavery to today, as each of them fashioned

Had a baby and named that child
Toshi Georgiana.

Loved that Toshi up so.
Yes, I loved that Toshi up.

So some mornings, I start all over.
Holding tight to little Toshi,
I whisper a story that came before her . . .

Jacqueline Woodson tells a story based on her own family history in **Show Way,** *illustrated by Hudson Talbott, who depicts this history through details in his art.*

a "show way" quilt in different artistic ways. While the original quilts literally "showed the way" to escaping slaves, from great-grandma Soonie onward, each woman fashioned her "quilt" in a unique manner—Jacqueline's is books. The metaphor of strength, determination, pride, and fierce love shines from the words and Talbott's detailed illustrations—all held together by a quilt motif.

We now turn to a close look at an outstanding piece of historical fiction, Avi's **Crispin: The Cross of Lead** (i–a).

✳   ✳   ✳

A CLOSE LOOK AT

Crispin: The Cross of Lead

Avi's fiftieth book and winner of the 2003 Newbery Medal, **Crispin: The Cross of Lead** (i–a), is an outstanding example of historical fiction. Set in medieval England, this is a riveting adventure, an intriguing mystery, and a moving coming-of-age story.

A great deal of research underlies the story of **Crispin**, research so meticulous and precise that both small details and the larger historical context are accurate. Avi reveals what people of the time wore, how and what they ate, how they spoke, how they thought, and how the feudal system operated, among other things. All of this information is woven seamlessly into the story so that it is unobtrusive. To prepare to write this book, Avi listened to lectures, read countless works on the Middle Ages, visited England, and read and listened to literature from the period. His familiarity with the time and place is evident in the setting, plot, character development, and themes that permeate this novel.

This attention to detail is apparent in the setting, integral to the story; without it the events could not have occurred. The character of Crispin is forged by when and where he lived. Avi provides many details of time and place. The book begins with the date—England, A.D. 1377—and the sentence, "The day after my mother died, the priest and I wrapped her body in a gray shroud and carried her to the village church." Within the first four pages, the scene is set: a dismal, dreary, wet, muddy village where people worked in the fields and were cruel to Crispin. We discover that the village is part of a manor owned by a lord and managed by an evil steward, John Aycliffe. We learn that punishment is swift and severe, that when someone died a death tax was owed the lord, that God and the church were a central part of life, and that Crispin wore a gray wool tunic and leather shoes. We learn that Crispin believes that God directs every action, even that of tripping and falling onto a stone. And a careful reader will realize that Crispin has no name other than "Asta's son."

As the story develops and Crispin leaves his village, the sights, sounds, tastes, and smells of medieval England come vividly to life as readers travel along the road with Crispin and his companion, Bear. As Crispin sees new sights, and wonders about what he sees, Bear offers explanations. Through Crispin's comments and questions,

and Bear's answers, the setting is elaborated in a natural manner.

One of the most difficult stylistic aspects of historical fiction is the language the characters speak. It is difficult to strike a balance between authentic and understandable, especially when the language a character would actually speak is as different from modern English as the Middle English of the medieval period. Avi manages to capture a cadence of speech that marks the language as different from modern English without making it difficult to understand. He also uses words appropriate to the period—steward, reeve, pestilence—that are easily understood within the context of the story. Finally, there are Bear's songs, songs that reflect the language of the time and enrich the setting.

As the protagonist, Crispin is a fully developed, dynamic character. We understand his feelings, values, and attitudes, and they reflect the milieu in which he lives. His growth across the story is tremendous: from an ignorant, fearful, unnamed slave who knew nothing of his heritage to a courageous, curious, free man who knows who he is and is sure that his name is Crispin. When Crispin flees the village, he is running because of fear, trying to get to a city and obtain his freedom, but he has little idea of how to get there or what freedom really means. When he stumbles upon Bear, a huge, red-bearded juggler, his life begins to improve. As he travels with him, Crispin begins to realize that Bear juggles ideas as well as balls, and for the first time in his life, Crispin begins to question, to think for himself. As Bear explains the political realities of the day, Crispin begins to sense possibilities he has never considered and to question things he has taken for granted—such as the right of one human being to own another. Bear challenges Crispin to think for himself, and the boy begins to rely more on his own judgment than on the rules of others or their assumptions about what God wants done. Crispin's quest for freedom—of both mind and body—is thoroughly shaped by his historical context.

The story is told through Crispin's first-person point of view. This enables Avi to apprise the reader of what Crispin is thinking. Thus, when Crispin is frightened and confused, the reader is also confused and aware of danger. When Crispin slowly begins to figure out why Aycliffe is chasing him, when his new experiences cause him to question old ideas, the reader is privy to those thoughts and realizations. This allows us to know Crispin well and to believe in his transformation.

The story opens with a series of major events: the death of Crispin's mother, his realization that Aycliffe wants him killed, learning that he has a name and that his mother could read and write, and his subsequent discovery of the body of the village priest. These events both create an immediate interest in what might happen

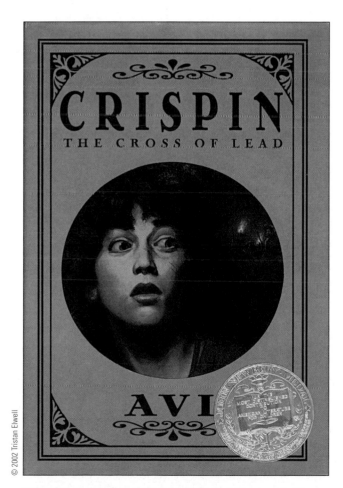

When his mother dies, Crispin embarks on a journey of self-discovery.

Profile

Avi

W riting] is hard. And writing very well is very hard. Never believe any writer who suggests otherwise. Scratch the surface of any successful author. Just below—in fetal position, sucking a thumb—is an insecure writer. For all of us writing well is always a struggle.

Avi knows what it means to write well. Since 1975, he has engaged in the struggle to create award-winning literature for children. His fiftieth book, *Crispin: The Cross of Lead*, won the 2003 Newbery Medal. In his acceptance speech, Avi suggested that a successful story is one that the writer begins and the reader completes. For Avi, the best literature contains gaps that challenge readers to consider, for the first time, aspects of themselves or their surroundings that are familiar but unexamined. "Great writing," he said, "reveals what we know—but never noticed before. Great writing identifies that most elusive of all things—that which

we have seen but had not noticed, that which did not seem to exist until it was named."

Avi has invited readers to complete gaps in many historical fiction pieces. Some of his popular titles include *The True Confessions of Charlotte Doyle*, which won a Newbery Honor in 2000, and his two books about Crispin. Avi discussed the challenge of writing historical fiction. "We don't know fully what life was like," he says, "and you have to build a whole style and language to convey something. In other words, the whole thing is a stylistic construction, and you almost invent the language." In writing *Crispin*, Avi first composed his text "in verse." "[B]ut it would have been six hundred pages," Avi laughed. "So I took the linguistic structure and recast it back into a traditional narrative."

Avi describes the challenge of writing *Crispin* in a way that would enable readers to complete the gaps in a story that takes place in the late 1300s. "I think the problem of writing historical fiction for young

people in particular is how to convey the strictures of that earlier society," he said. "The rules of life in the fourteenth century are so radically different from today that you have to create a context that is understandable." Avi found that music was one way for twentieth-century readers to see themselves in Crispin. "Music," says Avi, "is something kids do relate to, and figuring out that there was music at that time is a way for them to connect."

Avi works hard to help kids connect with books. "I've published at least one book a year," he said in his Newbery acceptance speech. "Since *Crispin* I've written and published more. But though I may tire at the end of the day, I never tire of this great enterprise." By creating texts in which readers help complete his stories, Avi has contributed books that strengthen readers' aesthetic experiences of literature. Watch the interview with Avi on the companion website and visit Avi at www.Avi-writer.com.

and propel Crispin out of his village and into the wider world. His journey from village to city is exciting not only because he is seeing and learning new things but because he is being pursued by Aycliffe for some unknown reason. The combination of adventure and mystery serves to heighten the tension and propel the plot toward its rousing conclusion.

Although Crispin knows that Aycliffe has declared him a "wolf's head," which means that anyone can kill him and claim a reward, he does not know why. In fact, there is a large price on his head, though Crispin can't imagine why he is worth anything. As Crispin begins to realize that Aycliffe's pursuit has something to do with who Crispin really is, he also begins to see that his own actions have consequences. As the plot and the mystery unfold, Crispin learns from his experiences and grows accordingly. This unity of character and action works to make the plot believable and the character of Crispin fully human.

Crispin's quest for freedom is shaped by his historical context, but it echoes across the ages. This quest is one that all humans pursue. We might call it growing up or becoming free from the constraints of childhood and the control of adults. It is often a larger freedom that we struggle for, such as the freedom of independent thought, the freedom of equality, or perhaps the freedom to live in peace and to develop and grow as human beings. Crispin is seeking all these freedoms, in spite of terrible odds, and his attainment of freedom is a triumph. His journey to self-discovery is literal as well as figurative, and one that young readers recognize and share. Teaching Idea 8.2 offers ways to help students explore the theme of self-knowledge.

In *Crispin: The Cross of Lead*, the seamless interweaving of setting, plot, and character as they center around a universal theme of the search for freedom and self-awareness is supported by impeccable writing that offers just enough flavor of the times.

Teaching Idea 8.2

Thematic Exploration: Self-Knowledge

One of the themes that is woven through the story of Crispin is his discovery of who he is. He discovers this literally as he learns his name and the truth about his mother and his heritage. This is one kind of self-knowledge that he acquires during the course of the story. He also discovers his own interests, desires, abilities, and strengths, coming to know his emotional self. Ask students to consider the knowledge they have of themselves. They might want to create a coat of arms for Crispin or for their own family with emblems that signify important aspects of their lives; Crispin might include, for example, a cross on his coat of arms. They might want to write a list poem or an acrostic, or name poem, for Crispin or for themselves, in which they list character traits. Crispin's name poem might begin "Courageous / Ready to learn / Inquisitive." Or they might simply write a journal entry discussing what Crispin discovered about himself or what they have discovered about themselves. This activity can also be linked to other books and other genres that explore this same theme.

History through Historical Fiction

Historical fiction can be organized and studied in many ways: as a genre, by theme, by chronological period, or according to the topics in a social studies curriculum. In any case, well-written stories will "establish human and social circumstances in which the interaction of historical forces may be known, felt, and observed" (Blos, 1992). We present historical fiction chronologically, and then consider how to explore particular historical settings as well as important themes across history.

PREHISTORIC AND ANCIENT TIMES

Prehistoric times, the ancient period before written records were kept, are wrapped in the shrouds of antiq-uity. Scientists theorize about the daily life and culture of ancient peoples by observing fragments of life and making inferences from shards of pottery, weapons, or bits of bone. Authors draw from the findings of archaeologists, anthropologists, and paleontologists to create vivid tales of life as it might have been.

Many novels of prehistoric times are set in distant lands around the Mediterranean Sea or in ancient Britain. The best fiction about prehistoric people does more than re-create possible settings and events of the past. It engages itself with themes basic to all persons everywhere: the will to survive, the need for courage and honor, the growth of understanding, the development of compassion. Peter Dickinson's series **The Kin**, which includes *Suth's Story*, *Noli's Story*, *Po's Story*, and *Mana's Story* (I–A), takes readers back two hundred thousand years but grapples with issues important today. War and peace, the power of language and the thought it enables, loving relationships, and community are some of the themes that connect these stories with our own times.

Stories of ancient times often focus on life in the Mediterranean civilizations. Julius Lester's *Pharaoh's Daughter: A Novel of Ancient Egypt* (A) is a fictional account of the biblical story of Moses that contains well-developed characters and complex themes. Susan Fletcher writes imaginatively of life in a Persian harem during the time of Scheherazade in *Shadow Spinner* (A), a suspenseful story with a resourceful female protagonist and intriguing details of time.

Rosemary Sutcliff's novels of ancient Britain, such as the recently reissued *Frontier Wolf* (A), are masterful evocations of their time; they also provide sensitive insights into the human spirit. Each story reverberates with an eternal truth and lasting theme. Sutcliff's heroes live and die for values and principles that we embrace today. Much like high fantasy, a very different genre, her stories reveal the eternal struggle between goodness—that which we value—and evil—the forces that work to destroy it.

THE MIDDLE AGES

The dissolution of the Roman Empire signaled the beginning of that part of the medieval period sometimes referred to as the Middle Ages, spanning roughly from 500 to the early 1500s A.D. There is some recorded history of these times, and writers breathe life into the shadowy figures of the history of this period. Although not technically a novel because it is actually a collection of brief plays, Laura Amy Schlitz's *Good Masters! Sweet Ladies! Voices from a Medieval Village* (I) won the Newbery Medal. This gathering of monologues and dialogues from fictional children from ages ten through fifteen is filled with details of life in medieval England, a variety of topics, wonderful period vocabulary, and a great deal of humor. Robert Byrd's illustrations add beautifully to the overall effect. In a gripping adventure for older readers, Michael Cadnum chose to re-create an actual historical event in Norman England, one shrouded in mystery to this day, in his *The King's Arrow* (A), a story filled with action, violence, and gritty details.

Others construct novels that blend fact and legend, as in Michael Morpurgo's retelling of *Sir Gawain and the Green Knight* (I–A). In the past ten years, there have been a number of outstanding narratives set in the Middle Ages, both fantasy and literary lore, as discussed in Chapter 6, and more realistic fictional narratives. Elizabeth Wein links ancient Britain and ancient Africa in her acclaimed Arthurian/Aksumite cycle. The books, *The Winter Prince*, *A Coalition of Lions*, *The Sunbird*, *The Lion Hunter*, and *The Empty Kingdom* (A) move from sixth-century Great Britain to sixth-century Africa as Goewin, princess of Britain, travels to African Aksum (today's Eritrea and Ethiopia) and helps forge an alliance between ancient Britain and the African kingdom.

Steeped in Arthurian legend but based on facts about the history of Britain and Ethiopia, these riveting narratives postulate a believable connection between the two ancient kingdoms, forged by unforgettable characters. Are they fantasy, or are they historical fiction? One could argue for both, as we do, by discussing them in Chapter 6 as well. The same blurring of genre lines can be seen in Kevin Crossley-Holland's **Arthur** trilogy, *The Seeing Stone*, *At the Crossing Places*, and *King of the Middle March* (I–A), because of the close connection with Arthurian legend. There is no fantasy in *Crossing to Paradise* (I–A), where Gatty's story is told as she journeys to the Holy Land and back home, where we first met her in *The Seeing Stone*, profoundly changed by her quest. K. M. Grant's *Blood Red Horse* (A), also set during the Crusades and containing some elements of fantasy, is an exciting adventure tale, a romance, and a terrific horse story, while also illuminating the effect of the Crusades on relations between the Arabs and the west, effects that permeate our lives today.

Avi's *Crispin: The Cross of Lead* and *Crispin: At the Edge of the World* are exciting adventure stories as Crispin follows his quest. He finds great friendship, enlightenment, and tragedy as he encounters the world beyond Britain when he, Bear, and the girl they have befriended are shipwrecked on the Brittany coast of France. In both books the sights, sounds, tastes, and smells, as well as the customs and beliefs of the period, are so vivid that readers are left with the feeling of having traveled through time. Karen Cushman's *The Midwife's Apprentice* (I–A), winner of the 1996 Newbery Medal, also weaves an array of details about daily life in Britain into a compelling narrative. The mundane, often distasteful details of the lives of the common folk in the Middle Ages form the rich background against which a young girl discovers her worth. Cushman's other two books set in the Middle Ages, *Matilda Bone* and *Catherine, Called Birdy* (A), are also filled with details that sweep readers into the midst of life in England at that time. Readers who have enjoyed Avi's and Cushman's books might want to go on to read Odo Hirsch's *Yoss* (A), a novel of the Middle Ages for slightly older readers that explores many of the themes that appear in *Crispin*.

Other fine stories explore the medieval period in other parts of the world. Constance Leeds's *The Silver Cup* (I) is set in Germany in 1095. Rich with details of time and place, this story portrays a friendship between two young women—one Christian and one Jewish—as they struggle against the intolerance of their cultures. Frances Temple's *The Beduins' Gazelle* (A) is set in the midst of a war between Beduin tribes in 1302. Jill Paton Walsh tells the story of the fall of Constantinople in 1453 in *The Emperor's Winding Sheet* (I–A). Tracy Barrett's *Anna of Byzantium* (A) is a graphic novel of the life of a brilliant woman in the eleventh-century Byzantine Empire, a difficult time in history for strong women. Janet Rupert's *The African Mask* (A) is set in eleventh-century Nigeria. Linda Sue Park's *A Single Shard* (A), set in medieval Korea, won a Newbery Medal for her exquisite description of time and place and development of a protagonist whom readers come to care about. Mette Newth's *The Transformation* (A), set in Greenland in the mid-1400s, explores the impact of Christian Europeans on the beliefs and culture—indeed, on the well-being—of the Inuit. This is a novel that presents a place and time that is unfamiliar to most readers, considers profound questions of theology and culture, and is also a riveting adventure as well as a tender love story.

• • THE RENAISSANCE AND • • THE AGE OF EXPLORATION

Whether in real life or in books, mysterious or dangerous explorations of the unknown mesmerize us all. Accounts of navigation of the New World intrigue today's children as much as travels to the moon or Mars do. Explorers of the past and present need the same kind of courage and willingness to face the unknown. Stories of explorations range from tales of the early Vikings to those set in the age of European exploration—Columbus and after.

In 1992, the five-hundredth anniversary of Columbus's famous 1492 voyage brought forth many books to mark the anniversary. These books also reflected a growing trend in children's literature: some told the "other side" of the story, presenting Columbus from the point of view of the Native Americans who were present when he landed, or of Europeans who were skeptical of his motives. Books like Jane Yolen's *Encounter* (I–A) and Pam Conrad's

Pedro's Journal (I) help present a more balanced picture of the impact of the age of exploration. The powerful writing and clever structure of Michael Dorris's *Morning Girl* (I) allows young readers to experience "first-hand" the shock of Columbus's invasion of the Taino Indian islands.

Michael Cadnum's *Ship of Fire* (I–A) is based on actual events during Sir Francis Drake's raid on the Spanish port of Cadiz in 1587. The protagonist, a young doctor, not only finds adventure and acts courageously but also is forced to question the English hero, Drake. Is he truly a hero or simply a pirate, stealing for Queen Elizabeth? These questions elevate this exciting novel beyond just an adventure story.

The Renaissance is a fascinating time in history, but few books for children explore this era in Europe, and even fewer are set in other parts of the world. Pilar Molina Llorente's *The Apprentice* (I) is set in Renaissance Florence and depicts the lives of middle-class merchants and famous artists alike. Linda Sue Park sets *The Kite Fighters* (I) in Seoul, Korea.

• • COLONIAL THROUGH POST–REVOLUTIONARY WAR TIMES

Immigrants began sailing to America in the late sixteenth century, some seeking adventure and financial gain, some escaping religious persecution, some traveling as missionaries, and some seeking political freedom. Economic and social conditions made the New World attractive to people who were willing to sacrifice the known for the possibilities of a promising unknown. The settlements by the English at Roanoke, Jamestown, Plymouth, and Boston are vivid settings for stories based on early colonial life. Historical fiction set after Europeans came to North America is plentiful, with most books by North American writers set here rather than in Europe or beyond.

By the end of the seventeenth century, the early settlers were well established in their new communities and were stern guardians of their religious views, pious behavior, and moral standards. The hysteria that gripped the people of Salem, Massachusetts, in the days of the witch hunts grew out of the political, economic, and social forces of the community. Kathryn Lasky's *Beyond the Burning Time* (A) explores some of the hidden passions that might have stoked the fires of Salem, and brings to life the way people lived, believed, and sometimes died in that place and time. In her classic *The Witch of Blackbird Pond* (I–A), winner of the 1959 Newbery Medal, Elizabeth George Speare reveals how guilt by association occurs in Old Salem when a young girl and the old woman she has befriended are accused of witchcraft. Both books artfully blend fact and fiction to create a vivid picture of people and their lives during colonial times.

The history of America is incomplete without stories of Native Americans. In the past their story was told, if at all, by European Americans who often characterized them in stereotyped ways. A growing number of writers now give more accurate portrayals of Native American cultures and a more objective picture of the five-hundred-year clash between the European and Native American cultures. Stories for younger children may present a simple view of the interaction between Europeans and Native Americans, but this view should not rely on stereotypes. Stories for older readers often consider the complexities inherent in the clash between two cultures, such as Elizabeth George Speare's compelling novel about the faltering friendship of a white boy and an Indian boy in the 1700s, *The Sign of the Beaver* (I–A). Although some people criticize Speare for her non-Native point of view, others find the book to be a rewarding catalyst for discussion about the clash of cultures.

Stories that reflect a Native American point of view concerning these times are still scarce, however, as are those that depict the lives and struggles of the many Africans brought as slaves before the turn of the century. Notable exceptions include Michael Dorris's *Guests* and *Sees Behind Trees* (I), as well as Joseph Bruchac's *The Arrow over the Door* (I). In Joyce Rockwood's *To Spoil the Sun* (A), the story of the devastation of smallpox is vivid and moving. Rain Dove, a young Cherokee girl, finds her life destroyed when the disease arrives along with the white man.

The eighteenth century was an interesting and tumultuous time, with disease wreaking havoc in Europe and ships carrying people around the globe with greater and greater frequency. L. A. Meyer captures the dangers and excitement of mid-eighteenth-century life in *Bloody Jack: Being an Account of the Curious Adventures of Mary "Jacky" Faber, Ship's Boy* and its sequel, *Curse of the Blue Tattoo: Being an Account of the Misadventures of Jacky Faber, Midshipman and Fine Lady* (I–A). These tales of high adventure on the seas differ from most others in one remarkable way—the protagonist is female. Based on a true event, Mary Hooper's *Newes from the Dead* (A) recounts the experience of young Anne Green, hanged but not killed in seventeenth-century England. Told in the alternating voices of Anne and a medical student, this novel is well researched and documented with a bibliography and author's note.

There was also great upheaval in many countries around the world during this time, including Great Britain. Jane Yolen and Robert Harris again combine their talents in *Prince Across the Water* (I–A), set during the Scottish rebellion to replace King George with Bonnie Prince Charlie. The age-old desire of young men to go to war to prove their mettle plays itself out against a meticulously detailed setting and a thorough understanding of the role of clan and honor in the Highlander culture of the day. Another collaboration between Yolen and Harris, *The Queen's Own Fool: A Novel of Mary Queen of Scots* (I–A), brings another exciting piece of Scottish history to young readers.

Wars wrapped the globe in this period, and the American Revolutionary War was one of the most significant. Stories of this war were once quite one–sided: the Tories, or loyalists, were bad, the Patriots good. A more balanced picture began to appear in the 1970s with *My Brother Sam Is Dead* (A), and this trend has continued. Since then, the divided loyalties in colonial families or communities and the true horror of war have usually been foregrounded in fiction about this era. Janet Lunn, one of Canada's best-known writers for children, explores just these topics in *The Hollow Tree* (A), a gripping account of a young girl's harrowing journey north from New Hampshire to Canada to join other loyalist families even though her own family is divided in its allegiance.

Recently, several books that tell part of the story of the American Revolution through the eyes of a slave have highlighted the irony of a country fighting for freedom while enslaving others. M. T. Anderson's *The Astonishing Life of Octavian Nothing, Traitor to the Nation, Volume I: The Pox Party* (A), winner of the National Book Award and a Printz Honor book, and *Volume II: The Kingdom on the Waves* (A) are crossover books that straddle the young adult and adult market. Nevertheless, they represent a new direction in historical fiction of this period as sweeping epics that explore issues of race and class even as they explore issues of freedom. In *Chains* (A), a novel for younger adolescents, Laurie Halse Anderson holds up the institution of slavery against the Patriots' desire for freedom from Britain. Here we take a close look at *Chains*.

✳   ✳   ✳

A CLOSE LOOK AT
Chains

Laurie Halse Anderson's *Chains* (A) is an unflinching look at the life of a young black girl during the early days of the American Revolution, revealing through her experiences the larger historical issues of the time. Thirteen-year-old Isabel and her fragile younger sister, Ruth, expect to be freed when their old mistress dies; she had promised to do so when Isabel's mother was dying. To her dismay, she is, instead, sold into slavery to a mean-tempered woman and her Loyalist husband, the Locktons, and taken by ship from Rhode Island to New York City. Central issues of how class and race influenced colonial life are evident from the beginning. In just the first few chapters we meet a former indentured servant, a white woman, who reluctantly tries

to help Isabel in the only way she can—by buying her. Later in the novel, a wealthy woman who has grown fond of Isabel seeks to do the same. Although well-intentioned, neither thinks of *freeing* the girls, only buying them and treating them humanely.

As the story progresses, we are introduced to the political complexity of the time, with avid Tories fighting both verbally and physically with avid Patriots, and a large group in the middle, not sure where their sympathies lie. Although there are more sympathetic characters who are Patriots, Anderson does not gloss over the dimensionality of the movement for independence. When, for example, Isabel takes a considerable risk to spy on her master, she does so because she thinks that the Patriots she is helping will reward her with freedom. They don't; nor do the British when she appeals to them after they have taken the city. Freedom, it seems, is freedom for whites only.

Anderson raises class issues as well, beginning with the formerly indentured woman who tried to help Isabel, the character of the Lockton's white cook, and the clearly

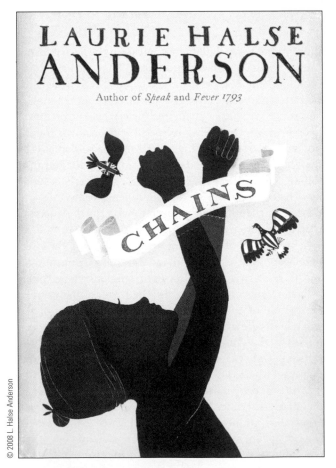

Laurie Halse Anderson highlights the irony that underscored the Patriots' fight for freedom even as they ignored the thriving institution of slavery in **Chains***.*

drawn social lines between the wives of enlisted British troops and wives of officers. Differences between the way captured Patriots were treated—the officers sent to work for Loyalist establishments, the enlisted men thrown in prison where many died of cold, starvation, and disease— also highlight the class issues that existed at the time. It is perhaps through this issue that the fundamental flaw in the Patriots' cause is most visible: they rebelled against the class system of England, but they did not extend their quest for freedom across racial lines.

The characters, especially Isabel, are multidimensional and generally reflect the inherent contradictions in the struggle for freedom. Isabel, like many other slaves, wonders if the British, who had abolished slavery in England, would be better than the Patriots, but finds that not to be the case. The plot is packed with the historical events of this tumultuous time as well as events in Isabel's life, and the setting is carefully detailed, even down to the peculiar and unsavory smells. Each chapter opens with a quote culled from varied sources that highlights the thought of the time and serves to comment on the action in the chapter, often ironically. Most welcome is the handbill at the end of the story stating that a second book, *Forge*, is coming soon. End material containing an interview with Anderson and acknowledgements clarify what is from the historical record and what is fiction.

Profiles

Laurie Halse Anderson

*A*merican history has been a life-long passion for Laurie. If she were to become a teacher, it is what she'd teach. (Officially Long Official Biography of Laurie Halse Anderson, by Stephanie Holcomb Anderson.)

Laurie Halse Anderson's first book was published in 1996, although she began writing before that. When *Speak* was published in 1999 it was a Printz Honor Award winner and a finalist for the National Book Award, as well as being a *New York Times* bestseller. Since then, she has "shifted into high gear" and has published six novels, including *Fever 1793* and *Chains*. Her **Vet Volunteers** series is immensely popular with young readers. She has also written a number of nonfiction titles including *Independent Dames: What You Never Knew About the Women and Girls of the American Revolution*. Laurie Halse Anderson plans to alternate between historical fiction and contemporary young adult novels for the next several years. Visit her at www.writer lady.com.

Louise Erdrich

*L*ouise Erdrich is a versatile, gifted writer for adults and young readers. Her novel for adults, *Love Medicine*, is often studied in high school English classes. Her series for young readers, beginning with *The Birchbark House*, a National Book Award finalist, is inspired by research and stories from her Ojibwe (also known as Chippewa) family. The second book in the series, *The Game of Silence*, won the Scott O'Dell Award for Historical Fiction. *The Porcupine Year* is the third book in the planned, multibook series. Louise Erdrich owns a bookstore for children and adults, Birch Bark Books, in Minneapolis.

• • WESTWARD EXPANSION • • AND THE CIVIL WAR

After the American Revolution, the nineteenth century saw the citizens of the new United States continue to move westward. National identity was seriously challenged; the question of slavery became a national debate; and immigrants from Europe, Africa, and Asia (both voluntary and involuntary) brought their despair and sometimes their hopes and dreams to a new land. It was an interesting century, filled with amazing contradictions. As the United States grew, the native peoples' lands continued to shrink, and their cultures were almost obliterated. As the nation expanded, indentured Chinese, lured to America by the promise of work, were exploited as they built the transcontinental railroad. As the new nation prospered, Africans and others continued to be ripped from their homelands, forcibly transported, and doomed to endure a life of slavery. As the nation became industrialized, the quality of life improved for some and grew worse for many. Children's books explore these contradictions from many viewpoints, telling the story of the growth of a nation and the consequences of that growth.

The Westward Migration

Americans were on the move from the beginning. Those moving called it expansion; those who were displaced saw it as invasion. In either case, life required great physical strength and, often, the ability to endure loneliness. People worked hard by necessity, providing their own food, clothing, shelter, and entertainment. Themes of loneliness, hardship, and acceptance of what life brings are threaded through many excellent novels about the pioneers and their struggle to tame a wild land.

These themes are evident in Joyce Carol Thomas's descriptions of the courage and dignity of a young black woman determined to own her own land. *I Have Heard of a Land* (P–I) presents the inspiring story of one woman who symbolizes all who homesteaded the American West, braving isolation, the wilderness, and nature's vagaries to forge a home for themselves. Loretta Ellsworth's *The Shrouding Woman* (I), set on the prairie, presents a quiet story of grief and recovery along with a description of a job that is all but extinct today—the shrouding of the dead by women trained to do so. In *Prairie Whispers* (I), Frances Arrington uses the setting to create a mood of foreboding and isolation. *Nothing Here But Stones: A Jewish Pioneer Story* (I–A), by Nancy Oswald, tells the fictional story of a real group of Russian Jews who struggled to create a new home in the Colorado mountains.

Going west was an adventure story to many, and Will Hobbs's *Jason's Gold* (A) is a spine-tingling account of a young boy's adventures in the Klondike during the Alaskan gold rush. Michael Cadnum explores a similar story in the California gold fields in *Blood Gold* (I–A). This gripping adventure story takes readers from Panama to San Francisco by ship and then on to the gold fields, as the young narrator pursues an acquaintance who left his pregnant girlfriend in Philadelphia. The suspense is high, the plot twists and turns, and the settings are vivid.

During these times, the clash of cultural values between European settlers and Native Americans resulted in numerous conflicts, from grisly battles in which hundreds were killed to more personal conflicts in which individuals who had come to know each other as friends had to choose between friendship and loyalty to their own people.

The famous 1804–1805 voyage of Merriweather Lewis and William Clark is emblematic of the interest the U.S. government had in expanding westward. Until recently, stories of their expedition were told from the viewpoint of the two leaders or the soldiers who accompanied them. However, with the minting of the Sacajawea "gold" dollar came not one but several stories about this brave Native American woman who helped lead Lewis and Clark through a large part of the upstream Missouri River and into the Rocky Mountains. Joseph Bruchac's *Sacajawea* (I–A) is a brilliant, thoughtful recounting of the voyage told in alternating points of view—Sacajawea's and William Clark's. Clark's chapters begin with excerpts from the diaries he kept on the journey; Sacajawea's begin with stories that her people told. Each brings a unique perspective to the grand adventure, and their mutual respect and growing friendship are evident.

The two hundredth anniversary of this epic journey occurred in 2004–2005, accompanied by the appearance of more books. Kate McMullan tells the story of the journey from the point of view of the youngest member of the group in *My Travels with Capts. Lewis and Clark by George Shannon* (I–A). McMullan used not only public records but also family documents—she is a direct descendant of George Shannon—to create a first-rate adventure story. The story is also filled with great detail about people and places and is a chronicle of the growth of a boy called Pup because he was so young. Stephen Ambrose also creates a fictional diary of George Shannon in *This Vast Land* (A). Allan Wolf tells the same story from the perspective of thirteen participants on the journey, one of which is the dog, Seaman, in *New Found Land: Lewis and Clark's Voyage of Discovery* (A).

Fortunately, some stories about the westward expansion reflect the views of someone other than the white settlers. Laurence Yep writes of the life of the Chinese laborers in *The Traitor: 1885* (I–A), part of his **Gold Mountain Chronicles** series. Cornelia Cornelissen tells of the forcible removal of the Cherokee to Oklahoma in *Soft Rain: A Story of the Cherokee Trail of Tears* (I). In the first three books of a planned cycle of novels, Louise Erdrich tells of the effects of encroachment by whites on the Ojibwe people in *The Birchbark House*, a National Book Award winner, *The Game of Silence*, a Scott O'Dell Award winner, and *The Porcupine Year* (I). Teaching Idea 8.3 offers a way to help students notice how varying perceptions of events influence the way we think of those events. We now take a close look at *The Porcupine Year* along with the other books in this ongoing series.

Teaching Idea 8.3

Discussion: Compare Perceptions of a Historical Event

Collect several books, both historical fiction and nonfiction, that describe a historical event such as the first Thanksgiving, the westward expansion on the Great Plains, or the Civil War. Read these with your students. Compare them, considering such questions as the following:

- Who is telling the story?
- What is the narrator's perception of the events?
- What factors influence that perception?
- How do perceptions differ across books?

An effective follow-up activity is to ask students to role-play from different perspectives.

* * *

A CLOSE LOOK AT

The Porcupine Year

Beginning with *The Birchbark House* (I), Louise Erdrich chronicles the life and times of a young Ojibwe girl, Omakayas, and her extended family. In the first book of the series, we spend a year with seven-year-old Omakayas, a year that begins with small joys, such as her older sister and the beautiful place she lives, and small irritations, such as her younger brother, Pinch. As the year passes, her community is stricken by smallpox, an often-fatal disease introduced by white settlers who are also encroaching on the Ojibwe lands. In *The Game of Silence*, several canoes filled with people driven from their land join Omakayas's people, even as her people are being forced by the gov-ernment to leave their beloved island. *The Porcupine Year* continues the story as Omakayas and her extended family set off through Minnesota rivers and lakes to their destination, Lake of the Woods, on the border between the United States and Canada.

The setting of the north woods, rivers, and lakes in all of the novels is lovingly described; it is evident that Erdrich cherishes the places that she writes about. Set within this natural beauty, the social setting in which Omakayas lives her life seems almost idyllic, until the larger society—the encroaching white settlers—disrupts the community's life with disease and forces them to leave their island to seek an uncertain future. At the same time, Omakayas is growing from child to woman, learning her own gifts and responsibilities, and beginning to discover her own strength.

The Porcupine Year is a year in which Omakayas, her family, and a few others take everything they can carry that will help them settle into a new life and travel from the shores of Lake Superior to join their relatives on an island in Lake of the Woods. They are well prepared but meet with danger and disaster along the way. As they are dying from starvation when caught by winter after being robbed of their food, tools, and weapons, Omakayas saves them by following her heart. Her strength of character has been building throughout the three novels, with each new challenge representing an occasion for growth, and by the time she and her family reach their destination, she has transformed, heart and body, into a woman.

All three novels are full of the small details of life—how they dressed, ate, hunted, gardened, interacted with one another, worked together as a team—and Ojibwe words, with a glossary and pronunciation guide to aid non-fluent readers. Both heighten the experience of joining with Omakayas on her adventures, as she journeys toward her new future and adulthood.

Louise Erdrich continues the story of Omakayas and her family in The Porcupine Year, *the third book in her series based on her family history.*

Slavery, the Civil War, and Its Aftermath

Slavery was a part of American life from early colonial days until long after the Emancipation Proclamation. Many chapters of American history are grim, and those involving slavery and the Civil War are among the worst. Slavery shamed a nation of people who professed to believe in freedom, and the war was a long, savage contest that tore the country apart and caused many deaths. Historical fiction of this period describes antebellum life as well as the turmoil and tragedy of the bloody war years. The years preceding the Civil War were a bleak period in American history, although individual acts of compassion and heroism did occur. A notable children's book that has captured the antebellum period is Ann Turner's picturebook *Nettie's Trip South* (I–A), which depicts the horror of slavery as seen through the eyes of a white girl from the North who is on a train trip to the South. In another picturebook, Elisa Carbone tells the fictional story of a real person, James Smith, in *Night Running: How James Escaped with the Help of His Faithful Dog* (P–I). Full-bleed double-page spreads by E. B. Lewis pull the reader into this story of courage and love between boy and dog. There are many other outstanding picturebooks that tell stories of escaping slaves and the Underground Railroad.

Julius Lester uses the multiple voices of enslaved Africans and their owners to depict an actual event—the largest auction of slaves in American history on March 2 and 3, 1859, in Savannah, Georgia. *Day of Tears* (A), Lester's 2006 Coretta Scott King Award–winning novel in dialogue, is a stunning indictment of the institution of slavery and those who participated in it.

Avi's novel of the Civil War, *Iron Thunder: The Battle Between the Monitor & the Merrimac* (I) is set in Brooklyn, New York, during the war. In an interesting portrayal of the class differences that existed at that time, Avi creates a memorable character, thirteen-year-old Tom, whose father is killed fighting for the Union. Tom takes a job in the ironworks where the "iron-clad" Monitor is being constructed and, in the process, sets himself on a perilous course. A confrontation with Confederate spies, the opportunity to join the Monitor's crew, and detailed, vivid battle scenes contribute to the fast-paced plot.

Although *The River Between Us* (A) begins and ends in 1916, Richard Peck re-creates life during the Civil War in a small Illinois town on the Mississippi River. When fifteen-year-old Howard, his father, and his two younger brothers arrive in Grand Tower, Illinois, to visit his grandparents and Great Aunt Delphine and Grand Uncle Noah, he and the reader are immediately swept up in Grandma Tilly's stories and transported into the world of the Civil War. Border states, such as Illinois, and especially the southern regions of those states, reflected the larger division in the country. Further, the Mississippi was the main thoroughfare for the center of the country, and North and South mingled, even after the beginnings of the war, through the trade between New Orleans and the North. This setting is integral to the story that Grandma Tilly unfolds of the mysterious Calinda and the beautiful Delphine who came north from New Orleans on one of the last riverboats. With this story, Peck raises questions about how the United States considers race and what it meant to be a free person of color in that time and place.

Mildred Taylor reached back in time in her ongoing chronicle of the Logan family in *The Land* (A), the story of Paul-Edward, Cassie Logan's grandfather. The son of a white man and his former slave, Paul-Edward is privileged and educated, but also a young black man in the post–Civil War South. Blacks distrust his whiteness,

whites discriminate against him because of his blackness, and he needs to find in himself the strength to craft the life that he wants because society is determined to thwart him. Taylor, arguably one of our most important contemporary authors, is unflinching in her examination of what life was like for African Americans in the postwar era.

• • IMMIGRATION AND • • THE INDUSTRIAL REVOLUTION

Continuing the Logan family saga, Mildred Taylor's *The Well: David's Story* (A) is set in the rural South in the early twentieth century and tells the story of David, the son of Paul-Edward. Focused on discrimination and injustice, Taylor's story is emotionally draining and raises important issues for older readers to think about and discuss. As in *The Land*, the social, political, and physical setting is richly detailed.

With the aftereffects of the Civil War at work in the South and the continued westward expansion, the East was changing as well. Millions of immigrants came from distant lands, dreaming of freedom and hoping to create a better life. Their stories are familiar stories, repeated over and over at family gatherings where young children cluster around their elders. Historical fiction contains a wealth of immigrant stories for all ages. Many books describe the conditions that led families to leave their country and migrate to America; others focus on the difficulties and hardships endured during and after immigration.

Patricia Reilly Giff sets *Nory Ryan's Song* (I–A) in 1845 in Ireland, just at the beginning of the potato famine. Although Nory is only twelve, her strength of character and gritty determination help her save her family and friends from starvation before she begins her own journey to America. That journey and its happy ending are described in the sequel, *Maggie's Door* (I–A). Nory is a mother as her story continues in *Water Street* (I–A), set in Brooklyn in the late nineteenth century as the famous bridge is being built. Karen Hesse's *Brooklyn Bridge* (I–A) is set in the same location in the early twentieth century. The famous bridge stands as a metaphor for bridges between old and new worlds, between generations, and between friends in this combination of romance, comedy, and ghost story.

In *A House of Tailors* (I–A), Patricia Reilly Giff relates the story of thirteen-year-old Dina, who flees Germany after being accused of spying against the Germans during the Franco-Prussian War. Dina hopes to leave her work as a seamstress, but when she arrives in Brooklyn in 1870, she finds that her uncle's house is as full of sewing as her father's was. As Dina adjusts to life in America, she also comes to value her talent as a seamstress and to realize that although she may love her American life, she will always long to return to Germany. This duality in the immigrant experience is beautifully captured by Allen Say in his Caldecott Medal–winning picturebook, *Grandfather's Journey* (P–I–A), set in the first half of the twentieth century.

Turn-of-the-century Japan is the setting for Alan Gratz's *Samurai Shortstop* (A), a multilayered novel that explores honor, familial duty, and generational differences. The protagonist struggles with older boys in his boarding school, his father's aversion to all things Western, and his own love of baseball as he seeks to honor his family's samurai values in an increasingly modern Japan.

While the West was being settled and immigrants were pouring into the thriving cities of the East, rural and small-town America seemed quiet and peaceful. Several stories set around the turn of the century give a glimpse of life as it was lived in small towns in the East, away from the high drama of life on the frontier or in bustling urban centers. Gary Schmidt bases the Newbery Honor book *Lizzie Bright and the Buckminster Boy* (I–A) on a true story. In 1911, Maine officials forced African American, Native American, and foreign-born residents to leave Malaga Island because they wanted to use the island as a tourist attraction. Schmidt takes this incident and weaves the story of Turner Buckminster III, son of the new congregational preacher, and Lizzie Bright Griffin, granddaughter of Malaga's African American preacher. The gripping drama contains multiple conflicts—not the least between Turner and his father—that reveal both the worst and the best sides of humanity, as townspeople engage in a struggle for human dignity that is sparked by the desire for money and power.

In *Sweetgrass Basket* (A), Marlene Carvell uses prose poems and alternating voices to tell the story of two Mohawk sisters sent by their widowed father to boarding school in Carlisle, Pennsylvania. Based on a true story, this fictional interpretation is heartbreaking. Deborah Hopkinson's *Into the Firestorm: A Novel of San Francisco, 1906* (I), is a carefully researched story of one boy's experience in the famous fire. Choosing between self-preservation and helping others becomes a defining moment in young Nick's life. Another famous fire is at the climax of Margaret Peterson Haddix's *Uprising* (A), which portrays the abysmal working conditions at the Triangle Shirtwaist Factory in New York City. Three main characters, a young Italian immigrant, a Russian immigrant who tries to organize the women in the factory, and a wealthy young woman who becomes involved in the struggle of these young women for safe and humane working conditions, allow Haddix to present a tapestry of the way people lived in that time and place. Katherine Paterson's *Bread and Roses, Too* (A) tells the moving story of the 1912 "Bread and Roses" mill strike in Lawrence, Massachusetts. Her compelling characterization,

as always, puts a human face on history. Her earlier book, *Lyddie* (I–A), is set in the 1840s in the Lawrence mills.

·· WORLD WAR I ·· AND ITS AFTERMATH

There are not many books set during World War I, in either picturebook or novel form, but the books that do exist are outstanding. Recently, there have been several books that examine both the events and the nature of this war from the perspective of those left behind as well as those on the front lines. In Iain Lawrence's *Lord of the Nutcracker Men* (I–A), young Johnny's world has been profoundly affected. With his father in France and his mother working in a distant munitions plant, Johnny must leave London for the safety of his aunt's countryside home. He takes with him the nutcracker men and toy soldiers that his father made for him before leaving, and his army grows with each soldier that his father carves and sends him from the front. As the war continues, both the soldiers and the letters from his father get more and more frightening, while Johnny learns to take responsibility for himself. Although Johnny's anguish is foregrounded, his father's letters also reveal the true horrors of the front.

Michael Morpurgo's *Private Peaceful* (A) moves from the front to the idyllic past of turn-of-the-century rural England as Private Thomas (Tommo) Peaceful spends a sleepless night trying to remember his past. His memories, told in a series of vignettes, recount his childhood and adolescence in the company of his older brother, Charlie, and their best friend, Molly. The brothers are so close that even though Tommo loves Molly, Charlie's marriage to her does not destroy their relationship. When Charlie goes to war, Tommo lies about his age to follow him. Morpurgo explores the brutality of not only the war but the people who engage in it. The ending is a profound condemnation of the killing of others, for any reason.

In the summer of 1925, it was hot—very hot—in New York City, the setting of Walter Dean Myers's *Harlem Summer* (A). Sixteen-year-old Mark needs a summer job, anything that will keep him from having to work for his uncle, an undertaker. He takes a job downtown at *The Crisis* publishing office, wondering how he fits in with the "new Negroes" working there—people such as Dr. W.E.B. DuBois and Langston Hughes. And besides, it's just a job; his real passion is his saxophone and the music of Fats Waller. When Fats gets Mark involved in gangster activity and into the bad graces of the notorious Dutch Schultz, Mark must figure out how to solve his problem, quickly. Poignant and humorous, this is a terrific coming-of-age story and an entertaining glimpse of life in Harlem in 1925. Jen Bryant's *Ringside, 1925: Views from the Scopes Trial* (A) offers another view of the way thought was changing in the United States.

• • THE GREAT DEPRESSION • •

Stories of the Depression years portray America in times of trouble. The beginning of the period is generally considered to be the stock market crash of 1929. Then, stories of ruined businessmen jumping from skyscrapers filled the headlines of daily newspapers. Now, stories for children describe the grim effects of living in poverty. Mildred Taylor's books about Cassie Logan and her family, *Song of the Trees* (I), *Roll of Thunder, Hear My Cry* (A), *Let the Circle Be Unbroken* (A), *The Friendship* (A), and *Mississippi Bridge* (A), show rural poverty and prevailing racism. Young Cassie and her extended family, including Paul-Edward's widow (Cassie's grandmother) and David Logan (her father), live on their own farm. Owning their own land was unusual for African Americans in Mississippi at that time, and it is a source of pride for Cassie. However, she doesn't really understand why her father has to leave the family to find work to pay the taxes. Nor does she understand the prevalent racism that surrounds her, because she has been protected by her loving family. In the Newbery Medal–winning *Roll of Thunder, Hear My Cry* Taylor vividly portrays the physical, social, and political setting through Cassie's eyes as Cassie begins to discover the truth about where she lives and the compelling reasons for holding on to their land. The Logan saga is the most complete chronicle of the Jim Crow era available for young readers. As such, it illuminates key threads of our history and identity as a nation.

Jen Bryant builds on a specific incident—the kidnapping and subsequent death of the Lindbergh baby in 1932—in *The Trial* (I–A). This novel in poems introduces us to twelve-year-old Katie and the world of small-town New Jersey during the Depression as seen through Katie's eyes. Katie finds herself inside the courtroom at the Hauptmann trial, helping her Uncle Jeff, a reporter who needs help taking notes because he has broken his arm. Because Katie, in all her innocence, is there, we can see the trial through fresh eyes, eyes that wonder about guilt and innocence.

Karen Hesse's Newbery Medal–winning *Out of the Dust* (A), also discussed in Chapter 4, is unrelenting in its depiction of life in the Oklahoma dust bowl; the story is softened only by the sensitivity of its heroine and its own poetic form. Told through the poems of young Billie Jo, the novel captures the combination of hope and despair that reflects the time and place; it also captures the pain of adolescence at any time, in any place.

Other stories set during this time are less grim. In Gennifer Choldenko's *Al Capone Does My Shirts* (I–A), Moose worries about his father losing his job and their home, but he also copes with his sister's autism and their mother's emotional trauma; the daily life of his family, living on Alcatraz; and his increasing maturity. Although Christopher Paul Curtis's Newbery Medal–winning *Bud,*

Not Buddy (I) does involve death, homelessness, and racism, its overall tone is one of hope mixed with poignant humor. Richard Peck's Newbery Medal–winning *A Year Down Yonder* and Newbery Honor–winning *A Long Way from Chicago: A Novel in Stories* (I–A) are set in the Depression-era small-town Midwest. In both books, the characterization and humor, as well as the sense of place and time, are outstanding. Teaching Idea 8.4 offers suggestions for exploring the theme of homelessness, a common occurrence during the Depression, across different genres.

• • WORLD WAR II • • AND ITS AFTERMATH

The years 1933 to 1946 encompassed Adolf Hitler's rise and fall in Germany and Japanese military activity in the Pacific, as well as the maneuvering of the Soviet Union to annex other countries. World War II brought into vivid awareness humanity's potential inhumanity, particularly toward our fellow human beings. The horrors of the period were so unthinkable that it was several decades before the story was told in books for young people. The children who read these books today are reading about the world of their grandparents and great-grandparents; these stories connect with many family histories.

Stories Set in Europe and Asia

The familiar adage that those who do not know the past are condemned to repeat it is adequate cause for attending to the tragedy of the Holocaust. The books describing Hitler's reign of terror, with its effects ultimately on all people, are a good place to begin. Many emphasize—some in small ways, others in larger—that in the midst of inhumanity there can be small acts of human kindness.

Despite their grimness, some books are affirmative: young people work in underground movements, strive against terrible odds, plan escapes, and struggle for survival. Some books show heroic resistance, in which characters fight back or live with dignity and hope in the face of a monstrous future. Jane Yolen's *The Devil's Arithmetic* (A) is a graphic, moving account of being a Jew in Poland during the Nazi persecution. Using the fantasy device of a time slip, Yolen plunges her young protagonist into the life that her aunt and her aunt's best friend endured at the hands of the Nazis. A less graphic book appropriate for upper elementary-school readers is Lois Lowry's Newbery Medal–winning *Number the Stars* (I). Lowry tells the story of how one Danish family saves the lives of their friends, the Rosens. The contrast between the implications of Nazi rule for the Jewish Ellen and the Christian Annemarie is striking.

Norway is the setting for Mary Casanova's *The Klipfish Code* (I)—the story of two children sent to the safety

Teaching Idea **8.4**

Genre Study: Compare Treatment of a Theme across Genres

Select a theme that crosses the boundaries of time, such as the effects of homelessness on people's lives. Gather primary sources, such as current or historical newspapers and magazines and contemporary and historical fiction and nonfiction. Ask students to read and respond to their reading, then to compare these experiences to their reading of a textbook or encyclopedia on the same topic. Discuss the different ways of knowing—cognitive and emotional—that these readings generate.

The following are titles that deal with homelessness during the Great Depression and today:

Contemporary Fiction

Bunting, Eve, *Fly Away Home* (1991) (I)

Fox, Paula, *Monkey Island* (1991) (A)

Johnson, Lindsay Lee, *Soul Moon Soup* (2002) (I–A)

Tolan, Stephanie, *Sophie and the Sidewalk Man* (1992) (I)

Historical Fiction

Bartoletti, Susan Campbell, *Christmas Promise* (2001) (P)

Choldenko, Gennifer, *Al Capone Does My Shirts* (2004) (I–A)

Curtis, Christopher Paul, *Bud, Not Buddy* (1999) (I)

DeFelice, Cynthia, *Nowhere to Call Home* (1999) (I–A)

Peterson, Jeanne Whitehouse, *Don't Forget Winona* (2000) (I)

Nonfiction

Coombs, Karen Mueller, *Children of the Dust Days* (2000) (I)

Wroble, Lisa, *Kids During the Great Depression* (1999) (I)

---

of an island to live with their grandfather and aunt, and how the war came with them. As the children struggle to adjust to a very different life, and to cope with the loneliness and fear of not knowing what is happening to their parents, young Marit decides to act to aid her country, doing what she can to hinder the Nazis during the occupation. William Durbin's *The Winter War* (I–A), set during the Soviet invasion of Finland in 1939, portrays the cunning and heroism of the Finns—some of them young boys—who used the snow and cold and their skill on skis to defeat the invading army. Both of these books portray heroic acts, but neither glorifies war.

Karen Hesse, intrigued by an article she read, began to research the Warsaw ghetto and Jewish resistance in Poland and wrote *The Cats in Krasinski Square* (I), a picturebook with a spare, poetic text and muted, lovely illustrations. The illustrations fill in details of time and place, and Hesse's words convey fear, determination, and the small joys of life in this story of resistance.

The Book Thief (A), a book that has become a favorite of young—and older—adults, is narrated by Death as Death tells the story of a young German foster child living outside of Munich. This 550-page novel by the award-winning Australian writer Markus Zusak is a moving and powerful statement of the humanity that can be found within the inhumanity of war.

Stories about life in Europe after the war explore how people began to mend their shattered lives. Mirjam Pressler's *Halinka* (A) explores the emotional damage of war through the eyes of a young girl sent to a home for troubled girls in Germany in the postwar years. This story, translated from the German, is truly a universal tribute to the power of love.

Despite the fact that American armed forces fought for four years in the Pacific, few children's and adolescent novels are set in this locale. Roland Smith's *Elephant Run* (I), set in Burma, is a war story and a thrilling adventure as well as an animal story—in this case, elephants. Padma Venkatraman's *Climbing the Stairs* (A), a novel set in the India of 1941 during the British occupation, is a coming-of-age story within a country, and a world, in turmoil.

A novel set in Korea under the control of the Japanese, Linda Sue Park's *When My Name Was Keoko* (A), chronicles the life of the children of a Korean scholar, revealing the small, quiet triumphs and the abiding fear of an oppressed people. Set within the larger historical context of the war, the struggles of Sun-hee, forced to take the Japanese name of Keoko, and her brother Tae-yul, renamed Nobuo, are revealed in alternating first-person points of view. What is happening in Korea is mirrored in the family's life, and the hope at the end of the novel is only slightly dimmed by the communist threat in the north.

discover our own connections with humanity throughout history, to make sense of our present through our past, and to think about our future in new ways.

Historical Fiction in the Classroom

History is made by people—people with strengths and weaknesses who experience victories and defeats. It reflects what they do, what they say, and what they are. Authors of books set in the past want young readers to understand that history is full of human beings—real people like themselves. Today's youth don't know a world without computers, technology, rapid transportation, and modern communication. When they read good historical fiction, however, they can imagine themselves living in another time and place. They can speculate about how they would have reacted and how they would have felt. They can read about ordinary people acting heroically. By doing so, they begin to understand the impact one person can have on history.

Historical fiction can help children discover their own place in the history of their world; it can give them a sense of the historical importance of their own lives. Well-written historical fiction can make the past alive, real, and meaningful to children who are living today and who will shape the world of tomorrow.

Reading historical fiction can help children realize that they are players on the historical stage and that their lives, too, will one day become part of history. As they read historical fiction, they come to realize the human drama inherent in history as well as the common themes that reach across time and cultures. Historical fiction offers students opportunities that history textbooks do not. Students who read trade books in addition to textbooks learn more than students who do not.

There are many ways to explore historical fiction with young readers. Here, we briefly describe two of them: presenting historical eras through multiple genres and exploring themes through historical fiction in combination with other genres.

Historical fiction can be linked to other genres: poetry, folklore, fantasy, biography, and nonfiction can be combined with historical fiction in the study of a particular time and place. For example, teachers who want their students to come to know about life in medieval England might want to combine folklore (such as the legends that surround King Arthur) with fantasy set in that period, as well as with books that combine fantasy with historical fiction (such as the novels of Elizabeth Wein and Kevin Crossley-Holland) and historical fiction (such as *Crispin*, *Yoss*, *Catherine, Called Birdy*, and *The Midwife's Apprentice*). Together,

these books provide a series of reading experiences that leave young readers so steeped in the time and place that they understand how people lived and thought, and how that influenced subsequent generations.

The first time one fifth-grade teacher tried using historical fiction, poetry, biography, and nonfiction instead of the social studies text for the study of the American Revolution, she was unsure of the possible outcomes. She asked students to read one novel, some poetry, one biography, and one informational book on that historical period. In addition, they read an encyclopedia account of one of the events described in the novel. The students then critically examined the presentations in the various sources. The teacher modeled the process, and they worked in collaborative learning groups to discuss their findings. The class concluded that no single book could have given them the basis for understanding that they gained from their wide reading. The children begged their teacher to use the same approach for the next social studies unit.

Another teacher worked with her third-grade children to develop a study plan for a unit on early settlers in America. She filled the room with many sources of information, including books, records, poetry, films, and pictures. The students spent several days exploring the material and making suggestions about topics that interested them. Their list included the pilgrims, Plymouth Rock, the *Mayflower*, and the first Thanksgiving. The group organized the ideas into reasonably logical categories, and students chose topics they wanted to pursue, identified sources of information, and began the research for the study. Examining the past in this way helped students begin to understand human behavior, the ways that people and societies interact, the concept of humans as social beings, and the values that make people human.

When studying the same period of time with his eighth-grade students, another teacher successfully combined historical fiction set in colonial times with some of the excellent nonfiction available about those times, such as *Sir Walter Ralegh and the Quest for El Dorado* (A) by Marc Aronson. This allowed his students to understand how the political systems and religious thought in England influenced the structures and thought of colonial America.

Thematically organized instruction is yet another way to explore historical fiction. History is always repeating itself, and many stories set in the past explore issues that are important to people today. Understanding human nature and social patterns can result from thinking about themes found in historical fiction and linking them to books in other genres and to our own lives. People have common needs; these universal needs can be identified as themes that permeate social interactions. For example, the quest for freedom and respect, the struggle between good

Teaching Idea 8.5

Explore Themes in Historical Fiction

Grouping historical fiction by theme allows students to see how people from diverse times and places grapple with common issues. You can also work with contemporary fiction and fantasy that consider the same themes. Here we present titles that explore aspects of prejudice, but historical fiction can be organized around many themes and also linked with other genres.

Bunting, Eve, *Spying on Miss Muller* (1995) (A)

Byars, Betsy, *Keeper of the Doves* (2002) (I)

Curtis, Christopher Paul, *The Watsons Go to Birmingham—1963* (1995) (I–A)

Franklin, Kristine, *The Grape Thief* (2003) (A)

Hesse, Karen, *Witness* (2001) (A)

Mochizuki, Ken, *Heroes* (1995) (I)

Taylor, Mildred, *The Friendship* (1987) (A)

_____, *Mississippi Bridge* (1990) (A)

_____, *Roll of Thunder, Hear My Cry* (1976) (A)

Wolff, Virginia Euwer, *Bat 6* (1998) (I–A)

---

and evil or between love and hate, and the determination to seek a better life are themes that are as old as time and as current as today. Historical fiction contains the stories of many people caught up in such struggles. Reading a number of books that explore the same theme across different periods of history allows students to understand the similarities of human needs across time; looking at books that explore the same theme in different cultures allows students to understand the similarities of human needs across peoples.

Prejudice, for example, is an issue that permeates many of the books discussed in this chapter, many of the books of contemporary realism discussed in Chapter 7, and even some of the fantasy and science fiction novels discussed in Chapter 6. You will find issues of prejudice in the biographies of people who faced racism and sexism and in the nonfiction accounts of segregation, women in the workforce, and life for immigrants, to name but a few subjects. The cultural dislocation experienced by immigrants is both a timeless and a contemporary issue. The contemporary fiction presented in Chapter 7 can be combined with historical fiction about the immigrant experience to explore this theme. Teaching Idea 8.5 offers ideas for thematic study.

The possibilities for thematic combinations across genres as well as within the historical fiction genre are many, as are the times and places that young readers can explore. There are resources available to help teachers identify books to use. An annotated bibliography published yearly by the Children's Book Council and the National Council for the Social Studies, *Notable Children's Trade Books in the Field of Social Studies*, is one such resource. This is available from either organization and is also published in the April/May issue of the journal *Social Education*. Other resources, such as the National Council of Teachers of English publication *Adventuring with Books*, present books by theme. These and other resources mentioned in Chapter 1 and Appendix B will help you construct powerful reading experiences for your students.

• • • SUMMARY • • •

When teachers put wonderful stories set in the past into the hands of children, the past comes alive for those students. By reading historical fiction, students see that history was lived by people who—despite their different dress, customs, and habits—were a lot like we are. Whether they are confronting the plague in Europe during the Middle Ages, fleeing from soldiers in the American West, or watching a young father go to war, today's readers can vicariously experience the events of the past. When children are immersed in a compelling story, history comes to life. It is only then that it becomes real and important, that it becomes meaningful for young readers.

✸ Indicates some aspect of diversity

Prehistoric Times

Crowley, Marjorie, *Dar and the Spear Thrower* (1994) (I)
✸ Dickinson, Peter, *Mana's Story* (1999) (I–A)
✸ _____, *Noli's Story* (1998) (I–A)
✸ _____, *Po's Story* (1998) (I–A)
✸ _____, *Suth's Story* (1998) (I–A)
Steele, William, *The Magic Amulet* (I–A)
✸ Sutcliff, Rosemary, *Warrior Scarlet* (1994) (A)

Ancient Times

✸ Barrett, Tracy, *Anna of Byzantium* (1999) (A)
Behn, Harry, *The Faraway Lurs* (1963) (I–A)
Carter, Dorothy, *His Majesty, Queen Hatshepsut* (1987) (I)
✸ Fletcher, Susan, *Shadow Spinner* (1998) (A)
Haugaard, Erik Christian, *The Samurai's Tale* (1984) (A)
✸ Lester, Julius, *Pharaoh's Daughter* (2002) (A)
Speare, Elizabeth George, *The Bronze Bow* (1961) (A)
Sutcliff, Rosemary, *The Eagle of the Ninth* (1993) (A)
_____, *The Lantern Bearers* (1994) (A)
_____, *The Shining Company* (1992) (A)

The Middle Ages

Avi, *Crispin: The Cross of Lead* (2002) (I–A)
Burkert, Nancy Ekholm, *Valentine and Orson* (1989) (A)
Cadnum, Michael, *The Book of the Lion* (2002) (A)
Cushman, Karen, *Catherine, Called Birdy* (1994) (A)
_____, *Matilda Bone* (2000) (A)
_____, *The Midwife's Apprentice* (1995) (I–A)
De Angeli, Marguerite, *The Door in the Wall* (1949) (I)
Gray, Elizabeth Vining, *Adam of the Road* (1942) (A)
Hirsch, Odo, *Yoss* (2004) (A)
Hoobler, Dorothy, and Thomas Hoobler, *The Demon in the Teahouse* (2001) (I)
Hunter, Mollie, *The King's Swift Rider* (1998) (A)
Jinks, Catherine, *Pagan in Exile* (2004) (A)
✸ Kelly, Eric, *The Trumpeter of Krakow* (1928) (A)
McCaffrey, Anne, *Black Horses for the King* (1996) (A)
✸ McCaughrean, Geraldine, *The Kite Rider* (2002) (A)
Morpurgo, Michael, *Sir Gawain and the Green Knight* (2004) (I–A)
✸ Newth, Mette, *The Dark Light* (1998) (A)
✸ _____, *The Transformation* (2000) (A)
✸ Park, Linda Sue, *A Single Shard* (2001) (A)
Sauerwein, Leigh, *Song for Eloise* (2003) (A)
Springer, Nancy, *I Am Mordred* (1998) (A)
✸ Temple, Frances, *The Beduins' Gazelle* (1996) (A)
✸ _____, *The Ramsay Scallop* (1994) (A)
✸ Walsh, Jill Paton, *The Emperor's Winding Sheet* (2004) (I–A)
✸ Wein, Elizabeth, *A Coalition of Lions* (2003) (A)

✸ _____, *The Sunbird* (2004) (A)
✸ _____, *The Winter Prince* (1993) (A)
✸ Yolen, Jane, and Robert Harris, *Girl in a Cage* (2002) (I–A)

The Renaissance and the Age of Exploration

Blackwood, Gary, *The Shakespeare Stealer* (1998) (I)
Cadnum, Michael, *Ship of Fire* (2003) (I–A)
Chibbaro, Julie, *Redemption* (2005) (A)
✸ Conrad, Pam, *Pedro's Journal* (1991) (I)
Cooper, Susan, *King of Shadows* (1999) (I)
✸ Dorris, Michael, *Morning Girl* (1992) (I)
Garden, Nancy, *Dove and Sword: A Novel of Joan of Arc* (1995) (I–A)
Konigsburg, E. L., *A Proud Taste for Scarlet and Miniver* (1973) (A)
✸ Park, Linda Sue, *The Kite Fighters* (2000) (I)
✸ Yolen, Jane, *Encounter* (1992) (I–A)
Yolen, Jane, and Robert Harris, *The Queen's Own Fool* (2000) (A)

Colonial through Post–Revolutionary War Times

Anderson, Laurie Halse, *Fever 1793* (2000) (I–A)
Aronson, Marc, *Sir Walter Ralegh and the Quest for El Dorado* (2000) (A)
Avi, *Encounter at Easton* (1980) (I)
_____, *The Fighting Ground* (1984) (I)
_____, *Night Journeys* (1979) (I)
Bowen, Gary, *Stranded at Plimoth Plantation 1626* (1994) (I)
✸ Bruchac, Joseph, *The Arrow over the Door* (1998) (I)
Carbone, Elisa, *Storm Warriors* (2001) (I)
✸ Clifton, Lucille, *The Times They Used to Be* (2000) (I–A)
Collier, James Lincoln, and Christopher Collier, *My Brother Sam Is Dead* (1974) (A)
_____, *War Comes to Willie Freeman* (1983) (I)
✸ Dorris, Michael, *Guests* (1994) (I)
✸ _____, *Sees Behind Trees* (1996) (I)
Fleischman, Paul, *Saturnalia* (1990) (A)
Forbes, Esther, *Johnny Tremain* (1969) (A)
Fritz, Jean, *Early Thunder* (1967) (A)
Jacques, Brian, *The Angel's Command* (2003) (I)
Krensky, Stephen, *The Printer's Apprentice* (1995) (I)
Lasky, Kathryn, *Beyond the Burning Time* (1996) (A)
Levitin, Sonia, *Roanoke: A Novel of the Lost Colony* (1973) (I–A)
✸ Lunn, Janet, *The Hollow Tree* (2000) (A)
Martin, Jacqueline Briggs, *Grandmother Bryant's Pocket* (1996) (P)
Meyer, L. A., *Bloody Jack: Being an Account of the Curious Adventures of Mary "Jacky" Faber, Ship's Boy* (2002) (I–A)
_____, *Curse of the Blue Tattoo: Being an Account of the Misadventures of Jacky Faber, Midshipman and Fine Lady* (2004) (I–A)
Monjo, F. N., *The House on Stink Alley* (1977) (I)
✸ Petry, Ann, *Tituba of Salem Village* (1964) (I)

Rinaldi, Ann, *A Break with Charity: A Story about the Salem Witch Trials* (1992) (A)
☀ Rockwood, Joyce, *To Spoil the Sun* (2003) (I–A)
☀ Speare, Elizabeth George, *The Sign of the Beaver* (1983) (I–A)
_____, *The Witch of Blackbird Pond* (1958) (I–A)
Updale, Eleanor, *Montmorency: Thief, Liar, Gentleman?* (2003) (I–A)
Yolen, Jane, and Robert Harris, *Prince Across the Water* (2004) (I–A)

Slavery, the Civil War, and Its Aftermath

Alcott, Louisa May, *Little Women* (1968) (A)
Armstrong, Jennifer, *The Dreams of Mairhe Mehan* (1996) (I–A)
_____, *Mairy Mehan Awake* (1997) (I–A)
_____, *Steal Away* (1992) (A)
Beatty, Patricia, *Charlie Skedaddle* (1987) (A)
_____, *Jayhawker* (1991) (A)
_____, *Turn Homeward, Hannalee* (1984) (A)
_____, *Who Comes with Cannons?* (1992) (A)
Blos, Joan, *A Gathering of Days: A New England Girl's Journal, 1830–32* (1969) (A)
Climo, Shirley, *A Month of Seven Days* (1987) (A)
Collier, James Lincoln, and Christopher Collier, *With Every Drop of Blood* (1994) (A)
☀ Cox, Clinton, *Undying Glory* (1991) (I–A)
Elliott, Laura M., *Annie Between the States* (2004) (I–A)
Fleischman, Paul, *Bull Run* (1993) (I–A)
☀ Fox, Paula, *The Slave Dancer* (1997) (A)
Fritz, Jean, *Brady* (1960) (I–A)
Gaeddert, Louann, *Breaking Free* (1994) (I–A)
Gauch, Patricia Lee, *Thunder at Gettysburg* (1975) (I)
Hahn, Mary Downing, *Hear the Wind Blow: A Novel of the Civil War* (2003) (A)
☀ Hansen, Joyce, *The Heart Calls Home* (1999) (A)
☀ _____, *Out from this Place* (1988) (A)
☀ _____, *Which Way Freedom?* (1986) (A)
Hesse, Karen, *A Light in the Storm: The Civil War Diary of Amelia Martin* (1999) (I)
☀ Hopkinson, Deborah, *Sweet Clara and the Freedom Quilt* (1993) (P)
Houston, Gloria, *Bright Freedom's Song* (1998) (I–A)
Hunt, Irene, *Across Five Aprils* (1964) (A)
☀ Hurmence, Belinda, *Tancy* (1984) (I–A)
☀ Johnson, Dolores, *Now Let Me Fly: The Story of a Slave Family* (1993) (I)
☀ Johnston, Tony, *The Wagon* (1996) (I)
Keith, Harold, *Rifles for Watie* (1957) (A)
☀ Lester, Julius, *Day of Tears* (2005) (I–A)
☀ _____, *Long Journey Home* (1972) (A)
Lyons, Mary E., *Letters from a Slave Girl: The Story of Harriet Jacobs* (1992) (A)
Monjo, F. N., *The Drinking Gourd* (1993) (P–I)
Paulsen, Gary, *Soldier's Heart* (1998) (A)
☀ Peck, Richard, *The River Between Us* (2003) (A)
☀ Polacco, Patricia, *Pink and Say* (1994) (I–A)
Reeder, Carolyn, *Shades of Gray* (1989) (A)
☀ Ruby, Lois, *Soon to Be Free* (2000)
☀ _____, *Steal Away Home* (1994) (A)
☀ Siegelson, Kim, *Trembling Earth* (2004) (I–A)
☀ Taylor, Mildred, *The Land* (2001) (A)
☀ Turner, Ann, *Nettie's Trip South* (1987) (I–A)
☀ Winter, Jeanette, *Follow the Drinking Gourd* (1988) (P–I)

Westward Migration

Ambrose, Stephen, *This Vast Land* (2003) (A)
Armstrong, Jennifer, *Black-Eyed Susan* (1995) (I)
Arrington, Francis, *Bluestem* (2000) (I)
_____, *Prairie Whispers* (2003) (I)
Avi, *The Barn* (1994) (I–A)
Beatty, Patricia, *Wait for Me, Watch for Me, Eula Bea* (1978) (A)
Brink, Carol Ryrie, *Caddie Woodlawn* (1935) (I–A)
☀ Burks, Brian, *Runs with Horses* (1995) (A)
Cadnum, Michael, *Blood Gold* (2004) (I–A)
Coerr, Eleanor, *Buffalo Bill and the Pony Express* (1995) (P)
_____, *The Josephina Story Quilt* (1986) (P)
Conrad, Pam, *Prairie Songs* (1985) (A)
Cushman, Karen, *The Ballad of Lucy Whipple* (1996) (A)
_____, *Rodzina* (2003) (I)
Ellsworth, Loretta, *The Shrouding Woman* (2002) (I)
☀ Erdrich, Louise, *The Birchbark House* (1999) (I)
☀ _____, *The Game of Silence* (2005) (I)
☀ _____, *The Porcupine Year* (2008) (I)
Figley, Marty Rhodes, *The Schoolchildren's Blizzard* (2004) (P)
Fritz, Jean, *The Cabin Faced West* (1958) (I)
☀ Goble, Paul, *Death of the Iron Horse* (1987) (I)
Gray, Dianne, *Holding Up the Earth* (2000) (A)
_____, *Together Apart* (2002) (A)
Harvey, Brett, *Cassie's Journey: Going West in the 1860s* (1988) (P–I)
_____, *My Prairie Christmas* (1990) (P–I)
_____, *My Prairie Year: Based on the Diary of Elenore Plaisted* (1986) (P–I)
Howard, Ellen, *The Chickenhouse House* (1991) (P–I)
_____, *Edith Herself* (1987) (P–I)
_____, *Sister* (1999) (P–I)
Irwin, Hadley, *Jim-Dandy* (1994) (I–A)
Johnston, Tony, *The Quilt Story* (1997) (P)
LaFaye, Alexandra, *Worth* (2004) (I–A)
MacLachlan, Patricia, *Caleb's Story* (2001) (P–I)
_____, *More Perfect Than the Moon* (2004) (P–I)
_____, *Sarah, Plain and Tall* (1985) (P–I)
_____, *Skylark* (1994) (P–I)
_____, *Three Names* (1991) (P)
McCaughrean, Geraldine, *Stop the Train!* (2003) (P)
McMullan, Kate, *My Travels with Capts. Lewis and Clark by George Shannon* (2004) (I–A)
☀ Meyer, Carolyn, *Where the Broken Heart Still Beats* (1992) (A)
☀ Myers, Walter Dean, *The Righteous Revenge of Artemis Bonner* (1995) (I–A)
☀ O'Dell, Scott, *Sing Down the Moon* (1970) (A)
☀ _____, *Thunder Rolling in the Mountains* (1992) (A)
☀ Oswald, Nancy, *Nothing Here But Stones* (2004) (I)
Paulsen, Gary, *Call Me Francis Tucket* (1995) (I)
Turner, Ann, *Dakota Dugout* (1985) (P–I)
_____, *Grasshopper Summer* (1989) (I–A)
Van Leeuwen, Jean, *Bound for Oregon* (1994) (I–A)
_____, *Going West* (1991) (P)
Warner, Sally, *Finding Hattie* (2001) (I)
☀ Whelan, Gloria, *Next Spring an Oriole* (1987) (I)
_____, *Night of the Full Moon* (1993) (I)
Wilder, Laura Ingalls, **Little House** series (1932–1943) (I)
Wolf, Allan, *New Found Land: Lewis and Clark's Voyage of Discovery* (2004) (A)
☀ Yep, Laurence, *The Traitor: 1885* (2003) (I–A)

The New Century

Blos, Joan, *Brooklyn Doesn't Rhyme* (1994) (I)
Boling, Katharine, *January 1905* (2004) (I–A)
Byars, Betsy, *Keeper of the Doves* (2002) (I)
Cameron, Eleanor, *Julia and the Hand of God* (1977) (I)
_____ , *Julia's Magic* (1984) (I)
_____ , *The Private Worlds of Julia Redfern* (1988) (I)
_____ , *A Room Made of Windows* (1971) (I)
_____ , *That Julia Redfern* (1982) (I)
Crew, Linda, *Brides of Eden: A True Story Imagined* (2001) (A)
DeFelice, Cynthia, *Lostman's River* (1994) (A)
Donnelly, Jennifer, *A Northern Light* (2003) (A)
Fleischman, Paul, *The Borning Room* (1991) (A)
✳ Giff, Patricia Reilly, *A House of Tailors* (2004) (I–A)
✳ _____ , *Maggie's Door* (2003) (I–A)
✳ _____ , *Nory Ryan's Song* (2000) (I–A)
Hahn, Mary Downing, *Anna on the Farm* (2001) (I)
Hall, Donald, *Lucy's Christmas* (1994) (P)
_____ , *Lucy's Summer* (1995) (P)
✳ Howard, Elizabeth Fitzgerald, *Aunt Flossie's Hats (and Crab Cakes Later)* (1990) (P)
✳ _____ , *Chita's Christmas* (1989) (P)
✳ _____ , *Papa Tells Chita a Story* (1995) (P)
✳ Ibbotson, Eva, *The Star of Kazan* (2004) (I)
Jocelyn, Marthe, *Mable Riley: A Reliable Record of Humdrum, Peril, and Romance* (2004) (I)
✳ Levinson, Riki, *I Go with My Family to Grandma's* (1986) (P)
✳ _____ , *Watch the Stars Come Out* (1985) (P)
✳ Levitin, Sonia, *Journey to America* (1970) (I)
✳ _____ , *Silver Days* (1989) (I)
Lovelace, Maud Hart, *Betsy-Tacy* (1940) (I)
_____ , *Betsy-Tacy and Tib* (1941) (I)
✳ Lowry, Lois, *The Silent Boy* (2003) (I–A)
Martin, Jacqueline Briggs, *The Camp, the Ice, and the Boat Called Fish* (2001) (I)
_____ , *On Sand Island* (2003) (P)
✳ Mayerson, Evelyn, *The Cat Who Escaped from Steerage* (1990) (I)
✳ McDonald, Megan, *The Potato Man* (1994) (P–I)
✳ McKissack, Patricia, *Mirandy and Brother Wind* (1998) (P)
Moeri, Louise, *The Devil in Ol' Rosie* (2001) (I)
Nagell, Judy, *One Way to Ansonia* (1985) (A)
Oneal, Zibby, *A Long Way to Go* (1990) (A)
✳ Paterson, Katherine, *Lyddie* (1991) (A)
Peck, Richard, *The Teacher's Funeral: A Comedy in Three Parts* (2004) (I–A)
✳ Sandin, Joan, *The Long Way to a New Land* (1981) (P)
✳ _____ , *The Long Way Westward* (1989) (P)
✳ Schmidt, Gary, *Lizzie Bright and the Buckminster Boy* (2004) (I–A)
Skurzynski, Gloria, *The Tempering* (1983) (A)
✳ Taylor, Mildred, *The Well: David's Story* (1995) (A)

World War I and Its Aftermath

Doyle, Brian, *Mary Ann Alice* (2001) (I–A)
✳ Franklin, Kristine, *The Grape Thief* (2003) (A)
Harlow, Joan Hiatt, *Thunder from the Sea* (2004) (I)
Houston, Gloria, *The Year of the Perfect Christmas Tree* (1988) (P–I)
Kinsey-Warnock, Natalie, *The Night the Bells Rang* (1991) (I)
Lawrence, Iain, *Lord of the Nutcracker Men* (2001) (I–A)

✳ Morpurgo, Michael, *Private Peaceful* (2004) (A)
Rostkowski, Margaret, *After the Dancing Days* (1986) (A)
Smith, Barry, *Minnie and Ginger* (1990) (P)
Whelan, Gloria, *The Impossible Journey* (2003) (I)
Wulffson, Don, *Soldier X* (2001) (A)

The Great Depression

Avi, *Smugglers' Island* (1983) (I)
Bryant, Jen, *The Trial* (2004) (I)
✳ Disher, Garry, *The Bamboo Flute* (1992) (I–A)
Durbin, William, *The Darkest Evening* (2004) (A)
French, Jackie, *Somewhere around the Corner* (1994) (A)
Griffin, Adele, *Hannah, Divided* (2002) (I)
Hale, Marian, *The Truth about Sparrows* (2004) (I–A)
Hesse, Karen, *Out of the Dust* (1997) (A)
Houston, Gloria, *Littlejim* (1990) (I–A)
Levinson, Riki, *Boys Here—Girls There* (1993) (I)
✳ Mitchell, Margaree King, *Uncle Jed's Barbershop* (1993) (P–I)
✳ Parkinson, Siobhan, *Kathleen: The Celtic Knot* (2003) (I)
Peterson, Jeanne Whitehouse, *Don't Forget Winona* (2000) (I)
Reeder, Carolyn, *Grandpa's Mountain* (1991) (I–A)
_____ , *Moonshiner's Son* (1993) (A)
✳ Taylor, Mildred, *Let the Circle Be Unbroken* (1981) (A)
✳ _____ , *Mississippi Bridge* (1990) (A)
✳ _____ , *The Road to Memphis* (1990) (A)
✳ _____ , *Roll of Thunder, Hear My Cry* (1976) (A)
✳ _____ , *Song of the Trees* (1985) (I)
Turner, Ann, *Dust for Dinner* (1995) (P)
Wells, Rosemary, *Wingwalker* (2002) (I)

World War II and Its Aftermath

Ackerman, Karen, *When Mama Retires* (1992) (P)
Avi, *Who Was That Masked Man, Anyway?* (1992) (A)
✳ Bunting, Eve, *Spying on Miss Muller* (1995) (A)
✳ Chotjewitz, David, *Daniel Half Human and the Good Nazi* (2004) (A)
Cormier, Robert, *Other Bells for Us to Ring* (1990) (I–A)
✳ Degens, T., *On the Third Ward* (1990) (A)
✳ _____ , *Transport 451-R* (1974) (A)
✳ Doyle, Brian, *Boy O'Boy* (2003) (I–A)
✳ Gallico, Paul, *The Snow Goose* (1967) (A)
✳ Hautzig, Esther, *The Endless Steppe* (1995) (A)
Holt, Kimberly Willis, *My Louisiana Sky* (1998) (I)
Houston, Gloria, *But No Candy* (1992) (P)
✳ Innocenti, Robert, *Rose Blanche* (1985) (I–A)
Janeczko, Paul, *Worlds Afire* (2004) (A)
Johnston, Julie, *Hero of Lesser Causes* (1992) (I–A)
Kerr, Judith, *When Hitler Stole Pink Rabbit* (1971) (I–A)
Kositsky, Lynne, *The Thought of High Windows* (2004) (I–A)
✳ Laird, Christa, *But Can the Phoenix Sing?* (1993) (A)
✳ _____ , *Shadow of the Wall* (1990) (A)
Lawrence, Iain, *B for Buster* (2004) (N)
✳ Levitin, Sonia, *Room in the Heart* (2003) (A)
Lingard, Joan, *Between Two Worlds* (1991) (A)
_____ , *Tug of War* (1989) (A)
✳ Lowry, Lois, *Number the Stars* (1989) (I)
Magorian, Michelle, *Back Home* (1984) (A)
_____ , *Good Night, Mr. Tom* (1981) (A)
✳ Matas, Carol, *After the War* (1996) (A)
✳ _____ , *Daniel's Story* (1993) (A)

Mazer, Harry, *A Boy At War: A Novel of Pearl Harbor* (2001) (A)
☀ Mochizuki, Ken, *Baseball Saved Us* (1993) (I)
Morpurgo, Michael, *Waiting for Anya* (1991) (A)
☀ Mosher, Richard, *Zazoo* (2001) (A)
☀ Oppenheim, Shulamith Levey, *The Lily Cupboard* (1992) (P)
☀ Orlev, Uri, *The Island on Bird Street* (1983) (A)
☀ _____, *The Lady with the Hat* (1995) (A)
☀ _____, *Lydia, Queen of Palestine* (1993) (A)
☀ _____, *The Man from the Other Side* (1991) (A)
☀ Park, Linda Sue, *When My Name Was Keoko* (2002) (A)
Pearson, Kit, *The Lights Go On Again* (1993) (I–A)
_____, *Looking at the Moon* (1991) (I–A)
_____, *The Sky Is Falling* (1990) (I–A)
☀ Pressler, Mirjam, *Halinka* (1998) (A)
☀ _____, *Malka* (2002) (A)
☀ Recorvitz, Helen, *Where Heroes Hide* (2002) (I)
☀ Reiss, Johanna, *The Upstairs Room* (1987) (A)
Rylant, Cynthia, *I Had Seen Castles* (1993) (A)
Schmidt, Gary, *Mara's Stories: Glimmers in the Darkness* (2001) (I–A)
☀ Spinelli, Jerry, *Milkweed* (2003) (A)
Stevenson, James, *Don't You Know There's a War On?* (1992) (P)
Thesman, Jean, *Molly Donnelly* (1993) (A)
☀ Uchida, Yoshiko, *The Invisible Thread* (1991) (A)
☀ _____, *Journey Home* (1978) (A)
☀ _____, *Journey to Topaz* (1971) (A)
Vos, Ida, *Anna Is Still Here* (1993) (I–A)
_____, *Dancing on the Bridge of Avignon* (1995) (A)
_____, *Hide and Seek* (1991) (I–A)
☀ Watkins, Yoko Kawashima, *My Brother, My Sister, and I* (1994) (A)
☀ _____, *So Far from the Bamboo Grove* (1986) (A)
Westall, Robert, *The Kingdom by the Sea* (1983) (A)
Yolen, Jane, *All Those Secrets of the World* (1991) (P–I)
☀ _____, *The Devil's Arithmetic* (1988) (A)

The 1950s through the 1980s: Political and Social Turmoil

Almond, David, *The Fire-Eaters* (2004) (A)
☀ Baille, Allan, *Little Brother* (1992) (A)
Bunting, Eve, *The Wall* (1990) (I)
☀ Crowe, Chris, *Mississippi Trial, 1955* (2002) (A)
☀ Curtis, Christopher Paul, *The Watsons Go to Birmingham—1963* (1995) (I–A)
Dahlberg, Maurine, *Escape to West Berlin* (2004) (I–A)
Geisert, Bonnie, *Prairie Summer* (2002) (I)
☀ Harrington, Janice, *Going North* (2004) (I)
☀ Ho, Minfong, *The Clay Marble* (1991) (A)
☀ _____, *Gathering the Dew* (2003) (A)
☀ _____, *Rice Without Rain* (1990) (A)
Lyon, George Ella, *Sonny's House of Spies* (2004) (I)
☀ Martin, Ann, *A Corner of the Universe* (2002) (I)
_____, *Here Today* (2004) (I)
McCord, Patricia, *Pictures in the Dark* (2004) (I–A)
☀ McKissack, Patricia, *Tippy Lemmey* (2003) (P)
☀ Mochizuki, Ken, *Baseball Saved Us* (1993) (I)
☀ _____, *Heroes* (1995) (I)
☀ Myers, Walter Dean, *Fallen Angels* (1988) (A)
Nelson, Theresa, *And One for All* (1989) (A)
☀ Nelson, Vaunda Micheaux, *Mayfield Crossing* (1993) (A)
☀ Oughton, Jerrie, *Music from a Place Called Half Moon* (1995) (I–A)
☀ Paek, Min, *Aekyung's Dream* (1988) (P)
Paterson, Katherine, *Park's Quest* (1988) (A)
Paulsen, Gary, *Harris and Me* (1993) (A)
Rostkowski, Margaret, *The Best of Friends* (1989) (A)
Sherlock, Patti, *Letters from Wolfie* (2004) (A)
☀ Smothers, Ethel Footman, *Moriah's Pond* (1994) (I–A)
Thesman, Jean, *Rachel Chance* (1990) (A)
White, Ruth, *Buttermilk Hill* (2004) (I)
_____, *Tadpole* (2003) (I)
☀ Wiles, Deborah, *Freedom Summer* (2001) (I)

Biography and Memoir

But even if drastic social conditions produced a new leader like Hitler, there's no reason the world should extend the same leeway to him that it did toward his predecessor. With the hindsight of history, it's clear that the Führer's rise to power could have been stopped, or at least braked, at many places along the way. If the moderate political parties in Germany had put aside their differences and joined forces against him, he might have been defeated at the polls in the crucial elections of the early 1930s. Later, if France and Britain had taken a strong stand, he might not have dared to reoccupy the Rhineland, or invade Austria and Czechoslovakia, or launch a Blitzkreig attack on Poland.

Above all, if more of Germany's Jews—not to mention the religious and political leaders of other countries—had taken seriously what Hitler wrote in Mein Kampf when it first appeared, the worst effects of the Holocaust might have been lessened if not averted entirely. So many ifs. The trick will be to apply them before rather than after the fact, should another Hitler come to power in a time of crisis.

At the end of the political testament he dictated in the last days of his life, Adolf Hitler refused to accept the reality of Germany's defeat. Instead, he said the six-year war the country had waged would one day be recognized as "the most glorious and valiant manifestation of a nation's will to existence." Going further, he predicted that National Socialism would rise again, and that the sacrifices he and his soldiers had made in the struggle against "international Jewry" would be vindicated at last.

The challenge to the world's peoples couldn't be clearer. Now and in the future, every possible step must be taken to ensure that the Führer's final predictions never come true.

—JAMES CROSS GIBLIN,
The Life and Death of Adolf Hitler,
pp. 222–223

When Susan decided to read Giblin's Sibert Award–winning biography of Hitler with her eighth-grade class, she sent a letter home to the parents of her students, explaining why they would be spending time learning and talking about the life of a man whom most people consider evil. In that letter she talked about how a study of Hitler's life related to the history that students were learning in social studies, and also about how she had developed a thematic organization for the semester that centered around tolerance. She didn't know a more powerful example of what happens when people act on their prejudice than the Holocaust, she told them, and she wanted to read this biography to spark conversations about the consequences of acts of bigotry against others. She wanted her students to link what happened in Germany to the experiences of Native Americans and African Americans, almost all immigrant groups that came to the United States, and to religious, racial, and social intolerance today. Her letter was so persuasive that all parents gave permission, and her students embarked on a study of power gone terribly wrong.

As they discussed the information that Giblin presents, the students came to realize that Hitler was not born a monster, but that his attitudes and experiences, as well as the times in which he lived, made him into one. Perhaps more than anything else, this shook their confidence as they realized that human beings are capable of evil on both a small and a grand scale.

Defining Biography and Memoir

Biographies, autobiographies, and memoirs are narratives; they all tell the story of the life or a portion of the life of a real person. Autobiographies and memoirs are written by the subject himself or herself. Biographies and autobiographies range from mostly fictional to authentic—the genre straddles the boundary between fiction and nonfiction. Memoirs are interpretive accounts in which facts and events in the life of the author are selected, arranged, and constructed in order to bring out a particular theme or personality trait. Memoirs certainly contain facts, but they are based upon and interpreted through memory.

Biographies and memoirs may be episodic; that is, the author may highlight a particular part or parts of a life to illustrate the subject's character or to explore an especially important event in the life of the subject. In episodic biographies, writers can present a number of details within a manageable length, providing young readers the details they relish without sacrificing authenticity. Some-

times episodic biographies center around the early years of the subject, as in Catherine Brighton's *Keep Your Eye on the Kid: The Early Years of Buster Keaton* (P), in which she uses comic book frames to reflect the action. She also includes a brief bibliography, a list of Keaton's films, and an author's note, so that readers can discover more about the life of this man as an adult. Judith St. George focuses on the early years of Abraham Lincoln in *Stand Tall, Abe Lincoln* (P–I), illustrated by Matt Faulkner.

Robert Burleigh's *Langston's Train Ride* (I) is an excellent example of an episodic biography that focuses on a pivotal event in the life of the subject. For Langston Hughes, this event was the train trip when he wrote his beautiful poem "The Negro Speaks of Rivers" and realized that he was a poet. Through the device of Langston's reflection about his life as he traveled, Burleigh is able to present other facts about him as well. Jeanette Winter's small biography *Beatrix: Various Episodes from the Life of Beatrix Potter* (P) is simple, yet full of details of the life and thoughts of this special writer. Winter presents several key episodes in Potter's life and uses Potter's own words in her letters and journals to portray her subject.

Other biographies are more complete, spanning the entire life of a subject. Some, for primary- and intermediate-grade readers, are simplified, presenting what is in effect an outline of the subject's life. Oversimplification can result in an incomplete picture of both the individual and the times (Saul, 1986). David Adler's many biographies for primary-grade readers are examples of simplified biography. Even though they are factual, they contain few details and are most useful as an introduction to important people in history; some argue that their very simplification amounts to distortion. On the other hand, Barbara Kerley's Sibert Honor–winning *What to Do about Alice? How Alice Roosevelt Broke the Rules, Charmed the World, and Drove Her Father Teddy Crazy* (P–I) presents the life of this interesting woman from childhood through adulthood in a manner that intrigues young readers. Even biographies for younger readers can rely on fact and original source material, as Kerley's does. Biographies for older readers are even more inclusive of fact and source documents. We discuss some of those biographies, such as Russell Freedman's *Lincoln: A Photobiography* (I–A) and James Cross Giblin's *The Life and Death of Adolf Hitler* (A) later in this chapter.

Biographies also vary according to presentation. Some biographies focus on a single individual, whereas others are collective biographies, or biographies about several individuals. These usually focus around a theme or other unifying principle. Catherine Thimmesh has gathered brief biographical sketches of women in politics in *Madam President: The Extraordinary, True (and Evolving) Story of Women in Politics* (I) and arranged them so that young readers can learn about some important women and their accomplishments while also understanding the realities and possibilities of today. Laurie Halse Anderson chose to look at other "unsung" female heroes in *Independent Dames: What You Never Knew About the Women and Girls of the American Revolution* (P–I). Anderson's humorous text is complimented by Matt Faulkner's illustrations, and young readers learn about some amazing girls and women. A timeline, additional facts, bibliography, web resources, and an index add to the information presented in the text itself.

A Brief History of Biography and Memoir for Young Readers

Biography was once regarded as an opportunity for young people to read about people they might emulate. For example, they might strive to be as honest as Abraham Lincoln or as brave as Lewis and Clark. Biographers in the nineteenth and early twentieth centuries wrote only about the good qualities of their subjects. During this period of intense nationalism, these writers deified America's heroes in a conscious effort to provide children with a set of role models, even if the depictions of these role models were false. Early biographies often did not include source material; documentation was rare. It was also difficult to separate fact from opinion because most biographers did not attempt to do so. Accuracy was less important than story, it seemed. Further, most of the early biographies were about white men of fame, and many were in multivolume series.

Fortunately, contemporary biographers are more likely to consider their subjects in a less adulatory and more realistic manner. We now view biography not as an opportunity for moral enlightenment, but as a chance for children to learn about themselves as they learn about the lives and times of people who made or are making a significant impact on the world (Herman, 1978). With this altered view of the role of biography have come books that focus on people who are not heroes. Today, there are biographies of ordinary, contemporary people living out their lives, such as Claire Nivola's *Planting the Trees of Kenya: The Story of Wangari Maathai* (P), a brilliantly told and illustrated story of the Kenyan woman who rallies the women of her country to plant trees. Eventually, they are joined by men and children, and even soldiers. Wangari Maathai, a contemporary hero, won the Nobel Peace Prize in 2004. There are also biographies of villains, such as James Cross Giblin's *The Life and Death of Adolf Hitler* (A). The genre has also grown to encompass the diversity that exists in the world. Perhaps it has not grown quickly enough, but it is no longer as difficult to find excellent biographies of African American, Native American, Asian American, Latino, and international subjects. Biographies of all kinds of people allow young readers to understand both history and the contemporary world.

Still today, some very engaging biographies are biographical fiction, consisting almost entirely of imagined conversations and reconstructed events in the life of an individual. Francesco D'Adamo's *Iqbal* (I–A) is a fictionalized account of the life of an actual person, thirteen-year-old Iqbal, who worked to change the conditions of the child laborers who create Pakistani rugs. Joseph Bruchac's *Pocahontas* (I–A), told in alternating chapters by Pocahontas and John Smith, is another intriguing work of biographical fiction. Both books are classified as fiction, but they are based in part on factual evidence about a real person's life.

Today, memoirs are an increasingly popular form of writing in which an individual explores his or her own life; they are truthful, without necessarily being completely true. Francisco Jiménez's memoirs, *The Circuit: Stories from the Life of a Migrant Child* and *Breaking Through* (I–A), are stories about his life as a migrant child.

They are classified as fiction. In contrast, Chris Crutcher's *King of the Mild Frontier: An Ill-Advised Autobiography* (A) is classified as nonfiction, yet both are stories about their lives as recalled by the authors. The line is a fine one and is made even more complicated by such books as Milton Meltzer's *Lincoln: In His Own Words* and *Frederick Douglass: In His Own Words* (A), in which the author uses selections from the speeches and writings of his subjects, connected by his own commentary, to create a form very much like a memoir.

Today, most biographies for young readers are authentic biographies, well-documented stories about individuals in which even the dialogue is based on some record of what was actually said or written by particular people at particular times. Russell Freedman is an accomplished biographer, and his work, such as the Newbery Medal–winning *Lincoln: A Photobiography* (I–A), is filled with archival photographs, documented through multiple sources, and written with passion and verve. We take a close look at his Sibert Award–winning *The Voice That Challenged a Nation: Marian Anderson and the Struggle for Equal Rights* (I–A) later in this chapter.

Today's biographers also often rely on illustrations to convey information, whether in picturebooks or full-length formats. Picturebook biographies present a subject through both text and art. In Rosemary Bray's *Martin Luther King* (P–I), Malcah Zeldis's folk art paintings brilliantly depict the important moments of King's life, and evoke the spirit of the times and of the man himself. Illustrated biographies often make use of archival photographs and other documents, such as newspaper clippings, to present visual information that complements and extends the text. Melissa Sweet's mixed-media illustrations for Jen Bryant's Caldecott Honor–winning *A River of Words: The Story of William Carlos Williams* (I) earned a spot on the *New York Times* top ten illustrated books for 2008. This terrific book is filled with Williams' own words, with lines from his poems often incorporated into the accompanying illustrations.

Any good biography illuminates the interaction between an individual and historical events, demonstrating how a person's time and culture influence his or her life even as that person influences his or her time and culture. Today, we are fortunate to have vivid and accurate portrayals of the *people* of history, stories that make history come alive for young readers.

Considering Quality in Biography and Memoir

Biographies and memoirs are stories of people's lives and, like all narratives, are evaluated in terms of the characterization, the presentation of plot and setting, the style of the writing, the unifying theme, and, in the case of picturebooks or illustrated books, the quality and contribution of the illustrations. As biographies, they are also subject to special considerations because they are portraits of real people, complete with both strengths and weaknesses. Further, biographies and memoirs must present accurate depictions of the time and place in which the subject lived. Even biographical fiction and memoirs should be grounded in fact and should present authentic information about a person's life and times in an engaging style. Figure 9.1 presents a brief list of criteria for evaluating biography and memoir.

• • ACCURACY • •

Increasingly, biographers for young readers rely heavily on primary sources; good biographies are always grounded in fact. Biographies need to present both a vivid and an accurate picture of the life and the times of the subject. As is true of historical fiction, accuracy is a complex criterion. Careful biographers do not go beyond the facts as we know them today, but they do interpret these facts through the eyes of the present. Consider, for example, how early biographies of Rosa Parks present her as a woman who

*Melissa Sweet's mixed-media illustrations that incorporate the poet's own words truly illuminate the work of the poet in **A River of Words: The Story of William Carlos Williams** by Jen Bryant.*

Figure 9.1

Considering Quality in Biography and Memoir

Accuracy and Social Details

✧ The story is grounded in fact. Source material is noted for biography. For a memoir, there is enough truthful information to make it worth reading.

✧ The facts and story line are seamlessly integrated.

✧ The details are vivid, accurate, and linked to the individual's accomplishments.

Portrayal of the Subject

✧ The subject's character is well developed and multidimensional.

✧ The author avoids stereotypes.

Style

✧ The writing style is comprehensible and engaging.

✧ Complex topics are explained adequately.

Theme

✧ There is a unifying theme that highlights the special qualities of the subject.

Illustrations

✧ The illustrations help the reader visualize the time and place.

✧ The illustrations illuminate the character of the subject.

sat down in the front of the bus because she was tired. Later portraits, such as **Rosa Parks: My Story** (I), reflect society's acknowledgment of the careful organization of the civil rights movement and present her action as the planned, deliberate attempt to confront unjust practices and laws that it was.

Authentic biographies are anchored by primary sources: letters, diaries, collected papers, and photographs. They usually contain lists of sources the author consulted and address the author's process. Biographical fiction goes well beyond what is known about a subject; it would be a mistake to think of it as a factual resource. Memoirs, too, are not meant to be a source of facts, but rather an evocation of a subject's life in the subject's own

words. Both biographical fiction and memoir, however, should be truthful.

Russell Freedman's **Lincoln: A Photobiography** (I–A) exemplifies what an authentic biography should be. Freedman is always careful to distinguish fact from opinion and truth from legend. He presents a significant amount of interesting historical detail. His text includes many direct quotations from Lincoln, all set off with quotation marks. These quotations, the historical facts, and social details are all taken from sources listed at the end of the book. Freedman follows the text with a sampling of Lincoln's famous quotations, with sources indicated, along with the sources for the quotations that begin each chapter. After these are a list and description of historic sites having to do with Lincoln's life, a description of source books about Lincoln, acknowledgments, and a useful five-page index. This end material and the photographs of historical documents that appear throughout the text all attest to the integrity and thoroughness of this biography.

In an interesting departure from the norm, Candace Fleming uses archival material not only to support but actually to format her book **Ben Franklin's Almanac: Being a True Account of the Good Gentleman's Life** (I–A). Fleming patterns her book on Franklin's own *Poor Richard's Almanack*, organizing her information around the major interests in Franklin's life—science, public service, family, time in France—and including reproductions of etchings, paintings, and cartoons of the time along with Franklin's own words. The originality in the design of the book is matched by the authenticity of its content.

Judging the accuracy of a biographer's presentation is not easy unless one happens to be an expert on the subject. Asking yourself the following questions can help you judge the accuracy of a biography: What sources did the author use? Are these sources documented? Does the account of the subject's life seem truthful according to what you already know? Are unnecessary generalizations about the people of the time or stereotypes of gender, ethnic, or racial groups evident? With memoirs, it is slightly different, as the "sources" for most memoirs are, in fact, memories, or perhaps diaries, with supporting detail from family and friends.

• • SETTING AND PLOT • •

A subject's personality and accomplishments are more understandable when they are presented against a rich and vivid depiction of the social details of life. Readers enjoy these social details, relishing the minutiae of another person's life. Further, settings need to depict the cultural forces that influenced the development of the subject's character and accomplishments. Careful biographers find a balance between telling everything and telling just enough to portray a person's life accurately, in an interesting manner. Many subjects of biographies for children had lives that were touched with pain, suffering, and great hardship; many great achievements were won at great cost. These issues must be carefully but honestly presented in biographies for young readers.

Good examples of this can be found in many biographies of Dr. Martin Luther King, Jr. The times that shaped Dr. King were not easy times; he grew up in a country deeply divided by racism. In any biography of King written for young readers, the social climate needs to be honestly portrayed in a way that is understandable to children without being overwhelming. Balancing the needs of the audience and the accuracy of the story is especially difficult when writing for primary-grade readers. Rosemary Bray's **Martin Luther King** is an outstanding example of the achievement of this balance, in part because of the strength of the illustrations. So, too, are Doreen Rappaport's **Martin's Big Words: The Life of Dr. Martin Luther King** (P), with illustrations by Bryan Collier, and **My Brother Martin: A Sister Remembers Growing Up with the Rev. Dr. Martin Luther King Jr.** (P–I), written by King's sister Christine King Farris. Tonya Bolden's **M.L.K.: Journey of a King** (I–A) combines a riveting text with more than eighty photographs to highlight King's philosophy of nonviolence and loving one's neighbor.

Peter Sís's moving memoir, **The Wall: Growing Up Behind the Iron Curtain** (I–A), a Caldecott Honor book, depicts his personal history through young adulthood as it was shaped by life in Soviet-occupied Czechoslovakia during the Cold War. Through text and brilliant illustrations, Sís presents a moving portrait of one boy's struggle for freedom as well as his artistic freedom of expression, which represents the struggle of the Czech nation itself.

Whether complete or episodic, authentic biography or memoir, the particular events that shaped a subject's life form the basis of a biographical plot. Although some present the subject's entire lifetime, good biographers do not plod through tedious detail about everything that happened in that life. Biographers have an array of facts available to them; how they select from those facts and craft an engaging story is up to them. Certainly, whatever events are presented as facts should be accurate.

Good authors document their facts and also differentiate between fact and opinion, or fact and legend. Diane Stanley and Peter Vennema do an excellent job of this in their biography **Bard of Avon: The Story of William Shakespeare** (I). In a foreword, they alert their readers to the problems of fact they encountered; not much is known about the details of Shakespeare's early life. In their text, they make careful use of qualifying words and phrases, such as *if so* and *perhaps*, to alert readers to theory, opinion, and educated guesses.

By selecting key events in a subject's life and presenting them vividly, biographers illuminate their subject and keep a reader's interest with plots that blend factual background with a good story.

• • PORTRAYAL • • OF SUBJECT

Good biographers consider their subjects as individuals rather than as paragons, and individuals are multidimensional. The strengths *and* weaknesses of individuals are presented in excellent biographies, such as **This Land Was Made for You and Me: The Life and Songs of Woody Guthrie** (A) by Elizabeth Partridge. Guthrie's failings as well as his strengths and the harsh times in which he created his songs are vividly portrayed. Good biographies also avoid implying that the greatness of the subject was implicit from birth. They avoid weaving background knowledge or prescient knowledge of latent talents into unlikely conversations (Herman, 1978). Exaggerating the good qualities of a subject results in *hagiography*—the telling of the life of a saint—or the creation of a legend. Biographies are about real people, not legendary figures. The same is true of memoirs: fine authors seek to depict themselves and the events that shaped them as honestly as possible.

The biographer's point of view and interest in the subject should be apparent, as should the biographer's purpose. The same subject may be treated differently by different biographers. Teaching Idea 9.1 explores this idea.

• • STYLE • •

Authors make choices about what they say and how they say it. Even when a story is well-grounded in verifiable fact, as in authentic biography, it still represents an author's choice of facts, structure, and language. Good biographies incorporate the language and customs of the times. The dialogue should reflect how the subject is likely to have talked with enough authenticity that readers get a true picture but are not overwhelmed by archaic or idiosyncratic speech patterns. For example, Joseph Bruchac's biography of Sitting Bull, **A Boy Called Slow: The True Story of Sitting Bull** (I), is told in the cadence of the storyteller and includes some Lakota words. Robert Burleigh captures Langston Hughes's voice by quoting from his poetry in **Langston's Train Ride** (I), and Deborah Kogan Ray uses William Bartram's journals in **The Flower Hunter: William Bartram, America's First Naturalist** (P–I). Look for language that rings true to the characters but is not overwhelmingly archaic or full of dialect.

• • THEME • •

The theme of a biography is the unifying element behind the story. Facts are merely facts until they are subordinated to a theme and a structure that allows them to

Teaching Idea 9.1

Compare Biographies about One Person

Ask your students to compare and evaluate different biographies about the same person by having them do the following:

1. Choose two biographies about the same person and read them.

2. Decide which biography gives the best idea of what the person was really like. How does it accomplish this?

3. Decide which tells the most about the person's accomplishments.

4. Decide which is more informative and which is more interesting.

Students can also compare biographies written from different perspectives:

1. Compare a biography written before 1980 with one written within the past five years.

2. Describe the differences in the way the subject is viewed or the way similar events are reported.

3. Decide which is more informative and which is more interesting.

make a statement with universal application and appeal. Fighting against injustice, struggling for independence, or working for human rights happens around the world and in many different ways. Each individual story builds its own theme; combined, the stories highlight the resilience and courage of human beings. Look for books that contain a theme with universal application and appeal.

• • ILLUSTRATIONS • •

If the biography is a picturebook, the illustrations must present the setting and the subject in an accurate manner. Illustrations often provide the interesting details that the brief text of a picturebook biography lacks. For example, in **Woody Guthrie: Poet of the People** (P–I), Bonnie Christensen captures the mood of the time and presents many small details in her powerful illustrations.

Biographers also make use of archival photographs, when they are available, to highlight their subject's personalities and lives. Orbis Pictus Award–winning **Through My Eyes** (I–A) by Ruby Bridges contains reproductions of

photographs taken during the tense times when schools in the South were forcibly integrated. They allow readers to compare the innocence and courage of a young girl with the hatred and ugliness of the adults who opposed integration. Look for illustrations that include interesting details and illuminate the character of the subject.

We now take a close look at James Cross Giblin's **The Life and Death of Adolf Hitler** (A), an authentic, chronological biography for older readers that exemplifies these qualities of excellence.

✳   ✳   ✳

A CLOSE LOOK AT

The Life and Death of Adolf Hitler

In 2003, the American Library Association bestowed the Sibert Award for nonfiction on James Cross Giblin's stunning biography of one of history's greatest villains. The award committee recognized both Giblin's accuracy and his artistry.

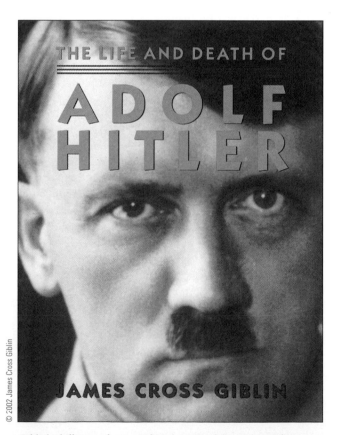

© 2002 James Cross Giblin

Giblin's chilling and remorseless account of the making of a monstrous dictator ends with the hope that the world never sees another Hitler.

Giblin chose to tell the story of Hitler's entire life, from birth to death, but he carefully selected facts that would build on one another to present an accurate and vivid picture. Giblin frames Hitler's life in the present, thereby increasing a reader's perception of the relevance of this biography. He begins with a discussion of why we don't know where Hitler's remains are, the evolution of the idea of dictatorship, and the questions that frame the book: "What sort of man could plan and carry out such horrendous schemes? How was he able to win support for his deadly ventures? And why did no one try to stop him until it was almost too late?" (pp. 2–3). In like manner, he ends the book with a discussion of the neo-Nazi movement of today and the hope that the world will never see another Hitler. The framing of the story of Hitler's life by chapters that are contemporary supports one of Giblin's primary themes—that this could happen again.

As the successive chapters unfold, Giblin not only recounts Hitler's life but sets it within the context of European history at the time. Because one of his theses is that Hitler was shaped by the time and place in which he lived, Giblin takes great pains to explain the attitudes, opportunities, and beliefs that surrounded Hitler as a boy and a young man. He describes life in Vienna, where Hitler had hoped to become an artist, and the excitement of Munich just before World War I, through the rise of Hitler and the Nazi party and the World War II years. As he paints a broad picture of the setting and the historical events, Giblin also includes small details that bring the bigger picture into manageable focus. We learn of Hitler's infatuation with his niece, and then with Eva Braun; we are privy to the scene in which he became a vegetarian. These small details serve to heighten the tension between Adolf the human being and Hitler the monster.

There is no danger of hagiography in this portrayal of the subject; it is clear from the outset that Giblin considers Hitler to be a very evil man, but a man nonetheless. As he presents Hitler's life, he highlights events that might be considered influential or perhaps even causal in the development of this dictator. We discover that Hitler's father beat him; that he was extraordinarily close to his mother, who died when he was a young man; that he experienced debilitating failure early in life; and that he was attracted to beautiful young women but had difficulty developing relationships. Hitler's eccentricities hinted at an emotionally disturbed young man; his magnetism and oratorical skills propelled him to the forefront of the Nazi party in the chaos of postwar Germany. Thus, Giblin's portrayal of Hitler emphasizes the transformation from child to dictator and the interaction of personality and social milieu.

Giblin is careful to distinguish between fact and supposition. For example, he states, "It's not clear what role, if any, Adolf Hitler played in the Munich revolution and its suppression." Giblin also presents speculations as to why, other than because of the prevailing attitude of the times, Hitler might have developed such hatred for the Jewish people. For example, he mentions that some suggest that it was because the doctor who treated his mother during her final illness was Jewish; Giblin also notes, however, that Hitler had "nothing but praise" for the doctor.

Giblin faces the particular difficulty of reporting the thoughts of a man whose ideas are repugnant. At times

Profile

James Cross Giblin

I try to write books that I would have enjoyed reading when I was the age of my readers.

James Cross Giblin is best known for his nonfiction writing. Among his long list of nonfiction titles are award-winning biographies, including *Charles A. Lindbergh: A Human Hero* and *The Amazing Life of Benjamin Franklin*. In 2003, Giblin won the Robert F. Sibert Award for *The Life and Death of Adolf Hitler*.

When asked in a *Publishers Weekly* interview (Frederick, 2002) why he chose to write about Adolf Hitler, Giblin referred to his childhood experiences. "I was six," said Giblin, "when Hitler invaded Poland. At 12, I remember our teacher bringing a radio into the classroom so we could hear Germany surrender in May of 1945. My childhood was shaped by the war, and Hitler was a big part of that. In going back to write about him, it was almost like reliving an important chunk of my past."

Giblin feels that an author's fascination with his or her subjects leads to good nonfiction books for children. "In writing nonfiction, as with other types of books," noted Giblin, "I believe it's absolutely essential for the author to be enthusiastic about his or her topic. Only then can one hope to generate enthusiasm in readers. . . . I only hope my pleasure communicates itself to young readers," he said, "and makes them want to read more books. If it does, I'll be repaying the debt I owe all the fine writers who nurtured my love of reading when I was a child" (Crowell Junior Books, n.d.). With his contribution of more than twenty exemplary informational books for children, James Cross Giblin is fulfilling his debt while expanding the literary lives of young readers.

he reminds the reader that what Hitler thought was not true, or even close to accurate, as in the scene in which Hitler wonders what happened to the patriotic spirit of Munich by the third year of World War I: "He soon decided he'd found the answer: the Jews. 'The offices were filled with Jews,' he wrote in *Mein Kampf*. 'Nearly every clerk was a Jew, and nearly every Jew was a clerk. I was amazed at this plethora of warriors of the chosen people and could not help but compare them with their rare representatives at the front.' (Which was not an accurate observation: Many Jews served with distinction in the German army in the First World War.)"

Each chapter in the text is filled with quotes from various sources, and the end material contains source notes for each chapter, both supporting Giblin's scholarship and extending to readers the possibility of exploring the source material themselves. The chapters are also filled with archival photographs that support the text and add visual interest.

The liberal use of photographs, generous trim size, and 12-point font make this a physically attractive book. The cover, in which Hitler's eyes stare directly at the reader in an eerie and unsettling manner, presages the disturbing nature of the story that Giblin tells. And he tells it well, with chapters that spill naturally from one to the other, each chapter ending with a thought or question that the subsequent chapter takes up. Scholarship, artistry, and passion are evident throughout the book, and it comes as no surprise to read in the introduction to the source notes and bibliography that Giblin has had a lifelong fascination with Hitler.

One of the themes that permeate this biography is that Hitler was not always Hitler. He began life, as we all did, as a baby. The first line of chapter 2 makes this theme explicit: "It's hard to find hints in the young Adolf Hitler of the cruel dictator he was to become" (p. 4). Giblin's portrait of this deeply disturbed man who was also a charismatic leader serves to remind us that this could happen again and that it's crucial not to forget the lesson this dictator's life has taught us.

Variety in Biographical Subjects

Looking at biography in terms of historical period is perhaps the most common way of using biography in the classroom. Like historical fiction, biography can help students envision what life was like in the past, and we discuss this later in the chapter. Here, however, we categorize biography according to the people that the biographies portray. Because the subject is the reason for biography,

we look to the subject as a way to classify biographical narratives.

Doing so also makes it easier to talk about biography in terms of broad human themes. Political and military leaders seek either to control or to lead their people toward specific goals; issues of power, vision, and honor permeate the biographies of these leaders. Philosophers and religious leaders seek to articulate principles on which we might live; their lives are spent considering the role of human beings and higher entities. Many of these leaders exemplify or demonstrate their principles simply by living a holy life, however that might be defined, thus convincing others of the truth of their ideas. Artists of all kinds—musicians, dancers, writers, painters, craftsmen, filmmakers, and entertainers—all try to present their inner visions to the world; they often struggle to realize their talent and to find acceptance for their innovations. Scientists and inventors, too, seek to discover, understand, and create new ideas and opportunities for their fellow human beings; they often face a long struggle for recognition, during which they must persevere to reach their goals. Adventurers and explorers, propelled by their innate curiosity, spend their lives exploring new places and new challenges. Sports heroes work hard to attain a level of excellence that allows them to succeed. And the extraordinary ordinary people who live lives with dignity and strength change the world, one person at a time. An exploration of all these types of biographical subjects can inspire readers to think about their own place in the world today.

• • POLITICAL AND • • MILITARY LEADERS

For good or for ill, political and military leaders help shape the course of history. One such leader is the subject of Diane Stanley's **Saladin: Noble Prince of Islam** (1). Her portrayal of this courageous yet merciful man brings to life a person and a time in history that is not well-known to most of the Western world. Stanley carefully describes major events in the history of the Middle East through to the time of the Second Crusade, the world into which Saladin was born. Through charisma and courage, Saladin succeeded in uniting the Arab world to fight against the barbarians of the West and regain Jerusalem. As he did so, he distinguished himself by his generous and merciful treatment of those he fought. Throughout the text, Stanley reminds readers that three faiths—Jewish, Muslim, and Christian—share the same regard for the Holy Land, then and now.

A political leader who never held office, Frederick Douglass inspired a movement toward abolition and became one of the greatest, if not the greatest, African Americans of the nineteenth century. Peter Burchard's

Frederick Douglass: For the Great Family of Man (A) chronicles the life of this American hero, from his childhood as a slave, to his rise to prominence as counselor to presidents, to his death. Although Burchard portrays Douglass's great strengths and influence, he also depicts his personal struggles. Douglass was, in many ways, an icon of the century that moved from slavery to a taste of freedom in the post-Reconstruction South. He died knowing that the promise of emancipation had not truly been fulfilled. A biography from the same era, Candace Fleming's *The Lincolns: A Scrapbook Look at Abraham and Mary* (I) is, like the first two "scrapbooks" she created, a treat for young readers, who can read a bit or a lot and come away with a better understanding not only of the two subjects, but of the times they influenced and were influenced by. Reproductions of visual and textual primary sources, notes, a bibliography, timeline, and an index bolster the information Fleming provides.

Tonya Bolden's *Up Close: W.E.B. Du Bois: A Twentieth-Century Life* (A) chronicles the career of this talented writer and political activist who spent most of his ninety-five years fighting for justice. This and other volumes in this series are very inviting to young adolescent readers, with their small trim size, interesting subjects, and outstanding writing.

Kathleen Krull's biography, *Hillary Rodham Clinton: Dreams Taking Flight* (P), illustrated by Amy June Bates,

introduces this remarkable woman to young readers. We now take a close look at a biography of another contemporary political leader, Barack Obama, the 44th president of the United States.

* * *

A CLOSE LOOK AT

Barack Obama: Son of Promise, Child of Hope

Most often, biographies that are quickly produced about new heroes are rough portraits at best, but Nikki Grimes's biography, *Barack Obama: Son of Promise, Child of Hope* (P–I), illustrated by Bryan Collier, is a notable exception to this rule. Grimes cleverly contextualizes her biography by having a mother, appropriately named "Hope," try to explain to her son just who Barack Obama is. The mother and son are not well off; the text states that they "live in a tenement," and they are African American. Collier's illustrations reveal that the television they are watching is old, the wallpaper is haphazardly applied, and the kitchen table and chairs are not new. Within this framework, Hope tells her son the story of Obama's life. Grimes quietly underscores the fact that he is biracial, with a "mama, white as whipped cream" and a "daddy, black as ink." Small inserts

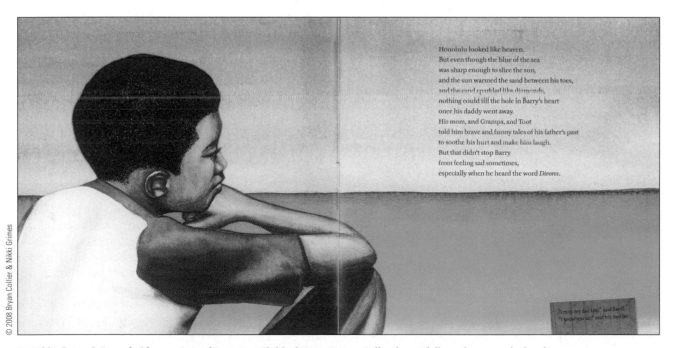

*In Nikki Grimes's **Barack Obama: Son of Promise, Child of Hope**, Bryan Collier beautifully underscores the loneliness of the young Barack Obama when his father went away.*

Profile

Nikki Grimes

B ooks were my soul's delight. Even so, in one sense, the stories I read betrayed me. Too few gave me back my mirror image. Fewer still spoke to, or acknowledged, the existence of the problems I faced as a black foster child from a dysfunctional and badly broken home. I couldn't articulate it then, but I sensed a need for validation which the books I read did not supply. "When I grow up," I thought, "I'll write books about children who look and feel like me."

Nikki Grimes is a woman of many talents. She is a photographer, singer, dancer, jewelry-maker, artist, and a writer of poetry, novels, biographies, nonfiction, and picturebooks. It seems she's done it all! She began composing verse at the age of six and recently won the National Council of Teachers of English Award for excellence in poetry for children. She has written many award-winning books of poetry and prose, also winning Coretta Scott King Awards and Honors across many genres. In addition to her writing for children, she writes articles for magazines for adults and poems for adults as well. She wrote her biography of Barack Obama in two weeks; it spent much longer than that on the *New York Times* bestseller list! Visit Nikki Grimes at www.nikki grimes.com.

capture the interchange between mother and child as the story progresses, reminding the reader of the context. We see young Barack playing with diverse children in Hawaii, learn that he was called "Barry," and see his loneliness when his father left the family. Obama's diverse roots and experiences are highlighted further as we follow him to Indonesia, watch him reuniting with his father for a brief time, and then struggle with the eternal adolescent questions: Who am I and what will I become?

We witness Obama's decision to carry his father's name, Barack, rather than Barry, while also learning that he felt himself to be biracial, even as he traveled to Africa to find his place in his father's family. With the book's publication date coinciding with the Democratic National Convention, Grimes chose to end Obama's story with a crowd chanting "Yes, we can!" while the young boy whose mother is telling him Obama's story asks his mother if it's okay that he, too, wants to be president. Although Grimes's refrain of Obama's hope might be seen as an unwarranted attribution of prescience on his part, it springs directly from her primary source, Obama's memoir, *Dreams from My Father*. Author and illustrator notes, bibliography and additional sources, a timeline, and a family tree provide additional information.

Biographies such as this allow students to consider subjects' unique strengths, as described in Teaching Idea 9.2.

Teaching Idea 9.2

Thematic Connection: Self-Knowledge

There are many biographies in which one of the pivotal events is the subject's recognition of his or her own talent or strength. This is evident in Francisco Jiménez's *Breaking Through* (I–A), Robert Burleigh's *Langston's Train Ride* (I), and William Miller's *Zora Hurston and the Chinaberry Tree* (P–I) as well as many other books. As you read books such as these with your students, ask them to consider how the subject's realization altered his or her life. Then ask them to think about themselves. Do they have a dream? A special talent? A special strength?

• • PHILOSOPHERS AND • •
RELIGIOUS LEADERS

As we live in an increasingly interconnected world, it is increasingly important to understand the thought and beliefs of other people. Books about philosophers and religious leaders help introduce young readers to timeless ideas and new ones. Many great philosophers and religious leaders have left their mark on the world. Born more than 2,500 years ago, Confucius was one of them. Russell Freedman celebrates his influence in *Confucius: The Golden Rule* (I). Although Confucius was born poor and had a homely appearance, his charm and intelligence helped him become a revered teacher and philosopher. His progressive ideals, such as equality and treating others as oneself, have been studied and argued for more than twenty-five centuries. Freedman teaches us not only who Confucius was but how he thought and how his precepts have echoed across time, as, for example, Jesuit missionaries read his teachings during the sixteenth century and realized the similarities between Confucius's thinking and their own Christian precepts. The liberal use of quotations from the *Analects* of Confucius help present the man while also stimulating the minds of readers: "Do you want to know what knowledge is? When you know something, recognize that you know it, and when you don't know something, recognize that you don't know it. That's knowledge."

• • SCIENTISTS • •
AND INVENTORS

Just as philosophers seek to articulate their particular beliefs and share them with the world, scientists and inventors seek to discover, understand, and create new knowledge and possibilities. Often their search begins with careful observation of the world around them. Galileo observed the heavens and came to the conclusion that the Earth was not the center of the universe. Peter Sís uses his considerable talents as an artist to present the genius of Galileo in *Starry Messenger: Galileo Galilei* (I). The story can be read in several ways. Sís's spare text reveals the basic details of Galileo's life, his illustrations present the main ideas of the text, and Galileo's own words present his experiences and ideas. All together, this is a remarkable introduction to the man who, in spite of punishment by the Pope, puzzled out the workings of the solar system by observing the stars and changed the way we see the world.

Jane Goodall's name is known all over the world as the woman who studied chimpanzees in Tanzania's Gombe Reserve, and, today, as the woman who roams the globe speaking about the importance of conservation today. Sudipta Bardhan-Quallen's contribution to the outstanding **Up Close** series, *Up Close: Jane Goodall* (A) is a detailed look at the life's work of this remarkable woman, one who sparked controversy when she became attached to the very animals that she studied. The harsh reality of her struggle to fund her work, the criticism her work engendered, and her difficulty juggling her professional and personal lives are balanced by a portrait of a woman and a scientist who continues to work tirelessly to help the world understand the importance of taking care of our wild places. An index, bibliography, source notes, and photographs bolster Bardhan-Quallen's text.

• • ADVENTURERS • •
AND EXPLORERS

It is not unusual for scientists to also be explorers as they pursue their scientific questions by traveling in search of answers. Such is the case with John Wesley Powell, who led the first recorded expedition down the Green and Colorado rivers as he mapped and studied the flora and fauna of a large portion of the Grand Canyon in 1869. In Deborah Kogan Ray's *Down the Colorado: John Wesley Powell, the One-Armed Explorer* (I), single pages of text with facing illustrations chronicle Powell's early life through his service in the Civil War. As he explores the Grand Canyon, double-page illustrations and quotes from Powell's journals and letters allow the reader to also experience the majesty of the canyon. A map, timeline, author's note, chronology, and bibliography add important information about the man and his journey.

Those who leave home to confront physical challenges or explore unknown places often become heroes. Grand exploits, such as climbing Mt. Everest or crossing the South Pole by dogsled, capture the imagination of the world. Sometimes, however, the adventure lies closer to home. Mordicai Gerstein's Caldecott Medal–winning *The Man Who Walked between the Towers* (P–I) presents the extraordinary feat of Philippe Petit's walk on a wire strung between the almost completed towers of the World Trade Center in August 1974. Defying the rules, as well as gravity, Petit did something extraordinary, something that captured the imagination of the world.

• • PRACTITIONERS • •
OF THE ARTS

There are many wonderful biographies of painters, sculptors, musicians, filmmakers, dancers, artisans, and writers who have successfully presented their visions to the world. The success is often hard won, however, and stories about these individuals often portray their struggles as thoroughly as they celebrate their successes.

Increasingly, those who write for children and young adults are creating autobiographies and memoirs that allow young readers to see the struggles of authors they admire. Our nation's "ambassador of children's literature," and an author beloved by many elementary school children, Jon Scieszka has offered his story to readers in *Knucklehead: Tall Tales & Mostly True Stories About Growing Up Scieszka* (I–A). It is certainly not surprising that the approximately three dozen brief "true" tales from his childhood are funny, but they are also poignant, offering a loosely chronological look at his experiences growing up as one of six brothers and how that shaped the man he is today. Biographies about writers are important resources for exploring what it means to be a writer and for extending children's knowledge of the authors whose works they enjoy reading.

The artist Alexander Calder is the subject of Tanya Lee Stone's *Sandy's Circus: A Story About Alexander Calder* (P–I), illustrated by Boris Kulikov. In this biography for younger readers, Stone focuses on Calder's early years when he made things out of the many bits and pieces that his parents provided for him. Studying both engineering and art, he continued his childhood passion and eventually created his famous circus, in which small figures made of wire, wood, cloth, and other scrap materials came alive as the springs, strings, and levers he built made them "leap, run, and dance." The illustrations do full justice to Calder's creativity, and an author's note, sources, and a photograph of Calder performing his circus offer additional information to curious readers. In a biography in verse written for older readers, Carmen T. Bernier-Grand presents the life of artist Frida Kahlo. *Frida: ¡Viva la vida! Long Live Life!* (I–A), a Pura Belpré Honor book, uses reproductions of Kahlo's paintings to illuminate the emotions presented in the biographical poems.

Sometimes those who have great artistic talent use their talent to do more than delight or entertain. Marian Anderson was one such artist, and two recent biographies present her life and times and celebrate the profound impact she had on the struggle for civil rights over the course of her long life (1897–1993). Pam Muñoz Ryan's picturebook biography *When Marian Sang: The True Recital of Marian Anderson, the Voice of a Century* (I) presents Marian's early life with simplicity and honesty, depicting a young African American girl with great talent being denied access to the training she needed because of the racist attitudes prevalent in the United States at that time. These trials and tribulations make all the more satisfying her brilliant performance on the steps of the Lincoln Memorial in Washington, D.C. Brian Selznick's brilliant illustrations frame the story as a play—the curtain closed at the beginning, yet remaining open in the final, triumphant scene of Marian's debut with the Metropolitan Opera. Now, we take a close look at a more detailed biography of Anderson for older readers, Russell Freedman's *The Voice That Challenged a Nation: Marian Anderson and the Struggle for Equal Rights* (I–A).

Standing on the steps of the Lincoln Memorial, Marian Anderson sings to a crowd of 75,000 people.

*In this picture from **The Voice That Challenged a Nation**, the soaring columns at the Lincoln Memorial seem to dwarf Marian Anderson, but her voice rang out across the Mall and the nation itself.*

A CLOSE LOOK AT

The Voice That Challenged a Nation: Marian Anderson and the Struggle for Equal Rights

In this detailed biography for older readers, Russell Freedman's perspective on Anderson's life is clear from the very beginning, when the book opens with the concert at the Lincoln Memorial in 1939: seventy-five thousand people standing in front of the memorial on a cool Easter Sunday, an ovation, a moment of silence, and then Marian singing. This dramatic introduction is followed by an effectively brisk recounting of her childhood and young adulthood, focusing on her dedication to her talent and on the obstacles she had to overcome. The emphasis, however, is on Marian as a singer; Freedman does not presume to

cast her as an active player in the civil rights movement that was just beginning to develop, but rather as an artist whose great talent put her in a position to make a powerful statement simply by using that talent, as she did.

By beginning his biography with Anderson's performance on the steps of the Lincoln Memorial, and ending with a consideration of Anderson's own words in which she makes it clear that she was a singer, not an activist, Freedman places Anderson's amazing talent against the cultural milieu of the United States at that time. This juxtaposition highlights the magnificence of Anderson's achievements while also illuminating the pernicious effect of the racism that was rampant at that time. Indeed, every aspect of Anderson's life, as presented by Freedman, was touched by racism. Freedman depicts this in such a matter-of-fact way that the emphasis is clearly on Anderson's strength and commitment to her music.

Both a Sibert Medal and Newbery Honor winner, the book is filled with archival photographs that support and extend the engaging story, as do the chapter notes, bibliography, discography, and index that close the book.

• • SPORTS HEROES • •

Sports heroes, like famous artists, often have the opportunity to work for a better world because of the esteem in which others hold them. Jackie Robinson epitomizes both the talent that it takes to be a heroic sports figure and the dedication that is necessary to use that position to benefit others. Sharon Robinson's moving tribute to her father, *Promises to Keep: How Jackie Robinson Changed America* (I–A), combines narrative reconstruction of the major events in his life with family photographs and letters. She presents the life of the man who broke the color barrier in major league baseball and who then went on to become an activist in politics and the struggle for civil rights. Although not all sports heroes have the opportunity to affect the world in the manner Jackie Robinson did, good sports biographies are more than just sources of information about heroic exploits in the sports arena.

Muhammad Ali is the subject of two recent biographies that contextualize his outstanding physical abilities with his moral courage as he confronted the racism that surrounded him, especially after he refused to serve in the Vietnam War. Jonah Winter's *Muhammad Ali: Champion of the World* (P), illustrated by François Roca, borrows from Genesis as he "introduces" Jack Johnson and Joe Louis, predecessors—great in their own right—to Ali, the champion of the world. The variations in font make the text visually as well as verbally powerful, and highlight the "fight" that Ali had with the world, while Roca's realistic oil paintings offer visual depictions of Ali's accomplishments. Charles R. Smith, Jr.'s biography for older readers, *Twelve Rounds to Glory: The Story of Muhammad Ali* (A), illustrated by Bryan Collier, tells much the same story in more detail. The rhyming text—much like Ali's signature rhymes—clearly indicates Smith's admiration for the man, both as boxer and as human being, as he highlights not only the fights, but Ali's outspokenness against racism, against the Vietnam War, and his final fight with Parkinson's disease.

• • EXTRAORDINARY ORDINARY PEOPLE • •

Not everyone has a recognizable, outstanding talent. Most people are actually quite ordinary. Sometimes, however, the dignity and grace with which ordinary people live their lives make them extraordinary. Memoirs such as Alan Govenar's *Osceola: Memories of a Sharecropper's Daughter* (I), authentic biographies like Alison Leslie Gold's *A Special Fate: Chiune Sugihara: Hero of the Holocaust* (A), and biographical fiction such as Joseph Bruchac's *Sacajawea* (I–A) depict the acts of ordinary people. The heroes of these stories are not sports or movie stars, politicians or generals, artists or philosophers, but persons whose strength of character makes them extraordinary in some way. Sacajawea's knowledge, bravery, and intelligence made her an integral part of Lewis and Clark's expedition instead of just the wife of one of their interpreters. Osceola Mays's courage and strength allowed her to triumph over poverty and a cruelly racist society. Chiune Sugihara's sense of decency and personal courage led him to defy his government and save thousands of Jews of eastern Europe during World War II. In Claire A. Nivola's *Planting the Trees of Kenya: The Story of Wangari Maathai* (P), young readers find a story about someone who changed the world (and won a Nobel Peace Prize) by doing something quite mundane: planting a tree.

Profile

Russell Freedman

*T*he truth is, when I sit down to write, I simply want to capture the reader's attention and tell a story about a person, an event, or a series of events that for some reason happen to interest me. I want to lose myself in the world where those events took place, and through the transformative power of language, make that world, that person, those events live again for my readers.

Russell Freedman was selected as the May Hill Arbuthnot Honor Lecturer because of his outstanding and lasting contributions to children's literature. He has published approximately fifty books for young readers and has received numerous awards in addition to the Arbuthnot Honor, including Newbery Honors, Orbis Pictus and Boston Globe–Horn Book Awards and Honors, and a Newbery Medal for *Lincoln: A Photobiography*. *The Voice that Challenged a Nation* won both a Newbery Medal and the Sibert Medal.

Freedman does extensive research when writing, visiting libraries, museums, and monuments, and does at least four drafts of each manuscript. Reading one of his books means experiencing the passion, knowledge, and brilliant style that he brings to his work.

Sometimes it surprises us that people who are now considered famous or heroic, such as Ruby Bridges, Rosa Parks, or Malcolm X, were in fact people with no particular reputation, talent, or position that would indicate eventual fame. There were many women like Elizabeth Cady Stanton, women who wanted the right to vote, but Stanton stood up and fought for her rights, as Tanya Lee Stone depicts in *Elizabeth Leads the Way: Elizabeth Cady Stanton and the Right to Vote* (P–I), with illustrations by Rebecca Gibbon. Today, Stanton's name is forever linked with the cause that she worked for.

Others whose lives are worth reading and thinking about still aren't famous—but they are exemplary. Quietly told stories of people who did not create headlines can also have a strong and lasting impact on young readers. The memoir *Leon's Story* (I–A), written by Leon Walter Tillage and illustrated with collage art by Susan L. Roth, won a Boston Globe–Horn Book Award for nonfiction. In this small book, Tillage tells the story of his life as the son of an African American sharecropper, growing up in North Carolina during the 1940s. As a young boy, he learns to endure the racism and bigotry of his surroundings while keeping intact his own dignity and sense of worth. His experiences lead him directly to being involved in the civil rights movement.

Biography and Memoir in the Classroom

Biography can help young readers develop their concepts of historical time; they can discover ideas and empathize with historical characters. Those who read biographies learn that all people have the same basic needs and desires. They begin to see their lives in relation to those of the past, learn a vast amount of social detail about the past, and consider the human problems and relationships of the present in the light of those in the past.

Biography can enliven a social studies curriculum; in conjunction with historical fiction and nonfiction, it can illuminate a time and place by telling the story of an individual. It can also support studies in music and art; many fine biographies of artists and musicians explore both their lives and their creative endeavors. An exploration of themes is enriched by including biographies.

Memoirs can serve as models for young readers as they develop their own or those of an older friend or family member. Other biographies serve as excellent examples of how to use source material to craft an engaging and accurate story. Some provide access to primary source material for students to use in their own research. A biography collection is an important part of any classroom or school library.

• • BUILDING A • • BIOGRAPHY COLLECTION

A collection of biographies needs to be wide in scope and representative of diverse people. If there are biographies of women and people of color that speak to your subject, be sure to include them in your collection. If there are not, you may want to consider with your students why there are no biographies of, for example, ancient female explorers, and why biographies of modern female explorers are now available. Taking into account the biographies and memoirs of ordinary people that are available today, consider with your students why someone might become the subject of a biography, a concept explored in Teaching Idea 9.3. Using this approach, children can begin to see how the world has changed and how historical and current social conditions influence individuals' potential.

• • USING BIOGRAPHY • • WITH OTHER GENRES TO STUDY AN ERA

As we discuss in other chapters, it is often quite effective to read across genres. When you do this, students not only learn about the focus of study but also further develop their understanding of genre constraints and possibilities. If, for example, you link literature with social studies, you can combine historical fiction, biography, and nonfiction to study a particular time or place. Experiences in each genre offer readers different opportunities that, taken together, can help them learn not only the "facts" about particular people and particular places but also the human story that has become history.

If you want students to really understand the reasons for and the impact of the civil rights movement, for example, you might want to read biographies of Gandhi, Martin Luther King, Jr., and Malcolm X. Trace the development of Gandhi's ideas in the work of King, and compare King with Malcolm X. Then bring in the stories of such people as Rosa Parks, Leon Tillage, and Ruby Bridges, some poetry from Langston Hughes (and his biographies), and historical fiction such as *Roll of Thunder, Hear My Cry* (A) or *The Watsons Go to Birmingham—1963* (I–A). Nonfiction, such as Chris Crowe's *Getting Away with Murder: The True Story of the Emmett Till Case* (A) supplements biography to provide added facts, while the stories told in biographies enhance the fiction.

• • ORGANIZING • • BIOGRAPHY BY THEME

Biography, like fiction, includes stories of people who explore their world, fight for freedom, revolt against

Teaching Idea 9.3

Who Becomes a Biographical Subject?

Ask your students to consider what types of people are most likely to become the subjects of biographies. Which people are most likely to have several biographies written about them? Ask students to consider whether the subjects of biography have changed in the past thirty years. Have them follow this procedure:

1. Go to the library or search on the Internet to find out how many biographies have been written about a particular individual. List authors, titles, and dates of publication.

2. Check the school library holdings to ascertain what kinds of people are subjects of biographies written within the past thirty years. List subjects, authors, titles, and dates of publication.

3. Summarize the data from items 1 and 2 and make generalizations based on the data.

4. Discuss the findings, considering these questions: Who is in favor? Who is not? What kinds of people are the subjects of biographies or memoirs in any given year? Are there any observable trends?

oppression, immigrate, establish new nations, and struggle for survival and human rights. Biographies can complement historical and realistic fiction that develop similar themes, or themes can be explored primarily through biographies. There are several biographical series—for example, the **Extraordinary People** series, published by Children's Book Press; the **Black Americans of Achievement** series, published by Chelsea; and Enslow's **African-American Biography**, **Hispanic Biography**, **World Writers**, and **Historical Americans** series—which present biographies about various people engaged in similar struggles. There are also collective biographies, mentioned earlier in this chapter, which present brief biographies of a number of people who are linked in some way.

You can collect books that illustrate a particular theme, such as the struggle for human rights. By studying the lives of diverse people from around the world and across history, students can come to understand the universal struggles of humankind. Why do people around the world struggle for human rights? How are these struggles similar across nations and time? How do they vary according to age and culture? Exploring these kinds

of questions can lead to a better understanding of humanity and one's place in it.

For example, you might want to consider the human desire to explore new places. Many biographies focus on explorers, both ancient and modern. Sir Walter Raleigh explored the New World; Sally Ride explored space. The theme of exploration can be widened to include those who explore the boundaries of science. Those people who have made scientific and technological breakthroughs are curious, dedicated individuals, just as many geographic explorers are. Biographies of famous scientists and inventors can enrich students' concepts of what it means to be an explorer. Artists and musicians who break new ground can also be considered explorers. Thus, a general theme like exploration or human rights can be woven from many varying biographies and even complemented by fiction and nonfiction.

Biographies of artists and musicians also can support the study of art and music. They can be compared in terms of the driving force that shaped the lives of their subjects: What caused them to pursue their talents with such passion and success? Biographies of female artists and musicians can be explored as examples of triumph over discrimination and then related to the general theme of human rights.

A great number of writers and illustrators of books for children have written biographies and memoirs, including a series of autobiographies for primary-grade readers published by Richard Owens. These biographies can be read for any number of purposes—to discover information about the writers, to learn about the effect of the time and place in which the writer lived on the writer's work, to develop an understanding of what it means to be a writer, and to extend knowledge of the authors whose works children enjoy reading.

Biography has become one of the most diverse, interesting, and popular genres in literature for young readers. Wise adults build on children's fascination with real stories and the details about the lives of others by using biography to explore both contemporary and historical people, events, and ideas.

• • • SUMMARY • • •

Biographies and memoirs tell the stories of the people who shaped and are shaping our history. Reading these books helps children and adolescents understand that people make history and that these people have strengths and weaknesses, as we all do. Understanding the humanity behind the greatness allows readers to dream of their own accomplishments and to know they are possible.

Booklist

✳ Indicates some aspect of diversity

Political and Military Leaders

✳ Andronik, Catherine, *Hatshepsut, His Majesty, Herself* (2001) (I)

✳ Bolden, Tanya, *Up Close: W.E.B. Du Bois: A Twentieth-Century Life* (2008) (A)

✳ Bolden, Tanya, *M.L.K.: Journey of a King* (2008) (I–A)

✳ Bruchac, Joseph, *A Boy Called Slow: The True Story of Sitting Bull* (1994) (P–I)

✳ _____, *Crazy Horse's Vision* (2000) (P)

✳ Burchard, Peter, *Frederick Douglass: For the Great Family of Man* (2003) (A)

_____, *Lincoln and Slavery* (1999) (A)

Cooper, Ilene, *Jack: The Early Years of John F. Kennedy* (2003) (I–A)

Donnelly, Matt, *Theodore Roosevelt: Larger Than Life* (2003) (A)

Fleming, Candace, *Ben Franklin's Almanac: Being a True Account of the Good Gentleman's Life* (2003) (I–A)

_____, *The Lincolns: A Scrapbook Look at Abraham and Mary* (2008) (I)

_____, *Our Eleanor: A Scrapbook Look at Eleanor Roosevelt's Remarkable Life* (2005) (I)

Freedman, Russell, *Lincoln: A Photobiography* (1987) (I–A)

Fritz, Jean, *And Then What Happened, Paul Revere?* (1973) (I)

_____, *Can't You Make Them Behave, King George?* (1977) (I)

_____, *The Great Little Madison* (1989) (A)

_____, *Traitor: The Case of Benedict Arnold* (1981) (A)

_____, *What's the Big Idea, Ben Franklin?* (1976) (I)

_____, *Why Don't You Get a Horse, Sam Adams?* (1974) (I)

_____, *Will You Sign Here, John Hancock?* (1976) (I)

Giblin, James Cross, *The Amazing Life of Benjamin Franklin* (2000) (I)

✳ _____, *The Life and Death of Adolf Hitler* (2002) (A)

✳ Gormley, Beatrice, *Barack Obama: Our 44th President* (2008) (P–I)

✳ Grimes, Nikki, *Barack Obama: Son of Promise, Child of Hope* (2008) (P–I)

Gulotta, Charles, *Extraordinary Women in Politics* (1998) (I)

Kerley, Barbara, *What to Do About Alice: How Alice Roosevelt Broke the Rules, Charmed the World, and Drove Her Father Crazy* (2008) (P–I)

✳ King Farris, Christine, *My Brother Martin: A Sister Remembers Growing Up with the Rev. Dr. Martin Luther King Jr.* (2003) (P–I)

Kraft, Betsy Harvey, *Theodore Roosevelt: Champion of the American Spirit* (2003) (A)

Krull, Kathleen, *Harvesting Hope: The Story of Cesar Chavez* (2003) (P–I)

_____, *Hillary Rodham Clinton: Dreams Taking Flight* (2008) (P)

_____, *Lives of Extraordinary Women: Rulers, Rebels (and What the Neighbors Thought)* (2000) (I)

_____, *Lives of the Presidents: Fame, Shame (and What the Neighbors Thought)* (1998) (I)

Marrin, Albert, *The Great Adventure: Theodore Roosevelt and the Rise of Modern America* (2007) (A)

_____, *Old Hickory: Andrew Jackson and the American People* (2004) (A)

_____, *Sitting Bull and His World* (2000) (A)

Mills, Judie, *Robert Kennedy* (1998) (A)

Murphy, Jim, *The Real Benedict Arnold* (2007) (A)

✳ Myers, Walter Dean, *Malcolm X: A Fire Burning Brightly* (2000) (I–A)

✳ _____, *Malcolm X: By Any Means Necessary* (1993) (I–A)

Rappaport, Doreen, *Abe's Honest Words: The Life of Abraham Lincoln* (2008) (I)

✳ Rumford, James, *Sequoyah: The Cherokee Man Who Gave His People Writing* (2004) (I)

St. George, Judith, *Stand Tall, Abe Lincoln* (2008) (P–I)

_____, *You're on Your Way, Teddy Roosevelt* (2004) (P–I)

✳ Stanley, Diane, *Saladin: Noble Prince of Islam* (2002) (I)

Thimmesh, Catherine, *Madame President: The Extraordinary, True (and Evolving) Story of Women in Politics* (2004) (I)

Thomas, Jane Resh, *Behind the Mask: The Life of Queen Elizabeth* (1998) (A)

Philosophers and Religious Leaders

✳ Demi, *Buddha* (1996) (I)

✳ _____, *The Dalai Lama: A Biography of the Tibetan Spiritual and Political Leader* (1998) (I)

✳ _____, *Gandhi* (2001) (I)

✳ _____, *Muhammad* (2003) (I)

✳ Freedman, Russell, *Confucius: The Golden Rule* (2002) (I)

Scientists and Inventors

Armstrong, Jennifer, *Audubon: Painter of Birds in the Wild Frontier* (2003) (P–I)

Bardhan-Quallen, Sudipta, *Up Close: Jane Goodall* (2008) (A)

Brown, Don, *Odd Boy Out: Young Albert Einstein* (2004) (P)

Collins, Mary, *Airborne: A Photobiography of Wilbur and Orville Wright* (2003) (I)

Davies, Jacqueline, *The Boy Who Drew Birds: A Story of John James Audubon* (2004) (P–I)

Fisher, Leonard Everett, *Alexander Graham Bell* (1999) (I)

Gerstein, Mordicai, *Sparrow Jack* (2003) (I)

✳ Krensky, Stephen, *A Man for All Seasons: The Life of George Washington Carver* (2008) (P–I)

Krull, Katherine, *They Saw the Future: Oracles, Psychics, Scientists, Great Thinkers, and Pretty Good Guessers* (1999) (I)

Lasky, Katherine, *The Man Who Made Time Travel* (2003) (I)

Matthews, Tom, *Always Inventing: A Photobiography of Alexander Graham Bell* (1999) (I)

Old, Wendie, *To Fly: The Story of the Wright Brothers* (2002) (I–A)

Ray, Deborah Kogan, *Down the Colorado: John Wesley Powell, the One-Armed Explorer* (2007) (I)

_____, *The Flower Hunter: William Bartram, America's First Naturalist* (2004) (P–I)

Reef, Catherine, *Sigmund Freud: Pioneer of the Mind* (2001) (A)

Severance, John, *Einstein: Visionary Scientist* (1999) (I)

Sís, Peter, *Starry Messenger: Galileo Galilei* (1996) (I)

_____, *The Tree of Life: A Book Depicting the Life of Charles Darwin: Naturalist, Geologist and Thinker* (2003) (I–A)

Adventurers and Explorers

Aronson, Marc, *Sir Walter Ralegh and the Quest for El Dorado* (2000) (A)

※ Blumberg, Rhoda, *York's Adventures with Lewis and Clark: An African-American's Part in the Great Expedition* (2004) (I)

※ Grimes, Nikki, *Talkin' about Bessie: The Story of Aviator Elizabeth Coleman* (2002) (I)

Ray, Deborah Kogan, *Down the Colorado: John Wesley Powell, the One-Armed Explorer* (2007) (I)

Weatherford, Carole Boston, *I, Matthew Henson: Polar Explorer* (2008) (P–I)

Zaunders, Bo, *Feathers, Flaps, and Flops: Fabulous Early Fliers* (2001) (I)

Artists, Artisans, and Filmmakers

Bernier-Grand, Carmen, *Frida: ¡Viva la vida! Long Live Life!* (2008) (I–A)

Brighton, Catherine, *Keep Your Eyes on the Kid: The Early Years of Buster Keaton* (2008) (P)

Brown, Don, *Mack Made Movies* (2003) (P–I)

Debon, Nicolas, *Four Pictures by Emily Carr* (2003) (I–A)

Greenberg, Jan, *Romare Bearden: Collage of Memories* (2003) (P–I)

Greenberg, Jan, and Sandra Jordan, *Action Jackson* (2002) (P–I)

_____, *Andy Warhol: Prince of Pop* (2004) (A)

_____, *Christo and Jeanne-Claude: Through the Gates and Beyond* (2008) (I)

Ross, Michael Elsohn, *Salvador Dalí and the Surrealists: Their Lives and Ideas* (2003) (A)

Slaymaker, Melissa Eskridge, *Bottle Houses: The Creative World of Grandma Prisbrey* (2004) (P)

Stone, Tanya Lee, *Sandy's Circus: A Story About Alexander Calder* (2008) (P)

Stanley, Diane, *Michelangelo* (2000) (I)

Wallner, Alexandra, *Grandma Moses* (2004) (P)

Warhola, James, *Uncle Andy's: A Fabulous Visit with Andy Warhol* (2003) (P)

Musicians and Dancers

Anderson, M. T., *Strange Mr. Satie* (2003) (P)

Christensen, Bonnie, *Woody Guthrie: Poet of the People* (2001) (P–I)

Freedman, Russell, *Martha Graham: A Dancer's Life* (1998) (A)

※ _____, *The Voice That Challenged a Nation: Marian Anderson and the Struggle for Equal Rights* (2004) (I–A)

Gerstein, Mordicai, *What Charlie Heard* (2002) (P–I)

※ Lang, Lang, and Michael French, *Playing with Flying Keys* (2008) (A)

※ Parker, Robert Andrew, *Piano Starts Here: The Young Art Tatum* (2008) (P–I)

Partridge, Elizabeth, *This Land Was Made for You and Me: The Life and Songs of Woody Guthrie* (2002) (A)

※ Pinkney, Andrea Davis, *Duke Ellington: The Piano Prince and His Orchestra* (1998) (I)

※ _____, *Ella Fitzgerald: The Tale of a Vocal Virtuosa* (2002) (P–I)

Rappaport, Doreen, *John's Secret Dreams: The Life of John Lennon* (2004) (P–I)

Reich, Susanna, *Clara Schumann: Piano Virtuoso* (1999) (I)

※ Ryan, Pam Muñoz, *When Marian Sang: The True Recital of Marian Anderson: The Voice of a Century* (2002) (P–I)

Sís, Peter, *Play, Mozart, Play!* (2006) (P)

※ Tallchief, Maria, and Rosemary Wells, *Tallchief: America's Prima Ballerina* (1999) (I)

※ Weatherford, Carole Boston, *Before John Was a Jazz Giant: A Song of John Coltrane* (2008) (P)

Winter, Jeanette, *Sebastian: A Book about Bach* (1999) (P)

Writers

Bryant, Jen, *A River of Words: The Story of William Carlos Williams* (2008) (I)

※ Burleigh, Robert, *Langston's Train Ride* (2004) (I)

※ Cooper, Floyd, *Coming Home: From the Life of Langston Hughes* (1994) (I)

Crutcher, Chris, *King of the Mild Frontier: An Ill-Advised Autobiography* (2003) (A)

Fleischman, Sid, *The Trouble Begins at 8: A Life of Mark Twain in the Wild, Wild West* (2008) (A)

Gantos, Jack, *Hole in My Life* (2002) (A)

※ Herrera, Juan Felipe, *The Upside Down Boy/El Niño de Cabeza* (2000) (P)

Kerley, Barbara, *Walt Whitman: Words for America* (2004) (I)

Krull, Kathleen, *The Boy on Fairfield Street: How Ted Geisel Grew Up to Become Dr. Seuss* (2004) (P–I)

_____, *The Road to Oz: Twists, Turns, Bumps, and Triumphs in the Life of L. Frank Baum* (2008) (P–I)

Lasky, Kathryn, *A Brilliant Streak: The Making of Mark Twain* (1998) (I)

Lowry, Lois, *Looking Back: A Book of Memories* (1998) (I)

※ Murphy, Jim, *Pick and Shovel Poet: The Journeys of Pascal D'Angelo* (2000) (I–A)

※ Myers, Walter Dean, *Bad Boy: a Memoir* (2001) (A)

Paulsen, Gary, *Guts: The True Stories behind Hatchet and the Brian Books* (2001) (I–A)

Nobleman, Marc Tyler, *Boys of Steel: The Creators of Superman* (2008) (I–A)

Scieszka, Jon, *Knucklehead: Tall Tales & Mostly True Stories About Growing Up Scieszka* (2008) (I–A)

Spinelli, Jerry, *Knots in My Yo-Yo String: The Autobiography of a Kid* (1998) (I)

Stanley, Diane, and Peter Vennema, *Bard of Avon: The Story of William Shakespeare* (1992) (I)

Winter, Jeanette, *Beatrix: Various Episodes from the Life of Beatrix Potter* (2003) (P)

Younger, Barbara, *Purple Mountain Majesties: The Story of Katharine Lee Bates and "America the Beautiful"* (1998) (P)

Sports Heroes

※ Bolden, Tonya, *The Champ: the Story of Muhammad Ali* (2004) (I)

※ Bruchac, Joseph, *Jim Thorpe's Bright Path* (2004) (I)

※ Cooper, Floyd, *Jump! From the Life of Michael Jordan* (2004) (P–I)

Debon, Nicolas, *The Strongest Man in the World: Louis Cyr* (2007) (I)

Hopkinson, Deborah, *Girl Wonder: A Baseball Story in Nine Innings* (2003) (P)

Krull, Kathleen, *Wilma Unlimited: How Wilma Rudolph Became the World's Fastest Woman* (1996) (P–I)

Myers, Walter Dean, *The Greatest: Muhammad Ali* (2001) (I–A)

Robinson, Sharon, *Promises to Keep: How Jackie Robinson Changed America* (2004) (I–A)

Smith, Charles R., Jr., *Twelve Rounds to Glory: The Story of Muhammad Ali* (2007) (A)

Winter, Jonah, *Muhammad Ali: Champion of the World* (2008) (P)

Wise, Bill, *Louis Sockalexis: Native American Baseball Pioneer* (2007) (I)

Extraordinary Ordinary People

Anderson, Laurie Halse, *Independent Dames: What You Never Knew About the Women and Girls of the American Revolution* (2008) (P–I)

al-Windawi, Thura, *Thura's Diary: My Life in Wartime Iraq* (2004) (I–A)

Bang, Molly, *Nobody Particular: One Woman's Fight to Save the Bays* (2000) (I–A)

Barakat, Ibtisam, *Tasting the Sky: A Palestinian Childhood* (2007) (I–A)

Bridges, Ruby, *Through My Eyes* (1999) (I–A)

Brown, Don, *Kid Blink Beats the World* (2004) (P–I)

Bruchac, Joseph, *Pocahontas* (2003) (I–A)

_____, *Sacajawea* (2000) (I–A)

Coleman, Evelyn, *The Riches of Osceola McCarty* (1998) (I)

D'Adamo, Francesco, *Iqbal* (2003) (I–A)

Dash, Joan, *The World at Her Fingertips: The Story of Helen Keller* (2001) (A)

Engle, Margarita, *The Surrender Tree: Poems of Cuba's Struggle for Freedom* (2008) (A)

Erdich, Liselotte, *Sacagawea* (2003) (P–I)

Fradin, Dennis Brindell, and Judith Bloom Fradin, *Fight On!: Mary Church Terrell's Battle for Integration* (2003) (I)

_____, *Ida B. Wells: Mother of the Civil Rights Movement* (2000) (I–A)

Gold, Alison Leslie, *A Special Fate: Chiune Sugihara: Hero of the Holocaust* (2000) (A)

Greenfield, Eloise, *How They Got Over: African Americans and the Call of the Sea* (2003) (P)

Grovenar, Alan, *Osceola: Memories of a Sharecropper's Daughter* (2001) (I)

Halfman, Janet, *Seven Miles to Freedom: The Robert Smalls Story* (2008) (P–I)

Hamilton, Virginia, *Anthony Burns: The Defeat and Triumph of a Fugitive Slave* (1988) (A)

_____, *Many Thousand Gone: African Americans from Slavery to Freedom* (1993) (I–A)

Hurst, Carol Otis, *Rocks in His Head* (2001) (P–I)

Jiménez, Francisco, *Breaking Through* (2001) (I–A)

_____, *The Circuit: Stories from the Life of a Migrant Child* (1997) (I–A)

Lobel, Anita, *No Pretty Pictures: A Child of War* (1998) (A)

Marx, Trish, *One Boy from Kosovo* (2000) (I)

McCully, Emily Arnold, *Manjiro: The Boy Who Risked His Life for Two Countries* (2008) (P)

_____, *My Heart Glow: Alice Cogswell, Thomas Gallaudet, and the Birth of American Sign Language* (2008) (P)

Monceaux, Morgan, and Ruth Katcher, *My Heroes, My People: African Americans and Native Americans in the West* (1999) (I)

Nivola, Claire, *Planting the Trees of Kenya: The Story of Wangari Maathai* (2008) (P)

Pinkney, Andrea Davis, *Let It Shine: Stories of Black Women Freedom Fighters* (2000) (I–A)

Pressler, Mirjam, *Anne Frank: A Hidden Life* (2000) (A)

Say, Allen, *Music for Alice* (2004) (P–I)

Siegal, Aranka, *Memories of Babi* (2008) (I–A)

Steig, William, *When Everybody Wore a Hat* (2003) (P)

Stone, Tanya Lee, *Elizabeth Leads the Way: Elizabeth Cady Stanton and the Right to Vote* (2008) (P)

Tillage, Leon Walter, *Leon's Story* (1997) (I–A)

Warren, Andrea, *Escape from Saigon: How a Vietnam War Orphan Became an American Boy* (2004) (I–A)

Wolf, Bernard, *Coming to America: A Muslim Family's Story* (2003) (P)

Nonfiction

The Garbage Patch

What would happen if you released a floating object (any floating object will do) from a handful of different locations along the Pacific coasts of Asia and North America and then followed those objects as they drifted around the ocean for thirty years? An experiment of this nature would, of course, be almost impossible to carry out in real life.

—LOREE GRIFFIN BURNS,
**Tracking Trash: Flotsam, Jetsam,
and the Science of Ocean Motion**, *p. 33*

Rene's fourth/fifth-grade class has embarked on a study of ocean currents and they are doing much more than learning what and where ocean currents are. Rene is using this opportunity to help her students learn to think like scientists, to see what scientists in the field do, and to think about ways they can help improve life on this planet. She knows that page 40 of the book has ideas for what individuals can do. She's also planning to read the adaptation of Al Gore's *An Inconvenient Truth: The Crisis of Global Warming* (1) with her students, and she has many other books about various aspects of ecology on the bookshelves. She has also planned some "experiments" that her students can do so that they can learn to do "lab reports." Using the richness of nonfiction children's literature, she's brought her science curriculum alive, and her students are working with great enthusiasm.

Defining Nonfiction

Children and adolescents have a desire to *know*, and when they discover that books are a place to find answers, they embark on a journey of lifelong learning. They turn to nonfiction literature to feed their hunger for facts, ideas, and concepts. The term *nonfiction* describes books of information and fact about any topic. Nonfiction, or informational, books are distinguished from fiction by their emphasis. Although both may tell a story, and both may include fact, in nonfiction, the facts and concepts are uppermost, with storytelling perhaps used as an expressive technique; in fiction, the story is uppermost, with facts sometimes used to support it. The key lies in the emphasis of the writer, which in nonfiction should be on the facts and concepts being presented. It is these that must be truthful, verifiable, and understandable.

The nonfiction now being published has great appeal to young readers. Writers select topics that interest children, and many of the topics they select fit nicely into an existing school curriculum. Nonfiction today includes books with spacious, well-designed pages and intriguing illustrations that enhance and extend the reader's understanding of the topic. The texts present writing at its best: interesting language used in varied ways. Metaphor and descriptive language allow readers to link what they are reading about with what they already know. The structure of nonfiction varies widely. Some books use fantasy devices and parallel texts to interest young readers. Others use a narrative frame to impart information. And there are many other structures that clever writers use to support their goal—to impart information to their readers. This was not always the case.

A Brief History of Nonfiction for Young Readers

Although the horn books of the mid-sixteenth century were designed to instruct children in reading and religion, the first widely adopted book of nonfiction was John Amos Comenius's compendium of information that he believed every child should know, *Orbis Sensualium Pictus (Illustrated World of the Senses)*. Comenius, a Moravian churchman, advocated relating education to everyday life by emphasizing contact with objects in the environment and systematizing all knowledge. His *Orbis Pictus* was the first book in which pictures were as important as the text—the first picturebook.

In the United States in the early nineteenth century, there were series such as the **Boy's and Girl's Library** that were a combination of fact and fiction; by mid-century biographical series such as the **Makers of History** books were read by both children and adults seeking to fill in the gaps in their own education (Marcus, 2008). Other biographical series followed; with the end of World War II came the debut of the **Landmark** series, a few biographies mostly focused on important episodes in American history. Following Sputnik, other series such as Crowell's **Let's Read and Find Out** books became extremely popular. These combined interesting information, often about science topics, within an easy-to-read framework.

Nonfiction as we know it today began to come into its own in the 1980s, with advances in printing that allowed nonfiction writers to illustrate their books in a variety of ways, including photography. Books such as the science series for elementary school readers introduced by John Wiley and Sons were snatched up by schools and parents eager to feed their children's hunger to know about the world. The power of a photograph was showcased in the books of Seymour Simon, which contained NASA photographs, and in Russell Freedman's work in science and history. The **Magic School Bus** series began in 1986, to great popular acclaim. At the same time, the topics, events, and experiences that nonfiction covered were increasingly diverse. Tom Feelings's *The Middle Passage: White Ships/ Black Cargo* (A) and other historical nonfiction told stories of women, African Americans, Asian Americans, and Native Americans, of workers as well as bosses, and of the myriad "unsung" historical events (Marcus, 2008).

When Milton Meltzer questioned the obvious bias of award committees toward fiction in his "Where Do All the Prizes Go? The Case for Nonfiction" (1976), professionals in the field took notice. The Boston Globe–Horn Book Award added a separate category for nonfiction in 1976, and the International Reading Association's Children's Book Award did as well in 1995. The Orbis Pictus Award, established in 1990 by the National Council of Teachers of English, and the Robert F. Sibert Award, established in 2001 by the American Library Association, honor outstanding nonfiction titles, including biography. A list of all of the books winning the latter two awards appears at the end of this chapter. Nonfiction is now recognized as the artistic achievement that it can be.

Nonfiction available today is appealing, attractive, and abundant. Most collections in elementary school libraries and in the children's sections of public libraries are 60 to 70 percent nonfiction—a surprise to most people. Today's young readers enjoy the interesting information, gorgeous design, arresting illustrations, and outstanding writing.

Considering Quality in Nonfiction

Each year, committees of subject area specialists and children's literature specialists select the outstanding examples of books in their respective disciplines. The work, coordinated by the Children's Book Council, involves the National Science Teachers Association, the National Council for the Social Studies, the International Reading Association, and the National Council of Teachers of English. Lists of outstanding books that can enhance teaching and learning in each discipline are published in the professional journals of each organization.

The science committee, for example, evaluates books using three criteria: (1) the book must be accurate and readable; (2) its format and illustrations must be pleasing; and

(3) the information must be consistent with current scientific knowledge. In areas of controversy, a book should present different points of view, and information should not be distorted by personal biases or values. Facts must be clearly distinguished from theories, generalizations must be supported by facts, and significant facts must not be omitted. If experiments are a feature of a book, the science committee considers whether they lead to an understanding of basic principles. Moreover, experiments discussed in the book must be appropriate for the reader's age group and must be both feasible and safe. The committee eschews anthropomorphized animals and plants. It also rejects books that are racist or sexist or that extol violence.

The Orbis Pictus Award for Outstanding Nonfiction for Children is an award for nonfiction of all types, and thus the criteria are broad enough to be applicable to books from varied disciplines. The award committee considers four criteria: accuracy, organization, design, and style. The following discussion expands on those criteria. Figure 10.1 contains a checklist of general criteria for evaluating all types of nonfiction.

• • ACCURACY • •

The criterion of accuracy comprises several facets. First, the facts presented must be current and complete, with a balance between fact and theory, if appropriate, and authenticity of detail. If applicable, varying points of view should be presented. Second, stereotypes should be avoided. Third, the scope of the book should be appropriate to the target audience and to the topic being presented. Fourth, the author's expertise and research should be demonstrated in reference lists, acknowledgments, notes describing the research process, and other documentation.

In excellent nonfiction, facts and theories are clearly distinguished. Highly qualified writers state clearly and succinctly what is known and what is conjectured; they do not mislead by stating as fact what is still a theory or hypothesis. Careful writers use qualifying phrases when they are tentative about the information. For example, some will use such phrases as "many scientists [or historians] believe," "probably could not," "we think that," and "the evidence to date suggests" to indicate that experts in the field are not certain about all things. Good writers also describe the changing status of information about a topic.

In *Wolves* (P), reissued in 2009, Seymour Simon lets his readers know what is fact and what is supposition: "Wolves make all kinds of sounds besides howling; they bark, growl, whine, and squeak. Barking *seems to be* a warning when a wolf is surprised at its den. Growling *is* common among pups when they play." A careful reader realizes that scientists *suppose* that barking serves as a warning, but *know* that pups growl when they play. In

Pale Male: Citizen Hawk of New York City (P–I), Janet Schulman carefully states "Birdwatchers *believe* . . ." when discussing the possibility that one of Pale Male's descendants also nests in the city.

Nonfiction writers with integrity acknowledge other opinions of value; they present different views about their topic, discussing their strengths and weaknesses, if this type of discussion is appropriate for the topic or the intended audience. For example, many books about dinosaurs for older readers present differing ideas about the extinction of the dinosaurs; those for younger readers simply use verbs such as *think* or *suppose* to indicate that they are presenting theory rather than fact. In books for older readers, multiple facets of the topic are presented, requiring readers to carefully consider what they are reading.

Figure 10.1

Considering Quality in Nonfiction

Accuracy

✦ Facts are current and complete. When appropriate there is a balance of fact and theory, with differing viewpoints represented.

✦ The scope is appropriate to both the intended audience and the subject.

✦ The author's expertise and resources are apparent.

Organization

✦ Ideas are clearly developed, presented in a logical sequence, and in an understandable and appropriate fashion.

✦ The author indicates interrelationships between facts and between facts and theories.

Design

✦ The format of the book is attractive and reader-friendly, with appropriate illustrations that are strategically placed.

✦ Illustrations illuminate the facts and concepts.

Style

✦ The writing is interesting, revealing the author's enthusiasm about the subject.

✦ The terminology is appropriate. The writer uses rich language that stimulates a reader's curiosity.

Marc Aronson's *Race: A History Beyond Black and White* (A) is a book that pushes young readers to consider multiple facets of ideas—one that asks them to be critical thinkers. Al Gore's *An Inconvenient Truth: The Crisis of Global Warming* (I) presents enough information, an array of fact and theory, that older children can understand the reasoning behind the warnings from many scientists.

The appropriateness of the scope of a book is related to its target audience. What might be said about a topic for very young children is quite different from what might be said about the same topic for older children. For example, in Laurence Pringle's *Everybody Has a Belly Button* (N–P), the topic of human reproduction is explored in a manner that is appropriate for young children. The information presented is accurate, but the level of detail is minimal in both text and illustration. It is easy to see the difference that a target audience can make when looking at Janet Schulman's *Pale Male: Citizen Hawk of New York City*, written for intermediate readers, and Jeanette Winter's *The Tale of Pale Male: A True Story* (P), written for a younger audience.

In *Shutting Out the Sky: Life in the Tenements of New York, 1880–1924* (I–A), Deborah Hopkinson tells the story of the vast wave of immigrants that came to this country at the turn of the century. Her book is crammed with facts, and she makes them meaningful to and understandable by young readers through her vivid writing, her re-creation of the voices of young people who lived through this era, and her liberal use of period photographs. In her afterword, she speaks directly to her readers, telling them why she wrote the book and inviting them to find and tell their own family stories. The further reading and bibliography that she provides helps them understand both this particular era and Hopkinson's process.

When evaluating accuracy in nonfiction, consider the author's expertise, the sources the author used, the presentation of fact and theory, and the acknowledgment of alternative viewpoints, as appropriate to the scope of the book.

• • ORGANIZATION • •

The organization of a book refers to the logical development of the content. Ideas should be presented according to a clear sequence and pattern that reflects the structure of the text. Interrelationships among facts or events should be clearly indicated.

How content is organized and presented affects the overall value of a piece of nonfiction. Good informational books are clearly organized. A brief look through a piece of nonfiction reveals how the content of a book is arranged. Does it illuminate concepts and build understanding? If appropriate, does it have a table of contents to show readers what it contains? Some books need

additional features, such as a glossary, a subject index (and perhaps an author index as well), a bibliography for further reading, and appendixes with further information. Readers are able to retrieve information or build on the information presented in the book by going to other sources.

The unity of a book results from the relationships among the ideas in the text. The degree of unity hinges on how the author has organized ideas to convey information. Careful, logical development of concepts is essential. Ideas should follow a logical pattern, moving, for example, from simple to complex or general to specific. Well-organized texts also make use of helpful transitions that guide the reader from one idea to the next. And all elements should tie to a central theme.

In Phillip Hoose's *The Race to Save the Lord God Bird* (I–A), the bulk of the chapters are arranged chronologically, a logical organization in a recounting of the extinction of a species over time. Before the chronology begins, however, we read an introduction, "A Bird of the Sixth Wave," that briefly describes the first five waves of extinction and foregrounds how the current, sixth, wave is different. Hoose then presents the prologue, a vivid recounting of a naturalist's discovery of several ivory-billed woodpeckers in 1809, all of which he kills, one especially tragically. In Chapter 1, the story jumps ahead almost one hundred years to discuss ivory-billed woodpecker specimens that had been collected in 1899; Hoose writes of his discovery of these specimens and of the questions this encounter raised about the fate of these magnificent birds. With this extended introduction setting the predominant theme—extinction and what it means for all of us—the chronology begins. This is more than just the story of the futile attempt to save the ivory-billed woodpecker, more than the stories of the biologists and ornithologists who tried to track, understand, and save the bird, but a story of the impact of extinction on our world. Written with passion, beautifully organized, and bolstered by reproductions of period photographs and art, *The Race to Save the Lord God Bird* is an outstanding work of nonfiction. The end material includes a timeline, glossary, source notes, and index.

Catherine Thimmesh's *Team Moon: How 400,000 People Landed Apollo 11 on the Moon* (I), winner of the Sibert Award, begins at the end—and it should! Readers know that Apollo 11 took the first human beings to the moon, so there is no suspense anyway; and it is the perfect introduction to this book, which documents the work behind the scenes. Thimmesh cleverly inserts the speech prepared for Nixon in case the astronauts were unable to return to Earth, but quickly qualifies those remarks. From there, the drama, fraught with tension even though we know the happy ending, unfolds.

A book's organization, of course, should be related to its intended audience. Responsible writers respect their

Teaching Idea 10.1

Genre Study: Noting the Aesthetic in Nonfiction

So much nonfiction today is beautiful as well as educational. As you work with students who are reading nonfiction, help them get into the habit of noticing how their books are designed. The best way to do this is for *you* to notice and comment on books. Point out an especially beautiful photograph or illustration, commenting not only on its informational value but also on its aesthetic quality. Note the way archival material is placed in a text, even as you comment on what you learn from it. In the case of nonfiction picturebooks, look at the illustrations as "pictures on a wall" as well as funds of information.

You and your students can talk about the art in nonfiction in terms of line, shape, texture, color, and design, just as you would a picture storybook.

You can do the same with the writing in nonfiction. Note the metaphors that an author uses, commenting on their beauty along with their explanatory power. Discuss how an author "hooks" you, just as you would discuss the "hook" at the beginning of a story. If you note the artistry in the nonfiction that you and your students read, they will too.

readers and know that children, no matter what their age, can understand important ideas and concepts if they are presented clearly, in an organized fashion. Look for books that have a logical development, with a clear sequence of ideas organized in an identifiable pattern.

• • DESIGN • •

The design of an excellent nonfiction book is attractive, with illustrations that complement the text. These illustrations are of an appropriate medium and format to support and extend the ideas and concepts developed in the text. Further, this illustrative material is appropriately placed.

Nonfiction books should be as appealing in layout and design as fiction books. Verbal information can be elaborated by photographs, diagrams, maps, sketches, graphs, or other visual support. The illustrations help readers visualize the information contained in the text. Effective layout means that illustrations appear in close proximity to the text they illuminate, headings and subheadings are clearly presented, and the amount of text and illustration on a page does not make the page appear crowded or overwhelming.

Many design variations are available today. In the **Eyewitness** series and the **Visual Timeline** series, each double-page spread has clear color photographs, small explanatory notes for each photograph, a brief introduction, and drawings. David Macaulay's *Mosque* (I–A), like his earlier architectural books, is a combination of lucid text and meticulous drawings to pore over. In *The Way We Work* (I), Macaulay turns his talents to an explanation of the human body, making our bodies' systems understandable with straightforward, often humorous text as well as pencil and watercolor illustrations that reveal details of

our insides in a remarkably understated yet accurate manner. Humor laces the illustrations as well.

Frogs (P), by Nic Bishop, invites young readers to pay attention right from the start through the cover photograph, a close-up of a frog with a bit of green plant in its mouth. The superb photographs throughout the book are matched by an attractive and attention-grabbing design consisting of clever use of color, various fonts and sizes of type, and a double gatefold time-lapse photograph of a frog leaping into and completing a dive.

Look for books in which the design enhances the presentation of information and is visually appealing. Teaching Idea 10.1 suggests an easy way for teachers to help students notice the beauty in many works of nonfiction.

• • STYLE • •

A work of nonfiction is also judged by style, or how the information is presented. The writing should be interesting and stimulating, and should reveal the author's enthusiasm for the subject. Appropriate terminology and rich language should generate curiosity and wonder in young readers.

Even when a book deals with hard facts, graceful language and a fresh vision are important components of excellent literature. Descriptive words used in interesting yet precise ways are a mark of good nonfiction. The tone of the book reveals the thrust and significance of an author's work as well as the author's relationship to the subject. The literary value of a nonfiction book depends in large part on how much passion an author brings to the work. It is clear from the photographs and the interesting presentation of information in *Frogs* that Nic Bishop is passionate about his work. The humor in David Macaulay's

The Way We Work: Getting to Know the Amazing Human Body adds an unexpected and very welcome tone to the way that information is presented.

Sophie Webb's books, *My Season with Penguins: An Antarctic Journal* (P–I) and *Looking for Seabirds: Journal from an Alaskan Voyage* (I), convey Webb's delight in her world through lively text and appealing watercolor illustrations. They also present a model of a field-based research journal, complete with Webb's humorous commentary on life in the field. Another strength of these books is Webb's dual perspective as both artist and scientist, with each complementing the other.

Nonfiction writers often use a narrative structure to tell the story of a person, event, or series of events. Jim Murphy uses this technique brilliantly in his many outstanding works of nonfiction, including *An American Plague: The True and Terrifying Story of the Yellow Fever Epidemic of 1793* (I–A), which won a Newbery Honor, an award rarely bestowed on a work of nonfiction. Jennifer Armstrong's riveting *Shipwreck at the Bottom of the World: The Extraordinary True Story of Shackleton and the* Endurance (I) is another outstanding work of nonfiction that employs a narrative frame.

Many nonfiction writers directly address their audience, using the pronoun *you* to draw readers into the book. Other authors offer readers ideas for doing their own experiments or research, or challenge them to evaluate ideas and arguments based on the facts presented. This technique creates active readers. Look for books that contain language that both conveys and generates excitement about the subject.

We now take a close look at *Tracking Trash: Flotsam, Jetsam, and the Science of Ocean Motion* (I), by Loree Griffin Burns.

A CLOSE LOOK AT

Tracking Trash: Flotsam, Jetsam, and the Science of Ocean Motion

A Boston Globe–Horn Book Honor book, *Tracking Trash: Flotsam, Jetsam, and the Science of Ocean Motion* is a good example of nonfiction at its best. The focus is timely and appealing, the information is both interesting and accurate, the organization is straightforward and allows for exploration of various facets of the topic, and the design and style are inviting to young readers. An effective blend of stories of people being scientists and the science behind what they do makes for a very appealing book.

End material that includes titles of books that young readers might enjoy, websites they can explore, acknowledgements, and bibliographic notes, as well as the author's credentials, would be enough to convince any reader of the accuracy of the information presented in this book. Even so, it is the photographs and charts and the actual words of the scientists who were involved in this scientific work that are most convincing. By going to the sources and telling the story using their words, with appropriate photographs, Burns builds a convincing case for the veracity of her text.

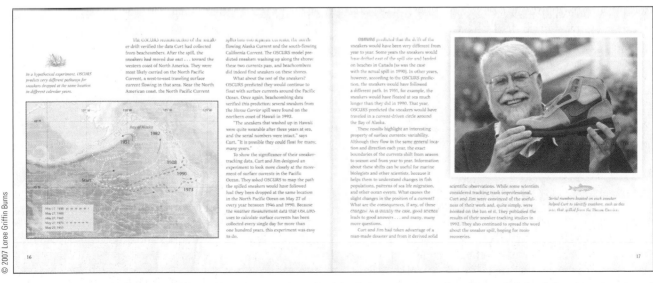

Diagrams offer visual support for the scientific concepts presented, while photographs personalize the people behind the science in Tracking Trash: Flotsam, Jetsam, and the Science of Ocean Motion.

Loree Griffin Burns

I write books about science for children . . . and I love my job.

Loree Griffin Burns majored in biology in college, then went on to earn her PhD. She enjoys meeting other scientists, either in person or through research connections, and she is passionate about sharing the great things that research scientists can do. ***Tracking Trash: Flotsam, Jetsam, and the Science of Ocean Motion*** is her first book for children, and it won the International Reading Association's Author Award for nonfiction in 2008, as well as a Boston Globe–Horn Book Honor Award. Visit Loree at www.loreegriffinburns.com.

In five brief chapters brimming with photographs, Burns tells the story of how Dr. Curtis Ebbesmeyer got involved in studying flotsam and jetsam in his work as an oceanographer: his mother told him about sneakers washing up on North Pacific beaches and he set out to see what was happening. Chapter 2 recounts the scientific career of W. James Ingraham, oceanographer at the National Oceanic and Atmospheric Administration, who developed a computer program to calculate surface current motion in the North Pacific Ocean. The two men collaborated and published the results of their studies of the sneaker spill. Chapter 3 recounts what they did when there was a second major spill, this time of bathtub toys. Chapter 4 adds more information about currents and the garbage that floats in the ocean, while Chapter 5 discusses the "monster dumps" of garbage that scientists have found. At the end of each chapter, there is a brief explanation of a scientific concept that is important to understand, or a call to action on the part of the reader.

Design and style work together to make this an engaging book. Diagrams that, for example, explain the patterns of currents, photographs of people, sneakers, and bathtub toys, the first page of the *Beachcombers' Alert* newsletter, and photographs of the trash itself—as well as the damage it can cause—are informative and engaging. Throughout, there is a pattern of smart people noticing things and asking good questions. At the end of Chapter 2, Burns makes her theme explicit when she says: "As is usually the case, good science leads to good answers . . . and many, many more questions."

Common Subjects in Nonfiction

So many wonderful books are available today that young readers can use nonfiction trade books to explore almost any topic that interests them. Here we discuss nonfiction (excluding biography, which is covered in Chapter 9) that presents information about a multitude of topics in science, mathematics, social studies, language study, and the fine arts. Teaching Idea 10.2 applies to any nonfiction topic that is available for young readers.

• • SCIENCE • • AND MATHEMATICS

Science books are so popular that there are several series of science books for young readers. These include the **Let's Read and Find Out** series for newly independent readers and the **Magic School Bus** series, as well as the **Magic Tree House** series, now accompanied by "nonfiction companions," or **Magic Tree House Research Guides**, and other series such as the **National Geographic Science Chapters** and the **Scientists in the Field** series. These series introduce young readers to the vast world of science and to the scientific enterprise.

Science, like any other discipline, evolves over time, and books for children reflect the changes in the discipline. Advances in science and technology also affect children's books. Sally Ride and Tam O'Shaughnessy present some of the interesting information that has been gathered during recent space explorations in *Exploring Our Solar System* (I–A). Some books about timely topics such as space exploration have to be revised in light of new information. Seymour Simon's wonderful series about the solar system, updated whenever new information makes it necessary, includes *Our Solar System* (I), first published in 1992 with a new edition in 2007. It is illustrated with stunning photographs taken during the many space explorations that have occurred in the past several years. His *Destination: Mars* (I), an updated version published in 2000, became necessary because of recent exploration of and thinking about the red planet, and includes new photographs. These and other books in the series are outstanding resources for readers interested in space.

As what we know changes, new topics emerge. The past several years have produced books about climate change such as Al Gore's *An Inconvenient Truth:*

Teaching Idea 10.2

Make an Alphabet Book or Glossary

Every discipline, topic, or subject area has a vocabulary of its own. In order to read and comprehend text, students exploring a new area need to become familiar with its vocabulary. One way to develop vocabulary related to a particular topic is to create an ABC book or a glossary, depending on the topic. This can be done as an individual or group project, and it is a good alternative to the standard "report" by which students demonstrate their expertise.

1. Have students explore a new area of study by having them read widely in nonfiction trade books.

2. Have students select an area within the broader topic in which they would like to specialize.

3. Have students list all the new or important words related to the topic under study.

4. Have students create a book that has a letter on each page, listing topical vocabulary that begins with that letter.

5. Have students draw pictures, list synonyms (if appropriate), and write definitions for each word. Use each word in a sentence that explains something about the topic.

6. Have students read the book to peers or younger students and display the handmade books in the classroom.

The Crisis of Global Warming, Lynn Cherry and Gary Braasch's *How We Know What We Know about Our Changing Climate: Scientists and Kids Explore Global Warming* (I), and Laurie David and Cambria Gordon's *The Down-to-Earth Guide to Global Warming* (I). Restoration of ecosystems is explored in two exceptional books about wolves. Jean Craighead George's *The Wolves Are Back* (P), with gorgeous illustrations by Wendell Minor, and Dorothy Hinshaw Patent's *When the Wolves Returned: Restoring Nature's Balance in Yellowstone* (P–I), illustrated with photographs by Dan and Cassie Hartman, are both interesting reports of the restoration of diversity, with the resulting costs and benefits to Yellowstone.

Topics such as human beings, plants, animals and their habitats, and dinosaurs have remained popular over the years. These include the food web, as in April Pulley Sayre's *Trout Are Made of Trees* (N–P), illustrated by Kate Endle, in which readers learn about the food web in a deciduous forest ecosystem. Appended Internet resources, information about the trout life cycle, and ways to help the environment all provide additional possibilities for young readers. Gail Gibbons's many nonfiction books for young readers cover a wide variety of topics. In *Corn* (P), she combines a simple text, additional information in text boxes, and her signature illustrations. A specific creature is the focus of Sarah C. Campbell's *Wolfsnail: A Backyard Predator* (N–P), illustrated with photos by the author and Richard P. Campbell. In this book, we follow the wolfsnail, a predator, as it tracks its food, a garden snail. Additional information includes a description of wolfsnail habits, life cycle and human-influenced habitat, and a glossary. Helen Frost explores one of nature's most harmonious relationships in *Monarch and Milkweed* (P), with jewel-like illustrations by Leonid Gore illuminating the text.

Martin Jenkins introduces very young readers to the five species of great apes in *Ape* (N–P), with detailed pencil-and-oil illustrations by Vicky White. Interesting variations in font and size allow different readings, with more detailed information appearing in "footnotes" on the expansive pages. Steve Jenkins combines two favorite topics—color and animals—in *Living Color* (P), a visually dazzling book filled with information about animal coloration and vivid cut-paper collage that is, in a word, colorful. Jenkins and Robin Page collaborate to present sibling relationships in the animal kingdom, relationships much like those that young readers have with their own siblings. *Sisters & Brothers: Sibling Relationships in the Animal World* (P), is visually interesting, factual, and humorous.

Prehistoric animals also continue to be popular subjects in nonfiction. Charlotte Lewis Brown explores the probable cause of the extinction of dinosaurs in her *The Day the Dinosaurs Died* (P), illustrated by Phil Wilson. This **I Can Read** book allows newly emergent readers the opportunity to read for themselves the drama of the asteroid hit and the death and destruction that follow. In another book for primary-grade readers, Robert Sabuda and Matthew Reinhart offer a terrific pop-up book that explores the size and features of prehistoric creatures in *Encyclopedia Prehistorica: Mega Beasts* (P). Caroline Arnold takes a look at *Giant Sea Reptiles of the Dinosaur Age* (I), with illustrations by Laurie Caple. Sandra Markle's *Outside and Inside Woolly Mammoths* (I), a part of her excellent **Outside and Inside** series, pulls readers into the science behind the ideas about mammoth physiology and habitat, including the possibility of cloning one of the beasts. Endmatter includes an index, glossary, reading list, and websites. A humorous but accurate account of prehistoric life, Hannah Bonner's *When Fish Got Feet, Sharks Got Teeth, and Bugs Began to Swarm: A Cartoon Prehistory of Life Long before Dinosaurs* (I–A) offers older readers a look at concepts in biology, paleontology, and geology through lucid text and clever, comic illustrations. Paleontologist Thomas R. Holtz, Jr. offers a very informative volume for older readers, *Dinosaurs: The Most Complete, Up-to-Date Encyclopedia for Dinosaur Lovers of All Ages* (I–A), illustrated by Luis V. Rey.

The human body is another topic for many science nonfiction books, and two top nonfiction writers have created books that both inform and delight. Seymour Simon's *The Human Body* (P–I) combines full-page false-color images, photomicrographs, diagrams of the interior of the human body, and brisk prose to present information on the twelve body systems and the senses in a way that captivates young readers. He has also written individual books about the body's systems, such as *The Brain: Our Nervous System* (P–I) and *The Heart: Our Circulatory System* (P–I), both reissues. David Macaulay and Richard Walker's *The Way We Work: Getting to Know the Amazing Human Body* (I–A), illustrated by Macaulay, first introduces basic biology and chemistry cellular concepts, and then takes a tour of the systems of the human body. Nicola Davies's exploration of human parasites in *What's Eating You?: Parasites—The Inside Story* (P–I), illustrated by Neal Layton, takes a comic but very accurate look at something that most of us don't want to think about. Becky Balnes focuses on the outside of the body in *Your Skin Holds You In* (N–P), with thirteen brief sentences describing skin and several smaller-print sentences sprinkled through the double-page spreads to provide additional information. The illustrations invite exploration and questions, as does the endmatter. In a very real way, this book encourages very young readers to conduct scientific inquiry.

The scientific method itself is presented in several books for young readers, such as Stephen Swinburne's *The Woods Scientist* (I), part of the acclaimed **Scientists in the Field** series. In other books in this outstanding series, Sy Montgomery focuses on how scientists study particular species in *The Snake Scientist* and *The Tarantula Scientist* (I). Fran Hodgkins's *The Whale Scientists: Solving the Mystery of Whale Strandings* (I) is a **Scientists in the Field** book that presents the ongoing research in an as-yet-unsolved scientific mystery. Many of Jim Arnosky's books, such as *Field Trips: Bug Hunting, Animal Tracking, Bird-Watching, and Shore Walking with Jim Arnosky* (I) and *The Brook Book: Exploring the Smallest Streams* (P) are intended to help young readers learn to be keen observers.

Partly biographical, Pamela Turner's *Life on Earth—and Beyond: An Astrobiologist's Quest* (I–A), explains NASA scientist Chris McKay's career as a field scientist studying the microscopic life that exists in extreme environments. The science is fascinating, but it is the excitement of the cycle of questions, explanations, and more questions—the shape of a field scientist's life—that is extraordinary. An index, further reading, movies, and Internet resources are appended. Donna M. Jackson explores the edges of sensory perception in *Phenomena: Secrets of the Senses* (I–A). Quotes from researchers coupled with first-person accounts and factual explanations enable her to draw a distinction between what we know and what we think, and how intuitions and alternate explanations of phenomena can result in careful research that then results in knowledge.

A list of outstanding science trade books can be obtained from the Children's Book Council and is also published in the spring in *Science and Children*, a journal of the National Science Teachers Association for elementary- and middle-school teachers. Other journals, such as *The Reading Teacher, Language Arts*, and *The Horn Book Magazine*, regularly review books that consider science topics. The Orbis Pictus Award and Sibert Award lists are also useful resources. Now, we take a close look at a science book that takes a complicated topic and makes it understandable to young children. *Our Family Tree: An Evolution Story* (P) begins at the beginning of life on Earth and presents a basic outline of the complicated theory of evolution in a manner that young children can understand.

✳   ✳   ✳

A CLOSE LOOK AT

Our Family Tree: An Evolution Story

Although the text is minimal and the description of evolution is not detailed, Lisa Westberg Peters presents accurate facts. The end of the book contains a double-page spread with scientific explanations of nine of the major ideas in the book, another double-page spread that presents a timeline of evolution from single cells to modern humans, and a final page in which both Peters and illustrator Lauren Stringer talk about where they got their information and who reviewed the manuscript. Just as Peters meticulously researched before writing, so too did Stringer in preparation for creating her illustrations. Both text and illustrations were checked and rechecked for accuracy. The central concepts that underlie evolutionary theory—change, adaptation, chance, and interdependence—are also clearly and accurately presented.

The text is organized chronologically, a logical way to present the "story" of evolution. The minimal space of a picturebook format prohibits a full explanation, so Peters very carefully chose what information to present. Keeping the intended audience in mind, Peters compresses vast amounts of time, saying, for example, "As the seas rose and fell, our family changed again." The timeline at the end of the book indicates the number of years that this took, but within the text, that detail is not crucial, only the fact that it happened. Because Peters wanted to

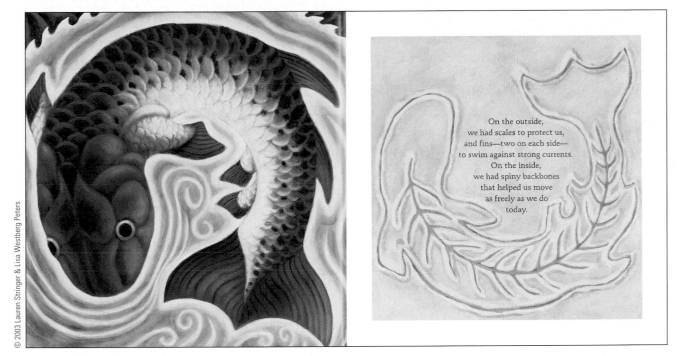

On the outside,
we had scales to protect us,
and fins—two on each side—
to swim against strong currents.
On the inside,
we had spiny backbones
that helped us move
as freely as we do
today.

*Full-color paintings accompanied by paintings of sand drawings allowed Lauren Stringer to combine scientific fact and beauty in her illustrations for **Our Family Tree: An Evolution Story** by Lisa Westberg Peters.*

make evolution understandable by young children, she chose to introduce it by connecting the idea of evolution to the image of a human family tree. Stringer begins her illustrations on the title page with an image of a mother and two children—a family—on the beach, where one of them picks up a piece of driftwood and begins to draw their family tree. The text and illustrations end with the same image and the same immediacy. This organizational frame allows young readers to understand the larger idea of "family" that evolutionary theory suggests.

The book is beautifully illustrated and designed. Stringer pays close attention to details. For example, the first four images of the family on the beach are enclosed in circles that mirror the shape of our beginnings as single-celled creatures. As the text progresses, Stringer juxtaposes sand sketches of the scientific details that the text is presenting. The genetic code is sketched in the sand, as are the backbone of the fish, the lungs of the amphibian, and the rest of the major points in our evolution that are described in the text. Through the sand sketches, Stringer portrays details without making them too graphic; the accompanying full-color paintings reflect the more general information presented in the text. The sand drawings reappear just before the end of the book in a double-page spread that recapitulates the major stages of evolution.

Although many nonfiction books directly address the reader with the pronoun *you*, Peters uses the first-person pronouns, *we, our*, and *us* to reinforce the idea of the fam-

ily of man. The title is *Our* Family Tree rather than *The* Family Tree. The book begins, "All of us are part of an old, old family," and as Peters tells the story of evolution, it is happening to us. "We" were tiny round cells. "We" eventually developed big brains. This technique serves to heighten the sense of connectedness, illuminate a central concept of evolution, and keep the reader engaged. Finally, choosing to use a narrative frame to present the idea of evolution—"an evolution story"—creates a familiar structure in which to embed new ideas. Stringer's illustrations build on the story frame by depicting the progression of the day and the elaboration of the drawings that the family makes on the beach, ending with sunset as they walk away together, the sun behind them, their shadows ahead.

Fewer nonfiction books support a study of mathematics than support either science or social studies, although several are published each year. Mathematics programs today reflect a philosophy in which fiction and nonfiction literature fit naturally. Today, we present mathematical problems in context, draw on children's background knowledge to solve them, and model strategies for alternate ways to solve problems.

Many mathematics lessons begin with a story—a story with a problem that can be solved through a mathematical process. Teachers invite children to propose as many different strategies as possible to try to solve the problem. Together, they apply each strategy and evaluate

Profile

Lisa Westberg Peters

I wanted to write about evolution. I knew that this subject pulled on my emotions and made me wonder what it means to be human. Whatever I wrote, I wanted to make room for that emotion and that sense of wonder.

Many of Peters's books for children reflect her passion for researching and writing about the natural world. *Our Family Tree* developed over the course of thirteen years, during which Peters studied geology and garnered information about evolution through reading, lectures, and field trips. "The subjects of evolution and earth and life history were all so new to me," comments Peters (2004). "Everything was startlingly fresh. I'm a curious person, so whenever I learn something new, it always leads me to ask more questions. Many writers are natural researchers and it's a trip to a candy store to sit in a library poring over the books."

To create an outstanding picture-book about evolution, Peters had to combine curiosity with creativity. "The hardest part of this process," says Peters (2004), "was finding a way to translate what I was learning into a text that might be accessible and appealing to even the youngest readers. This was the part that took the longest time—more than a dozen years." In her article for *Riverbank Review*, Peters writes that "[the] family album approach provided the frame of reference I was looking for, since children often see family albums at home or make family trees at school." She goes on to explain that "despite having found a familiar frame of reference, I knew I would be entering territory foreign to most children. I wanted to engage readers by writing a clear, simple story, not a list of facts. As a picture-book writer, I also needed to write a story that offered plenty of visual opportunities and inspiration to an artist, because images would play a critical role in introducing this subject to children" (2003, pp. 11–12).

Although the illustrator, Lauren Stringer, and Peters did not directly collaborate to make decisions about the book's appearance, they did communicate about the text in a way that helped *Our Family Tree* develop into a uniquely unified piece of nonfiction. "The text was finished before Lauren knew about the project," explains Peters (2004). "Once she accepted the project, she needed time and distance from me to learn about the subject and to make the book her own. However, we communicated regularly. I often sent her relevant clippings with images that might be helpful to her. We both sent each other letters and postcards. From the time I first met her and talked about the book," notes Peters, "I felt she had the right soul to illustrate *Our Family Tree*."

With Stringer's meticulously researched illustrations, Peters's depiction of humanity's long ancestry is both aesthetically engaging and scientifically accurate. The book's artistic value and the questions it asks about the world combine to make *Our Family Tree* an exemplary piece of nonfiction for children.

Watch the interview with Lisa on our companion website.

---

its accuracy and efficiency. They learn that there are alternative ways to come up with the right answer. Stories that are structured around numbers and counting, such as Pat Hutchins's classic, *The Doorbell Rang* (P), are especially useful for primary teachers who want to link mathematics and reading.

There are also many beautiful counting books and books that allow children to practice numeral recognition, such as Stephen Johnson's *City by Numbers* (P). These books encourage children to develop their visual skills as they look for numerals or count items on the artistically beautiful pages. Other books explain mathematical concepts, such as Bruce McMillan's *Eating Fractions* (P–I). McMillan illustrates fractions with mouthwatering photographs of children sharing—and eating—food. The concept of one-fourth is understandable when it means the difference between a whole pizza and only part of one!

Measurement and size are explored in Steve Jenkins's *Actual Size* (P–I) and *Prehistoric Actual Size* (P–I). Jenkins's amazing cut-paper collages appear again in these oversize books containing life-size illustrations of creatures, or parts thereof. The white backdrop emphasizes the relative sizes of the creatures in the books as compared to each other, and invites young readers to compare themselves to the creatures depicted. Just how big is a gorilla's hand, anyway? Ben Hillman's *How Big Is It?: A Big Book All about Bigness* (P) combines a conversational text and manipulated photographs that allow young readers to see the actual size of twenty-two animals, objects, and places.

Jon Scieszka's *Math Curse* (I), illustrated by Lane Smith, is a wonderfully funny book that underscores how we use mathematics in our daily lives and presents interesting mathematical puzzles for children to figure out. The outrageous humor in the book is so infectious that children enthusiastically engage in the mental arithmetic the book calls for.

The journal *Teaching Children Mathematics* reviews books that relate to mathematics instruction, as do *Language Arts, The Reading Teacher*, and *The Horn Book Magazine*.

Profile

Lauren Stringer

W hen I finally began paint-ing the original paintings for [*Our Family Tree*] I had memorized my research enough that it came from inside me. I felt as if I had taken walks through the Devonian swamps and across the arid landscape of Pangaea. When I painted the dancing volcanoes, I knew I would be able to blend my personal vision with the scientific facts and still be accurate. I knew I had done my research well when I felt a deep connection to each of our ancestors and could picture in my mind where they lived, how they moved about, and what they ate. The day I painted the Permian Extinc-tion I found myself in tears thinking about such an enormous loss of life on this earth.

"Upon first reading *Our Family Tree*," notes Stringer (2004), "I loved it and was terrified by it at the same time. I knew I would need to do a tremen-dous amount of research before I could even begin to paint this book in my own way. I am not a science

illustrator, nor do I have a science/biology background, so I knew I would have to start with the 'ABC's' of evolution." Researching the illus-trations for Peters's nonfiction book about evolution was a monumental task, leading Stringer on a journey from the children's science sections of libraries to the academic offices of anthropologists and geologists.

The journals and studio wall space Stringer usually uses to collect and organize artifacts and sketches for new books proved too small a space to contain the four-and-a-half bil-lion years' worth of information she needed in order to illustrate *Our Family Tree*. Her research began to sprawl:

It became very clear early on that there was not enough room to sort and organize all my research and images on one wall. Just outside my studio on the second floor of our old Victorian house is a long wall that goes down the hall and turns to con-tinue down the stairs. I hung sheets of paper on this wall to create a timeline that was 4 feet high by 20 feet long, placing Lisa's text at intervals that

coincided with geological eras. I then began to collage images found from books on evolution, art history books, biology books, present day ancestors who still resemble ancient ancestors (e.g., the salamander for the amphib-ian stage that evolved lungs for us to breathe with). With this timeline I could make note of when the land-scape was frozen and arid because of glaciers or when it was more tropical and hot. I could see when the first deciduous trees and the first flowers evolved. These details were extremely important because often, when I'm working on a book, I will decide to add a flower or a tree for color or texture—but what if they didn't exist yet?! (2004)

Stringer's artistic impression of her scientific findings makes even our most distant ancestors seem famil-iar. Her ability to synthesize research with artistic vision culminates in a nonfiction text for children that is both accurate and aesthetically engaging.

Watch the interview with Lauren on our companion website.

• • SOCIAL STUDIES • •

Just as in science, the content of social studies evolves as changes in the world result in new configurations of countries and people. New communications technology makes the world seem much smaller than it used to be and increases our interest in other people and places. Children have more books than ever to select from as they pursue their interests in the past and present.

Many nonfiction books cover such topics as geogra-phy and maps, life in the past, and the social structures and customs of various cultures, past and present. Children are quite naturally interested in others, where they come from, and in the world around them; this natural curiosity and openness to people makes them receptive to books that explore the global community, past and present.

Sound historical detective work marks Scott Reynolds Nelson's *Ain't Nothing but a Man: My Quest to Find the Real John Henry* (I), written in collaboration with Marc Aronson. The reader, along with Nelson, follows the clues

as Nelson finds them—photographs, census data, prison records, and other sources—and learns that John Henry might have been a convict, and most likely died of silico-sis and was buried along with hundreds of other African American convicts forced to work on the railroad. Doreen Rappaport creates a pseudo-biography of the Statue of Liberty in *Lady Liberty: A Biography* (P–I), with illustra-tions by Matt Tavares, through the fictional accounts of various people who worked on the statue. From the sculp-tor Auguste Bartholdi to the ten-year-old who donated her two roosters for fundraising, the accounts are both vivid and moving.

Faraway places and people are brought close in good nonfiction. Ted and Betsy Lewin visited Mongo-lia to see the Naadam, a sporting event held through-out Mongolia. In *Horse Song: The Naadam of Mongolia* (P–I), they focus on a race in which young boys gallop for fourteen miles across the Gobi Desert on their stal-lions. The watercolor illustrations are gorgeous as well as informative, the text succinct and vivid, and the end material provides interesting additional information about a nomadic culture so remote that most of us will never experience it.

Current issues in social studies find their way into children's books, as Judith St. George's *So You Want to Be President?* (I–A) aptly demonstrates. David Small's funny cartoon-style illustrations perfectly match the witty text in which St. George imparts information about the office, offers humorous tidbits, and makes some forthright political statements. Deborah Ellis focuses on North America in *Off to War: Voices of Soldiers' Children* (I–A), in which she interviews American and Canadian children whose parents have been sent to Iraq or Afghanistan.

History is also an important subject in nonfiction. American history is presented from fresh perspectives in such books as Tom Feelings's *Middle Passage: White Ships/ Black Cargo* (A) and Patricia and Fredrick McKissack's *Christmas in the Big House, Christmas in the Quarters* (I). Russell Freedman's *Who Was First?: Discovering the Americas* (I–A) invites readers to consider how the Americas have been "discovered" by many people at many times in history. He presents historical theories with accompanying evidence that both supports and refutes them. Anita Silvey presents the stories of those that history has ignored in *I'll Pass for Your Comrade: Women Soldiers in the Civil War* (I–A). The women she focuses on defied the social norms of their time to risk their lives as soldiers on both sides, even though they could not vote, could not own property, and were generally considered to be the property of their fathers or husbands. History that we all think we know, such as that of the American Revolution, is presented in a fresh way in *Let It Begin Here!* (I) by Don Brown, and in Russell Freedman's *Washington at Valley Forge* (I).

Places, how they evolved, and how people lived there are another important topic in social studies. An American icon is the focus of a collection of portraits from 108 contemporary writers and artists, *Our White House: Looking In, Looking Out* (I–A). A patchwork of general history of the White House; interesting, unique stories about it; and major events that occurred are followed by support material that includes a website, www .ourwhitehouse.org. Mark Foster tells the story of a fictional whaling town in New England in *Whale Port* (I) with arresting double-page-spread bird's-eye views of the town as it grows. Single-page depictions of the inside of workplaces, houses, and other buildings with accompanying text, small sketches, and labels create a book full of information that readers spend time with, looking closely at the interesting details. Richard Michelson's *Tuttle's Red Barn: The Story of America's Oldest Family Farm* (P) chronicles social and economic changes over four centuries. Azarian's woodcuts are worth poring over for details of dress, buildings, tools, and other artifacts.

World War II is the setting for Susan Campbell Bartoletti's *Hitler Youth: Growing Up in Hitler's Shadow* (A), a deeply disturbing but also moving account of some of the young people caught up in the Hitler Youth movement. Voices of those who were enthusiastic Hitler Youth members, those who were part of the resistance, and those persecuted by the Third Reich help Bartoletti create a book that sparks discussion of values and the consequences of one's actions.

New facts about history are presented in Chris Crowe's *Getting Away with Murder: The True Story of the Emmett Till Case* (A), in which the 1955 murder of a young black boy and the speedy acquittal of his white murderers is portrayed. Crowe also discusses how this incident galvanized people across the nation and helped provoke the civil rights movement of the 1960s. In *Nobody Gonna Turn Me 'Round: Stories and Songs of the Civil Rights Movement* (I), with illustrations by Shane W. Evans, Doreen Rappaport completes a trilogy of books that recount pivotal events of the 1950s and 1960s.

Books such as these are easy to find. The Children's Book Council's "Notable Trade Books in Social Studies" list is available from the council and published in the April/May issue of the journal *Social Education*; they are reviewed in journals such as *The Horn Book Magazine*, *Language Arts*, and *The Reading Teacher*. Now, we take a close look at another book that presents an important historical event, the rise and fall of Negro League Baseball, Kadir Nelson's Sibert Award–winning *We Are the Ship: The Story of Negro League Baseball* (I–A).

✳ ✳ ✳

A CLOSE LOOK AT

We Are the Ship: The Story of Negro League Baseball

Kadir Nelson's artistry—and the history—in this book begins with the cover, a full-color oil painting of Josh Gibson framed with a thin cream band and topped by a deep brown background for the title, presented in off-white and cream. All is bordered by a vivid red frame. The end pages, a deep, rich brown, continue the palette of a book that is all about color, the color of the skin of certain human beings who were not allowed to play major league baseball because of it. The copyright and dedication pages, on a cream background that continues throughout the book, contain quotes from various individuals involved in Negro League baseball, including Rube Foster, the founder of the Negro National League, from whom the title is drawn: "We are the ship; all else the sea." The foreword by Hank Aaron, with a full-color portrait of

© 2008 Kadir Nelson

Oil paintings based on archival photographs make vivid the personalities of the players in Negro League Baseball in Kadir Nelson's We Are the Ship: The Story of Negro League Baseball.

"first colored world series," which unfolds into a double gatefold portrait of the members of the two teams that played that game. Each chapter is filled with details that make the time and the characters come alive.

A pattern is established in the first chapter and continues throughout the book. Nelson creates a narrator who represents "everyman" in the League, using the pronouns "we," "us," and "our," which evoke feelings of both isolation and fraternity. Isolated from the white National League, the Negro League was a cohesive unit, a close-knit brotherhood of competitors. The narrative voice has an oral quality, as if the reader were listening to a story told by a former member of the league, and serves to draw the reader into the personalities of the players as well as the history of the times.

The racism that controlled baseball—and much else—in America from the mid-1860s to the late 1940s, when Jackie Robinson signed with the Brooklyn Dodgers, is unflinchingly portrayed. Despite the ugliness of that racism, the tone of the book is never bitter, but rather matter-of-fact, while clearly condemning and even poking fun at the systematic exclusion of talented athletes because they were black. The final words in the book demonstrate the tone throughout:

> People ask all the time if we're bitter because we weren't given the chance to play baseball in the major leagues for all of those years. Some of us are, but most of us aren't. Most Negroes back then had to work in factories, wash windows, or work on some man's plantation, and they didn't get paid much for it. We were fortunate. We got to play baseball for a living, something we would have done even if we hadn't gotten paid for it. When you can do what you love to do and get paid for it, it's a wonderful thing.
>
> We look at guys like Bob Gibson and Ken Griffey, Jr., and smile, because we made it possible

him on the facing page, contextualizes the story about to unfold, as he began his career in the Negro Leagues but played there for only a very brief time before moving to the majors once Jackie Robinson broke the color barrier.

The story of the Negro League unfolds in ten chapters, nine "innings" plus "extra innings" that trace the origin, development, and end of the league. Appropriately, the first inning, "Beginnings" is graced with a gorgeous oil painting of Smokey Joe Williams. Throughout the book, Nelson's paintings, based on archival photographs, vividly portray the people about whom he is writing. At the end of the first chapter is a facsimile painting of a ticket to the

Profile

Kadir Nelson

m *y focus is to create images of people who demonstrate a sense of hope and nobility. I want to show the strength and integrity of the human being and the human spirit.*

Kadir Nelson began drawing at the age of three, and painting at age ten.

He explains that it's "part of [his] DNA." His talent won him a scholarship at Pratt Institute in Brooklyn, New York, and, upon graduating, he began his professional career as an artist, working with a variety of publishers and production studios

In 1999, he began to illustrate picturebooks, and at present almost twenty of them are still in print. He has won a Coretta Scott King Illus-

trator Award, a Caldecott Honor, and a NAACP Image Award. *We Are the Ship,* his authorial debut, won the Sibert Award, the Coretta Scott King Author Award, and a King Illustrator Honor Award. Visit Kadir at www.kadirnelson.com.

Teaching Idea 10.3

Thematic Connection: Learning about Family History

Students are always interested in finding out about themselves and their families and friends. Ask students to interview their older family members about family history. Then, after students have described that history—either orally or in writing—have them use their research skills, with the help of the school librarian, to find nonfiction books that offer information about some aspect of that history. For example, if a student's great-grandparents emigrated from eastern Europe at the turn of the century, look for books that present that history. If a student's uncle fought in the Vietnam conflict, look for books about that war. Students' family histories can then be put in the context of what the students discovered through their research. For upper-elementary and middle-school students, this can take the form of a paper—one that is grounded in personal history.

for these guys to play in the majors. If there had been no such thing as a Negro League, there would have been no Jackie Robinson or Willie Mays or Hank Aaron. These guys stand on our shoulders. We cleared the way for them and changed the course of history. And knowing that satisfies the soul. How can you be bitter about something like that? (pp. 77–78)

An interesting topic revealed with both passion and accuracy through a compelling narrative and brilliant oil paintings makes this an outstanding piece of nonfiction. The author's note, bibliography and filmography, chapter notes regarding sources for the paintings, and an index, offer young readers a way to pursue the history of the Negro Leagues further. Teaching Idea 10.3 offers suggestions for how to help students explore and present their own family histories.

LANGUAGE, LITERATURE, AND THE ARTS

Children's books that explore language are wonderful resources for an integrated language arts curriculum. Alphabet books, books about traditional parts of speech, histories of language, and books about writing are becoming more plentiful. Don Robb's *Ox, House, Stick: The History of Our Alphabet* (I), illustrated by Anne Smith, traces

the transformations of each letter, weaving in history and interesting bits of information. Punctuation takes on a new dimension in Robin Pulver's *Punctuation Takes a Vacation* (P), a primary-grade version of the popular adult book *Eats, Shoots and Leaves*.

Books like Brian Cleary's *Hairy, Scary, Ordinary: What Is an Adjective?* (P) explore the parts of speech. Ruth Heller is known for her brightly illustrated, eye-catching books about the parts of speech, including *Mine, All Mine: A Book about Pronouns* (P–I). The rhyming text is surrounded by double-page illustrations visually depicting the pronouns. Heller's books give concrete and intriguing examples of what many students feel is boringly remote. Robin Pulver explores grammar in *Silent Letters Loud and Clear* (P–I), illustrated by Lynn Rowe Reed, and Loreen Leedy has fun with similes in *Crazy Like a Fox: A Simile Story* (P–I).

A series of books by Marvin Terban explores wordplay, such as *Guppies in Tuxedos: Funny Eponyms* (I). Jon Agee's books, such as *Elvis Lives! and Other Anagrams* (I), are also interesting to students exploring what we can do with the English language. Loreen Leedy and Pat Street present interesting sayings in *There's a Frog in My Throat! 440 Animal Sayings a Little Bird Told Me* (P) with illustrations to increase the fun.

Studies of books and authors often accompany composition instruction. These studies work best if they transcend the usual biographical information to get at the essence of what writers and illustrators do—create books. Leonard Marcus does just that in many books, including *The Wand in the Word: Conversations with Writers of Fantasy* (I–A) and *Pass It Down: Five Picture Book Families Make Their Mark* (I–A). Marcus explores how authors and illustrators work together to create picturebooks in *Side by Side: Five Favorite Picture-Book Teams Go to Work* (I–A). These books help students not only understand the complexities of the writing process but also recognize the artistry of the books they read and enjoy. Used in combination with the memoirs and biographies described in Chapter 9, they offer young readers an opportunity to get to know some of their favorite writers and illustrators. Outstanding books for teaching the English language arts are selected each year by a committee of the National Council of Teachers of English and published in *Language Arts*.

In addition to the many fine biographies of musicians and artists also explored in Chapter 9, a variety of nonfiction books explore aspects of music and art. Just as other subject areas are enhanced when well-written and beautifully designed books become a part of the curriculum, the study of art and music is made more vivid when accompanied by beautiful books.

Several series books that explore elements of art, including Philip Yenawine's *Lines* (P–I), and books that help readers learn to look at paintings, such as Gladys Blizzard's *Come Look with Me: Animals in Art* (I), are excellent resources for those interested in learning more about fine art. Jean Tucker introduces children to photography in *Come Look with Me: Discovering Photographs with Children* (I), another book in the **Come Look with Me** series. The **Looking at Paintings** series, by Peggy Roalf, is organized around what a viewer sees in a painting. Two books in this series are *Children* and *Flowers* (I). Each volume contains nineteen full-color reproductions of paintings accompanied by a text that presents a history of the artist and information about technique and style.

The Painter's Eye: Learning to Look at Contemporary American Art (A) is a fascinating book that explains complicated concepts in an understandable fashion. Jan Greenberg and Sandra Jordan define and give examples of the elements of art and principles of design that artists use to create paintings. They also present the postwar American artists themselves through conversations, photographs, and brief anecdotes about their childhoods and their work. The text begins with a useful table of contents and includes brief biographies of the artists, a list and description of the paintings discussed, a glossary, a bibliography, an index, and suggestions for further reading. Greenberg and Jordan's *The Sculptor's Eye: Looking at Contemporary American Art* (A) is an excellent introduction to the concepts of contemporary sculpture.

A number of books explain different artistic processes and the creation of different products, inviting children to create collages, make paper, or design structures. Others explore bridges, buildings, and other objects as architectural art. Thomas Nau presents the innovative photographs of an American artist in *Walker Evans: Photographer of America* (I–A). Nau arranges the photographs chronologically and discusses the art lucidly, asking viewers to interpret the photograph itself.

Books about music and dance also are available. Ashley Bryan visually interprets music through his brilliantly colored, cut-paper illustrations in *Let It Shine: Three Favorite Spirituals* (I). Walter Dean Myers explores music in *Blues Journey* (I) and *Jazz* (I), both brilliantly illustrated by Christopher Myers. Historical events, great musicians, forms, and instruments are all touched on. These books are so compelling that they seem to be music themselves. Siena Cherson Siegel explores another art form in her memoir, *To Dance: A Ballerina's Graphic Novel* (I), illustrated by Mark Siegel. In *Dance* (P), Bill T. Jones and Susan Kuklin add few words to visually stunning photographs of Jones dancing.

Whether the subject is science, mathematics, social studies, language, or the arts, many beautiful nonfiction children's books present more depth of information than can be contained within the pages of a textbook. The well-written texts of these books do not just inform; they provide models of effective nonfiction prose. The illustrations illuminate concepts and present information visually, bringing life and vitality to the topic under scrutiny. Children learn about the world from the many fine nonfiction books that are available, as they learn how to be critical consumers of information.

Nonfiction in the Classroom

Adults selecting books for young readers often give short shrift to nonfiction, assuming that stories and poetry are more appealing or are in some way superior to nonfiction. They aren't. Many young readers prefer nonfiction to fiction; their insatiable curiosity about the world is fueled by nonfiction books. As they mature, many continue to prefer nonfiction, wanting to read to learn. Excellent nonfiction books allow children to learn about a particular topic, and when that matches children's interests, reading nonfiction is fun, just as reading fiction is fun.

We learn best by fitting new information into a coherent frame or schema. When children seek out information for themselves, identify what is relevant, and use it for meaningful goals, they become more efficient at storing and retrieving facts. Furthermore, nonfiction is readily available on virtually any topic and for almost any level of understanding. This rich and vast array of materials generates an interest and excitement that encourages children to find out about their world.

Reading for information relates to other language uses; it is part of the scheme of the total language system. Children do read to learn in assigned textbooks, but they read to learn with enthusiasm and excitement in specialized, excellent nonfiction. Compared to a textbook, a trade book can reveal the point of view of the author more directly, focus on an individual or a topic with a sharper light, and present specialized information that often gives readers a broader understanding. Trade books provide reading and learning opportunities for readers of all ages and skill levels. Textbooks, written with a generic grade-level student in mind, cannot. Trade books also provide the opportunity for greater depth of study, as they offer more information about individual topics than any one textbook could hold. Excellent nonfiction provides many rich opportunities for learning.

Learning is more than the laying on of discrete areas of information; it requires an active response from students, an interpretation or reconstruction of new information in relation to what they already know. Rather than simply teaching a body of facts for students to memorize, effective teachers help students learn to think critically.

Teaching Idea **10.4**

Read First, Write Later

Teachers often discover that students' science and social studies reports sound all too much like the entries in their encyclopedias. The ideas offered here will help students learn to write in their own voice, use a variety of resources, and synthesize information instead of copying it from an encyclopedia.

Collect many resources on science and social studies topics for the classroom library. Keep in mind the following suggestions for enriching students' learning experience:

✿ Have your students keep journals as they read, in which they write down what they are learning *and* what they think about what they are learning. They can do this by using the left-hand side of each double-page spread for notes and the right-hand side for comments.

✿ At regular intervals, have students answer these questions in writing: "What do I know already?" "What do I want to learn?"

✿ Have students explain to a classmate what they have learned and what they are still trying to find out.

✿ Be sure that students use a variety of books to search for answers to their questions. As they read for this purpose, have them take notes about their discoveries.

✿ When they have read widely, talked about their discoveries, and written about what they are learning and how they feel about it, then it is time for them to draft a report. Talk with them about the importance of writing it in their own voice. Give them guidelines for what you want them to produce.

Teaching Idea 10.4 offers some suggestions for helping students recognize what they are learning from nonfiction texts, put it in their own words, and determine what they still need to know as they become experts about a particular topic in preparation for writing about it.

Critical reading and thinking are basic to a lifetime of learning. The schemata we develop as we read to learn influences all subsequent knowledge. Thinking readers, called critical readers, evaluate new information in light of what they already know, compare many sources instead of accepting only one point of view, and make judgments about what they read. If one goal of education is to develop informed, thinking, participating citizens, then helping children learn to read critically is essential.

The person who believes that anything found in print is the truth—the whole truth—is at a disadvantage relative to one who has learned to check sources, compare reports, and evaluate. Young readers do not question what they read when they are given one textbook that is held up as embodying the final and complete truth on its subject. They do learn to question and evaluate as they read if we encourage them to make comparisons among different sources, including nonfiction trade books. We can encourage critical thinking by asking students to see what different books have to say about the same topic, or to use their own knowledge and experiences to judge the quality of an idea or piece of information.

Readers of all ages can verify information found in books by checking it against observations made in real life. They can also assess an author's qualifications, look at the documentation provided, and critically evaluate the books they read, much as we suggest in Figure 10.1, the evaluation checklist at the beginning of this chapter. Many of the nonfiction books we've discussed here encourage readers to adopt a critical stance based on research and observation, collect and analyze data, draw conclusions, make inferences, and test hypotheses. Books that draw the reader into research help develop an observant critical stance that spills over from books into daily life.

• • • SUMMARY • • •

There are many outstanding books of nonfiction on virtually any topic for a wide range of readers. Awards such as the Orbis Pictus and the Sibert establish criteria that recognize quality in nonfiction. When children are given excellent nonfiction books to explore topics of interest, they learn a great deal about those topics. They learn more than they would from textbooks or encyclopedias alone because the intriguing formats of nonfiction books make them intrinsically more interesting to read and because trade books contain more detailed information. When reading nonfiction, children also have the opportunity to experience well-written, organized expository prose that can then serve as a model for their own informational writing. Further, reading several nonfiction books provides a perfect opportunity to think critically—evaluating and verifying information by making comparisons with experience and with other books.

Because the subjects, and the examples, of excellent nonfiction for young readers are almost inexhaustible, here we present the titles that have won the Sibert and Orbis Pictus Awards. These titles include both biography and other types of nonfiction; all are excellent.

The Robert Sibert Award Books

2001

Sir Walter Ralegh and the Quest for El Dorado, by Marc Aronson (Clarion)

HONOR BOOKS: *The Longitude Prize*, by Joan Dash, illustrated by Susan Petricic (Farrar, Straus & Giroux); *Blizzard*, by Jim Murphy (Scholastic); *My Season with Penguins: An Antarctic Journal*, by Sophie Webb (Houghton Mifflin); *Pedro and Me: Friendship, Loss, and What I Learned*, by Judd Winick (Henry Holt)

2002

Black Potatoes: The Story of the Great Irish Famine, 1845–1850, by Susan Campbell Bartoletti (Houghton Mifflin)

HONOR BOOKS: *Surviving Hitler: A Boy in the Nazi Death Camps*, by Andrea Warren (HarperCollins); *Vincent van Gogh*, by Jan Greenberg and Sandra Jordan (Delacorte Press); *Brooklyn Bridge*, by Lynn Curlee (Atheneum)

2003

The Life and Death of Adolf Hitler, by James Cross Giblin (Clarion)

HONOR BOOKS: *Six Days in October: The Stock Market Crash of 1929*, by Karen Blumenthal (Atheneum); *Hole in My Life*, by Jack Gantos (Farrar, Straus & Giroux); *Action Jackson*, by Jan Greenberg and Sandra Jordan, illustrated by Robert Andrew Parker (Roaring Brook Press); *When Marian Sang*, by Pam Muñoz Ryan, illustrated by Brian Selznick (Scholastic)

2004

An American Plague: The True and Terrifying Story of the Yellow Fever Epidemic of 1793, by Jim Murphy (Clarion)

HONOR BOOK: *I Face the Wind*, by Vicki Cobb, illustrated by Julia Gorton (HarperCollins)

2005

The Voice That Challenged a Nation: Marian Anderson and the Struggle for Equal Rights, by Russell Freedman (Clarion)

HONOR BOOKS: *Sequoyah: The Cherokee Man Who Gave His People Writing*, by James Rumford (Houghton Mifflin); *The Tarantula Scientist*, by Sy Montgomery, illustrated by Nic Bishop (Houghton Mifflin); *Walt Whitman: Words for America*, by Barbara Kerley, illustrated by Brian Selznick (Scholastic); *People Writing* by James Rumford (Houghton Mifflin)

2006

Secrets of a Civil War Submarine: Solving the Mysteries of the H. L. Hunley, by Sally M. Walker (Carolrhoda Books)

HONOR BOOK: *Hitler Youth: Growing Up in Hitler's Shadow*, by Susan Campbell Bartoletti (Scholastic)

2007

Team Moon: How 400,000 People Landed Apollo 11 on the Moon, by Catherine Thimmesh (Houghton Mifflin)

HONOR BOOKS: *Freedom Riders: John Lewis and Jim Zwerg on the Front Lines of the Civil Rights Movement*, by Ann Bausum (National Geographic); *To Dance: A Ballerina's Graphic Novel*, by Siena Cherson Siegel (Simon & Schuster); *Quest for the Tree Kangaroo: An Expedition to the Cloud Forest of New Guinea*, by Sy Montgomery (Houghton Mifflin)

2008

The Wall: Growing Up Behind the Iron Curtain, by Peter Sís (Farrar/Frances Foster)

HONOR BOOKS: *Lightship*, by Brian Floca (Simon & Schuster); *Nic Bishop Spiders*, by Nic Bishop (Scholastic)

2009

We Are the Ship: The Story of Negro League Baseball, by Kadir Nelson (Jump at the Sun/Hyperion)

HONOR BOOKS: *Bodies from the Ice: Melting Glaciers and Rediscovery of the Past*, by James M. Deem (Houghton Mifflin); *What to Do About Alice?: How Alice Roosevelt Broke the Rules, Charmed the World, and Drove Her Father Teddy Crazy!*, by Barbara Kerley, illustrated by Edwin Fotheringham (Scholastic)

The Orbis Pictus Award Books

1990

The Great Little Madison, by Jean Fritz (Putnam)

HONOR BOOKS: *The Great American Gold Rush*, by Rhoda Blumberg (Bradbury Press); *The News about Dinosaurs*, by Patricia Lauber (Bradbury Press)

1991

Franklin Delano Roosevelt, by Russell Freedman (Clarion)

HONOR BOOKS: *Arctic Memories*, by Normee Ekoomiak (Henry Holt); *Seeing Earth from Space*, by Patricia Lauber (Orchard Books)

1992

Flight: The Journey of Charles Lindbergh, by Robert Burleigh and Mike Wimmer (Philomel)

Honor Books: *Now Is Your Time! The African-American Struggle for Freedom*, by Walter Dean Myers (HarperCollins); *Prairie Vision: The Life and Times of Solomon Butcher*, by Pam Conrad (HarperCollins)

1993

Children of the Dust Bowl: The True Story of the School at Weedpatch Camp, by Jerry Stanley (Crown)

Honor Books: *Talking with Artists*, by Pat Cummins (Bradbury Press); *Come Back, Salmon*, by Molly Cone (Sierra Club Books)

1994

Across America on an Emigrant Train, by Jim Murphy (Clarion)

Honor Books: *To the Top of the World: Adventures with Arctic Wolves*, by Jim Brandenburg (Walker); *Making Sense: Animal Perception and Communication*, by Bruce Brooks (Farrar, Straus & Giroux)

1995

Safari Beneath the Sea: The Wonder of the North Pacific Coast, by Diane Swanson (Sierra Club Books)

Honor Books: *Wildlife Rescue: The Work of Dr. Kathleen Ramsay*, by Jennifer Owings Dewey (Boyds Mills Press); *Kids at Work: Lewis Hine and the Crusade against Child Labor*, by Russell Freedman (Clarion); *Christmas in the Big House, Christmas in the Quarters*, by Patricia and Fredrick McKissack (Scholastic)

1996

The Great Fire, by Jim Murphy (Scholastic)

Honor Books: *Dolphin Man: Exploring the World of Dolphins*, by Laurence Pringle, photos by Randall S. Wells (Atheneum); *Rosie the Riveter: Women Working on the Home Front in World War II*, by Penny Colman (Crown)

1997

Leonardo da Vinci, by Diane Stanley (Morrow Junior Books)

Honor Books: *Full Steam Ahead: The Race to Build a Transcontinental Railroad*, by Rhoda Blumberg (National Geographic Society); *The Life and Death of Crazy Horse*, by Russell Freedman (Holiday House); *One World, Many Religions: The Way We Worship*, by Mary Pope Osborne (Knopf)

1998

An Extraordinary Life: The Story of a Monarch Butterfly, by Laurence Pringle, illustrated by Bob Marstall (Orchard Books)

Honor Books: *A Drop of Water: A Book of Science and Wonder*, by Walter Wick (Scholastic); *A Tree Is Growing*, by Arthur Dorros, illustrated by S. D. Schindler (Scholastic); *Charles A. Lindbergh: A Human Hero*, by James Cross Giblin (Clarion); *Kennedy Assassinated! The World Mourns: A Reporter's Story*, by Wilborn Hampton (Candlewick Press); *Digger: The Tragic Fate of the California Indians from the Missions to the Gold Rush*, by Jerry Stanley (Crown)

1999

Shipwreck at the Bottom of the World: The Extraordinary True Story of Shackleton and the Endurance, by Jennifer Armstrong (Crown)

Honor Books: *Black Whiteness: Admiral Byrd Alone in the Antarctic*, by Robert Burleigh, illustrated by Walter Lyon Krudop (Atheneum); *Fossil Feud: The Rivalry of the First American Dinosaur Hunters*, by Thom Holmes (Messner); *Hottest, Coldest, Highest, Deepest*, by Steve Jenkins (Houghton Mifflin); *No Pretty Pictures: A Child of War*, by Anita Lobel (Greenwillow)

2000

Through My Eyes, by Ruby Bridges and Margo Lundell (Scholastic)

Honor Books: *At Her Majesty's Request: An African Princess in Victorian England*, by Walter Dean Myers (Scholastic); *Clara Schumann: Piano Virtuoso*, by Susanna Reich (Clarion); *Mapping the World*, by Sylvia Johnson (Atheneum); *The Snake Scientist*, by Sy Montgomery, illustrated by Nic Bishop (Houghton Mifflin); *The Top of the World: Climbing Mount Everest*, by Steve Jenkins (Houghton Mifflin)

2001

Hurry Freedom: African Americans in Gold Rush California, by Jerry Stanley (Crown)

Honor Books: *The Amazing Life of Benjamin Franklin*, by James Cross Giblin, illustrated by Michael Dooling (Scholastic); *America's Champion Swimmer: Gertrude Ederle*, by David Adler, illustrated by Terry Widener (Harcourt); *Michelangelo*, by Diane Stanley (HarperCollins); *Osceola: Memories of a Sharecropper's Daughter*, by Alan Govenar, illustrated by Shane W. Evans (Jump at the Sun); *Wild and Swampy*, by Jim Arnosky (HarperCollins)

2002

Black Potatoes: The Story of the Great Irish Famine, 1845–1850, by Susan Campbell Bartoletti (Houghton Mifflin)

Honor Books: *The Cod's Tale*, by Mark Kurlansky, illustrated by S. D. Schindler (Putnam); *The Dinosaurs of Waterhouse Hawkins: An Illuminating History of Mr. Waterhouse Hawkins, Artist and Lecturer*, by Barbara Kerley, illustrated by Brian Selznick (Scholastic); *Martin's Big Words: The Life of Dr. Martin Luther King, Jr.*, by Doreen Rappaport, illustrated by Bryan Collier (Hyperion)

2003

When Marian Sang: The True Recital of Marian Anderson: The Voice of a Century, by Pam Muñoz Ryan, illustrated by Brian Selznick (Scholastic)

Honor Books: *Confucius: The Golden Rule*, by Russell Freedman, illustrated by Frédéric Clément (Levine Books); *The Emperor's Silent Army: Terracotta Warriors of Ancient China*, by Jane O'Connor (Viking); *Phineas Gage: A Gruesome but True Story about Brain Science*, by John Fleischman (Houghton Mifflin); *Tenement: Immigrant Life on the Lower East Side*, by Raymond Bial (Houghton Mifflin); *To Fly: The Story of the Wright Brothers*, by Wendie Old, illustrated by Robert Andrew Parker (Clarion)

2004

An American Plague: The True and Terrifying Story of the Yellow Fever Epidemic of 1793, by Jim Murphy (Clarion)

HONOR BOOKS: *Empire State Building: When New York Reached for the Skies*, by Elizabeth Mann, illustrated by Alan Witschonke (Mikaya Press); *In Defense of Liberty: The Story of America's Bill of Rights*, by Russell Freedman (Holiday House); *Leonardo: Beautiful Dreamer*, by Robert Byrd (Dutton); *The Man Who Made Time Travel*, by Kathryn Lasky, illustrated by Kevin Hawkes (Farrar, Straus & Giroux); *Shutting Out the Sky: Life in the Tenements of New York, 1880–1924*, by Deborah Hopkinson (Orchard Books)

2005

York's Adventures with Lewis and Clark: An African-American's Part in the Great Expedition, by Rhoda Blumberg (HarperCollins)

HONOR BOOKS: *Actual Size*, by Steve Jenkins (Houghton Mifflin); *The Race to Save the Lord God Bird*, by Phillip Hoose (Farrar, Straus & Giroux); *Secrets of the Sphinx*, by James Cross Giblin (Scholastic); *Seurat and La Grande Jatte: Connecting the Dots*, by Robert Burleigh (Abrams Books for Young Readers); *The Voice That Challenged a Nation: Marian Anderson and the Struggle for Equal Rights*, by Russell Freedman (Clarion Books)

2006

Children of the Great Depression, by Russell Freedman (Clarion Books)

HONOR BOOKS: *ER Vets: Life in an Animal Emergency Room*, by Donna Jackson (Houghton Mifflin); *Forbidden Schoolhouse: The True and Dramatic Story of Prudence Crandall and Her Students*, by Suzanne Jurmain (Houghton Mifflin); *Genius: A Photobiography of Albert Einstein*, by Marfe Ferguson Delano (National Geographic); *Hitler Youth: Growing Up in Hitler's Shadow*, by Susan Campbell Bartoletti (Scholastic); *Mosquito Bite*, by Alexandra Siy and Dennis Kunkel (Charlesbridge Publishing)

2007

Quest for the Tree Kangaroo: An Expedition to the Cloud Forest of New Guinea, by Sy Montgomery, photographs by Nic Bishop (Houghton Mifflin)

HONOR BOOKS: *Gregor Mendel: The Friar Who Grew Peas*, by Cheryl Bardoe (Abrams Books for Young Readers); *Freedom Walkers: The Story of the Montgomery Bus Boycott*, by Russell Freedman (Holiday House); *John Muir: America's First Environmentalist*, by Kathryn Lasky (Candlewick Press); *Something Out of Nothing: Marie Curie and Radium*, by Carla Killough McClafferty (Farrar, Straus & Giroux); *Team Moon: How 400,000 People Landed Apollo 11 on the Moon*, by Catherine Thimmesh (Houghton Mifflin)

2008

M.L.K.: Journey of a King, by Tonya Bolden (Abrams Books for Young Readers)

HONOR BOOKS: *Black and White Airmen: Their True History*, by John Fleischman (Houghton Mifflin); *Spiders*, by Nic Bishop (Scholastic); *Helen Keller: Her Life in Pictures*, by George Sullivan (Scholastic); *Muckrakers*, by Ann Bausum (National Geographic); *Venom*, by Marilyn Singer (Darby Creek Publishing) music, through the use of children's books. Teachers who use this approach link curriculum areas by teaching reading and writing in conjunction with a topic in a particular area. They select children's books about that area and use them as the texts through which students practice reading skills and strategies. For example, many primary grades focus on the community in their social studies curriculum. Using that focus to develop a thematic unit around the idea of belonging to a number of different communities can allow teachers to integrate their curriculum in a way that makes it meaningful to their students' lives. The books are resources for reading, information gathering, and stimulating discussions, and act as models as students craft their own writing.

Although you can certainly find curriculum guides and book study guides that provide step-by-step ideas for building a curriculum around literature, we encourage you to think for yourself. Think about your students—what they are interested in, what they know how to do, what they need to learn, and how they like to learn. Then think

about your curriculum—what you need to teach, how much time you have to teach it, and what materials you have available. Consider how literature can help you create meaningful and effective learning experiences for your students. One essential tool in this enterprise is a classroom library. Teaching Idea 11.2 presents guidelines for building a classroom library that will support a literature-based curriculum for the primary grades.

Cengage Learning/Wadsworth

Even toddlers benefit from spending time with books, looking at them on their own, and hearing them read by others.

Teaching Idea 11.2

Create a Classroom Library

Research shows that when there is a classroom library, students read fifty percent more books than when there is not. Classroom libraries provide easy access to books, magazines, and other materials. To make sure your classroom library is attractive and inviting, follow these guidelines.

Collect books that are:

- Good examples of literature.
- Written about the curriculum topics being studied.
- Related to the current literature focus.
- Suitable for recreational reading.
- About diverse people and cultures.
- "Touchstone" books, enduring favorites.

Organize books:

- In consultation with students.
- In a simple manner.
- In a way that accommodates routine changes in focus.
- So that book covers, not spines, are visible when possible.

Include such support materials as:

- Story props, including flannel boards and felt board stories and figures.
- Tapes, DVDs, CD-ROMs.
- Puppets.
- Posters, bulletin boards, dust jackets.

Provide a comfortable, quiet space:

- Where students can read privately or sit and relax.
- That is away from vigorous activity.
- That features an appealing display of books.

There are many ways to enact a literature-based literacy curriculum. Such a curriculum varies along many dimensions, including curricular goals, learning activities, and selection of books. In a study of how literature-based programs look in varied classrooms, Hiebert and Colt (1989) describe how the programs vary along two main dimensions: the instructional format and the selection of literature. The variations are linked to the amount of teacher control in each dimension, ranging from teacher-led instruction to independent application in terms of instructional format, and from teacher-selected to student-selected material in terms of literature.

Some programs are marked by a high degree of teacher control; teachers select the materials and lead the instruction. Other programs are marked by student selection of materials and student direction of their own learning with less teacher intervention. All sorts of variations and combinations of student independence and teacher direction are possible. In some cases, you will want to select materials that will help students learn something they need to know in order to progress in the curriculum. In other cases, you and your students will negotiate what is to be explored, how it will be explored, and which materials will be used. Often, students will independently select books and decide what to do with them, either within parameters that you have set or entirely on their own.

For about thirty years, research has explored the ways in which teachers enact a literature-based curriculum. Some of the many books, classic and current, about this topic are listed in Figure 11.1. Journals such as *Language Arts* and *The Reading Teacher* contain articles written by classroom teachers and by university researchers that inform us about the difficulties and benefits of literature-based instruction. Many language arts and reading textbooks also explain in great detail ways of structuring such a curriculum. Later in this chapter, we present the ways some particular primary-grade teachers structured their curriculum using literature; we do the same for intermediate- and middle-school teachers in Chapter 12. As you read these two chapters, think about the children and the books you know, and how you might adapt these ideas for your own classroom.

Reading Aloud

One primary way that teachers help children grow as engaged, responsive readers is to read aloud. Reading aloud is one of the most common and easiest means of sharing books. It is a pleasurable experience for all when done well, and it has a positive impact on students' reading development. Reading aloud not only helps young children become readers, but also helps older children become better readers. Reading aloud extends students' horizons, introduces them to literature they might not read on their own, offers alternate worlds and lifestyles for them to think about, increases the experiential base from which to view the world, and models good reading (Galda & Cullinan, 2003). Reading aloud to young children also demonstrates print and book-handling concepts such as left-to-right and top-to-bottom directionality, page turning, and the role of print and pictures in telling a story or presenting a concept. The many reasons for reading aloud are summarized here. Reading aloud:

- Introduces new vocabulary
- Displays interesting sentence patterns
- Presents a variety of forms of language
- Shows various styles of written language
- Develops a sense of story, poetry, or exposition
- Motivates children to read more
- Provides ideas for students' writing
- Enriches students' general knowledge
- Models the sound of fluent reading
- Adds pleasure to the day

Reading aloud to children creates a "space" in the school day that allows teachers to encourage a number of types of cognitive and affective growth. In a school climate where many teachers may feel under pressure to spend little time in storybook read-alouds, this intellectual and emotional richness provides an argument to justify what we know is a potentially meaningful literacy experience for children. Some of the "spaces" created by reading aloud to children are the following:

- *A supportive, intimate, and emotionally rich space*—to share personal experience that relates to stories, to laugh and cry together, to consider foundational questions about what it means to be human. In this space, both teachers and children feel comfortable to express themselves honestly and openly. Through the medium of story, children may talk about sensitive or complicated issues in an uninhibited and deep way.
- *A space for play, pleasure, and spontaneity*—unleashing children's creativity and sense of fun. Children become immersed in the world of the story or use the story as the platform for an expression of their own imagination. Children and teachers alike can participate in these playful and exuberant "performances." There is concern, these days, about the absence of time to play in young children's lives—preschool and kindergarten have become much more prescriptive and skill-oriented, for example, and a lot of play seems rather individual—for example in video games and

Figure **11.1**

Resources for a Literature-based Curriculum for Elementary Grades

See also Figure 2.1, *Resources for Finding and Studying Culturally Diverse Literature*, and Figure 4.3, *Resources for the Poetry Teacher.*

Bamford, Rosemary, and Janice Kristo, editors, *Making Facts Come Alive: Choosing Quality Nonfiction Literature K–8*

Blatt, Gloria, editor, *Once upon a Folktale: Capturing the Folklore Process with Children*

Bosma, Betty, *Fairy Tales, Fables, Legends, and Myths*

Cullinan, Bernice E., editor, *Invitation to Read: More Children's Literature in the Reading Program*

Daniels, Harvey, and Nancy Steineke, *Mini-Lessons for Literature Circles*

Daniels, Harvey, and Steven Zemelman, *Subjects Matter: Every Teacher's Guide to Content-Area Reading*

Edinger, Monica, *Fantasy Literature in the Elementary Classroom: Strategies for Reading, Writing, and Responding*

Galda, Lee, Shane Rayburn, and Lisa Stanzi, *Looking through the Faraway End: Creating a Literature-Based Curriculum with Second Graders*

Hancock, Marjorie, *A Celebration of Literature and Response: Children, Books, and Teachers in K–8 Classrooms*

Hefner, Christine, and Kathryn Lewis, *Literature-Based Science: Children's Books and Activities to Enrich the K–5 Curriculum*

Hickman, Janet, and Bernice E. Cullinan, *Children's Literature in the Classroom: Weaving Charlotte's Web*

Hickman, Janet, Bernice E. Cullinan, and Susan Hepler, *Children's Literature in the Classroom: Extending Charlotte's Web*

Hill, Bonnie, Nancy Johnson, and Katherine Schlick Noe, editors, *Literature Circles and Response*

Holland, Kathleen, Rachel Hungerford, and Shirley Ernst, editors, *Journeying: Children Responding to Literature*

Lattimer, Heather, *Thinking through Genre: Units of Study in Reading and Writing Workshops 4–12*

Laughlin, Mildred, and Terri Street, *Literature-Based Art and Music: Children's Books and Activities to Enrich the K–5 Curriculum*

Martinez, Miriam, and Nancy Roser, *What a Character!: Character Study as a Gateway to Literary Understanding*

McMahon, Susan, and Taffy Raphael, editors, *The Book Club Connection: Literacy Learning and Classroom Talk*

Moss, Jay, *Teaching Literature in the Elementary School: A Thematic Approach*

Peterson, Ralph, and Maryann Eeds, *Grand Conversations: Literature Groups in Action*

Roser, Nancy, and Miriam Martinez, editors, *Book Talk and Beyond: Children and Teachers Respond to Literature*

Samway, Katharine, and Gail Whang, *Literature Study Circles in a Multicultural Classroom*

Schlick Noe, Katherine, and Nancy Johnson, *Getting Started with Literature Circles*

Short, Kathy, *Literature as a Way of Knowing*

Short, Kathy, and Kathleen Pierce, editors, *Talking about Books: Creating Literate Communities*

Sorensen, Marilou, and Barbara Lehman, editors, *Teaching with Children's Books: Paths to Literature-Based Instruction*

Young, Terrell, *Happily Ever After: Sharing Folk Literature with Elementary and Middle School Students*

Zarnowski, Myra, and Arlene Gallagher, editors, *Children's Literature and Social Studies: Selecting and Using Notable Books in the Classroom*

---

so forth. The read-aloud situation creates a space for "school-sanctioned" play, especially if the read-alouds are interactive and follow the children's interpretive trajectories rather than the teacher's. The "spaces" and time for play are extremely limited in many preschool, kindergarten, and primary classrooms; however, viewing the read-aloud as such a playful space provides a way of subverting the tightly scripted programs that so often characterize current literacy curricula.

✎ *A space for imagining, speculating, critiquing, and reflecting.* Read-alouds provide occasions for children to share alternative interpretations, put themselves in the place of story characters for vicarious experiences, and assume different stances and perspectives, "stretching" their cognitive abilities. One of the chief joys of stories is to see the world from a different lens, and thereby to increase children's capacities for imagining the world from an entirely different perspective. In turn, this capacity allows children to critique their own worlds and to imagine a more just and equitable society.

- *A space for creating an interpretive community.* During read-alouds, children have the opportunity to socially construct meaning. Together, children and the teacher work cooperatively to build and shape literary interpretation. This cooperative meaning-building makes children feel that they are part of a dynamic literary community where everyone's voice is heard and respected.
- All in all, read-alouds provide *a space for responding to "art"* in the broadest sense of that term. Children pursue the impulse to interpret and know; the impulse to personalize and connect stories to their own lives; and the impulse to imaginatively liberate themselves from the contingencies of life. This is what all art does: it allows us to know in new ways, perceive ourselves and others in new ways, and it frees our imaginative capacities.

There are some guidelines to consider when selecting books to read aloud, the most important of which is to select books that are well written. Books of quality abound, as we discuss in Chapters 3 through 10, and it is a waste of precious time to read second-rate materials. Good books pique children's interest and invite them to read them—or others like them—independently. Sometimes teachers will read an inferior book "because the children love it," but students will love good books even more. Select books that will influence and expand children's literary tastes.

Find out which books are already familiar by asking children to list their favorites and then build from there, selecting old favorites as well as books that children will probably not discover on their own. Use read-aloud time to share the special books that you want your students to know. Introduce children to all of an author's books by reading aloud from one of them and telling them where to find the rest.

Reading from outstanding examples of all types of literature can help expand children's literary tastes. Reading some books slightly above students' reading abilities extends their language; they usually comprehend more than they can read. Most books can be understood on several levels, but do consider your students' capabilities as you choose. Select books that you want to make part of the whole-class experience, books that you want to become part of the shared knowledge in your classroom.

When reading aloud to children, know your material before you begin. Preparation is important, especially when reading poetry, where the phrasing and cadence carry so much of the meaning. Preparation also helps you decide on the mood and tone that you want to set and allows you to learn special names or refrains. It is important to be thoroughly familiar with the content of the material you read aloud.

When reading, use a natural voice, with inflections and modulations befitting the book. Avoid greatly exaggerated voice changes and overly dramatic gestures, unless the book calls for that. Read slowly, enunciate clearly, project your voice directly, and maintain eye contact with your listeners as much as possible. Teachers who read aloud with their noses in the book soon lose their audience. Some brief guidelines for reading aloud are:

- Read the book ahead of time; be familiar with it.
- Give a brief description of the book, why you chose it, or how it relates to something you are doing as a class to establish a context for the listeners.
- Begin reading aloud slowly; quicken the pace as listeners are drawn into the book.
- Look up from the book frequently to maintain eye contact.
- Interpret dialogue meaningfully.
- Read entire books, if possible, or read a chapter or more per day to sustain meaning.
- If reading a picturebook, hold the book so that the children can "read" the illustrations while listening to the text.
- Make reading aloud a highlight in the day, and ask for your students' complete attention.

Media adaptations of books are also an important part of primary-grade classrooms. Teaching Idea 11.3 suggests how to make sure the adaptations you use are of excellent quality.

Supporting Children's Growing Literary Understanding

Sensitive teachers help children make connections between their own lives and the books they read. Cochran-Smith (1984) documented how one preschool teacher did this with her class as she demonstrated how to make connections between text and life and between life and text. Wolf and Heath (1992) describe the way two children incorporate the literature that is read to them into their own lives. Asking questions and making connections to books helps children become avid readers. When teachers demonstrate how to do this, students learn that the stuff of their own lives is sometimes mirrored in the books they read.

Teaching Idea 11.3

Select Media for Your Classroom

✦ Set your goals. Think about why you want to use media. If you want to extend your students' time with print, then you will want material that is connected to books you have in your classroom library or that includes text. If you want to use media to help students practice visual literacy skills or to encourage them to compare across media, then you will want to find materials that suit these goals.

✦ Consider the literary value of the original work; a good film, tape, or video cannot improve a bad book.

✦ Consider if the medium is appropriate to the literary work. Does it enrich and expand the work?

✦ Consider the audience. Are the book and media materials appropriate for your students? Adaptations that dilute a work of art to make it accessible to a younger audience are inauthentic and misleading.

✦ Consider the quality of the materials. Media materials should be technically excellent; clear sound and visual reproduction are vital.

✦ Check the American Library Association website (www.ala.org) for their Notable Children's Recordings, Notable Children's Videos, and Great Interactive Software for Kids lists.

Connections between life and text are at the core of children's experiences with literature, but connections among and between books and popular culture texts are important as well. As children read and listen to stories, they begin to build their personal storehouse of literary understanding. They begin to recognize thematic connections across stories, similarities in plot structures and characterization, and distinctive styles in text and illustration. Teachers can encourage this kind of understanding by drawing on their knowledge of how literature works and by planning a literature curriculum that contains books selected specifically to help students make connections among texts—connections that result in a deeper understanding of what literature is and how it works.

Teachers enhance their students' growing literary understandings when they structure opportunities for students to make links across books, or *intertextual* connections. Learning about the world of literature is an ongoing process as students come to recognize similarities and differences in plot structures, characters, and themes. As

with connecting books to life, connecting books to other books adds dimension to future reading and responding. Wide reading (many varied books) and deep reading (many books in a particular genre, by a particular author, with a particular structure, and so on) acquaint children with the world of literature and help them learn a lot about specific aspects of that world.

Oral Language and Literature

Oral language is central to many book extension activities in the primary grades. These range from the spontaneous recommendation of a book by its reader to discussions during or following a read-aloud, to dramatic reenactment, storytelling, or choral speaking. Good for all students, oral activities offer English language learners and students not ready to read support for developing oral language as they interact with literature. Effective oral language activities may be extensive or brief, but they always help children share and explore their responses to the books they read.

• • DISCUSSION • •

Book discussions are wonderful ways to help children learn about literature and how it works. These discussions, often spontaneous, present moments that allow teachers to explore books with students. We invite you to reread the opening vignette of this chapter, where we reproduce part of a discussion of David Wiesner's *The Three Pigs*, in which the pigs have the opportunity of visiting several stories after being blown out of their own familiar tale. Specifically, we invite you to analyze what the teacher does (and does not do) to orchestrate the discussion.

First, the teacher seems to follow the children's lead, encouraging them to listen to one another's ideas and praising them rather than asking questions or making statements that position her as the prime knower; in fact, she stays out of the way of the children's meaning-making and encourages the children to talk to one another a great deal. These exchanges among children are called "cross-talk" by linguists because they are not directed to the teacher, but among the children themselves as they construct an interpretation. There is some struggle, as Wiesner's story does not follow the traditional versions with which the children are familiar, but the teacher is quite comfortable with this struggle. In essence, she hands the power of meaning-making over to the children. We suggest that, when children are given this power, they tend to rise to the occasion and come up with an interpretation that makes sense without a great deal of scaffolding from the teacher. This is not to say tern. Especially at the beginning of the year, the picture-books that Betty selected were often patterned, predictable texts that supported the reading development of the many emergent and beginning readers in her classroom.

Patterned, Predictable Texts

We know that children become literate in different ways and at different rates of development. We also know that children who have experience with literature before they come to school begin school with an advantage. They are already emergent readers, readers who have some concepts about how print works. One of the best ways that preschool and early elementary teachers can help children develop these concepts is to read to them. When the books that are read are highly patterned and thus predictable, it is easier for children to figure out how print works (Holdaway, 1979).

Children search for patterns as they learn. They like to find things that match, words that rhyme, and phrases that are repeated. Many books are predictable because of their repetitive sequences, cumulative sequences, rhyme and rhythm, or familiar cultural sequences such as numbering, days of the week, or months of the year. Betty often read from books like these. When she could, she used enlarged versions of these stories so that students could see the words. Then she was able to help them make connections between sounds and print, and learn about concepts of print, such as top to bottom, left to right, and the functions of capitals, periods, and white spaces.

Patterned stories also formed the basis of rich oral language activities as students learned structures and patterns that they called upon to do storytelling and drama. These performances were quite interactive; if a student forgot an important word or phrase, his peers were happy to supply it for him. These patterned stories also made their way into the students' own stories, both oral and written. Sharing time, which once had focused on brief accounts of events from the children's lives, eventually featured elaborate accounts of these events, with students incorporating book language and patterns into their own stories. In their writing, students often borrowed stock characters, basic plot structures, or literary phrases. These "borrowings" helped build the students' resources and abilities for both oral and written language production.

Easy Readers and Transitional Chapter Books

As is the case in many classrooms, Betty's students were not all at the same reading level, so her collection included picturebooks that were more difficult than the patterned texts we have discussed. It also included some easy reading for newly independent readers, such as Arnold Lobel's **Frog and Toad** series, and transitional chapter books of many genres.

As the most advanced readers in the class grew ready for more extended text, Betty introduced the class to the **Frog and Toad** series. After she read aloud from one of the books, she told students that several other books were written about the same characters; she made sure students knew where they were on the shelves. As the more advanced readers began to read them, they often had an attentive audience, with two or three of their peers gathered around them. As the students in the class came

Spending time with good books is the best way to become an avid reader.

to know the stories well through repeated readings, the struggling readers were able to "read" them as well, calling on their memory and the illustrations to supplement their reading skills. By the end of the year, everyone had read all of this and other series.

The more advanced readers moved on to transitional chapter books, which gave them the opportunity to read extended text over time. Because the texts of these books are arranged in chapters, these students felt a sense of accomplishment—they could now read chapter books. It also gave them practice in reading stories that were a bit more complex than many of the picturebooks they were familiar with. No students abandoned picturebooks altogether. Betty's collection was so extensive that even the most fluent reader could find a picturebook with a challenging text. As readers became increasingly fluent, they moved on to longer versions of transitional chapter books, and eventually into longer novels with an episodic structure.

Betty's literature-based literacy instruction offered her students the opportunity to read, write, speak, and listen for meaningful purposes. Quite often these purposes were related to the positive value these students had learned to place on being engaged with a good book.

• • USING LITERATURE • •
TO INTEGRATE THE
CURRICULUM

Karen Bliss's first-grade class was experiencing literature-based instruction of a different kind. Using the science curriculum as a basis, Karen created and maintained a single theme across the year as she and her students explored the idea of interdependence. This theme involved a study of oceans for the first seven months of the school year. Her students were so interested in what they were doing that their reading, writing, listening, and speaking activities, as well as most of their social studies and science, were linked to their exploration of the oceans of the world. They learned geography, wrote extensively about the oceans and seas and the various continents they border, read extensively from fiction, nonfiction, and poetry, and painted many beautiful pictures of the oceans and their inhabitants. Their language activities were motivated and purposeful as they read books to research and wrote to explain. One of their big projects was a group-authored book on penguins, an animal they had become intrigued with during their studies. Working together and independently, they read children's books about penguins, wrote about penguins based on the models they found in the trade books they were reading, revised their writing, and published a class book about penguins. A parent made copies of the book for each student and for the classroom and school libraries. As they were learning

about science and geography—and penguins—they were also learning to read, write, speak, and listen with fluency and effectiveness.

By structuring the content of the learning tasks within a thematic framework and exploring them through quality children's literature, Karen built in integration and meaningfulness. Excellent children's books are easy to find for almost any theme you might want to explore. Whether you link thematic study to the science or social studies curriculum, or both, as Karen did, or to the language arts curriculum, a thematic organization offers children the opportunity to learn about language while they are learning through the language of literature.

• • LITERATURE STUDY • •
WITH PRIMARY-GRADE
READERS

The children in Lisa Stanzi's second-grade reading group were learning about reading and writing, as well as listening and speaking, as they engaged in the study of literature. Lisa's elementary school had an unusual way of organizing reading instruction. For seventy minutes each morning, students in a particular grade level were grouped according to ability, with each group receiving instruction from one teacher. Each of the two second-grade teachers worked with a group, and specialists worked with the other groups. Lisa's group consisted of five students from her own class and six to seven from the other second-grade class; all were reading at or above grade level. In spite of this, the group was quite heterogeneous in many ways. Some were struggling at a second-grade reading level; others were fluent at a fourth-grade level. The students were from many parts of the world—China, India, and Africa, as well as the United States. Several were English language learners. Further, they all had varying levels of experience with books.

Lisa was in the process of moving from a basal-based reading curriculum to a more literature-based curriculum, hoping to transform her "reading" group into something that looked more like a book discussion group or literature study group. To accomplish this, she gathered hundreds of trade books that supported the six themes that appeared in the system-mandated basal reader and planned her lessons around the literature in the basal text, the books she offered the children for independent reading, and those she read aloud. The books ranged from very easy to more difficult picturebooks, fiction, poetry, and nonfiction, and included easy readers and transitional chapter books with a range of difficulty. When she introduced the first whole-class chapter book in November, Lisa read it aloud; by the end of the year, the students were reading chapters at home in the evening in preparation for the next day's discussion. Every day for seventy

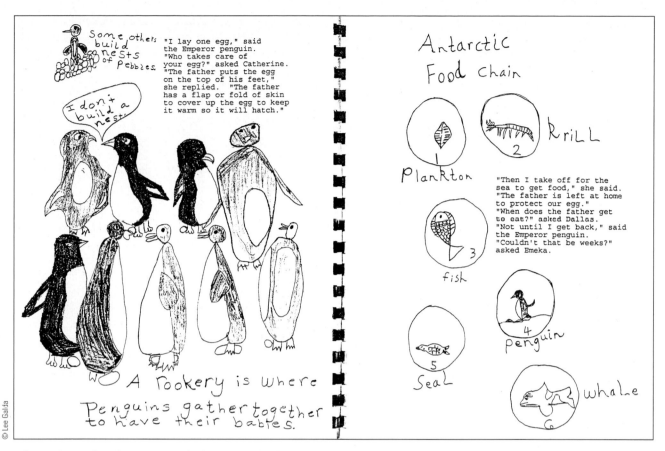

After reading and studying a series of informational books, Karen's class collaborated on their own book about penguins.

minutes, her "literature group," as they called themselves, read, wrote, and talked about literature (Galda, Rayburn, & Stanzi, 2000).

Lisa taught reading and the language arts through literature, using both the stories, poems, and nonfiction found in the basal text and the hundreds of trade books that the children read. Oral discussion of literature was at the heart of her reading program, and she spent a significant amount of time helping her students learn to talk about books. Although Lisa worked on decoding skills and strategies with those students who needed this work, as well as on vocabulary development, her focus was on comprehension strategies, which are directly linked to children's being able to read and respond to a book. In this way she was much like Betty, incorporating reading instruction when her students were engaged in reading children's books and responding to students' strengths and weaknesses. She also taught her students about literature by teaching them about literary elements, about how to make connections between what they read and their own lives, and about how to make connections among texts.

Lisa's students learned about what authors do by talking about the books they were reading. They studied authors and their work across the year. Teaching Idea 11.5 suggests a way in which children can get to know a favorite author or illustrator. They also explored genre characteristics and conventions, trying to distinguish between fantasy and realism, historical and contemporary settings, fiction and nonfiction. They did all of this by reading widely, writing in response journals, and discussing what they read. They delighted in noticing and discussing an author's particular use of a literary element such as plot, setting, characterization, and theme.

On one spring morning, the group talked about the relationships that the characters in Sid Fleischman's *The Whipping Boy* (I) have with each other; they hypothesized about characters' motives for some of their actions. Sarah commented that she thought the prince didn't want to go back to his castle. Chris thought that the prince really liked another character, and Brett agreed that they might become friends. Cameron moved the discussion to another level with his perceptive comment: "On the inside he likes him, but on the outside he's just mean." They went

Teaching Idea   11.5

Study the Life and Work of an Author or Illustrator

Students become interested in authors' and illustrators' lives when they discover connections between writers' and artists' life experiences and their work.

✿ Choose an author or illustrator whose work students like, and read as many of the person's books as possible.

✿ Help students make some generalizations about the person's work.

✿ Make a comparison chart or display that demonstrates similarities and differences across several books.

✿ Locate biographical information about the person. Many children's book authors and illustrators have wonderful websites that you can find simply by typing their names into a search engine.

✿ Read and discuss the information you and your students gather.

✿ Make some generalizations about how the person's life influenced his or her work.

✿ Prepare a display in which students depict the connections they found between the person's life and work.

on to discuss the characters and their own experiences as they wrestled with the idea that a person can be different on the inside from the way he or she is on the outside. Discussions like this one prompted Chris to make a comment that revealed the heart of what Lisa did with books when he said, "In here we read differently. Here we think about what we read." These eight-year-olds had, by the end of the year, a very sophisticated understanding of theme and relished a discussion that centered on themes they found in the books they read. Teaching Idea 11.6 contains ideas for exploring themes in literature.

Lisa also helped her students develop their visual literacy skills as she taught them how to "read" the illustrations in their basal reader and in the books in the classroom. In many group discussions, the children pored over illustrations as they sought to determine a mood, defend a theme, or describe a setting or character.

Lisa's young readers spent the year honing their reading skills while engaging in often passionate discussions

of the stories, poems, novels, and nonfiction books they read. They read many books, made many connections across books and with their own lives, and learned a lot about themselves and about literature. They were able to do this because their teacher created a literature-based reading program that allowed time to read, choice of reading material, and a room full of good books.

Assessment

When literature abounds in classrooms, there is less time for traditional assessment procedures than when children are busy working on "gradable" products, such as worksheets. There is, however, more opportunity for what some teachers describe as "authentic" assessment. This type of assessment involves observing children as they are reading and responding to literature, examining the work they produce as part of their reading and responding, and talking with them about what they are doing. It also involves assessing yourself as a teacher—looking critically at your planning, at the daily life of your classroom, and at your students' literacy development to determine what is and is not effective practice. The focus is on what children can do and are doing, as teachers gather artifacts, observe student behaviors, listen to students talk, and record what goes on.

You will want to keep records that represent what your students are doing in the classroom and how they are performing. These records may include artifacts that children produce, such as reading logs or response journals. Children's response activities often involve products, such as pictures they paint or writing they produce. Save these so that you can inform yourself about students' understanding of and response to the books they are reading. Reading tests, such as informal reading inventories or standardized tests, become part of the record as well.

Notes from observation of students as they select books and as they read and respond to books provide a picture of what they are actually doing in the classroom. Watch to see if your students select books they can read and are likely to enjoy. If they are not yet reading fluently, see if they can retell the story through the illustrations. Find out how your students select books and whom they ask for suggestions. Discover whom they read with and where they like to read. Keep track of how your students respond to the books they read and examine the kinds of things they do. Notice the writing they do in response, and note how often they choose art or dramatic activities as response options. Watch students as they engage in these activities, looking for demonstrations of their

Teaching Idea **11.6**

Connecting Books: Exploring Themes

During the course of the school year, Lisa and her students considered many thematic connections. This was easy because her curriculum was thematically organized. They began the year by talking about families as portrayed in the picturebooks they were reading, exploring the idea "What makes a family?" As they continued to read and talk about books, they frequently linked them by theme because that was something that Lisa did as she talked with them. You can do this with your students. If you comment that a book reminds you of another book because they are both "about the same thing," and then discuss the themes, your students will emulate your behavior.

In the late fall and early winter, Lisa's students discussed Patricia MacLachlan's *Arthur, for the Very First Time*, in which a young boy begins to understand the feelings he has about becoming a big brother. At this point these second-grade readers began to talk, just a little, about themselves in relation to the books they were reading. Many of them could connect to Arthur because they, too, had experienced feeling sad or angry without knowing

why. As one boy put it, "It helps when you understand how you feel." This was the beginning of a yearlong consideration of how important it is to "know thyself," a discussion that culminated with their talk about Sid Fleischman's *The Whipping Boy*. The following are tips for leading your students into a consideration of theme:

✿ Begin talking about themes with the picturebooks you read.

✿ Group books by theme. Allow the children to physically manipulate the books as they consider how they connect.

✿ Introduce brief novels by reading aloud and discussing the themes as a group.

✿ Ask children to think about themes through both writing and discussion prompts.

✿ Continue to explore thematic connections across the school year, linking books to books, and books to the children's own lives.

engagement with and understanding of the books they read. As you observe, jot down brief notes about what you are seeing. If you use mailing labels to write on, you can affix them to a sheet of paper in each child's record. As you keep adding notes, you build a picture of each child's reading behaviors.

Notes from listening to their conversations about literature provide information about students' comprehension and response, just as an analysis of their oral reading provides information about their decoding strategies. Listening to children discuss books is a good way to assess their development as readers. Note the kinds of things they talk about, whether they attend to others' ideas, and whether others' ideas enrich their own reading and responding. This helps you know what you need to focus on in your instruction. Ask individual children to read aloud to you on a regular basis and note the skills and strategies they call on as they decode unfamiliar text. This helps tell you what you need to teach.

As you engage in these assessment activities, you will find that you learn things about your students that inform the instructional decisions you make. You will find yourself teaching more effectively as you focus on students rather than on a standard curriculum. This focus is crucial to a literature-based literacy curriculum.

• • • SUMMARY • • •

There are many ways to structure literature-based instruction for young children. Reading aloud and oral language activities, time to read, a rich choice of reading material, and a purposeful classroom are basic to a successful program. Some teachers use literature to teach reading, writing, listening and speaking. They seek out patterned, predictable texts, easy readers, and transitional chapter books to provide their students with rich literary experiences. Other teachers use children's books to support a thematic organization that links several areas of the curriculum. The books become a resource for practicing the English language arts, and they provide learning content about a particular theme. Still other teachers teach students about literature through literature-based instruction, even as they teach them how to read, write, and respond—and to discuss the books they read. There are as many ways to structure literature-based instruction as there are teachers and classrooms full of children. In all cases, however, teachers pay careful attention to what their students are doing, assessing their progress in order to plan instruction.

Chapter

12

Response-centered, Literature-based Instruction in Intermediate Grades and Middle School

This chapter was revised and updated by Lauren Aimonette Liang.

Dr. Death faced me across the kitchen table. He touched my hand with his long curved fingers. I caught the scent of tobacco that surrounded him. I saw the black spots on his skin. Dad was telling him the story: my disappearance in the night, my sleepwalking. I heard in his voice how scared he still was, how he thought he'd lost me. I wanted to tell him again that I was all right, everything was all right.

—DAVID ALMOND, *Skellig*, p. 122

Skellig calls attention to the blurred line between reality and fantasy, causing young readers to wonder just who or what Skellig really is.

The students in George's sixth-grade class are scattered around the room in small groups, heatedly discussing David Almond's *Skellig* (I–A), a Michael L. Printz Honor book. They have just finished the part where Michael and Mina visit Skellig in the night, and Michael's father awakes to find him gone. They are trying to decide just what or who Skellig is. Is he an angel? A vagrant? A figment of Mina and Michael's overactive imaginations? An apparition sent to comfort Michael during his newborn sister's medical crisis?

Because there is so much to think and talk about, so many things to figure out, George is reading this brief novel aloud so that everyone is, quite literally, on the same page. The surreal story has gripped everyone, and students ask George to go back a few chapters to reread some of the earlier descriptions of Skellig. Many students have asked their parents to buy them their own copy of the book; others are hoping that it will be offered through the book club that their class participates in. Later, George will ask his students to talk about the genre that *Skellig* belongs in, another query that will provoke lively discussion.

Reading and talking together about books that provoke strong responses are making these sixth-grade students more avid readers. These activities are also helping them become better readers because their desire to understand and be able to participate in class discussions is strong. These students are lucky to have the opportunity to engage with good books on a regular basis, to have time to talk about them with their peers, and to have opportunities to respond in journals, projects, and more formal papers. Both fluent and still struggling readers are caught up in the ideas that Almond is exploring and are actively creating meaning as they read. And they're enjoying it!

Response-centered Literature Instruction

There are many ways to make literature a central part of intermediate-grade and middle-school instruction. Chapter 2 discussed a transactional view of reading literature and the goals of a response-centered curriculum. In this chapter, we explore different instructional frameworks that focus on developing intermediate- and middle-school students' responses and literary understanding as they engage with books.

As discussed in Chapter 2, the primary goal of a response-centered curriculum is to engage readers in the act of reading responsively. The focus is not on the works of literature, nor on the topics or skills, but on "the mind of the reader as it meets the book—the response" (Purves, Rogers, & Soter, 1990). A response-centered curriculum recognizes and encourages diversity among readers, recognizes and encourages connections among readers, and "recognizes that response is joyous" (Purves, Rogers, & Soter, 1990, p. 56). In this curriculum, the teacher provides a variety of books, time to read and explore them, time to talk and write about them, and time to draw and dramatize from them. In addition, teachers provide opportunities for students to enjoy the collaborative company of peers with whom to explore similarities and differences in responses. The teacher also helps students find the language with which to articulate their responses, and challenges them to understand why they respond as they do (Purves, Rogers, & Soter, 1990).

A second goal is to build on the engagement that a response-centered curriculum fosters in order to develop children's awareness of the world of literature and of how words work (Benton, 1984) in literature. This goal is focused on helping children learn language and learn about it and its use in literature through reading. Although this is especially important in the primary grades, it also remains a central focus in a response-centered curriculum for the intermediate- and middle-school grades in a more advanced manner.

A third goal is to give children the opportunity to learn about themselves and their world through books, to learn *through* language. The virtual experiences possible through story, the emotional expansion that is possible with poetry, and the exposure to information about the world that comes from nonfiction all increase children's knowledge of themselves and their worlds. And this increased knowledge widens children's horizons and makes even more learning possible.

The three essential ingredients of a response-based curriculum—time and choice, reading aloud, and activities that support children's developing understanding of literature—are all elements in the frameworks discussed next. First, we will look at two ways to organize a response-based literature curriculum for the entire year, and then explore some methods for teaching individual books with a focus on students' responses. In each case, the suggested instruction allows for students' need for time to read, choices about how they read and respond, and scaffolding as they grow in their understanding of how literature works.

Teaching Literature across the Year

We know that children need both time to read and choices about what to read, how to read, and whom to read with.

> Allowing children time to be with books in the classroom, rather than assigning them to a certain number of books to be read on their own time, teaches them to value books. When time is set aside for reading and responding to literature, students know that this is viewed as important by their teacher. So, too, does reading to and with a class help to convince students of the value and the pleasures of reading. (Galda, 1988, p. 100)

The difficulty is finding a way to create this time and space for choice in the school day on a regular basis, especially in the upper-elementary and middle-school grades when an increasing amount of complex content must be covered. The amount of independent reading children do in school, particularly when the texts are appropriately challenging, is significantly related to gains in reading achievement (Kuhn et al. 2006; Samuels & Wu, 2003).

However, researchers estimate that the typical primary-school child reads silently only seven or eight minutes per day. By the middle grades, silent reading time averages only fifteen minutes per school day. No one can become skilled at anything practiced only seven to fifteen minutes a day (Taylor, Frye, & Maruyama, 1990; West, Stanovich, & Mitchell, 1993).

We might think that we can solve the problem of tight schedules and too little time for reading in the classroom by assigning reading as homework. Research has found that students are more likely to read outside of school if the teacher reads aloud in school and if they have a period of independent silent reading during school (Fielding, Wilson, & Anderson, 1986). If we want students to read, we must tempt them with good stories, poems, and nonfiction, and show them that we value reading by devoting a significant amount of time to it in the classroom. However, it is also important that students have time to respond to what they have read with peers, with their teachers, and on their own. Further, students need opportunities to make choices about what they read. As we discussed earlier, responses and preferences are highly individualistic. Although you as a teacher need to be able to help students select books they will like and that are appropriately challenging, and although you can and should make suggestions and assign books and response activities at times, children also need to be able to make their own choices about the books they read. They also should be able to make choices at times about what they want to do when they are finished with a book. Some children might like to write, others to talk, and others to sit quietly and think.

Teachers help students become knowledgeable about themselves as readers by providing both guidance and the freedom to choose books. Some teachers choose to use literature frameworks such as Reading Workshop, which allows children a fairly full range of choice; they can frequently choose nearly any book that they would like to read. Other teachers use frameworks like Book Club, which encourages teachers to provide revolving curriculum-based classroom collections for children to choose from. Whatever the approach, the idea that they can choose what they want to read has changed the way many children feel about reading.

As children become confident readers, they learn with teacher scaffolding to recognize what books they can read and what books they might like to read. They begin to know which authors and illustrators they like. And they learn where to go for recommendations about books—to the teacher, the librarian, family and friends, other students in their class. Good readers know how to find books for themselves.

Year-long programs or frameworks for a response-based literature curriculum are often built around this

Reading with friends means that students can discuss what they read, and that increases both pleasure and understanding.

important notion of time and choice. The two described here, Book Club and Reading Workshop, are widely used in the intermediate and middle grades.

· · BOOK CLUB · ·

Book Club (McMahon, Raphael, Goatley, et al. 1997) was developed by classroom teachers in conjunction with university researchers. It is structured to include multiple opportunities for language use and easily accommodates thematic studies in a language arts curriculum or links between language arts and other curricular areas. The developers of Book Club also created a corollary program, Book Club for Middle School (Raphael, Kehus, & Damphousse, 2001), for middle-grade students. The elements and background in the Book Club for Middle School program are the same as those in the original Book Club, but the sample units, themes, and lessons are geared specifically toward middle-school classrooms.

Book Club is grounded in a sociocultural perspective on language and learning and in response theory, discussed in Chapter 2. A sociocultural perspective reflects an understanding that language first develops through social interaction and eventually becomes internalized as thought. During this interaction, learning occurs when individuals work on tasks in the company of more knowledgeable others who guide them. Through this interaction, individuals develop their own sense of self and of others, and they learn to use language in particular forms within particular contexts (McMahon et al., 1997). Because readers are reading and responding to literature in Book Club, this perspective includes the idea that readers read within a social context and construct their responses over time as they read and share their thinking with others. These theoretical concepts shape the structure of Book Club. This includes reading, writing, small-group discussions, whole-class interactions, and multiple opportunities for instruction.

Reading

If we want our students to read more, then we have to provide time for them to read during the school day. Book Club does just this. The reading in Book Club differs from the traditional independent silent reading because the books are selected by the teacher or by both the teacher and the students, in an effort to explore a theme or curricular area. Criteria for selection include literary quality, substance, age-appropriateness, thematic connection, and difficulty; the book must be sufficiently engaging and stimulating that students will want to think, write, and talk about it.

The whole class may be reading the same book, or the class may divide into smaller groups, or book clubs, with each book club reading a different book, all relating

what they have learned is a powerful step toward the practice of self-evaluation, a necessary skill for independent learners. See Strickland, Galda, & Cullinan (2004) for more extended discussion of assessment and of teaching with literature.

• • • SUMMARY • • •

There are many ways to structure response-centered, literature-based instruction in the intermediate grades and middle school. Some teachers chose to use year-long frameworks such as Book Club or Reading Workshop. Both frameworks allow for social interaction around literary events, time spent reading, and opportunities for students to respond in writing and by talking with peers. Other teachers might chose to work on response-centered instruction more in depth with individual books throughout the year. These teachers might use the SRE (Scaffolded Reading Experience) framework to foster students' under-

standing and enjoyment of the book and promote deep understanding. Over time, these experiences with individual books help students begin to make intertextual connections that build their general literary understanding.

Teachers also might infuse literature into their curriculum in other ways. Many teachers combine literature study and writing, using the books students read as resources for and examples of good writing. Others work toward transforming the curriculum they teach by using literature that provides students with alternative perspectives. All of these ways of incorporating literature into the curriculum are supported by assessment practices that keep teachers informed about how their students are performing.

Teaching with a response-centered, literature-based approach helps readers think about themselves and their world and expand their ideas about people, places, history, current events, and important issues. It helps students learn to read and think critically, considering multiple points of view. Books and the right kind of teaching can transform much more than the curriculum. They can transform lives.

Selected Children's and Adolescent Book Awards

American Library Association Awards

• • • The John Newbery Medal • • • and Honor Books

The John Newbery Medal, established in 1922 and named for an eighteenth-century British publisher and bookseller, the first to publish books for children, is given annually for the most distinguished contribution to literature for children published in the United States in the preceding year. This award is administered by the Association for Library Service to Children, a division of the American Library Association.

1922

The Story of Mankind, by Hendrik Willem van Loon (Liveright)

HONOR BOOKS: *The Great Quest*, by Charles Hawes (Little, Brown); *Cedric the Forester*, by Bernard Marshall (Appleton); *The Old Tobacco Shop*, by William Bowen (Macmillan); *The Golden Fleece and the Heroes Who Lived before Achilles*, by Padraic Colum (Macmillan); *Windy Hill*, by Cornelia Meigs (Macmillan)

1923

The Voyages of Doctor Doolittle, by Hugh Lofting (HarperCollins)

HONOR BOOKS: No record

1924

The Dark Frigate, by Charles Hawes (Little, Brown)

HONOR BOOKS: No record

1925

Tales from Silver Lands, by Charles Finger (Doubleday)

HONOR BOOKS: *Nicholas*, by Anne Carroll Moore (Putnam); *Dream Coach*, by Anne Parrish (Macmillan)

1926

Shen of the Sea, by Arthur Bowie Chrisman (Dutton)

HONOR BOOK: *Voyagers*, by Padraic Colum (Macmillan)

1927

Smoky, the Cowhorse, by Will James (Scribner's)

HONOR BOOKS: No record

1928

Gay-Neck: The Story of a Pigeon, by Dhan Gopal Mukerji (Dutton)

HONOR BOOKS: *The Wonder Smith and His Son*, by Ella Young (Longman); *Downright Dencey*, by Caroline Snedeker (Doubleday)

1929

The Trumpeter of Krakow, by Eric P. Kelly (Macmillan)

HONOR BOOKS: *Pigtail of Ah Lee Ben Loo*, by John Benett (Longman); *Millions of Cats*, by Wanda Gág (Coward-McCann); *The Boy Who Was*, by Grace Hallock (Dutton); *Clearing Weather*, by Cornelia Meigs (Little, Brown); *Runaway Papoose*, by Grace Moon (Doubleday); *Tod of the Fens*, by Elinor Whitney (Macmillan)

1930

Hitty, Her First Hundred Years, by Rachel Field (Macmillan)

HONOR BOOKS: *A Daughter of the Seine*, by Jeanette Eaton (HarperCollins); *Pran of Albania*, by Elizabeth Miller (Doubleday); *Jumping-Off Place*, by Marian Hurd McNeely (Longman); *Tangle-Coated Horse and Other Tales*, by Ella Young (Random House); *Vaino*, by Julia Davis Adams (Dutton); *Little Blacknose*, by Hildegarde Swift (Harcourt)

1931

The Cat Who Went to Heaven, by Elizabeth Coatsworth (Macmillan)

HONOR BOOKS: *Floating Island*, by Anne Parrish (HarperCollins); *The Dark Star of Itza*, by Alida Malkus (Harcourt); *Queer Person*, by Ralph Hubbard (Doubleday); *Mountains Are Free*, by Julia Davis Adams (Dutton); *Spice and the Devil's Cave*, by Agnes Hewes (Knopf); *Meggy Macintosh*, by Elizabeth Janet Gray (Doubleday); *Garram the Hunter*, by Herbert Best (Doubleday); *Ood-Le-Uk the Wanderer*, by Alice Lide and Margaret Johansen (Little, Brown)

1932

Waterless Mountain, by Laura Adams Armer (Random House)

HONOR BOOKS: *The Fairy Circus*, by Dorothy P. Lathrop (Macmillan); *Calico Bush*, by Rachel Field (Macmillan); *Boy of the South Seas*, by Eunice Tietjens (Coward-McCann); *Out of the Flame*, by Eloise Lownsbery (Longman); *Jane's Island*, by Marjorie Allee (Houghton Mifflin); *Truce of the Wolf and Other Tales of Old Italy*, by Mary Gould Davis (Harcourt)

1933

Young Fu of the Upper Yangtze, by Elizabeth Foreman Lewis (Winston)

HONOR BOOKS: *Swift Rivers*, by Cornelia Meigs (Little, Brown); *The Railroad to Freedom*, by Hildegarde Swift (Harcourt); *Children of the Soil*, by Nora Burglon (Doubleday)

1934

Invincible Louisa, by Cornelia Meigs (Little, Brown)

HONOR BOOKS: *The Forgotten Daughter*, by Caroline Snedeker (Doubleday); *Swords of Steel*, by Elsie Singmaster (Houghton Mifflin); *ABC Bunny*, by Wanda Gág (Coward-McCann); *Winged Girl of Knossos*, by Erik Berry (Appleton); *New Land*, by Sarah Schmidt (McBride); *Big Tree of Bunlahy*, by Padraic Colum (Macmillan); *Glory of the Seas*, by Agnes Hewes (Knopf); *Apprentice of Florence*, by Ann Kyle (Houghton Mifflin)

1935

Dobry, by Monica Shannon (Viking)

HONOR BOOKS: *Pageant of Chinese History*, by Elizabeth Seeger (Random House); *Davy Crockett*, by Constance Rourke (Harcourt); *A Day on Skates*, by Hilda Van Stockum (HarperCollins)

1936

Caddie Woodlawn, by Carol Ryrie Brink (Macmillan)

HONOR BOOKS: *Honk the Moose*, by Phil Stong (Trellis); *The Good Master*, by Kate Seredy (Viking); *Young Walter Scott*, by Elizabeth Janet Gray (Viking); *All Sail Set*, by Armstrong Sperry (Winston)

1937

Roller Skates, by Ruth Sawyer (Viking)

HONOR BOOKS: *Phoebe Fairchild: Her Book*, by Lois Lenski (Stokes); *Whistler's Van*, by Idwal Jones (Viking); *Golden Basket*, by Ludwig Bemelmans (Viking); *Winterbound*, by Margery Bianco (Viking); *Audubon*, by Constance Rourke (Harcourt); *The Codfish Musket*, by Agnes Hewes (Doubleday)

1938

The White Stag, by Kate Seredy (Viking)

HONOR BOOKS: *Pecos Bill*, by James Cloyd Bowman (Little, Brown); *Bright Island*, by Mabel Robinson (Random House); *On the Banks of Plum Creek*, by Laura Ingalls Wilder (HarperCollins)

1939

Thimble Summer, by Elizabeth Enright (Holt)

Honor Books: *Nino*, by Valenti Angelo (Viking); *Mr. Popper's Penguins*, by Richard and Florence Atwater (Little, Brown); *"Hello the Boat!"*, by Phyllis Crawford (Holt); *Leader by Destiny: George Washington, Man and Patriot*, by Jeanette Eaton (Harcourt); *Penn*, by Elizabeth Janet Gray (Viking)

1940

Daniel Boone, by James Daugherty (Viking)

Honor Books: *The Singing Tree*, by Kate Seredy (Viking); *Runner of the Mountain Tops*, by Mabel Robinson (Random House); *By the Shores of Silver Lake*, by Laura Ingalls Wilder (HarperCollins); *Boy with a Pack*, by Stephen W. Meader (Harcourt)

1941

Call It Courage, by Armstrong Sperry (Macmillan)

Honor Books: *Blue Willow*, by Doris Gates (Viking); *Young Mac of Fort Vancouver*, by Mary Jane Carr (HarperCollins); *The Long Winter*, by Laura Ingalls Wilder (HarperCollins); *Nansen*, by Anna Gertrude Hall (Viking)

1942

The Matchlock Gun, by Walter D. Edmonds (Putnam)

Honor Books: *Little Town on the Prairie*, by Laura Ingalls Wilder (HarperCollins); *George Washington's World*, by Genevieve Foster (Scribner's); *Indian Captive: The Story of Mary Jemison*, by Lois Lenski (HarperCollins); *Down Ryton Water*, by Eva Roe Gaggin (Viking)

1943

Adam of the Road, by Elizabeth Janet Gray (Viking)

Honor Books: *The Middle Moffat*, by Eleanor Estes (Harcourt); *Have You Seen Tom Thumb?*, by Mabel Leigh Hunt (HarperCollins)

1944

Johnny Tremain, by Esther Forbes (Houghton Mifflin)

Honor Books: *These Happy Golden Years*, by Laura Ingalls Wilder (HarperCollins); *Fog Magic*, by Julia Sauer (Viking); *Rufus M.*, by Eleanor Estes (Harcourt); *Mountain Born*, by Elizabeth Yates (Coward-McCann)

1945

Rabbit Hill, by Robert Lawson (Viking)

Honor Books: *The Hundred Dresses*, by Eleanor Estes (Harcourt); *The Silver Pencil*, by Alice Dalgliesh (Scribner's); *Abraham Lincoln's World*, by Genevieve Foster (Scribner's); *Lone Journey: The Life of Roger Williams*, by Jeannette Eaton (Harcourt)

1946

Strawberry Girl, by Lois Lenski (HarperCollins)

Honor Books: *Justin Morgan Had a Horse*, by Marguerite Henry (Rand McNally); *The Moved-Outers*, by Florence Crannel Means (Houghton Mifflin); *Bhimsa, the Dancing Bear*, by Christine Weston (Scribner's); *New Found World*, by Katherine Shippen (Viking)

1947

Miss Hickory, by Carolyn Sherwin Bailey (Viking)

Honor Books: *Wonderful Year*, by Nancy Barnes (Messner); *Big Tree*, by Mary and Conrad Buff (Viking); *The Heavenly Tenants*, by William Maxwell (HarperCollins); *The Avion My Uncle Flew*, by Cyrus Fisher (Appleton); *The Hidden Treasure of Glaston*, by Eleanore Jewett (Viking)

1948

The Twenty-One Balloons, by William Pène du Bois (Viking)

Honor Books: *Pancakes-Paris*, by Claire Huchet Bishop (Viking); *Li Lun, Lad of Courage*, by Carolyn Treffinger (Abingdon); *The Quaint and Curious Quest of Johnny Longfoot*, by Catherine Besterman (Bobbs); *The Cow-Tail Switch and Other West African Stories*, by Harold Courlander (Holt); *Misty of Chincoteague*, by Marguerite Henry (Rand McNally)

1949

King of the Wind, by Marguerite Henry (Rand McNally)

Honor Books: *Seabird*, by Holling C. Holling (Houghton Mifflin); *Daughter of the Mountains*, by Louise Rankin (Viking); *My Father's Dragon*, by Ruth Stiles Gannett (Random House); *Story of the Negro*, by Arna Bontemps (Knopf)

1950

The Door in the Wall, by Marguerite de Angeli (Doubleday)

Honor Books: *Tree of Freedom*, by Rebecca Caudill (Viking); *The Blue Cat of Castle Town*, by Catherine Coblentz (Random House); *Kildee House*, by Rutherford Montgomery (Doubleday); *George Washington*, by Genevieve Foster (Scribner's); *Song of the Pines*, by Walter and Marion Havighurst (Winston)

1951

Amos Fortune, Free Man, by Elizabeth Yates (Aladdin)
HONOR BOOKS: *Better Known as Johnny Appleseed*, by Mabel Leigh Hunt (HarperCollins); *Gandhi: Fighter without a Sword*, by Jeanette Eaton (Morrow); *Abraham Lincoln, Friend of the People*, by Clara Ingram Judson (Follett); *The Story of Appleby Capple*, by Anne Parrish (HarperCollins)

1952

Ginger Pye, by Eleanor Estes (Harcourt)
HONOR BOOKS: *Americans before Columbus*, by Elizabeth Baity (Viking); *Minn of the Mississippi*, by Holling C. Holling (Houghton Mifflin); *The Defender*, by Nicholas Kalashnikoff (Scribner's); *The Light at Tern Rock*, by Julia Sauer (Viking); *The Apple and the Arrow*, by Mary and Conrad Buff (Houghton Mifflin)

1953

Secret of the Andes, by Ann Nolan Clark (Viking)
HONOR BOOKS: *Charlotte's Web*, by E. B. White (HarperCollins); *Moccasin Trail*, by Eloise McGraw (Coward-McCann); *Red Sails to Capri*, by Ann Weil (Viking); *The Bears on Hemlock Mountain*, by Alice Dalgliesh (Scribner's); *Birthdays of Freedom, Vol. 1*, by Genevieve Foster (Scribner's)

1954

. . . and now Miguel, by Joseph Krumgold (HarperCollins)
HONOR BOOKS: *All Alone*, by Claire Huchet Bishop (Viking); *Shadrach*, by Meindert DeJong (HarperCollins); *Hurry Home, Candy*, by Meindert DeJong (HarperCollins); *Theodore Roosevelt, Fighting Patriot*, by Clara Ingram Judson (Follett); *Magic Maize*, by Mary and Conrad Buff (Houghton Mifflin)

1955

The Wheel on the School, by Meindert DeJong (HarperCollins)
HONOR BOOKS: *The Courage of Sarah Noble*, by Alice Dalgliesh (Scribner's); *Banner in the Sky*, by James Ullman (HarperCollins)

1956

Carry on, Mr. Bowditch, by Jean Lee Latham (Houghton Mifflin)
HONOR BOOKS: *The Secret River*, by Marjorie Kinnan Rawlings (Scribner's); *The Golden Name Day*, by Jennie Lindquist (HarperCollins); *Men, Microscopes, and Living Things*, by Katherine Shippen (Viking)

1957

Miracles on Maple Hill, by Virginia Sorensen (Harcourt)
HONOR BOOKS: *Old Yeller*, by Fred Gipson (HarperCollins); *The House of Sixty Fathers*, by Meindert DeJong (HarperCollins); *Mr. Justice Holmes*, by Clara Ingram Judson (Follett); *The Corn Grows Ripe*, by Dorothy Rhoads (Viking); *Black Fox of Lorne*, by Marguerite de Angeli (Doubleday)

1958

Rifles for Watie, by Harold Keith (Crowell)
HONOR BOOKS: *The Horsecatcher*, by Mari Sandoz (Westminster); *Gone-Away Lake*, by Elizabeth Enright (Harcourt); *The Great Wheel*, by Robert Lawson (Viking); *Tom Paine, Freedom's Apostle*, by Leo Gurko (HarperCollins)

1959

The Witch of Blackbird Pond, by Elizabeth George Speare (Houghton Mifflin)
HONOR BOOKS: *The Family under the Bridge*, by Natalie Savage Carlson (HarperCollins); *Along Came a Dog*, by Meindert DeJong (HarperCollins); *Chucaro: Wild Pony of the Pampa*, by Francis Kalnay (Harcourt); *The Perilous Road*, by William O. Steele (Harcourt)

1960

Onion John, by Joseph Krumgold (HarperCollins)
HONOR BOOKS: *My Side of the Mountain*, by Jean Craighead George (Dutton); *America Is Born*, by Gerald W. Johnson (Morrow); *The Gammage Cup*, by Carol Kendall (Harcourt)

1961

Island of the Blue Dolphins, by Scott O'Dell (Houghton Mifflin)
HONOR BOOKS: *America Moves Forward*, by Gerald W. Johnson (Morrow); *Old Ramon*, by Jack Schaefer (Houghton Mifflin); *The Cricket in Times Square*, by George Selden (Farrar, Straus & Giroux)

1962

The Bronze Bow, by Elizabeth George Speare (Houghton Mifflin)

HONOR BOOKS: *Frontier Living*, by Edwin Tunis (World); *The Golden Goblet*, by Eloise McGraw (Coward-McCann); *Belling the Tiger*, by Mary Stolz (HarperCollins)

1963

A Wrinkle in Time, by Madeleine L'Engle (Farrar, Straus & Giroux)

HONOR BOOKS: *Thistle and Thyme*, by Sorche Nic Leodhas (Holt); *Men of Athens*, by Olivia Coolidge (Houghton Mifflin)

1964

It's Like This, Cat, by Emily Cheney Neville (HarperCollins)

HONOR BOOKS: *Rascal*, by Sterling North (Dutton); *The Loner*, by Ester Wier (McKay)

1965

Shadow of a Bull, by Maia Wojciechowska (Simon & Schuster)

HONOR BOOK: *Across Five Aprils*, by Irene Hunt (Follett)

1966

I, Juan de Pareja, by Elizabeth Borton de Treviño (Farrar, Straus & Giroux)

HONOR BOOKS: *The Black Cauldron*, by Lloyd Alexander (Holt); *The Animal Family*, by Randall Jarrell (Pantheon); *The Noonday Friends*, by Mary Stolz (HarperCollins)

1967

Up a Road Slowly, by Irene Hunt (Follett)

HONOR BOOKS: *The King's Fifth*, by Scott O'Dell (Houghton Mifflin); *Zlateh the Goat and Other Stories*, by Isaac Bashevis Singer (HarperCollins); *The Jazz Man*, by Mary H. Weik (Simon & Schuster)

1968

From the Mixed-Up Files of Mrs. Basil E. Frankweiler, by E. L. Konigsburg (Simon & Schuster)

HONOR BOOKS: *Jennifer, Hecate, Macbeth, William McKinley, and Me, Elizabeth*, by E. L. Konigsburg (Simon & Schuster); *The Black Pearl*, by Scott O'Dell (Houghton Mifflin); *The Fearsome Inn*, by Isaac Bashevis Singer (Scribner's); *The Egypt Game*, by Zilpha Keatley Snyder (Simon & Schuster)

1969

The High King, by Lloyd Alexander (Holt)

HONOR BOOKS: *To Be a Slave*, by Julius Lester (Dial); *When Shlemiel Went to Warsaw and Other Stories*, by Isaac Bashevis Singer (Farrar, Straus & Giroux)

1970

Sounder, by William H. Armstrong (HarperCollins)

HONOR BOOKS: *Our Eddie*, by Sulamith Ish-Kishor (Pantheon); *The Many Ways of Seeing: An Introduction to the Pleasures of Art*, by Janet Gaylord Moore (World); *Journey Outside*, by Mary Q. Steele (Viking)

1971

Summer of the Swans, by Betsy Byars (Viking)

HONOR BOOKS: *Kneeknock Rise*, by Natalie Babbitt (Farrar, Straus & Giroux); *Enchantress from the Stars*, by Sylvia Louise Engdahl (Simon & Schuster); *Sing Down the Moon*, by Scott O'Dell (Houghton Mifflin)

1972

Mrs. Frisby and the Rats of NIMH, by Robert C. O'Brien (Simon & Schuster)

HONOR BOOKS: *Incident at Hawk's Hill*, by Allan W. Eckert (Little, Brown); *The Planet of Junior Brown*, by Virginia Hamilton (Macmillan); *The Tombs of Atuan*, by Ursula Le Guin (Simon & Schuster); *Annie and the Old One*, by Miska Miles (Little, Brown); *The Headless Cupid*, by Zilpha Keatley Snyder (Simon & Schuster)

1973

Julie of the Wolves, by Jean Craighead George (HarperCollins)

HONOR BOOKS: *Frog and Toad Together*, by Arnold Lobel (HarperCollins); *The Upstairs Room*, by Johanna Reiss (HarperCollins); *The Witches of Worm*, by Zilpha Keatley Snyder (Simon & Schuster)

1974

The Slave Dancer, by Paula Fox (Bradbury)

HONOR BOOKS: *The Dark Is Rising*, by Susan Cooper (McElderry)

1975

M. C. Higgins, the Great, by Virginia Hamilton (Macmillan)

HONOR BOOKS: *Figgs and Phantoms*, by Ellen Raskin (Dutton); *My Brother Sam Is Dead*, by James Lincoln and Christopher Collier (Four Winds); *The Perilous Guard*, by Elizabeth Marie Pope (Houghton Mifflin); *Philip Hall Likes Me. I Reckon Maybe*, by Bette Greene (Dial)

1976

The Grey King, by Susan Cooper (McElderry)
HONOR BOOKS: *The Hundred Penny Box*, by Sharon Bell Mathis (Viking); *Dragonwings*, by Laurence Yep (HarperCollins)

1977

Roll of Thunder, Hear My Cry, by Mildred Taylor (Dial)
HONOR BOOKS: *Abel's Island*, by William Steig (Farrar, Straus & Giroux); *A String in the Harp*, by Nancy Bond (McElderry)

1978

Bridge to Terabithia, by Katherine Paterson (HarperCollins)
HONOR BOOKS: *Ramona and Her Father*, by Beverly Cleary (Morrow); *Anpao: An American Indian Odyssey*, by Jamake Highwater (HarperCollins)

1979

The Westing Game, by Ellen Raskin (Dutton)
HONOR BOOKS: *The Great Gilly Hopkins*, by Katherine Paterson (HarperCollins)

1980

A Gathering of Days: A New England Girl's Journal, 1830–32, by Joan Blos (Scribner's)
HONOR BOOK: *The Road from Home: The Story of an Armenian Girl*, by David Kherdian (Greenwillow)

1981

Jacob Have I Loved, by Katherine Paterson (HarperCollins)
HONOR BOOKS: *The Fledgling*, by Jane Langton (Harper-Collins); *A Ring of Endless Light*, by Madeleine L'Engle (Farrar, Straus & Giroux)

1982

A Visit to William Blake's Inn: Poems for Innocent and Experienced Travelers, by Nancy Willard (Harcourt)

HONOR BOOKS: *Ramona Quimby, Age 8*, by Beverly Cleary (Morrow); *Upon the Head of the Goat: A Childhood in Hungary, 1939–1944*, by Aranka Siegel (Farrar, Straus & Giroux)

1983

Dicey's Song, by Cynthia Voigt (Simon & Schuster)
HONOR BOOKS: *The Blue Sword*, by Robin McKinley (Greenwillow); *Doctor De Soto*, by William Steig (Farrar, Straus & Giroux); *Graven Images*, by Paul Fleischman (HarperCollins); *Homesick: My Own Story*, by Jean Fritz (Putnam); *Sweet Whispers, Brother Rush*, by Virginia Hamilton (Philomel)

1984

Dear Mr. Henshaw, by Beverly Cleary (Morrow)
HONOR BOOKS: *The Wish Giver: Three Tales of Coven Tree*, by Bill Brittain (HarperCollins); *A Solitary Blue*, by Cynthia Voigt (Simon & Schuster); *The Sign of the Beaver*, by Elizabeth George Speare (Houghton Mifflin); *Sugaring Time*, by Kathryn Lasky (Macmillan)

1985

The Hero and the Crown, by Robin McKinley (Greenwillow)
HONOR BOOKS: *The Moves Make the Man*, by Bruce Brooks (HarperCollins); *One-Eyed Cat*, by Paula Fox (Bradbury); *Like Jake and Me*, by Mavis Jukes (Knopf)

1986

Sarah, Plain and Tall, by Patricia MacLachlan (HarperCollins)
HONOR BOOKS: *Commodore Perry in the Land of Shogun*, by Rhoda Blumberg (Lothrop, Lee & Shepard); *Dogsong*, by Gary Paulsen (Bradbury)

1987

The Whipping Boy, by Sid Fleischman (Greenwillow)
HONOR BOOKS: *On My Honor*, by Marion Dane Bauer (Clarion); *A Fine White Dust*, by Cynthia Rylant (Bradbury); *Volcano*, by Patricia Lauber (Bradbury)

1988

Lincoln: A Photobiography, by Russell Freedman (Clarion)
HONOR BOOKS: *Hatchet*, by Gary Paulsen (Bradbury); *After the Rain*, by Norma Fox Mazer (Morrow)

1989

Joyful Noise: Poems for Two Voices, by Paul Fleischman (HarperCollins)

HONOR BOOKS: *In the Beginning: Creation Stories from around the World*, by Virginia Hamilton (Harcourt); *Scorpions*, by Walter Dean Myers (HarperCollins)

1990

Number the Stars, by Lois Lowry (Houghton Mifflin)

HONOR BOOKS: *Afternoon of the Elves*, by Janet Taylor Lisle (Orchard); *Shabanu: Daughter of the Wind*, by Suzanne Fisher Staples (Knopf); *The Winter Room*, by Gary Paulsen (Orchard)

1991

Maniac Magee, by Jerry Spinelli (Little, Brown)

HONOR BOOK: *The True Confessions of Charlotte Doyle*, by Avi (Orchard)

1992

Shiloh, by Phyllis Reynolds Naylor (Simon & Schuster)

HONOR BOOKS: *Nothing but the Truth*, by Avi (Orchard); *The Wright Brothers: How They Invented the Airplane*, by Russell Freedman (Holiday House)

1993

Missing May, by Cynthia Rylant (Orchard)

HONOR BOOKS: *What Hearts*, by Bruce Brooks (Harper-Collins); *The Dark Thirty: Southern Tales of the Supernatural*, by Patricia McKissack (Knopf); *Somewhere in the Darkness*, by Walter Dean Myers (Scholastic)

1994

The Giver, by Lois Lowry (Houghton Mifflin)

HONOR BOOKS: *Crazy Lady!*, by Jane Leslie Conly (HarperCollins); *Dragon's Gate*, by Laurence Yep (Harper-Collins); *Eleanor Roosevelt: A Life of Discovery*, by Russell Freedman (Clarion)

1995

Walk Two Moons, by Sharon Creech (HarperCollins)

HONOR BOOKS: *Catherine, Called Birdy*, by Karen Cushman (Clarion); *The Ear, the Eye and the Arm*, by Nancy Farmer (Orchard)

1996

The Midwife's Apprentice, by Karen Cushman (Clarion)

HONOR BOOKS: *The Great Fire*, by Jim Murphy (Scholastic); *The Watsons Go to Birmingham—1963*, by Christopher Paul Curtis (Delacorte); *What Jamie Saw*, by Carolyn Coman (Front Street); *Yolanda's Genius*, by Carol Fenner (McElderry)

1997

The View from Saturday, by E. L. Konigsburg (Simon & Schuster)

HONOR BOOKS: *A Girl Named Disaster*, by Nancy Farmer (Orchard); *The Moorchild*, by Eloise McGraw (McElderry); *The Thief*, by Megan Whalen Turner (Greenwillow); *Belle Prater's Boy*, by Ruth White (Farrar, Straus & Giroux)

1998

Out of the Dust, by Karen Hesse (Scholastic)

HONOR BOOKS: *Lilly's Crossing*, by Patricia Reilly Giff (Delacorte); *Ella Enchanted*, by Gail Carson Levine (HarperCollins); *Wringer*, by Jerry Spinelli (HarperCollins)

1999

Holes, by Louis Sachar (Farrar, Straus & Giroux)

HONOR BOOK: *A Long Way from Chicago*, by Richard Peck (Dial)

2000

Bud, Not Buddy, by Christopher Paul Curtis (Delacorte)

HONOR BOOKS: *Getting Near to Baby*, by Audrey Coloumbis (Delacorte); *26 Fairmount Avenue*, by Tomie dePaola (Putnam); *Our Only May Amelia*, by Jennifer L. Holm (HarperCollins)

2001

A Year Down Yonder, by Richard Peck (Dial)

HONOR BOOKS: *Hope Was Here*, by Joan Bauer (Putnam); *The Wanderer*, by Sharon Creech (HarperCollins); *Because of Winn-Dixie*, by Kate DiCamillo (Candlewick); *Joey Pigza Loses Control*, by Jack Gantos (Farrar, Straus & Giroux)

2002

A Single Shard, by Linda Sue Park (Clarion)

HONOR BOOKS: *Everything on a Waffle*, by Polly Horvath (Farrar Straus & Giroux); *Carver: A Life in Poems*, by Marilyn Nelson (Front Street)

2003

Crispin: The Cross of Lead, by Avi (Hyperion)

HONOR BOOKS: House of the Scorpion, by Nancy Farmer (Simon & Schuster); *Pictures of Hollis Woods*, by Patricia Reilly Giff (Random House); *Hoot*, by Carl Hiaasen (Knopf); *A Corner of the Universe*, by Ann Martin (Scholastic); *Surviving the Applewhites*, by Stephanie Tolan (HarperCollins)

2004

The Tale of Despereaux: Being the Story of a Mouse, a Princess, Some Soup, and a Spool of Thread, by Kate DiCamillo (Candlewick)

HONOR BOOKS: *Olive's Ocean*, by Kevin Henkes (Greenwillow); *An American Plague: The True and Terrifying Story of the Yellow Fever Epidemic of 1793*, by Jim Murphy (Clarion)

2005

Kira-Kira, by Cynthia Kadohata (Simon & Schuster)

HONOR BOOKS: *Lizzie Bright and the Buckminster Boy*, by Gary Schmidt (Clarion); *Al Capone Does My Shirts*, by Gennifer Choldenko (Putnam); *The Voice That Challenged a Nation: Marian Anderson and the Struggle for Equal Rights*, by Russell Freedman (Clarion)

2006

Criss Cross, by Lynne Rae Perkins (HarperCollins)

HONOR BOOKS: *Whittington*, by Alan Armstrong, illustrated by S. D. Schindler (Random House); *Hitler Youth: Growing Up in Hitler's Shadow*, by Susan Campbell Bartoletti (Scholastic); *Princess Academy*, by Shannon Hale (Bloomsbury); *Show Way* by Jacqueline Woodson, illustrated by Hudson Talbott (G. P. Putnam's Sons)

2007

The Higher Power of Lucky by Susan Patron, illustrated by Matt Phelan (Simon & Schuster)

HONOR BOOKS: *Penny from Heaven*, by Jennifer L. Holm, (Random House); *Hattie Big Sky*, by Kirby Larson (Delacorte); *Rules*, by Cynthia Lord (Scholastic)

2008

Good Masters! Sweet Ladies! Voices from a Medieval Village, by Laura Amy Schlitz (Candlewick)

HONOR BOOKS: Elijah of Buxton, by Christopher Paul Curtis (Scholastic); *The Wednesday Wars*, by Gary D. Schmidt (Clarion); *Feathers*, by Jacqueline Woodson (Putnam)

2009

The Graveyard Book, by Neil Gaiman (HarperCollins)

HONOR BOOKS: The Underneath, by Kathi Appelt (Simon & Schuster); *The Surrender Tree: Poems of Cuba's Struggle for Freedom*, by Margarita Engle (Holt); *Savvy*, by Ingrid Law (Dial); *After Tupac and D Foster*, by Jacqueline Woodson (Putnam)

• • • The Randolph Caldecott Medal • • • and Honor Books

The Randolph Caldecott Medal, established in 1938 and named for a nineteenth-century British illustrator of books for children, is given annually to the illustrator of the most distinguished picturebook for children published in the United States in the preceding year. This award is administered by the Association for Library Service to Children, a division of the American Library Association.

1938

Animals of the Bible, by Helen Dean Fish, illustrated by Dorothy P. Lathrop (Lippincott)

HONOR BOOKS: *Seven Simeons*, by Boris Artzybasheff (Viking); *Four and Twenty Blackbirds*, by Helen Dean Fish, illustrated by Robert Lawson (Stokes)

1939

Mei Li, by Thomas Handforth (Doubleday)

HONOR BOOKS: *The Forest Pool*, by Laura Adams Armer (Longman); *Wee Gillis*, by Munro Leaf, illustrated by Robert Lawson (Viking); *Snow White and the Seven Dwarfs*, by Wanda Gág (Coward-McCann); *Barkis*, by Clare Newberry (HarperCollins); *Andy and the Lion*, by James Daugherty (Viking)

1940

Abraham Lincoln, by Ingri and Edgar Parin D'Aulaire (Doubleday)

HONOR BOOKS: *Cock-a-Doodle Doo . . .*, by Berta and Elmer Hader (Macmillan); *Madeline*, by Ludwig Bemelmans (Viking); *The Ageless Story*, by Lauren Ford (Dodd, Mead)

1941

They Were Strong and Good, by Robert Lawson (Viking)

HONOR BOOK: *April's Kittens*, by Clare Newberry (HarperCollins)

1942

Make Way for Ducklings, by Robert McCloskey (Viking)

HONOR BOOKS: *An American ABC*, by Maud and Miska Petersham (Macmillan); *In My Mother's House*, by Ann Nolan Clark, illustrated by Velino Gerrera (Viking); *Paddle-to-the-Sea*, by Holling C. Holling (Houghton Mifflin); *Nothing at All*, by Wanda Gág (Coward-McCann)

1943

The Little House, by Virginia Lee Burton (Houghton Mifflin)

HONOR BOOKS: *Dash and Dart*, by Mary and Conrad Buff (Viking); *Marshmallow*, by Clare Newberry (HarperCollins)

1944

Many Moons, by James Thurber, illustrated by Louis Slobodkin (Harcourt)

HONOR BOOKS: *Small Rain: Verses from the Bible*, selected by Jessie Orton Jones, illustrated by Elizabeth Orton Jones (Viking); *Pierre Pigeon*, by Lee Kingman, illustrated by Arnold E. Bare (Houghton Mifflin); *The Mighty Hunter*, by Berta and Elmer Hader (Macmillan); *A Child's Good Night Book*, by Margaret Wise Brown, illustrated by Jean Charlot (Scott); *Good Luck Horse*, by Chih-Yi Chan, illustrated by Plao Chan (Whittlesey)

1945

Prayer for a Child, by Rachel Field, illustrated by Elizabeth Orton Jones (Macmillan)

HONOR BOOKS: *Mother Goose*, illustrated by Tasha Tudor (Walck); *In the Forest*, by Marie Hall Ets (Viking); *Yonie Wondernose*, by Marguerite de Angeli (Doubleday); *The Christmas Anna Angel*, by Ruth Sawyer, illustrated by Kate Seredy (Viking)

1946

The Rooster Crows, illustrated by Maud and Miska Petersham (Macmillan)

HONOR BOOKS: *Little Lost Lamb*, by Golden MacDonald, illustrated by Leonard Weisgard (Doubleday); *Sing Mother Goose*, by Opal Wheeler, illustrated by Marjorie Torrey (Dutton); *My Mother Is the Most Beautiful Woman in the World*, by Becky Reyher, illustrated by Ruth Gannett (Lothrop, Lee & Shepard); *You Can Write Chinese*, by Kurt Weise (Viking)

1947

The Little Island, by Golden MacDonald, illustrated by Leonard Weisgard (Doubleday)

HONOR BOOKS: *Rain Drop Splash*, by Alvin Tresselt, illustrated by Leonard Weisgard (Lothrop, Lee & Shepard); *Boats on the River*, by Marjorie Flack, illustrated by Jay Hyde Barnum (Viking); *Timothy Turtle*, by Al Graham, illustrated by Tony Palazzo (Viking); *Pedro, the Angel of Olvera Street*, by Leo Politi (Scribner's); *Sing in Praise: A Collection of the Best Loved Hymns*, by Opal Wheeler, illustrated by Marjorie Torrey (Dutton)

1948

White Snow, Bright Snow, by Alvin Tresselt, illustrated by Roger Duvoisin (Lothrop, Lee & Shepard)

HONOR BOOKS: *Stone Soup*, by Marcia Brown (Scribner's); *McElligot's Pool*, by Dr. Seuss (Random House); *Bambino the Clown*, by George Schreiber (Viking); *Roger and the Fox*, by Lavinia Davis, illustrated by Hildegard Woodward (Doubleday); *Song of Robin Hood*, edited by Anne Malcolmson, illustrated by Virginia Lee Burton (Houghton Mifflin)

1949

The Big Snow, by Berta and Elmer Hader (Macmillan)

HONOR BOOKS: *Blueberries for Sal*, by Robert McCloskey (Viking); *All around the Town*, by Phyllis McGinley, illustrated by Helen Stone (Lippincott); *Juanita*, by Leo Politi (Scribner's); *Fish in the Air*, by Kurt Wiese (Viking)

1950

Song of the Swallows, by Leo Politi (Scribner's)

HONOR BOOKS: *America's Ethan Allen*, by Stewart Holbrook, illustrated by Lynd Ward (Houghton Mifflin); *The Wild Birthday Cake*, by Lavinia Davis, illustrated by Hildegard Woodward (Doubleday); *The Happy Day*, by Ruth Krauss, illustrated by Marc Simont (HarperCollins); *Bartholomew and the Oobleck*, by Dr. Seuss (Random House); *Henry Fisherman*, by Marcia Brown (Scribner's)

1951

The Egg Tree, by Katherine Milhous (Scribner's)

HONOR BOOKS: *Dick Whittington and His Cat*, by Marcia Brown (Scribner's); *The Two Reds*, by William Lipkind, illustrated by Nicholas Mordvinoff (Harcourt); *If I Ran the Zoo*, by Dr. Seuss (Random House); *The Most Wonderful Doll in the World*, by Phyllis McGinley, illustrated by Helen Stone (Lippincott); *T-Bone, the Baby Sitter*, by Clare Newberry (HarperCollins)

1952

Finders Keepers, by William Lipkind, illustrated by Nicholas Mordvinoff (Harcourt)

HONOR BOOKS: *Mr. T. W. Anthony Woo*, by Marie Hall Ets (Viking); *Skipper John's Cook*, by Marcia Brown (Scribner's); *All Falling Down*, by Gene Zion, illustrated by Margaret Bloy Graham (HarperCollins); *Bear Party*, by William Pène du Bois (Viking); *Feather Mountain*, by Elizabeth Olds (Houghton Mifflin)

1953

The Biggest Bear, by Lynd Ward (Houghton Mifflin)

HONOR BOOKS: *Puss in Boots*, by Charles Perrault, illustrated and translated by Marcia Brown (Scribner's); *One Morning in Maine*, by Robert McCloskey (Viking); *Ape in a Cape*, by Fritz Eichenberg (Harcourt); *The Storm Book*, by Charlotte Zolotow, illustrated by Margaret Bloy Graham (HarperCollins); *Five Little Monkeys*, by Juliet Kepes (Houghton Mifflin)

1954

Madeline's Rescue, by Ludwig Bemelmans (Viking)

HONOR BOOKS: *Journey Cake, Ho!*, by Ruth Sawyer, illustrated by Robert McCloskey (Viking); *When Will the World Be Mine?*, by Miriam Schlein, illustrated by Jean Charlot (Scott); *The Steadfast Tin Soldier*, by Hans Christian Andersen, illustrated by Marcia Brown (Scribner's); *A Very Special House*, by Ruth Krauss, illustrated by Maurice Sendak (HarperCollins); *Green Eyes*, by A. Birnbaum (Capitol)

1955

Cinderella, or the Little Glass Slipper, by Charles Perrault, translated and illustrated by Marcia Brown (Scribner's)

HONOR BOOKS: *Books of Nursery and Mother Goose Rhymes*, illustrated by Marguerite de Angeli (Doubleday); *Wheel on the Chimney*, by Margaret Wise Brown, illustrated by Tibor Gergely (Lippincott); *The Thanksgiving Story*, by Alice Dalgliesh, illustrated by Helen Sewell (Scribner's)

1956

Frog Went A-Courtin', edited by John Langstaff, illustrated by Feodor Rojankovsky (Harcourt)

HONOR BOOKS: *Play with Me*, by Marie Hall Ets (Viking); *Crow Boy*, by Taro Tashima (Viking)

1957

A Tree Is Nice, by Janice May Udry, illustrated by Marc Simont (HarperCollins)

HONOR BOOKS: *Mr. Penny's Race Horse*, by Marie Hall Ets (Viking); *1 Is One*, by Tasha Tudor (Walck); *Anatole*, by Eve Titus, illustrated by Paul Galdone (McGraw-Hill); *Gillespie and the Guards*, by Benjamin Elkin, illustrated by James Daugherty (Viking); *Lion*, by William Pène du Bois (Viking)

1958

Time of Wonder, by Robert McCloskey (Viking)

HONOR BOOKS: *Fly High, Fly Low*, by Don Freeman (Viking); *Anatole and the Cat*, by Eve Titus, illustrated by Paul Galdone (McGraw-Hill)

1959

Chanticleer and the Fox, adapted from Chaucer, illustrated by Barbara Cooney (Crowell)

HONOR BOOKS: *The House That Jack Built*, by Antonio Frasconi (Harcourt); *What Do You Say, Dear?*, by Sesyle Joslin, illustrated by Maurice Sendak (Scott); *Umbrella*, by Taro Yashima (Viking)

1960

Nine Days to Christmas, by Marie Hall Ets and Aurora Labastida, illustrated by Marie Hall Ets (Viking)

HONOR BOOKS: *Houses from the Sea*, by Alice E. Goudey, illustrated by Adrienne Adams (Scribner's); *The Moon Jumpers*, by Janice May Udry, illustrated by Maurice Sendak (HarperCollins)

1961

Baboushka and the Three Kings, by Ruth Robbins, illustrated by Nicolas Sidjakov (Parnassus)

HONOR BOOK: *Inch by Inch*, by Leo Lionni (Obolensky)

1962

Once a Mouse . . ., by Marcia Brown (Scribner's)

HONOR BOOKS: *The Fox Went Out on a Chilly Night*, by Peter Spier (Doubleday); *Little Bear's Visit*, by Else Holmelund Minarik, illustrated by Maurice Sendak (HarperCollins); *The Day We Saw the Sun Come Up*, by Alice E. Goudey, illustrated by Adrienne Adams (Scribner's)

1963

The Snowy Day, by Ezra Jack Keats (Viking)

HONOR BOOKS: *The Sun Is a Golden Earring*, by Natalie M. Belting, illustrated by Bernarda Bryson (Holt); *Mr. Rabbit and the Lovely Present*, by Charlotte Zolotow, illustrated by Maurice Sendak (HarperCollins)

1964

Where the Wild Things Are, by Maurice Sendak (HarperCollins)

HONOR BOOKS: *Swimmy*, by Leo Lionni (Pantheon); *All in the Morning Early*, by Sorche Nic Leodhas, illustrated by Evaline Ness (Holt); *Mother Goose and Nursery Rhymes*, illustrated by Philip Reed (Atheneum)

1965

May I Bring a Friend?, by Beatrice Schenk de Regniers, illustrated by Beni Montresor (Atheneum)

HONOR BOOKS: *Rain Makes Applesauce*, by Julian Scheer, illustrated by Marvin Bileck (Holiday); *The Wave*, by Margaret Hodges, illustrated by Blair Lent (Houghton); *A Pocketful of Cricket*, by Rebecca Caudill, illustrated by Evaline Ness (Holt)

1966

Always Room for One More, by Sorche Nic Leodhas, illustrated by Nonny Hogrogian (Holt)

HONOR BOOKS: *Hide and Seek Fog*, by Alvin Tresselt, illustrated by Roger Duvoisin (Lothrop); *Just Me*, by Marie Hall Ets (Viking); *Tom Tit Tot*, by Evaline Ness (Scribner's)

1967

Sam, Bangs and Moonshine, by Evaline Ness (Holt)

HONOR BOOK: *One Wide River to Cross*, by Barbara Emberley, illustrated by Ed Emberley (Prentice)

1968

Drummer Hoff, by Barbara Emberley, illustrated by Ed Emberley (Prentice)

HONOR BOOKS: *Frederick*, by Leo Lionni (Pantheon); *Seashore Story*, by Taro Yashima (Viking); *The Emperor and the Kite*, by Jane Yolen, illustrated by Ed Young (World)

1969

The Fool of the World and the Flying Ship, by Arthur Ransome, illustrated by Uri Shulevitz (Farrar, Straus & Giroux)

HONOR BOOK: *Why the Sun and the Moon Live in the Sky*, by Elphinstone Dayrell, illustrated by Blair Lent (Houghton)

1970

Sylvester and the Magic Pebble, by William Steig (Windmill)

HONOR BOOKS: *Goggles!*, by Ezra Jack Keats (Macmillan); *Alexander and the Wind-Up Mouse*, by Leo Lionni (Pantheon); *Pop Corn and Ma Goodness*, by Edna Mitchell Preston, illustrated by Robert Andrew Parker (Viking); *Thy Friend, Obadiah*, by Brinton Turkle (Viking); *The Judge*, by Harve Zemach, illustrated by Margot Zemach (Farrar, Straus & Giroux)

1971

A Story, a Story, by Gail E. Haley (Atheneum)

HONOR BOOKS: *The Angry Moon*, by William Sleator, illustrated by Blair Lent (Atlantic/Little); *Frog and Toad Are Friends*, by Arnold Lobel (HarperCollins); *In the Night Kitchen*, by Maurice Sendak (HarperCollins)

1972

One Fine Day, by Nonny Hogrogian (Macmillan)

HONOR BOOKS: *If All the Seas Were One Sea*, by Janina Domanska (Macmillan); *Moja Means One: Swahili Counting Book*, by Muriel Feelings, illustrated by Tom Feelings (Dial); *Hildilid's Night*, by Cheli Durán Ryan, illustrated by Arnold Lobel (Macmillan)

1973

The Funny Little Woman, retold by Arlene Mosel, illustrated by Blair Lent (Dutton)

HONOR BOOKS: *Anansi the Spider*, adapted and illustrated by Gerald McDermott (Holt); *Hosie's Alphabet*, by Hosea, Tobias, and Lisa Baskin, illustrated by Leonard Baskin (Viking); *Snow-White and the Seven Dwarfs*, translated by Randall Jarrell, illustrated by Nancy Ekholm Burkert (Farrar, Straus & Giroux); *When Clay Sings*, by Byrd Baylor, illustrated by Tom Bahti (Scribner's)

1974

Duffy and the Devil, by Harve Zemach, illustrated by Margot Zemach (Farrar, Straus & Giroux)

HONOR BOOKS: *Three Jovial Huntsmen*, by Susan Jeffers (Bradbury); *Cathedral: The Story of Its Construction*, by David Macaulay (Houghton)

1975

Arrow to the Sun, adapted and illustrated by Gerald McDermott (Viking)

Honor Book: *Jambo Means Hello*, by Muriel Feelings, illustrated by Tom Feelings (Dial)

1976

Why Mosquitoes Buzz in People's Ears, retold by Verna Aardema, illustrated by Leo and Diane Dillon (Dial)

Honor Books: *The Desert Is Theirs*, by Byrd Baylor, illustrated by Peter Parnall (Scribner's); *Strega Nona*, retold and illustrated by Tomie dePaola (Prentice Hall)

1977

Ashanti to Zulu: African Traditions, by Margaret Musgrove, illustrated by Leo and Diane Dillon (Dial)

Honor Books: *The Amazing Bone*, by William Steig (Farrar, Straus & Giroux); *The Contest*, retold and illustrated by Nonny Hogrogian (Greenwillow); *Fish for Supper*, by M. B. Goffstein (Dial); *The Golem*, by Beverly Brodsky McDermott (Lippincott); *Hawk, I'm Your Brother*, by Byrd Baylor, illustrated by Peter Parnall (Scribner's)

1978

Noah's Ark, illustrated by Peter Spier (Doubleday)

Honor Books: *Castle*, by David Macaulay (Houghton Mifflin); *It Could Always Be Worse*, retold and illustrated by Margot Zemach (Farrar, Straus & Giroux)

1979

The Girl Who Loved Wild Horses, by Paul Goble (Bradbury)

Honor Books: *Freight Train*, by Donald Crews (Greenwillow); *The Way to Start a Day*, by Byrd Baylor, illustrated by Peter Parnall (Scribner's)

1980

Ox-Cart Man, by Donald Hall, illustrated by Barbara Cooney (Viking)

Honor Books: *Ben's Trumpet*, by Rachel Isadora (Greenwillow); *The Garden of Abdul Gasazi*, by Chris Van Allsburg (Houghton Mifflin)

1981

Fables, by Arnold Lobel (HarperCollins)

Honor Books: *The Bremen-Town Musicians*, by Ilse Plume (Doubleday); *The Grey Lady and the Strawberry Snatcher*, by Molly Bang (Four Winds); *Mice Twice*, by Joseph Low (McElderry); *Truck*, by Donald Crews (Greenwillow)

1982

Jumanji, by Chris Van Allsburg (Houghton Mifflin)

Honor Books: *Where the Buffaloes Begin*, by Olaf Baker, illustrated by Stephen Gammell (Warne); *On Market Street*, by Arnold Lobel, illustrated by Anita Lobel (Greenwillow); *Outside over There*, by Maurice Sendak (HarperCollins); *A Visit to William Blake's Inn*, by Nancy Willard, illustrated by Alice and Martin Provensen (Harcourt)

1983

Shadow, by Blaise Cendrars, translated and illustrated by Marcia Brown (Scribner's)

Honor Books: *When I Was Young in the Mountains*, by Cynthia Rylant, illustrated by Diane Goode (Dutton); *A Chair for My Mother*, by Vera B. Williams (Greenwillow)

1984

The Glorious Flight: Across the Channel with Louis Blériot, by Alice and Martin Provensen (Viking)

Honor Books: *Ten, Nine, Eight*, by Molly Bang (Greenwillow); *Little Red Riding Hood*, retold and illustrated by Trina Schart Hyman (Holiday House)

1985

St. George and the Dragon, retold by Margaret Hodges, illustrated by Trina Schart Hyman (Little, Brown)

Honor Books: *Hansel and Gretel*, retold by Rika Lesser, illustrated by Paul O. Zelinsky (Dodd, Mead); *Have You Seen My Duckling?*, by Nancy Tafuri (Greenwillow); *The Story of Jumping Mouse*, by John Steptoe (Lothrop, Lee & Shepard)

1986

The Polar Express, by Chris Van Allsburg (Houghton Mifflin)

Honor Books: *The Relatives Came*, by Cynthia Rylant, illustrated by Stephen Gammell (Bradbury); *King Bidgood's in the Bathtub*, by Audrey Wood, illustrated by Don Wood (Harcourt)

1987

Hey, Al, by Arthur Yorinks, illustrated by Richard Egielski (Farrar, Straus & Giroux)

HONOR BOOKS: *The Village of Round and Square Houses*, by Ann Grifalconi (Little, Brown); *Alphabetics*, by Suse MacDonald (Bradbury); *Rumpelstiltskin*, adapted and illustrated by Paul O. Zelinsky (Dutton)

1988

Owl Moon, by Jane Yolen, illustrated by John Schoenherr (Philomel)

HONOR BOOK: *Mufaro's Beautiful Daughters: An African Tale*, adapted and illustrated by John Steptoe (Lothrop, Lee & Shepard)

1989

Song and Dance Man, by Karen Ackerman, illustrated by Stephen Gammell (Knopf)

HONOR BOOKS: *The Boy of the Three Year Nap*, by Allen Say (Houghton Mifflin); *Free Fall*, by David Wiesner (Lothrop, Lee & Shepard); *Goldilocks and the Three Bears*, adapted and illustrated by James Marshall (Dial); *Mirandy and Brother Wind*, by Patricia McKissack, illustrated by Jerry Pinkney (Knopf)

1990

Lon Po Po: A Red Riding-Hood Story from China, adapted and illustrated by Ed Young (Philomel)

HONOR BOOKS: *Bill Peet: An Autobiography*, by Bill Peet (Houghton Mifflin); *Color Zoo*, by Lois Ehlert (Lippincott); *Hershel and the Hanukkah Goblins*, by Eric Kimmel, illustrated by Trina Schart Hyman (Holiday House); *The Talking Eggs*, by Robert D. San Souci, illustrated by Jerry Pinkney (Dial)

1991

Black and White, by David Macaulay (Houghton Mifflin)

HONOR BOOKS: *"More More More," Said the Baby: 3 Love Stories*, by Vera B. Williams (Greenwillow); *Puss in Boots*, by Charles Perrault, translated by Malcolm Arthur, illustrated by Fred Marcellino (Farrar, Straus & Giroux)

1992

Tuesday, by David Wiesner (Clarion)

HONOR BOOK: *Tar Beach*, by Faith Ringgold (Crown)

1993

Mirette on the High Wire, by Emily Arnold McCully (Putnam)

HONOR BOOKS: *The Stinky Cheese Man and Other Fairly Stupid Tales* by Jon Scieszka and Lane Smith, illustrated by Lane Smith; (Viking); *Working Cotton*, by Sherley Anne Williams, illustrated by Carole Byard (Harcourt); *Seven Blind Mice*, by Ed Young (Philomel)

1994

Grandfather's Journey, by Allen Say (Houghton Mifflin)

HONOR BOOKS: *In the Small, Small Pond*, by Denise Fleming (Holt); *Owen*, by Kevin Henkes (Greenwillow); *Peppe the Lamplighter*, by Elisa Bartone, illustrated by Ted Lewin (Lothrop, Lee & Shepard); *Raven: A Trickster Tale from the Pacific Northwest*, by Gerald McDermott (Harcourt); *Yo! Yes?*, by Chris Raschka (Orchard)

1995

Smoky Night, by Eve Bunting, illustrated by David Diaz (Harcourt)

HONOR BOOKS: *John Henry*, by Julius Lester, illustrated by Jerry Pinkney (Dial); *Swamp Angel*, by Anne Isaacs, illustrated by Paul O. Zelinsky (Dutton); *Time Flies*, by Eric Rohmann (Crown)

1996

Officer Buckle and Gloria, by Peggy Rathmann (Putnam)

HONOR BOOKS: *Alphabet City*, by Stephen Johnson (Viking); *The Faithful Friend*, by Robert D. San Souci, illustrated by Brian Pinkney (Simon & Schuster); *Tops and Bottoms*, by Janet Stevens (Harcourt); *Zin! Zin! Zin! A Violin*, by Lloyd Moss, illustrated by Marjorie Priceman (Simon & Schuster)

1997

Golem, by David Wisniewski (Clarion)

HONOR BOOKS: *Hush! A Thai Lullaby*, by Minfong Ho, illustrated by Holly Meade (Orchard); *The Graphic Alphabet*, by David Pelletier (Orchard); *The Paperboy*, by Dav Pilkey (Orchard); *Starry Messenger*, by Peter Sís (Farrar, Straus & Giroux)

1998

Rapunzel, by Paul O. Zelinsky (Dutton)

HONOR BOOKS: *Harlem*, by Walter Dean Myers, illustrated by Christopher Myers (Scholastic); *The Gardener*, by Sarah Stewart, illustrated by David Small (Farrar, Straus & Giroux); *There Was an Old Lady Who Swallowed a Fly*, by Simms Taback (Viking)

1999

Snowflake Bentley, by Jacqueline Briggs Martin, illustrated by Mary Azarian (Houghton Mifflin)

HONOR BOOKS: *Duke Ellington*, by Andrea Davis Pinkney, illustrated by Brian Pinkney (Hyperion); *No, David!*, by David Shannon (Blue Sky Press); *Snow*, by Uri Shulevitz (Farrar, Straus & Giroux); *Tibet: Through the Red Box*, by Peter Sís (Farrar, Straus & Giroux)

2000

Joseph Had a Little Overcoat, by Simms Taback (Viking)

HONOR BOOKS: *The Ugly Duckling*, by Hans Christian Andersen, illustrated by Jerry Pinkney (Morrow); *A Child's Calendar*, by John Updike, illustrated by Trina Schart Hyman (Holiday House); *Sector 7*, by David Wiesner (Clarion); *When Sophie Gets Angry—Really, Really Angry . . .* , by Molly Bang (Blue Sky Press)

2001

So You Want to Be President?, by Judith St. George, illustrated by David Small (Philomel)

HONOR BOOKS: *Casey at the Bat: A Ballad of the Republic Sung in the Year 1888*, by Ernest Lawrence Thayer, illustrated by Christopher Bing (Handprint Books); *Click, Clack, Moo: Cows That Type*, by Doreen Cronin, illustrated by Betsy Lewin (Simon & Schuster); *Olivia*, by Ian Falconer (Simon & Schuster)

2002

The Three Pigs, by David Wiesner (Clarion)

HONOR BOOKS: *The Dinosaurs of Waterhouse Hawkins*, by Barbara Kerley, illustrated by Brian Selznick (Scholastic); *Martin's Big Words: The Life of Dr. Martin Luther King, Jr.*, by Doreen Rappaport, illustrated by Bryan Collier (Hyperion); *The Stray Dog*, by Marc Simont (HarperCollins)

2003

My Friend Rabbit, by Eric Rohmann (Roaring Brook Press)

HONOR BOOKS: *The Spider and the Fly*, by Mary Howitt, illustrated by Tony DiTerlizzi (Simon & Schuster); *Hondo & Fabian*, by Peter McCarty (Holt); *Noah's Ark*, by Jerry Pinkney (SeaStar Books)

2004

The Man Who Walked between the Towers, by Mordicai Gerstein (Roaring Brook Press)

HONOR BOOKS: *Ella Sarah Gets Dressed*, by Margaret Chodos-Irvine (Harcourt); *What Do You Do with a Tail Like This?*, by Steve Jenkins and Robin Page (Houghton Mifflin); *Don't Let the Pigeon Drive the Bus!*, by Mo Willems (Hyperion)

2005

Kitten's First Full Moon, by Kevin Henkes (Greenwillow)

HONOR BOOKS: *The Red Book*, by Barbara Lehman (Houghton Mifflin); *Coming On Home Soon*, by Jacqueline Woodson, illustrated by E. B. Lewis (Putnam); *Knuffle Bunny: A Cautionary Tale*, by Mo Willems (Hyperion)

2006

The Hello, Goodbye Window, by Norton Juster, illustrated by Chris Raschka (Hyperion)

HONOR BOOKS: *Rosa*, by Nikki Giovanni, illustrated by Bryan Collier (Holt); *Zen Shorts*, by Jon J. Muth (Scholastic); *Hot Air: The (Mostly) True Story of the First Hot-Air Balloon Ride*, by Marjorie Priceman (Simon & Schuster); *Song of the Water Boatman and Other Pond Poems*, by Joyce Sidman, illustrated by Beckie Prange (Houghton Mifflin)

2007

Flotsam, by David Wiesner (Clarion)

HONOR BOOKS: Gone Wild: An Endangered Animal Alphabet, by David McLimans (Walker); *Moses: When Harriet Tubman Led Her People to Freedom*, by Carole Boston Weatherford, illustrated by Kadir Nelson (Hyperion)

2008

The Invention of Hugo Cabret, by Brian Selznick (Scholastic)

HONOR BOOKS: *Henry's Freedom Box: A True Story from the Underground Railroad*, by Ellen Levine, illustrated by Kadir Nelson (Scholastic); *First the Egg*, by Laura Vaccaro Seeger (Roaring Brook Press); *The Wall: Growing Up Behind the Iron Curtain*, by Peter Sís (Farrar, Straus & Giroux); *Knuffle Bunny Too: A Case of Mistaken Identity*, by Mo Willems (Hyperion)

2009

The House in the Night, by Susan Marie Swanson, illustrated by Beth Krommes (Houghton Mifflin)

HONOR BOOKS: A Couple of Boys Have the Best Week Ever, by Marla Frazee (Harcourt); *How I Learned*

Geography, by Uri Shulevitz (Farrar, Straus & Giroux), *A River of Words: The Story of William Carlos Williams*, by Jen Bryant, illustrated by Melissa Sweet (Eerdmans)

• • • The Coretta Scott King Award • • •
and Honor Books

These awards, administered by the Social Responsibilities Round Table and the American Library Association, recognize an outstanding African American author and illustrator whose work commemorates and fosters the life, work, and dreams of Dr. Martin Luther King, Jr., as well as honoring the courage and determination of Coretta Scott King to continue to work for peace and world brotherhood. Prior to 1974, the Coretta Scott King Award was given to authors only.

1970

AUTHOR AWARD: *Martin Luther King, Jr.: Man of Peace*, by Lillie Patterson (Garrand)

1971

AUTHOR AWARD: *Black Troubador: Langston Hughes*, by Charlemae Rollins (Rand McNally)

1972

AUTHOR AWARD: *17 Black Artists*, by Elton C. Fax (Dodd, Mead)

1973

AUTHOR AWARD: *I Never Had It Made*, by Jackie Robinson as told to Alfred Duckett (Putnam)

1974

AUTHOR AND ILLUSTRATOR AWARDS: *Ray Charles*, by Sharon Bell Mathis, illustrated by George Ford (Crowell)

1975

AUTHOR AWARD: *The Legend of Africania*, by Dorothy Robinson (Johnson)
ILLUSTRATOR AWARD: No award given

1976

AUTHOR AWARD: *Duey's Tale*, by Pearl Bailey (Harcourt)
ILLUSTRATOR AWARD: No award given

1977

AUTHOR AWARD: *The Story of Stevie Wonder*, by James Haskins (Lothrop, Lee & Shepard)
ILLUSTRATOR AWARD: No award given

1978

AUTHOR AWARD: *Africa Dream*, by Eloise Greenfield (Crowell)
AUTHOR HONOR BOOKS: *The Days When the Animals Talked: Black Folk Tales and How They Came to Be*, by William J. Faulkner (Follett); *Marvin and Tige*, by Frankcina Glass (St. Martin's Press); *Mary McCleod Bethune*, by Eloise Greenfield (Crowell); *Barbara Jordan*, by James Haskins (Dial); *Coretta Scott King*, by Lillie Patterson (Garrard); *Portia: The Life of Portia Washington Pittman, the Daughter of Booker T. Washington*, by Ruth Ann Steward (Doubleday)
ILLUSTRATOR AWARD: *Africa Dream*, illustrated by Carole Byard, text by Eloise Greenfield (Crowell)

1979

AUTHOR AWARD: *Escape to Freedom*, by Ossie Davis (Viking)
AUTHOR HONOR BOOKS: *Benjamin Banneker*, by Lillie Patterson (Abingdon); *I Have a Sister—My Sister Is Deaf*, by Jeanne Whitehouse Peterson (HarperCollins); *Justice and Her Brothers*, by Virginia Hamilton (Greenwillow); *Skates of Uncle Richard*, by Carol Fenner (Random House)
ILLUSTRATOR AWARD: *Something on My Mind*, illustrated by Tom Feelings, text by Nikki Grimes (Dial)

1980

AUTHOR AWARD: *The Young Landlords*, by Walter Dean Myers (Viking)
AUTHOR HONOR BOOKS: *Movin' Up*, by Berry Gordy (HarperCollins); *Childtimes: A Three-Generation Memoir*, by Eloise Greenfield and Lessie Jones Little (HarperCollins); *Andrew Young: Young Man with a Mission*, by James Haskins (Lothrop, Lee & Shepard); *James Van Der Zee: The Picture Takin' Man*, by James Haskins (Africa World Press); *Let the Lion Eat Straw*, by Ellease Southerland (Scribner's)
ILLUSTRATOR AWARD: *Cornrows*, illustrated by Carole Byard, text by Camille Yarbrough (Coward-McCann)

1981

AUTHOR AWARD: *This Life*, by Sidney Poitier (Knopf)

AUTHOR HONOR BOOK: *Don't Explain: A Song of Billie Holiday*, by Alexis De Veaux (HarperCollins)

ILLUSTRATOR AWARD: *Beat the Story Drum, Pum-Pum*, by Ashley Bryan (Simon & Schuster)

ILLUSTRATOR HONOR BOOKS: *Grandmama's Joy*, illustrated by Carole Byard, text by Eloise Greenfield (Collins); *Count on Your Fingers African Style*, illustrated by Jerry Pinkney, text by Claudia Zaslavsky (Crowell)

1982

AUTHOR AWARD: *Let the Circle Be Unbroken*, by Mildred Taylor (Dial)

AUTHOR HONOR BOOKS: *Rainbow Jordan*, by Alice Childress (Coward-McCann); *Lou in the Limelight*, by Kristin Hunter (Scribner's); *Mary: An Autobiography*, by Mary E. Mebane (Viking)

ILLUSTRATOR AWARD: *Mother Crocodile*, by John Steptoe (Delacorte)

ILLUSTRATOR HONOR BOOK: *Daydreamers*, illustrated by Tom Feelings, text by Eloise Greenfield (Dial)

1983

AUTHOR AWARD: *Sweet Whispers, Brother Rush*, by Virginia Hamilton (Philomel)

AUTHOR HONOR BOOK: *This Strange New Feeling*, by Julius Lester (Dial)

ILLUSTRATOR AWARD: *Black Child*, by Peter Magubane (Knopf)

ILLUSTRATOR HONOR BOOKS: *All the Colors of the Race*, illustrated by John Steptoe, text by Arnold Adoff (Lothrop, Lee & Shepard); *I'm Going to Sing: Black American Spirituals*, illustrated by Ashley Bryan (Simon & Schuster); *Just Us Women*, illustrated by Pat Cummings, text by Jeanette Caines (HarperCollins)

1984

AUTHOR AWARD: *Everett Anderson's Goodbye*, by Lucille Clifton (Holt)

SPECIAL CITATION: *The Words of Martin Luther King, Jr.*, compiled by Coretta Scott King (Newmarket Press)

AUTHOR HONOR BOOKS: *The Magical Adventures of Pretty Pearl*, by Virginia Hamilton (HarperCollins); *Lena Horne*, by James Haskins (Coward-McCann); *Bright Shadow*, by Joyce Carol Thomas (Avon); *Because We Are*, by Mildred Pitts Walter (Lothrop, Lee & Shepard)

ILLUSTRATOR AWARD: *My Mama Needs Me*, illustrated by Pat Cummings, text by Mildred Pitts Walter (Lothrop, Lee & Shepard)

1985

AUTHOR AWARD: *Motown and Didi*, by Walter Dean Myers (Viking)

HONOR BOOKS: *Circle of Gold*, by Candy Dawson Boyd (Apple); *A Little Love*, by Virginia Hamilton (Philomel)

ILLUSTRATOR AWARD: No award given

1986

AUTHOR AWARD: *The People Could Fly: American Black Folktales*, by Virginia Hamilton (Knopf)

AUTHOR HONOR BOOKS: *Junius Over Far*, by Virginia Hamilton (HarperCollins); *Trouble's Child*, by Mildred Pitts Walter (Lothrop, Lee & Shepard)

ILLUSTRATOR AWARD: *The Patchwork Quilt*, illustrated by Jerry Pinkney, text by Valerie Flournoy (Dial)

ILLUSTRATOR HONOR BOOK: *The People Could Fly: American Black Folktales*, illustrated by Leo and Diane Dillon, text by Virginia Hamilton (Knopf)

1987

AUTHOR AWARD: *Justin and the Best Biscuits in the World*, by Mildred Pitts Walter (Lothrop, Lee & Shepard)

AUTHOR HONOR BOOKS: *Lion and the Ostrich Chicks and Other African Folk Tales*, by Ashley Bryan (Simon & Schuster); *Which Way Freedom*, by Joyce Hansen (Walker)

ILLUSTRATOR AWARD: *Half a Moon and One Whole Star*, illustrated by Jerry Pinkney, text by Crescent Dragonwagon (Macmillan)

ILLUSTRATOR HONOR BOOKS: *Lion and the Ostrich Chicks and Other African Folk Tales*, by Ashley Bryan (Simon & Schuster); *C.L.O.U.D.S.*, by Pat Cummings (Lothrop, Lee & Shepard)

1988

AUTHOR AWARD: *The Friendship*, by Mildred Taylor (Dial)

AUTHOR HONOR BOOKS: *An Enchanted Hair Tale*, by Alexis De Veaux (HarperCollins); *The Tales of Uncle Remus: The Adventures of Brer Rabbit*, by Julius Lester (Dial)

ILLUSTRATOR AWARD: *Mufaro's Beautiful Daughters: An African Tale*, by John Steptoe (Lothrop, Lee & Shepard)

ILLUSTRATOR HONOR BOOKS: *What a Morning! The Christmas Story in Black Spirituals*, illustrated by Ashley Bryan, selected by John Langstaff (Macmillan); *The Invisible Hunters: A Legend from the Miskito Indians of Nicaragua*, illustrated by Joe Sam, compiled by Harriet Rohmer, Octavio Chow, and Morris Vedaure (Children's Book Press)

1989

AUTHOR AWARD: *Fallen Angels*, by Walter Dean Myers (Scholastic)

AUTHOR HONOR BOOKS: *A Thief in the Village and Other Stories*, by James Berry (Orchard); *Anthony Burns: The Defeat and Triumph of a Fugitive Slave*, by Virginia Hamilton (Knopf)

ILLUSTRATOR AWARD: *Mirandy and Brother Wind*, illustrated by Jerry Pinkney, text by Patricia McKissack (Knopf)

ILLUSTRATOR HONOR BOOKS: *Under the Sunday Tree*, illustrated by Amos Ferguson, text by Eloise Greenfield (HarperCollins); *Storm in the Night*, illustrated by Pat Cummings, text by Mary Stolz (HarperCollins)

1990

AUTHOR AWARD: *A Long Hard Journey: The Story of the Pullman Porter*, by Patricia and Frederick McKissack (Walker)

AUTHOR HONOR BOOKS: *Nathaniel Talking*, by Eloise Greenfield, illustrated by Jan Spivey Gilchrist (Black Butterfly); *The Bells of Christmas*, by Virginia Hamilton (Harcourt); *Martin Luther King, Jr., and the Freedom Movement*, by Lillie Patterson (Facts on File)

ILLUSTRATOR AWARD: *Nathaniel Talking*, illustrated by Jan Gilchrist, text by Eloise Greenfield (Black Butterfly)

ILLUSTRATOR HONOR BOOKS: *The Talking Eggs*, illustrated by Jerry Pinkney, text by Robert D. San Souci (Dial)

1991

AUTHOR AWARD: *The Road to Memphis*, by Mildred Taylor (Dial)

AUTHOR HONOR BOOKS: *Black Dance in America*, by James Haskins (Crowell); *When I Am Old with You*, by Angela Johnson (Orchard)

ILLUSTRATOR AWARD: *Aida*, illustrated by Leo and Diane Dillon, told by Leontyne Price (Harcourt)

1992

AUTHOR AWARD: *Now Is Your Time! The African American Struggle for Freedom*, by Walter Dean Myers (HarperCollins)

AUTHOR HONOR BOOKS: *Night on Neighborhood Street*, by Eloise Greenfield, illustrated by Jan Spivey Gilchrist (Dial)

ILLUSTRATOR AWARD: *Tar Beach*, by Faith Ringgold (Crown)

ILLUSTRATOR HONOR BOOKS: *All Night, All Day: A Child's First Book of African American Spirituals*, by Ashley Bryan (Simon & Schuster); *Night on Neighborhood Street*, illustrated by Jan Spivey Gilchrist, text by Eloise Greenfield (Dial)

1993

AUTHOR AWARD: *The Dark Thirty: Southern Tales of the Supernatural*, by Patricia McKissack (Knopf)

AUTHOR HONOR BOOKS: *Mississippi Challenge*, by Mildred Pitts Walter (Bradbury); *Sojourner Truth: Ain't I a Woman?*, by Patricia and Frederick McKissack (Scholastic); *Somewhere in the Darkness*, by Walter Dean Myers (Scholastic)

ILLUSTRATOR AWARD: *The Origin of Life on Earth: An African Creation Myth*, illustrated by Kathleen Atkins Wilson, retold by David Anderson (Sights Productions)

ILLUSTRATOR HONOR BOOKS: *Little Eight John*, illustrated by Wil Clay, text by Jan Wahl (Lodestar); *Sukey and the Mermaid*, illustrated by Brian Pinkney, text by Robert D. San Souci (Four Winds); *Working Cotton*, illustrated by Carole Byard, text by Sherley Anne Williams (Harcourt)

1994

AUTHOR AWARD: *Toning the Sweep*, by Angela Johnson (Orchard)

AUTHOR HONOR BOOKS: *Brown Honey in Broomwheat Tea*, by Joyce Carol Thomas, illustrated by Floyd Cooper (HarperCollins); *Malcolm X: By Any Means Necessary*, by Walter Dean Myers (Scholastic); *Soul Looks Back in Wonder*, edited by Phyllis Fogelman, illustrated by Tom Feelings (Dial)

ILLUSTRATOR AWARD: *Soul Looks Back in Wonder*, illustrated by Tom Feelings, edited by Phyllis Fogelman (Dial)

ILLUSTRATOR HONOR BOOKS: *Brown Honey in Broomwheat Tea*, illustrated by Floyd Cooper, by Joyce Carol Thomas (HarperCollins); *Uncle Jed's Barbershop*, illustrated by James Ransome, text by Margaree King Mitchell (Simon & Schuster)

1995

AUTHOR AWARD: *Christmas in the Big House, Christmas in the Quarters*, by Patricia and Frederick McKissack (Scholastic)

AUTHOR HONOR BOOKS: *The Captive*, by Joyce Hansen (Scholastic); *I Hadn't Meant to Tell You This*, by Jacqueline Woodson (Delacorte); *Black Diamond: Story of the Negro Baseball League*, by Patricia and Frederick McKissack (Scholastic)

ILLUSTRATOR AWARD: *The Creation*, illustrated by James Ransome, text by James Weldon Johnson (Holiday House)

ILLUSTRATOR HONOR BOOKS: *The Singing Man*, illustrated by Terea D. Shaffer, text by Angela Shelf Medearis (Holiday House); *Meet Danitra Brown*, illustrated by Floyd Cooper, text by Nikki Grimes (Lothrop, Lee & Shepard)

1996

AUTHOR AWARD: *Her Stories: African American Folktales, Fairy Tales, and True Tales*, by Virginia Hamilton, illustrated by Leo and Diane Dillon (Blue Sky Press)

AUTHOR HONOR BOOKS: *The Watsons Go to Birmingham—1963*, by Christopher Paul Curtis (Delacorte); *Like Sisters on the Homefront*, by Rita Williams-Garcia (Delacorte); *From the Notebooks of Melanin Sun*, by Jacqueline Woodson (Scholastic)

ILLUSTRATOR AWARD: *The Middle Passage: White Ships/ Black Cargo*, by Tom Feelings (Dial)

ILLUSTRATOR HONOR BOOKS: *Her Stories*, illustrated by Leo and Diane Dillon, text by Virginia Hamilton (Blue Sky Press); *The Faithful Friend*, illustrated by Brian Pinkney, text by Robert D. San Souci (Simon & Schuster)

1997

AUTHOR AWARD: *Slam*, by Walter Dean Myers (Scholastic)

AUTHOR HONOR BOOKS: *Rebels against Slavery: American Slave Revolts*, by Patricia and Frederick McKissack (Scholastic)

ILLUSTRATOR AWARD: *Minty: A Story of Harriet Tubman*, illustrated by Jerry Pinkney, text by Alan Schroeder (Dial)

ILLUSTRATOR HONOR BOOKS: *The Palm of My Heart: Poetry by African American Children*, illustrated by Gregorie Christie, edited by Davida Adedjouma (Lee & Low); *Running the Road to ABC*, illustrated by Reynold Ruffins, text by Denize Lauture (Simon & Schuster); *Neeny Coming, Neeny Going*, illustrated by Synthia Saint James, text by Karen English (Bridgewater Books)

1998

AUTHOR AWARD: *Forged by Fire*, by Sharon M. Draper (Simon & Schuster)

AUTHOR HONOR BOOKS: *Bayard Rustin: Behind the Scenes of the Civil Rights Movement*, by James Haskins (Hyperion); *I Thought My Soul Would Rise and Fly: The Diary of Patsy, a Freed Girl*, by Joyce Hansen (Scholastic)

ILLUSTRATOR AWARD: *In Daddy's Arms I Am Tall: African Americans Celebrating Fathers*, illustrated by Javaka Steptoe, text by Alan Schroeder (Lee & Low)

ILLUSTRATOR HONOR BOOKS: *Ashley Bryan's ABC of African American Poetry*, by Ashley Bryan (Simon & Schuster); *Harlem*, illustrated by Christopher Myers, text by Walter Dean Myers (Scholastic); *The Hunterman and the Crocodile*, by Baba Wagué Diakité (Scholastic)

1999

AUTHOR AWARD: *Heaven*, by Angela Johnson (Simon & Schuster)

AUTHOR HONOR BOOKS: *Jazmin's Notebook*, by Nikki Grimes (Dial); *Breaking Ground, Breaking Silence: The Story of New York's African Burial Ground*, by Joyce Hansen and Gary McGowan (Holt); *The Other Side: Shorter Poems*, by Angela Johnson (Orchard)

ILLUSTRATOR AWARD: *I See the Rhythm*, illustrated by Michele Wood, text by Toyomi Igus (Children's Book Press)

ILLUSTRATOR HONOR BOOKS: *I Have Heard of a Land*, illustrated by Floyd Cooper, text by Joyce Carol Thomas (HarperCollins); *The Bat Boy and His Violin*, illustrated by E. B. Lewis, text by Gavin Curtis (Simon & Schuster); *Duke Ellington: The Piano Prince and His Orchestra*, illustrated by Brian Pinkney, text by Andrea Davis Pinkney (Hyperion)

2000

AUTHOR AWARD: *Bud, Not Buddy*, by Christopher Paul Curtis (Delacorte)

AUTHOR HONOR BOOKS: *Francie*, by Karen English (Farrar, Straus & Giroux); *Black Hands, White Sails: The Story of African-American Whalers*, by Patricia and Frederick McKissack (Scholastic); *Monster*, by Walter Dean Myers (HarperCollins)

ILLUSTRATOR AWARD: *In the Time of the Drums*, illustrated by Brian Pinkney, text by Kim L. Siegelson (Hyperion)

ILLUSTRATOR HONOR BOOKS: *My Rows and Piles of Coins*, illustrated by E. B. Lewis, text by Tololwa M. Mollel (Clarion); *Black Cat*, by Christopher Myers (Scholastic)

2001

AUTHOR AWARD: *Miracle's Boys*, by Jacqueline Woodson (Putnam)

AUTHOR HONOR BOOKS: *Let It Shine! Stories of Black Women Freedom Fighters*, by Andrea Davis Pinkney, illustrated by Stephen Alcorn (Harcourt)

ILLUSTRATOR AWARD: *Uptown*, by Bryan Collier (Holt)

ILLUSTRATOR HONOR BOOKS: *Freedom River*, by Bryan Collier (Hyperion); *Only Passing Through: The Story of Sojourner Truth*, illustrated by R. Gregory Christie, written by Anne Rockwell (Random House); *Virgie Goes to School with Us Boys*, illustrated by E. B. Lewis, written by Elizabeth Fitzgerald Howard (Simon & Schuster)

2002

AUTHOR AWARD: *The Land,* by Mildred Taylor (Fogelman)

AUTHOR HONOR BOOKS: *Money-Hungry,* by Sharon G. Flake (Hyperion); *Carver: A Life in Poems,* by Marilyn Nelson (Front Street)

ILLUSTRATOR AWARD: *Goin' Someplace Special,* illustrated by Jerry Pinkney, written by Patricia McKissack (Simon & Schuster)

ILLUSTRATOR HONOR BOOKS: *Martin's Big Words,* illustrated by Bryan Collier, written by Doreen Rappoport (Hyperion)

2003

AUTHOR AWARD: *Bronx Masquerade,* by Nikki Grimes (Dial)

AUTHOR HONOR BOOKS: *The Red Rose Box,* by Brenda Woods (Putnam); *Talkin' about Bessie: The Story of Aviator Elizabeth Coleman,* by Nikki Grimes (Orchard)

ILLUSTRATOR AWARD: *Talkin' about Bessie: The Story of Aviator Elizabeth Coleman,* illustrated by E. B. Lewis, written by Nikki Grimes (Orchard)

ILLUSTRATOR HONOR BOOKS: *Rap a Tap Tap: Here's Bojangles—Think of That,* illustrated by Leo and Diane Dillon (Blue Sky Press); *Visiting Langston,* illustrated by Bryan Collier (Holt)

2004

AUTHOR AWARD: *The First Part Last,* by Angela Johnson (Simon & Schuster)

AUTHOR HONOR BOOKS: *Days of Jubilee: The End of Slavery in the United States,* by Patricia and Frederick McKissack (Scholastic); *Locomotion,* by Jacqueline Woodson (Putnam); *The Battle of Jericho,* by Sharon M. Draper (Simon & Schuster)

ILLUSTRATOR AWARD: *Beautiful Blackbird,* by Ashley Bryan (Simon & Schuster)

ILLUSTRATOR HONOR BOOKS: *Almost to Freedom,* illustrated by Colin Bootman, written by Vaunda Micheaux Nelson (Carolrhoda Books); *Thunder Rose,* illustrated by Kadir Nelson, written by Jerdine Nolen (Silver Whistle)

2005

AUTHOR AWARD: *Remember: The Journey to Integration,* by Toni Morrison (Houghton Mifflin)

AUTHOR HONOR BOOKS: *The Legend of Buddy Bush,* by Sheila Moses (McElderry); *Who Am I without Him? Short Stories about Girls and the Boys in Their Lives,* by Sharon Flake (Hyperion); *Fortune's Bones: The Manumission Requiem,* by Marilyn Nelson (Front Street)

ILLUSTRATOR AWARD: *Ellington Was Not a Street,* illustrated by Kadir Nelson, written by Ntozake Shange (Simon & Schuster)

ILLUSTRATOR HONOR BOOKS: *God Bless the Child,* illustrated by Jerry Pinkney, written by Billie Holiday and Arthur Herzog Jr. (Amistad); *The People Could Fly: The Picturebook,* illustrated by Leo and Diane Dillon, written by Virginia Hamilton (Knopf)

2006

AUTHOR AWARD: *Day of Tears: A Novel in Dialogue,* by Julius Lester (Hyperion/Hyperion)

AUTHOR HONOR BOOKS: *Maritcha: A Nineteenth-Century American Girl,* by Tonya Bolden (Abrams); *Dark Sons,* by Nikki Grimes (Hyperion); *A Wreath for Emmett Till,* by Marilyn Nelson, illustrated by Philippe Lardy (Houghton Mifflin)

ILLUSTRATOR AWARD: *Rosa,* illustrated by **Bryan Collier,** written by Nikki Giovanni (Holt)

ILLUSTRATOR HONOR BOOKS: *Brothers in Hope: The Story of the Lost Boys of Sudan,* by R. Gregory Christie (Lee & Low)

2007

AUTHOR AWARD: *Copper Sun,* by Sharon Draper (Simon & Schuster)

AUTHOR HONOR BOOKS: *The Road to Paris,* by Nikki Grimes, (Putnam/Penguin)

ILLUSTRATOR AWARD: *Moses: When Harriet Tubman Led Her People to Freedom,* illustrated by Kadir Nelson, written by Carole Boston Weatherford (Hyperion)

ILLUSTRATOR HONOR BOOKS: *Jazz,* illustrated by Christopher Myers, written by Walter Dean Myers (Holiday House); *Poetry for Young People: Langston Hughes,* illustrated by Benny Andrews, edited by David Roessel and Arnold Rampersad (Sterling)

2008

AUTHOR AWARD: *Elijah of Buxton,* by Christopher Paul Curtis (Scholastic)

AUTHOR HONOR BOOKS: *November Blues,* by Sharon M. Draper (Simon & Schuster); *Twelve Rounds to Glory: The Story of Muhammad Ali,* by Charles R. Smith Jr., illustrated by Bryan Collier (Candlewick)

ILLUSTRATOR AWARD: *Let it Shine,* by Ashley Bryan (Simon & Schuster)

ILLUSTRATOR HONOR BOOKS: *The Secret Olivia Told Me,* by Nancy Devard, written by N. Joy (Just Us Books); *Jazz On A Saturday Night,* by Leo and Diane Dillon (Scholastic/Blue Sky Press)

AUTHOR AWARD: *We Are the Ship: The Story of Negro League Baseball*, by Kadir Nelson (Hyperion)

AUTHOR HONOR BOOKS: *Keeping the Night Watch*, by Hope Anita Smith (Holt), *The Blacker the Berry*, by Joyce Carol Thomas (Amistad/HarperCollins), *Becoming Billie Holiday*, by Carole Boston Weatherford (Wordsong/ Boyds Mills)

ILLUSTRATOR AWARD: *The Blacker the Berry*, illustrated by Floyd Cooper, written by Joyce Carol Thomas (Amistad/ HarperCollins)

ILLUSTRATOR HONOR BOOKS: *We Are the Ship: The Story of Negro League Baseball*, by Kadir Nelson (Hyperion), *The Moon Over Star*, by Jerry Pinkney, text by Dianna Hutts Aston (Dial), *Before John Was a Jazz Giant*, by Sean Qualls, text by Carole Boston Weatherford (Holt)

• • • The Pura Belpré Award • • •

The Pura Belpré Award, established in 1996, presented biennially until 2009 when it became an annual award, honors a Latino/Latina writer and illustrator whose work best portrays, affirms, and celebrates the Latino cultural experience in an outstanding work of literature for children and youth. It is cosponsored by the Association for Library Service to Children, a division of the American Library Association, and the National Association to Promote Library Services to the Spanish Speaking, an ALA affiliate. The award is named in honor of Pura Belpré, the first Latina librarian in the New York Public Library. As children's librarian, storyteller, and author, she enriched the lives of Puerto Rican children in the United States through her pioneering work of preserving and disseminating Puerto Rican folklore.

1996

NARRATIVE AWARD: *An Island Like You: Stories of the Barrio*, by Judith Ortiz Cofer (Orchard, 1995)

NARRATIVE HONOR BOOKS: *The Bossy Gallito/El Gallo de Bodas: A Traditional Cuban Folktale*, by Lucía González, illustrated by Lulu Delacre (Scholastic, 1994); *Baseball in April and Other Stories*, by Gary Soto (Harcourt, 1994)

ILLUSTRATION AWARD: *Chato's Kitchen*, illustrated by Susan Guevara, text by Gary Soto (Putnam, 1995)

ILLUSTRATION HONOR BOOKS: *Pablo Remembers: The Fiesta of the Day of the Dead*, by George Ancona (Lothrop, Lee & Shepard, 1993) (also available in a Spanish-language edition; *Pablo Recuerda: La Fiesta de Día de los Muertos*); *The Bossy Gallito/El Gallo de Bodas: A Traditional Cuban Folktale*, illustrated by Lulu Delacre, text by Lucía González (Scholastic, 1994); *Family Pictures/Cuadros de Familia*, by Carmen Lomas Garza, Spanish text by Rosalma Zubizarreta (Children's Book Press, 1990)

1998

NARRATIVE AWARD: *Parrot in the Oven: Mi Vida*, by Victor Martinez (HarperCollins, 1996)

NARRATIVE HONOR BOOKS: *Laughing Tomatoes and Other Spring Poems/Jitomates Risuenos y Otros Poemas de Primavera*, by Francisco X. Alarcón, illustrated by Maya Christina Gonzalez (Children's Book Press, 1997); *Spirits of the High Mesa*, by Floyd Martinez (Arte Público Press, 1997)

ILLUSTRATION AWARD: *Snapshots from the Wedding*, illustrated by Stephanie Garcia, text by Gary Soto (Putnam, 1997)

ILLUSTRATION HONOR BOOKS: *In My Family/En Mi Familia*, by Carmen Lomas Garza (Children's Book Press, 1996); *The Golden Flower: A Taino Myth from Puerto Rico*, illustrated by Enrique O. Sánchez, text by Nina Jaffe (Simon & Schuster, 1996); *Gathering the Sun: An Alphabet in Spanish and English*, illustrated by Simon Silva, text by Alma Flor Ada, Spanish text by Rosa Zubizarreta (Lothrop, Lee & Shepard, 1997)

2000

NARRATIVE AWARD: *Under the Royal Palms: A Childhood in Cuba*, by Alma Flor Ada (Simon & Schuster, 1998)

NARRATIVE HONOR BOOKS: *From the Bellybutton of the Moon and Other Summer Poems/Del Ombligo de la Luna y Otro Poemas de Verano*, by Francisco X. Alarcón, illustrated by Maya Christina Gonzalez (Children's Book Press, 1998); *Laughing Out Loud, I Fly: Poems in English and Spanish*, by Juan Felipe Herrera, illustrated by Karen Barbour (HarperCollins, 1998)

ILLUSTRATION AWARD: *Magic Windows*, by Carmen Lomas Garza (Children's Book Press, 1999)

ILLUSTRATION HONOR BOOKS: *Barrio: Jose's Neighborhood*, by George Ancona (Harcourt, 1998); *The Secret Stars*, illustrated by Felipe Dávalos, text by Joseph Slate (Cavendish, 1998); *Mama and Papa Have a Store*, by Amelia Lau Carling (Dial, 1998)

2002

NARRATIVE AWARD: *Esperanza Rising*, by Pam Muñoz Ryan (Scholastic, 2000)

NARRATIVE HONOR BOOKS: *Breaking Through*, by Francisco Jiménez (Houghton Mifflin, 2001); *Iguanas in the Snow*, by Francisco X. Alarcón, illustrated by Maya Christina Gonzalez (Children's Book Press, 2001)

ILLUSTRATION AWARD: *Chato and the Party Animals*, illustrated by Susan Guevara, text by Gary Soto (Putnam, 2000)

ILLUSTRATION HONOR BOOKS: *Juan Bobo Goes to Work*, illustrated by Joe Cepeda, retold by Marisa Montes (HarperCollins, 2000)

2004

NARRATIVE AWARD: *Before We Were Free*, by Julia Alvarez (Random House, 2002)

NARRATIVE HONOR BOOKS: *Cuba 15*, by Nancy Osa (Delacorte, 2003), *My Diary from Here to There/Mi Diario de Aquí Hasta Allá*, by Amada Irma Pérez (Children's Book Press, 2002)

ILLUSTRATION AWARD: *Just a Minute: A Trickster Tale and Counting Book*, by Yuyi Morales (Chronicle, 2003)

ILLUSTRATION HONOR BOOKS: *First Day in Grapes*, illustrated by Robert Casilla, text by L. King Pérez (Lee & Low, 2002); *The Pot That Juan Built*, illustrated by David Diaz, text by Nancy Andrews-Goebel (Lee & Low, 2002); *Harvesting Hope: The Story of Cesar Chavez*, illustrated by Yuyi Morales, text by Kathleen Krull (Harcourt, 2003)

2006

NARRATIVE AWARD: *The Tequila Worm*, by Viola Canales (Random House, 2005)

NARRATIVE HONOR BOOKS: *César: ¡Sí, Se Puede! Yes, We Can!*, by Carmen T. Bernier-Grand, illustrated by David Diaz (Marshall Cavendish, 2004); *Doña Flor: A Tall Tale About a Giant Woman with a Great Big Heart*, by Pat Mora, illustrated by Raul Colón (Random House, 2005); *Becoming Naomi León*, by Pam Munoz Ryan (Scholastic, 2004)

ILLUSTRATION AWARD: *Doña Flor: A Tall Tale About a Giant Woman with a Great Big Heart*, illustrated by Raul Colon, text by Pat Mora (Random House, 2005)

ILLUSTRATION HONOR BOOKS: *Arrorró, Mi Niño: Latino Lullabies and Gentle Games*, illustrated by Lulu Delacre (Lee & Low, 2004); *César: ¡Sí, Se Puede! Yes, We Can!*, illustrated by David Diaz, text by Carmen T. Bernier-Grand (Marshall Cavendish, 2004); *My Name Is Celia/Me Llamo Celia: The Life of Celia Cruz/ La Vida de Celia Cruz*, illustrated by Rafael Lopez, text by Monica Brown (Rising Moon, 2004)

2008

NARRATIVE AWARD: *The Poet Slave of Cuba: A Biography of Juan Francisco Manzano*, by Margarita Engle, illustrated by Sean Qualls (Holt, 2006)

NARRATIVE HONOR BOOKS: *Frida: ¡Viva la vida! Long Live Life!*, by Carmen T. Bernier-Grand, (Marshall Cavendish, 2007); *Martina the Beautiful Cockroach: A Cuban Folktale*, by Carmen Agra Deedy, illustrated by Michael Austin (Peachtree, 2007); *Los Gatos Black on Halloween*, by Marisa Montes, illustrated by Yuyi Morales (Holt, 2006)

ILLUSTRATION AWARD: *Los Gatos Black on Halloween*, illustrated by Yuyi Morales, text by Marisa Montes (Holt, 2006)

ILLUSTRATION HONOR BOOKS: *My Name is Gabito: The Life of Gabriel García Márquez/Me llamo Gabito: la vida de Gabriel García Márquez*, illustrated by Raul Colon, text by Monica Brown, (Rising Moon, 2007); *My Colors, My World/Mis colores, mi mundo*, illustrated and text by Maya Christina Gonzalez (Children's Book Press, 2007)

2009

NARRATIVE AWARD: *The Surrender Tree: Poems of Cuba's Struggle for Freedom*, by Margarita Engle (Holt)

NARRATIVE HONOR BOOKS: *Just in Case*, by Yuri Morales (Roaring Brook), *Reaching Out*, by Francisco Jimenez (Houghton Mifflin), *The Storyteller's Candle/La velita de los cuentos*, by Lucia Gonzalez, illustrated by Lulu Delacre (Children's Book Press)

ILLUSTRATION AWARD: *Just in Case*, by Yuri Morales (Roaring Brook)

ILLUSTRATION HONOR BOOKS: *Papa and Me*, illustrated by Rudy Gutierrez, written by Arthur Dorros (HarperCollins), *The Storyteller's Candle/La velita de los cuentos*, by Lulu Delacre, written by Lucia Gonzalez (Children's Book Press), *What Can You Do with a Rebozo*, illustrated by Amy Cordova, written by Carmen Tafolla, (Ten Speed Press)

● ● ● The Robert F. Sibert Award ● ● ●

The Robert F. Sibert Award, established in 2001, is sponsored by Bound to Stay Bound Books, Inc., in honor of its longtime president, Robert F. Sibert. It is administered by the Association of Library Service to Children, a division of the American Library Association, and seeks outstanding informational books written and illustrated to present, organize, and interpret verifiable, factual material for children. The complete list of award winners can be found at the end of Chapter 10.

● ● ● The Laura Ingalls Wilder Medal ● ● ●

The Laura Ingalls Wilder Medal, established in 1954 and named for its first winner, the author of the **Little House** books, is given to an author or illustrator whose books, published in the United States, have made a substantial and lasting contribution to literature for children. Between 1960 and 1980, the Wilder Award was given every five years. From 1980 to 2001, it was awarded every three years. Beginning in 2001, it has been awarded every two years. This award is administered by the Association for Library Service to Children, a division of the American Library Association.

1954	Laura Ingalls Wilder
1960	Clara Ingram Judson
1965	Ruth Sawyer
1970	E. B. White
1975	Beverly Cleary
1980	Theodor S. Geisel (Dr. Seuss)
1983	Maurice Sendak
1986	Jean Fritz
1989	Elizabeth George Speare
1992	Marcia Brown
1995	Virginia Hamilton
1998	Russell Freedman
2001	Milton Meltzer
2003	Eric Carle
2005	Laurence Yep
2007	James Marshall
2009	Ashley Bryan

• • • The Margaret A. Edwards Award • • •

The Margaret A. Edwards Award, established in 1988, honors an author's lifetime achievement for writing books that have been popular over a period of time. The annual award is administered by the Young Adult Library Services Association, a division of the American Library Association, and sponsored by *School Library Journal*. It recognizes an author's work in helping adolescents become aware of themselves and addressing questions about their role and importance in relationships, society, and in the world.

1988	S. E. Hinton
1990	Richard Peck
1991	Robert Cormier
1992	Lois Duncan
1993	M. E. Kerr
1994	Walter Dean Myers
1995	Cynthia Voigt
1996	Judy Blume
1997	Gary Paulsen
1998	Madeleine L'Engle
1999	Anne McCaffrey
2000	Chris Crutcher

2001	Robert Lipsyte
2002	Paul Zindel
2003	Nancy Garden
2004	Ursula Le Guin
2005	Francesca Lia Block
2006	Jacqueline Woodson
2007	Lois Lowry
2008	Orson Scott Card
2009	Laurie Halse Anderson

• • • The Michael L. Printz Award • • •

The Michael L. Printz Award, established in 2000, is administered by the Young Adult Library Services Association, a division of the American Library Association. The award honors the author of an outstanding young adult book.

2000

Monster, by Walter Dean Myers (HarperCollins)

HONOR BOOKS: *Skellig*, by David Almond (Delacorte); *Speak*, by Laurie Halse Anderson (Farrar, Straus & Giroux); *Hard Love*, by Ellen Wittlinger (Simon & Schuster)

2001

Kit's Wilderness, by David Almond (Delacorte)

HONOR BOOKS: *Many Stones*, by Carolyn Coman (Front Street); *The Body of Christopher Creed*, by Carol Plum-Ucci (Harcourt); *Angus, Thongs, and Full-Frontal Snogging*, by Louise Rennison (HarperCollins); *Stuck in Neutral*, by Terry Trueman (HarperCollins)

2002

Step from Heaven, by An Na (Front Street)

HONOR BOOKS: *The Ropemaker*, by Peter Dickinson (Delacorte); *Heart to Heart: New Poems Inspired by Twentieth-Century American Art*, by Jan Greenberg (Abrams); *Freewill*, by Chris Lynch (HarperCollins); *True Believer*, by Virginia Euwer Wolff (Simon & Schuster)

2003

Postcards from No Man's Land, by Aidan Chambers (Dutton)

HONOR BOOKS: *The House of the Scorpion*, by Nancy Farmer (Simon & Schuster); *My Heartbeat*, by Garret Freymann-Weyr (Houghton Mifflin); *Hole in My Life*, by Jack Gantos (Farrar, Straus & Giroux)

2004

The First Part Last, by Angela Johnson (Simon & Schuster)
HONOR BOOKS: *A Northern Light*, by Jennifer Donnelly (Harcourt); *Keesha's House*, by Helen Frost (Farrar, Straus & Giroux); *Fat Kid Rules the World*, by K. L. Going (Putnam); *The Earth, My Butt and Other Big Round Things*, by Carolyn Mackler (Candlewick)

2005

How I Live Now, by Meg Rosoff (Random House)
HONOR BOOKS: *Airborn*, by Kenneth Oppel (EOS); *Chanda's Secrets*, by Allan Stratton (Annick); *Lizzie Bright and the Buckminster Boy*, by Gary Schmidt (Clarion)

2006

Looking for Alaska, by John Green (Dutton)
HONOR BOOKS: *Black Juice*, by Margo Lanagan (Allen & Unwin); *I Am the Messenger*, by Markus Zusak (Random House); *John Lennon: All I Want Is the Truth*, a Photographic Biography, by Elizabeth Partridge (Viking); *A Wreath for Emmett Till*, by Marilyn Nelson (Houghton Mifflin)

2007

American Born Chinese, by Gene Luen Yang (Macmillan)
HONOR BOOKS: *The Astonishing Life of Octavian Nothing, Traitor to the Nation: Volume I: The Pox Party*, by M. T. Anderson (Thorndike Press); *An Abundance of Katherines*, by John Green (Penguin); *Surrender*, by Sonya Hartnett (Candlewick); *The Book Thief*, by Markus Zusak (Knopf)

2008

The White Darkness, by Geraldine McCaughrean (HarperTempest)
HONOR BOOKS: *Dreamquake: Book Two of the Dreamhunter Duet*, by Elizabeth Knox (Frances Foster Books); *One Whole and Perfect Day*, by Judith Clarke (Front Street); *Repossessed*, by A. M. Jenkins (HarperTeen); *Your Own, Sylvia: A Verse Portrait of Sylvia Plath*, by Stephanie Hemphill (Knopf)

2009

Jellicoe Road, by Melina Marchetta (HarperCollins)
HONOR BOOKS: *The Astonishing Life of Octavian Nothing, Traitor to the Nation, Volume II: The Kingdom on the Waves*, by M. T. Anderson (Candlewick); *The Disreputable History of Frankie Landau-Banks*, by E. Lockhart

(Hyperion); *Nation*, by Terry Pratchett (HarperCollins); *Tender Morsels*, by Margo Lanagan (Knopf)

• • • Geisel Award • • •

The (Theodore Seuss) Geisel Award, established in 2006, is given annually to the author and illustrator of the most distinguished American book for beginning readers published in English in the United States during the preceding year.

2006

Henry and Mudge and the Great Grandpas, by Cynthia Rylant, illustrated by Sucie Stevenson (Simon & Schuster)
HONOR BOOKS: *Hi! Fly Guy*, by Tedd Arnold (Scholastic); *A Splendid Friend, Indeed*, by Suzanne Bloom (Boyds Mills); *Cowgirl Kate and Cocoa*, by Erica Silverman, illustrated by Betsy Lewin (Harcourt); *Amanda Pig and the Really Hot Day*, by Jean Van Leeuwen, illustrated by Ann Schweninger (Dial)

2007

Zelda and Ivy: The Runaways, by Laura McGee Kvasnosky (Candlewick)
HONOR BOOKS: *Mercy Watson Goes for a Ride*, by Kate DiCamillo, illustrated by Chris Van Dusen (Candlewick), *Move Over, Rover!*, by Karen Beaumont, illustrated by Jane Dyer (Harcourt); *Not a Box*, by Antoinette Portis (HarperCollins)

2008

There Is a Bird on Your Head, by Mo Willems (Hyperion)
HONOR BOOKS: *First the Egg*, by Laura Vaccaro Seeger (Roaring Brook); *Hello, Bumblebee Bat*, by Darrin Lunde, illustrated by Patricia J. Wynne (Charlesbridge); *Jazz Baby*, by Lisa Wheeler, illustrated by R. Gregory Christie (Harcourt); *Vulture View*, by April Pulley Sayre, illustrated by Steve Jenkins (Holt)

2009

Are You Ready to Play Outside?, by Mo Willems (Hyperion)
HONOR BOOKS: *Chicken Said, "Cluck!"*, by Judyann Ackerman Grant, illustrated by Sue Truesdell (HarperCollins); *One Boy*, by Laura Vaccaro Seeger (Roaring Brook); *Stinky*, by Eleanor Davis (Little Lit Library); *Wolfsnail: A Backyard Predator*, by Sarah C. Campbell, illustrated by Sarah C. Campbell and Richard P. Campbell (Boyds Mills)

National Council of Teachers of English Awards

• • • The Award for Excellence • • • in Poetry for Children

The NCTE Award for Excellence in Poetry for Children, established in memory of Jonathan Cullinan (1969–1975), is given to a living American poet in recognition of an outstanding body of poetry for children. The award is administered by the National Council of Teachers of English and was given annually from 1977 to 1982; currently, the award is presented every three years. The poet receives a citation. A medallion designed by Karla Kuskin is available for use on dust jackets of all the poet's books. An archival collection of the poets' books is housed at the Children's Literature Research Center, Andersen Library, at the University of Minnesota. Another collection is housed at Boston Public Library in the David McCord Room.

1977   David McCord
1978   Aileen Fisher
1979   Karla Kuskin
1980   Myra Cohn Livingston
1981   Eve Merriam

1982   John Ciardi
1985   Lilian Moore
1988   Arnold Adoff
1991   Valerie Worth
1994   Barbara Esbensen
1997   Eloise Greenfield
2000   X. J. Kennedy
2003   Mary Ann Hoberman
2006   Nikki Grimes
2009   Lee Bennett Hopkins

• • • The Orbis Pictus Award • • • and Honor Books

The Orbis Pictus Award, established in 1990, is administered by the National Council of Teachers of English and honors the author of an outstanding nonfiction book. The complete list of award winners can be found at the end of Chapter 10.

International Reading Association Awards

• • • The IRA Children's Book Award • • •

The IRA Children's Book Award, established in 1975, sponsored by the Institute for Reading Research and administrated by the International Reading Association, is presented for a children's book published in the preceding year by an author who shows unusual promise. Since 1987, the award has been presented for both picturebooks and novels. Currently, the award is given for both fiction and nonfiction in each of three categories: primary, intermediate, and young adult. Books originating in any country are eligible. For books written in a language other than English, the IRA committee first determines if the book warrants an English translation and, if so, extends to it an additional year of eligibility.

1975

Transport 7-41-R, by T. Degens (Viking)

1976

Dragonwings, by Laurence Yep (HarperCollins)

1977

A String in the Harp, by Nancy Bond (McElderry)

1978

A Summer to Die, by Lois Lowry (Houghton Mifflin)

1979

Reserved for Mark Anthony Crowder, by Alison Smith (Dutton)

1980

Words by Heart, by Ouida Sebestyen (Little, Brown)

1981

My Own Private Sky, by Delores Beckman (Dutton)

1982

Good Night, Mr. Tom, by Michelle Magorian (Penguin, Great Britain; HarperCollins, USA)

1983

The Darkangel, by Meredith Ann Pierce (Little, Brown)

1984

Ratha's Creature, by Clare Bell (Simon & Schuster)

1985

Badger on the Barge, by Janni Howker (Greenwillow)

1986

Prairie Songs, by Pam Conrad (HarperCollins)

1987

PICTUREBOOK: *The Line Up Book*, by Marisabina Russo (Greenwillow)
NOVEL: *After the Dancing Days*, by Margaret Rostkowski (HarperCollins)

1988

PICTUREBOOK: *Third Story Cat*, by Leslie Baker (Little, Brown)
NOVEL: *The Ruby in the Smoke*, by Philip Pullman (Knopf)

1989

PICTUREBOOK: *Rechenka's Eggs*, by Patricia Polacco (Philomel)
NOVEL: *Probably Still Nick Swansen*, by Virginia Euwer Wolff (Holt)

1990

PICTUREBOOK: *No Star Nights*, by Anna Egan Smucker (Knopf)
NOVEL: *Children of the River*, by Linda Crew (Delacorte)

1991

PICTUREBOOK: *Is This a House for Hermit Crab?*, by Megan McDonald (Orchard)
NOVEL: *Under the Hawthorn Tree*, by Marita Conlon-McKenna (O'Brien Press)

1992

PICTUREBOOK: *Ten Little Rabbits*, by Virginia Grossman (Chronicle)
NOVEL: *Rescue Josh McGuire*, by Ben Mikaelsen (Hyperion)

1993

PICTUREBOOK: *Old Turtle*, by Douglas Wood (Pfeiffer-Hamilton)
NOVEL: *Letters from Rifka*, by Karen Hesse (Holt)

1994

PICTUREBOOK: *Sweet Clara and the Freedom Quilt*, by Deborah Hopkinson, illustrated by James Ransome (Knopf)
NOVEL: *Behind the Secret Window: A Memoir of a Hidden Childhood*, by Nelly Toll (Dutton)

1995

PICTUREBOOK: *The Ledgerbook of Thomas Blue Eagle*, by Gay Matthaei and Jewel Grutman, illustrated by Adam Cvijanovic (Thomasson-Grant)
NOVEL: *Spite Fences*, by Trudy Krisher (Bantam)
NONFICTION: *Stranded at Plimoth Plantation 1626*, by Gary Bowen (HarperCollins)

1996

PICTUREBOOK: *More Than Anything Else*, by Marie Bradby and Chris Soentpiet (Orchard)
NOVEL: *The King's Shadow*, by Elizabeth Adler (Farrar, Straus & Giroux)
NONFICTION: *The Case of the Mummified Pigs and Other Mysteries in Nature*, by Susan Quinlan (Boyds Mills Press)

1997

PICTUREBOOK: *The Fabulous Flying Fandinis*, by Ingrid Slyder (Cobblehill Books)
NOVEL: *Don't You Dare Read This, Mrs. Dunphrey*, by Margaret Peterson Haddix (Simon & Schuster)

NONFICTION: *The Brooklyn Bridge*, by Elizabeth Mann (Mikaya Press)

1998

YOUNGER READER: *Nim and the War Effort*, by Milly Lee and Yangsook Choi (Farrar, Straus & Giroux)

OLDER READER: *Moving Mama to Town*, by Ronder Thomas Young (Orchard)

NONFICTION: *Just What the Doctor Ordered: The History of American Medicine*, by Brandon Marie Miller (Lerner)

1999

YOUNGER READER: *My Freedom Trip: A Child's Escape from North Korea*, by Frances and Ginger Park (Boyds Mills Press)

OLDER READER: *Choosing Up Sides*, by John Ritter (Philomel)

NONFICTION: *First in the Field: Baseball Hero Jackie Robinson*, by Derek Dingle (Hyperion)

2000

YOUNGER READER: *The Snake Scientist*, by Sy Montgomery (Houghton Mifflin)

OLDER READER: *Bud, Not Buddy*, by Christopher Paul Curtis (Delacorte); *Eleanor's Story: An American Girl in Hitler's Germany*, by Eleanor Ramrath Garner (Peachtree)

NONFICTION: *Molly Bannaky*, by Alice McGill (Houghton Mifflin)

2001

YOUNGER READER: *Stranger in the Woods*, by Carl R. Sams II and Jean Stoick (Carl R. Sams II Photography)

OLDER READER: *Jake's Orphan*, by Peggy Brooke (DK Publishing); *Girls Think of Everything*, by Catherine Thimmesh (Houghton Mifflin)

NONFICTION: *My Season with Penguins*, by Sophie Webb (Houghton Mifflin)

2002

PRIMARY FICTION: *Silver Seeds*, by Paul Paolilli and Dan Brewer (Viking)

PRIMARY NONFICTION: *Aero and Officer Mike*, by Joan Plummer Russell (Boyds Mills Press)

INTERMEDIATE FICTION: *Coolies*, by Yin (Philomel)

INTERMEDIATE NONFICTION: *Pearl Harbor Warriors*, by Dorinda Makanaonalani Nicholson and Larry Nicholson (Woodson House)

YOUNG ADULT FICTION: *A Step from Heaven*, by An Na (Front Street)

YOUNG ADULT NONFICTION: *A Race against Nuclear Disaster at Three Mile Island*, by Wilborn Hampton (Candlewick)

2003

PRIMARY FICTION: *One Leaf Rides the Wind*, by Celeste Davidson Mannis (Viking)

PRIMARY NONFICTION: *The Pot That Juan Built*, by Nancy Andrews-Goebel (Lee & Low)

INTERMEDIATE FICTION: *Who Will Tell My Brother?*, by Marlene Carvell (Hyperion)

INTERMEDIATE NONFICTION: *If the World Were a Village: A Book about the World's People*, by David Smith (Kids Can Press)

YOUNG ADULT FICTION: *Mississippi Trial, 1955*, by Chris Crowe (Fogelman Books)

YOUNG ADULT NONFICTION: *Headin' for Better Times: The Arts of the Great Depression*, by Duane Damon (Lerner)

2004

PRIMARY FICTION: *Mary Smith*, by Andrea U'ren (Farrar, Straus & Giroux)

PRIMARY FICTION: *Uncle Andy's: A Faabbbulous Visit with Andy Warhol*, by James Warhola (Penguin Books)

INTERMEDIATE FICTION: *Sahara Special*, by Esmé Raji Codell (Hyperion)

INTERMEDIATE NONFICTION: *Carl Sandburg: Adventures of a Poet*, by Penelope Niven (Harcourt)

YOUNG ADULT FICTION: *Buddha Boy*, by Kathe Koja (Farrar, Straus & Giroux)

YOUNG ADULT NONFICTION: *At the End of Words: A Daughter's Memoir*, by Miriam Stone (Candlewick)

2005

PRIMARY FICTION: *Miss Bridie Chose a Shovel*, by Leslie Conner, illustrated by Mary Azarian (Houghton Mifflin)

PRIMARY NONFICTION: *Eliza and the Dragonfly*, by Susie Calwell Rinehart, illustrated by Anisa Claire Hovemann (Dawn)

INTERMEDIATE FICTION: *The Golden Hour*, by Maiya Williams (Amulet)

INTERMEDIATE NONFICTION: *Buildings in Disguise*, by Joan Marie Arbogast (Wordsong)

YOUNG ADULT FICTION: *Emako Blue*, by Brenda Woods (G. P. Putnam's Sons)

YOUNG ADULT NONFICTION: *The Burn Journals*, by Brent Runyon (Knopf)

2006

PRIMARY FICTION: *Russell the Sheep*, by Rob Scotton (HarperCollins)

PRIMARY NONFICTION: *Night Wonders*, by Jane Ann Peddicord (Charlesbridge)

INTERMEDIATE FICTION: *The Bicycle Man*, by David L. Dudley (Clarion)

INTERMEDIATE NONFICTION: *Americans Who Tell the Truth*, by Robert Shetterly (Dutton)

YOUNG ADULT FICTION: *Black and White*, by Paul Volponi (Viking Press)

YOUNG ADULT NONFICTION: *JAZZ ABZ: An A to Z Collection of Jazz Portraits*, by Wynton Marsalis and Paul Rogers (Candlewick)

2007

PRIMARY FICTION: *Tickets to Ride: An Alphabetical Amusement*, by Mark Rogalski (Running Press Kids)

PRIMARY NONFICTION: *Theodore*, by Frank Keating (Simon & Schuster)

INTERMEDIATE FICTION: *Blue*, by Joyce Moyer Hostetter (Boyds Mills Press)

INTERMEDIATE NONFICTION: *Something Out of Nothing: Marie Curie and Radium*, by Carla Killough McClafferty (Farrar, Straus & Giroux)

YOUNG ADULT FICTION: *Leonardo's Shadow: Or, My Astonishing Life as Leonardo da Vinci's Servant*, by Christopher Grey (Simon & Schuster)

YOUNG ADULT NONFICTION: *The Poet Slave of Cuba: A Biography of Juan Francisco*, by Margarita Engle Manzano (Holt)

2008

PRIMARY FICTION: *One Thousand Tracings: Healing the Wounds of World War II*, by Lita Judge (Hyperion)

PRIMARY NONFICTION: *Louis Sockalexis: Native American Baseball Pioneer*, by Bill Wise, illustrated by Bill Farnsworth (Lee & Low)

INTERMEDIATE FICTION: *The Silver Cup*, by Constance Leeds (Viking)

INTERMEDIATE NONFICTION: *Tracking Trash: Flotsam, Jetsam, and the Science of Ocean Motion*, by Loree Griffin Burns (Houghton Mifflin)

YOUNG ADULT FICTION: *Red Glass*, by Laura Resau (Random House)

YOUNG ADULT NONFICTION: *Tasting the Sky: A Palestinian Childhood*, by Ibtisam Barakat (Farrar, Straus & Giroux)

International Awards

• • • The Library Association Carnegie Medal • • •

Instituted in 1936 to mark the centenary of the birth of Andrew Carnegie, philanthropist and benefactor of libraries, the Library Association Carnegie Medal is awarded annually for an outstanding book for children written in English receiving its first publication in the United Kingdom during the preceding year.

1936	Arthur Ransome, *Pigeon Post*
1937	Eve Garnet, *The Family from One End Street*
1938	Noel Streatfeild, *The Circus Is Coming*
1939	Eleanor Doorly, *The Radium Woman* (biography of Marie Curie)
1940	Kitty Barne, *Visitors from London*
1941	Mary Treadgold, *We Couldn't Leave Dinah*
1942	"B.B." (D. J. Watkins-Pitchford), *The Little Grey Men*
1943	No award
1944	Eric Linklater, *The Wind on the Moon*
1945	No award
1946	Elizabeth Goudge, *The Little White Horse*
1947	Walter de la Mare, *Collected Stories for Children*
1948	Richard Armstrong, *Sea Change*
1949	Agnes Allen, *The Story of Your Home* (NONFICTION)
1950	Elfrida Vipont, *The Lark on the Wing*
1951	Cynthia Harnett, *The Wool-Pack*
1952	Mary Norton, *The Borrowers*
1953	Edward Osmond, *A Valley Grows Up* (NONFICTION)
1954	Ronald Welch, *Knight Crusaders*
1955	Eleanor Farjeon, *The Little Bookroom*
1956	C. S. Lewis, *The Last Battle*
1957	William Mayne, *A Grass Rope*
1958	Philippa Pearce, *Tom's Midnight Garden*

1959	Rosemary Sutcliff, *The Lantern Bearers*
1960	Ian W. Cornwall and Howard M. Maitland, *The Making of Man* (NONFICTION)
1961	Lucy M. Boston, *A Stranger at Green Knowe*
1962	Pauline Clark, *The Twelve and the Genii*
1963	Hester Burton, *Time of Trial*
1964	Sheena Porter, *Nordy Bank*
1965	Philip Turner, *The Grange at High Force*
1966	No award
1967	Alan Garner, *The Owl Service*
1968	Rosemary Harris, *The Moon in the Cloud*
1969	K. M. Peyton, *The Edge of the Cloud*
1970	Edward Blishen and Leon Garfield, *The God Beneath the Sea*
1971	Ivan Southall, *Josh*
1972	Richard Adams, *Watership Down*
1973	Penelope Lively, *The Ghost of Thomas Kempe*
1974	Mollie Hunter, *The Stronghold*
1975	Robert Westall, *The Machine Gunners*
1976	Jan Mark, *Thunder and Lightnings*
1977	Gene Kemp, *The Turbulent Term of Tyke Tyler*
1978	David Rees, *The Exeter Blitz*
1979	Peter Dickinson, *Tulku*
1980	Peter Dickinson, *City of Gold*
1981	Robert Westall, *The Scarecrows*
1982	Margaret Mahy, *The Haunting*
1983	Jan Mark, *Handles*
1984	Margaret Mahy, *The Changeover*
1985	Kevin Crossley-Holland, *Storm*
1986	Berlie Doherty, *Granny Was a Buffer Girl*
1987	Susan Price, *The Ghost Drum*
1988	Geraldine McCaughrean, *A Pack of Lies*
1989	Anne Fine, *Goggle-Eyes*
1990	Gillian Cross, *Wolf*
1991	Berlie Doherty, *Dear Nobody*
1992	Anne Fine, *Flour Babies*
1993	Robert Swindells, *Stone Cold*
1994	Theresa Breslin, *Whispers in the Graveyard*
1995	Philip Pullman, *Northern Lights*
1996	Melvin Burgess, *Junk*
1997	Tim Bowler, *River Boy*
1998	David Almond, *Skellig*
1999	Aiden Chambers, *Postcards from No Man's Land*
2000	Beverly Naidoo, *The Other Side of Truth*
2001	Terry Pratchett, *The Amazing Maurice and His Educated Rodents*

2002	Sharon Creech, *Ruby Holler*
2003	Jennifer Donnelly, *A Gathering Light*
2004	Frank Cottrell Boyce, *Millions*
2005	Mal Peet, *Tamar*
2007	Meg Rosoff, *Just in Case*
2008	Philip Reeve, *Here Lies Arthur*

● ● ● The Hans Christian Andersen Award ● ● ●

The Hans Christian Andersen Award, established in 1956, is given biennially and administered by the International Board on Books for Young People. It is given to one author and, since 1966, to one illustrator in recognition of his or her entire body of work. A medal is presented to the recipient.

1956

Eleanor Farjeon, Great Britain

1958

Astrid Lindgren, Sweden

1960

Erich Kästner, Germany

1962

Meindert DeJong, USA

1964

René Guillot, France

1966

AUTHOR: Tove Jansson, Finland
ILLUSTRATOR: Alois Carigiet, Switzerland

1968

AUTHORS: James Krüss, Germany, and José Maria Sanchez-Silva, Spain
ILLUSTRATOR: Jiri Trnka, Czechoslovakia

1970

AUTHOR: Gianni Rodari, Italy
ILLUSTRATOR: Maurice Sendak, USA

1972

AUTHOR: Scott O'Dell, USA
ILLUSTRATOR: Ib Spang Olsen, Denmark

1974

AUTHOR: Maria Gripe, Sweden
ILLUSTRATOR: Farshid Mesghali, Iran

1976

AUTHOR: Cecil Bodker, Denmark
ILLUSTRATOR: Tatjana Mawrina, USSR

1978

AUTHOR: Paula Fox, USA
ILLUSTRATOR: Otto S. Svend, Denmark

1980

AUTHOR: Bohumil R'ha, Czechoslovakia
ILLUSTRATOR: Suekichi Akaba, Japan

1982

AUTHOR: Lygia Bojunga Nunes, Brazil
ILLUSTRATOR: Zbigniew Rychlicki, Poland

1984

AUTHOR: Christine Nöstlinger, Austria
ILLUSTRATOR: Mitsumasa Anno, Japan

1986

AUTHOR: Patricia Wrightson, Australia
ILLUSTRATOR: Robert Ingpen, Australia

1988

AUTHOR: Annie M. G. Schmidt, Holland
ILLUSTRATOR: Dusan Kallay, Czechoslovakia

1990

AUTHOR: Tormod Haugen, Norway
ILLUSTRATOR: Lisbeth Zwerger, Austria

1992

AUTHOR: Virginia Hamilton, USA
ILLUSTRATOR: Kveta Pacovská, Czechoslovakia

1994

AUTHOR: Michio Mado, Japan
ILLUSTRATOR: Jörg Müller, Switzerland

1996

AUTHOR: Uri Orlev, Israel
ILLUSTRATOR: Klaus Ensikat, Germany

1998

AUTHOR: Katherine Paterson, USA
ILLUSTRATOR: Tomi Ungerer, France

2000

AUTHOR: Ana Maria Machado, Brazil
ILLUSTRATOR: Anthony Browne, United Kingdom

2002

AUTHOR: Aidan Chambers, United Kingdom
ILLUSTRATOR: Quentin Blake, United Kingdom

2004

AUTHOR: Martin Waddell, Ireland
ILLUSTRATOR: Max Velthuijs, The Netherlands

2006

AUTHOR: Margaret Mahy, New Zealand
ILLUSTRATOR: Wolf Erlbruch, Germany

2008

AUTHOR: Jurg Schubiger, Switzerland
ILLUSTRATOR: Roberto Innocenti, Italy

• • • The Mildred L. Batchelder Award • • •

The Mildred L. Batchelder Award, established in 1966, is given by the Association of Library Service to Children of the American Library Association to the publisher of the most outstanding book of the year that is a translation, published in the United States, of a book that was first published in another country. In 1990, honor books were added to this award. The original country of publication is given here.

1968

The Little Man, by Erich Kastner, translated by James Kirkup, illustrated by Rick Schreiter (Knopf), Germany

1969

Don't Take Teddy, by Babbis Friis-Baastad, translated by Lise Somme McKinnon (Scribner's), Norway

1970

Wildcat under Glass, by Alki Zei, translated by Edward Fenton (Holt), Greece

1971

In the Land of Ur, by Hans Baumann, translated by Stella Humphries (Pantheon), Germany

1972

Friedrich, by Hans Peter Richter, translated by Edite Kroll (Holt), Germany

1973

Pulga, by S. R. Van Iterson, translated by Alison and Alexander Gode (Morrow), Netherlands

1974

Petros' War, by Alki Zei, translated by Edward Fenton (Dutton), Greece

1975

An Old Tale Carved out of Stone, by A. Linevsky, translated by Maria Polushkin (Crown), Russia

1976

The Cat and Mouse Who Shared a House, by Ruth Hurlimann, translated by Anthea Bell, illustrated by the author (Walck), Germany

1977

The Leopard, by Cecil Bødker, translated by Gunnar Poulsen (Simon & Schuster), Denmark

1978

Konrad, by Christine Nostlinger, illustrated by Carol Nicklaus (Watts), Germany

1979

Rabbit Island, by Jörg Steiner, translated by Ann Conrad Lammers, illustrated by Jörg Müller (Harcourt), Germany

1980

The Sound of the Dragon's Feet, by Alki Zei, translated by Edward Fenton (Dutton), Greece

1981

The Winter When Time Was Frozen, by Els Pelgrom, translated by Maryka and Rafael Rudnik (Morrow), Netherlands

1982

The Battle Horse, by Harry Kullman, translated by George Blecher and Lone Thygesen-Blecher (Bradbury), Sweden

1983

Hiroshima No Pika, by Toshi Maruki (Lothrop, Lee & Shepard), Japan

1984

Ronia, the Robber's Daughter, by Astrid Lindgren, translated by Patricia Crampton (Viking), Sweden

1985

The Island on Bird Street, by Uri Orlev, translated by Hillel Halkin (Houghton Mifflin), Israel

1986

Rose Blanche, by Christophe Gallaz and Roberto Innocenti, translated by Martha Coventry and Richard Graglia (Creative Education), Italy

1987

No Hero for the Kaiser, by Rudolf Frank, translated by Patricia Crampton (Lothrop, Lee & Shepard), Germany

1988

If You Didn't Have Me, by Ulf Nilsson, translated by Lone Tygesen-Blecher and George Blecher, illustrated by Eva Eriksson (McElderry), Sweden

1989

Crutches, by Peter Hatling, translated by Elizabeth D. Crawford (Lothrop, Lee & Shepard), Germany

1990

Buster's World, by Bjarne Reuter, translated by Anthea Bell (Dutton), Denmark

1991

Two Long and One Short, by Nina Ring Aamundsen (Houghton Mifflin), Norway

1992

The Man from the Other Side by Uri Orlev, translated by Hillel Halkin (Houghton Mifflin), Israel

1993

No award

1994

The Apprentice, by Molina Llorente, translated by Robin Longshaw (Farrar, Straus & Giroux), Spain

1995

The Boys from St. Petri, by Bjarne Reuter, translated by Anthea Bell (Dutton), Denmark

1996

The Lady with the Hat, by Uri Orlev, translated by Hillel Halkin (Houghton Mifflin), Israel

1997

The Friends, by Kazumi Yumoto, translated by Cathy Hirano (Farrar, Straus & Giroux), Japan

1998

The Robber and Me, by Josef Holub, edited by Mark Aronson, translated by Elizabeth Crawford (Holt), Germany

1999

Thanks to My Mother, by Schoschana Rabinovici, translated by James Skofield (Dial), Germany

2000

The Baboon King, by Anton Quintana, translated by John Nieuwenhuizen (Walker), Holland

2001

Samir and Yonatan, translated by Arthur A. Levine (Scholastic), Israel

2002

How I Became an American, by Karin Gündisch (Cricket), Germany

2003

The Thief Lord, by Cornelia Funke (Scholastic), Germany

2004

Run, Boy, Run, by Uri Orlev (Houghton Mifflin) Israel

2005

The Shadows of Ghadames, by Joëlle Stolz (Delacorte), France

2006

An Innocent Soldier, by Josef Holub (Levine), Germany

2007

The Pull of the Ocean, by Jean-Claude Mourlevat (Delacorte), France

2008

Brave Story, by Miyuki Miyabe (VIZ Media), Japan

2009

Moribito: Guardian of the Spirit, by Nahoko Uehashi (Scholastic), Japan

Other Awards

• • • The Ezra Jack Keats Award • • •

This award, first presented in 1985, is administered by the Ezra Jack Keats Foundation and the New York Public Library. The award was originally given biennially to a promising new writer. Beginning in the year 2001, the award has been given annually to an illustrator as well as to a writer. The award honors work done in the tradition of Ezra Jack Keats, using the criteria of appeal to young children, storytelling quality, relation between text and illustration, positive reflection of families, and the multicultural nature of the world. The award is presented at the Early Childhood Resource and Information Center of the New York Public Library. Funded by the Ezra Jack Keats Foundation, the recipient receives a monetary award and a medallion.

1985

The Patchwork Quilt, by Valerie Flournoy, illustrated by Jerry Pinkney (Dial)

1987

Jamaica's Find, by Juanita Havill, illustrated by Anne Sibley O'Brien (Houghton Mifflin)

1989

Anna's Special Present, by Yoriko Tsutsui, illustrated by Akiko Hayashi (Viking)

1991

Tell Me a Story, Mama, by Angela Johnson, illustrated by David Soman (Orchard)

1993

Tar Beach, by Faith Ringgold (Crown)

1995

Taxi! Taxi!, by Cari Best, illustrated by Dale Gottlieb (Little, Brown)

1997

Calling the Doves, by Juan Felipe Herrera, illustrated by Elly Simmons (Children's Book Press)

2001

WRITER: *Henry Hikes to Fitchburg*, by D. B. Johnson (Houghton Mifflin)

ILLUSTRATOR: *Uptown*, by Bryan Collier (Holt)

2002

WRITER AND ILLUSTRATOR: *Freedom Summer*, by Deborah Wiles; illustrated by Jerome Lagarrigue (Simon & Schuster)

2003

WRITER AND ILLUSTRATOR: *Ruby's Wish*, by Shirin Yim Bridges, illustrated by Sophie Blackall (Chronicle)

2004

WRITER: *Yesterday I Had the Blues*, by Jeron Ashford Frame (Ten Speed Press)

ILLUSTRATOR: *My Name Is Yoon*, illustrated by Gabi Swiatkowska (Farrar, Straus & Giroux)

2005

WRITER: *Going North*, by Janice Harrington (Farrar, Straus & Giroux)

ILLUSTRATOR: *The Night Eater*, illustrated by Jerome Lagarrigue (Scholastic)

2006

WRITER: *My Best Friend*, by Mary Ann Rodman (Viking)

ILLUSTRATOR: *Silly Chicken*, illustrated by Yunmee Kyong (Viking)

2007

WRITER: *For You Are A Kenyan Child*, by Kelly Cunnane (Simon & Schuster)

ILLUSTRATOR: *Mystery Bottle*, illustrated by Kristen Balouch (Hyperion)

2008

WRITER: *Leaves*, by David Ezra Stein (G. P. Putnam's Sons)

ILLUSTRATOR: *The Apple Pie that Papa Baked*, illustrated by Jonathan Bean (Simon & Schuster)

• • • The Boston Globe–Horn Book Awards • • •

The Boston Globe–Horn Book Awards have been presented annually since 1967 by the *Boston Globe* newspaper and *The Horn Book Magazine*. Through 1975, two awards were given, one for outstanding fiction and one for outstanding picturebook. In 1976, the award categories were changed to fiction or poetry, nonfiction, and picturebook. A monetary gift is awarded to the winner in each category.

1967

FICTION: *The Little Fishes*, by Erik Christian Haugaard (Houghton Mifflin)

PICTUREBOOK: *London Bridge Is Falling Down!*, illustrated by Peter Spier (Doubleday)

1968

FICTION: *The Spring Rider*, by John Lawson (Crowell)

FICTION HONOR BOOKS: *Young Mark*, by E. M. Almedingen (Farrar); *Dark Venture*, by Audrey White Beyer (Knopf); *Smith*, by Leon Garfield (Pantheon); *The Endless Steppe*, by Esther Hautzig (Crowell)

PICTUREBOOK: *Tikki Tikki Tembo*, by Arlene Mosel, illustrated by Blair Lent (Holt)

PICTUREBOOK HONOR BOOKS: *Gilgamesh: Man's First Story*, retold and illustrated by Bernarda Bryson (Holt); *Rosie's Walk*, by Pat Hutchins (Macmillan); *Jorinda and Joringel*, text by Jacob and Wilhelm Grimm, illustrated by Adrienne Adams (Scribner's); *All in Free but Janey*, text by Elizabeth Johnson, illustrated by Trina Schart Hyman (Little, Brown)

1969

FICTION: *A Wizard of Earthsea*, by Ursula Le Guin (Houghton Mifflin)

FICTION HONOR BOOKS: *Flambards*, by K. M. Peyton (World); *Turi's Poppa*, by Elizabeth Borton de Treviño (Farrar, Straus & Giroux); *The Pigman*, by Paul Zindel (HarperCollins)

PICTUREBOOK: *The Adventures of Paddy Pork*, by John S. Goodall (Harcourt)

PICTUREBOOK HONOR BOOKS: *New Moon Cove*, by Ann Atwood (Scribner's); *Monkey in the Jungle*, text by Edna Mitchell Preston, illustrated by Clement Hurd (Viking); *Thy Friend, Obadiah*, by Brinton Turkle (Viking)

1970

FICTION: *The Intruder*, by John Rowe Townsend (Lippincott)

FICTION HONOR BOOK: *Where the Lilies Bloom*, by Vera and Bill Cleaver (Lippincott)

PICTUREBOOK: *Hi, Cat!*, by Ezra Jack Keats (Macmillan)

PICTUREBOOK HONOR BOOK: *A Story, a Story*, by Gail Haley (Simon & Schuster)

1971

FICTION: *A Room Made of Windows*, by Eleanor Cameron (Little, Brown)

FICTION HONOR BOOKS: *Beyond the Weir Bridge*, by Hester Burton (Crowell); *Come by Here*, by Olivia Coolidge (Houghton Mifflin); *Mrs. Frisby and the Rats of NIMH*, by Robert C. O'Brien (Simon & Schuster)

PICTUREBOOK: *If I Built a Village*, by Kazue Mizumura (HarperCollins)

PICTUREBOOK HONOR BOOKS: *If All the Seas Were One Sea*, by Janina Domanska (Macmillan); *The Angry Moon*, retold by William Sleator, illustrated by Blair Lent (Little, Brown); *A Firefly Named Torchy*, by Bernard Waber (Houghton Mifflin)

1972

FICTION: *Tristan and Iseult*, by Rosemary Sutcliff (Dutton)

PICTUREBOOK: *Mr. Gumpy's Outing*, by John Burningham (Holt)

1973

FICTION: *The Dark Is Rising*, by Susan Cooper (McElderry)

FICTION HONOR BOOKS: *The Cat Who Wished to Be a Man*, by Lloyd Alexander (Dutton); *An Island in a Green Sea*, by Mabel Esther Allan (Simon & Schuster); *No Way of Telling*, by Emma Smith (McElderry)

PICTUREBOOK: *King Stork*, by Trina Schart Hyman (Little, Brown)

PICTUREBOOK HONOR BOOKS: *The Magic Tree*, by Gerald McDermott (Holt); *Who, Said Sue, Said Whoo?*, by Ellen Raskin (Simon & Schuster); *The Silver Pony*, by Lynd Ward (Houghton Mifflin)

1974

FICTION: *M. C. Higgins, the Great*, by Virginia Hamilton (Macmillan)

FICTION HONOR BOOKS: *And Then What Happened, Paul Revere?*, by Jean Fritz (Coward-McCann); *The Summer after the Funeral*, by Jane Gardam (Macmillan); *Tough Chauncey*, by Doris Buchanan Smith (Morrow)

PICTUREBOOK: *Jambo Means Hello*, by Muriel Feelings, illustrated by Tom Feelings (Dial)

PICTUREBOOK HONOR BOOKS: *All Butterflies*, by Marcia Brown (Scribner's); *Herman the Helper*, by Robert Kraus, illustrated by Jose Aruego and Ariane Dewey (Windmill); *A Prairie Boy's Winter*, by William Kurelek (Houghton Mifflin)

1975

FICTION: *Transport 7-41-R*, by T. Degens (Viking)

FICTION HONOR BOOK: *The Hundred Penny Box*, text by Sharon Bell Mathis, illustrated by Leo and Diane Dillon (Viking)

PICTUREBOOK: *Anno's Alphabet*, by Mitsumasa Anno (HarperCollins)

PICTUREBOOK HONOR BOOKS: *She Come Bringing Me That Little Baby Girl*, text by Eloise Greenfield, illustrated by John Steptoe (Lippincott); *Scram, Kid!*, text by Ann McGovern, illustrated by Nola Langner (Viking); *The Bear's Bicycle*, text by Emilie Warren McLeod, illustrated by David McPhail (Little, Brown)

1976

FICTION: *Unleaving*, by Jill Paton Walsh (Farrar, Straus & Giroux)

FICTION HONOR BOOKS: *A String in the Harp*, by Nancy Bond (McElderry); *A Stranger Came Ashore*, by Mollie Hunter (HarperCollins); *Dragonwings*, by Laurence Yep (HarperCollins)

NONFICTION: *Voyaging to Cathay: Americans in the China Trade*, by Alfred Tamarin and Shirley Glubok (Viking)

NONFICTION HONOR BOOKS: *Will You Sign Here, John Hancock?*, text by Jean Fritz, illustrated by Trina Schart Hyman (Coward-McCann); *Never to Forget: The Jews of the Holocaust*, by Milton Meltzer (HarperCollins); *Pyramid*, by David Macaulay (Houghton Mifflin)

PICTUREBOOK: *Thirteen*, by Remy Charlip and Jerry Joyner (Four Winds Press)

PICTUREBOOK HONOR BOOKS: *The Desert Is Theirs*, text by Byrd Baylor, illustrated by Peter Parnall (Scribner's); *Six Little Ducks*, by Chris Conover (Crowell); *Song of the Boat*, text by Lorenz Graham, illustrated by Leo and Diane Dillon (Crowell)

1977

FICTION: *Child of the Owl*, by Laurence Yep (HarperCollins)

FICTION HONOR BOOKS: *Blood Feud*, by Rosemary Sutcliff (Dutton); *Roll of Thunder, Hear My Cry*, by Mildred Taylor (Dial); *The Machine Gunners*, by Robert Westall (Greenwillow)

NONFICTION: *Chance, Luck and Destiny*, by Peter Dickinson (Little, Brown)

NONFICTION HONOR BOOKS: *Watching the Wild Apes*, by Betty Ann Kevles (Dutton); *The Colonial Cookbook*, by Lucille Recht Penner (Hastings); *From Slave to Abolitionist*, by Lucille Schulberg Warner (Dial)

PICTUREBOOK: *Grandfa' Grig Had a Pig and Other Rhymes without Reason from Mother Goose*, by Wallace Tripp (Little, Brown)

PICTUREBOOK HONOR BOOKS: *Anno's Counting Book*, by Mitsumasa Anno (Crowell); *Ashanti to Zulu: African Traditions*, text by Margaret Musgrove, illustrated by Leo and Diane Dillon (Dial); *The Amazing Bone*, by William Steig (Farrar, Straus & Giroux)

SPECIAL CITATION: *The Changing City and the Changing Countryside*, by Jörg Müller (McElderry)

1978

FICTION: *The Westing Game*, by Ellen Raskin (Dutton)

FICTION HONOR BOOKS: *Ramona and Her Father*, by Beverly Cleary (Morrow); *Anpao: An American Indian Odyssey*, by Jamake Highwater (Lippincott); *Alan and Naomi*, by Myron Levoy (HarperCollins)

NONFICTION HONOR BOOKS: *Settlers and Strangers: Native Americans of the Desert Southwest and History as They Saw It*, by Betty Baker (Macmillan); *Castle*, by David Macaulay (Houghton Mifflin)

NONFICTION: *Mischling, Second Degree: My Childhood in Nazi Germany*, by Ilse Koehn (Greenwillow)

PICTUREBOOK: *Anno's Journey*, by Mitsumasa Anno (Philomel)

PICTUREBOOK HONOR BOOKS: *The Story of Edward*, by Philippe Dumas (Parents); *On to Widecombe Fair*, text by Patricia Lee Gauch, illustrated by Trina Schart Hyman (Putnam); *What Do You Feed Your Donkey On? Rhymes from a Belfast Childhood*, collected by Collette O'Hare, illustrated by Jenny Rodwell (Collins)

1979

FICTION: *Humbug Mountain*, by Sid Fleischman (Little, Brown)

FICTION HONOR BOOKS: *All Together Now*, by Sue Ellen Bridgers (Knopf); *Silas and Ben-Godik*, by Cecil Bodker (Delacorte)

NONFICTION: *The Road from Home: The Story of an Armenian Girl*, by David Kherdian (Greenwillow)

NONFICTION HONOR BOOKS: *The Iron Road: A Portrait of American Railroading*, text by Richard Snow, photos by David Plowden (Four Winds); *Self-Portrait: Margot Zemach*, by Margot Zemach (Addison-Wesley); *The Story of*

American Photography: An Illustrated History for Young People, by Martin Sandler (Little, Brown)

PICTUREBOOK: *The Snowman*, by Raymond Briggs (Random House)

PICTUREBOOK HONOR BOOKS: *Cross-Country Cat*, text by Mary Calhoun, illustrated by Erik Ingraham (Morrow); *Ben's Trumpet*, by Rachel Isadora (Greenwillow)

1980

FICTION: *Conrad's War*, by Andrew Davies (Crown)

FICTION HONOR BOOKS: *The Night Swimmers*, by Betsy Byars (Delacorte); *Me and My Million*, by Clive King (Crowell); *The Alfred Summer*, by Jan Slepian (Macmillan)

NONFICTION: *Building the Fight against Gravity*, text by Mario Salvadori, illustrated by Saralinda Hooker and Christopher Ragus (McElderry)

NONFICTION HONOR BOOKS: *Childtimes: A Three-Generation Memoir*, text by Eloise Greenfield, illustrated by Jerry Pinkney, and with photos (Crowell); *Stonewall*, text by Jean Fritz, illustrated by Stephen Gammell (Putnam); *How the Forest Grew*, text by William Jaspersohn, illustrated by Chuck Eckart (Greenwillow)

PICTUREBOOK: *The Garden of Abdul Gasazi*, by Chris Van Allsburg (Houghton Mifflin)

PICTUREBOOK HONOR BOOKS: *The Gray Lady and the Strawberry Snatcher*, by Molly Bang (Greenwillow); *Why the Tides Ebb and Flow*, text by John Chase Bowden, illustrated by Marc Brown (Houghton Mifflin)

SPECIAL CITATION: *Graham Oakley's Magical Changes*, by Graham Oakley (Simon & Schuster)

1981

FICTION: *The Leaving*, by Lynn Hall (Scribner's)

FICTION HONOR BOOKS: *Ida Early Comes over the Mountain*, by Robert Burch (Viking); *Flight of the Sparrow*, by Julia Cunningham (Pantheon); *Footsteps*, by Leon Garfield (Delacorte)

NONFICTION: *The Weaver's Gift*, text by Kathyrn Lasky, photos by Christopher Knight (Warne)

NONFICTION HONOR BOOKS: *You Can't Be Timid with a Trumpet: Notes from the Orchestra*, by Betty English (Lothrop, Lee & Shepard); *The Hospital Book*, text by James Howe, photos by Mal Warshaw (Random House); *Junk Food, Fast Food, Health Food: What America Eats and Why*, by Lila Perl (Clarion)

PICTUREBOOK: *Outside over There*, by Maurice Sendak (HarperCollins)

PICTUREBOOK HONOR BOOKS: *Where the Buffaloes Begin*, text by Olaf Baker, illustrated by Stephen Gam-

mell (Warne); *On Market Street*, text by Arnold Lobel, illustrated by Anita Lobel (Greenwillow); *Jumanji*, by Chris Van Allsburg (Houghton Mifflin)

1982

FICTION: *Playing Beatie Bow*, by Ruth Park (Simon & Schuster)

FICTION HONOR BOOKS: *The Voyage Begun*, by Nancy Bond (Simon & Schuster); *Ask Me No Questions*, by Ann Schlee (Holt); *The Scarecrows*, by Robert Westall (Greenwillow)

NONFICTION: *Upon the Head of the Goat: A Childhood in Hungary, 1939–1944*, by Aranka Siegal (Farrar, Straus & Giroux)

NONFICTION HONOR BOOKS: *Lobo of the Tasaday*, by John Nance (Pantheon); *Dinosaurs of North America*, text by Helen Roney Sattler, illustrated by Anthony Rao (Lothrop, Lee & Shepard)

PICTUREBOOK: *A Visit to William Blake's Inn: Poems for Innocent and Experienced Travelers*, by Nancy Willard, illustrated by Alice and Martin Provensen (Harcourt)

PICTUREBOOK HONOR BOOK: *The Friendly Beasts: An Old English Christmas Carol*, by Tomie dePaola (Putnam)

1983

FICTION: *Sweet Whisper, Brother Rush*, by Virginia Hamilton (Philomel)

FICTION HONOR BOOKS: *Homesick: My Own Story*, by Jean Fritz (Putnam); *The Road to Camlann*, by Rosemary Sutcliff (Dutton); *Dicey's Song*, by Cynthia Voigt (Simon & Schuster)

NONFICTION: *Behind Barbed Wire: The Imprisonment of Japanese Americans during World War II*, by Daniel Davis (Dutton)

NONFICTION HONOR BOOKS: *Hiroshima No Pika*, by Toshi Maruki (Lothrop, Lee & Shepard); *The Jewish Americans: A History in Their Own Words: 1650–1950*, by Milton Meltzer (Crowell)

PICTUREBOOK: *A Chair for My Mother*, by Vera B. Williams (Greenwillow)

PICTUREBOOK HONOR BOOKS: *Friends*, by Helme Heine (McElderry); *Yeh-Shen: A Cinderella Story from China*, text by Ai-Ling Louie, illustrated by Ed Young (Philomel); *Doctor De Soto*, by William Steig (Farrar, Straus & Giroux)

1984

FICTION: *A Little Fear*, by Patricia Wrighton (McElderry)

FICTION HONOR BOOKS: *Archer's Goon*, by Diana Wynne Jones (Greenwillow); *Unclaimed Treasures*, by Patricia

MacLachlan (HarperCollins); *A Solitary Blue*, by Cynthia Voigt (Simon & Schuster)

NONFICTION: *The Double Life of Pocahontas*, by Jean Fritz (Putnam)

NONFICTION HONOR BOOKS: *Queen Eleanor: Independent Spirit of the Medieval World: A Biography of Eleanor of Aquitaine*, by Polly Schoyer Brooks (Lippincott); *Children of the Wild West*, by Russell Freedman (Clarion); *The Tipi: A Center of Native American Life*, by David and Charlotte Yue (Knopf)

PICTUREBOOK: *Jonah and the Great Fish*, by Warwick Hutton (McElderry)

PICTUREBOOK HONOR BOOKS: *Dawn*, by Molly Bang (Morrow); *The Guinea Pig ABC*, by Kate Duke (Dutton); *The Rose in My Garden*, text by Arnold Lobel, illustrated by Anita Lobel (Greenwillow)

1985

FICTION: *The Moves Make the Man*, by Bruce Brooks (HarperCollins)

FICTION HONOR BOOKS: *Babe: The Gallant Pig*, by Dick King-Smith (Crown); *The Changeover: A Supernatural Romance*, by Margaret Mahy (McElderry)

NONFICTION: *Commodore Perry in the Land of the Shogun*, by Rhoda Blumberg (Lothrop, Lee & Shepard)

NONFICTION HONOR BOOKS: *Boy*, by Roald Dahl (Farrar, Straus & Giroux); *1812: The War Nobody Won*, by Albert Marrin (Simon & Schuster)

PICTUREBOOK: *Mama Don't Allow*, by Thacher Hurd (HarperCollins)

PICTUREBOOK HONOR BOOKS: *Like Jake and Me*, text by Mavis Jukes, illustrated by Lloyd Bloom (Knopf); *How Much Is a Million?*, text by David M. Schwartz, illustrated by Stephen Kellogg (Lothrop, Lee & Shepard); *The Mysteries of Harris Burdick*, by Chris Van Allsburg (Houghton Mifflin)

SPECIAL CITATION: *1, 2, 3*, by Tana Hoban (Greenwillow)

1986

FICTION: *In Summer Light*, by Zibby Oneal (Viking)

FICTION HONOR BOOKS: *Prairie Songs*, by Pam Conrad (HarperCollins); *Howl's Moving Castle*, by Diana Wynne Jones (Greenwillow)

NONFICTION: *Auks, Rocks, and the Odd Dinosaur: Inside Stories from the Smithsonian's Museum of Natural History*, by Peggy Thomson (Crowell)

NONFICTION HONOR BOOKS: *Dark Harvest: Migrant Farmworkers in America*, text by Brent Ashabranner, photos by Paul Conklin (Dodd, Mead); *The Truth about Santa Claus*, by James Cross Giblin (Crowell)

PICTUREBOOK: *The Paper Crane*, by Molly Bang (Greenwillow)

PICTUREBOOK HONOR BOOKS: *Gorilla*, by Anthony Browne (Knopf); *The Trek*, by Ann Jonas (Greenwillow); *The Polar Express*, by Chris Van Allsburg (Houghton Mifflin)

1987

FICTION: *Rabble Starkey*, by Lois Lowry (Houghton Mifflin)

FICTION HONOR BOOKS: *Georgia Music*, by Helen V. Griffith (Greenwillow); *Isaac Campion*, by Janni Howker (Greenwillow)

NONFICTION: *The Pilgrims of Plimoth*, by Marcia Sewall (Simon & Schuster)

NONFICTION HONOR BOOKS: *Being Born*, text by Sheila Kitzinger, photos by Lennart Nilsson (Grosset & Dunlap); *The Magic Schoolbus at the Waterworks*, text by Joanna Cole, illustrated by Bruce Degen (Scholastic); *Steamboat in a Cornfield*, by John Hartford (Crown)

PICTUREBOOK: *Mufaro's Beautiful Daughters*, by John Steptoe (Lothrop, Lee & Shepard)

PICTUREBOOK HONOR BOOKS: *In Coal Country*, text by Judith Hendershot, illustrated by Thomas B. Allen (Knopf); *Cherries and Cherry Pits*, by Vera B. Williams (Greenwillow); *Old Henry*, text by Joan Blos, illustrated by Stephen Gammell (Morrow)

1988

FICTION: *The Friendship*, by Mildred Taylor (Dial)

FICTION HONOR BOOKS: *Granny Was a Buffer Girl*, by Berlie Doherty (Orchard); *Joyful Noise: Poems for Two Voices*, by Paul Fleischman (HarperCollins); *Memory*, by Margaret Mahy (McElderry)

NONFICTION: *Anthony Burns: The Defeat and Triumph of a Fugitive Slave*, by Virginia Hamilton (Knopf)

NONFICTION HONOR BOOKS: *African Journey*, by John Chiasson (Bradbury); *Little by Little: A Writer's Education*, by Jean Little (Viking)

PICTUREBOOK: *The Boy of the Three-Year Nap*, text by Diane Snyder, illustrated by Allen Say (Houghton Mifflin)

PICTUREBOOK HONOR BOOKS: *Where the Forest Meets the Sea*, by Jeannie Baker (Greenwillow); *Stringbean's Trip to the Shining Sea*, text by Vera B. Williams, illustrated by Jennifer and Vera B. Williams (Greenwillow)

1989

FICTION: *The Village by the Sea*, by Paula Fox (Orchard)

FICTION HONOR BOOKS: *Eva*, by Peter Dickinson (Delacorte); *Gideon Ahoy!*, by William Mayne (Delacorte)

NONFICTION: *The Way Things Work*, by David Macaulay (Houghton Mifflin)

NONFICTION HONOR BOOKS: *The Rainbow People*, by Laurence Yep (HarperCollins); *Round Buildings, Square Buildings, and Buildings That Wiggle Like a Fish*, by Philip M. Isaacson (Knopf)

PICTUREBOOK: *Shy Charles*, by Rosemary Wells (Dial)

PICTUREBOOK HONOR BOOKS: *Island Boy*, by Barbara Cooney (Viking); *The Nativity*, illustrated by Julie Vivas (Harcourt)

1990

FICTION: *Maniac Magee*, by Jerry Spinelli (Little, Brown)

FICTION HONOR BOOKS: *Saturnalia*, by Paul Fleischman (HarperCollins); *Stonewords*, by Pam Conrad (HarperCollins)

NONFICTION: *The Great Little Madison*, by Jean Fritz (Putnam)

NONFICTION HONOR BOOK: *Insect Metamorphosis: From Egg to Adult*, text by Ron and Nancy Goor, photos by Ron Goor (Simon & Schuster)

PICTUREBOOK: *Lon Po Po: A Red Riding-Hood Story from China*, by Ed Young (Philomel)

PICTUREBOOK HONOR BOOK: *Chicka Chicka Boom Boom*, text by Bill Martin Jr. and John Archambault, illustrated by Lois Ehlert (Simon & Schuster)

SPECIAL CITATION: *Valentine and Orson*, by Nancy Ekholm Burkert (Farrar, Straus & Giroux)

1991

FICTION: *The True Confessions of Charlotte Doyle*, by Avi (Orchard)

FICTION HONOR BOOKS: *Paradise Cafe and Other Stories*, by Martha Brooks (Joy Street); *Judy Scuppernong*, by Brenda Seabrooke (Cobblehill Books)

NONFICTION: *Appalachia: The Voices of Sleeping Birds*, text by Cynthia Rylant, illustrated by Barry Moser (Harcourt)

NONFICTION HONOR BOOKS: *The Wright Brothers: How They Invented the Airplane*, by Russell Freedman (Holiday House); *Good Queen Bess: The Story of Elizabeth I of England*, text by Diane Stanley and Peter Vennema, illustrated by Diane Stanley (Four Winds)

PICTUREBOOK: *The Tale of the Mandarin Ducks*, by Katherine Paterson, illustrated by Leo and Diane Dillon (Dutton)

PICTUREBOOK HONOR BOOKS: *Aardvarks, Disembark!*, by Ann Jonas (Greenwillow); *Sophie and Lou*, by Petra Mathers (HarperCollins)

1992

FICTION: *Missing May*, by Cynthia Rylant (Orchard)

FICTION HONOR BOOKS: *Nothing but the Truth*, by Avi (Orchard); *Somewhere in the Darkness*, by Walter Dean Myers (Scholastic)

NONFICTION: *Talking with Artists*, by Pat Cummings (Bradbury)

NONFICTION HONOR BOOKS: *Red Leaf, Yellow Leaf*, by Lois Ehlert (Harcourt); *The Handmade Alphabet*, by Laura Rankin (Dial)

PICTUREBOOK: *Seven Blind Mice*, by Ed Young (Philomel)

PICTUREBOOK HONOR BOOK: *In the Tall, Tall Grass*, by Denise Fleming (Holt)

1993

FICTION: *Ajeemah and His Son*, by James Berry (HarperCollins)

FICTION HONOR BOOK: *The Giver*, by Lois Lowry (Houghton Mifflin)

NONFICTION: *Sojourner Truth: Ain't I a Woman?*, by Patricia and Fredrick McKissack (Scholastic)

NONFICTION HONOR BOOK: *Lives of the Musicians: Good Times, Bad Times (and What the Neighbors Thought)*, text by Kathleen Krull, illustrated by Kathryn Hewitt (Harcourt)

PICTUREBOOK: *The Fortune Tellers*, by Lloyd Alexander, illustrated by Trina Schart Hyman (Dutton)

PICTUREBOOK HONOR BOOKS: *Komodo!*, by Peter Sís (Greenwillow); *Raven: A Trickster Tale from the Pacific Northwest*, by Gerald McDermott (Harcourt)

1994

FICTION: *Scooter*, by Vera B. Williams (Greenwillow)

FICTION HONOR BOOKS: *Flour Babies*, by Anne Fine (Little, Brown); *Western Wind*, by Paula Fox (Orchard)

NONFICTION: *Eleanor Roosevelt: A Life of Discovery*, by Russell Freedman (Clarion)

NONFICTION HONOR BOOKS: *Unconditional Surrender: U. S. Grant and the Civil War*, by Albert Marrin (Simon & Schuster); *A Tree Place and Other Poems*, text by Constance Levy, illustrated by Robert Sabuda (McElderry)

PICTUREBOOK: *Grandfather's Journey*, by Allen Say (Houghton Mifflin)

PICTUREBOOK HONOR BOOKS: *Owen*, by Kevin Henkes (Greenwillow); *A Small Tall Tale from the Far Far North*, by Peter Sís (Knopf)

1995

FICTION: *Some of the Kinder Planets*, by Tim Wynne-Jones (Orchard)

FICTION HONOR BOOKS: *Jericho*, by Janet Hickman (Greenwillow); *Earthshine*, by Theresa Nelson (Orchard)

NONFICTION: *Abigail Adams, Witness to a Revolution*, by Natalie Bober (Simon & Schuster)

NONFICTION HONOR BOOKS: *It's Perfectly Normal: Changing Bodies, Growing Up, Sex, and Sexual Health*, text by Robie H. Harris, illustrated by Michael Emberley (Candlewick); *The Great Fire*, by Jim Murphy (Scholastic)

PICTUREBOOK: *John Henry*, by Julius Lester, illustrated by Jerry Pinkney (Dial)

PICTUREBOOK HONOR BOOK: *Swamp Angel*, text by Anne Isaacs, illustrated by Paul O. Zelinsky (Dutton)

1996

FICTION: *Poppy*, by Avi, illustrated by Brian Floca (Orchard)

FICTION HONOR BOOKS: *The Moorchild*, by Eloise McGraw (McElderry); *Belle Prater's Boy*, by Ruth White (Farrar, Straus & Giroux)

NONFICTION: *Orphan Train Rider: One Boy's True Story*, by Andrea Warren (Houghton Mifflin)

NONFICTION HONOR BOOKS: *The Boy Who Lived with the Bears: And Other Iroquois Stories*, text by Joseph Bruchac, illustrated by Murv Jacob (HarperCollins); *Haystack*, text by Bonnie and Arthur Geisert, illustrated by Arthur Geisert (Houghton Mifflin)

PICTUREBOOK: *In the Rain with Baby Duck*, text by Amy Hest, illustrated by Jill Barton (Candlewick)

PICTUREBOOK HONOR BOOKS: *Fanny's Dream*, text by Caralyn Buehner, illustrated by Mark Buehner (Dial); *Home Lovely*, by Lynne Rae Perkins (Greenwillow)

1997

FICTION AND POETRY: *The Friends*, by Kazumi Yumoto, translated by Cathy Hirano (Farrar, Straus & Giroux)

FICTION AND POETRY HONOR BOOKS: *Lily's Crossing*, by Patricia Reilly Giff (Delacorte); *Harlem*, by Walter Dean Myers, illustrated by Christopher Myers (Scholastic)

NONFICTION: *A Drop of Water: A Book of Science and Wonder*, by Walter Wick (Scholastic)

NONFICTION HONOR BOOKS: *Lou Gehrig: The Luckiest Man*, by David Adler, illustrated by Terry Widener (Harcourt); *Leonardo da Vinci*, by Diane Stanley (Morrow)

PICTUREBOOK: *The Adventures of Sparrowboy*, by Brian Pinkney (Simon & Schuster)

PICTUREBOOK HONOR BOOKS: *Home on the Bayou: A Cowboy's Story*, by G. Brian Karas (Simon & Schuster); *Potato: A Tale from the Great Depression*, by Kate Lied, illustrated by Lisa Campbell Ernst (National Geographic Society)

1998

FICTION AND POETRY: *The Circuit: Stories from the Life of a Migrant Child*, by Francisco Jiménez (University of New Mexico Press)

FICTION AND POETRY HONOR BOOKS: *While No One Was Watching*, by Jane Leslie Conly (Holt); *My Louisiana Sky*, by Kimberly Willis Holt (Holt)

NONFICTION: *Leon's Story*, by Leon Walter Tillage, illustrated by Susan L. Roth (Farrar, Straus & Giroux)

NONFICTION HONOR BOOKS: *Martha Graham: A Dancer's Life*, by Russell Freedman (Clarion); *Chuck Close up Close*, by Jan Greenberg and Sandra Jordan (DK Publishing)

PICTUREBOOK: *And If the Moon Could Talk*, by Kate Banks, illustrated by Georg Hallensleben (Farrar, Straus & Giroux)

PICTUREBOOK HONOR BOOKS: *Seven Brave Women*, by Betsy Hearne, illustrated by Bethanne Andersen (Greenwillow); *Popcorn: Poems*, by James Stevenson (Greenwillow)

1999

FICTION: *Holes*, by Louis Sachar (Farrar, Straus & Giroux)

FICTION HONOR BOOKS: *The Trolls*, by Polly Horvath (Farrar, Straus & Giroux); *Monster*, by Walter Dean Myers, illustrated by Christopher Myers (HarperCollins)

NONFICTION: *The Top of the World: Climbing Mount Everest*, by Steve Jenkins (Houghton Mifflin)

NONFICTION HONOR BOOKS: *Shipwreck at the Bottom of the World: The Extraordinary True Story of Shackleton and the* Endurance, by Jennifer Armstrong (Crown); *William Shakespeare and the Globe*, by Aliki (HarperCollins)

PICTUREBOOK: *Red-Eyed Tree Frog*, by Joy Cowley, illustrated by Nic Bishop (Scholastic)

PICTUREBOOK HONOR BOOKS: *Dance*, by Bill T. Jones and Susan Kuklin, illustrated by Susan Kuklin (Hyperion); *The Owl and the Pussycat*, by Edward Lear, illustrated by James Marshall (HarperCollins)

SPECIAL CITATION: *Tibet: Through the Red Box*, by Peter Sís (Farrar, Straus & Giroux)

2000

FICTION: *The Folk Keeper*, by Franny Billingsley (Simon & Schuster)

FICTION HONOR BOOKS: *King of Shadows*, by Susan Cooper (McElderry); *145th Street: Short Stories*, by Walter Dean Myers (Delacorte)

NONFICTION: *Sir Walter Ralegh and the Quest for El Dorado*, by Marc Aronson (Clarion)

NONFICTION HONOR BOOKS: *Osceola: Memories of a Sharecropper's Daughter*, collected and edited by Alan Govenar, illustrated by Shane W. Evans (Hyperion); *Sitting Bull and His World*, by Albert Marrin (Dutton)

PICTUREBOOK: *Henry Hikes to Fitchburg*, by D. B. Johnson (Houghton Mifflin)

PICTUREBOOK HONOR BOOKS: *Buttons*, by Brock Cole (Farrar, Straus & Giroux); *A Day, a Dog*, by Gabrielle Vincent (Front Street)

2001

FICTION AND POETRY: *Carver: A Life in Poems*, by Marilyn Nelson (Front Street)

FICTION AND POETRY HONOR BOOKS: *Everything on a Waffle*, by Polly Horvath (Farrar, Straus & Giroux); *Troy*, by Adèle Geras (Harcourt)

NONFICTION: *The Longitude Prize*, by Joan Dash, illustrated by Dusan Petricic (Farrar, Straus & Giroux)

NONFICTION HONOR BOOKS: *Rocks in His Head*, by Carol Otis Hurst, illustrated by James Stevenson (Greenwillow); *Uncommon Traveler: Mary Kingsley in Africa*, by Don Brown (Houghton Mifflin)

PICTUREBOOK: *Cold Feet*, by Cynthia DeFelice, illustrated by Robert Andrew Parker (DK Publishing)

PICTUREBOOK HONOR BOOKS: *Five Creatures*, by Emily Jenkins, illustrated by Tomek Bogacki (Farrar, Straus & Giroux); *The Stray Dog*, retold and illustrated by Marc Simont (HarperCollins)

2002

FICTION AND POETRY: *Lord of the Deep*, by Graham Salisbury (Delacorte)

FICTION AND POETRY HONOR BOOKS: *Amber Was Brave, Essie Was Smart*, by Vera B. Williams (Greenwillow); *Saffy's Angel*, by Hilary McKay (McElderry)

NONFICTION: *This Land Was Made for You and Me: The Life and Songs of Woody Guthrie*, by Elizabeth Partridge (Viking)

NONFICTION HONOR BOOKS: *Handel, Who Knew What He Liked*, by M. T. Anderson, illustrated by Kevin Hawkes (Candlewick); *Woody Guthrie: Poet of the People*, by Bonnie Christensen (Knopf)

PICTUREBOOK: *"Let's Get a Pup!" Said Kate*, by Bob Graham (Candlewick)

PICTUREBOOK HONOR BOOKS: *I Stink!*, by Kate McMullan, illustrated by Jim McMullan (HarperCollins); *Little Rat Sets Sail*, by Monika Bang-Campbell, illustrated by Molly Bang (Harcourt)

2003

FICTION AND POETRY: *The Jamie and Angus Stories*, by Anne Fine, illustrated by Penny Dale (Candlewick)

FICTION AND POETRY HONOR BOOKS: *Feed*, by M. T. Anderson (Candlewick); *Locomotion*, by Jacqueline Woodson (Putnam)

NONFICTION: *Fireboat: The Heroic Adventures of the John J. Harvey*, by Maira Kalman (Putnam)

NONFICTION HONOR BOOKS: *To Fly: The Story of the Wright Brothers*, by Wendie C. Old, illustrated by Robert Andrew Parker (Clarion); *Revenge of the Whale: The True Story of the Whaleship* Essex, by Nathaniel Philbrick (Putnam)

PICTUREBOOK. *Big Momma Makes the World*, by Phyllis Root, illustrated by Helen Oxenbury (Candlewick)

PICTUREBOOK HONOR BOOKS: *Dahlia*, by Barbara McClintock (Farrar, Straus & Giroux); *Blues Journey*, by Walter Dean Myers, illustrated by Christopher Myers (Holiday House)

2004

FICTION AND POETRY: *The Fire Eaters*, by David Almond (Delacorte)

FICTION AND POETRY HONOR BOOKS: *God Went to Beauty School*, by Cynthia Rylant (HarperTempest); *The Amulet of Samarkand: The Bartimaeus Trilogy, Book One*, by Jonathan Stroud (Hyperion)

NONFICTION: *An American Plague: The True and Terrifying Story of the Yellow Fever Epidemic of 1793*, by Jim Murphy (Clarion)

NONFICTION HONOR BOOKS: *Surprising Sharks*, by Nicola Davies, illustrated by James Croft (Candlewick); *The Man Who Went to the Far Side of the Moon: The Story of Apollo 11 Astronaut Michael Collins*, by Bea Uusma Schyffert (Chronicle)

PICTUREBOOK: *The Man Who Walked Between the Towers*, by Mordicai Gerstein (Roaring Brook Press)

PICTUREBOOK HONOR BOOKS: *The Shape Game*, by Anthony Browne (Farrar, Straus & Giroux); *Snow Music*, by Lynne Rae Perkins (Greenwillow)

2005

FICTION AND POETRY: *The Schwa Was Here*, by Neal Schusterman (Dutton)

FICTION AND POETRY HONOR BOOKS: *Kalpana's Dream*, by Judith Clarke (Front Street); *A Wreath for Emmett Till*, by Marilyn Nelson (Houghton)

NONFICTION: *The Race to Save the Lord God Bird*, by Phillip Hoose (Kroupa/Farrar)

NONFICTION HONOR BOOKS: *Good Brother, Bad Brother*, by James Cross Giblin (Clarion); *Michael Rosen's Sad Book*, by Michael Rosen, illustrated by Quentin Blake (Candlewick)

PICTUREBOOK: *Traction Man Is Here!*, by Mini Grey (Knopf)

PICTUREBOOK HONOR BOOKS: *That New Animal*, by Emily Jenkins, illustrated by Pierre Pratt (Foster/Farrar); *The Hello, Goodbye Window*, by Norton Juster, illustrated by Chris Raschka (di Capua/Hyperion)

2006

FICTION AND POETRY: *The Miraculous Journey of Edward Tulane*, by Kate DiCamillo, illustrated by Bagram Ibatoulline (Candlewick)

FICTION AND POETRY HONOR BOOKS: *Yellow Elephant: A Bright Bestiary* (Harcourt) by Julie Larios, illustrated by Julie Paschkis; Yellow Star, by Jennifer Roy (Marshall Cavendish)

NONFICTION: *If You Decide to Go to the Moon*, by Faith McNulty, illustrated by Steven Kellogg (Scholastic)

NONFICTION HONOR BOOK: *A Mother's Journey*, by Sandra Markle, illustrated by Alan Marks (Charlesbridge); *Wildfire*, by Taylor Morrison (Lorraine/Houghton)

PICTUREBOOK: *Leaf Man*, by Lois Ehlert (Harcourt)

PICTUREBOOK HONOR BOOKS: *A True Story in Which a Baby Hippo Loses His Mama during a Tsunami, but Finds a New Home, and a New Mama*, by Jeanette Winter (Harcourt); *Sky Boys: How They Built the Empire State Building*, by Deborah Hopkinson, illustrated by James E. Ransome (Schwartz & Wade/Random)

2007

FICTION AND POETRY: *The Astonishing Life of Octavian Nothing, Traitor to the Nation, Volume I: The Pox Party*, by M. T. Anderson (Candlewick)

FICTION AND POETRY HONOR BOOKS: *Clementine*, by Sara Pennypacker, illustrated by Marla Frazee (Hyperion); *Rex Zero and the End of the World*, by Tim Wynne-Jones (Kroupa/Farrar)

NONFICTION: *The Strongest Man in the World: Louis Cyr*, by Nicolas Debon (Groundwood)

NONFICTION HONOR BOOKS: *Tracking Trash: Flotsam, Jetsam, and the Science of Ocean Motion*, by Loree Griffin Burns (Houghton); *Escape!*, by Sid Fleischman (Greenwillow)

PICTUREBOOK: *Dog and Bear: Two Friends, Three Stories*, by Laura Vaccaro Seeger (Porter/Roaring Brook)

PICTUREBOOK HONOR BOOKS: *365 Penguins* by Jean-Luc Fromental, illustrated by Joelle Jolivet (Abrams); *Wolves*, by Emily Gravett (Simon)

2008

PICTUREBOOK: *At Night*, by Jonathan Bean (Farrar)

PICTUREBOOK HONOR BOOKS: *Fred Stays with Me!*, by Nancy Coffelt, illustrated by Tricia Tusa (Little); *A Couple of Boys Have the Best Week Ever*, by Marla Frazee (Harcourt)

FICTION AND POETRY: *The Absolutely True Diary of a Part-Time Indian*, by Sherman Alexie, illustrated by Ellen Forney (Little)

FICTION AND POETRY HONOR BOOKS: *Shooting the Moon* by Frances O'Roark Dowell (Simon & Schuster); *Savvy*, by Ingrid Law (Walden/Dial)

NONFICTION: *The Wall*, by Peter Sís (Foster/Farrar)

NONFICTION HONOR BOOK: *Frogs*, by Nic Bishop (Scholastic); *What to Do About Alice?*, by Barbara Kerley, illustrated by Edwin Fotheringham (Scholastic)

• • • The Lee Bennett Hopkins Poetry Award • • •

The Lee Bennett Hopkins Poetry Award, established in 1993 and administered by Penn State University, is given annually to a living American poet for a volume of poetry, either an original collection or an anthology. In 1999, the Penn State University group decided to choose honor books for the award.

1993

Sing to the Sun, by Ashley Bryan (McElderry)

1994

Spirit Walker, by Nancy Wood (Doubleday)

1995

Beast Feast, by Douglas Florian (Greenwillow)

1996

Dance with Me, by Barbara Juster Esbensen (HarperCollins)

1997

Voices from the Wild, by David Bouchard (Chronicle)

1998

The Great Frog Race, by Kristine O'Connell George (Clarion)

1999

The Other Side: Shorter Poems, by Angela Johnson (Orchard)
HONOR BOOK: *A Crack in the Clouds*, by Constance Levy (McElderry)

2000

What Have You Lost?, edited by Naomi Shihab Nye (Greenwillow)
HONOR BOOKS: *An Old Shell*, by Tony Johnston (Farrar, Straus & Giroux); *The Rainbow Hand*, by Janet S. Wong (McElderry)

2001

Light Gathering Poems, edited by Liz Rosenberg (Holt)
HONOR BOOK: *Stone Bench in an Empty Park*, edited by Paul Janeczko (Orchard)

2002

Pieces: A Year in Poems and Quilts, by Anna Grossnickle Hines (Greenwillow)
HONOR BOOKS: *A Humble Life: Plain Poems*, by Linda Oatman High, illustrated by Bill Farnsworth (Eerdmans); *A Poke in the I: A Collection of Concrete Poems*, by Paul Janeczko, illustrated by Chris Raschka (Candlewick); *Short Takes: Fast-Break Basketball Poetry*, by Charles R. Smith Jr. (Dutton)

2003

Splash! Poems of Our Watery World, by Constance Levy, illustrated by David Soman (Orchard)
HONOR BOOKS: *Girl Coming in for a Landing: A Novel in Poems*, by April Halprin Wayland, illustrated by Elaine Clayton (Knopf); *Becoming Joe DiMaggio*, by Maria Testa (Candlewick); *The Song Shoots out of My Mouth*, by Jaime Adoff, illustrated by Martin French (Dutton)

2004

The Wishing Bone and Other Poems, by Stephen Mitchell, illustrated by Tom Pohrt (Candlewick)
HONOR BOOKS: *Animal Sense*, by Diane Ackerman, illustrated by Peter Sís (Knopf); *Blues Journey*, by Walter Dean Myers, illustrated by Christopher Myers (Holiday House); *The Pond God and Other Stories*, by Samuel Jay Keyser, illustrated by Robert Shetterly (Front Street); *The Way a Door Closes*, by Hope Anita Smith, illustrated by Shane W. Evans (Holt)

2005

Here in Harlem, by Walter Dean Myers (Holiday House)
HONOR BOOKS: *Is This Forever, or What?: Poems and Paintings from Texas*, by Naomi Shihab Nye (Greenwillow); *Creature Carnival*, by Marilyn Singer (Hyperion)

2006

Song of the Water Boatman & Other Pond Poems, by Joyce Sidman (HMC)
HONOR BOOKS: *A Maze Me*, Naomi Shihab Nye (Greenwillow); *A Wreath for Emmett Till*, by Marilyn Nelson (Houghton Mifflin)

2007

Jazz, by Walter Dean Myers (Harcourt)
HONOR BOOKS: *Behold the Bold Umbrellaphant and Other Poems*, by Jack Prelutsky (Greenwillow); *The Braid*, by Helen Frost (Farrar, Strauss, and Giroux); *Tour America*, by Diane Siebert (Chronicle)

2008

Birmingham—1963, by Carole Boston Weatherford (Wordsong)
HONOR BOOKS: *Blue Lipstick*, by John Grandits (Clarion); *This Is Just to Say*, by Joyce Sidman (Houghton Mifflin)

How to Update Current Listings and Find Other Awards

There are almost two hundred different awards given for children's and adolescent books; each has its own unique selection process and criteria. Some awards are chosen by adults, some by children, and some by young adults; some are international, some state or regional; some are for a lifetime of work, some for one book. We used the comprehensive listing of various award winners in *Children's Books: Awards and Prizes*, published by the Children's Book Council. This publication is updated periodically. We also used websites of professional organizations for the most up-to-date information: www.ala.org, www.reading.org, and www.ncte.org, among others.

Resources

• • • Book Selection Aids • • •

Adventuring with Books: Grades Pre-K–6 (13th edition), edited by Amy A. McClure and Janice V. Kristo (National Council of Teachers of English, 2002). A comprehensive list of books selected for their merit and potential use in the classroom. Approximately two thousand new books are annotated with several hundred from previous editions listed by genre. New editions are prepared periodically.

Best Science and Technology Reference Books for Young People, edited by H. Robert Malinowsky (Greenwood, 1991). Reviews science and technology resources and recommends grade levels for sci-tech reference books.

Books to Help Children Cope with Separation and Loss (4th edition), compiled by Masha Kabakow Rudman, Kathleen Dunne Gagne, and Joanne E. Bernstein (Bowker, 1993). 514 pages. Discussion of bibliotherapy with annotated lists of books grouped by category, such as adoption, divorce, and disabilities.

Children's Books: Awards and Prizes, compiled and edited by the Children's Book Council (1996). 497 pages. A comprehensive list of honors awarded to children's books. Awards chosen by adults and children are grouped by state, national, and international designations.

Children's Books fror Other Countries, edited by Carl M. Tomlinson (Scarecrow Press, 1998). An annotated bibliography of more than seven hundred titles for children, containing both translated books and books from English-speaking countries other than the United States, published between 1950 and 1996.

Children's Books in Print (Bowker, annual). A comprehensive index of all children's books in print at time of publication. Author, title, and illustrator indexes give pertinent publishing information. A directory of publishers and addresses is included.

Children's Catalog (Wilson, annual). A comprehensive catalog classified by Dewey decimal system, with nonfiction, fiction, short stories, and easy books. Five-year cumulations and annual supplements available.

Children's Literature Review (Gale Research). Articles about authors and topics of interest with excerpts from reviews of the works of each author. Since 1976, new volumes have been added periodically.

Continuum Encyclopedia of Children's Literature, edited by Bernice E. Cullinan and Diane G. Person (Giniger/Continuum International, 2005). A comprehensive collection of author and illustrator biographies, and topic and genre entries about children's literature in the major English-speaking countries.

Elementary School Library Collection (25th edition), edited by Linda Homa (Bro-Dart, 2000). A comprehensive bibliography of print and nonprint materials for school media collections. Dewey decimal subject classification, age level, and brief annotations.

For Reading Out Loud!, by Elizabeth Segel and Margaret Mary Kimmel (Bantam Dell, 1991). A guide to selecting books for sharing with young people and techniques for sharing them. Subject, title, and author index.

Hey! Listen to This: Stories to Read Aloud, edited by Jim Trelease (Penguin, 1992). Selections from literature to read to primary-grade children. Trelease adds intriguing background information about each excerpt.

Jewish Children's Books: How to Choose Them, How to Use Them, by Marcia Posner (Hadassah, 1986). 48 pages. Summaries, themes, discussion guides, questions and activities, and further resources are given for more than thirty books.

Kaleidoscope: A Multicultural Booklist for Grades K–8 (4th edition), edited by Nancy Hansen-Krening, Elaine M. Aoki, and Donald T. Mizokawa (National Council of Teachers of English, 2003). Hundreds of fiction and nonfiction texts for elementary and middle-school students, featuring culturally diverse populations.

Library Services for Hispanic Children: A Guide for Public and School Librarians, edited by Adela Artola Allen (Oryx Press, 1987). 201 pages. Articles on professional issues related to library service for Hispanic children. Annotated bibliographies of children's books in English about Hispanics, recent noteworthy children's books in Spanish, computer software, and resources about Hispanic culture for librarians.

The New Read-Aloud Handbook (5th edition), by Jim Trelease (Penguin, 2001). An enthusiastic argument for why we should read to children, techniques for reading aloud, and a treasury of more than a thousand books that work well as read-alouds.

Newbery and Caldecott Medal Books: 1986–2000: A Comprehensive Guide to the Winners (Horn Book/Association for Library Service to Children, 2001). A continuing collaboration features book summaries, selected excerpts, reviews, acceptance speeches, and biographical essays about the winners.

Pass the Poetry, Please (3rd edition), by Lee Bennett Hopkins (HarperCollins, 1998). A well-informed author describes engaging interviews with outstanding poets. Hopkins includes comments from interviews and insights into the poets' work, and suggests ways to use poetry with children.

Read to Me: Raising Kids Who Love to Read (2nd edition), by Bernice E. Cullinan (Scholastic, 2006). A book that encourages parents to make reading a central part of children's lives and shows them how to do it.

Selected Jewish Children's Books, compiled by Marcia Posner (Jewish Book Council, 1991). Annotated list of books containing Jewish content and values, categorized by topic and age levels.

Subject Guide to Children's Books in Print (Bowker, annual). Approximately 140,000 titles are grouped under seven thousand subject categories. This indispensable reference helps you find books on specific topics.

Subject Index to Poetry for Children and Young People, compiled by Violet Sell (Core Collection Books, 1982). 1,035 pages. An index of poetry organized by subject with a code for title and author.

With Women's Eyes: Visitors to the New World, 1775–1918, edited by Marion Tinling (University of Oklahoma Press, 1993). 204 pages. Twenty-seven European women who visited America between 1775 and 1918 tell about their experiences.

The World Through Children's Books, edited by Susan Stan (Scarecrow, 2002). An annotated bibliography of more than seven hundred titles for children containing both translated books and books from English-speaking countries other than the United States, and including books written by authors residing in the United States but set in other countries, published between 1996 and 2000.

General Reference Books about Authors and Illustrators

Author Talk: Conversations with Judy Blume, Bruce Brooks, Karen Cushman, Russell Freedman, Lee Bennett Hopkins, James Howe, Johanna Hurwitz, E. L. Konigsburg, Lois Lowry, Ann M. Martin, Nicholasa Mohr, Gary Paulsen, Jon Scieszka, Seymour Simon, and Laurence Yep, by Leonard S. Marcus (Simon & Schuster, 2000). Interviews with well-known children's writers.

Caldecott Medal Books: 1938–1957, by Bertha Mahony Miller and Elinor Whitney Field (Horn Book, 1958). Artists' acceptance speeches and biographical articles of the Caldecott Medal winners. See also more recent editions.

Celebrating Children's Books, edited by Betsy Hearne and Marilyn Kaye (Lothrop, Lee & Shepard, 1981). Articles about their craft by the foremost authors writing for children today. The essays in this collection appear in honor of Zena Sutherland.

Children's Book Illustration and Design (Vol. 1, 1992; Vol. 2, 1998), edited by Julie Cummins (PBC International). Each book is a showcase for the work of about eighty illustrators of children's books selected by a knowledgeable critic.

From Writers to Students: The Pleasures and Pains of Writing, edited by Jerry Weiss (International Reading Association, 1979). 113 pages. Interviews with nineteen noted authors who reveal the inside story on their writing, including Judy Blume, Mollie Hunter, Milton Meltzer, Mary Rodgers, and Laurence Yep.

Illustrators of Children's Books: 1744–1945, edited by Bertha E. Mahony, Louise Payson Latimer, and Beulah Folmsbee (Horn Book, 1947). 527 pages. *Illustrators of Children's Books: 1946–1956*, edited by Bertha Mahony Miller, Ruth Hill Viguers, and Marcia Dalphin (Horn Book, 1958). 229 pages. *Illustrators of Children's Books: 1957–1966*, edited by Lee Kingman, Joanna Foster, and Ruth Giles Lontoft (Horn Book, 1968). 295 pages. *Illustrators of Children's Books: 1967–1976*, edited by Lee Kingman, Grace Allen Hogarth, and Harriet Quimby (Horn Book, 1978). 290 pages. *Illustrators of Children's Books: 1977–1986*, edited by Lee Kingman (Horn Book, 1987). Biographical sketches and discussion of artists' techniques.

Meet the Authors and Illustrators, by Deborah Kovacs and James Preller (Scholastic, 1991). Sixty creators of favorite children's books talk about their work.

Newbery and Caldecott Medal Books: 1956–1965, edited by Lee Kingman (Horn Book, 1965). 300 pages. *Newbery and Caldecott Medal Books: 1966–1975*, edited by Lee Kingman (Horn Book, 1975). *Newbery and Caldecott Medal Books: 1976–1985*, edited by Lee Kingman (Horn Book, 1987). *Newbery Medal Books: 1922–1955*, edited by Bertha Mahony Miller and Elinor Whitney Field (Horn Book, 1955). Acceptance speeches and biographical sketches about the winners.

Oxford Companion to Children's Literature, compiled by Humphrey Carpenter and Mari Prichard (Oxford University Press, 1984). Includes nearly two thousand entries, more than nine hundred of which are biographical sketches of authors, illustrators, printers, and publishers. Other entries cover topic and genre issues and plot summaries of major works.

Pauses: Autobiographical Reflections of 101 Creators of Children's Books, by Lee Bennett Hopkins (HarperCollins, 1995). Biographical information and excerpts from interviews with authors and illustrators.

Secret Gardens, by Humphrey Carpenter (Houghton Mifflin, 1985). A book about the authors who wrote during the years called the golden age of children's literature in the late nineteenth and early twentieth centuries.

Something about the Author (Gale Research). In more than 120 volumes, extensive biographical information, photographs, publication records, awards received, and quotations about thousands of authors and illustrators of children's books.

Speaking for Ourselves: Autobiographical Sketches by Notable Authors of Books for Young Adults, edited by Donald R. Gallo (National Council of Teachers of English, 1990). Includes brief first-person statements from writers about writing and a bibliography for each writer.

Speaking for Ourselves, Too, edited by Donald R. Gallo (National Council of Teachers of English, 1993). More autobiographical sketches by notable authors of books for adolescents. Also includes brief first-person statements from writers about writing and a bibliography for each writer.

Speaking of Poets: Interviews with Poets Who Write for Children and Young Adults, edited by Jeffrey S. Copeland (National Council of Teachers of English, 1993). *Speaking of Poets: Interviews with Poets Who Write for Children and Young Adults 2*, edited by Jeffrey S. and Vicki L. Copeland (National Council of Teachers of English, 1994). Brief biographies and substantial interviews, followed by individual bibliographies.

Talking with Artists (Vol. 1, 1992, Vol. 2, 1995, Vol. 3, 1999), edited by Pat Cummings (Bradbury). Children's book illustrators talk about their work.

Periodicals about Children's Literature

Book Links: Connecting Books, Libraries, and Classrooms, American Library Association, published six times a year. Features booklists, interviews, teaching guides, and theme-related bibliographies to help teachers and librarians bring literature to children in ways that make connections across the curriculum.

Bookbird: A Journal of International Children's Literature, edited by Siobhán Parkinson and Valerie Coghlan; past editor-in-chief Meena G. Khorana. A refereed journal published quarterly by the International Board on Books for Young People, Nonnenweg 12 Postfach, CH-4004 Basel, Switzerland. The journal provides a forum to exchange experience and information among readers and writers in fifty nations of the world. Includes analyses of children's literature in particular regions—for example, children's literature of Latin America.

Booklist, American Library Association, published biweekly September through August, once each in July and August. Reviews children's, adolescent, and adult books and nonprint materials. Periodic bibliographies on a specific subject, reference tools, and commentary on issues are invaluable.

Bulletin of the Center for Children's Books, Graduate School of Library and Information Science of the University of Illinois at Urbana-Champaign, distributed by the University of Illinois Press, published monthly, except August. One of the few journals to include critical starred reviews of books rated as * (books of special distinction), R (recommended), Ad (additional), M (marginal), NR (not recommended), SpC (special collection), SpR (special reader). Curriculum use and developmental values are assigned when appropriate.

CBC Features. Children's Book Council, published semiannually. A newsletter about current issues and events, free and inexpensive materials, materials for Children's Book Week, topical bibliographies, and essays by publishers and authors or illustrators.

Children and Libraries: The Journal of the Association for Library Service to Children. Articles of interest to teachers and librarians on current issues, specialized bibliographies, acceptance speeches by the Newbery and Caldecott Award winners, conference proceedings, and organizational news.

Children's Literature Association Quarterly. Children's Literature Association. Book reviews and articles on British and American children's literature, research, teaching children's literature, theater, and conference proceedings. Special sections on current topics of interest, poetry, censorship, awards, and announcements.

The Horn Book Magazine, published bimonthly. A review journal with intelligent commentary by the editor and invited writers, and articles by creators of children's books, publishers, critics, teachers, and librarians. Ratings include starred reviews for outstanding books and comprehensive reviews of recommended books. Also includes Newbery and Caldecott acceptance speeches, biographical sketches of winners, and Boston Globe–Horn Book Award winners. Announces children's literature conferences and events. Cumulative indexes with ratings for all books published appear in *The Horn Book Guide* twice a year.

Language Arts. A journal published monthly from September through May by the National Council of Teachers of English. A book review column reviews current recommended books for children. Profiles on authors and illustrators; articles on using books in the classroom, response to literature, and writing as an outgrowth of reading literature.

The New York Times Book Review. Includes occasional columns of reviews written by authors, illustrators, or reviewers. Special section in spring and fall features children's books; annual list of the ten best illustrated books of the year.

Publishers Weekly. Published by Reed Elsvier with a spring and fall special edition on children's books. Diane Roback is senior children's book editor, Jennifer M. Brown is forecasts editor, and Joy Bean is associate editor. Both positive and negative reviews of books and news articles of interest to publishers, teachers, librarians, and authors. Interviews with authors, illustrators, and publishers are regular features.

The Reading Teacher. International Reading Association, published nine times a year. A column of reviews of current children's books is a regular feature. Articles appear on the use of books in the classroom, special bibliographies,

cross-cultural studies, and research using children's books in reading programs.

Scholastic Instructor, edited by Terry Cooper, Scholastic, published eight times a year. Teachers and librarians write feature articles about trends, new books, and authors and illustrators of note. Bernice E. Cullinan is editor of the primary-grade poetry column; Paul Janeczko is editor of the intermediate-grade poetry column. Conducts an annual poetry writing contest for children.

School Library Journal. Published eleven times a year. Includes articles on current issues and reviews of children's books written by practicing librarians. Information is given about conferences and library services. Also includes an annual "Best Books of the Year" column and a cumulative index of starred reviews.

School Library Media Research: Refereed Research Journal of the American Association of School Librarians. Published online at www.ala.org. Includes research articles on censorship, using books in the classroom, research, library services, and current issues.

Science and Children. Published eight times a year by the National Science Teachers Association. Monthly column of reviews of informational books on science topics, plus an annual list of recommended books chosen by NSTA/ Children's Book Council Liaison Committee.

Young Adult Library Services: The Journal of the Young Adult Library Services Association. Articles of interest to teachers and librarians on current issues, specialized bibliographies, acceptance speeches by the Printz Award winner, conference proceedings, and organizational news.

Note: Each professional organization and journal publisher has an online website. Check the Internet for listings of current events and features.

Publishers, Book Clubs, Organizations, and Magazines

• • • Publishers • • •

Harry N. Abrams, Inc.
www.abramsbooks.com

Addison-Wesley and Benjamin Cummings
www.aw-bc.com

Africa World Press and The Red Sea Press
www.africanworld.com

Arte Público Press
www.arte.uh.edu

Atheneum (*see* Simon & Schuster)

Avon Books (*see* HarperCollins)

Bantam Doubleday Dell Books for Young Readers (*see* Random House)

Black Classic Press
www.blackclassic.com

Blue Sky Press (*see* Scholastic)

Boyds Mills Press
www.boydsmillspress.com

Bradbury Press (see Simon & Schuster)

Candlewick Press
www.candlewick.com

Carolrhoda Books (*see* Lerner)

Cavendish Children's Books
www.marshallcavendish.com

Children's Book Press (*see* Scholastic)

Clarion (*see* Houghton Mifflin)

Cricket Books
www.cricketmag.com

Crown (*see* Random House)

Delacorte Press (*see* Random House)

Dial Books for Young Readers (*see* Penguin Putnam)

Disney Books
http://disney.go.com/disneybooks/index.html

DK Publishing
www.dk.com

Doubleday (*see* Random House)

Dutton (*see* Penguin Putnam)

Wm. B. Eerdmans Publishing
www.eerdmans.com/youngreaders

Farrar, Straus & Giroux
www.fsgbooks.com

Phyllis Fogelman Books (*see* Penguin Putnam)

Four Winds Press (*see* Simon & Schuster)

Front Street Books
www.frontstreetbooks.com

David R. Godine Publisher
www.godine.com

Golden Books Children's Publishing Group (*see* Random House)

Greenwillow (*see* HarperCollins)

Grolier Publishing (*see* Scholastic)

Grosset & Dunlap (*see* Penguin Putnam)

Groundwood Books
www.groundwoodbooks.com

Hachette Book Group
www.hachettebookgroup.com

Harcourt Trade Publishers
www.harcourtbooks.com

HarperCollins Children's Books
www.harperchildrens.com

HarperTempest (*see* HarperCollins)

Henry Holt & Co.
www.henryholt.com

Holiday House
www.holidayhouse.com

Houghton Mifflin
www.hmco.com

Hyperion Books for Children
www.hyperionbooksforchildren.com

Jewish Publication Society
www.jewishpub.org

Jump at the Sun (*see* Hyperion)

Just Us Books
www.justusbooks.com

The Kane Press
www.kanepress.com

Kane/Miller Book Publishers
www.kanemiller.com

Kids Can Press Ltd.
www.kidscanpress.com

Alfred A. Knopf (see Random House)

Lee & Low Books
www.leeandlow.com

Lerner Publications
www.lernerbooks.com

Lippincott (see HarperCollins)

Little, Brown and Company (see Hachette Book Group)

Lothrop, Lee & Shepard (see HarperCollins)

Margaret McElderry Books (see Simon & Schuster)

The Millbrook Press (see Lerner Publications Co.)

Mondo Publishing
www.mondopub.com

Morrow (see HarperCollins)

North-South Books
www.northsouth.com

Orchard Books (see Scholastic)

Richard C. Owen Publishers
www.rcowen.com

Oxford University Press
www.oup.com/us

Pantheon (see Random House)

Peachtree Publishers Ltd.
www.peachtree-online.com

Penguin Putnam
www.penguinputnam.com

Philomel Books (see Penguin Putnam)

Piñata Books (see Arte Público Press)

Pleasant Company Publications
www.pleasantcopublications.com

Rand McNally
www.randmcnally.com

Random House
www.randomhouse.com

Rizzoli/Universe International Publications
www.rizzoliusa.com

Scholastic
www.scholastic.com

Sierra Club Books
www.sierraclub.org/books

Silver Moon Press
www.silvermoonpress.com

Simon & Schuster
www.simonsays.com

Third World Press
www.thirdworldpressinc.com

Tristan Publishing (formerly Waldman House Press)
2300 Louisiana Avenue North, Suite B,
Golden Valley, MN 55427

Viking (see Penguin Putnam)

Walker & Co.
www.walkerbooks.com

Frederick Warne (see Penguin Putnam)

Franklin Watts Inc.
www.wattspub.co.uk

Albert Whitman & Co.
www.awhitmanco.com

Winston-Derek Publishers Group
P.O. Box 90883
Nashville, TN 37203

Wordsong (see Boyds Mills Press)

• • • Paperback Book Clubs • • •

Scholastic Book Clubs
www.scholastic.com

TrollCarnival Book Clubs (see Scholastic)
www.trollcarnival.com

Trumpet Book Club (see Scholastic)

• • • Professional Organizations • • •

American Library Association
www.ala.org

Children's Book Council
www.cbcbooks.org

International Reading Association
www.reading.org

National Council of Teachers of English
www.ncte.org

• • • Children's Magazines and Newspapers • • •

Chickadee
Age range: 6–9. Introduces the world of science, nature, and technology to young children through engaging stories and well-developed illustrations.
www.owlkids.com/chickadee

Cicada
Age range: 9–18. A literary magazine for teenagers with fiction and poetry written by adults and teens.
www.cricketmag.com

Click: Opening Windows for Young Minds
Age range: 3–7. Published ten times a year by the publishers of *Cricket Magazine* and *Smithsonian Magazine*, and contains 36 pages that visualize a child's world.
www.cricketmag.com

Cobblestone
Age range: 8–14. This is a magazine of American history containing stories of the past for middle school students.
www.cobblestonepub.com

Creative Kids
Age range: 8–14. Games, art, stories, poetry, and opinion by and for kids. Creative Kids Magazine, Prufrock Press, 5926 Balcones Dr., Suite 220, Austin, TX 78731

Cricket
Age range: 8–14. Contains quality literature in folktales, fantasy, science fiction, history, biographies, poems, science, and sports stories.
www.cricketmag.com

Current Events
Age range: 11–16. Contains articles on current events that students in

social studies classes in middle schools, and junior-high, and early senior-high schools can understand. www.weeklyreader.com

Current Science

Age range: 11–16. Filled with current science discoveries and issues that students in middle schools, and junior-high, and early senior-high schools can understand. www.weeklyreader.com

Dream/Girl

Age range: 8–18. Established in 1997 to provide girls with arts and literary information. www.dgarts.com

Faces

Age range: 8–14. Anthropologists of the American Museum of Natural History advise editors about the lifestyles, beliefs, and customs of cultures throughout the world. www.cobblestonepub.com

Highlights for Children

Age range: 2–12. The flagship general-interest magazine that combines learning and fun in 42 pages filled with stories, poems, information, hidden pictures, cartoons, and crafts. www.highlights.com

Junior Scholastic

Age range: Grades 6–8. A classroom magazine published eighteen times during the school year that features social studies events and issues. www.scholastic.com

Ladybug

Age range: 2–6. Contains a collection of stories, poems, songs, and games for young children. A parent's companion suggests additional activities, crafts, and books. www.cricketmag.com

Merlyn's Pen: The National Magazine of Student Writing

Age range: Grades 6–9. Published four times a year, the magazine contains stories, poems, and expository pieces written by teens in the United States. www.merlynspen.org

The Mini Page

Age range: 5–12. A four-page educational newspaper inserted in five hundred newspapers, often part of Newspaper in Education Week programs. Universal Press Syndicate, 4520 Main Street, Kansas City, MO 64111-7701

National Geographic World

Age Range: 8–14. Contains natural history, science, diverse cultural groups, and outdoor adventure captured in excellent photographs and engaging writing. www.nationalgeographic.com

Odyssey

Age range: 10–16. Features current events about space exploration and astronomy in each 48-page, fully illustrated, theme-related issue. www.odysseymagazine.com

Owl: The Discovery Magazine for Kids

Age range: 8 and older. Each 32-page issue contains nature, science, animals, technology, games, puzzles, pull-out poster, and a comic strip. www.owlkids.com

Ranger Rick

Age range: 6–12. Each 48-page issue contains nature stories, information, poems, animal life histories, natural history, riddles, crafts, and activities in well-illustrated pages. Animal lovers are regular readers. www.nwf.org

Science World

Age range: Grades 7–10. This 24-page news magazine is published biweekly during the school year. It features current research in life, earth, astronomy, space, physical, and health sciences. www.scholastic.com

Sesame Street

Age range: 2–6. This appealing magazine features stories, games, and activities to introduce the alphabet, numbers, and problem solving. Its stories reinforce social skills using

characters from the television program (free with *Parenting* magazine). Sesame Street Magazine, Box 52000, Boulder, CO 80321-2000

Skipping Stones

Age range: 8–18. Published bimonthly, this nonprofit children's magazine celebrates cultural richness with stories, articles, and photos from all over the world. www.skippingstones.org

Spider

Age range: 6–9. Intended for independent readers, the magazine contains stories, poems, informational articles, multicultural tales, activities, and well-illustrated pages that appeal to primary-grade readers. www.cricketmag.com

Spire Magazine

Age range: 8–18. A biannual magazine dedicated to publishing traditionally marginalized and young writers and artists. www.spirepress.org

Sports Illustrated for Kids

Age range: 8–14. This magazine, modeled on its adult predecessor, introduces young readers to professional and amateur sports events and sports heroes. www.sikids.com

Stone Soup: The Magazine by Young Writers and Artists

Age range: 6–14. This magazine publishes poems, stories, art, and expository pieces written by children. www.stonesoup.com.

Storyworks Magazine

Age range: Grades 3–5. Good stories, poems, plays, nonfiction, word games, author interviews, news briefs about books, and student-written book reviews excite readers and teachers. www.scholastic.com

Teen Voices

Age range: 13–18. Written by and about teenage and young adult women. www.teenvoices.com

Time for Kids
Age range: Grades 4–6. This weekly classroom news magazine presents current events in language that intermediate-grade students can understand. A teacher's edition suggests ways to extend the learning. www.timeforkids.com

U*S* Kids
Age range: 6–11. Stories, articles, and activities in this 42-page full-color magazine interest children in their world and the people who live in it. Games, interactive activities, and puzzles with a historical focus combine learning and pleasure. www.cbhi.org/cbhi/magazines

Weekly Reader
Age range: Grades K–6. This graded series of classroom newspapers contains current news, activities, and recreational reading. www.weeklyreader.com

Your Big Backyard
Age range: 8–12. Outstanding photography and illustrations attract readers to this nature and conservation magazine. www.nwf.org

Zillions: The Consumer Report for Kids
Age range: 8–14. The place kids learn how to determine when a bargain is a bargain; they become wise consumers (online only). www.zillions.com

• • • Reference • • •

Magazines for Kids and Teens: A Resource for Teachers, Parents, Librarians, and Kids. Editor Don Stoll. Foreword by Jim Trelease. Published by International Reading Association and EdPress Association, 1997.

Glossary of Terms

Alliteration The repetition of initial consonant sounds at close intervals.

Allusion A reference to a literary work, character, or setting contained in another literary work.

Assonance The repetition of vowel sounds at close intervals.

Biography The story of an actual person's life, or part of a life history, written by someone other than the subject.

Case The front and back fixed covers of a book, usually thick cardboard or cloth-covered board.

Censorship The act of limiting access to books and other sources of information in order to control others.

Character A personality in literature.

Characterization Means by which the author establishes the credibility of a personality created by words, usually through physical description, character's actions, words, thought, and feelings

Climax Peak of action that brings about resolution of the conflict.

Composition The way in which an artist achieves unity in art through balance, repetition, variety, emphasis, and spatial order.

Connotation The private, individual resonance of a particular word.

Consonance The repetition at close intervals of two or more consonants in combination with different vowels.

Contemporary realistic fiction Stories whose settings, characters, and events are plausible in today's world.

Convention Standard formulas and elements, often found in folklore.

Crossover book A book published for one audience and read by another.

Dedication page A page that contains a note by the author and sometimes illustrator, honoring some person or persons.

Denotation The public, shared meaning of a word.

Double-page spreads Art that extends across both pages of a particular opening.

Dust jacket A removable cover that surrounds the front and back fixed covers (the case) of a book, folded inside at the front and back to keep it in place.

End rhyme Poetic lines in which rhyming words appear at the end of the line.

Endpages or endpapers The inside of the front and back board cover, consisting of two parts: a pastedown (affixed to the inside back or front cover) and the flyleaf (the part of the endpage that is not pasted down).

End-stopped Poetic lines in which the grammatical sense is contained within a single line.

Epics A cycle of hero tales written in verse that center on a legendary hero.

Fables A brief tale, usually with animal characters, that presents an unambiguous moral.

Fairy tales Brief, fanciful folktales containing magic.

Fantasy Stories with worlds, characters, and/or events that could not exist in reality as we know it.

Figurative language Language that goes beyond the literal meaning of a word, usually by comparison with something else. Includes **simile, metaphor**, and **personification**.

Flap The part of the dust jacket that is folded inside the front and back covers (the case) of a book.

Flyleaf The part of the endpage that is not pasted down, opposite the **pastedown**.

Folklore Traditional stories from the oral tradition of the past.

Folksongs Songs that portray the values and life styles of those who created them

Folktales Brief, fanciful narratives, originally spoken rather than written, that convey a lesson.

Front matter All of the fine print about copyright, ISBN number, Library of Congress cataloguing data that appears in a book.

Genre Category of literature.

Gutter The middle of the spread where the pages are bound.

Hagiography Excessive praise or erroneous attribution of good qualities to a biographical subject.

Half-title page A page containing only the title of the book.

Hero tales Stories of the courageous deeds of humans, often portrayed as superhuman, as they struggle against one another, gods, or monsters.

Historical fiction Stories whose realistic settings, characters, and events reconstruct life in the past.

Hue The various rainbow of colors.

Illustrated books Books in which visual images add interest to a text but are clearly subordinated to the words.

Imagery Use of words that arrest the senses.

Improvisation Dramatizing beyond the basic story line, based on inferences about character and plot.

Intensity The relative use of shade and tint in pure hues.

Interpretation An oral, dramatic reading of a story.

Intertextual connections Linking books to other books and types of text (film, music, etc.).

Legends Hero tales that are not technically epics.

Library edition An edition created especially for libraries in which the dust jacket is often omitted.

Line A mark on paper or a place where different colors meet.

Link rhyme When the final word or syllable of one line rhymes with the first word or syllable of the second rhyme.

Medium The material used in the production of a work. Plural is **media**.

Memoir Interpretive accounts of facts and events in the life of the author.

Metaphor An inferred comparison between two unlike entities.

Meter The measure of metrical language in poetry.

Motif Recurring element in literature; a conventional situation, device, or incident; prevailing idea or design.

Mythology Tales that explain natural phenomena, the deities, and human behavior, expressing the beliefs of ancient cultures.

Narrative A story; the recounting of events in temporal order.

Nonfiction Informational books that explain a subject or concept using facts.

Nursery rhymes Brief, fanciful rhythmic verses, originally oral, for very young children.

Onomatopoeia Words created from natural sounds associated with the object or action designated.

Opening The new image that is visible as each page is turned.

Pantomime Conveying a story or meaning solely through facial expressions, shrugs, gestures, and other body language.

Pastedown The part of the endpage that adheres to the cover, opposite the flyleaf

Personification Representation of a thing or abstraction as possessing human traits.

Picturebooks Books in which meaning is created through the unity, harmony, or synergy of the words and illustrations.

Plot Sequence and relationship of events.

Poetry Expression of imaginative thoughts and perceptions through condensed language.

Point of view The voice through which a story is told or concept explored.

Pourquoi stories Brief, often humorous tales that explain natural phenomena.

Publishing information Front matter that appears at the back of a book.

Readers' theatre Reading aloud student-generated scripts created from stories.

Recto The right-hand page of a folded sheet or bound book.

Re-enacting Usually following a read-aloud session, with only brief planning children dramatize the story they have just heard.

Resolution Action following climax; solution of the central problem.

Rhyme Words whose ending sounds are alike.

Rhythm The recurrence of specific beats of stressed and unstressed syllables.

Role-playing Assuming a role and interacting with others in role to explore specific aspects of stories.

Run-on line When the grammatical sense of one line of poetry carries over into the next; also known as enjambment.

Saturated Colors that are intense rather than subdued.

Science fiction Stories based on extending scientific possibilities to their logical outcomes.

Setting Time and place of story events.

Shade Color created with the addition of black to the pure hue.

Shape An area or form with a definite outline.

Shape poems Poetry in which the words are arranged in a shape that reflects the meaning.

Signature A bundle of pages that are sewn or pasted together, usually in numbers of 8 (or 16, if both sides are counted). The standard-size picturebook contains two signatures, or 32 pages.

Simile A comparison between two unlike entities using "like" or "as."

Social and cultural dimensions of reading The social and cultural milieu of the author, the reader, and the act of reading.

Soft-cover edition A paperback edition containing no dust jacket and often no endpages.

Stock response Evaluation of a book solely in terms of one's own limited view of the world.

Style How an author writes; the vocabulary, syntax, and structure of a text.

Tall tales Brief, fanciful narratives that exaggerate human accomplishments.

Technique The method artists use to create art with the chosen medium.

Theme Central or dominating idea that holds the work together. In nonfiction, it may be the topic; in poetry, fiction, and drama, it is an abstract concept that is made vivid through character, plot, and image.

Tint Color created with the addition of white (or water in the case of watercolors or acrylics) to the pure hue.

Title page A page containing the title, the names of the author and illustrator, the name of the publisher, the city, and the date the book was published.

Trade edition The edition found in the children's section of a bookstore.

Transactional reading Reading in which the reader shapes the meaning in conjunction with the text.

Transformational reading Reading in which the reader's values, ideas, beliefs, or knowledge are changed as a result of that reading.

Trim size The overall size and proportion of a book.

Value The amount of light and dark in a color.

Verso The left-hand page of a folded sheet or bound book.

Word order In poetry, the arrangement of words.

Professional References

Alexander, L. (1970). Identifications and identities. *Wilson Library Bulletin, 45*(2), 144–148.

Anderson, Laurie Halse. www.writerlady.com, accessed December 15, 2008. (See Laurie Halse Anderson profile in Chapter 8.)

Apol, L. (1998). "But what does this have to do with kids?": Literary theory and children's literature in the teacher education classroom. *Journal of Children's Literature, 24*(2), 32–46.

Appelt, Kathi. (2002). *Poems from homeroom: A writer's place to start.* New York: Holt.

Atwell, N. (1998). *In the middle: New understandings about writing, reading, and learning.* Portsmouth, NH: Heinemann.

_____. (2007). *The reading zone: How to help kids become skilled, passionate, habitual, critical readers.* New York: Scholastic.

Avi. Newbery Medal acceptance speech, Toronto, June 22, 2003.

Bader, B. (2003a). Multiculturalism takes root. *The Horn Book Magazine, 79,* 143–162.

_____. (2003b). Multiculturalism in the mainstream. *The Horn Book Magazine, 79,* 265–291.

_____. (2006). Krik, krik, krik: How Aardema & Co. attuned us to African folklore. *The Horn Book Magazine, 82,* 651–658.

Baker, D. F. (2006). Special effects: What makes a good fantasy? *The Horn Book Magazine, 82,* 621–625.

_____. (2007). Why is the Cold War hot? *The Horn Book Magazine, 83,* 655–660.

Banks, J. A., & Banks, C.A.M. (1993). *Multicultural education: Issues and perspectives* (Third edition). Boston: Allyn & Bacon.

Beach, R., Thein, A. H., & Parks, D. (2007). Perspective-taking as transformative practice in teaching multicultural literature to white students. *English Journal, 97*(2), 54–60.

_____. (2008). *High school students' competing social worlds: Negotiating identities and allegiances in response to multicultural literature.* New York: Erlbaum.

Benton, M. (1984). The methodology vacuum in teaching literature. *Language Arts, 61,* 265–275.

_____. (1992). *Secondary worlds: Literature teaching and the visual arts.* Buckingham, UK: Open University Press.

Benton, M., & Benton, P. (2008). Forty years on: Touchstones now. *Children's Literature in Education, 39,* 135–140.

Bishop, R. S. (Ed.). (1994). *Kaleidoscope: A multicultural booklist for grades K–8.* Urbana, IL: National Council of Teachers of English.

_____. (1997). Multicultural literature for children: Making informed choices. In V. J. Harris (Ed.), *Teaching multicultural literature in grades K–8* (pp. 37–54). Norwood, MA: Christopher-Gordon.

_____. (2007). *Free within ourselves: The development of African American children's literature.* Portsmouth, NH: Heinemann.

Blos, J. (1992). Perspectives on historical fiction. In R. Ammon & M. Tunnell (Eds.), *The story of ourselves: Teaching history through children's literature* (pp. 11–17). Portsmouth, NH: Heinemann.

Bogdan, D. (1990). In and out of love with literature: Response and the aesthetics of total form. In D. Bogdan & S. Straw (Eds.), *Beyond communication: Reading comprehension and criticism* (pp. 109–137). Portsmouth, NH: Heinemann.

Booth, D., & Moore, B. (1988). *Poems please! Sharing poetry with children.* Markham, Ontario: Pembroke.

Botkin, B. A. (1944). *A Treasury of American Folklore.* New York: Crown.

Britton, J. (1970). *Language and learning.* London: Penguin.

Brown, B. and Glass, M. (1991). *Important words: A book for poets and writers.* Portsmouth, N.H.: Boynton/Cook.

Bruchac, J. (1997). *Tell me a tale: A book about storytelling.* San Diego: Harcourt Brace.

Campbell, P. (2004). Vetting the verse novel. *The Horn Book Magazine, 80,* 611–616.

Carrington, V., & L. A. (2003). Reading homes and families: From postmodern to modern? In A. van Kleeck, S. A. Stahl, & E. B. Bauer (Eds.), *On reading books to children: Parents and teachers* (pp. 231–252). Mahwah, NJ: Lawrence Erlbaum.

Carter, B. (2005). Privacy please. *The Horn Book Magazine, 81,* 525–534.

Chatton, B. (1993). *Using poetry across the curriculum: A whole language approach.* Phoenix, Ariz.: Oryx.

Cherland, M. (1992). Gendered readings: Cultural restraints upon response to literature. *The New Advocate, 5,* 187–198.

Cochran-Smith, M. (1984). *The making of a reader.* Norwood, NJ: Ablex.

Coles, R. (1989). *The call of stories: Teaching and the moral imagination*. Boston: Houghton Mifflin.

Cooke, C. L. (2002). *The effects of scaffolding multicultural short stories on students' comprehension and attitudes*. Paper presented at the 51st Annual Meeting of the National Reading Conference, Miami, FL.

Cooper, S. (1996). *Dreams and wishes: Essays on writing for children* (pp. 57–71). New York: Simon & Schuster.

Corso, G. (1983). Comment. In P. B. Janeczko (Ed.), *Poetspeak* (p. 11). New York: Bradbury.

Cox, M. R. (1893). *Cinderella: Three hundred and forty-five variants*. New York: David Nutt/Folklore Society.

Crispin: The cross of lead. Teacher's guide. (2003). Hyperion Books for Children Lesson Plan Series. New York: Hyperion.

Crowell Junior Books. (n.d.). James Cross Giblin promotional brochure. New York.

Cullinan, B., Scala, M., Schroder, V., & Lovett, A. (1995). *Three voices: An invitation to poetry across the curriculum*. York, ME: Stenhouse.

Cummings, P. (Ed.). (1992). *Talking with artists* (Vol. 1). New York: Bradbury.

———. (Ed.). (1995). *Talking with artists* (Vol. 2). New York: Simon & Schuster.

Cummins, J. (2004). Accessing the international children's digital library. *The Horn Book Magazine, 80*, 145–151.

Cunningham A. E., & Stanovich, K. E. (1998). What reading does for the mind. *American Educator, Spring/Summer*, 8–15.

de la Mare, W. (1942). *Peacock pie*. London: Faber & Faber.

Denman, Gregory A. (1988). *When you've made it your own: Teaching poetry to young people*. Portsmouth, NH: Heinemann.

Dyson, A. H. (2003). *The brothers and sisters learn to write: Popular literacies in childhood and school culture*. New York: Teachers College Press.

Egoff, S. (1981). *Thursday's child: Trends and patterns in contemporary children's literature*. Chicago: American Library Association.

Eisner, Will. (2008). *Comics and sequential art*. New York: W. W. Norton

Enciso, P. (1994). Cultural identity and response to literature: Running lessons from Maniac McGee. *Language Arts, 71*, 524–533.

Esbensen, B. J. (1975). *A celebration of bees: Endless opportunities for inspiring children to write poetry*. Minneapolis, MN: Winston.

Farmer, N. (n.d.). *Meet the Writers*. www.barnesandnoble.com/writers. Accessed July 21, 2004.

Farmer, P. (1979). *Beginnings: Creation myths of the world*. New York: Atheneum.

Feitelsen, D., Kita, B., & Goldstein, Z. (1986). Effects of listening to series stories on first graders' comprehension and use of language. *Research in the Teaching of English, 20*, 339–356.

Fielding, L., Wilson, P. T., & Anderson, R. (1986). A new focus on free reading: The role of trade books in reading instruc-tion. In T. E. Raphael & R. E. Reynolds (Eds.), *The contexts of school-based literacy* (pp. 149–160). New York: Random House.

Fish, S. (1980). *Is there a text in this class? The authority of interpretive communities*. Cambridge, MA: Harvard University Press.

Fisher, C. J. & Natarella, M.A. (1982). Young children's preferences in poetry: A national survey of first-, second-, and third-graders. *Research in the Teaching of English, 16*(4), 339–354.

Fitzgerald, J., & Graves, M.F. (2004). *Scaffolding reading experiences for English language learners*. Norwood, MA: Christopher-Gordon.

Fletcher, R. (2002). *Poetry matters: Writing a poem from the inside out*. New York: HarperTrophy.

Fox, D., & Short, K. (Eds.). (2003). *Stories matter: The complexity of cultural authenticity in children's literature*. Urbana, IL: National Council of Teachers of English.

Fox, M. (1993). *Radical reflections: Passionate opinions on teaching, learning and living*. San Diego: Harcourt Brace.

Frederick, H. V. (2002). PW talks with James Cross Giblin. *Publishers Weekly*. http://static.highbeam.com/p/publishers weekly/april012002. Accessed July 16, 2004.

Frost, R. (1939). The figure a poem makes. *Collected poems of Robert Frost*. NY: Holt Rinehart Winston.

Frye, N. (1970). *The educated imagination*. Bloomington: Indiana University Press.

Galda, L. (1982). Assuming the spectator stance: An examination of the responses of three young readers. *Research in the Teaching of English, 16*, 1–20.

———. (1988). Readers, texts, and contexts: A response-based view of literature. *New Advocate, 1*, 92–102.

———. (1990). A longitudinal study of the spectator stance as a function of age and genre. *Research in the Teaching of English, 24*, 261–278.

———. (1998). Mirrors and windows: Reading as transformation. In T. E. Raphael & K. H. Au (Eds.), *Literature-based instruction: Reshaping the curriculum* (pp. 1–12). Norwood, MN: Christopher-Gordon.

———. (2007). *Talent, turmoil, and tension: Adolescent literature today*. (May) Annual Couper Lecture, Binghamton University, the State University of New York.

Galda, L., & Cullinan, B. E. (2003). Literature for literacy: What research says about the benefits of using trade books in the classroom. In J. Flood, D. Lapp, J. R. Squire, & J. M. Jensen (Eds.), *Handbook of research on teaching the English language arts* (Second edition, pp. 640–648). Old Tappan, NJ: Macmillan.

Galda, L., & Graves, M. F. (2006). *Reading and responding in the middle grades*. Boston: Allyn & Bacon.

Galda, L., Ash, G. E., & Cullinan, B. E. (2000). Children's literature. In M. L. Kamil, P. B. Mosenthal, P. D. Pearson, & R. Barr (Eds.), *Handbook of reading research* (vol. III, pp. 361–379). Mahwah, NJ: Erlbaum.

Galda, L., Rayburn, J. S., & Stanzi, L. C. (2000). *Looking through the faraway end: Creating a literature-based reading curriculum with second graders.* Newark, DE: International Reading Association.

Galda, L., Shockley, B. S., & Pellegrini, A. D. (1995). Sharing lives: Reading, writing, talking, and living in a first grade classroom. *Language Arts, 72,* 334–339.

Giff, P. R., Viking Penguin Children's Books, n.d. (See Patricia Reilly Giff profile in Chapter 7.)

Goodman, K. S. (1985). Transactional psycholinguistics model: Unity in reading. In H. Singer & R. B. Ruddell (Eds.), *Theoretical models and processes of reading* (Third edition, pp. 813–840). Newark, DE: International Reading Association.

Graves, D. (1992). *Explore poetry: The reading/writing teacher's companion.* Portsmouth, NH: Heinemann; Toronto: Irwin.

Graves, M. F., & Graves, B. B. (2003). *Scaffolding reading experiences to promote success.* (Second edition), Norwood, MA: Christopher-Gordon.

Graves, M. F., Graves, B. B., & Braaten, S. (1996). Scaffolded reading experiences for inclusive classrooms. *Educational Leadership, 53*(5), 14–16.

Grimal, P. (1965). *Larousse world mythology.* Seacaucus, NJ: Chartwell.

Grossman, F. (1991). *Listening to the bells: Learning to read poetry by writing poetry.* Portsmouth, NH: Boynton/Cook.

Guthrie, J., & Wigfield, A. (2000). Motivation and engagement in reading. In M. L. Kamil, P. B. Mosenthal, P. D. Pearson, & R. Barr (Eds.), *Handbook of reading research* (vol. III, pp. 403–422). Mahwah, NJ: Erlbaum.

Hamilton, V. (1993). Everything of value: Moral realism in the literature for children. *Journal of Youth Services in Libraries, 6,* 364–377.

Hansen, S. (2004). *Fourth and fifth graders' poetry preferences before and after classroom poetry experiences: A case study.* (Plan B project submitted to the faculty of the Graduate School of the University of Minnesota in partial fulfillment for the requirements for the degree of Master of Arts.)

Hansen-Krening, N., Aoki, E.M., & Mizokawa, D. T. (Eds.) (2003). *Kaleidoscope: A multicultural booklist for grades K–8* (Fourth edition). Urbana, IL: National Council of Teachers of English.

Harrison, D. L., & Cullinan, B. (1999). *Easy poetry lessons that dazzle and delight.* New York: Scholastic.

Heard, G. (1989). *For the good of the earth and sun: Teaching poetry.* Portsmouth, NH: Heinemann.

———. (1995). *Writing toward home: Tales and lessons to find your way.* Portsmouth, NH: Heinemann.

———. (1999). *Awakening the heart: Exploring poetry in elementary and middle school.* Portsmouth, NH: Heinemann.

Hearne, B. (2006). Something new. *The Horn Book Magazine, 82,* 542–545.

Hemphill, L. (1999). Narrative style, social class, and response to poetry. *Research in the Teaching of English, 33,* 275–302.

Herman, G. B. (1978). "Footprints in the sands of time": Biography for children. *Children's Literature in Education, 9*(2), 85–94.

Hewitt, G. (1998). *Today you are my favorite poet: Writing poems with teenagers.* Portsmouth, NH: Heinemann.

Hickman, J. (1981). A new perspective on response to literature: Research in an elementary school setting. *Research in the Teaching of English, 115,* 343–354.

Hiebert, E. H., & Colt, J. (1989). Patterns of literature-based reading instruction. *The Reading Teacher, 43,* 14–20.

Holdaway, D. (1979). *The foundations of literacy.* Sydney: Ashton Scholastic.

Hopkins, Lee Bennett. (1987). *Pass the poetry, please.* New York: Harper & Row.

———. (1995). *Pauses: Autobiographical reflections of 101 creators of children's books.* New York: HarperCollins.

Hunt, J. (2007). Epic fantasy meets sequel prejudice. *The Horn Book Magazine, 83,* 645–653.

———. (2007). Redefining the young adult novel. *The Horn Book Magazine, 83,* 141–147.

Isaacs, K. T. (2007). Building bridges from both sides. *The Horn Book Magazine, 83,* 419–426.

Iser, W. (1978). *The act of reading: A theory of aesthetic response.* Baltimore: The Johns Hopkins University Press.

Jackson, J. (1992). Paper presented at the Holmes' Hunter lecture. University of Georgia: Athens.

Janeczko, P. (1983). *Poetspeak: In their work, about their work: A selection.* Scarsdale, NY: Bradbury.

———. (1990). *The place my words are looking for: What poets say about and through their work.* New York: Bradbury.

———. (2002). *Seeing the blue between: Advice and inspiration for young poets.* Cambridge, MA: Candlewick.

Kennedy, X. J., & Kennedy, D. M. (1982). *Knock at a star: A child's introduction to poetry.* Boston: Little, Brown.

Koertge, R. (2006). What makes a good poem? Tell the truth, but tell it slant. *The Horn Book Magazine, 82,* 535–539.

Kuhn, M. et al. (2006). Teaching children to become fluent and automatic readers. *Journal of Literacy Research, 38,* 357–388.

Kuskin, K. (1980). *Dogs and dragons, trees and dreams.* New York: Harper & Row.

Langer, J. A. (1990). The process of understanding: Reading for literary and informative purposes. *Research in the Teaching of English, 24,* 229–260.

Larrick, N. (1991). *Let's do a poem: Introducing poetry to children through listening, singing, chanting, impromptu choral reading, body movement, dance, and dramatization; including 98 favorite songs and poems.* New York: Delacorte.

Larson, L. C. (2007). *A case study exploring the "new literacies" during a fifth-grade electronic reading workshop.* Doctoral dissertation, Kansas State University.

Lehr, S. S. (1991). *The child's developing sense of theme: Responses to literature.* New York: Teacher's College Press.

Lehr, S. (Ed.). (2001). *Beauty, brains, and brawn: The construction of gender in children's literature.* Portsmouth, NH: Heinemann.

Lester, J. (2004). *On writing for children and other people*. New York: Dial.

Lewis, C. (1997). The social drama of literature discussion in a fifth/sixth grade classroom. *Research in the Teaching of English, 31,* 163–204.

———. (2000). Limits of identification: The personal, pleasurable, and critical in reader response. *Journal of Literacy Research, 32,* 253–266.

———. (2001). *Literacy practices as social acts: Power, status, and cultural norms in the classroom.* Mahwah, NJ: Erlbaum.

Liang, L. A. (2004). *Scaffolding middle school students' comprehension of and response to narrative text.* Paper presented at the meeting of the National Reading Conference, San Antonio, TX.

Livingston, M. Cohn. (1990). *Climb into the bell tower.* New York: Harper & Row.

———. (1991). *Poem-making: Ways to begin writing poetry.* New York, NY: HarperCollins.

Locus Online. (2004). (January) Excerpts from an interview with Nancy Farmer. www.locusmag.com/2004/Issues/01Farmer .html. Accessed July 21, 2004.

Lunge-Larsen, L. (2004). *Folklore for today's children.* Speech given for Book Week at the University of Minnesota, Minneapolis.

MacDonald, M. R. & Sturm, B. W. (2001). *The storytellers' sourcebook: A subject, title, and motif index to folklore collections for children, 1983–1999.* Detroit: Gale.

MacLean, M., Bryant, P. E., & Bradley, L. (1987). Rhymes, nursery rhymes and reading in early childhood. *Merrill-Palmer Quarterly, 33,* 225–281.

Maloch, B. (2002). Scaffolding student talk: One teacher's role in literature discussion groups. *Reading Research Quarterly, 37,* 94–112.

Many, J. E., & Wiseman, D. L. (1992). The effects of teaching approach on third-grade students' response to literature. *Journal of Reading Behavior, 24,* 265–287.

Marcus, L. S. (2008). *Minders of make-believe: Idealists, entrepreneurs, and the shaping of American children's literature.* New York: Houghton Mifflin.

Martin, R. (1999). Why folktales? *Storytelling Magazine.* www .rafemartin.com/articles.htm#folk. Accessed October 23, 2004.

Martinez-Roldan, M. (2003). Building worlds and identities: A case study of the role of narratives in bilingual literature discussions. *Research in the Teaching of English, 37,* 491–526.

McClure, A. (1985). *Children's responses to poetry in a supportive literary context.* Unpublished doctoral dissertation, Ohio State University.

McClure, A., Harrison, P., & Reed, S. (1990). *Sunrises and songs: Reading and writing poetry in an elementary classroom.* Portsmouth, NH: Heinemann.

McGee, L. M. (1992). An exploration of meaning construction in first graders' grand conversations. In C. K. Kinzer & D. J. Leu (Eds.), *Literacy research, theory, and practice: Views from many perspectives* (pp. 177–186). Forty-first yearbook of the National Reading Conference. Chicago: National Reading Conference.

McGinley, W., & Kamberelis, G. (1996). "Maniac Magee and Ragtime Tumpie": Children negotiating self and world through reading and writing. *Research in the Teaching of English, 30,* 75–113.

McIntyre, E., Kyle, D. W., & Moore, G. H. (2006). A primary-grade teacher's guidance toward small-group dialogue. *Reading Research Quarterly, 41,* 36–66.

McMahon, S., Raphael, T. E., Goatley, V. J., et al. (1997). *The book club connection: Literacy learning and classroom talk.* New York: Teachers College Press.

McVitty, W. (1985). *Word magic: Poetry as a shared adventure.* Rozelle, Australia: Primary English Teaching Association.

Meltzer, M. (1976). Where do all the prizes go? The case for nonfiction. *The Horn Book Magazine, 52,* 21–22.

Michaels, J. (2004). Pulp fiction. *The Horn Book Magazine, 80,* 299–306.

Mills, L. C. (2002). The portrayal of mental disability in children's literature: An ethical appraisal. *The Horn Book Magazine, 78,* 531–542.

Moeller, K., & Allen, J. B. (2000). Connecting, resisting, and searching for safer places: Students respond to Mildred Taylor's *The Friendship. Journal of Literacy Research, 32,* 145–186.

Moll, L. (1994). Literacy research in community and classrooms: A sociocultural approach. In R. B. Ruddell, M. R. Ruddell, & H. Singer (Eds.), *Theoretical models and processes of reading* (Fourth edition, pp. 179–207). Newark, DE: International Reading Association.

National Council of Teachers of English. (1983). Statement on censorship and professional guidelines. *The Bulletin, 9* (1–2), 17–18.

Nodelman, P. (1996). *The pleasures of children's literature* (Second edition). White Plains, NY: Longman.

———. (1997). Fear of children's literature: What's left (or right) after theory? In S. L. Beckett (Ed.), *Reflections of change: Children's literature since 1945.* Westport, CT: Greenwood.

Nodelman, P., & Reimer, M. (2003). *The pleasure of children's literature* (Third edition). Boston: Allyn & Bacon.

Nye, N. S., & Bryan, A. (2000). *Salting the ocean: 100 poems by young poets.* New York: Greenwillow.

Odland, Norine. (1982). Profile: John Ciardi. *Language Arts, 59,* 872–874.

Ohio Reading Road Trip. (n.d.). James Cross Giblin. www.ohio readingroadtrip.org/giblin/index.html. Accessed March 7, 2005.

Opie, I., & Opie, P. (1951). *The Oxford dictionary of nursery rhymes.* London: Oxford University Press.

———. (1974). *Classic fairy tales.* London: Oxford University Press.

Pantaleo, S. (2008). *Exploring student response to contemporary picturebooks.* Toronto: University of Toronto Press.

Payton Walsh, J. (2007). A ghostly quartet. *The Horn Book Magazine, 80,* 245–252.

Peacock, S. (Ed.). Nikki Grimes. (2007). In *Something about the Author, 174,* 61–69. New York: Gale Research.

———. Kathi Appelt. (2002). In *Something about the Author,* vol. 129, p. 27–29.

———. (Ed.). (2002). Lauren Stringer. In *Something about the author: Facts and pictures about authors and illustrators of books for young people, 129,* 186–188. New York: Gale Research.

———. (Ed.). (2001). Kate DiCamillo. In *Something about the Author: Facts and Pictures about Authors and Illustrators of Books for Young People, 121,* 74–75. New York: Gale Research.

———. (Ed.). (2001). James Cross Giblin. In *Something about the Author: Facts and Pictures about Authors and Illustrators of Books for Young People, 122,* 89–93. New York: Gale Research.

———. (2000). Nancy Farmer. In *Something about the author: Facts and pictures about authors and illustrators of books for young people, 117,* 56–59. New York: Gale Research.

Pellowski, A. (1984). *The story vine: A source book of unusual and easy-to-tell stories from around the world.* Old Tappan, NJ: Macmillan.

Peters, L. W. (2003). The evolution of Our Family Tree. *Riverbank Review, 6*(1), 10–12.

———. (2004). Personal email correspondence, August 22.

———. (n.d.). Biography. www.lisawestbergpeters.com/bio.html. Accessed March 2, 2005.

Pillar, A. M. (1983). Aspects of moral judgment in response to fables. *Journal of Research and Development in Education, 16 (3),* 37–40.

Pressley, M., Dolezal, S. E., Raphael, L. M., Mohan, L., Roehrig, A. D., & Bogner. L. (2003). *Motivating primary grade students.* New York: Guilford.

Propp, V. (1958). *Morphology of the folktale.* Minneapolis: University of Minnesota Press.

Purves, A. C., Rogers, T., & Soter, A. D. (1990). *How porcupines make love II: Teaching a response-centered literature curriculum.* New York: Longmans.

Raphael, T. E., Florio-Ruane, S., & George, M. (2001). Book club plus: A conceptual framework to organize literacy instruction. *Language Arts, 79,* 159–168.

Raphael, T. E., Florio-Ruane, S., George, M., et al. (2004). *Book club plus: A literacy framework for the primary grades.* Lawrence, MA: Small Planet Communications.

Raphael, T. E., Kehus, M., & Damphousse, K. (2001). *Book club for middle school.* Lawrence, MA: Small Planet Communications.

Reid, A. H. (n.d.). Nancy Farmer. *Meet the Writers.* www.barnesandnoble.com/writers. Accessed July 21, 2004.

Ringrose, C. (2007). A journey backwards: History through style in children's fiction. *Children's Literature in Education, 38,* 207–218.

Robinson, L. (2008). Travels through time and genre. In L. Robinson & Z. Charles (Eds.), *Over rainbows and down rabbit holes: The art of children's books* (pp. 16–34). Santa Barbara, CA & Amherst, MA: Santa Barbara Museum of Art & The Eric Carle Museum of Picture Book Art.

Rosenberg, L. (2005). Reviewing poetry. *The Horn Book Magazine, 81,* 375–378.

Rosenblatt, L. M. (1938/1976). *Literature as exploration.* New York: Noble & Noble.

———. (1978). *The reader, the text, the poem: The transactional theory of literary work.* Carbondale: Southern Illinois University Press.

Roser, N. L., Martinez, M., Furhken, C., et al. (2007). Characters as guides to meaning. *The Reading Teacher, 60,* 548–559.

Russell Freedman. (2006). The Past isn't past: How history speaks and what it says to the next generation (May Hill Arbuthnot Honor lecture). *Children and Libraries,* 21–28.

Samuels, S. J., & Wu, Y. C. (2003). *How the amount of time spent on independent reading affects reading achievement: A response to the National Reading Panel.* www.tc.umn.edu/~samue001. Retrieved November 13, 2008.

Saul, W. (1986). Living proof: Children's biographies of Marie Curie. *School Library Journal, 33,* 103–108.

Sawyer, R. (1962). *The Way of the Storyteller.* New York: Viking.

Schwarcz, J. (1985). *Ways of the illustrator.* Chicago: American Library Association.

Sebesata, S. E., & Monson, D. L. (2003). Reading preferences. In J. Flood, D. Lapp, J. R. Squire, & J. M. Jensen, (Eds.), *Handbook of research on teaching the English language arts* (Second edition, pp. 835–847). Old Tappan, NJ: Macmillan.

Seeger, P., & Jacobs, P. D. (2000). *Pete Seeger's storytelling book.* San Diego: Harcourt.

Shapiro, K., & Beum, R. (1975). *A prosody handbook.* New York: Harper & Row.

Short, K. G., & Pierce, K. M. (Eds.). (1990). *Talking about books: Creating literate communities.* Portsmouth, NH: Heinemann.

Shulevitz, U. (1985). *Writing with pictures: How to write and illustrate children's books.* Lakewood, NJ: Watson-Guptill.

Silvey, A. (2004). *100 best books for children.* New York: Houghton Mifflin.

Sipe, L. R. (1998). Individual literary response styles of first and second graders. In T. Shanahan and F. V. Rodriguez-Brown (Eds.), *Forty-seventh yearbook of the National Reading Conference* (pp. 76–89). Chicago: National Reading Conference.

———. (1999). Children's response to literature: Author, text, reader, context. *Theory into Practice,* 38, 120–129.

———. (2000). "Those two gingerbread boys could be brothers": How children use intertextual connections during storybook readalouds. *Children's Literature in Education, 31,* 73–90.

———. (2008). *Storytime! Young children's literary understanding in the classroom.* New York: Teachers College Press.

Sipe, L. R., & McGuire, C. E. (2006). Young children's resistance to stories. *The Reading Teacher, 60,* 6–13. Portsmouth, NH: Heinemann.

Sipe, L. R., & McGuire, C. E. (in press). "The stinky cheese man" and other fairly postmodern picturebooks for children. In S. Lehr, (Ed.), *Shattering the looking glass: challenge, risk, and controversy in children's literature* (pp. 273–288). Norwood, MA: Christopher-Gordon.

Sloan, G. D. (2009). Northrop Frye in the elementary classroom. *Children's Literature in Education.*

Sloyer, S. (1982). *Readers theatre: Story dramatization in the classroom.* Urbana, IL: National Council of Teachers of English.

Stan, S. (Ed.). (2002). *The world through children's books.* Lapham, MD: Scarecrow.

Staples, S. F. (2008). Speech given at the International Reading Association Annual Meeting, Book and Author Luncheon, Atlanta, GA.

Stephens, J. (1992). *Language and ideology and children's fiction.* London: Longman.

Stevenson, D. (2006). Finding literary goodness in a pluralistic world. *The Horn Book Magazine, 82,* 511–517.

Stewart, S. L. (2008). Beyond borders: Reading "other" places in children's literature. *Children's Literature in Education, 39,* 95–105.

Stott, J. C. (1987). Spiraled sequence story curriculum: A structuralist approach to teaching fiction in the elementary grades. *Children's Literature in Education, 18,* 148–163.

Strickland, D. L., Galda, L., & Cullinan, B. E. (2004). *Language arts: learning and teaching.* Belmont, CA: Wadsworth.

Stringer, L. (2004). Personal email correspondence, September 8.

Sumara, D. J. (1996). *Private readings in public: Schooling and the literary imagination.* New York: Peter Lang.

Sutherland, R. (1985). Hidden persuaders: Political ideologies in literature for children. *Children's Literature in Education, 16,* 143–157.

Taxel, J. (1984). The American Revolution in children's fiction: An analysis of historical meaning and narrative structure. *Curriculum Inquiry, 14*(1), 7–55.

Taylor, B. M., Frye, B., Maruyama, G. (1990). Time spent reading and reading growth. *American Educational Research Journal, 27,* 351–362.

Terry, A. (1974). *Children's poetry preferences: A national survey of upper elementary grades.* Urbana, IL: National Council of Teachers of English.

Thomas, J. T., Jr. (2007). *Poetry's playground: The culture of contemporary American children's poetry.* Detroit: Wayne State University Press.

Thompson, S. (1955/1958). *Motif-index of folk-literature.* (Vols. 1–5). Bloomington: Indiana University Press.

Tolkien, J.R.R. (1938/1964). *Tree and leaf.* London: Unwin Books.

Tomlinson, C. (Ed.). (1998). *Children's books from other countries.* Lapham, MD: Scarecrow.

———. (2002). An overview of international children's literature. In S. Stan (Ed.), *The world through children's books* (pp. 3–26). Lapham, MD: Scarecrow.

Varley, P. (2002). As good as reading? Kids and the audiobook revolution. *The Horn Book Magazine, 78,* 251–262.

Weiss, M. J., & Weiss, H. S. (1997). *From one experience to another: Award-winning authors sharing real-life experiences through fiction.* New York: Tom Doherty Associates.

Werlin, N. (2006). Working with fear: What makes a good . . . thriller? *The Horn Book Magazine, 82,* 529–532.

West, R., Stanovich, K., & Mitchell, H. (1993). Reading in the real world and its correlates. *Reading Research Quarterly, 28,* 34–50.

White, M. L. (1988). Profile: Arnold Adoff. *Language Arts, 65,* 584–588.

Wolf, S. A., & Heath, S. B. (1992). *The braid of literature: Children's worlds of reading.* Cambridge, MA: Harvard University Press.

Wood, K. D., Roser, N. L., & Martinez, M. (2001). Collaborative literacy: lessons learned from literature. *The Reading Teacher, 55,* 102–111.

Yolen, Jane. (2000). *Touch magic: Fantasy, faerie and folklore in the literature of childhood.* Little Rock, AR: August House.

Zipes, Jack. (1979/2002). *Breaking the magic spell: Radical theories of folk and fairy tales.* Lexington University Press of Kentucky.

Children's Literature References

Aardema, Verna. (1975). *Why Mosquitoes Buzz in People's Ears: A West African Tale*. Illustrated by Leo Dillon and Diane Dillon. New York: Dial.

_____. (1981). *Bringing the Rain to Kapiti Plain: A Nandi Tale*. Illustrated by Beatriz Vidal. New York: Dial.

_____. (1988). *Princess Gorilla and a New Kind of Water*. Illustrated by Victoria Chess. New York: Dial.

_____. (1991). *Borreguita and the Coyote: A Tale from Ayutla, Mexico*. Illustrated by Petra Mathers. New York: Random House.

_____. (1994). *Misoso: Once upon a Time: Tales from Africa*. Illustrated by Reynold Ruffins. New York: Knopf.

_____. (1996). *The Lonely Lioness and the Ostrich Chicks: A Masai Tale*. Illustrated by Yumi Heo. New York: Knopf.

Abbot, Jacob. (1854). *Rollo's Tour in Europe*. Boston: W. J. Reynolds.

Ablow, Gail. (2007). *A Horse in the House and Other Strange but True Animal Stories*. Illustrated by Kathy Osborn. Cambridge, MA: Candlewick.

Ada, Alma Flor. (1995). *Mediopollito/Half-Chicken*. Illustrated by Kim Howard. New York: Doubleday.

_____. (1997). *Gathering the Sun: An Alphabet in Spanish and English*. Illustrated by Simon Silva. New York: HarperCollins.

_____. (1999). *Three Golden Oranges*. Illustrated by Reg Cartwright. New York: Atheneum.

Ada, Alma Flor, Isabel Campoy, & Alice Schertle. (2003). *¡Pío Peep!: Traditional Spanish Nursery Rhymes*. Illustrated by Vivi Escrivá. New York: HarperCollins.

Adams, Richard. (1972). *Watership Down*. New York: Macmillan.

Addams, Charles. (1967). *The Charles Addams Mother Goose*. New York: Windmill.

Adler, David A. (1986). *Martin Luther King Jr.: Free at Last*. New York: Holiday House.

_____. (1994). *A Picture Book of Sojourner Truth*. New York: Holiday House.

_____. (2007). *Bones and the Birthday Mystery*. Illustrated by Barbara Johansen Newman. New York: Viking.

Adler, Joseph. (2000). *America's Champion Swimmer: Gertrude Ederle*. Illustrated by by Terry Widener. San Diego, CA: Harcourt.

Adlington, L. J. (2008). *Cherry Heaven*. New York: Greenwillow.

Adoff, Arnold. (1973). *Black Is Brown Is Tan*. Illustrated by Emily Arnold McCully. New York: HarperCollins.

_____. (1975). *Make a Circle, Keep Us In: Poems for a Good Day*. Illustrated by Arnold Himler. New York: Dell.

_____. (1979). *Eats: Poems*. Illustrated by Susan Russo. New York: Lothrop, Lee & Shepard Books.

_____. (1982). *All the Colors of the Race: Poems*. Illustrated by John Steptoe. New York: HarperCollins.

_____. (1986). *Sports Pages*. Illustrated by Steve Kuzma. New York: J. B. Lippincott.

_____. (1989). *Chocolate Dreams: Poems*. Illustrated by Turi McCombie. New York: Lothrop, Lee & Shepard.

_____. (1995). *My Black Me: A Beginning Book of Black Poetry*. New York: Penguin.

_____. (1997). *I Am the Darker Brother: An Anthology of Modern Poems by African Americans*. New York: Simon & Schuster.

Adoff, Jamie. (2004). *Names Will Never Hurt Me*. New York: Dutton.

Agee, Jon. (2003). *Elvis Lives! and Other Anagrams*. New York, Farrar, Straus & Giroux.

Agee, Jon. (2003). *Z Goes Home*. New York: Hyperion.

Ahlberg, Allan. (1999). *The Bravest Ever Bear*. Illustrated by Paul Howard. Cambridge, MA: Candlewick.

_____. (2004). *The Improbable Cat*. New York: Delacorte.

Ahlberg, Janet, & Allan Ahlberg. (1978). *Each Peach Pear Plum*. New York: Penguin.

_____. (1986). *The Jolly Postman or Other People's Letters*. Boston: Little, Brown.

Ajmera, Maya. (2004). *Be My Neighbor*. Illustrated by John D. Ivanko. Watertown, MA: Charlesbridge.

Alarcon, Francisco X. (2008). *Animal Poems of the Iguazú/ Animalario del Iguazú*. Illustrated by Maya Cristina Gonzalez. San Francisco: Children's Book Press.

Alcott, Louisa May. (1868/1968). *Little Women*. New York: Little, Brown.

Alexander, Elizabeth, & Marilyn Nelson. (2007). *Miss Crandall's School for Young Ladies & Little Misses of Color: Poems*. Illustrated by Floyd Cooper. Hornsdale, PA.: Wordsong.

Alexander, Lloyd. (1964). *The Book of Three*. New York: Holt, Rinehart & Winston.

Alexander, Lloyd. (1965). *The Black Cauldron*. New York: Holt, Rinehart & Winston.

_____. (1966). *The Castle of Llyr*. New York: Holt, Rinehart & Winston.

_____. (1967). *Taran Wanderer*. New York: Holt, Rinehart & Winston.

_____. (1968). *The High King*. New York: Holt, Rinehart & Winston.

_____. (1969/1999). *The Book of Three*. New York: Holt.

_____. (1973). *Foundling and Other Tales of Prydain*. New York: Holt, Rinehart & Winston.

_____. (2002). *The Rope Trick*. New York: Dutton Children's Books.

_____. (2007). *Golden Dream of Carlo Cuchio*. New York: Holt.

Alexie, Sherman. (2007). *The Absolutely True Diary of a Part-Time Indian*. Illustrated by Ellen Forney. New York: Little, Brown.

Aliki, (1986). *Feelings*. New York: HarperCollins.

_____. (1988). *How a Book Is Made*. New York: HarperCollins.

_____. (1998). *Marianthe's Story: Painted Words, Spoken Memories*. New York: Greenwillow.

Allen, Jonathan. (2008). *I'm Not Scared*. London: Boxer Books.

Alley, Zoe. (2008). *There's a Wolf at the Door*. Illustrated by R. W. Alley. Roaring Brook.

Almond, David. (1999). *Skellig*. New York: Delacorte.

_____. (2001). *Heaven Eyes*. Waterville: Thorndike.

_____. (2001). *Kit's Wilderness*. New York: Dell.

_____. (2004). *The Fire-Eaters*. New York: Knopf.

_____. (2008). *Savage*. Illustrated by Dave Mckean. Cambridge, MA: Candlewick.

Alter, Stephen. (2007). *The Phantomisles*. London: Bloomsbury/Walker.

al-Windawi, Thura. (2004). *Thura's Diary: My Life in Wartime Iraq*. New York: Viking.

Amateau, Gigi. (2008). *Chancey of the Maury River*. Cambridge, Mass: Candlewick.

Ambrose, Stephen. (2003). *This Vast Land*. New York: Random House.

Ammon, Richard. (2007). *An Amish Year*. Illustrated by Pamela Patrick. Honesdale, PA: Windsong.

Anaya, Rudolfo. (1999) *My Land Sings: Stories from the Rio Grande*. Illustrated by Amy Cordova. New York: Morrow.

Anderson, Peggy Perry. (2006). *Chuck's Truck*. Boston: Houghton Mifflin.

Anderson, Ho Che. (2003). *King*. Washington: Fantagraphics.

Anderson, Laurie Halse. (1999). *Speak*. New York: Farrar, Straus & Giroux.

_____. (2000). *Fever 1793*. New York: Simon & Schuster.

_____. (2007). *Twisted*. New York: Viking.

_____. (2008). *Chains*. New York: Simon & Schuster.

_____. (2008). *Independent Dames: What You Never Knew About the Women and Girls of the American Revolution*. Illustrated by Matt Faulkner. New York: Simon & Schuster.

Anderson, M. T. (1999). *Burger Wuss*. Cambridge, MA: Candlewick.

_____. (2002). *Feed*. Cambridge, MA: Candlewick.

_____. (2003). *Strange Mr. Satie*. Illustrated by Petra Mathers. New York: Viking.

_____. (2006). *The Astonishing Life of Octavian Nothing, Traitor to the Nation, Volume 1: The Pox Party*. Cambridge, MA: Candlewick.

_____. (2008). *The Astonishing Life of Octavian Nothing, Traitor to the Nation, Volume II: The Kingdom on the Waves*. Cambridge, MA: Candlewick.

Anderson, Sara. (2007). *Fruit*. Brooklyn, NY: Handprint.

Andronik, Catherine. (2001). *Hatshepsut, His Majesty, Herself*. Illustrated by Joseph Daniel Fiedler. New York: Atheneum.

Angelou, Maya. (2008). *Amazing Peace: A Christmas Poem*. Illustrated by Steve Johnson & Lou Fancher. New York: Schwartz & Wade Books.

Anno, Mitsumasa. (1986). *Anno's Counting Book*. New York: HarperCollins.

_____. (1989). *Anno's Aesop: A Book of Fables by Aesop and Mr. Fox*. New York: Orchard.

_____. (1993). *Anno's Journey*. New York: Philomel.

_____. (1993). *Anno's Twice Told Tales: The Fisherman and His Wife & the Four Clever Brothers*. New York: Putnam.

Anonymous. (1971). *Go Ask Alice*. New York: Simon & Schuster.

Antieau, Kim. (2007). *Broken Moon*. New York: McElderry.

Appelt, Kathi. (2008). *The Underneath*. Illustrated by David Small. New York: Atheneum.

Applegate, Katherine. (2007). *The Buffalo Storm*. Illustrated by Jan Ormerod. New York: Clarion.

Ardizzone, Edward. (1955). *Little Tim and the Brave Sea Captain*. New York: Walck.

Armstrong, Jennifer. (1996). *The Dreams of Mairhe Mehan*. New York: Knopf.

_____. (1997). *Mary Mehan, Awake*. New York: Knopf.

_____. (1998). *Shipwreck at the Bottom of the World: The Extraordinary True Story of Shackleton and the Endurance*. New York: Crown.

_____. (2002). *Shattered: Stories of Children and War*. New York: Knopf.

_____. (2003). *Audubon: Painter of Birds in the Wild Frontier*. Illustrated by Jos. A Smith. New York: H. N. Abrams.

_____. (2006). *Once Upon a Banana*. Illustrated by David Small. New York: Simon & Schuster.

Arnold, Caroline. (2006). *The Terrible Hodag and the Animal Catchers*. Illustrated by John Sanford. Honesdale, PA: Windsong.

_____. (2007). *Giant Sea Reptiles of the Dinosaur Age*. Illustrated by Laurie Caple. New York: Clarion.

_____. (2007). *Wiggle and Waggle*. Illustrated by Mary Peterson. Watertown, MA: Charlesbridge.

Arnold, Marsha Diane. (2006). *Roar of a Snore*. Illustrated by Pierre Pratt. New York: Dial.

Arnold, Tedd. (2007). *There Was an Old Lady Who Swallowed Fly Guy*. New York: Scholastic.

Arnosky, Jim. (2000). *Wild and Swampy*. New York: HarperCollins.

———. (2002). *Field Trips: Bug Hunting, Animal Tracking, Bird-Watching, Shore Walking with Jim Arnosky*. New York: HarperCollins.

———. (2008). *The Brook Book: Exploring the Smallest Streams*. New York: Dutton.

Aronson, Marc. (2000). *Sir Walter Ralegh and the Quest for El Dorado*. New York: Clarion.

———. (2007). *Race: A History Beyond Black and White*. New York: Atheneum.

Arrington, Frances. (2000). *Bluestem*. New York: Philomel.

———. (2003). *Prairie Whispers*. New York: Philomel.

Asch, Frank. (2004). *Mr. Maxwell's Mouse*. Illustrated by Devin Asch. Toronto: Kids Can Press.

Asimov, Isaac. (1966). *Fantastic Voyage: A Novel*. Boston: Houghton Mifflin.

Aston, Dianna. (2006). *An Egg Is Quiet*. Illustrated by Sylvia Long. San Francisco: Chronicle.

———. (2007). *A Seed Is Sleepy*. Illustrated by Sylvia Long. San Francisco: Chronicle.

Atkins, Catherine. (2003). *Alt Ed*. New York: Putnam.

Atkins, Jeannine. (2007). *Anne Hutchinson's Way*. Illustrated by Michael Dooling. New York: Clarion.

Atwater-Rhodes, Amelia. (2007). *Wolfcry*. New York: Random House.

Auch, Mary Jane & Herm Auch. (2007). *Beauty and the Beaks: A Turkey's Cautionary Tale*. New York: Holiday House.

Avi. (1984). *S.O.R. Losers*. Scarsdale, NY: Bradbury.

———. (1990). *The True Confessions of Charlotte Doyle*. New York: Scholastic.

———. (1992). *Who Was That Masked Man, Anyway?* New York: HarperCollins.

———. (1997). *Poppy*. Illustrated by Brian Floca. New York: HarperCollins.

———. (1998). *Perloo the Bold*. Illustrated by Marcy Reed. New York: Scholastic.

———. (1999). *Poppy and Rye*. Illustrated by Brian Floca. New York: Camelot.

———. (2000). *Ereth's Birthday*. Illustrated by Brian Floca. New York: HarperCollins.

———. (2000). *Ragweed: A Tale for Dimwood Forest*. Illustrated by Brian Floca. New York: HarperCollins.

———. (2002). *Crispin: The Cross of Lead*. New York: Hyperion.

———. (2003). *Silent Movie*. Illustrated by C. B. Mordan. New York: Simon & Schuster.

———. (2008). *Crispin: At the Edge of the World*. New York: Hyperion.

———. (2008). *The End of the Beginning: Being the Adventures of a Small Snail (and an Even Smaller Ant)*. Illustrated by Tricia Tusa. San Diego, CA: Harcourt.

———. (2008). *Iron Thunder: The Battle Between the Monitor & the Merrimac*. New York: Hyperion.

Avi, & Rachel Vail. (2004). *Never Mind! A Twin Novel*. New York: HarperCollins.

Avi, Cathy Shute, & Katherine Paterson. (2006). *Best Shorts: Favorite Short Stories for Sharing*. Boston: Houghton Mifflin.

Azarian, Mary. (2000). *A Gardener's Alphabet*. Boston: Houghton Mifflin.

Babbitt, Natalie. (1969). *Search for Delicious*. New York: Farrar, Straus & Giroux.

———. (1975). *Tuck Everlasting*. New York: Farrar, Straus & Giroux.

———. (2007). *Jack Plank Tells Tales*. New York: Scholastic.

Baek, Matthew. (2008). *Be Gentle with the Dog, Dear!* New York: Penguin.

Bagert, Brod. (2007). *Hormone Jungle: Coming of Age in Middle School*. Gainesville, FL: Maupin House.

Bailey, Linda. (2007). *Goodnight, Sweet Pig*. Illustrated by Josée Masse. Tonawanda, NY: Kids Can Press.

Baker, Jeannie. (1988). *Where the Forest Meets the Sea*. New York: HarperCollins.

———. (1991). *Window*. New York: Greenwillow.

———. (2004). *Home*. New York: Greenwillow.

———. (2005). *The Hidden Forest*. New York: Walker.

Balliett, Blue. (2004). *Chasing Vermeer*. Illustrated by Brett Helquist. New York: Scholastic.

———. (2006). *The Wright 2*. Illustrated by Brett Helquist. New York: Scholastic.

———. (2008). *The Calder Game*. Illustrated by Brett Helquist. New York: Scholastic.

Balnes, Becky. (2008). *Your Skin Holds You In*. Washington, DC: National Geographic Society.

Bang, Molly. (1996). *Ten, Nine, Eight*. New York: HarperCollins.

———. (1999). *When Sophie Gets Angry—Really, Really, Angry. . . .* New York: Scholastic.

———. (2000). *Nobody Particular: One Woman's Fight to Save the Bays*. New York: Holt.

———. (2006). *In My Heart*. New York: Little, Brown.

Bang-Campbell, Monika. (2008). *Little Rat Makes Music*. Illustrated by Molly Bang. San Diego, CA: Harcourt.

Bania, Michael. (2004). *Kumak's Fish: A Tall Tale from the Far North*. Portland, OR: Alaska Northwest.

Banks, Kate. (2006). *Max's Words*. Illustrated by Boris Kulikov. New York: Farrar, Straus & Giroux.

———. (2007). *Fox*. Illustrated by Georg Hallensleben. New York: Farrar, Straus & Giroux.

———. (2007). *Lenny's Space*. New York: Farrar/Foster.

Banyai, Istvan. (1998). *Zoom*. New York: Penguin.

———. (1999). *Re-Zoom*. New York: Penguin.

———. (2005). *The Other Side*. San Francisco: Chronicle.

Barakat, Ibtisam. (2007). *Tasting the Sky: A Palestinian Childhood*. New York: Farrar, Straus & Giroux.

Bardhan-Quallen, Sudipta, (2008). *Up Close: Jane Goodall*. New York: Viking.

Bardoe, Cheryl. (2006). *Gregor Mendel: The Friar Who Grew Peas*. New York: Abrams.

Barklem, J. Illustrated by (1980). *Brambly Hedge*. New York: HarperCollins.

Barner, Bob. (2007). *Penguins, Penguins, Everywhere!* San Francisco: Chronicle.

Barrett, Tracy. (1999). *Anna of Byzantium*. New York: Delacorte.

Barrie, James M. (1950). *Peter Pan*. New York: Scribner.

Barron, T. A. (1998). *Fires of Merlin*. New York: Philomel.

_____. (2002). *Mirror of Merlin*. New York: Ace.

_____. (2004). *The Great Tree of Avalon: Child of the Dark Prophecy*. New York: Philomel.

_____. (2007). *The Day the Stones Walked*. Illustrated by William Low. New York: Philomel.

_____. (2007). *Wings of Merlin*. New York: Philomel.

Barrows, Annie. (2008). *Ivy and Bean Take Care of the Babysitter*. Illustrated by Sophie Blackall. San Francisco: Chronicle.

Bartoletti, Susan Campbell. (2001). *Black Potatoes: The Story of the Great Irish Famine, 1845–1850*. Boston: Houghton Mifflin.

_____. (2001). *Christmas Promise*. New York: Blue Sky Press.

_____. (2005). *Hitler Youth: Growing Up in Hitler's Shadow*. New York: Scholastic.

Bass, L. G. (2004). *Sign of the Qin: Outlaws of the Moonshadow Marsh, Book One*. New York: Hyperion.

Bateman, Donna. (2007). *Deep in the Swamp*. Illustrated by Brian Lies. Watertown, MA: Charlesbridge.

Bateman, Teresa. (2007). *Fiona's Luck*. Illustrated by Kelly Murphy. Watertown, MA: Charlesbridge.

Bates, Katharine Lee. (2004). *America the Beautiful*. Illustrated by Chris Gall. London: Little, Brown.

Bauer, Cat. (2000). *Harley, Like a Person*. Deleray Beach, FL: Winslow.

Bauer, Joan. (1998). *Rules of the Road*. New York: Putnam.

_____. (2000). *Hope Was Here*. New York: Putnam.

_____. (2002). *Stand Tall*. New York: Putnam.

Bauer, Marion Dane. (1986). *On My Honor*. New York: Clarion.

_____. (1992). *Ghost Eye*. Illustrated by Trina Schart Hyman. New York: Scholastic.

_____. (2004). *The Double-Digit Club*. New York: Holiday House.

Bausum, Ann. (2006). *Freedom Riders: John Lewis and Jim Zwerg on the Front Lines of the Civil Rights Movement*. Washington D. C.: National Geographic Society.

_____. (2007). *Muckrakers*. Washington, D. C: National Geographic Society.

Bean, Jonathan. (2007). *At Night*. New York: Farrar, Straus & Giroux.

Beatty, Patricia. (1984). *Turn Homeward, Hannalee*. New York: Morrow.

_____. (1987). *Charlie Skedaddle*. New York: Morrow.

_____. (1992). *Who Comes with Cannons?* New York: Morrow.

Beaty, Andrea. (2007). *Iggy Peck, Architect*. Illustrated by David Roberts. New York: Abram's Books.

_____. (2008). *Cicada Summer*. New York: Amulet.

Beaumont, Karen. (2006). *Move Over, Rover!* Illustrated by Jane Dyer. San Diego, CA: Harcourt.

Bell, Clare. (1988/2007). *Ratha's Creature*. New York: Penguin.

Bell, Hilari. (2004). *The Goblin Wood*. New York: HarperCollins.

_____. (2007). *Last Knight: A Knight and Rogue Novel*. New York: Eos.

_____. (2008). *Rogue's Home*. New York: Eos.

Bemelmans, Ludwig. (1939/1962). *Madeline*. New York: Viking.

Berger, Carin. (2008). *The Little Yellow Leaf*. New York: HarperCollins.

Bergman, Mara. (2007). *Oliver Who Would Not Sleep!* Illustrated by Nick Maland. New York: Arthur A. Levine.

Bernier-Grand, Carmen T. (1994). *Juan Bobo: Four Tales from Puerto Rico*. Illustrated by Ernesto Ramos Nieves. New York: HarperCollins.

_____. (2008). *Frida: ¡Viva la vida! Long Live Life!* Tarrytown, NY: Cavendish

Bertrand, Diane Gonzales. (2007). *We Are Cousins/Somos primos*. Illustrated by Christina E. Rodriguez. Houston: Pinata.

Bial, Raymond. (2002). *Tenement: Immigrant Life on the Lower East Side*. Boston: Houghton Mifflin.

Bianco, Margery Williams. (1981). *The Velveteen Rabbit*. Philadelphia: Running Press.

Bierhorst, John. (1987). *Doctor Coyote: A Native American Aesop's Fables*. Illustrated by Wendy Watson. New York; London: Macmillan.

_____. (2000). *Is My Friend at Home? Pueblo Fireside Tales*. Illustrated by Wendy Watson. New York: Farrar, Straus & Giroux.

_____. (2000). *The People with Five Fingers: A Native Californian Creation Tale*. Illustrated by Robert Andrew Parker. Tarrytown, NY: Cavendish.

Billingsley, Franny. (1999). *The Folk Keeper*. New York: Atheneum.

Birdsall, Jeanne. (2008). *The Penderwicks of Gardam Street*. New York: Random House.

Bishop, Nic. (2007). *Spiders*. New York: Scholastic.

_____. (2008). *Frogs*. New York: Scholastic.

Blackwood, Gary. (2004). *The Shakespeare Stealer Series*. New York: Dutton.

Blades, Ann. (1971). *Mary of Mile 18*. Plattsburg, NY: Tundra.

Blake, William. (1789). *Songs of Innocence and Experience*. Princeton, NJ: William Blake Trust/Princeton University Press.

Bley, Anette, (2007). *And What Comes After a Thousand?* La Jolla, CA: Kane Miller.

Blizzard, Gladys. (1992). *Come Look with Me: Animals in Art*. Charlottesville, VA: Thomasson-Grant.

Blomberg, Loda. (1989). *The Great American Gold Rush*. Scarsdale, NY: Bradbury.

Bloor, Edward. (1997). *Tangerine*. San Diego, CA: Harcourt.

———. (1999). *Crusader*. San Diego, CA: Harcourt.

Bloor, Thomas. (2000). *The Memory Prisoner*. New York: Dial.

Blos, Joan. (1969). *A Gathering of Days: A New England Girl's Journal, 1830–32*. New York: Scribner.

Blumberg, Rhoda. (1996). *Full Steam Ahead: The Race to Build a Transcontinental Railroad*. Washington, D.C: National Geographic Society.

———. (2004). *York's Adventures with Lewis and Clark: An African-American's Part in the Great Expedition*. New York: HarperCollins.

Blume, Judy. (1970). *Are You There God? It's Me, Margaret*. Englewood Cliffs, NJ: Bradbury.

———. (1971). *Then Again, Maybe I Won't*. Scarsdale, NY: Bradbury.

———. (1974). *The Pain and the Great One*. Scarsdale, NY: Bradbury.

———. (1975). *Forever*. Scarsdale, NY: Bradbury.

———. (1981). *Tiger Eyes*. Scarsdale, NY: Bradbury.

———. (2003) *Tales of a Fourth-Grade Nothing*. New York: Dutton.

Blumenthal, Karen. (2002). *Six Days in October: The Stock Market Crash of 1929*. New York: Atheneum.

Bodeen, S. A. (2008). *The Compound*. New York: Feiwel & Friends.

Bolden, Tonya. (2004). *The Champ: The Story of Muhammad Ali*. Illustrated by Gregory Christie. New York: Random House.

———. (2007). *M.L.K.: The Journey of a King*. Illustrated by Bob Adelman. New York: Abrams.

———. (2008). *Up Close: W.E.B. Du Bois: A Twentieth-Century Life*. New York: Viking.

Boling, Katharine. (2004). *January 1905*. Orlando, FL: Harcourt.

Bond, Michael. (2008). *Paddington Here and Now*. Illustrated by R. W. Alley. New York: HarperCollins.

Bond, Nancy. (1994). *Truth to Tell*. New York: McElderry.

Bonner, Hannah. (2007). *When Fish Got Feet, Sharks Got Teeth, and Bugs Began to Swarm: A Cartoon Prehistory of Life Long Before Dinosaurs*. Washington, DC: National Geographic Society.

Borden, Louise. (2006). *Across the Blue Pacific: A World War II Story*. Illustrated by Robert Andrew Parker. Boston: Houghton Mifflin.

Bosse, Malcolm. (1980). *Cave Beyond Time*. New York: Harper & Row.

Boston, Lucy M. (1954/2002). *The Children of Green Knowe*. San Diego, CA: Harcourt.

Bowen, Betsy. (2002). *Antler, Bear, Canoe: A Northwoods Alphabet*. Boston: Houghton Mifflin.

Bowler, Tim. (2003). *Storm Catchers*. New York: McElderry.

Bowsher, Melodie. (2007). *My Lost and Found Life*. London: Bloomsbury.

Boyne, John. (2007). *The Boy in the Striped Pajamas*. New York: Random House.

Bradby, Marie. (2004). *Some Friend*. New York: Atheneum.

Bradley, Alex. (2007). *Hot Lunch*. New York: Dutton.

Brande, Robin. (2007). *Evolution, Me & Other Freaks of Nature*. New York: Knopf.

Brandenburg, Jim. (1993). *To the Top of the World: Adventures with Arctic Wolves*. New York: Walker.

Brashares, Ann. (2001). *The Sisterhood of the Traveling Pants*. New York: Delacorte.

———. (2003). *The Second Summer of the Sisterhood*. New York: Delacorte.

Bray, Rosemary. (1995). *Martin Luther King*. Illustrated by Malcah Zeldis. New York: Greenwillow.

Breen, Steve. (2007). *Stick*. New York: Dial.

Brett, Jan. (1989). *The Mitten: A Ukrainian Folktale*. New York: Putnam.

———. (1994). *Town Mouse, Country Mouse*. New York: Putnam.

Bridges, Ruby. (1999). *Through My Eyes*. New York: Scholastic.

Briggs, Raymond. (1970). *Jim and the Beanstalk*. New York: Coward-McCann.

———. (2006). *The Puddleman*. London: Red Fox.

Brighton, Catherine. (2008). *Keep Your Eyes on the Kid: The Early Years of Buster Keaton*. Brookfield, CT: Roaring Brook Press.

Brink, Carol Ryrie. (1935/1973). *Caddie Woodlawn*. Illustrated by Trina Schart Hyman. New York: Simon & Schuster.

Broach, Elise. (2008). *Masterpiece*. Illustrated by Kelly Murphy. New York: Holt.

Brooks, Bruce. (1984). *The Moves Make the Man*. New York: Harper & Row.

———. (1990). *Everywhere*. New York: Harper & Row.

———. (1992). *What Hearts: A Laura Geringer Book*. New York: HarperCollins.

———. (1993). *Making Sense: Animal Perception and Communication*. New York: Farrar, Straus & Giroux.

———. (1999). *Vanishing*. New York: Laura Geringer Books.

———. (2001). *All That Remains*. New York: Atheneum.

Brooks, Gwendolyn. (1963). *Selected Poems* New York: Harper & Row.

Brooks, Kevin. (2007). *Being*. New York: Scholastic.

———. (2008). *Black Rabbit Summer*. New York: Scholastic.

Brooks, Martha. (1994). *Traveling on into the Light and Other Stories*. New York: Orchard.

———. (2000). *Being with Henry*. New York: Dorling Kindersley.

———. (2002). *True Confessions of a Heartless Girl*. Toronto: Groundwood.

Brooks, William. (1990). *A Telling of the Tales*. Illustrated by Richard Egielski. New York: Harper & Row.

Brown, Charlotte Lewis. (2006). *The Day the Dinosaurs Died*. Illustrated by Phil Wilson. New York: HarperCollins.

Brown, Dee. (1993). *Wounded Knee: An Indian History of the American West*. Adapted by Amy Ehrlich. New York: Henry Holt.

Brown, Don. (2003). *Mack Made Movies*. Brookfield, CT: Roaring Brook Press.

_____. (2004). *Kid Blink Beats the World*. Brookfield, CT: Roaring Brook Press.

_____. (2008). *Odd Boy Out: Young Albert Einstein*. Boston: Houghton Mifflin.

_____. (2007). *Dolley Madison Saves George Washington*. Boston: Houghton Mifflin.

_____. (2008). *Let It Begin Here!* Brookfield, CT: Roaring Brook Press.

Brown, Jackie. (2004). *Little Cricket*. New York: Hyperion.

Brown, Lisa. (2006). *How to Be*. New York: HarperCollins.

Brown, Marc. (1987). *Play Rhymes*. New York: Dutton.

Brown, Marcia. (1989). *Once a Mouse*. New York: Simon & Schuster.

Brown, Margaret Wise. (1947). *Goodnight Moon*. Illustrated by Clement Hurd. New York: Harper.

_____. (2004). *Where Have You Been?* Illustrated by Leo and Diane Dillon. New York: HarperCollins.

Browne, Anthony. (1983/2002). *Gorilla*. Cambridge, MA: Candlewick.

_____. (1987). *Piggybook*. New York: Knopf.

_____. (1990). *Changes*. New York: Knopf.

_____. (1997). *The Tunnel*. New York: Walker Books.

_____. (1998/2001). *Voices in the Park*. New York: DK Publishing.

_____. (1999). *Willy's Pictures*. Cambridge, MA: Candlewick.

_____. (2001). *My Dad*. New York: Farrar, Straus & Giroux.

_____. (2004). *Into the Forest*. Cambridge, MA: Candlewick.

_____. (2005). *My Mom*. New York: Farrar, Straus & Giroux.

_____. (2007). *My Brother*. New York: Farrar, Straus & Giroux.

Bruchac, Joseph. (1994). *A Boy Called Slow: The True Story of Sitting Bull*. Illustrated by Rocco Baviera. New York: Philomel.

_____. (1995). *The Boy Who Lived with the Bears and Other Iroquois Stories*. Illustrated by Murv Jacob. New York: HarperCollins.

_____. (1995). *Gluskabe and the Four Wishes*. Illustrated by Christine Nyburg Shrader. New York: Dutton.

_____. (1995). *The Story of the Milky Way: A Cherokee Tale*. Illustrated by Virginia A. Stroud. New York: Dial.

_____. (1996). *Between Earth and Sky: Legends of Native American Sacred Places*. Illustrated by Thomas Locker. San Diego, CA: Harcourt.

_____. (1998). *The Arrow over the Door*. New York: Dial.

_____. (2000). *Crazy Horse's Vision*. Illustrated by S. D. Nelson. New York: Lee & Low.

_____. (2000). *Sacajawea*. San Diego, CA: Silver Whistle.

_____. (2001). *The Heart of a Chief*. New York: Penguin.

_____. (2003). *Pocahontas*. Orlando, FL: Silver Whistle.

_____. (2004). *The Dark Pond*. New York: HarperCollins.

_____. (2004). *Jim Thorpe's Bright Path*. Illustrated by S. D. Nelson. New York: Lee & Low Books.

_____. (2008). *Sacajawea*. New York: Harcourt.

Bruel, Robert O. (2007). *Bob and Otto*. Illustrated by Nick Bruel. New Milford, CN: Roaring Brook Press.

Brugman, Alyssa. (2007). *Being Bindy*. New York: Random House.

Brusca, María Cristina, & Tona Wilson. (1995). *When Jaguars Ate the Moon and Other Stories about Animals and Plants of the Americas*. New York: Holt.

Bryan, Ashley. (1986). *Lion and the Ostrich Chicks*. New York: Atheneum.

_____. (1998). *Ashley Bryan's African Tales, Uh-Huh*. New York: Atheneum.

_____. (2002). *Beautiful Blackbird*. New York: Simon & Schuster.

_____. (2007). *Let It Shine*. New York: Simon & Schuster.

Bryant, Jen. (2004). *The Trial*. New York: Knopf.

_____. (2007). *Pieces of Georgia*. New York: Random House.

_____. (2008). *Ringside, 1925: Views from the Scopes Trial*. New York.

_____. (2008). *A River of Words: The Story of William Carlos Williams*. Illustrated by Melissa Sweet. Grand Rapids, MI: Eerdmans.

Buckingham, Royce. (2007). *Demonkeeper*. New York: Penguin.

Bucknall, Caroline. (1986). *Three Little Pigs*. New York: Dial.

Bunge, Daniela. (2006). *The Scarves*. Translated by Kathryn Bishop. New York: Minedition.

_____. (2007). *Cherry Time*. New York: Penguin.

Bunting, Eve. (1990). *The Wall*. Illustrated by Ronald Himler. New York: Clarion.

_____. (1991). *Fly Away Home*. Boston: Houghton Mifflin.

_____. (1994). *Smoky Night*. Illustrated by David Diaz. San Diego, CA: Harcourt.

_____. (2006). *One Green Apple*. Illustrated by Ted Lewin. New York: Clarion.

_____. (2007). *Hurry! Hurry!*. Illustrated by Jeff Mack. San Diego, CA: Harcourt.

Burchard, Peter. (1999). *Lincoln and Slavery*. New York: Atheneum.

_____. (2003). *Frederick Douglass: For the Great Family of Man*. New York: Atheneum.

Burgess, Melvin. (1998). *Smack*. New York: Holt.

Burkert, Nancy Elkholm. (1972). *Snow White*. New York: Farrar, Straus & Giroux.

Burks, Brian. (1995). *Runs with Horses*. San Diego, CA: Harcourt.

_____. (1998). *Walks Alone*. San Diego, CA: Harcourt.

Burleigh, Robert. (1991). *Flight: The Journey of Charles Lindbergh*. New York: Philomel.

_____. (1998). *Black Whiteness: Admiral Byrd Alone in the Antarctic*. New York: Atheneum.

_____. (2004). *Langston's Train Ride*. Illustrated by Leonard Jenkins. New York: Orchard.

_____. (2004). *Seurat and La Grande Jatte: Connecting the Dots*. New York: Abrams Books for Young Readers.

Burman, Ben Lucien. (1952). *High Water at Catfish Bend*. New York: Messner.

Burnett, Frances Hodgson. (1962). *The Secret Garden*. New York: HarperCollins.

Burnford, Sheila, and Carl Burger. (1961) *The Incredible Journey*. Boston: Little, Brown.

Burns, Loree Griffin. (2007). *Tracking Trash: Flotsam, Jetsam, and the Science of Ocean Motion*. Boston: Houghton Mifflin.

Butler, John. (2007). *Can You Growl Like a Bear?* Atlanta, GA: Peachtree.

Byars, Betsy. (1970). *The Summer of the Swans*. New York: Viking.

———. (1986). *The Not-Just-Anybody Family*. New York: Dell.

———. (1994). *The Dark Stairs: A Herculeah Jones Mystery*. New York: Viking.

———. (2002). *Keeper of the Doves*. New York: Viking.

Byars, Betsy, Betsy Duffey and Laurie Myers. (2004). *The SOS File*. Illustrated by Arthur Howard. New York: Holt.

———. (2007). *Dog Diaries: Secret Writings of the WOOF Society*. Illustrated by Erik Brooks. New York: Holt.

Bynum, Janie. (2006). *Nutmeg and Barley: A Budding Friendship*. Cambridge, MA: Candlewick.

Byrd, Robert. (2003). *Leonardo: Beautiful Dreamer*. New York: Dutton.

Cadnum, Michael. (2002). *The Book of the Lion*. New York: Viking.

———. (2003). *Ship of Fire*. New York: Viking.

———. (2004). *Blood Gold*. New York: Viking.

———. (2004). *Starfall: Phaeton and the Chariot of the Sun*. New York: Orchard.

———. (2008). *The King's Arrow*. New York: Viking.

Cali, Davide. (2007). *Piano Piano*. Illustrated by Eric Héliot. Watertown, MA: Charlesbridge.

Campbell, Sarah C. (2008). *Wolfsnail: A Backyard Predator*. Illustrated by Richard P. Campbell. Honesdale, PA: Boyds Mills.

Carbone, Elisa Lynn. (2008). *Night Running: How James Escaped with the Help of His Faithful Dog*. Illustrated by E. B. Lewis. New York: Random House.

Carbone, Elisa. (2001). *Storm Warriors*. New York: Knopf.

Carle, Eric. (1981). *The Very Hungry Caterpiller*. New York: Philomel.

———. (1989). *The Very Busy Spider*. New York: Philomel.

Carlson, Lori M. (2005). *Moccasin Thunder: American Indian Stories for Today*. New York: HarperCollins.

Carmi, Daniella. (2000). *Samir and Yonatan*. New York: Levine.

Carroll, Lewis. (1865/1992). *Alice's Adventures in Wonderland*. Illustrated by John Tenniel. New York: Morrow.

———. (1871/1977). *Through the Looking Glass*. Illustrated by John Tenniel. New York: St. Martin's Press.

———. (2007). *Jabberwocky*. Illustrated by Christopher Myers. New York: Hyperion.

———. (2008). *Alice in Wonderland*. Illustrated by Lisbeth Zwerger. London: Penguin.

Cart, Michael. (2003). *Necessary Noise: Stories about Our Families as They Really Are*. Illustrated by Charlotte Noruzi. New York: HarperCollins.

Carvell, Marlene. (2005). *Sweetgrass Basket*. New York: Dutton.

Casanova, Mary. (1995). *Moose Tracks*. New York: Hyperion.

———. (1997). *Wolf Shadows*. New York: Hyperion.

———. (2007). *The Klipfish Code*. Boston: Houghton Mifflin.

———. (2007). *Some Dog!*. Illustrated by Ard Hoyt. New York: Farrar, Straus & Giroux.

———. (2007). *To Catch a Burglar*. Illustrated by Omar Rayyan. New York: Aladdin.

Cassedy, Sylvia. (1983). *Behind the Attic Wall*. New York: T. Y. Crowell.

———. (1989). *Lucie Babbidge's House*. New York: T. Y. Crowell.

Cassedy, Sylvia, & Kunihiro Suetake. (1992). *Red Dragonfly on My Shoulder*. Illustrated by Molly Bang. New York: HarperCollins Publishers.

Castellucci, Cecil. (2007). *Plain Janes*. Illustrated by Jim Rugg. New York: DC/Minx.

Catalanotto, Peter. (2007). *Ivan the Terrier*. New York: Atheneum Books.

Catalanotto, Peter, & Pamela Schembri. (2008). *The Veteran's Day Visitor*. New York: Holt.

Cazet, Denys. (1998). *Minnie and Moo Go to the Moon*. New York: DK Publishing.

Cech, John. (2007). *The Elves and the Shoemaker*. Illustrated by Kirill Chelushkin. Falls Church, VA: Sterling.

Cecil, Laura. (1995). *The Frog Princess*. Illustrated by Emma Chichester Clark. New York: Greenwillow.

Chaconas, Dori. (2007). *Virginnie's Hat*. Illustrated by Holly Meade. Cambridge, MA: Candlewick.

Chen, Chih-Yuan. (2003). *On My Way to Buy Eggs*. La Jolla, CA: Kane Miller.

———. (2004). *Guji Guji*. La Jolla, CA: Kane Miller.

Cheng, Andrea. (2003). *The Key Collection*. New York: Holt.

———. (2004). *Honeysuckle House*. Asheville, NC: Front Street.

———. (2008). *Where the Steps Were*. Honesdale, PA: Wordsong.

Cherry, Lynn, & Gary Braasch. (2008). *How We Know What We Know About Our Changing Climate: Scientists and Kids Explore Global Warming*. Nevada City, CA: Dawn.

Chibbaro, Julie. (2005). *Redemption*. London: Simon & Schuster.

Child, Lauren. (2000). *Beware of the Storybook Wolves*. New York: Scholastic.

———. (2002). *Who's Afraid of the Big Bad Book?* New York: Hyperion.

———. (2007). *Clarice Bean, Don't Look Now*. Cambridge, MA: Candlewick.

Chodos-Irvine, Margaret. (2003). *Ella Sarah Gets Dressed*. San Diego, CA: Harcourt.

Chodos-Irvine, Margaret. (2006). *Best Best Friends*. San Diego, CA: Harcourt.

Choldenko, Gennifer. (2006). *Al Capone Does My Shirts*. New York: Putnam.

_____. (2007). *If a Tree Falls at Lunch Period*. New York: Harcourt.

Chotjewitz, David. (2004). *Daniel Half Human and the Good Nazi*. New York: Atheneum.

Christelow, Eileen. (2007). *Five Little Monkeys Go Shopping*. Boston: Clarion.

Christensen, Bonnie. (2001). *Woody Guthrie: Poet of the People*. New York: Knopf.

Christopher, John. (1967). *The City of Gold and Lead*. Old Tappan, NJ: Macmillan.

_____. (1967). *The White Mountains*. Old Tappan, NJ: Macmillan.

_____. (1970). *The Pool of Fire*. Old Tappan, NJ: Macmillan.

_____. (1988). *When the Tripods Came*. New York: Dutton.

Church, Caroline Jayne. (2007). *Digby Takes Charge*. New York: McElderry.

Ciardi, John. (1959). *The Reason for the Pelican*. Philadelphia: Lippincott.

_____. (1961). *I Met a Man*. Boston: Houghton Mifflin

_____. (1961). *The Man Who Sang the Sillies*. Philadelphia: Lippincott

_____. (1962). *You Read to Me, I'll Read to You*. Philadelphia: Lippincott.

_____. (1964). *You Know Who*. Philadelphia: Lippincott.

_____. (1966). *The Monster Den: Or Look What Happened at My House—and to It*. Philadelphia: Clarion.

Cisneros, Sandra. (1997). *Hairs/Pelitos*. Illustrated by Terry Ybanez. New York: Knopf.

Cleary, Brian P. (2000). *Hairy, Scary, Ordinary: What Is an Adjective? (Words Are Categorical Series)*. Illustrated by Jenya Prosmitsky. Minneapolis: Lerner.

Clement-Moore, Rosemary. (2007). *Prom Dates from Hell*. New York: Delacorte.

Clements, Andrew. (1996). *Frindle*. Illustrated by Brian Selznick. New York: Simon & Schuster.

_____. (1999). *The Landry News*. Illustrated by Sal Murdocca. New York: Simon & Schuster.

_____. (2000). *The Janitor's Boy*. New York: Simon & Schuster.

_____. (2001). *The School Story*. Illustrated by Brian Selznick. New York: Simon & Schuster.

_____. (2002). *Things Not Seen*. New York: Philomel.

_____. (2008). *Lost and Found*. Illustrated by Mark Elliott. New York: Atheneum.

Clifton, Lucille. (2000). *The Times They Used to Be*. New York: Delacorte.

Climo, Shirley. (1989). *The Egyptian Cinderella*. Illustrated by Ruth Heller. New York: Crowell.

_____. (1993). *The Korean Cinderella*. Illustrated by Ruth Heller. New York: HarperCollins.

_____. (1994). *Stolen Thunder: A Norse Myth*. Illustrated by Alexander Koshkin. New York: Clarion.

_____. (1995). *Atalanta's Race: A Greek Myth*. Illustrated by Alexander Koshkin. New York: Clarion.

_____. (1995). *The Little Red Ant and the Great Big Crumb: A Mexican Fable*. Illustrated by Francisco X. Mora. New York: Clarion.

_____. (2002). *Tuko and the Birds: A Tale from the Philippines*. Illustrated by Francisco X. Mora. New York: Holt.

_____. (2005). *Monkey Business: Stories from Around the World*. Illustrated by Erik Brooks. New York: Holt.

_____. (1996). *The Irish Cinderella*. New York: HarperCollins.

Cline-Ransome, Lisa. (2007). *Pelé: Soccer's First Star*. Illustrated by James Ransome. New York: Random House.

Cobb, Vicki. (2003). *I Face the Wind*. New York: Scholastic.

Codell, Esme Raji. (2003). *Sahara Special*. New York: Hyperion.

_____. (2004). *Sing a Song of Tuna Fish: Hard-to-Swallow Stories from Fifth Grade*. New York: Hyperion.

Cofer, Judith. (2004). *Call Me Maria*. New York: Orchard.

Coffelt, Nancy. (2007). *Fred Stays with Me!* Illustrated by Tricia Tusa. Boston: Little, Brown.

Cohn, Rachel, & David Levithan. (2007). *Nick & Norah's Infinite Playlist*. New York: Random House.

Cole, Brock. (1987). *The Goats*. New York: Farrar, Straus & Giroux.

_____. (2007). *Good Enough to Eat*. New York: Farrar, Straus & Giroux. Brookfield, CN: Roaring Brook Press.

Coleman, Evelyn. (1998). *The Riches of Osceola McCarty*. Morton Grove, IL: Albert Whitman.

Coleman, Michael. (1996). *Weirdo's War*. London: Orchard.

Colfer, Eoin. (2001). *Artemis Fowl*. New York: Hyperion.

_____. (2008). *Airman*. New York: Hyperion.

Collier, Bryan. (2003). *Uptown*. New York: Holt.

Collier, James Lincoln, and Christopher Collier. (1974). *My Brother Sam Is Dead*. Old Tappan, NJ: Macmillan.

Collins, Mary. (2003). *Airborne: A Photobiography of Wilbur and Orville Wright*. Washington, D. C.: National Geographic Society.

Collins, Suzanne. (2007). *Gregor and the Code of Claw*. New York: Scholastic.

_____. (2008). *The Hunger Games*. New York: Scholastic.

Collodi, Carlo. (1883/1993). *Pinocchio*. Illustrated by Lorenzo Mattotti. New York: Lothrop, Lee & Shephard.

Colman, Penny. (1995). *Rosie the Riveter: Women Working on the Home Front in World War II*. New York: Crown.

Coloumbis, Audrey. (1999). *Getting Near to Baby*. New York: Putnam.

Compton, Kenn, & Joanne Compton. (1993). *Jack the Giant Chaser: An Appalachian Tale*. New York: Holiday House.

Cone, Molly. (1992). *Come Back, Salmon*. San Francisco: Sierra Club.

Conly, Jane Leslie. (1995). *Trout Summer*. New York: Holt.

_____. (1998). *While No One Was Watching*. New York: Holt.

Connolly, James E. (1985). *Why the Possum's Tail Is Bare and Other North American Indian Nature Tales*. Illustrated by Andrea Adams. Owings Mills, MD.: Stemmer House.

Conrad, Pam. (1985). *Prairie Songs*. Illustrated by Darryl Zudeck. New York: Harper & Row.

_____. (1991). *Pedro's Journal*. Honesdale, PA: Caroline House.

_____. (1991). *Prairie Vision: The Life and Times of Solomon Butcher*. New York: HarperCollins.

_____. (1996). *The Tub People*. New York: HarperCollins.

_____. (1996). *Zoe Rising*. New York: Laura Geringer Books.

Consentino, Ralph. (2006). *The Marvelous Misadventures of . . . Fun Boy*. New York: Viking.

Coombs, Kate. (2006). *The Secret-Keeper*. Illustrated by Heather M. Solomon. New York: Antheneum.

Cooney, Barbara. (1982). *Chanticleer and the Fox*. New York: HarperCollins.

_____. (1985). *Miss Rumphius*. New York: Penguin.

Cooney, Caroline B. (2007). *Diamonds in the Shadow*. New York: Delacorte.

_____. (2007). *Enter Three Witches: A Story of Macbeth*. New York: Scholastic.

Cooper, Elisha. (2006). *Beach*. New York: Orchard.

Cooper, Floyd. (1994). *Coming Home: From the Life of Langston Hughes*. New York: Philomel.

_____. (2004). *Jump! From the Life of Michael Jordan*. New York: Philomel.

Cooper, Helen. (2007). *Delicious!* New York: Farrar, Straus & Giroux.

Cooper, Ilene. (2003). *Jack: The Early Years of John F. Kennedy*. New Yyork: Dutton.

Cooper, Susan. (1966). *Over Sea, Under Stone*. San Diego, CA: Harcourt.

_____. (1973). *The Dark Is Rising*. Illustrated by Alan E. Cober. New York: Atheneum.

_____. (1973). *Greenwitch*. New York: McElderry.

_____. (1974). *The Grey King*. New York: McElderry.

_____. (1977). *Silver on the Tree*. New York: McElderry.

_____. (2006). *Victory*. New York: Simon & Schuster.

Corbet, Robert. (2002). *Fifteen Love*. London: A & U.

Corcoran, Barbara. (1993). *Wolf at the Door*. New York: Atheneum.

Cormier, Robert. (1974). *The Chocolate War*. New York: Knopf.

_____. (2001). *The Rag and Bone Shop*. New York: Delacorte.

Cornelissen, Cornelia. (1999). *Soft Rain: A Story of the Cherokee Trail of Tears*. New York: Delacorte.

Cottin, Menena. (2008). *The Black Book of Colors*. Toronto: Groundwood.

Couloumbis, Audrey. (1999). *Getting Near to Baby*. New York: Putnam.

Cousins, Lucy. (1996). *Katy Cat and Beaky Boo*. Illustrated by Lucy Cousins. Cambridge, MA: Candlewick.

Coville, Bruce. (1991). *Jeremy Thatcher, Dragon Hatcher*. San Diego, CA: Harcourt.

Coville, Bruce. (1992). *Jennifer Murdley's Toad*. Illustrated by Gary Lippincott. San Diego, CA: Harcourt.

Cowley, Joy. (2008). *Chicken Feathers*. Illustrated by David Elliot. New York: Philomel.

Coy, John. (2007). *Crackback*. New York: Scholastic.

_____. (2008). *Box Out*. New York: Scholastic.

Crawford, Elizabeth D. (1983). *Little Red Cap*. Illustrated by Lisbeth Zwerger. New York: North-South Books.

Creagh, Carson. (2005). *Things with Wings*. New York: Barnes and Noble.

Creech, Sharon. (1994). *Walk Two Moons*. New York: HarperCollins.

_____. (1997). *Chasing Redbird*. New York: HarperCollins.

_____. (2000). *The Wanderer*. New York: HarperCollins.

_____. (2001). *Love That Dog*. New York: HarperCollins.

_____. (2002). *Ruby Holler*. New York: Joanna Cotler Books.

_____. (2003). *Granny Torrelli Makes Soup*. London: Bloomsbury.

_____. (2004). *Heartbeat*. New York: HarperCollins.

_____. (2007). *Castle Corona*. Illustrated by David Diaz. New York: Joanna Cotler Books.

_____. (2008). *Hate That Cat*. New York: Joanna Cotler Books.

Cresswell, Helen. (1977). *Ordinary Jack*. New York: Macmillan.

Crew, Linda. (2001). *Brides of Eden: A True Story Imagined*. New York: HarperCollins.

Crews, Donald. (1978). *Freight Train*. New York: Greenwillow.

_____. (1992). *Shortcut*. New York: Greenwillow.

Crews, Nina. (2004). *The Neighborhood Mother Goose*. New York: Greenwillow.

_____. (2006). *Below*. New York: Holt.

Criswell, Patti Kelley. (2007). *The Book Club Kit*. Illustrated by Ali Douglass. Middleton, WI: American Girl.

Cronin, Doreen. (2000). *Click Clack Moo: Cows That Type*. Illustrated by Betsy Lewin. New York: Simon & Schuster.

Cross, Gillian. (1994). *New World*. New York: Holiday House.

_____. (2004). *The Dark Ground: Book One*. New York: Dutton.

_____. (2005). *The Black Room: Book Two*. New York: Dutton.

_____. (2007). *Nightmare Game: Book Three*. New York: Dutton.

Crossley-Holland, Kevin. (1968). *Beowulf*. Translated by Bruce Mitchell. New York: Farrar, Straus & Giroux.

_____. (1998). *The World of King Arthur and His Court: People, Places, Legend and Lore*. Illustrated by Peter Malone. New York: Dutton.

_____. (2001). *The Seeing Stone*. New York: Scholastic.

_____. (2002). *At the Crossing Places*. New York: Scholastic.

_____. (2004). *King of the Middle March*. New York: Scholastic.

_____. (2008). *Crossing to Paradise*. New York: Levine.

Crowe, Chris. (2002). *Mississippi Trial, 1955*. New York: P. Fogelman Books.

_____. (2003). *Getting Away with Murder: The True Story of the Emmett Till Case*. New York: Penguin.

Cruise, Robin. (2007). *Only You*. Illustrated by Margaret Chodos-Irvine. San Diego, CA: Harcourt.

Crum, Shutta. (2007). *A Family for Old Mill Farm*. New York: Clarion.

Crutcher, Chris. (1983). *Running Loose*. New York: Greenwillow.

_____. (1993). *Staying Fat for Sarah Byrnes*. New York: Greenwillow.

_____. (1995). *Ironman*. New York: Greenwillow.

_____. (2001). *Whale Talk*. New York: Greenwillow.

_____. (2003). *King of the Mild Frontier: An Ill-Advised Autobiography*. New York: Greenwillow.

_____. (2007). *Deadline*. New York: Greenwillow.

Cullinan, Bernice. (1996). *A Jar of Tiny Stars: Poems by NCTE Award-Winning Poets*. Illustrated by Andi Macleod and Marc Nadel. Honesdale, PA.: Wordsong.

Cummings, Priscilla. (2004). *Red Kayak*. New York: Dutton.

Cummins, Pat. (1992). *Talking with Artists*. Scarsdale, NY: Bradbury.

Cunnane, Kelly. (2006). *For You Are a Kenyan Child*. Illustrated by Ana Juan. New York: Antheneum.

Curlee, Lynn. (2001). *Brooklyn Bridge*. New York: HarperCollins.

_____. (2008). *Mythological Creatures: A Classical Bestiary: Tales of Strange Beings Fabulous Creatures, Fearsome Beasts, & Hideous Monsters from Ancient Greek Mythology*. New York: Atheneum.

Curry, Jane Louise. (1998). *Dark Shade*. New York: McElderry.

Curtis, Christopher Paul. (1995). *The Watsons Go to Birmingham—1963*. New York: Delacorte.

_____. (2004). *Bud, Not Buddy*. New York: Delacorte.

_____. (2007). *Elijah of Buxton*. New York: Scholastic.

Cushman, Karen. (1994). *Catherine, Called Birdy*. New York: Clarion.

_____. (1995). *The Midwife's Apprentice*. New York: Clarion.

_____. (1996). *The Ballad of Lucy Whipple*. New York: Clarion.

_____. (2000). *Matilda Bone*. New York: Clarion.

_____. (2003). *Rodzina*. New York: Clarion.

_____. (2008). *The Loud Silence of Francine Green*. New York: Clarion.

D'Adamo, Francesco. (2003). *Iqbal*. New York: Atheneum.

D'Aulaire, Ingri, and Edgar Parin d'Aulaire. (1955/1966). *Columbus*. Sandwich Village, MA: Beautiful Feet Books.

Dadey, Debbie. (2007). *The Worst Name in the Third Grade*. New York: Scholastic.

Dahl, Roald. (1961). *James and the Giant Peach*. New York: Knopf.

_____. (1964). *Charlie and the Chocolate Factory*. Illustrated by Joseph Schindelman. New York: Knopf.

_____. (1988). *Matilda*. New York: Viking Kestrel.

Dahlberg, Maurine. (2004). *Escape to West Berlin*. New York: Farrar, Straus & Giroux.

Daly, Niki. (2006). *Happy Birthday, Jamela!* New York: Farrar, Straus & Giroux.

_____. (2007). *Pretty Salma: A Little Red Riding Hood Story from Africa*. New York: Clarion.

Danziger, Paula. (2007). *Amber Brown*. New York: Penguin.

Dash, Joan. (2000). *The Longitude Prize*. New York: Farrar, Strauss, & Giroux.

_____. (2001). *The World at Her Fingertips: The Story of Helen Keller*. New York: Scholastic.

David, Laurie, & Cambria Gordon. (2007). *The Down-to-Earth Guide to Global Warming*. New York: Scholastic.

Davidson Mannis, Celeste. (2003). *The Queen's Progress: An Elizabethan Alphabet*. Illustrated by Bagram Ibatoulline. New York: Penguin.

Davies, Edith. (2001). *Pat the Bunny*. New York: Random House.

Davies, Jacqueline. (2004). *The Boy Who Drew Birds: A Story of John James Audubon*. Boston: Houghton Mifflin.

_____. (2006). *The Night Is Singing*. Illustrated by Kyrsten Brooker. New York: Dial.

Davies, Nicola. (2005). *Surprising Sharks*. Illustrated by James Croft. Cambridge, MA: Candlewick.

_____. (2007). *What's Eating You? Parasites—The Inside Story*. Illustrated by Neal Layton. Cambridge, MA: Candlewick.

_____. (2008). *White Owl, Barn Owl*. Illustrated by Michael Foreman. New York: Walker.

Davol, Marguerite W. (1997). *The Paper Dragon*. Illustrated by Robert Sabuda. New York: Simon & Schuster.

de Angeli, Marguerite. (1949). *The Door in the Wall*. New York: Doubleday.

de Brunhoff, Jean. (1933). *The Story of Babar*. New York: Random House.

de Brunhoff, Laurent. (2003). *Babar's Museum of Art*. New York: Abrams.

de la Mare, Walter. (1968). *Songs of Childhood*. Mineola, NY: Dover.

de la Peña, Matt. (2008). *Mexican Whiteboy*. New York: Delacorte.

de Regniers, Beatrice Schenk. (1972). *Red Riding Hood*. Illustrated by Edward Gorey. New York: Atheneum.

de Varennes, Monique. (2007). *The Jewel Box Ballerinas*. Illustrated by Ana Juan. New York: Schwartz & Wade.

Debon, Nicolas. (2003). *Four Pictures by Emily Carr*. Toronto: Groundwood.

_____. (2007). *The Strongest Man in the World: Louis Cyr*. Toronto: Groundwood.

Deedy, Carmen Agra. (2007). *Martina the Beautiful Cockroach: A Cuban Folktale*. Illustrated by Michael Austin. Atlanta, GA: Peachtree.

DeFelice, Cynthia. (1999). *Nowhere to Call Home*. New York: Farrar, Straus & Giroux.

_____. (2006). *One Potato, Two Potato*. Illustrated by Andrea U'Ren. New York: Farrar, Straus & Giroux.

Degen, Bruce. (1995). *Jamberry*. New York: HarperCollins.

Degens, T. (1974). *Transport 451-R*. New York: Viking.

_____. (1990). *On the Third Ward*. New York: Harper & Row.

deGroat, Diane. (2007). *Last One In Is a Rotten Egg!* New York: HarperCollins.

Delaney, Joseph. (2007). *Night of the Soul Stealer.* New York: Greenwillow.

Delano, Marfe Ferguson. (2005). *Genius: A Photobiography of Albert Einstein.* Washington, DC: National Geographic Society.

Del Vecchio, Gene. (2007). *The Sword of Anton.* Gretna, LA: Pelican.

Dematons, Charlotte. (2004). *The Yellow Balloon.* Honesdale, PA: Boyds Mills Press.

Demi. (1987). *A Chinese Zoo: Fables and Proverbs.* San Diego, CA: Harcourt.

———. (1990). *The Empty Pot.* New York: Holt.

———. (1990). *The Magic Boat.* New York: Holt.

———. (1994). *Firebird.* New York: Holt.

———. (1996). *Buddha.* New York: Holt.

———. (1998). *The Dalai Lama: A Biography of the Tibetan Spiritual and Political Leader.* New York: Holt.

———. (2001). *Gandhi.* New York: McElderry.

———. (2003). *Muhammad.* New York: McElderry.

———. (2004). *The Hungry Coat: A Tale from Turkey.* New York: McElderry.

———. (2007). *The Legend of Lao Tzu and the Tao Te Ching.* New York: Simon & Schuster.

Denise, Anika. (2007). *Pigs Love Potatoes.* Illustrated by Denise Christopher. New York: Philomel.

dePaola, Tomie. (1975). *Strega Nona.* New York: Simon & Schuster.

———. (1978). *Pancakes for Breakfast.* San Diego, CA: Harcourt.

———. (1985). *Tomie dePaola's Mother Goose.* London: Methuen Children's.

Dessen, Sarah. (1998). *Someone Like You.* New York: Viking.

———. (2000). *Dreamland.* New York: Viking.

———. (2004). *The Truth about Forever.* New York: Viking.

Deuker, Carl. (1993). *Heart of a Champion.* Boston: Joy Street.

———. (2000). *Night Hoops.* New York: HarperCollins.

———. (2007). *Gym Candy.* Boston: Houghton Mifflin.

Dewey, Jennifer. (1994). *Wildlife Rescue: The Work of Dr. Kathleen Ramsay.* Honesdale, PA: Wordsong.

Diakité, Baba Wagué. (2007). *Mee-Ann And The Magic Serpent.* Toronto: Groundwood.

Diakité, Penda. (2006). *I Lost My Tooth in Africa.* Illustrated by Baba Wagué Diakité. New York: Scholastic.

DiCamillo, Kate. (2000). *Because of Winn-Dixie.* Cambridge, MA: Candlewick.

———. (2003). *The Tale of Despereaux: Being the Story of a Mouse, a Princess, Some Soup, and a Spool of Thread.* Illustrated by Timothy Basil Ering. Cambridge, MA: Candlewick.

Dickinson, Peter. (1988). *Eva.* New York: Delacorte.

———. (1998). *Noli's Story.* New York: Grosset & Dunlap.

———. (1998). *Po's Story.* New York: Grosset & Dunlap.

———. (1998). *Suth's Story.* New York: Grosset & Dunlap.

———. (1999). *Mana's Story.* New York: Grosset & Dunlap.

———. (2007). *Angel Isle.* New York: Random House.

Diehl, David. (2007). *Sports A to Z.* New York: Lark.

Dillon, Eilís. (1954/2006). *The Lost Island.* New York: NYR Children's Collection.

Dillon, Leo, & Diane Dillon. (1998). *To Everything There Is a Season.* New York: Scholastic.

———. (2007). *Mother Goose: Numbers on the Loose.* San Diego, CA: Harcourt.

Divakaruns, Chitra Banerjee. (2003). *The Conch Bearer.* Brookfield, Conn: Roaring Brook Press.

DK Publishing. (2007). *Dinosaurium.* New York: DK Publishing.

———. (2007). *Night Sky Atlas.* New York: DK Publishing.

Doctorow, Cory. (2008). *Little Brother.* New York: HarperCollins.

Dodds, Dayle Ann. (2003). *Where's Pup?* Illustrated by Pierre Pratt. New York: Penguin.

———. (2006). *Teacher's Pets.* Illustrated by Marylin Hafner. Cambridge, MA: Candlewick.

Dodge, Mary Mapes. (1915). *Hans Brinker; or The Silver Skates.* York: Scribner.

Doeden, Matt. (2007). *Crazy Cars.* Minneapolis, MN: Lerner.

Doherty, Berlie. (2008). *The Girl Who Saw Lions.* Amsterdam: Facet.

Donaldson, Julia. (2007). *One Ted Falls Out of Bed.* Illustrated by Anna Currey. New York: Holt.

Donnelly, Jennifer. (2003). *A Northern Light.* New York: Farrar, Straus & Giroux.

Donnelly, Matt. (2003). *Theodore Roosevelt: Larger Than Life.* North Haven, CT: Linnet Books.

Donnio, Sylviane. (2007). *I'd Really Like To Eat A Child.* Illustrated by Dorothée de Monfreid. New York: Random House.

Dorris, Michael. (1992). *Morning Girl.* New York: Hyperion.

———. (1994). *Guests.* New York: Hyperion.

———. (1996). *Sees Behind Trees.* New York: Hyperion.

Dorros, Arthur. (1995). *Isla.* (1999). Illustrated by Elisa Kleven. New York: Penguin.

———. (1997). *A Tree Is Growing.* New York: Scholastic.

———. (1997). *Abuela.* Illustrated by Elisa Kleven. New York: Penguin.

———. (2004). *Under the Sun.* New York: Amulet.

Dowd, Siobhan. (2007). *The London Eye Mystery.* New York: David Fickling.

Dowell, Frances O'Roark. (2004). *The Secret Language of Girls.* New York: Aladdin.

———. (2007). *Phineas L. MacGuire . . . Gets Slimed!* Illustrated by Preston McDaniels. New York: Atheneum.

Downes, Belinda. (1996). *A Stitch in Rhyme: A Nursery Rhyme Sampler with Embroidered Illustrations.* New York: Knopf.

Doyle, Brian. (2001). *Mary Ann Alice.* Toronto: Douglas & McIntyre.

Doyle, Malachy. (2000). *Tales from Old Ireland*. Illustrated by Niamh Sharkey. New York: Barefoot.

Draper, Sharon. (2003). *The Battle of Jericho*. New York: Atheneum.

———. (2006). *Copper Sun*. New York: Atheneum.

———. (2008). *Fire from the Rock*. New York: Dutton.

Dronzek, Laura. (2007). *Rabbit's Gift*. Illustrated by George Shannon. San Diego, CA: Harcourt.

Dubosarsky, Ursula. (2007). *The Red Shoe*. New York: Roaring Brook Press.

Duder, Tessa. (1987). *In Lane Three, Alex Archer*. Boston: Houghton Mifflin.

Duey, Kathleen. (2007). *Skin Hunger*. New York: Atheneum.

Duffey, Betsy. (1994). *Coaster*. New York: Viking.

———. (1999). *Alien for Rent*. New York: Delacorte.

———. (1999). *Cody Unplugged*. New York: Viking.

Duke, Kate. (2007). *The Tale of Pip and Squeak*. New York: Dutton.

Dunbar, Polly. (2007). *Penguin*. Cambridge, MA: Candlewick.

Duncan, Lois. (1981). *Stranger with My Face*. Boston: Little, Brown.

Dunmore, Helen. (2008). *The Tide Knot*. New York: HarperCollins.

Dunrea, Olivier. (2008). *Boo-Boo*. Boston: Houghton Mifflin.

———. (2008). *Peedie*. Boston: Houghton Mifflin.

DuPrau, Jean. (2003). *The City of Ember*. New York: Yearling.

———. (2005). *The People of Sparks*. New York: Random House.

DuPrau, Jeanne. (2008). *The Diamond of Darkhold*. New York: Random House.

Durbin, William. (2004). *The Darkest Evening*. New York: Orchard.

———. (2008). *The Winter War*. New York: Random House.

Duvosin, Roger. (1961). *Veronica*. New York: Knopf.

Earls, Nick. (1999). *48 Shades of Brown*. Boston: Graphia.

Easton, Kelly. (2007). *White Magic: Spells to Hold You*. New York: Random House.

Eaton, Maxwell, III. (2007). *Best Buds*. New York: Knopf.

Edgeworth, Maria. (1864). *The Purple Jar*. Routledge.

Edmonds, Walter D. (1941). *The Matchlock Gun*. New York: Putnam.

Edwards, David. (2007). *The Pen That Pa Built*. Illustrated by Ashley Wolff. Berkeley, CA: Ten Speed Press.

Edwards, Pamela Duncan. (2001). *Boston Tea Party*. Illustrated by Henry Cole. New York: Putnam.

———. (2003). *The Wright Brothers*. Illustrated by Henry Cole. New York: Hyperion.

Edwards, Wallace. (2007). *The Painted Circus*. Tonawanda, NY: Kids Can Press.

Egielski, Richard. (2000). *The Gingerbread Boy*. New York: HarperCollins.

Ehlert, Lois. (1989). *Color Zoo*. New York: HarperCollins.

———. (1989). *Eating the Alphabet: Fruits & Vegetables from A to Z*. San Diego, CA: Harcourt.

———. (1990). *Color Farm*. New York: HarperCollins.

———. (1991). *Red Leaf, Yellow Leaf*. San Diego, CA: Harcourt.

———. (1994). *Mole's Hill*. San Diego, CA: Harcourt.

———. (2005). *Leaf Man*. San Diego, CA: Harcourt.

———. (2008). *Oodles of Animals*. San Diego, CA: Harcourt.

Ekoomiak, Normee. (1988). *Arctic Memories*. New York: Holt.

Eliot, T. S. (1959/1982). *Old Possum's Book of Practical Cats*. San Diego, CA: Harcourt Brace.

Elliott, David. (2008). *On the Farm*. Illustrated by Holly Meade. Cambridge, MA: Candlewick.

Elliott, Laura M. (2004). *Annie between the States*. New York: Katherine Tegen Books.

Elliott, Patricia. (2007). *Ambergate*. New York: Little, Brown.

Ellis, Deborah. (2000). *The Breadwinner*. Toronto: Douglas & McIntyre.

———. (2004). *Parvanna's Journey*. Oxford: Oxford University Press.

———. (2008). *Off to War: Voices of Soldier's Children*. Toronto: Groundwood.

Ellsworth, Loretta. (2002). *The Shrouding Woman*. New York: Holt.

Emberley, Barbara. (1967). *Drummer Hoff*. Illustrated by Ed Emberley. Upper Saddle River, NJ: Prentice Hall.

Endle, Kate. (2008). *Trout Are Made of Trees*. Watertown, MA: Charlesbridge.

Engdahl, Sylvia Louise. (1970). *Enchantress from the Stars*. Illustrated by Rodney Shackell. New York: Atheneum.

———. (1971). *The Far Side of Evil*. New York: Firebird.

England, Kathryn. (2007). *Grandfather's Wrinkles*. Illustrated by Richard McFarland. Brooklyn, NY: Flashlight.

Engle, Margarita. (2006). *The Poet Slave of Cuba: A Biography of Juan Francisco Manzano*. Illustrated by Sean Qualls. New York: Holt.

———. (2008). *The Surrender Tree: Poems of Cuba's Struggle for Freedom*. New York: Holt.

English, Karen. (2004). *Hot Day on Abbott Avenue*. Illustrated by Javaka Steptoe. New York: Clarion.

———. (2007). *Francie*. New York: Square Fish.

Erdich, Liselotte. (2003). *Sacagawea*. Illustrated by Julie Buffalohead. Minneapolis: Carolrhoda.

Erdrich, Louise. (1996). *Grandmother's Pigeon*. Illustrated by Jim LaMarche. New York: Hyperion.

———. (1999). *The Birchbark House*. New York: Hyperion.

———. (2005). *The Game of Silence*. New York: HarperCollins.

———. (2008). *The Porcupine Year*. New York: HarperCollins.

Ericsson, Jennifer. (2007). *A Piece of Chalk*. Illustrated by Michelle Shapiro. New Milford, Conn.: Roaring Brook.

Ernst, Lisa Campbell. (1995). *Little Red Riding Hood: A Newfangled Prairie Tale*. New York: Simon & Schuster.

———. (2004). *The Turn-Around, Upside-Down Alphabet Book*. New York: Simon & Schuster.

Esbensen, Barbara Juster. (1984). *Cold Stars and Fireflies*. New York: HarperCollins.

_____. (1986). *Words with Wrinkled Knees: Animal Poems.* New York: Crowell.

_____. (1989). *Ladder to the Sky: How the Gift of Healing Came to the Ojibway Nation.* Illustrated by Helen Davie. Boston: Little, Brown.

_____. (1992). *Who Shrank My Grandmother's House? Poems of Discovery.* Illustrated by Eric Beddows. Toronto: University of Toronto Press.

Evans, John D. (2007). *Diary of a Renaissance Man.* Oak Park, IL: The Evans Poetry Collection.

Evans, Lady Hestia. (2007). *Mythology.* Dugald A. Steer (Ed.). Cambridge, MA: Candlewick.

Falconer, Ian. (2000). *Olivia.* New York: Simon & Schuster.

_____. (2007). *Olivia Helps with Christmas.* New York: Atheneum.

Faller, Regis. (2006). *The Adventures of Polo.* New Milford, CT: Roaring Brook Press.

_____. (2007). *Polo The Runaway Book.* New Milford, CT: Roaring Book Press.

Farjeon, Eleanor. (1951). *Poems for Children.* Philadelphia: Lippincott.

_____. (1960). *The Children's Bells: A Selection of Poems.* New York: H. Z. Walck.

Farley, Walter. (1947/2008). *The Black Stallion.* Illustrated by Milton Menasco. New York: Random House.

Farmer, Nancy. (2002). *The House of the Scorpion.* New York: Atheneum.

_____. (2004). *The Sea of Trolls.* New York: Atheneum.

_____. (2006). *Clever Ali.* Illustrated by Gail de Marcken. New York: Orchard.

_____. (2007). *The Land of the Silver Apples.* New York: Atheneum.

_____. (2009). *Islands of the Blessed.* New York: Atheneum.

Farndon, John. (2007). *Do Not Open.* New York: Dorling Kindersley.

Faulkner, William J. (1995). *Brer Tiger and the Big Wind.* Illustrated by Roberta Wilson. New York: Morrow.

Feelings, Tom. (1993). *Soul Looks Back in Wonder.* New York: Dial.

_____. (1995). *Middle Passage: White Ships/Black Cargo.* New York: Dial.

Feiffer, Jules. (1997). *Meanwhile.* New York: HarperCollins.

_____. (1999). *Bark, George.* New York: Balzer & Bray.

Feinstein, John. (2007). *Cover Up: Mystery at the Super Bowl.* New York: Knopf.

Felin, M. Sindy. (2007). *Touching Snow.* New York: Atheneum.

Felix, Monique. (1988). *The Story of a Little Mouse Trapped in a Book.* La Jolla, CA: Green Tiger.

Fergus, Maureen. (2007). *Exploits of a Reluctant (But Extremely Goodlooking). Hero.* Tonawanda, NY: Kids Can Press.

Ferris, Jean. (1998). *Love Among the Walnuts.* San Diego, CA: Harcourt.

_____. (2002). *Once Upon a Marigold.* San Diego, CA: Harcourt.

Field, Eugene. (2008). *Wynken, Blynken and Nod.* Illustrated by Giselle Potter. New York: Random House.

Fienberg, Anna. (2007). *Number 8.* New York: Walker.

Figley, Marty Rhodes. (2004). *The Schoolchildren's Blizzard.* Minneapolis, MN: Carolrhhoda.

Fine, Anne. (1992). *Flour Babies.* Boston: Little, Brown.

_____. (2002). *The Jamie and Angus Stories.* Illustrated by Penny Dale. Cambridge, MA: Candlewick.

_____. (2007). *Jamie and Angus Together.* Illustrated by Penny Dale. Cambridge, MA: Candlewick.

Fisher, Aileen Lucia. (1962). *Like Nothing at All: Out in the Dark and Daylight.* Illustrated by Leonard Weisgard. New York: HarperCollins.

_____. (1980). *Anybody Home?* Illustrated by Susan Bonners. Ohio: Crowell.

_____. (1983). *Rabbits, Rabbits.* Illustrated by Gail Niemann. New York: Harper & Row.

_____. (1991). *Always Wondering.* Illustrated by Joan Sandin. New York: HarperCollins.

_____. (2001). *Sing of the Earth and Sky: Poems about Our Planet and the Wonders Beyond.* Illustrated by Karmen Thompson. Honesdale, PA: Wordsong.

Fisher, Aileen. (1988). *The House of a Mouse.* Illustrated by Joan Sandin. New York: HarperCollins.

Fisher, Catherine. (2003). *Snow-Walker.* New York: Greenwillow.

_____. (2003). *The Oracle Betrayed.* New York: Greenwillow.

Fisher, Leonard Everett. (1984). *Olympians: Great Gods and Goddesses of Ancient Greece.* New York: Holiday House.

_____. (1990). *The Oregon Trail.* New York: Holiday House.

_____. (1991). *The ABC Exhibit.* New York: Atheneum.

Fitzhugh, Louise. (1964). *Harriet the Spy.* New York: Harper & Row.

Flaherty, A. W. (2007). *The Luck of the Loch Ness Monster: A Tale of Picky Eating.* Illustrated by Scott Magoon. Boston: Houghton Mifflin.

Flake, Sharon. (2004). *Who Am I without Him? Short Stories about Girls and the Boys in their Lives.* New York: Hyperion.

_____. (2007). *Broken Bike Boy and the Queen of 33rd Street.* Illustrated by Colin Bootman. New York: Hyperion.

Fleischman, John. (2002). *Phineas Gage: A Gruesome but True Story about Brain Science.* Boston: Houghton Mifflin.

_____. (2007). *Black and White Airmen: Their True History.* Boston: Houghton Mifflin.

Fleischman, Paul. (1986). *I Am Phoenix: Poems for Two Voices.* Illustrated by Ken Nut. (Eric Beddowes). New York: HarperCollins.

_____. (1988). *Joyful Noise: Poems for Two Voices.* New York: HarperCollins.

_____. (1991). *The Borning Room.* New York: HarperCollins.

_____. (1991). *Time Train.* New York: HarperCollins.

_____. (1998). *Whirligig.* New York: Holt.

_____. (1999). *Weslandia.* Cambridge, MA: Candlewick.

Fleischman, Paul. (2000). *Big Talk: Poems for Four Voices*. Illustrated by Beppe Giacoppe. Cambridge, MA: Candlewick.

_____. (2001). *Seek*. Chicago: Cricket.

_____. (2007). *Glass Slipper, Gold Sandal: A Worldwide Cinderella*. Illustrated by Julie Paschkis. New York: Holt.

Fleischman, Sid. (1978). *McBroom and the Beanstalk*. Boston: Little, Brown.

_____. (1986). *The Whipping Boy*. New York: Greenwillow.

_____. (2008). *The Trouble Begins at 8: A Life of Mark Twain in the Wild, Wild West*. New York: Greenwillow.

Fleming, Candace. (2003). *Ben Franklin's Almanac: Being a True Account of the Good Gentleman's Life*. New York: Atheneum.

_____. (2005). *Our Eleanor: A Scrapbook Look at Eleanor Roosevelt's Remarkable Life*. New York: Simon & Schuster.

_____. (2008). *The Lincolns: A Scrapbook Look at Abraham and Mary*. New York: Random House.

Fleming, Denise. (1995). *On the Day You Were Born*. San Diego, CA: Harcourt.

_____. (1996). *Lunch*. New York: Holt.

_____. (1998). *In the Small, Small Pond*. New York: Holt.

_____. (2000). *The Everything Book*. New York: Holt.

_____. (2000). *Where Once There Was a Wood*. New York: Holt.

_____. (2001). *Barnyard Banter*. New York: Holt.

_____. (2002). *Alphabet Under Construction*. New York: Holt.

_____. (2002). *Mama Cat Has Three Kittens*. New York: Holt.

_____. (2006). *The Cow Who Clucked*. New York: Holt.

Fletcher, Ralph. (1998). *Flying Solo*. New York: Clarion.

_____. (2001). *Uncle Daddy*. New York: Holt.

Fletcher, Susan. (1998). *Shadow Spinner*. New York: Atheneum.

_____. (2007). *Dadblamed Union Army Cow*. Illustrated by Kimberly Bulcken Root. New York: Clarion.

Flinn, Alex. (2004). *Nothing to Lose*. New York: HarperCollins.

Floca, Brian. (2003). *The Racecar Alphabet*. New York: Simon & Schuster.

_____. (2007). *Lightship*. New York: Simon & Schuster.

Florian, Douglas. (1997). *In the Swim: Poems and Paintings*. San Diego, CA: Harcourt Brace.

_____. (1999). *Winter Eyes*. New York: Greenwillow.

_____. (2002). *Summersaults: Poems and Paintings*. New York: Greenwillow.

_____. (2003). *Autumblings*. New York: Greenwillow.

_____. (2006). *Handsprings*. New York: Greenwillow.

Forbes, Esther. (1943). *Johnny Tremain*. Boston: Houghton Mifflin.

Forester, Victoria. (2008). *The Girl Who Could Fly*. New York: Feiwel.

Foster, Mark. (2007). *Whale Port*. Illustrated by Gerald Foster. Boston: Houghton Mifflin.

Fox, Diane, & Christyan Fox. (2007). *Tyson The Terrible*. London: Bloomsbury/Walker.

Fox, Mem. (1989). *Wilfred Gordon McDonald Partridge*. Illustrated by Julie Vivas. La Jolla: Kane Miller.

_____. (1992). *Hattie and the Fox*. Illustrated by Patricia Mullins. New York: Simon & Schuster.

_____. (1997). *Whoever You Are*. San Diego, CA: Harcourt.

_____. (2004). *Where Is the Green Sheep?* Illustrated by Judy Horacek. San Diego, CA: Harcourt.

Fox, Paula. (1984). *The One-Eyed Cat*. Scarsdale, NY: Bradbury.

_____. (1991). *Monkey Island*. New York: Orchard.

Fradin, Dennis Brindell, & Judith Bloom Fradin. (2000). *Ida B. Wells: Mother of the Civil Rights Movement*. New York: Clarion.

_____. (2003). *Fight On! Mary Church Terrell's Battle for Integration*. New York: Clarion.

Frame, Jeron Ashford. (2008). *Yesterday I Had the Blues*. Illustrated by Christie R. Gregory. Berkeley, CA: Ten Speed Press.

Franco, Betsy. (2003). *Mathmatickles!* Illustrated by Steven Salermo. New York: McElderry.

Frank, Anne. (1952). *The Diary of a Young Girl*. New York: Modern Library.

Frank, E. R. (2000). *Life Is Funny*. New York: DK Publishing.

Frank, Lucy. (1995). *I Am an Artichoke*. New York: Holiday House.

Franklin, Kristine. (2003). *The Grape Thief*. Cambridge, MA: Candlewick.

Frasier, Debra. (1991). *On the Day You Were Born*. San Diego, CA: Harcourt.

_____. (2002). *Out of the Ocean*. New York: Voyager.

_____. (2004). *The Incredible Water Show*. San Diego, CA: Harcourt.

_____. (2007). *Miss Alaineus: A Vocabulary Disaster*. New York: Voyager.

Frazee, Marla. (2006). *Roller Coaster*. New York: Voyager.

_____. (2008). *A Couple of Boys Have the Best Week Ever*. Orlando: Harcourt.

Fredericks, Mariah. (2007). *Love*. New York: Atheneum.

Freedman, Deborah. (2007). *Scribble*. New York: Random House.

Freedman, Russell. (1987). *Lincoln: A Photobiography*. New York: Clarion.

_____. (1990). *Franklin Delano Roosevelt*. New York: Clarion.

_____. (1992). *An Indian Winter*. New York: Holiday House.

_____. (1994). *Kids at Work: Lewis Hine and the Crusade against Child Labor*. New York: Clarion.

_____. (1996). *The Life and Death of Crazy Horse*. New York: Holiday House.

_____. (2002). *Confucius: The Golden Rule*. Illustrated by Frederic Clement. New York: Levine.

_____. (2003). *Defense of Liberty: The Story of America's Bill of Rights*. New York: Holiday House.

_____. (2004). *The Voice That Challenged a Nation: Marian Anderson and the Struggle for Equal Rights*. New York: Clarion.

_____. (2005). *Children of the Great Depression*. New York: Clarion.

Freedman, Russell. (2006). *Freedom Walkers: The Story of the Montgomery Bus Boycott*. New York: Holiday House.

_____. (2007). *Who Was First? Discovering the Americas*. New York: Clarion.

_____. (2008). *Washington at Valley Forge*. New York: Holiday House.

French, Vivian. (2008). *The Robe of Skulls*. Cambridge, MA: Candlewick.

Freymann, Saxton. (2006). *Baby Food*. Illustrated by Joost Elfers. New York: Scholastic.

_____. (2006). *Dog Food*. Illustrated by Joost Elfers. New York: Scholastic.

_____. (2006). *Fast Food*. Illustrated by Joost Elfers. New York: Scholastic.

Friedman, Ina R. (1987). *How My Parents Learned To Eat*. Illustrated by Allan Say. San Anselmo, CA: Sandpiper.

Friend, Catherine. (2001). *The Perfect Nest*. Illustrated by John Manders. Cambridge, MA: Candlewick.

Friend, Natasha. (2007). *Lush*. New York: Scholastic.

Frisch, Aaron, & Gary Kelley. (2008). *Dark Fiddler: The Life and Legend of Nicolo Paganini*. Mankato, MN: Creations Edition.

Fritz, Jean. (1973). *And Then What Happened, Paul Revere?* Illustrated by Margot Tomes. New York: Coward, McCann & Geoghegan.

_____. (1974). *Why Don't You Get a Horse, Sam Adams?* Illustrated by Trina Schart Hyman. New York: Coward, McCann & Geoghegan.

_____. (1976). *What's the Big Idea, Ben Franklin?* Illustrated by Margot Tomes. New York: Putnam & Grosset Group.

_____. (1976). *Will You Sign Here, John Hancock?* Illustrated by Trina Schart Hyman. New York: Coward. McCann & Geoghegan.

_____. (1977). *Can't You Make Them Behave, King George?* Illustrated by Tommie de Paola & Margot Tomes. New York: Coward, McCann & Geoghegan.

_____. (1989). *The Great Little Madison*. New York: Putnam.

Frost, Helen, & Leonid Gore. (2008). *Monarch and Milkweed*. New York: Atheneum.

Frost, Helen. (2006). *The Braid*. Detroit: Thorndike.

_____. (2008). *Diamond Willow*. New York: Farrar, Straus & Giroux.

_____. (2008). *Monarch and Milkweed*. Illustrated by Leonid Gore. New York: Atheneum.

Funke, Cornelia. (2002). *The Thief Lord*. New York: Scholastic.

_____. (2003). *Inkheart*. New York: Scholastic.

_____. (2004). *Dragon Rider*. New York: Scholastic.

_____. (2005). *Inkspell*. New York: Scholastic.

_____. (2006). *The Wildest Brother*. Illustrated by Kerstin Meyer. New York: Scholastic.

_____. (2008). *Inkdeath*. New York: Scholastic.

Furlong, Monica. (2004). *Colman*. New York: Random House.

_____. (2004). *Juniper*. New York: Random House.

_____. (2004). *Wise Child*. New York: Random House.

Gag, Wanda. (1928). *Millions of Cats*. New York: Coward-McCann.

Gaiman, Neil. (1993). *Sandman*. New York: St. Martin's Press.

_____. (2008). *Coraline*. New York: HarperCollins.

_____. (2008). *The Graveyard Book*. Illus David McKean. New York: HarperCollins.

Gaiman, Neil, & Reaves, Michael. (2007). *InterWorld*. New York: Eos.

Galdone, Paul. (1969). *The Monkey and the Crocodile: A Jataka Tale from India*. New York: Seabury.

_____. (1986). *Three Little Kittens*. New York: Clarion.

Gall, Chris. (2006). *Dear Fish*. New York: Little, Brown.

_____. (2008). *There's Nothing to Do on Mars*. New York: Little, Brown.

Galloway, Priscilla. (1995). *Truly Grim Tales*. New York: Delacorte.

Gantos, Jack. (1999). *Jack on the Tracks: Four Seasons of Fifth Grade*. New York: Farrar, Straus & Giroux.

_____. (2000). *Joey Pigza Loses Control*. New York: Farrar, Straus & Giroux.

_____. (2002). *Hole in My Life*. New York: Farrar, Straus & Giroux.

_____. (2007). *I Am Not Joey Pigza*. New York: Farrar, Straus & Giroux.

Garden, Nancy. (1982). *Annie on My Mind*. New York: Farrar, Straus & Giroux.

Gardner, Lyn. (2007). *Into the Woods*. New York: David Fickling Books.

Garza, Carmen Lomas. (1997). *In my Family/En mi familia*. Danbury, CT: Children's Book Press.

Gauthier, Gail. (2003). *Saving the Planet and Stuff*. New York: Putnam.

_____. (2007). *A Girl, a Boy, and a Monster Cat*. Illustrated by Joe Cepeda. New York: Putnam.

Gee, Joshua. (2007). *Encyclopedia Horrifica*. New York: Scholastic.

Geisel, Theodore. (1957). *The Cat in the Hat*. New York: Random House.

_____. (1989). *And to Think I Saw It on Mulberry Street*. New York: Random House.

Geisert, Arthur. (2008). *Hogwash*. Boston: Houghton Mifflin.

Geisert, Bonnie. (2002). *Prairie Summer*. Illustrated by Arthur Geisert. Boston: Hougton Mifflin.

Geist, Ken, & Julia Gorton. (2007). *Three Little Fish and the Big Bad Shark*. New York: Cartwheel.

Gelman, Rita Golden. (2004). *Doodler Doodling*. Illustrated by Paul Zelinsky. New York: HarperCollins.

George, Jean Craighead. (1959). *My Side of the Mountain*. New York: Dutton.

_____. (1972). *Julie of the Wolves*. New York: Harper & Row.

_____. (1980). *The Cry of the Crow*. New York: Harper & Row.

_____. (2008). *The Wolves Are Back*. Illustrated by Wendell Minor. New York: Penguin.

George, Kristine O'Connell. (2001). *Toasting Marshmallows: Camping Poems*. Illustrated by Kate Kiesler. New York: Clarion.

_____. (2004). *Hummingbird Nest: A Journal of Poems*. Illustrated by Barry Moser. Orlando, FL: Harcourt.

_____. (2005). *Fold Me a Poem*. Illustrated by Lauren Stringer. San Diego, CA: Harcourt.

George, Madeleine. (2008). *Looks*. New York: Viking.

Geras, Adele. (2001). *Troy*. San Diego, CA: Harcourt.

_____. (2006). *Ithaka*. Orlando, FL: Harcourt.

Gerasole, Isabella, & Olivia Gerasole. (2007). *The Spatulatta Cookbook*. New York: Scholastic.

Gershator, Phyllis. (2005). *Sky Sweeper*. Illustrated by Holly Meade. New York: Farrar, Straus & Giroux.

Gerson, Mary-Joan. (1994). *Why the Sky Is Far Away: A Nigerian Folktale*. Illustrated by Carla Golembe. Boston: Little, Brown.

_____. (1995) *People of Corn: A Mayan Story*. Illustrated by Carla Golembe. Boston: Little, Brown.

Gerstein, Mordicai. (2002). *What Charlie Heard*. New York: Farrar, Straus & Giroux.

_____. (2003). *The Man Who Walked Between the Towers*. Brookfield, CT: Roaring Brook Press.

_____. (2003). *Sparrow Jack*. New York: Frances Foster Books.

Gibbons, Gail. (2008). *Corn*. New York: Holiday House.

Giblin, James Cross. (1997). *Charles A. Lindbergh: A Human Hero*. New York: Clarion.

_____. (2000). *The Amazing Life of Benjamin Franklin*. Illustrated by Michael Dooling. New York: Scholastic.

_____. (2002). *The Life and Death of Adolf Hitler*. New York: Clarion.

_____. (2004). *Secrets of the Sphinx*. New York: Scholastic.

Giff, Patricia Reilly. (2000). *Nory Ryan's Song*. New York: Delacorte.

_____. (2002). *Pictures of Hollis Woods*. New York: Random House.

_____. (2003). *Maggie's Door*. New York: Random House.

_____. (2004). *A House of Tailors*. New York: Random House.

_____. (2008). *Eleven*. New York: Random House.

_____. (2008). *Water Street*. New York: Yearling.

Gifford, Peggy. (2008). *Moxy Maxwell Does Not Love Stuart Little*. New York: Swartz & Wade Books.

Giganti, Paul, Jr. (1988). *How Many Snails? A Counting Book*. Illustrated by Donald Crews. New York: Greenwillow.

Giles, Gail. (2007). *What Happened to Cass McBride?* London: Little, Brown.

Gilmore, Kate. (1999). *The Exchange Student*. Boston: Houghton Mifflin.

Gilson, Jamie. (1987). *Hobie Hanson, You're Weird*. Illustrated by Elise Primavera. New York: Lothrop, Lee & Shepard.

Giovanni, Nikki. (2006). *Rosa*. Illustrated by Bryan Collier. New York: Holt.

Giovanni, Nikki, & Tony Medina. (2008). *Hip Hop Speaks to Children: A Celebration of Poetry*. Naperville, IL: Sourcebooks: Jabberwocky.

Gipi. (2007). *Garage Band*. New York: Roaring Book Press.

Global Fund for Children. (2007). *Global Babies*. Watertown, MA: Charlesbridge.

Goble, Paul. (1983). *Star Boy*. New York: Simon & Schuster.

_____. (1988). *Her Seven Brothers*. New York: Simon & Schuster.

_____. (1992). *Crow Chief: A Plains Indian Story*. New York: Orchard.

_____. (1994). *Adopted by the Eagles: A Plains Indian Story of Friendship and Treachery*. New York: Simon & Schuster.

_____. (1998) *Iktomi and the Coyote*. New York: Scholastic.

_____. (2003). *Mystic Horse*. New York: HarperCollins.

Godwin, Laura. (1998). *Forest*. Illustrated by Stacey Schuett. New York: HarperCollins.

Going, K. L. (2003). *Fat Kid Rules the World*. New York: Putman.

Going, K. L. (2007). *Garden of Eve*. Orlando, FL: Harcourt.

Gold, Alison Leslie. (2000). *A Special Fate: Chiune Sugihara: Hero of the Holocaust*. New York: Scholastic.

Golding, Julia. (2007). *The Secret of the Sirens*. Tarrytown, NY: Cavendish.

_____. (2008). *The Diamond of Drury Lane*. New York: Holt.

Goldish, Meish. (2007). *Dogs*. Illustrated with photographs. New York: Bearport.

Goldstein, Bobbye S. (1992). *Inner Chimes: Poems on Poetry*. Honesdale, PA: Wordsong.

Gonzalez, Lucia. (1994). *The Bossy Gallito: A Traditional Cuban Folktale*.

Gonzalez, Maya Christina. (2007). *My Colors, My World/Mis Colores, Mi Mundo*. Danbury, CT: Children's Book Press.

Goodall, John. (1988). *Little Red Riding Hood*. New York: McElderry.

Goodman, Susan. (2003). *Skyscraper: From the Ground Up*. Illustrated by Michael Doolittle. Boston: Hornbook.

Goodrich, Samuel. (1827). *The Tales of Peter Parley About America*. New York: Garland.

Gorbachev, Valeri. (2007). *Red Red Red*. New York: Philomel.

Gore, Al. (2007). *An Inconvenient Truth: The Crisis of Global Warming*. New York: Penguin.

Gore, Leonid. (2007). *Danny's First Snow*. New York: Simon & Schuster.

Gorman, Carol. (1999). *Dork in Disguise*. New York: HarperCollins.

Gormley, Beatrice. (2008). *Barack Obama: Our 44th President*. New York: Aladdin.

Govenar, Allan. (2000). *Osceola: Memories of a Sharecropper's Daughter*. Illustrated by Shane W. Evans New York: Hyperion.

Graff, Lisa. (2007). *The Thing About Georgie*. New York: HarperCollins.

Graham, Joan Bransfield. (1994). *Splish Splash*. Boston: Houghton Mifflin.

_____. (1999). *Flicker Flash*. Boston: Houghton Mifflin.

Grahame, Kenneth. (1908/1961). *Wind in the Willows*. New York: Scribner.

Gran, Julia. (2007). *Big Bug Surprise*. New York: Scholastic.

Grandits, John. (2007). *Blue Lipstick: Concrete Poems*. New York: Clarion.

Grant, K. M. (2005). *Blood Red Horse*. New York: Walker.

Gratz, Alan. (2008). *Samurai Shortstop*. New York: Penguin.

Graves, Bonnie. (1998). *No Copycats Allowed*. Illustrated by Abby Carter. New York: Hyperion.

_____. (2002). *Taking Care of Trouble*. Illustrated by Robin Preiss-Glasser. New York: Dutton.

Graves, Keith. (2006). *The Unexpectedly Bad Hair of Barcelona Smith*. New York: Philomel.

Gravett, Emily. (2006). *Wolves*. New York: Simon & Schuster.

_____. (2007). *Meerkat Mail*. New York: Simon & Schuster.

_____. (2008). *Monkey and Me*. New York: Simon & Schuster.

Gray, Dianne. (2000). *Holding Up the Earth*. Boston: Hougton Mifflin.

_____. (2002). *Together Apart*. Boston: Houghton Mifflin.

Gray, Elizabeth Janet. (1942). *Adam of the Road*. New York: Viking.

Greaves, Margaret. (1990). *Tattercoats*. Illustrated by Margaret Chamberlain. New York: Clarkson N. Potter.

Greenberg, Jan. (2003). *Romare Bearden: Collage of Memories*. New York: Abrams.

Greenberg, Jan, & Sandra Jordan. (1991). *The Painter's Eye: Learning to Look at Contemporary American Art*. New York: Delacorte.

_____. (1993). *The Sculptor's Eye. Looking at Contemporary American Art*. New York: Delacorte.

_____. (2001). *Vincent van Gogh*. New York: Delacorte.

_____. (2002). *Action Jackson*. Brookfield, CN: Roaring Brook Press.

_____. (2004). *Andy Warhol: Prince of Pop*. New York: Delacorte.

_____. (2008). *Cristo and Jeanne-Claude: Through the Gates and Beyond*. New York: Roaring Brook Press.

Greene, Ellin. (1996). *Ling-Li and the Phoenix Fairy: A Chinese Folktale*. Illustrated by Zong-Zhou Wang. New York: Clarion.

Greene, Stephanie. (1999). *Owen Foote: Frontiersman*. New York: Clarion.

Greenfield, Eloise. (1978). *Honey, I Love and Other Love Poems*. New York: Crowell.

_____. (1988). *Under a Sunday Tree*, Illustrated by Amos Ferguson. New York: Harper & Row.

_____. (1989). *Nathaniel Talking*. Illustrated by Jan Spivey Gilchrist. Danbury, CT: Writers & Readers Publishing, Inc.

_____. (1991). *Night on a Neighborhood Street*. Illustrated by Jan Spivey Gilchrist. New York: Dial.

_____. (1992). *Koya Delaney and the Good Girl Blues*. New York: Scholastic.

_____. (2003). *How They Got Over: African Americans and the Call of the Sea*. Illustrated by Jan Spivey Gilchrist. New York: HarperCollins.

Greenfield, Eloise, & Jan Spivey Gilchrist. (2006). *The Friendly Four*. New York: HarperCollins/Amistad.

Gregor, C. Shana. (1996). *Cry of the Benu Bird: An Egyptian Creation Story*. Boston: Houghton Mifflin.

Gretchen, Sylvia. (1990). *Hero of the Land of Snow*. Illustrated by Julie Witwer. Berkley: Dharma.

Grey, Mini. (2005). *Traction Man Is Here*. New York: Knopf.

_____. (2006). *The Adventures of the Dish and the Spoon*. New York: Knopf.

_____. (2007). *Ginger Bear*. New York: Knopf.

_____. (2008). *Traction Man Meets Turbo Dog*. New York: Knopf.

Griego, Margot C., Betsy L. Bucks, Sharon S. Gilbert, & Laura H. Kimball, editors and translators. (1981). *Tortillitas Para Mama and Other Nursery Rhymes, Spanish and English*. Illustrated by Barbara Cooney. New York: Holt.

Griffin, Adele. (2002). *Hannah, Divided*. New York: Hyperion.

Griffith, Helen. (1999). *Cougar*. New York: Greenwillow.

Grimes, Nikki. (1994). *Meet Danitra Brown*. Illustrated by Floyd Cooper. New York: HarperCollins.

_____. (1996). *Come Sunday* Grand Rapids, MI.: William B. Eerdmans.

_____. (2001). *Danitra Brown Leaves Town*. Illustrated by Floyd Cooper. New York: HarperCollins.

_____. (2001) *A Pocketful of Poems*. New York: Clarion.

_____. (2002). *Bronx Masquerade*. New York: Dial.

_____. (2002). *My Man Blue*. Illustrated by Jerome Lagarrigue. New York: Penguin.

_____. (2002). *Talkin' about Bessie: The Story of Aviator Elizabeth Coleman*. Illustrated by Earl B. Lewis. New York: Orchard.

_____. (2004). *What Is Goodbye?* Illustrated by Raul Colón. New York: Hyperion.

_____. (2005). *Danitra Brown, Class Clown*. Illustrated by E. B. Lewis. New York: HarperCollins.

_____. (2005). *It's Raining Laughter*. Illustrated by Miles C. Pinkney. Honesdale, PA: Boyds Mills Press.

_____. (2008). *Barack Obama: Son of Promise, Child of Hope*. Illustrated by Bryan Collier. New York: Simon & Schuster.

_____. (2008). *Oh, Brother!* Illustrated by Mike Benny. New York: HarperCollins.

_____. (2008). *The Road to Paris*. New York: Penguin.

Grimm, Jacob, & Wilhelm Grimm. (2004). *The Annotated Brothers Grimm*, translated and edited by Maria Tatar. New York: W.W. Norton.

Grossman, Virginia. (1991). *Ten Little Rabbits*. Illustrated by Sylvia Long. San Francisco: Chronicle.

Grunwell, Jeanne Marie. (2003). *Mind Games*. Boston: Houghton Mifflin.

Guarino, Deborah. (1989). *Is Your Mama a Llama?* Illustrated by Steven Kellogg. New York: Scholastic.

Gulotta, Charles. (1998). *Extraordinary Women in Politics*, from the **Extraordinary People** series. New York: Children's Press.

Gunning, Monica. (1993). *Not a Copper Penny in Me House*. Illustrated by Frane Lessac. Honesdale, PA: Boyds Mills Press.

Guthrie, Woody. (2004). *New Baby Train*. Illustrated by Marla Frazee. London: Little, Brown.

Gutierrez, Elisa. (2005). *Picturescape*. Vancouver, Canada: Simply Read Books.

Guy, Ginger Foglesong. (2007). *Perros! Perros! Dogs! Dogs! A Story in English and Spanish*. Illustrated by Sharon Glick. New York: Greenwillow.

Haas, Jessie. (1993). *Beware the Mare*. Illustrated by Martha Haas. New York: Greenwillow.

_____. (2001). *Runaway Radish*. Illustrated by Margot Apple. New York: Greenwillow.

Haddix, Margaret Peterson. (1998). *Among the Hidden*. New York: Simon & Schuster.

_____. (2002). *Among the Betrayed*. New York: Simon & Schuster.

_____. (2002). *Among the Imposters*. New York: Simon & Schuster.

_____. (2003). *Among the Barons*. New York: Simon & Schuster.

_____. (2004). *Say What?* New York: Simon & Schuster.

_____. (2007). *Uprising*. New York: Simon & Schuster.

Haddon, Mark. (2003). *The Curious Incident of the Dog in the Night-Time*. New York: Doubleday.

Hahn, Mary Downing. (2001). *Anna on the Farm*. New York: Clarion.

_____. (2003). *Hear the Wind Blow: A Novel of the Civil War*. New York: Clarion.

_____. (2008). *All the Lovely Bad Ones*. New York: Clairon.

Hale, Marian. (2004). *The Truth about Sparrows*. New York: Holt.

Hale, Shannon, & Dean Hale. (2008). *Rapunzel's Revenge*. Illustrated by Nathan Hale. Bloomsbury.

Haley, Gail E. (1970). *A Story, a Story*. New York: Atheneum.

_____. (1992). *Mountain Jack Tales*. New York: Dutton.

_____. (1998). *Jack and the Fire Dragon*. New York: Crown.

Halfman, Janet. (2008). *Seven Miles to Freedom: The Robert Smalls Story*. Illustrated by Duane Smith. New York: Lee & Low.

Hall, Lynn. (1992). *The Soul of the Silver Dog*. San Diego, CA: Harcourt.

Hamilton, Martha, & Weiss, Mitch. (2007). *Priceless Gifts: A Folktale from Italy*. Illustrated by John Kanzler. Little Rock, AR: August House.

Hamilton, Virginia. (1967). *Zeely*. New York: Macmillan.

_____. (1971/2002). *The Planet of Junior Brown*. New York: Simon & Schuster.

_____. (1974). *M. C. Higgins, the Great*. New York: Macmillan.

_____. (1983). *The Magical Adventures of Pretty Pearl*. New York: Harper & Row.

_____. (1985/2004). *The People Could Fly: American Black Folktales*. Illustrated by Leo and Diane Dillon. New York: Random House.

_____. (1988). *In the Beginning: Creation Stories from around the World*. Illustrated by Barry Moser. San Diego, CA: Harcourt Brace Jovanovich.

_____. (1990). *The Dark Way: Stories from the Spirit World*. Illustrated by Lambert Davis. San Diego, CA: Harcourt Brace Jovanovich.

_____. (1993). *Plain City*. New York: Blue Sky Press.

_____. (1993). *Many Thousand Gone: African Americans from Slavery to Freedom*. Illustrated by Leo Dillon & Diane Dillon. New York: Knopf.

_____. (1995). *Her Stories: African American Folktales, Fairy Tales, and True Tales*. Illustrated by Leo Dillon and Diane Dillon. New York: Blue Sky Press.

_____. (1996). *When Birds Could Talk and Bats Could Sing: The Adventures of Bruh Sparrow, Sis Wren, and their friends*. Illustrated by Barry Moser. New York: Blue Sky Press.

_____. (1998). *Second Cousins*. New York: Blue Sky Press.

_____. (1999). *Bluish*. New York: Blue Sky Press.

_____. (2003). *Bruh Rabbit and the Tar Baby Girl*. Illustrated by James Ransome. New York: Blue Sky.

_____. (2004). *Wee Winnie Witch's Skinny*. Illustrated by Barry Moser. New York: Scholastic.

Hampton, Wilburn. (1997). *Kennedy Assassinated! The World Mourns: A Reporter's Story*. Cambridge, MA: Candlewick.

Hannigan, Katherine. (2004). *Ida B: And Her Plan to Maximize Fun, Avoid Disaster and (Possibly) Save the World*. New York: Greenwillow.

Hardcastle, Henry and Dugald A. Steer (Eds). (2007). *Explorer: A Daring Guild for Young Adventurers*. Illustrated by Milivoj Ceran and Alastair Graham. Cambridge, MA: Candlewick.

Harding, Frances. (2007). *Well Witched*. New York: HarperCollins.

Harley, Avis. (2000). *Fly with Poetry: An ABC of Poetry*. Honesdale, PA.: Wordsong.

_____. (2001). *Leap into Poetry: More ABC's of Poetry*. Honesdale, PA.: Wordsong.

_____. (2008). *The Monarch's Progress: Poems with Wings*. Honesdale, PA: Wordsong.

Harlow, Joan Hiatt. (2004). *Thunder from the Sea*. New York: Simon & Schuster.

Harrington, Jane. (2007). *Extreme Pets!* New York: Scholastic.

Harrington, Janice N. (2004). *Going North*. Illustrated by Jerome Lagarrigue. New York: Farrar, Straus & Giroux.

_____. (2007). *The Chicken-Chasing Queen of Lamar County*. Illustrated by Shelley Jackson. New York: Farrar, Straus & Giroux.

Harrison, David L. (2007). *Piggy Wiglet and the Great Adventure*. Illustrated by Karen Stormer Brooks. Honesdale, PA: Wordsong.

Harrison, David, & Bernice Cullinan. (1999). *Easy Poetry Lessons That Dazzle and Delight*. New York: Scholastic.

Hartinger, Brent. (2003). *Geography Club*. New York: HarperCollins.

Hastings, Selina. (1992). *The Firebird*. Illustrated by Reg Cartwright. Cambridge, MA: Candlewick.

Hautman, Pete. (1998). *Stone Cold*. New York: Simon & Schuster.

———. (2001). *Hole in the Sky*. New York: Simon & Schuster.

Hawkes, Kevin. (2007). *The Wicked Big Toddlah*. New York: Random House.

Hawkins, Colin, & Jacqui Hawkins. (2004). *Fairytale News*. Cambridge, MA: Candlewick.

Hawthorne, Nathaniel. (1851/1893). *A Wonder Book for Boys and Girls*. Boston: Houghton Mifflin.

Hayes, Joe. (2000). *Little Gold Star/Estrellita de Oro: A Cinderella Cuento*. Illustrated by Gloria Osuna Perez and Lucia A. Perez. El Paso, TX: Cinco Puntos Press.

———. (2004). *La Llorona/The Weeping Woman: An Hispanic Legend Told in Spanish and English*. Illustrated by Vicki Trego Hill and Mona Pennypacker. El Paso, TX: Cinco Puntos.

Heard, Georgia. (1992). *Creatures of Earth, Sea, and Sky: Poems*. Illustrated by Jennifer Dewey. Honesdale, PA: Wordsong.

Hearne, Betsy. (1996). *Eliza's Dog*. Illustrated by Erica Thurston. New York: McElderry.

———. (2001). *Wishes, Kisses, and Pigs*. New York: Simon & Schuster.

———. (2003). *The Canine Connection: Stories about Dogs and People*. New York: McElderry.

Heiman, Diane, & Liz Suneby. (2007). *See What You Can Be*. Illustrated by Tracey Wood. Middleton, WI: American Girl.

Heins, Ethel. (1995). *The Cat and the Cook and Other Fables of Krylov*. Illustrated by Anita Lobel. New York: Greenwillow.

Heller, Ruth. (1997). *Mine, All Mine: A Book about Pronouns*. New York: Grosset & Dunlap.

Hemphill, Stephanie. (2007). *Your Own, Sylvia: A Verse Portrait of Sylvia Plath*. New York: Knopf.

Henderson, Kathy. (2006). *Lugalbanda: The Boy Who Got Caught Up in a War*. Illustrated by Jane Ray. Cambridge, MA: Candlewick.

Henkes, Kevin. (1988). *Chester's Way*. New York: Greenwillow.

———. (1991). *Chrysanthemum*. New York: Greenwillow.

———. (1993). *Owen*. New York: Greenwillow.

———. (1995). *Protecting Marie*. New York: Greenwillow.

———. (1999). *The Birthday Room*. New York: Greenwillow.

———. (2003). *Olive's Ocean*. New York: Greenwillow.

———. (2007). *A Good Day*. New York: Greenwillow.

———. (2008). *Bird Lake Moon*. New York: Greenwillow.

Hennessy, B. G. (2006). *The Boy Who Cried Wolf*. Illustrated by Boris Kulikov. New York: Simon & Schuster.

Henry, Marguerite. (1947). *Misty of Chincoteague*. Illustrated by Wesley Dennis. Chicago: Rand McNally.

———. (1948). *King of the Wind*. Illustrated by Wesley Dennis. Chicago: Rand McNally.

Hermes, Patricia. (1998). *Cheat the Moon: A Novel*. Boston: Little, Brown.

Hermsen, Ronald. (2007). *The Story of Giraffe*. Illustrated by Guido Pigni. Honesdale, PA: Front Street.

Herrera, Juan Felipe. (2000). *The Upside Down Boy/El Niño de Cabeza*. Illustrated by Elizabeth Gomez. San Francisco: Children's Book Press.

Herrick, Steven. (2008). *Naked Bunyip Dancing*. Illustrated by Beth Norling. Asheville, NC: Front Street Press.

Hesse, Karen. (1994). *Sable*. Illustrated by Marcia Sewall. New York: Holt.

———. (1997). *Out of the Dust*. New York: Scholastic.

———. (1999). *A Light in the Storm: The Civil War Diary of Amelia Martin*. New York: Scholastic.

———, (2003). *Witness*. New York: Scholastic.

———. (2004). *The Cats in Krasinski Square*. Illustrated by Wendy Watson. New York: Scholastic.

———. (2008). *Brooklyn Bridge*. New York: Feiwel & Friends.

———. (2008). *Spuds*. Illustrated by Wendy Watson. New York: Scholastic.

Hiassen, Carl. (2002). *Hoot*. New York: Knopf.

Hickey, Caroline. (2007). *Cassie Was Here*. New York: Roaring Brook Press.

Higgins, F. E. (2007). *Black Book of Secrets*. New York: Feiwel and Friends.

Hillenbrand, Jane. (2006). *What a Treasure!* Illustrated by Will Hillenbrand. New York: Holiday House.

Hillman, Ben.(2007). *How Big Is It? A Big Book All about Bigness*. New York: Scholastic.

Hills, Tad. (2006). *Duck & Goose*. New York: Random House.

———. (2007). *Duck, Duck, Goose*. New York: Random House.

Hinton, S. E. (1995). *The Outsiders*. Carmel, CA: Hampton-Brown.

Hirahara, Naomi. (2008). *1001 Cranes*. New York: Delacorte.

Hirsch, Odo. (2004). *Yoss*. New York: Random House.

Ho, Minfong. (1990). *Rice without Rain*. New York: Lothrop, Lee & Sheperd.

———. (1991). *The Clay Marble*. New York: Farrar, Straus & Giroux.

———. (1996). *Hush! A Thai Lullaby*. Illustrated by Holly Meade. New York: Orchard.

———. (2003). *Gathering the Dew*. New York: Orchard.

Ho, Minfong, & Saphan Ros. (1995). *The Two Brothers*. Illustrated by Jean Tseng and Mou-sien Tseng. New York: Lothrop, Lee & Shepard.

———. (1996). *Brother Rabbit: A Cambodian Tale*. Illustrated by Jennifer Hewitson. New York: Lothrop, Lee & Shepard.

Hoban, Tana. (1970). *Shapes and Things*. New York: Macmillan.

———. (1990). *Exactly the Opposite*. New York: Greenwillow.

———. (1996). *Just Look*. New York: Greenwillow.

———. (1996). *Of Color and Things*. New York: HarperCollins.

———. (1996). *Shapes, Shapes, Shapes*. New York: HarperCollins.

Hoban, Tana. (2000). *Cubes, Cones, Cylinders, and Spheres*. New York: HarperCollins.

Hobbs, Will. (1998). *The Maze*. New York: Morrow.

———. (2000). *Jason's Gold*. New York: HarperCollins.

———. (2008). *Go Big or Go Home*. New York: HarperCollins.

Hoberman, Mary Ann. (1991). *Fathers, Mothers, Sisters, Brothers: A Collection of Family Poems*. Illustrated by Marylin Hafner. Boston: Joy Street.

———. (1998). *The Llama Who Had No Pajama: 100 Favorite Poems*. Illustrated by Betty Fraser. San Diego, CA: Harcourt.

———. (2007). *A House Is a House for Me*. Illustrated by Betty Fraser. New York: Penguin.

———. (2007). *I'm Going to Grandma's*. Illustrated by Tiphanie Beeke. San Diego, CA: Harcourt.

Hoberman, Mary Ann, & Norman Hoberman. (1957). *All My Shoes Come in Twos*. New York: Little, Brown.

Hodges, Margaret, & Margery Evernden. (1993). *Of Swords and Sorcerers: The Adventures of King Arthur and His Knights*. Illustrated by David Frampton. New York: Scribner.

Hodges, Margaret. (1984). *St. George and the Dragon*. Illustrated by Trina Schart Hyman. Boston: Little, Brown.

———. (1990). *The Kitchen Knight: A Tale of King Arthur*. Illustrated by Trina Schart Hyman. New York: Holiday House.

———. (2004). *Merlin and the Making of the King*. Illustrated by Trina Schart Hyman. New York: Holiday House.

———. (2006). *Dick Whittington and His Cat*. Illustrated by Melisande Potter. New York: Holiday House.

Hodgkins, Fran. (2007). *The Whale Scientists: Solving the Mystery of Whale Strandings*. Boston: Houghton Mifflin.

Hoffman, Alice. (2003). *Green Angel*. New York: Scholastic.

Hogrogian, Nonny. (1971). *One Fine Day*. New York: Macmillan.

———. (1981). *Cinderella*. New York: Greenwillow.

Holling, Holling C. (1941). *Paddle-to-the-Sea*. Boston: Houghton Mifflin.

Holm, Jennifer L. (2007). *Middle School Is Worse Than Meatloaf*. Illustrated by Elicia Castaldi and Ginee Seo. New York: Atheneum.

Holm, Jennifer L., & Matthew Holm. (2006). *Babymouse*. New York: Random House.

———. (2007). *Babymouse: Camp Babymouse*. New York: Random House.

———. (2007). *Babymouse: Heartbreaker*. New York: Random House.

———. (2007). *Babymouse Puppy Love*. New York: Random House.

Holman, Felice. (1974). *Slake's Limbo*. New York: Scribner.

Holmberg, Bo R. (2008). *A Day with Dad*. Illustrated by Eva Eriksson. Cambridge, MA: Candlewick.

Holmes, Thom. (1998). *Fossil Feud: The Rivalry of the First American Dinosaur Hunters*. Parsippany, NJ: Messner.

Holt, Kimberly Willis. (1998). *My Louisiana Sky*. New York: Holt.

———. (2003). *Keeper of the Night*. New York: Holt.

———. (2006). *When Zachary Beaver Came to Town*. New York: Holt.

———. (2007). *Piper Reed: Navy Brat*. Illustrated by Christine Davenier. New York: Holt.

———. (2008). *Piper Reed: The Great Gypsy*. New York: Holt.

Holtz, Thomas R., Jr., (2007). *Dinosaurs: The Most Complete, Up-to-Date Encyclopedia for Dinosaur Lovers of All Ages*. Illustrated by Luis V. Rey. New York: Random House.

Holub, Josef. (2007). *An Innocent Soldier*. New York: Scholastic.

Hoobler, Dorothy, & Thomas Hoobler. (2001). *The Demon in the Teahouse*. New York: Philomel.

Hooks, William H. (1987). *Moss Gown*. Illustrated by Donald Carrick. New York: Clarion.

———. (1989). *The Three Little Pigs and the Fox*. Illustrated by S. D. Schindler. New York: Macmillan.

Hooper, Mary. (2008). *Newes from the Dead*. New York: Holt.

Hoose, Phillip. (2004). *The Race to Save the Lord God Bird*. New York: Farrar, Straus & Giroux.

Hope, Laura Lee. (1950). *The Bobbsey Twins*. New York: Grosset & Dunlap.

Hopkins, Lee Bennett. (1999). *Pauses: Autobiographical Reflections of 101 Creators of Children's Books*. New York: HarperCollins.

———. (2004). *Wonderful Words*. Illustrated by Karen Barbour. New York: Simon & Schuster.

———. (2008). *Americans at War*. Illustrated by Stephen Alcorn. New York: Simon & Schuster.

———. (2008). *Sky Magic*. Illustrated by Mariusz Stawarski. New York: Dutton.

Hopkinson, Deborah. (1993/2003). *Sweet Clara and the Freedom Quilt*. Illustrated by James Ransome. New York: Random House.

———. (2003). *Girl Wonder: A Baseball Story in Nine Innings*. Illustrated by Terry Widener. New York: Atheneum Books.

———. (2003). *Shutting Out the Sky: Life in the Tenements of New York, 1880–1924*. New York: Orchard.

———. (2005). *Under the Quilt of Night*. Illustrated by James Ransome. New York: Simon & Schuster.

———. (2006). *Sky Boys: How They Built the Empire State Building*. Illustrated by James E. Ransome. New York: Random House.

———. (2008). *Abe Lincoln Crosses a Creek*. Illustrated by John Hendrix. New York: Random House.

———. (2008). *Into the Firestorm: A Novel of San Francisco*. New York: Yearling Press.

Horacek, Petr. (2007). *Butterfly, Butterfly*. Cambridge, MA: Candlewick.

Horniman, Joanne. (2003). *Mahalia*. New York: Knopf.

Hort, Lenny. (2003). *The Seals on the Bus*. Illustrated by G. Brian Caras. New York: Holt.

Houston, Gloria. (1998). *Bright Freedom's Song*. San Diego, CA: Harcourt.

Howard, Elizabeth Fitzgerald. (1989). *Chita's Christmas Tree*. New York: Simon & Schuster.

_____. (1990). *Aunt Flossie's Hats*. New York: Clarion.

_____. (1995). *Papa Tells Chita a Story*. New York: Alladin.

Howard, Ellen. (1991). *The Chickenhouse House*. New York: Atheneum.

_____. (1999). *Sister*. New York: Atheneum.

Howe, James. (1979). *Bunnicula*. Illustrated by Alan Daniel. New York: Simon & Schuster.

Howe, James. (1985). *What Eric Knew*. New York: Atheneum.

Howe, John. (1989). *Jack and the Beanstalk*. Boston: Little, Brown.

Huck, Charlotte. (1989). *Princess Furball*. Illustrated by Anita Lobel. New York: Greenwillow.

_____, (2001). *The Black Bull of Norroway: A Scottish Tale*. Illustrated by Anita Lobel. New York: Greenwillow.

Hughes, Langston. (2000). *The Book of Rhythms*. Illustrated by Matt Wawiorka. New York: Oxford.

_____. (2008). *The Dream Keeper and Other Poems*. Illustrated by Brian Pinkney. New York: Knopf.

Hughes, Monica. (1981). *Keeper of the Isis Light*. New York: Atheneum.

_____. (1990). *Invitation to the Game*. New York: Simon & Schuster.

_____. (1995). *The Golden Aquarians*. New York: Simon & Schuster.

Hughes, Pat. (2007). *Seeing the Elephant: A Story of the Civil War*. Illustrated by Ken Stark. New York: Farrar, Straus & Giroux.

Huneck, Stephen. (2000). *Sally Goes to the Beach*. New York: Abrams.

Hunt, Irene. (1964). *Across Five Aprils*. Chicago: Follett.

Hurst, Carol Otis. (2001). *Rocks in His Head*. Illustrated by James Stevenson. New York: Greenwillow.

Hurwitz, Johanna. (1979). *Aldo Applesauce*. Illustrated by John C. Wallner. New York: Morrow.

_____. (1985). *Adventures of Ali Baba Bernstein*. Illustrated by Gail Owens. New York: Morrow.

_____. (1992). *Roz and Ozzie*. Illustrated by Eileen McKeating. New York: Morrow.

_____. (2000). *One Small Dog*. Illustrated by Diane De Groat. New York: HarperCollins.

Hutchins, Hazel. (2004). *A Second Is a Hiccup: A Child's Book of Time*. Illustrated by Kady MacDonald Denton. New York: Levine.

Hutchins, Pat. (1971). *Changes, Changes*. New York: Simon & Schuster.

_____. (1985). *The Very Worst Monster*. New York: Greenwillow.

_____. (1986). *The Doorbell Rang*. New York: Greenwillow.

_____. (1988). *Where's the Baby?* New York: Greenwillow.

Huth, Holly Young. (2000). *The Son of the Sun and the Daughter of the Moon: A Saami Folktale*. Illustrated by Anna Vojtech. New York: Atheneum.

Hutton, Warwick. (1989). *Theseus and the Minotaur*. New York: McElderry.

_____. (1994). *Persephone*. New York: McElderry.

_____. (1995). *Odysseus and the Cyclops*. New York: McElderry.

Hyman, Trina Schart. (1983). *Little Red Riding Hood*. New York: Holiday House.

Ibbotson, Eva. (2004). *The Haunting of Granite Falls*. Illustrated by Kevin Hawkes. New York: Dutton.

_____. (2004). *The Star of Kazan*. New York: Dutton.

_____. (2008). *The Dragonfly Pool*. Illustrated by Kevin Hawkes. New York: Dutton.

Innocenti, Robert. (1985). *Rose Blanche*. Mankato, MN: Creative Editions.

Inns, Christopher. (2006). *Peekaboo Panda and Other Animals*. London: MacMillan.

Irving, Washington. (2007). *The Legend of Sleepy Hollow*. Illustrated by Gris Grimley. New York: Simon & Schuster.

Isadora, Rachel. (1989). *The Princess and the Frog*. New York: Greenwillow.

_____. (1990). *Babies*. New York: Greenwillow.

_____. (2000). *1 2 3 Pop!* New York: Viking.

_____. (2000). *Listen to the City*. New York: Penguin.

_____. (2001). *ABC Pop!* New York: Penguin.

_____. (2006). *What a Family!* New York: Putnam.

_____. (2007). *The Twelve Dancing Princesses*. New York: Putnam.

_____. (2007). *The Princess and the Pea*. New York: Putnam.

_____. (2007). *Yo, Jo!* San Diego, CA: Harcourt.

_____. (2008). *Uh-Oh!* San Diego, CA: Harcourt.

_____. (2008). *The Fisherman and His Wife*. New York: Putnam.

Issa, Kobayashi (1973). *Don't Tell the Scarecrow and Other Japanese Poems*. New York: Scholastic.

_____. (2007). *Today and Today*. Illustrated by G. Brian Karas. New York: Scholastic.

Jackson, Donna M. (2008). *Phenomena: Secrets of the Senses*. New York: Little, Brown.

Jackson, Donna. (2005). *ER Vets: Life in an Animal Emergency Room*. Boston: Houghton Mifflin.

Jacobs, Joseph. (1965). *Tom Tit Tot*. Illustrated by Evaline Ness. New York: Scribner.

_____. (1989). *Tattercoats*. Illustrated by Margot Tomes. New York: Putman.

Jacques, Brian. (1998). *Redwall*. New York: Ace.

_____. (1999). *Marlfox*. New York: Philomel.

_____. (2001). *Lord Brocktree*. New York: Ace.

_____. (2003). *The Angel's Command*. New York: Philomel.

Jaffe, Nina. (1996). *The Golden Flower: A Taino Myth from Puerto Rico*. Illustrated by Enrique O. Sanchez. New York: Simon & Schuster.

Jaffrey, Madhur. (1985). *Seasons of Splendour: Tales, Myths, and Legends of India*. Illustrated by Michael Foreman. New York: Atheneum.

James, Mary. (1990). *Shoebag*. New York: Scholastic.

James, Simon. (2008). *Baby Brains*. Cambridge, MA: Candlewick.

Janeczko, Paul. (1993). *A Poke in the I: A Collection of Concrete Poems*. Illustrated by Christopher Rashka. Cambridge, MA: Candlewick.

_____. (1993). *Looking for Your Name: A Collection of Contemporary Poems*. New York: Orchard.

_____. (2000). *Stone Bench in an Empty Park*. Illustrated by Henri Silberman. New York: Orchard.

_____. (2001). *Dirty Laundry Pile: Poems in Different Voices*. Illustrated by Melissa Sweet. New York: HarperCollins.

_____. (2004). *Worlds Afire*. Cambridge, MA: Candlewick.

_____. (2005). *A Kick in the Head: An Everyday Guide to Poetic Forms*. Cambridge, MA: Candlewick.

_____. (2007). *Hey, You! Poems to Skyscrapers, Mosquitoes, and Other Fun Things*. Illustrated by Robert Rayevsky. New York: HarperCollins.

Janeczko, Paul B., & J. Patrick Lewis (2006). *Wing Nuts: Screwy Haiku*. Illustrated by Tricia Tusa. New York: Little, Brown.

_____. (2008). *Birds on a Wire*. Illustrated by Gary Lippincott. Honesdale, PA: Wordsong.

Jango-Cohen, Judith. (2007). *Real-Life Sea Monsters*. Illustrated by Ryan Durney. Minneapolis, MN: Lerner.

Jansson, Tove. (1989). *Finn Family Moomintroll*. New York: Farrar, Straus & Giroux.

Jarrie, Martin. (2005). *ABC USA*. New York: Sterling.

Jay, Allison. (2005). *ABC: A Child's First Alphabet Book*. New York: Penguin.

Jeffers, Oliver. (2006). *Lost and Found*. New York: Philomel.

Jenkins, Emily. (2006). *Love You When You Whine*. Illustrated by Sergio Ruzzier. New York: Farrar, Straus & Giroux.

Jenkins, Martin. (2007). *Ape*. Illustrated by Vicky White. Cambridge, MA: Candlewick.

Jenkins, Steve. (1995). *Biggest, Strongest, Fastest*. Boston: Houghton Mifflin.

_____. (1995). *Looking Down*. Boston, MA: Houghton Mifflin.

_____. (1998). *Hottest, Coldest, Highest, Deepest*. Boston: Houghton Mifflin.

_____. (1999). *The Top of the World: Climbing Mount Everest*. Boston: Houghton Mifflin.

_____. (2004). *Actual Size*. Boston: Houghton Mifflin.

_____. (2005). *Animals in Flight*. Boston: Houghton Mifflin.

_____. (2005). *Prehistoric Actual Size*. Boston: Houghton Mifflin

_____. (2007). *Living Color*. Boston: Houghton Mifflin.

Jenkins, Steve, & Robin Page. (2003). *What Do You Do with a Tail Like This?* Illustrated by Steve Jenkins. Boston: Houghton Mifflin.

_____. (2006). *Move!* Illustrated by Steve Jenkins. Boston: Houghton Mifflin.

_____. (2008). *How Many Ways Can You Catch a Fly?* Illustrated by Steve Jenkins. Boston: Houghton Mifflin.

_____. (2008). *Sisters & Brothers: Sibling Relationships in the Animal World*. Boston: Houghton Mifflin.

Jennings, Richard. (2007). *Ferret Island*. Boston: Houghton Mifflin.

Jensen, Nancy Orr Johnson. (2007). *Helen, Ethel & the Crazy Quilt: Based on the 1890 Letters Between Helen Keller and Ethel Orr*. Illustrated by Dawn Peterson. Mahomet, IL: Mayhaven.

Jiménez, Francisco. (1997). *The Circuit: Stories from the Life of a Migrant Child*. Albuquerque: University of New Mexico Press.

_____. (1998). *La Mariposa*. Boston: Houghton Mifflin.

_____. (2001). *Breaking Through*. Boston: Houghton Mifflin.

Jinks, Catherine. (2004). *Pagan in Exile*. Cambridge, MA: Candlewick.

Jocelyn, Marthe. (2004). *Mable Riley: A Reliable Record of Humdrum, Peril, and Romance*. Cambridge, MA: Candlewick.

Johnson, Angela. (1993). *When I Am Old with You*. Illustrated by David Soman. New York: Scholastic.

_____. (1998). *Gone from Home: Short Takes*. New York: DK Publishing.

_____. (1998). *Songs of Faith*. New York: Orchard.

_____. (2003). *The First Part Last*. New York: Simon & Schuster.

_____. (2003). *I Dream of Trains*. Illustrated by Loren Long. New York: Simon & Schuster.

_____. (2007). *Lily Brown's Paintings*. Illustrated by E. B. Lewis. New York: Orchard.

_____. (2007). *Wind Flyers*. Illustrated by Loren Long. New York: Simon & Schuster.

Johnson, D. B. (2000). *Henry Hikes to Fitchburg*. Boston: Houghton Mifflin.

_____. (2002). *Henry Builds a Cabin*. Boston: Houghton Mifflin.

_____. (2003). *Henry Climbs a Mountain*. Boston: Houghton Mifflin.

_____. (2004). *Henry Works*. Boston: Houghton Mifflin.

_____. (2007). *Four Legs Bad, Two Legs Good!* Boston: Houghton Mifflin.

Johnson, David A. (2006) *Snow Sounds: An Onomatopoeic Story*. Boston: Houghton Mifflin Company.

Johnson, Dolores. (1993). *Now Let Me Fly: The Story of a Slave Family*. New York: Macmillan.

Johnson, Lindsay Lee. (2002). *Soul Moon Soup*. Asheville, NC: Front Street.

Johnson, Paul Brett. (1999). *Old Dry Frye: A Deliciously Funny Tall Tale*. New York: Scholastic.

_____. (2006). *On Top of Spaghetti*. New York: Scholastic.

Johnson, Stephen T. (1995). *Alphabet City*. New York: Penguin.

_____. (2003). *City by Numbers*. New York: Viking.

Johnson, Sylvia. (1999). *Mapping the World*. New York: Atheneum.

Johnson-Davies, Denys. (2005). *Goha, the Wise Fool*. Illustrated by Hany El Saed Ahmed. New York: Philomel.

Johnston, Tony. (1996). *The Wagon*. New York: Tambourine.

_____. (1997). *The Quilt Story*. Logan, IA: Perfection Learning.

Jonas, Ann. (1989). *Color Dance*. New York: Greenwillow.

Jones, Bill T., & Susan Kuklin. (1998). *Dance*. New York: Hyperion.

Jones, Diana Wynne. (2008). *House of Many Ways*. New York: Greenwillow.

_____. (2004). *The Merlin Conspiracy*. New York: Greenwillow.

Jones, Sylvie. (2007). *Who's in the Tub?* Illustrated by Pascale Constantin. Maplewood, NJ: Blue Apple.

Jongman, Mariken. (2008). *Rits*. Asheville, NC: Front Street.

Jonnell, Lynne. (2007). *Emmy and the Incredible Shrinking Rat*. Illustrated by Jonathan Bean. New York: Holt.

_____. (2008). *Emmy and the Home for Troubled Girls*. Illustrated by Jonathan Bean. New York: Holt.

Joosse, Barbara. M. (1998). *Ghost Trap: A Wild Willie Mystery*. Illustrated by Sue Truesdell. Boston: Houghton Mifflin Harcourt.

_____. (1991). *Mama, Do You Love Me?* Illustrated by Barbara Lavallee. San Francisco: Chronicle.

Joseph, Lynn, (1994). *The Mermaid's Twin Sister: More Stories from Trinidad*. Illustrated by Donna Perrone. New York: Clarion.

Joyce, William. (1985). *George Shrinks*. New York: Harper & Row.

Juby, Susan. (2007). *Another Kind of Cowboy*. New York: HarperCollins.

Judge, Lila. (2007). *One Thousand Tracings: Healing the Wounds of World War II*. New York. Hyperion.

Jungman, Ann. (1992). *Cinderella and the Hot Air Balloon*. Illustrated by Russell Ayto. London: F. Lincoln.

Jurmain, Suzanne. (2005). *Forbidden Schoolhouse: The True and Dramatic Story of Prudence Crandall and Her Students*. Boston: Houghton Mifflin.

Juster, Norman. (2006). *The Hello, Goodbye Window*. Illustrated by Chris Raschka. New York: Hyperion.

_____. (2008). *Sourpuss and Sweetie Pie*. Illustrated by Chris Raschka. New York: Michael Di Capua Books.

Juster, Norton. (1961). *The Phantom Tollbooth*. New York: Epstein & Carroll.

Kaaberbol, Lene. (2000). *The Shamer's Daughter*. New York: Holt.

Kadohata, Cynthia. (2006). *Kira-Kira*. New York: Alladin.

_____. (2007). *Cracker!* New York: Atheneum.

_____. (2008). *Outside Beauty*. New York: Simon & Schuster.

Kajikawa, Kimiko. (2000). *Yoshi's Feast*. Illustrated by Yumi Heo. New York: DK Publishing.

Kalman, Maira. (1992). *Max in Hollywood, Baby*. New York: Viking.

Kamm, Katja. (2006). *Invisible*. New York: North-South Books.

Kanevsky, Polly. (2006). *Sleepy Boy*. Illustrated by Stephanie Anderson. New York: Atheneum.

Kantor, Melissa. (2004). *Confessions of a Not It Girl*. New York: Hyperion.

Katz, Michael Jay. (1990). *Ten Potatoes in a Pot and Other Counting Rhymes*. Illustrated by June Otani. New York: HarperCollins.

Keats, Ezra Jack. (1962). *The Snowy Day*. New York: Viking.

_____. (1973). *Pssst! Doggie*. New York: Orchard.

_____. (1976). *The Snowy Day*. New York: Penguin.

Keenan, Sheila, (2000). *Gods, Goddesses and Monsters: A Book of World Mythology* New York: Scholastic.

_____. (2007). *Animals in the House*. New York: Scholastic.

Keller, Laurie. (2007). *Do Unto Otters: A Book about Manners*. New York: Holt.

Kelley, K. C. (2007). *Hottest Nascar Machines*. Berkeley Heights, NJ: Enslow.

Kellogg, Steven. (1984). *Paul Bunyan*. New York: Morrow.

_____. (1986). *Best Friends*. New York, NY: Dial.

_____. (1986). *Pecos Bill*. New York: Morrow.

_____. (1987). *Prehistoric Pinkerton*. New York: Dial.

_____. (1991). *Jack and the Beanstalk*. New York: Morrow.

Kendall, Carol. (1959). *The Gammage Cup*. San Diego, CA: Harcourt.

_____. (2000). *The Whisper of Glocken: A Novel of the Minnipins*. Illustrated by Imero Gobotto. New York: Odyssey.

Kennedy, X. J. (1975). *One Winter Night in August and Other Nonsense Jingles*. Illustrated by David M. McPhail. New York: Simon & Schuster.

Kennedy, X. J., & Dorothy Kennedy. (1992). *Talking Like the Rain*. Illustrated by Jane Dyer. Boston: Little, Brown.

Kerley, Barbara. (2001). *The Dinosaurs of Waterhouse Hawkins: An Illuminating History of Mr. Waterhouse Hawkins, Artist and Lecturer*. Illustrated by Brian Selznick. New York: Scholastic.

_____. (2004). *Walt Whitman: Words for America*. Illustrated by Brian Selznick. New York: Scholastic.

_____. (2008). *What to Do About Alice: How Alice Roosevelt Broke the Rules, Charmed the World, and Drove Her Father Teddy Crazy*. Illustrated by Edwin Fotheringham. New York: Scholastic.

Kerr, M. E. (1972). *Dinky Hocker Shoots Smack*. New York: Harper & Row.

_____. (2000). *What Became of Her*. New York: HarperCollins.

Kerrin, Jessica Scott. (2007). *Martin Bridge: Sound the Alarm!* Illustrated by Joseph Kelly. Tonawanda, NY: Kids Can Press.

Kessler, Liz. (2008). *Philippa Fisher's Fairy Godsister*. Illustrated by Katie May. Cambridge, MA: Candlewick.

Khalsa, Dayal Kaur. (1995). *How Pizza Came to Queens*. New York: Clarkson Potter.

Kherdian, David. (1992). *Feathers and Tails: Animal Fables from around the World*. Illustrated by Nonny Hogrogian. New York: Philomel.

Khing, T. T. (2007). *Where Is the Cake?* New York: Abrams.

Kilaka, John. (2006). *True Friends: A Tale from Tanzania*. Groundwood.

Kim, Derek Kirk. (2007). *Good as Lily*. Illustrated by Jesse Hamm. New York: Minx.

Kimmel, Eric A. (1995). *The Adventures of Hershel of Ostropol*. Illustrated by Trina Schart Hyman. New York: Holiday House.

_____. (1996). *Count Silvernose: A Story from Italy*. Illustrated by Omar Rayyan. New York: Holiday House.

_____. (2000). *The Two Mountains: An Aztec Legend*. Illustrated by Leonard Everett Fisher. New York: Holiday House.

_____. (2004). *Cactus Soup*. Illustrated by Phil Huling. Tarrytown, NY: Cavendish.

_____. (1988). *Anansi and the Moss-Covered Rock*. Illustrated by Janet Stevens. New York: Holiday House.

_____. (2003). *Three Samurai Cats: A Story from Japan*. Illustrated by Mordicai Gerstein. New York: Holiday House.

Kimmell, Elizabeth Cody. (2000). *Visiting Miss Caples*. New York: Dial.

_____. (2008). *Suddenly Supernatural: School Spirit*. Boston: Little, Brown.

Kindersley, Anabel, & Barnabas Kindersley. (1995). *Children Just Like Me*. New York: DK Publishing.

Kindl, Patrice. (2001). *Goose Chase*. Boston: Houghton Mifflin.

Kinerk, Robert. (2007). *Clorinda Takes Flight*. Illustrated by Steven Kellogg. New York: Simon & Schuster.

King Farris, Christine. (2003). *My Brother Martin: A Sister Remembers Growing Up with the Rev. Dr. Martin Luther King Jr*. Illustrated by Chris K. Soentpiet. New York: Simon & Schuster.

Kingsley, Charles. (1863/1995). *The Water Babies*. New York: Penguin.

King-Smith, Dick. (1985). *Babe, the Gallant Pig*. New York: Crown.

_____. (1988). *Martin's Mice*. New York: Crown.

_____. (1992). *The Topsy Turvy Storybook*. Illustrated by John Eastwood. London: Gollancz.

_____. (1998). *The Water Horse*. New York: Crown.

Kinney, Jeff. (2008). *Diary of a Wimpy Kid*. London: Penguin.

_____. (2008). *Diary of a Wimpy Kid: Rodrick Rules*. New York: Abrams.

Kipling, Rudyard. (1912). *Just So Stories*. Garden City, NC: Doubleday.

Kitamora, Satoshi. (1995). *From Acorn to Zoo: And Everything in Between in Alphabetical Order*. New York: Farrar, Straus & Giroux.

_____. (2000). *Me and My Cat*. New York: Farrar, Straus & Giroux.

Klages, Ellen. (2008). *The Green Glass Sea*. New York: Viking.

_____. (2008). *White Sand, Red Menace*. New York: Viking.

Kline, Suzy. (2008). *Horrible Harry Cracks The Code*. Illustrated by Frank Remkiewicz. New York: Penguin.

Klinting, Lars. (2007). *What Do You Want?* Translated by Maria Lundin. Toronto: Groundwood.

Klise, Kate. (2007). *Imagine Harry*. Illustrated by M. Sarah Klise. San Diego, CA: Harcourt.

Knight, Eric. (1938). *Lassie Come-Home*. New York: Holt, Rinehart & Winston.

Knox, Elizabeth. (2007). *Dreamquake: Book Two of the Dragonhunter Duet*. New York: Farrar, Straus & Giroux.

Knutson, Barbara. (1987). *Why the Crab Has No Head*. Minneapolis: Carolrhoda.

_____. (1990). *How the Guinea Fowl Got Her Spots*. Minneapolis: Carolrhoda.

_____. (1993). *Sungura and Leopard: A Swahili Trickster Tale*. Boston: Little, Brown.

Koertge, Ron. (2002). *Stoner and Spaz*. Cambridge, MA: Candlewick.

_____. (2003). *Shakespeare Bats Cleanup*. Cambridge, MA: Candlewick.

_____. (2006). *Margaux with an X*. Cambridge, MA: Candlewick.

_____. (2007). *Strays*. Cambridge, MA: Candlewick.

Koja, Kathe. (2003). *Buddha Boy*. New York: Frances Foster Books.

_____. (2004). *The Blue Mirror*. New York: Farrar, Straus & Giroux.

_____. (2007). *Kissing the Bee*. New York: Farrar Foster.

Konigsburg, E. L. (1967). *From the Mixed-Up Files of Mrs. Basil E. Frankweiler*. New York: Atheneum.

_____. (2000). *Silent to the Bone*. New York: Atheneum.

_____. (2004). *The Outcasts of 19 Schuyler Place*. Waterville, ME: Thorndike.

Koren, Edward. (1972). *Behind the Wheel*. New York: Holt, Reinhart & Winston.

Korman, Gordon. (2000). *No More Dead Dogs*. New York: Hyperion.

Kositsky, Lynne. (2004). *The Thought of High Windows*. Toronto: Kids Can Press.

Koss, Amy Goldman. (2000). *The Girls*. New York: Dial.

_____. (2001). *Stranger in Dadland*. New York: Dial.

Kraft, Betsy Harvey. (2003). *Theodore Roosevelt: Champion of the American Spirit*. New York: Clarion.

Kratter, Paul. (2004). *The Living Rain Forest*. Boston: Charlesbridge.

Kraus, Joanna H. (2007). *A Night of Tamales & Roses*. Illustrated by Elena Caravela. Summit, NJ: Shenanigan Books.

Krensky, Stephen. (2007). *Big Bad Wolves At School*. Illustrated by Brad Sneed. New York: Simon & Schuster.

_____. (2007). *Ghosts*. Minneapolis, MN: Lerner.

_____. (2008). *A Man for All Seasons: The Life of George Washington Carver*. Illustrated by Wil Clay. New York: HarperCollins.

Krishnaswami, Uma. (2004). *Naming Maya*. New York: Farrar, Straus & Giroux.

Kromhout, Rindert. (2007). *Little Donkey and the Birthday Present*. Illustrated by Annemarie van Haeringen. Translated by Marianne Martens. New York: North-South.

Krull, Kathleen. (1996). *Wilma Unlimited: How Wilma Rudolph Became the World's Fastest Woman*. Illustrated by David Diaz. San Diego, CA: Harcourt Brace.

_____. (1999). *They Saw the Future: Oracles, Psychics, Scientists, Great Thinkers, and Pretty Good Guessers*. Illustrated by Kyrsten Brooker. New York: Atheneum.

_____. (2000). *Lives of Extraordinary Women: Rulers, Rebels (and What the Neighbors Thought)*. Illustrated by Kathryn Hewitt. San Diego, CA: Harcourt.

_____. (2003). *Harvesting Hope: The Story of Cesar Chavez*. Illustrated by Yuyi Morales. San Diego, CA: Harcourt Brace.

_____. (2004). *The Boy on Fairfield Street: How Ted Geisel Grew Up to Become Dr. Seuss*. Illustrated by Steve Johnson, Lou Fancher, and Dr. Seuss. New York: Random House.

_____. (2008). *Hillary Rodham Clinton: Dreams Taking Flight*. Illustrated by Amy June Bates. New York: Simon & Schuster.

_____. (2008). *The Road to Oz: Twists, Turns, Bumps, and Triumphs in the Life of L. Frank Baum*. Illustrated by Kevin Hawkes. New York: Knopf.

Kundhardt, Dorothy. (2001). *Pat the Bunny*. New York: Golden Books.

Kurlansky, Mark. (2001). *The Cod's Tale*. Illustrated by S. D. Schindler. New York: Putnam.

Kurtz, Jane. (2000). *Faraway Home*. Illustrated by E. B. Lewis. San Diego, CA: Harcourt.

_____. (2001). *Jakarta Missing*. New York: Greenwillow.

_____. (2003). *Saba: Under the Hyena's Foot*. Middleton, WI: Pleasant.

Kurzweil, Allen. (2003). *Leonard and the Spitting Image*. Illustrated by Bret Bertholf. New York: Greenwillow.

Kuskin, Karla. (1975). *Near the Window Tree: Poems and Notes*. New York: Harper & Row.

_____. (1980). *Dogs and Dragons, Trees and Dreams: A Collection of Poems*. New York: Harper & Row.

_____. (1997). *The Upstairs Cat*. New York: Clarion.

_____. (1998). *The Sky Is Always in the Sky*. Illustrated by Isabelle Dervaux. New York: Laura Geringer Books.

_____. (2000). *I Am Me*. New York: Simon & Schuster.

_____. (2003). *Moon, Have You Met my Mother? The Collected Poems of Karla Kuskin*. Illustrated by Sergio Ruzzier. New York: Laura Geringer Books.

Kwon, Yoon-duck. (2007). *My Cat Copies Me*. La Jolla, CA: Kane Miller.

L'Engle, Madeleine. (1960). *Meet the Austins*. New York: Vanguard.

_____. (1962). *A Wrinkle in Time*. New York: Farrar, Straus & Giroux.

_____. (1965). *The Arm of the Starfish*. New York: Ariel.

_____. (1973). *A Wind in the Door*. New York: Farrar, Straus & Giroux.

_____. (1978). *A Swiftly Tilting Planet*. New York: Farrar, Straus & Giroux.

_____. (1994). *Troubling a Star*. New York: Farrar, Straus & Giroux.

LaFaye, Alexandra. (2004). *Worth*. New York: Simon & Schuster.

Lagerlof, Selma. (1991). *The Wonderful Adventures of Nils*. Minneapolis, MN: Skandisk.

Lakin, Patricia. (2007). *Max & Mo Go Apple Picking*. Illustrated by Brian Floca. New York: Aladdin.

_____. (2007). *Rainy Day*. Illustrated by Scott Nash. New York: Dial.

Lanagan, Margo. (2007). *Red Spikes*. New York: Knopf.

Landau, Elaine. (2007). *Big Cats*. Berkeley Heights, NJ: Enslow.

Lang, Lang, & Michael French. (2008). *Lang Lang: Playing with Flying Keys*. New York: Delacorte.

Langley, John. (1995). *Little Red Riding Hood*. London: HarperCollins.

Langström, Lena. (2006). *Boo and Baa Have Company*. Illustrated by Olof Landström. Translated by Joan Sandin. New York: Macmillan.

Larios, Julie. (2006). *Yellow Elephant: A Bright Bestiary*. Illustrated by Julie Paschkis. San Diego, CA: Harcourt.

LaRochelle, David. (2005). *Absolutely, Positively Not*. New York: Scholastic.

_____. (2007). *The End*. Illustrated by Richard Egielski. New York: Levine.

Lasky, Kathryn. (1996). *Beyond the Burning Time*. New York: Scholastic.

_____. (1999). *Elizabeth I: Red Rose of the House of Tudor*. New York: Scholastic.

_____. (2003). *The Man Who Made Time Travel*. Illustrated by Kevin Hawkes. New York: Farrar, Straus & Giroux.

_____. (2006). *John Muir: America's First Environmentalist*. Cambridge, MA: Candlewick.

Lattimore, Deborah Nourse. (1989). *Why There Is No Arguing in Heaven: A Mayan Myth*. New York: Harper & Row.

Lauber, Patricia. (1986). *The Eruption and Healing of Mt. St. Helens*. New York: Aladdin.

_____. (1989). *The News about Dinosaurs*. Boston: Houghton Mifflin.

_____. (1990). *Seeing Earth from Space*. New York: Orchard.

Law, Ingrid. (2008). *Savvy*. New York: Dial.

Lawrence, Iain. (2001). *Lord of the Nutcracker Men*. New York: Delacorte.

_____. (2004). *B for Buster*. New York: Delacorte.

_____. (2005). *The Convicts: The Curse of the Jolly Stone Trilogy, #1*. New York: Random House.

_____. (2005). *The Cannibals: The Curse of the Jolly Stone Trilogy, #2*. New York: Random House.

_____. (2007). *The Castaways: The Curse of the Jolly Stone Trilogy, #3*. New York: Random House.

_____. (2008). *Gemini Summer*. New York: Yearling.

Lawrence, Louise. (2002). *Children of the Dust*. London: Random House.

Lawson, Robert. (1944). *Rabbit Hill*. New York: Viking.

Le Guin, Ursula. (1968). *A Wizard of Earthsea*. Illustrated by Ruth Robbins. Boston: Houghton Mifflin.

_____. (1971). *The Tombs of Atuan*. New York: Bantam.

Le Guin, Ursula. (1972). *The Farthest Shore*. New York: Bantam.

_____. (1990). *Tehanu: The Last Book of Earthsea*. New York: Atheneum.

_____. (2004). *Gifts*. Orlando, FL: Harcourt.

_____. (2007). *Powers*. Orlando, FL: Harcourt.

Leaf, Munro. (1936). *The Story of Ferdinand*. Illustrated by Robert Lawson. New York: Penguin.

Lear, Edward. (1846/1980) *A Book of Nonsense*. New York: Metropolitan Museum of Art and Viking.

Lee, Suzy. (2008). *Wave*. San Francisco: Chronicle.

Leeds, Constance. (2007). *The Silver Cup*. New York: Viking.

Leedy, Loreen, (2008). *Crazy Like a Fox: A Simile Story*. New York: Holiday House.

Leedy, Loreen, & Pat Street. (2003). *There's a Frog in My Throat! 440 Animal Sayings a Little Bird Told Me*. New York: Holiday House.

Lehman, Barbara. (2004). *The Red Book*. Boston: Houghton Mifflin.

_____. (2006). *Museum Trip*. Boston: Houghton Mifflin.

_____. (2007). *Rainstorm*. Boston: Houghton Mifflin.

_____. (2008). *Trainstop*. Boston: Houghton Mifflin.

Lennon, Joan. (2007). *Questors*. New York: McElderry.

Lester, Alison. (1997). *The Quicksand Pony*. Boston: Houghton Mifflin.

Lester, Julius. (1987). *The Tales of Uncle Remus: The Adventures of Brer Rabbit*. Illustrated by Jerry Pinkney. New York: Dial.

_____. (1988). *More Tales of Uncle Remus: Further Adventures of Brer Rabbit, His Friends, Enemies, and Others*. Illustrated by Jerry Pinkney. New York: Dial.

_____. (1989). *How Many Spots Does a Leopard Have? And Other Tales*. Illustrated by David Shannon. New York: Scholastic.

_____. (1990). *Further Tales of Uncle Remus: The Misadventures of Brer Rabbit, Brer Fox, Brer Wolf, the Doodang, and Other Creatures*. Illustrated by Jerry Pinkney. New York: Dial.

_____. (1994). *John Henry*. Illustrated by Jerry Pinkney. New York: Penguin.

_____. (2000). *Sam and the Tigers*. Illustrated by Jerry Pinkney. New York: Penguin.

_____. (2001). *When Dad Killed Mom*. San Diego, CA: Silver Whistle.

_____. (2002). *Pharaoh's Daughter: A Novel of Ancient Egypt*. New York: HarperCollins.

_____. (2005). *Day of Tears*. New York: Hyperion.

_____. (2005). *The Old African*. New York: Penguin.

_____. (2007). *Cupid*. Orlando, FL: Harcourt.

Lester, Mike. (2000). *A Is for Salad*. New York: Grosset & Dunlap.

Levin, Betty. (1998). *Look Back, Moss*. New York: Greenwillow.

Levine, Anna. (1999). *Running on Eggs*. New York: Cricket.

Levine, Ellen. (2007). *Henry's Freedom Box*. Illustrated by Kadir Nelson. New York: Scholastic.

Levine, Gail Carson. (1997). *Ella Enchanted*. New York: HarperCollins.

_____. (2003). *The Two Princesses of Bamarre*. Illustrated by Pauline Baynes. New York: HarperCollins.

_____. (2008). *Ever*. New York: HarperCollins.

Levithan, David. (2003). *Boy Meets Boy*. New York: Knopf.

Levitin, Sonia. (2003). *Room in the Heart*. New York: Dutton.

_____. (2007). *Junk Man's Daughter*. Illustrated by Guy Porfirio. Chelsea, MI: Sleeping Bear.

Lewin, Ted. (1997). *Fair!* New York: HarperCollins.

Lewin, Ted, & Betsy Lewin. (2008). *Horse Song: The Naadam of Mongolia*. New York: Lee & Low.

Lewis, C. S. (1952). *The Voyage of the Dawn Treader*. New York: HarperCollins.

_____. (1953). *The Silver Chair*. Illustrated by Pauline Baynes. New York: HarperCollins.

_____. (1956). *The Last Battle*. Illustrated by Pauline Baynes. New York: Macmillan.

_____. (1983). *The Magician's Nephew*. Illustrated by Pauline Baynes. New York: HarperCollins.

_____. (1994). *The Horse and His Boy*. Illustrated by Pauline Baynes. New York: HarperCollins.

_____. (1994). *The Lion, the Witch, and the Wardrobe*. Illustrated by Pauline Baynes. New York: HarperCollins.

_____. (1994). *Prince Caspian*. Illustrated by Pauline Baynes. New York: HarperCollins.

Lewis, J. Patrick. (1998). *Doodle Dandies: Poems That Take Shape*. Illustrated by Lisa Desimini. New York: Atheneum.

_____. (2004). *Scien-Trickery: Riddles in Science*. Illustrated by Franz Remkiewicz. Orlando, FL: Silver Whistle.

_____. (2007) *The Brother's War: Civil War Voices in Verse*. Washington, D. C.: National Geographic Society.

Lewis, Maggie. (1999). *Morgy Makes His Move*. Boston: Houghton Mifflin.

Liao, Jimmy (2006). *The Sound of Colors*. Boston: Little, Brown.

Lies, Brian. (2006). *Bats at the Beach*. Boston: Houghton Mifflin.

Liestman, Vicki. (1991). *Columbus Day*. Minneapolis: Carolrhoda.

Light, John. (2007). *The Flower*. Illustrated by Lisa Evan. Swindon, UK: Child's Play International.

Lillegard, Dee. (2007). *Who Will Sing a Lullaby?* Illustrated by Dan Yaccarino. New York: Knopf.

Lin, Grace. (2007). *Lissy's Friends*. New York: Viking.

_____. (2008). *The Year of the Rat*. New York: Little, Brown.

Lindbergh, Reeve. (2007). *My Little Grandmother Often Forgets*. Illustrated by Kathryn Brown. Cambridge, MA: Candlewick.

Lindgren, Astrid. (1950). *Pippi Longstocking*. New York: Viking.

Lionni, Leo. (1985). *Frederick's Fables*. New York: Random House.

Lipsyte, Robert. (1967/1997). *The Contender*. New York: HarperCollins.

_____. (1991). *The Brave*. New York: HarperCollins.

_____. (2007). *Yellow Flag*. New York: HarperCollins.

Lisle, Holly. (2008). *The Ruby Key*. New York: Orchard.

Lisle, Janet Taylor. (1989). *Afternoon of the Elves*. New York: Orchard.

_____. (1991). *Lampfish of Twill*. Illustrated by New York: Orchard.

_____. (1999). *The Lost Flower Children*. New York: Philomel.

_____. (2002). *The Art of Keeping Cool*. New York: Aladdin.

_____. (2002). *How I Became a Writer and Oggie Learned to Drive*. New York: Philomel.

_____. (2008). *Highway Cats*. Illustrated by David Frankland. New York: Philomel.

Livingston, M. C. (1979). *O Sliver of Liver and Other Poems*. New York: Atheneum.

_____. (1991). *Lots of Limericks*. Illustrated by Rebecca Perry. New York: McElderry.

_____. (1991). *Poem-Making: Ways to Begin Writing Poetry*. New York: HarperCollins.

_____. (1993). *Abraham Lincoln: A Man for All the People*. Illustrated by Samuel Perry. New York: Holiday House.

_____. (1994). *Keep on Singing: A Ballad of Marion Anderson*. Illustrated by Samuel Byrd. New York: Holiday House.

_____. (1994). *Riddle-Me Rhymes*. Illustrated by Rebecca Perry. New York: Simon & Schuster.

_____. (1995). *Call Down the Moon*. New York: Simon & Schuster.

Ljungkvist, Laura. (2006). *Follow the Line*. New York: Penguin.

_____. (2007). *Follow the Line through the House*. New York: Penguin.

Llorente, Pilar Molina. (1994). *The Apprentice*. New York: Farrar, Straus & Giroux.

Lloyd-Jones, Sally. (2007). *How To Be a Baby . . . by Me, the Big Sister*. Illustrated by Sue Heap. New York: Random House.

Lobel, Anita. (1998). *No Pretty Pictures: A Child of War*. New York: Greenwillow Books.

_____. (2002). *One Lighthouse, One Moon*. New York: HarperCollins.

Lobel, Arnold. (1970). *Frog and Toad Are Friends*. New York: Harper & Row.

_____. (1983). *The Book of Pigericks: Pig Limericks*. New York: Harper & Row.

_____. (1986). *Random House Book of Mother Goose*. New York: Random House.

Lockhart, E. (2007). *The Boy Book*. New York: Random House.

_____. (2007). *Fly on the Wall*. New York: Random House.

Lodge, Bernard. (2008). *Custard Surprise*. Illustrated by Tim Bowers. New York: HarperCollins.

Lofting, Hugh. (1920). *The Story of Doctor Dolittle*. New York: F. A. Stokes.

_____. (1997). *The Story of Doctor Dolittle*. Illustrated by Michael Hague. New York: HarperCollins.

Logue, Mary. (2000). *Dancing with an Alien*. New York: HarperCollins.

Longfellow, Henry Wadsworth. (1983). *Hiawatha*. Illustrated by Susan Jeffers. New York: Dial.

_____. (1990). *Paul Revere's Ride*. Illustrated by Ted Rand. New York: Dutton.

_____. (2001). *The Midnight Ride of Paul Revere*. Illustrated by Christopher Bing. Brooklyn: Handprint.

Look, Lenore. (1999). *Love as Strong as Ginger*. Illustrated by Stephen Johnson. New York: Simon & Schuster.

Lorbiecki, Marybeth. (2007). *Paul Bunyan's Sweetheart*. Illustrated by Renée Graef. Chelsea, MI: Sleeping Bear Press.

Louie, Ai-Ling. (1982). *Yeh Shen: A Cinderella Story from China*. Illustrated by Ed Young. New York: Philomel.

Lovelace, Maud Hart. (1940). *Betsy-Tacy*. New York: Crowell.

Low, William. (2007). *Old Penn Station*. New York: Holt.

Lowell, Pamela. (2007). *Returnable Girl*. Tarrytown, NY: Cavendish.

Lowell, Susan. (2000). *Cindy Ellen: A Wild Western Cinderella*. Illustrated by Jane K. Manning. New York: HarperCollins.

Lowry, Lois. (1977). *A Summer to Die*. Boston: Houghton Mifflin.

_____. (1979). *Anastasia Krupnik*. Illustrated by Diane De Groat. Boston: Houghton Mifflin.

_____. (1987). *Rabble Starkey*. Boston: Houghton Mifflin.

_____. (1989). *Number the Stars*. Boston: Houghton Mifflin.

_____. (1993). *The Giver*. Boston: Houghton Mifflin.

_____. (1998). *Looking Back: A Book of Memories*. Boston: Houghton Mifflin.

_____. (2000). *Gathering Blue*. Boston: Houghton Mifflin.

_____. (2002). *Gooney Bird Greene*. Illustrated by Middy Thomas. Boston: Houghton Mifflin.

_____. (2003). *The Silent Boy*. Boston: Houghton Mifflin.

_____. (2004). *Messenger*. Boston: Houghton Mifflin.

_____. (2005). *Gooney Bird and the Room Mother*. Illustrated by Middy Thomas. Boston: Houghton Mifflin.

_____. (2007). *Gooney the Fabulous*. Illustrated by Middy Thomas. Boston: Houghton Mifflin.

_____. (2008). *The Willoughbys*. Boston: Houghton Mifflin.

Luján, Jorge Elias. (2004). *Rooster/Gallo*. Illustrated by Manuel Monroy. Ontario, Canada: Groundwood.

Lunge-Larsen, Lise. (2001). *The Race of the Birkebeiners*. Illustrated by Mary Azarian. Boston: Houghton Mifflin.

_____. (2004). *The Hidden Folk: Stories of Fairies, Dwarves, Selkies, and Other Secret Beings*. Illustrated by Beth Krommes. Boston: Houghton Mifflin.

Lunn, Janet. (2000). *The Hollow Tree*. New York: Viking.

Lupton, Hugh. (2003). *Pirican Pic and Pirican Mor*. Cambridge, MA: Barefoot.

Lynch, Chris. (1993). *Shadow Boxer*. New York: HarperCollins.

_____. (1994). *Ice Man*. New York: HaperCollins.

_____. (2005). *Inexcusable*. New York: Atheneum.

Lyon, George Ella. (1990). *Come a Tide*. Illustrated by Stephen Gammell. New York: Scholastic.

_____. (2000). *One Lucky Girl*. Illustrated by Irene Trivas. New York: DK Publishing.

Lyon, George Ella. (2004). *Sonny's House of Spies*. New York: Atheneum.

_____. (2004). *Weaving the Rainbow*. Illustrated by Stephanie Anderson. New York: Atheneum.

Lyons, Mary E. (1992). *Letters from a Slave Girl: The Story of Harriet Jacobs*. New York: Scribner.

_____. (1995). *The Butter Tree: Tales of Bruh Rabbit*. Illustrated by Mireille Vautier. New York: Holt.

Macaulay, David. (1988). *The Way Things Work*. Boston: Houghton Mifflin.

_____. (1990). *Black and White*. Boston: Houghton Mifflin.

_____. (1995). *Shortcut*. Boston: Houghton Mifflin.

_____. (2003). *Mosque*. Boston: Houghton Mifflin.

_____. (2008). *The Way We Work: Getting to Know the Amazing Human Body*. Illustrated by Richard Walker. Boston: Houghton Mifflin.

MacDonald, George. (1871/1989). *At the Back of the North Wind*. New York: Morrow.

MacDonald, Ross. (2003). *Achoo! Bang! Crash! The Noisy Alphabet*. Brookfield, CT: Roaring Brook Press.

MacDonald, Suse. (1986). *Alphabatics*. New York: Simon & Schuster.

_____. (1990). *Once upon Another: The Tortoise and the Hare/ The Lion and the Mouse*. Illustrated by Bill Oakes. New York: Dial.

MacLachlan, Patricia. (1980). *Arthur, for the Very First Time*. New York: HarperCollins.

_____. (1985). *Sarah, Plain and Tall*. New York: Harper & Row.

_____. (1988). *The Facts and Fictions of Minna Pratt*. New York: Harper & Row.

_____. (1991). *Journey*. New York: Delacorte.

_____. (1991). *Three Names*. New York: HarperCollins.

_____. (1993). *Baby*. New York: Delacorte.

_____. (1994). *Skylark*. New York: HarperCollins.

_____. (2001). *Caleb's Story*. New York: Joanna Cotler Books.

_____. (2004). *More Perfect Than the Moon*. New York: Joanna Cotler Books.

MacLeod, Doug. (2007). *I'm Being Stalked by a Moonshadow*. Asheville, NC: Front Street.

MacLeod, Elizabeth. (2007). *I Heard a Little Baa*. Illustrated by Louise Phillips. Toronto: Kids Can Press.

Maestro, Betsy. (1990). *The Discovery of the Americas*. New York: Lothrup, Lee, & Low.

Magoon, Scott. (2007). *I've Painted Everything*. Boston: Houghton Mifflin.

Maguire, Gregory. (2007). *What-the-Dickens: The Story of a Rogue Fairy*. Cambridge, MA: Candlewick.

Mahy, Margaret. (1990). *The Great White Man-Eating Shark: A Cautionary Tale*. Illustrated by Johnathan Allen. New York: Dial.

_____. (2003). *Alchemy*. New York: McElderry.

Makhijani, Pooja. (2007). *Mama's Saris*. Illustrated by Elena Gomez. Boston: Little, Brown.

Mammano, Julie. (2007). *Rhinos Who Rescue*. San Francisco: Chronicle.

Manes, Stephen. (1982). *Be a Perfect Person in Just Three Days!* Illustrated by Tom Huffman. New York: Clarion.

Mann, Elizabeth. (2003). *Empire State Building: When New York Reached for the Skies*. Illustrated by Alan Witschonke. New York: Miyaka.

Manna, Anthony, & Christodoula Mitakidou. (1997). *Mr. Semolina-Semolinus: A Greek Folktale*. Illustrated by Giselle Potter. New York: Atheneum.

Manning, Maurie. (2003). *The Aunts Go Marching*. Illustrated by Sandra D'Antonio. Honesdale, PA: Boyds Mills Press.

Manning, Mick, & Brita Granstrom. (2007). *Dino-Dinners*. New York: Holiday House.

Marcantonio, Patricia Santos. (2005). *Red Ridin' in the Hood: and Other Cuentos*. Illustrated by Renato Alarcao. New York: Farrar, Straus & Giroux.

Marchetta, Melina. (1992). *Looking for Alibrandi*. New York: Orchard.

_____. (2008). *Jellicoe Road*. New York: HarperCollins.

Marcus, Leonard. (1990). *Mother Goose's Little Misfortunes*. Illustrated by Amy Swartz. New York: Simon & Schuster.

_____. (2006). *Side by Side: Five Favorite Picture-Book Teams Go to Work*. New York: Walker.

_____. (2006). *Pass It Down: Five Picture Book Families Make Their Mark*. New York: Walker.

_____. (2006). *The Wand in the Word: Conversations with Writers of Fantasy*. Cambridge, MA: Candlewick.

Marillier, Juliet. (2007). *Wildwood Dancing*. New York: Knopf.

Mark, Jan. (2004). *Useful Idiots*. Oxford: David Fickling.

Markle, Sandra. (2006). *A Mother's Journey*. Illustrated by Alan Marks. Watertown, MA: Charlesbridge.

_____. (2007). *Outside and Inside Woolly Mammoths*. New York: Walker.

Marrin, Albert. (2000). *Sitting Bull and His World*. New York: Dutton.

_____. (2004). *Old Hickory: Andrew Jackson and the American People*. New York: Dutton.

_____. (2007). *The Great Adventure: Theodore Roosevelt and the Rise of Modern America*. New York: Dutton.

Marsden, Carolyn. (2007). *Bird Springs*. New York: Viking.

Marsden, John. (1993). *Tomorrow, When the War Began*. Boston: Houghton Mifflin.

_____. (2007). *While I Live*. New York: Scholastic.

Marshall, James. (1972). *George and Martha*. Boston: Houghton Mifflin.

_____. (1989) *The Three Little Pigs*. New York: Dial.

_____. (1993). *Pocketful of Nonsense*. New York: Artists and Writers Guild Book.

Martel, Yann. (2001). *The Life of Pi*. San Diego, CA: Harcourt.

Martignacco, Carole. (2006). *The Everything Seed: A Story of Beginnings*. Berkeley, CA: Ten Speed Press.

Martin, Bill, Jr. (1997). *Polar Bear, Polar Bear, What Do You Hear?* Illustrated by Eric Carle. New York: Holt.

_____. (2006). *Fire! Fire! Said Mrs. McGuire.* Illustrated by Vladimir Radunsky. San Diego, CA: Harcourt.

_____. (2007). *Brown Bear, Brown Bear, What Do You See?* Illustrated by Eric Carle. New York: Holt.

Martin, Bill, Jr., & John Archambault. (1989). *Chicka Chicka Boom Boom.* Illustrated by Lois Ehlert. New York: Simon & Schuster.

Martin, Jacqueline Briggs. (1998). *Snowflake Bentley.* Illustrated by Mary Azarian. Boston: Houghton Mifflin.

_____. (2001). *The Camp, the Ice, and the Boat Called Fish.* Boston: Houghton Mifflin.

_____. (2003). *On Sand Island.* Boston: Houghton Mifflin.

Martin, Rafe. (1985). *Foolish Rabbit's Big Mistake.* Illustrated by Ed Young. New York: Putnam.

_____. (1992). *The Rough-Face Girl.* Illustrated by David Shannon. New York: Putnam.

_____. (1993). *The Boy Who Lived with the Seals.* Illustrated by David Shannon. New York: Putnam.

Martin, Sarah Catherine. (1991). *Old Mother Hubbard and Her Wonderful Dog.* Illustrated by James Marshall. New York: Farrar, Straus & Giroux.

Maruki, Toshi. (1982). *Hiroshima No Pika.* New York: HarperCollins.

Marvel. (2007). *The Amazing Spider-Man Pop Up*, Caroline Repchuk (Ed.). Cambridge, MA: Candlewick.

Marx, Trish. (2000). *One Boy from Kosovo.* Illustrated by Cindy Karp. New York: Lothrop & Shepard.

Mash, Robert. (2007). *Extreme Dinosaurs.* Illustrated by Stuart Martin. New York: Atheneum.

Mass, Wendy. (2004). *Leap Day.* New York: Little, Brown.

Matthews, Tina. (2007). *Out of the Egg.* Boston: Houghton Mifflin.

Matthews, Tom. (1999). *Always Inventing: A Photobiography of Alexander Graham Bell.* Washington, DC: National Geographic Society.

Mayer, Bill (2008). *All Aboard: A Traveling Alphabet.* New York: McElderry.

Mayer, Mercer. (2003). *Frog Goes to Dinner.* New York: Dial.

_____. (2003). *Frog, Where Are You?* New York: Dial.

_____. (2003). *One Frog Too Many.* New York: Dial.

Mayo, Margaret. (2006). *Roar!* Illustrated by Alex Ayliffe. New York: Orchard.

Mazer, Harry. (2001). *A Boy At War: A Novel of Pearl Harbor.* New York: Simon & Schuster.

Mazer, Norma Fox. (2007). *Has Anyone Seen My Emily Greene?* Illustrated by Christine Davenier. Cambridge, MA: Candlewick.

_____. (2008). *The Missing Girl.* New York: HarperCollins.

McAllister, Angela. (2007). *Mama and Little Joe.* Illustrated by Terry Milne. New York: McElderry.

McBrantney, Sam. (2005). *One Voice, Please: Favorite Read-aloud Stories*. Illustrated by Russell Ayto. Cambridge, MA: Candlewick.

McCaffrey, Anne. (1976). *Dragonsong.* New York: Atheneum.

_____. (1977). *Dragonsinger.* New York: Atheneum.

_____. (1979). *Dragondrums.* New York: Atheneum.

_____. (2007). *A Closer Look.* New York: Greenwillow.

McCarty, Peter. (2007). *Fabian Escapes.* New York: Holt.

McCaughrean, Geraldine. (2002). *Gilgamesh the Hero.* Oxford: Oxford University Press.

_____. (2002). *My Grandmother's Clock.* Illustrated by Stephen Lambert. Boston: Houghton Mifflin.

_____. (2002). *The Kite Rider.* New York: HarperCollins.

_____. (2003). *Stop the Train!* New York: HarperCollins.

_____. (2007). *White Darkness.* New York: HarperTempest.

McCaulay, David. (1987). *Why the Chicken Crossed the Road.* Boston: Houghton Mifflin.

McClafferty, Carla Killough. (2006). *Something Out of Nothing: Marie Curie and Radium.* New York: Farrar, Straus & Giroux.

McClintock, Barbara. (2005). *Cinderella.* New York: Scholastic.

McCloskey, Robert. (1941). *Make Way for Ducklings.* New York: Viking.

_____. (1999). *Time of Wonder.* New York: Penguin.

McCord, David M. (1977). *One at a Time.* Illustrated by Henry Bugbee Kane. Boston: Little, Brown.

McCord, David T. W. (1952). *Far and Few: Rhymes of the Never Was and Always Is.* Illustrated by Henry B. Kane. Boston: Little, Brown.

McCord, Patricia. (2004). *Pictures in the Dark.* New York: Bloomsbury.

McCormick, Patricia. (2000). *Cut.* Asheville, NC: Front Street.

_____. (2006). *Sold.* New York: Hyperion.

McCully, Emily Arnold. (1997). *Mirette on the High Wire.* New York: Penguin.

_____. (2003). *Picnic.* New York: HarperCollins.

_____. (2004). *Squirrel and John Muir.* New York: Farrar, Straus & Giraux.

_____. (2007). *The Escape of Oney Judge: Martha Washington's Slave Finds Freedom.* New York: Farrar, Straus & Giroux.

_____. (2008). *Manjiro: The Boy Who Risked His Life for Two Countries.* New York: Farrar, Straus &, Giroux.

McCully, Emily Arnold. (2008). *My Heart Glow: Alice Cogswell, Thomas Gallaudet, and the Birth of American Sign Language.* New York: Hyperion.

McCurdy, Michael. (1994). *Escape from Slavery: The Boyhood of Frederick Douglass in His Own Words.* New York: Knopf.

McDermott, Gerald. (1974). *Arrow to the Sun: a Pueblo Indian Tale.* New York: Viking.

_____. (1978). *The Stonecutter.* New York: Penguin.

_____. (1992). *Zomo the Rabbit: A Trickster Tale from West Africa.* San Diego, CA: Harcourt.

_____. (1993). *Raven: A Trickster Tale from the Pacific Northwest.* San Diego, CA: Harcourt.

_____. (1994). *Coyote: A Trickster Tale from the American Southwest.* San Diego, CA: Harcourt.

_____. (1996). *Zomo the Rabbit.* San Diego, CA: Harcourt.

McDermott, Gerald. (1999). *The Fox and the Stork*. San Diego, CA: Harcourt.

———. (2001). *Raven*. San Diego, CA: Harcourt.

McGhee, Alison. (2004). *Snap*. Cambridge, MA: Candlewick.

McGill, Alice. (1999). *Molly Bannaky*. Illustrated by Chris K. Soentpiet. Boston: Houghton Mifflin.

———. (2004). *Sure as Sunrise: Stories of Bruh Rabbit and His Walkin' Talkin' Friends*. Illustrated by Don Tate. Boston: Houghton Mifflin.

———. (2008). *Way Up and Over Everything*. Illustrated by Jude Daly. Boston: Houghton Mifflin Harcourt.

McGuirk, Leslie. (2007). *Tucker's Spooky Halloween*. Cambridge, MA: Candlewick.

McKay, Hilary. (1991). *The Exiles*. New York: McElderry.

———. (1993). *The Exiles at Home*. New York: McElderry.

———. (1998). *The Exiles in Love*. New York: McElderry.

———. (2002). *Saffy's Angel*. New York: McElderry.

———. (2003). *Indigo's Star*. New York: McElderry.

———. (2008). *Forever Rose*. New York: McElderry.

McKinley, Robin. (1982). *The Blue Sword*. London: Futura.

———. (1985). *The Hero and the Crown*. New York: Greenwillow.

———. (1988). *The Outlaws of Sherwood*. New York: Greenwillow.

———. (1997). *Rose Daughter*. New York: Greenwillow.

———. (1999). *Beauty*. New York: HarperCollins.

———. (2000). *Spindle's End*. New York: Putnam.

———. (2007). *Dragonhaven*. New York: Putnam.

McKissack, Patricia C. (1986). *Flossie and the Fox*. Illustrated by Rachel Isadora. New York: Dial.

———. (1988). *Mirandy and Brother Wind*. New York: Knopf.

———. (1992). *The Dark-Thirty: Southern Tales of the Supernatural*. Illustrated by J. Brian Pinkney. New York: Knopf.

———. (2003). *Tippy Lemmey*. New York: Alladin.

———. (2005). *Precious and Boo Hag*. Illustrated by Kyrsten Brooker. New York: Simon & Schuster.

———. (2007). *Friendship for Today*. New York: Scholastic.

———. (2007). *A Song for Harlem: Scraps of Time, 1928*. Illustrated by Gordon C. James. New York: Viking.

———. (2008). *The Homerun King: Scraps of Time, 1937*. Illustrated by Gordon C. James. New York: Viking.

———. (2008). *Stitchin' and Pullin': A Gee's Bend Quilt*. Illustrated by Cozbi Cabrera. New York: Random House.

McKissack, Patricia C., & Fredrick McKissack. (1994). *Christmas in the Big House, Christmas in the Quarters*. New York: Scholastic.

McLaughlin, Patricia, & Emily MacLaughlan Charest. (2006). *Once I Ate a Pie*. New York: HarperCollins.

McLeod, Bob. (2006). *SuperHero ABC*. New York: HarperCollins.

McLimans, David. (2006). *Gone Wild*. New York: Walker.

McMillan, Bruce. (1991). *Eating Fractions*. New York: Scholastic.

———. (2007). *How the Ladies Stopped the Wind*. Illustrated by Gunella. Boston: Houghton Mifflin.

McMullan, Kate. (2003). *Papa's Song*. Illustrated by Jim McMullan. New York: Farrar, Straus & Giroux.

———. (2004). *My Travels with Capts. Lewis and Clark by George Shannon*. New York: Cutler Books.

McNamara, Margaret. (2007). *The Luck of the Irish*. Illustrated by Mike Gordon. New York: Aladdin.

McNulty, Faith. (2005). *If You Decide to Go to the Moon*. Illustrated by Steven Kellogg. New York: Scholastic.

McPhail, David. (2006). *Boy on the Brink*. New York: Holt.

Mead, Alice. (1995). *Junebug*. New York: Farrar, Straus & Giroux.

Meddaugh, Susan. (1995). *Hog-Eye*. Boston: Houghton Mifflin.

Meltzer, Milton. (1990). *Columbus and the World around Him*. New York: Watts.

———. (1993). *Lincoln: In His Own Words*. San Diego, CA: Harcourt.

———. (1995). *Frederick Douglass: In His Own Words*. San Diego, CA: Harcourt.

Menchin, Scott. (2007). *Taking A Bath with the Dog and Other Things That Make Me Happy*. Cambridge, MA: Candlewick.

Merriam, Eve. (1962). *There Is No Rhyme for Silver*. New York: Atheneum.

———. (1964). *It Doesn't Always Have to Rhyme*. New York: Atheneum.

———. (1992). *The Singing Green: New and Selected Poems for All Seasons*. Illustrated by Kathleen Collins Howell. New York: Morrow.

———. (1994). *Higgle Wiggle: Happy Rhymes*. New York: Morrow.

———. (1995). *Halloween ABC*. Illustrated by Lane Smith. New York: Aladdin.

Merrill, Jean. (1987). *The Pushcart War*. New York: Dell.

Messinger, Carla, & Susan Katz. (2007). *When The Shadbush Blooms*. Illustrated by David Kanietakeron Fadden. Berkeley, CA: Ten Speed Press.

Meyer, Louis A. (2002). *A. Bloody Jack: Being an Account of the Curious Adventures of Mary "Jacky" Faber, Ship's Boy*. San Diego, CA: Harcourt.

———. (2004). *Curse of the Blue Tattoo: Being an Account of the Misadventures of Jacky Faber, Midshipman and Fine Lady*. San Diego, CA: Harcourt.

Meyer, Stephenie. (2007). *New Moon*. London: Little, Brown.

Michelson, Richard. (2006). *Across the Alley*. Illustrated by E. B. Lewis. New York: Penguin.

———. (2007). *Tuttle's Red Barn: The Story of America's Oldest Family Farm*. Illustrated by Mary Azarian. New York: Putnam.

———. (2008). *As Good As Anybody*. Illustrated by Raul Colón. New York: Random House.

Mickelson, Ben. (2002). *Red Midnight*. New York: HarperCollins.

Micklethwait, Lucy. (1993). *A Child's Book of Art*. New York: DK Publishing.

Milgrim, David. (2006). *Time to Get Up, Time to Go*. New York: Clarion.

Miller, William. (1994). *Zora Hurston and the Chinaberry Tree*. Illustrated by Cornelius Van Wright and Ying-Hwa Hu. New York: Lee & Low.

Mills, Claudia. (2007). *Being Teddy Roosevelt*. Illustrated by R. W. Alley. New York: Farrar, Straus & Giroux.

———. (2008). *The Totally Made-Up Civil War Diary of Amanda MacLeish*. New York: Farrar, Straus & Giroux.

Mills, Judie. (1998). *Robert Kennedy*. Brookfield, CT: Millbrook.

Milne, Alan Alexander. (1926). *Winnie-the-Pooh*. Illustrated by Ernest H. Shepard. New York: Penguin.

Milne, Alan Alexander. (1924). *When We Were Very Young*. New York: Dutton.

———. (1926). *Winnie-the-Pooh*. Illustrated by Ernest H. Shepard. New York: Penguin.

———. (1927). *Now We Are Six*. New York: Dutton.

Minarik, Else. (1957). *Little Bear*. New York: Harper.

Miranda, Anne. (1997). *To Market, to Market*. Illustrated by Janet Stevens. San Diego, CA: Harcourt.

Mitchell, Margaree King. (1993). *Uncle Jed's Barbershop*. New York: Simon & Schuster.

Mitchell, Stephen. (2008). *Genies, Meanies, and Magic Rings: Three Tales from the Arabian Nights*. Illustrated by Tracey Campbell Pearson. New York: Walker.

Mochizuki, Ken. (1993). *Baseball Saved Us*. Illustrated by Dom Lee. New York: Lee & Low.

———. (1995). *Heroes*. Illustrated by Dom Lee. New York: Lee & Low.

Moeri, Louise. (2001). *The Devil in Ol' Rosie*. New York: Atheneum.

Mollel, Tololwa M. (1990). *The Orphan Boy: A Maasai Story*. Illustrated by Paul Morin. New York: Clarion.

———. (1998). *Shadow Dance*. Illustrated by Donna Perrone. New York: Clarion.

———. (2000). *Subira Subira*. Illustrated by Linda Saport. New York: Clarion.

Monceaux, Morgan, & Ruth Katcher. (1999). *My Heroes, My People: African Americans and Native Americans in the West*. New York: Frances Foster.

Monroe, Mary Alice. (2007). *Turtle Summer*. Mount Pleasant, SC: Sylvan Dell.

Montgomery, L. M. (1935/1983). *Anne of Green Gables*. New York: Grosset & Dunlap.

Montgomery, Sy. (1999). *The Snake Scientist*. Illustrated by Nic Bishop. Boston: Houghton Mifflin.

———. (2004). *The Tarantula Scientist*. Boston: Houghton Mifflin.

———. (2006). *Quest for the Tree Kangaroo: An Expedition to the Cloud Forest of New Guinea*. Boston: Houghton Mifflin.

———. (1999). *The Snake Scientist*. Boston: Houghton Mifflin.

Moore, Clement Clarke. (1823/1992) *A Visit from St. Nicholas*. Illustrated by Elmer and Berta Hader. New York: Santley Rosen Associates.

Moore, Lilian. (1982). *Something New Begins: New and Selected Poems*. New York: Simon & Schuster.

———. (1984). *I Feel the Same Way*. New York: Simon & Schuster.

———. (1992). *Adam Mouse's Book of Poems*. Illustrated by Kathleen Gary McCord. New York: Simon & Schuster.

———. (1997). *Poems Have Roots*. New York: Simon & Schuster.

Moore, Martha. (1995). *Under the Mermaid Angel*. New York: Delacorte.

Moore, Perry. (2007). *Hero*. New York: Hyperion.

Mora, Pat. (2005). *Doña Flor*. Illustrated by Raul Colón. New York: Knopf.

Morales, Yuyi. (2003). *Just a Minute: A Trickster Tale and Counting Book*. San Francisco: Chronicle.

———. (2007). *Little Night*. Brookfield, CT: Roaring Brook Press.

Morgan, Michaela. (2007). *Bunny Wishes*. Illustrated by Caroline Jayne Church. Frome, Somerset, UK: Chicken House.

Moriarty, Jaclyn. (2004). *The Year of Secret Assignments*. New York: Levine.

Morley, Jacqueline. (1999). *Egyptian Myths*. Illustrated by Giovani Caselli. Lincolnwood, IL: Peter Bedrick Books.

Morpurgo, Michael. (1999). *Kensuke's Kingdom*. London: Heinemann Young.

———. (2004). *Private Peaceful*. New York: Scholastic.

———. (2004). *Sir Gawain and the Green Knight*. Cambridge, MA: Candlewick.

Morris, Carla. (2007). *The Boy Who Was Raised by Librarians*. Illustrated by Brad Sneed. Atlanta, GA: Peachtree.

Morris, Gerald. (1998). *The Squire's Tale*. Boston: Houghton Mifflin.

———. (1999). *The Squire, His Knight, and His Lady*. Boston: Houghton Mifflin.

———. (2000). *The Savage Damsel and the Dwarf*. Boston: Houghton Mifflin.

———. (2001). *Parsifal's Page*. Boston: Houghton Mifflin.

———. (2003). *The Ballad of Sir Dinadan*. Boston: Houghton Mifflin.

———. (2004). *The Princess, the Crone, and the Dung-Cart Knight*. Boston: Houghton Mifflin.

Morrison, Taylor. (2006). *Wildfire*. Boston: Houghton Mifflin.

Morse, Jenifer. (2007). *Scholastic Book of World Records 2008*. New York: Scholastic.

Moser, Barry. (2001). *The Three Little Pigs*. Boston: Little, Brown.

Moses, Shelia P. (2007). *Sallie Gal and the Wall-a-kee Man*. Illustrated by Niki Daly. New York: Scholastic.

Moses, Will (2001) *Johnny Appleseed: The Story of a Legend*. New York: Philomel.

Mosher, Richard. (2001). *Zazoo*. New York: Clarion.

Moss, Lloyd. (2000). *Zin! Zin! A Violin*. Illustrated by Marjorie Priceman. New York: Aladdin.

Mould, Chris. (2008). *Something Wickedly Weird: The Icy Hand*. Roaring Brook Press.

Mould, Chris. (2008). *Something Wickedly Weird: The Wooden Mile*. Roaring Brook Press.

Mourlevat, Jean-Claude. (2006). *The Pull of the Ocean*. New York: Delacorte.

Muntean, Michaela. (2006). *Do Not Open This Book!* New York: Scholastic.

Murdock, Catherine Gilbert. (2008). *Princess Ben*. Boston: Houghton Mifflin.

Murphy, Jim. (1993). *Across America on an Emigrant Train*. New York: Clarion.

_____. (1995). *The Great Fire*. New York: Scholastic.

_____. (2000). *Blizzard! The Storm That Changed America*. New York: Scholastic.

_____. (2000). *Pick and Shovel Poet: The Journeys of Pascal D'Angelo*. New York: Clarion.

_____. (2007). *The Real Benedict Arnold*. New York: Clarion.

_____. (2003). *An American Plague: The True and Terrifying Story of the Yellow Fever Epidemic of 1793*. New York: Clarion.

Murrie, Steve, & Matthew Murrie. (2007). *Every Minute on Earth*. Illustrated by Mary Anne Lloyd. New York: Scholastic.

Muth, Jon. (2003). *Stone Soup*. New York: Scholastic.

Myers, Christopher. (2005). *Lies and Other Tall Tales*. Collected by Zora Neale Hurston. New York: HarperCollins.

Myers, Walter Dean. (1988). *Fallen Angels*. New York: Scholastic.

_____. (1991). *Now Is Your Time! The African America Struggle for Freedom*. New York: HarperCollins.

_____. (1993). *Malcolm X: By Any Means Necessary*. New York: Scholastic.

_____. (1995). *The Righteous Revenge of Artemis Bonner*. Columbus, OH: Zaner-Bloser.

_____. (1996). *Slam!* New York: Scholastic.

_____. (1997). *Harlem*. Illustrated by Christopher Myers. New York: Scholastic.

_____. (1999). *At Her Majesty's Request: An African Princess in Victorian England*. New York: Scholastic.

_____. (1999). *Coraline*. New York: HarperCollins.

_____. (1999). *Monster*. Illustrated by Christopher Myers. New York: HarperCollins.

_____. (2000) *145th Street Stories*. New York: Delacorte.

_____. (2000). *Malcolm X: A Fire Burning Brightly*. Illustrated by Leonard Jenkins. New York: HarperCollins.

_____. (2001). *Bad Boy: A Memoir*. New York: HarperCollins.

_____. (2001). *The Greatest: Muhammad Ali*. New York: Scholastic.

_____. (2003). *The Beast*. New York: Scholastic.

_____. (2003). *Blues Journey*. Illustrated by Christopher Myers. New York: Holiday House.

_____. (2004). *Here in Harlem: Poetry in Many voices*. New York: Holiday House.

_____. (2004). *Shooter*. New York: HarperCollins.

_____. (2006). *Jazz*. Illustrated by Christopher Myers. New York: Holiday House.

_____. (2007). *Harlem Summer*. New York: Scholastic.

_____. (2007). *What They Found: Love on 145th Street*. New York: Random House.

Myracle, Lauren. (2007). *Twelve*. New York: Penguin.

Na, An. (2001). *A Step from Heaven*. Asheville, NC: Front Street.

Nadimi, Suzan (2007). *The Rich Man and the Parrot*. Illustrated by Ande Cook. Morton Grove, IL: Whitman.

Naidoo, Beverly. (1999). *The Other Side of Truth*. New York: HarperCollins.

Namioka, Lensey. (1995). *Yang the Third and Her Impossible Family*. Illustrated by Kees de Kiefte. Boston: Little, Brown.

_____. (2007). *Mismatch*. New York: Random House.

Nanji, Shenaaz. (2008). *Child of Dandelions*. Honesdale, PA: Wordsong.

Napoli, Donna Jo. (1992). *The Prince of the Pond*. New York: Dutton.

_____. (1993). *The Magic Circle*. New York: Dutton.

_____. (1996). *Zel*. New York: Dutton.

_____. (1999). *Crazy Jack*. New York: Delacorte.

_____. (1999). *Spinners*. New York: Dutton.

_____. (2000). *Beast*. New York: Dutton.

_____. (2003). *Breath*. New York: Atheneum.

National Geographic Society. (2007). *Sea Monsters: A Prehistoric Adventure*. Washington, DC: National Geographic Society.

Nau, Thomas. (2007). *Walker Evans: Photographer of America*. New York: Roaring Brook Press.

Naylor, Phyllis Reynolds. (1991). *Shiloh*. New York: Atheneum.

_____. (1995). *Alice the Brave*. New York: Atheneum.

_____. (1995). *Ice*. New York: Atheneum.

_____. (1998). *Achingly Alice*. New York: Atheneum.

_____. (1999). *Alice on the Outside*. New York: Atheneum.

_____. (2000). *The Grooming of Alice*. New York: Atheneum.

_____. (2001). *Alice Alone*. New York: Atheneum.

_____. (2004). *Lovingly Alice*. New York: Atheneum.

_____. (2007). *Dangerously Alice*. New York: Atheneum.

_____. (2008). *Almost Alice*. New York: Atheneum.

NCBLA, & David McCullough. (2008). *Our White House: Looking In, Looking Out*. Cambridge, MA: Candlewick.

Nelson, Kadir. (2008). *We Are the Ship: The Story of the Negro Baseball League*. New York: Hyperion.

Nelson, Marilyn. (2001). *Carver: A Life in Poems*. Asheville, NC: Front Street.

_____. (2005). *A Wreath for Emmett Till*. Illustrated by Philippe Lardy. Boston: Houghton Mifflin.

Nelson, Scott Reynolds, & Mark Aronson. (2008). *Ain't Nothing but a Man: My Quest to Find the Real John Henry*. Washington, DC: National Geographic Society.

Nelson, Theresa. (1998). *The Empress of Elsewhere*. New York: DK Publishing.

_____. (2003). *Ruby Electric*. New York: Atheneum.

Nelson, Vaunda Micheaux. (1993). *Mayfield Crossing*. New York: Putnam.

_____. (1995). *Possibles*. New York: Putnam.

Nesbit, E. (1999). *Five Children and It*. Illustrated by Paul O. Zelinsky. New York: William Morrow.

———. (2006). *Lionel and the Book of Beasts*. Illustrated by Michael Hague. New York: HarperCollins.

Newbery, John. (1765). *The Renowned History of Little Goody Two Shoes*. London: John Newbery.

———. (1744/1967). *A Little Pretty Pocket-Book: Intended for the Instruction and Amusement of Little Master Tommy and Pretty Miss Polly*. San Diego, CA: Harcourt.

Newbery, Linda. (2007). *At the Firefly Gate*. New York: David Fickling Books.

Newth, Mette. (1998). *The Dark Light*. New York: Farrar, Straus & Giroux.

———. (2000). *The Transformation*. New York: Farrar, Straus & Giroux.

Nicholls, Sally. (2008). *Ways to Live Forever*. New York: Levine.

Nikola-Lisa, W. (1995). *Bein' with You This Way*. Illustrated by Michael Bryant. New York: Lee & Low.

Niland, Deborah. (2006). *Annie's Chair*. New York: Walker.

Nilsson, Per. (2003). *Heart's Delight*. Asheville, NC: Front Street.

Nivola, Claire. (2008). *Planting the Trees of Kenya: The Story of Wangari Maathai*. Illustrated by Rebecca Gibbon. New York: Holt.

Nix, Garth. (1995). *Sabriel*. New York: HarperCollins.

———. (2001). *Lirael*. New York: HarperCollins.

———. (2003). *Abhorsen*. New York: HarperCollins.

Nixon, Joan Lowry. (1995). *Spirit Seeker*. New York: Delacorte.

———. (1998). *The Haunting*. New York: Delacorte.

Noble, Trinka Hakes. (2007). *The Legend of Cape May Diamond*. Illustrated by E. B. Lewis. Farmington Hills, MI: Sleeping Bear.

Nobleman, Marc Tyler. (2008). *Boys of Steel: The Creators of Superman*. Illustrated by Ross MacDonald. New York: Knopf.

Nolen, Jerdine. (2007). *Pitching in for Eubie*. Illustrated by E. B. Lewis. New York: HarperCollins.

Norman, Howard. (2004). *Between Heaven and Earth: Bird Tales from around the World*. Illustrated by Leo Dillon and Diane Dillon. San Diego, CA: Harcourt.

Norton, Mary. (1953). *The Borrowers*. Illustrated by Beth and Joe Krush. San Diego, CA: Harcourt.

Noyes, Deborah. (2007). *Red Butterfly: How a Princess Smuggled the Secret of Silk Out of China*. Illustrated by Sophie Blackall. Cambridge, MA: Candlewick.

———. (2007). *When I Met the Wolf Girls*. Illustrated by August Hall. Boston: Houghton Mifflin.

Nye, Naomi Shihab. (1994). *Sitti's Secrets*. Illustrated by Nancy Carpenter. New York: Four Winds.

———. (1997). *Habibi*. New York: Simon & Schuster.

———. (2001). *19 Varieties of Gazelle: Poems of the Middle East*. New York: Greenwillow.

———. (2008). *Honeybee*. New York: Greenwillow.

Nyeu, Tao. (2008). *Wonder Bear*. New York: Dial.

Oberman, Sheldon. (1994). *The Always Prayer Shaw*. Illustrated by Ted Lewin. Honesdale, PA: Boyds Mills Press.

O'Brien, Robert C. (1971). *Mrs. Frisby and the Rats of NIMH*. Illustrated by Zena Bernstein. New York: Atheneum.

———. (1975). *Z for Zachariah*. New York: Atheneum.

O'Conner, George. (2004). *Kapow!* New York: Simon & Schuster.

O'Connor, Barbara. (2003). *Fame and Glory in Freedom, Georgia*. New York: Frances Foster.

———. (2007). *How to Steal a Dog*. New York: Farrar, Straus & Giroux..

O'Connor, Jane. (2002). *Emperor's Silent Army: Terracotta Warriors of Ancient China*. New York: Viking.

———. (2007). *Ready, Set, Skip!* Illustrated by Ann James. New York: Viking.

O'Dell, Kathleen. (2004). *Ophie out of Oz*. New York: Dial.

O'Dell, Scott. (1960). *Island of the Blue Dolphins*. Boston: Houghton Mifflin.

———. (1970). *Sing Down the Moon*. Boston: Houghton Mifflin.

O'Dell, Scott, & Elizabeth Hall. (1992). *Thunder Rolling in the Mountains*. Boston: Houghton Mifflin.

Offill, Jenny. (2006). *17 Things I'm Not Allowed to Do Anymore*. Illustrated by Nancy Carpenter. New York: Random House.

Old, Wendie. (2002). *To Fly: The Story of the Wright Brothers*. Illustrated by Robert A. Parker. New York: Clarion.

Onishi, Satoru. (2007). *Who's Hiding?* La Jolla, CA: Kane Miller.

Onyefulu, Obi. (1994). *Chinye: A West African Folk Tale*. Illustrated by Evie Safarewicz. New York: Viking.

Opie, Iona, (1988). *Tail Feathers from Mother Goose: The Opie Rhyme Book*. Boston: Little, Brown.

———. (1996). *My Very First Mother Goose*. Illustrated by Rosemary Wells. Cambridge, MA: Candlewick.

———. (1999). *Here Comes Mother Goose*. Illustrated by Rosemary Wells. Cambridge, MA: Candlewick.

Opie, Iona, & Peter Opie. (1951). *The Oxford Dictionary of Nursery Rhymes*. Oxford: Claredon.

———. (1992). *I Saw Esau: The Schoolchild's Pocket Book*. Illustrated by Maurice Sendak. Cambridge, MA: Candlewick.

Oppel, Kenneth. (2000). *Sunwing*. New York: Simon & Schuster.

———. (2003). *Firewing*. New York: Simon & Schuster.

———. (2004). *Airborn*. New York: Eos.

———. (2007). *Darkwing*. Illustrated by Keith Thompson. New York: Eos.

———. (2007). *Silverwing*. New York: Simon & Schuster.

Orgel, Doris. (1994). *Ariadne, Awake!* Illustrated by Barry Moser. New York: Viking.

Ormerod, Jan, & David Lloyd. (1990). *The Frog Prince*. New York: Lothrop, Lee & Shepard.

Osborne, Mary Pope. (1991). *American Tall Tales*. Illustrated by Michael McCurdy. New York: Knopf.

———. (1996). *Favorite Norse Myths*. Illustrated by Troy Howell. New York: Scholastic.

Osborne, Mary Pope. (1996). *One World, Many Religions: The Way We Worship*. New York: Random House

———. (2000). *Kate and the Beanstalk*. Illustrated by Giselle Potter. New York: Atheneum.

———. (2002). *The Land of the Dead*. New York: Hyperion.

———. (2002). *The One-Eyed Giant*. New York: Hyperion.

———. (2003). *The Gray-Eyed Goddess*. New York: Hyperion.

———. (2003). *Sirens and Sea Monsters*. New York: Hyperion.

———. (2004). *Return to Ithaca*. New York: Hyperion.

———. (2007). *Monday with a Mad Genius*. Illustrated by Sal Murdocca. New York: Random House.

Oswald, Nancy. (2004). *Nothing Here But Stones: A Jewish Pioneer Story*. New York: Holt.

Oughton, Jerrie. (1992). *How the Stars Fell into the Sky: A Navajo Tale*. Illustrated by Lisa Desimini. Boston: Houghton Mifflin.

Owens, Mary Beth. (1988). *A Caribou Alphabet*. Gardiner, ME: Tilbury House.

———. (2007). *Panda Whispers*. New York: Dutton.

Oxenbury, Helen. (1983). *ABC of Things*. New York: Random House.

———. (1991). *Goodnight, Good Morning*. New York: Dial.

Paolini, Christopher. (2003). *Eragon*. New York: Knopf.

———. (2005). *Eldest*. New York: Knopf.

———. (2008). *Brisinger*. New York: Knopf.

Park, Linda Sue. (2000). *The Kite Fighters*. Boston: Houghton Mifflin.

———. (2001). *A Single Shard*. New York: Clarion.

———. (2002). *When My Name Was Keoko*. New York: Clarion.

———. (2004). *The Firekeeper's Son*. Illustrated by Julie Downing. Boston: Houghton Mifflin.

———. (2007). *Tap Dancing on the Roof: Sijo (Poems)*. Illustrated by Istvan Banyai. New York: Clarion.

———. (2008). *Keeping Score*. New York: Clarion.

Parker, Robert Andrew. (2008). *Piano Starts Here: The Young Art Tatum*. New York: Schwartz & Wade.

Parker, Robert B. (2008). *The Boxer and the Spy*. New York: Philomel.

Parkinson, Siobhan. (2003). *Kathleen: The Celtic Knot*. Middleton, WI: Pleasant.

———. (2007). *Blue Like Friday*. New York: Roaring Brook Press.

Parks, Rosa. (1992). *Rosa Parks: My Own Story*. New York: Dial.

Parks, Van Dyke. (1987). *Jump Again! More Adventures of Brer Rabbit*. Illustrated by Barry Moser. San Diego, CA: Harcourt.

———. (1989). *Jump on Over! The Adventures of Brer Rabbit and His Family*. Illustrated by Barry Moser. San Diego, CA: Harcourt.

Parks, Van Dyke, & Malcolm Jones.(1986). *Jump! The Adventures of Brer Rabbit*. Illustrated by Barry Moser. San Diego, CA: Harcourt.

Partridge, Elizabeth. (2002).*This Land Was Made for You and Me: The Life and Songs of Woody Guthrie*. New York: Viking.

Patent, Dorothy Hinshaw. (2008). *When the Wolves Returned: Restoring Nature's Balance in Yellowstone*. Illustrated by Dan and Cassie Hartman. New York: Walker.

Paterson, Katherine. (1952). *Charlotte's Web*. Illustrated by Garth Williams. New York: Harper.

———. (1977). *Bridge to Terabithia*. Illustrated by Donna Diamond. New York: HarperCollins.

———. (1978). *The Great Gilly Hopkins*. New York: HarperCollins/Crowell.

———. (1980). *Jacob Have I Loved*. New York: HarperCollins/Crowell.

———. (1990). *The Tale of the Mandarin Ducks*. Illustrated by Leo Dillon and Diane Dillon. New York: Lodestar.

———. (1991). *Lyddie*. New York: Lodestar.

———. (1994). *Flip-Flop Girl*. New York: Dutton.

———. (1999). *Preacher's Boy*. New York: Clarion.

———. (2002). *The Same Stuff as Stars*. New York: Clarion.

———. (2008). *Bread and Roses, Too*. New York: Sandpiper.

Paton Walsh, Jill. (1982). *The Green Book*. Illustrated by Lloyd Bloom. New York: Farrar, Straus & Giroux.

Patron, Susan. (2008). *The Higher Power of Lucky*. New York: Alladin.

Patterson, James. (2006). *School's Out—Forever*. New York: Little, Brown.

Paulsen, Gary. (1985). *Dog Song*. New York: Simon & Schuster.

———. (1987). *Hatchet*. New York: Atheneum.

———. (1989). *The Winter Room*. New York: Orchard.

———. (1994). *Mr. Tucket*. New York: Delacorte.

———. (1996). *Brian's Winter*. New York: Delacorte.

———. (1998). *Soldier's Heart*. New York: Delacorte.

———. (1999). *Brian's Return*. New York: Delacorte.

———. (2001). *Guts: The True Stories behind Hatchet and the Brian Books*. New York: Delacorte.

———. (2007). *The Amazing Life of Birds*. New York: Random House.

———. (2007). *Lawn Boy*. New York: Random House.

Paye, Won-Ldy, & Margaret Lippert. (2002). *Head, Body, Legs: A Tale from Liberia*. New York: Holt.

———. (2003). *Mrs. Chicken and the Hungry Crocodile*. Illustrated by Julie Paschkis. New York: Holt.

Pearce, Philippa. (1958). *Tom's Midnight Garden*. Philadelphia: Lippincott.

Pearson, Mary. (2008). *The Adoration of Jenna Fox*. New York: Holt.

Pearson, Tracey Campbell. (2006). *The Moon*. New York: Farrar, Straus & Giroux.

Peck, Richard. (1998). *Strays Like Us*. New York: Dial.

———. (2002). *A Year Down Yonder*. New York: Penguin.

———. (2003). *The River Between Us*. New York: Dial.

———. (2004). *A Long Way from Chicago: A Novel in Stories*. New York: Penguin.

_____. (2004). *The Teacher's Funeral: A Comedy in Three Parts*. Waterville, ME: Thorndike.

Peck, Robert. (2004). *Bro*. New York: Harper.

Pelletier, David. (1996). *The Graphic Alphabet*. New York: Orchard.

Pemberton, Bonnie. (2007). *The Cat Master*. Tarrytown, NY: Cavendish.

Pendziwol, Jean E. (2005). *The Red Sash*. Illustrated by Nicolas Debon. Berkeley, CA: Groundwood.

Pennebaker, Ruth. (2000). *Both Sides Now*. New York: Holt.

Pennypacker, Sara. (2007). *The Talented Clementine*. Illustrated by Marla Frazee. New York: Hyperion.

_____. (2008). *Clementine*. Illustrated by Marla Frazee. New York: Hyperion.

_____. (2008). *Clementine's Letter*. New York: Hyperion.

Pérez, Amada Irma. (2007). *Nana's Big Surprise/Nana, Qué Sorpresa!* Illustrated by Maya Christina Gonzalez. San Francisco: Children's Book Press.

Perham, Molly. (1993). *King Arthur: The Legends of Camelot*. Illustrated by Julek Heller. New York: Viking.

Perkins, Lynne Rae. (1999). *All Alone in the Universe*. New York: Greenwillow.

_____. (2003). *Snow Music*. New York: Greenwillow.

_____. (2005). *America the Beautiful*. Illustrated by Chris Gall. New York: Penguin.

_____. (2005). *Criss Cross*. New York: Greenwillow.

_____. (2005). *The First Part Last*. New York: Greenwillow.

_____. (2007). *Pictures From Our Vacation*. New York: Greenwillow.

Perkins, Mitale. (2004). *Monsoon Summer*. New York: Delacorte.

Perrault, Charles. (1989) *Beauty and the Beast,* adapted by Jan Brett. New York: Clarion.

_____. (1989). *Cinderella and Other Tales from Perrault*. Illustrated by Michael Hague. New York: Holt.

Peters, Kimberly Joy. (2007). *Painting Caitlyn*. Montreal: Lobster.

Peters, Lisa Westberg. (2003). *Our Family Tree: An Evolution Story*. Illustrated by Lauren Stringer. San Diego, CA: Harcourt.

_____. (2005). *Cold Little Duck, Duck, Duck*. Illustrated by Sam Williams. New York: HarperCollins.

Peterson, Jeanne Whitehouse. (2000). *Don't Forget Winona*. New York: Joanna Cotler Books.

Peterson, John. (1967). *The Littles*. New York: Scholastic.

Petrucha, Stefan. (2007). *Nancy Drew Graphic Novels #9: Ghost in the Machinery*. Illustrated by Sho Murase. New York: Papercutz.

Philbrick, Rodman. (2004). *The Young Man and the Sea*. New York: Blue Sky Press.

Philip, Neil. (1987). *Tale of Sir Gawain*. Illustrated by Charles Keeping. Cambridge, MA: James Clarke.

Philip, Neil. (1994). *King Midas*. Illustrated by Isabelle Brent. Boston: Little, Brown.

_____. (1999). *Celtic Fairy Tales*. Illustrated by Isabelle Brent. New York: Viking.

_____. (2003). *Horse Hooves and Chicken Feet: Mexican Folktales*. Illustrated by Jacqueline Mair. New York: Clarion.

Pierce, Meredith Ann. (1982). *Dark-Angel*. Boston: Little, Brown.

_____. (1990/2007). *A Gathering of Gargoyles*. Boston: Little, Brown.

_____. (2001). *Treasure at the Heart of Tanglewood*. New York: Viking.

Pierce, Tamora. (1983). *Alanna, the First Adventure*. New York: Atheneum.

_____. (1984). *In the Hand of the Goddess*. New York: Atheneum.

_____. (1986). *The Woman Who Rides Like a Man*. New York: Atheneum.

_____. (1988). *Lioness Rampant*. New York: Atheneum.

_____. (1992). *Wild Magic*. New York: Atheneum.

_____. (1994). *Wolf Speaker*. New York: Atheneum.

_____. (1997). *The Emperor Mage*. New York: Random House.

_____. (2000). *Magic Steps*. New York: Scholastic.

_____. (2001). *Squire*. New York: Random House.

_____. (2001). *Street Magic*. New York: Scholastic.

_____. (2003). *Shatterglass*. New York: Scholastic.

_____. (2003). *Trickster's Choice*. New York: Random House.

Pigni, Guido, & Ronald Hermsen. (2007). *The Story of Giraffe*. Honesdale, PA: Front Street.

Pilkey, Dav. (1996). *Paperboy*. New York: Scholastic.

_____. (1997). *Captain Underpants*. New York: Blue Sky Press.

Pinkney, Andrea Davis. (1998). *Duke Ellington: The Piano Prince and His Orchestra*. Illustrated by Brian Pinkney. New York: Hyperion.

_____. (2000). *Let It Shine: Stories of Black Women Freedom Fighters*. San Diego, CA: Harcourt Brace.

_____. (2002). *Ella Fitzgerald: The Tale of a Vocal Virtuosa*. Illustrated by Brian Pinkney. New York: Hyperion.

_____. (2006). *Peggony-Po: A Whale of a Tale*. Illustrated by Brian Pinkney. New York: Hyperion.

Pinkney, Brain. (2000). *The Adventures of Sparrowboy*. New York: Simon & Schuster.

Pinkney, Jerry. (1999). *The Ugly Duckling*. New York: HarperCollins.

_____. (2000). *Aesop's Fables*. New York: SeaStar.

_____. (2006). *The Little Red Hen*. New York: Penguin.

_____. (2007). *Little Red Riding Hood*. New York: Little, Brown.

Pinkwater, Daniel. (2007). *Neddiad*. Boston: Houghton Mifflin.

_____. (2008). *Bear's Picture*. Illustrated by D.B. Johnson. Boston: Houghton Mifflin.

Piper, Watty. (1954). *The Little Engine That Could*. New York: Platt & Munk.

Pitzer, Susanna. (2006). *Not Afraid of Dogs*. Illustrated by Larry Day. New York: Walker.

Piven, Hanoch. (2004). *What Presidents Are Made Of*. New York: Simon & Schuster.

Pixton, Kaaren. (2006). *Farm Charm*. Missouri: Tybook.

Plummer, Louise. (1995). *The Unlikely Romance of Kate Bjorkman*. New York: Delacorte.

_____. (2000). *A Dance for Three*. New York: Delacorte.

Plum-Ucci, Carol. (2000). *The Body of Christopher Creed*. San Diego, CA: Harcourt.

Polacco, Patricia. (1994). *Pink and Say*. New York: Philomel.

_____. (1995). *Babushka's Mother Goose*. New York: Philomel.

_____. (1998). *My Rotten, Red-Headed Older Brother*. New York: Aladdin.

_____. (2000). *The Butterfly*. New York: Philomel.

Pollock, Penny. (1995). *The Turkey Girl: A Zuni Cinderella Story*. Illustrated by Ed Young. Boston: Little, Brown.

Pomerantz, Charlotte. (1983). *Posy*. New York: Greenwillow.

Portis, Antoinette. (2006). *Not a Box*. New York: HarperCollins.

Potter, Beatrix. (1902/2000). *The Tale of Peter Rabbit*. New York: Warne.

Powell, Randy. (1999). *Tribute to Another Dead Rock Star*. New York: Farrar, Straus & Giroux.

_____. (2001). *Run If You Dare*. New York: Farrar, Straus & Giroux.

_____. (2002). *Three Clams and an Oyster*. New York: Farrar, Straus & Giroux.

Pratchett, Terry. (2003). *The Wee Free Men*. New York: HarperCollins.

_____. (2004). *A Hat Full of Sky*. London: Coral.

_____. (2008). *Johnny and the Bomb*. New York: HarperCollins.

_____. (2008). *Nation*. New York: HarperCollins.

Pratt, Kristin Joy. (1992). *A Walk in the Rain Forest*. Nevada City, CA: Dawn.

_____. (1994). *A Swim through the Sea*. Nevada City, CA: Dawn.

Prelutsky, Jack. (1974). *Circus*. Illustrated by Arnold Lobel. New York: Macmillan.

_____. (1992). *The Headless Horseman Rides Tonight: More Poems to Trouble Your Sleep*. Illustrated by Arnold Lobel. New York: HarperCollins.

_____. (2007). *Good Sports: Rhymes about Running, Jumping, Throwing, and More*. Illustrated by Chris Raschka. New York: Knopf.

_____. (2008). *My Dog May Be a Genius*. Illustrated by James Stevenson. New York: Greenwillow.

Pressler, Mirjam. (1998). *Halinka*. Translated by Elizabeth D. Crawford. New York: Holt.

_____. (2000). *Anne Frank: A Hidden Life*. New York: Dutton Children's Books.

_____. (2002). *Malka*. Translated by Brian Murdock. New York: Philomel.

_____. (2007). *Let Sleeping Dogs Lie*. Asheville, NC: Front Street.

Prevost, Guillaume. (2007). *The Book of Time*. Translated by William Rodarmor. New York: Levine.

Price, Charlie. (2007). *Lizard People*. New York: Roaring Brook Press.

Price, Susan. (2000). *The Sterkarm Handshake*. New York: HarperCollins.

_____. (2004). *The Sterkarm Kiss*. New York: HarperCollins.

Prince, April Jones. (2006). *What Do Wheels Do All Day?* Illustrated by Giles Laroche. Boston: Houghton Mifflin.

Prineas, Sarah. (2008). *The Magic Thief*. New York: HarperCollins.

Pringle, Laurence. (1995). *Dolphin Man: Exploring the World of Dolphins*. New York: Atheneum.

_____. (1997). *An Extraordinary Life: The Story of a Monarch Butterfly*. New York: Orchard.

_____. (1997). *Everybody Has a Belly Button*. Honesdale, PA: Boyds Mills Press.

Provensen, Alice. (1990). *The Buck Stops Here: The Presidents of the United States*. New York: HarperCollins.

Prue, Sally. (2001). *Cold Tom*. New York: Scholastic.

_____. (2002). *The Devil's Toenail*. New York: Scholastic.

Pullman, Philip. (1995). *The Golden Compass*. New York: Knopf.

_____. (1997). *The Subtle Knife*. New York: Knopf.

_____. (2000). *The Amber Spyglass*. New York: Knopf.

_____. (2000). *I Was a Rat*. New York: Knopf.

_____. (2007). *His Dark Materials*. New York: Random House.

_____. (2008). *Once Upon a Time in the North*. New York: Random House.

_____. (2008). *The Ruby in the Smoke*. New York: Random House.

_____. (2008). *The Shadow in the North*. New York: Random House.

_____. (2008). *The Tiger in the Well*. New York: Random House.

_____. (2008). *The Tin Princess*. New York: Random House.

Pulver, Robin. (2003). *Punctuation Takes a Vacation*. Illustrated by Lynn Rowe Reed. New York: Holiday House.

_____. (2008). *Silent Letters Loud and Clear*. Illustrated by Lynn Rowe Reed. New York: Holiday House.

Pyle, Kevin C. (2007). *Blindspot*. New York: Holt.

Qamar. Amjed. (2008). *Beneath My Mother's Feet*. New York: Atheneum.

Quan, Elizabeth. (2007). *Once Upon a Full Moon*. Toronto: Tundra.

Quattlebaum, Mary. (2006). *Sparks Fly High: The Legend of Dancing Point*. New York: Farrar, Straus & Giroux.

Quigley, Mary. (2007). *Granddad's Fishing Buddy*. Illustrated by Stéphanie Jorisch. New York: Dial.

Rallison, Janette. (2007). *It's a Mall World After All*. New York: Walker.

Ramirez, Antonio. (2006). *Napi Goes to the Mountain*. Illustrated by Domi. Toronto: Groundwood.

Rankin, Laura. (1991). *The Handmade Alphabet*. New York: Dial.

Ransom, Jeanie Franz. (2007). **What Do Parents Do? (When You're Not Home)**. Illustrated by Cyd Moore. Atlanta, GA: Peachtree.

Ransome, Arthur. (1916/1968). *The Fool of the World and the Flying Ship: A Russian Tale*. Illustrated by Uri Shulevitz. New York: Farrar, Straus & Giroux.

Rappaport, Doreen. (2000). *Freedom River*. Illustrated by Bryan Collier. New York: Hyperion.

_____. (2001). *Martin's Big Words: The Life of Dr. Martin Luther King, Jr*. Illustrated by Bryan Collier. New York: Hyperion.

_____. (2004). *John's Secret Dreams: The Life of John Lennon*. Illustrated by Bryan Collier. New York: Hyperion.

_____. (2006). *Nobody Gonna Turn Me 'Round: Stories and Songs of the Civil Rights Movement*. Illustrated by Shane W. Evans. Cambridge, MA: Candlewick.

_____. (2007). *Martin's Big Words*. Illustrated by Bryan Collier. New York: Hyperion.

_____. (2008). *Abe's Honest Words: The Life of Abraham Lincoln*. Illustrated by Kadir Nelson. New York: Hyperion.

_____. (2008). *Lady Liberty: A Biography*. Illustrated by Matt Tavares. Cambridge, MA: Candlewick.

Raschka, Christopher. (1993). *Yo! Yes?* New York: Orchard.

_____. (2002). *John Coltrane's Giant Steps*. New York: Simon & Schuster.

Rascol, Sabina. (2004). *The Impudent Rooster*. Illustrated by Holly Berry. New York: Dutton.

Rash, Andy. (2004). *Agent A to Agent Z*. New York: Levine.

Raskin, Ellen. (1978). *The Westing Game*. New York: Penguin.

Rathman, Peggy. (1994). *Goodnight, Gorilla*. New York: Putnam.

_____. (1995). *Officer Buckle and Gloria*. New York: Penguin.

Raven, Margot Theis. (2006). *Night Boat to Freedom*. Illustrated by E. B. Lewis. New York: Farrar, Straus & Giroux.

Ravishankar, Anushka, & Christiane Pieper. (2007). *Elephants Never Forget!* Boston: Houghton Mifflin.

Rawlings, Marjorie. (2002). *The Yearling*. New York: Simon & Schuster.

Ray, Deborah Kogan. (2004). *The Flower Hunter: William Bartram, America's First Naturalist*. New York: Farrar, Straus & Giroux.

_____. (2007). *Down the Colorado: John Wesley Powell, the One-Armed Explorer*. New York: Farrar, Straus & Giroux.

Ray, Mary Lyn. (2001). *Mud*. Illustrated by Lauren Stringer. San Diego, CA: Harcourt.

Recorvits, Helen. (2002). *Where Heroes Hide*. New York: Farrar, Straus & Giroux.

_____. (2003). *My Name Is Yoon*. Illustrated by Gabi Swiatkowska. New York: Farrar, Straus & Giroux.

Reef, Catherine. (2001). *Sigmund Freud: Pioneer of the Mind*. New York: Clarion.

Reeve, Philip. (2001). *Mortal Engines*. New York: HarperCollins.

_____. (2003). *Predator's Gold*. New York: HarperCollins.

_____. (2007). *A Darkling Plain*. New York: Eos.

_____. (2007). *Starcross*. London: Bloomsbury.

Reibstein, Mark.(2008). *Wabi Sabi*. Illustrated by Ed Young. New York: Little, Brown.

Reich, Susanna. (1999). *Clara Schumann: Piano Virtuoso*. New York: Clarion.

Reiser, Lynn. (1993). *Margaret and Margarita*. New York: HarperCollins.

_____. (2003). *Ten Puppies*. New York: HarperCollins.

_____. (2006). *Hardworking Puppies*. San Diego, CA: Harcourt.

_____. (2007). *My Way/A mi manera: A Margaret and Margarita Story*. New York: Greenwillow.

Rennison, Louise. (1988). *Angus, Thongs and Full-Frontal Snogging: Confessions of Georgia Nicholson*. New York: HarperCollins.

Rex, Adam. (2007). *The True Meaning of Smekday*. New York: Hyperion.

Rey, H. A. (1957). *Curious George Gets a Medal*. Boston: Houghton Mifflin.

Reynolds, Peter. (2003). *The Dot*. Cambridge, MA: Candlewick.

_____. (2004). *Ish*. Cambridge, MA: Candlewick.

Richardson, E. E. (2007). *The Intruders*. New York: Random House.

Ride, Sally, & Tam O'Shaughnessy. (2003). *Exploring Our Solar System*. New York: Crown.

Ries, Lori. (2007). *Fix It, Sam*. Illustrated by Sue Ramá. Watertown, MA: Charlesbridge.

Rinaldi, Ann. (1999). *My Heart Is on the Ground: The Diary of Nannie Little Rose, a Sioux Girl, Carlisle Indian School, PA 1880*. New York: Scholastic.

Riordan, Rick. (2007). *The Titan's Curse*. New York: Hyperion.

_____. (2008). *The Battle of the Labyrinth*. New York: Hyperion.

Roalf, Peggy. (1993). *Children*. New York: Hyperion.

_____. (1993). *Flowers*. New York: Hyperion.

Robb, Don. (2007). *Ox, House, Stick: The History of Our Alphabet*. Illustrated by Anne Smith. Watertown, MA: Charlesbridge.

Robberecht, Thierry. (2007). *Sam Tells Stories*. Illustrated by Philippe Goossens. New York: Clarion.

Robbins, Ken. (1991). *Bridges*. New York: Dial.

_____. (2004). *Seeds*. New York: Simon & Schuster.

_____. (2007). *Pumpkins*. New York: Square Fish.

Roberts, Willo Davis. (1975). *The View from the Cherry Tree*. New York: Atheneum.

_____. (1989). *What Could Go Wrong?* New York: Atheneum.

Robinson, Sharon. (2004). *Promises to Keep: How Jackie Robinson Changed America*. New York: Scholastic.

Rocco, John. (2007). *Wolf! Wolf!* New York: Hyperion.

Rockhill, Dennis. (2007). *Polar Slumber*. New York: Raven Tree.

Rockwell, Anne. (2000). *Only Passing Through: The Story of Sojourner Truth*. Illustrated by Gregory Christie. New York: Knopf.

Rockwell, Anne. (2001). *The Boy Who Wouldn't Obey: A Mayan Legend*. New York: Greenwillow.

Rockwood, Joyce. (2003). *To Spoil the Sun*. New York: Holt.

Rodanas, Kristina. (1991). *Dragonfly's Tale*. New York: Clarion.

———. (1994). *Dance of the Sacred Circle: A Native American Tale*. Boston: Little, Brown.

Rodda, Emily. (2001). *Rowan of Rin*. New York: Greenwillow.

Rodowsky, Colby. (1994). *Hannah in Between*. New York: Farrar, Straus & Giroux.

———. (1995). *Sydney, Invincible*. New York: Farrar, Straus & Giroux.

———. (1999). *Not My Dog*. Illustrated by Thomas Yezerski. New York: Farrar, Straus & Giroux.

Rogers, Gregory. (2007). *Midsummer Knight*. New Milford, Conn.: Roaring Brook Press.

Rohmann, Eric. (2002). *My Friend Rabbit*. Brookfield, CT: Roaring Brook Press.

Root, Phyllis. (2002). *Big Momma Makes the World*. Illustrated by Helen Oxenbury. Cambridge, MA: Candlewick.

———. (2004). *If You Want to See a Caribou*. Illustrated by Jim Meyer. Boston: Houghton Mifflin.

———. (2007). *Aunt Nancy and the Bothersome Visitors*. Illustrated by David Parkins. Cambridge, MA: Candlewick.

Rose, Deborah Lee. (2000). *Into the A, B, Sea: An Ocean Alphabet*. Illustrated by Steve Jenkins. New York: Scholastic.

Rosen, Michael. (1989). *We're Going on a Bear Hunt*. New York: McElderry.

———. (1991). *How the Animals Got Their Colors: Animal Myths from around the World*. Illustrated by John Clementson. San Diego, CA: Harcourt.

Rosenberg, Liz. (2001). *Roots and Flowers: Poets and Poems on Family*. New York: Holt.

———. (2002). *17: A Novel in Prose Poems*. Chicago: Cricket.

Rosenberg, Liz, & Deena November. (2005). *I Just Hope It's Lethal: Poems of Sadness, Madness, and Joy*. Boston: Houghton Mifflin.

Rosenberry, Vera. (2004). *Vera Rides a Bike*. New York: Holt.

Rosenthal, Amy Krouse. (2006). *One of Those Days*. Illustrated by Rebecca Doughty. New York: Putnam.

Rosoff, Meg. (2004). *How I Live Now*. New York: Random House.

Ross, Gayle. (1995). *How Turtle's Back Was Cracked: A Traditional Cherokee Tale*. Illustrated by Murv Jacob. New York: Dial.

Ross, Michael Elsohn. (2003). *Salvador Dali and the Surrealists: Their Lives and Ideas*. Chicago: Chicago Review Press.

Rostkowski, Margaret. (1986). *After the Dancing Days*. New York: Harper & Row.

Roth, Susan. (2004). *Hard Hat Area*. New York: Bloomsbury.

Rotner, Shelley. (2006). *Senses at the Seashore*. Minneapolis: Millbrook.

Rowling, J. K. (1998). *Harry Potter and the Sorcerer's Stone*. Illustrated by Mary Grandpré. New York: Scholastic.

———. (1999). *Harry Potter and the Chamber of Secrets*. Illustrated by Mary Grandpré. New York: Scholastic.

———. (1999). *Harry Potter and the Prisoner of Azkaban*. Illustrated by Mary Grandpré. New York: Scholastic.

———. (2000). *Harry Potter and the Goblet of Fire*. Illustrated by Mary Grandpré. New York: Scholastic.

———. (2003). *Harry Potter and the Order of the Phoenix*. Illustrated by Mary Grandpré. New York: Scholastic.

Rubenstein, Gillian. (1993). *Galax-Arena: A Novel*. New York: Simon & Schuster.

———. (2001). *Under the Cat's Eye: A Tale of Morph and Mystery*. New York: Simon & Schuster.

Ruby, Lois. (1994). *Steal Away Home*. New York: Macmillan.

———. (2000). *Soon to Be Free*. New York: Simon & Schuster.

Ruffin, Frances E. (2007). *Medical Detective Dogs*. Illustrated with photographs. New York: Bearport.

———. (2007). *Military Dogs*. Illustrated with photographs. New York: Bearport.

Rumford, James. (2004). *Sequoyah: The Cherokee Man Who Gave His People Writing*. Boston: Houghton Mifflin.

———. (2007). *Beowulf, a Hero's Tale Retold*. Boston: Houghton Mifflin.

Running Wolf, Michael B., & Patricia Clark Smith. (2000). *On the Trail of Elder Brother: Glous'gap Stories of the Micmac Indians*. New York: Presea.

Runyon, Brent. (2007). *Maybe*. New York: Random House.

Rupert, Janet. (2005). *The African Mask*. New York: Backinprint.com.

Russo, Marisabina. (2002). *House of Sports*. New York: Greenwillow.

Russon, Penni. (2007). *Breathe*. New York: Greenwillow.

Ryan, Pam Muñoz. (1999). *Amelia and Eleanor Go for a Ride*. Illustrated by Brian Selznick. New York: Scholastic.

———. (2002). *When Marian Sang: The True Recital of Marian Anderson: The Voice of a Century*. Illustrated by Brian Selznick. New York: Scholastic.

———. (2004). *Becoming Naomi Leon*. New York: Scholastic.

Ryden, Hope. (1988). *Wild Animals of Africa ABC*. New York: Dutton.

Rylant, Cynthia. (1992). *Missing May*. New York: Orchard.

———. (1996). *Henry and Mudge*. Illustrated by Sucie Stevenson. New York: Simon & Schuster.

———. (2001). *Scarecrow*. Illustrated by Lauren Stringer. San Diego, CA: Harcourt.

———. (2007). *Snow*. Illustrated by Lauren Stringer. New York: Harcourt.

Sabuda, Robert, & Matthew Reinhart. (2007). *Encyclopedia Prehistorica: Mega Beasts*. Cambridge, MA: Candlewick.

Sabuda, Robert. (1992). *Saint Valentine*. New York: Simon & Schuster.

———. (1995). *Arthur and the Sword*. New York: Atheneum.

———. (1997). *King Tutankhamen's Gift*. New York: Simon & Schuster.

_____. (2000). *The Wonderful Wizard of Oz*. New York: Simon & Schuster.

_____. (2003). *Alice's Adventures in Wonderland*. New York: Simon & Schuster.

_____. (2005). *Winter's Tale*. New York: Simon & Schuster.

_____. (2007). *The Chronicles of Narnia*. New York: HarperCollins.

Sachar, Louis. (1987). *There's a Boy in the Girls' Bathroom*. New York: Knopf.

_____. (1998). *Holes*. New York: Farrar, Straus & Giroux.

_____. (2000). *Marvin Redpost #7: Super Fast, Out of Control!* Illustrated by Amy Wummer. New York: Random House.

_____. (2007). *Small Steps*. New York: Random House.

Said, S. F. (2005). *Varjak Paw*. Illustrated by Dave McKean. New York: Random House.

Saint-Exupery, Antoine de. (1943). *The Little Prince*. San Diego, CA: Harcourt.

Sakai, Komako. (2006). *Emily's Balloon*. San Francisco: Chronicle.

Salisbury, Graham. (2001). *Lord of the Deep*. New York: Delacorte.

Salley, Coleen. (2004). *Why Epossumondas Has No Hair on His Tail*. Illustrated by Janet Stevens. San Diego, CA: Harcourt.

_____. (2006). *Epossumondas Saves the Day*. Illustrated by Janet Stevens. Orlando, FL: Harcourt.

Salmansohn, Karen. (2007). *Girl Wonders*. Berkeley, CA: Ten Speed Press.

San Jose, Christine. (1994). *Cinderella*. Illustrated by Debrah Santini. Honesdale, PA: Caroline House.

San Souci, Robert D. (1989). *The Talking Eggs*. Illustrated by Jerry Pinkney. New York: Dial.

_____. (1991). *Larger Than Life: The Adventures of American Legendary Heroes*. Illustrated by Andrew Glass. New York: Doubleday.

_____. (1992). *Sukey and the Mermaid*. Illustrated by J. Brian Pinkney. New York: Four Winds.

_____. (1993). *Young Guinevere*. Illustrated by Jamichael Henterly. New York: Doubleday.

_____. (1994). *Sootface: An Ojibwa Cinderella Story*. Illustrated by Daniel San Souci. New York: Delacorte.

_____. (1995). *The Faithful Friend*. Illustrated by J. Brian Pinkney. New York: Simon & Schuster.

_____. (1998). *Cendrillon: A Caribbean Cinderella*. Illustrated by Brian Pinkney. New York: Simon & Schuster.

_____. (2000). *Cinderella Skeleton*. Illustrated by David Catrow. San Diego, CA: Harcourt.

_____. (2000) *Six Foolish Fishermen*. Illustrated by Doug Kennedy. New York: Hyperion.

San Souci, Robert D. & Jane Yolen. (1993). *Cut from the Same Cloth: American Women of Myth, Legend, and Tall Tale*. Illustrated by J. Brian Pinkney. New York: Philomel.

Sanderson, Brandon. (2007). *Alcatraz versus the Evil Librarians*. New York: Scholastic.

_____. (2008). *Alcatraz versus the Scrivener's Bones*. New York: Scholastic.

Sandin, Joan. (2007). *At Home in a New Land*. New York: HarperCollins.

Sandler, Michael. (2007). *Race Horses*. New York: Bearport.

Sauerwein, Leigh. (2003). *Song for Eloise*. Ashville, NC: Front Street.

Savadier, Elivia. (2007). *Time to Get Dressed!* New York: DK Publishing.

Say, Allen. (1993). *Grandfather's Journey*. Boston: Houghton Mifflin.

_____. (1999). *Tea with Milk*. Boston: Houghton Mifflin.

_____. (2002). *Home of the Brave*. Boston: Walter Lorraine Books.

_____. (2004). *Music for Alice*. Boston: Houghton Mifflin.

Sayre, April Pulley. (2008). *Trout Are Made of Trees*. Illustrated by Kate Endle. Watertown, MA: Charlesbridge.

Schaefer, Lola M. (2007). *Frankie Stein*. Illustrated by Kevan Atteberry. Tarrytown, NY: Cavendish.

Schertle, Alice. (2007). *Very Hairy Bear*. Illustrated by Matt Phelan. San Diego, CA: Harcourt.

Schlitz, Laura Amy. (2007). *The Bearskinner: A Tale of the Brothers Grimm*. Cambridge, MA: Candlewick.

_____. (2007). *Good Masters! Sweet Ladies! Voices from a Medieval Village*. Illustrated by Robert Byrd. Cambridge, MA: Candlewick.

Schmidt, Gary. (2001). *Mara's Stories: Glimmers in the Darkness*. New York: Holt.

_____. (2004). *Lizzie Bright and the Buckminster Boy*. New York: Clarion.

_____. (2007). *The Wednesday Wars*. New York: Clarion.

_____. (2008). *Trouble*. New York: Clarion.

Schneider, Christine. (2004). *I'm Bored!* Illustrated by Herve Pinel. New York: Clarion.

Schnur, Steven. (2001). *Summer: An Alphabet Acrostic*. Illustrated by Leslie Evans. Boston: Houghton Mifflin.

_____. (2002). *Winter: An Alphabet Acrostic*. Illustrated by Leslie Evans. Boston: Houghton Mifflin.

Schories, Pat. (2004). *Breakfast for Jack*. Asheville, NC: Front Street.

Schulman, Janet. (2008). *Pale Male: Citizen Hawk of New York City*. Illustrated by Meilo So. New York: Random House.

Schwartz, Amy. (2003). *What James Likes Best*. New York: Simon & Schuster.

Schwartz, David M. (1998). *G is for Googol: A Math Alphabet Book*. Illustrated by Marissa Moss. New York: Ten Speed Press.

_____. (2001). *Q is for Quark: A Science Alphabet Book*. Illustrated by Kim Doner. New York: Ten Speed Press.

Scieszka, Jon. (1989). *The True Story of the Three Little Pigs*. Illustrated by Lane Smith. New York: Viking.

Scieszka, Jon. (1991). *The Frog Prince Continued*. Illustrated by Steve Johnson. New York: Viking.

———. (1992). *The Stinky Cheese Man and Other Fairly Stupid Tales*. Illustrated by Lane Smith. New York: Viking.

———. (1994). *The Book That Jack Wrote*. New York: Viking.

———. (1995). *Math Curse*. Illustrated by Lane Smith. New York: Viking.

———. (1999). *It's All Greek to Me*. New York: Viking.

———. (2004). *Science Verse*. Illustrated by Lane Smith. New York: Viking.

———. (2005). *Seen Art?* New York: Viking.

———. (2008). *Knucklehead: Tall Tales & Mostly True Stories about Growing Up Scieszka*. New York: Viking.

Searl, Duncan. (2007). *Wolves*. Illustrated with photographs. New York: Bearport.

Sedgwick, Marcus. (2001). *Floodland*. New York: Delacorte.

Seeger, Karen Vaccaro. (2007). *First the Egg*. New Milford, CT: Roaring Brook Press.

Seeger, Laura Vaccaro. (2003). *The Hidden Alphabet*. New Milford, CT: Roaring Brook Press.

———. (2006). *Black? White! Day? Night!—A Book of Opposites*. New Milford, CT: Roaring Brook Press.

———. (2007). *Dog and Bear: Two Friends, Three Stories*. New Milford, CN: Roaring Brook Press.

———. (2007). *First the Egg*. New Milford, CT: Roaring Brook Press.

Seidler, Tor. (2002). *Brothers Below Zero*. New York: L. Geringer.

———. (2008). *Gully's Travels*. Illustrated by Brock Cole. New York: Scholastic.

Selden, George. (1987). *Old Meadow*. Illustrated by Garth Williams. New York: Farrar, Strauss & Giroux.

———. (1989). *Tucker's Countryside*. Illustrated by Garth Williams. New York: Random House.

———. (1997). *Cricket in Times Square*. Illustrated by Garth Williams. New York: Dell.

Sellier, Marie. (2007). *Legend of the Chinese Dragon*. Illustrated by Catherine Louis and Wang Fei. New York: North-South Press.

Selznick, Brain. (2007). *The Invention of Hugo Cabret*. New York: Scholastic.

Sendak, Maurice. (1963). *Where the Wild Things Are*. New York: HarperCollins.

———. (1989). *Outside Over There*. New York: HarperCollins.

———. (2006). *Mommy?* Paper engineering by Matthew Reinhart; Scenario by Arthur Yorinks. New York: HarperCollins.

Service, Pamela. (2007). *Tomorrow's Magic*. New York: Random House.

Seuling, Barbara. (2007). *Robert and the Happy Endings*. Illustrated by Paul Brewer. Peterborough, NH: Cricket.

Seuss, Dr. (1957). *The Cat in the Hat*. New York: Random House.

———. (1971). *The Lorax*. New York: Random House.

Severance, John. (1999). *Einstein: Visionary Scientist*. New York: Clarion.

Sewall, Marcia. (1990). *People of the Breaking Day*. New York: Atheneum.

Sfar, Joann. (2007). *Professor's Daughter*. London: Macmillan.

Shah, Idries. (1998). *Neem the Half-Boy*. Illustrated by Natasha Delmar. Cambridge, MA: Hoopoe Books.

———. (2000). *The Boy without a Name*. Illustrated by Mona Karon. Boston: Hoopoe.

———. (2000). *The Clever Boy and the Terrible, Dangerous Animal*. Illustrated by Rose Mary Santiago. Boston: Hoopoe.

———. (2003). *The Old Woman and the Eagle*. Illustrated by Natasha Delmar. Boston: Hoopoe.

Shange, Ntozake. (2004). *Ellington Was Not a Street*. New York: Simon & Schuster.

Shannon, David. (1998). *No, David!* New York: Scholastic.

———. (1999). *David Goes to School*. New York: Scholastic.

———. (2002). *David Gets in Trouble*. New York: Scholastic.

Shannon, George. (1996). *Tomorrow's Alphabet*. Illustrated by Donald Crews. New York: Greenwillow.

———. (2001). *More True Lies: 18 Tales for You to Judge*. Illustrated by John O'Brien. New York: Greenwillow.

———. (2007). *Rabbit's Gift*. Illustrated by Laura Dronzek. San Diego, CA: Harcourt.

Sharmat, Marjorie. (1972). *Nate the Great*. Illustrated by Marc Simont. New York: Coward, McCann & Geoghegan.

Shea, Pegi Deitz Shea. (1996). *The Whispering Cloth*. Illustrated by Anita Riggio and You Yang. Honesdale, PA: Boyds Mills Press.

Shearer, Alex. (2008). *Canned*. New York: Scholastic.

Sheen, Dong Il, & Jae-So Lin. (2002). *Yellow Umbrella*. La Jolla, CA: Kane Miller.

Shepard, Aaron. (2006). *One Eye! Two Eyes! Three Eyes! A Very Grimm Fairy Tale*. Illustrated by Gary Clement. New York: Atheneum.

Shepard, Sara. (2007). *Pretty Little Liars*. New York: HarperCollins.

Sherlock, Patti. (2004). *Letters from Wolfie*. New York: Viking.

Sheth, Kashmera. (2004). *Blue Jasmine*. New York: Hyperion.

Shulevitz, Uri. (1988). *Dawn*. New York: Farrar, Straus & Giroux.

———. (1998). *Snow*. New York: Farrar, Straus & Giroux.

———. (2006). *So Sleepy Story*. New York: Farrar, Straus & Giroux.

Shumacher, Julie. (2004). *Grass Angel*. New York: Delacorte.

———. (2008). *Blackbox*. New York: Delacorte.

Shusterman, Neal. (2003). *Full Tilt*. New York: Simon & Schuster.

———. (2007). *Everlost*. New York: Simon & Schuster.

———. (2007). *Unwind*. New York: Simon & Schuster.

Shyer, Marlene Fanta. (1978). *Welcome Home, Jellybean*. New York: Scribner.

Sidman, Joyce. (2003). *The World According to Dog: Poems and Teen Voices*. Boston: Houghton Mifflin.

———. (2006). *Butterfly Eyes and Other Secrets of the Meadow: Poems*. Illustrated by Beth Krommes. Boston: Houghton Mifflin.

_____. (2006) *Meow Ruff*. Illustrated by Michelle Berg. Boston: Houghton Mifflin.

_____. (2007). *This Is Just to Say: Poems of Apology and Forgiveness*. Illustrated by Pamela Zagarenski. Boston: Houghton Mifflin.

Sidney, Margaret. (1963). *The Five Little Peppers and How They Grew*. New York: Grosset & Dunlap.

Siegal, Aranka. (2008). *Memories of Babi*. New York: Farrar, Straus & Giroux.

Siegel, Siena Cherson. (2006). *To Dance: A Ballerina's Graphic Novel*. New York: Simon & Schuster.

Siegelson, Kim. (2004). *Trembling Earth*. New York.

Sierra, Judy. (1996). *Nursery Tales around the World*. Illustrated by Stefano Vitale. New York: Clarion.

_____. (1996). *Wiley and the Hairy Man*. Illustrated by J. Brian Pinkney. New York: Lodestar.

_____. (2000). *The Beautiful Butterfly: A Folktale from Spain*. Illustrated by Victoria Chess. New York: Clarion.

_____. (2006). *Thelonius Monster's Sky-High Fly Pie*. Illustrated by Edward Koren. New York: Knopf.

Silverman, Erica. (1999). *Raisel's Riddle*. Illustrated by Susan Gaber. New York: Farrar, Straus & Giroux.

_____. (2007). *Cowgirl Kate and Cocoa: School Days*. Illustrated by Betsy Lewin. San Diego, CA: Harcourt.

Silverstein, Shel. (1964). *The Giving Tree*. New York: Harper & Row.

_____. (1974). *Where the Sidewalk Ends: Poems and Drawings*. New York: Harper & Row.

Silvey, Anita. (2008). *I'll Pass for Your Comrade: Women Soldiers in the Civil War*. Boston: Houghton Mifflin Harcourt.

Siméon, Jean-Pierre. (2007). *This is a Poem that Heals Fish*. Illustrated by Olivier Tallec. Brooklyn: Enchanted Lion.

Simon, Seymour. (1987/2000). *Destination: Mars*. New York: HarperCollins.

_____. (1992/2007). *Our Solar System*. New York: HarperCollins.

_____. (1993). *Wolves*. New York: HarperCollins.

_____. (2006). *The Brain: Our Nervous System*. New York: HarperCollins.

_____. (2006). *The Heart: Our Circulatory System*. New York: HarperCollins.

_____. (2008). *The Human Body*. New York: HarperCollins.

Singer, Isaac Bashevis. (1966). *Zlateh the Goat and Other Stories*. Illustrated by Maurice Sendak. New York: Harper & Row.

_____. (1968). *When Shlemiel Went to Warsaw and Other Stories*. Illustrated by Margot Zemach. New York: Farrar, Straus & Giroux.

_____. (1976). *Naftali the Storyteller and His Horse, Sus*. Illustrated by Margot Zemach. New York: Farrar, Straus & Giroux.

Singer, Marilyn. (1998). *Stay True: Short Stories for Strong Girls*. New York: Scholastic.

_____. (2007). *Venom*. Plain City, OH: Darby Creek.

Sís, Peter. (1996). *Starry Messenger: Galileo Galilei*. New York: Farrar, Straus & Giroux.

_____. (1998). *Tibet through the Red Box*. New York: Farrar, Straus & Giroux.

_____. (2000). *Dinosaur!* New York: Greenwillow.

_____. (2001). *The Three Golden Keys*. New York: HarperCollins.

_____. (2003). *The Tree of Life: A Book Depicting the Life of Charles Darwin: Naturalist, Geologist and Thinker*. New York: Farrar, Straus & Giroux.

_____. (2006). *Play, Mozart, Play*. New York: HarperCollins.

_____. (2007). *The Train of States*. New York: HarperCollins.

_____. (2007). *The Wall: Growing Up Behind the Iron Curtain*. New York: Farrar, Straus & Giroux.

Siy, Alexandria and Dennis Kunkel. (2005). *Mosquito Bite*. Watertown, MA: Charlesbridge.

Skurzynski, Gloria. (1983). *The Tempering*. New York: Clarion.

Slade, Arthur. (2003). *Dust*. New York: Random House.

Slaymaker, Melissa Eskridge. (2004). *Bottle Houses: The Creative World of Grandma Prisbrey*. Illustrated by Julie Paschkis. New York: Holt.

Sleator, William. (1985). *Singularity*. New York: Dutton.

_____. (2007). *Hell Phone*. New York: Abrams.

Slepian, Jan. (2001). *The Alfred Summer*. New York: Philomel.

Slier, Debby. (1995). *The Real Mother Goose: Book of American Rhymes*. New York: Scholastic.

Slobodkina, Esphyr. (1985). *Caps for Sale: A Tale of a Peddler, Some Monkeys and Their Monkey Business*. New York: HarperCollins.

Smee, Nicola. (2006). *Clip-Clop*. London: Boxer.

Smith, Alexander McCall. (2007). *Max & Maddy and the Bursting Balloons Mystery*. Illustrated by Macky Pamintuan. New York: Knopf.

_____. (2007). *Max & Maddy and the Chocolate Money Mystery*. Illustrated by Macky Pamintuan. New York: Knopf.

Smith, Charles R., Jr. (2007). *Twelve Rounds to Glory: The Story of Muhammad Ali*. Illustrated by Bryan Collier. Cambridge, MA: Candlewick.

Smith, Cynthia Leitich. (2002). *Indian Shoes*. Illustrated by Jim Madsen. New York: HarperCollins.

_____. (2007). *Tantalize*. Cambridge, MA: Candlewick.

Smith, Hope Anita. (2008). *Keeping the Night Watch*. Illustrated by E. B. Lewis. New York: Holt.

Smith, James. (2008). *Night Running: How James Escaped with the Help of His Faithful Dog*. New York: Random House.

Smith, Jeff. (2007). *Bone #5: Rock Jaw*. New York: Graphix.

_____. (2007). *Bone #6: Old Man's Cave*. New York: Graphix.

Smith, Roland. (2007). *Elephant Run*. New York: Hyperion.

_____. (2007). *Peak*. New York: Harcourt.

Sneve, Virginia Driving Hawk. (2007). *Lana's Lakota Moons*. Lincoln, NE: Bison.

Snicket, Lemony. (1999). *Series of Unfortunate Events*. New York: HarperCollins.

So, Meilo. (2004). *Gobble, Gobble, Slip, Slop: A Tale of a Very Greedy Cat*. New York: Knopf.

Sobol, Donald J. (2007). *Encyclopedia Brown Cracks the Case*. New York: Penguin.

Sobol, Donald, & Greg Andrews. (1983). *Encyclopedia Brown Takes the Cake: a Cook and case book*. Illustrated by Ib Ohlsson. New York: Simon & Schuster.

Sommer, Carl. (2007). *Dare To Dream!* Illustrated by Jorge Martinez, Greg Budwine and Kennon James. Houston, TX: Advance.

———. (2007). *The Richest Poor Kid*. Illustrated by Jorge Martinez. Houston, TX: Advance.

———. (2007). *Spike the Rebel!* Illustrated by Enrique Vignolo. Houston, TX: Advance.

Sones, Sonya. (2001). *What My Mother Doesn't Know*. New York: Simon & Schuster.

———. (2004). *One of Those Hideous Books Where the Mother Dies*. New York: Simon & Schuster.

Sonnenblick, Jordan. (2007). *Zen and the Art of Faking It*. New York: Scholastic.

Soto, Gary. (1993). *Too Many Tamales*. Illustrated by Ed Martinez. New York: Putnam.

———. (1997). *Buried Onions*. San Diego, CA: Harcourt Brace.

———. (2007). *Mercy on these Teenage Chimps*. New York: Harcourt.

———. (2008). *Facts of Life*. Orlando, FL: Harcourt.

Souhami, Jessica. (1995). *The Leopard's Drum: An Ashanti Tale from West Africa*. Boston: Little, Brown.

———. (1999). *No Dinner! The Story of the Old Woman and the Pumpkin*. Tarrytown, NY: Cavendish.

———. (2006). *Sausages*. London: Frances Lincoln Children's Books.

Speare, Elizabeth George. (1958). *The Witch of Blackbird Pond*. Boston: Houghton Mifflin.

———. (1961). *The Bronze Bow*. Boston: Houghton Mifflin.

———. (1983). *The Sign of the Beaver*. Boston: Houghton Mifflin.

Speck, Katie. (2007). *Maybelle in the Soup*. Illustrated by Paul Ratz de Tagyos. New York: Holt.

Spiegelman, Art. (1996). *Maus: A Survivor's Tale, Volume I: My Father Bleeds History*. New York: Knopf.

Spier, Peter. (2007). *The Fox Who Went Out on a Chilly Night*. Pine Plains, NY: Live Oak Media.

Spinelli, Eileen. (2007). *Callie Cat, Ice Skater*. Illustrated by Anne Kennedy. Morton Grove, IL: Albert Whitman.

———. (2007). *Heat Wave*. Illustrated by Betsy Lewin. San Diego, CA: Harcourt.

———. (2007). *Summerhouse Time*. Illustrated by Joanne Lew-Vriethoff. New York: Knopf.

Spinelli, Jerry. (1996). *Crash*. New York: Knopf.

———. (1998). *Knots in My Yo-Yo String: The Autobiography of a Kid*. New York: Knopf.

———. (2002). *Star Girl*. New York: Knopf.

———. (2003). *Milkweed*. New York: Knopf.

———. (2007). *Eggs*. New York: Little, Brown.

Spinner, Stephanie. (2002). *Quiver*. New York: Knopf.

Springer, Nancy. (1998). *I Am Mordred: A Tale from Camelot*. New York: Philomel.

———. (2001). *I Am Morgan LeFay: A Tale from Camelot*. New York: Philomel.

———. (2001). *Rowan Hood: Outlaw Girl of Sherwood Forest*. New York: Philomel.

Spyri, Johanna. (1884). *Heidi*. New York: Platt & Peck.

St. George, Judith. (2000). *So You Want to Be President?* Illustrated by David Small. New York: Philomel.

———. (2004). *You're on Your Way, Teddy Roosevelt*. Illustrated by Matt Faulkner. New York: Philomel.

———. (2008). *Stand Tall, Abe Lincoln*. Illustrated by Matt Faulkner. New York: Philomel.

Stanley, Diane. (1990). *Fortune*. New York: Morrow.

———. (1996). *Leonardo da Vinci*. New York: Morrow.

———. (1997). *Rumpelstiltskin's Daughter*. New York: Scholastic.

———. (2000). *Michelangelo*. New York: HarperCollins.

———. (2002). *Joan of Arc*. New York: HarperCollins.

———. (2002). *Saladin: Noble Prince of Islam*. New York: HarperCollins.

Stanley, Diane, & Peter Vennema. (1992). *Bard of Avon: The Story of William Shakespeare*. New York: Morrow.

Stanley, Jerry. (1992). *Children of the Dust Bowl: The True Story of the School at Weedpatch Camp*. New York: Crown.

———. (1997). *Digger: The Tragic Fate of the California Indians from the Missions to the Gold Rush*. New York: Crown.

———. (2000). *Hurry Freedom: African Americans in Gold Rush California*. New York: Crown.

Staples, Suzanne Fisher. (1989). *Shabanu*. New York: Knopf.

———. (1993). *Haveli*. New York: Knopf.

Stead, Rebecca. (2007). *First Light*. New York: Random House.

Steffensmeier, Alexander. (2007). *Millie Waits for the Mail*. New York: Walker.

Steig, Jeanne. (1998). *A Handful of Beans: Six Fairy Tales*. Illustrated by William Steig. New York: HarperCollins.

———. (2001). *A Gift from Zeus: Sixteen Favorite Myths*. Illustrated by William Steig. New York: Joanna Cotler Books.

———. (2004). *Tales from Gizzard's Grill*. Illustrated by Sandy Turner. New York: Joanna Cotler Books.

———. (1969). *Sylvester and the Magic Pebble*. New York: Windmill.

———. (1986). *Brave Irene*. New York: Farrar, Straus & Giroux.

———. (1986). *Caleb and Kate*. New York: Farrar, Straus & Giroux.

———. (1993). *The Amazing Bone*. New York: Farrar, Straus & Giroux.

———. (1998). *Pete's a Pizza*. New York: HarperCollins.

———. (2003). *When Everybody Wore a Hat*. New York: Johanna Cotler Books.

Stein, David Ezra. (2007). *Leaves*. New York: Putnam.

Stein, Mathilde. (2007). *Mine!* Illustrated by Mies van Hout. Honesdale, PA: Lemniscaat.

Steptoe, John. (1969). *Stevie*. New York: Harper & Row.

Stevens, April. (2007). *Waking Up Wendell*. Illustrated by Tad Hills. New York: Random House.

Stevens, Janet. (1984). *The Tortoise and the Hare: An Aesop Fable*. New York: Holiday House.

_____. (1987). *The Town Mouse and the Country Mouse: An Aesop Fable*. New York: Holiday House.

_____. (1995). *Tops and Bottoms*. San Diego, CA: Harcourt.

_____. (1996). *Old Bag of Bones: A Coyote Tale*. New York: Holiday House.

Stevens, Susan Crummel. (2006). *Ten Gallon Bart*. Illustrated by Dorothy Donohue. Tarrytown, NY: Cavendish.

Stevenson, James. (1995). *The Bones in the Cliff*. New York: Greenwillow.

Stevenson, Robert Louis. (1885). *A Child's Garden of Verses*. New York: Philomel.

Stewart, Paul & Chris Riddell. (2007). *Hugo Pepper*. New York: David Fickling Books.

Stewart, Sarah. (2004). *The Friend*. Illustrated by David Small. New York: Farrar, Straus & Giroux.

Stewart, Trenton Lee. (2008). *The Mysterious Benedict Society and the Perilous Journey*. New York: Little, Brown.

Stine, R. L. (2007). *Goosebumps Graphix 3: Scary Summer*. Illustrated by Ted Naifeh, Dean Haspiel and Kyle Baker. New York: Graphix.

Stone, Tanya Lee. (2007). *A Bad Boy Can Be Good for a Girl*. New York: Random House.

_____. (2008). *Elizabeth Leads the Way: Elizabeth Cady Stanton and the Right to Vote*. Illustrated by Rebecca Gibbon. New York: Holt.

_____. (2008). *Sandy's Circus: A Story About Alexander Calder*. Illustrated by Boris Kulikov. New York: Viking.

Storace, Patricia. (2007). *Sugar Cane: A Caribbean Rapunzel*. Illustrated by Raúl Colón. New York: Hyperion.

Storrie, Paul D. (2007). *Beowulf*. Illustrated by Ron Randall. Minneapolis, MN: Lerner.

_____. (2007). *Yu the Great*. Illustrated by Sandy Carruthers. Minneapolis, MN: Lerner.

Stratton, Allan. (2004). *Chanda's Secrets*. Toronto: Annick.

_____. (2008). *Chanda's Wars*. New York: HarperCollins.

Stryer, Andrea Stenn. (2007). *Kami and the Yaks*. Illustrated by Bert Dodson. Palo Alto, CA: Bay Otter.

Sturges, Philemon. (2007). *How Do You Make A Baby Smile?* Illustrated by Bridget Strevens-Marzo. New York: HarperCollins.

Sullivan, George. (2007). *Helen Keller: Her Life in Pictures*. New York: Scholastic.

Sutcliff, Rosemary. (1992). *The Shining Company*. New York: Farrar, Straus & Giroux.

_____. (1993). *The Eagle of the Ninth*. New York: Farrar, Straus & Giroux.

_____. (1994). *The Lantern Bearers*. New York: Farrar, Straus & Giroux.

_____. (1994). *Warrior Scarlet*. New York: Farrar, Straus & Giroux.

_____. (2007). *Frontier Wolf*. Honesdale, PA: Front Street.

Sutherland, Zena. (1990). *The Orchard Book of Nursery Rhymes*. Illustrated by New York: Orchard.

Swallow, Pamela Curtis. (2005). *Groundhog Gets a Say*. Illustrated by Denise Brunkus. New York: Putman.

Swanson, Diane. (1994). *Safari beneath the Sea: The Wonder of the North Pacific Coast*. San Francisco: Sierra Club.

Swanson, Susan. (2008). *The House in the Night*. Illustrated by Beth Krommes. Boston: Houghton Mifflin.

Swinburne, Stephen. (2002). *The Woods Scientist*. Boston: Houghton Mifflin.

Swope, Sam. (2004). *Jack and the Seven Deadly Giants*. New York: Farrar, Straus & Giroux.

Taback, Simms. (1997). *There Was an Old Lady Who Swallowed a Fly*. New York: Viking.

_____. (1999). *Joseph Had a Little Overcoat*. New York: Viking.

Tafuri, Nancy. (2007). *The Busy Little Squirrel*. New York: Simon & Schuster.

Tallchief, Maria, & Rosemary Wells. (1999). *Tallchief: America's Prima Ballerina*.

Tamaki, Mariko. (2008). *Skim*. Toronto: Groundwood.

Tan, Shaun. (2007). *The Arrival*. New York: Levine.

_____. (2009). *Tales from Outer Suburbia*. New York: Scholastic.

Tankard, Jeremy. (2007). *Grumpy Bird*. New York: Scholastic.

Tarcov, Edith H. (1974). *Frog Prince*. Illustrated by James Marshall. New York: Scholastic.

Tarshis, Lauren. (2007). *Emma-Jean Lazarus Fell Out of a Tree*. New York: Dial.

Tashiro, Chisato. (2007). *Five Nice Mice*. Translated by Sayko Uchida and Kate Westerlund. New York: Minedition/Penguin.

Tashjian, Janet. (1999). *Multiple Choice*. New York: Holt.

Taylor, Ann, & Jane Taylor. (1804). *Original Poems for Infant Minds by Several Young Persons*. New York: Garland.

Taylor, G. P. (2004). *Shadowmancer*. New York: Putnam.

Taylor, Mildred. (1976). *Roll of Thunder, Hear My Cry*. New York: Dial.

_____. (1981). *Let the Circle Be Unbroken*. New York: Dial.

_____. (1985). *Song of the Trees*. New York: Dial.

_____. (1987). *The Friendship*. New York: Dial.

_____. (1990). *Mississippi Bridge*. New York: Dial.

_____. (1990). *The Road to Memphis*. New York: Dial.

_____. (1995). *The Well: David's Story*. New York: Dial.

_____. (2001). *The Land*. New York: Fogelman Books.

Tchana, Katrin H. (2002). *Sense Pass King: A Story from Cameroon*. New York: Holiday House.

_____. (2006). *Changing Woman and Her Sisters: Stories of Goddesses from around the World*. Illustrated by Trina Schart Hyman. New York: Holiday House.

Tekavec, Heather. (2006). *What's That AWFUL Smell?* Illustrated by Margaret Spengler. New York: Penguin.

Temple, Frances. (1994). *The Ramsay Scallop*. New York: Orchard.

_____. (1996). *The Beduin's Gazelle*. New York: HarperCollins.

Terban, Marvin. (1988). *Guppies in Tuxedos: Funny Eponyms*. Illustrated by Giulio Maestro. Boston: Houghton Mifflin.

Thayer, Ernest L. (2007). *Casey at the Bat*. Illustrated by Joe Morse. Tonawanda, NY: Kids Can Press.

Thesman, Jean. (1990). *Rachel Chance*. Boston: Houghton Mifflin.

_____. (1999). *The Rain Catchers*. Boston: Houghton Mifflin.

_____. (2000). *Calling the Swan*. New York: Viking.

_____. (2004). *Singer*. New York: Viking.

Thimmesh, Catherine. (2004). *Madam President: The Extraordinary, True (and Evolving). Story of Women in Politics*. Illustrated by Douglas B. Jones. Boston: Houghton Mifflin.

_____. (2006). *Team Moon: How 400,000 People Landed Apollo 11 on the Moon*. Boston: Houghton Mifflin.

Thomas, Jan. (2007). *What Will Fat Cat Sit On?* San Diego, CA: Harcourt.

Thomas, Jane Resh. (1998). *Behind the Mask: The Life of Queen Elizabeth*. New York: Clarion.

Thomas, Joyce Carol. (1993). *Brown Honey in Broomwheat Tea*. Illustrated by Floyd Cooper. New York: HarperCollins.

_____. (1995). *Gingerbread Days*. New York: HarperCollins.

_____. (1998) *I Have Heard of a Land*. Illustrated by Floyd Cooper. New York: HarperCollins.

_____. (2000). *Hush Songs: African American Lullabies*. New York: Hyperion.

_____. (2008). *The Blacker the Berry*. Illustrated by Floyd Cooper. New York: HarperCollins.

Thomas, Pamela. (2000). *Brooklyn Pops Up*. New York: Simon & Schuster.

Thompson, Colin. (2007). *The Short and Incredibly Happy Life of Riley*. Illustrated by Amy Lissiat. La Jolla, CA: Kane Miller.

Thompson, Kate. (2007). *New Policeman*. New York: Greenwillow.

_____. (2007). *Origins*. New York: Bloomsbury.

_____. (2008). *The Last of the High Kings*. New York: Greenwillow.

Thong, Roseanne. (2007). *Tummy Girl*. Illustrated by Sam Williams. New York: Holt.

Tillage, Leon Walter. (1997). *Leon's Story*. Illustrated by Susan L. Roth. New York: Farrar, Straus & Giroux.

Tinkham, Kelly A. (2007). *Hair for Mama*. Illustrated by Amy June Bates. New York: Dial.

Titus, Eve. (1956). *Anatole*. New York: Whittlesey House.

_____. (1957). *Anatole and the Cat*. New York: Whittlesey House.

Tjong-Khing, Thé. (2007). *Where is the Cake?* New York: Abram's.

Tolan, Stephanie. (2002). *Surviving the Applewhites*. New York: HarperCollins.

Tolkien, J.R.R. (1937). *The Hobbit*. New York: Random House.

_____. (1954–1955). *The Lord of the Rings* **trilogy**. London: Allen & Unwin.

Tomlinson, Heather. (2008). *Aurelie: A Faerie Tale*. New York: Holt.

Townley, Roderick. (2001). *The Great Good Thing*. New York: Atheneum.

_____. (2002). *Into the Labyrinth*. New York: Atheneum.

Travers, P.L. (1952). *Mary Poppins*. New York: Harcourt, Brace.

Trivizas, Eugene. (1993). *Three Little Wolves and the Big Bad Pig*. Illustrated by Helen Oxenbury. New York: McElderry.

Troughton, Joanna. (1976). *How the Birds Changed Their Feathers: A South American Indian Folktale*. London: Blackie.

_____. (1986). *How Rabbit Stole the Fire: A North American Indian Folktale*. London: Blackie.

_____. (1989). *How Stories Came into the World: A Folk Tale from West Africa*. London: Blackie.

Trueman, Terry. (2000). *Stuck in Neutral*. New York: HarperCollins.

_____. (2003). *Inside Out*. New York: HarperCollins.

_____. (2004). *Cruise Control*. New York: HarperCollins.

Tucker, Ann. (1987). *Come Look with Me: Discovering Photographs with Children*. Charlottesville, VA: Thomasson-Grant.

Turner, Ann. (1987). *Nettie's Trip South*. Illustrated by Ronald Himler. Old Tappan, NJ: Macmillan.

Turner, Pamela. (2008). *Life on Earth—and Beyond: An Astrobiologist's Quest*. Watertown, MA: Charlesbridge.

Uchida, Yoshiko. (1978). *Journey Home*. New York: Atheneum.

_____. (1991). *The Invisible Thread*. Englewood Cliffs, NJ: Messner.

Uehashi, Nahoko. (2008). *Moeibito: Guardian of the Spirit*. Translated by Cathy Hirano. New York: Scholastic.

Ungar, Richard. (2007). *Even Higher*. Toronto: Tundra.

Ungerer, Tomi. (2009). *The Moon Man*. London, UK: Phaidon.

Updale, Eleanor. (2003). *Montmorency: Thief, Liar, Gentleman?* New York: Orchard.

Ursu, Anne. (2007). *Siren Song: The Cronus Chronicles, Book Two*. New York: Atheneum.

Vail, Rachel. (1998). *Over the Moon*. Illustrated by Scott Nash. New York: Orchard.

_____. (2007). *You, Maybe: The Profound Asymmetry of Love in High School*. New York: HarperCollins.

Van Allsburg, Chris. (1979). *The Garden of Abdul Gasazi*. Boston: Houghton Mifflin.

_____. (1981). *Jumanji*. Boston: Houghton Mifflin.

_____. (1983). *The Wreck of the Zephyr*. Boston: Houghton Mifflin.

_____. (1984). *The Mysteries of Harris Burdick*. Boston: Houghton Mifflin.

_____. (1985). *The Polar Express*. Boston: Houghton Mifflin.

_____. (1986). *The Stranger*. Boston: Houghton Mifflin.

_____. (1991). *The Wretched Stone*. Boston: Houghton Mifflin.

_____. (1994). *The Garden of Abdul Gasazi*. Boston: Houghton Mifflin.

_____. (1995). *Bad Day at Riverbend*. Boston: Houghton Mifflin.

_____. (2002). *Zathura*. Boston: Houghton Mifflin.

Van Draanen, Wendelin. (1998). *Sammy Keyes and the Skeleton Man*. New York: Knopf.

_____. (2001). *Sammy Keyes and the Hollywood Mummy*. New York: Knopf.

_____. (2004). *Sammy Keyes and the Psycho Kitty Queen*. Illustrated by Dan Yaccarino. New York: Knopf.

Van Fleet, Matthew. (2007). *Dog*. Illustrated by Brian Stanton. New York: Simon & Schuster.

Van Laan, Nancy. (1995). *In a Circle Long Ago: A Treasury of Native Lore from North America*. Illustrated by Lisa Desimini. New York: Apple Soup.

_____. (1995). *Sleep, Sleep, Sleep: A Lullaby for Little Ones around the World*. Illustrated by Holly Meade. Boston: Little, Brown.

_____. (1998). *With a Whoop and a Holler: A Bushel of Lore from Way Down South*. Illustrated by Scott Cook. New York: Atheneum.

Vande Velde, Vivian. (2007). *Remembering Raquel*. New York: Harcourt.

_____. (2008). *Stolen*. Tarrytown, NY: Cavendish.

Varon, Sara. (2006). *Chicken and Cat*. New York: Scholastic.

Vaughan, Brian. (2008). *Pride of Baghdad*. London: Titan.

Venkatraman, Padma. (2008). *Climbing the Stairs*. New York: Putnam.

Vennema, Peter. (1988). *Shaka, King of the Zulus*. Illustrated by Diane Stanley. New York: HarperCollins.

Vogel, Carole Garbuny. (1999). *Legends of Landforms: Native American Lore and the Geology of the Land*. Brookfield, CT: Millbrook.

Voigt, Cynthia. (1981). *Homecoming*. New York: Atheneum.

_____. (1996). *Bad Girls*. New York: Scholastic.

Waddell, Martin. (2006). *Sleep Tight, Little Bear*. Illustrated by Barbara Firth. New York: Walker.

_____. (2008). *Skyscraper: From the Ground Up*. Illustrated by John Lawrence. Cambridge, MA: Candlewick.

Waldman, Neil. (1999). *The Starry Night*. Honesdale, PA: Wordsong.

Walker, Alice. (2007) *Why War Is Never a Good Idea*. New York: HarperCollins.

Walker, Paul Robert. (1993). *Big Men, Big Country: A Collection of American Tall Tales*. Illustrated by James Bernardin. San Diego, CA: Harcourt.

Walker, Sally M. (2005). *Secrets of a Civil War Submarine: Solving the Mysteries of the H. L. Hunley*. Minneapolis: Carolrhoda.

Wallace, Rich. (1996). *Wrestling Sturbridge*. New York: Knopf.

_____. (1997). *Shots on Goal*. New York: Knopf.

_____. (2000). *Playing without the Ball: A Novel in Four Quarters*. New York: Knopf.

_____. (2003). *Losing Is Not an Option*. New York: Knopf.

Wallner, Alexandra. (2004). *Grandma Moses*. New York: Holiday House.

Walsh, Ellen Stoll. (1989). *Mouse Paint*. San Diego, CA: Harcourt.

_____. (2007). *Mouse Shapes*. San Diego, CA: Harcourt.

Walsh, Jill Paton. (2004). *The Emperor's Winding Sheet*. Ashville, NC: Front Street.

Walter, Mildred Pitts. (1999). *Suitcase*. New York: Lothrop, Lee & Shepard.

Ward, Helen. (1999). *The Hare and the Tortoise: A Fable from Aesop*. Brookfield, CT: Millbrook.

Ward, Helen. (2004). *Unwitting Wisdom: An Anthology of Aesop's Fables*. San Francisco: Chronicle.

_____. (2008). *Varmints*. Cambridge, MA: Candlewick.

Warhola, James. (2003). *Uncle Andy's: A Fabulous Visit with Andy Warhol*. New York: Putnam.

Warner, Sally. (2001). *Finding Hattie*. New York: HarperCollins.

Warren, Andrea. (2004). *Escape from Saigon: How a Vietnam War Orphan Became an American Boy*. New York: Farrar, Straus & Giroux.

Warren, Sandra. (2001). *Surviving Hitler: A Boy in the Nazi Death Camps*. New York: Simon & Schuster.

Washington, Donna. (2003). *A Pride of African Tales*. Illustrated by James Ransome. New York: HarperCollins.

Watkins, Yoko Kawashima. (1986). *So Far from the Bamboo Grove*. New York: Lothrop, Lee & Shepard.

_____. (1994). *My Brother, My Sister, and I*. New York: Bradbury.

Watson, Wendy. (1989). *Wendy Watson's Mother Goose*. New York: Lothrop, Lee & Shepard.

Watt, Mélanie. (2007). *Chester*. Toronto: Kids Can Press.

_____. (2008). *Chester's Back!* Toronto: Kids Can Press.

Wattenberg, Jane. (2000). *Henny Penny*. New York: Scholastic.

Waugh, Sylvia. (2003). *Who Goes Home?* New York: Delacorte.

Weatherford, Carole Boston. (2008). *I, Matthew Henson: Polar Explorer*. Illustrated by Eric Velasquez. New York: Walker.

_____. (2008). *Before John Was a Jazz Giant: A Song of John Coltrane*. New York: Holt.

Weaver, Tess. (2007). *Cat Jumped In!* Illustrated by Emily Arnold McCully. New York: Clarion.

Weaver, Will. (2007). *Defect*. New York: Farrar, Straus & Giroux.

Webb, Sophie. (2000). *My Season with Penguins: An Antarctic Journal*. Boston: Houghton Mifflin.

_____. (2004). *Looking for Seabirds: Journal from an Alaskan Voyage*. Boston: Houghton Mifflin.

Weeks, Sarah. (2000). *Guy Time*. New York: HarperCollins.

_____. (2006). *Ruff! Ruff! Where's Scruff?* Illustrated by David A. Carter. San Diego, CA: Harcourt.

_____. (2008). *Pip Squeak*. Illustrated by Jane Manning. New York: HarperCollins.

Weill, Cynthia & K.B. Basseches. (2008). *AbeCedarios: Mexican Folk Art ABCs in English and Spanish*. Photographs by Moisés Jiménez and Armando Jiménez. El Paso. TX: Cinco Puntos Press.

Wein, Elizabeth. (1993). *The Winter Prince*. New York: Atheneum.

———. (2003). *A Coalition of Lions*. New York: Viking.

———. (2004). *The Sunbird*. New York: Viking.

———. (2007). *The Lion Hunter*. New York: Viking.

———. (2008). *The Empty Kingdom*. New York: Viking.

Weitzman, Jacqueline Preiss. (2002). *You Can't Take a Balloon into the National Gallery*. Illustrated by Robin Preiss Glasser. New York: Penguin.

Wells, Rosemary. (1979). *Max's First Word*. New York: Dial.

———. (1980). *When No One Was Looking*. New York: Dial.

———. (1995). *Lassie Come-Home: Eric Knight's Original 1938 Classic*. Illustrated by Susan Jeffers. New York: Holt.

———. (2002). *Wingwalker*. New York: Hyperion.

———. (2006). *Max's ABC*. New York: Viking.

———. (2007). *Max Counts His Chickens*. New York: Viking.

———. (2008). *Max's ABC*. New York: Penguin.

———. (2008). *Max's Bunny Business*. New York: Penguin.

———. (2008). *My Kindergarten*. New York: Hyperion.

Werlin, Nancy. (1998). *The Killer's Cousin*. New York: Delacorte.

———. (2004). *Double Helix*. New York: Dial.

———. (2008). *The Rules of Survival*. New York: Penguin.

Westerfeld, Scott. (2007). *Extras*. New York: Simon & Schuster.

———. (2007). *Specials*. New York: Simon & Schuster.

Weston, Carrie. (2007). *If A Chicken Stayed for Supper*. Illustrated by Sophie Fatus. New York: Holiday House.

Weston, Robert Paul. (2008). *Zorgamazoo*. New York: Penguin.

Wetherford, Carole Boston. (2006). *Moses: When Harriet Tubman Led her People to Freedom*. Illustrated by Kadir Nelson. New York: Hyperion.

Whatley, Bruce. (2001). *Wait! No Paint!* New York: HarperCollins.

Wheeler, Lisa. (2006). *Castaway Cats*. Illustrated by Ponder Goembel. New York: Antheneum.

———. (2007). *Dino-Hockey*. Illustrated by Barry Gott. Minneapolis, MN: Lerner.

———. (2007). *Jazz Baby*. Illustrated by R. Gregory Christie. San Diego, CA: Harcourt.

Whelan, Gloria. (2003). *The Impossible Journey*. New York: HarperCollins.

White, E. B. (1952). *Charlotte's Web*. Illustrated by Garth Williams. New York: HarperCollins.

White, Ruth. (2003). *Tadpole*. New York: Farrar. Straus & Giroux.

———. (2004). *Buttermilk*. New York: Farrar, Straus & Giroux.

———. (2007). *Way Down Deep*. New York: Farrar Straus & Giroux.

White, T. H. (1958). *The Once and Future King*. New York: Putnam.

White, Trudy. (2007). *Could You? Would You?* La Jolla, CA: Kane Miller.

Wick, Walter. (1997). *A Drop of Water: A Book of Science and Wonder*. New York: Scholastic.

Wiesner, David. (1988). *Free Fall*. New York: HarperCollins.

———. (1991). *Tuesday*. New York: Clarion.

———. (1999). *Sector 7*. New York: Clarion.

———. (2001). *The Three Pigs*. New York: Clarion.

———. (2006). *Flotsam*. New York: Clarion.

Wilce, Ysabeau. (2007). *Flora Sequnda: Being the Magical Mishaps of a Girl*. Orlando, FL: Harcourt.

Wild, Margaret. (2007). *Piglet and Papa*. Illustrated by Stephen Michael King. New York: Abrams.

———. (2007). *Woolvs in the Sitee*. Illustrated by Anne Spudvilas. Honesdale, PA: Front Street/Boyds Mills Press.

Wilder, Laura Ingalls. (1953). *Little House in the Big Woods*. Illustrated by Garth Williams. New York: Harper.

Wildsmith, Brian. (1994). *Jack and the Meanstalk*. Illustrated by Rebecca Wildsmith. New York: Knopf.

Wiles, Deborah. (2001). *Freedom Summer*. New York.

———. (2007). *Aurora County All-Stars*. New York: Harcourt.

Willard, Nancy. (1981). *A Visit to William Blake's Inn: Poems for Innocent and Experienced Travelers*. New York: Harcourt Brace Jovanovich.

———. (2003). *Cinderella's Dress*. Illustrated by Jane Dyer. New York: Scholastic.

Willems, Mo. (2003). *Don't Let the Pigeon Drive the Bus!* New York: Hyperion.

———. (2004). *Knuffle Bunny*. New York: Hyperion.

———. (2004). *The Pigeon Finds a Hot Dog*. New York: Hyperion.

———. (2006). *Don't Let the Pigeon Stay Up Late!* New York: Hyperion.

———. (2006). *Edwina, The Dinosaur Who Didn't Know She Was Extinct*. New York: Hyperion.

———. (2007). *I Am Invited to a Party!* New York: Hyperion.

———. (2007). *Knuffle Bunny Too: A Case of Mistaken Identity*. New York: Hyperion.

———. (2007). *My Friend Is Sad*. New York: Hyperion.

———. (2007). *There Is a Bird on Your Head!* New York: Hyperion.

———. (2007). *Today I Will Fly!* New York: Hyperion.

Willey, Margaret. (2001). *Clever Beatrice: An Upper Peninsula Conte*. Illustrated by Heather Solomon. New York: Atheneum.

———. (2004). *Clever Beatrice and the Best Little Pony*. Illustrated by Heather Solomon. New York: Atheneum.

Williams, Dar. (2004). *Amalee*. New York: Scholastic.

Williams, Marcia. (1996). *King Arthur and the Knights of the Round Table*. Cambridge, MA: Candlewick.

———. (2000). *Bravo, Mr. William Shakespeare*. Cambridge, MA: Candlewick.

———. (2004). *Tales from Shakespeare*. Cambridge, MA: Candlewick.

Williams, Vera B. (1982). *A Chair for My Mother*. New York: Greenwillow Books.

———. (1996). *"More More More" Said the Baby*. New York: HarperCollins.

Williams-Garcia, Rita. (2001). *Every Time a Rainbow Dies*. New York: HarperCollins.

Wilson, April. (1999). *Magpie Magic*. New York: Dial.

Wilson, Jacqueline. (2008). *Best Friends*. Illustrated by Nick Sharratt. New York: Roaring Brook Press.

Wilson, N. D. (2007). *Leepike Ridge*. New York: Random House.

_____. (2007). *100 Cupboards*. New York: Random House.

Winick, Judd. (2000). *Pedro and Me: Friendship, Loss, and What I Learned*. New York: Holt.

Winter, Jeanette. (1988). *Follow the Drinking Gourd*. New York: Knopf.

_____. (1999). *Sebastian: A Book about Bach*. San Diego, CA: Harcourt Brace.

_____. (2003). *Beatrix: Various Episodes from the Life of Beatrix Potter*. New York: Farrar, Straus & Giroux.

_____. (2007). *The Tale of Pale Male: A True Story*. San Diego, CA: Harcourt.

Winter, Jonah. (2008). *Muhammad Ali: Champion of the World*. Illustrated by Francois Roca. New York: Random House.

_____. (2008). *Roberto Clemente: Pride of the Pittsburg Pirates*. Illustrated by Raul Colón. New York: Simon & Schuster.

_____. (2008). *Steel Town*. Illustrated by Terry Widener. New York: Simon & Schuster.

Wise, Bill. (2007). *Louis Sockalexis: Native American Baseball Pioneer*. Illustrated by Bill Farnsworth. New York: Lee & Low.

Wisniewski, David. (1990). *Elfwyn's Saga*. Illustrated by Lee Salsbery. New York: Lothrop, Lee & Shephard.

_____. (1991). *Rain Player*. New York: Clarion.

_____. (1996). *Golem*. Boston: Houghton Mifflin.

Wittlinger, Ellen. (2000). *What's in a Name?* New York: Simon & Schuster.

_____. (2004). *Heart on My Sleeve*. New York: Simon & Schuster.

_____. (2007). *Parrotfish*. New York: Simon & Schuster.

Wolf, Allan. (2004). *New Found Land: Lewis and Clark's Voyage of Discovery*. Cambridge, MA: Candlewick.

Wolf, Bernard. (2003). *Coming to America: A Muslim Family's Story*. New York: Lee & Low.

Wolff, Virginia Euwer. (1993). *Make Lemonade*. New York: Holt.

_____. (2000). *Bat 6*. New York.

_____. (2001). *True Believer*. New York: Atheneum.

Wong, Janet S. (2003). *Minn and Jake*. Illustrated by Genevieve Cote. New York: Farrar, Straus & Giroux.

_____. (2007). *The Dumpster Diver*. Illustrated by David Roberts. Cambridge, MA: Candlewick.

Wood, Don. (2008). *Into the Volcano*. New York: Blue Sky Press.

Woods, Brenda. (2004). *Emako Blue*. New York: Putnam.

Woodson, Jacqueline. (1990). *Last Summer with Maizon*. New York: Delacorte.

_____. (1994). *From the Notebooks of Melanin Sun*. New York: Blue Sky Press.

_____. (1994). *I Hadn't Meant to Tell You This*. New York: Delacorte.

_____. (1997). *The House You Pass on the Way*. New York: Delacorte.

_____. (2000). *Miracle's Boys*. New York: Putnam.

_____. (2001). *The Other Side*. Illustrated by E. B. Lewis. New York: Putnam.

_____. (2003). *Locomotion*. New York: Putman.

_____. (2004). *Coming on Home Soon*. Illustrated by E. B. Lewis. New York: Putnam.

_____. (2005). *Show Way*. Illustrated by Hudson Talbott. New York: Putnam.

_____. (2007). *Feathers*. New York: Penguin.

_____. (2008). *After Tupac and D Foster*. New York: Putman.

_____. (2009). *Peace, Locomotion*. New York: Putnam.

Worth, Valerie. (1994). *All the Small Poems and Fourteen More*. Illustrated by Natalie Babbitt. New York: Farrar, Straus & Giroux.

_____. (2007). *Animal Poems*. Illustrated by Steve Jenkins. New York: Farrar, Straus & Giroux.

Wright, Betty Ren. (1994). *The Ghost Comes Calling*. New York: Scholastic.

_____. (1998). *A Ghost in the Family*. New York: Scholastic.

Wulffson, Don. (2001). *Soldier X*. New York: Viking.

Wyeth, Sharon Dennis. (1998). *Something Beautiful*. New York: Doubleday.

Wynne-Jones, Tim. (1998). *Stephen Fair: A Novel*. New York: DK Publishing.

_____. (2007). *Rex Zero and the End of the World*. New York: Farrar, Straus & Giroux.

_____. (2007). *Rex Zero, King of Nothing*. New York: Farrar, Straus & Giroux.

Xiong, Blia. (1989). *Nine-in-One Grr! Grr! A Folktale from the Hmong People*. Illustrated by Nancy Hom. San Francisco: Children's Book Press.

Yaccarino, Dan. (2007). *Every Friday*. New York: Holt.

Yang, Gene Luen. (2006). *American Born Chinese*. New York: First Second/Roaring Brook Press.

Yates, Elizabeth. (1950). *Amos Fortune: Free Man*. New York: Dutton.

Yates, Philip. (2003). *Ten Little Mummies: An Egyptian Counting Book*. Illustrated by G. Brian Caras. New York: Viking.

Yee, Lisa. (2003). *Millicent Min, Girl Genius*. New York: Levine.

Yee, Wong Herbert. (2007). *Abracadabra! Magic with Mouse and Mole*. Boston: Houghton Mifflin.

_____. (2007). *Tracks in the Snow*. New York: Square Fish.

_____. (2007). *Who Likes Rain?* New York: Holt.

Yeh, Phil. (2007). *Dinosaurs Across America*. New York: Nantier Beall Minoustchine.

Yenawine, Philip. (1991). *Lines*. New York: Museum of Modern Art.

Yep, Laurence. (1991). *Tongues of Jade*. Illustrated by David Weisner. New York: HarperCollins.

Yep, Laurence. (1991). *The Star Fisher*. New York: Morrow.

———. (1997). *Thief of Hearts*. New York: HarperCollins.

———. (2003). *The Traitor: 1885*. New York: HarperCollins.

Ylvisaker, Anne. (2009). *Little Klein*. Cambridge, MA: Candlewick.

Yolen, Jane. (1987). *Owl Moon*. Illustrated by John Schoenherr. New York: Philomel.

———. (1988). *The Devil's Arithmetic*. San Diego, CA: Harcourt.

———. (1990). *Tam Lin: An Old Ballad*. Illustrated by Charles Mikolaycak. San Diego, CA: Harcourt.

———. (1992). *Jane Yolen's Mother Goose Songbook*. Illustrated by Rosekrans Hoffman. Honesdale, PA: Caroline House.

———. (1992). *Encounter*. Illustrated by David Shannon. San Diego, CA: Harcourt.

———. (1992). *Street Rhymes around the World*. Honesdale, PA: Wordsong.

———. (1993). *All Those Secrets of the World*. Illustrated by Leslie Baker. St. Paul, MN: Turtleback.

———. (1994). *Sleep Rhymes around the World*. Honesdale, PA: Wordsong.

———. (1995). *Camelot*. Illustrated by Winslow Pels. New York: Philomel.

———. (1996). *Encounter*. Illustrated by David Shannon. San Diego, CA: Harcourt.

———. (1996). *Sky Scrape/City Scape: Poems of City Life*. Honesdale, PA: Wordsong.

———. (1998). *Merlin*. New York: Scholastic.

———. (1998). *Passager*. New York: Scholastic.

———. (1999). *Hobby*. Honesdale, PA: Boyd Mills Press.

———. (2000). *Color Me a Rhyme: Nature Poems for Young People*. Illustrated by Jason Stemple. Honesdale, PA: Wordsong.

———. (2000). *Not One Damsel in Distress: World Folktales for Strong Girls*. Illustrated by Susan Guevara. San Diego, CA: Silver Whistle.

———. (2001). *The Dragon's Boy*. New York: HarperCollins.

———. (2003). *Mightier Than the Sword: World Folktales for Strong Boys*. Illustrated by Raul Colón. San Diego, CA: Harcourt.

———. (2003). *Sword of the Rightful King: A Novel of King Arthur*. San Diego, CA: Harcourt.

———. (2004). *Fine Feathered Friends: Poems for Young People*. Hornsdale, PA.: Wordsong.

———. (2007). *How Do Dinosaurs Go to School?* Illustrated by Mark Teague. New York: Blue Sky Press.

Yolen, Jane, & Andrew Fusek Peters. (2007). *Here's a Little Poem: A Very First Book of Poetry*. Illustrated by Polly Dunbar. New York: Walker.

Yolen, Jane, & Robert Harris. (2001). *The Queen's Own Fool: A Novel of Mary, Queen of Scots*. Illustrated by Cynthia Von Buhler. New York: Philomel.

———. (2002). *Girl in a Cage*. New York: Philomel.

———. (2004). *Prince across the Water*. New York: Philomel.

Yorinks, Arthur. (1999). *The Alphabet Atlas*. Illustrated by Adrienne Yorinks. Delray Beach, FL: Winslow.

———. (2007). *The Witch's Child*. Illustrated by Jos. A. Smith. New York: Abrams.

Young, Ed. (1989). *Lon Po Po: A Red Riding Hood Story from China*. New York: Philomel.

———. (1992). *Seven Blind Mice*. New York: Philomel.

———. (1998). *The Lost Horse: A Chinese Folktale*. San Diego, CA: Harcourt Brace.

———. (2001). *Monkey King*. New York: HarperCollins.

———. (2004). *The Sons of the Dragon King: A Chinese Legend*. New York: Atheneum.

———. (2006). *My Mei Mei*. New York: Philomel.

Young, Steve. (2007). *15 Minutes*. New York: HarperCollins.

Yumoto, Kazumi. (1996). *The Friends*. Illustrated by Cathy Hirano. New York: Farrar, Straus & Giroux.

Zaunders, Bo. (2001). *Feathers, Flaps, and Flops: Fabulous Early Fliers*. Illustrated by Roxie Munro. New York: Dutton.

Zee, Ruth Vander, & Marian Sneider. (2007). *Eli Remembers*. Illustrated by Bill Farnsworth. Grand Rapids, MI: Eerdmans.

Zeifert, Harriet. (2000) *Little Red Riding Hood*. Illustrated by Emily Bolam. New York: Penguin.

Zeises, Lara. (2004). *Contents under Pressure*. New York: Delacorte.

Zelinsky, Paul O. (1986). *Rumpelstiltskin*. New York: Penguin.

———. (1990). *The Wheels on the Bus*. New York: Dutton.

———. (1997). *Rapunzel*. New York: Penguin.

Zemach, Harve. (1973). *Duffy and the Devil: A Cornish Tale*. Illustrated by Margot Zemach. New York: Farrar, Straus & Giroux.

Zemach, Margot. (1988). *The Three Little Pigs: An Old Story*. New York: Farrar, Straus & Giroux.

———. (1997). *Hush Little Baby*. San Francisco, CA: Chronicle.

Zephaniah, Benjamin. (2004). *Gangsta Rap*. New York: Bloomsbury.

Zevin, Gabrielle. (2007). *Memoirs of a Teenage Amnesiac*. New York: Farrar, Straus & Giroux.

Zimmer, Tracie Vaughn. (2007). *Reaching for Sun*. London: Bloomsbury.

Zindel, Paul. (1968). *The Pigman*. New York: HarperCollins

Zolotow, Charlotte. (1972). *William's Doll*. Illustrated by William Pene DuBois. New York: HarperCollins.

———. (1995). *The Old Dog*. Illustrated by James Ransome. New York: HarperCollins.

Zuckerman, Linda. (2007). *Taste for Rabbit*. New York: Levine.

Zusak, Marcus. (2000). *Fighting Ruben Wolfe*. New York: Scholastic.

———. (2001). *Getting the Girl*. New York: Levine.

———. (2006). *The Book Thief*. New York: Random House.

Text Credits

This page constitutes an extension of the copyright page. We have made every effort to trace the ownership of all copyrighted material and to secure permission from copyright holders. In the event of any question arising as to the use of any material, we will be pleased to make the necessary corrections in future printings. Thanks are due to the following authors, publishers, and agents for permission to use the material indicated.

CHAPTER 4

138: Excerpt from "Bedside Reading" from *Carver: A Life in Poems* by Marilyn Nelson (Front Street, an imprint of Boyds Mills Press, 2001). Reprinted with the permission of Boyds Mills Press, Inc. Copyright © 2001 by Marilyn Nelson. 139: From Paul Janeczko, "Seeing the Blue Between," © 2002 Candlewick Press. Reprinted by permission of Kristine O'Connell George. 145: From *Fathers, Mothers, Sisters, Brothers* by Mary Ann Hoberman. Copyright © 1991 by Marilyn Hafner (illustrations). By permission of Little, Brown and Company (Inc.). 146: From *Looking For Your Name*, © 1993 Orchard Books. Reprinted by permission of Lee Sharkey. 151: Reprinted with the permission of Simon & Schuster Books for Young Readers, an imprint of Simon & Schuster Children's Publishing Division from *Circus* by Jack Prelutsky. © 1974 Jack Prelutsky. 151: Reprinted with the permission of Simon & Schuster Books for Young Readers, an imprint of Simon & Schuster Children's Publishing Division from *Circus* by Jack Prelutsky. © 1974 Jack Prelutsky. 152: "Galoshes" from *Stories To Begin On* by Rhoda W. Bacmeister, illustrated by Tom Maley, copyright 1940 by E. P. Dutton, renewed © 1968 by Rhoda W. Bacmeister. Used by permission of Dutton Children's Books, an division of Penguin Putman Books for Young Readers Group, a memeber of Penguin Group (USA) Inc., 345 Hudson Street, New York, NY 10014. All rights reserved. 153: From *One at a Time* by David McCord. Copyright © 1965, 1966 by David McCord. By permission of Little, Brown and Company (Inc.). 153: Copyright © 1996 by Jane Yolen. First appeared in *Sky Scrape/City Scape*, published by Boyds Mills Press. Reprinted by per-

mission of Boyds Mills Press. 153: Reprinted with permission of David Harrison. 154: From Gwendolyn Brooks, "We Real Cool." Reprinted by permission of Brooks Permissions. 155: Text copyright © by Georgia Heard, illustrations copyright © 1992 by Jennifer Owings Dewey, from "Creatures of the Earth, Sea, and Sky." Published by Wordsong, Boyds Mills Press, Inc. Reprinted by permission. 155: From *It Doesn't Always Have to Rhyme* by Eve Merriam. Copyright © 1964 Eve Merriam. © renewed 1992. All rights reserved. Used by permission of Marian Reiner. 155: Sarah Hansen, "Rising" from *Sky Magic*, Dutton Juvenile Publishers. Reprinted by permission of the author. 155–156: "Dandelion" from *All the Small Poems and Fourteen More* by Valerie Worth. © 1987, 1994 by Valerie Worth. Used by permission of Farrar, Straus and Giroux, LLC. 156: Text copyright © 1986 by Barbara Juster Esbensen from *Words With Wrinkled Knees* by Barbara Juster Esbensen. Published by Boyds Mills Press, Inc. Reprinted by permission. 156: From *Fold Me a Poem*, text © 2005 by Kristine O'Connell George, illustrations © 2005 by Lauren Stringer, reproduced by permission of Houghton Mifflin Harcourt Publishing Co. 158: Reprinted by Harold Ober Associates Incorporated. Copyright © 1957 by Eleanor Farjeon. From *The Children's Bells*. 159: From *Splish Splash* by Joan Bransfield Graham. Text © 1994 by Joan Bransfield Graham. Reprinted by permission of Houghton Mifflin Harcourt Publishing Co. All rights reserved. 160: Text and illustration from "The Salmon" in *The Swim*, © 1997 by Douglas Florian, reprinted by permission of Houghton Mifflin Publishing Company. 161: Kobayashi Issa, *Don't Tell the Scarecrow*. 161–162: "What My Bed Says" by Myra Cohn Livingston, from *O Sliver of Liver and Other Poems* by Myra Cohn Livingston. © 1979 by Myra Cohn Livingston. Used by permission of Marion Reiner. 161: From *Tap Dancing on the Roof* by Linda Sue Park. Text © 2007 by Linda Sue Park. Reprinted by permission of Clarion Books, an imprint of Houghton Mifflin Harcourt Publishing Company. All rights reserved. 162: Rebecca Kai Dotlich, "Whispers to the Wall" from *A Kick in the Head* by Paul Janeczko, © 2005 Candlewick Press. Reprinted by permission of Curtis Brown, Ltd. 163: Reprinted by permission of Avis Harley.

Illustration and Photo Credits

CHAPTER 4

CHAPTER 5

Author and Title Index

Note:
· Titles in bold indicate series books.
· Titles in bold italics indicate individual children's books.
· Titles in italics indicate books or periodicals about children's literature.
· Page numbers in italics indicate author profiles.
· Page numbers followed by *(2)* or *(3)* indicate two or three separate discussions.

Subject Index

Note:
- Titles in bold italics indicate children's books.
- Titles in italics indicate books or periodicals about children's literature.
- Page numbers in italics indicate text features including figures, profiles, and teaching ideas.
- Page numbers followed by *(2), (3), (4),* or *(5)* indicate two, three, four, or five separate references.

thinking:
poetry and, 164
reading and critical thinking, 319–320, 356–357
thoughts of characters, 259
three little pigs stories, 20, 198, 328–330
booklist, 204
The Three Pigs: first-grade class discussion, 328–330
thrillers, 241
booklist, 250
tightrope walk between the towers story, 92, 295
Till, Emmett:
case story, 298, 316
poetry for, 158–159
Tillage, Leon Walter: memoir, 298
time and choice needs of readers, 348
time concept, 107
time slips in fantasy, 212, 272
booklist, 225–226
time to read vs. time for testing, 25–26
title page of picturebooks, 91
Tolkien, J.R.R., 18, 40
Tomlinson, Carl, 22
"Touch it with your pencil..." (poem), 156
Tracking Trash: Flotsam, Jetsam, and the Science of Ocean Motion, 304
close look at, 309–310
trade books:
science trade books, 312
vs. textbooks, 319
trade editions of picturebooks, 98, 99
transactional view of reading literature, 36–38
transformation approach to multicultural education, 357–358
transformation tales, 181, 182
transforming the curriculum: in social studies, 356–359
transgendered characters, 7
transitional chapter books, 340
translated books:
award for (see Batchelder Award)
dearth in the U.S., 7, 22
publishers of, 8
A Treasury of American Folklore, 197
tree planting stories, 188, 286, 297
trickster tales, 174, 175, 181, 185–186
trim size of picturebooks, 94
"The Truth About Sharks" (short story), 353–355
Tuck Everlasting, 212
discussion group questions, 213
two-voice poetry, 148–149, 154, 271

Uncle Remus stories, 185–186
The Underneath, 206–207, 223
close look at, 210–211
understanding life:
reading and, 34–35, 39, 41, 42–43, 299, 335–336
studying lives and, 299
See also self-discovery through reading
understanding literature: life experience and, 39, 40–41, 154
See also teaching ideas
the unexpected in books, 9
United States Board on Books for Young People (USBBY), 22
unity of art, 70
unity of books, 307
urchin verse, 141
USBBY. *See* United States Board on Books for Young People

Van Allsburg, Chris: life works, 116
variant folktales, 188–191
booklist, 204
variants of stories:
folktales, 188–191, 204
reading aloud, 128
variety in art, 70
verse:
epics, 195
free (see free verse)
linked verse, 158, 162
picturebook booklist, 134–135
vs. poetry, 139
See also poetry
verse novels, 19, 157–158
booklist, 173
contemporary realistic fiction, 237, 239, 242
historical fiction, 138, 141, 272(2)
videos of books, 22
Vietnam wartime stories, 45, 124, 258, 275
violence theme, 246
booklist, 250
hanging stories, 123, 265, 316
See also war stories
Virginia Hamilton Award winner, 245

Walsh, Jill Payton, 34
war: children of soldiers book, 316
war stories, 246
booklist, 250
children in, 19, 240, 246, 271, 272–275, 275
Cold War period stories, 275
consequences of war, 214, 246, 250 (see also children in, *above*)
Revolutionary War, 266–267
Scottish rebellion, 265–266

Vietnam wartime stories, 45, 124, 258, 275
See also World War I period stories; World War II period stories
Washington, Booker T., 150
watercolor in picturebook art, 72–73, 83
booklist, 79
We Are the Ship: The Story of Negro League Baseball:
close look at, 316–318
"We Real Cool..." (poem), 154
websites:
of authors, 29
on censorship, 27
for kids, 23
for language arts standards, 26
for selecting children's books, 29
Werlin, Nancy, 241
Westward expansion stories, 267–269, 358
booklist, 279
whaling town history, 316
"What My Bed Says" (poem), 161–162
"what's on my mind?" questions, 337
whimsy in nursery rhymes, 183
"Whispers to the Wall" (poem), 162
Whitbread Book of the Year Award: winners, 17, 20, 249
White, Mary Lou, 151
White House history, 316
Wiesner, David: *The Three Pigs,* 328–330
Wild, Margaret:
profile, 125
Woolvs in the Sitee, 124–126
The Wild Rumpus bookstore, 4
"Will You Walk into My Parlor?...", 140
Williams, William Carlos: biography of, 287
Winklejohann, Sister Rosemary, 141
Wolf, S. A., 335
wolf books, 306, 311
wolf stories, 215
wolfsnail book, 311
woman characters. *See* female characters
women in politics stories, 286
Clinton biography, 293
women of the American Revolution, 286
women soldiers of the Civil War, 316
woodcuts in picturebook art, 73
booklist, 79
Woolvs in the Sitee: close look at, 124–126

word patterns in poetry, 153–154
word pictures in poetry, 154–156
word–picture relationships in picturebooks, 92–94
quality criteria, *100*
teaching, 95
wordless books, 12, 56, 83, 88, 94, 112–113, 119, 123, 337
wordplay books, 318
works of art: nonfiction books as, 18
world folktales booklists, 200–202
The World through Children's Books, 22
World War I period stories, 271
booklist, 280
World War II period stories, 272–275
booklist, 280–281
the world we wish for: folktales as expressive of, *190*
Worth, Valerie, 155
"Dandelion", 155–156
profile, *151*
writer's notebook: keeping, 232
writers. *See* authors
writing:
in Book Club, 350
picturebook creation studies, 318
reading and, 33–34, *320,* 355–356
reading poetry and, 163–164
resources on, *356*
writing nonfiction, 291
writing poetry:
reading poetry and, 355–356
teaching, *148, 167*
Wynne-Jones, Tim, 18

Yolen, Jane, 18, 40, 175, 209, *215*
"Sky Scrape/City Scape", 153
Young Adult Choices Awards, 41
winners in 2008, *49*
young adult literature. *See* adolescent literature
young readers:
appreciating reader-response differences between teachers and, *42*
and fables, 192
fantasy for, 12
fiction profitability, 6
picturebooks: for emerging readers, 112–116; for young children, 104–112
poetry books for, *168–169*
resistance to texts, 39, 45–46
teaching to compare old and new books, 10, 13
See also readers

Zipes, Jack, 176

Touchstones in the History of Children's Literature

1950S

1959   PHILIPPA PEARCE
Tom's Midnight Garden

1957   DR. SEUSS
The Cat in the Hat

1956   GWENDOLYN BROOKS
Bronzeville Boys and Girls

1952   ANNE FRANK
*Anne Frank:
The Diary of a Young Girl*

1952   MARY NORTON
The Borrowers

1952   E. B. WHITE
Charlotte's Web
ILLUSTRATED BY GARTH
WILLIAMS

1950   BEVERLY CLEARY
Henry Huggins

1950   C. S. LEWIS
*The Lion, the Witch,
and the Wardrobe*

1940S

1947   MARGARET WISE BROWN
Goodnight Moon

1947   ALVIN TRESSELT
White Snow, Bright Snow
ILLUSTRATED BY ROGER
DUVOISIN

1945   LOIS LENSKI
Strawberry Girl

1944   ROBERT LAWSON
Rabbit Hill

1943   JAMES THURBER
Many Moons
ILLUSTRATED BY MARC SIMONT

1942   VIRGINIA LEE BURTON
The Little House

1941   ROBERT MCCLOSKEY
Make Way for Ducklings

1941   H. A. REY
Curious George

1930S

1939   LUDWIG BEMELMANS
Madeline

1938   VIRGINIA LEE BURTON
*Mike Mulligan and
His Steam Shovel*

1937   J. R. R. TOLKIEN
The Hobbit

1935   CAROL RYRIE BRINK
Caddie Woodlawn

1934   PAMELA TRAVERS
Mary Poppins

1932   LAURA INGALLS WILDER
*Little House in the
Big Woods*
ILLUSTRATED BY GARTH WILLIAMS

1920S

1926   A. A. MILNE
Winnie-the-Pooh
ILLUSTRATED BY E. H. SHEPARD

1922   MARGERY WILLIAMS
The Velveteen Rabbit
ILLUSTRATED BY WILLIAM
NICHOLSON

1900S

1911   FRANCES HODGSON
BURNETT
The Secret Garden

1908   LUCY M. MONTGOMERY
Anne of Green Gables

1908   KENNETH GRAHAME
Wind in the Willows

1904   JAMES M. BARRIE
Peter Pan

1903   KATE DOUGLAS WIGGIN
*Rebecca of Sunnybrook
Farm*

1903   LESLIE BROOKE
Johnny Crow's Garden

1902   BEATRIX POTTER
The Tale of Peter Rabbit

1900   L. FRANK BAUM
The Wizard of Oz
ILLUSTRATED BY W. W. DENSLOW

1800S

1899   E. NESBIT
*The Story of the Treasure
Seekers*

1894   RUDYARD KIPLING
The Jungle Book

1891   CARLO COLLODI
Pinocchio

1891   JAMES WHITCOMB RILEY
Rhymes of Childhood

1888   ROBERT BROWNING
The Pied Piper of Hamlin